THE THEORY AND MEASUREMENT
OF DEMAND

THE THEORY
AND MEASUREMENT OF
DEMAND

By HENRY SCHULTZ

THE UNIVERSITY OF CHICAGO PRESS

CHICAGO & LONDON

THE UNIVERSITY OF CHICAGO PRESS, CHICAGO 60637

The University of Chicago Press, Ltd., London

Copyright 1938 by The University of Chicago. All rights reserved. Published 1938. Sixth Impression 1972. Printed in the United States of America

International Standard Book Number: 0–226–74083–8
Library of Congress Catalog Card Number: 38–19565

PREFACE

It is a notorious fact that the "givens" of economic science are, in fact, unknown and must be determined empirically. Economic theorists explain changes in prices and in purchases and sales—in fact, the entire working of the pricing process—in terms of the traders' demand functions, supply functions, and "liquidity preferences," which must be assumed as known. Actually, they are unknown, and it is this void in our knowledge which is responsible for much of the aridity of present-day economics.

The main objectives of this book are: (1) to derive the concrete, statistical demand functions of sixteen agricultural commodities; (2) to compare the "elasticities" and the time shifts of these functions; (3) to develop a theory of demand for completing and competing goods; and (4) to submit this theory to a statistical test. The treatment begins with a résumé of the modern mathematical theory of demand. It then compares and evaluates the various methods and procedures which have been suggested for deriving demand curves from statistics. From these it selects the more promising methods and applies them to the problem of determining the American demand functions for sugar, corn, cotton, hay, wheat, potatoes, oats, barley, rye, buckwheat; and for beef, pork, and mutton; and the Canadian demand functions for sugar, tea, and coffee. Finally, it develops a theory of demand for related goods, the keystone of which is the "Law of Rational Consumer Behavior," which is explained and tested in chapters xviii and xix. This law frees the statistical study of demand from much of its former empiricism, gives it greater significance and utility, and opens up many new problems.

This work is part of a larger study of price determination which was begun in 1928–29. Its progress was frequently slowed down, if not actually halted, by the pressure of teaching and administrative duties, by an unusually high marriage rate among my assistants, and by an attack of low spirits. None of these factors, however, impeded the completion of the book as much as did the several revisions on the part of the Bureau of Agricultural Economics of the underlying production and price series which were published in the *Yearbooks of Agriculture* for 1932–35 and in *Agricultural Statistics* for 1936. (As this book goes to press we note that further revisions appear in *Agricultural Statistics* for 1937.) The appearance of a revised series for a commodity often led me to discard former analyses and to recompute the equations from the new data, only to discover a year or two later that the revisions were not final! This began to consume such an exasperating amount of time and energy that I finally decided to let some of the completed analyses stand and to satisfy myself with an investigation of the maximum changes that would be brought about in the derived constants through the substitution of the new series for the old (see chap. v).

No one is more aware than I of the shortcomings of this work—the lack of adequate data at certain points and the unevenness of treatment of the statistical chapters. Furthermore, as the work has progressed, my understanding of the problem and of the methods has deepened, so that the treatment would be at many points more adequate were the investigation to be undertaken now. In spite of its shortcomings, however, it is the only work which attempts to unify the theoretical-quantitative, the empirical-quantitative, and the historical approaches to the study of demand on so large a scale. I may, therefore, be pardoned for calling attention to some of its distinctive features.

1. It gives a simple, yet quite adequate, summary of the general theory of utility, exchange, and demand and its latest developments—something which is not to be found in existing treatises. (See chaps. i, xviii, and xix.)

2. The statistical chapters of Parts II and III not only give the elasticities and the time shifts of the demand curves of a very important group of commodities but also analyze the factors affecting the prices of the same commodities. This feature should appeal to all those who have a practical interest in the production and marketing of these goods as well as to general economists and statisticians.

3. The elasticities and the time shifts of the demand curves for the different commodities are derived by several methods and subjected to various comparisons, so that the reader may get an idea of the consistency of the various results. (See chaps. xvi and xvii.)

4. Chapters xviii and xix present the modern theory of demand for completing and competing goods, subject it to a statistical test, and develop a measure of the extent to which human behavior in the market place is rational or consistent. The applications to the analyses of the American demands for barley, corn, hay, and oats; and for beef, pork, and mutton; and of the Canadian demands for sugar, tea, and coffee should be of interest not only to economic specialists but also to students of the commodities or industries concerned.

5. The mathematical appendix (Appen. C) provides a brief explanation of the statistical methods and procedures which are very useful, if not indispensable, in demand and price analyses, and which, together with the nontechnical explanations given in the body of the book, should also constitute a good basis for advanced courses in least squares, correlation, and sampling.

I have attempted so to write this book that the gist of the technical discussions shall be intelligible to nonmathematical readers. With this end in view, I have taken pains to define the more important terms and illustrate the more important procedures in the first statistical chapter (chap. vi) and to provide nontechnical summaries of the mathematical developments in the other chapters as well. The various statistical chapters of Part II may, therefore, be read as independent monographs by practical students of the commodity or industry in question without fear that their efforts will be entirely unrewarded. In the chapters on the demands for sugar, corn, cotton, and wheat (chaps. vi, vii, viii, and x), and in the summary chapter xvii, I have also given brief indications of the bearing of the statistical findings on the Agricultural Adjustment Act, the "Ever Normal Granary," and related programs.

HENRY SCHULTZ

UNIVERSITY OF CHICAGO

ACKNOWLEDGMENTS

A book of this nature, based as it is on a study of hundreds of statistical series and thousands of graphical and mathematical analyses, not to mention the considerable amount of historical and mathematical research, would have been impossible without the co-operation of a staff of assistants at various stages in its preparation.

In its earlier phase, in 1928–30, Ardis T. Monk, Ramona Simpson Knick, and Yue Kei Wong were responsible for a large amount of the exploratory statistical research. During different times between October, 1928, and June, 1931, these pioneers were joined or succeeded by four graduate students—Harry Pelle Hartkemeier, Roswell Whitman, Lester S. Kellogg, and Virginius F. Coe— who, as part-time research assistants, worked for about one year on the statistical equations. In its second phase, which extended from 1930 to 1934 and in which most of the computations were made, Frances Gibson McIntyre, Edith Mohn Foster, and Janet Murray were responsible for the painstaking statistical research. For a period of nine months they also had the part-time assistance of two graduate students—Francis McIntyre and Sidney Sufrin. In the third and final phase, which began in 1934 and which saw the revisions of some of the earlier computations as well as the completion of the analyses for Part III, I was also favored with a succession of splendid assistants. In the fall of 1934, when I returned from a year's stay abroad and was faced with the prospect of having to train and build up an entirely new staff of assistants in order to finish the work, Milton Friedman, a former graduate student of mine, came to my rescue and for a year continued to render invaluable assistance. In the fall of 1935, Friedman was succeeded by Jacob L. Mosak, who, together with Elizabeth J. Slotkin, exhibited an unusual combination of thoroughness, persistence, and skill in handling the remaining statistical analyses and in putting the material into readily usable form. The difficult task of typing and preparing the manuscript for the printer was carried out by Anne Mitchell and Dorothy Hampton, whose collegiate and statistical training saved the text from stenographic shipwreck. Other helpful assistants from time to time have been Margaret Hancock, Elizabeth Millies, Erika Schoenberg, and Anne M. Lescisin. To all of these collaborators I acknowledge a grateful and large obligation. Much of whatever merit this book may have is due to them.

The reader will, I am sure, also join me in heartily thanking the three assistants who are responsible for the graphs—Lester Kellogg, who assisted in the planning of the three-dimensional diagrams and who drew the first set; Yue Kei Wong, who drew the remaining three-dimensional diagrams as well as most of the other charts; and H. Gregg Lewis, who drew the rest. I hope that their beautiful work will facilitate an understanding of some of the more important economic and statistical notions which occur in all statistical studies of demand.

To Dr. O. C. Stine and his co-workers of the Bureau of Agricultural Economics of the United States Department of Agriculture my thanks are due for special compilations to supplement the basic series published in the *Yearbook of Agriculture*, and for their uniform courtesy, patience, and scientific attitude in handling the many inquiries which I addressed to them. To all others who supplied data, or made suggestions, and to the authors and publishers who gave permission to quote from their works, due acknowledgments are made in the appropriate places in the text.

My heaviest intellectual indebtedness is due to Professor Henry Ludwell Moore, who first aroused my interest in the statistical analysis of demand and to whose general scientific approach I have remained faithful. As a token of gratitude I have dedicated this book to him.

To the University of Chicago Press I wish to express my heartfelt appreciation for its co-operation in finding satisfactory solutions to the difficult typographical and financial problems presented by this book.

Finally, I wish to acknowledge with deep gratitude the continued financial and moral support of the Social Science Research Committee of the University of Chicago which has made possible the preparation and publication of this work.

H. S.

SUGGESTIONS TO READERS

1. The *cursory* reader will find the gist of the book in Sections I, III (C and D), and IV of Chapter I; Sections I and II of Chapter II; the concluding sections of Chapters III and IV; Sections I, II, and V of Chapter V; Sections I, II, V, and VI of Chapter VI, and the explanations of the charts in Sections III and IV; the charts and the concluding summaries of Chapters VII–XV, but especially those of Chapters VII, VIII, and X; the concluding summaries of Chapters XVII, XVIII, and XIX; and Chapter XX.

2. The *general* reader will be interested in all the nonmathematical parts of Chapters I, II, IV; in all of Chapter V; in the nonmathematical parts of Chapter VI and of at least two other statistical chapters, but preferably Chapters VII, VIII, and X; in the nonmathematical parts of Chapters XVII, XVIII, and XIX, and in all of Chapter XX. He will also be interested in the diagrams of the various chapters.

3. *Students of mathematical economics* should read Chapters I, XVIII, XIX, and XX.

4. *Those interested in statistical analysis* should read Chapters I, II, IV, V, VI, XVII, XVIII, and XIX, and especially Appendix C.

The table of contents which precedes each chapter, and the Index, should facilitate the use of the book for reference purposes.

In any one chapter the graphs of all equations with the *same dependent variable* are drawn to the same scale, so that the slopes of the curves are directly comparable.

TABLE OF CONTENTS

PART I.   THEORETICAL FOUNDATION

PART II.   STATISTICAL FINDINGS

PART III.   INTERRELATIONS OF DEMAND

TABLE OF CONTENTS

APPENDIXES

BIBLIOGRAPHY

INDEXES

LIST OF ILLUSTRATIONS

[In any one chapter the graphs of all equations with *the same dependent variable* are drawn to the same scale, so that the slopes of the curves are directly comparable.]

LIST OF TEXT TABLES

LIST OF APPENDIX TABLES

LIST OF STATISTICAL FORMS

PART I

THEORETICAL FOUNDATION

CHAPTER I

THE PURE THEORY OF DEMAND CURVES

CHAPTER I

THE PURE THEORY OF DEMAND CURVES

If the price of a given crop is reduced by 1 per cent, will sales increase by more than 1 per cent, or by less than 1 per cent? Is a large crop worth more or less than a small crop? What, in short, is the elasticity of demand for the crop? What is the shape of the demand curve? Is it essentially fixed, or is it subject to change? With the passage of time, does the curve retain its height, or does it shift upward or downward? If it does shift, at what rate? What are the factors affecting the demand for the commodity in question? What relations exist between the demand curves for substitutes? If there are different statistical and mathematical procedures for attacking these problems, do they all lead to the same conclusions?

The main object of this book is to derive concrete, statistical answers to these and other questions for each of the following ten crops: corn, cotton, hay, wheat, sugar, potatoes, oats, barley, rye, and buckwheat; as well as to explore the interdependence of the demands for such groups of related commodities as (1) sugar, tea, and coffee and (2) beef, mutton, and pork. In order, however, to understand the significance and the limitations of these answers, it is necessary that we first obtain a clear understanding of the meaning and properties of the theoretical law of demand.

I. DEVELOPMENT OF THE DEMAND CONCEPT

A century ago the law of demand—or, rather, the law of price which embraces it—was commonly stated as follows: "The price of goods varies directly as the quantity demanded and inversely as the quantity supplied."[1]

If it be permissible to translate this statement into mathematical symbols, it means that

$$(1.1) \qquad P \propto \frac{D}{S},$$

where P stands for price, D for quantity demanded, and S for quantity supplied.[2]

---

[1] Thus, Jean Baptiste Say: "Le prix d'une marchandise ne baisse-t-il pas en proportion de ce qu'elle est plus offerte, et ne monte-t-il pas en proportion de ce qu'elle est plus demandée?" (*Catéchisme d'économie politique* [4th ed.; Paris, 1835], chap. xi, p. 104).

[2] Dr. P. N. Rosenstein-Rodan calls to my attention the fact that the formula $P = D/S$ actually appears in the following early works: Pietro Verri, *Meditazioni sull'economia politica* (1st ed.; Livorno,

5

But what meaning can we give to the term "quantity demanded"? Obviously, "the quantity of a commodity demanded *at a certain price*." And what do we mean by the term "quantity supplied"? Obviously, "the quantity supplied *at a certain price*." A consumer cannot tell how much he will purchase, and a producer cannot tell how much he will sell, unless the price of the commodity in question is specified. The foregoing "law" taken at its face value now assumes this meaning: "Price varies directly as the quantity demanded, which depends on price, and inversely as the quantity supplied, which also depends on price"—clearly an ambiguous statement.

In 1838, Cournot brushed aside such "meaningless and sterile statements" as the foregoing and stated the law of demand in the following unambiguous terms: "Let us admit," he said, ". . . . that the sales or the annual demand D is, for each article, a particular function $F(p)$ of the price p of such article. To know the form of this function would be to know what we call the *law of demand* or *of sales*."[3]

1771); L. M. Valeriani, *Del prezzo delle case tutte mercatabili* (Bologna, 1806); *Operette concernenti quella parte del gius delle genti e pubblico che dicesi pubblica economia* (Bologna, 1815–24); and Francesco Fuoco, *Saggi economici* (Pisa, 1825–27). Verri's formula was reproduced without acknowledgment in the book of his friend, General Henry Lloyd, entitled *An Essay on the Theory of Money* (London, 1771), which was published anonymously.

[3] Augustin Cournot, *Researches into the Mathematical Principles of the Theory of Wealth*, trans. Bacon (New York, 1897), p. 47. While W. Whewell in 1829 anticipated Cournot in the clear recognition of the fact that "the increase in price . . . . must be a *function* of the defect of supply, and may be in this manner introduced into the calculation" (the italics are Whewell's), in his mathematical work he, nevertheless, satisfied himself with the assumption that "the increase of price is proportional to the deficiency of supply," using the term "proportional" in its strict mathematical sense. He justified his procedure on the ground that the special type of dependence seemed sufficiently accurate for small changes. See his "Mathematical Exposition of Some Doctrines of Political Economy," *Transactions of the Cambridge Philosophical Society*, III (1830), 201; "Mathematical Exposition of Some of the Leading Doctrines in Mr. Ricardo's 'Principles of Political Economy and Taxation,'" *ibid.*, IV (1833), 163–64. In a third paper entitled "Mathematical Exposition of Some Doctrines of Political Economy. Second Memoir" (*ibid.*, IX, Part I [1856], 128–49; "Third Memoir," Part II, pp. [1]–[7]), Whewell restated in mathematical form some of the theories of J. S. Mill and developed a criterion which serves essentially the same purpose as the coefficient of the elasticity of demand. The first memoir was read in 1829, the second in 1831, and the third in 1850.

My friend and colleague, Professor Jacob Viner, argues that some of the early nonmathematical economists also had the correct schedule notion of demand and supply and that, when they used expressions similar to those criticized by Cournot, they meant to say in nonmathematical terms that the quantity demanded is a decreasing function of price, and the quantity supplied is an increasing function of price, although they did not generally think of price as the independent variable. While this is undoubtedly true of some of them, as is evident from the existence of the much-quoted "Gregory King's Law," the fact remains that the schedule or functional concept of demand had a slow development; that even John Stuart Mill, whose *Principles* was published ten years after Cournot's *Recherches*, had no consistently clear notion of a demand function, although the concept is essentially at hand in his discussion of international values (*Principles*, Book III, chap. xviii); and that Cournot was the first economist to give the schedule concepts of demand and supply their exact mathematical formulation and to illustrate them graphically. In his second book on economics, *Principes de la*

Mathematically, Cournot's law is

$$(1.2) \qquad\qquad D = F(p) \, .$$

Alfred Marshall developed this concept at great length and popularized it.[4] It may, therefore, be called the Cournot-Marshall law of demand.

But how can we obtain the form of the function $F(p)$? Conceptually, this appears easy. We can ask a group of potential buyers how much of a given commodity each one of them would buy if the price were p'; how much each would buy if the price were p'', etc. We can then add up all the quantities that would be purchased at each price and thus obtain a demand schedule. The mathematical formula which describes or summarizes this schedule, or which expresses the relation between changes in price and corresponding changes in the quantity taken, is the function $F(p)$ of the price p of the article in question. It is generally assumed that $F(p)$ is a decreasing function of p; that is, that more will be bought when prices are low than when they are high.

In this hypothetical deduction of the law of demand we have tacitly assumed that each purchaser can tell us readily the amount of the commodity which he would purchase at each price in a unit of time. Is this in accordance with the facts? If, for example, our hypothetical potential buyer be a poor housewife, and if she be asked how many pounds of porterhouse steak she would buy in a week if the price were, say, sixty cents a pound, will she not also want to know the prices of the various cheaper cuts of meat, as well as the prices of potatoes, beans, and other foods? In general, is it possible for any buyer to make up his demand schedule for a commodity without knowing the prices of competing commodities? To ask these questions is to answer them. In general, a purchaser cannot decide how much he will buy of a given commodity

---

théorie des richesses, which was published in Paris in 1863, or twenty-five years after his *Recherches*, Cournot saw fit to criticize at even greater length the statements of the law of supply and demand that were current in his day. In his own words: "... quand les auteurs ont dit (d'une voix si unanime) que le prix est *en raison inverse de la quantité offerte*, ils ont énoncé une vérité triviale s'ils ont seulement voulu dire que l'offre avilit la marchandise, et un théorème manifestement faux, s'ils ont pris ces mots de *raison inverse* dans le sens précis qu'on leur donne en mathématiques. ...

"Et quand les auteurs ajoutent, avec la même unanimité, que le prix est *en raison directe de la quantité demandée*, ils disent une chose plus visiblement encore fausse ou dépourvue de sens: fausse, si l'on veut dire que le prix doublera ou triplera quand la quantité se débitera effectivement en quantité double ou triple; dépourvu de sens, si l'on n'entend par demande qu'un désir vague d'acheter la chose au cas qu'on puisse l'avoir à très-bon marché, ce qui conduit dans les encans tant de gens qui n'achètent pas" (*ibid.*, p. 94).

The vague and sterile statement of the "law" which Cournot criticized a century ago is still to be found in many modern textbooks on economics. It must be admitted, however, that the explanations which accompany this "law" sometimes remove something of its ambiguity. It appears that in the modern texts the inexact formulation is repeated more as a traditional formula than as a reasoned proposition.

[4] *Principles of Economics* (8th ed.; London, 1920), Book III. All references will be to this edition.

unless he knows not only the price of the commodity in question but also the prices of related (theoretically, of all) goods.

In mathematical terms this means that the quantity of any commodity purchased in a given interval of time must be expressed as a function not only of its price but also of all other prices, or

$$(1.3) \qquad\qquad D = f(p_1, p_2, p_3, \ldots, p_n) ,$$

where D is the quantity of the commodity demanded, p_1 its price, and p_2, $p_3, \ldots, p_n$ the prices of all other commodities.[5]

Equation (1.3) is due to Léon Walras, who, in 1873, was the first to write the demand for any commodity as a function of the prices of all commodities.[6] It is the law of demand of the Lausanne school.[7] It is only through such a general formulation that all prices may be determined by a system of simultaneous equations and that an insight may be had into the tremendous complexity of our price economy.

To realize the importance of this achievement, it is only necessary to recall that textbooks on economics are still being written by authors who are greatly troubled by the so-called problem of "circular reasoning" in price theory. Knowing that a change in the price of one commodity may bring about a change in the price of a second, and that the change in the price of the second commodity may in turn bring about a change in the price of a third, etc., these authors ask, "If the price of coal is a cause of the cost of transportation,

---

[5] Cournot, Walras, Pareto, and most other mathematical economists make the price of the commodity (or the system of prices considered) the independent variable in the demand equation. This practice is convenient in the treatment of general equilibrium, and it has the merit of suggesting that, *to the individual purchaser*, price fluctuations are independent of any action that he can take. All he can do is to adjust himself to them. However, Marshall and most English and American economists do not follow this practice. They make the quantity the independent variable in the demand equation. For the purpose of this exposition we shall follow the practice initiated by Cournot.

[6] *Eléments d'économie politique pure* (4th ed. ["édition définitive"]; Lausanne and Paris, 1900), pp. v–vii, and esp. n. 1, p. vii; see also pp. 122–33 and 208–15. (In 1926 a reprint of the 1900 edition was published, "revue et augmentée par l'auteur," but except for some minor changes it is identical with the earlier edition. See my paper "Marginal Productivity and the General Pricing Process," *Journal of Political Economy*, XXXVII [1929], 516.)

[7] On the difference between the ordinary and the general mathematical statement of the law of demand see Vilfredo Pareto, "Economie mathématique" in *Encyclopédie des sciences mathématiques*, Tome I, Vol. IV, Fasc. 4 (1911), pp. 593–94, 614–20, and esp. pp. 628–30; *Manuel d'économie politique* (Paris, 1909), pp. 579 ff.; Walras, *op. cit.*, pp. 122–24, 208–15; Gustav Cassel, *The Theory of Social Economy* (New York, 1924), chap. iv: "The Mechanism of Pricing"; Henry L. Moore, "A Theory of Economic Oscillations," *Quarterly Journal of Economics*, XLI (1926), 1–29. For a criticism of Pareto's *Manuel* which has a bearing on his treatment of the law of demand see Knut Wicksell's "Vilfredo Pareto's *Manuel d'économie politique*," *Zeitschrift für Volkwirtschaft, Sozialpolitik und Verwaltung*, XXII (1913), 132–51, and esp. p. 138. The relation between the distribution of income and the law of demand is discussed by Pareto in "La Legge della domanda," *Giornale degli economisti*, X (2d ser., January, 1895), 59–68.

how can the cost of transportation in turn be a cause of the price of coal?" To them the problem of pricing is thus insoluble. They do not seem to know that over fifty years ago Walras showed how the pricing problem is perfectly soluble. Walras' solution involves the substitution of the concept of mutual determination for that of causation.

The law of demand of the mathematical school (1.3) includes the Cournot-Marshall law of demand (1.2) as a special case. To obtain the latter from the former, we make use of the only valid nonexperimental method for keeping the "other things" constant, which may be stated as follows:· First, take all the factors (variables) into consideration; second, assign constant values to all variables except the price and the quantity of the commodity in question. This means that we must first determine the equation connecting the quantity demanded and all the prices and then assign constant values to all the variables except the two under consideration. And it may well be that the demand curve thus obtained will depend upon the magnitude of the constants which are assigned to the other variables.[8] Thus the demand curve for wheat when the price of rye is kept constant at seventy-five cents a bushel may be considerably different from what it is when the price of rye is kept constant at a dollar and fifty cents a bushel. Also, the relations between the variables may be such that a variation in one of them will involve a variation in one or more of the others.

The designation of the ordinary demand curve as a special case of the general demand function, from which it is derived by assigning constant values to all the variables except the price and quantity under consideration, marks a distinct improvement over the classical and neo-classical conception of this curve. The neo-classical economists, though they talked about other variables, never took the pains first to introduce them into their demand equation and then to assign them constant values. These economists never thought to raise the question whether it was always possible to keep other things constant, nor did they ever face the problem of the levels at which each of the "other things" might be kept constant. Theirs was the *ceteris paribus* postulate of classical fame, which must not be confused with the method of mathematical ignoration described above.

The means by which we were led from the vague and indefinite statement of the law of demand represented by (1.1) to the general formulation represented by (1.3) is the procedure of hypothetically asking each prospective purchaser in a given market, "How much will you buy of this commodity?" and of analyzing the probable replies. In this procedure we have assumed that all our "subjects" can give ready answers to our question, under the conditions

---

[8] In pure theory this interdependence *always* exists. However, the presence of other variables affects the slope as well as the location of the demand curve only when the general demand function (see eq. [1.3]) contains terms involving two or more of the variables.

explained above. As a matter of fact, this assumption is not generally valid. A good many, if not most, of our "subjects"—a term which may be stretched to include ourselves—will not be able to tell how much of a given commodity they would buy under given price conditions. And if they were compelled or induced to give an answer, it would not be a safe guide to their actual conduct. Most persons simply *do not know* how their consumption of a given commodity would be affected if prices were to move much above or below their accustomed range, and even within the accustomed range there may be a great deal of uncertainty. They must *experience* a given set of price relations in its proper institutional setting in order to make up their minds as to the quantities they will purchase. In short, the way to deduce the demand function for a commodity is to observe the behavior of consumers in masses in the market, i.e., to observe market transactions.[9]

But each market transaction represents a unique combination of circumstances—a "point" on our demand "curve" or surface. To obtain the probable form of the demand function, we must have numerous observations; and, in order to obtain the requisite number of observations, data covering a considerable period must, as a rule, be used. During the interval, however, important dynamic changes take place in the market. The pragmatic approach must, therefore, deal with variables (situations) which are functions of *time*. Our law of demand then becomes

$$(\text{1.4}) \qquad\qquad D = F(p_1, p_2, \ldots, p_n, t) \,,$$

where the p's have the same meaning as in (1.3), and t stands for time—a catch-all for those factors which change slowly and smoothly with time. If, in this dynamic law of demand, we give t a fixed value t_0, representing the particular date in which we happen to be interested, we obtain the Walrasian statical law of demand (1.3) as a special case. If we also give constant values to all the p's except p_1, we obtain the Cournot-Marshall statical law of demand as another special case. In any inductive investigation, however, the statical laws of demand may only be approached, never realized.

From the foregoing it is clear that by asking the question, "How much will you buy of this commodity?" and by analyzing the answers that may be given to it, we are compelled to abandon the earlier statements of the law of demand and to reach its most general formulation as represented by (1.4).

The method employed to deduce (1.4) serves as an illustration of what Professor Bridgman in his stimulating book, *The Logic of Modern Physics*, has called "the operational procedure" for determining the meaning of a concept.

[9] This is not to be understood as excluding scientific experiments in the study of demand.

After criticizing the view that the meaning of terms can be stated by referring to their intrinsic properties, he explains his own position in these words:

> The new attitude toward a concept is entirely different. We may illustrate by considering the concept of length: what do we mean by the length of an object? We evidently know what we mean by length if we can tell what the length of any and every object is, and for the physicist nothing more is required. To find the length of an object, we have to perform certain physical operations. The concept of length is therefore fixed when the operations by which length is measured are fixed: that is, the concept of length involves as much as and nothing more than the set of operations by which length is determined. In general, we mean by any concept nothing more than a set of operations: *the concept is synonymous with the corresponding set of operations.* If the concept is physical, as of length, the operations are actual physical operations, namely, those by which length is measured; or if the concept is mental, as of mathematical continuity, the operations are mental operations, namely those by which we determine whether a given aggregate of magnitudes is continuous. It is not intended to imply that there is a hard and fast division between physical and mental concepts, or that one kind of concept does not always contain an element of the other; this classification of concept is not important for our future considerations.
>
> We must demand that the set of operations equivalent to any concept be a unique set, for otherwise there are possibilities of ambiguity in practical applications which we cannot admit.[10]

And again:

> If a specific question has meaning, it must be possible to find operations by which an answer may be given to it. It will be found in many cases that the operations cannot exist, and the question therefore has no meaning. For instance, it means nothing to ask whether a star is at rest or not.[11]

As economists we will do well to study the implications of Professor Bridgman's distinction between concepts which are defined in terms of *operations* and those which are defined in terms of *properties* of things. Although we may not always succeed in drawing a distinct line of demarcation between the two concepts in economics, and although we may be unwilling to grant, on general philosophical grounds, that the distinction is valid for pure mental concepts such as mathematical continuity, as Professor Bridgman claims,[12] the very attempt to make such a distinction between operational and nonoperational concepts will clarify our own thinking; for some of the most important of the concepts with which we work are definitely of the latter variety. Thus, utility is

[10] P. W. Bridgman, *The Logic of Modern Physics* (New York, 1927), pp. 5–6. (Italics are his.) I am grateful to Professor Bridgeman and to his publishers, the Macmillan Company, for permission to quote.

[11] *Ibid.*, p. 28.

[12] For a discussion of this question see the paper by Professor Edwin Burtt, "Two Basic Issues in the Problem of Meaning and of Truth," in *Essays in Honor of John Dewey* (New York, 1929), esp. p. 72.

commonly defined as the "property" which a good has to satisfy a want. Similarly, "the representative firm" is defined by Marshall as

one which has had a fairly long life, and fair success, which is managed with normal ability, and which has normal access to the economies, external and internal, which belong to that aggregate volume of production; account being taken of the class of goods produced, the conditions of marketing them and the economic environment generally.[13]

As long as a concept remains nonoperational, it is vain to hope that it will yield to the quantitative approach. The restatement and extension of the earliest concept of demand into forms which have meaning in terms of operations, which has been attempted in the foregoing pages, is the first step in the direction of the derivation of concrete, statistical laws of demand.

II. THE PLACE OF DEMAND IN THE MODERN THEORY OF UTILITY

The "mental experiments" by which we have deduced the general law of demand (1.3) tell us, however, very little about the form of the function and the interrelations of the independent variables. (This applies a fortiori to the more complex equation [1.4].) True, we have assumed that, when all the other variables are fixed, the quantity demanded decreases as the price increases—an assumption which is preferred by some economists because it appears to have its roots in experience and is free, therefore, from certain "metaphysical notions" which have no place in a scientific economics. But experience also yields instances in which the quantity demanded increases with an increase in its price, i.e., in which the demand curve is positively inclined. Furthermore, experience tells us very little about the other properties of the two types of curves. We must, therefore, consider the questions: (1) What are the conditions which give rise to each type of curve? (2) What are the other characteristics of these curves? To throw light on these questions, it is necessary to make certain simplifying assumptions (hypotheses) about the market behavior of individuals, work out the implications and consequences of these assumptions, and then observe to what extent they are justified by the actual behavior of prices and quantities. Let us make the simplifying assumption that the market behavior of human beings is dictated by considerations of utility and see what light this throws on the form of the demand and supply functions.

First it is necessary to assure the reader who may have a "complex" against utility analysis in economics that the theory with which we are immediately concerned is not, in all probability, that which he has in mind. It does not necessarily assume that utility is a measurable quantity; it does not attempt to compare the utilities (satisfactions) of different persons; and it does not restore metaphysical entities previously discarded. In fact, it is not, or need not be, a subjective theory at all. Its keystone is the notion of indifference curves,

---

[13] *Op. cit.*, p. 317.

with the related notion of index functions—concepts which can be defined in terms of operations, and which have a clear, objective, measurable basis. The development and application of these concepts is one of Pareto's fundamental contributions to economic science.[14]

A. INDIFFERENCE CURVES AND INDICES OF UTILITY

The notion of indifference curves, with the related notions of contract curves and lines of preference, was introduced by F. Y. Edgeworth, who was the first to write the utility of a commodity as a function not only of the quantity of it possessed but also of the quantities of other commodities.[15] Edgeworth started out with the notion of utility, which he assumed to be a known and measurable quantity, and deduced from it the notion of indifference curves. Pareto[16] inverted the problem: starting out with the notion of indifference curves, *a notion given directly by experience*, he showed how we can, with their aid, proceed to determine economic equilibrium and to obtain certain functions which will represent ophelimity (utility) if it exists. In any event, we can obtain indices of ophelimity.

Edgeworth's procedure may be illustrated as follows: Let x and y represent, respectively, the quantities of two commodities (X) and (Y) possessed or consumed by an individual in a unit of time. Let $U = F(x, y)$ represent the total utility or ophelimity derived from any combination of x and y. Then $U = F(x, y)$ may be thought of as a surface, U denoting the length of the ordinate drawn from any point on the xy-plane to the surface. This surface, which need not extend indefinitely over the plane, is usually concave downward like a dome, with a single maximum point.

The partial derivatives

(2.1)
$$\frac{\partial F}{\partial x}, \quad \frac{\partial F}{\partial y},$$

[14] The nonmathematical reader may now find it more convenient to turn to Sec. III, C, p. 50, where the main argument is taken up again, returning to the omitted pages for such definitions, equations, and conclusions, as he may need in order to follow the main argument.

[15] *Mathematical Psychics* (London, 1881). One advantage of the indifference-curve approach, which will not be developed in the text, "is that it is applicable to the particular cases of imperfect competition; where the conceptions of *demand and supply at a price* are no longer appropriate" (*ibid.*, p. 31).

[16] *Manuel*, § 32, pp. 263–65, and the Mathematical Appendix. As a matter of fact, Professor Irving Fisher anticipated Pareto in recognizing the weak point in Edgeworth's assumption and in seeking to give utility an objective basis. In Part II of his "Mathematical Investigations in the Theory of Value and Prices" (*Transactions of Connecticut Academy of Arts and Sciences*, IX, Part I [New Haven, 1892], 1-124 [a reprint of it was published in New Haven in 1926]), he developed a theory of indifference curves which is very similar to Pareto's theory of choice, but Professor Fisher did not develop the implications of his theory as fully and as thoroughly as did Pareto.

In his first works, the *Cours* (1896–97), and the articles in the *Giornale degli economisti* (1892–97), Pareto used the notion of utility or ophelimity. In his *Manuale di economia politica* (Milan, 1907) the concept of ophelimity is replaced by that of an index of utility. In his *Manuel*, p. 659, the concept is generalized still further. For a summary of his theory see his article "Economie mathématique," *op. cit.*, pp. 591–640.

will be designated, respectively, as the *marginal degrees of utility* (or, more briefly, as the *degrees of utility*) of the two commodities. Each of these quantities may be a function of both x and y. The quantities

$$(2.2) \qquad \frac{\partial F}{\partial x}\, dx\,, \qquad \frac{\partial F}{\partial y}\, dy\,,$$

will be designated as the *marginal utilities* of the two commodities.[17]

Let the surface $U = F(x, y)$ be cut by planes parallel to the plane of the x- and y-axes. Each intersection forms a curve which may be called an *indifference* curve. It is the locus of points representing all possession- or consumption-combinations of x and y which have a given total utility for the individual. In Figure 1 the number attached to each curve represents the amount of this utility. The curves may be looked upon as contour lines, the numbers attached to them being the elevations above sea-level (zero utility). The difference between any two numbers is the difference between the total utilities of the combinations in question.

Analytically, the differential equation of an indifference curve is

$$(2.3) \qquad \frac{\partial F}{\partial x}\, dx + \frac{\partial F}{\partial y}\, dy = dU = 0\,.$$

Pareto argues that the total utility function is not known and may not even exist. What we do know or can obtain are the indifference curves. Thus, we may ask a person who possesses, say, 100 apples and 100 nuts, "How many nuts would just induce you to part with 10 apples? with 20 apples?" etc. "How many apples would just compensate you for the loss of 10 nuts? 20 nuts?" etc. The responses of the individual will give us the various combinations of apples and nuts which give him the same satisfaction as the possession of 100 apples and 100 nuts. Let the combinations be:

Nuts	160	140	120	100	80	60
Apples	70	80	90	100	140	180

---

[17] It is desirable to have different expressions for the derivative $\dfrac{\partial F}{\partial x}$ of the total utility surface $F(x, y)$, and for the differential increment $\dfrac{\partial F}{\partial x}\, dx$. The terms "marginal degree of utility" and "marginal utility" are due to Alfred Marshall (*op. cit.*, Mathematical Appendix, n. 1). W. Stanley Jevons refers to the first as the "degree of utility" and more commonly as the "final degree of utility" (*Theory of Political Economy* [4th ed.; 1924], pp. 50–51 and 98–99); he gives no name for the second quantity. However, as Marshall correctly observes, "there is room for doubt as to which mode of expression is the more convenient: no question of principle is involved in the decision."

It is also desirable to introduce a corresponding distinction in the theory of cost. If $y = \varphi(x)$ be the total money cost of producing x units, then I suggest that by analogy $\dfrac{dy}{dx} \equiv \dfrac{d\varphi(x)}{dx} = \varphi'(x)$ should be referred to as the "marginal degree of cost," and $\dfrac{dy}{dx}\, dx \equiv \dfrac{d\varphi(x)}{dx}\, dx = \varphi'(x)dx$ as the "marginal cost."

Similar series may be obtained by starting out with another original combination, say, 200 apples and 200 nuts. Such series are called *indifference* series.[18]

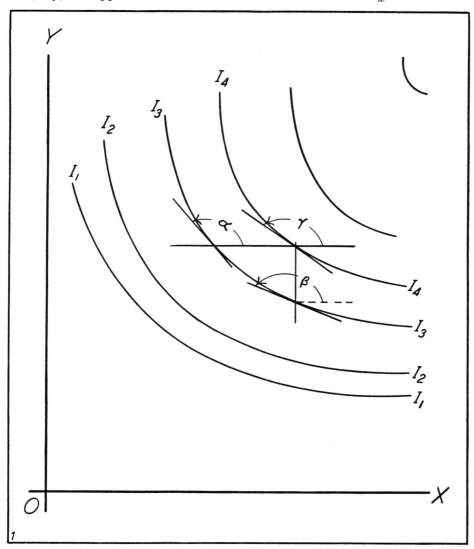

FIG. I.—A typical indifference map of a consumer

If the quantities of the commodities can be assumed to vary by infinitesimal amounts, the indifference series may be represented by indifference curves. A

[18] A psychological experiment designed to determine the shape of a simple indifference curve was conducted in 1930 by the writer's colleague, Professor L. L. Thurstone, of the department of psychology. See his article on "The Indifference Function," *Journal of Social Psychology*, II (1931), 139–67.

few typical indifference curves are shown in Figure 1, but the numbers attached to these curves no longer necessarily measure utility. *They are simply indices.*

Analytically, the new conception may be stated as follows: Instead of the utility surface $U = F(x, y)$, we have a surface of an *index* of utility corresponding to any combination of x and y,

$$(2.4) \qquad I = \varphi(x, y) \,.$$

By putting $I = 1, 2, 3, \ldots$, successively, we obtain the indifference curves $1, 2, 3, \ldots$, respectively. All that they show is that one series of combinations, say that marked by 4, is preferred by the person in question to that marked by any lower figure such as 3 or 2. The difference between any two figures does not necessarily *measure* differences in utility.

That differences between the indices of two indifference curves do not necessarily measure differences between utilities, or that a knowledge of the indifference curves does not always permit the deduction of the utility surface (if it exists), is evident from the fact that there are any number of utility surfaces whose horizontal sections, when projected on the xy-plane, form one and the same family of indifference curves. Since in practice we know only the projections, i.e., the indifference curves, the index surface I must remain somewhat arbitrary. That is, when we have obtained one system of indices

$$(2.5) \qquad I = \varphi(x, y, z, \ldots) \,,$$

we have an infinity of others, given by the equation

$$(2.6) \qquad I = F(\varphi) \,,$$

where F is an arbitrary function, restricted only by the condition that F' must be positive. Pareto calls $F(\varphi)$ an index function (*fonction-indice*) of utility.

The fact that it is, in general, impossible to determine the utility surfaces does not, however, prevent us from solving the problem of economic equilibrium. Indifference curves, which might be obtained by experiment, are sufficient (together with the other well-known conditions) to determine the various unknowns of the problem.

In the modern mathematical theory of exchange, the index function with its indifference curves takes the place formerly occupied by the total utility function. There is, however, no general unequivocal correspondence between the indifference curves (or the *varieties*[19] in hyperspace, in the case of four or

---

[19] "Varieties are to be regarded as generalizations of curves and surfaces, a curve being a variety of one dimension, while a surface is a variety of two dimensions" (E. P. Lane, *Projective Differential Geometry of Curves and Surfaces* [Chicago, 1932], p. 256).

more commodities) which are (in theory) given by experience, and the utilities which the individual enjoys from the consumption of the several commodities. This correspondence does exist—abstracting from a scale constant—(1) when the order of consumption of the various commodities is indifferent, and the utility of each commodity depends only on the quantity of that commodity; or (2) when the pleasure is different, depending on the order of consumption, and it is possible to determine what that order is going to be.

There remain two cases: (1) when the order of consumption is indifferent, and the utility of each commodity depends on the quantities of all the other goods; (2) when the order of consumption influences the pleasure but is not known. In these cases there exists no such unequivocal correspondence between the indifference curves and the utilities. In the first case only the index function and not the utility surface can be obtained from the indifference curves. In the second neither the utility function nor the index function even exists so long as the path to be taken is not determined; so long as it is not known, for example, whether the individual will eat his dessert at the beginning or at the end of his dinner.[20] However, when there are only two commodities, the function I always exists, whether the order of consumption be indifferent or not.

What, then, can be done about the difficulty presented by the order of consumption which appears to undermine the very basis of our theory? It seems to me that an answer to this question is essentially at hand in the fact that economic theory can approximate the facts of economic experience only if there is a routine in economic affairs (including the routine of change); when there is no routine, there can be no economic law. But if it is reasonable to assume a routine, is it not also reasonable to assume that the order in which the various courses of a dinner are consumed is known? It appears, therefore, that too much attention has been attached in utility analysis to the problem of the order of consumption. Although it was introduced into economics by the eminent mathematician, Professor Vito Volterra,[21] and although it was discussed at length by Pareto, it has little or no significance in an economy dominated by routine. Professor Edwin B. Wilson, following an entirely different line of argument, even goes so far as to say that "the whole discussion

[20] Pareto, *Manuel*, Appendix, pp. 539–57, and esp. § 19. For a recent critical discussion of the problem of index functions, see G. C. Evans, *Mathematical Introduction to Economics* (New York, 1930), chaps. xi and xii, and his paper "The Role of Hypothesis in Economic Theory," *Science* (N.S.), LXXV, No. 1943 (1932), 321–24; and my review of Evans' book in the *Journal of the American Statistical Association*, XXVI (1931), 484–91.

[21] See Volterra's review of Pareto's *Manuale di economia politica* in the *Giornale degli economisti*, XXXII (2d ser., 1906), 296–301, and Pareto's discussion of this point in the same journal, XXXIII (2d ser., 1906), 15–30, and in the Mathematical Appendix to his *Manuel*, esp. pp. 546–57.

of the order of integration, a point that naturally occurs to the mathematician, can be thrown out of court by the economist."[22]

A still stronger reason for neglecting the difficulty presented by the order of consumption is that there is generally an interval of time between the act of purchase and the act of consumption. All goods are essentially capital goods, i.e., they yield services over long or short intervals of time. Thus, even such a consumer's good as bread may be looked upon as yielding a service over a period of time, no matter how brief. When we buy goods, we buy the right to enjoy or to consume their services at some later time in the manner most agreeable to us. Now, while the order of consumption of the various services may have an influence on the pleasure derived from them, it does not follow that the order of purchase will have such an influence. And from the point of view of the theory of exchange it is purchase and sale rather than consumption that are of primary interest.

We shall assume, therefore, that the order of consumption is known and that, consequently, the index of utility $I = \varphi(x, y, z, \ldots)$ always exists.

B. PROPERTIES OF THE INDICES OF UTILITY
AND THE INDIFFERENCE CURVES

The properties of the index function I and of the indifference curves have not as yet been definitely established. Following Pareto,[23] we may, nevertheless, list some of them as having a high degree of probability.

Experience suggests that within the region in which we are generally interested, the index function $I = \varphi(x, y)$ is such that it increases with an increase in any of the quantities, or

$$(2.7) \qquad \varphi_x > 0, \qquad \varphi_y > 0,$$

where φ_x, φ_y, denote the first derivatives of φ with respect to x, y, respectively. *This is the first property of the index.* It means that total utility increases with an increase in any of the quantities x, y, consumed or possessed.

To obtain the other properties of the index function, it is convenient first to consider the properties of the indifference curves. We shall list four:

1. First, we know from experience that in general it is necessary to compen-

[22] See Wilson's review of Pareto's *Manuel* in the *Bulletin of the American Mathematical Society*, XVIII (1912), 469. Professor Wilson might have added that Pareto was of the same opinion. See *Manuel*, pp. 249–51.

[23] *Manuel*, pp. 572–79. For a discussion and illustrations of the indifference curves for various commodities—completing, competing, and independent—see chap. iv of the *Manuel*, as well as A. L. Bowley, *The Mathematical Groundwork of Economics* (Oxford, 1924), pp. 14–18; Fisher, *op. cit.*, pp. 64–78; R. G. D. Allen, "The Nature of Indifference Curves," *Review of Economic Studies*, I (1934), 110–21; and J. R. Hicks and R. G. D. Allen, "A Reconsideration of the Theory of Value," *Economica*, XIV (1934), 52–76 and 196–219.

sate an individual for a diminution in his stock of (Y) by increasing his stock of (X). Hence, if x and y are the coordinates of an indifference curve, we must have

(2.8)
$$\frac{dy}{dx} < 0 \, .$$

This is the first characteristic of indifference curves.

2. Subject to only a few exceptions, the variable quantity dy which one is disposed to give, along a curve of indifference, for a constant quantity dx, diminishes as x increases. We have, then, for the second characteristic of indifference curves,

(2.9)
$$\frac{d^2y}{dx^2} > 0 \, ,$$

which means that the negative slope $\frac{dy}{dx}$ of the indifference curve increases (or that its absolute value decreases) as x increases. The geometric interpretation of this condition is that the curve is concave upward.

3. But dy decreases more slowly as x increases. We have then—always subject to a few exceptions—as the third characteristic of indifference curves,

(2.10)
$$\frac{d^3y}{dx^3} < 0 \, .$$

4. For a large class of commodities the indifference curves are such that, when we pass from one curve to another,

(2.11)
$$\delta_x \frac{dy}{dx} > 0 \, , \qquad \delta_y \frac{dy}{dx} < 0 \, ,$$

where δ_x is the variation in $\frac{dy}{dx}$ along a line parallel to the axis of x, and δ_y is the variation in $\frac{dy}{dx}$ along a line parallel to the axis of y. The first of the conditions (2.11) means that, as we pass from one curve to another where the quantity x is greater and the quantity y is the same, the ratio $\frac{dy}{dx}$, which is negative, increases (its absolute value decreases). The second of these conditions means that, as we pass from one curve to another where the quantity of y is greater and the quantity of x is the same, the ratio $\frac{dy}{dx}$, which is negative, decreases (its absolute value increases).

The meaning of the characteristics (2.11) may be illustrated by the following example. Suppose that an individual has 100 apples (X) and 100 nuts (Y)

and that, when he proceeds *to another indifference curve*, he has 200 apples and 100 nuts. If the individual is such that the increase in the stock of apples does not decrease his desire for more nuts, he will be disposed to give more apples for one nut (and fewer nuts for one apple) in the second position than in the first.

In Figure 1 this is illustrated geometrically by the inequalities:

$$\tan \gamma > \tan \alpha ,$$

$$\tan \gamma < \tan \beta .$$

With these four properties of the indifference curves in mind, we may proceed to consider the characteristics of the indices of utility.

The first characteristic of the index has already been mentioned. It is given by

(2.7) $$\varphi_x > 0 , \qquad \varphi_y > 0 .$$

That these derivatives must all have the same sign can also be deduced from (2.8). In the index

$$I = \varphi(x, y) ,$$

y is an implicit function of x, and, consequently, by the fundamental theorem of implicit functions,

(2.12) $$\frac{dy}{dx} = -\frac{\varphi_x}{\varphi_y} .$$

Since the left term of this equation is negative, by virtue of (2.8), the right term is also negative, and φ_x, φ_y must have the same sign. We have already assumed that the sign is positive.

The second characteristic of the index of utility is that

(2.13) $$\begin{cases} \dfrac{\varphi_{xx}\,\varphi_y - \varphi_{xy}\,\varphi_x}{\varphi_y^2} < 0 , \\[2em] \dfrac{\varphi_{yy}\,\varphi_x - \varphi_{xy}\,\varphi_y}{\varphi_y^2} < 0 , \end{cases}$$

where φ_{xx} stands for the second derivative of φ with respect to x; φ_{yy} for the second derivative of φ with respect to y, etc. This characteristic may be obtained from the inequalities (2.11) by substituting therein the value of $\dfrac{dy}{dx}$ derived from (2.12). This gives

(2.14) $$-\frac{\partial}{\partial x}\left(\frac{\varphi_x}{\varphi_y}\right) > 0 , \qquad -\frac{\partial}{\partial y}\left(\frac{\varphi_x}{\varphi_y}\right) < 0 ,$$

which, when expanded in accordance with the rule for differentiating a quotient, leads to (2.13).

In the very important case where φ_x depends only on x, φ_y only on y, etc., we have $\varphi_{xy} = 0$, and, since φ_x and φ_y are positive, the inequalities (2.13) become

(2.15) $$\varphi_{xx} < 0, \qquad \varphi_{yy} < 0.$$

This special case of the second characteristic of the indices is the mathematical statement of the well-known principle of decreasing marginal degree of utility. When $\varphi_{xy} < 0$, (2.15) must hold if (2.13) is to be satisfied. But, as will be shown later, this is the case for which (2.13) does not necessarily hold. When $\varphi_{xy} > 0$, we cannot specify the sign of φ_{xx} and φ_{yy}. It follows that we cannot assert the universal validity of the principle of decreasing marginal degree of utility. Though it is a fundamental principle, it cannot be taken as an axiom.

From inequality (2.9) it follows that

(2.16) $$\frac{d}{dx}\left(-\frac{\varphi_x}{\varphi_y}\right) = -\frac{\varphi_y^2\varphi_{xx} - 2\varphi_x\varphi_y\varphi_{xy} + \varphi_x^2\varphi_{yy}}{\varphi_y^3} > 0.$$

This is not, however, a new condition on the index of utility, for it can be obtained from the inequalities (2.13) by multiplying the first by (φ_y/φ_y), the second by (φ_x/φ_y), and then adding.[24]

An important property of the conditions (2.12), (2.13), and (2.16) is that they are invariant with respect to sign under the transformation of φ into $I = F(\varphi)$ and thus are valid for any index of utility.

Though the foregoing conditions on the indifference curves and indices of utility have been derived on the assumption that there are but two commodities, they are also valid for three or more commodities $(x, y, z, \ldots)$. All that we have to do is to write $\frac{\partial}{\partial x}$ for $\frac{d}{dx}$ in (2.12) and (2.16). On the surface this change makes the left-hand member of (2.16) identical with (2.14). There

[24] It should be noted that (2.16) is somewhat more general than (2.13), for, while (2.16) can be deduced from (2.13), the reverse is not the case—(2.13) cannot be deduced from (2.16).

Pareto also gives, as a third characteristic of the index of utility, the inequalities

$$\varphi_{xxx} > 0, \qquad \varphi_{yyy} > 0,$$

stating that this condition can be derived from the inequality (2.10) when $\varphi_{xy} = 0$. He gives no proof of this statement, and I have been unable to construct one. The only condition I have been able to derive from (2.10) and $\varphi_{xy} = 0$ is the following complicated inequality:

$$\frac{1}{\varphi_y^5}[-\varphi_y^4\varphi_{xxx} - 3\varphi_x\varphi_y^2\varphi_{xx}\varphi_{yy} - 3\varphi_x^3\varphi_{yy}^2 + \varphi_x^3\varphi_y\varphi_{yyy}] < 0,$$

and it does not seem that Pareto's conclusion follows from it.

is, however, an essential difference between the operations indicated by the two partial derivatives which is masked by the identity of the symbols employed.[25] Geometrically, the difference between the two operations is that in (2.13) we are considering the rate of change of the slope as it is moved along a line parallel to one of the axes, as in Figure 1, while in (2.16) we are considering the rate of change of the slope as it is moved along a given indifference curve.

C. CLASSIFICATION OF COMMODITIES

The characteristics of the indices of utility enable us easily to classify commodities according to their relations in consumption. We may distinguish three groups, according as the values of $\varphi_{xy} \gtreqless 0$:

1. The commodities $(X), (Y), (Z), \ldots$, are said to be *independent* in consumption if φ_x (index of the marginal degree of utility of x) depends only on x, φ_y depends only on y, etc. Then we have

$$(2.17) \qquad \varphi_{xy} = 0, \quad \varphi_{xz} = 0, \ldots, \varphi_{yz} = 0, \ldots$$

2. The commodities $(X), (Y), (Z), \ldots$, are said to be *completing* (complementary) in consumption if the *same quantity* of any one of them yields a higher marginal degree of utility when the commodities are consumed jointly than when they are consumed separately. Thus, within certain limits, the marginal degree of utility of the same amount of bread is increased as we increase the quantity of butter. For such commodities we have, in general,

$$(2.18) \qquad \varphi_{xy} > 0, \quad \varphi_{xz} > 0, \ldots, \varphi_{yz} > 0, \ldots$$

A very large number of economic goods have approximately this characteristic.

3. The commodities $(X), (Y), (Z), \ldots$, are said to be *competing* (rivals) in consumption if the same quantity of any one of them yields a lower marginal degree of utility when they are consumed jointly than when they are consumed separately. For this very important group, which has received the special attention of Menger and the other members of the Austrian school, we have

$$(2.19) \qquad \varphi_{xy} < 0, \quad \varphi_{xz} < 0, \ldots, \varphi_{yz} < 0, \ldots$$

Examples of competing commodities are butter and oleomargarine, wine and beer.[26]

[25] Mathematically, the difference may be stated as follows: The expression $-(\varphi_y/\varphi_x)$ is a function of $x, y, z, \ldots$. Call it $G(x, y, z, \ldots)$. Then in (2.12) we consider all the variables $(x, y, z, \ldots)$ independent. The partial derivatives of G give (2.13). In (2.16), on the other hand, we consider y as a function of x and all the other variables as independent. That is, we differentiate partially $G[x, y(x), z, \ldots]$ and obtain (2.16).

[26] For corresponding criteria of independent, completing, and competing goods in terms of the properties of the demand functions see my "Interrelations of Demand," *Journal of Political Economy*, XLI (1933), 468–512, and chaps. xviii and xix.

Since the publication of this paper, Dr. J. R. Hicks, Professor Harold Hotelling, Mr. R. G. D. Allen, and Dr. P. N. Rosenstein-Rodan have called my attention to the fact that, if we cannot as-

For independent and completing goods, the characteristic (2.13) always holds. The same characteristic also holds for competing goods, except, possibly, when one or the other of the commodities is possessed almost to satiation, i.e., when φ_x or φ_y is close to zero.

In the case of independent and completing goods, a commodity made up of fixed proportions of (X), (Y), (Z), . . . —say, a sandwich or a cocktail—may be considered as a simple commodity with respect to the characteristic (2.15). For this group of goods (2.15) is equivalent to

$$(2.20) \quad d^2\varphi \equiv d(\varphi_x dx + a\varphi_y dx + \beta\varphi_z dx + \ldots)$$
$$\equiv (\varphi_{xx} + a^2\varphi_{yy} + \ldots + 2a\varphi_{xy} + \ldots + 2a\beta\varphi_{yz} + \ldots)dx^2 < 0 ,$$

where a, β, . . . , are the fixed proportions defined by the relations $y = ax$, $z = \beta x$, ... This inequality leads to new characteristics of the indices of utility, one of which involves the satisfaction of (2.15) for each of the component commodities.[27]

---

sume that utility is measurable, then neither the form nor the sign of φ_{xy} is determinate. For, suppose that we have only an index of utility $I = \varphi(x, y)$. Then, by (2.6) we have an infinity of other indices, given by $I = F[\varphi(x, y)]$. But,

$$\frac{\partial^2 I}{\partial x \partial y} = \varphi_{xy} F'(\varphi) + \varphi_x \varphi_y F''(\varphi) ,$$

and this expression varies with the form assumed for $F(\varphi)$. I shall treat the problems raised by this difficulty in the chapters on the interrelations of demand. For the remainder of the present chapter I shall assume that F is a linear function of φ. This is equivalent to the assumption that utility is measurable (see Pareto, *Manuel*, pp. 545–46; O. Lange, "The Determinateness of the Utility Function," *Review of Economic Studies*, I [1934], 218–25; E. H. Phelps Brown, H. Bernardelli, and O. Lange, "Notes on the Determinateness of the Utility Function," *ibid.*, II [1934], 66–77). The suggestion that F be restricted to a linear function of φ was also made by M. Georges Lutfalla, of Paris.

Criteria for independent, completing, and competing goods may also be deduced from a consideration of the changes in the *ratios* of the marginal degrees of utility of any two commodities. See the later chapters on the interrelations of demand; Pareto, *Manuel*. pp. 573–74; W. E. Johnson, "Pure Theory of Utility Curves," *Economic Journal*, XXIII (1913), 483–513; Allen, "The Foundations of a Mathematical Theory of Exchange," *Economica*, XII (1932), 221–22; "A Comparison between Different Definitions of Complementary and Competitive Goods," *Econometrica*, II (1934), 168–75; and "Nachfragefunktionen für Güter mit korreliertem Nutzen," *Zeitschrift für Nationalœkonomie*, V, Heft 4 (1934), 486–506; Hicks and Allen, *op. cit.*, pp. 52–76 and 196–219.

[27] See Pareto, *Manuel*, Mathematical Appendix, §§ 47–48, 121–25, and "Economie mathématique," *loc. cit.*, p. 613. In each of these references there are troublesome misprints. In § 47, p. 576, of the *Manuel*, eqs. (63) and (64) should be interchanged. In the article, "Economie mathématique," the last inequality in eq. (25), p. 613, should be reversed, and also φ_{xx} should be omitted from the denominator of the expression given for $\dfrac{\partial m}{\partial p_y}$ in § 35, p. 630.

The second-order condition (2.20) is of particular importance in the consideration of the stability of the equilibrium of exchange. Professor Harold Hotelling has also used a similar condition to derive interesting theorems in connection with the incidence of taxation. See his "Edgeworth's Taxation Paradox and the Nature of Demand and Supply Functions," *Journal of Political Economy*, XL (1932), 577–616.

In practice there are no very clear lines of demarcation separating one class of commodities from another. The three classes merge into one another almost imperceptibly in the market. Thus the same two commodities may be completing to one individual, and competing or independent to another. Furthermore, the same individual may consider the same two commodities as completing under one set of conditions and competing or independent under another. Nevertheless, this classification will turn out to be very useful in later investigations. As will be shown in the chapters on "Interrelations of Demand,"[28] the classification of commodities according as $\varphi_{xy} \gtreqless 0$, taken in conjunction with certain other relations of pure theory, yield conditions on the demand functions for related goods which have interesting and significant applications.

D. THE EQUILIBRIUM OF EXCHANGE

Equilibrium exists when there is a balance between the desires of the individuals, on the one hand, and the obstacles which must be overcome to satisfy them, on the other.

The term "obstacles" is used by Pareto to designate any impediments—social, natural, or economic—to the satisfaction of a want. Thus, the Eighteenth Amendment to the Constitution and the Volstead Act constituted a legal or social obstacle to many persons. Again, the fact that a commodity cannot be produced except by using up other commodities is a physical obstacle. Also, if it is desired to divide a given quantity among several individuals, the fact that this quantity is fixed constitutes an economic obstacle. The best known of all obstacles is, however, the fact that we cannot get something for nothing—the truth of which was forcibly brought home to several millions of Americans by the stock-market crash of October, 1929. This fact finds its general expression in *price*. Equilibrium, then, exists when the intensity of the desires of individuals is exactly balanced by the prices which must be paid to satisfy them.

I. ONE INDIVIDUAL, TWO COMMODITIES

As a simple illustration of the balance between desires and obstacles, we may consider the equilibrium of an individual who has x_0 units of the commodity (X) and y_0 units of the commodity (Y), and who wishes to acquire additional units of (Y). Of course, y_0 may be equal to zero. Let the initial quantities (x_0, y_0) be the coordinates of the point O' in Figure 2, and let the intensity of desire of the individual for every combination of the quantities x and y be represented by the indices attached to the indifference curves in the same diagram.

If there were no obstacles, the individual would proceed to the highest in-

[28] See chap. xviii, Sec. III and chap. xix, Sec. IV.

difference curve (or to the highest point M on the utility surface). That is to say, he would not necessarily give up any of (X) but would acquire as much of

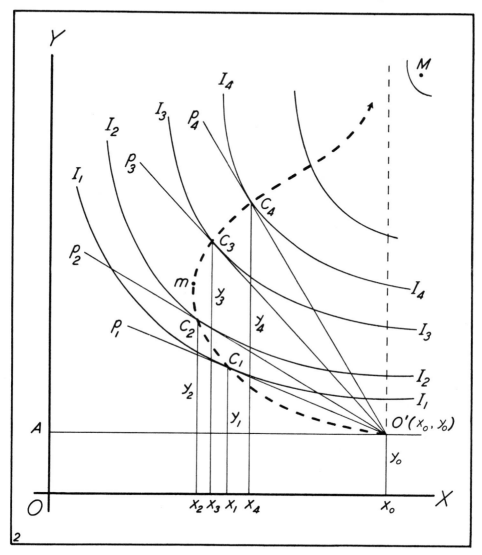

FIG. 2.—An individual's equilibrium purchases of two commodities under various price conditions and his curve of supply and demand.

both commodities as would be necessary to satisfy completely his desires for them. But this is possible only when both commodities are *free goods;* and the problem then ceases to have economic significance. It becomes an economic problem only when an obstacle is introduced which prevents the individual from reaching the highest point M on the utility surface.[29]

Let us suppose, then, that the obstacle consists of the fact that the individual is constrained to move along the straight line $O'p_1$. Where will he stop? That is, how much of (X) will he give up, and how much of (Y) will he receive? The answer is that he will stop at the point c_1, at which the line $O'p_1$ is tangent to the indifference curve I_1; for this is the highest point on the utility surface that he can reach under the circumstances. The coordinates (x_1, y_1) of that point show that he will give up (supply) $x_1 - x_0$ units[30] of (X), retaining x_1 units in his possession, and that he will receive (demand) $y_1 - y_0$ units of (Y). When he has effected this exchange, his utility is at a relative maximum. This is shown graphically by the fact that the index I_1, on which point c_1 is located, is the highest index which the individual can reach under the circumstances. To move away from this point—the motion still being confined to the path $O'p_1$— is to proceed to a lower index. The point c_1 is, then, the equilibrium position of the individual. At that point the intensity of his desire for the two articles is exactly balanced by the obstacle which he must overcome. The geometrical illustration of this fact is that at the point c_1 the slope of the obstacle (path) and that of the indifference curve are equal to each other.

Suppose next that the path which the individual is constrained to follow is $O'p_2$. Where will he stop? By the same reasoning it follows that he will stop at c_2, the point at which the new obstacle is tangent to an indifference curve. At this point his utility will be at a relative maximum under the new conditions. The coordinates (x_2, y_2) of this point show that he will give up (supply) $x_2 - x_0$ units of (X) and receive (demand) $y_2 - y_0$ units of (Y).

Similarly, it can be shown that, if the obstacles were $O'p_3$, or $O'p_4$, the equilibrium points would be c_3 or c_4, respectively. At each of these points the obstacle is tangent to an indifference curve. At each of these points the utility of the individual is a relative maximum.

If we connect these points of tangency, we obtain the curve $O'c_1c_2c_3c_4$. The point of intersection of this curve with the path the individual is compelled to follow gives the quantity of (Y) demanded and the quantity of (X) supplied. The former is equal to $(y-y_0)$, the difference between the ordinate of the point of intersection and the original quantity of (Y). The latter, which is taken to be negative, is equal to $(x-x_0)$, the difference between the abscissa and the original quantity of (X). Consequently, *the curve $O'c_1c_2c_3c_4$ is the*

[29] For the sake of brevity the term "utility surface" will also be used to designate the surface of the index of utility.

[30] When $x_1 - x_0$ is negative, as it is in the present example, it indicates that the quantity is *supplied*. When this is positive, it indicates that the quantity is *demanded*. This is also true for all other quantities, such as $y-y_0$, $z-z_0$, etc. When (Y) is demanded, y_0 may be zero, and that is generally the case; but when it is supplied, y_0 must be a positive quantity.

curve of the demand for y and of the supply of x as a function of the slope of the path (obstacle) followed by the individual.

What is the economic significance of this slope?

Reference to Figure 2 will show that the greater the angle which the path makes with the axis of x, the greater is the quantity of (Y) which can be obtained for a given quantity of (X). Thus, when the path is $O'p_1$, the individual supplies (x_1-x_0) units of (X) (the quantity supplied having a negative sign) and receives in exchange (y_1-y_0) units of (Y). But if the path were $O'p_2$, he would have received a *greater* quantity of (Y) for the *same* quantity (x_1-x_0) of (X). Our individual would have said that the *price per unit* of his commodity (X) in terms of (Y) was greater than before, or that the price per unit of (Y) in terms of (X) was less than before. *The inclination of the path measures, therefore, the prices of the commodities.* The greater the angle $AO'p$ which the path makes with the horizontal axis, the greater the price of (X) in terms of (Y), and the smaller the price of (Y) in terms of (X). If the slope were measured by the angle which the line makes with the axis of Y, the reasoning would be exactly the same, but the conclusion would have to be stated as follows: The smaller the angle which the path makes with this axis, the greater the price of (X) in terms of (Y) and the smaller the price of (Y) in terms of (X). We may, therefore, define the two prices as follows:

$$(2.21a) \qquad p_{x \cdot y} = -\frac{y-y_0}{x-x_0} = -\frac{\Delta y}{\Delta x}, \qquad p_{y \cdot x} = -\frac{x-x_0}{y-y_0} = -\frac{\Delta x}{\Delta y}$$

where $p_{x \cdot y}$ is the price of (X) in terms of (Y) and $p_{y \cdot x}$ is the price of (Y) in terms of (X).

If, now, we replace the finite increments Δx and Δy by dx and dy, making use of the assumption that the goods in question are infinitely divisible, we obtain

$$(2.21b) \qquad\qquad p_{x \cdot y} = -\frac{dy}{dx}, \qquad p_{y \cdot x} = -\frac{dx}{dy},$$

which are the limiting values of the average prices $-\dfrac{\Delta y}{\Delta x}$ and $-\dfrac{\Delta x}{\Delta y}$, and which would hold even if $O'p_1$, $O'p_2$, . . . , were curves instead of straight lines.

It follows, therefore, that $O'c_1c_2c_3c_4$ . . . is the curve of the demand for (Y) and of the supply of (X) as a function of the prices of the two commodities.

Pareto refers to this curve as the "curve of supply and demand." Professor Bowley refers to it simply as "the offer curve."[31]

Regarding this curve, the following observations are in order:

1. It is re-entrant: it curls back to the right. This, however, is not a gen-

[31] *Op. cit.*, § 1.

eral property; it depends on the form of the indifference curves (or of the index function). This property is supposed to be typical of the supply curve of labor. The meaning of such a supply curve is that a rise of price does not always create an increase of supply. At first it does, but beyond the point m, where the curve begins to curl back, a rise in price evidently results in reducing the supply.

2. If the initial quantities x_0 and y_0 were different, the curve of demand and supply would also be different. In fact, by varying the initial quantities, we can obtain a family of demand and supply curves corresponding to the family of indifference curves.

3. For our immediate purpose, however, the important fact to be kept in mind is that, given the initial quantities (x_0, y_0), the individual is in equilibrium when the path which he must follow is tangent to an indifference curve.

2. ONE INDIVIDUAL, MANY COMMODITIES

The extension of the theory of exchange to three or more commodities cannot be shown geometrically, for we have to deal with surfaces and varieties[32] in hyperspace. Recourse must be had to other methods of analysis.

Let there be n commodities[33] (X), (Y), (Z), . . . ; let the tastes or the desires of an individual for these commodities be represented by the index function

$$(2.22) \qquad I = \varphi(x, y, z, \ldots) ;$$

and let the obstacles which he must overcome in order to satisfy his desires be represented by

$$(2.23) \qquad f(x, y, z, \ldots) = 0 .$$

The problem is to determine the quantity of each commodity which the individual will demand or supply.

From what has been said before, the quantities will be given by the point of tangency of the two n-dimensional surfaces (2.22) and (2.23). The Pareto equations which express the solution are:

$$(2.24) \qquad \varphi_x = \frac{1}{p_y} \varphi_y = \frac{1}{p_z} \varphi_z = \ldots ,$$

$$(2.25) \qquad (x - x_0) + p_y(y - y_0) + p_z(z - z_0) + \ldots = 0 ,$$

where the commodity (X) is taken as the standard commodity (Walras' *numéraire*), in terms of which the prices of all the other commodities are ex-

---

[32] For definition see n. 19.

[33] Pareto designates the number of commodities by m. I am deviating from his notation for the reason that he later uses the same symbol for the marginal degree of utility of money.

pressed (but which itself has no utility other than that which arises from its ordinary properties as a commodity), so that

$$(2.26) \qquad p_x = 1, \qquad p_y = p_{y \cdot x}, \qquad p_z = p_{z \cdot x}, \ldots,$$

and where $x_0, y_0, z_0, \ldots$, represent the quantities of the various commodities in the possession of the individual when he comes to the market, and $x, y, z, \ldots$, are the corresponding quantities remaining in his possession at any stage in the exchange. When any commodity (Y) is demanded, $(y - y_0)$ is positive.

There are $n - 1$ equations in (2.24). Together with (2.25) they constitute n equations equal in number to the n unknowns, i.e., the n quantities of (X), (Y), (Z), $\ldots$, which the individual will demand or supply at the point of equilibrium.

Equations (2.24) and (2.25) are fundamental. They play a role in the study of economic equilibrium which is analogous to that of the equations of Lagrange in the study of mechanical equilibrium.

The general meaning of (2.24) is that, given the obstacles which he must overcome, the desires or tastes of the individual are satisfied. His weighted marginal degrees of utility are equal to each other, the weights being the reciprocals of the prices. To divide the marginal degree of utility by the price is to make the unit of the commodity the "dollar's worth." These equations mean, therefore, that at the margin, the utility of a "dollar's worth" is the same for all commodities.

Equation (2.25) is the solution of (2.23); the former is the explicit statement of the latter when prices are constant. It means that the individual's budget balances, that he gives in proportion to what he receives, and that he receives in proportion to what he gives. It is true at any stage of the exchange, while equation (2.24) is true only at equilibrium.

a) Relation between the income and the demand of an individual.—Equation (2.25) also gives an illuminating insight into the relation of income to demand. Writing it in the form

$$(2.27) \qquad x + p_y y + p_z z + \ldots = x_0 + p_y y_0 + p_z z_0 + \ldots,$$

and recalling that $x_0, y_0, z_0, \ldots$, are the quantities which the individual possesses at the beginning of the exchange, we observe that the right side of this equation represents the sum of these quantities expressed in terms of money, or the money value of the *wealth* of the individual. The left side of the equation represents the wealth of the individual at the end of the exchange. From the equation we see that the wealth of the individual, expressed in money, must be constant, no matter what may be the quantities of the various commodities which the individual buys and the prices which he pays for them.

If he comes to the market with only x_0 units (dollars) of (X) and with nothing of the other commodities, we represent this situation by putting $y_0 = z_0 = \ldots = 0$. The individual will then supply $x - x_0$ units of money and demand the quantities $y, z, \ldots$, of the commodities $(Y), (Z), \ldots$, at the prices which he finds in the market. Equation (2.25) then becomes

(2.28a) $$p_y y + p_z z + \ldots = x_0 - x,$$

which expresses the fact that the value of the goods purchased is equal to the amount of money spent. It may also be written in the form corresponding to (2.27):

(2.28b) $$x + p_y y + p_z z + \ldots = x_0,$$

which states that the value of the goods purchased, plus the unexpended balance (x), is equal to the *wealth* (x_0) of the individual.

This interpretation of the right side of (2.27) or of (2.28b) as representing the wealth of the individual is, however, valid only for a single exchange. If instead of thinking of these equations as relating to a single exchange, we think of them—as well as of (2.24)—as describing the *average* of many similar situations, each extending over sufficiently long periods, but not involving secular changes in the utility function, then $x_0 + p_y y_0 + p_z z_0 + \ldots$ (or x_0 in equation [2.28b]) is equal to the *income* of the individual in the average or typical period. Equation (2.27) now reads,

(2.28c) $$\text{Value of goods purchased} = \text{Income} .^{34}$$

Since equations (2.28b) and (2.24) must hold simultaneously, it is clear that the equilibrium purchases and sales of the individual depend not only on the prices but also on his income.

In the case of two commodities (X) and (Y) the relation between changes in income and the corresponding changes in the quantities demanded may be illustrated by a simple diagram (see Fig. 3).

For convenience, let us express the prices p_x and p_y of the two commodities in terms of some third commodity—say, paper money—which does not have direct utility. Then we need not consider the effects of changes in the quantity of the third commodity on the indifference curves of (X) and (Y). Equation (2.28c) then becomes

(2.29) $$x p_x + y p_y = r$$

or

$$\frac{x}{r/p_x} + \frac{y}{r/p_y} = 1 ,$$

[34] With this interpretation x, in eqs. (2.28a) and (2.28b), no longer represents the unexpended balance but the amount saved. When the purchases consume the entire income, $x = 0$.

where r stands for the income of the individual, which we assume is spent entirely on the two commodities. By varying r and observing the corresponding

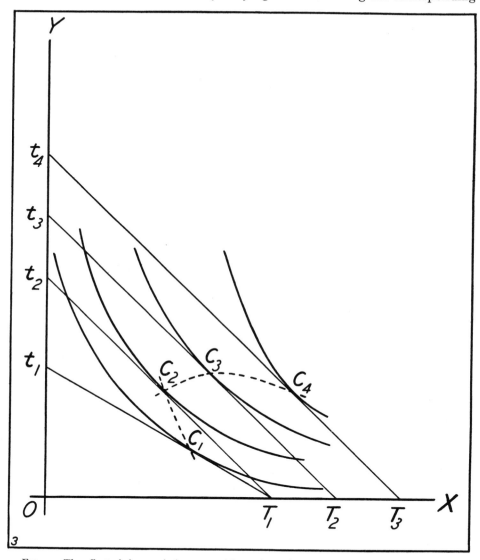

FIG. 3.—The effect of changes in income and in market prices on an individual's purchases of two commodities.

variations in the points of tangency of the line (2.29) to the indifference curves, we obtain a measure of the effects of changes in income on demand.

In Figure 3 the abscissa $OT = r/p_x$ represents the amount of (X) which can be bought for the income r, the ordinate Ot represents the amount of (Y)

which can be bought for the same income. The slope of the line tT (i.e., the tangent of the angle tTO) represents the ratio of the price p_x to p_y.

When two price lines such as $T_2 t_3$ and $T_3 t_4$ are parallel, they represent a variation in the income r while the prices p_x and p_y are kept constant, the ratio of the higher income to the lower being given by the ratio OT_3 to OT_2.

When two price lines such as $T_1 t_1$ and $T_1 t_2$ cut the x-axis at the same point T_1, they represent constant values of r and p_x and with varying values of p_y, the ratio of the higher price to the lower being given by the ratio of $T_1 t_2$ to $T_1 t_1$.

In this diagram a rise in income such as to shift the point of tangency from C_2 to C_3 leads to an increase in the purchase of both (X) and (Y); a rise in income such as to shift the point of tangency from C_3 to C_4 leads to an increase in the purchase of (X) and to a decrease in the purchase of (Y). In such a case (X) is called the "superior" good and (Y) the "inferior." An increase in the purchase of (X) and a decrease in the purchase of (Y) may also be brought about by keeping the income fixed and changing the price ratios. Thus a rotation of the price line from T_1t_2 to T_1t_1, which indicates a rise in the price of (Y) relative to (X), leads to an increase in the purchase of (X) and a decrease in the purchase of (Y).

By connecting such points as C_2, C_3, and C_4, we may show the effect of changes in income on the demand for (X) and (Y) while the prices remain constant. By connecting such points as C_1 and C_2, we may show the effect on the demand for (X) and (Y) of a change in the price of one of the commodities—say (Y)—while the income and the price of the other commodity remain fixed.[35]

This analysis can be extended to three or more commodities. The price line then becomes the plane whose equation is (2.28b). A change in income with fixed prices is represented by shifting the position of the plane without changing its inclination to the axes. The locus of the points of tangency of the plane to the indifference surfaces, as income is varied, will represent the functional relationship between income and the quantities of various commodities purchased. A change in price ratios is represented by a change in the inclination of the plane. These relationships can be expressed analytically by means of equations (2.24) and (2.28b).[36]

3. MANY INDIVIDUALS, MANY COMMODITIES

There remains to be considered the general case of exchange with fixed prices among many individuals.

---

[35] This explanation as well as Fig. 3 is adapted from Johnson, *op. cit.*, pp. 488–92. The relations detailed above have an important bearing on the theory of index numbers of cost of living and on many other economic problems. See H. Staehle, "International Comparison of Food Costs," *International Comparisons of Cost of Living* ("Studies and Reports of the International Labour Office," Ser. N [Statistics], No. 20), esp. Appen. I, pp. 74–92.

[36] See Sec. III, A, below.

Let the number of individuals be θ and identified as follows: $1, 2, 3, \ldots, \theta$. Let the number of commodities $(X), (Y), (Z), \ldots$, be n as before. Assuming that each individual takes the market prices for granted and does not (and cannot) directly influence them, we have for each of them a group of equations corresponding to equations (2.24) and (2.25):

(2.30)
$$\left\{ \begin{aligned} \varphi_{1x} &= \frac{1}{p_y}\varphi_{1y} = \frac{1}{p_z}\varphi_{1z} = \ldots \\ \varphi_{2x} &= \frac{1}{p_y}\varphi_{2y} = \frac{1}{p_z}\varphi_{2z} = \ldots \\ &\cdot\quad\cdot\quad\cdot\quad\cdot\quad\cdot\quad\cdot\quad\cdot \\ \varphi_{\theta x} &= \frac{1}{p_y}\varphi_{\theta y} = \frac{1}{p_z}\varphi_{\theta z} = \ldots \end{aligned} \right.$$

(2.31)
$$\left\{ \begin{aligned} (x_1 - x_{10}) + p_y(y_1 - y_{10}) + p_z(z_1 - z_{10}) + \ldots &= 0 \\ (x_2 - x_{20}) + p_y(y_2 - y_{20}) + p_z(z_2 - z_{20}) + \ldots &= 0 \\ \cdot\quad\cdot\quad\cdot\quad\cdot\quad\cdot\quad\cdot\quad\cdot\quad\cdot\quad\cdot\quad&\cdot\quad\cdot \\ (x_\theta - x_{\theta 0}) + p_y(y_\theta - y_{\theta 0}) + p_z(z_\theta - z_{\theta 0}) + \ldots &= 0 \end{aligned} \right.$$

There are $\theta(n-1)$ equations in (2.30) and θ equations in (2.31), or θn equations in all, by means of which we can determine the θn quantities of the commodities exchanged by the θ individuals, *if the* $n - 1$ *prices are given.*

But the fact that the prices are considered as given by each individual does not necessarily mean that they remain fixed. The very efforts of the individuals to adjust their purchases and sales to the prevailing prices will give rise to forces which will modify them. It follows, therefore, that from the point of view of the market as a whole the prices are as much of an unknown as are the quantities that are exchanged, and the two sets of unknowns must be determined simultaneously. How is this done? By fixing or specifying the total amount of each commodity that is available during the period of the exchange. The mathematical translation of this procedure consists in the addition of the following set of $(n-1)$ equations[37] to those of (2.30) and (2.31):

(2.32)
$$\left\{ \begin{aligned} (y_1 - y_{10}) + (y_2 - y_{20}) + \ldots + (y_\theta - y_{\theta 0}) &= 0 \\ (z_1 - z_{10}) + (z_2 - z_{20}) + \ldots + (z_\theta - z_{\theta 0}) &= 0 \\ \cdot\quad\cdot\quad\cdot\quad\cdot\quad\cdot\quad\cdot\quad\cdot\quad\cdot\quad&\cdot\quad\cdot\quad\cdot \end{aligned} \right.$$

[37] It appears at first that there should be n equations in (2.32), one for each commodity. However, such a set of n equations embodies but $(n-1)$ new conditions, for one of them can be deduced from (2.31) and (2.32). Thus, if we sum the equations in (2.31), we obtain

$$\sum_{i=1}^{\theta}(x_i - x_{i0}) + p_y\sum_{i=1}^{\theta}(y_i - y_{i0}) + p_z\sum_{i=1}^{\theta}(z_i - z_{i0}) + \ldots = 0.$$

But by (2.32) every term except the first is zero. The resultant equation is identically the one omitted from (2.32).

These equations express the fact that the total stock of each commodity is the same after the exchange as before.

Equations (2.30), (2.31), and (2.32) are the fundamental equations which determine simultaneously the equilibrium quantities that will exchange hands, and the equilibrium price of each commodity, in the general case of exchange when there are θ traders and n commodities. They are the fundamental equations of mathematical economics.[38]

4. THE MARGINAL DEGREE OF UTILITY OF MONEY EXPENDITURE

In the foregoing development the commodity of comparison (X) has been assumed to possess direct utility for each individual. The final utilities φ_{1x}, φ_{2x}, . . . , in (2.30) have then a significance independent of the process of exchange. Suppose, however, that the commodity in question is one which has no direct utility—say, paper money, its importance being due solely to its use as a medium of exchange. What meaning can we give to the notion of marginal degree of utility of money? Equations (2.24) suggest an answer to this question. We can define it as *the common equilibrium value of* $\dfrac{\varphi_x}{p_x}, \dfrac{\varphi_y}{p_y}, \dfrac{\varphi_z}{p_z},$ . . . , or

$$(2.33) \qquad m = \frac{\varphi_x}{p_x} = \frac{\varphi_y}{p_y} = \frac{\varphi_z}{p_z} = \ldots ,$$

the prices being expressed in terms of "money," a commodity which does not necessarily have direct utility. This definition makes the marginal degree of utility of money a function of the equilibrium prices and of the initial quantities (income) possessed by the individual. The notion has, therefore, meaning only after the equilibrium has been attained and differs from the marginal degree of utility of a direct good.[39] The marginal degree of utility of money should not be confused with the marginal degree of utility of the cash balance (Walras' *encaisse désirée*), although the two notions are related.

5. THE STABILITY OF THE EQUILIBRIUM

To discuss the stability of this equilibrium, we should have to consider whether the second-order condition

$$d^2\varphi < 0$$

[38] Lack of space prevents a consideration of the way in which the equilibrium is attained, and whether the different paths (successive exchanges) which an individual may follow necessarily lead to the same position of equilibrium. For a discussion of this question see Walras, *op. cit.*, *passim*, and esp. Leçons 21, 25, 30, and 35; Edgeworth, *Papers Relating to Political Economy*, II, 310–11.

[39] For a more detailed discussion of this concept see François Divisia, *Economique rationnelle* (Paris, 1928), pp. 416–33; and Allen, "On the Marginal Utility of Money and Its Application," *Economica*, XIII (1933), esp. 187–94. For a discussion of the meaning which can be given to the utility of an indirect or producers' good which is not necessarily used as a medium of exchange, see Divisia, *op. cit.*, pp. 393–97; and Maurice Fréchet, "Sur l'existence d'un indice de désirabilité des

is or is not satisfied for each individual; but a consideration of this question is beyond the scope of this chapter. It will be sufficient for our immediate purposes simply to point out the limitations of this equilibrium. These have been well summarized by Professor Bowley:

The whole solution is statical. If exchanges were established at the rates given by the equations, no forces would disturb them till some of the constants involved (such as the number of persons) changed. The questions at once arise whether there is more than one set of solutions and whether the equilibrium is stable.

There is nothing in the nature of the case to prevent multiple solutions, but in practice if we had any numerical values there is not likely to be difficulty in knowing which set is appropriate.

. . . .

Though the solution is statical it is generally possible (as in most statical problems) to determine in what direction the system will move if there is a given change in any of the constants. . . . But an actual solution, when defined changes take place continually over a period, would involve complicated analysis, and little progress has as yet been made in such an investigation.[40]

Equations (2.32) also bring into clear relief the difference between the theory of exchange and the theory of production. Put

(2.34)
$$\begin{cases} x_{10} + x_{20} + \ldots = X_0 \\ y_{10} + y_{20} + \ldots = Y_0 \\ \cdot \quad \cdot \quad \cdot \quad \cdot \quad \cdot \quad \cdot \quad \cdot \end{cases}$$

Then (2.32) may be written as

(2.35)
$$\begin{cases} x_1 + x_2 + \ldots = X_0 \\ y_1 + y_2 + \ldots = Y_0 \\ \cdot \quad \cdot \quad \cdot \quad \cdot \quad \cdot \quad \cdot \quad \cdot \end{cases}$$

In the theory of exchange the sums X_0, Y_0, Z_0, . . . , of the initial quantities are given and constant. In the theory of production we must replace the constant quantities X_0, Y_0, Z_0, . . . , by the variable quantities X, Y, Z, ...

---

biens indirects," *Comptes rendus des séances de l'académie des sciences*, CLXXXVII (1928), 589–91. See also Pareto, *Cours*, II, 210–15, § 859.

[40] *Op. cit.*, p. 53. When the goods compete with or complete one another, the probability of multiple solutions is greatly increased. This proposition is ably argued by Dr. P. N. Rosenstein-Rodan in his "La Complementarietà: prima delle tre tappe del progresso della teoria economica pura," *Riforma sociale*, XLIV (1933), 257–308.

In two important papers published in 1935 and 1936, Dr. A. Wald showed, however, how the Walras-Cassel equations—they differ from the Pareto equations in several respects—should be modified so as to yield unique positive solutions. See his "Über die eindeutige positive Lösbarkeit der neuen Produktionsgleichungen," *Ergebnisse eines mathematischen Kolloquiums*, ed. Karl Menger (Leipzig and Wien), VI (1933–34), 12–20; and "Über die Produktionsgleichungen der ökonomischen Wertlehre II," *ibid.*, VII (1934–35), 1–6.

III. GENERAL LAWS OF INDIVIDUAL DEMAND AND SUPPLY

In Section I, we derived the general statical law of demand (1.3) by a series of "mental experiments" which make no use of the notion of utility. That law simply states that the demand for a commodity is a function not only of its price but also of all other prices. The method followed leaves it to experience to tell us the nature of the function, as well as the interrelations among the independent variables, but bare experience is a slow and sometimes incoherent and ambiguous teacher. Thus, experience suggests that, when all the other variables are fixed, the quantity demanded generally decreases as price increases, but it does not tell us when this ceases to be true, and it leaves us in almost complete darkness with respect to the other characteristics of the demand function. To get more light on these difficulties, we assumed that each individual behaves in accordance with the principle of decreasing marginal degree of utility and traced the bearing of this hypothesis on the nature of our demand function (Sec. II). We could not, however, proceed directly to the consideration of the consequences of this hypothesis. We found it necessary, by way of preparation, to clear up some of the misunderstandings that have centered around the theory of utility and to develop briefly, though critically and along rigorous lines, the modern mathematical theory of choice which is based on the notions of indifference curves and indices of utility, and which forms the foundation for the three general equations of exchange—the systems (2.30), (2.31), and (2.32). Now that the foundation has been laid, we can proceed to give Pareto's derivation of the law of demand (and supply) for any commodity as a function of all the prices, all the utility indices, and all the initial quantities (income). We shall then attempt to answer the following questions: (1) What are the interrelations of demand, prices, and income? (2) Which conditions give rise to a negatively sloping curve and which give rise to a positively sloping curve? (3) What other light, if any, does the modern theory of choice throw on the characteristics of the theoretical demand curve? (4) What guidance does pure theory offer to the economist who wishes to derive concrete, statistical demand curves?

The problem of deriving the general laws of demand (and supply) may be stated as follows:

From (2.30) and (2.31) let us select the general equations of exchange for a particular individual. Upon suppressing the identifying subscript (for convenience, since it is no longer necessary), we obtain equations (2.24) and (2.25), which we have already considered.

Let the prices be expressed in terms of money, as in (2.29), so that p_x is not necessarily equal to unity. Then, making use of (2.33), we may write equations (2.24) in the symmetrical form

$$(3.1) \qquad \varphi_x = m p_x, \qquad \varphi_y = m p_y, \qquad \varphi_z = m p_z, \ldots .$$

The solution of this system, together with

$$(3.2) \qquad p_x(x - x_0) + p_y(y - y_0) + p_z(z - z_0) + \ldots = 0,$$

will give us the equilibrium quantities $(x - x_0)$, $(y - y_0)$, $(z - z_0)$, ..., which the individual will demand or supply at the prices p_x, p_y, p_z, ..., which are assumed to be fixed.

Since his tastes (utility functions) are assumed to undergo no modification, a change in the system may be brought about either through a change in the prices or through a change in his income, r, which is the money value of the quantities x_0, y_0, z_0, ..., in his possession:

$$(3.3) \qquad r \equiv p_x x_0 + p_y y_0 + p_z z_0 + \ldots = p_x x + p_y y + p_z z + \ldots .$$

If the price p_y should change to p_y', the new situation will be given by the same equations (3.1) and (3.2) in which, however, p_y will be replaced by p_y'. Solving these equations, we get a new series of values $(x - x_0)$, $(y - y_0)$, ..., for the quantities demanded and supplied. Proceeding in this manner, we can obtain the effect of a given change in p_y on the marginal degree of utility of money (m), on the quantity $(y - y_0)$ of the commodity in question (Y) that will be demanded or supplied, and on the quantity $(x - x_0)$ of any other commodity (X) that will be demanded or supplied. Similarly, if the income r should change to r', we can obtain the effect that this would have on the same variables.

What we desire to know, however, is whether it is possible to derive the desired results without having to undertake the exceedingly laborious and practically impossible task of solving the set of equations every time there is a change in the price p_y or in the income r. More specifically, our problem is this: Suppose that the price p_y of (Y) is increased by dp_y, or that the income r is increased by dr. What are the values of the partial derivatives

$$\frac{\partial m}{\partial p_y}, \quad \frac{\partial x}{\partial p_y}, \quad \frac{\partial y}{\partial p_y}, \ldots ,$$

$$\frac{\partial m}{\partial r}, \quad \frac{\partial x}{\partial r}, \quad \frac{\partial y}{\partial r}, \ldots ,$$

subject to the condition that (3.1) and (3.2) [or (3.1) and (3.3)] are identically satisfied? Though we are primarily interested in $\frac{\partial y}{\partial p_y}$, it will also be desirable to have the values of the other expressions.

A. THE GENERAL EQUATIONS

The solution of this problem was first given by Pareto in 1892,[41] but was simplified, extended, and put in more elegant form by the Russian statistician

[41] "Considerazioni sui principii fondamentali dell'economia pura," *Giornale degli economisti,* IV (2d ser., 1892), 389–420; V (1892), 119–57; VI (1893), 1–37; VII (1893), 279–321; *Cours,* Vol. II,

and economist, Professor Eugen Slutsky, in a remarkable paper in 1915.[42] Following Slutsky's general procedure, but deviating as little as possible from Pareto's symbolism, since his works are more easily accessible, we may give the solution in three steps: (1) the variation of demand with price, (2) the variation of demand with income, and (3) the interrelations of demand, price, and income.

1. VARIATION OF DEMAND (OR SUPPLY) WITH PRICE

Differentiate (3.2) and (3.1) with respect to p_y, remembering that the prices are independent variables. This gives the following set of $(n + 1)$ equations:

$$(3.4) \begin{cases} -(y - y_0) = & 0 & + p_x \dfrac{\partial x}{\partial p_y} + p_y \dfrac{\partial y}{\partial p_y} + p_z \dfrac{\partial z}{\partial p_y} + \cdots \\[2mm] 0 & = -p_x \dfrac{\partial m}{\partial p_y} + \varphi_{xx} \dfrac{\partial x}{\partial p_y} + \varphi_{xy} \dfrac{\partial y}{\partial p_y} + \varphi_{xz} \dfrac{\partial z}{\partial p_y} + \cdots \\[2mm] m & = -p_y \dfrac{\partial m}{\partial p_y} + \varphi_{xy} \dfrac{\partial x}{\partial p_y} + \varphi_{yy} \dfrac{\partial y}{\partial p_y} + \varphi_{yz} \dfrac{\partial z}{\partial p_y} + \cdots \\[2mm] 0 & = -p_z \dfrac{\partial m}{\partial p_y} + \varphi_{xz} \dfrac{\partial x}{\partial p_y} + \varphi_{yz} \dfrac{\partial y}{\partial p_y} + \varphi_{zz} \dfrac{\partial z}{\partial p_y} + \cdots \\ \cdots \cdots \cdots \cdots \cdots \cdots \cdots \cdots \cdots \cdots \cdots \end{cases}$$

from which to determine the $(n + 1)$ unknown partial derivatives: $\dfrac{\partial m}{\partial p_y}, \dfrac{\partial x}{\partial p_y}, \dfrac{\partial y}{\partial p_y}, \cdots$

Let M be the determinant of (3.4):

$$(3.5) \qquad M = - \begin{vmatrix} 0 & p_x & p_y & p_z & \cdots \\ p_x & \varphi_{xx} & \varphi_{xy} & \varphi_{xz} & \cdots \\ p_y & \varphi_{xy} & \varphi_{yy} & \varphi_{yz} & \cdots \\ p_z & \varphi_{xz} & \varphi_{yz} & \varphi_{zz} & \cdots \\ \cdots & \cdots & \cdots & \cdots & \cdots \end{vmatrix},$$

and let M_{ij} be the cofactor corresponding to the element of the ith row and the jth column of M, M_{ij} being equal to M_{ji} on account of the symmetry of M.

§ 977; *Manuel*, Appendix, §§ 52–62, 579–91; and "Economie mathématique," *op. cit.*, Tome I, Vol. IV, Fasc. 4 (1911), §§ 32–36.

[42] "Sulla teoria del bilancio del consumatore," *Giornale degli economisti*, LI (1915), 1–26. The importance of this paper appears to have been overlooked until 1933, when it was discovered by Valentino Dominedo, of the University of Bocconi, by Mr. J. R. Hicks, and by myself. See Professor Dominedo's scholarly paper, "Considerazioni intorno alla teoria della domanda," *Giornale degli economisti e rivista di statistica*, LXXIII (January, 1933), 30–48, and *ibid.* (November, 1933), pp. 765–807. The reference to Slutsky appears on p. 790.

The solution of the simultaneous equations may then be written in the following simple form:

$$(3.6) \qquad \frac{\partial m}{\partial p_y} = \frac{(y - y_0)M_{11} - mM_{31}}{M},$$

$$(3.7) \qquad \frac{\partial x}{\partial p_y} = \frac{-(y - y_0)M_{12} + mM_{32}}{M},$$

$$(3.8) \qquad \frac{\partial y}{\partial p_y} = \frac{-(y - y_0)M_{13} + mM_{33}}{M}.$$

These equations are analogous to the equations (74), (75), and (76) given on page 581 of Pareto's *Manuel*.

Interest naturally centers on the differential equation (3.8), which expresses the rate of change of the individual's demand (or supply) for (Y) with respect to its price, as a function of all the prices, all the initial quantities (income), and all the degree of utility functions. If we solve this equation, we obtain

$$(3.9) \qquad y = f_y(p_y, p_z, \ldots, x_0, y_0, \ldots),$$

which is the general demand function of the individual. Adding the quantities demanded by all the individuals in the market, we get

$$(3.10) \qquad \Sigma y = Y = f_Y(p_y, p_z, \ldots, R),$$

which is the general market demand function for (Y), corresponding to the general statical law of demand (1.3) which was deduced by a different procedure and without reference to the theory of utility. In this equation R is a function of the constants $x_0, y_0, \ldots$, and represents the size and the distribution of the income of the economy.[43] The individual incomes are the initial conditions which determine the constants of integration.

2. VARIATION OF DEMAND WITH INCOME

In obtaining equations (3.6), (3.7), and (3.8), we used equation (3.2), in which the income of the individual is expressed in terms of the quantities of the various commodities in his possession at the beginning of the exchange process. As we shall see later, this procedure enables us to study the effect of a change in the price of a given commodity on the quantity of it that is supplied, as well as on the quantity that is demanded. In analyzing the effect of a change in income on demand, it is, however, more convenient to express income in terms of money and use (3.3) rather than (3.2). Thus, differentiating (3.3) and

[43] In practice the process of obtaining the market demand function from the individual demand function of the type (3.9) would be complicated by the difficulty of giving a clear, unambiguous definition of social income, for this need not equal the sum of the nominal incomes of the individuals.

(3.1) with respect to r, and remembering that the market prices are assumed to be unaffected by changes in the individual's income, we obtain the following set of $(n + 1)$ simultaneous equations:

(3.11)
$$
\begin{cases}
1 = 0 \quad + p_x \frac{\partial x}{\partial r} + p_y \frac{\partial y}{\partial r} + p_z \frac{\partial z}{\partial r} + \dots \\[2mm]
0 = -p_x \frac{\partial m}{\partial r} + \varphi_{xx} \frac{\partial x}{\partial r} + \varphi_{xy} \frac{\partial y}{\partial r} + \varphi_{xz} \frac{\partial z}{\partial r} + \dots \\[2mm]
0 = -p_y \frac{\partial m}{\partial r} + \varphi_{xy} \frac{\partial x}{\partial r} + \varphi_{yy} \frac{\partial y}{\partial r} + \varphi_{yz} \frac{\partial z}{\partial r} + \dots \\[2mm]
0 = -p_z \frac{\partial m}{\partial r} + \varphi_{xz} \frac{\partial x}{\partial r} + \varphi_{yz} \frac{\partial y}{\partial r} + \varphi_{zz} \frac{\partial z}{\partial r} + \dots \\[2mm]
\quad \cdot \quad \cdot \quad \cdot \quad \cdot \quad \cdot \quad \cdot \quad \cdot \quad \cdot \quad \cdot \quad \cdot
\end{cases}
$$

from which to determine the $(n + 1)$ unknown partial derivatives $\dfrac{\partial m}{\partial r}, \dfrac{\partial x}{\partial r}, \dfrac{\partial y}{\partial r}, \dots$.

The determinant of (3.11) is the same as that of (3.4) and is given by (3.5). In terms of this determinant, M, the solution is

(3.12)
$$
\frac{\partial m}{\partial r} = -\frac{M_{11}}{M},
$$

(3.13)
$$
\frac{\partial x}{\partial r} = \frac{M_{12}}{M},
$$

(3.14)
$$
\frac{\partial y}{\partial r} = \frac{M_{13}}{M}.
$$

3. INTERRELATIONS OF DEMAND, PRICE, AND INCOME

If we re-write equations (3.6), (3.7), and (3.8) in the form they would take if the individual's income were considered as exclusively monetary (i.e., if we set $y_0 = 0$ in those equations), and make use of the results just obtained, we have,

(3.15)
$$
\frac{\partial m}{\partial p_y} = -m \frac{\partial y}{\partial r} - y \frac{\partial m}{\partial r},
$$

(3.16)
$$
\frac{\partial x}{\partial p_y} = m \frac{M_{32}}{M} - y \frac{\partial x}{\partial r},
$$

(3.17)
$$
\frac{\partial y}{\partial p_y} = m \frac{M_{33}}{M} - y \frac{\partial y}{\partial r}.
$$

Equations (3.13), (3.14), (3.16), and (3.17) can all be proved to be invariant under the transformation of φ into $F(\varphi)$, that is, they are independent of the assumption that utility is uniquely measurable.[44] Equations corresponding to (3.12) to (3.17) are not to be found in Pareto; they are due to Slutsky.

The interrelations of the several variables which enter in these equations are expressed in terms of absolute changes and involve, therefore, the units in terms of which the variables happen to be measured. We may, however, write these equations in a form which is independent of the units of measurement, by making use of the notion of "elasticity" of one variable (say, a) with respect to another related variable (say, β), which has been defined as the ratio of the relative change in a to the relative change in β, with which it is associated, when the changes are infinitesimal. In symbols,

$$(3.18) \qquad \eta_{a\beta} = \frac{\partial a}{\partial \beta} \cdot \frac{\beta}{a} .$$

Expressing (3.15), (3.16), and (3.17) in terms of elasticities, and simplifying, we obtain

$$(3.19) \qquad \eta_{mp_y} = -k_y(\eta_{yr} + \eta_{mr})$$

$$(3.20) \qquad \eta_{xp_y} = m \frac{M_{32}}{M} \frac{p_y}{x} - k_y\eta_{xr}$$

$$(3.21) \qquad \eta_{yp_y} = m \frac{M_{33}}{M} \frac{p_y}{y} - k_y\eta_{yr}$$

where $k_y = yp_y/r$ is the proportion of his total income which the individual spends on y.

Equations (3.15), (3.16), and (3.17) give, respectively, the change in the degree of utility of money, m, and in the quantities x and y demanded that would result from a *unit* change in the price p_y of (Y), if the other prices and the money income of the individual were kept fixed. When multiplied by dp_y, they give the *total* change in m, x, and y that would result from a change dp_y in the price p_y.

The right-hand member of each of these equations indicates that the change in the variable in question brought about by the change dp_y in the price p_y may be considered as composed of two parts. The first of these, which is measured by the first term of the right-hand member of the equation, is the change in the variable in question that would result if the price change dp_y were accompanied by such a compensating adjustment of money income as to keep real

---

[44] The invariance is suggested by the fact that eq. (3.3) and the $(n - 1)$ equations which can be obtained from (3.1) by eliminating m are all invariant under the transformation.

income apparently unchanged.[45] The second part, measured by the second term of the right-hand member of the equation, gives the additional change in the variable, which arises from the fact that money income is not so adjusted but is held constant.

The apparent change in the real income of the individual which would arise from an (inverse) change dp_y in price is given by $dr = y\,dp_y$, for if this amount be added (algebraically) to his money income he will be able to buy the same quantities of the various commodities at the new set of prices as he had at the old. (Such a combination of an income change $y\,dp_y$ with a price change dp_y may be designated "a compensated variation of price.") It is evident, however, that although he is able to do so the individual will not in fact buy the same quantities as he had previously, for the fall (or rise) in the price of (Y) modifies the price ratios, and under these conditions he will find it to his advantage to increase (or decrease) his purchases of (Y) at the expense of the other commodities.[46] Now $m(M_{33}/M)dp_y$ is the change in the quantity of (Y) demanded corresponding to the compensated variation dp_y.[47] (This change is always negative for a rise in price, and positive for a fall.)[48] Similarly, $m(M_{32}/M)dp_y$ and $-m\dfrac{\partial y}{\partial r}\,dp_y$ are, respectively, the changes in the quantity of any other commodity (X) demanded, and in the marginal degree of utility of money corresponding to the compensated variation dp_y in the price of (Y). These quantities may be called the "direct changes" in demand.

[45] By the real income of an individual I mean the utility which he derives from the combination of economic goods and services which he consumes during a given interval of time. Two combinations represent the same real income and are said to be *equivalent* if they lie on the same indifference curve. The money income which leaves the real income of an individual *actually* unchanged in a new price situation is such as will induce him to buy a combination of goods which he considers *equivalent* to the original. The money income which leaves the real income of an individual *apparently* unchanged in a new price situation may be defined as one which enables him to buy *the identical* combination of goods as the original. The apparent money income minus the original money income may be called the *apparent loss or gain*, according as it is positive or negative.

[46] It can be shown that by following this procedure he will land on a higher indifference curve; i.e., he will enjoy a greater utility.

[47] The proof is as follows:
When p_y and r are both allowed to change, then

$$dy = \frac{\partial y}{\partial p_y}\,dp_y + \frac{\partial y}{\partial r}\,dr\,.$$

In the case of a compensated variation in price, $dr = y\,dp_y$. Substituting this in the equation just written and at the same time substituting for $\dfrac{\partial y}{\partial p_y}$ its value from (3.17), we obtain:

$$dy = m\left(\frac{M_{33}}{M} - y\frac{\partial y}{\partial r}\right)dp_y + y\frac{\partial y}{\partial r}\,dp_y = m\frac{M_{33}}{M}\,dp_y\,.$$

See Slutsky, *op. cit.*, p. 14.

[48] See *ibid.*, p. 13, for a proof of this statement.

The remainder of the total change in each of the variables m, x, and y resulting from a change dp_y in p_y—we may call this the "indirect change"—must be attributed to the apparent gain or loss $dr = y \, dp_y$ in the real income. The residual change in m, x, and y corresponding to a price change dp_y is given, respectively, by $-\dfrac{\partial m}{\partial r}(y \, dp_y)$, $-\dfrac{\partial x}{\partial r}(y \, dp_y)$, and $-\dfrac{\partial y}{\partial r}(y \, dp_y)$, that is, by the second terms of (3.15), (3.16), and (3.17) when these equations are multiplied by dp_y.[49]

The interrelations of demand, price, and income deduced above lend themselves to a simple graphical illustration if we assume that the individual consumes only two commodities, (X) and (Y); for then his system of choices may be represented by a two-dimensional indifference map and his budget equation by the straight line

$$x p_x + y p_y = r \, .$$

In Figure 4 let the money income r of the individual be proportional to OT_1[50] and let the prices p_x and p_y be in the ratio of Ot_1 to OT_1. His equilibrium position is then given by C_1, the point at which the budget line $t_1 T_1$ is tangent to the indifference curve I_1. At this point he demands x_1 units of (X) and y_1 units of (Y).

Now, while keeping r and p_x fixed, let us decrease the price of y from p_y to p'_y, so that $p'_y = p_y + dp_y$. Graphically, this is done by pivoting the line $t_1 T_1$ on the point T_1 and turning it clockwise until it intersects the Y-axis at a point t'_1 such that $Ot'_1/Ot_1 = p_y/(p_y + dp_y)$. By decreasing the price of (Y) by this amount, we increase the ratio of the price of (X) to the price of (Y) from Ot_1/OT_1 to Ot'_1/OT_1. Under the new conditions the individual finds it to his advantage to shift his position from C_1 to C_3, the point at which the line $t'_1 T_1$ is tangent to the indifference curve I_3. The quantity of (Y) which he demands in the new equilibrium position is increased by $(y_3 - y_1) = \dfrac{\partial y}{\partial p_y} \, dp_y$, and the quantity of (X) by $(x_3 - x_1) = \dfrac{\partial x}{\partial p_y} \, dp_y$.[51]

In equations (3.16) and (3.17), the movement from C_1 to C_3 is considered

[49] That $-\dfrac{\partial y}{\partial r}(y \, dp_y)$ gives the change to be attributed to the apparent gain or loss in real income follows from the fact that $\dfrac{\partial y}{\partial r} \, dr$ measures the change in the quantity of (Y) purchased corresponding to a change dr in income, and in the situation here considered $dr = -y \, dp_y$. The reason why dr is here the negative of what it was in n. 47 is that there we were varying income from its original value to the value that would compensate the variation in price, whereas here we are proceeding from this adjusted income to the original one.

[50] As explained on p. 31, OT_1 is the number of units of (X) that can be purchased with the total income r, i.e., $OT_1 = r/p_x$ or $r = OT_1 \cdot p_x$.

[51] It is possible for one, but not both, of these quantities to be negative.

as taking place in two steps: (1) that from C_1 to C_2 and (2) that from C_2 to C_3. The first shows what the change in the individual's equilibrium position would

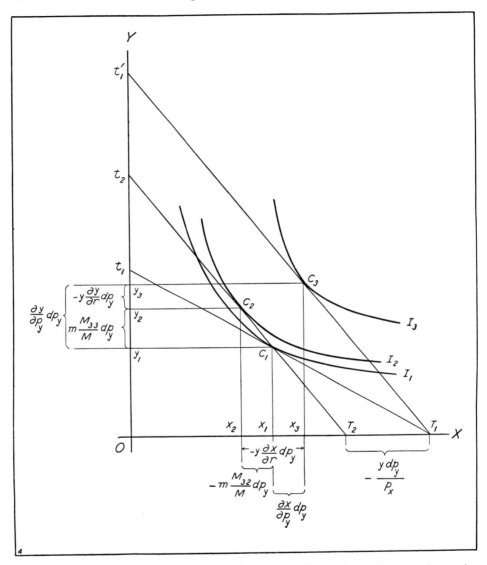

FIG. 4.—Interrelations of demand, price, and income: An illustration of the economic meaning of equations (3.16) and (3.17) in the case of two commodities.

be if the increase in his real income arising from the reduction in the price of (Y) were offset by a compensating reduction of $-ydp_y = T_1T_2 \cdot p_x$ in his money income. Graphically, the new position of equilibrium is found by moving the line $t_1'T_1$ parallel to itself until it intersects C_1, the original equilibrium position, and determining the point C_2 at which this line is tangent to another indifference curve I_2. The transformation of the line t_1T_1 into the line t_2T_2 represents "a compensated variation in price," and the point C_2 the equilibrium position corresponding to such a variation. At this point the individual would demand y_2 units of (Y) and x_2 units of (X). His demand for (Y), whose price has fallen, would increase by $(y_2 - y_1) = m(M_{33}/M)dp_y$ units; and his demand for (X), whose price, though fixed in absolute value, has risen relatively to that of (Y), would decrease by $(x_1 - x_2) = -m(M_{32}/M)dp_y$ units. These are the quantities which we have called "direct changes" in demand. They are the changes in the consumption of (Y) and (X) which would result from a change of dp_y in the price of (Y), if the real income of the individual were kept apparently unchanged.

Since, however, the individual experiences in fact no compensating reduction in his money income when the price of (Y) is reduced, his real income rises. He will not, therefore, remain at C_2; he will move to C_3. The increase in the quantity of (Y) demanded as a result of this change is $(y_3 - y_2) = -y\dfrac{\partial y}{\partial r}\,dp_y$, and the corresponding increase in the quantity of (X) demanded is $-y\dfrac{\partial x}{\partial r}\,dp_y$. These are the quantities which we have called "indirect changes" in demand.[52]

The total change in the demand for (Y) corresponding to the change of dp_y in p_y is, then,

$$(y_3 - y_1) = (y_3 - y_2) + (y_2 - y_1),$$

and the corresponding total change in the demand for (X) is

$$(x_3 - x_1) = (x_3 - x_2) + (x_2 - x_1).$$

These equations constitute a geometrical translation of (3.17) and (3.16).

If we multiply $m(M_{33}/M)$ by p_y/y, the resultant expression, which is the first term of the right-hand member of (3.21), is the elasticity of the demand for (Y) with respect to a compensated variation in the price of (Y). Similarly, the first terms in the right-hand members of (3.20) and (3.19)—$m(M_{32}/M)(p_y/x)$ and $-k_y\eta_{yr}$—give, respectively, the elasticity of demand of any other commodity (X), and the elasticity of the marginal degree of utility of money, m, with respect to a compensated variation in the price of (Y). The second terms of (3.19), (3.20), and (3.21), involving as they do the elasticities of the variables with respect to income, measure the effect on these variables of the apparent change in real income.

[52] It is possible for one, but not both, of these quantities to be negative.

The important conclusions just presented were first derived by Slutsky[53] but have since been reached independently by Hicks and Allen in a very important paper. These writers do not, however, employ the concept of the elasticity of demand with respect to a compensated variation in price. They introduce, instead, the analogous notion of the elasticity of substitution,[54] which enables them to state the economic significance of (3.20) and (3.21) in these words:

The increase in demand for a commodity (Y) which results from a fall in its price . . . . [can be looked upon] as consisting of two parts, one of which is due to the increase in the real income which a fall in the price of (Y) entails, the other to the opportunity of substituting (Y) for other goods which results from the fall in the *relative* price of (Y).[55]

Equations (3.19), (3.20), and (3.21) are fundamental. They constitute the capstone of the entire theoretical structure which connects demand, income, and price. As Slutsky pointed out,[56] they form a category of laws which is comparatively rare in the social sciences; that is, they enable us to derive quantitatively definite relations between observable magnitudes which can be verified by properly planned statistical investigations.[57] They should constitute the point of departure for all statistical studies of demand.

B. SPECIAL CASES

To get more information from (3.6) to (3.8) and (3.12) to (3.14), it is convenient to consider separately: (1) the demand for independent commodities, (2) the demand for dependent commodities, and (3) the demand for one of a large number of independent commodities.

[53] In his words: "If price increases by dp_y, the value ydp_y can be said to be an *apparent loss*, since, in order to make possible the purchase of the same quantities of all the goods that had formerly been bought, the income should have to increase by $dr = ydp_y$. But the individual, though having the possibility of preserving unchanged the preceding budgetary equation [*bilancio*], will no longer consider it preferable to any other, and there will take place some kind of . . . . variations of demand. . . . .

"The increment dp_y of price, accompanied by an increment of income equal to the apparent loss, can be said to be the *compensated variation* of price. In such a case $m(M_{33}/M)$ and $m(M_{32}/M)$ can be regarded as . . . . variations of demand for each unit of the compensated variation of price" (*op. cit.*, p. 14). I have taken the liberty of modifying Slutsky's symbols.

[54] In our terms, the Hicks-Allen elasticity of substitution between (Y) and the pair (X, Z) is equal to the negative of $1/(1 - k_y)$ times the elasticity of demand for (Y) with respect to a compensated variation in the price of (Y). Similarly, their elasticity of complementarity of (X) with (Y) against (Z) is equal to the negative of $1/k_y$ times the elasticity of demand for (X) with respect to a compensated variation in the price of (Y). Hicks and Allen do not explicitly define the elasticities of substitution and complementarity for more than three variables.

[55] Hicks and Allen, *op. cit.*, p. 66. I have taken the liberty of substituting Y for X (italics are theirs). Eqs. (3.19) and (3.20) correspond to the Hicks-Allen eqs. (16) as given on p. 209 of their article. In their paper, however, price elasticity is taken as opposite in sign to the elasticity used above, although income elasticity is defined the same way as above.

[56] *Op. cit.*, p. 15.　　　　　　　　　　[57] See chap. xix.

I. INDEPENDENT COMMODITIES

In this case

$$\varphi_{xy} = 0, \qquad \varphi_{xz} = 0, \qquad \dots, \qquad \varphi_{yz} = 0, \dots$$

and the formulas (3.6), (3.7), (3.8), and (3.12), (3.13), (3.14), take the simpler form

$$(3.22) \qquad \frac{\partial m}{\partial p_y} = -\frac{(y - y_0) + m\,\dfrac{p_y}{\varphi_{yy}}}{T} = -\frac{(y - y_0) + \dfrac{\varphi_y}{\varphi_{yy}}}{T}$$

$$(3.23) \qquad \frac{\partial x}{\partial p_y} = \frac{\partial m}{\partial p_y} \cdot \frac{p_x}{\varphi_{xx}}$$

$$(3.24) \qquad \frac{\partial y}{\partial p_y} = \frac{-(y - y_0)p_y + m\left(T - \dfrac{p_y^2}{\varphi_{yy}}\right)}{T\varphi_{yy}}$$

$$(3.25) \qquad \frac{\partial m}{\partial r} = \frac{1}{T}$$

$$(3.26) \qquad \frac{\partial x}{\partial r} = \frac{p_x}{T\varphi_{xx}}$$

and

$$(3.27) \qquad \frac{\partial y}{\partial r} = \frac{p_y}{T\varphi_{yy}},$$

where

$$T = -\frac{M}{M_{11}} = \frac{p_x^2}{\varphi_{xx}} + \frac{p_y^2}{\varphi_{yy}} + \dots.$$

We also have

$$(3.28) \qquad \frac{\partial[p_y(y - y_0)]}{\partial p_y} = -\frac{\partial m}{\partial p_y}\left(T - \frac{p_y^2}{\varphi_{yy}}\right),$$

the multiplier of $\dfrac{\partial m}{\partial p_y}$ being negative, since T is negative and numerically greater than p_y^2/φ_{yy}.

We must distinguish between demand and supply.

a) *Variations of demand with price.*—From these equations we draw the following conclusions:

1. When the commodity (Y) is demanded, we always have

$$\frac{\partial y}{\partial p_y} < 0,$$

or the quantity demanded decreases when price increases.

This follows from (3.24). The prices, p_x, p_y, p_z, ..., are essentially positive. Also $(y - y_0) > 0$, since (Y) is demanded. The quantity $m = \varphi_x p_x$, and the functions φ_y, φ_z, ..., which are the first derivatives of the total utility function, are also essentially positive. The functions φ_{xx}, φ_{yy}, φ_{zz}, ..., however, are always negative by the principle of diminishing marginal degree of utility. Lastly, T is negative, since φ_{xx}, φ_{yy}, φ_{zz}, ..., are negative. Hence $\dfrac{\partial y}{\partial p_y} < 0$.

2. The sign of $\dfrac{\partial m}{\partial p_y}$ cannot be determined, since its numerator consists of a positive term and a negative term. It is evident from (3.28), however, that $\dfrac{\partial m}{\partial p_y}$ and $\dfrac{\partial[p_y(y - y_0)]}{\partial p_y}$ have the same sign. This last expression gives the rate of change in the individual's expenditure for (Y), as a function of p_y. [It would measure the rate of change in the receipts for (Y) if that commodity were supplied.] It follows, therefore, that the index of the marginal degree of utility of money will increase, remain constant, or decrease, according as the individual increases, maintains constant, or decreases his rate of expenditure for (Y).[58] Another, and perhaps more significant, statement of this proposition is that an increase in the price of (Y) is compatible with any one of the following conditions: (a) an increase in the marginal degree of utility of money and an increase in the consumer outlay on (Y); (b) an unchanged marginal degree of utility of money and an unchanged consumer outlay on (Y); and (c) a decrease in the marginal degree of utility of money and a decrease in the consumer outlay on (Y).

$b)$ *Variations of supply with price.*—For supply the conclusions are not so positive. They may be stated as follows:

1. When the commodity (Y) is supplied, nothing can be said about the sign of $\dfrac{\partial y}{\partial p_y}$. This quantity may increase and then decrease, passing through zero. It should be borne in mind, however, that the supply function considered here is that which arises when the total stock of the commodity is fixed. The property of the supply function which has just been indicated is not, therefore, to be understood as holding in the normal case where the stock of the commodity can be varied by production.

2. When (Y) is supplied, we always have

$$\frac{\partial m}{\partial p_y} < 0, \qquad \frac{\partial z}{\partial p_y} > 0, \qquad \frac{\partial[p_y(y - y_0)]}{\partial p_y} < 0.$$

[58] A rate of expenditure which remains constant while price changes implies unitary elasticity of demand: $\eta = \dfrac{\partial y}{\partial p_y} \cdot \dfrac{p_y}{y} = -1$. But a constant rate of expenditure is implied by a constant marginal degree of utility of money. Hence $\dfrac{\partial m}{\partial p_y} = 0$ involves unitary elasticity of demand.

c) Variations of demand with income.—From equations (3.25), (3.26), and (3.27) it follows that:

$$\frac{\partial m}{\partial r} < 0, \qquad \frac{\partial x}{\partial r} > 0, \qquad \frac{\partial y}{\partial r} > 0.$$

The last two inequalities mean that when the commodities are independent in consumption an increase in income always brings about an increase in the quantity purchased of each commodity. It follows that the marginal degree of utility of money must decrease, which is the meaning of the first inequality.

2. DEPENDENT COMMODITIES

In this case $\varphi_{yz} \gtrless 0$, depending upon whether the commodities (Y) and (Z) are completing or competing.

When the commodities are *completing,* $\varphi_{yz} > 0$; and the conclusions are the same as for independent goods.

When the commodities are *competing,* $\varphi_{yz} < 0$, and the conclusions change. *When (Y) is demanded, the quantity y may increase with p_y, or the demand curve may be positively inclined.* The economic explanation of this fact is that when the goods are competing an increase in income may bring about a *decrease* in the consumption of (Y), so that, when there is a fall in the price of this commodity, the decrease in the quantity of it demanded owing to the apparent rise in real income may be greater than the increase owing to the compensated fall in price. Mathematically, this means that the positive second term of the right-hand member of (3.17) may be greater in absolute value than the negative first term, yielding a positive value for the left-hand member, the slope of the demand curve.

3. A LARGE NUMBER OF INDEPENDENT COMMODITIES

When we have a large number of commodities whose consumptions are independent of one another, the quantity T in equations (3.22) to (3.27) may have a very large absolute value, while none of its terms may be very large. We may then assume that T approaches $-\infty$ as the number of commodities increases, and thus consider the marginal degree of utility of money m as approximately constant, so that $\dfrac{\partial m}{\partial p_y}$ and $\dfrac{\partial m}{\partial r}$ equal zero. The hypothesis that T is $-\infty$ has the important advantage of introducing a great simplification into the equations (3.23), (3.26), and (3.27), for $\dfrac{\partial x}{\partial p_y}, \dfrac{\partial z}{\partial p_y}, \dots, \dfrac{\partial x}{\partial r}, \dfrac{\partial y}{\partial r}, \dots$, may then be neglected, and equation (3.24) becomes

(3.29)
$$\frac{\partial y}{\partial p_y} = \frac{m}{\varphi_{yy}}.$$

As is well known, this assumption is the keystone of Marshall's theory of demand. In fact, equation (3.29) is the differential equation of his law of demand, of which more later.

C. THE ECONOMIC SIGNIFICANCE OF THE MATHEMATICAL RESULTS

The upshot of the foregoing mathematical analysis may be stated as follows: (1) Even when the quantity of a commodity that is demanded is a function of all the prices, an increase in its price will reduce, and an increase in income will increase, the amount taken as long as the commodity in question does not compete in consumption with any other commodity. (2) When the consumption of a commodity is related to that of another, an increase in its price may *increase*, and an increase in income *decrease*, the quantity taken. (3) The Cournot-Marshall law of demand is a special case of the general law of demand.

Let us now examine the economic significance of these results.

1. THE SCOPE OF THE GENERAL LAW OF DEMAND

With the development of his general law of demand Pareto has corrected, completed, and extended the work of Walras and others on the relation of utility to demand; with the explicit introduction of income into the demand function Slutsky and, later, Hicks and Allen have rendered a similar service to Pareto. Given the utility functions of the various commodities, we have learned how to express the demand for any one of them as a function of all the prices and of income (eqs. [3.8] and [3.24]), and have seen that it is only when the commodities do not compete with each other that the quantity demanded will always decrease as price increases. Since, however, the independence of consumption is tacitly assumed by all writers on demand, and since they have always maintained that the demand curve is negatively sloped, it may be asked, "Is not Pareto's proof an elaboration of the obvious?"

The answer is that, although the quantity of any independent commodity that is demanded will decrease as price increases, both under the Cournot-Marshall law of demand as well as under the general law of demand of Pareto, the amount of the decrease is not necessarily the same in the two cases. The introduction of the other prices into the demand equation generally changes the response of consumption to price. Pareto himself expressed the difference in these words:

One must not confuse this general proposition, obtained for the case where the price of a commodity depends on all the quantities exchanged, and vice versa, where the quantity exchanged of a commodity depends on all the prices, with the apparently similar propositions obtained when the assumption is made that the price of a commodity depends solely on the quantity of that commodity that is bought or sold. A table in which there is listed in one place the price of a commodity and in another the quantity which an individual will buy or sell, without taking into account other commodities, does not correspond to reality; it is simply a hypothetical case.[59]

[59] *Manuel*, p. 583.

2. THE POSITIVELY SLOPING DEMAND CURVE

Pareto's proof that under certain conditions the quantity of a commodity that is demanded may increase as its price increases has played an important role in statistical economics. Commenting on this proof, Professor Zawadzki asks:

What is the value of such a conclusion? Is it not in flagrant contradiction with the facts? It is easy to imagine theoretical cases in which the demand should decrease upon a diminution in the price. Theory should, therefore, be able to give an account of them. Do they actually occur (and under the statical hypothesis) otherwise than by way of exception? What may be their importance? Here are some questions, and one might ask several others to which theory does not provide us with answers. In this example, we put our fingers, as it were, on the strength and the weakness of mathematical economics. We have a most general formula which embraces even the extremely rare cases, but we are not able to pass on to the particular cases or even to distinguish the exception from the rule.[60]

Professor Moore argues, however, that the positively sloping demand curve is the typical demand curve for producers' goods in a dynamic society,

because if we assume that all demand curves are of the same negative type, we are confronted with an impossibility at the very beginning of our investigation. Upon the assumption that all demand curves are of the negative type, it would be impossible for general prices to fall while the yield per acre of crops is decreasing. In consequence of the decrease in the yield per acre, the price of crops would ascend, the volume of commodities represented by pig-iron would decrease, and upon the hypothesis of the universality of the descending type of demand curves, the prices of commodities like pig-iron would rise. In a period of declining yield of crops, therefore, there would be a rise of prices, and in a period of increasing yield of crops there would be a fall of prices. But the facts are exactly the contrary.[61]

Taking pig iron as a representative producers' good, he finds that the correlation between the percentage change in the product (x) and the percentage change in the price (y) is $r = +0.537$, and that the law of demand is $y = +0.5211x - 4.58$, thus showing that the price rises with an increase of the product and falls with a decrease.

While the questions raised by Zawadzki and Moore cannot as yet be definitely answered, the following remarks are nevertheless in order:

1. The phenomenon of a positively sloping demand curve means that, where commodities are competing in consumption and where a rise in income will cause a fall in the consumption of one of the articles, a rise in the price of that article may cause an increase in its consumption. Thus, a rise in the price of bread may so impoverish the poorer classes that they cannot afford more "superior" goods, such as meat, and must eat more bread.[62]

2. The phenomenon in question was commented upon by some of the early economists. Thus Simon Gray, writing under the pseudonym of George Purves,

[60] Wl. Zawadzki, *Les Mathématiques appliquées à l'économie politique* (Paris, 1914), p. 186.

[61] *Economic Cycles: Their Law and Cause* (New York, 1914), pp. 110–16. See also his *Forecasting the Yield and Price of Cotton* (New York, 1917), p. 150.

[62] See Pareto, *Cours*, II, 338–39, § 977 and note; Marshall, *op. cit.*, p. 132.

observed as early as 1817–18 that "the working classes consume more bread when it is dear than when it is cheap."[63] We now know that this is not inconsistent with the principle of diminishing utility.

3. A necessary condition for the positively sloping demand curve for a commodity seems to be that it should be one of a pair which are correlated by way of rivalry ($\varphi_{xy} < 0$) and that the expenditure for it should form a considerable portion of the income of the individual. The smaller the relative outlay on a given commodity, the less the probability that its demand curve has a positive slope (see eqs. [3.17] and [3.21]).

4. The problem of a positively sloping demand curve may arise in statistical work when an attempt is made to deduce the demand for a commodity on the part of the very poor, from budget statistics giving quantities, prices, and income. When, however, the demand relates to the entire country, the existence of such a function is extremely improbable. Furthermore, the difficulty of the apparently positively sloping demand curve for producers' goods which has troubled Professor Moore has yielded to a different statistical attack.[64]

5. In any event, the difficulties connected with the time variable in the statistical study of demand are so serious as to overshadow the extremely small probability that a commodity which is consumed by rich and poor alike has a positively sloping demand curve. The statistical economist will be justified, therefore, in assuming that, when his data relate to a large market in which the demand of the very poor is incorporated with that of others, the quantity taken must decrease as price increases, when the disturbing factors are held constant, and that, when his statistical results contradict this assumption, there is something wrong either with his data or with his analysis.

3. THE COURNOT-MARSHALL DEMAND CURVE

Marshall defines this law in these terms:

There is . . . . one general *law of demand:*—The greater the amount to be sold, the smaller must be the price at which it is offered in order that it may find purchasers; or, in other words, the amount demanded increases with a fall in price, and diminishes with a rise in price.

And again: "The one universal rule to which the demand curve conforms is that it is *inclined negatively* throughout the whole of its length."[65] We have

---

[63] Article on Simon Gray in Palgrave's *Dictionary of Political Economy* (London, 1926), II, 257. I am indebted to my friend and colleague, Professor Jacob Viner, for calling my attention to this reference. It is interesting to observe that the *Dictionary* gives this quotation from Gray as an example of his "radical fallacies."

[64] See Roswell H. Whitman, "Statistical Investigations in the Demand for Iron and Steel" (University of Chicago dissertation). For a summary see his "The Problem of Statistical Demand Techniques for Producers' Goods: An Application to Steel," *Journal of Political Economy*, XLII (1934), 577–94, and "The Statistical Law of Demand for a Producer's Good as Illustrated by the Demand for Steel," *Econometrica*, IV (1936), 138–52.

[65] *Op. cit.*, p. 99 (italics Marshall's).

seen, however, that this law is neither "general" nor "universal"; that it is true only when certain conditions are realized.

In fact, the very reservations which Marshall himself points out contradict the universality of this law. Thus, he tells us that the usual statement of the law of demand does not take "account of the fact that, the more a person spends on anything the less power he retains of purchasing more of it or of other things, and the greater is the value of money to him (in technical language every fresh expenditure increases the marginal value of money to him)."[66] When, however, account is taken of the varying marginal utility of money, Marshall himself warns us that it is possible for the demand curve for food, on the part of the "poorer laboring families," to be positively inclined. But, in the statement of the law of demand, he has said, "The one universal rule to which the demand curve conforms is that it is *inclined negatively* throughout the whole of its length."[67]

Marshall also assumes, in giving definite form to the law of demand for any one commodity, that the prices of all other commodities remain constant. This is the well-known *ceteris paribus* assumption; but, as Edgeworth pointed out,

demand curves as usually understood involve a postulate which is frequently not fulfilled; namely, that while the price of the article under consideration is varied, the prices of all other articles remain constant. This postulate fails in the case of rival commodities such as beef and mutton. The price of one of these cannot be supposed to rise or fall considerably without the price of the other being affected. The same is true of commodities for which there is a "joint demand" as for malt and hops. And in the case of a necessary of life the price cannot be supposed to increase indefinitely without the prices of other articles falling, owing to the retrenchment of expenditure on articles other than necessaries. . . . . It is true indeed that the postulate which has been stated might be dispensed with. But this can only be done at the sacrifice of two of the characteristic advantages which demand curves offer to the theorist. First, unless this postulate is granted, it is hardly conceivable that, when the prices of several articles are disturbed concurrently, the collective demand curve may be predicted by ascertaining the disposition of the individual—a conception which, as employed by Prof. Walras (*Eléments d'économie politique*, Art. 50), aids us to apprehend the workings of a market. Secondly, when the prices of all commodities but one are not supposed fixed, there no longer exists that exact correlation between the demand curve and the interest of consumers in low prices which Prof. Marshall has formulated as "consumer's rent."[68]

It is clear, therefore, that there is nothing "universal" about this law. But its extreme simplicity and the ease with which it can be manipulated, coupled with the good approximate description which it provides in many instances of actual economic behavior, have earned for it a secure place among the funda-

[66] *Ibid.*, p. 132.

[67] *Ibid.*, p. 99, n. 2. This inconsistency was first pointed out by Professor Moore. See his *Forecasting the Yield and the Price of Cotton*, p. 150.

[68] "Demand Curves" in Palgrave's *Dictionary*, pp. 543–44. Also quoted by Moore, *Forecasting the Yield and the Price of Cotton*, pp. 148–49.

mental laws of economics. This is another illustration of the fact that in science it is often more important that a law be simple than that it be true. Nevertheless, as Pareto pointed out,[69] it may lead to erroneous and unacceptable results.

D. ADVANTAGES DERIVED FROM THE UTILITY APPROACH TO THE STUDY OF DEMAND

In the beginning of Section II the theory of utility was brought into the analysis of demand, with the hope that it would throw some light on certain problems which could not be solved by a purely objective, behavioristic, operational approach. The discussion which followed brought out, I hope, the substantial contributions which the theory of utility has made to the theory of demand.[70] It has provided us with a rational foundation for the law of demand, and with a generalization of the law, which brings out the interdependence of the various economic factors. It has enabled us to classify commodities into useful and significant categories and to explain both the negatively and the positively sloping demand curves, thus providing us with a useful background for statistical work.

But this is not all. The theory of utility can also be used as a means of determining whether certain forms of demand equations are consistent with given assumptions. Thus, Pareto has shown[71] that it is inadmissible to use Marshall's constant elasticity demand curve

$$yp_y^n = c \, ,$$

where y = quantity, p_y = price, and n and c are constants, to represent the demand for a commodity in a market in which several independent commodities are exchanged, except in the special case when $n = 1$. Further researches on the best form of the demand function will, I believe, also lead to interesting and useful results.

But the most important contribution of the theory of utility to the study of demand still remains to be mentioned. I have in mind the conditions which the theory of utility gives on the demand functions for individual and related commodities. These conditions, which will be discussed in chapters xviii and xix, enable us to determine whether the behavior of consumers is consistent or rational, and whether commodities compete with or complete one another. They also have an important bearing on the theory of incidence of taxation.

In short, we cannot conveniently dispense with the theory of utility. In the

---

[69] *Cours*, I, 36, § 84.

[70] For a discussion of other aspects of the theory of utility see Jacob Viner, "The Utility Concept in Value Theory and Its Critics," *Journal of Political Economy*, XXXIII (1925), 369–87, 638–59; and Dr. P. N. Rosenstein-Rodan, "Grenznutzen," *Handwörterbuch der Staatswissenschaften* (4th ed.; Jena, 1927).

[71] "Economie mathématique," *op. cit.*, pp. 617–20.

slippery field of statistical economics, we must seek the support of both theory and observation.

IV. THE PROBLEM OF THE DYNAMIC LAW OF DEMAND

Instructive as our excursion into the modern theory of utility has proved, it has been confined solely to the more or less well-beaten path of economic statics. From this point of view, the general demand function (3.9), with its special cases, is no significant improvement over the demand function (1.3) which was deduced without specific reference to utility. Both functions are static. But, as we have already remarked in Section I, in order to obtain the probable form of the statistical demand function, we must have numerous observations; and in order to obtain the requisite number of observations, data covering a considerable period must, as a rule, be used. During the interval, however, important dynamic changes take place in the market. We must, therefore, deal with variables (situations) which are functions of time. Our law of demand then becomes

$$(4.1) \qquad\qquad x_1 = F(y_1, y_2, \ldots, y_n, R, t) ,$$

where x_1 is the quantity of the commodity that is demanded, y_1 its price, $y_2, \ldots, y_n$ the other prices or influencing factors, R the size and distribution of income, and t is time—a catch-all for the resultant of those factors which cannot conveniently be measured separately, but which change more or less slowly and smoothly.[72]

The question naturally arises whether the fundamental equations of exchange (2.24) and (2.25) cannot be so "dynamicized" as to yield the dynamic demand function (3.16) as a necessary consequence, just as they yielded the general statical demand function (1.4). For if that were possible, we should have the exact form of (4.1) as a function of the utility curves, the prices, the rate of saving, and time. Even if the values of the utility functions and the other necessary elements could not be determined, a study of their forms and their interrelations would, nevertheless, throw a flood of light on the nature of the dynamic law of demand and its rate of shift through time.[73]

The answer is that although it is possible formally to "dynamicize" the fundamental equations of exchange (2.24) and (2.25)—as well as the other equa-

[72] This equation is identical with (1.4), except for slight changes in notation. The present notation is the one that will actually be used in the computations. These y's (prices) should not be confused with the y's (quantities) of Secs. II and III. The previous notation, which is Pareto's, has been used to facilitate reference to his works.

[73] I am far from suggesting that the abrupt changes in demand which are due to innovations and inventions could be profitably studied in this manner. Historical change cannot be conveniently subsumed in a mathematical formula.

tions of statical equilibrium—the modifications have not yet proved of much heuristic value.[74]

For the study of the dynamics of demand, we need to know not only the *direction* of change of the system—this is given by the statical equations (2.24) and (2.25)—but also its *velocity*. This means that the quantities consumed, as well as some of the other elements, must be considered as *vectors* which are functions of time.

Now every economic system presents considerable resistance to the internal or external forces which tend to modify it. When the accidental movements which originate in the economy are completely neutralized by the movements in the opposite direction to which they give rise, we have a statical equilibrium. When the entire economy is carried along by a general movement which modifies it slowly and regularly, we have a dynamic equilibrium.[75]

The dynamic problem of a physical system may be stated as follows: "I know that I have a set of bodies (whether atoms, billiard balls, or planets) placed in such and such places, and moving in such and such ways now; where will they be and how moving at any later time?"[76]

The dynamic problem of demand may also be stated in similar terms:[77] We have a number of individuals with such and such desires (utility functions), subject to such and such obstacles, and consuming and producing and saving at such and such rates now. What will be their consumptions, and how will their demand curves be moving at any later time?

The solution of the physical problem, Newton showed, may be separated into two parts: the first quite general, which could be solved completely, and the second special to each case. He gave the general rules for determining

---

[74] Pareto, *Cours*, Vol. II, chap. i: "Principes généraux de l'évolution sociale," esp., § 586, n. 1 and § 592, n. 1; *ibid.*, § 928, nn. 1 and 2; "Le nuove teorie economiche," *Giornale degli economisti*, Ser. II, XXIII (1901), 235–59, esp. the Appendix, which gives the equations of dynamic equilibrium. See also E. Barone, "Sul trattamento di questioni dinamiche," *ibid.*, IX (1894), 407 ff. In his *Manuel*, p. 216, Pareto warns us, however, that "note 2 of § 928 of the *Cours* rests on erroneous conclusions, and should be entirely changed."

[75] It has been suggested that statics be distinguished from dynamics in terms of the form of the equations used to characterize the system studied. If the variables contained in the equations all refer to a single instant of time, the system is to be called static; if to different instants of time, the system is to be called dynamic. See Georges Lutfalla, "Compte rendu de la III⁰ réunion européene de la société internationale d'économétrie," *Revue d'économie politique*, II (1934), 414–15. The suggested definition does not, however, dispose of the difficulties discussed in this section.

[76] C. G. Darwin, *The New Conceptions of Matter* (London, 1931), p. 24.

[77] Economic equilibrium is probably more akin to chemical or to biological than to mechanical equilibrium. But the latter is simpler, and its laws have been more fully worked out. That is why it is generally used as a basis of comparison. For a comparison of the mechanical and economic notions of equilibrium, see Luigi Amoroso, *Lezioni di economia matematica* (Bologna, 1921), pp. 460–72. For a discussion of the various notions of both mechanical and biological equilibria see the stimulating book by A. J. Lotka, *Elements of Physical Biology* (Baltimore, 1925).

where the system will be at the next instant of time; these are the equations of motion. The second part is a matter that is special to every problem, but there exist certain fundamental general principles which are extremely helpful in the solution. They are called the "conservation laws." The first of these is the principle of the conservation of momentum, which asserts that, in any isolated system, the total momentum is constant. This is implied by Newton's third law, which states that "to every action there is an equal and opposite reaction; or, the mutual actions of two bodies are always equal and oppositely directed." The second of these is the conservation of angular momentum, which asserts that the total angular momentum of a system is absolutely invariable, no matter what interchanges there may be between the elements of the system.[78] The third principle is that of the conservation of energy and is the most important of all.[79] It asserts that the energy of an isolated system can never increase, or that it is impossible to make a machine work without providing it with power.[80]

But what equations of motion and what laws of conservation of comparable scope do we have in economics? To ask the question is to answer it. There are none that have the definiteness and universal demonstrability of the corresponding physical laws. Our economic laws of change are simply empirical extrapolations of the present situation; they do not enable us to determine with certainty what, for example, the demand and supply situation will be at the next instant of time.

With respect to the second problem—namely, how will the demand curve move at a *finite* time later—we are even more helpless. True, we can write down equations which are analogous to the laws of conservation, to the principle of virtual movements, etc.; and we can think of the total utility function—if it exists—as corresponding to the energy potential whose partial derivatives measure the forces which guide the movements of the individual. But, unfortunately, we know neither the values nor the forms of the required functions.

The best that we can do at the present stage of our knowledge is to make a study of a series of statical equilibria, isolate their routine of change, if it

---

[78] Professor Darwin illustrates the concept of angular momentum in these words: "If I whirl a stone around at the end of a string, keeping some slack in the hand, and then pay out the slack, the stone will go slower as the string gets longer. This illustrates the conservation of another quantity, angular momentum, which applies especially for motions round a centre or axle. The angular momentum of the stone is technically defined as the joint product of its mass, speed, and of the length of the string. As the angular momentum has got to stay constant, when the string is lengthened the speed must diminish. The most important example of angular momentum is that of the planets round the sun." (*op. cit.*, p. 26).

[79] Recent investigations indicate, however, that it may have to be discarded when dealing with certain atomic transformations.

[80] Darwin, *op. cit.*, p. 27. See also Ernst Mach, *The Science of Mechanics*, English trans. (Chicago, 1919), chap. iii.

exists, and hope that this routine will continue to operate in the future. Such a routine of change is represented by the "dynamic" demand function

$$(4.1) \qquad\qquad x_1 = F(y_1, y_2, \ldots, y_n, R, t) \, .$$

In the nature of the case, it cannot have any of the heuristic properties of the laws of mechanics.

But the determination of the routine of change in human affairs is, nevertheless, a vitally important and, as we shall see in the following chapters, an exceedingly difficult task.

CHAPTER II

THE DERIVATION OF DEMAND CURVES FROM TIME SERIES

CHAPTER II

THE DERIVATION OF DEMAND CURVES FROM TIME SERIES

I. STATEMENT OF THE PROBLEM

The problem of deriving demand curves from statistics has been well stated by the late Professor Allyn A. Young. "Economic theory," said he, "has never professed to deal with the temporal succession or the spatial distribution of unique combinations of circumstances, while statistics has to deal, in the first instance, with nothing else."[1] In geometric terms the problem is simply this: The statistical data by themselves give only one observation—a point—on the unknown demand curve or surface for each time interval. We are required, nevertheless, to deduce the concrete, statistical equation of the entire surface. If the form of the dynamic demand function

$$(1.1) \qquad x_1 = F(y_1, \ldots, y_n, R, t)$$

and the interrelations of the variables entering into it were known, the difficulty to which Professor Young refers would not be so serious; but they are not. Is there a way out?

The answer is obvious. It is impossible to derive a demand curve from statistics without making some assumptions regarding the nature of the theoretical function and the interrelations of the variables. As Professor Pigou put it:

It is . . . . impossible to derive the demand curve as a whole or any part of the demand curve (save the single given point) in respect of any time interval unless we marry to the statistical data some hypothesis or hypotheses external to them and derived from elsewhere [p. 386].[2]

One hypothesis which we must make and which is common to all of the methods used for deriving demand curves is that the unknown theoretical demand curve can be approximated by a more or less simple empirical equation. The other hypotheses which we make depend in part, at least, on the data at our disposal which fall into two main classes—time series of prices and quantities and family-budget data.

If we wish to work with time series, we must take the dynamic demand function (1.1) as our point of departure and assume either that tastes remain constant or that they change regularly and smoothly with time. In addition to

[1] "English Political Economy," *Economica*, VIII (1928), 10.

[2] A. C. Pigou, "The Statistical Derivation of Demand Curves," *Economic Journal*, XL (1930), 384–400, and reprinted in A. C. Pigou and Dennis H. Robertson, *Economic Essays and Addresses* (London, 1931), pp. 62–83.

these hypotheses which are basic to *all* time-series methods, we must make certain subsidiary assumptions as to the properties of the demand curve and the way in which it shifts its position from time to time. Thus, if we assume that in (1.1) the prices of all the other commodities have only a negligible effect upon the commodity in question, we obtain

$$x_1 = G(y_1, t) \, ,$$

which is a Cournot-Marshall demand curve shifting its position from time to time; and which represents quite satisfactorily the demand conditions obtaining in a large group of agricultural commodities. If, furthermore, we assume that the foregoing demand curve is one of constant elasticity and that its rate of shift is the same in each time interval, we have the foundations of Professor Pigou's approach. It is to differences in these subsidiary assumptions that we can trace the differences among the various methods that are in actual use.

If, however, we prefer to work with family-budget data, we must face the fact that such data are not generally available for a consecutive number of years, so that the most that they can yield is the shape of a demand curve at a particular "point" in time—the year covered by the data; they cannot throw light on the way in which the curve shifts its position from time to time. Under these circumstances, we cannot use the general *dynamic* demand function (1.1), but must take as our point of departure the general *static* demand function

$$(1.2) \qquad\qquad x_1 = f(y_1, \ldots, y_n, R) \, ,$$

in which time does not enter but in which the quantity of the commodity demanded is expressed as a function of all the prices $y_1, \ldots, y_n$ and of the income R of the consumers.[3] Moreover, since the data refer to a large number of individual families, we must make some hypothesis as to the comparability of families. In addition to this hypothesis, which is basic to all methods using budget data, we must make subsidiary assumptions about the interrelations of the variables in (1.2). Thus we may assume that the utility of a commodity depends only on the quantity of that commodity, or that all the utility functions are of the same type, or that certain prices have no effect on the consumption of the commodity, or that the effect of changes in other prices may be measured by index numbers, or that an increase in income is equivalent to a general lowering of prices—and study the fecundity of these assumptions when applied to the data at our disposal. The particular assumptions made will determine the method to be used.

Logically there is no significant difference between the time-series and the family-budget approach, since equation (1.2) is only a special case of equation

---

[3] Eq. (1.2) is simply eq. (3.11) of chap. i written in the symbols subsequently adopted.

(1.1). But the fact that the family-budget data may be taken as referring to a "point" in time is sufficiently important to justify a separate treatment of each type of approach. This chapter will deal with those methods which have been applied to time series and which make the dynamic demand function (1.1) their point of departure. More specifically, it will review the more important hypotheses and methods which are associated with the names of Professors Henry L. Moore, Wassily Leontief, and A. C. Pigou. Chapter iii will deal with the methods for deriving demand curves from family-budget data. In it we shall pay particular attention to the methods suggested by Professors A. C. Pigou, Ragnar Frisch, and René Roy, and Dr. Jacob Marschak.

II. HISTORICAL NOTE

The statistical study of demand is a new field in economics and may be said to be the creation of only one man—Professor Henry L. Moore. Although Marshall wrote, as far back as 1885, "I believe that inductions with regard to the elasticity of demand, and deductions based on them, have a great part to play in economic science,"[4] and although the great Cournot, Marshall's main source of inspiration, had expressed a similar conviction over half a century before,[5] it was not until 1914 that the first definitive attack on the problem of deriving the elasticity of demand from statistics was made. In that year Professor Henry L. Moore published his *Economic Cycles: Their Law and Cause*,[6] in which he obtained equations expressing the relations between the quantities demanded and the prices of corn, hay, oats, and potatoes; determined the precision of these equations as formulas for estimating prices; and measured the elasticity of demand for each crop. True, we now know that Moore's attempt to derive the numerical values of the elasticities of demand of different commodities was anticipated by Professor Pigou[7] in 1910, and by Professor Tschayanow[8] in 1912, who adopted an entirely different method of approach; and that, in the same year in which Moore's book appeared, Professor R. A.

[4] Alfred Marshall, "On the Graphic Method of Statistics," *Jubilee Volume of the Royal Statistical Society* (London, 1885), p. 260.

[5] Augustin Cournot, *Researches into the Mathematical Principles of the Theory of Wealth* (1838), trans. N. T. Bacon (2d ed.; New York, 1927), § 24.

[6] New York, 1914.

[7] "A Method of Determining the Numerical Value of Elasticities of Demand," *Economic Journal*, XX (1910), 636–40; and reprinted in his *Economics of Welfare* (London, 1920), Appen. II. Care should be taken not to confuse this method with that developed in his latest contribution to this subject, "The Statistical Derivation of Demand Curves," *loc. cit.*, which will be analyzed later in this chapter.

[8] Alexander Tschayanow, *Essays on the Theory of Labor Economics* (in Russian)(Moscow, 1912), reprinted in the collection, *Essays on Agricultural Economics* (in Russian) (Moscow, 1923), quoted in Jacob Marschak, *Elastizität der Nachfrage* ("Beiträge zur ökonomischen Theorie," No. 2 [Tübingen, 1931]), p. 53. See also Tschayanow's *Die Lehre von der bäuerlichen Wirtschaft* (Berlin, 1923).

Lehfeldt published an estimate of the elasticity of demand for wheat.[9] Further-more, Moore's own procedures were essentially at hand in 1891 in a book by two American business men, Arthur B. and Henry Farquhar,[10] and more es-pecially in a paper by Professor Rodolfo Benini,[11] published in 1907, in which the latter went so far as to derive the demand for coffee in Italy as a function of its price and the price of sugar, by the method of multiple correlation; and in Dr. Marcel Lenoir's important book, *Etudes sur la formation et le mouvement des prix*, which was published in 1913.[12] But none of these predecessors of Moore attracted much attention, none covered so wide a field, and none succeeded so well in wringing fresh knowledge from the accumulated masses of data.

Moore's methods have been used in most of the work since done in the statis-tical study of demand. They have served as the point of departure for the work of such well-known statisticians as Dr. Mordecai Ezekiel, Mr. L. H. Bean, Professors G. F. Warren, F. A. Pearson, and Holbrook Working, and Dr. E. J. Working. Practically all the price analyses which have been carried on by the statisticians of the federal and state governments have been directly or in-directly influenced by Moore's work.[13]

Very recently, however, several other attacks on the problem of deriving the elasticity of demand from statistics have come to the forefront. Though they differ among themselves, they have this characteristic in common: they are attempts to derive the demand curve and the elasticity of demand from income data or from family-budget data rather than from time series of prices and quantities,[14] and they take as their point of departure the general static equation (1.2). They may be said to constitute a revival and a development of the point of view and method exemplified in Professor Pigou's *first* attack

[9] "The Elasticity of Demand for Wheat," *Economic Journal*, XXIV (1914), 212–17. For a com-ment on Professor Lehfeldt's procedure see my *Statistical Laws of Demand and Supply with Special Application to Sugar* (Chicago, 1928), pp. 211–12.

[10] *Economic and Industrial Delusions* (New York, 1891), pp. 205–8. For a brief summary of their procedure see my *Der Sinn der statistischen Nachfragekurven* ("Veröffentlichungen der Frankfurter Gesellschaft für Konjunkturforschung," Heft 10), ed. Dr. Eugen Altschul (Bonn, 1930), Appen. III.

[11] "Sull'uso delle formole empiriche nell'economia applicate," *Giornale degli economisti*, XXXV (1907 II), 1052–63. See also his "Una possibile creazione del metodo statistico: L'economia politica induttiva," *ibid.*, XXXVI (1908 II), 11–34.

As far as I can determine, the first economist to call attention to Benini's work was Professor H. L. Moore. See his "The Statistical Complement of Pure Economics," *Quarterly Journal of Economics*, XXIII (1908–9), 24–25. See also Professor Umberto Ricci, "Elasticità dei bisogni, della domanda e dell'offerta," *Giornale degli economisti*, LXIV (1924), 513–14, § 54. Fuller references to Benini's work may be found in Professor C. Bresciani-Turroni's "Über die Elastizität des Verbrauchs ägyptischer Baumwolle," *Weltwirtschaftliches Archiv*, XXXIII (1931), 48; and in Professor Felice Vinci's scholarly paper "L'Elasticità dei consumi," *Rivista italiana di statistica*, III (1931), 30–91.

[12] Paris, 1913.   [13] For references see the bibliography at the end of the book.

[14] For a clear and suggestive statement of the relation between changes in income and changes in demand see Vilfredo Pareto, *Cours d'économie politique* (Lausanne, 1896), Vol. II, §§ 973–89.

on this problem in 1910. Among the economists and statisticians whose names are connected with these methods are Professor Ragnar Frisch (1926 and 1932),[15] Professor Irving Fisher (1927),[16] Professor René Roy (1930),[17] and Dr. Jacob Marschak (1931),[18] not to mention the methodological works of Professors Ricci, Gini, Vinci, and of others.[19]

III. PROFESSOR MOORE'S PROCEDURES

Professor Moore's contributions to the solution of the problem are three: (1) he restated the hypothetical, statical law of demand in a form admitting of concrete, inductive treatment; (2) he devised ingenious statistical techniques, such as the method of link relatives and the method of trend ratios, for handling the time variable, and was among the first to apply the method of multiple correlation to the study of demand; and (3) he succeeded in deducing for the first time the statistical demand curves for several important commodities, and in measuring their elasticities of demand.

A. HIS UNDERLYING ASSUMPTIONS

Three tacit assumptions appear to underlie Moore's procedures: The first is that there exists a routine in the demand behavior of human beings in the market. The second assumption is that the statistical data of consumption and prices are such as to reflect this routine of demand. The third assumption is that the unknown theoretical demand function can be approximated by various empirical curves, which can be fitted to the data.

The first assumption implies that during the period covered by the data there have been no significant changes in the tastes and desires of the con-

---

[15] "Sur un problème d'économie pure," *Norsk Matematisk Forenings Skrifter*, Ser. 1, No. 16 (1926); and his latest book, *New Methods of Measuring Marginal Utility* ("Beiträge zur ökonomischen Theorie," No. 3 [Tübingen, 1932]). For a review of this book see my paper, "Frisch on the Measurement of Utility," *Journal of Political Economy*, XLI (1933), 95–116.

[16] "A Statistical Method for Measuring 'Marginal Utility' and Testing the Justice of a Progressive Income Tax," in *Economic Essays Contributed in Honor of John Bates Clark*, ed. Jacob H. Hollander (New York, 1927), pp. 157–93. In a circular letter which accompanied the reprint of this paper, Professor Fisher writes: "Although the publication of my own method comes later, I had, in unpublished lectures, employed it at least as early as 1912. In an article entitled 'Is "Utility" the Most Suitable Term for the Concept It Is Used To Denote?' in the *American Economic Review*, June, 1918, I referred to the intention of publishing this method; but publication was put off from year to year in the hope of first making a full statistical application."

[17] "La Demande dans ses rapports avec la répartition des revenus," *Metron*, VIII, No. 3 (1930), 101–53; and "Les Lois de la demande," *Revue d'économie politique*, XLV (1931), 1190–1218, also reprinted in *Etudes économétriques* (Paris: Recueil Sirey, 1935), pp. 82–110.

[18] *Op. cit.* Marschak's monograph contains a good succinct analysis of the methods of Pigou, Tschayanow, Frisch, and Fisher, but not of Roy. His criticism of Frisch is, however, based on a misconception which I point out in my review of his book in the *Weltwirtschaftliches Archiv*, XXXVII, Heft 1 (1933), 29*–38*.

[19] See references in n. 11.

sumers, so that the "dynamic" market demand function which depends on them also holds for the entire period. More specifically, the assumption is that there have been no abrupt, significant changes in the *shapes* of the utility functions. When an abrupt change occurs in the tastes and desires of the consumers, the routine of change is destroyed and the statistical data may be misleading.

The reasonableness of this assumption must, of course, be investigated in each case by a careful analysis of all the known facts relating to the industry or commodity in question. Failure to make such an investigation has often either obscured the true relation or led to erroneous or absurd results.[20]

The second assumption, which is basic to *any* attempt to derive demand curves from statistics, implies not only the existence of a routine of demand on the part of consumers but also *the absence of a single equilibrium position which is maintained throughout the period under consideration*. For, if there had existed such an equilibrium between demand and supply, the data would not give us sufficient observations on the demand function to determine its probable shape. This implication is of the greatest importance in the derivation and interpretation of statistical demand curves. We cannot, however, undertake an analysis of it without first obtaining at least a general notion of Moore's statistical procedures. For in his actual work theory and practice are intertwined, and one can scarcely be understood apart from the other.

The third assumption requires in general that the demand curve and its derivatives shall be continuous within the range in which we are interested.

[20] See, e.g., the paper by Elizabeth Waterman Gilboy, "The Leontief and Schultz Methods of Deriving 'Demand' Curves," *Quarterly Journal of Economics*, XLV (1931), 218–61. Disregarding oft-repeated warnings that no statistical method can be relied upon always to give satisfactory results in the statistical study of demand, and that before embarking on such a study an investigation should be made of the economics of the industry or commodity in question, Mrs. Gilboy attempted to get demand curves by applying the link-relative method indiscriminately to certain price-quantity series of coffee, copper, and sugar, to English import and export indices, to iron and steel exports, and to cotton exports, and got what she was apparently looking for—absurd results.

But was it really necessary to do so much computing in order to show that "absurd results may be found by the indiscriminate application of a technical method" (p. 253)? As she herself admits, a preliminary economic analysis of the industries and commodities in question, coupled with an investigation into the adequacy and reliability of the statistical series for the purpose in view, would have been much more useful and enlightening. (I have made such an analysis for coffee and found the results particularly interesting.)

Without wishing to cast the slightest suspicion on Mrs. Gilboy's intentions, I must, nevertheless, take this opportunity to warn the interested reader that her paper betrays a misunderstanding of my procedures in several particulars, that the account of them given therein is consequently misleading, and that much ado is made about certain questions or difficulties which were first raised in my writings. The interested reader will, therefore, do well to read my *Der Sinn der statistischen Nachfragekurven* (Bonn, 1930), and my *Statistical Laws of Demand and Supply* (Chicago, 1928), along with Mrs. Gilboy's criticisms. I may add that the former book is not available in English and is not published by the University of Chicago Press, as Mrs. Gilboy claims. She used one of the copies of the English manuscript which I had planographed for distribution to a few friends.

This assumption is necessary to validate the particular statistical procedures employed by Moore.

B. HIS STATISTICAL PROCEDURES

The procedures that Moore introduced consist in the treatment of the problem statistically by the following methods: the method of multiple correlation, the method of relative changes, the method of trend ratios, and combinations of these.[21]

The first problem that must be faced in deriving a demand curve is the handling of the long-time disturbing factors; these must be eliminated in order that price-quantity data may be conceived of as homogeneous. To perform this elimination in a simple manner, Professor Moore uses two statistical devices: the method of relative changes and the method of trend ratios.

I. THE METHOD OF RELATIVE CHANGES

The method of relative changes consists in finding the functional relationship not between the absolute prices and absolute quantities but between the relative change in the price of the commodity and the relative change in the quantity demanded.

By taking the relative change in the amount of the commodity that is demanded, instead of the absolute quantities, the effects of increasing population are approximately eliminated; and by taking the relative change in the corresponding prices instead of the corresponding absolute prices, the errors due to a fluctuating general price level are partially removed. If the observations should cover the period of a major cycle of prices, and the commodity under investigation should be a staple commodity . . . . , the above method of deriving the demand curve will give an extremely accurate formula summarizing the relation between variations in price and variations in the amount of the commodity that is demanded.[22]

As a measure of relative change we may take either the *percentage change* in the value from one year to the next or the *ratio* of the given year's value to that of the preceding year (link relatives).

Using the method of percentage changes, Professor Moore deduced, for the first time (in 1914), the laws of demand for corn, hay, oats, and potatoes.[23]

[21] Henry Ludwell Moore's path-blazing contributions to demand theory, arranged in chronological order, are as follows: *Economic Cycles: Their Law and Cause* (New York, 1914), chap. iv, "The Law of Demand"; *Forecasting the Yield and the Price of Cotton* (New York, 1917), 100–115, and chap. v, "The Law of Demand for Cotton"; "Empirical Laws of Demand and Supply and the Flexibility of Prices," *Political Science Quarterly*, XXXIV (1919), 546–67; "Elasticity of Demand and Flexibility of Prices," *Journal of the American Statistical Association*, XVIII (1922), 8–19; "A Moving Equilibrium of Demand and Supply," *Quarterly Journal of Economics*, XXXIX (1925), 357–71; "Partial Elasticity of Demand," *ibid.*, XL (1926), 393–401; and "A Theory of Economic Oscillations," *ibid.*, XLI (1926), 1–29.

In the first two references there are full and suggestive comparisons between his approach and that of Alfred Marshall. In the last reference there is a comparison between his approach and that of Léon Walras. For a synthesis of Professor Moore's theories see his latest book, *Synthetic Economics* (New York, 1929).

[22] Moore, *Economic Cycles*, pp. 69–70.   [23] *Ibid.*, chap. iv.

2. THE METHOD OF TREND RATIOS

The method of trend ratios derives the demand curve not from the absolute prices and corresponding absolute quantities but from the ratios of these prices and quantities to their respective trends. The rationale of this method rests on the following considerations:

If, during the period when our observations were taken, "all other things" had remained equal as theory demands, we should have no secular trend either of prices or of quantities. The existence of a secular trend in either series is *prima facie* evidence that "all other things" did not remain equal, that there were one or more disturbing factors or elements. It is the "disturbing elements" which give rise to the trend and which create a different "normal" from time to time. Hence it follows that, by taking the ratio of the actual (observed) prices to normal or trend prices, we eliminate, to a first approximation, the effect of the long-time disturbing elements on the price of the commodity under consideration. Likewise, by taking the ratio of the corresponding quantities to their trend, we eliminate approximately all the long-time disturbing factors influencing the supply. By taking the ratios of our variables to their respective trends, we are practically overcoming the chief difficulties which, according to Edgeworth and others, lie in the way of deriving statistical laws of demand. For our data, though extending over a period of years, may, when thus adjusted, be conceived of as approximately representing observations taken at a given point in time.[24]

The first use of the method of trend ratios in the study of demand was in 1922, when Professor Moore applied it to deduce the demand curve for potatoes and to illustrate the application of his "typical equation to the law of demand."[25]

3. THE METHOD OF MULTIPLE CORRELATION

Once the data have been adjusted for the influence of long-time disturbing forces by the use of link relatives or trend ratios, Moore is in a position to at-

[24] For further discussion of the methods of link relatives and trend ratios see Wirth F. Ferger, "The Static and the Dynamic in Statistical Demand Curves," *Quar. Jour. of Econ.*, XLVII (1932), 36–62. Professor Ferger makes the interesting point that, when link relatives of prices are correlated with the link relatives of the corresponding quantities, the inquiry is, Do *rising* prices decrease, and *falling* prices increase, the quantity demanded? On the other hand, the correlation of trend ratios of prices and quantities is an attempt to answer the question, Do *high* prices decrease, and *low* prices increase, the quantity demanded?

[25] Moore, "Elasticity of Demand and Flexibility of Prices," *op. cit.*, pp. 8–19. The use of ratios-to-trend (as well as deviations-from-trend) for eliminating long-time factors, and thus isolating short-time fluctuations, was, however, suggested and described by Warren M. Persons in 1910, who mentions their previous application in J. P. Norton's *Statistical Studies in the New York Money Market* (New York, 1902). See his paper, "The Correlation of Economic Statistics," *Quarterly Publications of the American Statistical Association*, XII (1910), 317–18.

tack directly the problem of obtaining an approximate expression for the law of demand, which now becomes

$$(3.1) \qquad\qquad X_1 = \Phi(Y_1, \ldots, Y_n),$$

where the variables are those of (1.1) adjusted for time changes. Thus, if the adjustment is by the method of trend ratios, $X_i = x_i/f(t_i)$, where t stands for time; and $Y_i = y_i/f(t_i)$.

Moore then experiments with different types of function Φ and of interrelations of $X_1, Y_1, \ldots, Y_n$, and selects those types which enable him to determine X_1 with the degree of accuracy sufficient for the problem in hand.

As a first approximation he chooses the simplest possible function

$$(3.2) \qquad\qquad \begin{aligned} X_1 &= \Phi(Y_1, \ldots, Y_n) \\ &= a_0 + a_{11} Y_1 + a_{12} Y_2 + \ldots + a_{1n} Y_n. \end{aligned}$$

As both the form of the function Φ and the interrelations of $X_1, Y_1, \ldots, Y_n$ are assumed to be linear, the method of multiple correlation immediately suggests itself for determining the values of $a_0, a_{11}, \ldots, a_{1n}$ and the relation between X_1 and the right-hand members of (3.2).

An excellent illustration is afforded by Moore's derivation of the law of demand for cotton in the United States for the period 1890–1913.[26] It is:

$$Y_1 = 7.11 - 0.97X_1 + 1.60P_2,$$

where Y_1 is the percentage change in the price of cotton, X_1 is the percentage change in the amount produced, and P_2 is the percentage change in the index of general prices. (The changes are measured from the corresponding values for the year immediately preceding.) This formula enables us to say what the probable change in the price of cotton will be when we know the probable changes in the production of cotton and in the level of general prices.

The degree of accuracy with which this formula enables us to estimate changes in the price of cotton is measured by the standard error $S = \sigma\sqrt{1 - R^2}$ (where R is the coefficient of multiple correlation), which shows the limits within which approximately two-thirds of the observations will fall. Moore's computations show that

$$R = 0.859, \quad \text{and} \quad S = 13.56.$$

[26] *Forecasting the Yield and the Price of Cotton*, pp. 155–61. I have taken the liberty to modify the symbols used by Professor Moore. Moore's use of price as the dependent variable is not to be interpreted as meaning that he necessarily questions the legitimacy of the theoretical development of this chapter, in which it is more convenient to use quantity as the dependent variable.

"This is a very high coefficient of correlation, and consequently the forecasting formula makes possible the prediction of the changes in the price of cotton with a relatively high degree of precision."[27]

For his purposes Moore found the linear demand function (3.2) quite satisfactory; but it is clear that if in other applications the linear function should fail to give good results, that is, if the error involved in estimating X_1 from the linear function should turn out to be too large for the problem under consideration, we must either include more factors in (3.2) or else take as a second approximation to our function some more general equation, as

$$(3.3) \qquad \begin{aligned} X_1 = \Phi(Y_1, \ldots, Y_n) &= a_{00} \\ &+ a_{11} Y_1 + b_{11} Y_1^2 + \ldots \\ &+ a_{12} Y_2 + b_{12} Y_2^2 + \ldots \\ &+ \ldots + \ldots + \ldots \\ &+ \text{product terms}, \end{aligned}$$

and determine the parameters of this equation and the correlations between X_1 and the right-hand members of (3.3).

The procedure which Moore introduced of adjusting the several variables for secular or cyclical influences before introducing them into his demand equation is not, however, always likely to lead to a good description of the interrelations of the factors that are involved. As B. B. Smith first showed,[28] the introduction of time as an *explicit* variable may greatly improve the accuracy of the estimate of the dependent variable.[29] The introduction of time as an explicit variable is, of course, equivalent to expanding the demand function (1.1) instead of (1.2) into a Taylor series:

$$(3.4) \qquad \begin{aligned} x_1 = F(y_1, \ldots, y_n, t) &= a_{00} \\ &+ a_{11} y_1 + b_{11} y_1^2 + \ldots \\ &+ a_{12} y_2 + b_{12} y_2^2 + \ldots \\ &+ \ldots + \ldots + \ldots \\ &+ a_{1t} t + b_{1t} t^2 + \ldots \\ &+ \text{product terms}. \end{aligned}$$

[27] *Ibid.*, p. 158.

[28] Bradford B. Smith, "The Error in Eliminating Secular Trend and Seasonal Variation before Correlating Time Series," *Jour. Amer. Statist. Assoc.*, XX (1925), 543–45. Smith is, however, in error when he claims (p. 545) that "on theoretical considerations, correlation coefficients secured by *simultaneous*, or multiple, correlation methods will be as high or higher, and never less, than those resulting from any possible sequence of *consecutive* elimination of the influence of independent factors from the dependent, ... *before* correlating. . . . ." (Italics are Smith's.) This is not true in general as can be seen from the statistical experiments of chap. xvii, Tables 47 and 48. For a discussion of this question see Ragnar Frisch and Frederick V. Waugh, "Partial Time Regressions as Compared with Individual Trends," *Econometrica*, I (1933), 387–401.

[29] Although in his actual work Moore never used this method of dealing with time, yet the possibility of doing so is clearly indicated in his discussion of the method of multiple correlation.

If many variables are to be included, the demand function may become quite complicated, and the question arises: "How can we deal with very complicated functions in any practical problem?" The answer is that, although *in theory* it is necessary to deal with the demand function in all its complexity in order to show that the price problem is soluble, *in practice* only a small advantage is gained by considering more than the first few highly associated variables.[30]

Equations (3.2), (3.3), and (3.4) are examples of what Moore calls a "dynamic law of demand in its complex form." These equations, however, also include an approximation to the *static* law of demand as a special case. Thus, if in these equations we single out Y_1 (or y_1) as the important variable in relation to X_1 (or x_1) and assign constant values to all the other variables, we have examples of *approximations* to the static (Cournot-Marshall) law of demand. Thus, when the variables are all expressed in *percentage changes*, then the constant values which must be assigned to $Y_2, Y_3, \ldots, Y_n$ to obtain the static law are all equal to zero, since "the general hypothesis in mind when the static law of demand is formulated is that there shall be no changes in other economic factors."[31]

As an illustration of this procedure, we may cite Moore's solution of the problem: "What is the relation between the changes in the price of cotton and the changes in the amount demanded when there are no changes in the purchasing power of money?"[32]

Since in his formula

$$Y_1 = 7.11 - 0.97X_1 + 1.60P_2$$

the variables are all percentage changes, Moore puts $P_2 = 0$, and thus obtains an answer to his problem. "The equation $Y_1 = 7.11 - 0.97 X_1$ expresses the relation between the changes in the price of cotton and the changes in the amount of cotton demanded *when the purchasing power of money remains constant*."[33] The standard error of estimate of this formula is $S = 15.38$, as compared with $S = 13.56$ by the three-constant formula.[34]

The procedure of first introducing the more important (theoretically, *all*) factors influencing X_1 into our demand equation and then assigning constant values to all the variables except the price and the quantity under consideration is, in fact, the *only procedure* by which the Cournot-Marshall law of demand may be deduced either conceptually or statistically. This becomes clear

---

[30] Moore, *Forecasting the Yield and the Price of Cotton*, p. 162.

[31] *Ibid.*, p. 152.   [32] *Ibid.*, p. 158.   [33] *Ibid.*, pp. 158–59.

[34] The fact that the standard error of the three-constant formula is less than that of the two-constant formula does not necessarily mean that the first equation constitutes a significant improvement over the latter, which has one more degree of freedom.

if we recall two fundamental assumptions in the Cournot-Marshall (and current) treatment of demand. There is first the assumption that *all other things being equal,* an increase in the supply of a commodity will lead to a corresponding fall in its price. There is second the assumption that the concrete problem of the relation of the price and the supply of a commodity will be simplified by attacking first the constituent elements of the question rather than by attacking the problem in its full concreteness.

Neither assumption is satisfactory nor indeed admissible. *The "other things" that are supposed to remain equal are seldom mentioned and are never completely enumerated;* and consequently the assumption that, other unmentioned and unenumerated factors remaining constant, the law of demand will be of a certain type, is really tantamount to saying that under conditions which are unanalyzed and unknown, the law of demand will take the supposed definite form. *The burden of proof is upon anyone using this method to show that the assumption does not at least involve a physical impossibility.* [Italics mine.]

The second of the above two assumptions is not more satisfactory than the first. It reproduces the defects of the first assumption with others superadded. The movement of prices results from changes in many factors: According to the statical method, the method of *ceteris paribus,* the proper course to follow in the explanation of the phenomenon is to investigate in turn, theoretically, the effect upon price of each factor, *ceteris paribus,* and then finally to make a synthesis! But if in case of the relation of each factor to price the assumption *ceteris paribus* involves large and at least questionable hypotheses does one not completely lose himself in a maze of implicit hypotheses when he speaks of a final synthesis of the several effects?[35]

The various methods—multiple correlation, relative changes, and trend ratios—are not mutually exclusive. The competent statistician will know how to combine them to the best advantage. Nor is any one of them necessarily superior to all the others. They must all be valued according to their efficacy in enabling us to lay bare the true relationship between the phenomena under consideration.

C. THE CHARACTERISTICS OF THE DATA AND THE SIGNIFICANCE OF THE STATISTICAL RESULTS

With the salient features of Moore's procedures in mind, we are ready for a consideration of the question suggested by his second tacit assumption, namely, What must be the characteristics of the statistical data so as to yield a routine of change of demand, rather than one of supply, or of the resultant of both demand and supply? Since the statistical data—the time series of prices and quantities—are always taken as the coordinates of points of intersection of a demand curve with a supply curve, the foregoing question may be restated as follows: Is it possible to deduce statistically the theoretical demand (or supply) curve when we know only the coordinates of the points of intersection of the

---

[35] Moore, *Economic Cycles,* pp. 66–67. A more extensive and even more suggestive analysis of the limitations of the statical law of demand is found in his *Forecasting the Yield and the Price of Cotton,* pp. 147–51.

theoretical (unknown) demand curve with the theoretical (unknown) supply curve at different points of time?

I. FOUR MAIN TYPES OF RELATION

To simplify the analysis, we shall assume that the theoretical curves are of the Cournot-Marshall type, and we shall consider the following main types of relation which may exist between them and the effect that this relation may have on the statistical results.[36]

a) Fixed supply curve and shifting demand curve.—Figure 5*A* shows a fixed theoretical supply curve and a demand curve which, while retaining a constant elasticity, moves steadily to the right.

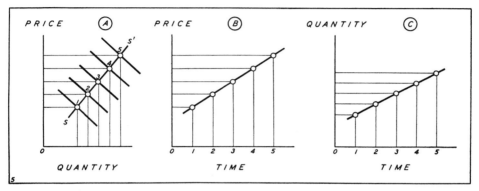

FIG. 5.—Fixed supply curve and shifting demand curve, with historical curves of price and quantity to which they may give rise.

From the data given in Figure 5*A* we may construct a price-time curve (Fig. 5*B*) and a quantity-time curve (Fig. 5*C*), on the assumption that equal time intervals, say, one year, elapse between the successive shiftings of the theoretical supply curve. Time is the abscissa in both Figure 5*B* and Figure 5*C*, but the ordinates of 5*B* are the prices (ordinates) of 5*A* and the ordinates of 5*C* are the quantities (abscissas) of 5*A*.

Figures 5*B* and 5*C* represent the original statistical series from which the economist would attempt to deduce concrete statistical demand and supply curves. Figure 5*B* shows a perfect positively sloping price trend, while Figure 5*C* shows a perfect positively sloping quantity trend. By "a perfect trend" I mean one that fits all the observations—one that has no "scatter."

What will our statistical economist do with the series?

[36] For a more detailed discussion of the relation between the Cournot-Marshall and the statistical demand and supply curves from a somewhat different point of view see Elmer J. Working, "What Do Statistical 'Demand Curves' Show?" *Quar. Jour. of Econ.*, XLI (1927), 212–35, and Philip G. Wright's review of my *Statistical Laws of Demand and Supply*, in *Jour. Amer. Statist. Assoc.*, XXIV (1929), 207–15, as well as his *The Tariff on Animal and Vegetable Oils* (New York, 1928), Appen. B. But this Appendix contains many troublesome misprints.

He cannot use the method of trend ratios because all the price-trend ratios and all the quantity-trend ratios have the value 1.0; and the resulting scatter would consist of only one point having for its coordinates 1.0 and 1.0. He would not use the method of link relatives because both the price-link relatives and the quantity-link relatives are subject to negative secular movements; and to correlate data from which the secular trend has not been eliminated is to run the risk of obtaining a "spurious" correlation. He would not correlate the original data of prices and quantities as they stand, for the same reason: the correlation might be spurious, since no allowance has been made for secular changes. Suppose now that, baffled in his efforts to get a concrete demand curve by "accepted" statistical methods, he decides that when the data do not fluctuate about their (fitted) trends, as is the case in the problem under con-

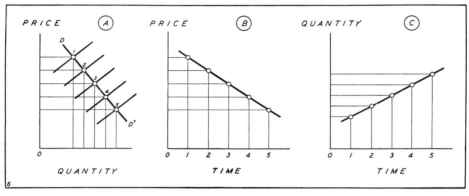

FIG. 6.—Fixed demand curve and shifting supply curve, with historical curves of price and quantity to which they may give rise.

sideration (see Figs. 5B and 5C), it is legitimate to correlate the original data. Will he not then get the theoretical curve SS' (Fig. 5A) that remains fixed? He will. *But he will not know how to interpret it. He will not know whether it is a short-time, reversible supply curve, or a long-time, irreversible supply curve.* The price trend (Fig. 5B) would probably suggest the latter interpretation.

What can our economist do? Without additional information, *absolutely nothing!*

b) *Fixed demand curve and shifting supply curve.*—A similar analysis of the case presented in Figure 6A, where the demand curve remains constant while the supply curve moves progressively to the right, shows that our statistical economist will simply fail to get any results, although he will not be misled by his methods. He cannot use the method of trend ratios because all the price-trend ratios and all the quantity-trend ratios have the value 1.0. He probably will not use the method of link relatives because the price relatives have a positive secular trend while the quantity relatives have a negative secular trend;

and to correlate two series which are subject to secular movements is to run the risk of obtaining a spurious correlation. If he does correlate the data of Figures 6B and 6C as they stand, he will, of course, obtain the negatively sloping curve DD' of Figure 6A. *But he will not know whether it is a short-time, reversible demand curve, a long-time, irreversible demand curve, or a long-time, irreversible supply curve!* The chances are that the first interpretation will not be entertained for the reason that the data of Figures 6B and 6C are not subject to short-time fluctuations.[37]

c) *Shifting demand curve and shifting supply curve.*—When both theoretical demand and supply curves move, an endless variety of price-time curves and quantity-time curves is possible, depending upon (1) whether the shifts of the theoretical curves are correlated or uncorrelated; (2) whether a shift of the demand curve to the right is accompanied by a shift of the supply curve to the right, and vice versa; or (3) whether a shift of the demand curve to the right is accompanied by a shift of the supply curve to the left, and vice versa. *The fluctuations in the resulting price-time curves and quantity-time curves may appear to be so arbitrary as to defy all attempts to deduce from them any demand or supply curve; or they may be such as to lead to a demand curve or to a supply curve whose elasticity is considerably different from that of the corresponding theoretical curve.* The reader can easily verify this statement by imagining the demand curves and the supply curves to have shifted in any desired manner and by studying the resulting scatter diagrams. This is illustrated by Figure 7. By varying only the slopes of the supply curves of this figure, it is possible to construct (hypothetical) demand and supply movements which will "explain" almost any combination of actual fluctuations in prices and consumption. Some of these are shown in parts B and C of Figure 7. The *degrees of freedom* of the theoretical demand and supply curves are infinite.

When both curves have shifted, it is, therefore, impossible to deduce their forms statistically from the data of consumption and prices. We must have more information.

d) *Fixed demand curve and fixed supply curve.*—It is necessary to recollect, however, that there is an important implicit assumption in the foregoing example, namely, that all changes in supply occur *simultaneously* with the changes in the prices which call them forth. It is known, however, that for many commodities changes in supply which occur at a subsequent period are much more important than those which occur simultaneously with the price change. This greatly simplifies the study of supply because it reduces the number of degrees of freedom of the theoretical demand and supply curves. More particularly, if a fixed time interval elapses between changes in price and corresponding

---

[37] While the conclusions in both cases (*a*) and (*b*) are based on examples in which the curve which shifts does so in a regular manner, they are still valid even if the shifting is irregular.

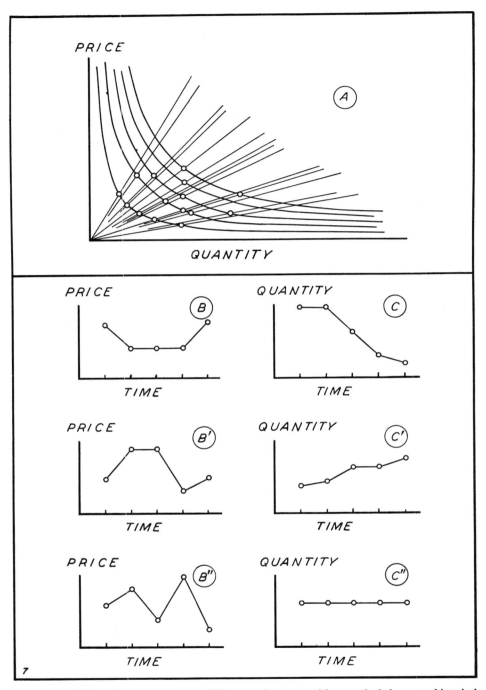

FIG. 7.—Shifting demand curve and shifting supply curve, with several of the many historical curves of price and quantity to which they may give rise.

changes in supply, and if the theoretical demand and supply curves remain fixed, it is possible to deduce both of these curves from the same data of prices and quantities.

In Figure 8, let D_1D_1' be the theoretical demand curve and S_1S_1' the theoretical supply curve for a given commodity.[38] Let the conditions of production be such that a high or low price for any year (or other time interval) calls forth a high or low output in the *following* year, or period. Furthermore, let the quantity produced in any year be equal to the quantity consumed in the same year.[39]

If demand and supply curves were always in equilibrium, it would be impossible statistically to deduce their equations. For "equilibrium," in the strict sense of the term, denotes either that exchange has come to a standstill or that the *same* quantity changes hands at the *same* price in different periods of time. The statistical records of such transactions are the same year in and year out: they always give the coordinates of the same equilibrium point. From such records no demand and supply curves can be deduced.

But, in any real market, demand and supply are rarely in exact equilibrium, partly because the equilibrium has to be found by a series of trials and errors, and partly because there are numerous forces at work which tend to upset it as soon as it is established. It is these movements about the point of equilibrium which enable us to deduce statistically both the demand curve D_1D_1' and the supply curve S_1S_1'.

Let the quantity produced and available in a given year be oq_1. As this is less than the equilibrium quantity, the demand price will be aq_1. But this high price will, by our assumption, call forth the output oq_2 in the following year. When such an output is placed on the market, the demand price will drop to cq_2. This will reduce the output in the third year to oq_3. The price will then rise to eq_3. This process, which is brought into operation as soon as the equilibrium is upset, will continue until the equilibrium has been re-established.

The interesting result of this process is that it gives rise to a series of observations on *both* (unknown) curves. Thus the points a and c are observations on the demand curve, while the points b and d are observations on the supply curve. When a sufficiently large number of such observations are available, the statistician can determine the demand curve D_1D_1' and the supply curve S_1S_1'. He can determine the demand curve by relating the price for any given

[38] For corresponding graphs relating to monopoly see Erich Schneider, "Über den Einfluss von Änderungen der Nachfrage auf die Monopolpreisbildung," *Archiv f. Sozialw. u. Sozialpol.*, LXIV, Heft 2 (1930), 281–315. For an analytic statement of the oscillations shown in Fig. 8 see J. Tinbergen, "L'Utilization des équations fonctionnelles et des nombres complexes dans les recherches économiques," *Econometrica*, I (1933), 38–39.

[39] These last two statements imply that the "instantaneous" supply curves, whose intersections with the demand curve give us our observations, are straight lines perpendicular to the quantity axis. They are fixed only for the period (here a year) which it is assumed must elapse before producers respond to a change in price. This "instantaneous" curve must be distinguished from the supply curve S_1S_1' which is here assumed fixed for the whole period in question.

year to the quantity for the same year, and he can determine the supply curve by relating the price for any given year to the quantity for the following year.

In any concrete problem, however, the points will not always fall exactly either on the unknown demand curve or on the unknown supply curve. It is desirable, therefore, to look upon the points a, b, c, etc., as averages of many observations.

In this example the price-time curve and the quantity-time curve each show a *decreasing* amplitude with time, or a tendency to stable equilibrium (Figs. B_1 and C_1). This is due to the fact that in Figure A_1 the supply curve is less elastic than the demand curve. If the supply curve is more elastic than the demand curve, as in Figure A_2, the tendency is to get farther and farther away from the equilibrium position, and the price-time curve and the quantity-time curve will each be subject to an *increasing* amplitude with time (Figs. B_2 and C_2). If, finally, the elasticity of supply is exactly equal (numerically) to the elasticity of demand (Fig. A_3), the price-time curve and the quantity-time curve will each have a constant amplitude.

In Figure 8 the price and quantity scales are logarithmic, so that the straight lines represent demand and supply curves of *constant* elasticity. If the demand and supply curves are straight lines on an arithmetic scale, they will yield oscillations of decreasing, increasing, or constant amplitude according as the *slope* of the supply curve is in absolute value greater than, less than, or equal to, the slope of the demand curve.

The assumption in each of the three cases is that producers react mechanically to a given price change; that they do not learn from experience. Such a behavior is not to be ruled out as extremely improbable. It is approximately represented by the response that American producers of potatoes,[40] corn,[40] and cabbage[41] make to price changes. It is probable, however, that in the demand-supply adjustments of most commodities the number of steps by which equilibrium is established is less than that indicated by the continuous lines ab, bc, etc. The process is more nearly like that indicated by the dotted lines ab', $b'c'$, etc. (Fig. A_1).

But whether or not there exists a tendency for an equilibrium to be established between demand and supply, and whether the steps by which equilibrium is established are few or many, are matters which are not nearly so important for present purposes as is the fact that the process of adjustment yields observations on both the demand curve and the supply curve.

Thus far we have assumed that the two unknown curves D_1D_1' and S_1S_1' re-

[40] See Harry Pelle Hartkemeier, *The Supply Function for Agricultural Commodities: A Study of the Effect of Price and Weather on the Production of Potatoes and Corn* ("University of Missouri Studies," Vol. VII, No. 4 [1932]).

[41] R. H. Whitman, "The Cabbage Industry and the Price System," an unpublished study.

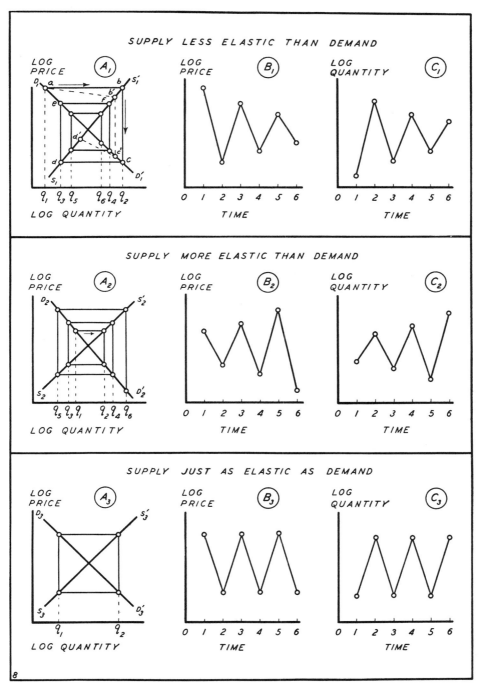

FIG. 8.—Fixed demand curve and fixed supply curve, with historical curves of price and quantity to which they may give rise.

main fixed and have shown that, when an interval elapses between changes in price and corresponding changes in supply, it is possible to deduce both curves statistically. This conclusion also holds even when both curves are subject to secular movements, the necessary conditions being: (1) that the curves retain their shape, (2) that each curve shift in some regular manner, and (3) that there exist a time interval between changes in price and changes in supply.

The importance of such a demand-supply relationship lies in that it admits of a straightforward statistical "verification." If by correlating prices and output (consumption) for synchronous years (or other intervals) we obtain a high negative correlation; and if by correlating the same data but with output lagged by, say, one year, we get a high positive correlation; *and if these correlations have meaning in terms of the industry or commodity under consideration*, the statistical demand and supply curves thus obtained are probably very close approximations to the theoretical curves.[42] It is assumed, of course, that the data have been adjusted for secular changes and other disturbing factors.

2. SUMMARY OF FINDINGS

The upshot of the foregoing analysis of the four cases of demand-supply relations may be summarized in these propositions:

1. When the theoretical supply curve remains fixed, and the demand curve moves in any manner, it should be possible to get the (fixed) supply curve from the statistical data; but without "outside evidence" the statistician cannot tell whether it is a short-time, reversible supply curve, or a long-time, irreversible supply curve!

2. When the theoretical demand curve remains fixed, and the theoretical supply curve moves in any manner, it should be possible to get the (fixed) demand curve from the statistical data; but without "outside evidence" the statistician cannot tell whether it is a short-time, reversible demand curve, or a long-time, irreversible supply curve!

3. When both theoretical curves move, the data of output and prices may lead (*a*) to no demand curve or supply curve, or (*b*) to a demand curve or supply curve with an elasticity different from that of the theoretical curves. In this case, even more than in the preceding cases, outside evidence is needed in order intelligently to interpret the statistical results.

4. But the assumption that the two curves can shift in any direction independently of each other is not, in general, a reasonable assumption, for it overlooks the interdependence of economic phenomena which is shown, in part, by the general demand equation (1.1). Furthermore, a pair of demand and supply curves which can shift in any direction constitute an ideal "model" or "pattern" with so many *degrees of freedom* that it can "fit" or "explain" perfectly

[42] A similar conclusion was reached by Mordecai Ezekiel in his interesting paper, "Statistical Analyses and the 'Laws' of Price," *Quar. Jour of Econ.*, XLII (1928), 199–227.

any phenomenon from the price of eggs to the toboggan slide of the stock market. But such a Protean model cannot be deduced from the statistics of quantities exchanged or produced and prices paid. The statistical method can yield significant results only when it is applied to such data as can be "explained" in terms of theoretical demand and supply curves which do not change at all, or which change in a regular manner, i.e., when the demand-supply conditions are subject to a *routine of change*.

5. A very simple illustration of a routine of change occurs where both theoretical curves remain fixed or change very slowly; *and when there is a fixed time interval between changes in price and corresponding changes in supply*. This is our Case IV. In such cases it is possible to obtain fairly good approximations to both theoretical curves from the same price and quantity series.

D. THE BEARING OF THESE FINDINGS ON MOORE'S FUNDAMENTAL ASSUMPTION

The light that these findings throw on Moore's second and most important assumption is clear. When he assumes that the data are such as to yield a routine of demand, he is assuming in fact that during the period covered by the statistics of prices and quantities one of the following relations must have existed between the theoretical (and unknown) demand and supply curves: Either (1) the demand curve remained fixed, and the supply curve moved; or (2) both curves moved, but the movements of the demand curve were very small compared with those of the supply curve, so that *on the average* the statistics of the quantities and prices are observations on the relatively fixed demand curve;[43] or, (3) both curves remained fixed, or changed very slowly, but there was a fixed time interval between changes in price and corresponding changes in the quantity supplied.

In fairness to the constructive critics of Moore's methods, I must, however, hasten to observe that these assumptions are only implied, not expressed, in Moore's writings; or, rather, that they are subsumed under his general thesis that the assumptions underlying Marshall's derivation of his law of demand are neither satisfactory nor indeed admissible,[44] and that the only valid procedure for deriving Marshall's demand curve *even conceptually* is first to derive the general dynamic law of demand of which it is a special case. There is only one procedure for "keeping other things constant," as Marshall's theory demands, and that is first to take the "other things" into consideration in the general formulation of the law of demand and then to assign constant values to all the other variables except the price and the quantity of the commodity in question. But among these other variables are to be found the various "disturbing fac-

---

[43] Strictly speaking, the condition must also be added that the shiftings of the two curves are uncorrelated with one another.

[44] See pp. 71–72.

tors," such as changes in population, changes in income, etc., which bring about the shifts in the demand and supply curves. When measures or indices of these disturbing factors are available, it may be possible either to derive the general demand equation which would give the Cournot-Marshall demand curve as a special case or to apply corrections directly to the prices and quantities of the commodity in question, and obtain approximately the same result. It is this aspect of Moore's theory which has escaped the attention of most of his critics.

In justice to Moore, I must, however, record the fact that several years before the question was raised in the literature he was well aware of the implications for his procedure of shifts in the theoretical demand and supply curves. Indeed, I discussed it with him as far back as 1924. But he could not, as do most of his critics, accept the Cournot-Marshall demand curve at its face value. He questioned the assumptions underlying it, and he did not wish to give it much prominence in his own theoretical structure. To him the problem was much more complex, namely, how to derive the general dynamic demand function from statistical observations. If all the variables entering into it were known and measurable, the Cournot-Marshall demand curve could be derived as a special case and the manner of its shifting explained. Since, however, it is impossible in a statistical investigation to take all the relevant factors into account or to make allowance for them, Moore preferred to call his statistical curves "dynamic curves." But he did not mean to suggest that his statistically derived curve had no relation at all to Marshall's—when the latter can be given an unambiguous meaning. Indeed, it may be a very good approximation to it. But the burden of proof is on the investigator. He must decide, on the basis of all the known facts of the industry or commodity in question, what interpretation to give to it. With this view I have been, and am still, in hearty agreement.

Part of the difficulty which students of Moore's methods have had with his underlying assumption is, I am sure, traceable to his claim that the demand curve for a producers' good, of which pig iron is an example, is positively inclined in a dynamic society. The improbability of this view has tended to give the impression that Moore and his followers would call the result of *any* correlation between the price of a commodity and the quantity of it that is produced or consumed a demand curve, whether it be positively sloping or negatively sloping, reasonable or unreasonable. This is indeed regrettable, for, although we may not be inclined to accept his conclusion on the demand for producers' goods, we must, nevertheless, admit that it was not reached without the inspiration of pure theory.[45] Furthermore, Moore's fundamental contributions to the statistical study of demand, which have opened up a new, difficult, and useful field of research, are quite independent of this part of his work.

[45] See chap. i, p. 51.

In recent years two other attacks on the problem of deriving statistical demand curves from time series of quantities and prices have been suggested. These are connected with the names of Dr. Wassily Leontief, now of Harvard University, and Professor A. C. Pigou. We turn to an examination of these methods.

IV. PROFESSOR LEONTIEF'S METHOD

Leontief's method[46] lays most claim to rationality, being based directly on certain preconceptions of economic theory. Moreover, it has been applied to as many as forty-six series relating to seven different commodities.

The chief feature which differentiates his method from all others is his attempt to derive the elasticities of both demand and supply by a single calculation from the same set of unadjusted statistics of prices and corresponding quantities. According to Leontief, it is not only unnecessary but even undesirable to make allowance for changes in the purchasing power of money, in the prices of substitutes, and in other disturbing factors. There is no place in his procedure for adjusted data, link relatives, trend ratios, the "lag" method, multiple and partial correlation, and the other devices which are used by Moore and his followers. These are judged to be "empirical," leading neither to pure demand curves nor to pure supply curves, and are at best only imperfect substitutes for his procedure.

A. HIS UNDERLYING ASSUMPTIONS

Leontief's method is based on the following assumptions:

1. Each market transaction represents the intersection of an instantaneous (Cournot-Marshall) demand curve with a theoretical instantaneous supply curve, and these curves change their positions from time to time.

2. For each of these curves the elasticity is approximately constant.

3. The shiftings of the demand and supply curves are independent of one another, and do not affect the shape (elasticity) of the curves.

The implication of the first assumption is that one must determine not only the elasticities of demand and supply but also the extent to which the theoretical curves have shifted from time to time.

The meaning of the second assumption is that the demand and supply curves appear as straight lines when plotted on double-logarithmic paper.

The geometrical translation of the third assumption is that a shift of the

---

[46] Wassily Leontief, "Ein Versuch zur statistischen Analyse von Angebot und Nachfrage," *Weltwirtschaftliches Archiv*, XXX, Heft 1 (July, 1929), 1*–53*. The present discussion of Leontief's method is taken with some slight changes from my little book, *Der Sinn der statistischen Nachfragekurven*, Appen. II. The period covered by the data used in the statistical illustrations of this discussion (1890–1914) does not agree with the period generally used in the statistical chapters of the present book (1896–1914), but as the conclusions reached are quite independent of the length of the period, it is hardly advisable to recompute the coefficients of elasticity.

demand curve to the right is just as likely to be associated with a shift of the supply curve to the left as to the right.

B. HIS STATISTICAL PROCEDURE

The actual statistical procedure is very simple. It consists of fitting two straight lines to the scatter of the logarithms of the observations. Since the shiftings of the theoretical curves are assumed to be independent of each other, it follows that if one of the curves, say, the supply curve, be given, the demand curve can be found from it.[47] A convenient method of doing this—and it is the one adopted by Leontief—is to take as the demand curve the line which minimizes the sum of the squares of the deviations about it *measured parallel to the supply curve;* and vice versa. But neither curve is given. It follows that from one scatter diagram of quantities and prices we can deduce an infinite number of pairs of curves related in this manner. To get a unique solution, Leontief arranges his observations in chronological order, divides them into two equal parts, fits a pair of lines to the scatter of each half, imposing the condition (developed by Dr. Robert Schmidt in his Mathematical Appendix to Leontief's article) that the two scatters should have one pair of curves in common.[48] One of these curves is taken as the demand curve, and the other as the supply curve.

[47] See Leontief, *op. cit.*, pp. 24*–25*.

[48] The formulas for determining the slopes (elasticities) of the two lines are, respectively,

$$\eta_1 = \frac{\lambda_1 x_1 - a x_2}{\lambda_1 z_1 - a z_2},$$

$$\eta_2 = \frac{\lambda_2 x_1 - a x_2}{\lambda_2 z_1 - a z_2},$$

where x_1 and x_2 are the sums of the squares of the x's (logarithms of quantities) of the two periods, y_1 and y_2 are the sums of the squares of the y's (logarithms of prices), and z_1 and z_2 are the sums of the products of the x's and the y's, all variables being measured from their respective means. The other terms are defined as follows:

$$a = x_1 y_1 - z_1^2$$
$$b = x_1 y_2 + x_2 y_1 - 2 z_1 z_2$$
$$c = x_2 y_2 - z_2^2$$

and λ_1 and λ_2 are the roots of the quadratic

$$\lambda^2 - b\lambda + ac = 0.$$

Since the publication of my *Der Sinn der statistischen Nachfragekurven*, from which the discussion in the text is taken, Ragnar Frisch in his *Pitfalls in the Statistical Construction of Demand and Supply Curves* ("Veröffentlichungen der Frankfurter Gesellschaft für Konjunkturforschung" [N.F.], Heft 5), ed. Dr. Eugen Altschul (Leipzig, 1933), has shown how Leontief's results may be deduced in a much simpler manner, and without the use of least squares. (I have taken the liberty to modify Frisch's symbols so as to conform with those used in the first part of this note.)

Let

$$x(t) - \eta_1 y(t) = u(t)$$
$$x(t) - \eta_2 y(t) = v(t)$$

be the demand and supply curves, respectively, where t is time, u and v are the shifts, η_1 and η_2 are the elasticities of the demand and supply curves, the u's and v's as well as the x's and y's being meas-

The two curves thus found represent the "average" demand and supply curves. The distance of the observations (points) for each year from the average demand curve (measured parallel to the supply curve) and the distance of the same point from the supply curve (measured parallel to the demand curve) are taken by Leontief as the respective amounts by which the demand and supply curves for that year have shifted from their average positions.

The average, or general, elasticity which relates to the entire period covered by the data is not, however, the only elasticity deduced by Leontief. By taking moving averages of his data, and by applying the same procedure to the smoothed data, he also determines coefficients which have a different significance, and which must be interpreted from a different point of view.

Leontief illustrates his method by deriving forty-six elasticities of demand and an equal number of elasticities of supply.

The foregoing summary gives only the bare outlines of the method, containing no reference to the reservations and qualifications with which it is presented. For a full explanation the reader is referred to the original paper.

C. ILLUSTRATIONS AND COMPARISONS

Leontief does not compare his method with the methods of Moore and his followers by applying all of them to one and the same problem. We shall, therefore, supply this deficiency by subjecting the sugar data used in my *Der Sinn der statistischen Nachfragekurven* to an analysis by the Leontief method.

The scatter diagram of Figure 9 represents the logarithms of the total consumption of sugar, and the logarithms of the money prices from 1890 to 1914. The correlation between the two series of logarithms is $r = -0.058 \pm 0.199$. The low correlation is indicated by the large angle between the two lines of regression $A'A'$ and AA, whose equations are, respectively,

(4.1) $$\log x = 3.56180 - 0.17120 \log y$$

and

(4.2) $$\log y = 3.68804 - 0.01997 \log x .$$

---

ured from their respective means. Multiply one of these equations by the other and then sum over time. The result is

$$\eta_1 \eta_2 \, \Sigma y^2 - (\eta_1 + \eta_2)\Sigma xy + \Sigma x^2 = \Sigma uv .$$

Since the shifts in u and v are assumed independent, the right-hand member of this equation is zero. But from this one equation it is impossible to determine the two unknowns, η_1 and η_2. If, however, the data be divided into two parts, there result two equations:

$$\eta_1 \eta_2 - (\eta_1 + \eta_2) \frac{z_1}{y_1} + \frac{x_1}{y_1} = 0 ,$$

$$\eta_1 \eta_2 - (\eta_1 + \eta_2) \frac{z_2}{y_2} + \frac{x_2}{y_2} = 0 ,$$

sufficient to determine the two unknowns. The values of η_1 and η_2 thus obtained are identical with those secured by using Leontief's method.

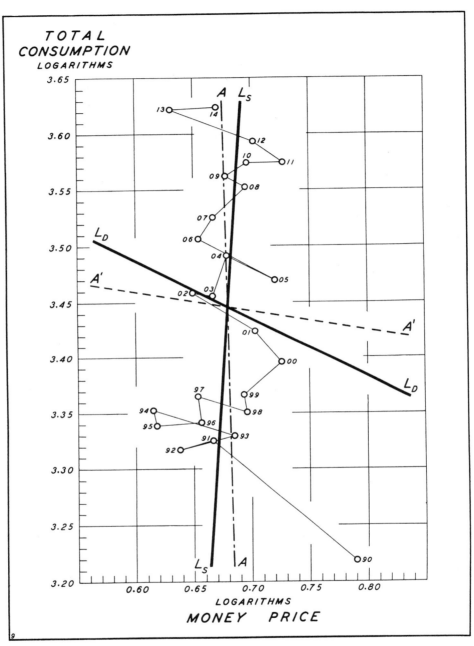

FIG. 9.—Leontief's curves of demand, $L_D L_D$, and supply, $L_S L_S$, obtained from the total consumption and money prices of sugar in the United States, 1890–1914, compared with the two lines of regression, $A'A'$ and AA.

Leontief's procedure for deriving elasticities of demand and supply calls for a division of the observations into two equal parts. As, in the present problem, there is an odd number of pairs of observations (25), we have considered the first thirteen pairs (1890–1902) as constituting the first part, and the last twelve pairs (1903–14) as the second part. By performing the computations as explained in Leontief's paper, we obtained for his curves

(4.3) $$\log x = 3.79570 - 0.51562 \log y$$

and

(4.4) $$\log x = -6.74573 + 15.00600 \log y .$$

These are the lines $L_D L_D$ and $L_S L_S$ in Figure 8. There is nothing in the mathematics of Leontief's procedure to necessitate that the slopes of the two curves obtained by his method should be of opposite sign, or to enable us to distinguish the demand curve from the supply curve. Since, however, one of the curves of this example (eq. [4.3]) happens to have a negative slope, and the other (eq. [4.4]) a positive slope, it is perhaps reasonable to call the first the "demand curve" and the second the "supply curve."

From (4.4) we get for Leontief's elasticity of demand $\eta_1 = -0.5156$, and from (4.4) we get for his elasticity of supply $\eta_2 = +15.006$.

What do these figures mean? The figure $\eta_1 = -0.52$ may perhaps be taken as an approximation to the mean elasticity of demand derived by the methods discussed in this study, which, as I have shown elsewhere, varied from -0.21 to -0.78. But his figure $\eta_2 = 15.0$, which means that a 1 per cent increase in price will call forth a 15 per cent increase in the output, appears to be devoid of economic meaning.

It cannot measure the short-time elasticity of supply, for the following reasons: (a) The data relate to consumption, not to production, and consumption figures cannot, in the present problem, lead to an elasticity of supply which has meaning because the United States is not a self-contained economy with respect to sugar.[49] It derives its supply partly from domestic production, partly from imports from insular possessions, but mostly from imports from the rest of the world. (b) When the supplies coming to the United States from the various

[49] This example is not unfair to Leontief, for in his own examples he derives both coefficients of elasticity sometimes from the statistics of consumption and prices, and sometimes from the data of production and prices, without considering the problems which arise when the economy under consideration is not a self-contained economy. See the table on pp. 42*-43* of his paper.

sources are studied separately, we find that their elasticities vary from $+0.56$ to $+1.05$.[50] This is a far cry from an elasticity of supply of 15.0! (c) There was not a single instance on record during the twenty-five years from 1890 to 1914 where the relative annual increase (or decrease) in production, in consumption, or in imports was accompanied by a relative increase (or decrease) in price in the ratio of 15 to 1. Certainly, no one who has studied the sugar industry in the United States will claim that a 1 per cent change in price is likely to call forth a 15 per cent change in supply *in the same year*.

It cannot measure the long-time elasticity of supply for the reason that the total consumption of sugar between 1890 and 1914 increased by 155 per cent, while the price of sugar *decreased* by 24 per cent. This would lead to a ratio of -6.5, which differs both in sign and in magnitude from Leontief's figure of $+15.0$.[51] One may perhaps select a pair of years during which the relative change in consumption and price was in the ratio of 15 to 1. But is this the meaning that Leontief would wish to give to his figure?

We are inclined to conclude, therefore, that *both* of Leontief's coefficients of elasticity are numerical accidents having no economic meaning. An additional reason for this belief is the sheer arbitrariness of his procedure. There is no more reason for dividing his observations into two equal parts in order to get a solution than there is for dividing them into two unequal parts. In the present example, where the number of pairs of observations is odd (25), we included the thirteenth pair of observations (i.e., the price and the quantity for 1902), in the first part, and obtained the results $\eta_1 = -0.52$, and $\eta_2 = +15.0$. Had we, however, included the observations for 1902 in the second part, the corresponding values would have been $\eta_1 = -0.43$, and $\eta_2 = +9.04$. Still greater differences might be obtained by dividing the period in yet another manner.

It may be thought that, since the correlation between the unadjusted series used in this example is practically zero, the determination of the elasticities of

---

[50] See my *Statistical Laws of Demand and Supply with Special Application to Sugar*, chap. v, and Table XI, p. 201. The elasticities of supply there given are derived from "lines of mutual regression." The use of the ordinary "regression of x on y," or the "regression of y on x," would have led to somewhat different elasticities of supply.

[51] If we find the average annual increase of consumption and price by fitting compound-interest curves to the data, we obtain

$$x = 2789.4e^{0.0348t}$$

and

$$y = 4.776e^{0.00065t}$$

where x is measured in thousands of tons, y in cents, and t in years from 1902 as the origin. The first equation tells us that consumption increased at the rate of 3.48 per cent per annum. The second equation tells us that prices increased at the rate of 0.065 of 1 per cent per annum. This would lead to a long-time "elasticity of supply" of $+53.5$ instead of -6.5!

demand and supply is left too much to chance, and that the result is, therefore, not a fair test of Leontief's method.

Although the obvious answer is that Leontief himself deduces elasticities of demand and supply from pairs of series between which the correlation appears to be just as low as between the data of the present example, and although Leontief does not require that there should be any correlation between the two variables (price and quantity), it is nevertheless instructive to apply his method to a case where the correlation is high.

The scatter diagram of the logarithms of per capita consumption and the logarithms of real prices is such a case. The correlation between the two series of logarithms is $r = -0.904 \pm 0.037$. Figure 10 is a graphic illustration of this series. The two lines of regression are $A'A'$ and AA, and their respective equations are

$$(4.5) \qquad \log x = 2.40974 - 0.80062 \log y$$

and

$$(4.6) \qquad \log y = 2.58637 - 1.02006 \log x .$$

Grouping the observations in the same way as in the previous example, we obtain, respectively, for Leontief's lines L_DL_D and L_SL_S the equations

$$(4.7) \qquad \log x = 2.52493 - 0.96522 \log y$$

and

$$(4.8) \qquad \log x = 1.89095 - 0.05927 \log y .$$

Here both of Leontief's lines are negatively inclined, leading to $\eta_1 = -0.9652$, and $\eta_2 = -0.0593$, instead of $\eta_1 = -0.5156$, and $\eta_2 = +15.006$, as obtained from the unadjusted data.

The results give rise to several questions. Which of these two negatively sloping curves is the demand curve, and which is the supply curve? Are they short-time, reversible demand and supply curves; or long-time, irreversible demand and supply curves? If these are short-time curves, does not the negatively sloping supply curve mean that we have a condition of unstable equilibrium? How can Leontief explain a negatively sloping supply curve in terms of his fundamental assumptions? Leontief meets cases where both curves have the same sign for their slopes in his own examples. But he does not attempt to explain them. He does not seem to realize that the fact that his method may lead to two negatively sloping curves is inconsistent with the fundamental assumption of his theory, which is that the supply curve must be positively inclined.

It may be argued, however, that both per capita consumption and real price are subject to secular movements; that Leontief erred when he decided not to

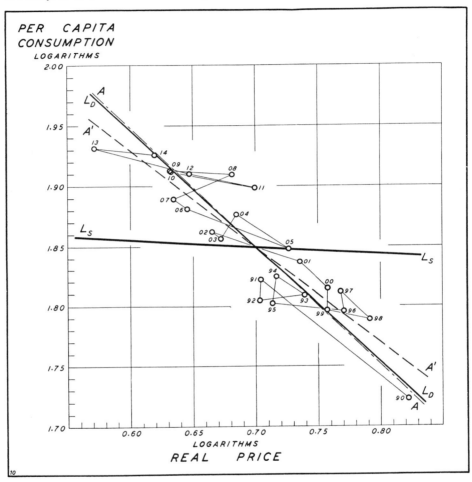

Fig. 10.—Leontief's curves of demand, L_DL_D, and supply, L_SL_S, obtained from the per capita consumption and real prices of sugar in the United States, 1890–1914, compared with the two lines of regression, $A'A'$ and AA.

eliminate the trends from his series; and that, if the two series were adjusted for secular changes, Leontief's method would not lead to ridiculous results.[52]

[52] This argument was actually made by H. J. Wadleigh, a former co-worker of Leontief's at Kiel, and later a Fellow in the Department of Economics at the University of Chicago. I am indebted to Mr. Wadleigh for discussing Leontief's method with me.

Figure 11 is designed to throw light on this question. It is the scatter diagram of the logarithms of the *trend ratios* of per capita consumption and real prices.

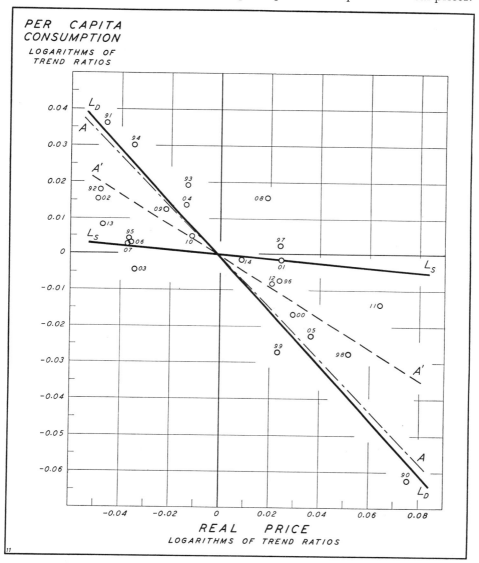

FIG. 11.—Leontief's curves of demand, L_DL_D, and supply, L_SL_S, obtained from the trend ratios of the per capita consumption and the real prices of sugar in the United States, 1890–1914, compared with the two lines of regression, $A'A'$ and AA.

The coefficient of correlation between the two series is $r = -0.782 \pm 0.078$, and the equations of the two lines of regression, $A'A'$ and AA, are, respectively

$$\log X = -0.00086 - 0.43215 \log Y$$

and

$$\log Y = -0.00166 - 1.41662 \log X .$$

It will be observed that the fit of these lines to the data is very good.

By dividing the series in the same manner as in the preceding examples, we obtain for Leontief's curves, $L_D L_D$ and $L_S L_S$, respectively, the equations

(4.9) $\log X = -0.00122 - 0.75020 \log Y$

and

(4.10) $\log X = -0.00043 - 0.05757 \log Y ,$

from which $\eta_1 = -0.75$, and $\eta_2 = -0.06$. Neither of Leontief's lines can be said to fit the data.

Again we ask, What do these figures mean? Which is the elasticity of demand, and which is the elasticity of supply? Why does Leontief's method lead to such divergent results, when the methods which he criticizes—trend ratios, link relatives, multiple correlation—whether applied to the adjusted or to the unadjusted data, all give practically the same value for the elasticities of demand? How can he explain two negatively sloping curves, when his fundamental assumption is that the supply curve must be positively inclined? What *economic meaning* can he give to his coefficient of elasticity of supply which varies from -0.06 to $+15.0$?

D. APPRAISAL

Leontief's difficulties have their roots in his economic analysis of the demand-supply problem as well as in the limitations of the statistical methods which he employs.

I. LIMITATIONS OF THE ECONOMIC ARGUMENT

By making the conventional assumption that the Cournot-Marshall demand and supply curves can shift in any direction, and that the shiftings of the two curves are independent of one another, he throws overboard the fundamental principle of the general theory of equilibrium, i.e., that the demand for any one commodity is a function not only of its price but of all other prices, and is led to adopt a pattern possessing so many degrees of freedom that it can "explain" any price and quantity series, including the errors which generally abound in such data. Thus, suppose that we wittingly introduce large errors or deviations into the series of consumption and prices. This would generally make it impossible to deduce demand and supply curves from such data by the correlation approach, or by any of the other methods used by Moore and his followers. By Leontief's method, however, these errors could be "explained" as coordinates and points of intersection of hypothetical demand and supply curves which can shift in any direction. If it seems strange that it should be possible to get such ridiculous results by Leontief's method without doing violence to the assumptions underlying it, the explanation lies in the fact that by it one cannot determine how much of a given price change results from such known and measurable factors as growth of population, changes in the prices of substitutes, and variation in the purchasing power of money; how much from factors which have not been taken into account; and how much from errors or deficiencies in the data. By Leontief's method these errors are treated on a par with the true causal factors, and are explained in the same way, i.e., as the coordinates of the points of intersection of shifting demand and supply curves.

Another difficulty in Leontief's economic analysis must be noted. He implicitly assumes that the supply and demand curves shift *simultaneously*. Is this a reasonable assumption for an agricultural commodity like potatoes? We know that in the United States a high price for potatoes in any one year is, on the average, associated with a high production in the following year; and that a low price in any one year is associated with a low production in the following year. Since Leontief rejects the "lag" method and derives two curves from prices and quantities for synchronous years, what meaning can he give to the "supply curve" thus obtained?

2. LIMITATIONS OF THE STATISTICAL PROCEDURE

Turning now to the technical and statistical aspects of Leontief's method, we are also struck with several shortcomings:

1. As Dr. Robert Schmidt points out in his Mathematical Appendix to Leontief's paper, the mathematical solution leads to two curves only when the ellipses of the two scatters into which Leontief breaks up his series are not similar to each other, and the corresponding axes are not parallel to one another. But when the scatter for the first period is significantly[53] different from that of the second, is this not an indication that the data are not homogeneous, and that, therefore, each period should be studied separately?[54]

[53] Of course, the chances that in any concrete problem the two scatters will be *perfectly* similar are very small.

[54] Since the appearance of these lines in 1930, Professor Ragnar Frisch has published a memoir entitled, *Pitfalls in the Statistical Construction of Demand and Supply Curves*, in which he gives an algebraic statement of the difficulty which arises when the two scatters are similar and in which he develops the necessary conditions for Leontief's procedure to have meaning. Frisch is, however, in error when he writes (p. 35): "Schultz has carried out a series of numerical computations comparing the Leontief coefficients with those obtained by the Moore-Schultz method. *From this empirical comparison* he concludes that there must be something wrong with Leontief's method." (Italics are mine.) As the reader will observe, the points which I make in this paragraph are not based on the statistical results which I have presented. They were, in fact, suggested by a study of the mathematics of Leontief's method as given in Dr. Robert Schmidt's Mathematical Appendix. See also Wassily Leontief, "Pitfalls in the Construction of Demand and Supply Curves: A Reply," *Quar. Jour. of Econ.*, XLVIII (1934), 352–63; "More Pitfalls in Demand and Supply Analysis"; Ragnar Frisch, "A Reply"; Wassily Leontief, "A Final Word"; Jacob Marschak, "Some Comments," *ibid.*, XLVIII (1934), 749–67.

2. Leontief's method breaks down whether either the theoretical demand curve or the theoretical supply curve has more than two parameters or "constants." He assumes that the elasticities of his underlying theoretical curves are constant, not so much because that is a simple, convenient assumption to make,[55] but because the assumption of a more complicated curve would spell the failure of his entire method.

3. There is no way of verifying Leontief's assumption that the elasticities of his underlying curves are constant. One may, for example, assume that the underlying theoretical demand and supply curves are straight lines (on arithmetic scale), and, since a straight line has also two parameters, one can apply Leontief's method to the absolute data (instead of to the logarithmic) and obtain the equations of these lines. One can make an equally good "explanation" of the observed scatter in terms of the shiftings of these straight lines, whose elasticities vary from point to point. By Leontief's procedure one can thus "explain" the actual data either as the coordinates of points of intersection of two straight lines, or of two constant-elasticity curves (straight lines on a double logarithmic scale). There is no way of telling which explanation is in better agreement with the facts.

4. As Leontief himself recognizes ("Ein Versuch . . . . ," p. 38*), his fundamental assumption that the shifts in the demand and supply curves are independent of each other is contradicted by the statistical results which he obtains for several of his series. His attempt to resolve this contradiction in terms of various "levels" of elasticity is not convincing.

5. Leontief's failure to allow for changes in the purchasing power of money, and to separate secular movements from short-time movements either by eliminating the secular trends from his series or by using any of the other methods referred to in this study, would lead him to spurious results, even if his method were otherwise beyond reproach. Furthermore, he contradicts himself when, after arguing against the practice of eliminating trends, he proceeds to derive his coefficients of elasticity from moving averages. What is a moving average if not a kind of trend?

6. Even if the foregoing shortcomings be waived, the fact remains that Leontief's method can neither separate nor measure the intensity of the various price-making forces, as is possible by the correlation approach.

For these and other reasons,[56] the conclusion emerges that Leontief's method

---

[55] See, however, Pareto's discussion of this point in the *Encyclopédie des sciences mathématiques,* Tome I, Vol. IV, Fasc. 4, § 23, 619–20.

[56] Three minor points must be noted:

1. Leontief argues ("Ein Versuch . . . . ," *op. cit.,* p. 4*, n. 3) that "Jeder Schritt in der mathematischen Ebene muss ökonomisch interpretiert werden können, wenn er nicht seinen Sinn verlieren soll." Surely, this is asking for the impossible. The mathematical solution is, in most cases, more general than is necessary for the concrete problem under consideration. The conditions of the

is an extremely arbitrary method, and that the results obtained by it are apt to be arithmetical accidents.

Students of the subject will, however, always be grateful to Leontief for his bold and painstaking attempt to deduce the true statical, Cournot-Marshall demand and supply curves from statistics. His efforts will not have been wasted if they serve to convince economists and statisticians of the futility of trying to obtain these curves without first examining, by means of "mental experiments," whether and to what extent the Cournot-Marshall law of supply and demand has meaning in terms of operations. Such an examination may possibly lead to a new statement of the law of supply and demand. If so, this will not be the first time in the history of science that an important goal has been reached through the re-formulation of an earlier principle. The Principle of Least Action, which according to the eminent physicist, Professor Max Planck, is "the chief law of physics, the pinnacle of the whole system," exercised no appreciable effect on the advance of science until it was restated by H. von Helmholtz in a form admitting of quantitative application.[57]

Perhaps the principal difference between Leontief's procedure and that connected with the name of Moore is simply this: Leontief looks at a scatter diagram of prices and quantities and sees in it traces of unrelated, arbitrary shiftings of hypothetical demand and supply curves; the latter seeks to discover in it a "routine of change," such as will be illustrated in the statistical chapters of this book.[58]

---

problem must be studied with a view of selecting that solution which is significant for the purpose in view.

2. He misunderstands (*ibid.*, p. 20*, n. 1) the rationale of a method of curve-fitting used by the present writer in his book, *Statistical Laws of Demand and Supply.* He thinks that the method consists of fitting a curve by minimizing the sum of the squares of the perpendicular deviations of the points from the curve. The method is much more general. *It enables us to assign weights to both variables in any ratio*—something which is not possible by the ordinary methods. It is only when the observations in x are given the same weight as those in y that the method makes the sum of the squares of the normal deviations a minimum (see p. 38 of that book and Sec. III, chap. iv, and Sec. I, Appen. C, of this work). Furthermore, my method, just like Leontief's method, leads to *two* curves, one of them being "the line of *best* fit," and the other "the line of *worst* fit." The latter is rejected.

3. Leontief ("Ein Versuch . . . . ," *op. cit.*, p. 42*) applies his method to an index of production of twelve crops. If, in constructing the index, the crops are weighted according to their *values*, then the elasticities of demand and supply do not represent the relative change in *quantity* corresponding to a relative change in price. The whole subject requires further investigation.

[57] See Max Planck, *A Survey of Physics* (London, 1925), essay entitled "The Principle of Least Action."

[58] In fairness to Leontief, I asked him to comment on the foregoing analysis of his method and to advise me of any revisions of it which he may have had occasion to make. I quote from his reply (November 1, 1933):

"1) I have not introduced any changes in the statistical computation itself, but two reliability measures have been added, which enable me to give a more definite interpretation of the results

V. PROFESSOR PIGOU'S SECOND METHOD

Professor Pigou has made two contributions to the statistical study of demand, the first of which was published in 1910[59] and the second in 1930.[60] The first method is designed for use in connection with family-budget data and will be considered in chapter iii. Here we shall consider only his second contribution.

Pigou is critical both of Moore's approach and of Leontief's. Identifying the former with the method of link relatives and the method of trend ratios as used in my *Statistical Laws of Demand and Supply*—he does not refer to the method of multiple correlation, which is also employed in that book—he argues that both these methods require for their justification the assumption that the demand curves may be treated without serious error as straight lines and that their movements conform to certain conditions. It is not, however, easy to make explicit precisely what these conditions are. A mathematical machine is grinding out results; but the *exact* nature of what was put into the machine at the beginning is, at all events to non-expert readers, somewhat obscure. This is true in a still higher degree of the more complicated method of deriving demand curves employed in his interesting article in the *Weltwirtschaftliches Archiv* of July, 1929, by Dr. Wassily Leontief. A more serious difficulty is that, while the objective sought by these writers in respect of any interval—year or month—is avowedly the *most probable* demand curve, not the actual demand curve, no explicit calculation is made of the probable error to which the results attained are subject. We are not told, nor, I think, can we easily ascertain, within what limits the actual demand curve is more likely than not to lie. This is a very important matter, because some sort of data must obviously allow of a more reliable conclusion being drawn than is possible with other sorts.[61]

---

obtained. The first of these two measures characterizes the *difference in the shape* of the two distributions (ellipses) on which the whole computation is based.

[Here he gives formulas.]

"The second measure refers to the total price-quantity distribution and describes the *relative reliability of each of the two curves separately*. It may also be described as indicating the relative intensity of shifts of the two curves.

[Here he gives formulas.]

"Applying this criterion to your examples of the use of my method on the sugar data, you will find that the 'supply' curves are absolutely unreliable.

. . . .

"2) I agree with you that trends have to be eliminated.

"3) Your objection concerning time-lags is perfectly justified. I think, however, that in most cases in which such a lag makes the discovery of one of the two curves impossible, the nonsensical result will automatically reveal itself: The 'impossible' curve will have a tendency to assume a vertical or horizontal position, which reads: 'no relation.'

"4) I agree that there is no sense in trying to measure the fit of my curves. I hope, however, that you will agree with me that in the case where the choice of any *particular type* of curve (which is to be fitted) is more or less free, the *goodness of fit* is far from being indicative of the quality of the result.

. . . .

"5) I still feel that a choice of logarithmic shifts is more than a purely statistical assumption."

I am delighted at this agreement with Professor Leontief on so many points.

[59] "A Method of Determining the Numerical Value of Elasticities of Demand," *op. cit.*, pp. 636–40, and reprinted in *Economics of Welfare*, Appen. II.

[60] "The Statistical Derivation of Demand Curves," *op. cit.*, pp. 384–400, and reprinted in Pigou and Robertson, *op. cit.*, pp. 62–83.

[61] "The Statistical Derivation of Demand Curves," *op. cit.*, pp. 390–91. (Italics are Pigou's.)

A. HIS DEFINITIONS AND ASSUMPTIONS

Like Leontief, Pigou works with the Cournot-Marshall demand curve. Thus he defines demand curves for the purpose of his study as curves giving "the quantities of a commodity that a market will buy during a short interval, say a year, in response to different average prices proper to the interval."[62] He is careful to point out, however, the fact that the quantity of any commodity demanded may be a function not only of its price but also of *"the conditions of supply* of several other things" (italics are Pigou's), but he assumes that in each interval these conditions are constant. In his own words,

if t be the distance of any interval from some basal moment, we write, ignoring the fact that our intervals are in practice of finite duration,

$$x_i = f(y_i, t) .$$

In respect of a given interval t has some constant value, say T; and, when this is given, all the other conditions relevant to the quantity demanded, except only the price of our commodity, are conceived as frozen solid. So interpreted, the statement that there is, in respect of our commodity, a single definite demand curve in respect of each interval is true, no matter how many substitutes and so on there may be for it.[63]

Since the statistical data by themselves give only one observation—a single point—on the theoretical demand curve for each time interval, it is clear that it is impossible to derive the demand curve as a whole or any part of it "unless we marry to the statistical data some hypothesis or hypotheses external to them and derived from elsewhere."[64] The hypotheses which Pigou finally adopts are: (1) that the demand curve is likely to have a smooth and not a kinky appearance in each interval; and (2) that it shifts steadily over different periods of time, the rate of shift being equal in two (small) successive intervals.

More specifically, Pigou assumes (1) that the demand curve for each interval is a curve of constant elasticity (i.e., a straight line when plotted on double-logarithmic paper); and (2) that its rate of shift is such that the distance between the first and the second position (on a logarithmic scale) is the same as between the second and the third.

B. HIS STATISTICAL PROCEDURE

The procedure which enables him to marry these hypotheses to the data is the geometric proposition that through three noncollinear points only three triads of parallel straight lines can be drawn which are equidistant from one another vertically (which also implies horizontally).[65] If, however, we specify the point which shall lie on the middle line, then only one triad is possible.

[62] *Ibid.*, p. 384.

[63] *Ibid.*, p. 385. I have taken the liberty to modify some of Professor Pigou's symbols.

[64] *Ibid.*, p. 386.

[65] Professor Pigou does not consider the question of the collinearity of the points and also states that only *two* triads of lines are possible. These slips have been pointed out by Professor Wirth Ferger, "Notes on Pigou's Method of Deriving Demand Curves," *Economic Journal*, XLII (1932),

Figure 12 is an illustration of this proposition, the "straight lines" being constant-elasticity curves drawn with the logarithms of the quantities as abscissas and the logarithms of the prices as ordinates. If the three points represent by their coordinates observed quantities and prices for three chronologically successive years (or other periods), the problem is to determine the slope of the lines so that they will be equidistant from one another vertically (which also implies horizontally), the middle line passing through the second point.[66]

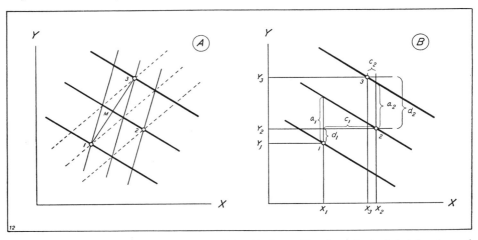

FIG. 12.—Illustration of the theory underlying Professor Pigou's method of deriving demand curves from market data. *A:* The three triads of equidistant parallel lines which can be drawn through the three points *1, 2, 3.* (If we specify that point *2* shall lie on the middle line, only one triad [the heavy lines] can be drawn.)   *B:* Method of determining the slope of the triad in a case favorable to the Pigou theory. (See the text.)

Let the coordinates of the three points be, respectively, (X_1, Y_1), (X_2, Y_2), (X_3, Y_3)—the capital letters designating logarithms—and let

$$d_1 = Y_1 - Y_2 \qquad c_1 = X_1 - X_2$$
$$d_2 = Y_2 - Y_3 \qquad c_2 = X_2 - X_3 .$$

Write also a_1 and a_2 for the vertical distance of the first line above the second, and of the second above the third. Then the slope of the lines is given by the expression

(5.1)
$$\frac{d_1 - a_1}{c_1} = \frac{d_2 - a_2}{c_2} .$$

17–26; by Dr. J. M. Cassels, "A Critical Consideration of Professor Pigou's Method for Deriving Demand Curves," *ibid.*, XLIII (1933), 575–87; and by R. G. D. Allen, "A Critical Examination of Professor Pigou's Method of Deriving Demand Elasticity," *Econometrica*, II (1934), 249–57.

[66] As has been pointed out by Ferger, Cassels and Allen, this can be done graphically in a very simple manner. In Fig. 12*A* draw the line connecting the points 1 and 3; now draw a line through *M*, the midpoint of 13, and the point 2. This gives the middle line of the triad. The other two may now be drawn parallel to this one. By a similar procedure we can obtain the other two triads.

This is obviously equal to

$$(5.2) \qquad \frac{(d_1 - a_1) - (d_2 - a_2)}{c_1 - c_2} = \frac{(d_1 - d_2) - (a_1 - a_2)}{c_1 - c_2}.$$

But when the vertical distance between the first line and the second is equal to that between the second and the third, then $a_1 - a_2 = 0$, and the slope reduces to the form

$$(5.3) \qquad \frac{d_1 - d_2}{c_1 - c_2}.$$

Substituting for the d's and c's their values, we have

$$(5.4) \qquad \frac{(Y_1 - Y_2) - (Y_2 - Y_3)}{(X_1 - X_2) - (X_2 - X_3)}.$$

The reciprocal of this quantity is the elasticity of demand.[67] Pigou's method of deriving demand curves from time series of quantities and prices may, therefore, be stated as follows:

1. Make up a table of the logarithms of the successive quantities (X_i) and of the logarithms of the successive prices (Y_i).
2. Compute the quantities

$$(5.5) \qquad \frac{(X_i - X_{i+1}) - (X_{i+1} - X_{i+2})}{(Y_i - Y_{i+1}) - (Y_{i+1} - Y_{i+2})} \qquad (i = 1, 2, \ldots, n).$$

These may be all negative, or all positive, or some may be negative and the others positive. Pigou's interpretation of the three cases is as follows:

When in respect of any interval the figure obtained in this manner is positive, it cannot measure the elasticity of demand for the relevant triad; a swing in demand must have occurred between the second and third intervals widely different from that which occurred between the first and second. When the figure attained is negative, it *may* measure this elasticity. If the distances between the first and second and between the second and third lines in the triad are equal, it *does* measure it.[68]

3. If the negative figures exceed the positive figures, and if all figures are grouped fairly closely about a given value, and if the data are not suspected on other grounds, then consider each quantity as an "observation" on the elasticity

---

[67] Professor Pigou attaches a ± to this quantity and states that "thus two triads of lines can be drawn through our three points, the slope of the lines in each triad being equal numerically but of opposite sign" (p. 391). But, as Professor Wirth F. Ferger pointed out in his interesting paper, "Notes on Pigou's Method of Deriving Demand Curves," *op. cit.*, pp. 17–26, this is an erroneous statement, since the sign of the slope is given unambiguously by the formula as it stands.

[68] "Statistical Derivation of Demand Curves," *op. cit.*, pp. 393–94. For a very good reason, Professor Pigou rejects the interpretation of the positive figures as observations on the supply curve. See his comment at the end of Professor Ferger's paper referred to in n. 68.

of demand, subject to an "error" due to a deviation from equality between the distance of the second line in the triad from the first and the distance of the

TABLE 1

ILLUSTRATION OF THE PIGOU METHOD OF DERIVING STATISTICAL DEMAND CURVES*

Year	X_i	$X_i - X_{i+1}$	$(X_i - X_{i+1})$ minus $(X_{i+1} - X_{i+2})$	Y_i	$Y_i - Y_{i+1}$	$(Y_i - Y_{i+1})$ minus $(Y_{i+1} - Y_{i+2})$	Col. (3) Col. (6)
	(1)	(2)	(3)	(4)	(5)	(6)	(7)
1890........	1.72263	....	....	0.82236	....	....	....
1891........	1.82151	−0.09888	....	0.70424	0.11812	....	....
1892........	1.80482	0.01669	−0.11557	0.70355	0.00069	0.11743	−0.984
1893........	1.80889	−0.00407	0.02076	0.73190	−0.02835	0.02904	0.715
1894........	1.82413	−0.01524	0.01117	0.71675	0.01515	−0.04350	−0.257
1895........	1.80209	0.02204	−0.03728	0.71357	0.00318	0.01197	−3.114
1896........	1.79588	0.00621	0.01583	0.77093	−0.05736	0.06054	0.261
1897........	1.81158	−0.01570	0.02191	0.76827	0.00266	−0.06002	−0.365
1898........	1.78888	0.02270	−0.03840	0.79120	−0.02293	0.02559	−1.501
1899........	1.79657	−0.00769	0.03039	0.75740	0.03380	−0.05673	−0.536
1900........	1.81425	−0.01768	0.00999	0.75793	−0.00053	0.03433	0.291
1901........	1.83696	−0.02271	0.00503	0.74617	0.01176	−0.01229	−0.409
1902........	1.86216	−0.02520	0.00249	0.66521	0.08096	−0.06920	−0.036
1903........	1.85065	0.01151	−0.03671	0.67237	−0.00716	0.08812	−0.417
1904........	1.87679	−0.02614	0.03765	0.68485	−0.01248	0.00532	7.077
1905........	1.84819	0.02860	−0.05474	0.72681	−0.04196	0.02948	−1.857
1906........	1.88138	−0.03319	0.06179	0.64562	0.08119	−0.12315	−0.502
1907........	1.88930	−0.00792	−0.02527	0.63478	0.01084	0.07035	−0.359
1908........	1.90956	−0.02026	0.01234	0.68151	−0.04673	−0.05757	0.214
1909........	1.91275	−0.00319	−0.01707	0.63195	0.04956	−0.09629	0.177
1910........	1.91169	0.00106	−0.00425	0.63286	−0.00091	0.05047	−0.084
1911........	1.89875	0.01294	−0.01188	0.69975	−0.06689	0.06598	−0.180
1912........	1.91009	−0.01134	0.02428	0.64748	0.05227	−0.11916	−0.204
1913........	1.93146	−0.02137	0.01003	0.57171	0.07577	−0.02350	−0.427
1914........	1.92583	0.00563	−0.02700	0.61972	−0.04801	0.12378	−0.218

* In this table I have corrected several arithmetical errors which have crept into Professor Pigou's computations and which I communicated to him in 1930. These errors necessitated a minor modification in the conclusions. I have also inserted cols. (3) and (6), which do not appear in his Table II.

third line from the second. An average of these observations should give a good approximation to the theoretical value of the coefficient of elasticity.

C. ILLUSTRATION

Pigou applies his method to two sets of data studied in my *Statistical Laws of Demand and Supply*, namely, the total consumption and the money price of sugar in the United States, 1890–1914, and the corresponding per capita consumption and the real (deflated) prices; and to one set of data studied by Leontief, namely, the monthly sales and prices of copper in the United States, January, 1909–December, 1913. For our purposes it will be sufficient to consider only one of these applications, and we shall take the one relating to the per capita consumption and real prices of sugar.

In Table 1, the figure in column 7 is positive for 1893, 1896, 1900, 1904, 1908, and 1909. In every figure except those for 1896 and 1909 the positive value is consequent upon both the price difference and the quantity difference (cols. 2 and 5) being negative. "This suggests," writes Professor Pigou, "that there has been manifest a general tendency towards an accelerated upward movement of the demand curves; and this suggests in turn that any figures derived on the assumption that the distances between the curves proper to the adjacent intervals are constant will exaggerate the elasticity of demand."[69] Of the seventeen negative figures in column 7, the minimum (numerically) is −0.036, and the maximum is −3.114. The middle nine figures lie between −0.218 and −0.536. The arithmetic mean of the negative figures is −0.674. The median— an average preferred by Professor Pigou—is −0.409. Professor Pigou's interpretation of these findings is:

We are entitled, ... to conclude with confidence that the elasticity of demand is not less than −0.250 and not greater than −0.550. It probably lies somewhere in the neighbourhood of −0.4. This conclusion may be compared with those reached by Dr. Schultz. He finds an elasticity of demand under normal conditions of consumption of −0.5; and further that, even when conditions of consumption differ substantially from normal, the coefficient of elasticity is still numerically less than 1.0.[70]

D. APPRAISAL

Any appraisal of Pigou's solution of the problem of the statistical derivation of demand curves must begin with the observation that his criticism of the Moore-Schultz approach, a criticism which appears to constitute the *raison d'être* of his own solution, is based on a misunderstanding. That criticism, it will be recalled, is that (1) the link-relative method and the trend-ratio method require for their justification the assumption that the demand curves are straight lines and that their movements conform to certain unknown conditions; and that (2) no explicit calculation is made of the probable error to which the results are subject, nor can one be easily ascertained. But a careful reading of my *Statistical Laws of Demand and Supply*, the very book to which Pigou refers, would disprove the first part of his criticism (see esp. the graphs on pp. 57 and 83). The use of any type of demand function is perfectly compatible with the method of link relatives and with the method of trend ratios. Furthermore, the conditions to which the movements of the demand curves conform when these methods are used can easily be shown.[71]

The second part of his criticism is even less valid than the first. Probable errors (or, rather, standard errors) in the least-square sense can be derived for the elasticity of demand or for the entire demand function.[72] True, I did not give any probable errors in my *Statistical Laws of Demand and Supply*, but the

[69] *Ibid.*, pp. 396–97.

[70] *Ibid.*, p. 400. See my *Statistical Laws of Demand and Supply*, p. 92.   [71] See chap. xvi.

[72] See my papers, "The Standard Error of the Coefficient of Elasticity of Demand," *Jour. Amer. Statist. Assoc.*, XXVIII (1933), 64–69 which is reproduced with some modifications in Appen. D, and "The Standard Error of a Forecast from a Curve," *ibid.*, XXV (1930), 139–85.

reason for adopting this policy was not the impossibility of computing them but rather that

> when the observations are as few as those on which these correlations are based, it is not advisable to give "probable errors," though recourse may be had to the powerful tools provided in R. A. Fisher's *Statistical Methods for Research Workers* (London, 1925), for testing the significance of constants computed from small samples. Such conclusions as are [drawn] . . . . . from the various correlations for supply are based more on the variety of methods and data used than on the significance of any coefficient of correlation (or other constant) with respect to its probable error.[73]

In my *Der Sinn der statistischen Nachfragekurven*, however, I gave the probable errors of the elasticities of demand. Pigou's criticism is, therefore, not well taken.[74]

But the fact that Pigou's contribution was motivated by a misconception of someone else's approach does not necessarily mean that it is unsound. As a matter of fact, it is an extremely neat and direct attack on the whole problem. But, like all other methods, it has certain limitations which must be kept clearly in mind.

1. It is based on the assumption that the demand curve may be written as

$$x = f(y, t) ,$$

and that the other factors can be conceived as "frozen" while we vary y and observe the corresponding variation in x. We have seen, however, that it is generally impossible to "freeze" the other factors without first taking them into account.

2. Unlike the methods developed by Moore and his followers, it can be applied only to linear demand functions, or to functions which can be reduced to linear form.

3. It cannot allow for, or separately measure, the intensity of the various factors which generally affect the demand for a commodity. This is a very serious limitation. Suppose, for example, that the negative elasticities which are expected in, or postulated by, Pigou's method had been obscured by the action of certain disturbing factors, and that, therefore, most or all of the observed elasticities—the figures in the last column of Table 1—are positive. The Pigou method then breaks down completely. The method of multiple correlation may, however, give a perfect solution in this case.

4. It is not applicable to those cases in which the underlying theoretical demand curve changes its direction of motion. But this limitation is clearly recognized by Professor Pigou.

5. It breaks down completely if in the three successive sets of observations the three price-quantity points are collinear, for the slope is then indetermi-

[73] *Statistical Laws of Demand and Supply*, p. 151, n. 16.

[74] I am pleased to report that Professor Pigou has in a letter retracted this criticism.

nate.[75] It follows, therefore, that it breaks down practically even in those cases in which the successive points are almost collinear. The closer they are to being collinear, the greater is the error in the computed slope.[76]

6. Back of Pigou's approach there is the tacit assumption that the relative positions of the observed points (prices and quantities) are such as to yield the slope of the theoretical demand curve. This corresponds to Moore's assumption that the data are such as to yield a routine of demand. But when this assumption is borne out by the facts, then several other methods are also applicable, some of them being considerably superior to that under discussion. Thus, even before Pigou's method was published, I showed[77] that the same data which Pigou used for his illustration can also be described excellently by the following simple demand hypothesis:

$$x = 141.4y^{-(0.4302\pm0.0683)} \, e^{(0.0092\pm0.0013)t}$$

where x is the per capita consumption of sugar, and y the corresponding real price. This equation tells us that during the period 1890–1914, the elasticity of demand was

$$\eta = \frac{\partial x}{\partial y}\frac{y}{x} = -0.4302 \, ,$$

[75] In practice difficulties will also arise if the three lines are parallel to one of the axes. For in this case we shall obtain an infinite or a zero value for the elasticity and this will preclude the use of the arithmetic or geometric mean. This is one of the reasons why Pigou chooses the median as the least objectionable average.

[76] The foregoing conclusions are in substantial agreement with those reached independently by Dr. John M. Cassels in his paper, "A Critical Consideration of Professor Pigou's Method for Deriving Demand Curves," *op. cit.*, pp. 575–87, to which the reader is referred for detailed developments and illustrations. (I learned of Cassels' forthcoming paper from Professor Pigou in November, 1933, when I communicated to him the substance of the present analysis.) Cassels finds the relation between the theoretical demand and supply curves and the statistical curve obtained by the Pigou method (on the assumption that the theoretical demand curve shifts continually in one direction) to be as follows:

"The more constant the rate of shifting of the supply curve the greater will be the error in the results obtained. If the supply curve (assumed to be a straight line on the chart) remained fixed while the demand curve moved at a precisely constant rate, the result would be indeterminate, i.e., the figure obtained to represent the slope would be zero. If the supply curve remained fixed while the demand curve moved unequal distances, the slope obtained would be that of the supply curve. If both moved at precisely constant rates, the slope would again be indeterminate. If both moved at approximately constant rates, the second observation would give a point close to the middle point between the other two . . . . and the triad slope would deviate widely from that of the demand curve. Actually the conditions required to give the most dependable results would be those in which the supply curve had swung back and forth from one extreme to the other between each pair of successive observations, while the demand curve moved at an approximately constant rate" (p. 581).

". . . . in cases where the direction [of motion] was reversed while the observations were being made, there is not even a semblance of logical relationship between the derived slopes and the slopes of the real demand curves that we are trying to discover" (p. 582). See also Allen, "A Critical Examination . . . . ," *loc. cit.*

[77] See my *Der Sinn der statistischen Nachfragekurven*, pp. 68 and 70, n. 23.

with a standard error of 0.0683 units, and that the demand curve shifted its position upward at the average rate of 0.92 per cent per annum,[78] for

$$\frac{1}{x}\frac{\partial x}{\partial t} = 0.0092$$

with a standard error of 0.0013. The fit of this demand surface to the data is excellent,[79] the observed values of x differing from the computed values by less than 3 per cent on the average, the maximum deviation being only 6 per cent. The correlation between the observed and the computed consumption is 0.9720. Now I submit that this is a more informative, more precise, and more interesting description of the observed routine of demand than is provided by Pigou's method.

[78] As it stands, the figure measures the rate of shift per *unit* per annum. To express the rate as a *per cent* per annum, the figure, with its standard error, must be multiplied by 100.

[79] The data may also be represented excellently by a function of the type $x = a + by + ct$. For graphs of the two functions (fitted to the data for 1896–1914), see chap. vi, Figs. 24 and 26, pp. 201 and 203.

CHAPTER III

THE DERIVATION OF DEMAND CURVES
FROM FAMILY-BUDGET DATA

CHAPTER III

THE DERIVATION OF DEMAND CURVES FROM FAMILY-BUDGET DATA

Four main methods for deriving demand curves from family-budget data and from utility functions have been suggested. They are connected with the names of Professor Pigou (1910), Professor Frisch (1926 and 1930), Dr. Marschak (1931), and Professor Roy (1930 and 1931). As I have already pointed out in the introduction to chapter ii, they differ considerably among themselves, their only common characteristic being that they are all based implicitly or explicitly on the general static demand equation (3.10) of chapter i. It is convenient to take them up in the order given above.

I. PROFESSOR PIGOU'S 1910 METHOD

This method[1] differs radically from that described in chapter ii, in that it is derived from the theory of utility and makes use of budget data.

A. HIS ASSUMPTIONS AND PROCEDURE

Suppose that we have tables giving the expenditure of a group of working people classified according to the wages (or income) received.

Let

$$(1.1) \qquad \begin{cases} u_1 = u_1(x) \\ u_2 = u_2(x) \end{cases}$$

be the marginal degree of utility (or, more briefly, the degree of utility) functions for the quantity x of a given commodity "for typical men" in two successive wage groups 1 and 2. Let these functions be independent of the quantities of all the other commodities and therefore of the degree of utility of money.

If we denote the degree of utility of money to the two groups by μ_1 and μ_2, respectively, we have, from equations (2.30) or (2.33) of chapter i,

$$(1.2) \qquad \begin{cases} \mu_1 = \dfrac{u_1(x_1)}{p} \\ \mu_2 = \dfrac{u_2(x_2)}{p} \,, \end{cases}$$

---

[1] A. C. Pigou, "A Method of Determining the Numerical Value of Elasticities of Demand," *Economic Journal*, XX (1910), 636–40. Reprinted in *Economics of Welfare* (London, 1920), Appen. II. I have taken the liberty to modify some of Professor Pigou's symbols. All references will be to the article.

where x_1 and x_2 are the equilibrium quantities of the commodity consumed by each group, and p is the price, which must be the same to both groups.

If the wage-grouping be small, say, one shilling, then according to Pigou, "we may [also] fairly assume that the tastes and temperament of the people in any two adjacent groups are approximately the same,"[2] and we may write

$$(1.3) \qquad\qquad u_1(x) = u_2(x) = u(x) .$$

Making use of this relation, we obtain from (1.2),

$$(1.4) \qquad\qquad p = \frac{u(x_1)}{\mu_1} = \frac{u(x_2)}{\mu_2} .$$

But if x_2 differs only slightly from x_1, we have, by the theorem of the mean,

$$(1.5) \qquad\qquad u(x_2) = u(x_1) + (x_2 - x_1)u'(x_1) ,$$

whence,

$$u'(x_1) = \frac{u(x_2) - u(x_1)}{x_2 - x_1} = \frac{p(\mu_2 - \mu_1)}{x_2 - x_1}$$

or, making use of (1.4),

$$(1.6) \qquad\qquad u'(x) = \frac{1}{x_2 - x_1} \frac{\mu_2 - \mu_1}{\mu_1} u(x_1) .$$

We know, however, that the elasticity of the consumption x_1 with respect to the utility $u(x_1)$ is

$$(1.7) \qquad\qquad E(x_1, u) = \frac{u(x_1)}{x_1 u'(x_1)} .$$

Comparing (1.7) with (1.6), we see that

$$(1.8) \qquad\qquad E(x_1, u) = \frac{x_2 - x_1}{x_1} \frac{\mu_1}{\mu_2 - \mu_1} ,$$

in which the variables must be given their equilibrium values, since equation (1.4), which was used in deriving (1.8), is true only under equilibrium conditions.

But [argues Pigou] since a small change in the consumption of any ordinary commodity on which a small proportion of a man's total income is spent cannot involve any appreciable change in the marginal [degree of] utility of money to him, the elasticity of the utility curve in respect of any consumption x_1 is equal to the elasticity of the demand curve in respect to that consumption.[3]

[2] *Ibid.*, p. 637.   [3] *Ibid.*, pp. 637–38.

Therefore he concludes that the elasticity of demand with respect to price for the commodity in question in the lowest wage group, when x_1 units of it are consumed, is also given by the foregoing formula. We may, therefore, write

$$(1.9) \qquad \eta(x_1) = \frac{x_2 - x_1}{x_1} \frac{\mu_1}{\mu_2 - \mu_1} .$$

Similar equations will enable us to determine the corresponding elasticities of demand in each of the other wage groups.

By the foregoing process the elasticity of demand in any one wage group may be obtained for all the commodities consumed in that wage group. Thus, if the group consumes y_1 units of the commodity (Y), we have

$$(1.10) \qquad \eta(y_1) = \frac{y_2 - y_1}{y_1} \frac{\mu_1}{\mu_2 - \mu_1} ,$$

or

$$(1.11) \qquad \frac{\eta(y_1)}{\eta(x_1)} = \frac{\dfrac{y_2 - y_1}{y_1}}{\dfrac{x_2 - x_1}{x_1}} .$$

Hence

$$(1.12) \qquad \eta(y_1) = \eta(x_1) \frac{y_2 - y_1}{y_1} \frac{x_1}{x_2 - x_1} .$$

It follows, therefore, that any one of these elasticities of demand can be determined in terms of any other without reference to μ_1 and μ_2.

By way of illustration Pigou uses formula (1.11) to deduce "the ratio of the elasticity of demand for clothes to that for food for [several groups of workers],"[4] and obtains the following results:

Earnings of Workmen	Ratio of the Elasticities
Under 20s........................	1.16
From 20s. to 25s....................	1.31
From 25s. to 30s....................	1.62
From 30s. to 35s....................	1.25
From 35s. to 40s....................	2.46

B. APPRAISAL

Comment on Pigou's method must begin with the observation that, even if his assumptions be granted, his procedure can yield only the ratio of two elasticities of demand. To obtain the absolute values of the elasticities, we must first be able to derive the elasticity of demand of the commodity of comparison by some other method. But it is difficult to grant his most important assump-

[4] *Ibid.*, p. 639.

tion, namely, that "since a small change in the consumption of any ordinary commodity on which a small proportion of a man's total income is spent cannot involve any appreciable change in the marginal [degree of] utility of money to him, the elasticity of the utility curve . . . . is equal to the elasticity of the demand curve . . . . ,"[5] for there is a basic contradiction in his development. While it is plausible to assume that the degree of utility of money is constant when income remains fixed and the price of one commodity varies,[6] it is not legitimate to make this assumption when prices are fixed and income varies. This latter assumption implies that $\mu_2 = \mu_1$, in which case the utility elasticity which is given by the right-hand member of (1.8) becomes infinite, and this contradicts the assumption of diminishing degree of utility. But the proposition that "the elasticity of the utility curve . . . . is equal to the elasticity of the demand curve" is, as Pigou states, valid only when the degree of utility of money is constant. It follows that Pigou's result (1.11) cannot be interpreted as the ratio of two price elasticities. What Pigou does in effect is to derive the utility elasticity on the assumption that degree of utility of money is not constant ($\mu_2 \neq \mu_1$), then equates this utility elasticity to the demand elasticity on the assumption that the degree of utility of money is constant, and then divides out the factor ($\mu_2 - \mu_1$), stating that the error involved is small.

It may be asked why, if this criticism is valid, Pigou's statistical results appear consistent and reasonable. The answer is that Pigou's final result (1.11) has a perfectly valid interpretation, but it is not that which is given by him. *It is the ratio of the elasticities of demand of* x *and* y *with respect to income.*[7] These (arc) elasticities, measured from the points x_1 and y_1, are by definition

$$(1.13) \qquad E(x_1, r_1) = \frac{\dfrac{x_2 - x_1}{x_1}}{\dfrac{r_2 - r_1}{r_1}} ,$$

and

$$(1.14) \qquad E(y_1, r_1) = \frac{\dfrac{y_2 - y_1}{y_1}}{\dfrac{r_2 - r_1}{r_1}} ,$$

respectively, where r_1 and r_2 are the two incomes. These expressions are similar in form to (1.8) and (1.10) and can be obtained from them by substituting

---

[5] *Ibid.*, pp. 637–38.

[6] This assumption if taken strictly implies unitary elasticity of demand, as Pigou states. See Milton Friedman, "Professor Pigou's Method for Measuring Elasticities of Demand from Budgetary Data," *Quarterly Journal of Economics*, L (1935), 151–63, and A. C. Pigou, Milton Friedman, and N. Georgescu-Roegen, "Marginal Utility of Money and Elasticities of Demand," *ibid.*, pp. 532–39.

[7] I am indebted to Mr. Milton Friedman for this interpretation.

r_1 and r_2 for μ_1 and μ_2. If now we divide the second of these expressions by the first, we obtain

(1.15)
$$\frac{E(y_1, r_1)}{E(x_1, r_1)} = \frac{\dfrac{y_2 - y_1}{y_1}}{\dfrac{x_2 - x_1}{x_1}},$$

the right-hand member of which is identical with the right-hand member of (1.11). Pigou's equation (1.11) is, therefore, the ratio of the two elasticities of demand *with respect to income*. In the light of this interpretation his statistical results seem both reasonable and interesting.[8]

II.   PROFESSOR FRISCH'S METHODS

Frisch's contributions have for their primary object the measurement of the degree of utility of money and not the derivation of statistical demand curves. But his fundamental procedure yields as a by-product the Cournot-Marshall demand curve. It is, therefore, desirable to obtain a clear notion of the rationale of his procedure.

Although Frisch's main work relating to this subject was not published until 1932,[9] it is essentially a development of a paper which he published in 1926.[10] Frisch must, therefore, be considered as the first economist after Pigou to suggest a method for deriving demand curves from family-budget data.

A.   DEFINITIONS AND ASSUMPTIONS

Let u be the marginal degree of utility[11] of the commodity (X)—sugar, for example—and let it depend only on the quantity x of (X) (measured in pounds) that is bought or consumed in a unit of time, so that

(2.1)
$$u = u(x) .$$

Let p be the price in dollars per pound of the same commodity, $\xi = xp$ the money expenditure per unit of time, and μ the degree of utility of a "dollar's worth" of x, or of $1/p$ pounds, so that

(2.2)
$$\mu = \frac{u(x)}{p} .$$

---

[8] It may be objected that the procedure by which (1.15) was obtained seems arbitrary. Why not substitute for μ some other variable, say, the price of another commodity, and obtain (1.15)? The answer is that by Pigou's assumptions the only variable elements are income, the quantity of each commodity consumed, and, consequently, the degree of utility of each commodity. It follows that the only elasticities that have meaning—unless we make additional assumptions—are those with respect to income or to utility.

[9] Ragnar Frisch, *New Methods of Measuring Marginal Utility* ("Beiträge zur ökonomischen Theorie," No. 3 [Tübingen, 1932]).

[10] "Sur un problème d'économie pure," *Norsk Matematisk Forenings Skrifter*, Ser. 1, No. 16 (1926), pp. 1–40.

[11] Frisch employs "marginal utility" for what I call "marginal degree of utility."

Since u is assumed to be a function of x only, μ will be a function of ξ and p, and (2.2) may be written as

$$(2.3) \qquad \mu(\xi, p) = \frac{1}{p}\, u\!\left(\frac{\xi}{p}\right).$$

Let ρ be the nominal income of the consumer in question measured in dollars per unit of time, and P be the "price of living." Then

$$(2.4) \qquad r = \frac{\rho}{P}$$

is the deflated income. Let ω be the degree of utility of money measured per dollar, and let it depend only on the size of the income; and let w be the degree of utility of money measured per unit of real purchasing power. Since w measures the utility of P-times as many dollars as does ω, we have

$$(2.5) \qquad \omega = \frac{w}{P},$$

which corresponds to (2.2).

Just as the degree of utility of a dollar's worth of sugar was considered as a function of ξ and p—see (2.3)—so the degree of utility ω of money measured per dollar may be considered as a function of ρ and P, and we have

$$(2.6) \qquad \omega(\rho, P) = \frac{w}{P} = \frac{1}{P}\, w\!\left(\frac{\rho}{P}\right),$$

where ρ/P is substituted for r. This equation corresponds to (2.3). When the price of living, P, is put equal to unity, we get a function $\omega(\rho, 1)$ of a single variable, and we have

$$(2.7) \qquad \omega(\rho, 1) = w(\rho),$$

or, what amounts to the same thing,

$$(2.8) \qquad \omega(r, 1) = w(r).$$

The relative change in the degree of utility of real income, $w(r)$, corresponding to a small relative change in the real income r, is called the *flexibility of the degree of utility of money*, or the money flexibility, and is written as

$$(2.9) \qquad \check{w} = \check{w}(r) = \frac{\dfrac{dw(r)}{w(r)}}{\dfrac{dr}{r}} = \frac{d \log w(r)}{d \log r}.$$

The average or "arc" money flexibility corresponding to a finite change in the real income from r_1 to r_2 may be written as

$$(2.10) \qquad \breve{w}(r_1, r_2) = \frac{\log w(r_1) - \log w(r_2)}{\log r_1 - \log r_2}.$$

The objectives of Frisch's book are to determine the properties of the functions w and $\breve{w}$ and their numerical values for given values of r.

B. THE SURFACE OF CONSUMPTION

The basis of Frisch's procedures is the classic formula (2.24) of chapter i, which states that at equilibrium the individual distributes his expenditures in such a way that a dollar's worth of any commodity yields the same utility as a dollar's worth of any other commodity. In order not to confuse the symbols of chapter i with those used by Frisch, we may re-write that equation in the form:

$$(2.11) \qquad \frac{u_1(a)}{p_a} = \frac{u_2(b)}{p_b} = \frac{u_3(c)}{p_c} = \cdots,$$

where $u_1(a)$, $u_2(b)$, $\ldots$ are the degree of utility functions of the quantities a, b, $\ldots$ of the commodities (A), (B), $\ldots$, and p_a, p_b, $\ldots$ are the prices.

If any one of these commodities—say, (A)—is taken as the unit of comparison in terms of which all the others are expressed, its price is by definition[12] $p_a = 1$.

In the problem at hand, the individual buys x units of (X) in exchange for money, ρ. We have, then, by (2.11)

$$(2.12) \qquad \omega(\rho, P) = \frac{u(x)}{p},$$

where p is the price of x. If we introduce the expression for ω from (2.6), this becomes

$$(2.13) \qquad \frac{w\left(\dfrac{\rho}{P}\right)}{P} = \frac{u(x)}{p},$$

[12] In this equation the assumption has been made, for convenience, that money has direct utility to the individual and is represented by $u_1(a)$. When the utility of money is not direct but is derived from the commodities for which it is exchanged, it can be given meaning only in terms of the equilibrium position of the individual, for it is equal to the *common equilibrium value of*

$$\frac{u_2(b)}{p_b}, \frac{u_3(c)}{p_c}, \cdots$$

It is then a function of the expenditure of the individual and of all the prices. Frisch makes the assumption that it is a function of only two variables—the individual's expenditure and the price of living. But, as was shown by R. G. D. Allen, in his paper, "On the Marginal Utility of Money and Its Application," *Economica*, XIII (1933), 186–209, this assumption is entirely arbitrary and can in no way be regarded as an approximation.

or, putting $\rho/P = r$, by (2.4)

(2.14)
$$\frac{w(r)}{P} = \frac{u(x)}{p} \, .$$

If we further put

(2.15)
$$a = \frac{P}{p} \, ,$$

we obtain finally for the equilibrium equation

(2.16)
$$w(r) = au(x) \, .$$

This equation is the keystone of Frisch's structure. It expresses the relation between the degree of utility of money and the degree of utility of the "commodity of comparison"—say, sugar—and represents a surface in a, x, and r, which Frisch calls "the surface of consumption."

If we had a number of observations relating to the same individual in different price and income situations, we could construct a surface of consumption for that individual. Since, however, different sets of observations on a single individual are generally not available, Frisch assumes that $u(x)$ and $w(r)$ are of the same shape for all persons, but that each curve has a personal factor independent of x and r; and that, furthermore, the shape of these curves is independent of time and place.

Figure 13 is a sketch of a three-dimensional model of such a surface of consumption "built on the actual numerical results obtained by the translation method," which will be referred to later. It is based, with the author's permission, on the photograph shown on page 17 of his book.[13] It is a graphic representation of equation (2.16). Of the two horizontal axes, the one extending from the foremost point (origin) to the right measures the deflated (real) income r, and the one extending from the origin backward to the left measures the inverted real price a. The vertical axis measures the consumption x of the "commodity of comparison" corresponding to any combination of a and r.

It is of interest to study the curves obtained by slicing the surface with the following three systems of planes: (1) vertical planes parallel to the (a, x) axes; (2) vertical planes parallel to the (x, r) axes; (3) horizontal planes, that is, planes parallel to the (a, r) axes.

The first set of curves shows how the quantity consumed varies as a function of the inverted price when the (real) income r is kept constant. It is a system of ordinary demand curves in which the reciprocal of p is substituted for p itself. To each (fixed) income there corresponds an inverted demand curve.

[13] Frisch explains that the model belongs to Professor Irving Fisher, to whom he dedicates this work and to whose encouragement and generosity he pays tribute.

The second set of curves shows how the consumption of the commodity increases with the real income when the price is kept constant. It represents the "Engel curves." To each (fixed) price there corresponds one Engel curve.

The third set of curves are contour lines which indicate the "altitude" of the surface above the (a, r) plane. They show the relation between changes in real income and the corresponding changes in the real (inverted) price per unit of sugar which the individual is willing to pay, when the quantity of sugar that is

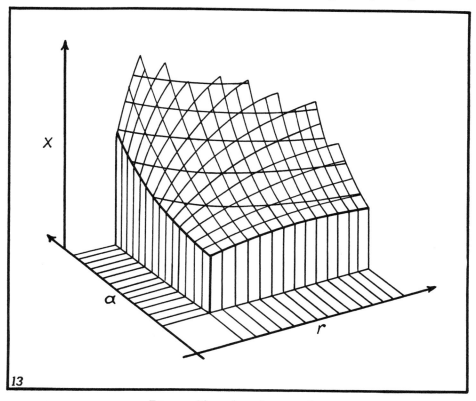

FIG. 13.—The surface of consumption

consumed is kept constant. To each (fixed) quantity there corresponds one curve, or contour line. These contour lines Frisch has named "isoquants" because any one of them shows how r and a vary together when the quantity x is kept constant.

A part from a scale constant along the a-axis, any such isoquant is simply the curve of the degree of utility for money, $w = w(r)$.

The proof is simple. From (2.16)

$$(2.17) \qquad a = \frac{1}{u(x)} \, w(r) \, .$$

But when x is given a constant value $x = x_0$, $u(x) = u(x_0)$, and the equation becomes

$$(2.18) \qquad a = Cw(r) ,$$

where $C = 1/u(x_0)$ is a constant. But apart from this constant factor, this is nothing else than the curve of the degree of utility for money,[14] $w = w(r)$.

All the isoquants are, therefore, similar to one another in the sense that any one of them can be obtained from another by multiplying the ordinate by a constant.

C. APPRAISAL

Frisch develops three methods for deriving this curve from statistics.[15] For present purposes, however, it is not the utility curve but the demand curve which concerns us. And this curve can be obtained by fixing the income of the individual at a particular level and observing how his consumption of the commodity in question varies as its price is changed. Indeed, this procedure yields two different types of demand curves according as real or monetary income is fixed. If real income is fixed, the demand curve obtained by cutting the surface of consumption by a plane parallel to the (a, x) axes gives the relationship between the real price of x and the quantity bought. If monetary income is fixed, the demand curve obtained gives the relationship between the money price of x and the quantity bought.[16] When the statistical

---

[14] Similarly, when the income is given a constant value $r = r_0$, the degree of utility of income is fixed, or $w(r) = w(r_0) = K$, a constant, and the equation becomes

$$a' = Ku(x) ,$$

where $a' = 1/a = p/P$. But apart from the constant K, this is nothing else than the curve of the degree of utility of "sugar," $u = u(x)$.

[15] Those who have not the time to read the full explanations of these methods as given by Frisch will find a brief summary of them in my review article, "Frisch on the Measurement of Utility," *Journal of Political Economy*, XLI (1933), 95–116. (On p. 96 of this article I inadvertently reversed the definitions of w and ω. The definitions given in this book are Frisch's.) For a more technical discussion of Frisch's method see Abram Burk, "Real Income, Expenditure Proportionality, and Frisch's 'New Methods of Measuring Marginal Utility,' " *Review of Economic Studies*, IV, No. 1 (1936), 33–52. For some limitations to which Frisch's "consumption surface" is subject see the summary of a paper by Jacob Marschak in *Econometrica*, V, No. 1 (1937), 96–98.

[16] The first of these demand curves cannot, however, be transformed into the second merely by multiplying the real price (i.e., p_x/P) by some (assumed constant) value of P, for P (as also, money income) cannot be kept constant while p_x varies. This is evident from the fact that P is an index of *all* prices including the price of x; from this it follows, further, that as p_x changes we must vary the individual's money income in order to keep his real income constant. Nor can these changes in P and in money income be neglected as of minor significance quantitatively, inasmuch as it is precisely these changes which make possible an elasticity other than unit elasticity for the resultant demand curves. For if P and p are assumed constant, then the left-hand member of (2.13) and consequently all of the ratios in (2.11) are fixed, which means that the quantity consumed of any commodity other than x cannot vary, and this is equivalent to saying that the demand for x has an elasticity of one. Further-

data are available for the construction of a surface of consumption, and when the demand for the commodity in question is practically independent of the demands for other goods, there is no doubt but that this procedure will yield the Cournot-Marshall demand curve for the particular income level. From the individual demand curves thus obtained it is very easy to construct the market demand curve.

III. DR. MARSCHAK'S METHOD

The work[17] in which Marschak presents his method of deriving elasticities is also the first attempt at a systematic presentation and criticism of the writings of the other workers in the same field.[18] We shall, however, concern ourselves primarily with his own method.

A. HIS ASSUMPTIONS AND PROCEDURE

The rationale of Marschak's procedure may be briefly summarized as follows:

1. Family-budget data give the relation between the following three categories of quantities: (a) the money incomes of the various households during a specified period of time, (b) the quantities of the various goods and services on which these incomes were spent, and (c) the prices paid for these goods and services.

2. For households of a fixed size, the relation connecting these categories can be expressed by an empirical formula.[19] We may denote this relation by

$$(3.1) \qquad\qquad q = f\left(\frac{\rho}{p}\right),$$

in which q is the quantity of a given commodity that is consumed by the household, p its price, and ρ the money income of the household.[20]

3. The quantity consumed may be varied either by varying the income, or by varying the prices, or by varying both income and prices but by unequal

---

more, the second type of demand curve cannot be derived from the consumption curve merely by cutting it by a plane. Its equation can, however, be obtained from (2.16) and is

$$w\left(\frac{\rho_0}{P}\right) = \frac{P}{p_x}\, u(x),$$

where ρ_0 is the given money income. It must once again be borne in mind that P is a function of p_x and consequently when we fix the money income and vary p_x we cannot consider any of the variables, a, r, or x, as constant.

[17] Jacob Marschak, *Elastizität der Nachfrage* ("Beiträge zur ökonomischen Theorie," No. 2 [Tübingen, 1931]).

[18] See my review of this book in *Weltwirtschaftliches Archiv*, XXXVII, Heft 1 (January, 1933), 29*–38*.

[19] To facilitate a comparison with the formulas used by Frisch, I have taken the liberty to modify some of Marschak's symbols.

[20] To the best of my knowledge, the first author to use this formula was Vilfredo Pareto. See his "La Legge della domando," *Giornale degli economisti*, X (2d ser., 1895), 65.

relative amounts.[21] When the money income and all prices are varied by the same relative amount, there is *in the long run*[22] no change in the quantities consumed, since the ratio (ρ/p) is unchanged.

4. Since at the time of the budgetary survey the prices have fixed values, we may put $p = 1$, and the foregoing equation becomes

$$(3.2) \qquad\qquad\qquad q = f(\rho) ,$$

which shows that the quantity consumed depends only on the size of the income. This is the household curve.

5. This curve may also be taken as a "single" market demand curve if we assume that all prices rise and fall together (the *Parallel-reaktion* assumption), that the amount spent on any one commodity constitutes a small part of the entire budget, and that there are no important substitutes for the commodity in question. Under these assumptions, an increase in income by a small (theoretically, *infinitesimal*) relative amount is equivalent to a decrease in the price by the same amount and vice versa, so that the *same* (small) increase in consumption may be brought about either by decreasing the price or by increasing the income by the same relative amount. When the rise in income is large—say, 20 per cent—a correction (which is worked out by Marschak) must be applied before it can be considered as equivalent to a 20 per cent fall in general prices.

6. The final market demand curve is the sum of the demand curves of the individual households. If it can be assumed that each income class contains the same number, the effect of the distribution of income may be neglected, and the market demand curve is the demand function for the typical household, multiplied by the number of households. Otherwise a function relating the size of income to the number of households receiving it must be used. Marschak multiplies the single demand formula by $n(\rho)$, the function of the income distribution, and integrates the product between the limits of incomes included in the data. The market demand $\bar{q}$ then becomes

$$(3.3) \qquad\qquad\qquad \bar{q} = \int_{\rho_1}^{\rho_2} n(\rho) f\left(\frac{\rho}{p}\right) d\rho .$$

In his numerical work, Marschak simplifies the problem by assuming that the elasticity is constant at every point and independent of price.

In short, Marschak's demand curve is first an income curve. What he measures in the first instance is the elasticity of quantity with respect to income, not with respect to price. It is the assumption of *Parallel-reaktion* (together with

[21] See chap. i, pp. 36–50, esp. Fig. 4.

[22] Marschak admits that in the short run a general decrease in all prices may not be equivalent to an increase in income by the same percentage. See p. 55, n. 1, of his book.

the other necessary assumptions mentioned above) which enables him to look upon his income curve also as the *Spiegelbild*, or reflected image, of a demand curve and to consider the two elasticities as approximately equal (numerically).[23]

Using the German budgetary data for 1907, Marschak computes by his method the elasticities for seven classes of commodities. The average values of these coefficients are as shown in Table 2.

TABLE 2

ELASTICITIES OF DEMAND FOR SELECTED GROUPS OF COMMOD-
ITIES COMPUTED BY THE MARSCHAK METHOD FROM
THE GERMAN BUDGETARY DATA FOR 1907

Commodity Group	Elasticity of Demand*
Housing	0.98
Meat, fish, and bacon	0.71
Personal and household washables (*Wäsche*)	1.15
Tobacco	1.01
Heat and light	0.32
Sugar	0.38

* These are average values, taken from the last column of the table on p. 108 of Marschak's book.

B. APPRAISAL

Before proceeding to evaluate Marschak's method, it is desirable to point out the fact that his criticism of the demand curve that is derived from time series of prices and quantities is overdrawn. Marschak argues that such a statistical demand curve never succeeds in ruling the time element out of consumption and that therefore it represents not a market demand curve but a series of points on successive demand and supply curves. But he maintains that his own curve, based as it is on family budgets relating to the same period of time, may be considered as fairly representative for that period and is not subject to the influence of the time element. While I grant that a demand curve derived from family-budget data is likely to be relatively freer from the disturbing influence of the time element than is one based on market data, it seems to me, nevertheless, that Marschak overemphasizes the difference between the two curves. He appears to forget that his own method is also dependent on the time element—something which he has, himself, pointed out.[24]

When the real income of an individual has been modified through a change in all the prices, a time interval must generally elapse before he will adjust his consumption habits to his new income. Who is to say that the final equilibrium will be exactly as postulated in Marschak's theory? Marschak's procedure is based on the assumption that the underlying utility functions will not be changed through a change in prices, as long as the real income remains the

[23] A more descriptive title of the book would be "Elasticity of Income."

[24] See p. 55, n. 1, of Marschak's book.

same. Those who work with market data assume that during a given interval of time the demand curve retains its shape or changes it in the manner suggested by the data. Both assumptions must be fortified by "outside evidence."

But the significant question is not whether his criticism of the time-series approach is well taken—he has admitted in a letter that it is not—but whether his own method yields the ordinary static Cournot-Marshall demand curve. This question has been answered in the negative by Professor Frisch.[25] In a discussion of Marschak's method before the Lausanne meeting of the Econometric Society in 1931,[26] Frisch showed that from only one budget or quantity-income curve it is impossible to construct the Cournot-Marshall demand curve by Marschak's *Spiegelbildmethode*. When, however, two (or more) budget curves are available, we can deduce the flexibility of the degree of utility of money and, hence, the elasticity of demand of the commodity in question.[27] This does not mean, however, that Marschak's curves are without value. On the contrary, they are exceedingly important; but they must be interpreted properly. They are demand curves that would obtain if all prices rose and fell together.

IV. PROFESSOR ROY'S METHOD

Professor Roy's fundamental contribution[28] is the investigation of the relation which should exist between the distribution of income and the law of de-

---

[25] My own discussion of Pigou's method (see pp. 107–11) suggests the same answer, for Marschak's and Pigou's methods are fundamentally the same, and both obtain expressions for *income* elasticity rather than for *price* elasticity.

[26] See Jacques Moret and Ragnar Frisch, "Méthodes nouvelles pour mesurer l'utilité marginale," *Revue d'économie politique*, XLVI, Part II (1932), 14–28.

[27] Of this conclusion Dr. Marschak, who kindly read this section, writes as follows: "If there existed a function relating marginal utility of money to income (and, therefore, a 'flexibility of the marginal utility of money') then the income-elasticities of goods on which only a small part of income is spent would be nearly proportionate to their price-elasticities. Unfortunately, as I pointed out at the Namur meeting of the Econometric Society 1935 (see *Econometrica*, Vol. V, No. 1, 1937, pp. 96–97), the existence of a functional relation between income and marginal utility of money requires unrealistic assumptions. I am therefore even more sceptical than R. Frisch as to the usefulness of my old method for a direct derivation of demand curves. On the other hand, income-elasticities can be very useful for the analysis of demand from time series, as they permit the elimination of influences on demand of known changes in the amount and distribution of incomes and thus to account properly for what probably is the most important cause of shifts of a demand curve" (Letter of November 23, 1937).

While I am grateful to Dr. Marschak for this note, I doubt very much whether income elasticities alone will enable us to allow for changes in the *distribution* of income.

[28] René Roy, "La Demande dans ses rapports avec la répartition des revenus," *Metron*, VIII, No. 3 (1930), 101–53; "Les Lois de la demande," *Revue d'économie politique*, XLV (1931), 1190–1218, also reprinted in *Etudes économétriques* (Paris: Recueil Sirey, 1935), pp. 82–110; and *Contribution aux Recherches Econométriques* (Paris: Hermann & Cie, 1936). The first paper gives the theoretical developments; the second is essentially a summary and an application to a few statistical series. The third study is essentially a review of results obtained from the statistical analyses of demand in different countries. The present treatment is based primarily on the first paper.

mand for the group of first necessities, for the group of commodities other than first necessities, and for individual commodities. The fundamental principle to which he appeals is the relation which exists between Pareto's law of distribution of income and the law of demand for all commodities taken as a group. Since he is not in a position to verify his formulas, he wishes his studies to be considered more as an indication of a method to be followed rather than as an attempt to establish definitive conclusions.

A. DEFINITIONS AND ASSUMPTIONS

Roy makes use of the following notation:

	is the income
$n(r)dr$	is the number of persons whose income lies between r and $r + dr$
$\displaystyle\int_{r_1}^{r_2} n(r)dr$	is the number of persons whose income is between r_1 and r_2
$N(x) = \displaystyle\int_x^{\infty} n(r)dr$	is the number of persons whose income is greater than x
$R_0 = \displaystyle\int_0^{\infty} r \cdot n(r)dr$	is the total income of the community
$N = \dfrac{A}{x^a}$	is Pareto's law of distribution of income

On the basis of Pareto's statistical studies, Roy concludes that the constant a has a mean value of about 1.5. He therefore takes the law of distribution of income to be

$$N = \frac{A}{x^{3/2}},$$

realizing very well that this formula does not apply to the low-income range.

Roy assumes that during the period covered by the data there have been no changes in the size of the population and in the size of the income and in its distribution.

He furthermore assumes that each individual has a scale of preference for the various commodities. If his income diminishes while the prices remain constant, he will forego the use of those commodities which he considers least indispensable. When we are considering the demand of a group of individuals, this order of preference is observable not for individual commodities but for commodity groups. If we wish to find the way in which the total quantities of the various commodities in any one group vary with the prices of these goods, we must, therefore, make use of an index number Q of the quantities and of an index number P of the prices, such that the product PQ of these indices will represent the total expenditure on the group in question:

$$(4.1) \qquad\qquad PQ = k \cdot \Sigma(qp) \qquad\qquad (k = \text{constant}).$$

In this expression the symbol q represents the quantities of the commodities and services exchanged during an infinitesimally small period of time, and p the corresponding unit prices.

Differentiating and then dividing through by PQ, he obtains

$$(4.2) \qquad\qquad \frac{dP}{P} + \frac{dQ}{Q} = \frac{\Sigma(qdp)}{\Sigma(qp)} + \frac{\Sigma(pdq)}{\Sigma(pq)} .$$

The index of prices[29] is then defined by

$$(4.3) \qquad\qquad \frac{dP}{P} = \frac{\Sigma(qdp)}{\Sigma(qp)}$$

and the index of quantities[29] by

$$(4.4) \qquad\qquad \frac{dQ}{Q} = \frac{\Sigma(pdq)}{\Sigma(pq)} .$$

Finally, Roy assumes that each individual has a maximum consumption point, a point of satiety, q_i for each commodity; and that, subject to a few ex-

---

[29] Strictly speaking, eq. (4.2) yields

$$\frac{dP}{P} = \frac{\Sigma(qdp)}{\Sigma(qp)} + dF ,$$

and

$$\frac{dQ}{Q} = \frac{\Sigma(pdq)}{\Sigma(pq)} - dF ,$$

where F is an arbitrary function of p and q. But in order that dP/P should depend only on dp, F must not contain dq; and in order that dQ/Q should depend only on dq, F must not contain dp. Hence $dF = 0$. See François Divisia, *Economique rationnelle* (Paris, 1928), p. 268. Divisia first pointed out the advantages of the differential forms (4.3) and (4.4).

In his study, "Les Index économiques," *Revue d'économie politique*, XLI (1927), 1251–91, 1493–1527 (also published separately by Recueil Sirey, Paris, and reprinted in *Etudes économétriques*, pp. 5–79), Roy points out two important properties of such an index as (4.3):

1. If the unit of time be taken sufficiently small, the coefficients q might be considered as substantially constant, and the index becomes a weighted arithmetic mean, the weights being the same quantities q.

2. The index, being defined by an expression which is not a total differential, may take different values for the same values of the prices and the quantities. The index at any instant t referred to the index at any other instant t_0 as a base might be expressed as a curvilinear integral, along the price-time and the quantity-time curves. It follows from this that the value of the index at any instant t depends not only on the values of p and q at that instant and at the initial instant t_0 but also on all *the values taken by these variables during the entire time interval t_0, t.* See Divisia, *op. cit.*, pp. 272–73.

ceptions, this point of satiety is the same for all individuals, irrespective of their incomes.

B. THE DEMAND FUNCTION FOR A GROUP OF FIRST NECESSITIES

For any given value P of the price index, some persons will each be able to afford to consume the maximum quantity q_l, while the others will each consume less than q_l. Each individual in the first group will spend $q_l P$, and the expenditure of this group will be $q_l P$ times the number of individuals:

$$q_l P \int_{q_l P}^{\infty} n(r) dr .$$

The expenditure of the second (poorer) group will be

$$\int_{r_o}^{q_l P} r \cdot n(r) dr ,$$

where r_o is the lowest income. Hence the expenditure of the two groups will be

(4.5) $$QP = \int_{r_o}^{q_l P} r \cdot n(r) dr + q_l P \int_{q_l P}^{\infty} n(r) dr .$$

To obtain the law of demand, we must substitute the expression for $n(r)$ in the foregoing equation, integrate, and divide both sides by P (or by Q).

Since, by Roy's assumption,

$$\int_{x}^{\infty} n(r) dr = A x^{-a} ,$$

the expression for the number of individuals is

$$n(r) = a A r^{-(a+1)} .$$

Substituting in (4.5), Roy obtains

(4.6) $$QP = a A \int_{r_o}^{q_l P} r^{-a} dr + q_l P \cdot A \cdot (q_l P)^{-a} .$$

Integrating, and dividing both sides by P, he finally reaches the following expression for the law of demand for first necessities:

(4.7) $$Q = \frac{A}{a-1} \left[\frac{a}{r^{a-1}} \frac{1}{P} - \frac{1}{q_l^{a-1}} \frac{1}{P^a} \right] .$$

This expression holds only for values of P superior to $P_l = r_o/q_l$. When P_l reaches this lower limit, the minimum income r_o is sufficient to assure satiety q_ι for all the individuals, and the consumption no longer varies with prices less than P_ι, the surplus income going to the "superior" goods. A study of this curve shows that it has the properties exhibited by Figure 14A.

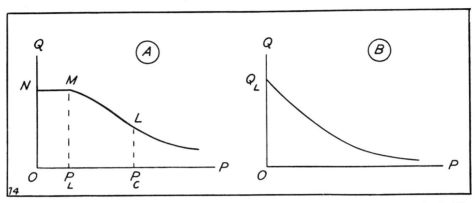

FIG. 14.—Theoretical demand curves for groups of commodities (according to Roy). A: The curve for a group of first necessities. B: The curve for a group of goods which are not first necessities. (The corresponding curves for single commodities resemble curves A and B, except that they have a finite price range.)

Roy also obtains an interesting expression for the elasticity of demand λ of (4.7).

From (4.5),

(4.8) $$\frac{d(QP)}{dP} = q_\iota \int_{q_\iota P}^{\infty} n(r)dr = Q_s ,$$

say, where Q_s is the consumption of all persons whose income is greater than $q_\iota P$. Therefore,

$$d(QP) \equiv QdP + PdQ = Q_s dP .$$

Whence,

(4.9) $$\lambda = \frac{-\dfrac{dQ}{Q}}{\dfrac{dP}{P}} = -\frac{Q_s - Q}{Q} ,$$

which is the ratio of the incomplete consumption to the actual consumption.

C. THE DEMAND FUNCTION FOR A GROUP OF GOODS WHICH ARE NOT FIRST NECESSITIES

Let ρ be that part of the income of an individual which is spent on the lower categories of goods,[30] ρ being greater than the minimum income r_0.

---

[30] Care should be taken not to confuse the meaning which ρ has in this connection with that which it has in Frisch's theory, namely, money income. In Roy's theory the distinction is not made between money and real income.

As in the case of first necessities, the expenditure on these goods falls into two parts: that spent by those who can afford to purchase the limiting quantity q_l and that spent by those who cannot afford to buy the limiting quantity.

The expenditure of the first group is

$$q_l P \int_{\rho + q_l P}^{\infty} n(r) dr ,$$

and the expenditure of the second group is

$$\int_{\rho}^{\rho + q_l P} (r - \rho) n(r) dr .$$

The expenditure of both groups is, therefore,

$$(4.10) \qquad QP = \int_{\rho}^{\rho + q_l P} (r - \rho) n(r) dr + q_l P \int_{\rho + q_l P}^{\infty} n(r) dr .$$

Substituting the explicit form for $n(r)$, integrating, and dividing by P, Roy obtains, after some simplifications,

$$(4.11) \qquad Q = \frac{A}{a - 1} \cdot \frac{1}{\rho^{a-1}} \cdot \frac{1}{P} \left[1 - \left(\frac{\rho}{\rho + q_l P} \right)^{a-1} \right] .$$

A study of this curve shows that it has the general form indicated by Figure 14B. The curve is like that which is generally assumed except that it is asymptotic to the axis of prices.

D. THE DEMAND FUNCTION FOR A SINGLE COMMODITY

To go from the demand for a group of commodities to that of a single commodity, we must, according to Roy, make an assumption about the way in which the income is allocated among the different groups of commodities, since this allocation is an expression of the scale of preference of the various commodities. Roy considers two hypotheses:

1. As the amount spent on any given class of commodities varies, the proportion of it devoted to each commodity remains unchanged.

2. As the amount spent on any given class of commodities varies, the quantities purchased of the various commodities are all increased or decreased by the same proportion.

The first hypothesis.—If $\Sigma(qp)$ is the sum spent on the group in question, then the first hypothesis is that

$$\frac{qp}{\Sigma(qp)} = a ,$$

$$\frac{q'p'}{\Sigma(qp)} = b ,$$

$$\cdot \quad \cdot \quad \cdot \quad \cdot \quad \cdot$$

where a and b are constants. In this case it can be shown[31] that the price index P is connected with the individual prices p, p', . . . by the logarithmic equation

(4.12) $$\log\left(\frac{P}{P_0}\right) = a \log\left(\frac{p}{p_0}\right) + b \log\left(\frac{p'}{p_0'}\right) + c \log\left(\frac{p''}{p_0''}\right) + \ldots$$

Since in deriving the Cournot-Marshall demand curve, the prices other than p, that of the commodity in question, are assumed to be constant, this equation enables us to relate p to P. Also, since $\Sigma(qp)$ is proportional to QP, qp is also proportional to QP, always. We thus obtain another equation, which, together with (4.12), enables us to express Q and P as functions of q and p, and hence the demand curve for the commodity in question.

It should be observed that the assumption that the other prices p', p'', . . . are constant does not necessarily involve the constancy of the quantities q', q'', . . . , since they are proportional to $\Sigma(qp)$. It is, therefore, possible to measure the effect of a change in the price of any given commodity on the changes in the quantities demanded of the other commodities.

The second hypothesis.—If we assume that q, q', q'', . . . remain proportional to their base values, then the quantity index Q remains also proportional to *each* of the quantities—which gives a very simple relation between Q and q.

But, on this hypothesis, the price index P is a linear function of the prices:

(4.13) $$\frac{P}{P_0} = a\left(\frac{p}{p_0}\right) + b\left(\frac{p'}{p_0'}\right) + c\left(\frac{p''}{p_0''}\right) + \ldots,$$

where a, b, c, . . . are the proportions of the total income spent on each commodity in the base year.

The Cournot-Marshall demand curve $q = q(p)$ may, therefore, be deduced from the function $Q = Q(P)$, by a simple change of the axes, which does not modify the general shape of the curve.

The foregoing equations also enable us to express q', q'', . . . as a function of p, since all these quantities vary proportionately to Q.

According to Roy, it is difficult to choose between these two hypotheses; statistical investigations are necessary for determining which of them is the most plausible. For small changes in the variables, both assumptions yield substantially equal results.

Roy concludes, therefore (without, however, giving the necessary mathematical developments), that the probable forms of the demand curves for individual commodities resemble the curves for groups of commodities (curves A and B, Fig. 14), except that the asymptotic branch must be replaced by one with a finite range for p; the first being the demand curve for a first necessity,

[31] See Roy, "Les Index économiques," *op. cit.*, pp. 1251–91, 1493–1527.

and the second the demand curve for a commodity other than a first necessity. In his statistical work he contents himself with the assumption that the demand curve is one of constant elasticity throughout the range of the observations, using a simplification of the method of link relatives.

The following example, which shows how he computed the elasticity for tobacco, is a good illustration of his procedure.[32] The data are as of April, 1923, when there was an increase in the price of the commodity on account of the imposition of a tax.

Index of the price of tobacco before the increase.   205
Index of the price of tobacco after the increase.   222
    Percentage change in price[33]. . . . . $+7.96$
Index of the consumption of tobacco before the increase. 69.933
Index of the consumption of tobacco after the increase. 66.355
    Percentage change in consumption[33]. . . . . -5.25

$$\text{Elasticity of demand} \equiv \frac{-5.25}{7.96} = \qquad -0.66$$

In this example it is not necessary to correct the data for secular and/or seasonal movements. Where such corrections are deemed necessary, Roy makes them.

With the meager data at his disposal, some such simple procedure as the foregoing is probably the only justifiable procedure, although it should be pointed out that it involves the same tacit assumptions which underlie Moore's procedure.

E. APPRAISAL

First it is necessary to observe that Roy's approach to the problem of deriving demand curves—and the same is also true of Marschak's—is essentially the one suggested by Pareto[34] in 1895, although neither Roy nor Marschak was aware of Pareto's contribution. After he had discovered his well-known law of distribution of income, Pareto made an investigation of the way in which the demand for a commodity depends on his law of the distribution of income and expressed the total demand as a function of the individual demands and the distribution of income.[35] Roy's formula (4.5) and Marschak's formula (3.3) are analogous to the one given by Pareto, but these authors have carried their investigations farther than did Pareto.

Coming to Roy's peculiar contributions, we are faced with several difficulties.

[32] See his "La Demande dans ses rapports avec la répartition des revenus," *op. cit.*, p. 146.

[33] Because of the relatively large magnitude of the tax, Roy uses the arithmetic means of the indices as a base for computing these percentages.

[34] *Op. cit.*, pp. 59–68.

[35] *Ibid.*, p. 65, eq. (3). The first student of statistical demand curves to call attention to the importance of Pareto's contribution was Henry L. Moore. See his "The Statistical Complement of Pure Economics," *Quar. Jour. of Econ.*, XXIII (1908–9), 24.

There is, first, the difficulty that Pareto's law of the distribution of income, which constitutes the keystone of his structure, is not valid for low-income ranges, and yet it is the consumers whose incomes fall within these ranges that have the greatest influence on the demand for first necessities and for other commodities as well. There is, second, the objection that the order or scale of preference in which an individual arranges the various commodities is a function of their prices and cannot, therefore, be used to explain the same prices. There is, finally, the objection that his assumption that the point of satiety, q_l, is the same for all individuals, irrespective of their incomes, is at best true for only a few commodities. But these and other objections that one might raise would be captious in view of the very modest claims which Roy makes for his formulas.

Finally it should be observed that verification of Roy's general formulas (4.7) and (4.11) must await the collection and preparation of adequate income-price-quantity data. But when such data become available, it will not be necessary to make Roy's assumptions. The Cournot-Marshall demand curve could then be derived quite directly from the empirically constructed Engel curves or from the surface of consumption.[36]

V.   CONCLUSION

The survey of the various methods of deriving statistical demand curves which has just been brought to a close should, I think, have convinced the reader of the truth of the proposition which I advanced in the beginning of chapter ii, namely, that it is impossible to derive a demand curve from statistical data without making some assumptions or hypotheses about the very curve which we are trying to derive. In this respect, the problem is like any other problem in induction.[37] According to the fundamental theorem of the theory of

---

[36] See pp. 114–15.

[37] If an event E may be explained by any one of the mutually exclusive hypotheses or causes

$$H_1, H_2, \ldots, H_n,$$

whose *a priori probabilities of existence* are

$$\pi_1, \pi_2, \ldots, \pi_n,$$

and whose *productive probabilities* are

$$p_1, p_2, \ldots, p_n,$$

then, when the event E has occurred, the *a posteriori* probability H_i/Eh that it had its origin in cause H_i ($i = 1, 2, \ldots, n$) under given conditions h, is

$$H_i/Eh = \frac{\pi_i p_i}{\pi_1 p_1 + \pi_2 p_2 + \ldots + \pi_n p_n}.$$

In nearly all problems which arise in practice, the *a priori* probability π_i is either unknown or known only within broad limits, and some assumption must be made with respect to it. The analysis of the effect on the *a posteriori* probability in question, of assigning different values to the *a priori* probability, constitutes one of the most important and interesting parts of the theory of induction.

induction, if we wish to know the probability that a given event had its origin in a given cause, we must first determine the *a priori* probability that the cause exists. Since this probability is generally not known, we must make the most plausible assumptions with respect to it.

The assumptions underlying the various procedures for deriving demand curves have already been detailed and need not be repeated. Here it is only necessary to point out the peculiar limitations and advantages of the two types of approach—the time-series approach and the family-budget-data approach.

The time-series approach suffers from the difficulty which it has in disentangling the "time factor" from the data. Furthermore, it is not very suitable for deriving the elasticities of demand for *classes* of commodities and services, such as clothing, housing, amusement, etc.; and it is applicable only when certain supply conditions prevail. It has, however, the advantage that it enables us to study the shifting of the demand curve through time.

The family-budget approach also has severe limitations. It does not enable us to derive the elasticities of demand of *intermediate* goods, or goods that are not consumed directly by human beings, such as hay, corn, rye, and wheat,[38] as well as iron, steel, copper, etc. It does not yield a measure of the rate of shift of the demand curve, since the data relate to a single "point" in time. It is not adapted for the analysis of the effects of substitutes. For example, it is extremely difficult, by this method, to express the demand for a commodity as a function not only of its price but also of the prices of its substitutes. The budget-data approach has, however, the advantage that its validity is independent of the mode of shifting of the supply curve.

It is greatly to be desired that the advantages and the limitations of the various methods of deriving the elasticity of demand of commodities and indices of the marginal utility of money should be thoroughly worked out. It would be a fine task for an adequately equipped research organization to make such a comparative study. It need not fear that its results will be without practical application, for they are likely to throw a flood of light on business-cycle phenomena and problems of taxation, to lead to a more realistic and useful type of economic theory, and to teach us how to wring fresh knowledge out of the accumulated masses of market and family-budget data.

[38] Bread is quite a different commodity from wheat. When we buy a loaf of bread, we buy milk, sugar, salt, wrapping, and service, in addition to wheat.

CHAPTER IV

ASSUMPTIONS, METHODS, AND PROCEDURES

CHAPTER IV

ASSUMPTIONS, METHODS, AND PROCEDURES

In this chapter I shall consider the general assumptions underlying my statistical work and indicate briefly the general type of analysis to which the data will be subjected, leaving a discussion of the detailed procedures to the statistical chapters which follow.

I. THE BASIC HYPOTHESES

The hypotheses which seem to me to be most plausible and suggestive are those which appear to underlie Professor Moore's procedures, namely, (1) that there exists a routine in the demand behavior of human beings; (2) that the statistical data of consumption and prices are such as to reflect this routine of demand; and (3) that the unknown theoretical demand function can be approximated by various empirical curves. The technical implications of these assumptions have already been discussed and need not be repeated.[1] The broader philosophical implications of the assumption that there is a routine in human behavior are, however, also extremely important and deserve at least a brief comment.

A. THEIR PHILOSOPHICAL IMPLICATIONS

There can be no foresight without an understanding of the role which routine plays in our lives. As Professor Whitehead put it:

Routine is the god of every social system; it is the seventh heaven of business, the essential component in the success of every factory, the ideal of every statesman. The social machine should run like clockwork. Every crime should be followed by an arrest, every arrest by a judicial trial, every trial by a conviction, every conviction by a punishment, every punishment by a reformed character. Or, you can conceive an analogous routine concerning the making of a motor car, starting with the iron in the ore, and the coal in the mine, and ending with the car driving out of the factory and with the president of the corporation signing the dividend warrants, and renewing his contracts with the mining corporations. In such a routine everyone from the humblest miner to the august president is exactly trained for his special job. Every action of miner or president is the product of conditioned reflexes, according to current physiological phraseology. When the routine is perfect, understanding can be eliminated, except such minor flashes of intelligence as are required to deal with familiar accidents, such as a flooded mine, a prolonged drought, or an epidemic of influenza.

A system will be the product of intelligence. But when the adequate routine is established, intelligence vanishes and the system is maintained by a coordination of conditioned reflexes. What is then required from the humans is receptivity of special training. No one, from president to miner, need understand the system as a whole. There will be no foresight, but there will be complete success in the maintenance of the routine.

[1] See chap. ii, pp. 65–67.

Now it is the beginning of wisdom to understand that social life is founded upon routine. Unless society is permeated, through and through, with routine, civilization vanishes. So many sociological doctrines, the products of acute intellects, are wrecked by obliviousness to this fundamental sociological truth. Society requires stability, foresight itself presupposes stability, and stability is the product of routine.[2]

"But," Professor Whitehead is careful to point out, "there are limits to routine, and it is for the discernment of these limits, and for the provision of the consequent action, that foresight is required."[3]

The fact that these limits exist and that now, more than in any previous generation, we are faced with fluid, shifting situations should also serve as a constant reminder that, no matter how well an economic law may fit the facts of a particular situation, it cannot be safely extrapolated to a new situation; economic laws even of the "dynamic" variety do not have the same heuristic properties as do physical laws.[4]

That the same conclusion also follows from other considerations is clearly shown by Professor Cohen.[5] In a suggestive discussion of the question, "Are there any social laws?" he approaches the issue by considering three types of laws:

1. The statement of a general fact that can be authenticated, as, for instance, the assertion that gold is yellow.

2. Empirical or statistical sequences, e.g., "Much sugar in a diet will be followed by decayed teeth."

3. The statement of universal abstract relations which can be connected systematically with other laws in the same field.

Referring to the third type of law he says:

Such laws we may indeed find in the social sciences, e.g. the laws governing the exchange of goods under free competition as worked out mathematically by Walras, Pareto, H. Schultz,[6] et al., but always these laws are on a plane of abstraction from which translation to actual experience is difficult and dangerous. The ideal entities represented by "free competition" and "economic man" are, to be sure, no more abstract than the ideal entities of physics, but nevertheless economics is a poorer basis for predicting actual events than is physics. For in physics the transition from laws governing rigid bodies to those applying to (say) lead bullets is made on the basis of new laws of compressibility or elasticity, while in

---

[2] Alfred N. Whitehead, "On Foresight," which constitutes the Introduction to W. B. Donham's *Business Adrift* (New York: McGraw-Hill, 1931), pp. xiii–xv. This essay is reprinted in A. N. Whitehead, *Adventures of Ideas* (New York: Macmillan, 1933), chap. vi. I am grateful to the author and publishers for permission to quote.

[3] *Ibid.*, p. xv.

[4] See chap. i, Sec. IV.

[5] Morris R. Cohen, *Reason and Nature: An Essay on the Meaning of Scientific Method* (New York: Harcourt, Brace & Co., 1931), Book III, chap. i: "The Social and the Natural Sciences." I am grateful to the author and publishers for permission to quote.

[6] See *The Meaning of Statistical Demand Curves.*

economics the transition from our laws of supply and demand in an ideal market to those determining (say) New York Stock Exchange transactions is still largely a matter of guess-work.[7]

The foregoing remarks should not, however, be taken—and Professor Cohen does not intend them to be taken—as disparaging the work of those who attempt to isolate routines of change of various degrees of generality and to state them in quantitative form. For it must constantly be kept in mind that all induction is essentially a leap in the dark. If, therefore, one is convinced that there is no routine in human behavior, one is certainly not likely to discover it. One must have a researcher's faith. Professor Cohen refers to the difficulty of the transition from the laws of supply and demand in an ideal market to those determining, say, New York Stock Exchange transactions. I venture the opinion that the transition is just as easy (or just as difficult) as in the case of the produce exchanges. The fact is that we know next to nothing about stock-exchange transactions from a scientific point of view. Millions upon millions of dollars have been spent on stock-exchange statistics for the purpose of extracting from them schemes for "beating the market," for developing get-rich-quick formulas, but not a cent for making the kind of scientific study that would be necessary to establish the truth or falsity of Professor Cohen's example. But the fact that stock-exchange transactions are considered as a particularly difficult field to which to apply the preconceptions of pure theory should be a challenge to statistical economists. Let them obtain the notebooks and other relevant records of the specialists in the various stocks.[8] Let them study the limitations of the "bids" and "offers" recorded therein as observations on the demand and supply functions. Let them secure the co-operation of the stock-exchange officials, in devising methods for observing them. From the improved data, let them, finally, construct approximations to the demand and supply functions. Then we shall *know* the extent to which the theoretical relations are verified in the stock market, and the role played by routine. Until such data are available, economists will be compelled to confine their scientific supply and demand analyses to the statistics of the commodity exchanges and more particularly to those relating to agricultural commodities.

B. THEIR REASONABLENESS

Now it happens that the more important agricultural commodities such as corn, wheat, cotton, etc., the demands for which will be studied later in this book, are produced and consumed under such conditions that the assumptions stated in the foregoing section are approximately realized. We may list three of

[7] Cohen, *op. cit.*, p. 358. Professor Cohen should not, however, necessarily associate the laws of exchange with free competition. Some of the most interesting and useful aspects of the laws of exchange are those which relate to barter, monopoly, duopoly, and oligopoly.

[8] I made several attempts to get such data but met with no success. See chap. xx, n. 22.

them: First, these commodities are staples of consumption, little affected by
the state of trade, by fashion, or by other abruptly changing factors. The demand curves for such commodities may, therefore, be assumed to be reasonably
stable. Second, they are produced as annual crops, which have to be marketed
within a certain period. The average price at which a given quantity is sold
can, therefore, be approximated more accurately than is possible for goods
which come to the market in a continuous flow.[9] Third, the commodities are
each produced by millions of independent producers who cannot individually
change the market price, but who may adjust their output to changes in the
market price—thus approximating the theoretical condition of perfect competition. This condition, taken in conjunction with the two preceding conditions,
suggests that, when the published data (quantities and prices) relating to
these staples are corrected for secular (and other) changes, they become essentially observations of the coordinates of points of intersection of a more or less
fixed demand curve with a moving supply curve. From such data it should be
possible to derive the concrete, statistical form of the demand curve.[10]

II. THE SUBSIDIARY ASSUMPTIONS

It is both an advantage and a limitation of the general hypotheses listed
above that they permit a very wide choice of auxiliary assumptions and methods of procedure in deriving the demand curve of a particular commodity.
Thus we still have to decide: (1) what assumptions to make about the form
of the demand function; (2) how to fit the function to the data; and (3) whether
to work with adjusted or unadjusted data.

In selecting the form that is to be given to the demand function, we have to
decide what variables to include in the equation and what functional relationship to assume among the variables.

A. THE VARIABLES INCLUDED IN THE DEMAND FUNCTION

When we say that the quantity of a commodity demanded is a function of a
particular set of variables, we are in effect defining the "state" of the system
to which we wish to confine our investigations. The following are a few of the
"states" which have practical significance.

(2.1) $$x = f(y)$$

(2.2) $$x = f(y_1, \ldots, y_n)$$

---

[9] But the increasing possibilities of storage and government subsidies to producers' associations
make this factor less important.

[10] See Chap. ii, Sec. III, C, pp. 72–83.

(2.3) $$x = f(y, t)$$

(2.4) $$x = f(y, R, t) \qquad \text{(R is income)}$$

(2.5) $$x = f(y_1, \ldots, y_n, t)$$

(2.6) $$x = f(y_1, \ldots, y_n, R, t)$$

(2.7) $$x = f\left(y, \frac{dy}{dt}\right)$$

(2.8) $$x = f\left(y, \frac{dy}{dt}, t\right)$$

(2.9) $$x = f(y, (t - T)) \qquad \text{(T is a constant)}$$

(2.10) $$x = f(y, (\tau)) \qquad (t - T \leq \tau \leq t) .$$

The foregoing equations relate the quantity of a commodity demanded either to its own price or to the prices of all the commodities in the group, and some of them also take income into account. In the first six equations the values of the variables relate to a single "point" (or year) in time, and in the first two of these it does not even matter which "point" is selected. In the last four equations, however, the quantity demanded at a given "point" in time depends not only on the values of the variables at that "point" but also on their values at preceding "points."

Assumption (2.1) is the first which should be tested when the data are free from secular[11] fluctuations. It is generally at variance with the facts if one or both of the variables has a secular trend. Even in such cases, however, it will be found that, when the data have been adjusted for these long-time fluctuations by using ratios to trend or link relatives, this simple function will give a surprisingly good approximation to the data. We shall make considerable use of it in connection with the methods of trend ratios and link relatives.

Equation (2.2) is the well-known general *statical* law of demand, but for work in connection with time series it has few advantages over (2.1). Most statistical series of quantities and prices are subject to secular fluctuations, and these are not generally removed through the introduction of the prices of other commodities as variables into our equations. Furthermore, the introduction of more than, say, four variables into a statistical equation is likely to yield diminishing returns. Where the situation warrants the use of the prices of related

[11] For some demand analyses it is also important that the data contain no cyclical and seasonal movements.

goods as variables in the demand equation, it is the general *dynamic* function (2.5) to which recourse must, as a rule, be had. In the investigations which follow, we shall, therefore, make only limited use of the statical hypothesis (2.2).[12]

The third assumption is one of the most useful for our purposes. It will play a leading role in our investigations.

Assumption (2.4) is more general than (2.3) but less general than (2.6). Where adequate data on income and its distribution are available, it should yield very accurate descriptions of fluctuations in demand. We shall make considerable use of it.

The fifth assumption will constitute the foundation of our investigation of the demands of related (completing and competing) goods. We shall see that it is possible to lay down certain conditions on (2.5) which simplify greatly this investigation.

Equation (2.6) is the general dynamic law of demand and is theoretically to be preferred to all the others. The range of its applicability is, however, greatly limited by the nature of the available data and the increasing unreliability of the results as the number of variables increases.

We come now to equations (2.7) to (2.10) in which not only the present but also the past values of the independent variables affect the quantity demanded. These are due to Professors Evans[13] and Roos.[14] But I have shown elsewhere[15] that the first two of these—i.e., (2.7) and (2.8)—do not describe the demand for such agricultural commodities as we are going to consider in this book. They may, however, be used to describe the demand for producers' goods, in which the speculative element is important,[16] but a considerable number of statistical investigations will have to be made before the range of its applicability can be ascertained.

Assumptions (2.9) and (2.10) are likely to be of greater importance in the

---

[12] See, however, chaps. xviii and xix.

[13] Griffith C. Evans, "The Dynamics of Monopoly," *American Mathematical Monthly*, XXXI (1924), 77–83; *Mathematical Introduction to Economics* (New York, 1930), pp. 143–64; "A Simple Theory of Economic Crises," *Journal of the American Statistical Association*, XXVI (March, 1931, Suppl.), 61–68; and "The Role of Hypothesis in Economic Theory," *Science*, LXXV, No. 1943 (March 25, 1932), 321–24.

[14] Charles F. Roos, "A Mathematical Theory of Competition," *American Journal of Mathematics*, XLVII (1925), 163–75; "A Dynamical Theory of Economics," *Journal of Political Economy*, XXXV (1927), 632–56; "A Mathematical Theory of Price and Production Fluctuations and Economic Crises," *ibid.*, XXXVIII (1930), 501–22.

[15] See my discussion of "A Simple Theory of Economic Crises," by G. C. Evans, in the *Jour. Amer. Statist. Assoc.*, XXVI (March, 1931, Suppl.), 68–72.

[16] See Roswell H. Whitman, "Statistical Investigations in the Demand for Iron and Steel" (University of Chicago dissertation, 1933).

study of supply[17] than in the study of demand, for it does not seem reasonable that *present* demand should be appreciably influenced by *past* prices.[18] But more statistical investigations will be needed to determine this question. We shall make very little use of these hypotheses.

To summarize: The assumptions which will prove most useful in working with absolute data are (2.3), (2.4), and (2.5), the last being particularly useful in the study of related demands. The one which will prove most useful in working with trend ratios and link relatives is (2.1).

Our next problem is to give specific form to these functions.

B. THE SPECIFIC FORM OF THE DEMAND FUNCTION

The functional relationship to be given to any set of variables which we select involves a delicate balancing of several factors. Professor Moore discusses the following grounds for selecting a curve: (*a*) its simplicity, (*b*) its fecundity, (*c*) its fit, (*d*) its facility of computation, and (*e*) its *a priori* validity.

a) The simplicity of the curve.—As Professor Moore points out, the impossibility of rigidly defining what is simple and what is complex has not escaped statisticians. In his own words:

It is quite possible that from a particular point of view the equation of one type of curve might be more simple than that of another type, and yet be more complex when viewed in another light. It might, for example, have fewer constants, and, from this point of view, be more simple than another equation with a greater number of parameters. But the evaluation of the constants in the first case might entail an extremely complex operation, while, in the latter case, no difficulty would be encountered. An inflexible definition of the simple, is, therefore, not offered, but it may be said that, in statistics, *simplicity is relative to the state of analysis and to the practical end in view.*[19]

b) The fecundity of the curve.—As an illustration, Moore cites the Gompertz formula for the number of persons l_x alive at age x as given in the life-table; namely, $l_x = kg^{c^x}$, where k, g, and c are constants to be determined from the special data. Although there are other curves which give a better graduation of the data, this one is, nevertheless, preferred by actuaries because

for the purpose of the actuary a dominant circumstance in favour of Gompertz's law is that it lends itself to problems of *joint survivorship*. The formula of Gompertz, and *this formula alone*, enables us to calculate the value of a joint life annuity from a table of the values of annuities on single lives, by finding a single life which may be substituted for the two or more joint lives.[20]

[17] See Harry Pelle Hartkemeier, *The Supply Function for Agricultural Commodities: A Study of the Effect of Price and Weather on the Production of Potatoes and Corn* ("University of Missouri Studies," Vol. VII, No. 4 [October 1, 1932]).

[18] See the references in nn. 16 and 17.

[19] "The Statistical Complement of Pure Economics," *Quarterly Journal of Economics*, XXIII (1908–9), 18. (Italics are Moore's.)

[20] F. Y. Edgeworth's article "On the Representation of Statistics by Mathematical Formulae," *Journal of the Royal Statistical Society*, LVI (December, 1898), 672. Quoted by Moore, *op. cit.*, p. 20. (Italics "this formula alone" are Moore's; other italics Edgeworth's.)

c) The fit of the data.—The notion of goodness of fit rests ultimately on aesthetic considerations. It cannot be given an unambiguous definition unless we first agree to use one of the various methods which have been suggested for measuring goodness of fit. For example, we may take as our criterion either the smallness of the absolute deviations of the points from the curve or the smallness of the relative deviations; and we may work with the first power, the second power, or with some other power of the deviations. Again, we may measure the deviations in a direction parallel to the axis of price, to the axis of quantity, or to neither. The different procedures do not necessarily lead to the same conclusion. Many controversies in statistics have turned on the questions whether a given criterion of goodness of fit is preferable to another, and whether the goodness of fit according to any criterion is a sufficient reason for regarding a particular curve as the curve appropriate to the data. I shall return to the criterion of goodness of fit in a later section.

d) The facility with which the constants of a curve may be computed.—This, again, is not an absolute criterion. The existence of machines or tables for facilitating computation according to a particular method of curve-fitting tends to insure the continued use of that method. Thus the *Tables for Statisticians and Biometricians* and the *Tracts for Computers*, which have been prepared under the supervision of Professor Karl Pearson for statisticians using his methods, will necessarily extend the use of those methods. Similarly, the forms which are now available for fitting curves by the method of least squares will lead the statistician to make frequent use of that method.

e) The "a priori validity."—As Moore points out, this is Edgeworth's phrase as well as his idea. According to Edgeworth, that type of curve is to be preferred for which there is an *a priori* demonstration that it will tend to correspond to the data and which actually does correspond very closely. The significance of the *a priori* validity is, according to Moore, the utilitarian doctrine that hypotheses are not to be wasted.

It is these five criteria—the simplicity of the formula, its fecundity, its closeness of fit, the ease with which it can be computed, and its *a priori* validity—which have usually guided the selection of a curve.

The bearing of these criteria on the problem of the specific form to be given to any of the demand assumptions discussed above can be illustrated by considering the comparatively simple function (2.3):

$$x = f(y, t) ,$$

as the conclusions reached for this case are easily extended to more complex cases.

Simple as this hypothesis is, it admits nevertheless of being represented by an infinitude of functions. To make progress in our investigation, we must subject it to certain conditions or restrictions. For our purposes we may formulate these in terms of the shape of the demand curve and the way in which it shifts its position from time to time.

By the shape of the demand curve we shall understand the form of the demand surface, $f(y, t)$, at a fixed point t_0 in time:

$$(2.11) \qquad x_{t_0}(y) = f(y, t_0) .$$

By the shift of the demand curve we shall understand the trace on the demand surface $f(y, t)$ corresponding to a fixed value y_0 of y:[21]

$$(2.12) \qquad x_{y_\bullet}(t) = f(y_0, t) .$$

The following are a few of the conditions which have practical significance:

(i) The shape of the demand curve should remain fixed as the curve shifts its position from time to time. Symbolically, the condition is that

$$(2.13) \qquad f(y, t) = Y(y) + T(t) .$$

This equation states that, when price is fixed, the *absolute* increment of the quantity purchased per unit of time is independent of the level at which price is fixed. The simplest function which has this property is the plane:

$$(2.14) \qquad f(y, t) = a + by + ct .$$

In this illustration the (Cournot-Marshall) demand curve, which is here taken as a straight line, retains its slope, b, as it shifts upward or downward to the right at the (constant) rate of c units of x per unit of time t.

(ii) The elasticity (but not the shape) of the (Cournot-Marshall) demand curve should remain fixed as the curve shifts its position from time to time. In symbolic form the condition is that

$$(2.15) \qquad f(y, t) = Y(y) \cdot T(t) ,$$

for, upon taking logarithms, this condition reduces to (2.13). This equation states that, when price is fixed, the *relative* increment of the quantity purchased per unit of time is independent of the level at which price is fixed. This seems a more probable assumption than (2.13). A simple function which has this property is

$$(2.16) \qquad f(y, t) = A y^\alpha e^{\beta t} .$$

[21] We might also define the shift as the trace corresponding to a fixed value of x.

This is the equation of a demand curve with constant elasticity, a, at every point, which elasticity is not affected by the shifting of the curve.[22]

(iii) Neither the shape nor the elasticity of the demand curve should remain fixed as the curve shifts. One such relationship may be expressed symbolically by

$$(2.17) \qquad f(y, t) = G(y) + H(t) + Y(y) \cdot T(t) .$$

This equation includes both (2.13) and (2.15) as special cases and states that the *absolute* increment of the quantity purchased per unit of time is composed of two parts, one of which is, and the other is not, independent of the level at which price is fixed. This situation is likely to arise when there is a minimum quantity that is demanded regardless of the price. A simple function having this property is

$$(2.18) \qquad f(y, t) = a + by + ct + dyt .$$

In this illustration, the demand curve, which is taken to be a straight line, changes its slope in a simple manner as it shifts its position to the right, for

$$\frac{\partial x}{\partial y} = b + dt .$$

Similarly, the rate of shift changes in a simple manner with price, for

$$\frac{\partial x}{\partial t} = c + dy .$$

Our problem is to determine expressions for the shape of the (Cournot-Marshall) demand curve, and for the way in which it shifts with time.

1. THE SHAPE OF THE DEMAND FUNCTION

The shape of the demand function has been given careful consideration by Professor Umberto Ricci, who has investigated the properties of many curves

[22] By logarithmic differentiation, the elasticity of the demand curve is

$$\frac{\partial x}{\partial y} \cdot \frac{y}{x} = a, \text{ a constant} ,$$

and the *relative* rate of shift of the curve is

$$\frac{1}{x} \cdot \frac{\partial x}{\partial t} = \beta, \text{ a constant} .$$

which have been suggested for use in statistical investigations.[23] Probably the most interesting of these is the curve

$$(2.19) \qquad x(y) = A(y + b)^a + c, \qquad \begin{matrix} A > 0, & a < 0, \\ b \gtrless 0, & c \gtrless 0, \end{matrix}$$

which is quite flexible and can, therefore, describe a variety of demand situations; and which permits the elasticity of demand to be either an increasing-decreasing, or a decreasing-increasing, function of price, thus yielding a price for which the total expenditure is a maximum—a property which is not possessed by constant-elasticity curves.[24] But this curve is difficult to fit. Furthermore, most price-quantity observations generally fall within a comparatively narrow range, and within this range many simpler curves give as good a fit as does the curve described by (2.19). For these reasons we shall use most frequently the straight line

$$(2.20) \qquad x(y) = a + by,$$

or the equilateral hyperbola

$$(2.21) \qquad x(y) = Ay^a,$$

in describing the shape of our demand curve, although we shall be compelled to use the more complex expression (2.19) in a few of our investigations. In each of these equations the parameters may, of course, be functions of t.

2. THE SHIFTING OF THE DEMAND FUNCTION

Only those forces acting over time in such a way as to cause the demand function to shift in some regular manner can be taken into account by $x(t)$. Of these, the most important are likely to be the growth of population and changes in taste and in income.

For staple agricultural commodities—and these are the ones with which we shall mainly be concerned—tastes are not likely to change very rapidly. It follows that the shifts of their demand curves are determined primarily by the growth of population and changes in income. In the case of such commodities

---

[23] "Elasticità dei bisogni, della domanda e dell'offerta," *Giornale degli economisti*, LXIV (1924), 413–31, 509–31 (for a list of errata to this article, see *ibid.*, LXVII [1927], 503–4); "La Loi de la demande individuelle et la rente de consommateur," *Revue d'économie politique*, XL (1926), 5–24 (for a list of errata to this article, see *ibid.*, p. 944); "Courbes de la demande et courbes de la dépense," *L'Egypte contemporaine*, XXII (1931), 556–88; and "Klassifikation der Nachfragekurven auf Grund des Elastizitätsbegriffes," *Archiv für Sozialwissenschaft und Sozialpolitik*, LXVI (1931), 36–61.

[24] Except for the trivial values $y = 0$ or $y = \infty$.

$x(t)$ is directly proportional either to the law of population growth or to some function of it.[25]

Now a formula which excellently describes the growth of population of the United States is the Verhulst-Pearl-Reed curve,[26] whose equation is

$$(2.22) \qquad\qquad P(t) = \frac{K}{1 + e^{a_1 + b_1 t}},$$

and which has the following properties: (1) it approaches a finite upper limit as t approaches plus infinity; (2) it approaches the lower limit zero as t approaches minus infinity; (3) it has a point of inflection, such that the rate of growth increases up to that point and decreases beyond it; (4) it is symmetrical about the point of inflection; and (5) it exhibits a declining rate of percentage increase throughout the range.

If then the shift of the demand curve is strictly proportional to the growth of population, the value of $x(t)$ is given by

$$(2.23) \qquad\qquad x(t) = k \cdot P(t) = k \frac{K}{1 + e^{a_1 + b_1 t}},$$

where k is the factor of proportionality.

It is more reasonable to suppose, however, that the shift of the demand curve is proportional not to the population itself but to some function of it. A particularly interesting function which suggests itself in this connection is the Reed saturation curve,[27] whose equation is

$$(2.24) \qquad\qquad T(t) = \frac{mK}{1 + e^{a_2 + b_2 t} + \dfrac{b_2}{b_2 - b_1} e^{a_1 + b_1 t}},$$

where m is the limiting number of units of the commodity per person, K the limiting number of persons, and a_1, a_2, b_1, and b_2 are constants, the first two being the same as in (2.22).

[25] Thus, if at a fixed price the absolute increment in quantity purchased is proportional to the absolute increment of population, and the factor of proportionality is independent of price, $x(t)$ will be given by (2.13) with $T(t)$ equal to some constant times the population $P(t)$ at time t. If the factor of proportionality depends on price in such a way that a given percentage increase in population will call forth the same percentage increase in the quantity at each price, then $x(t)$ will be given by (2.15) with $T(t)$ equal to $P(t)$. If the factor of proportionality depends on price in some other fashion, $x(t)$ will be given by (2.17) with $H(t)$ equal to zero and $T(t)$ equal to $P(t)$. If a part of the demand for the commodity is independent of price but is a function of population—say, $H[P(t)]$—then the increment to the quantity purchased resulting from a given increment of population will consist of one part which is independent of price and another part dependent on price, and $x(t)$ will be given by (2.17), with $H(t)$ equal to $H[P(t)]$ and $T(t)$ equal to $P(t)$.

[26] See Raymond Pearl, *Studies in Human Biology* (Baltimore, 1924), chaps. xxiv–xxv; and Henry Schultz, "The Standard Error of a Forecast from a Curve," *Jour. Amer. Statist. Assoc.*, XXV (1930), 139–85.

[27] Lowell J. Reed, "A Form of Saturation Curve," *Jour. Amer. Statist. Assoc.*, XX (1925), 390–96.

This curve is derived on the assumption that forces other than the growth of population are at work tending to increase the consumption of a commodity and that these forces *by themselves* would tend to cause consumption to vary in the manner described by the Verhulst-Pearl-Reed curve. In the population logistic (2.23) the upper limit to consumption is determined by the constant K. In this curve the upper limit to consumption is itself variable, being a function of the changing population, whose law of growth is taken as (2.22).

The curve defined by (2.24) is similar in shape to the population logistic (2.22). It rises rather slowly for a time, then more rapidly, and finally tapers off approaching an asymptote. It is not, however, symmetrical. Reed has used it to describe the growth of the number of registered passenger automobiles in the United States.[28]

If (2.24) be taken as the form of $x(t)$ and (2.21) as the form of $x(y)$, the demand function would become, by (2.11),

$$(2.25) \qquad f(y, t) = k \; \frac{mKy^\alpha}{1 + e^{a_2+b_2t} + \dfrac{b_2}{b_2 - b_1} e^{a_1+b_1t}} ,$$

where k is a constant.

[28] In some problems there may be more justification for considering the shifting of the demand curve as proportional to one of the following implicit functions of population:

$$f[P(t)] = kgc^t$$
$$f[P(t)] = ks^tgc^t$$

$$f[P(t)] = ke^{\frac{g}{\sqrt{\pi}}} \int_0^{t/T} e^{-\tau^2} d\tau$$

$$f[P(t)] = k(1 - R^t) .$$

All of these curves are (for suitable values of the parameters) asymptotic to a line parallel to the time axis.

The first of these is the Gompertz formula of actuarial fame. (See George King, *Textbook of the Institute of Actuaries* [London: C. & E. Layton, 1901], Part II, chap. vi.) Its use as a curve for representing economic trends was first suggested by Professor Henry L. Moore. It has been fitted to several important economic series. (See R. B. Prescott, "Laws of Growth in Forecasting Demand," *Jour. Amer. Statist. Assoc.*, XVIII [1922], 471–79; and Simon S. Kuznets, *Secular Movements in Production and Prices* [New York, 1930].)

The second curve is the Makeham modification of the Gompertz curve. (King, *op. cit.*; Leroy E. Peabody, "Growth Curves and Railway Traffic," *Jour. Amer. Statist. Assoc.*, XIX [1924], 476–83; and Henry Schultz, "An Extension of the Method of Moments," *ibid.*, XX [1925], 242–44.)

The third curve is the integral of the normal curve. It has been used to represent the population of England and Wales, the external trade of the United Kingdom, and the birth-rate of the German Empire. (See R. A. Lehfeldt, "The Normal Law of Progress," *Jour. Roy. Statist. Soc.*, LXXIX [1916], 329–32.)

The fourth curve is the Spillman-Mitscherlich law of growth which has been found to represent excellently a number of economic and biological series. (See W. J. Spillman, *The Law of Diminishing Returns* [Chicago, 1924].)

We shall not, however, make use of this hypothesis in our statistical investigations, for the following reasons: As we shall see in the next chapter,[29] the figures of production and consumption, and especially the data for the earlier years, are subject to considerable error. Although the year-to-year fluctuations are perhaps fairly reliable, their absolute magnitudes cannot be taken at their face value. Laws of growth derived from such data would, therefore, be quite unreliable and misleading. Furthermore, in order to study the changes in the elasticities of demand with time, we shall have occasion to break up the period from 1875 to 1929 into three parts—(I) 1875–95, (II) 1896–1914, and (III) 1915–29—and make a separate analysis of the data for each part. Now the longest of these periods is only twenty-one years and saw only two censuses of agriculture—hardly a sufficient basis for deriving a law of growth. Finally, and most important of all, the curve (2.25) is exceedingly difficult to fit, which renders it impracticable for our purposes. Instead we shall make frequent use of the following empirical hypotheses for $T(t)$:

$$(2.26) \quad \begin{cases} T(t) = c_0 + c_1 t \\ T(t) = c_0 + c_1 t + c_2 t^2 \\ T(t) = c_0 + c_1 t + c_2 t^2 + c_3 t^3 , \end{cases}$$

where the parameters may be functions of y. We shall find that, with few exceptions, these simple curves give very good descriptions of the shifting of our demand curves and are easy to fit to the data. Furthermore, they do not convey the impression of being underlying laws of growth. In a surprisingly large number of analyses, the simple linear term

$$T(t) = c_0 + c_1 t$$

will be found to give excellent results.

III. THE METHOD OF FITTING THE DEMAND FUNCTION

The problem of fitting a demand curve to data gives rise to several difficult mathematical questions. However, it is not our present purpose to enter upon a technical discussion of these mathematical questions but to indicate briefly the *economic implications* of some of the mathematical procedures which we must use.

In pure theory the demand curve is taken as a unique functional relation between the quantity sold and the price paid. Although in biology, as well as in certain other fields, the concept of *variation* or scatter about a central tendency, with the related concept of the regression of any one variable, upon any or all of the others, occupies a central role, it hardly enters into the theory of demand or the other fields of pure economics. Thus, while the average change in the

[29] Pp. 167–69.

stature of fathers corresponding to a change of one inch in the stature of their sons is not given by the same curve as that which represents the average change in the stature of sons corresponding to a change of one inch in the stature of their fathers, and while each of these two relations has a perfectly definite biological basis, in economics the average change in quantity corresponding to a given change in price and the average change in price corresponding to a given change in quantity are assumed to be given by one and the same regression or curve, for the simple reason that the relationship between the two variables is always taken to be of the unique, functional variety. As long as we confine our investigation to pure theory, the notion of a unique functional dependence between price and quantity is very helpful—indeed, quite indispensable. But as soon as we cross the boundaries of pure theory and begin to attack a concrete problem, we must deal with data which inevitably exhibit variation. Adjust the observations as you will, remove from them the effects of all the known disturbing factors, and they will still exhibit a considerable scatter, thus giving rise to the phenomenon of regression. The question arises, therefore, which of the two regressions—that of price on quantity or that of quantity on price—is to be taken as *the* demand curve?

The empirical statistician is hardly aware of this question. He arbitrarily selects one of the variables—generally price—as the dependent variable and determines the parameters of his curve so that the sum of the squares of the deviations of the observed prices from the computed prices is a minimum. He does not realize, however, that this procedure involves the assumption that an observed point fails to fall on the demand curve because of an "error" or deviation in the dependent variable y (price) alone, the independent variable x (consumption) being allowed no deviation. In fact, when he uses this method, he is considering the consumption figures so reliable that he gives them a weight infinitely greater than that which he assigns to the price observations.

Conversely, if our statistician determines the constants of his curve by minimizing the sum of the squares of the deviations of the observed consumption from the computed consumption, he is assuming that an observed point fails to fall on the demand curve because of an error or deviation in the dependent variable x (consumption), the independent variable y (price) being allowed no deviation. This procedure considers the *prices* so reliable that it gives them a weight infinitely greater than that given to the consumption figures. And, as is to be expected, the results obtained by the two procedures may be quite different.[30]

The question may be asked, Does not each regression have its place? Should we not take the regression in which price is the dependent variable when our primary purpose is to explain the factors affecting price, and the regression in

[30] See my *Statistical Laws of Demand and Supply* (Chicago, 1928), pp. 35–70, 178–86.

which quantity is the dependent variable when we are most interested in explaining the factors affecting consumption?

There would be no serious objection to this procedure if the formulas were to be confined to these purposes and never used for estimating elasticities of demand. If, however, we are asked to determine the effect of a change in conditions of supply—say, the imposition of a tariff—on prices, imports, and consumption, we need to know, among other things, the elasticity of demand of the commodity in question. And we cannot conveniently say to the legislator, "Your tariff will have one effect if the elasticity of demand is computed from the regression of price on quantity, and quite a different effect if it is derived from the regression of quantity on price!"

"Why not adopt a compromise between the two methods of fitting?" the reader will ask.

It is perfectly true that in practically all observations, both the quantity and the price series are subject to errors or deviations. It is evident, therefore, that a better-fitting or more probable demand curve will be obtained by taking both types of errors into consideration in the curve-fitting process. Unfortunately, this procedure can be easily applied only to the fitting of linear functions.[31] Mathematicians have not as yet succeeded in extending it to nonlinear

[31] The curve-fitting procedure, which assumes that there are errors in both variables, yields the two elementary regressions as special cases. This can be shown as follows:

Let the equation of the line be:

(i) $$a + bx - y = 0.$$

Let x_i and y_i be the observed values of consumption and price ($i = 1, 2, \ldots, n$), and let x_i' and y_i' be the corresponding adjusted or calculated values. The residuals are then:

(ii) $$\begin{cases} v_{x_i} = x_i - x_i' \\ v_{y_i} = y_i - y_i'. \end{cases}$$

Let w_x and w_y be the (constant) weights of x and y. The assumption that both variables are subject to error requires us to minimize

(iii) $$\varphi(a, b) \equiv \Sigma w_x v_{x_i}^2 + \Sigma w_y v_{y_i}^2.$$

Differentiating this partially with respect to a and b and setting the derivatives equal to zero we find that (i) is satisfied by the means of the variables, so that the intercept a can be readily determined, and that the slope b is given by one of the roots of the equation:

(iv) $$b^2 + b \left(g \frac{1}{r_{xy}} \cdot \frac{\sigma_x}{\sigma_y} - \frac{1}{r_{xy}} \cdot \frac{\sigma_y}{\sigma_x} \right) - g = 0,$$

where

(v) $$g = \frac{w_x}{w_y}.$$

The other root of (iv) gives the slope of the line of worst fit.

If $g \to \infty$, then (iv) yields

(vi) $$b = r_{xy} \frac{\sigma_y}{\sigma_x},$$

which is the slope of the regression of y on x.

[Footnote continued on opposite page.]

functions. It is extremely difficult, for example, to fit as simple a nonlinear function as the second-degree parabola $y = a + bx + cx^2$ by this procedure.[32] Furthermore, even in the case of linear functions, the method becomes extremely laborious when the number of variables exceeds two or three. Finally, the results obtained are not invariant with respect to the *units* in which the variables are measured.[33]

In view of these difficulties, we shall adopt the following procedures: We shall, first, treat consumption as the dependent variable and determine its regression on the other variables. Since the consumption series are subject to greater error than are the price series, this procedure should yield the more significant results. Second, we shall treat price as the dependent variable and determine its regression on consumption and all the other variables. Third, we shall study the corresponding relationships between these variables when they are expressed in the trend-ratio and in the link-relative forms.[34] Finally, we shall make a comparison of the elasticities of demand obtained by the various methods. The comparison should help us to determine the degree of confidence which we are justified in placing in our statistical findings.

IV. THE PROBLEM OF THE ADJUSTMENT OF THE DATA

The problem is whether it is better to work with total consumption and money prices, or with per capita consumption and "real" (deflated) prices. A

If $g \rightarrow 0$, then

(vii)
$$b = \frac{1}{r_{xy}} \frac{\sigma_y}{\sigma_x},$$

which is the slope of the regression of x on y referred to the same axis as that of the other elementary regression.

It is impossible to determine b without making an assumption regarding g. In my *Statistical Laws of Demand and Supply* (1928) the special assumption was made that $g = 1$. Geometrically, this means that we minimize the sum of the squares of the *perpendicular* deviations of the points from the line.

The extension of the method to linear functions of more than two variables is similar to the development traced above. We have then to make assumptions regarding the ratios of the weights of all but one of the variables to the weight of the remaining variable—say, y. For an application of this method to fitting linear functions in three variables see *ibid.*, pp. 178–86.

[32] See, however, the interesting attempt to fit this function when both variables are subject to random errors by G. Pietra in his papers, "Interpolating Plane Curves," *Metron*, III (1923–24), 311–28; and "Dell'interpolazione parabolica nel caso in cui entrambi i valori delle variabili sono affetti da errori accidentali," *ibid.*, IX, Nos. 3–4 (1932), 77–85.

[33] It is primarily for this reason that in my *Statistical Laws* I preferred to apply this method only to variables expressed in terms of link relatives or trend ratios.

For the latest discussion of this problem see Charles F. Roos, "A General Invariant Criterion of Fit for Lines and Planes Where All Variables Are Subject to Error," *Metron*, XIII, No. 1 (28–II–1937), 3–20, and Herbert E. Jones, "Some Geometrical Considerations in the General Theory of Fitting Lines and Planes," *Metron*, XIII, No. 1 (28–II–1937), 21–30.

[34] For the link relatives and for the trend ratios we also obtained the lines of *mutual* regression, i.e., the regressions which take into account errors in price as well as errors in consumption. But since these lines were generally close to the regressions of consumption on price, only the latter will be summarized in this work.

good theoretical case can be made out for the first procedure. It may be argued, for example, that to divide the consumption series by the figures for population and the price series by an index number of prices is to assume that there exists a relationship of proportionality between the deflator and the variable—which is not generally true; whereas if the two deflators are introduced as separate independent variables into our demand equation, the nature of their interrelations with the other independent variables could be more easily studied, and their influence on the quantity demanded more directly taken into account.

There is no denying the fact that the introduction of indices of population and of purchasing power of money as separate variables in our demand equation may prove advantageous in some cases. But competent mathematical statisticians have long felt that every effort should be made to reduce the number of variables in a statistical equation to a minimum. Thus, in his excellent textbook on statistics, Dr. Robert W. Burgess reaches this conclusion:

> Four-variable regression equations should . . . be used only with considerable caution, and the use of five or more variables is to be discouraged still more. At the best, these formulas give only an average relationship, the best there is, to be sure, of the first degree algebraically. But the assumption of the adequacy of a first-degree formula becomes increasingly dangerous as we increase the number of variables. . . . .
>
> In general, the writer believes that an intensive examination of two- or three-variable correlations, with full consideration of possible non-linear relationships, will be found more valuable than the cursory inspection implied by regression equations in four or more variables.[35]

Accordingly I have preferred to reduce the number of variables in the demand equations by dividing the total consumption series by the figures for population, and the money price series by an index number of prices, before submitting them to mathematical treatment. Most of the statistical chapters of this book constitute an analysis of such adjusted data.

For comparative purposes I have, however, also submitted the unadjusted data to a parallel mathematical treatment. Appendix B is a summary of the results obtained.

But the use of deflators does not necessarily iron out the secular movements of the series. In fact, the very process of deflating may introduce a secular trend into the data. If the adjusted data are subject to such trends, we may effect a further adjustment through the use of the trend-ratio method or of the link-relative method,[36] or by introducing time as an additional variable. In chapter xvii, a comparison will be made of the results yielded by the various methods.

[35] *Introduction to the Mathematics of Statistics* (Boston, 1927), p. 279.

[36] See chap. ii, pp. 67–68. These methods can, of course, be applied directly to the unadjusted data, and it is sometimes desirable to do so.

V. CONCLUDING SUMMARY

The statistical analysis to which the rest of the book will be devoted will proceed by stages as follows:

First, we shall derive two simple demand curves for each commodity, that is, demand curves of the type

$$(5.1) \qquad\qquad x = x(y, t)$$

and

$$(5.2) \qquad\qquad y = y(x, t) ,$$

which take no account of the prices of other goods. At this stage of the analysis, we shall experiment with different methods and procedures, typical examples of which are listed in Table 3.

TABLE 3

THE SIMPLER, TYPICAL METHODS, PROCEDURES, AND EQUATIONS USED IN DETERMINING THE STATISTICAL DEMAND CURVES OF SELECTED COMMODITIES*

I. The Time-Regression Method
   Type of demand equation assumed
   (1) $x(t) = a + by + ct$ $a > 0, \ b < 0, \ c \gtrless 0$
   (2) $x(t) = A y^a e^{\beta t}$ $A > 0, \ a < 0, \ \beta \gtrless 0$

II. The Method of Trend Ratios†
   Type of demand equation assumed
   (3) $X = a + bY$ $a > 0, \ b < 0$
   (4) $X = A Y^a$ $A > 0, \ a < 0$

III. The Method of Link Relatives†
   Type of demand equation assumed
   (5) $X = a + bY$ $a > 0, \ b < 0$
   (6) $X = A Y^a$ $A > 0, \ a < 0$

* For list of commodities, see chap. v, Table 4.
† Capital letters (X, Y) indicate trend ratios or link relatives in contrast with the lower-case letters (x, y), which indicate actual quantities and prices.

Second, we shall introduce an index of production (income) into the demand curves of some of the commodities, thereby obtaining functions of the type

$$(5.3) \qquad\qquad x = x(y, R, t)$$

and

$$(5.4) \qquad\qquad y = y(x, R, t) ,$$

and study the effect of this variable on the relations already found.

Finally, we shall select several groups of related commodities, express the demand for each commodity as a function not only of its price but also of the prices of the other goods and of income (or an index of it):

(5.5)
$$\begin{cases} x_1 = x_1(y_1, y_2, \ldots, R, t) \\ x_2 = x_2(y_1, y_2, \ldots, R, t) \\ \cdot \quad \cdot \quad \cdot \quad \cdot \quad \cdot \quad \cdot \quad \cdot \quad \cdot \quad \cdot \end{cases}$$

and

(5.6)
$$\begin{cases} y_1 = y_1(x_1, x_2, \ldots, R, t) \\ y_2 = y_2(x_1, x_2, \ldots, R, t) \\ \cdot \quad \cdot \quad \cdot \quad \cdot \quad \cdot \quad \cdot \quad \cdot \quad \cdot \quad \cdot \end{cases} ,$$

and analyze the relations which exist between the demands for completing and competing goods.

The reader should keep in mind the fact that the equations, methods, and procedures outlined above are typical, not exhaustive. In the statistical chapters which follow there will be found interesting and important modifications of them.

PART II

STATISTICAL FINDINGS

CHAPTER V

THE DATA AND THEIR LIMITATIONS

CHAPTER V

THE DATA AND THEIR LIMITATIONS

I. THE COMMODITIES

The commodities for which we shall derive concrete, statistical demand curves are sixteen in number. Of these, the first thirteen relate to the United

TABLE 4*

COMMODITIES SELECTED FOR DEMAND ANALYSIS, WITH THEIR VALUES IN 1915 AND 1925

COMMODITY	TOTAL VALUE (MILLIONS OF DOLLARS)		VALUE PER CAPITA (DOLLARS)	
	1915	1925	1915	1925
United States crops:				
Corn............................	1,723	1,966	17.22	16.99
Cotton...........................	631	1,464	6.31	12.65
Hay.............................	913	1,190	9.13	10.29
Wheat...........................	942	958	9.42	8.28
Sugar...........................	473	677	4.73	5.85
Potatoes.........................	222	600	2.22	5.19
Oats............................	560	566	5.59	4.89
Barley...........................	118	126	1.18	1.09
Rye.............................	45	36	0.45	0.31
Buckwheat.......................	12	12	0.12	0.11
Total.......................	5,639	7,595	....	....
United States meats:				
Pork............................	....	1,666	....	14.40
Beef and veal....................	....	1,003	....	8.67
Mutton and lamb.................	....	153	....	1.32
Total.......................	....	2,822	....	....
Canadian commodities:				
Sugar...........................	....	52	....	5.58
Tea.............................	....	19	....	2.03
Coffee...........................	....	6	....	0.68
Total.......................	....	77	....	....

* For all the commodities in the first group, except sugar, the data represent farm values and are taken from the *Agricultural Yearbook, 1931*. For the commodities in the second group the data represent gross income to farmers for hogs, cattle and calves, and sheep and lambs, and are taken from the *Statistical Abstract, 1931*, p. 671. For United States sugar and the Canadian commodities the data represent "consumption" multiplied by wholesale price. Sources for these data may be found in the relevant appendix tables.

States and the remaining three to Canada. Table 4 is a list of the commodities arranged by groups according to their approximate importance in 1915 and 1925.

The first group of commodities in Table 4 represents approximately 75 per cent of the total value of our crops in both 1915 and 1925, and approximately 45 per cent of the total value of our crops and animal products in the same years. The second group amounted to approximately 45 per cent of the total value of all animal products in 1925. The two groups combined represented

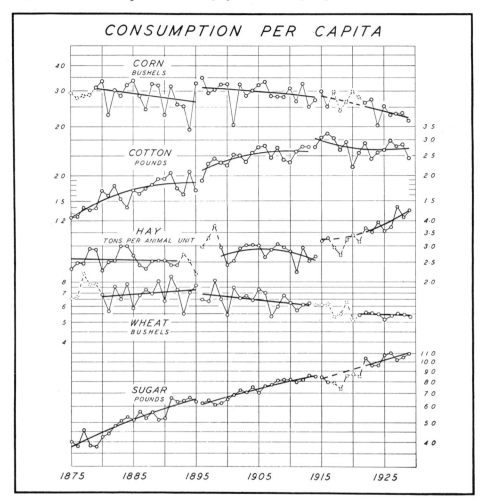

FIG. 15a.—The per capita consumption in the United States of the first five commodities listed in Table 4. The continuous curves show the trend of consumption by periods. The dotted circles indicate observations which were not used in the analysis.

approximately 60 per cent of the total value of the output of our farms in the same year.[1]

[1] These are estimates based upon the data given in the *Agricultural Yearbooks* for 1917 (p. 747) and 1926 (pp. 1201 and 1204) and in the *Statistical Abstract* for 1931 (pp. 670–71). Since the value given for sugar in Table 4 represents the consumption of sugar, and most of the sugar consumed is imported, the value of the sugar imports was subtracted from the total value of the crops listed in Table 4, before the percentages given above were computed.

The first group consists of ten apparently independent commodities; the demand for any one of them is not likely to depend significantly on the price

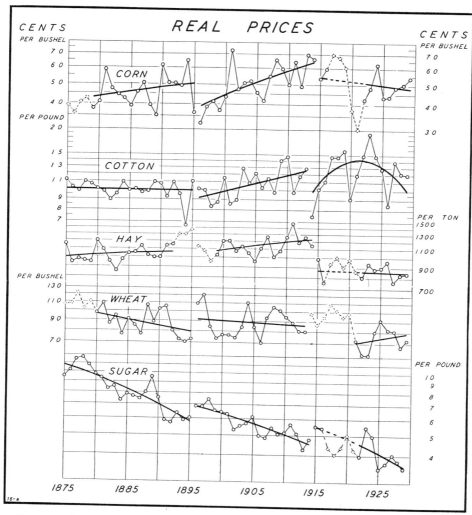

FIG. 16a. The real prices in the United States of the first five commodities listed in Table 4. The continuous curves show the price trends by periods. The dotted circles indicate observations which were not used in the analysis.

of any of the others. We shall, therefore, use the data for this group primarily for deriving various types of "simple" demand curves, i.e., those which take no account of the prices of the other goods. With this end in view we shall subject the data for each of these commodities to an analysis by the methods listed in Table 3 of chapter iv. This analysis will form the subject matter of Part II.

The second and the third groups consist of apparently related commodities. We shall use the data for these commodities (as well as for barley, corn, hay, and oats, which are also in the first group) primarily for analyzing the *interrela-*

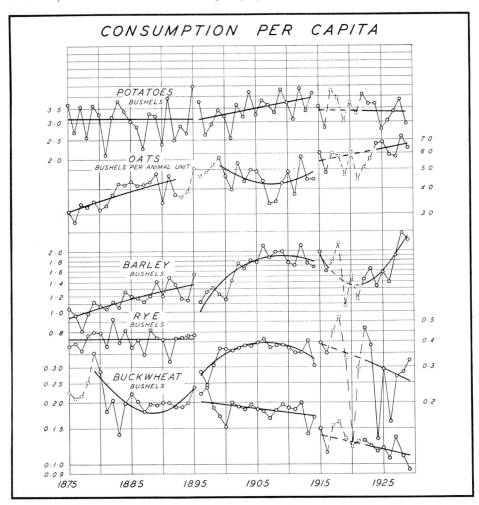

FIG. 15b.—The per capita consumption in the United States of the second five commodities listed in Table 4. The continuous curves show the trend of consumption by periods. The dotted circles indicate observations which were not used in the analysis.

tions of demand, or the extent to which any two members in a group compete with or complete each other in consumption. For each of these groups we shall deduce a demand function of the type (5.5) or (5.6) of chapter iv and compare the results with those suggested by theory. The analysis of these interrelations and comparisons will constitute the subject matter of Part III.

Figures 15 and 16 are a graphical representation of the adjusted quantities and prices of the first ten commodities of Table 4.[2] The data are all plotted to the same ratio scale so that the fluctuations in the different series are com-

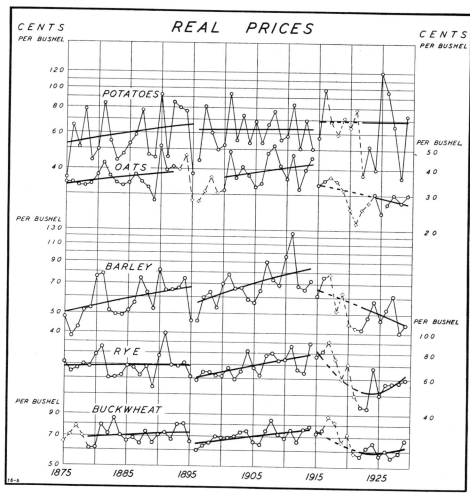

FIG. 16b.—The real prices in the United States of the second five commodities listed in Table 4. The continuous curves show the price trends by periods. The dotted circles indicate observations which were not used in the analysis.

parable with one another. In reducing the quantity series to a per capita basis, the population figures used were supplied by Clarence E. Batscheldt, geographer, Department of Commerce. In deflating the price series, the deflator used is the index of wholesale prices (1913 = 100) of the Bureau of Labor Statistics as extrapolated by Carl Snyder back to 1875.

[2] See Tables III–XII, Appen. A.

As can be seen from the diagrams, the data on these ten commodities cover the period from 1875 to 1929. But this period saw too many changes in our economic history to constitute a homogeneous period for our purposes. We shall, therefore, break it up into three parts as follows:

(I) 1875–95, the period of general falling prices
(II) 1896–1914, the period of general rising prices
(III) 1915–29 (omitting 1917–21), the period of the World War and "reconstruction"

and make a study of the data for each part, with the view of obtaining a better insight into the changes that have taken place in the shape of the demand curves and in the direction and rate of their shifting.

In each of the statistical chapters which follow, we shall also supplement the detailed analyses of the data prior to 1929 with a brief summary of the more important changes in demand that have taken place since 1929.

The following pages contain a discussion of the advantages and the limitations for our purposes of the data graphed in these diagrams. (For a more detailed discussion of the data on cotton and wheat see chaps. viii and x.) A description of the data relating to the other commodities of Table 4 will be given in Part III.

II. THE IDEAL DATA AND THE AVAILABLE APPROXIMATIONS

There are different types of demand curves which may be derived for one and the same commodity, such as the demand curve of the wholesaler, the demand curve of the retailer, and the demand curve of the final consumer. Most theoretical discussions of demand center around the demand curve of the final consumer. In our statistical studies, however, it is the demand curve of the wholesaler, dealer, and farmer which will receive the greatest attention. There are several reasons for this change of emphasis.

First, the wholesaler-dealer-farmer demand curve may be just as important and significant as the demand curve of the final consumer.

Second, there are many commodities for which there exists only the first type of demand curve. These are the raw materials which undergo several transformations before they reach the final consumer. Thus wheat is transformed into bread, pastries, etc.; corn into pork, lard, beef, milk, and alcohol. In theory this demand curve may be derived either directly from the quantities sold and prices paid for the raw materials in question or indirectly from the demand curves of the goods into which they have been transformed. There can be no doubt, however, but that at the present stage of our knowledge the indirect procedure is subject to almost insuperable difficulties. Thus, to take a very simple example, even if we had the demand curves of the various kinds of breads and pastries, we could not simply aggregate these curves and obtain the demand curve of wheat.[3] For bread is quite a different commodity from wheat. When we buy a loaf of bread—and the same is true *a fortiori* of cakes and pastries—we buy milk, sugar, shortening, salt, wrapping, and service, as well as wheat. Conversely, we should find it equally impossible as a practical procedure to derive the demand curve of bread from the demand curves of wheat and the other ingredients of bread.[4]

The commodities listed in Table 4 are essentially raw materials.[5] Therefore, the only type of demand curve that it seems practicable to derive for them is the wholesaler-dealer-farmer demand curve.

For deriving such a demand curve the primary data that are needed are *the quantities bought each year* (or other period) *by the wholesaler-dealer-farmer-consumers from the farmer-producers, and the corresponding average unit prices*, or, better still, the price per unit at which each transaction was made. Now such quantity and price series simply do not exist, and many of the difficulties which we shall encounter are traceable to this fact.

Perhaps the best approximation to our ideal quantity series would be either (1) yearly data on "total utilization," i.e., total production plus imports, plus stocks at the beginning of the year, minus exports, minus stocks at the end of the year, leaving the quantity used for food, feed, seed, and loss during the year—such as we shall use in the study of the demand for wheat; or (2) such direct consumption figures as are published by the Bureau of the Census on the takings of cotton by United States mills. For most of the commodities, however, such desirable series are simply not available or are available only for the most recent years. The only figures which we have for estimating the yearly consumption of all the crops except cotton, wheat, and oats are the total production and the import and export figures. There is reason to believe, however, that the stocks for most of these commodities are not large or, what is more important from our point of view, vary only slightly from year to year. Furthermore, the net exports of certain commodities—corn, hay, potatoes, oats, and buckwheat—seldom amount to as much as 5 per cent of production, so that for these commodities the statistics of production may be considered as approximating the quantities taken.[6]

[3] An indication of the proper procedure may be obtained from Dr. Erich Schneider's article, "Über die Nachfrage nach Produktionsmitteln und ihre Elastizität," *Jahrbücher für Nationalökonomie und Statistik*, 137. Band—III. Folge, Band 82 (1932), 801–14.

[4] However, I am not denying the fact that the demand curve of the wholesaler, dealer, and farmer ultimately depends on that of the final consumer and that the bilateral relation between the two deserves serious study.

[5] The more important exceptions are sugar, tea, and coffee.

[6] When total production is taken as an approximation to the quantity demanded, it should not be forgotten that the figures contain also the "reservation demand" of the producers, i.e., the quantities which do not exchange hands but which are consumed by the farmer-producers on the farm. As I have shown in my *Statistical Laws of Demand and Supply* (Chicago, 1928), pp. 16–23, a demand

Perhaps the best approximation to our ideal price series—the average annual price at which all the exchanges of the commodity between the farmer-producers and the wholesaler-dealer-processor-farmer-consumers have taken place —is the recently published season average price for all classes and grades produced in the United States which is weighted according to both the production in each state and the estimated sales during the marketing season. But this series was not available when our study was begun. Moreover, it extends back only to 1908 for some of our commodities and to 1919 for others. We therefore used the best approximation to this series, namely, the December 1 farm price, and except in the cotton, wheat, and oats analyses we did not deem it worth while to recompute our demand functions when the new series became available. The December 1 farm price series is also an average price for all classes and grades produced in the United States and—what is more important for our immediate purposes—is available for the entire period covered by our investigations. For sugar, however, there is no December 1 price series, and for barley the December 1 price series is subject to a serious limitation (see Sec. IV-B). In analyzing the demands for these commodities, we therefore used the New York wholesale price of sugar and the Chicago market price of barley.

The foregoing, then, are the quantity and price series selected as approximations to the unobtainable ideal series. The next question to be considered is their intrinsic accuracy. Within what margin of error do they represent the quantities designated by their titles—United States production and farm prices? No definite, numerical answer can be given to this question, but a description of the way in which the figures have been determined will help to indicate both their value and their limitations.

III. THE QUANTITY SERIES

The production estimates which form the basis for all our quantity series (except for sugar, cotton, and wheat) are those of the United States Department of Agriculture. Although the first federal appropriation for the collection of agricultural statistics was made as early as 1839,[7] it was only after the establishment of the Department of Agriculture in 1862 that the basis was laid for the

---

curve derived from such data has certain properties which distinguish it from the ordinary demand curve. Such a curve cannot be brought into juxtaposition with the ordinary supply curve in order to obtain the market price. The extent to which the statistical demand curves of this book are affected by the "reservation demand" of the producers must be determined in each case by a careful study of the data and methods used. The reservation demand does not enter at all into the demand for sugar and cotton. It should be added that both types of demand curves can be deduced from the indifference curves by the method explained in chap. i, pp. 24–50.

[7] In that year Congress appropriated $1,000 for the collection and distribution of seeds. This appropriation marks the beginning of the present Department of Agriculture. Similar appropriations continued to be made for the combined purpose of collecting agricultural statistics and distributing seeds, increasing in amount as the value and importance of the work came to be recognized. From

systematic collection of agricultural statistics, in the most general and comprehensive sense of that word.

The permanent annual record of agricultural statistics in the United States (which begins with 1863) is contained in the statistical appendix of the *Yearbook of the Department of Agriculture*, which has been issued annually since 1894. For the principal American crops and classes of livestock, this appendix gives the acreage, yield per acre, total production, average price, total value, and imports and exports, as well as other valuable data. It is primarily from these appendixes that our series are derived.

The production series are, as the Bureau of Agricultural Economics[8] emphasizes, not censuses but estimates, obtained by multiplying the estimated acreage by the estimated yield per acre. These estimates are based on an increasingly[9] large number of reports from voluntary farm correspondents, as well as regular paid state and field agents of the Bureau. In 1921, for instance, the crop-reporting staff of the Bureau consisted of forty-two agricultural statisticians distributed over the country, one in each state or group of states, who traveled throughout their territory getting information on all crop conditions. Each enlisted the services of from 250 to 1,500 crop correspondents, or "aids," whose reports, together with his own investigations, formed the basis for his detailed estimates of the crops in his state which he forwarded to the Washington office at the end of every month.

1839 to 1862 the work was handled by a small force in the Patent Office, but in 1862 it was transferred to the Department of Agriculture in accordance with the act, passed May 15, 1862, establishing the department. The first appropriation for collecting agricultural statistics by the Department was provided for by the act of February 25, 1863, which appropriated a lump sum for the work of the department amounting to $90,000. The then commissioner of agriculture allotted a part of this amount for collecting agricultural statistics and appointed a statistician for that purpose. For the fiscal year ending June 30, 1865, the first distinct and separate provision was made for collecting agricultural statistics for information and reports, and the amount of $20,000 was appropriated. See *The Crop and Livestock Reporting Service of the United States* (U.S. Department of Agriculture, Miscl. Publ. 171), pp. 3–4.

[8] Known at different times in its history also as the Division of Statistics, Bureau of Statistics, Bureau of Crop Estimates, Bureau of Markets and Crop Estimates.

The description given in the following pages of the methods for obtaining crop estimates is based on Lawrence F. Schmeckebier, *The Statistical Work of the National Government* (Baltimore, 1925), pp. 197–217; on the *Report on the Statistical Work of the U.S. Government*, H.D. 394 (67th Cong., 2d sess., 1922), which I assisted in writing; on an unpublished manuscript of the Bureau of Crop Estimates (1921), for which I am obliged to Mr. Nat C. Murray, former chief of that bureau; and on *The Crop and Livestock Reporting Service of the United States* (U.S. Department of Agriculture, Miscl. Publ. 171).

[9] The system of collecting crop information directly from farmers was first used in 1862, the year of the organization of the Department of Agriculture. The names of representative and competent men in each agricultural county were obtained through agricultural societies and members of Congress, and later through various other channels, including postmasters. A county reporter was thus secured to report monthly on printed blanks, basing his figures on his own observation and in-

A. METHOD OF ESTIMATING ACREAGE

In addition to the reports of the state agents, the Bureau received regular information directly from thousands of voluntary correspondents, classified as township reporters (35,000), county reporters (2,800), livestock reporters (16,000), mill and elevator reporters (22,000), and special lists reporting on particular crops, such as cotton, rice, potatoes, etc. Finally, more than 50,000 reported only for their own farms the actual number of acres grown of each crop and number of each class of livestock on the farm. This small census, in so far as these farms were representative of the country as a whole, served as a valuable index of the changes taking place in crop acreages and livestock from one year to another.

At the present time most of these returns from the county, township, and special reporters are received by mail by the agricultural statisticians in each state, who sort them by districts or by counties, tabulate, average, and summarize them separately for each class of reporter, for each crop and district, and then transmit the results to Washington by mail or by telegraph. The schedules received at the Washington office are sorted, tabulated, and averaged in the same way. With this information, the reports from the state agents, and such supplementary facts as weather conditions and crop reports issued by various state and private agencies, the crop-reporting board of the Bureau makes its monthly estimates.

It should be noted that the acreage estimates are made in terms of percentages of acreage of the preceding year, since, according to the experience of the Bureau, the local correspondents are much better able to estimate for their communities in this way than in terms of actual acres.

Before 1920 the relative acreage figures thus obtained used to be converted into absolute figures by being applied to the decennial census figures of acreage.

---

quiries, reinforced by similar reports from a few assistants situated in other parts of the county. Separate lists of such reporters were established by the state statistical agents during the period of their service and were continued by the field agents (agricultural statisticians).

In 1896 an additional list of township reporters was formed, followed later by special lists to report on particular subjects, as fruits, livestock, truck, and other special crops.

The system has so developed that recently (1931) there were 300,000 voluntary crop reporters on the active mailing lists of the Bureau.

A rough idea of the growth of the crop-reporting service may be obtained from the increase in the appropriations to the Bureau of Crop Estimates, which are shown in the following table:

APPROPRIATIONS OF THE BUREAU OF CROP ESTIMATES,
1881–1920, INCLUSIVE

Years Ending June 30 (5-Year Average)	Appropriation	Years Ending June 30 (5-Year Average)	Appropriation
1881–85................	$ 75,808	1901–5.................	$158,280
1886–90................	103,340	1906–10...............	233,904
1891–95................	142,052	1911–15...............	242,376
1896–1900.............	144,160	1916–20...............	328,140

For example, the census figure of 3,916,000 acres of corn in Ohio for 1909 was accepted by the Bureau of Agricultural Economics. In 1910 the Bureau estimated the acreage to be about 101 per cent of that of 1909, and therefore figured the total acreage in 1910 as 3,960,000. In 1911 the acreage was estimated to be about 1.5 per cent less than in 1910, giving, when applied to the 1910 acreage figure, 3,900,000 acres for 1911. This process would be continued from year to year, so that any bias in the yearly estimates would be cumulated. The next census, however, enabled the Bureau to make such readjustments or corrections as were necessary. Since 1920, however, the Bureau has used the acreage figures of the Fourteenth Census for some states but has developed a base figure of its own for the other states.

In addition to securing first, relative acreage figures, and then converting these into absolute figures, various estimates of absolute acreage are made as checks upon the results secured by the other method. These include estimates of actual acreage in sample farms, obtained by questionnaires, and by the measurement of the frontage of crops along a highway by a "crop meter" attached to an automobile speedometer.

B. METHOD OF ESTIMATING AVERAGE YIELD

The figures for average yield per acre are also estimates obtained from the reports of crop correspondents on the average yield per acre in their communities. From these reports weighted averages are computed for the separate states and for the country as a whole.

The data for total production are, as has already been indicated, the product of the estimated acreage by the estimated yield per acre. The errors (cumulative and other) in the components are, therefore, reflected in the error of the product. The Bureau believes, however, that its yield per acre estimates are not subject to serious cumulative errors, are comparable from year to year, and need not, therefore, be revised by the census.

In addition to the census, the Bureau utilizes other sources as checks which account for the rather frequent changes in the data which it publishes. Thus such information as receipts of crops at primary markets, railroad movements, exports, agricultural surveys, and enumerations by assessing officers, marketing organizations, and business institutions, especially selling agencies, are all examined for indications that they might give of the accuracy of the earlier estimates.

C. DISCREPANCIES IN THE ESTIMATES OF PRODUCTION

Nevertheless there still remain discrepancies between the Department of Agriculture and the census data on production of crops and livestock which for some years are rather large. Thus for buckwheat the Department estimate is 21 per cent higher than the census figure for 1909, and 11 per cent higher than that for 1924; for potatoes the estimates are 11 per cent higher than the census data for 1919, and 19 per cent higher than that for 1924; while for rye the Department's figures are higher by 20 and 18 per cent for the census years 1909 and 1924. Whether, however, these discrepancies cast doubt only on the reliability of the Department figures is a somewhat debatable question, as the following remarks of Dr. Joseph S. Davis indicate:

Some years ago, in plotting annual data on wheat acreage, as revised by the Department of Agriculture on the basis of census figures, I was struck by the fact that changes in trends occurred conspicuously at the census years—which I could hardly accept as inherently probable. . . . . The Department's published revision of annual estimates of crop acreage in New York state (Department Circular No. 373, April, 1926)—intended as a model for similar revisions of similar data for all the states—strongly suggests errors in census data for which no correction was attempted. The production data, which in many cases can be checked by data on disposition, derived in some cases from more adequate censuses of manufactures, are much more defective than the acreage statistics. If such figures are as defective as we suspect, the raw material for historical studies of many kinds, including newer types like price analyses and indexes of physical production, cannot safely be used for such purposes, and many such studies already made are weak in their very foundations.

Some of the worst difficulties arise in the 1890's, but latest figures do not command confidence. The published data of the agricultural census of 1925 leave one greatly troubled on this point. . . . . The Department's figures for acreage are 2 to 4 per cent higher than the census figures, for most crops, and much higher for several of the lesser crops (e.g., rye, ... , potatoes, ...). The production figures of the Department of Agriculture are much farther above those of the census—in wheat, 8 per cent, in most other crops considerably more. In each of these cases the Department's revised figures were published after the census data became available, and the difference represents a carefully considered judgment of the understatement in the census data, reached after close study of supplementary information. The Department's figures may not be correct; but there is reason to believe that the difference, in acreage at least, represents a conservative measure of the understatement in the census figures, rather than an overstatement by the Department of Agriculture; and in the case of certain crops the available checks on production estimates, readily available to outside investigators, appear to justify the higher figures of the Department.[10]

However, Mr. Leon E. Truesdell, of the Bureau of the Census, does not accept Dr. Davis' conclusion as appears from his reply to Dr. Davis:

There is material out of which one might make a sharp controversy in the differences between the census figures for crops in 1924 and the uniformly (and in some cases considerably) larger estimates published by the Department of Agriculture. For these estimates in their present form were made after the census figures became available and their continued use implies that they are considered to be in the nature of corrections of the census data.

This is not the place nor the time for any controversy, but in justice to the census figures I feel that I ought to express very positively the opinion that many of the estimates are far too high. It is doubtless true that there was some under-enumeration in 1925—some farms missed entirely and some schedules from which crop acreages were omitted. I cannot believe,

[10] "Some Observations on Federal Agricultural Statistics," *Jour. Amer. Statist. Assoc.*, XXIII (March, 1928, Suppl.), 6–8.

however, that the sum total of omissions of both types can have amounted to as much as 5 per cent in the case of any major crop, not to mention 10 or 15 or 40 per cent.

It is also true that duplication and other forms of overstatement get into reports of shipments and reports of stocks, and doubtless into some of the other data used to justify the use of production figures in excess of the census totals.[11]

In the course of our own study serious doubts as to the relative accuracy of the Department data in certain years led to their omission as observations in our computations. Thus the data for 1875–78 were omitted for corn and buckwheat; and the data for 1893–98 for hay and oats when animal units were used.[12]

It should be noted, however, that the remarks of Davis and Truesdell, as well as most of our computations, are based on data published prior to those given in the 1932 *Yearbook of Agriculture*. That *Yearbook* contains extensive revisions for most crops and most years since 1919—largely reductions in the previous estimates.[13] To have incorporated these changes would have meant a complete recomputation of our equations for the third period, which we did not feel justified in making.[14] As a test we simply took one of the commodities—oats—for which the changes were greatest and computed the demand equation from the unrevised and the revised data for the period 1915–29 (omitting 1917–23). The results are as follows:

(1) $\qquad$ Unrevised $\quad x = 197.015 - 1.375y - 1.074t \qquad R = 0.596$
$$(\pm 0.993)\ (\pm 0.999)$$

(2) $\qquad$ Revised $\quad x = 185.715 - 1.257y - 2.005t \qquad R = 0.704,$
$$(\pm 0.976)\ (\pm 1.001)$$

where x is the total production of oats, y the December 1 farm price, t time, the origins being at 0 for x and y and at 1922 for time, the figures preceded by $\pm$ being *standard* errors. The difference between the coefficients of price, it will be seen, is not significant; that between the coefficients of time is more marked but still within the range of the standard errors. The revised data yield, however, a higher coefficient of multiple correlation (R).

This example illustrates the fact that most of the discrepancies noted throw more doubt on the trend of the series used than on the year-to-year changes. If, through an error in determining the level of production in any one year, the true trend of production has been distorted, this will affect the rate of

[11] "Discussions of Dr. Davis' Paper, II," *Jour. Amer. Statist. Assoc.*, XXIII (March, 1928), 19.

[12] See Appen. A.

[13] The revisions of the estimates for the earlier years have not yet been completed, and even the 1932 revisions are being subjected to further revisions.

[14] Since this was written (1934), we have found it necessary to recompute the demand equations for cotton, wheat, and oats. For these we used the latest data available at the time of each analysis. The actual series used and specific references are given in chaps. viii, x, and xii, and in the tables of Appen. A relating to these commodities.

shifting of the demand curve derived from the data but not necessarily its shape or its elasticity. The latter depends primarily on the year-to-year fluctuations of the quantities and related prices.

IV. THE PRICE SERIES

The price series which we shall use fall into two groups: farm prices and produce-market and wholesale prices.

A. THE FARM PRICES

The history and method of collecting farm prices are detailed in a bulletin published by the U.S. Department of Agriculture.[15] We shall quote the more important passages:

Systematic collection of farm prices by the department began in 1867, when farm prices of crops and farm values of livestock as of January 1 were obtained from correspondents. In 1872 the date for reporting prices of crops was changed to December 1. After this change was made it became customary to consider the crop prices reported as of January 1, 1867–1872, as equivalent to the prices prevailing one month earlier (December 1 of the previous calendar year), and for many years past these prices have been published as of December 1, 1866–1871, making a full series of December 1 prices for crops. No change has been made in the date for reporting values of livestock. The prices of crops and the values of livestock for the period, 1866–1878, as now published have been reduced to a gold basis, using equivalents supplied by the United States Treasury Department.

The organization for gathering prices is the crop-estimating service, but that service is supplemented by special price reporters, of whom there were 7,600 in 1921 and 13,500 in 1933. These are mostly local merchants and dealers who report to the agricultural statisticians in their respective states the prices received by farmers for their produce or the prices paid by them for seed, feed, machinery, fertilizers, and other equipment and supplies.

The prices received by producers of farm products, commonly called "farm prices," represent the price-reporting estimate of the average price of all grades and classes of commodities being sold in the local farm market. . . . . The grades and classes vary from one season to another and even from one month to the next. . . . .

The farm price is seldom an f.o.b. price. In the case of potatoes, for example, there is usually some agency at the local market to buy from the producer, and these buyers must receive some compensation for their services. There is usually some spread between the farm price and the f.o.b. price. When the farmer sells direct to the consumer in a neighboring town the farm price and the retail price may be one and the same.

Strictly speaking, the actual farm price or "price at the farm" of a farm product is practically impossible to learn or obtain. The price which is usually obtained is the one the farmer receives at his local market. For most farm products there is no "at the farm" price. The price is made only when the product changes hands. The prices reported to the United States Department of Agriculture are the prices at which the products first changed hands when sold by the producer. The price of wheat as reported includes the cost to the farmer of han-

[15] Charles F. Sarle, *Reliability and Adequacy of Farm-Price Data* (U.S. Dept. Agric. Bull. 1480), pp. 5–6.

dling and delivering the wheat to the local elevator. The local handling cost may be relatively large with such products as . . . . cotton.

The State average of prices received by producers of farm products is made up of prices from both surplus-producing and deficit areas within the State. The farm price in areas of surplus production (J. W. Strowbridge, "Farm and Terminal Market Prices: Wheat, Corn, and Oats," U.S. Dept. Agric. Bull. 1083 (1922), 3–5) tends to be the primary-market price less the costs of marketing which arise from the time the product leaves the farmer's hands until it reaches the primary market. With such crops as cotton and wheat (in years when wheat is on an export basis) the farm price is the world price, as the Liverpool price is often called, less the cost of getting the product to Liverpool.[16]

As a consequence of the costs of transportation and marketing, the farm prices of many crops tend to fall into zones in much the same way as climatic data, with the zones of higher prices forming more or less concentric circles about the zones of lower prices.[17]

The farm price for a State is usually an average of prices received by farmers as they sell their product all along the line, from the price paid for the product entering the regular channels of trade to the retail price received by the farmer who sells direct to the consumer.[18]

It should also include the price received for that part of the crop which is sold for manufacturing purposes, as when potatoes are sold for making starch and potato flour, and when apples are sold for cider-making. Farm prices also include many seed prices.

It should be kept in mind that the farm price for a locality "is designed to express the general average of all sales made . . . . in the locality. . . . . If it is the local practice of the community for the farmer to sell potatoes in sacks or apples in boxes the farm price probably includes the cost of the container."[19]

The average price for the United States is determined as follows: The crop reporters report to the United States Department of Agriculture the price as of December 1 for their respective townships or districts. These prices are averaged, first, to form a state price and, second, to form the United States price. In determining the state farm price of an important crop, the price reports from each district are averaged, and these district averages are weighted by the number of acres of that crop raised in each district the last year for which data are available. The state prices are then weighted according to the latest estimate of the production of each crop and the United States average farm

[16] *Ibid.*, pp. 2–3.

[17] To the best of our knowledge, the pioneer studies of the geography of prices are Th. H. Engelbrecht, *Die geographische Verteilung der Getreidepreise in den Vereinigten Staaten von 1862 bis 1900* (Berlin: Paul Parey, 1903) and *Die geographische Verteilung der Getreidepreise in Indien von 1861 bis 1905* (Berlin: Paul Parey, 1908); and L. B. Zapoleon, *Geography of Wheat Prices* (U.S. Dept. Agric. Bull. 594 [1918]); *Geographical Phases of Farm Prices: Corn* (U.S. Dept. Agric. Bull. 696 [1918]); and *Geographical Phases of Farm Prices: Oats* (U.S. Dept. Agric. Bull. 755 [1919]).

[18] Sarle, *op. cit.*, p. 3.   [19] *Ibid.*, p. 5.

price determined. This series was begun as early as 1866 but is now being replaced by a season average price.

It is this series which we shall use for all our commodities except sugar and barley.

B. THE OTHER PRICES

The price series which we shall use for sugar is the average of daily quotations of the New York wholesale price of refined sugar, as given in Palmer's *Concerning Sugar* (a loose-leaf service of the U.S. Beet Sugar Assoc.).[20] This price was taken because New York was the dominant sugar market during the period covered by this investigation; prices in all markets throughout the United States were fixed by the New York price.

For barley it was found that the Chicago price (an August–July average of quotations for choice-to-fancy or fair-to-good malting grades in Chicago) and the farm price, instead of showing the customary general agreement, differed definitely as to direction of trend during the first period, 1875–95. This seemed to be due to a decided shift in regions of barley production. The average farm prices for the earlier years of the period were heavily weighted by the high prices of New York and California; those for the later years by the low prices of the Chicago region. The Chicago price seemed, therefore, to be more representative of the general trend of barley prices throughout the country than the farm price.

C. THE RELIABILITY OF THE FARM PRICES

The farm prices have not been subject to such numerous and large revisions as have the production figures. They are based on so many quotations—and this is true particularly of the prices of the major crops—that they are probably a good index of, or approximation to, our ideal series—the average price at which all the exchanges of the commodity between the producers and the consumers (wholesalers, dealers, processors, farmers) are made during the crop year. They are an average of all grades, varieties, and qualities and include prices from surplus-producing and deficit areas within any given state.[21]

But the December 1 farm prices of crops were developed primarily for the purpose of calculating, as of a given date, the value of the individual crops in the various states, and the question arises whether they constitute good averages for the year. The answer is that the monthly farm price series which was begun by the United States Department of Agriculture in 1909 probably yields a representative *annual* average which is preferable to the December 1 price.

---

[20] This service is no longer published. The data are based on statistics from official government sources and from Willett and Gray's *Weekly Statistical Sugar Trade Journal* (New York). The annual number published in January contains summaries of prices, consumption, and other series of interest to the trade.

[21] For a comparison of state farm prices and of farm prices with market prices see Sarle, *op. cit.*

But it is too short a series for our purposes. Nevertheless, it provides a test of the representativeness of the December 1 price. The correlations between the average of the monthly prices for the crop year and the December 1 price from 1909 to 1929 for some of the crops are as follows:

Buckwheat	0.9905	Corn	0.9790
Cotton	0.9905	Wheat	0.9745
Barley	0.9868	Rye	0.9729
Oats	0.9795	Potatoes	0.9558

The correlations are high, so that it seems reasonable to assume that the December 1 farm price is sufficiently representative of the period, the crop year.

V. SUMMARY

It is evident that the quantity and the price series do not correspond very closely to the ideal series and are not intrinsically very accurate, the quantity series being particularly suspect. Yet we believe that they are sufficiently accurate to yield good approximations to the demand curves of most of our commodities, and some indications of their shifts through time and their interrelations. In any event, no better data are available, and one way of bringing to light needed improvements in the present series is to subject them to just the type of analysis which we shall make in the following chapters.[22]

[22] For the actual series used, specific references to sources, and detailed comments, see Appen. A.

CHAPTER VI

THE DEMAND FOR SUGAR

CHAPTER VI

THE DEMAND FOR SUGAR

In the Preface to his well-known *Frequency Curves and Correlation*, Mr. W. Palin Elderton remarks that

the reader who goes through a book on a practical subject and does not work out examples is as certain to encounter imaginary and miss real difficulties as he is to fail to obtain any satisfactory knowledge of the subject.

The reader of a work on statistical economics ought to give particular heed to this advice, for few other fields are beset with so many imaginary, as well as real, difficulties. To facilitate his present task somewhat, we shall explain the derivation of the demand curve for sugar in a simple, nontechnical manner and, by making liberal use of graphs, lay bare a good part of the mathematical and statistical techniques that will be followed. This should serve as an introduction to the methods of analysis and enable us to condense the later chapters.

Sugar is selected for this purpose not because it is the most important commodity in our list—it ranks fifth in Table 4, chapter v—but because it has no substitutes of importance, which simplifies the theoretical problem, and because the statistical data relating to it have certain properties which make them desirable in this connection.

I. THE FACTS AND THE PROVISIONAL ASSUMPTIONS

Sugar provides about 13 per cent of all the energy obtained from food consumed by the people of the United States. . . . . The average amount eaten is [over] 2 pounds per week. This includes the sugar used in candies, sweet drinks, and other foods not prepared in the home. The amount which would be used in cooking and on the table averages about $1\frac{1}{2}$ pounds per person per week.[1]

The amount of sugar consumed is now higher in the United States than in most other countries, the per capita consumption having increased from 40.3 pounds in 1875 to 107.5 pounds in 1925. "There are no statistics to show how the increased per capita consumption is used, but it seems safe to assume that a considerable proportion goes into candies and sweet drinks."[2]

Of our total consumption of sugar in recent years, less than one-fourth is produced in Continental United States. In the five-year period from 1918 to

---

[1] Monograph on sugar in the *U.S. Department of Agriculture Yearbook* (1923), p. 151. This article, prepared by a group of experts, gives in less than one hundred pages an excellent introduction to the economic and technical aspects of the sugar industry.

[2] *Ibid.*, p. 151.

1922, Cuba supplied 50 per cent of our consumption; domestic producers of beet, 18 per cent; domestic producers of cane, 4.7 per cent; Hawaii, 11.4 per cent; Puerto Rico, 8.2 per cent; the Philippine Islands, 2.7 per cent; and other sources, 5 per cent.[3]

Table III of Appendix A records for the period 1875–1929, inclusive, the per capita consumption, the real price, and the value per capita of sugar in the United States, together with the link relatives and the trend ratios of the first two series. The basic (unadjusted) data and the deflators used in deriving these series are given in Tables I and II of the same appendix.

The reported total consumption for any year represents the domestic production plus the imports and minus the exports of that year. Domestic consumption is, therefore, made up of United States beet sugar, United States cane sugar, imported (dutiable and nondutiable) cane sugar, and sugars from foreign molasses, maple, etc. There are no data on stocks of sugar in the channels of trade except at Cuba and at refiners' ports in the United States. Our consumption series represents, therefore, the quantity demanded for stocks as well as for direct consumption.

The annual prices are yearly averages of daily quotations f.o.b. New York for fine granulated sugar in 100-pound bags, net cash. As was explained in the previous chapter, this price was taken because New York was the dominant sugar market during the period covered by this investigation; prices in all markets throughout the United States were fixed by the New York price. According to Willett and Gray, Inc., the source of our price and consumption series:

Refined sugar is, of course, not sold in heavy volume except on a relatively small number of days during the year on which there is an important change in prices, so that the daily average of raw and refined sugars which is not weighted does not truly represent an actual average price paid by refiners for raw sugars during the year nor the actual average price received by them for refined sugar sold during the year [*Weekly Statistical Sugar Trade Journal* (62d year), No. 2, January 13, 1938, p. 12].

Figure 17 is a graphic representation on a ratio scale of the three adjusted series—the per capita consumption, the real (deflated) price, and the per capita value—for each of the three periods. (The series of per capita values will be needed later in connection with the computation of the elasticity of demand.) Table 5 is a descriptive summary of the adjusted consumption and price series. We shall consider first the series for the first period and give most attention to two simple forms of the demand function.

A glance at Figure 17 shows that the consumption and the price series exhibit a rather high inverse correlation. The per capita consumption increased from 40.3 pounds in 1875 to 63.4 pounds in 1895, while real price declined from

---

[3] *Ibid.*, pp. 216–17.

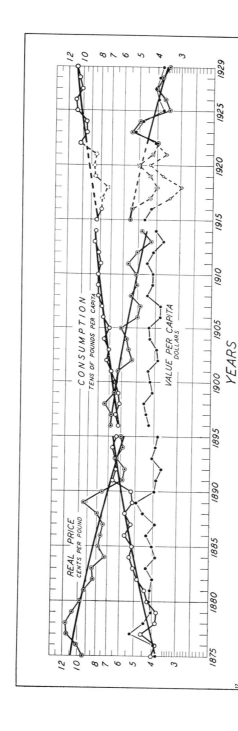

Fig. 17.—Sugar: The basic adjusted annual data used in deriving the demand curves for sugar in the United States, 1875–1929, with the computed trends by periods of the real prices and the per capita consumption. The observations connected by dotted lines in the third period are those which were not used in the computations.

9.485 cents to 6.017 cents in the same interval. The existence of this correlation is brought out clearly in the scatter diagram shown in Figure 18 in which the per capita consumption is plotted against the adjusted prices. The coefficient of correlation between the two series is −0.92. Lines AA and $A'A'$ show, respectively, the regression of consumption on price and of price on consumption.

TABLE 5

SUGAR: SUMMARY BY PERIODS OF THE ADJUSTED DATA USED IN
DERIVING THE DEMAND FUNCTIONS, 1875–1929

PERIOD*	PER CAPITA CONSUMPTION $x(t)$				DEFLATED PRICE $y(t)$				CORRELATION COEFFICIENT
	Descriptive Constants								r_{xy}
	Mean (Lb.)	Median (Lb.)	Stand-ard De-viation (Lb.)	Coeffi-cient of Varia-tion	Mean (Cents)	Median (Cents)	Stand-ard De-viation (Cents)	Coeffi-cient of Varia-tion	
I	51.8	51.8	9.207	17.76	8.313	8.054	1.780	21.42	−0.9156
II	73.8	75.3	7.735	10.47	5.700	5.521	0.826	14.49	−0.9205
III	98.8	102.1	9.751	9.87	4.364	4.004	0.830	19.02	−0.9007
	Equations of Trends								Origin
I	$x(t) = 51.8429 + 1.4147t$				$y(t) = 8.3130 - 0.2557t$				July 1, 1885
II	$x(t) = 73.8526 + 1.3558t$				$y(t) = 5.6999 - 0.1305t$				July 1, 1905
III	$x(t) = 95.9096 + 1.9269t$				$y(t) = 4.5808 - 0.1448t$				July 1, 1922

* I = 1875–95; II = 1896–1914; III = 1915–29 (excl. 1917–21).

As was shown in Part I of this book, and more especially in chapter iv, it is impossible to derive a demand curve from statistics without making use of certain hypotheses of a general economic and statistical nature, together with certain special subsidiary assumptions relating to the variables to be included in the demand function and the specific form to be given to it.

At first blush it might be thought that the simplest assumption justified by the data in question is that the quantity of sugar demanded depends only on its price:

(1.1) $$x = f(y) ,$$

or that

(1.2) $$y = f(x) .$$

It might be argued, for example, that the effect of two of the factors which are most responsible for the shifting of the demand curve, namely, changes in population and changes in the purchasing power of money, have been removed through the deflating of both the quantity and the price series; that the correla-

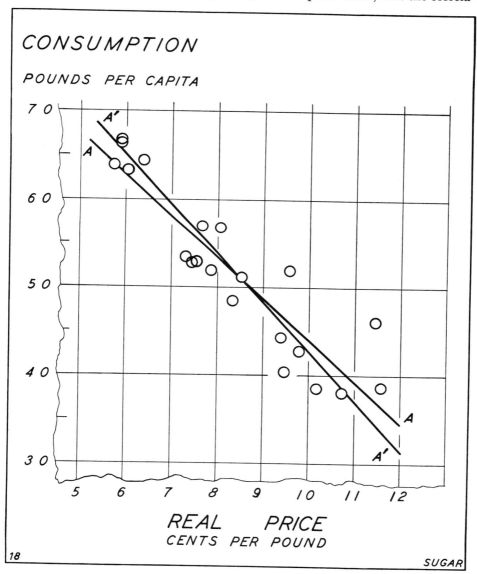

FIG. 18.—Sugar: Scatter diagram of the per capita consumption of sugar in the United States and the corresponding real price of sugar 1875–95. *AA* is the line of regression of per capita consumption on real price; *A'A'* that of real price on per capita consumption.

tion between the adjusted variables is very high, the correlation coefficient being $r = -0.92$; that there is no other factor which sensibly affects the demand for sugar; and that, consequently, one of the total regressions, either the line AA

$$x = 91.2099 - 4.7356y,$$

or the line $A'A'$

$$y = 17.4908 - 0.1770x,$$

should be considered as the specific form of the demand functions.

Of course, if one knows, or has good reason to believe, that the secular decrease in the price is the *cause* of the secular increase in consumption, and if one is not interested in short-time, reversible demand phenomena which may still be reflected in the data, the foregoing assumption would be quite valid. In general, however, it is better not to make use of this assumption. It is more reasonable to assume instead that, even if the data are corrected for changes in population and in the purchasing power of money, they still contain the effects of other factors which, though unknown or not admitting of measurement, change but slowly and smoothly with time. More specifically, it is preferable to begin with the hypothesis that time may be taken as an index of these other factors, so that the quantity demanded depends not only on its price but also on the time at which the particular price prevails.

In the problem before us, for example, it is fair to assume that the gross correlation between the price and the quantity of sugar is due in part, at least, to the long-time secular movements of the per capita consumption and the real prices and that the existence of such movements in any series ought to make us suspect the existence of disturbing factors which might produce spurious correlation, or which might give rise to long-time, *irreversible* demand or supply curves. One obvious factor which may cause such a spurious correlation is the growing taste for sugar which is suggested by the remarkable increase in the per capita consumption and which is not affected by the declining price trend. We must not, therefore, accept either the *gross* regression of consumption on price (line AA, Fig. 18) or the *gross* regression of price on consumption (line $A'A'$), as a bona fide, short-time, reversible demand curve. Rather, we must instead seek to determine the *net* regression between per capita consumption and real prices, i.e., the relation between that part of the per capita consumption which is independent of time and that part of the real price which is independent of time. It is only when the time variable is shown to be of negligible importance that this assumption reduces to the first.

Figure 19A, which illustrates the net regression of consumption on price— that of price on consumption will be studied later—enables us to test the reasonableness of the more general assumption. The scatter of the observations in Figure 19A is the same as Figure 18 except that it also shows the time (year

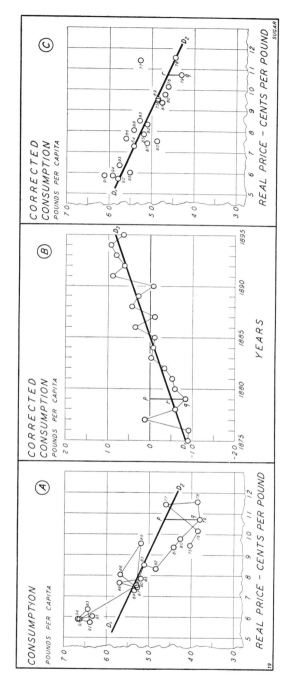

FIG. 19.—Sugar: Three aspects of the per capita demand for sugar during the period 1875–95 on the assumption that

$$x = 70.62 - 2.259y + 0.8371t.$$

A: Relation between the per capita consumption and the real prices when the data are not corrected for the effects of "time," with the demand curve D_1D_2 which results when such correction is made.

B: Relation between the per capita consumption and time when the former is corrected for the effects of changes in the real price. The slope of line D_1D_3 (fitted to the variables x and t when both are corrected for price) represents the mean rate of shift of the per capita demand curve D_1D_2.

C: The per capita demand curve for sugar, 1875–95. Line D_1D_2 shows the relation between that part of the per capita consumption of sugar in the United States which is independent of time and that part of the real price which is independent of time. In the scatter, however, only the ordinate is corrected for secular changes, the abscissa being uncorrected.

of occurrence) of each observation and the movements of the successive observations, which are connected by straight lines.

A glance at this chart shows that most of the lines are negatively inclined and that their slopes are, on the average, less steep than that of the entire scatter (see the regressions of Fig. 18). On the average, an increase in the price of sugar between any two years is accompanied by a decrease in consumption, and a decrease in price is accompanied by an increase in consumption in the same time interval. But the observations are not randomly distributed. An examination of the connecting lines shows that, with few exceptions, the later the observation, the higher its position on the chart. Thus, one of the lowest lines on the chart is that which connects the first two observations (1875–76), while one of the highest lines is that which connects the last two observations (1894–95). This indicates that consumption (x) is a function not only of price (y) but also of *time* (t)—a catch-all for the disturbing factors. We may therefore assume the general demand equation (3.30) of chapter i to be of the type

$$(1.3) \qquad\qquad\qquad\qquad x = f(y, t) \, .$$

II. THE GRAPHICAL SCAFFOLDING

To obtain a first approximation to the nature of this function, we proceed as follows: Through the point whose coordinates are the means of the two series we draw a line D_1D_2 with a slope which is representative of the slopes of the individual connecting lines. The line or curve[4] may be drawn in by inspection, for at this stage of the analysis extreme accuracy is not needed. If the line is well chosen, its slope will give, to a first approximation, the average or normal relation between consumption and price. In more technical terms, its slope will give the relation between that part of consumption which is independent of time and that part of price which is independent of time. The line may therefore be taken as a first approximation to our demand curve, which we assume has not changed in shape during the period in question. There remains to be explained why the lines connecting the successive observations are distributed in such a systematic manner about it.

Consider the observation for 1875. The "normal" per capita consumption as given by the curve corresponding to the observed real price of 9.485 cents, which obtained in that year, is 40.824 pounds. The observed consumption is 40.3 pounds. The observed consumption for 1875 is then 0.524 pounds *below* the average. By the same procedure we determine graphically for each year the difference (*positive or negative*) between the observed and the average or normal consumption. When these observations are plotted as a function of time, and a smooth curve is drawn through them by inspection, we have line D_1D_3 of

---

[4] Sometimes the scatter is such as to suggest that a curve rather than a straight line be drawn to represent the net relation between x and y.

Figure 19B, which gives to a first approximation the relation between (1) that part of consumption which is independent of price and (2) time.[5]

The final step in the graphic analysis consists of seeing how far we can reduce the scatter about the demand curve D_1D_2 of Figure 19A by assuming that the curve has shifted its position from year to year at the rate indicated by the curve D_1D_3 of Figure 19B. This will also tell us how far we have been justified in representing the demand for sugar by the straight line D_1D_2.

The procedure may be illustrated with the data for 1879. From Figure 19B, the normal amount by which the consumption for 1879 should deviate from that indicated by the demand curve D_1D_2 of Figure 19A for the price prevailing in that year (10.713 cents) is $-5.0228 = -\overline{pr}$ units. The observed amount was $-8.3215 = -\overline{pq}$ units. We therefore adjust the latter by the theoretical amount by which it should deviate from line D_1D_2. This puts the point for 1879, $3.2987 = \overline{r}$ units, *below* the demand curve (see Fig. 19C).[6] Similarly, we obtain the ordinates of all the points of Figure 19C.

A glance at the graph shows that the points lie very closely about the straight line D_1D_2 (which is the same as in Fig. 19A). There appear to be no systematic deviations about the line, and the fit is very good. The representation of the demand curve by the straight line D_1D_2 is therefore quite justified. The chances are very small that we shall get a better fit by trying a different curve.[7]

We may interpret the graphic procedure in algebraic terms as follows: An examination of the data graphed in Figures 17 and 18 led us to the conclusion that the quantity of sugar consumed depends on at least two variables, price and time. Having proceeded to an analysis of Figure 19, we saw that the relation between that part of consumption which is independent of time and that part of price which is independent of time, i.e., the net regression of consump-

[5] Theoretically, that part of time which is independent of price. But this has no meaning in the present problem.

[6] Mathematically, the process consists of adding to the computed consumption (ordinates of line D_1D_2) the difference between the observed and the normal deviations. In the present example, the difference is $-\overline{pq} - (-\overline{pr}) = -\overline{rq}$. This is equivalent to raising (or lowering) an observed point by the distance that the ordinate of curve D_1D_3 for that year is below (or above) the zero line.

[7] For methods of procedure when the observations give significant departures from the curves chosen in the first trial, see M. J. B. Ezekiel, "A Method of Handling Curvilinear Correlation for Any Number of Variables," *Jour. Amer. Statist. Assoc.*, XIX (1924), 431–53, and L. H. Bean, "A Simplified Method of Graphic Curvilinear Correlation," *ibid.*, XXIV (1929), 386–97. These methods are described more fully in Ezekiel's *Methods of Correlation Analysis* (New York, 1930), esp. chaps. xiv, xvi, xx, and xxi.

The present procedure differs from that of Ezekiel and Bean in that it uses the graphic method *simply as a scaffolding* in the process of deriving a suitable form of equation, linear or curvilinear, and then proceeds to a mathematical analysis of the data. Messrs. Ezekiel and Bean and their followers are generally content to stop with the graphic analysis. An important limitation of the graphic method is that it does not enable us to determine the standard errors of the parameters of the equation. See Henry Schultz, "The Standard Error of a Forecast from a Curve," *Jour. Amer. Statist. Assoc.*, XXV (1930), 139–85.

tion on price, may be represented to a first approximation by a straight line (line D_1D_2, Fig. 19A). We may let the equation to this line be

(2.1) $x_c = a' + by$,

where x_c stands for the consumption computed from this line. We then subtracted the computed consumption from the observed consumption (x_0), i.e., we found the difference

(2.2) $x' \equiv x_0 - x_c = x_0 - (a' + by)$

for each observed price y. In Fig. 19, for example, x' for 1879 is $-\overline{pq}$. The resulting series may be looked upon as being approximately freed from, or *adjusted for*, changes in price. It represents the effect on consumption of changes in the other variable—time. Then, by plotting each difference, x', against the year to which it relates,[8] and by passing a freehand curve through the data, we saw that a good approximation to the resulting series is the equation

(2.3) $x'_c = a'' + ct$.

Since by our assumption the consumption depends linearly on both price and time, we add (2.1) and (2.3) and obtain for our demand function

(2.4) $x = a + by + ct$, $(a = a' + a'')$,

where x is the consumption computed from both variables.

III. DEMAND FUNCTIONS WITH CONSUMPTION AS THE DEPENDENT VARIABLE

A. THE FIRST PERIOD, 1875–95

We have used the graphic procedure as a scaffolding to assist us in selecting a simple mathematical pattern or curve which will describe in a "mental shorthand" the relation between consumption, price, and time during the first period. We have found such a pattern in equation (2.4). Now that we have the pattern, we may dispense entirely with the graphic scaffolding and work directly with the algebraic curve or surface.

1. THE LINEAR FORM

Fitting the curve by minimizing the sum of the squares of the residuals:[9]

(3.1) $$\sum_{i=1}^{n} v_i^2 = \sum_{i=1}^{n} (a + by_i + ct_i - x_i)^2 ,$$

[8] Geometrically, this means that the coordinate system in 19A has been transformed into a new coordinate system in 19B, obtained by using the line D_1D_2 as the t axis.

[9] As we have shown in chap. iv, 147–49, this definition of a residual involves the assumption that an observed point fails to fall on the surface (2.4) because of an "error" or deviation in the dependent variable x (consumption) alone, the independent variables y (price) and t (time) being allowed no deviation. Later in this chapter we shall make y the dependent variable and assume that x and t are free from error.

we obtain

(3.2)
$$x = 70.62 - 2.259y + 0.8371t,$$

where x is measured in pounds, y in cents of the 1913 purchasing power, and t in years, the origins of x and y being at zero and the origin of t at July 1, 1885.

This equation means that, during the period 1875–95, an increase of 1 cent in the real annual price of sugar, other things being equal, was associated with a decrease of 2.259 pounds in the per capita consumption, for

$$\frac{\partial x}{\partial y} = -2.259.$$

But other things did not remain equal. The per capita consumption kept on increasing from year to year, as a result of changes in tastes and in other factors, at the average rate of 0.8371 pounds per annum, for

$$\frac{\partial x}{\partial t} = 0.8371.$$

This was shown by the slope of the curve $D_1 D_3$ of Figure 19B.

Curves $D_1 D_2$ and $D_1 D_3$ in Figures 19A and 19B, which have been referred to in the preceding pages as freehand curves, are really the graphic representations of the two parts of equation (3.2). But as these mathematically determined curves do not differ significantly from the freehand curves which were actually used in the preliminary statistical experimentations, they were made to do double duty in this exposition.

The equation of line $D_1 D_2$ is the first part of (3.2), or

(3.3)
$$x_c = 70.62 - 2.259y.$$

The equation[10] of the curve $D_1 D_3$, Figure 19B, is

(3.4)
$$x'_c = 0.8371t,$$

the origin being at the middle of the range (July 1, 1885), where

$$x' = x_0 - x_c = x_0 - (70.62 - 2.259y).$$

a) *The rate of shift of the demand curve.*—A much better graphical illustration of the properties of equation (3.2) is provided by Figure 20. In this diagram the relation between consumption and price of sugar and time is represented by a plane, formed by the shifting of the demand line $D_1 D_2$ to the right. The slope of the line remains constant (-2.259) from year to year, but its height

---

[10] In the present instance a'' (see eq. [2.3]) is zero because the origin of time is so chosen as to make its mean zero. In general, $a = \bar{x} - b\bar{y} - c\bar{t}$ and $a' = \bar{x} - b\bar{y}$, $a'' = -c\bar{t}$, where the barred letters indicate arithmetic means.

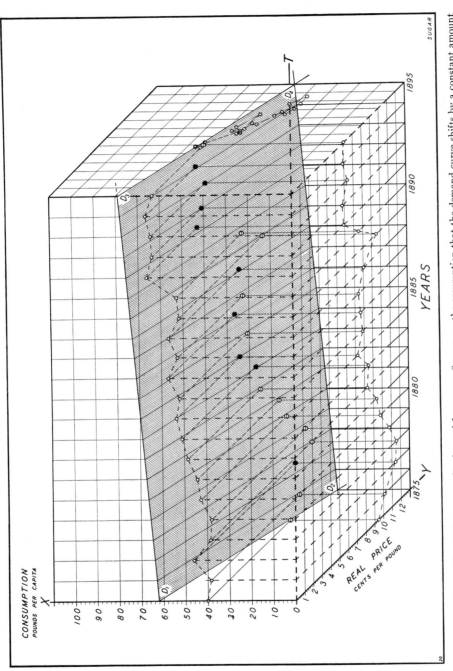

CONSUMPTION
POUNDS PER CAPITA

100
90
80
70
60
50
40
30
20
10
0

REAL PRICE
CENTS PER POUND

YEARS

1875 1880 1885 1890 1895

SUGAR

FIG. 20.—Sugar: The shifting per capita demand for sugar, 1875–95, on the assumption that the demand curve shifts by a constant amount per annum.

$$x = 70.62 - 2.259y + 0.8371t .$$

The heavy straight lines on this surface represent the successive annual demand curves for sugar.

● = Actual observations above the surface

⊕ = Actual observations below the surface

○ = Projections perpendicular to the vertical plane, XOT, and the horizontal plane, YOT

above the YOT-plane continues to rise at the rate of 0.8371 pounds per annum. This is shown by the shape of the shaded plane $D_1D_2D_3D_4$, which will be designated henceforth as D_1D_4.

The demand "curve" for the year $t = k$ is the line of intersection of the shaded plane with a plane which is parallel to the XOY-plane, and which has for its equation $t = k$. These intersections are represented by the heavier lines in the shaded surface.

The observations which lie above the surface are represented by black circles, those which lie below the surface are represented by shaded circles. The fit of the plane to the points is very good, the standard deviation of the observed from the computed consumption being somewhat less than 6 per cent. The correlation between the observed and the computed points is 0.95.

The orthogonal projections of the observations (circles) on the horizontal YOT-plane give the fluctuations in the price of sugar from 1875 to 1895. This series is also shown (on a ratio scale) by the upper curve of Figure 17.

The corresponding projections on the vertical XOT-plane give the fluctuations in the consumption of sugar during the same period. This series is also represented (on a ratio scale) in Figure 17 by the curve connecting the open circles.

The corresponding projections on any plane parallel to the XOY-plane give the scatter diagram in which consumption is plotted against price. In this diagram the projections are all shown on the vertical plane erected at the last year, 1895. This is the same scatter diagram which we studied in Figures 18 and 19A.

We are now in a better position to understand the geometrical significance of Figures 19B and 19C. Suppose that the entire Figure 20, *including the planes of reference*, had been tilted backward about the axis OT until the edge D_2D_4 coincided with the edge D_1D_3 (on our line of vision). Figure 19B shows in a general way how the points and the plane would appear.

Suppose next that we had taken a side view of the entire diagram. More definitely, suppose that we had tilted the diagram slightly backward about the axis OY until the line D_1D_2 coincided with the line D_3D_4. Figure 19C gives approximately this aspect. It should not be confused with the scatter diagram on the plane erected at 1895 (Fig. 20). In this diagram the points are perpendicular projections of the original observations. In Figure 19C the points are the perpendicular projections not onto the vertical plane at 1895, but onto a plane at right angles to the shaded plane D_1D_4.

The reader will do well to acquire an understanding of these relations and to keep them clearly in mind, for they will help him to gain a deeper insight into such economic notions as *ceteris paribus*, the shift of a demand curve, etc., which are only vaguely or imperfectly understood.

b) The elasticity of demand.—When the demand function is known, the elasticity of demand can be easily obtained. Since the demand curve for any year is a straight line, we know that the elasticity of demand varies from point to point, its absolute value being higher for high prices (or low consumption) than for low prices (or high consumption).[11] Furthermore, since the demand curve shifts its position in the manner indicated by Figure 20, the elasticity of demand also changes with time.

When the quantity demanded is a function of the single variable price, the elasticity of demand may be defined as the ratio of the relative change in quantity demanded to the relative change in price, when the relative changes are infinitesimal. In mathematical symbols,

$$(3.5) \qquad \eta_{xy} = \frac{\frac{dx}{x}}{\frac{dy}{y}} \equiv \frac{d \log x}{d \log y} \equiv \frac{dx}{dy} \cdot \frac{y}{x} \, .$$

If the quantity demanded is regarded as a function of more than one variable, we have to make use of the conception of partial elasticity of demand, which we owe to Professor Moore.[12] Thus, if the demand function is in the form of (2.4), the partial elasticity of demand for the commodity x with respect to y is by analogy with (3.5),

$$(3.6) \qquad \eta_{xy \cdot t} = \frac{\partial x}{\partial y} \cdot \frac{y}{x} \, .$$

In this notation the subscripts of η to the right of the dot represent the variables which are held constant, while those to the left of the dot are allowed to vary. When the coefficient of elasticity, η, is equal to unity in absolute value, the demand is neither elastic nor inelastic, the same amount will be spent regardless of the price, and the demand curve is a "constant outlay curve." When η is numerically greater than unity, the demand is elastic, and the lower the price, the greater the total expenditures on the commodity; when it is less than unity, the demand is inelastic, and the lower the price, the smaller the total expenditures.[13]

[11] See Henry Schultz, *Statistical Laws of Demand and Supply with Special Application to Sugar* (Chicago, 1928), p. 153, n. 20.

[12] Henry L. Moore, *Synthetic Economics* (New York, 1929), p. 55.

[13] The proof of these statements is as follows:
The total amount spent is given by xy. Now

$$\frac{d(xy)}{dy} = x(1 + \eta) \, ,$$

where η is defined by (3.6). This expression is negative for values of η between $-\infty$ and -1; zero, for η equal to -1; and positive for values of η between -1 and zero. That is, the total amount spent increases, remains constant, or decreases when price decreases (or when quantity increases), according as the elasticity of demand is numerically greater than, equal to, or less than, unity.

A rough-and-ready answer to the question whether the demand for a given commodity is elastic or inelastic may be obtained from a consideration of the graph of values per capita in Figure 17. When the demand is elastic, we know that a large crop (or supply) is worth more than a small crop. But a large crop means a smaller price per unit, on account of the negative slope of the demand curve. Consequently, when the demand is *elastic*, the year-to-year changes in total value will tend to be *negatively* correlated with the corresponding changes in price.[14] On the other hand, when the demand is *inelastic*, the changes in total value will be *positively* correlated with the corresponding changes in price. By comparing the value series with the price series (or with the quantity series), we can observe when the correlation changes sign. That year is generally one in which a disturbing factor has made its appearance.[15]

Confining our attention for the time being to the data for the first period, we observe that the year-to-year changes in the value series are negatively correlated with the corresponding changes in the quantity series and positively correlated with the corresponding changes in the price series. This indicates that the demand for sugar is inelastic. The problem is to determine the numerical value of the coefficient of elasticity.

Applying the definition to (3.2), we have

$$(3.7) \qquad \eta_{xy \cdot t} = \frac{\partial x}{\partial y} \cdot \frac{y}{x} = -2.259 \frac{y}{x} .$$

Though the variable t (time) does not enter in this equation, it must nevertheless be used (together with y) to compute the value of x from (3.2). It would be wrong to use the observed instead of the computed value of the dependent variable x in (3.6), for the reason that η must relate to a point on the curve, and the observed values of x do not generally lie on the curve.

The following example will illustrate the procedure for computing the elasticity of demand by (3.6). In 1875 the price was 9.485 cents. Substituting this figure for y in (3.2), and putting $t = -10$ in the same equation, because the origin of t is at 1885, we obtain for the theoretical consumption, $x = 40.824$ pounds per capita. Substituting these values of x and y in (3.6), we obtain $\eta_{xy \cdot t} = -0.52$.

This means that, if the price which prevailed in 1875 had been decreased (or increased) by 1 per cent, and *if the demand curve had remained fixed for one year*, there would have been an increase (or decrease) of 0.52 of 1 per cent in the annual consumption. If the relative price deviations were measured from a

---

[14] It is necessary to consider year-to-year changes in order to allow at least approximately for long-time secular movements.

[15] Professor C. Bresciani-Turroni has used this method to good advantage. See his "Über die Elastizität des Verbrauchs ägyptischer Baumwolle," *Weltwirtschaftliches Archiv*, XXXIII, Heft 1 (January, 1931), 46–86, or his "Relations entre la récolte et le prix du coton égyptien," *L'Egypte contemporaine*, XXI, 633–89.

higher or lower price than the one which actually obtained, the elasticity of demand would be different.[16]

But the demand curve has not remained fixed. It has shifted its position continuously to the right. That is, with the passage of time people have become more willing to consume a greater quantity of sugar at the same (money) price, or to pay a higher price for the same quantity.

What has been the effect of this shifting on the elasticity of demand? Table 6 gives an answer to this question. The three selected prices represent, respectively, the minimum observed price, the mean price for the entire period (or rather the price for 1882, which is very close to it), and the maximum observed price. The years selected are the terminal years and the middle year of the

TABLE 6

ELASTICITY OF THE PER CAPITA DEMAND FOR SUGAR IN THE
UNITED STATES FOR SELECTED YEARS AT THREE
DIFFERENT POINTS ON THE DEMAND CURVE

YEAR	ELASTICITY OF THE PER CAPITA DEMAND WHEN THE REAL PRICE IS			
	5.718*	8.319†	11.566‡	Observed§
1875	−0.26	−0.43	−0.72	−0.52
1885	−0.22	−0.36	−0.59	−0.34
1895	−0.20	−0.31	−0.49	−0.21

* Minimum observed price.
† Price for 1882 which is closest to the mean.
‡ Maximum observed price.
§ These prices are given in Table III, Appen. A.

period considered. The last column gives the elasticities of demand corresponding to the *observed* (real) price in each of the three years considered.

Assuming that the linear demand function (3.2) is the "true" demand function, then we may deduce the following interesting characteristics of the demand for sugar during the period from 1875 to 1895.

1. The elasticity of demand is numerically higher for high prices (and low consumption) than for low prices (and high consumption).

2. For comparable points on the demand curves, i.e., for equal prices, the elasticity of demand has been decreasing numerically since 1875.

3. The mean of the highest and the lowest values of the last column is −0.37, which agrees very well with the elasticity of demand deduced by other methods.[17] But the present procedure gives more detailed, and probably also more reliable, information about the changes in the elasticity of demand.

[16] The elasticity of demand is a function of the *time interval* between the successive observations on which the demand function is based. Thus the use of annual data might lead to a demand curve which is quite different from that based on monthly figures of the same series.

[17] By the method of trend ratios, the elasticity of demand for the same period corresponding to the means of the independent variables is also −0.37 (see chap. xvii, Table 48).

If the demand function (3.2) is not the true demand function for sugar but only an approximation to it, then the first two characteristics should not be considered as established, unless they have been verified by a different approach, since they may not be genuine but only the mathematical consequences of the particular form of the demand function in question. For it is a property of a linear demand function like (3.2) that the elasticity of the demand curve for any given year must be numerically higher for high prices than it is for low prices; and that, when the price is given any fixed value, it must decrease or increase (in absolute value) with time, according as the rate of shift of the curve is positive or negative.[18]

2. THE LOGARITHMIC FORM

The linear equation (2.4) is, however, only one of the many specific forms of curves which might be fitted to the data. While it gives a good fit, it has the disadvantage that it expresses the rate of shift of the demand curve as so many pounds, bushels, etc., per annum, thus making it difficult to compare the rate of shift of demand curves for different commodities. To overcome this limitation, it is necessary to express the rate of shift in relative terms which are independent of the units in which the commodity is measured.

A very simple, convenient form of demand function in which the rate of shift is so expressed is given by equation (2), Table 3, chapter iv, which, when fitted to the data for the first period, becomes

$$\log x = 2.0559 - 0.3828 \log y + 0.0068t,$$

or,

(3.8)
$$x = 113.7y^{-0.3828} e^{0.0156t},$$

where the origins of x (pounds) and y (real cents) are at o, and the origin of time (years) is at July 1, 1885.

Figure 21 shows three aspects of this function. It corresponds to Figure 19,

[18] The proof is simple. If the demand function is of the form (2.4), then

$$\eta = \frac{\partial x}{\partial y} \cdot \frac{y}{x} = \frac{by}{a + by + ct},$$

whence

$$\frac{\partial \eta}{\partial y} = \frac{b(a + ct)}{(a + by + ct)^2},$$

and

$$\frac{\partial \eta}{\partial t} = \frac{-bcy}{(a + by + ct)^2}.$$

From the first of these equations it follows that $\frac{\partial \eta}{\partial y}$ is always negative, since b is negative and $(a + ct)$ is positive (for otherwise any positive or zero price would involve negative consumption). This means that η decreases algebraically, or increases numerically, as the price y increases.

From the second equation it follows that, since b is negative, $\frac{\partial \eta}{\partial t}$ is of the same sign as c. Since η is always negative, this means that it increases or decreases algebraically (or that it decreases or increases numerically) according as the rate of shift c is positive or negative.

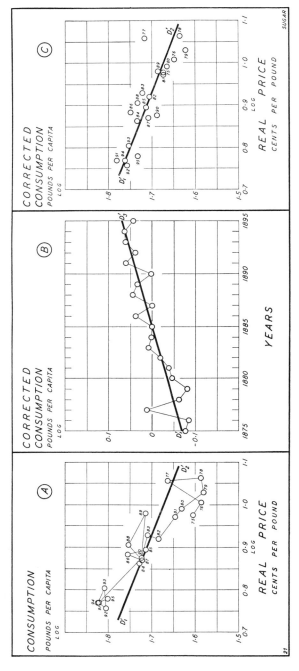

FIG. 21.—Sugar: Three aspects of the per capita demand for sugar during the period 1875–95 on the assumption that

$$x = 113.7\, y^{-0.3828} e^{0.0156 t}.$$

A: Relation between the per capita consumption and the real prices when the data are not corrected for the effects of "time," with the demand curve $D_1'D_2'$ which results when such correction is made.

B: Relation between the per capita consumption and time when the former is corrected for the effects of changes in the real price. The slope of line $D_1'D_3'$ (fitted to the variables x and t when both are corrected for price) represents the mean rate of shift of the per capita demand curve $D_1'D_2'$.

C: The per capita demand curve for sugar, 1875–95. Line $D_1'D_2'$ shows the relation between that part of the per capita consumption of sugar in the United States which is independent of time and that part of the real price which is independent of time. In the scatter, however, only the ordinate is corrected for secular changes, the abscissa being uncorrected.

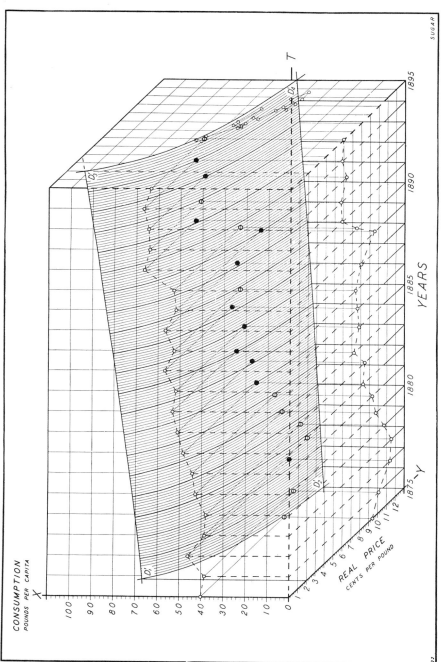

CONSUMPTION
POUNDS PER CAPITA

100
90
80
70
60
50
40
30
20
10
0

REAL PRICE
CENTS PER POUND

1 2 3 4 5 6 7 8 9 10 11 12

YEARS

1875 1880 1885 1890 1895

FIG. 22.—Sugar: The shifting per capita demand for sugar, 1875–95, on the assumption that the demand curve shifts by a constant percentage per annum.

$$x = 113.7 \, y^{-0.3828} e^{0.0156 t} \, .$$

The heavy straight lines on this surface represent the successive annual demand curves for sugar.

● = Actual observations above the surface

◍ = Actual observations below the surface

○ = Projections perpendicular to the vertical plane, XOT, and the horizontal plane, YOT

22

TABLE 7

SUGAR: THE CHARACTERISTICS OF THE PER CAPITA DEMAND FUNCTIONS

x = Per capita consumption in pounds
y = Deflated wholesale price in cents per pound
t = Time in years. For origins see Table 5

(Figures in parentheses are standard errors)

EQUATION No.	PERIOD*		Constant Term	y	w	t	t^3
1	I	$x=$	70.6200	−2.2588 (0.7322)	....	+0.8371 (0.2152)	....
2	II	$x=$	92.8952	−3.3408 (1.0090)	....	+0.9197 (0.1521)	....
3	III	$x=$	134.5059	−7.8031 (1.8199)	....	+0.0900† (0.0369)	....
4	I	$x=$	82.0195	−2.4758 (0.7297)	−0.0950 (0.0676)	+0.7900 (0.2123)	....
5	II	$x=$	120.5033	−4.6810 (0.7719)	−0.2033 (0.0566)	+1.0558 (0.1623)	−0.0047 (0.0022)
6	III	$x=$	165.2862	−7.0589 (1.7108)	−0.3314 (0.2073)	+0.0969† (0.0337)	....
			Constant Term	y'	w'	$‡Mt$	$‡Mt^3$
7	I	$x'=$	2.0559	−0.3828 (0.1224)	....	+0.0156 (0.0044)	....
8	II	$x'=$	2.0701	−0.2717 (0.0844)	....	+0.0124 (0.0022)	....
9	III	$x'=$	2.1980	−0.3118 (0.0775)	....	+0.0090§ (0.0025)	....
10	I	$x'=$	2.2919	−0.3972 (0.1248)	−0.1113 (0.1361)	+0.0152 (0.0044)	....
11	II	$x'=$	2.5308	−0.3489 (0.0771)	−0.2023 (0.0944)	+0.0150 (0.0028)	−0.00007 (0.00005)
12	III	$x'=$	2.8664	−0.2909 (0.0695)	−0.3392 (0.1956)	+0.0090§ (0.0023)	....

* I = 1875–95; II = 1896–1914; III = 1915–29 (excl. 1917–21).
† This is the coefficient of $(1 − 0.5^t)$. The value (0.5) was derived by inspection.

TABLE 7—*Continued*

WITH QUANTITY AS THE DEPENDENT VARIABLE, BY PERIODS, 1875–1929

w = W. M. Persons' "Index of Industrial Production and Trade," adjusted, weighted. Normal = 100

x', y', w' = Logs of x, y, w

(Figures in parentheses are standard errors)

| DESCRIPTIVE CONSTANTS | | | | | | EQUATION No. |
| Elasticity of Demand η | Quadratic Mean Error ϵ (Pounds) | Adjusted Multiple Correlation Coefficient R' | Percentage of Variance of Consumption Attributable to | | | |
			y	w	t	
−0.3622 (0.1553)	2.9472	0.9500	39.99	. . . .	51.23	1
−0.2578 (0.0930)	1.8170	0.9735	32.83	. . . .	62.52	2
−0.3388 (0.1130)	3.7239	0.9321	59.84	. . . .	29.95	3
−0.3970 (0.1580)	2.8707	0.9526	43.83	−0.05	48.35	4
−0.3613 (0.0780)	1.2477	0.9876	46.00	−3.30	55.38	5
−0.3060 (0.1038)	3.3685	0.9448	54.13	6.45	32.26	6
η	ϵ (Per Cent)	R'	y'	w'	t	
−0.3828 (0.1224)	94.4–106.0	0.9493	42.44	. . . .	48.66	7
−0.2717 (0.0844)	97.4–102.7	0.9703	33.63	. . . .	61.17	8
−0.3118 (0.0775)	96.6–103.6	0.9478	49.63	. . . .	42.47	9
−0.3972 (0.1248)	94.3–106.0	0.9483	44.04	−0.17	47.57	10
−0.3489 (0.0771)	97.8–102.2	0.9793	43.19	−2.69	56.33	11
−0.2909 (0.0695)	97.0–103.1	0.9594	46.27	5.83	42.60	12

‡ $M = \log_{10} e = 0.43429$.

§ This is the coefficient of $[1 − (2/3)^t]$. The value $(2/3)$ was derived by inspection.

except that it relates to the logarithms of consumption and price instead of to the actual figures. Had the equation (3.8) been drawn to the actual data as in Figure 19, the line $D_1'D_2'$ would have appeared as a curve of constant elasticity and the line $D_1'D_3'$ would have curved slightly upward. The surface $D_1'D_4'$ in Figure 22 is a graphic representation of this function and corresponds to Figure 20.

Equation (3.8) means that from 1875 to 1895 the elasticity of demand for sugar was

$$\eta_{xy \cdot t} = -0.3828 .$$

This is shown by the constancy of the slope of the line $D_1'D_2'$ (Figs. 19A and 19C) on a double logarithmic scale or by the properties of the curves $D_1'D_2'$ on Figure 22 which are plotted to an arithmetic scale. We interpret this to mean that, if the real price which prevailed in any year during the period had been decreased (or increased) by 1 per cent and *if the demand curve had remained fixed for one year*, there would have been an increase (or decrease) of approximately 0.38 of 1 per cent in the annual per capita consumption. Unlike the elasticity of demand deduced from equation (3.2), the value of this coefficient is constant for every point on the demand curve and is unaffected by the shifting of the curve to the right.[19]

Equation (3.8) also tells us that, even if the real price of sugar had been kept constant, the per capita consumption would have increased at the average momentary rate of 1.56 per cent per annum for

$$\frac{1}{x} \cdot \frac{\partial x}{\partial t} = 0.0156 .$$

This is shown graphically by the slope of the curve $D_1'D_3'$ or by that of the curve $D_2'D_4'$ (Fig. 22).

The relation between the two surfaces D_1D_4 and $D_1'D_4'$ is best shown in Figure 23. A glance at this figure shows that the surface $D_1'D_4'$ intersects the plane D_1D_4 twice: along the curve aa' as it dips below the plane and along the curve bb' as it emerges from under it. Unlike the plane D_1D_4, the surface $D_1'D_4'$ does not cut the vertical plane of reference XOT, but is asymptotic to it. However, in order better to show its relation to the plane, it was terminated at $D_1'D_3'$, which gives the consumption (x) for each year on the assumption that the price is kept constant at $y = 2$ cents.

Figure 23 also shows that within the range of variation of the data, there is

[19] In this curve, as well as in all the other curves listed in Table 7, the coefficient of elasticity of demand is independent of the rate of shift of the demand curve. Nevertheless, the italicized condition is necessary in order to emphasize the following facts: (1) It takes time for consumption to adjust itself to a price change; when the demand curve is derived from annual data, the necessary time interval is generally one year, or one season. (2) We are dealing here with a change in price, *ceteris paribus*.

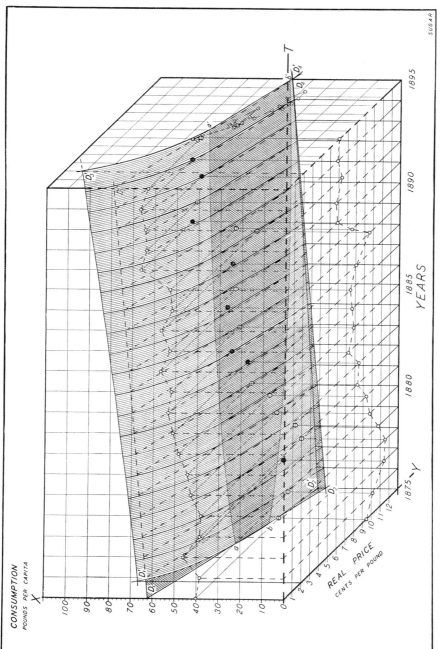

FIG. 23.—Sugar: The shifting per capita demand for sugar on two assumptions, 1875–95. (For an explanation of the diagram see the text.)

⊕ = Points falling between the two surfaces

(See Fig. 22 for meaning of other points.)

no appreciable difference between the constant elasticity demand curve $D_1'D_2'$ and the straight-line demand curve D_1D_2. Thus, if we confine our attention to the range of the variation of the data, we may replace the plane D_1D_4, which leads to a varying elasticity of demand, by the surface $D_1'D_4'$, which makes it constant at every point; and the fit of the latter is nearly as good as that of the former, the standard deviation of the observed from the computed points being between 5.5 and 6 per cent.

B. THE SECOND PERIOD, 1896–1914

The analysis of the data for the second period is similar to that for the first. Figures 24 and 25 relate to the second period. They correspond, respectively, to Figures 19 and 20 of the first period. The scatter diagram of the quantities and prices of the second period (Fig. 24A) is very similar to that of the first, the coefficients of correlation being almost identical. The equation of the demand function is

$$(3.9) \qquad\qquad x = 92.90 - 3.341y + 0.9197t ,$$

the origin of time being at July 1, 1905.

From this equation we see that, during the period from 1896 to 1914, an increase of 1 cent in the real price of sugar, other things being equal, was on the average associated with a decrease of 3.341 pounds in the per capita consumption. This relation is indicated by the slope of the demand curve D_1D_2 in Figures 24 and 25.

But other things did not remain equal. The per capita consumption kept on increasing at the average rate of 0.9197 pound per annum. This rate of shift of the demand curve is shown either by the slope of the line D_1D_3 in Figure 24B or by that of D_1D_3 or D_2D_4 in Figure 25.

It should be observed that both the slope of the demand curve and its rate of shift through time were greater (in absolute value) in the second period than they were in the first. The fit of the plane D_1D_4 to the observations is very good, the standard deviation of the points from the curve is only 2.5 per cent. This is a considerably better fit than that obtaining for the first period.

Figures 26 and 27 give the logarithmic form of the demand function for the second period. They correspond, respectively, to Figures 21 and 22. The equation of the surface is

$$(3.10) \qquad\qquad x = 117.5y^{-0.2717} e^{0.0124t} ,$$

which shows that both the elasticity of demand and the rate of shift were somewhat less in the second period than in the first.

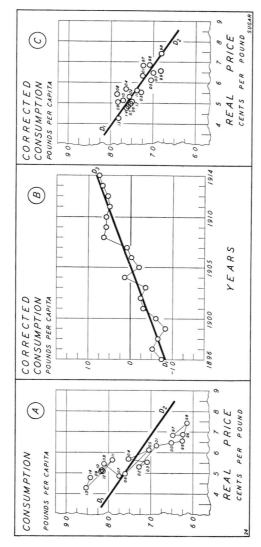

FIG. 24.—Sugar: Three aspects of the per capita demand for sugar during the period 1896–1914 on the assumption that

$$x = 92.90 - 3.341y + 0.9197t.$$

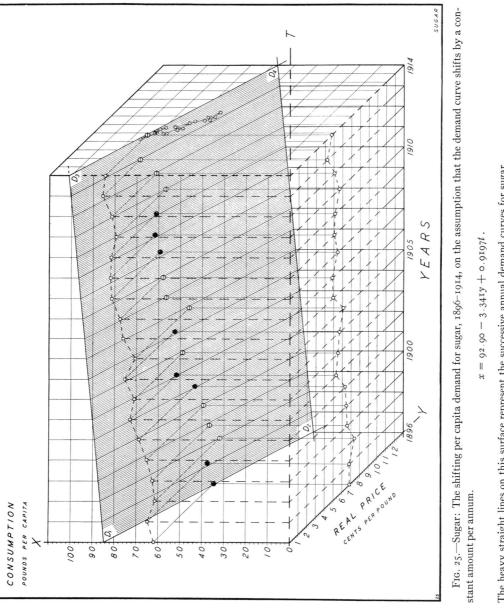

CONSUMPTION
POUNDS PER CAPITA

REAL PRICE
CENTS PER POUND

YEARS

SUGAR

FIG. 25.—Sugar: The shifting per capita demand for sugar, 1896–1914, on the assumption that the demand curve shifts by a constant amount per annum.

$$x = 92.90 - 3.341y + 0.9197t.$$

The heavy straight lines on this surface represent the successive annual demand curves for sugar.

● = Actual observations above the surface
⊖ = Actual observations below the surface
○ = Projections perpendicular to the vertical plane, XOT, and the horizontal plane, YOT

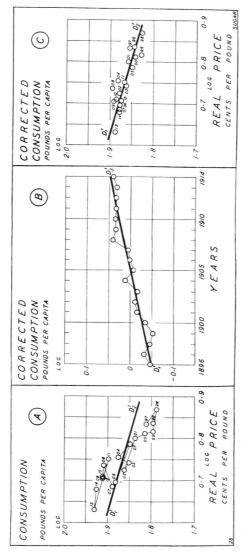

Fig. 26.—Sugar: Three aspects of the per capita demand for sugar during the period 1896-1914 on the assumption that

$$x = 117.5 \, y^{-0.2717} e^{0.0124 t}.$$

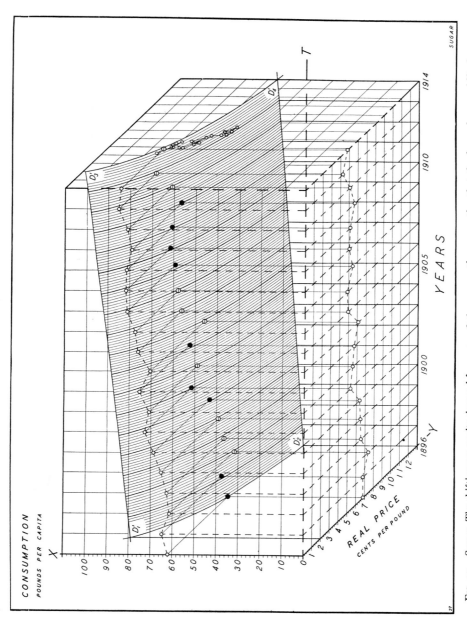

CONSUMPTION
POUNDS PER CAPITA

REAL PRICE
CENTS PER POUND

YEARS

SUGAR

FIG. 27.—Sugar: The shifting per capita demand for sugar, 1896–1914, on the assumption that the demand curve shifts by a constant percentage per annum.

$$x = 117.5 \, y^{-0.2717} \, e^{0.01240 t} \, .$$

● = Actual observations above the surface
⊖ = Actual observations below the surface
○ = Projections perpendicular to the vertical plane, XOT, and the horizontal plane, YOT

In Figure 28 the linear and the constant elasticity demand surfaces are brought into juxtaposition. As in the corresponding graph for the first period (Fig. 23) the fact emerges that most of the observations fall within the range of the intersections of the two surfaces (the heavily shaded area); within this range there is no appreciable difference between the surfaces.

C. THE THIRD PERIOD, 1915–29

Figures 29 and 30 relate to the third period (the dotted observations relate to the years 1917–21 and were not used in the computations), the former giving the three aspects of the linear demand surface and the latter those of the logarithmic demand surfaces. The equations of the two surfaces are, respectively:

(3.11) $$x = 134.51 - 7.8031y + 0.0900\,[1 - 0.5^t]$$

and

(3.12) $$x = 157.8y^{-0.3118}\,e^{0.0090\,[1-(2/3)^t]}.$$

Figures 29 and 30 correspond, respectively, to Figures 24 and 26 for the second period. These two diagrams bring out the following interesting facts:

1. The slope of the demand curve was much greater in the third period than in either of the other two.

2. The elasticity of demand remained, however, approximately constant during the three periods.

3. During the third period the demand curve ceased to shift upward but reached its "ceiling" (Fig. 29B).

Figure 31 is a graphic representation of the two demand surfaces. As we saw in Figures 23 and 28, there is no marked difference between the two surfaces within the range of the observations.

D. SUMMARY OF CHANGES IN THE DEMAND FOR SUGAR, 1875–1929

While the foregoing sketch makes it plain that the demand curve for sugar has undergone important structural changes in the fifty-five years from 1875 to 1929, it does not present them as an integrated whole and does not indicate which of them are significant and which are not. What we need is a comparative summary of the results obtained, coupled with some of the more useful statistical constants or measures of goodness of fit which will assist us in interpreting the statistical findings and in evaluating their significance.

Table 7 is designed to meet this need as well as to introduce a few additional (and more complex) functions which have been fitted to the sugar data.

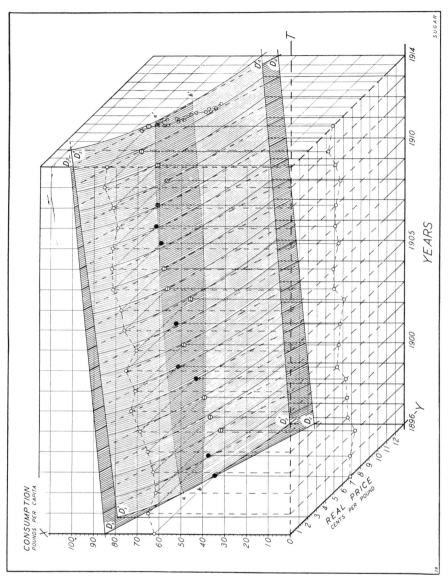

FIG. 28.—Sugar: The shifting per capita demand for sugar on two assumptions, 1896–1914. (For an explanation of the diagram see the text.)

⊕ = Points falling between the two surfaces

(See Fig. 27 for meaning of other points)

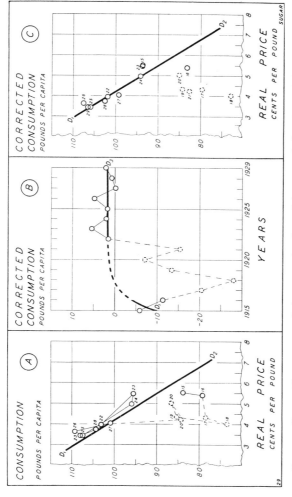

Fig. 29.—Sugar: Three aspects of the per capita demand for sugar during the period 1915–29 on the assumption that

$$x = 134.51 - 7.8031\,y + 0.0900\,(1 - 0.5^t).$$

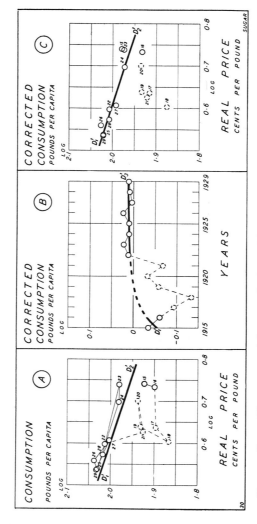

Fig. 30.—Sugar: Three aspects of the per capita demand for sugar during the period 1915–29 on the assumption that

$$x = 157.8 \, y^{-0.3118} e^{0.00901[1-(2/3)^t]}.$$

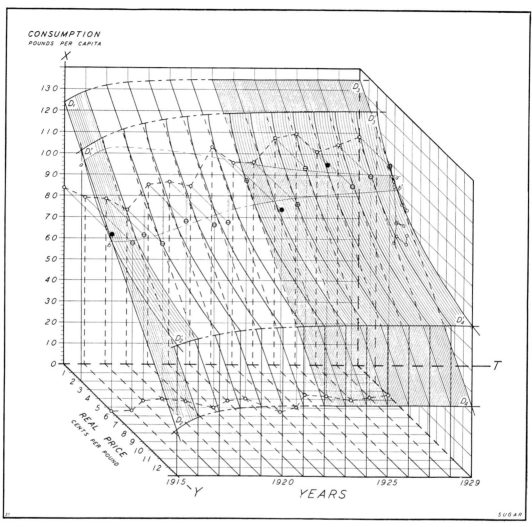

FIG. 31.—Sugar: The shifting per capita demand for sugar on two assumptions, 1915–29. (For an explanation of the diagram see the text.)

⊕ = Points falling between the two surfaces

(See Fig. 27 for meaning of other points.)

209

I. THE SUCCESSIVE DEMAND FUNCTIONS

The first three equations have already been explained in the text. The co-efficients of y show that an increase of 1 (deflated) cent in the price per pound of sugar brought about a decrease in the per capita consumption of 2.26 pounds in the first period, 3.34 in the second, and 7.80 in the third. These absolute changes can also be converted into relative changes or elasticities, by multiplying each of them by y/x. Substituting for y and x their mean values in each of the three periods, we obtain the following elasticities of demand: −0.36, −0.26, and −0.34. It is these figures which are given (to four significant figures) in the column headed "Elasticity of Demand."

From the coefficients of t in the same three equations we also see that during the first period the demand curve kept shifting upward at the rate of 0.84 of a pound per annum; that during the second period the upward rate of shift increased to 0.92 pound; and that during the third period, the rate of shift approached zero, the demand curve having reached its "ceiling" of approximately 110 pounds during the last part of this period. The fact that the demand curve for sugar is no longer shifting upward with time means that, while it is still true that in any one year a decrease in price will bring about an increase in consumption, producers of sugar can no longer count on an increase in per capita consumption even if prices are kept constant. This fact accounts for many of the difficulties that have confronted the industry since the war.

The third triad of equations represents the demand for sugar directly in terms of relative changes. Thus the coefficients of y' $(= \log y)$ show that the elasticities of demand for the three periods were: −0.38, −0.27, and −0.31, respectively. These agree very closely with the corresponding values obtained from the first three equations. The coefficients of t give the mean *relative* rates of shift of the demand curve. Thus, if we multiply each of them by 100, we find that during the first period the demand curve shifted upward at the rate of 1.56 per cent per annum; that during the second period the rate dropped to 1.24 per cent per annum; and that during the third period the rate dropped again, having practically reached the value zero by 1929.[20]

[20] It should be observed that the mean relative rate of shift of the demand curve is given by the coefficient of t only when the demand function is written in the form

$$x = Ay^b e^{ct}.$$

However, in the logarithmic equations of Table 7 this function is written as

$$x' = a + by' + cMt,$$

where $M = \log_{10} e$. When the equation is written in this form, the relative rate of shift, c, is obviously the coefficient of Mt.

It is, of course, inconsistent to represent the same shift by a constant *amount* per annum and by a constant *percentage* per annum, for an equal absolute increase corresponds to a decreasing percentage increase. This is also evident from Figures 19B and 21B; the scatter of the observations in the latter diagram suggests that the fit of $D_t'D_3'$ would have been improved if the curve were a parabola instead of a straight line. But in this case the improvement would hardly be of significance.

2. THE DESCRIPTIVE CONSTANTS[21]

a) The standard errors.—The goodness of fit of the demand curves to the data is measured by the various descriptive constants, which are also given in Table 7. Of these, probably the most important are the standard errors—the figures in the parentheses. The statement that a statistical constant has a value $\bar{b}$ with a standard error σ_b means that, if the constant be determined many times from random samples of relevant material, the observed value b obtained will differ in absolute value from $\bar{b}$ by less than σ_b in approximately 68 per cent of the number of samples. This is based on the assumption that the sampled values of b are normally distributed; the value σ_b ceases to have the same significance if the distribution be not normal.

When any statistical parameter is determined by the method of least squares from an infinitely large number of samples, the values obtained are normally distributed. The mean of this distribution is the "true" or "expected" value $\bar{b}$ of the parameter, and its standard deviation the "true" standard error σ_b of the same parameter.

When the "true" value of a statistical constant or parameter is known, and when the sampling distribution of this parameter follows the normal curve, the probability of obtaining a deviation from the "true" value less than any given multiple λ of the standard error of the constant in question can be calculated by finding the area under the normal curve between the "true" value $\bar{b}$ and $\lambda\sigma_b$ units to the right and to the left of it, i.e., by finding the area *inside* the range $\pm\lambda\sigma$. For example, if the observed values of the slope of the demand curve for the first period and its standard error (-2.2588 ± 0.7322) given in the first equation of Table 7 were the true values (or at least if they had been derived from a very large sample), then we should be justified in concluding, from the Tables of the Probability Integral, that in 68.27 per cent of further samples from relevant material the value of the slope obtained will be within the range -2.2588 ± 0.7322; and that in 95.45 per cent of the samples the value obtained will be within the range $-2.2588 \pm 2(0.7322)$. Perhaps a more significant way of stating these results is that, under this assumption, the slope obtained will differ from -2.2588 by *more than* 0.7322 in absolute value (or that it will lie *outside* the range of -1.5266 to -2.9910) in 31.73 per cent of the cases; and that it will differ from it by *more than* $2(0.7322)$ (or that it will fall *outside* the range of -0.7944 to -3.7232), in only 4.55 per cent of the cases. These are, respectively, the percentages of the total area of the normal curve outside the range $\pm\sigma$, and $\pm 2\sigma$. The greater the range adopted, the less probable it is that the sampled value will fall outside it.

Where only the standard error, but not the parameter, is accurately known,

---

[21] The descriptions which follow are nontechnical. A mathematical discussion of the derivation and properties of these constants and of related subjects will be found in Appen. C.

we may still make use of the Tables of the Probability Integral to answer the question whether the observed parameter differs significantly from any given hypothetical value. *And this is often the more significant question.* Thus, in the present illustration, what we wish to know is not so much how close -2.2588 is to the "true" value of the slope but whether the numerical value of the slope is significantly different from zero. Assuming, for the purpose of the illustration, that the standard error, 0.7322, derived from our one sample of twenty-one observations is the true value of that constant, we find that the deviation $o - (-2.2588)$ is 3.08 times the standard error. The area of the normal curve to the left and to the right of the range $\pm 3.08\sigma$ is only 0.207 per cent of the total; which means that, if the slope be determined many times from random samples of relevant material, for which the true value of the slope is zero, the value -2.2588 would be exceeded numerically in only 0.2 per cent of the cases.[22] Consequently, we should be justified in concluding that the true value of the slope is significantly different from zero.[23] By the same procedure we could test the significance of the departure of the slope of the demand curve from any other hypothetical value.

The foregoing procedure cannot, however, be applied to our data because the standard errors are derived from samples containing at most only twenty-one observations. Now while it is true that, even when the samples are small, the distribution of the deviations of the observed values from an expected (or "true") value is normal when the deviations are measured in terms of the *expected* standard error, it is definitely nonnormal when the deviations are expressed in terms of the *observed* standard error, especially when it is derived from only one small sample. The procedure generally recommended in such a case is to make use of "Student's"[24] distribution, which is the exact distribution of the *ratio* of the deviations of the observations on a given parameter from an assumed "true" value of the parameter, not to the *true*, i.e., σ_b, but to the *observed* standard error s_b *derived from the sample*, $[t = (\bar{b} - b)/s_b]$. This procedure, which has been treated most fully by Professor R. A. Fisher,[25] takes into account the size of the sample as well as the number of constants in the formula from which the constant b has been computed. As an illustration, we may assume that o is the correct numerical value $\bar{b}$ of the slope of the demand

[22] If we wish to test the hypothesis that the value obtained for the slope is significantly *negative*, we should compute only the area to the left of -3.08σ. The corresponding probability would, of course, be one-half of 0.00207.

[23] Of course, if on the basis of other evidence we have a sufficiently high degree of confidence in the validity of our hypothesis that the true value is zero, we would not reject it but conclude instead that the particular sample was a very unusual one.

[24] "Student" is the pseudonym of W. S. Gosset, a well-known writer on mathematical statistics.

[25] *Statistical Methods for Research Workers* (6th ed.; Edinburgh: Oliver & Boyd; New York: Van Nostrand, 1936).

curve for sugar during the twenty-one-year period from 1875 to 1895 and proceed to determine the probability of obtaining in random samples of twenty-
one observations from relevant material a slope which differs from o by at least
as much as the observed slope -2.2588.[26] This is, of course, the same hypothesis which we have just tested on the assumption that the observed standard error (0.7322) is the "true" standard error. Taking the ratio of the difference between these values to the observed standard error, we obtain

$$t = \frac{o - (-2.2588)}{0.7322} = 3.08 .$$

Subtracting the number of constants in the demand function from the number
of observations, we obtain $n = 21 - 3 = 18$ "degrees of freedom." Entering
Table IV of R. A. Fisher's *Statistical Methods for Research Workers* with $n = 18$,
we find that the probability, P_t, that t is numerically greater than 3.08 is less
than 0.01, the smallest probability in Fisher's table. By making use of an approximate formula, we find that $P_t = 0.0047$. The smaller the value of P_t, the
greater the significance of the difference between the two values tested. In the
present illustration the result means that, if the true slope of the demand curve
is o, a positive or negative deviation from it of not less than 3.08 times the observed standard error will be obtained in 0.47 per cent of random samples of
twenty-one observations each. It will be recalled that when we used the
Normal Probability Integral instead of Fisher's Table IV ("Student's" distribution), we obtained for the corresponding probability $P = 0.00207$, which
exaggerated the significance of the difference in question.

Although Fisher's and "Student's" t-test of significance constitutes a marked
improvement over the classical procedure—in fact, it is the only recourse when
we have no more reliable estimate of σ than that which can be obtained from
one small sample—it may prove misleading in practice. The hazard which attaches to its use is traceable to the fact that the distributions of $\bar{b} - b$ and
s_b are completely independent; in any sample $\bar{b} - b$ may be large and s_b small,
and conversely. This means that a very small value of P_t (which suggests that
the difference tested can hardly be imputed to chance) may be due to a fortui-
tously low value of s_b, which may thus lead us to an erroneous conclusion.
This does not mean, however, that the t-test is inherently misleading. It tests
objectively a certain value of t and accepts a perfectly definite hazard. More-

---

[26] The solution will be the same if we treat 2.2588 as the true value and o as the observed value.
It should, perhaps, be emphasized that we are really testing two hypotheses: first, that zero is the
true value and, second, that the distribution from which the sample is drawn is a normal one. An
extremely high t might then suggest either that zero is not the "true" value of the parameter or that
the distribution is not normal. The assumption of normality is made, for convenience, in practically
all sampling problems.

over, there is no disagreement between the *u*-test (i.e., the test when σ is known) and the *t*-test because in practice they would never be applied at the same time; each is supreme in its own sphere of application. But the contingency mentioned above is, nevertheless, a real one, notwithstanding the fact that it is part of the hazard which we have agreed to accept.[27] To guard against such a contingency—it cannot be completely avoided—*we must supplement our purely statistical tests of significance with all the theoretical and factual knowledge at our disposal.* Thus, no matter how statistically significant the net regression of the consumption of sugar on its own price may turn out to be, it must be rejected if it is positive, for we know that, except in the special situation discussed in chapter i, consumption cannot be increased as price increases.[28]

There is another and even more compelling reason why our standard errors give us little aid in drawing probable inferences: They are all derived from time series. Now time series, especially those relating to social and economic phenomena, are likely to violate in a marked degree the fundamental assumption which underlies the use of the methods sketched above, namely, that not only the successive items in the series but also the successive parts into which the series may be divided must be random selections from the *same* universe. Time series are, in fact, a group of successive items with a characteristic con-

[27] For a scholarly discussion of this question see W. Edwards Deming and Raymond T. Birge, "On the Statistical Theory of Errors," *Reviews of Modern Physics*, VI, No. 3 (July, 1934), 119–61; and their note bearing the same title in the *Physical Review*, XLVI, No. 11 (December 1, 1934), 1027. A reprint of this paper, published in 1937 by the Graduate School of the United States Department of Agriculture, Washington, D.C., contains additional notes and corrections.

[28] For other *economic* conditions which demand functions must satisfy, see Part III of this work.

Any attempt to supplement a purely statistical test of significance with other information is likely to lead one to the subject of *a posteriori* probability and its role in sampling theory. The following references should be helpful in a study of this subject.

Arthur L. Bowley, *F. Y. Edgeworth's Contributions to Mathematical Statistics* (London, 1928), chap. ii, pp. 6–28.

E. C. Molina and R. I. Wilkinson, "The Frequency Distribution of the Unknown Mean of a Sampled Universe," *Bell System Technical Journal*, VIII (1929), 632–45.

J. Neyman and Egon S. Pearson, "On the Use and Interpretation of Certain Test Criteria for Purposes of Statistical Inference," *Biometrika*, XXA (1928), 175–240 (the diagrams and tables of this paper, together with remarks on their use, will be found in *Tables for Statisticians and Biometricians*, ed. Karl Pearson, Part II, pp. clxxxi–clxxxvi, and Tables XXXV–XXXVII); "On the Problem of the Most Efficient Test of Statistical Hypotheses," *Philosophical Transactions of the Royal Society of London*, Ser. A, CCXXXI (1933), 289–337; "The Testing of Statistical Hypotheses in Relation to Probabilities a priori," *Proceedings of the Cambridge Philosophical Society*, XXIX, Part 4 (1933), 492–510; "Contributions to the Theory of Testing Statistical Hypotheses. (I) Unbiassed Critical Regions of Type A and Type A_1" and "Sufficient Statistics and Uniformly Most Powerful Tests of Statistical Hypotheses," *Statistical Research Memoirs* (Department of Statistics, University of London, University College, 1936), I, 1–37 and 113–37.

J. Neyman, "Sur la vérification des hypothèses statistiques composées," *Bulletin de la société mathématique de France*, LXIII (1935), 1–21; "Outline of a Theory of Statistical Estimation Based on the Classical Theory of Probability," *Philosophical Transactions of the Royal Society of London*, Ser. A, CCXXXVI (1937), 333–80.

formation. Such series, relating to a selected period in the past, cannot be considered as a random sample of any definable universe except in a very unreal sense. Nor are the successive items in the series independent of one another; they generally occur in sequences of rises and falls which do not repeat one another exactly, and which are often masked by many irregularities. The fact is that the "universe" of our time series does not "stay put," and the "relevant conditions" under which the sampling must be carried out cannot be re-created. Thus the (average) rate of shift of the demand curve for sugar during the period from 1896 to 1914 (second equation, Table 7) was 0.9197 pound per capita per annum. This figure is over six times as large as its standard error (0.1521). According to the theory of random sampling, the odds against our observing a *complete* cessation of the upward shift of the demand curve are 50,000,000 to 1.[29] Yet this exceedingly improbable event actually happened by 1929, and the economist is not surprised!

It is clear, then, that standard errors derived from time series relating to social and economic phenomena do not have the same heuristic properties that they have, or are supposed to have, in the natural sciences. Consequently, they must be used with extreme caution. They do *not* enable us to answer the question, "What is the probability that the true value of a given parameter will be found between such and such limits?" All that they enable us to answer is the much more restricted (and different) question, "If the observations constituting the sample are all independent of one another; if they are drawn at random from a normally distributed universe; and if the true value of the parameter is such and such: in how many cases out of 100 could the observed parameter have arisen as a result of the fluctuations of simple sampling?" In this restricted role they become one of the measures of goodness of fit. As such they are extremely useful and often indispensable.

No standard errors have been computed for the "constant terms" of the demand equations (Table 7), for the reason that the standard errors of these terms depend on the particular origins chosen for the independent variables and thus have little significance.

b) The elasticities of demand.—The elasticities yielded by the various demand functions are shown by the first column to the right of the equations (Table 7). The elasticities derived from the constant-elasticity demand surface (the third and the fourth sets of equations) are, of course, constant at every point on the surface; while those derived from the arithmetic demand surface (the first and the second sets of equations) vary from point to point. Before proceeding with a comparison of the results, we must, therefore, dispose of two questions: (1) At what point on each demand surface shall the elasticity of demand be

---

[29] See *Tables for Statisticians and Biometricians*, ed. Pearson, Part I, p. xliii, for the method of obtaining this approximation to the area under one tail of "Student's" distribution.

computed for the purpose of comparison? and (2) What is the standard error of the elasticity of demand?

The convention which is here adopted for comparing elasticities that vary from point to point on the demand surface is *to consider as comparable those points on two different demand surfaces, whose coordinates contain the mean values of their independent variables*. Thus, in the first equation of Table 7, the means of the independent variables are: $\bar{t} = 0 = 1885$, and $\bar{y} = 8.3130$ cents; and the corresponding value of the dependent variable, which is found by substituting these figures in that equation, is $\bar{x} = 51.84$ pounds. In the second equation the values of the three variables are: $\bar{t} = 0 = 1905$, $\bar{y} = 5.7000$ cents, $\bar{x} = 73.85$ pounds. For the third equation: $\bar{t} = 1.5 = $ January 1, 1924, $\bar{y} = 4.3636$ cents, and $\bar{x} = 98.80$ pounds.[30] This convention will facilitate the interperiod and the intraperiod comparisons of the elasticities of demand derived by different methods.

When the coefficient of the elasticity of demand is constant at every point on the demand curve, and the curve is fitted by the method of least squares, the standard error of this coefficient can be determined by the well-known least-square procedure.[31] It is these least-square standard errors which are attached to the constant coefficients of elasticity (the third and the fourth sets of equations of Table 7). But, when the coefficient of elasticity varies from point to point on the demand curve, its standard error is not given directly by the method of least squares but must be derived from the standard errors of the parameters and of the variables on which it depends. Its exact value cannot be determined. An upper limit to it has, however, been derived. It is this limiting value which has been attached to the elasticities of demand of the first and second sets of equations.[32] These standard errors are not, therefore, strictly comparable with those of the constant-elasticity equations (the third and fourth sets of equations). They exceed the latter by as much as 50 per cent.

The elasticities yielded by the arithmetic and by the logarithmic equations agree very closely. They show that the elasticity of demand for sugar has remained remarkably constant from period to period, its value being of the order −0.3 or −0.4 during each period. Their standard errors are, however, relatively large, being one-third or one-fourth of the value of the elasticities. This makes it impossible to say with a high degree of probability whether the difference between any two elasticities is statistically significant. It is better, how-

[30] It should be recalled that the years 1917–21 were omitted from the computations.

[31] See my "Standard Error of a Forecast from a Curve," *Jour. Amer. Statist. Assoc.*, XXV (1930), 139–85.

[32] See Appen. D, "The Standard Error of the Coefficient of Elasticity of Demand." After the book had gone to the press, my assistant, Mr. Jacob L. Mosak, succeeded in deriving the exact formula for the standard error of the elasticity of demand. It appears in the last section of Appen. D. A full treatment of this subject is given in a paper which he has submitted to the *Jour. Amer. Statist. Assoc.*

ever, to have a numerical, though approximate, value for the elasticity of demand of a commodity than none at all.

c) The quadratic mean errors.—A third measure of goodness of fit is the quadratic mean error ϵ, or the root-mean-square error of the observations about the demand surface, when allowance is made for the number of constants in the demand equation. In the language of the method of least squares, it is an approximation to the "standard error of a single observation of unit weight." It may be looked upon as the ordinary "standard error of estimate," S, corrected for the number of constants of the curve from which the estimates are made, and must, consequently, be greater than S. Thus, in the first equation, $\epsilon = \pm 2.9472$ pounds, while the corresponding value of S is ± 2.7286 pounds.

The ordinary "standard error of estimate," S, cannot be used to compare the goodness of fit of curves with different numbers of parameters. For, the larger the number of parameters in a least-squares regression surface, the smaller will be the value of S. The quadratic mean error, ϵ, is not subject to this limitation, for it reduces the total squared deviations about the regression surface to a per degree-of-freedom basis and need not decrease as the number of parameters increases. It is, therefore, particularly useful in comparing the goodness of fit of curves with different numbers of parameters.[33] The quadratic errors of the equations in the first set are all rather small, that for the second period amounting to only 1.8 pounds. They show that the curves fit the observations very well.

The ϵ for the logarithmic equation is, of course, also a logarithm. Thus, for the first equation of the third set in Table 7, $\epsilon = \pm 0.0252$ units. (This figure is not given in the table.) This means that, if the *logarithms* of x are normally distributed about this surface, approximately 68 per cent of them fall within a distance from the surface of ± 0.0252 units.

But this ϵ is not directly comparable with that derived from the first equation in the table, which is expressed in pounds per capita. We can overcome this difficulty by expressing the standard errors as ratios to the computed variable. The antilogarithms corresponding to -0.0252 and $+0.0252$ are, respectively, 0.9436 and 1.0597. This means that in 68 per cent of the cases the observed consumption will lie between 94.36 and 105.97 per cent of the computed consumption. It is these figures (rounded off to one decimal) which constitute the seventh entry in the column headed "ϵ."

To compare this result with that yielded by the standard error of the first equation of the first set, which is expressed in concrete units ($\epsilon = \pm 2.9472$

---

[33] When we compare the standard errors of different curves, we are primarily interested in the goodness of fit of the particular curves having *those particular constants.* When we compare the quadratic mean errors of different curves, we are interested in the goodness of fit of curves having *merely the form* of our functions (see W. Edwards Deming, "The Chi-Test and Curve Fitting," *Jour. Amer. Statist. Assoc.,* XXIX [1934], 372).

lb.), we may divide this figure by the mean consumption for the first period which, by Table 5, is 51.84 pounds. The result, ± 5.69 per cent, means that approximately 68 per cent of the observations will fall within 94.31 per cent and 105.69 per cent of the computed consumptions.

d) The corrected coefficients of multiple correlation.—The ordinary coefficient of multiple correlation, R, is the simple coefficient of correlation between the observed and the computed values of the dependent variable, x. When the distribution of each of the variables entering into a given equation is normal, R completes the description of the frequency surface in question. That is, when the means, the standard deviations, and the multiple (and simple) correlation coefficients are known, all the other properties of the frequency surface, such as the equations of regression, the standard errors of estimate, can be derived from these constants: the surface is perfectly described. When, however, the distributions are not normal, R does not have this property and is simply another measure of goodness of fit. Since the curves which we wish to compare do not have the same number of parameters, and since the number of observations is rather small, we have corrected R for the number of constants in the curve from which it is derived. The resulting constant, R', is always less than R. Thus, whereas R' deduced from the first equation is 0.9500, the corresponding value of R is 0.9551.[34]

All the R''s of Table 7 are very large, the smallest value being as high as 0.93. The fit of the demand curves to the data is, therefore, excellent.

e) The coefficients of determination.—The percentage of variance accounted for by each of the independent variables is a rough indication of the importance of the independent variables—price and time—as "determinants" of the quantity of sugar consumed (the dependent variable). Strictly speaking, when several factors have combined to produce a given result, it is no more possible

[34] The relation between R and R', S and ϵ, is as follows:

$$R = \left(1 - \frac{S^2}{\sigma^2}\right)^{1/2}, \qquad\qquad R' = \left(1 - \frac{\epsilon^2}{\mu^2}\right)^{1/2},$$

where

$$S^2 = \frac{1}{n}\sum_{i=1}^{n} v_i^2, \qquad\qquad \sigma^2 = \frac{1}{n}\sum_{i=1}^{n} (x_i - \bar{x})^2,$$

$$\epsilon^2 = \frac{n}{n-m}S^2 = \frac{1}{n-m}\sum_{i=1}^{n} v_i^2, \qquad \mu^2 = \frac{n}{n-1}\sigma^2 = \frac{1}{n-1}\sum_{i=1}^{n} (x_i - \bar{x})^2,$$

in which v_i is the residual of the dependent variable x_i and defined as in (3.1), $\bar{x}$ is the arithmetic mean of x_i, n the number of sets of observations, and m the number of parameters in the regression equation.

It may be shown that

$$R'^2 = \frac{1}{n-m}[(1 - m) + (n - 1)R^2],$$

from which it follows that R'^2 may be negative. A negative R'^2 is to be interpreted as zero correlation.

to tell how much of the given result is due to each of the factors than it is to tell which part of a glassful of water is due to the oxygen that is in it and which part to the hydrogen. However, by adopting certain conventions, it is possible under certain conditions to *impute* a "percentage of determination" to each factor. This imputation will, of course, depend on the particular hypothesis or theory which we adopt and/or on the number of variables which we wish to consider. Several measures of imputation suggest themselves. We may, for example, add the regression coefficients in our linear equation, paying no attention to their signs, and take the ratio of each term to the sum as a measure of the importance of each variable. However, it is mathematically more convenient to build our measure of imputation around the variance σ^2 of the dependent variable. We can illustrate this measure by referring to the first equation of Table 7. The coefficient of multiple correlation is $R = 0.9551$. We know that the square of this coefficient, or 0.9122, measures the proportion by which the square of the standard error of estimate of the per capita consumption has been reduced through the use of this equation, for $S^2 = \sigma^2 (1 - R^2)$. If this equation were not available, we could give only one and the same estimate of consumption (its arithmetic mean) for any combination of y and t; and the confidence which we would be justified in placing in such an estimate would be measured by the standard deviation of x. By using this equation to estimate the per capita consumption of sugar, we are able to reduce the square of the standard deviation by 91.22 per cent. To this reduction the price variable contributes 39.99 per cent, and the time variable 51.23 per cent. These are the figures which are entered in the last three columns of Table 7. The remaining 8.78 per cent—this figure is not entered in the table—is due either to factors which have not been taken into account, or to inaccuracies and deficiencies of the data, or to the impossibility of adequately representing the observations by the type of function selected. These figures thus measure the importance of the several factors as "determinants" of the quantity of sugar consumed.[35]

[35] The multiple correlation coefficient, defined in the previous note in terms of S^2 and σ^2, can also be defined in two other ways which display more clearly the influence of the individual variables. These definitions are:

$$R^2 = \beta_{xy \cdot t}\, r_{xy} + \beta_{xt \cdot y}\, r_{xt}$$
$$= \beta_{xy \cdot t}^2 + \beta_{xt \cdot y}^2 + 2\beta_{xy \cdot t}\beta_{xt \cdot y} r_{yt} ,$$

where the r's are the simple correlation coefficients between the variables indicated by the subscripts and where the β's are the regression coefficients of the equation relating x to y and t when the variables are all expressed in terms of their respective standard deviations. $\beta_{xy \cdot t}$ is the regression coefficient of x on y when t is kept constant, and $\beta_{xt \cdot y}$ is the regression coefficient of x on t when y is kept constant. We may then interpret the two terms of the first of the foregoing equations as expressing the portion of the total coefficient of determination (R^2) attributable to each variable independently, $\beta_{xy \cdot t} r_{xy}$ (39.99 per cent) being the portion attributable to price, and $\beta_{xt \cdot y} r_{xt}$ (51.23 per cent) the portion attributable to time.

The second equation suggests a slightly different way of interpreting the importance of the several variables. We may look upon $\beta_{xy \cdot t}^2$ as the portion of the reduction in variance attributable to the

E. EFFECT OF BUSINESS CONDITIONS ON THE CONSUMPTION OF SUGAR

The large role which time plays in our equations shows that our analysis of the factors affecting the demand for sugar is far from satisfactory. For time can hardly be looked upon as a causal factor.[36] Moreover, an examination of Figures 19B, 24B, and 29B suggests that the deviations of the points from the line are not random but *systematic*. This is particularly true of Figure 24B. They indicate the existence of a cyclical movement in consumption which cannot be explained by secular changes in the position of the demand curve D_1D_2. The most plausible assumption that suggests itself is that the demand for sugar is also affected by changes in income. Since no income data are available for the first two periods, we experimented with different indexes of production and trade with the hope of finding one which would give a plausible explanation of the fluctuations which still remain in the data and which would reduce the importance of the time variable.

The second and fourth sets of equations in Table 7 are a summary of some of these experiments. In these equations the additional variable w is Professor Persons' "Index of Industrial Production and Trade."[37]

To judge from the values of R' and of the percentage of the variance accounted for by this index, its use effects only a slight improvement in the results; the time variable is still very important. It appears, therefore, that the time variable is not simply a "carrier" of fluctuations in industry and trade. Our feeling is that it represents changes in taste.

We had expected to find that the *net* effect of an improvement in business conditions would be to increase the consumption of sugar. But the results belied our expectations. *All the regressions of x on w are negative.* That is, the effect of an improvement in business conditions, other things being equal, was to bring about a *decrease* in the consumption of sugar in each of the three periods. These findings were so contrary to expectations that we at first attributed them to the peculiarities of the index in question. Accordingly, we

---

direct effect of y, $\beta^2_{zt\cdot y}$ as the portion attributable to the *direct* effect of t, and $2\beta_{zy\cdot t}\beta_{zt\cdot y}r_{yt}$ as the portion to be attributed to the *joint* effect of the two variables. This last term may be negative. The meaning of a negative term is that part of the *direct* importance of each is really spurious, being due to the relationship existing between the two variables. Since

$$\beta_{zy\cdot t}r_{zy} = \beta^2_{zy\cdot t} + \beta_{zy\cdot t}\beta_{zt\cdot y}r_{yt},$$

and

$$\beta_{zt\cdot y}r_{zt} = \beta^2_{zt\cdot y} + \beta_{zy\cdot t}\beta_{zt\cdot y}r_{yt},$$

it is possible for either of these terms to be negative. These last two equations indicate the way in which the joint contribution is divided between the two variables: It is divided equally between them.

See Sewall Wright, "Correlation and Causation," *Journal of Agricultural Research*, XX (1921), 557–85; and S. Krichewsky, *Interpretation of Correlation Coefficients* (Cairo: Government Press, 1927). See also Appen. C, Sec. VI, C of this work.

[36] For different meanings which "time" has in economics see P. N. Rosenstein-Rodan, "The Role of Time in Economic Theory," *Economica* (N.S.), No. 1 (1934), pp. 77–97.

[37] Warren M. Persons, *Forecasting Business Cycles* (New York, 1931).

also experimented with the "Standard Statistics Composite Index of Industrial Production," Persons' "Unadjusted Index of Total Production," Persons' "Adjusted Index of Total Production," and Persons' "Index of Total Production Divided by Population."[38] But the use of these indexes simply confirmed the first findings: The net regression of the consumption of sugar on any of the indexes of industrial production is negative.

If there existed another—say, "superior"—commodity whose demand is so related to that of sugar that, as income increases, prices remaining constant, consumers buy more of that commodity and less of the "inferior" commodity —sugar—the phenomenon in question could thus be explained. But we do not know of such a commodity. Perhaps the difficulty can be explained by the negative correlation (if it exists) between sugar stocks, which are not taken into account in our consumption series, and business conditions. But this is only a guess. It may well be that, in attempting to explain the residual variations in the consumption of sugar through the introduction of variables other than price and time, we are attempting to build a mathematical structure on too shaky a factual foundation. There exists, however, a very important relation between income and demand, but an analysis of it must be postponed to Part III.

IV. DEMAND FUNCTIONS WITH THE DEFLATED PRICE AS THE DEPENDENT VARIABLE

In all the preceding analyses the consumption of sugar was taken as the dependent variable. That is, we assumed that the independent variables— price, time, etc.—are quite accurately known, and we used them to explain the fluctuations in the dependent variable. As we pointed out in chapter iv, there is a good reason for this assumption, for the statistics of prices are subject to less error than those of consumption. It is, nevertheless, also instructive to consider price as the dependent variable and to see the extent to which consumption, time, and the index of industrial production and trade account for the fluctuations in price.

Table 8 is a summary of the results obtained, arranged in four sets to correspond to those of Table 7. The third set of equations, which gives for each period the regression of the logarithm of price on the logarithm of consumption and on time, is also illustrated graphically in Figures 32, 33, and 34. These diagrams correspond, respectively, to Figures 21, 26, and 30, in which the logarithm of consumption is the dependent variable. Since the graphs of the arithmetic regressions (the first triad of equations) are almost identical with the logarithmic regressions of Figures 32, 33, and 34, they will not be reproduced.[39]

[38] *Standard Statistical Bulletin Basebook*, LXIII, No. 7 (January, 1932), 159, sec. 3 (January 1, 1923 = 100); and see Persons, *op. cit.*

[39] The agreement between the arithmetic and the logarithmic regressions when price is the dependent variable is just as close as when quantity is the dependent variable. Cf. Figs. 19 and 21; 24 and 26; and 29 and 30.

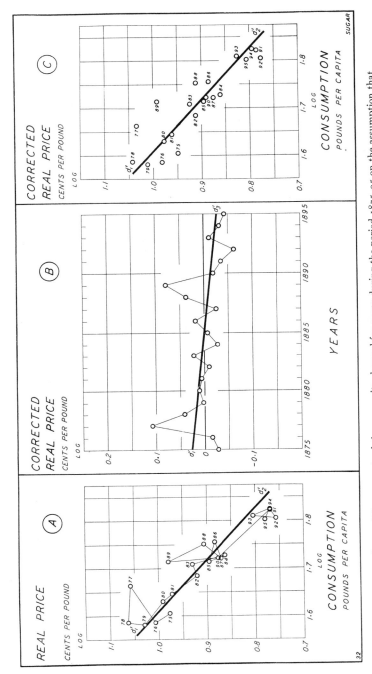

Fig. 32.—Sugar: Three aspects of the per capita demand for sugar during the period 1875–95 on the assumption that

$$y = 302.32 \ x^{-0.9198} e^{-0.0561t} .$$

222

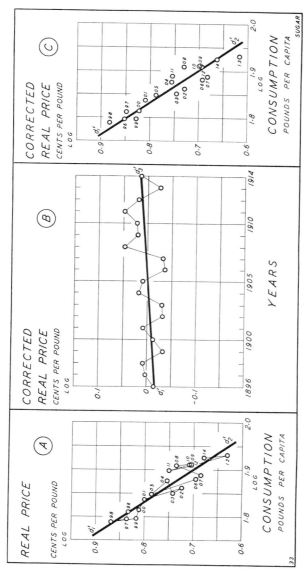

Fig. 33.—Sugar: Three aspects of the per capita demand for sugar during the period 1896–1914 on the assumption that

$$y = 2816.0 \, x^{-1.4461} e^{0.0012t} \, .$$

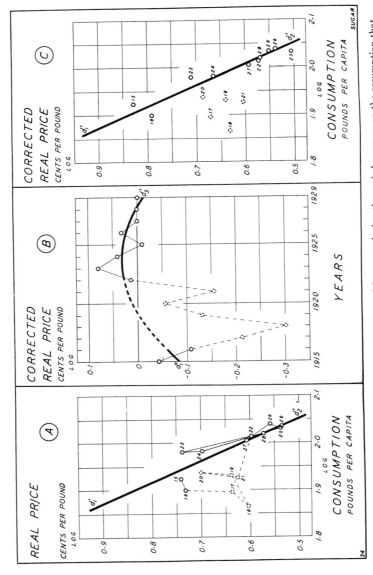

Fig. 34.—Sugar: Three aspects of the per capita demand for sugar during the period 1915–29 on the assumption that

$$y = 126430 \; x^{-2.2298} e^{0.01174 - 0.0035 t^2}.$$

224

An examination of Figures 32, 33, and 34 discloses the following interesting facts:

1. The observations giving the net regressions of price on time (Figures B) do not show nearly the same regular, consistent movement as we observed in the net regressions of consumption on time. Thus, during the first period (Fig. 32B), the corrected prices for 1877 and 1889 are much out of line and destroy the significance of the slight downward slope of the line $d_1'd_3'$. During the second period, the corrected prices exhibit a pronounced cyclical movement, although none of the observations is as extreme as those for 1877 and 1889. This cyclical movement appears to have no secular component, the slight upward inclination of the line $d_1'd_3'$ not being significant and being due entirely to the somewhat higher prices of 1908–14.

2. The distribution of the observations about the demand curves $d_1'd_2'$ (Figures C) is not random but follows the temporal order. In each period the observations for the earlier years are at the upper (left) end of the curve, and those for the later years are at the lower (right) end.

These facts indicate that there are important factors affecting the price of sugar which we have not yet taken into account. The hypothesis that suggests itself is that these factors are related to the fluctuations in income. Since we have no annual data on income for the first and second periods, we thought it advisable to experiment again with Warren M. Persons' "Index of Industrial Production and Trade."

The second and fourth sets of equations in Table 8 are a summary of these experiments. An examination of the regressions of y on w (and of y' on w') shows that changes in the index had no net effect on the fluctuations in the price of sugar during the first and third periods, but that they had a significant, though small, effect on the prices of the second period. The net relation between price and industrial production is, however, negative in all the periods, thus implying that the net effect of an increase in industrial production (and presumably in the demand for sugar) is to *decrease* the price of sugar. But what is the explanation of this phenomenon? Again we are faced with a quandary which will probably remain unsolved until reliable data on stocks of sugar become available.

Turning now to the descriptive constants, we find only one which we did not meet in Table 7, namely, the price flexibilities, φ. By a coefficient of price flexibility is understood the ratio of the relative change in price to the relative change in quantity with which it is associated, when the changes are infinitesimal:

$$\varphi = \frac{\partial y}{\partial x} \cdot \frac{x}{y} = \frac{\partial \log_e y}{\partial \log_e x} .$$

TABLE 8

SUGAR: THE CHARACTERISTICS OF THE PER CAPITA DEMAND FUNCTIONS

x = Per capita consumption in pounds
y = Deflated wholesale price in cents per pound
t = Time in years. For origins see Table 5

(Figures in parentheses are standard errors)

Equation No.	Period*		Constant Term	x	w	t	t^2	t^3
1	I	$y=$	16.2507	−0.1531 (0.0496)	....	−0.0391 (0.0755)	....	....
2	II	$y=$	14.6879	−0.1217 (0.0368)	....	+0.0345 (0.0519)	....	
3	III	$y=$	12.4888	−0.0825 (0.0305)	....	+0.0141 (0.0660)	....	
4	I	$y=$	19.5137	−0.1631 (0.0481)	−0.0272 (0.0171)	−0.0226 (0.0732)	....	
5	II	$y=$	21.0830	−0.1547 (0.0255)	−0.0403 (0.0094)	+0.1297 (0.0480)	....	−0.0007 (0.0004)
6	III	$y=$	14.6969	−0.0893 (0.0349)	−0.0151 (0.0297)	+0.0235 (0.0722)	....	
			Constant Term	x'	w'	†Mt	†Mt^2	†Mt^3
7	I	$y'=$	2.4805	−0.9198 (0.2941)	....	−0.0061 (0.0088)	....	....
8	II	$y'=$	3.4496	−1.4461 (0.4494)	....	+0.0042 (0.0087)	....	....
9	III	$y'=$	5.1018	−2.2298 (0.6307)	....	+0.0117 (0.0140)	−0.0035 (0.0016)	....
10	I	$y'=$	2.9181	−0.9402 (0.2954)	−0.2012 (0.2078)	−0.0053 (0.0088)	....	....
11	II	$y'=$	5.0052	−1.7028 (0.3762)	−0.5406 (0.1919)	+0.0170 (0.0099)	....	−0.00012 (0.00009)
12	III	$y'=$	6.8173	−2.5114 (0.7048)	−0.5754 (0.5997)	+0.0163 (0.0150)	−0.0037 (0.0016)	....

*I = 1875–95; II = 1896–1914; III = 1915–29 (excl. 1917–21).

TABLE 8—*Continued*

WITH PRICE AS THE DEPENDENT VARIABLE, BY PERIODS, 1875–1929

w = W. M. Persons' "Index of Industrial Production and
Trade," adjusted, weighted. Normal = 100

x', y', w' = Logs of x, y, w

(Figures in parentheses are standard errors)

DESCRIPTIVE CONSTANTS							EQUA-TION No.
Flexibility of Price φ	Maximum Value of η $1/\varphi$	Quadratic Mean Error ϵ (Cents)	Adjusted Multiple Correlation Coefficient R'	Percentage of Variance of Price Attributable to			
				x	w	t	
−0.9549 (0.4356)	−1.0473	0.7673	0.9072	72.51	....	11.57	1
−1.5768 (0.6111)	−0.6342	0.3468	0.9126	104.94	....	−19.80	2
−1.8667 (0.9348)	−0.5357	0.4296	0.8712	87.24	....	−5.98	3
−1.0170 (0.4303)	−0.9833	0.7368	0.9148	77.22	2.22	6.69	4
−2.0048 (0.4598)	−0.4988	0.2268	0.9636	133.42	13.00	−51.98	5
−2.0214 (1.0669)	−0.4947	0.4543	0.8547	94.46	−2.42	−10.01	6
φ	$1/\varphi$	ϵ (Per Cent)	R'	x'	w'	t	
−0.9198 (0.2941)	−1.0871	91.4–109.4	0.9144	70.39	....	14.86	7
−1.4461 (0.4494)	−0.6915	94.1–106.3	0.9101	98.73	....	−13.99	8
−2.2299 (0.6307)	−0.4485	91.9–108.9	0.9025	109.21	....	−21.58	9
−0.9402 (0.2954)	−1.0636	91.4–109.4	0.9141	71.95	1.05	13.01	10
−1.7028 (0.3762)	−0.5873	95.2–105.0	0.9434	116.26	10.05	−34.87	11
−2.5114 (0.7048)	−0.3982	91.8–109.0	0.9001	122.93	−3.41	−30.06	12

† $M = \log_{10} e = 0.43429$.

The reciprocal of a price flexibility is not necessarily equal to the elasticity of demand:

$$\eta = \frac{\partial x}{\partial y} \cdot \frac{y}{x} = \frac{\partial \log_e x}{\partial \log_e y},$$

computed from the regressions in which consumption is the dependent variable, because the concrete, statistical equations from which the two coefficients are computed cannot be transformed into one another. In fitting the equations of Table 7, we minimized the sum of the squares of the residuals of consumption (or of the logs of consumption), while in fitting the equations of Table 8, we minimized the sum of the squares of the residuals of price (or of the logs of price). Consequently, the equations of Table 8 cannot be converted (by simply putting consumption as the dependent variable) into the equations of Table 7, and vice versa. It follows, therefore, that the value of $1/\varphi$ computed from the regression of price on consumption will not be equal to η computed from the regression of consumption on price. The former should, however, give the maximum numerical value[40] of η. The numerical values of the φ's of Table 8 show marked increases from one period to the next. This appears to indicate that the elasticities of demand must have decreased in numerical value during the same time. The equations of Table 7 (third and fourth sets), which are more appropriate for computing elasticities of demand than are the corresponding equations of Table 8, lend some support to these findings.

[40] Denote the regression of x on y and of y on x, respectively, by

(i) $x = a + by,$

and

(ii) $y = a + \beta x.$

From elementary statistics we know that

$$b = \frac{\Sigma \bar{x}\bar{y}}{\Sigma \bar{y}^2} = r \frac{\sigma_x}{\sigma_y},$$

and

$$\beta = \frac{\Sigma \bar{x}\bar{y}}{\Sigma \bar{x}^2} = r \frac{\sigma_y}{\sigma_x},$$

where r is the coefficient of correlation, and σ_x and σ_y are the standard deviations of x and y. The elasticity of demand computed from the former is

(iii) $\eta = b \frac{y}{x} = r \frac{\sigma_x}{\sigma_y} \cdot \frac{y}{x},$

and the reciprocal of the price flexibility computed from the latter (for the same values of y on x) is

(iv) $\frac{1}{\varphi} = \frac{1}{\beta} \cdot \frac{y}{x} = \frac{1}{r} \frac{\sigma_x}{\sigma_y} \cdot \frac{y}{x}.$

Since $|r| \leq 1$, it follows that $\left| \frac{1}{\varphi} \right| \geq |\eta|$, the equality obtaining only when $|r| = 1$.

A comparison of the descriptive constants of Table 8 with those of the corresponding equations of Table 7 shows not a single instance in which the former equations are an improvement over the latter. The values of R' are all smaller, and values of ϵ are all larger, than in the corresponding equations of Table 7.[41] It is clear, then, that the demand for sugar is best approximated by those equations in which consumption is taken as the dependent variable.

V. SUMMARY

We began this chapter by illustrating the derivation of two simple demand functions for sugar for each of the three periods into which we divided our data. Then we introduced more variables into our equations and discussed the meaning and the limitations of the various descriptive constants which have enabled us to test the significance of the various parameters of the demand functions and to compare the goodness of fit of the different curves. Finally, we treated price as the dependent variable and discovered certain new problems which await solution. Throughout this analysis we have tried to keep in mind and to illustrate the truth of the proposition that the statistical data cannot yield significant results unless they are combined with sound economic theory.

It may seem that we have been too successful, for we have ended up with twenty-four equations, not to mention the link-relative and the trend-ratio results which are reserved for later analysis. Embarrassing as the multiplicity of our findings may be, they all agree that the demand for sugar exhibits both varying and fixed properties, which are briefly summarized in the following propositions.

1. The demand curve underwent important structural changes in the fifty-five years from 1875 to 1929. In the first period a reduction in the (deflated) price of sugar of 1 cent per pound increased the annual per capita consumption by 2.25 pounds; in the second period, by 3.34 pounds; and in the third, by 7.80 pounds.

2. The elasticity of demand for sugar has, however, remained fairly constant from period to period; a reduction in the price of 1 per cent increased the annual consumption by only 0.3 or 0.4 of 1 per cent in each of the three periods. There is slight evidence of a decrease in the numerical value of the elasticity of demand from −0.40 in the first period to −0.35 in the second and to −0.30 in the third. But the errors in the data are too great to warrant our attaching much significance to these slight changes.

3. During the first and second periods the demand curve shifted upward at the average annual rates of 0.84 pound and 0.92 pound, respectively, or at 1.56 and 1.24 per cent per annum. *During the third period the shift came to a standstill, the rate approximating zero. This is a very important change. It means that*

---

[41] Of course, only the ϵ's of the logarithmic equations of Tables 7 and 8 are comparable with one another.

the average consumer no longer buys increased quantities of sugar from one year to the next if the price is kept fixed; and that producers can no longer count on an increased per capita consumption unless prices are reduced or unless new uses for sugar are discovered in the arts. This fact looms large behind many of the difficulties which have confronted the industry since the war.

4. The factors affecting the consumption of sugar are, in the order of their importance, time, price, and business conditions, except in the third period when price is more important than time. The variable time is a catch-all for those factors which change slowly and smoothly and which we cannot measure directly. Of these, the changing taste for sugar is probably the most important. Changes in business conditions, as measured by Warren M. Persons' "Adjusted Index of Industrial Production and Trade," have only a very slight influence on consumption. Moreover, the net relation between this index and the consumption of sugar is negative, which suggests that an improvement in business conditions (and hence in the demand for sugar) brings about a *decrease* in the consumption of sugar. It is probable that this quandary would be resolved if we had annual data on stocks of sugar in the channels of trade during the first and second periods.

5. One of the results of the present inquiry is the demonstration that an acquisition of clear notions of the measures of such economic parameters as elasticity of demand and rate of shift of the demand curve is exceedingly difficult, if not quite impossible, without an understanding of the methods—economic, statistical, and graphical—by which they have been reached. The economic theory underlying this analysis has been developed in Part I; the statistical methods have been explained in this chapter and in the Mathematical Appendix (Appen. C). These methods, and especially the three-dimensional diagrams, should be carefully studied by all those who wish to get a deeper insight into the problem of the statistical analysis of demand and who wish to understand the statistical chapters which follow.

VI. THE BEARING OF THESE FINDINGS ON THE DEVELOPMENTS IN THE SUGAR INDUSTRY SINCE 1929

Probably the most important findings of this chapter are (1) that the demand for sugar is quite inelastic and (2) that by 1929 the demand curve had ceased to shift upward or had reached its "ceiling," so that the sugar industry can no longer count on a rising per capita consumption even when the price of sugar remains fixed—a condition to which it got accustomed during the last century. If these findings are valid, they have a significant bearing on the problems which are confronting the sugar industry today. There can be no serious doubt about the first finding. It emerges consistently from data relating to different periods and treated by different methods. But the second find-

ing is based on the data for the relatively short period of 1915–29, excluding
1917–21. Since several years have elapsed between the writing of this chapter
and its submission to the press—years in which the sugar industry has been
subjected to violent strains and stresses—it is desirable to test this conclusion
by an analysis of the data for the more recent years.

As this chapter goes to press, the latest year for which the values of all of
our basic series—consumption, price, and Persons' "Index of Industrial Production and Trade"—are available is 1936. Since the seven sets of observations from 1930 to 1936 are too few to admit of an independent demand analysis, we have decided to incorporate them with the data for the third period
(but to omit 1915–16, since these years are now relatively far away), and to
consider the fifteen years from 1922 to 1936 as our test period.

The data for our test are given in Tables I, IIa, and III of Appendix A.
Except for Persons' "Index of Industrial Production and Trade," which was
revised in 1933 after this chapter was written, the data which we shall use are
simply continuations of the series analyzed in the body of this chapter. As
in the previous analyses, we shall use both linear and logarithmic equations,
and we shall write first consumption and then price as the dependent variable.

The following four equations summarize the results obtained, the origin of
t being at July 1, 1929:

(6.1)
$$x = 108.83 - 6.0294y + 0.1644w - 0.4217t$$
$$\quad\quad\quad (1.3334)\quad (0.0519)\quad\;\; (0.2685)$$
$$\eta = -0.2416, \quad \epsilon = 2.4065 \text{ lb.}, \quad R' = 0.9145 .$$

(6.2)
$$x' = 1.9167 - 0.2582y' + 0.1209w' - 0.0048Mt$$
$$\quad\quad\quad (0.0617)\quad\;\; (0.0448)\quad\;\; (0.0028)$$
$$\eta = -0.2582, \quad \epsilon = 97.5 \text{ per cent—}102.6 \text{ per cent}, \quad R' = 0.9015 .$$

(6.3)
$$y = 13.615 - 0.1078x + 0.0122w - 0.0837t$$
$$\quad\quad\quad (0.0238)\quad\;\; (0.0089)\quad\;\; (0.0307)$$
$$\varphi = -2.6908, \quad \epsilon = 0.3218 \text{ cents}, \quad R' = 0.8294 .$$

(6.4)
$$y' = 5.0211 - 2.3792x' + 0.1683w' - 0.0211Mt$$
$$\quad\quad\quad (0.5684)\quad\;\; (0.1679)\quad\;\; (0.0072)$$
$$\varphi = -2.3792, \quad \epsilon = 92.5 \text{ per cent—}108.1 \text{ per cent}, \quad R' = 0.8108 .$$

The interpretation of such equations as the foregoing has been given several
times in the body of the chapter and need not be repeated again. Interest
naturally centers on the relation between these equations, which relate to the
period 1922–36, and the corresponding equations (6) and (12) of Tables 7 and 8

which relate to the period 1915–29, excluding 1917–21. A comparison of the two sets of equations brings to light two important differences:

1. Whereas in all previous analyses an improvement in business conditions was associated with a net *decrease* in sugar consumption, in equations (6.1) and (6.2) an improvement in business conditions brings about an *increase* in consumption. More specifically, an increase of one *unit* in Persons' index is associated with a net increase in the annual per capita consumption of 0.16 pound, other things being equal (eq. [6.1]). In relative terms, an increase of 1 per cent in the Persons' index is associated with an increase of 0.12 per cent in the per capita consumption under the same conditions (eq. [6.2]).[42]

2. When the observations from 1930 to 1936 are taken into account, as they are in equations (6.1) to (6.4), it appears that *the demand curve had not only reached its ceiling before 1929 but* that it *has also been shifting downward since 1922*. More specifically, equations (6.1) and (6.2) show that, since 1922 or thereabouts, consumers have been in the habit of reducing their purchases of sugar by approximately 0.42 pound per capita per annum, or by approximately 0.5 per cent per capita per annum. Of course, changes in sugar prices and in business conditions sometimes obscure this tendency, but there can be no serious doubt about its existence.

This fact, which is due to the "slim craze" and possibly also to the substitution of alcoholic beverages for soft drinks after the repeal of the prohibition amendment, has received little or no attention either from the sugar industry or from independent students of it. Writers on the subject have been unanimous in attributing the recent ills of the sugar industry to changes in supply conditions. Thus the former chief of the sugar section of the Agricultural Adjustment Administration[43] attributes the present crisis in sugar to three factors—the disruption of the industry by the World War, the rise in agrarian nationalism, and the technical revolution in sugar production—and refers to the pre-war conditions as normal or stable. That these are fundamental factors, no one will·deny. But he and other students of the problem will make a serious error if they continue to take for granted the former demand for sugar. *The sugar industry has always been characterized by a secular fall in real prices* (see Fig. 17). What differentiated the pre-war situation from the present is that throughout the period from 1875 to 1914, while the price of sugar was falling, the entire per capita demand curve was rising higher and higher (see Figs. 20 and 25, or Figs. 22 and 27). This situation no longer obtains. With the per capita demand curve shifting downward with time, any secular increase in consumption must come from an increase in population, and that increase is de-

---

[42] This change in the sign of the relation cannot be attributed to the revisions in Persons' index: the new and the old indexes have similar year-to-year fluctuations.

[43] John E. Dalton, *Sugar: A Case Study of Government Control* (New York, 1937), chaps. iv and v.

creasing at a rapid rate. True, some increase in consumption may also be expected from an improvement in business conditions. But no steady, long-run improvement in business conditions can be counted upon, and even in the short run an increase of 1 per cent in this factor is only one-half as effective in increasing the per capita consumption of sugar as is a decrease of 1 per cent in price (see eq. [6.2]).

The downward shift in the per capita demand curve for sugar also has an important bearing on the recent efforts of the government to control sugar production through crop reduction and marketing allotments, financed by the proceeds of processing taxes.

In the Agricultural Adjustment Act approved May 12, 1933, sugar beets and sugar cane were not made "basic agricultural commodities," primarily because the larger part of our consumption is imported from Hawaii, Puerto Rico, the Philippine Islands, and Cuba, and because the conflicting interests were unable to agree on a plan of "stabilization" which would be acceptable to the government. But in 1933 the very large prospective sugar crop in the United States and in its possessions and territories, the consequent threat to prices, and the collapse of the Cuban economy with the accompanying political upheaval and bloodshed gave rise to a demand for government action in behalf of the sugar industry. This found expression in a message to Congress dated February 8, 1934, in which the President outlined the nature of the sugar problem and recommended appropriate legislation. Congress embodied the President's recommendations in legislation passed in May, 1934. The essence of the Sugar Control Act was the limitation of production of sugar beets and cane in the producing areas and the limitation of sugar marketings under a quota system. The Secretary of Agriculture was directed to determine the nation's annual sugar requirements; to allot quotas among the various insular and foreign sugar-producing areas; to establish marketing allotments for individual processors; to levy a processing tax on sugar; and to enter into contracts with producers for acreage control.[44] The amount of bounty to be paid to continental producers was that which, when added to the farm price of beets and cane would assure a "fair exchange value" for these farm commodities. In the Philippines and Puerto Rico these payments were not so much "bounties" as compensation for reduction in production made necessary by the quota system.

During the year and a half that this plan was in effect, "surplus sugars" in the Continental United States and insular areas were eliminated. Also, the processing tax of one-half cent per pound which financed the sugar program did not of itself raise the price to the consumer, since the imposition of the tax was accompanied by a reduction in the tariff of an equal amount.

[44] See *Yearbook of Agriculture, 1935*, pp. 51–55; *ibid., 1936*, pp. 75–78; and Dalton, *op. cit.*, chaps. vii and viii.

On January 6, 1936, the Supreme Court, in invalidating the A.A.A., prohibited limitation of production coupled with direct payments to producers. *It did not, however, specifically outlaw production control through the quota system,* although doubt remains as to its legality. In 1936 Congress repealed the invalidated processing tax and benefit payment features of the Sugar Act, but extended its quota and allotment features through 1936 and 1937.

This leaves unaltered the basis of control prescribed by the Sugar Act, namely, an estimate of the "consumption requirements" of sugar for Continental United States, to be determined by the Secretary of Agriculture. It is in this connection that the nature of the demand curve for sugar becomes of great significance. The fact that the demand is getting progressively more inelastic, that a small crop is (within the observed range of the data) worth more than a large crop, should be an inducement to limitation of output. However, the fact that the per capita demand curve is shifting downward with time will make the task of control very difficult and expensive in the long run. For, if this downward shift does not come to a stop in the near future, the proposed schemes for raising the income of producers through a reduction in output will either be subjected to the strain of a secular decrease in consumption, or will demand enormous outlays from the Treasury. The sugar industry would, therefore, be well advised actively to promote new uses for sugar and persistently to seek ways of reducing costs of production.

CHAPTER VII

THE DEMAND FOR CORN

CHAPTER VII

THE DEMAND FOR CORN

I. THE POSITION OF CORN IN THE NATIONAL ECONOMY

Corn is the most important crop in the United States both in acreage and in value. From 1924 to 1929 the average acreage was 100 million acres or 156,250 square miles, an area exceeding that of Great Britain, Ireland, the Netherlands, and Belgium; and the average annual value was over 2 billion dollars, an amount exceeding the combined value of wheat and cotton.

Although corn is grown in every state of the Union, the acreage devoted to it is largest and the production is most intensive in the more favorable areas. These constitute the Corn Belt—a rather indefinite strip of land, varying from time to time, extending westward from mid-Ohio to mid-Nebraska; northward to southern Michigan, southern Wisconsin, southern Minnesota, and southern South Dakota; and southward to northern Missouri and eastern Kansas. In this belt is raised between 60 and 70 per cent of the corn crop. And there has been an increasing concentration of corn in it in the last twenty-five years. Thus the ratio of corn produced in the nine Corn Belt states[1] to the production in the thirty-nine other states increased from 1.28 in 1908 to 1.88 in 1929.[2] Most of this increase is, however, due to the continued expansion of the Corn Belt west and north which has been facilitated by the introduction of more drouth-resistant and early maturing varieties of corn, the use of larger implements, and some contraction of wheat acreage in regions in which it competes with corn.[3]

It [the Corn Belt] is the region of the country from which are obtained the major supply [of hogs] for the urban population outside the region and the bulk of our exported pork products. In this area lie eight of the ten principal markets for corn, seven of the nine principal stockyard markets, all of the first-size packing houses, and the majority of the second-size packing houses of the country. Hog products contribute close to 15 per cent of the calories of the national diet.[4]

[1] Iowa, Illinois, Indiana, Ohio, Missouri, Nebraska, South Dakota, Minnesota, and Wisconsin.

[2] See G. S. Shepherd, *The Trend of Corn Prices* (Agricultural Experiment Station, Iowa State College of Agriculture and Mechanic Arts, Bull. No. 284 [Ames, Iowa, July, 1931]), p. 326. This bulletin presents in condensed form the material in Research Bull. No. 140, *The Secular Movement of Corn Prices* (Iowa Agricultural Experiment Station [1931]).

[3] Shepherd, *op. cit.*, p. 314.

[4] Alonzo E. Taylor, *Corn and Hog Surplus of the Corn Belt* (Stanford University, 1932), p. 4. I am grateful to Dr. Taylor for permission to quote from his book as well as for his kindness in looking through the manuscript of this chapter.

Corn is the raw material upon which the gigantic livestock industry is dependent, so that even though it is not a cash crop—only about one-sixth of the total crop is sold for cash—it is nevertheless of paramount importance. According to estimates of the U.S. Department of Agriculture, more than 85 per cent of the crop harvested for grain is fed to livestock, and somewhat less than 10 per cent is used for human food, contributing nearly 7 per cent of the calories of the national diet.[5]

TABLE 9*

ESTIMATED DISPOSITION OF THE CORN HARVESTED FOR GRAIN
IN THE UNITED STATES, AVERAGE 1912–21
(Percentages of Total Crop)

Method of Disposition	On Farms	Not on Farms	Total
Fed to livestock:			
Hogs............................	40.0	....	....
Horses and mules..............	20.0	....	....
Cattle........................	15.0	....	....
Poultry.......................	4.0	....	....
Sheep.........................	1.0	....	....
Total.....................	80.0	5.5	85.5
Used domestically for human food..	3.5	6.5†	10.0
Exports as grain..................	....	1.5	1.5
Other uses........................	....	3.0	3.0
Total.....................	83.5	16.5	100.0

* See Taylor, *Corn and Hog Surplus of the Corn Belt*, p. 49. Adapted from *U.S.D.A. Yearbook of Agriculture* (1921), p. 165.
† Ground in merchant mills but not all used for food.

In addition to the use of corn as grain, the plant is also used extensively in the form of silage, fodder, and stover, as feed for animals. About 8.5 million acres are annually turned into these uses.

The Corn crop and the swine and cattle populations are intimately interrelated. With the exception of limited areas from which corn is largely sold as grain, because of the proximity of markets, swine are found most abundantly where corn production is greatest. In these areas, too, the finishing of cattle for market is a prominent industry. The six States, Iowa, Illinois, Nebraska, Missouri, Indiana, and Ohio, producing 48 per cent of the corn in 1921, had within their borders about 45 per cent of the swine of the country and over 25 per cent of the cattle other than milk cows on January 1, 1922. In addition these States produced 32 per cent of the chickens and 35 per cent of the hens' eggs produced in the United States in 1919.

Corn, therefore, consumed either directly or in the form of meat and other animal products, is the principal source of food of the American people.[6]

[5] *Ibid.*, p. 55.

[6] "The Corn Crop," *U.S.D.A. Yearbook of Agriculture* (1921), p. 165. (Italics inserted.)

The corn plant has also many industrial uses, ranging all the way from furfural to newsprint and building materials, to industrial alcohol and a variety of chemicals. But the proportion of the crop devoted to these uses is very small. Thus, the quantity of corn used in the production of alcohol and other distilled spirits and in the manufacture of cornstarch, glucose, etc., fluctuated from 50 million bushels in 1920 to a maximum of only 92 million bushels in 1928.[7]

The United States produced about 60 per cent of the world corn crop in 1924–29, which was approximately 4.5 billion bushels. Argentina was second in importance with 270 million bushels or 6 per cent of the total. Only about 300 million bushels, less than 7 per cent of the world-crop, enter international trade. During the same period, Argentina exported 76 per cent of her corn; the United States, 1 per cent.[8] Our imports are negligible.

II. DEFINITION OF THE DEMAND FOR CORN

In view of the fact that corn has many uses, whether as a food, feed, or an industrial raw material, the American demand for it must be defined in its broad sense, as the aggregate of the quantities which will be utilized for all purposes at a given price. According to this definition, the quantity demanded in any year should be given by the production of that year, plus the stocks at the beginning of the year, minus the stocks at the end of the year, plus the imports, and minus the exports. However, in the statistical analysis which follows, changes in stocks and in net exports will be neglected for the following reasons.

Data on the carry-over of corn are not available for the entire period covered by this study. It is only for the period beginning with 1897 that the United States Department of Agriculture has published annual estimates of "old stocks on farms November 1," which are "based on reported percentage of entire crop on farms, proportion merchantable, and per cent shipped out of county where grown."[9] Moreover, even if we were to confine our analysis to this period and to make use of the carry-over data, the corrections involved would be negligible. Thus, a computation shows that, when their signs are neglected, the differences between the stocks at the beginning of the year and the stocks at the end of the year averaged only 48 million bushels, or 1.89 per cent of the crop, during 1897–1914; and only 61 million bushels, or 2.23 per cent of the crop, during 1915–29 (excluding 1917–21).[10] These are small figures when compared with the admittedly large errors in the underlying production

[7] Shepherd, *The Secular Movement of Corn Prices*, p. 220, Tables VII and VIII.

[8] Theodore W. Schultz, *The Tariffs on Barley, Oats and Corn* (Tariff Research Committee, Madison, Wis.; Freeport, Ill.: Rawleigh Foundation, 1933), pp. 68–69.

[9] See *Agricultural Yearbook* for 1924, p. 606; for 1931, pp. 621–22.

[10] If signs of the differences are taken into account, the corresponding averages are 0.55 and 0.88 per cent.

series. Accordingly it was decided that the adjustment for changes in the size of the carry-over would constitute an unnecessary refinement.

Imports are certainly negligible, averaging only 0.04 of 1 per cent of production. Exports are also small, having amounted to 100 million bushels or more in only eleven years since 1879,[11] and having averaged 3.5 per cent of production during the first period, 3.7 per cent during the second, and 1.6 per cent during the third. It is probable, then, that the volume of exports also falls within the range of error in the production estimates. As Dr. Taylor puts it:

The reports on condition and yield tend to be misleading because corn is so often injured in the last fortnight of the growing period. It is very difficult to adjudge the proportion of soft corn, the amount cut for fodder, and the amount "hogged down." The stand, the moisture content, the variety, the bulk in the crib, and the ratio of corn on cob to shelled corn, all contribute to the variability of the crop estimate. The crop estimate ought to be revised in the spring on the basis of the loss of weight during the winter, but this is not practicable. *All in all, the plus-and-minus error in the corn-crop estimate may well be over 100 million bushels, a figure which bulks large against the corn crop passing to terminal markets and especially against the amount passing to export.*[12]

Accordingly, we decided also to neglect net exports and to consider the total corn demand (consumption) for any year as being approximately measured by the total production for the same year, feeling that the neglect of both carry-over and net exports will not materially affect the major findings of this investigation.

It is true, of course, that even if net exports and carry-over are each negligible, their sum is not necessarily negligible; and that, perhaps, both series should have been accepted at their face value and used to improve the estimate of consumption. But the fluctuations of the series thus corrected would differ so little from those of the uncorrected production series, and the errors in the latter are so great,[13] that it seemed a superrefinement to allow for net exports and the estimated carry-over. In any event, it is not advisable to make corrections of this nature until the U.S. Department of Agriculture has completed its revision of the basic production series.

III. FACTORS IN THE DEMAND FOR CORN

The demand for corn in the broad sense in which we have agreed to use the term is affected by a complex of factors. Probably the most important of these are:

  1. The size and economic status of the population
  2. The price of corn for the same crop year
  3. The general price level

[11] The highest figure, 210 million bushels, was reached in 1898.

[12] *Op. cit.*, p. 48. (Italics inserted.)   [13] See chap. v, pp. 167–70.

4. The prices of other cereals

5. General business conditions

6. The number of the different domestic animals receiving corn and the amount received by each kind

7. The prices of these animals

8. Other factors which we cannot, or do not, measure, but which change more or less slowly and smoothly with time, and which may be represented by the catch-all factor, time

All but (6) and (7) are the conventional factors which are introduced in the analysis of the demand for almost any staple agricultural commodity. Factors (6) and (7) are peculiar to corn.

That the size of the population has an influence on demand is of course always taken for granted, but that the distribution and economic status of the population may also affect demand is not so well known. Yet there is good reason for believing that the demand for corn has been seriously affected by these factors. Thus Taylor comes to the conclusion that the use of corn as a bread grain has fallen on account of the industrialization of the southern states, the elevation of the post-war plane of living (before the depression), the revulsion against corn bread as a war bread, and the circumstance that home baking is being supplanted by commercial baking, and corn bread does not lend itself to delivery-route handling.[14] However, it is neither possible nor practicable to take these factors directly into account. The most that our data will enable us to do is to make a rough allowance for only one factor—changes in the size of population. The method which we shall follow is to reduce the consumption data to a per capita basis. We shall make the usual assumption that the resultant of the other factors will be reflected, in part at least, in the time variable.

Of factors (2), (3), (4), and (5), the second and fifth will be introduced directly into our demand equations; the third will be approximately allowed for by deflating the December farm price of corn by the Bureau of Labor Statistics Index of Wholesale Prices for the same month; and the fourth will be studied in Part III, where an analysis will be made of the effect on the demand for corn of changes in the prices of such related goods as barley, hay, and oats.

Of the three remaining factors, the last is generally introduced in any analysis of demand to take care of unmeasured or unmeasurable secular factors.

The two groups of factors (6) and (7) are, however, peculiar to the demand for corn, since, as we have seen, 85 per cent of the crop is fed to livestock, but they are also the ones whose influence is most difficult to determine with a high

[14] *Op. cit.*, pp. 55–56.

degree of accuracy. This has been so well emphasized by Dr. Alonzo Taylor that it is desirable to quote him at some length:

> The amount of corn used as feedstuff is the product of two factors: the number of domesticated animals receiving corn and the amount of corn received by each animal during its lifetime. To evaluate these factors the country must be considered on a regional basis, or, better still, by states. The place of corn in the feeding program of hogs, cattle, sheep, and poultry varies widely from region to region and to some extent within regions from state to state. An increase in the count of swine, cattle, sheep, and poultry implies some increase in demand for corn as feedstuff, but not an increase necessarily proportional to augmentation in count of animals; the influence on demand for corn would be modified by the kind of animals involved, the regional distribution of the increase, and the availability and prices of other feedstuffs. An increase of cattle grown in Iowa has a different meaning in respect of demand for corn from an increase of cattle in California or an increase of cattle grown outside and shipped into Iowa. It is particularly in relation to hogs that increase in numbers implies increased demand for corn; but an increase in numbers of swine in Iowa has a different meaning for demand for corn than an increase in number of swine in California or in Pennsylvania. *Broadly considered, therefore, while increase in animal husbandry implies increase in demand for corn, the correlation cannot be close, for a variety of reasons which become apparent when one discerns the position of corn and other feedstuffs, state by state, in the animal husbandry of each region.*[15]

More important is the existence of a secular trend in the utilization of corn in animal husbandry. With each decade, less feedstuffs are required per unit population. Taylor lists four factors as accounting for this secular trend:

    1. The reduction of the death-rate in the newborn and during infancy

    2. The gradual replacement of animals of inferior strains by selected animals of superior strains

    3. The slaughter at earlier age which reduces the average term of life at market maturity

    4. The continuous improvement in the efficiency of rationing and feeding operations.[16]

Unfortunately, it is impossible to take all these factors into consideration. In the first place, most of the relevant data are lacking. The only series that are available which bear on the group of factors (6) and (7) are the U.S. Department of Agriculture estimates of the number of the various kinds of livestock[17] on January 1 of each year and the amount of corn consumed by each unit of livestock population in only one year—1914. Second, even if the relevant data were available, we could not have used them in our demand equation without giving up our announced plan of dividing the series into three periods,[18]

---

[15] *Ibid.*, pp. 50–51. (Italics inserted.)

[16] *Ibid.*, p. 51.

[17] Horses and mules, milch cows, other cattle, swine, and sheep.

[18] I = 1875–95; II = 1896–1914; III = 1915–29 (excluding 1917–21).

for then even the longest of the periods would not contain enough observations to enable us to determine the constants of the demand equation with a fair degree of probability. In fact, we could not even use an appreciable fraction of the numerous factors related to (6) and (7) without encountering the same difficulty. Thus, even if we neglected all factors except the five livestock populations, introduced these variables together with price and time into the demand equation, and attempted to fit it to the data for the first period, we should have only twenty-one observations from which to determine eight constants—hardly a sufficient basis.

In view of these and other considerations, we shall reduce the five population series to one by computing the number of "animal units" for each year. This is a weighted average of the estimated number of hogs, milch cows, other cattle, and horses and mules,[19] the weights being the per capita quantity of corn fed to these animals in 1914.[20]

The foregoing examination of the factors in the demand for corn and their statistical measurement suggest that all the factors listed in the beginning of this section deserve our consideration, although we must take care not to introduce too many variables into our demand equations, since the number of our observations in any one period is relatively small. Following the procedure outlined in chapter iv and used in chapter vi, we shall proceed with our analysis by stages as follows:

First, we shall write the per capita demand as a function of the deflated price and of time, using both the linear and logarithmic (constant-elasticity) demand functions.

Second, we shall introduce the index of business conditions into our equations and study such improvements as may result therefrom.

Third, we shall take consumption per animal unit as the dependent variable and subject it to the same analysis as that for the per capita consumption.

Fourth, we shall consider total consumption (=production) as the dependent variable and express it as a function of price, the number of animal units, and time.

Fifth, we shall repeat each of these analyses with price as the dependent variable and compare the results obtained.

In Part III we shall analyze the interrelations of demand, that is, the effect on the demand for corn of changes in the prices of related goods.

[19] See *U.S.D.A. Farmers' Bulletin*, No. 629 (October 16, 1914), p. 9. The number of sheep was neglected because the amount of corn fed to sheep is relatively small—1.2 bushels per animal per annum.

[20] See Table I of Appen. A.

IV. DEMAND FUNCTIONS WITH PER CAPITA CONSUMPTION
AS THE DEPENDENT VARIABLE[21]

Table IV of Appendix A records for the period 1875–1929, inclusive, the consumption (=production) per capita and per animal unit, the real price, and the value per capita of corn in the United States, together with the link relatives and the trend ratios of the per capita consumption and the deflated prices. The basic (unadjusted) data, the animal units series, and the deflators used in deriving these series are given in Tables II and I of the same appendix.

Figure 35 is a graphic representation on a ratio scale of the per capita consumption, the real price, and the per capita value series for each of the three periods. As was explained in chapter vi, the per capita values are useful in connection with the computation of the elasticity of demand. When the demand is *elastic*, the year-to-year changes in total value will tend to be *negatively* correlated with the corresponding changes in price. On the other hand, when the demand is *inelastic*, the changes in total value will be *positively* correlated with the corresponding changes in price. By comparing the value series with the price series (or with the quantity series), we can observe when the correlation changes sign. That year is generally one in which a disturbing factor has made its appearance.[22]

Since a study of the data led to serious doubts as to their relative accuracy for some years, the observations in question were omitted from the computations. These are the observations for 1875–78, which are indicated by the dotted lines on the graphs, and also the observations for 1893–98 in the animal unit series. The reason for the latter omission is that there is a break in the animal unit series for those years, which has resulted from adjustments apparently made by the United States Department of Agriculture in the number of horses and cattle in order to conform to the census figures for 1899.

Table 10 is a descriptive summary of the adjusted consumption and price series. We shall consider first the demand functions derived from the per capita consumption and real prices for the first period.

A. THE FIRST PERIOD, 1879–95

A glance at Figure 35 shows that, as in the case of the sugar series, the consumption and the price series are highly correlated with each other. The existence of this correlation is brought out very clearly in the scatter diagram shown in Figure 36, in which the per capita consumption is plotted against the adjusted prices. As shown in Table 10 the coefficient of correlation between the

---

[21] For a more detailed explanation of the methods used and for definitions of the technical terms employed see chap. vi.

[22] See chap. vi, n. 15.

TABLE 10

CORN: SUMMARY BY PERIODS OF THE ADJUSTED DATA USED IN
DERIVING THE DEMAND FUNCTIONS, 1879–1929

A. WITH CONSUMPTION* REDUCED TO A PER CAPITA BASIS

PERIOD†	PER CAPITA CONSUMPTION $x(t)$				DEFLATED PRICE‡ $y(t)$				CORRELATION COEFFICIENT
	Descriptive Constants								
	Mean (Bu.)	Median (Bu.)	Stand-ard De-viation (Bu.)	Coeffi-cient of Varia-tion	Mean (Cents)	Median (Cents)	Stand-ard De-viation (Cents)	Coeffi-cient of Varia-tion	r_{xy}
I	28.676	30.247	4.305	15.01	46.770	45.750	8.578	18.34	−0.8949
II	29.754	30.220	3.349	11.25	51.741	50.000	11.568	22.36	−0.8699
III	24.498	24.280	2.723	11.12	50.544	49.496	6.533	12.92	−0.2946

PERIOD	Equations of Trends	Origin
I	$x(t) = 28.6764 - 0.2642t$ $y(t) = 46.7698 + 0.4618t$	Jan. 1, 1888
II	$x(t) = 29.7540 - 0.1963t$ $y(t) = 51.7411 + 1.4104t$	Jan. 1, 1906
III	$x(t) = 25.1499 - 0.4347t$ $y(t) = 51.2028 - 0.4389t$	Jan. 1, 1923

B. WITH CONSUMPTION* REDUCED TO A PER ANIMAL UNIT BASIS

PERIOD§	CONSUMPTION PER ANIMAL UNIT $x(t)$				DEFLATED PRICE‡ $y(t)$				CORRELATION COEFFICIENT
	Descriptive Constants								
	Mean (Bu.)	Median (Bu.)	Stand-ard De-viation (Bu.)	Coeffi-cient of Varia-tion	Mean (Cents)	Median (Cents)	Stand-ard De-viation (Cents)	Coeffi-cient of Varia-tion	r_{xy}
I	68.139	70.237	8.533	12.52	46.023	44.958	7.467	16.22	−0.8694
II	84.639	85.421	9.327	11.02	54.428	51.373	10.514	19.32	−0.7906
III	87.851	90.388	7.598	8.65	50.544	49.496	6.533	12.92	−0.6666

PERIOD	Equations of Trends	Origin
I	$x(t) = 68.1393 - 0.3517t$ $y(t) = 46.0226 + 0.4943t$	July 1, 1886
II	$x(t) = 84.6391 + 0.2545t$ $y(t) = 54.4277 + 1.1374t$	July 1, 1907
III	$x(t) = 86.4578 + 0.9287t$ $y(t) = 51.2028 - 0.4389t$	Jan. 1, 1923

* Consumption taken as equal to production. See text.

† I = 1879–95; II = 1896–1914; III = 1915–29 (excl. 1917–21).

‡ The price series are the same in both Parts A and B of this table. The differences in the averages are due only to the different lengths of the first two periods.

§ I = 1879–92; II = 1899–1914; III = 1915–29 (excl. 1917–21).

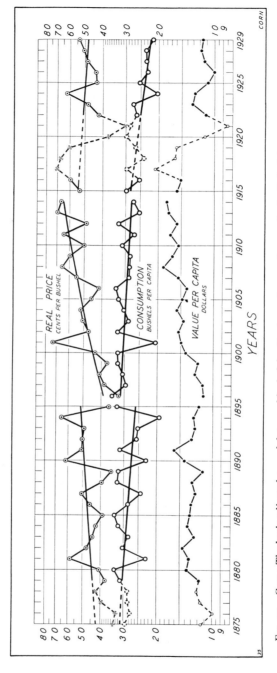

FIG. 35.—Corn: The basic adjusted annual data used in deriving the demand curves for corn in the United States, 1875–1929, with the computed trends by periods of the real prices and the per capita consumption. The dotted observations are those which were not used in the computations.

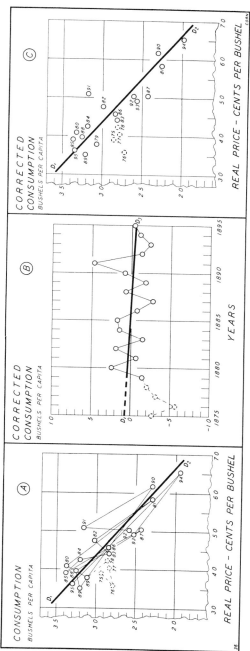

Fig. 36.—Corn: Three aspects of the per capita demand for corn during the period 1875–95 on the assumption that

$$x = 49.25 - 0.4398y - 0.0611t.$$

A: Relation between per capita consumption and real price when the data are not corrected for the effects of "time," with the demand curve D_1D_2 which results when such correction is made.

B: Relation between per capita consumption and time when the former is corrected for the effects of changes in the real price. The slope of line D_1D_3 (fitted to the variables x and t when both are corrected for price) represents the mean rate of shift of the per capita demand curve D_1D_2.

C: The per capita demand curve for corn, 1875–95. Line D_1D_2 shows the relation between that part of the per capita consumption of corn in the United States which is independent of time and that part of the real price which is independent of time. In the scatter, however, only the ordinate is corrected for secular changes, the abscissa being uncorrected.

247

two series is −0.89. From the chart we see that most of the lines connecting the earlier observations are negatively inclined and that their slopes are on the average just about as steep as that of the entire scatter. (The dotted circles show the observations not included in the computations.)

In Figure 36A, line D_1D_2 is the *net* regression of consumption on price. It gives the relation between that part of the per capita consumption which is linearly independent of time and that part of the real price which is linearly independent of time. It is a good approximation to the demand curve for corn.

To determine whether and how far we can reduce the scatter about the demand curve D_1D_2 by assuming that it has shifted its position from year to year, we take the differences between the computed and the observed consumption (i.e., the vertical deviations) and plot them as a function of time. The results are shown in Figure 36B. To these deviations there has been fitted the straight line D_1D_3. The slope of this line is slightly downward. It shows that the demand curve has, on the average, shifted downward during the period in question, but this slope is not significant, as it is exceeded by its standard error (see eq. 1 of Table 11 of which Fig. 36 is a graphic representation). When allowance is made for this slight downward shift, we obtain the reduced scatter of Figure 36C. In this particular example, the use of the additional variable time has brought about no significant improvement in the results.

Figure 37 corresponds to Figure 36, except that it relates to the logarithms of consumption and price instead of the actual figures, and is a graphical representation of the fourth equation[23] of Table 11. Had this equation been drawn to the actual data as in Figure 36, the line $D_1'D_2'$ would have appeared as a curve of constant elasticity, and the line $D_1'D_3'$ would have curved slightly upward.

Figure 38 shows different aspects of the three diagrams in Figures 36 and 37. The plane is a graphic representation of the first equation of Table 11, and the curved surface that of the fourth equation.

In Figure 38 each observation is shown in three dimensions. (The significance of the black and the white circles will be explained later.) For example, the first observation shows that in 1875 the price was thirty-nine cents a bushel and the consumption was twenty-nine bushels.

The orthogonal projections of the observations (circles) on the vertical plane XOT give the fluctuations in the per capita consumption of corn which were shown in Figure 35. The corresponding projections on the horizontal plane YOT give the fluctuations in the real price of corn, which were also shown in Figure 35. The corresponding projections on the vertical plane erected at the

[23] More correctly, of the antilogarithms of the fourth equation.

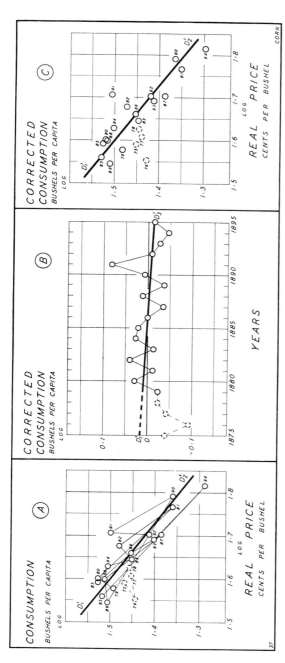

FIG. 37.—Corn: Three aspects of the per capita demand for corn during the period 1875–95 on the assumption that

$$x = 550.1 \ y^{-0.7749} e^{-0.0032t}.$$

A: Relation between per capita consumption and real price when the data are not corrected for the effects of "time," with the demand curve $D_1' D_2'$ which results when no correction is made.

B: Relation between per capita consumption and time when the former is corrected for the effects of changes in the real price. The slope of line $D_1' D_3'$ (fitted to the variables x' and t when both are corrected for price) represents the mean rate of shift of the per capita demand curve $D_1' D_2'$.

C: The per capita demand curve for corn, 1875–95. Line $D_1' D_2'$ shows the relation between that part of the per capita consumption of corn in the United States which is independent of time and that part of the real price which is independent of time. In the scatter, however, only the ordinate is corrected for secular changes, the abscissa being uncorrected.

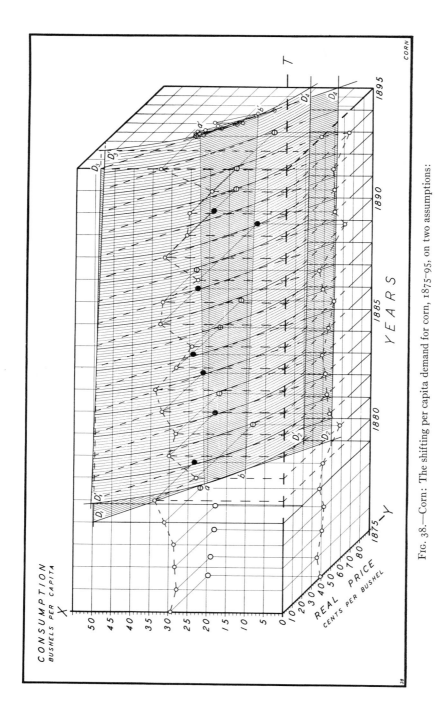

Fig. 38.—Corn: The shifting per capita demand for corn, 1875–95, on two assumptions:

$$x = 49.25 - 0.4398y - 0.0611t,$$

$$x = 550.1\, y^{-0.7749} e^{-0.0032t}.$$

The heavy straight lines on this surface represent the successive annual demand curves for corn

● = Actual observations above the surface
⊖ = Actual observations below the surface
○ = Projections perpendicular to the vertical plane, XOT, and the horizontal plane, YOT
⊕ = Points falling between the two surfaces

last year, 1895, give the scatter diagram of consumption on price, which was shown in Figure 36A.

The plane $D_1D_2D_3D_4$ (which will be designated henceforth as D_1D_4) is the demand surface which was fitted to the observations. (The curved plane $D_1'D_4'$ will be explained later.) This plane may be looked upon as formed by the shifting of the demand line D_1D_2 to the right. The observations which lie above both planes are represented by black circles; those which lie below both planes are represented by single-barred circles ($\ominus$); and those falling between the two planes are represented by double-barred circles ($\oplus$).

The equation of the plane D_1D_4 (see eq. 1, Table 11) tells us that, during the period 1879–95, an increase of 1 cent in the real price of corn, *other things being equal*, was associated with a decrease of 0.44 bushel in the per capita consumption, for

(4.1) $$\frac{\partial x}{\partial y} = -0.4398 .$$

This relation is indicated by the slope of the demand curve D_1D_2. It is this demand curve which is shown in Figures 36A and 36C.

But other things did not remain equal. The per capita consumption kept on decreasing at the average rate of 0.06 bushel per annum, for

(4.2) $$\frac{\partial x}{\partial t} = -0.0611 .$$

This rate of shift of the demand (which, however, is not significantly different from zero) is shown either by the slope of the line D_1D_3 of Figure 36B or by that of the line D_1D_3 or D_2D_4 of Figure 38.

As we have already explained in chapter vi, we are now in a better position to understand the geometrical significance of Figures 36B and 36C. Suppose that in Figure 38 the curved surface did not exist. Then suppose that the entire diagram, including the planes of reference, had been tilted backward about the axis OT until the edge D_2D_4 coincided with the edge D_1D_3 (on our line of vision). Figure 36B shows in a general way how the points and the plane would then appear.

Suppose next that—the curved surface still assumed to be out of the picture —we had taken a side view of the entire diagram. More definitely, suppose that we had tilted the diagram slightly forward about the axis OY until the line D_1D_2 coincided with line D_3D_4. Figure 36C gives approximately this aspect.

As can be seen from the descriptive constants of Table 11, the fit of the plane D_1D_4 to the observations is quite good. The quadratic mean error is only ± 2.09 bushels, which means that approximately two-thirds of the observations (points) fall within a distance of 2.09 bushels above and below the plane. The coefficient of multiple correlation, adjusted for the number of parameters in the equation, is 0.8817.

The partial elasticity of demand deduced from the first equation of Table 11 is

$$(4.3) \qquad \eta_{xy \cdot t} = \frac{\partial x}{\partial y} \cdot \frac{y}{x} = -0.4398 \frac{y}{x}.$$

It is clear that it varies from point to point on the demand curve. Though the variable t (time) does not enter into this equation, it must be used nevertheless (together with y) to compute the value of x from equation 1, Table 11. It would be wrong to use the observed instead of the computed value of the dependent variable, for the reason that the coefficient of the elasticity of demand *must relate to a point on the demand curve*, and the observed values of x do not generally lie on the curve.

The following example will illustrate the procedure for computing the elasticity of demand by (4.3). Taking the mean of t ($t = 0$ at 1887) and the mean of y ($\bar{y} = 46.7689$), and substituting these values in equation 1, Table 11, we obtain the theoretical per capita consumption of 28.6764 ($= \bar{x}$, the mean of x, since the equation is linear). Substituting these values of x and y in (4.3), we obtain

$$(4.4) \qquad \eta_{xy \cdot t} = -0.7173 \, .$$

This means that, if the real price which prevailed in 1887 had been decreased (or increased) by 1 per cent, and *if the demand curve had remained fixed for one year*, there would have been an increase (or a decrease) of 0.72 of 1 per cent in the annual per capita consumption.

The curved surface $D_1' D_4'$ (Fig. 38) is a graphic representation of the demand function which is shown (in logarithmic form) in the fourth equation of Table 11.

This equation gives directly the elasticity of demand, for

$$(4.5) \qquad \eta_{xy \cdot t} = \frac{\partial x}{\partial y} \cdot \frac{y}{x} = \frac{\partial x'}{\partial y'} = -0.7749 \, .$$

The fourth equation of Table 11 also tells us that, when the real price of corn is held constant, the per capita consumption decreases at the momentary rate of shift of 0.32 per cent per annum, for

$$(4.6) \qquad \frac{1}{x} \cdot \frac{\partial x}{\partial t} = \frac{\partial \log_e x}{\partial t} = -0.0032 \, .$$

This is shown graphically (on a natural scale) by the slope of the curve $D_1'D_3'$, or by that of the curve $D_2'D_4'$. But this rate of decrease is not statistically significant because it is exceeded by its standard error. We cannot assert, therefore, that the demand curve has on the average shifted either downward or upward during the period from 1879 to 1895.

A glance at Figure 38 shows that the curved surface $D_1'D_4'$ intersects the plane D_1D_4 twice: along the curve aa', as it dips below the plane, and along the curve bb', as it emerges from under it. Unlike the plane D_1D_4, the curved surface $D_1'D_4'$ does not cut the vertical plane of reference XOT but is asymptotic to it. However, in order better to show its relation to the plane, it was terminated at $D_1'D_3'$, which gives the consumption (x) for each year on the assumption that the price is kept constant at $y = 20$ cents.

Figure 38 also shows that within the range of variation of the data, there is no appreciable difference between the constant-elasticity demand curve $D_1'D_2'$ and the straight-line demand curve D_1D_2.

B. THE SECOND PERIOD, 1896–1914

The analysis for the second period is similar to that for the first. Figures 39, 40, and 41 relate to the second period and correspond, respectively, to Figures 36, 37, and 38 of the first period. These are, respectively, the graphic representations of the second and fifth equations of Table 11. From the second term in the first of these equations, we see that during 1896–1914 an increase of 1 cent in the real price of corn was associated with a decrease in consumption of 0.35 bushel, for

$$(4.7) \qquad \frac{\partial x}{\partial y} = -0.3468 .$$

This is the slope of the demand curve D_1D_2 (Fig. 39).

From the second term of the fifth equation we see that the elasticity of demand for corn is approximately -0.70, for

$$(4.8) \qquad \eta_{xy \cdot t} = \frac{\partial x}{\partial y} \cdot \frac{y}{x} = \frac{\partial x'}{\partial y'} = -0.6982 .$$

This is the *relative* change in the slope of the demand curve $D_1'D_2'$ (Fig. 41). It would be the actual value of the slope, if the logarithms of the data were plotted (as in Fig. 40) rather than the absolute figures.

A study of Figures 39B and 40B shows that during this period the demand curve shifted upward and to the right but at a varying rate.

The measure of the shift of D_1D_2 may be obtained by fixing y in the second equation of Table 11. Thus, if we put $y = 0$, we obtain the equation of the

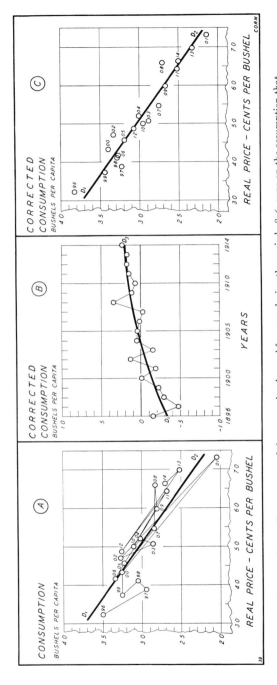

FIG. 39.—Corn: Three aspects of the per capita demand for corn during the period 1896–1914 on the assumption that

$$x = 48.07 - 0.3468y + 0.2929t - 0.0124t^2.$$

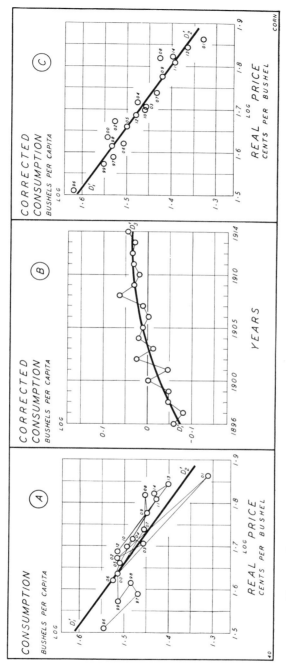

Fig. 40.—Corn: Three aspects of the per capita demand for corn during the period 1896–1914 on the assumption that

$$x = 468.8 \; y^{-0.6982} \; e^{0.01401t - 0.0009t^2}$$

255

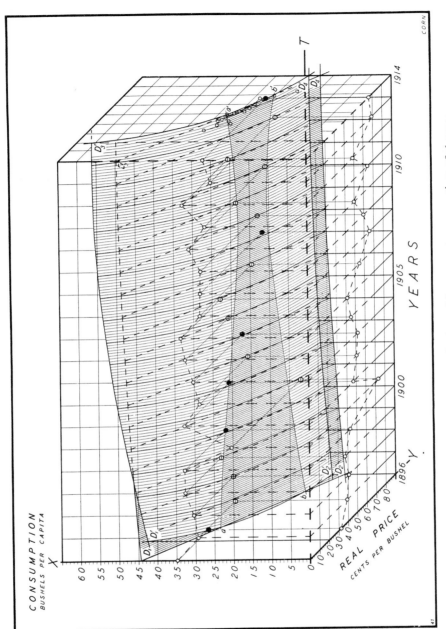

FIG. 41.—Corn: The shifting per capita demand for corn on two assumptions, 1896–1914:

$$x = 48.07 - 0.3468y + 0.2929t - 0.0124t^2,$$

and

$$x = 468.8 \ y^{-0.6982} e^{0.0140t - 0.0009t^2}.$$

curve D_1D_3. Similarly, if we put $y = 90$, we obtain the equation of the curve D_2D_4.[24]

In the same way the measure of shift of the demand curve $D_1'D_2'$ may be obtained by fixing y in the antilogarithm of the fifth equation of Table 11. Thus, by putting $y = 0$ we obtain the equation of the curve $D_1'D_3'$, and by putting $y = 90$ we obtain the equation of the curve $D_2'D_4'$.

From the second equation of Table 11 we obtain the rate of shift of the demand curve D_1D_2 in *absolute* terms. It is

$$(4.9) \qquad \frac{\partial x}{\partial t} = 0.2929 - 2(0.0124)t,$$

which shows that every year the curve shifted upward by 0.29 bushel but that this shift was subject to an annual retardation of 0.02 bushel.

From the antilogarithm of the fifth equation of Table 11 we obtain the *relative* rate of shift of the demand curve $D_1'D_2'$. It is

$$(4.10) \qquad \frac{1}{x} \cdot \frac{\partial x}{\partial t} = \frac{1}{M} \cdot \frac{\partial x'}{\partial t} = 0.0140 - 2(0.0009)t,$$

which means that the demand curve kept shifting upward at the average rate of 1.4 per cent per annum. However, this rate was not constant. It was subject to a retardation effect of 0.18 per cent per annum.

C. THE THIRD PERIOD, 1915–29

Figures 42, 43, and 44 give the corresponding information for the third period. The two surfaces of Figure 44 are a graphic representation of the third and sixth equations of Table 11.[25] The dotted circles in Figures 42 and 43 and the unshaded area in Figure 44 show the observations which were not included in the computations.

From these equations it is clear that during the third period important changes took place both in the elasticity of demand and in the rate of shift of the demand curve. The numerical value of the former decreased to 0.49, and the value of the latter dropped from an increasing rate of approximately 1.4 per cent per annum to a *decreasing* rate of 2.1 per cent. The change in elasticity may not be statistically significant, since the standard errors of these coefficients are relatively large. But there can be no reasonable doubt about the significance of the change in the rate of shift of the demand curve.

[24] The constant term in the equation of D_1D_3 in Fig. 39B was obtained by giving y its mean value.

[25] Or, rather, of the antilogarithm of the sixth equation.

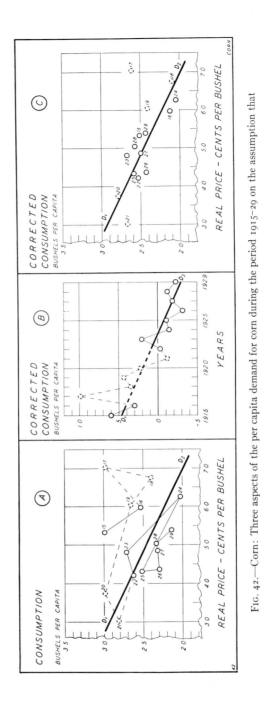

Fig. 42.—Corn: Three aspects of the per capita demand for corn during the period 1915–29 on the assumption that

$$x = 37.17 - 0.2348y - 0.5377t.$$

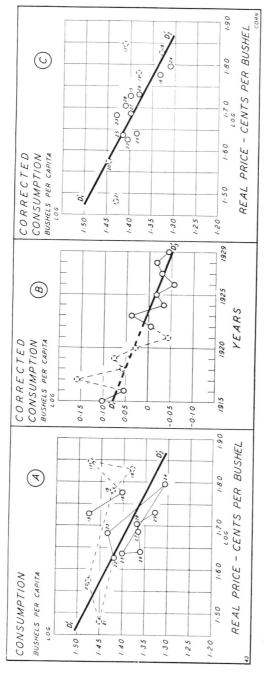

FIG. 43.—Corn: Three aspects of the per capita demand for corn during the period 1915–29 (excluding 1917–21) on the assumption that

$$x = 172.8y^{-0.4924}e^{-0.0213t}.$$

259

TABLE 11

CORN: DEMAND PER CAPITA: THE CHARACTERISTICS

x = Per capita consumption in bushels

y = Deflated December 1 farm price in cents per bushel

(Figures in parentheses are standard errors)

EQUATION No.	PERIOD*		Constant Term	y	t	t^2
					EQUATIONS	
1	I	$x=$	49.2472	−0.4398 (0.0614)	−0.0611 (0.1074)	....
2	II	$x=$	48.0692	−0.3468 (0.0322)	+0.2929 (0.0711)	−0.0124 (0.0109)
3	III	$x=$	37.1718	−0.2348 (0.0732)	−0.5377 (0.1062)	....
			Constant Term	y'	$†Mt$	$†Mt^2$
4	I	$x'=$	2.7404	−0.7749 (0.1100)	−0.0032 (0.0040)	....
5	II	$x'=$	2.6710	−0.6982 (0.0663)	+0.0140 (0.0027)	−0.0009 (0.0004)
6	III	$x'=$	2.2375	−0.4924 (0.1563)	−0.0213 (0.0044)	....
			Constant Term	x	t	t^2
7	I	$y=$	98.0099	−1.7868 (0.2492)	−0.0103 (0.2190)	....
8	II	$y=$	127.9152	−2.5241 (0.2459)	+0.9151 (0.1504)	−0.0358 (0.0292)
9	III	$y=$	114.9686	−2.5354 (0.7902)	−1.5410 (0.4782)	....
			Constant Term	x'	$†Mt$	$†Mt^2$
10	I	$y'=$	3.1241	−1.0066 (0.1429)	−0.0012 (0.0047)	....
11	II	$y'=$	3.5746	−1.2616 (0.1198)	+0.0210 (0.0026)	−0.0013 (0.0005)
12	III	$y'=$	3.3697	−1.1907 (0.3780)	−0.0287 (0.0092)	....

* I = 1879–95; II = 1896–1914; III = 1915–29 (excl. 1917–21).

TABLE 11—*Continued*

OF THE DEMAND FUNCTIONS, BY PERIODS, 1879–1929

t = Time in years. For origins see Table 10

x', y' = Logs of x, y

(Figures in parentheses are standard errors)

	DESCRIPTIVE CONSTANTS					EQUATION No.
	Elasticity of Demand η	Quadratic Mean Error ϵ (Bushels)	Adjusted Multiple Correlation Coefficient R'	Percentage of Variance of Consumption Attributable to		
				y	t	
....	−0.7173 (0.1853)	2.0931	0.8817	78.44	2.09	1
....	−0.5956 (0.1117)	1.2601	0.9305	104.21	−15.39	2
....	−0.4844 (0.2003)	1.4408	0.8649	16.59	63.82	3
	η	ϵ (Per Cent)	R'	y'	t	
....	−0.7749 (0.1100)	92.4–108.2	0.8793	77.10	3.05	4
....	−0.6982 (0.0663)	95.6–104.6	0.9318	106.79	−17.77	5
....	−0.4924 (0.1563)	94.2–106.2	0.8544	18.02	60.97	6
Flexibility of Price φ	Maximum Value of η $1/\varphi$	ϵ (Cents)	R'	Percentage of Variance of Price Attributable to		
				x	t	
−1.0956 (0.2928)	−0.9128	4.2189	0.8788	80.24	−0.16	7
−1.4220 (0.2678)	−0.7032	3.3996	0.9582	63.56	29.63	8
−1.2289 (0.5436)	−0.8138	4.7348	0.7261	31.13	32.10	9
φ	$1/\varphi$	ϵ (Per Cent)	R'	x'	t	
−1.0066 (0.1429)	−0.9935	91.4–109.4	0.8741	80.19	−0.83	10
−1.2616 (0.1198)	−0.7927	94.1–106.3	0.9649	55.92	38.34	11
−1.1907 (0.3780)	−0.8398	91.1–109.8	0.7169	32.44	29.75	12

† M = $\log_{10}e$ = 0.43429.

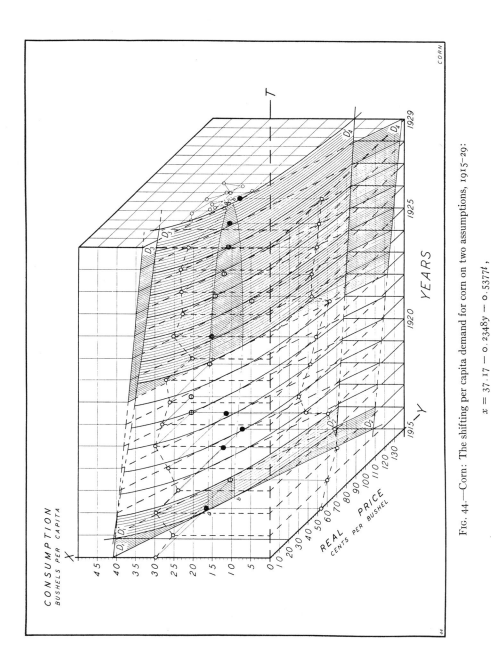

Fig. 44.—Corn: The shifting per capita demand for corn on two assumptions, 1915–29:

$$x = 37.17 - 0.2348y - 0.5377t,$$

and

$$x = 172.8\, y^{-0.4924} e^{-0.0213t}.$$

D. SUMMARY OF CHANGES IN THE DEMAND FOR CORN, 1879–1929

Table 11 gives a bird's-eye view of the more important changes which have taken place in the demand for corn from 1879 to 1929.

From the coefficients of y in the first three equations we see that an increase of 1 (deflated) cent in the price per bushel of corn brought about a decrease in the per capita consumption of 0.44 bushel in the first period, 0.35 bushel in the second, and 0.23 bushel in the third. These absolute changes can also be converted into relative changes or elasticities by multiplying each of them by y/x. Substituting for y and x their representative values,[26] we obtain in each of the three periods the following elasticities of demand: −0.72, −0.60, and −0.48, respectively. It is these figures which are given (to four significant figures) in the column headed "Elasticity of Demand."

From the coefficients of t in the same three equations we also see that, whereas during the first period the demand curve maintained an approximately constant height, during the second period it shifted upward at the average rate of 0.29 bushel per capita per annum, which shift was, however, subject to an annual retardation of 0.02 bushel per capita. During the third period, however, the demand curve began a precipitous downward shift at the remarkably high rate of 0.54 bushel per capita per annum.

The fact that the demand curve for corn was shifting downward with time means that, while it is still true that in any one year a decrease in price brought about an increase in per capita consumption, producers of corn would have been faced with a decrease in the per capita consumption even if prices had remained fixed. This fact is of capital importance to the farmers of the Corn Belt, for there is reason to believe that the downward shift of the demand curve has not yet been stopped.

The second triad of equations represents the demand for corn directly in terms of relative changes. Thus the coefficients of y' ($= \log y$) show that the elasticities of demand for the three periods were: −0.77, −0.70, −0.49, respectively. These agree fairly well with the corresponding values obtained from the first three equations.

The coefficients of t give the *relative* rates of shift of the demand curve. Thus, if we multiply each of them by 100, we find that during the first period the demand curve shifted downward by 0.32 per cent per annum, but this figure is not statistically significant. During the second period, however, the rate of shift jumped to 1.40 per cent per annum but was subject to a retardation effect of 0.18 per cent per annum. During the third period the rate became negative, amounting to −2.13 per cent per annum.

---

[26] As explained in chap. vi (III, D, 2, b), the representative value of y is taken as the arithmetic mean, and the representative value of x is obtained by substituting the mean values of the independent variables in the demand equation.

The fit of the demand surface to the data is very good. The scatters of the observations about the surface, measured by the quadratic mean error, were fairly small, fluctuating within approximately 8 per cent of the computed values for the first period, within 5 per cent of those for the second, and within 6 per cent of those for the third.

The coefficient of multiple correlation adjusted for the number of parameters in the demand functions were quite high, the lowest being 0.85 (third period), and the highest 0.93 (second period).

The fluctuations in the price of corn account for most of the variance in the per capita consumption of the first and second periods, but for only 17 per cent of the variance of the consumption during the third period, the variable "time" playing a predominant role in this period.

V. DEMAND FUNCTIONS WITH THE DEFLATED PRICE AS THE DEPENDENT VARIABLE

In all the preceding analyses the per capita consumption (=production) of corn was taken as the dependent variable. That is, we assumed that the independent variables—price and time—are quite accurately known, and we used them to explain the fluctuations in the dependent variable. As we pointed out in chapter iv, there is good reason for this assumption, for the statistics of prices are subject to less error than those of consumption. It is, nevertheless, also instructive to consider price as the dependent variable and see to what extent it is affected by fluctuations in consumption and by such other factors as are reflected in the variable time. Later, we shall also take into consideration the effects of industrial production and trade, of changes in the count of livestock, and of past prices.

We turn to the lower part of Table 11. The equations in this part give the regressions of price on consumption and time. Equations 7–9 are the arithmetic regressions; equations 10–12 are the corresponding logarithmic regressions.

The coefficients of x in equations 7–9 mean that an increase in the per capita consumption of one bushel was associated with a decrease in the deflated price of 1.79 cents in the first period, 2.52 cents in the second, and 2.54 cents in the third.

From the coefficients of t and t^2 in the same equations we see that although during the first period the demand curve maintained an approximately constant height—the slight downward shift of 0.01 cent per annum was negligible —during the second period it began shifting upward at the rate of 0.92 cent per annum but was subject to an annual retardation of 7 cents. During the third period, however, it changed its direction to a downward shift of 1.54 cents per annum. In other words, whereas during the period 1896–1914 a constant per capita production (= consumption) was associated with an average *increase* in the purchasing power of a bushel of corn of nearly 1 cent per annum, during the period 1915–29 the same conditions of production were associated with a *decrease* in the purchasing power of a bushel of corn of 1.54 cents per annum.

Equations 10–12 express the same relations in relative terms. Thus, the coefficients of x' give the price flexibilities or the relative change in the price of corn brought about by the relative change in the quantity in each of the three periods. (These figures are repeated in the column headed "Flexibility of Prices.") They show that during the first period an increase of 1 per cent in production (= consumption) was associated with a decrease in price of substantially the same percentage; that during the second period the corresponding decrease was 1.26 per cent, and during the third period it was 1.19 per cent.

The coefficients of t and t^2 in the same equations show that during the first period the demand curve remained fixed at a practically constant level; that during the second period it shifted upward at the rate of 2.10 per cent per annum but that this rate was subject to an annual retardation effect of 0.26 per cent; and that during the third period the curve began shifting downward, maintaining a rate of −2.87 per cent per annum.

Equations 10–12 of Table 11 are also illustrated graphically in Figures 45, 46, and 47. Since the graphs of the corresponding arithmetic regressions are very similar to these, they will not be reproduced. An examination of these diagrams and Table 11 discloses the following interesting facts:

1. The net regressions of price on time are roughly similar to those of consumption on time. Thus during the first period (Fig. 45B) the slope of the line $d'_1 d'_3$ is practically zero; during the second period (Fig. 46B) it increases at a decreasing rate as in Figure 40; and during the third period (Fig. 47B) it exhibits a pronounced negative slope as in Figure 43.

2. The reciprocals of the price flexibilities, which should give the corresponding maximum numerical values of the elasticities of demand, are all numerically less than unity, thus conforming in a general way to the results derived from the equations in which quantity (consumption) is the dependent variable, namely, *that the demand for corn is inelastic.*

3. The fit of these equations is in general just as good as that of equations 1–6, the quadratic mean error lying between 6 and 10 per cent of the computed surfaces.

4. Of the fluctuations in the price of corn as measured by its variance, the changes in consumption (= production) were responsible for 80 per cent during the first period, for 64 per cent during the second, and for only 31 per cent in the third. Evidently the factors other than consumption which influenced the price of corn have played an increasingly important role since the 1890's.

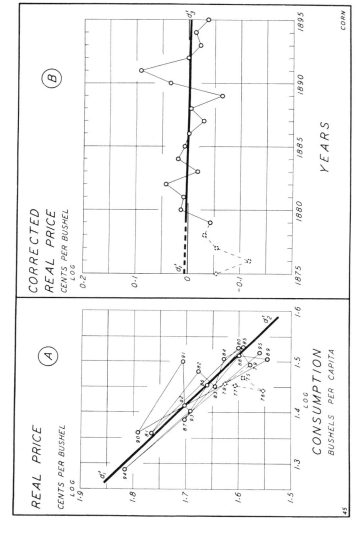

45

Fig. 45.—Corn: Two aspects of the per capita demand for corn during the period 1875–95 on the assumption

that

$$y = 1330.88\ x^{-1.0066}e^{-0.0012t}\ .$$

266

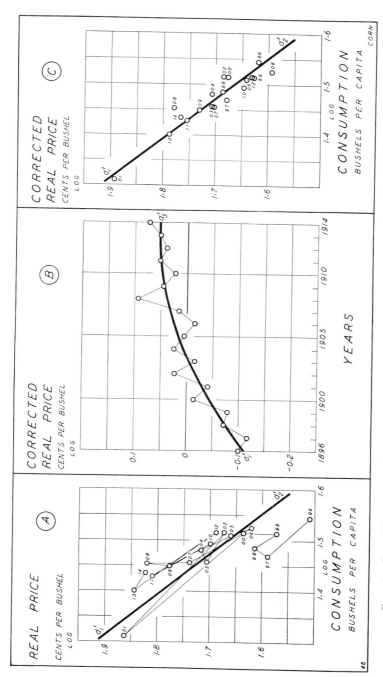

Fig. 46.—Corn: Three aspects of the per capita demand for corn during the period 1896–1914 on the assumption that

$$y = 3755.30 \; x^{-1.2616} e^{0.0210t - 0.0013t^2}.$$

267

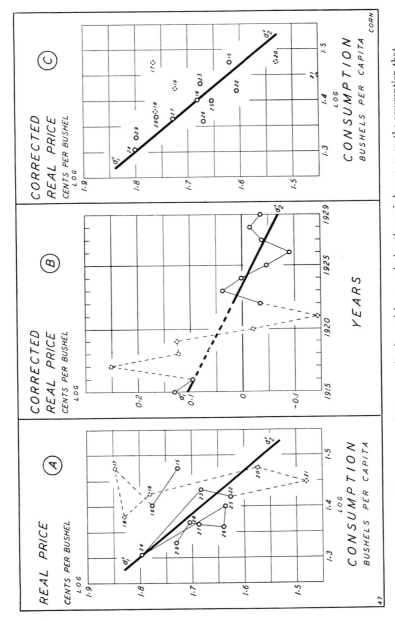

Fig. 47.—Corn: Three aspects of the per capita demand for corn during the period 1915–29 on the assumption that

$$y = 2342.80 \ x^{-1.1907} \ e^{-0.0287t}.$$

VI. EFFECT OF CHANGES IN BUSINESS CONDITIONS ON THE DEMAND AND PRICE OF CORN

The comparatively large role which time plays in our equations suggests the hypothesis that it is the resultant of two important factors which we have hitherto neglected, namely, the effect of business conditions and the number of domestic animals receiving corn and the amount of corn received during their lifetime. We are now ready to consider these hypotheses.

For reasons stated in chapter vi, we shall take for our measure of changes in business conditions Warren M. Persons' "Index of Industrial Production and Trade" (w) and introduce it into our demand equations. Table 12, which relates only to the logarithmic series, is a summary of the results obtained.

A glance at the coefficients of w' shows that they are all exceeded by their standard errors except those for the second period; and, of these, the regression of x' on y' is not significant. By introducing the variable w', we lower the value of the adjusted multiple correlation coefficient during the first and third periods (cf. Tables 11 and 12). The percentage of the variance of the dependent variable which is reduced as a result of the introduction of w' is negligible for the first and second periods. For the third period its value is fairly large but negative. The negative sign (-10.61 per cent) is due to the inclusion of the indirect effect of w' through its correlation with y' and t. Its direct effect, which is only 3.7 per cent, is not significant.

It appears, therefore, that changes in business conditions have no measurable effect on the demand for, or the price of, corn except possibly during the second period. But even for that period an improvement in business conditions is associated with a *decrease* in the price of, and in the demand for, corn, which is contrary to expectations. The results are, therefore, just as disappointing as those which we have already encountered in our analysis of the demand for sugar.[27]

VII. EFFECT OF CHANGES IN LIVESTOCK POPULATION ON THE DEMAND AND PRICE OF CORN

Since business conditions have no measurable effect on the demand for corn, and, since the most important determining factor in the amount of corn consumed is the size of the livestock population, it is desirable to see whether the introduction of this variable will reduce the importance of the time variable. We shall do this in two ways: (1) by reducing the total consumption (=production) to an animal unit basis and expressing the resulting variable as a function of price and time and (2) by treating total production as the dependent variable and expressing it as a function of the number of animal units as well as of price and of time.

Table 13 is a summary of the results obtained by the former method. It corresponds to Table 11 except for the substitution of consumption per animal

[27] See chap. vi, III, E.

TABLE 12

CORN: EFFECT OF CHANGES IN BUSINESS CONDITIONS ON THE PER CAPITA

x = Per capita consumption in bushels
y = Deflated December 1 farm price in cents per bushel
t = Time in years. For origins see Table 10

(Figures in parentheses are standard errors)

EQUA-TION No.	PERIOD*		Constant Term	y'	w'	$†Mt$	$†Mt^2$
1	I	$x' =$	2.4400	−0.7843 (0.1123)	+0.1574 (0.2054)	−0.0026 (0.0042)	. . . .
2	II	$x' =$	3.2653	−0.7168 (0.0662)	−0.2798 (0.2102)	+0.0150 (0.0027)	−0.0013 (0.0005)
3	III	$x' =$	3.0341	−0.5187 (0.1679)	−0.3718 (0.5647)	−0.0251 (0.0075)	. . . .
			Constant Term	x'	w'	$†Mt$	$†Mt^2$
4	I	$y' =$	2.7215	−1.0066 (0.1441)	+0.2005 (0.2313)	−0.0005 (0.0048)	. . . .
5	II	$y' =$	4.3970	−1.2463 (0.1151)	−0.4205 (0.2718)	+0.0220 (0.0026)	−0.0019 (0.0006)
6	III	$y' =$	4.8733	−1.1840 (0.3832)	−0.7483 (0.8291)	−0.0359 (0.0123)	. . . .

* I = 1879–95; II = 1896–1914; III = 1915–29 (excl. 1917–21).

TABLE 12—*Continued*

DEMAND: THE CHARACTERISTICS OF THE DEMAND FUNCTIONS, BY PERIODS, 1879–1929

w = W. M. Persons' "Index of Industrial Production
and Trade," adjusted, weighted. Normal = 100

x', y', w' = Logs of x, y, w

(Figures in parentheses are standard errors)

				DESCRIPTIVE CONSTANTS			
	Elasticity of Demand η	Quadratic Mean Error ϵ (Per Cent)	Adjusted Multiple Correlation Coefficient R'	Percentage of Variance of Consumption Attributable to			EQUA-TION No.
				y'	w'	t	
. . . .	−0.7843 (0.1123)	92.3–108.3	0.8754	78.04	0.54	2.44	1
. . . .	−0.7168 (0.0662)	95.7–104.5	0.9353	109.65	− 0.25	−19.14	2
. . . .	−0.5187 (0.1679)	93.9–106.5	0.8404	18.98	−10.61	72.04	3
Flexibility of Price φ	Maximum Value of η $1/\varphi$	ϵ (Per Cent)	R'	Percentage of Variance of Price Attributable to			
				x'	w'	t	
−1.0066 (0.1441)	−0.9934	91.4–109.5	0.8717	80.19	0.64	− 0.35	4
−1.2463 (0.1151)	−0.8024	94.4–106.0	0.9679	55.24	− 1.11	40.96	5
−1.1840 (0.3832)	−0.8446	90.9–110.0	0.7076	32.26	− 2.76	37.21	6

† $M = \log_{10} e = 0.43429$.

TABLE 13

CORN: DEMAND PER ANIMAL UNIT: THE CHARACTERISTICS

x = Consumption per animal unit in bushels
y = Deflated December 1 farm price in cents per bushel

(Figures in parentheses are standard errors)

EQUA-TION No.	PERIOD*		EQUATIONS			
			Constant Term	y	t	t^2
1	I	$x=$	114.8605	-1.0152 (0.1750)	$+0.1501$ (0.3241)	....
2	II	$x=$	135.8499	-0.9409 (0.1116)	$+1.0956$ (0.2545)	....
3	III	$x=$	124.9252	-0.8431 (0.2499)	$+0.6706$ (0.3403)	$+0.2015$ (0.0863)
			Constant Term	y'	$\dagger Mt$	$\dagger Mt^2$
4	I	$x'=$	3.0583	-0.7415 (0.1273)	$+0.0032$ (0.0050)	....
5	II	$x'=$	3.0686	-0.6621 (0.0838)	$+0.0158$ (0.0035)	....
6	III	$x'=$	2.7895	-0.5161 (0.1541)	$+0.0079$ (0.0040)	$+0.0026$ (0.0010)
			Constant Term	x	t	t^2
7	I	$y=$	96.6124	-0.7424 (0.1280)	$+0.2331$ (0.2709)	....
8	II	$y=$	130.4745	-0.8985 (0.1066)	$+1.1602$ (0.2156)	....
9	III	$y=$	113.7404	-0.7768 (0.2202)	$+0.3924$ (0.3874)	$+0.1979$ (0.0811)
			Constant Term	x'	$\dagger Mt$	$\dagger Mt^2$
10	I	$y'=$	3.5199	-1.0183 (0.1749)	$+0.0059$ (0.0057)	....
11	II	$y'=$	4.1337	-1.2501 (0.1582)	$+0.0236$ (0.0040)	....
12	III	$y'=$	4.1065	-1.2624 (0.3769)	$+0.0076$ (0.0074)	$+0.0041$ (0.0016)

* I = 1879–92; II = 1899–1914; III = 1915–29 (excl. 1917–21).

TABLE 13—*Continued*

OF THE DEMAND FUNCTIONS, BY PERIODS, 1879–1929

t = Time in years. For origins see Table 10

x', y' = Logs of x, y

(Figures in parentheses are standard errors)

	DESCRIPTIVE CONSTANTS					EQUA-TION No.
	Elasticity of Demand η	Quadratic Mean Error ϵ (Bushels)	Adjusted Multiple Correlation Coefficient R'	Percentage of Variance of Consumption Attributable to		
				y	t	
. . . .	−0.6857 (0.1964)	4.7112	0.8467	77.23	− 1.18	1
. . . .	−0.6050 (0.1310)	4.0683	0.9064	83.86	0.68	2
. . . .	−0.5087 (0.2007)	4.6136	0.8174	48.32	29.56	3
	η	ϵ (Per Cent)	R'	y'	t	
. . . .	−0.7415 (0.1273)	93.0–107.6	0.8466	77.46	− 1.43	4
. . . .	−0.6621 (0.0838)	94.6–105.7	0.8953	80.19	2.61	5
. . . .	−0.5161 (0.1541)	94.7–105.6	0.8134	47.35	30.09	6
Flexibility of Price φ	Maximum Value of η $1/\varphi$	ϵ (Cents)	R'	Percentage of Variance of Price Attributable to		
				x	t	
−1.0992 (0.3239)	−0.9097	4.0290	0.8542	73.77	3.36	7
−1.3972 (0.3075)	−0.7157	3.9755	0.9306	63.02	25.37	8
−1.4664 (0.5974)	−0.6820	4.4284	0.7658	60.22	12.21	9
φ	$1/\varphi$	ϵ (Per Cent)	R'	x'	t	
−1.0183 (0.1749)	−0.9821	91.8–108.9	0.8557	73.24	4.10	10
−1.2501 (0.1582)	−0.7999	92.7–107.8	0.9258	57.79	29.82	11
−1.2624 (0.3769)	−0.7921	91.7–108.9	0.7708	56.79	16.15	12

† M = log₁₀ e = 0.43429.

unit for consumption per capita. A comparison of the two tables brings out the following interesting facts:

1. Whereas in the third period the per capita demand curves (Table 11) shifted downward, the corresponding animal-unit demand curves of the same period (Table 13) shifted upward (cf. the change in the signs of the coefficients of t and t^2 for the third period in these tables). Perhaps the explanation of the positive shift of the animal-unit demand curves is to be found in the increase of corn consumption by cattle, which has been going on for years and which cannot be conveniently measured statistically. As Professor G. S. Shepherd tells us:

> The continued westward movement of agricultural settlement after 1866 cut into the western range areas, and shifted the emphasis from grass feeding on the western ranges to grain feeding in the feedlots of the Corn Belt. The 4 or 5-year-old Texas long-horn range steer was gradually displaced by Corn Belt baby beeves and 2-year-olds. This shift in emphasis meant that as the westward movement progressed, more corn was required per head of beef cattle. The cattle demand for corn therefore increased faster than the increase in the numbers of cattle on farms.[28]

2. Turning now to a comparison of the goodness of fit of the curves of the two tables, we find that with one significant exception, all the R'''s of Table 13 are lower than the corresponding R'''s of Table 11. That is, the equations of Table 13 give a somewhat worse fit than those of Table 11.

3. As judged by the percentage of the variance of the dependent variables which is attributable to time, the use of animal units as a deflator gives no better results than that obtained with population.[29]

Could the results be improved by treating the number of animal units as an independent variable? Table 14 enables us to test this hypothesis. A comparison of Tables 14 and 13 justifies the following observations:

1. As judged by the R'''s, the use of animal units as a separate independent variable results in a better fit of the curves to the data. With only two minor exceptions all the R'''s in Table 14 are higher than the corresponding R'''s of Table 13.

2. Apparently considerable percentages of variance of both total production (x) and deflated price (y) are attributable to the number of animal units (z). The figures given in the table include the direct as well as its joint contribution with the other independent variables to the variance of the dependent variable. When this variance is broken up into its components as is done in Table 15,[30] we find that the joint determination of z with y is negligible in all but the first period, and that of z with t is negligible in all but the first period, so that the total determination, as given in Table 14, masks the paths of influence. It can be safely asserted, however, that the introduction of the animal units did not diminish the importance of the time variable in the second period.

---

[28] *The Secular Movement of Corn Prices*, p. 197.   [29] A possible exception is the second period.

[30] The table relates only to the linear regressions. The results for the logarithmic (constant-elasticity) regressions are very similar.

VIII. CONCLUSIONS

Despite the paramount importance of the corn crop in our national economy, there have been but few mathematical investigations into the demand for corn.[31] In fact, even so comprehensive and informative a work as Taylor's *Corn and Hog Surplus of the Corn Belt* contains no statistical analysis of this important problem, the discussion being based largely "on accepted marketing experience."

The main findings of the present chapter center around the changes that have taken place in the shape, the elasticity, and the rate of shift of the demand curve for corn since 1879, and the factors which account for these changes.[32]

To repeat:

1. The net effect of a 1-cent rise in the (deflated) price per bushel of corn was to decrease the annual per capita consumption by 0.44 bushel in 1879–95, by 0.35 bushel in 1896–1914, and by 0.23 bushel in 1915–29 (omitting 1917–21). In terms of elasticities, the foregoing relations mean that the net effect of an increase of 1 per cent in price was to decrease consumption by approximately 0.8 per cent in the first period, by 0.7 per cent in the second, and by 0.5 per cent in the third. Since these coefficients of elasticity are all numerically less than unity, it follows that, in the observed range of crop variation, *a large crop was worth less than a small crop in each of the three periods.*

2. During the second and third periods, however, changes in the position (height) of the demand curve had a greater effect on consumption than did changes in price. *Even if price had been fixed, per capita consumption would not have been constant.* It would have increased by 0.29 bushel, or by 1.4 per cent per annum, in the second period (though this would have been subject to an annual retardation of 0.02 bushel or of 0.18 per cent); and it would have decreased by 0.54 bushel or by 2.13 per cent per annum in the third period.

[31] The pioneering study is that of Professor Henry L. Moore. See his *Economic Cycles: Their Law and Cause* (New York, 1914), chap. i. The more recent studies are: Henry A. Wallace, "Forecasting Corn and Hog Prices," constituting chap. xvii of W. M. Persons, W. T. Foster, and A. J. Hettinger, Jr., eds., *The Problem of Business Forecasting* (Boston, 1924); Sewall Wright, *Corn and Hog Correlations* (U.S.D.A. Bull. No. 1300 [January, 1925]); V. P. Timoshenko, "Correlations between Prices and Yields of Previous Years," *Journal of Political Economy*, XXXVI, No. 4 (1928), 510–15; G. F. Warren and F. A. Pearson, *Interrelationships of Supply and Price* (Cornell Agricultural Experiment Station Bull. No. 466 [Ithaca, 1928]), p. 51; G. S. Shepherd, *The Trend of Corn Prices* (Agricultural Experiment Station, Iowa State College of Agriculture and Mechanic Arts, Bull. No. 284 [Ames, Iowa, July, 1931]); and Geoffrey Shepherd and Walter W. Wilcox, *Stabilizing Corn Supplies by Storage* (*ibid.*, Bull. No. 368 [December, 1937]). Rex W. Cox, *Factors Influencing Corn Prices* (University of Minnesota Agricultural Experiment Station, University Farm, Tech. Bull. No. 81 [St. Paul, Minn., September, 1931]).

[32] The investigation into the effect on the demand for corn of changes in the prices of barley, hay, and oats has been postponed to Part III, which is devoted to a study of the general problem of related demands.

TABLE 14

CORN: TOTAL DEMAND: THE CHARACTERISTICS

x = Total Consumption in 100,000,000 bushels
y = Deflated December 1 Farm Price in cents per bushel
z = Animal units in millions

(Figures in parentheses are standard errors)

EQUA-TION No.	PERIOD*		Constant Term	y	z	t	t^2
				EQUATIONS			
1	I	$x=$	-1.3424	-0.2607 (0.0367)	$+1.2129$ (0.3900)	-0.2476 (0.2136)	. . . .
2	II	$x=$	34.6390	-0.2857 (0.0264)	$+0.2156$ (0.2166)	$+0.5622$ (0.1034)	. . . .
3	III	$x=$	26.9647	-0.2791 (0.0755)	$+0.4374$ (0.2031)	. . . .	$+0.0431$ (0.0279)
			Constant Term	y'	z'	$\dagger Mt$	$\dagger Mt^2$
4	I	$x'=$	0.6274	-0.7443 (0.1336)	$+1.3123$ (0.9814)	-0.0031 (0.0204)	. . . .
5	II	$x'=$	1.9296	-0.6854 (0.0370)	$+0.4450$ (0.3299)	$+0.0230$ (0.0054)	. . . .
6	III	$x'=$	1.5899	-0.5488 (0.1489)	$+0.5105$ (0.2428)	. . . .	$+0.0019$ (0.0011)
			Constant Term	x	z	t	t^2
7	I	$y=$	-1.6434	-3.2024 (0.4505)	$+4.0823$ (1.4176)	-0.8154 (0.7546)	. . . .
8	II	$y=$	118.9754	-3.1739 (0.2936)	$+0.5531$ (0.7339)	$+1.9384$ (0.3133)	. . . .
9	III	$y=$	77.4645	-2.4891 (0.6737)	$+1.2182$ (0.6363)	. . . .	$+0.1516$ (0.0765)
			Constant Term	x'	z'	$\dagger Mt$	$\dagger Mt^2$
10	I	$y'=$	0.7639	-1.0161 (0.1824)	$+1.5323$ (1.1468)	-0.0045 (0.0239)	. . . .
11	II	$y'=$	2.7977	-1.2721 (0.1408)	$+0.4838$ (0.4616)	$+0.0332$ (0.0066)	. . . .
12	III	$y'=$	2.3903	-1.2638 (0.3430)	$+0.7323$ (0.3826)	. . . .	$+0.0033$ (0.0015)

*I = 1879–92; II = 1899–1914; III = 1915–29 (excl. 1917–21).

TABLE 14—*Continued*

OF THE DEMAND FUNCTIONS, BY PERIODS, 1879–1929

t = Time in years. For origins see Table 10
x', y', z' = Logs of x, y, z

(Figures in parentheses are standard errors)

	DESCRIPTIVE CONSTANTS						
	Elasticity of Demand η	Quadratic Mean Error ϵ (100,000,000 Bu.)	Adjusted Multiple Correlation Coefficient R'	Percentage of Variance of Consumption Attributable to			EQUATION No.
				y	z	t	
....	−0.7088 (0.1727)	0.9810	0.9172	49.74	56.64	−18.58	1
....	−0.6072 (0.1090)	0.9492	0.9562	47.73	7.06	38.35	2
....	−0.5271 (0.1936)	1.4318	0.7719	59.02	16.27	−2.24	3
	η	ϵ (Per Cent)	R'	y'	z'	t	
....	−0.7443 (0.1336)	92.7–107.9	0.8632	50.38	33.69	−3.68	4
....	−0.6854 (0.0370)	95.2–105.0	0.9386	45.14	11.12	34.21	5
....	−0.5488 (0.1489)	94.7–105.5	0.7664	59.26	14.97	−1.73	6

Flexibility of Price φ	Maximum Value of η $1/\varphi$	ϵ (Cents)	R'	Percentage of Variance of Price Attributable to			
				x	z	t	
−1.1778 (0.2995)	−0.8490	3.4384	0.8962	61.71	34.89	−11.75	7
−1.4935 (0.2722)	−0.6695	3.1636	0.9566	47.26	3.56	42.38	8
−1.4489 (0.5600)	−0.6902	4.2758	0.7839	56.30	2.39	15.61	9
φ	$1/\varphi$	ϵ (Per Cent)	R'	x'	z'	t	
−1.0161 (0.1824)	−0.9842	91.4–109.3	0.8429	57.22	23.64	−3.14	10
−1.2721 (0.1408)	−0.7861	93.5–106.9	0.9420	42.70	6.38	41.90	11
−1.2638 (0.3430)	−0.7912	92.1–108.5	0.7927	53.37	2.37	19.48	12

† $M = \log_{10} e = 0.43429$.

TABLE 15

CORN: PERCENTAGE OF VARIANCE (σ^2) OF THE DEPENDENT VARIABLE IMPUTED TO EACH OF THE INDEPENDENT VARIABLES IN THE DEMAND EQUATIONS FOR THE THREE PERIODS*

x = Total production   z = Animal units
y = Deflated December 1 farm price   t = Time

Type of Imputation	Period I — Percentage of σ_x^2 Due to				Period II — Percentage of σ_x^2 Due to				Period III — Percentage of σ_x^2 Due to			
	y	z	t	Total	y	z	t	Total	y	z	t	Total
Direct	67.3	128.9	17.7	213.9	91.6	1.9	68.2	161.7	72.8	22.6	13.5	108.9
Joint												
y with z	−26.7	−26.7	....	−53.4	−4.5	−4.5	....	−9.0	−2.2	−2.2	....	−4.4
y with t	9.2	....	9.2	18.4	−39.4	....	−39.4	−78.8	−11.6	....	−11.6	−23.2
z with t	....	−45.5	−45.5	−91.0	....	9.6	9.6	19.2	....	−4.1	−4.1	−8.2
Total determination	49.8	56.7	−18.6	87.9	47.7	7.0	38.4	93.1	59.0	16.3	−2.2	73.1

Type of Imputation	Period I — Percentage of σ_y^2 Due to				Period II — Percentage of σ_y^2 Due to				Period III — Percentage of σ_y^2 Due to			
	x	z	t	Total	x	z	t	Total	x	z	t	Total
Direct	103.6	147.5	19.4	270.5	89.8	1.1	72.2	163.1	66.3	18.8	17.8	102.9
Joint												
x with z	−61.7	−61.7	....	−123.4	−5.1	−5.1	....	−10.2	−12.1	−12.1	....	−24.2
x with t	19.8	....	19.8	39.6	−37.4	....	−37.4	−74.8	2.1	....	2.1	4.2
z with t	....	−50.9	−50.9	−101.8	....	7.6	7.6	15.2	....	−4.3	−4.3	−8.6
Total determination	61.7	34.9	−11.7	84.9	47.3	3.6	42.4	93.3	56.3	2.4	15.6	74.3

* I = 1879–92; II = 1899–1914; III = 1915–29 (excl. 1917–21). The equations are given in Table 14.

3. If we look at the demand for corn from the point of view of the net effect on price of changes in the quantity, we find that an increase of 1 bushel in the annual per capita production reduced the deflated price by 1.79 cents in the first period, by 2.52 cents in the second, and by 2.54 cents in the third. The analogous relations in terms of price flexibilities are that the net effect of a 1 per cent increase in production was to reduce the real price by 1.01 per cent in the first period, by 1.26 per cent in the second, and by 1.19 per cent in the third.

4. If we measure the shift of the demand curve in terms of the change in price while production (=consumption) is held constant (rather than by the change in production while price is fixed), we find that it was quite negligible in the first period, that it moved upward at the rate of 0.92 cent per annum (subject to a retardation of 0.07 cent per annum) during the second period, and that this was changed to a downward shift of 1.54 cents per annum during the third period. In relative figures, the rates of shift of the demand curve during the three periods were: −0.12 per cent, +2.10 per cent (though subject to an annual retardation of 0.26 per cent), and −2.87 per cent, respectively.

5. The introduction of the number of animal units either as a deflator of consumption or as an independent variable in the demand equations does not reduce the importance of the time variable. This is probably due to the fact that the animal unit series, based as it is on very rough estimates, is a very poor index of the number of animals receiving corn and of the changes that have taken place in animal husbandry which affect the demand for corn. The introduction of this series does, however, impart an upward shift to the demand curve for the third period, but the explanation of this fact is probably to be found in the increase in the amount of corn fed to cattle consequent upon the reduction of the western range areas.

6. Changes in business conditions had no effect either on the quantity demanded or on the price of corn except possibly during the second period. Even in this period, the effect is contrary to expectations: an improvement in business conditions seems to be associated with a *decrease* in the demand for corn.

The most important of the foregoing findings is, of course, the fact that during 1915–29, the demand curve for corn was shifting downward at a precipitous rate. This is due to a variety of causes of which the following are probably the most important:

a) Changes in dietetic habits

b) The increase in the proportion of urban population with the accompanying extension of the field of sedentary occupations, which has reduced the consumption of certain energy-building foods, including corn

c) The advent of the auto and the truck and the accompanying decrease in the number of horses and mules *d*) The enormous improvement in feeding practices, which has resulted in a smaller requirement of corn per unit of animal population

e) The erection of higher and higher tariff walls—the Emergency Tariff Act of 1921, the Fordney-McCumber Tariff Act of 1922, and the Hawley-Smoot Tariff Act of 1930—which have made it increasingly difficult for foreign consumers to buy our pork and pork products

f)The substitution of wheat for corn in the cotton states

If these are the true causes—and they are generally recognized as such by the students of the subject—then it is fair to conclude that the downward shift of the demand curve has not yet come to a full stop, for the causes are still in operation.[33]

This is of paramount importance to the farmers of the Corn Belt and to the American people as a whole. It means that *at the same price less and less corn will be consumed with the passage of time, or that the same supply will command a smaller price from one year to the next.*

As an illustration, we may turn to equation 3 of Table 11. A simple computation shows that the (deflated) price which would have maximized total per capita receipts in 1915 is 87.17 cents per bushel, and the corresponding quantity of corn that would have been demanded (for all purposes) is 20.47 bushels per capita, yielding a maximum revenue of $17.84 times the population of 1915, or $1,785,000,000. At the same price, the quantity that would have been demanded in 1929 is 12.94 bushels per capita, yielding a revenue of $11.28 times the population[34] of 1929, or only $1,380,000,000.

The situation is really more serious than is indicated by this illustration. Even if it had been possible and practicable for corn farmers to produce *each year* the exact crop which would maximize the total receipts for that year, these receipts would still have shown a decline with time. Thus, whereas the optimum value of the crop for 1915 is, as we have seen, $1,785,000,000, the corresponding figure for 1929 is only $1,454,000,000.

This fact has an important bearing on the present agricultural policy with respect to corn. As long as the demand curve for corn continues to shift downward, such policies as those embodied in the A.A.A. will give only temporary relief, for it is only a matter of a few years before the downward shift of the

[33] A confirmation of this view is probably to be found in the fact that if we extrapolate the demand function (3) of Table 11 to 1934 and compute the theoretical value of the very small crop (10.879 bu. per capita) the result is $0.8450 × 10.879 bu. × population for 1934, or $1,167,000,000. *This exceeds by $225,000,000 the observed value of the corn crop,* both values being expressed in terms of the 1913 dollar. (B.L.S. Index of Wholesale Prices for December, 1934 is 118.) The other equations for the third period (Table 11) yield similar results.

[34] The population of the United States was 100,050,000 in 1915, and 122,359,000 in 1929. See Table I of Appen. A.

demand curve will counteract the gain obtained from the creation of an artificial scarcity. What is needed is an effective program for stopping this downward movement of the demand curve. In so far as this is due to our high tariff
wall, the desired program is, of course, a more liberal foreign-trade policy.
Such a policy would have the effect of extending the corn market, lowering
costs of production, raising farmers' income, and to that extent retard the
downward movement of the demand curve. In so far, however, as this movement is due to technical progress which has encountered an inelastic demand,
there is no program, no policy, which is likely to restore to corn its former purchasing power. In the absence of restriction, the adjustment would take place
through the substitution of more remunerative crops and through some shift
to the better-paid occupations, and this would result, in the long run, in a
higher general standard of living. Restriction puts an obstacle to this process
of adjustment. Like the tariff, it is a deliberate suppression of technical progress. If it should benefit the producers of corn—and this may turn out to be
impossible in the long run—it will do so by damaging producers of other commodities, by creating new vested interests, and by reducing the national income.[35]

[35] These lines were written in August, 1935, six months before the decision of the Supreme Court
invalidating the A.A.A.

CHAPTER VIII

THE DEMAND FOR COTTON

CHAPTER VIII

THE DEMAND FOR COTTON[1]

I. THE FACTUAL BACKGROUND

Cotton is the most important of the vegetable fibers of the world and the greatest commercial crop of the United States. The corn crop exceeds it in total value, but by far the greatest part of that crop is consumed on the farms where it is grown, whereas all of the cotton crop is sold off the farms.[2]

Cotton has been the mainstay of the South's economy. It is the chief and almost the only source of income of a large proportion of the farmers of the southern states. Anything which affects the profitableness of this crop greatly affects the economic life of these states.

A. THE EXTENT OF THE COTTON BELT

From the beginning of the nineteenth century until recent years, the world has drawn the bulk of its cotton supplies from one source, the Cotton Belt of the United States. This belt, which has moved westward with the expansion of the United States, now covers an area of about 700,000 square miles, which exceeds that of France, Germany, Italy, and Spain, and extends from the Atlantic Coast through North Carolina, South Carolina, Georgia, Florida, Alabama, Mississippi, Arkansas, western Tennessee, and northern Louisiana, into Texas and Oklahoma. Of the total area of the belt, approximately 10 per cent is under cotton cultivation, the average figure for 1924–25 to 1928–29 being 45,662,000 acres, or approximately 71,300 square miles. The distribution of this acreage by states for a few selected years (including those in which the A.A.A. was in effect) is shown in Table 16.

B. SOIL AND CLIMATE

The boundaries of the Cotton Belt are determined by physical and economic conditions.

[1] I am greatly indebted to Messrs. Maurice R. Cooper and L. H. Bean, of the Bureau of Agricultural Economics of the United States Department of Agriculture, for kindly reading the manuscript of this chapter and for valuable criticism and suggestions. They are not, however, responsible for the conclusions.

My thanks are also due to Alston H. Garside, economist for the New York Cotton Exchange, and to his publisher, Frederick A. Stokes Company, for permission to quote from his book, *Cotton Goes to Market.*

[2] An excellent summary of the economic situation with respect to cotton will be found in the *U.S.D.A. Yearbook, 1921,* pp. 323–406; Alston Hill Garside, *Cotton Goes to Market* (New York, 1935); John A. Todd, *The Cotton World* (London, 1927).

Areas have been tried out north of the areas in which cotton is now grown. Practically all possible available area for production in the United States has had a trial. Within the limits of suitable climatic conditions, production expands or contracts with changes in prices or in the profitableness of growing the crop.[3]

Although the most productive soils of the Cotton Belt are the bottoms of the Mississippi River and its tributaries, and the black prairies of Alabama, Mississippi, and Texas, the use of fertilizer also makes the sandy loams of the Coastal Plain and the red subsoil piedmont lands very productive. Within the Cotton Belt variations in the density of cotton acreage and in the average yield per acre over a period of years are due principally to the widely varying soil

TABLE 16*

COTTON ACREAGE OF THE UNITED STATES, BY STATES, FOR SELECTED YEARS

STATE	ABSOLUTE FIGURES (1,000 ACRES)				PERCENTAGE OF TOTAL			
	1913–14	1928–29	1933–34	1934–35	1913–14	1928–29	1933–34	1934–35
Total..............	35,206	42,434	29,383	26,866	100.00	100.00	100.00	100.00
Texas..............	12,352	16,887	11,069	10,097	35.09	39.80	37.67	37.58
Georgia............	4,711	3,274	2,162	2,142	13.38	7.72	7.36	7.97
Alabama...........	3,518	3,437	2,318	2,133	9.99	8.10	7.89	7.94
Oklahoma..........	3,242	4,007	2,860	2,647	9.21	9.44	9.73	9.85
Mississippi.........	2,961	3,875	2,830	2,530	8.41	9.13	9.63	9.42
South Carolina......	2,427	2,051	1,379	1,286	6.89	4.83	4.69	4.79
Arkansas...........	2,263	3,305	2,537	2,167	6.43	7.79	8.63	8.07
North Carolina......	1,377	1,620	1,072	970	3.91	3.82	3.65	3.61
Louisiana..........	1,117	1,836	1,295	1,189	3.17	4.33	4.41	4.43
Tennessee.........	811	1,042	883	759	2.30	2.45	3.01	2.82
All others.......	427	1,100	978	946	1.22	2.59	3.33	3.52

* Source: *Cotton Revisions, Acreage, Yield and Production, Crop Years 1866–1935* (U.S. Dept. Agric. [November, 1936]), pp. 1–28.

conditions; on the outer boundaries of the belt, production is determined largely by climatic factors.

The climate most suitable for the cotton plant is one in which the winter is sufficiently cold to destroy the hibernating pests, followed by an early spring of moderate rainfall, and by a moderately dry, hot summer with abundant sunshine. The autumn should be fairly dry and bright, and the first frost should be late.

The Cotton Belt has an average summer temperature of 77 degrees along the northern boundary. This temperature appears to be the limit, beyond which commercial production becomes unprofitable. In the southern portion of the Cotton Belt the summer temperature is 80 to 85 degrees. Along the northern margin of the Cotton Belt the last killing frost in spring occurs on an average about April 10, and the first killing frost in fall about October 25, so that the frostless season is about 200 days. In the southern portion of the Cotton Belt

[3] *U.S.D.A. Yearbook, 1921*, p. 330.

the last killing frost in spring occurs about March 10 on the average, and the first killing frost in fall seldom before November 25, the frostless season being 260 days or more in length.

The average annual precipitation in the Cotton Belt ranges from 23 inches in western Oklahoma and Texas to 55 inches in eastern North Carolina and 60 inches in southern Mississippi, but throughout much of the belt is between 30 and 50 inches. The spring rainfall ranges from 6 inches in western Texas to 16 inches in Arkansas and southern Mississippi, being heavier in the Mississippi Valley States than in Texas or the Southern Atlantic States. The summer rainfall is somewhat greater than that of the other seasons, especially in the southern and eastern portion of the belt, reaching a maximum of 20 inches in southern Mississippi and in eastern North and South Carolina, while in the black prairie region of central Texas the amount received averages only 8 inches. Autumn is the driest season of the year, practically all the important cotton regions receiving less than 10 inches of rain during the fall months. February and November are the wettest months in the Mississippi Valley States, in Alabama, and in northern Georgia. August is the wettest month in the Carolinas and May in Texas and Oklahoma. October and November are the driest months throughout practically the entire Cotton Belt.[4]

While this climate renders irrigation unnecessary, it has its own drawbacks which lie in its great extremes and its uncertainty. Thus the average yield per acre, which reached an all-time high of 219 pounds in 1894, dropped to 172 pounds in the following year. It was 186.7 pounds in 1920 but only 132.5 in 1921; 192.8 in 1926, but only 161.7 in 1927.[5]

C. CHANGES IN PRODUCTION

The history of the American crop dates practically from the discovery of the saw gin by Eli Whitney in 1793. The increasing supplies of American cotton made possible by this invention quickly replaced practically all others in the world-markets. Production increased from 3,000 bales of 500 pounds gross weight in 1790 to 10,000 in 1793, to 73,000 in 1800. By the middle of the century it was 2,136,000 bales, and in 1859, on the eve of the Civil War, it reached 4,310,000 bales. The Civil War almost wiped out the crop for the time being, and the economic conditions following the liberation of the slaves prevented its recovery to pre-war levels until 1875. From then until 1914 the crop increased rapidly, growing from 4,303,000 bales in 1875 to 7,147,000 bales in 1895 and to 16,135,000 bales in 1914.

During the first period (1875-95) the increase in production was largely from new lands. The expansion of railroads in Texas was followed by the rapid development of cotton production in the Black Waxy Prairie region. Production also increased in Arkansas and Oklahoma. The smaller increase in the eastern states was a product of both increased acreage and increased yield. The latter was largely the result of the extensive use of fertilizer, of improvements in the methods of cultivation, and of improvements in the varieties of cotton grown.

---

[4] *Ibid.*, pp. 341–43.　　　　　　[5] *Ibid.*, *1935*, pp. 425–26.

During the second period (1896–1914) Oklahoma and western Texas added a large acreage to the cotton-producing area.

This period is marked by the spread of the boll weevil, by the intensification of efforts to produce higher yields and better qualities, by the introduction of cotton into the irrigated districts of southern California and Arizona, by the great increase in the value of cotton seed, by the rapid development of cotton manufacturing in the South, and by increased competition from foreign countries.[6]

Following 1914, production was reduced considerably by the ravages of the boll weevil, the crop of 1921 (7,954,000 bales) being the smallest crop since 1895. By 1924, however, it regained its pre-war level and reached an all-time record of 17,977,000 bales in 1926.

In Table 17 there is a comparison of the American crop with the crops of the principal producing countries for three selected years. The table also gives a similar comparison of the consumption of cotton in each of the principal countries for the same years.

The sources of information in detail as to the production, consumption, and stocks of cotton have never been adequate or altogether satisfactory for many countries. The United States is the only country which has provided an efficient means of determining the supply and distribution of cotton within its borders. Comprehensive information for other countries is not available, but more or less accurate statistics on some phases of the cotton supply and distribution are compiled and published in a number of countries by governmental bureaus as well as by other agencies.[7]

D. COTTON-GINNING: DEFINITION OF TERMS

Owing to differences in climate, the various cotton-growing operations are performed about two months earlier in the southernmost than in the northernmost part of the Cotton Belt. The date when planting of cotton begins is from ten to twenty days after the last killing frost in spring. It is about March 1 in southern Texas, about April 1 in the middle of the belt, and about April 21 in the northern part of the belt. In any given district, planting is completed in two to four weeks. Picking normally begins around July 1 in southern Texas, about August 21 in the middle of the belt, and about September 11 along the northern border. The southern part of the belt has a long picking season; along the northern border the crop must be picked as early as possible to escape the frost.

After the beginning of August, the United States Department of Agriculture issues crop estimates at monthly intervals, and the Department of Commerce, through the Bureau of the Census, issues reports on ginnings at semimonthly intervals. Since all cotton has to be ginned to be commercially valuable, the

---

[6] *Ibid., 1921*, p. 334.

[7] *U.S. Department of Commerce Census Bulletin*, No. 171 (1933–34), p. 29.

TABLE 17*

WORLD-PRODUCTION AND MILL CONSUMPTION OF COTTON BY COUNTRIES, 1919–20, 1929–30, AND 1934–35

COUNTRY	PRODUCTION Absolute Figures†			PRODUCTION Percentages			MILL CONSUMPTION Absolute Figures†			MILL CONSUMPTION Percentages		
	1919–20	1929–30	1934–35	1919–20	1929–30	1934–35	1919–20	1929–30	1934–35	1919–20	1929–30	1934–35
Total world	19,260	26,927	23,047	100.0	100.0	100.0	18,451	24,993	25,384	100.0	100.0	100.0
United States	10,924	14,822‡	9,650‡	56.7	55.0	41.9	6,200	6,221‡	5,462‡	33.6	24.9	21.5
All foreign	8,336	12,105	13,397	43.3	45.0	58.1	12,251	18,772	19,922	66.4	75.1	78.5
India	4,316	5,120	4,475	22.4	19.0	19.4	1,646	2,105	2,544	8.9	8.4	10.0
China	1,100	1,825	2,150	5.7	6.8	9.3	§	2,265	2,457	...	9.1	9.7
Egypt	1,139	1,750	1,566	5.9	6.5	6.8	§	§	§	...	...	...
Continental Europe	...	...	...	...	...	...	3,660	7,911	7,023	19.8	31.7	27.7
United Kingdom	...	...	...	...	...	...	3,700	2,615	2,615	20.1	10.5	10.3
Japan	...	...	...	...	...	...	1,825	2,855	3,600	9.9	11.4	14.2
All others	1,781	3,410	5,206	9.3	12.7	22.6	1,420	1,021	1,683	7.7	4.0	6.6

* Source: For 1919, *Census Bull.*, No. 145, pp. 79 and 83; for 1929 and 1934, *Census Bull.*, No. 172, pp. 43–44.

† Unit: 1,000 bales of 500 lb. gross weight.

‡ In the census bulletins these figures were given in running bales.

§ No data available in the sources consulted.

last ginning report, issued in March, gives the size of the crop, though it is subject to revision in the final report which is issued in May.[2]

The cotton with the seed attached to it is called "seed cotton," and the cotton without the seed attached to it is called "lint" or simply "cotton." The ginner puts the lint into the form of a bale. Most of these are of the "flat" or "square" type, measuring about 54 by 27 by 48 inches and weighing about 500 pounds gross on the average. Since the bagging and the ties which surround the bale weigh about 22 pounds, the net weight of the bales is about 478 pounds. At some gins—and they form a small percentage of the total—the cotton is put up in the form of cylindrical bales, which are called "round" bales. These weigh about 250 pounds and are considered as "half-bales" in the statistical reports.

A valuable by-product of the cotton crop is the cottonseed, which yields growers about one-sixth as much income as they receive for the cotton itself. The seed which is not used for planting, feed, or fertilizer—and it constitutes a large part of the total—goes to an oil mill, where it undergoes a process called "delinting" or "cutting." This is really a second ginning process by which the short fibers or fuzz, which still adhere to the seed after the first ginning, are removed. The product of this ginning, or "linters," are packed in bales similar to the ordinary cotton bale and are used chiefly in the manufacture of explosives, absorbent cotton, low-grade yarns, and cellulose, and as batting, wadding, and stuffing material.

E. COTTON CLASSIFICATION

The problems encountered in the classification of cotton constitute an excellent illustration of the difficulties inherent in any attempt to give an unambigu-

[8] The collection and publication of cotton statistics was put on a systematic basis by the joint resolution of Congress approved February 9, 1905, which authorized and directed the director of the Census Bureau "to collect and publish in connection with the ginners' reports of cotton production provided for in section nine of an Act of Congress entitled 'An Act to provide for a permanent Census Office, approved March sixth, nineteen hundred and two,' statistics of the consumption of cotton, the surplus of cotton held by the manufacturers, and the quantity of cotton exported, the statistics to be summarized as of September first each year so as to show the cotton production and consumption of the preceding year" (*U.S. Census Bulletin*, No. 25 [1904–5], p. 7). This resolution called for "the collection and publication of the statistics of (1) cotton production as returned by ginners, (2) consumption of cotton in the United States, (3) supply of cotton held by manufacturers, and (4) quantity of cotton exported" (*ibid.*).

Since these facts alone do not show the complete distribution of the cotton crop or give an accurate conception of the cotton trade, the Bureau of the Census has associated with these data certain other statistics collected by the U.S. Department of Agriculture, the Bureau of Foreign and Domestic Commerce, and by trustworthy commercial agencies, and has prepared summary tables which carry the statistics of production and prices back to 1790 and the statistics of consumption back to 1826. The bulletins of the Bureau of the Census and the publications of the U.S. Department of Agriculture constitute the most important source of cotton statistics in the United States. Additional cotton statistics may be found in *Cotton Facts*, published by Shepperson Publishing Co. (first issue: 1878), and in the *Cotton Yearbook of the New York Cotton Exchange* (first issue: 1928).

ous definition of a commodity. For what is called "cotton" is not a homogeneous article but of thousands of varieties, differing in color, length, strength, fineness, and other characteristics. At Liverpool, one of the chief cotton markets of the world, thirty-eight types are recognized. From a manufacturing point of view the most convenient classification is according to the length of fiber or staple. On this principle, Professor J. A. Todd classifies the world's cottons into three broad groups as shown in Table 18.

TABLE 18*

CLASSIFICATION OF THE WORLD'S COTTON CROPS

Variety	Length of Staple	Approximate 1925–26 Crop (1,000 Bales of 500 Lb. Gross Wt.)	Percentage of Total
Group I, Long.....	1⅛″ and longer	2,644	9.2
Group II, Medium.	¾″–1⅛″	19,210	67.0
Group III, Short...	⅜″–¾″	6,810	23.8
Total........	....	28,664	100.0

* Adapted from the more detailed table given by John A. Todd, *The Cotton World* (London, 1927), p. 5.

In Group I fall the sea-island and the related Egyptian varieties, as well as the American long-staple cotton. In Group II falls the bulk of the American crop (15,000,000 bales). Group III is composed primarily of Indian (short-staple) and Chinese cottons. The four American cottons—sea island, American Egyptian, upland long-staple, and upland short-staple—thus fall in the first two groups.

Sea-island cotton is practically extinct in this country, the weevil having stopped its production, for it is a late-maturing cotton and hence particularly subject to weevil damage.[9]

American Egyptian cotton is grown in southern Arizona and constitutes less than 1 per cent of the total production of the United States. Thus the bulk of the American crop is upland cotton,[10] the long-staple ($1\frac{1}{8}$–$1\frac{3}{4}$ in.) variety forming 7 per cent, and the short-staple ($\frac{5}{8}$–1 in.) variety forming 92 per cent of the American production.

The official cotton standards of the United States for length of staple were

[9] Garside, *op. cit.*, p. 48.

[10] "The term upland originated in the very early days of cotton growing in this country, and it was then applied to that type of cotton which was grown on the higher land more or less distant from the seacoast, in distinction from the sea-island cotton which was grown near the coast or on islands off the coast. The word has completely lost its significance as designating the altitude or location of the land on which the cotton is produced. Upland cotton is now produced on lands of all altitudes, from the bottom lands of the Mississippi and other southern rivers to the foothills of the Blue Ridge Mountains in the Carolinas and the Ozark Mountains in Arkansas" (*ibid.*, pp. 48–49).

promulgated in 1918. They define the length of staple of any cotton as "the normal length by measurement without regard to quality or value, of a typical portion of its fibres under a relative humidity of the atmosphere of 65 per centum and a temperature of 70 degrees, Fahrenheit," and they establish the following standard lengths, expressed in inches or fractions of an inch: Below $\frac{3}{4}$; $\frac{3}{4}$; $\frac{13}{16}$; $\frac{7}{8}$; $\frac{15}{16}$; 1; then upward by thirty-seconds, disregarding any fraction less than a thirty-second.

The lengths of staple designated as $\frac{3}{4}$, $\frac{7}{8}$, 1, $1\frac{1}{8}$, $1\frac{1}{4}$, $1\frac{3}{8}$, $1\frac{1}{2}$, $1\frac{5}{8}$, and $1\frac{3}{4}$ inches, respectively, are each represented by a sample in the custody of the United States Department of Agriculture in a container marked "Original Official Cotton Standards of the United States Length of Staple" followed by the appropriate designation of such length of staple.

The standards also provide that, whenever the length of staple of cotton taken from one part of a bale is different from that taken from another part of the same bale, the length of staple of the cotton in such bale shall be that of the part which is the shorter.[11]

Although length of staple is the most important quality by which cotton is classified, it is not the only one. The other qualities are grouped by the cotton trade under two technical headings: "grade" and "character."

The term "grade" covers not only (a) the color, lustre, and brightness of the fibre, and (b) the nature and the amount of foreign matter in the lint, such as leaf, dust, twigs, and so forth, but also (c) those characteristics which result from the quality of the ginning, such as presence or absence of stringy cotton, gin-cut fibres, and so forth, these characteristics being termed "preparation." . . . . The term "character" indicates the degree of uniformity of length of the fibres, their strength, smoothness, and silkiness, and what is known as "body," this latter term meaning the degree to which the fibres tend to adhere to each other.[12]

The United States Department of Agriculture established its first standards for grade in 1909, but they were permissive and were not generally used. In 1914 it discontinued these standards and promulgated new ones, the use of which was made compulsory in trading in cotton for future delivery. Uniformity of description of American cotton in this country was finally effected through the passage of the Cotton Standards Act, approved March 4, 1923, effective August 1, 1923. The act made it unlawful to describe American cotton for grade or staple in interstate or foreign trade by a standard description other

[11] *Cotton Facts, 1931*, p. 38. See also *Regulations of the Secretary of Agriculture under the United States Cotton Futures Act* ("U.S.D.A., Bur. Agric. Econ., Service and Regulatory Announcements," No. 124 [effective May 1, 1931]); and *Regulations of the Secretary of Agriculture under the United States Cotton Standards Act* ("Service and Regulatory Announcements," No. 125 [effective May 1, 1931]). These supersede Service and Regulatory Announcements Nos. 105 and 115, respectively. See also *Proceedings of International Universal Cotton Standards Conference of 1929 and Items Relating to the Administration of the United States Cotton Futures and Cotton Standards Acts* ("Service and Regulatory Announcements," No. 117 [November, 1929]).

[12] Garside, *op. cit.*, pp. 51–52.

than that provided in the act. In the same year the United States standards were also adopted by the leading cotton exchanges of Europe, and they are therefore referred to as the "Universal Standards for American Cotton."[13]

According to these standards, American upland cotton is classified into eight color groups,[14] and each color group is further subdivided into several grades. Thus, for "white" cotton, the grades are: Middling Fair, Strict Good Middling, Good Middling, Strict Middling, Middling, Strict Low Middling, Low Middling, Strict Good Ordinary, and Good Ordinary.[15]

It will be observed that the grade names are built up and down from middling, and so it is customary to speak of middling as the basic grade. When the trade began to evolve these grade names 125 or 150 years ago, the term "middling" probably applied to the middle quality of American cotton, as American cotton was then running. At the present time, however, more of the cotton produced in this country is of the grades above middling than of the grades below middling, and hence middling grade cotton is somewhat below average. However, middling cotton constitutes a large section of the crop.[16]

Thus the average grade of the crop from 1923–24 to 1930–31 was as follows:

1923–24	Strict Low Middling to Middling	1927–28	Middling to Strict Middling
1924–25	Middling	1928–29	Strict Low Middling to Middling
1925–26	Strict Low Middling	1929–30	Strict Low Middling to Middling
1926–27	Strict Low Middling to Middling	1930–31	Middling[17]

The United States Department of Agriculture makes up type samples for goods and for staple called "official standard types" which it keeps in its vaults. Key copies of these standards are distributed to the trade.

The government has not formulated any classifications for "character," or issued any standard types for it.

[13] Beginning with January 1, 1936, however, cotton from the United States has ceased to be the only cotton constituting good delivery in Liverpool. According to the *New York Times* of January 5, 1936:

"The New Year ushered in the new contract of the Liverpool Cotton Association under which delivery of cotton of specified grade may be made without regard to the origin of the staple. Thus, for the first time since the association was organized more than fifty years ago, cotton from the United States is no longer the only cotton that constitutes good delivery in Liverpool—a market that ranks second only to New York in importance in the cotton trade. Agitation for a change in the contract was started in England more than a year ago, following the inauguration of price-pegging policies in the United States on a stricter basis than had been undertaken previously. In the circumstances, groups in this country have been unable to lodge protests in the matter with the Liverpool authorities —the situation might not have been altered had they done so. However, in this connection, it will be recalled that when the Commodity Exchange here considered last year the feasibility of making silk produced in countries other than Japan good delivery on contracts, the Japanese voiced strong protests. And the silk contract terms were not changed."

[14] Extra White, White, Spotted (Very Light Yellow Tinged), Yellow Tinged, Light Yellow Stained, Yellow Stained, Gray (Light Blue Stained), and Blue Stained.

[15] Garside, *op. cit.*, p. 57.

[16] *Ibid.*, pp. 58–59.

[17] *Cotton Facts, 1931*, p. 39.

II. THE DATA

A. SUPPLY AND DISTRIBUTION

Since our production of cotton greatly exceeds our consumption, a true picture of the demand-supply situation cannot be obtained without a knowledge of (1) production, carry-over, and imports, which constitute the total United States supply; (2) consumption, stocks, and exports, which constitute the distribution; and (3) prices. World production, supply, and consumption are also very useful. Complete and consistent statistics of all these series are, however, not available. Table IIb of Appendix A presents the best estimates of these series, reduced to equivalent 500-pound bales. In Table V of Appendix A the same series are reduced to a per capita basis.

It should be borne in mind that the series on production in equivalent 500-pound bales given in the Appendix tables is not the same as that which appears in *Census Bulletin*, No. 168, but has been obtained by converting the data on running bales which are given in the *Bulletin* into equivalent 500-pound bales, on the basis of the census data on average net weight per bale. This was done in order to render the data on production consistent with the other series which we have used (see n. ††, Table IIb, Appen. A).

Figures 48 and 49 are graphic representations of the more important series, the former relating to the unadjusted data and the latter to the adjusted data.

To get a correct idea of the limitations of these series and the uses to which they may be put, it is necessary to keep in mind the following definitions.

United States production.—By the production of cotton for any year is meant not the ginning which occurred in a given twelve-month period but the ginnings of that crop the bulk of which matured during the twelve months in question. For example, the figure 4,303,000 bales (of 500 lb. gross weight) which is entered in Table IIb, Appendix A, as the production for the twelve months beginning September 1, 1875, represents the total ginnings of the crop planted in the *spring* of 1875, no matter whether a part of this cotton was ginned before September 1, 1875, or after August 31, 1876. It does not include that part of the crop of 1874–75 which may have been ginned between September 1, 1875, and August 31, 1876; nor does it include that part of the crop of 1876–77 which may have been ginned before August 31, 1876. The former is included in the production figure for the year beginning September 1, 1874, while the latter is included in the production figure for the year beginning September 1, 1876.

Stocks and carry-over in the United States.—These series are available only since 1905. Stocks on hand at the end of the year include all stocks of cotton remaining in consuming establishments, in public storage or at compresses, and elsewhere at the close of the "cotton year." This figure is also the "carry-over" for the next year.

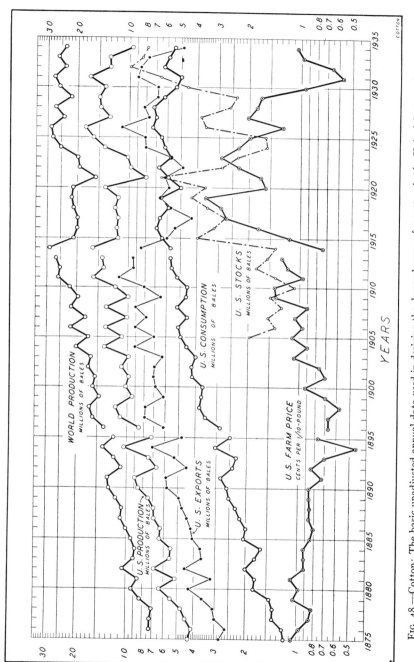

FIG. 48.—Cotton: The basic unadjusted annual data used in deriving the demand curves for cotton in the United States, 1875–1934

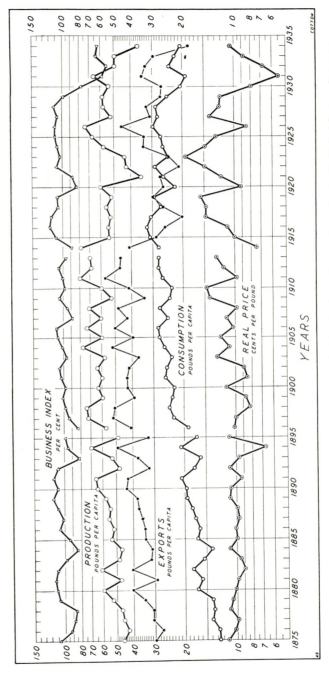

Fig. 49.—Cotton: The basic adjusted annual data used in deriving the demand curves for cotton in the United States, 1875–1934

United States consumption.—In the cotton trade "consumption" or demand has a technical meaning: "Cotton is usually counted as consumed when it is put into the first machine at the mill, this machine being the opener which loosens up the cotton as it is taken from the bale."[18] It is doubtful, however, whether the data designated as "consumption" for the earlier years actually represent consumption as thus defined or only purchases by the mills.

Total supply and total distribution in the United States.—A comparison of these series in Table IIb, Appendix A, shows that for any given year the total supply is not so large as the total distribution. While it is true that absolute agreement between these items cannot be expected, since the figures for production on the supply side "relate . . . . to the year of growth,"[19] i.e., to the ginnings of the crop of the stated year, while all other figures for that year refer to a twelve-month period beginning September 1,[20] this circumstance hardly accounts for the size of the discrepancy between these items. The explanation generally given is that the discrepancy is "due principally to the inclusion, in all distribution items, of the 'city crop,' which consists of rebaled samples and pickings from cotton damaged by fire and weather."[21] However, if the excess of distribution over supply (whether measured in running or 500-lb. equivalent bales) is plotted for each year since 1905, the magnitude of the series is seen to be decreasing—which is hardly to be expected of an item such as "city crop" during a period when both the production and the consumption of cotton were on the increase. What this fact seems to indicate is that canvassing of the ginners for figures on production and the gathering of data on consumption from the mills are becoming more complete and that consequently a better agreement between supply and distribution may be expected in the later years. The excess of total distribution over total supply is then due partly to the difference between the year of production and the year of consumption, imports, etc.; partly to the inclusion of the "city crop" in the distribution items; and mostly to the incompleteness and inaccuracies in the component series.

World-production.—The United States Department of Agriculture has published a series of the estimated total world cotton production for the years 1900–1924, and a revised series for the years 1916–34. For estimates of world-production in earlier years the series from Jones's *Handbook* as quoted in John

[18] Garside, *op. cit.*, title of photograph facing p. 317.

[19] *U.S. Census Bulletin*, No. 168 (1930–31), p. 57.

[20] In 1914 the beginning of the cotton year was changed to August 1. "The cotton exchanges and statistical bodies, both in this country and abroad, have very generally agreed upon a change in the 'cotton' year from the 12 months ending August 31 to the 12 months ending July 31, and their reports of the movement of cotton now relate to the year beginning August 1" (*U.S. Census Bulletin*, No. 128 [1913–14], p. 5).

[21] U.S. Dept. Agric., *Yearbook of Agriculture, 1935*, p. 430.

A. Todd's *The World's Cotton Crop* must be relied upon. One of the difficulties in arriving at a good estimate is the variation of the bale weight which ranges from an Indian bale of about 400 pounds average net weight to the Egyptian bale of 720–40 pounds net. In Table II*b*, Appendix A, all figures have been expressed in bales of approximately 478 pounds net, or 500 pounds gross, weight.

B. PRICES

For the purpose of deriving the demand curve for cotton, the price which we should like to have for each year is that which, if it had been maintained throughout the year, would have cleared the entire consumption. A good approximation to this ideal figure is probably the weighted average price paid by the mills (i.e., the consumers) for the cotton which they purchased. Such a series is not, however, available. The two[22] price series which may be taken as substitutes for it are: (1) The New York price of middling grade, $\frac{7}{8}$ inch staple, and (2) The United States farm price. The former is an unweighted average of daily quotations[23] and includes freight to New York. The latter is an average price of all grades sold in the whole of the United States. For the years beginning with 1908 it is also weighted by the quantity of cotton marketed.[24]

The limitations of the New York price are that (1) it relates to only one grade; (2) it is not weighted by sales; and (3) it relates to only one market. Since the greater portion of the domestic spinning industry is now in the South rather than in New England, the New York spot price is no longer an accurate index of the cost of cotton to the consumers.

The limitations of the farm price for our purposes are that (1) it is lower than the price paid by the mills, since it does not include transportation and handling charges; and (2), being a December price for the years 1875–1907, it probably does not reflect the changes in stocks, imports, and exports that take place after December[25] and may not, therefore, be a close approximation of the weighted average price for the season.

As was to be expected, the two series fluctuate sympathetically during the

[22] There is also the New Orleans price. But, in addition to being subject to most of the limitations of the New York price, it is not readily available for the first fourteen years of this study.

[23] For the years 1875 to August, 1900, the prices are an average of the daily quotations in the *Commercial and Financial Chronicle;* later figures are from the New York Cotton Exchange, except for the period September 23–November 16, 1914, when the exchange was closed and prices were obtained from the *Commercial and Financial Chronicle.*

[24] "The prices . . . . are averaged by district (most States being divided into about 9 districts), and the district averages are weighted by the number of acres in cotton in each district this giving the State farm price. . . . . At the end of the season the seasonal price for . . . . the United States is obtained by weighting the monthly prices of each State by the monthly marketings by States" (letter of Maurice R. Cooper, of the Bureau of Agricultural Economics, U.S. Department of Agriculture, April 8, 1932).

[25] This is not a serious difficulty, however, since statistics on stocks are not available before 1905.

entire period covered by the data, and the New York price is always higher
than the farm price. The difference between the two series is, however, greatest
during the first period (1875–96), when transportation and handling charges
constituted a larger part of the price paid by the consumers than they did in
the later periods.

Since the advantages and limitations of the New York price series are
counterbalanced by those of the farm price and since there was no *a priori*
reason for preferring one to the other, it was decided to conduct several preliminary demand analyses with both series. The experiment seemed to point
to the farm price as yielding more consistent results. Accordingly, it was decided to use it in all the demand investigations.[26]

III. FACTORS IN THE DEMAND FOR COTTON

The problem of deriving the demand curve for cotton differs from that of
deriving the demand curve for corn[27] in at least one important respect: there
is lacking in the demand function for cotton that symmetry between the quantity demanded and the price paid which we found in the demand for corn.
Corn is imported and exported in relatively negligible quantities, the United
States being practically a closed economy with respect to it. Moreover, the
carry-over is small, so that production and consumption may be taken as approximately equal to each other. Under these conditions, it is a priori a matter
of indifference whether we write the demand function for corn as

(3.1)
$$x_{dc} = x_{dc}(y, w, t) ,$$

or as

(3.2)
$$y = y(x_{dc}, w, t) ,$$

where x_{dc}=domestic consumption, y=price, w=an index of U.S. industrial
production and trade, and t=time. True, certain *statistical* considerations may
turn the scales in favor of one of the two hypotheses, for in fitting (3.1) we
generally minimize the sum of the squares of the x_{dc}-residuals, while in fitting
(3.2) we generally minimize the sum of the squares of the y-residuals, and one
of these procedures might be preferable to the other in a given situation.[28] But,

---

[26] Cotton, wheat, and oats are the only farm crops for which the demand analyses have been made
with the latest (1936) revised farm prices. Although most of the statistical analyses for cotton had
been made with the December price before the U.S. Department of Agriculture issued its revised
data, our desire to correlate total supply with an *average* annual price, led us to recompute our equations and substitute the revised and weighted farm price for the December price. The differences in
the results were not very great and probably did not warrant the additional labor involved in the
recomputations (see chap. v, pp. 172–73).

[27] See chap. vii.   [28] See chap. iv, pp. 146–49.

in theory at least, both equations (3.1) and (3.2) are equally valid representations of the unique functional relation connecting all the four variables:

(3.3) $$f(x_{dc}, y, w, t) = 0.$$

A different situation obtains, however, in the case of cotton. Of our total production, only two-fifths is consumed at home, the rest being sold abroad, where it competes with other cottons. Under these conditions it is no longer a matter of indifference whether we write the demand function for cotton in the form (3.1) or (3.2). The former is still a most reasonable hypothesis, for the effect on United States consumption of a given change in price is not likely to depend on the cause of the price change—whether it be a change in foreign or in domestic production or stocks. The latter (3.2) is, however, no longer very plausible, for the price of cotton is likely to be more affected by the American and foreign production and stocks than by the American consumption. Consequently, hypothesis (3.2) should be replaced either by

(3.4) $$y = y(x_{dp}, x_{fp}, w, t),$$

where x_{dp} = domestic production and x_{fp} = foreign production; or by

(3.5) $$y = y(x_{ds}, x_{fp}, w, t),$$

where x_{ds} = domestic supply (=production + stocks). Of course, foreign supply would be preferable to foreign production in (3.5), but data on world-stocks are available only in the post-war years. For these years there is also available an index of world industrial production compiled by N. J. Wall, of the United States Department of Agriculture. We shall, therefore, experiment with the hypothesis

(3.6) $$y = y(x_{ds}, x_{fs}, v, t),$$

for the years 1920–32, where x_{fs} = foreign supply, and v = Wall's index of world industrial production. It would have been desirable to study separately the effects on price of both domestic and foreign business conditions. However, the period is too short to permit the use of more variables in our equation.

There are, of course, many other factors not taken account of in the foregoing equations which affect the deflated price of cotton, such as shifts in the world demand and supply of other fibers, discoveries of new uses for cotton, and shifts in the foreign demand for American cotton. But these factors cannot be conveniently measured. In so far, however, as they change slowly and smoothly with time, their average effect may be subsumed under the catch-all variable t.

Our statistical analysis will then proceed by stages as follows:

First, we shall make use of hypothesis (3.1) and write the per capita United States consumption of cotton as a function of the deflated price, of W. M. Persons' "Index of United States Industrial Production and Trade," and of time, using as specific forms of (3.1) both linear and logarithmic (constant-elasticity) demand functions.

Second, we shall consider the deflated price as the dependent variable and express it as a function of the per capita domestic consumption, of the index

TABLE 19

Cotton: Summary by Periods of the Adjusted Data Used in Deriving the Demand Functions, 1875–1929

	Per Capita Domestic Consumption $x_{dc}(t)$				Deflated U.S. Farm Price $y(t)$				Correlation Coefficient
Period*	Descriptive Constants								r_{xy}
	Mean (Lb.)	Median (Lb.)	Standard Deviation (Lb.)	Coefficient of Variation	Mean (Cents)	Median (Cents)	Standard Deviation (Cents)	Coefficient of Variation	
I	16.4228	16.862	2.4411	14.86	10.0257	10.075	0.9710	9.69	−0.5059
II	24.9058	24.777	2.3357	9.38	10.8294	10.440	1.7654	16.30	+0.0128
III	27.5701	27.684	2.6549	9.63	12.5836	12.397	2.8950	23.01	−0.1262

	Equations of Trends		Origins
I	$x_{dc}(t) = 16.4228 + 0.3133t$	$\bar{y} = 10.0257 = $ Arithmetic mean	Mar. 1, 1886
II	$x_{dc}(t) = 24.9058 + 0.2979t$	$y(t) = 10.8294 + 0.1933t$	Sept. 1, 1905
III	$x_{dc}(t) = 26.8027 - 0.2150t$ $+ 0.0361t^2$	$y(t) = 14.2357 - 0.0777t^2$	Aug. 1, 1922

* I = 1875–95; II = 1896–1913; III = 1914–29.

of United States industrial production and trade, and of time, as in (3.2). *Although the use of consumption rather than production or stocks is, as we have just seen, not likely to yield a good explanation of the fluctuations in cotton prices, the results should nevertheless constitute a standard of comparison: all the other hypotheses should be in better agreement with the facts.*

Third, we shall experiment with the hypotheses (3.4), (3.5), and (3.6) and make a comparison of all the findings.

As in the two previous chapters, we shall break up the data into three periods: (I) 1875–95, (II) 1896–1913, and (III) 1914–29, and we shall also experiment with different subdivisions of the third period.

IV. DEMAND FUNCTIONS WITH PER CAPITA CONSUMPTION
AS THE DEPENDENT VARIABLE[29]

In Figure 49, to which reference has already been made, there are drawn the per capita domestic consumption and the real (deflated) price of cotton, W. M. Persons' "Index of United States Industrial Production and Trade," as well as two other related series, for each of the three periods. Table 19 is a descriptive summary of the per capita consumption and the real price.

Table 20 summarizes the more important changes which have taken place in the demand for cotton from 1875 to 1929. Let us consider first the linear regressions.

From the coefficients of y in the first three equations we see that, if w and t are held constant, an increase of 1 (deflated) cent in the price per pound of cotton brought about an average decrease in the per capita domestic consumption of 0.85 pound in the first period, 0.57 pound in the second, and 0.27 pound in the third. These absolute changes can also be converted into relative changes or elasticities by multiplying each one of them by y/x_{dc}. Substituting for y and x_{dc} their representative values,[30] we obtain in each of the three periods the following elasticities of demand: −0.51, −0.25, and −0.12, respectively. It is these figures which are given (to four significant figures) in the column headed "Elasticity of Demand." The absolute value of the coefficient of elasticity is thus seen to have been one-half as great in the second period as it was in the first, and one-half as great in the third as it was in the second.[31]

From the coefficients of w in the first three equations, we see that, other things being equal, an increase of one unit in the United States business index (adjusted for trend) was associated with an increase in the per capita domestic consumption of cotton of 0.10 pound in the first period, of 0.16 in the second, and of 0.24 in the third. And all these coefficients are considerably in excess of their standard errors and are, therefore, quite significant.[32]

From the coefficients of t (and t^2) in the first three equations we also see that the demand curve shifted upward and to the right during the first two periods, the average rate of shift being 0.26 pound per capita per annum (subject, however, to an annual retardation of approximately 0.02 lb. per capita) in the first

[29] For an explanation of the statistical methods used and for definitions of the technical terms see chap. vi.

[30] As explained in chap. vi (III, D, 2, b), the representative value of y is taken as the arithmetic mean, and the representative value of x_{dc} is obtained by substituting the mean values of the independent variables y, w, t, in the demand equation.

[31] For the interpretation which must be given to such statistically determined elasticities see chap. vi, pp. 215–17.

[32] That an improvement in business conditions should bring about an *increase* in the demand for cotton is what we should expect, since cotton is a raw material in several industries. It should be recalled, however, that we found either no relation at all or only a net *negative* relation between an improvement in business conditions and the consumption of sugar and corn (see chaps. vi and vii).

period, and 0.35 pound per capita in the second. During the third period, however, the shift assumed a *downward* course, the (negative) rate being 0.21 pound per capita per annum.[33]

The fact that the demand curve for cotton was shifting downward with time during 1914–29 means that, while it is still true that in any one year a decrease in the price of cotton, business conditions being kept fixed, brought about an increase in the per capita domestic consumption, *producers of cotton would have been faced with a decrease in the per capita domestic consumption from one year to the next even if prices had remained fixed throughout the entire period.* This fact may have a bearing on the present cotton situation.

The fit of each demand function to the data, as judged by the standard errors of the parameters, by the quadratic mean error, and by the adjusted multiple correlation coefficient, is quite good.

Of the total variance of the consumption $(\sigma^2_{x_{dc}})$ of cotton, the fluctuations in the price accounted *directly* for approximately 11 per cent in the first period, 19 per cent in the second, and 9 per cent in the third; the fluctuations in United States business conditions accounted *directly* for approximately 16 per cent in the first period, 19 per cent in the second, and 75 per cent in the third; and the fluctuations in the third independent variable, time, accounted *directly* for 43 per cent in the first period, 60 per cent in the second, and 13 per cent in the third. (These figures are not shown in Table 20.) Since, however, the independent variables are correlated with one another, each of them affects consumption both directly and *indirectly* through its effect on each of the other independent variables. The total (direct and indirect) imputed contribution of each of the independent variables to the variance of the dependent variable (consumption) is given in the last three columns of Table 20.

It should be observed that the variable "time" plays the most important role in the fluctuations of consumption in all but the third period—which suggests that we have not yet isolated and identified some very important variables affecting the demand for cotton.

The second triad of equations (Table 20) represents the demand for cotton directly in terms of relative changes (logarithms). Thus the coefficients of y' $(=\log y)$ show that the partial elasticities of demand for the three periods were −0.44, −0.24, and −0.12, respectively. These are also repeated in the column headed "Elasticity of Demand" and agree fairly well with the corresponding values derived from the first three equations.

The coefficients of w' give the *relative* change in domestic consumption corresponding to a given relative change in United States business conditions. They show that an improvement of 1 per cent in United States business condi-

[33] For definitions of the measures of the rate of shift and the rate of retardation of a demand curve see chap. vi, pp. 187–89 and vii, pp. 253–57.

TABLE 20

COTTON: THE CHARACTERISTICS OF THE PER CAPITA DEMAND FUNCTIONS

x_{dc} = Per capita domestic consumption in pounds
y = Deflated U.S. farm price in cents per pound
t = Time in years. For origins see Table 19

(Figures in parentheses are standard errors)

EQUATION No.	PERIOD*		Constant Term	y	w	t	t^2
1	I	$x_{dc} =$	15.3392	−0.8514 (0.2132)	+0.0989 (0.0211)	+0.2588 (0.0344)	−0.0088 (0.0063)
2	II	$x_{dc} =$	14.8649	−0.5740 (0.1978)	+0.1650 (0.0490)	+0.3478 (0.0708)	. . . .
3	III†	$x_{dc} =$	6.4026	−0.2727 (0.1177)	+0.2366 (0.0345)	−0.2100 (0.0710)	. . . .
			Constant Term	y'	w'	‡Mt	‡Mt^2
4	I	$x'_{dc} =$	0.5288	−0.4360 (0.1124)	+0.5653 (0.1206)	+0.0164 (0.0020)	−0.00084 (0.00037)
5	II	$x'_{dc} =$	0.2753	−0.2449 (0.0931)	+0.6880 (0.2000)	+0.0140 (0.0030)	. . . .
6	III	$x'_{dc} =$	− 0.2264	−0.1248 (0.0570)	+0.8936 (0.1365)	−0.0075 (0.0028)	. . . .

* I = 1875–95; II = 1896–1913; III = 1914–29.
† If the observations for 1914–21 be omitted, eq. 3 becomes:

$$x_{dc} = 1.6831 - 0.2138y + 0.2970w. \qquad R' = 0.7423.$$
$$\phantom{x_{dc} = 1.}(0.1908) \quad (0.1291)$$

TABLE 20—*Continued*

WITH QUANTITY AS THE DEPENDENT VARIABLE, BY PERIODS, 1875–1929

w = W. M. Persons' "Index of U.S. Industrial Production
and Trade," adjusted, weighted. Normal = 100

x', y', w' = Logs of x, y, w

(Figures in parentheses are standard errors)

	DESCRIPTIVE CONSTANTS						EQUA-TION No.
Elasticity of Demand η	Quadratic Mean Error ϵ (Pounds)	Adjusted Multiple Correlation Coefficient R'	Percentage of Variance of Consumption Attributable to				
			y	w	t		
−0.5097 (0.1664)	0.9112	0.9313	17.13	19.67	52.58		I
−0.2496 (0.1078)	1.1938	0.8679	− 0.56	29.12	51.13		2
−0.1245 (0.0669)	1.2801	0.8843	3.75	65.20	13.61		3
η	ϵ (Per Cent)	R'	y'	w'	t		
−0.4360 (0.1124)	94.8–105.5	0.9382	15.35	18.40	56.66		4
−0.2449 (0.0931)	95.1–105.2	0.8645	− 1.16	31.28	49.08		5
−0.1248 (0.0570)	95.2–105.1	0.8721	2.33	66.06	12.46		6

‡ $M = \log_{10} e = 0.43429$.

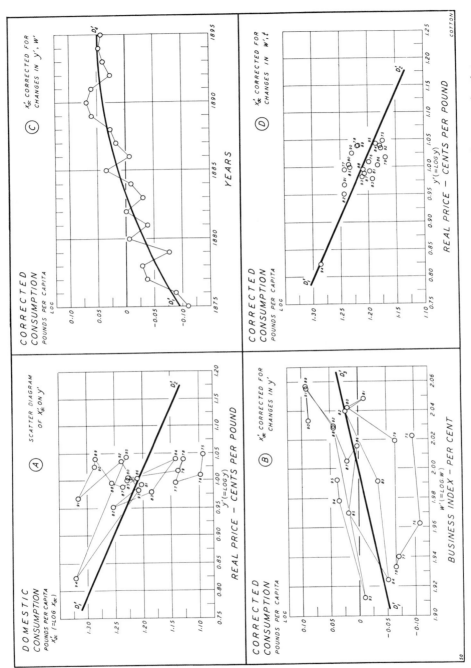

Fig. 50.—Cotton: Four aspects of the per capita demand for cotton during the period 1875–95 on the assumption that

$$x_{dc} = 3.3790 \ y^{-0.4360} \ w^{0.5653} \ e^{0.0164t - 0.00084t^2}.$$

See page 307 for further explanation.

tions as measured by Persons' "Index of Industrial Production and Trade" was associated with an increase of 0.57 per cent in the per capita consumption of cotton during the first period, of 0.69 in the second, and of 0.89 in the third. A 1 per cent change in business conditions thus had a greater net effect on the per capita consumption of cotton than did a 1 per cent change in the real price of cotton.

The coefficients of t (and t^2) in equations 4–6 (Table 20) give the *relative* rates of shift of the demand curve (see chap. vi, n. 20). Thus if we multiply each one of them by 100, we find that during the first period the per capita demand curve shifted upward and to the right at the average rate of 1.64 per cent per annum. However, this rate was not constant; it was subject to a retardation effect of 0.16 per cent per annum. During the second period the shift was also upward, amounting to 1.40 per cent per annum. During the third period, however, the shift of the demand curve assumed a downward course, the (negative) rate being 0.75 per cent per annum.

The fit of each of the logarithmic (constant-elasticity) curves is just as good as that of the corresponding arithmetic (linear) curves.

Figures 50, 51, and 52 are, respectively, graphic representations of equations 4, 5, and 6 of Table 20. We shall consider first Figure 50.

Figure 50A shows the scatter diagram of the logarithms of per capita consumption (x'_{dc}) on the logarithms of real price (y'). The line $D'_1D'_2$ is the *net* regression of x'_{dc} on y'. It gives the relation between that part of the logarithm of per capita consumption which is linearly independent of the logarithm of the United States business index and of time and that part of the logarithm of the real price which is linearly independent of the same variables. The slope of the line, which is given by the coefficient (-0.4360) of y' in equation 4, Table 20, shows that an increase of 1 per cent in the (deflated) price of cotton is associated

---

EXPLANATION OF FIGURE 50

A: Relation between per capita consumption and real price when the data are not corrected for the effects of business conditions and time, with the demand curve $D'_1D'_2$ which results when such corrections are made.

B: Relation between per capita consumption and business conditions when the former is corrected for the effects of changes in real price. The slope of line $D'_1D'_3$ represents the *net* relation between per capita consumption and business conditions.

C: Relation between per capita consumption and time when the former is corrected for the effects of changes in real price and business conditions. The slope of $D'_1D'_4$ (fitted to the variables x'_{dc} and t when both are corrected for price and business conditions) represents the mean rate of shift of the per capita demand curve $D'_1D'_2$.

D: The per capita demand curve for cotton, 1875–95. Line $D'_1D'_2$ shows the relation between that part of per capita consumption of cotton in the United States which is independent of business conditions and time and that part of real price which is independent of business conditions and time. In the scatter, however, only the ordinate is corrected for changes in business conditions and time, the abscissa being uncorrected.

with a decrease of approximately 0.44 per cent in the per capita consumption of cotton.

In Figure 50B, the differences between the computed and the observed values of x'_{dc} (i.e., the vertical deviations of the points from the line $D'_1D'_2$ in Fig. 50A) are plotted against w'. Line $D'_1D'_3$ gives the *net* relation between that part of x'_{dc} which is linearly independent of y' and of t and that part of w' which is linearly independent of the same variables. Its slope (the coefficient of w' in eq. 4, Table 20) shows that an increase of 1 per cent in the United States business index is associated with an increase of 0.57 per cent in the per capita domestic consumption of cotton.

In Figure 50C the residuals (the vertical deviations of the points from the line $D'_1D'_3$ in Fig. 50B) are plotted against time. The curve $D'_1D'_4$ drawn through these points measures the average rate of shift of the demand curve. It shows that during the first period the per capita consumption increased at the rate of 1.64 per cent per annum (the coefficient of t in eq. 4) but that it was subject to a retardation effect of 0.16 per cent per annum.

Figure 50D shows the scatter of the points about the demand curve $D'_1D'_2$ when allowance has been made for changes in w' and in t. We have already seen that the slope of this line, i.e., -0.4360, is the elasticity of demand.

Attention naturally centers on the extreme observation for 1894 (Figs. 50A and D). It is not the result of an error in the data. The explanation of the extremely low price and large consumption is to be found in the fact that in 1894, which was an excellent cotton year, the acreage was greatly increased, resulting in the largest crop ever gathered in the United States up to that time. This enormous crop greatly depressed the price, and the extremely low price brought about the large consumption. The situation, which was similar to that confronting the cotton producers in recent years, resulted in the calling of a planters convention at Jackson, Mississippi, on January 11, 1895, "to effect a reduction in acreage."[34]

Figure 51 relates to the second period and is a graphic representation of equation 5, Table 20. The meaning to be attached to each of the subdivisions of the diagram is similar to that of the corresponding subdivision of Figure 50 and need not, therefore, be repeated. It is important to observe, however, that the slope of the demand curve $D'_1D'_2$ (Figs. 51A and D) is only one-half of the slope of $D'_1D'_2$ in Figure 50. This is the graphic illustration of the fact that the elasticity of demand for cotton was, on the average, 50 per cent less (in numerical value) in the second period than in the first.

Another fact which is brought out clearly by Figure 51 is the nature of the

[34] James L. Watkins, *Production and Price of Cotton for 100 Years* ("U.S. Dept. Agric., Division of Statistics, Miscellaneous Series," Bull. No. 9 [1895]).

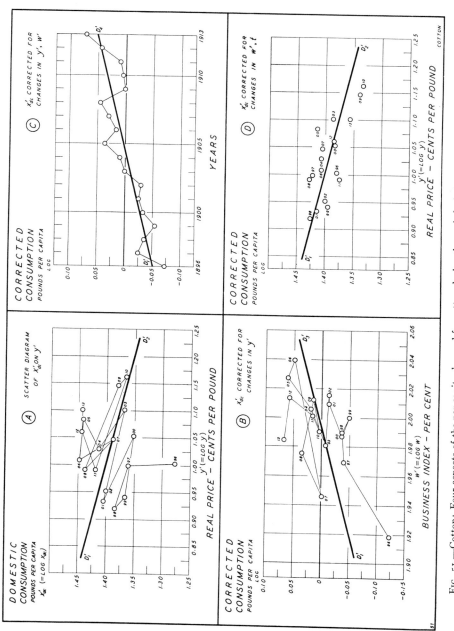

Fig. 51.—Cotton: Four aspects of the per capita demand for cotton during the period 1896–1913 on the assumption that

$$x_{dc} = 1.8851 \, y^{-0.2449} \, w^{0.6880} \, e^{0.01404 \, t} \, .$$

shift of the demand curve. Although it is clear from the net regressions of consumption on time in Figure 51*C* that the *average* shift of the demand curve is upward—this is given by the slope of the line $D'_1D'_4$—the actual movements of the demand curve fluctuated considerably *and in a systematic manner* about this average. In fact, the fluctuations appear to be of a cyclical nature. Evidently there were important factors in the demand for cotton during 1896–1913 which are not taken into account by our equations, or our equations are not of the right kind.

Figure 52, which is a graphic representation of equation 6, Table 20, relates to the third period. A comparison of this diagram with Figure 51 shows that, during the third period, important changes took place in all the three coefficients: the elasticity with respect to price, the elasticity with respect to business conditions, and the relative rate of shift of the demand curve.

The slope of $D'_1D'_2$ of Figure 52 (−0.12) is only one-half that of Figure 51 (−0.24).

The slope of $D'_1D'_3$ of Figure 52 is somewhat greater than that of the corresponding line of Figure 51. This indicates that the effect on consumption of a 1 per cent change in the index of business conditions was somewhat greater during the third period than during the second. In fact, it was 0.69 in the second and 0.89 in the third (see the coefficients of w' in Table 20).

The slope of $D'_1D'_4$ in Figure 52 is negative, while that in Figure 51 is positive. *This is by far the most important of the three changes.* The difference between the two slopes constitutes a graphic illustration of the fact that, whereas during the second period the per capita demand curve for cotton was shifting upward, during the third period it was shifting downward. During the period 1896–1913 the per capita domestic consumption of cotton would have increased on the average by 1.4 per cent per annum, even if no changes had taken place in the deflated price and in business conditions. During the period 1914–29 the per capita domestic consumption would have *decreased* by 0.75 per cent per annum, under the same conditions. *Abstracting from changes in United States business conditions, we thus find that at the same price American consumers bought less and less cotton (on a per capita basis) from one year to the next during this period.* This is an important factor in the present plight of the Cotton Belt.

V. FACTORS IN THE PRICE OF COTTON

In the preceding analyses, per capita domestic consumption of cotton was taken as the dependent variable. But, as we pointed out in Section III, there is lacking in the demand function for cotton that symmetry between the quantity demanded and the price paid which we found in the demand for corn: the fact that changes in consumption may be explained to a fairly high degree of approximation in terms of changes in price, in business conditions, and in time

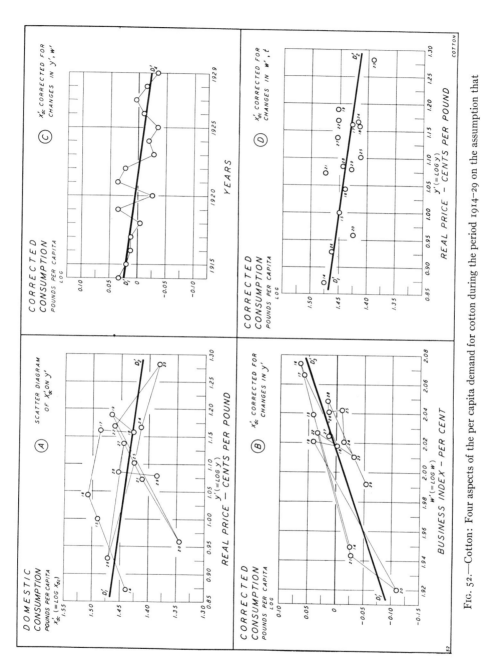

FIG. 52.—Cotton: Four aspects of the per capita demand for cotton during the period 1914–29 on the assumption that

$$x_{dc} = 0.5938 \, y^{-0.1248} \, w^{0.8936} \, e^{-0.0075t}.$$

(the shift of the demand curve) does not necessarily imply that changes in price can be explained by the same variables to the same degree of accuracy. In fact, we have reason to believe that the price of cotton is likely to be more affected by the American and foreign production and stocks than by American consumption. However, in the following analyses of the factors affecting the price of cotton we shall consider first the least probable hypothesis, namely, that the price of cotton depends only on the quantity consumed, on domestic business conditions, and on time:

(3.2) $$y = y(x_{dc}, w, t) ,$$

for this procedure will enable us to see the extent to which the more probable hypotheses (3.4), (3.5) and (3.6) are in better agreement with the facts.

The first six equations of Table 21 summarize the results obtained by using two specific forms of hypothesis (3.2): the linear form (eqs. 1–3) and the logarithmic or constant-elasticity form (eqs. 4–6).

By comparing the R''s of these six equations with the corresponding R''s of the first six equations of Table 20, which constituted a test of hypothesis (3.1), it becomes apparent that the arithmetic and the logarithmic regressions of y on x_{dc}, w, and t are not nearly so well in agreement with the facts as are the corresponding regressions of x_{dc} on y, w, and t. Perhaps the most useful information to be derived from the former regressions (Table 21) is the numerical value of the probable upper limit of the elasticity of domestic demand for cotton.[35]

We turn now to the more probable hypothesis

(3.4) $$y = y(x_{dp}, x_{fp}, w, t) .$$

Equations 7–9 of Table 21 are the results obtained by fitting one specific form of (3.4)—the logarithmic—to the data. In each of these equations total United States production (x_{dp}) has been substituted for per capita domestic consumption, and a new variable, foreign production (x_{fp}), has been added to the independent variables.

By comparing the R''s of these equations with the corresponding R''s of equations 4–6 of the same table, we see that, with the exception of the equation for the first period, hypothesis (3.4) gives a better fit to the data than does hypothesis (3.2). The low value of R' for the first period (0.5504) is, however, a disappointment. An explanation which suggests itself is that the statistics of production for the first period are less reliable than are the corresponding statistics of consumption. But we have no direct evidence in support of this hypothesis.

Although the value of R' is greater in this than in the previous set of equa-

---

[35] For an explanation of this property of $1/\varphi$ see chap. vi, p. 228.

tions, it cannot be considered as a satisfactory explanation of the factors affecting the price of cotton because the regression coefficient of price on foreign production is positive, indicating that an increase in foreign production brings
about an *increase* in the domestic price.[36] This finding is contrary to both
reason and experience. It results, in part, from the fact that the series for
foreign production is subject to large errors and, in part, from the fact that our
analysis does not include any measure of foreign business conditions, foreign
stocks, and other factors which affect the foreign demand for American cotton.
As we shall show later, when world business conditions and foreign supply are
introduced into the equation, the regression of price on the latter variable is
negative.

Another puzzling fact brought out by equations 7–9 of Table 21 is that, other
things being equal, an improvement in United States business conditions was
associated with a *decrease* in the price of cotton during the second period,
which contradicts the relation obtained for the first and third periods (cf. the
coefficients of w' in eqs. 7–9). But the coefficient of w' for the second period is
not very significant as compared with its standard error; consequently, it could
be omitted without greatly reducing the adjusted multiple correlation coefficient.

We turn next to the more probable hypothesis, namely, that the domestic
price depends on United States supply (=production+ stocks), foreign production, American business conditions, and time:

(3.5) $$y = y(x_{ds}, x_{fp}, w, t) \, .$$

Unfortunately, data on United States supply are available only since 1905.
This prevents us from dividing our series into three periods and from testing
the hypothesis on the data for each period. If we treat the observations for
1905–29 as homogeneous, and fit the logarithmic form of hypothesis (3.5) to
them, we obtain equation 10 of Table 21, of which Figure 53 is a graphic representation. Among the more important relations summarized by this equation
are the following:

1. Based on the experience of 1905–29, an increase of 1 per cent in the
domestic supply of cotton for any given year is, on the average, associated with
a decrease of 1.38 per cent in the domestic price, when foreign production and
United States business conditions are fixed (see line $d'_1 d'_2$, Figs. 53A and E).

2. The positive effect of changes in foreign production on the domestic price
of cotton is not altered by the substitution of domestic supply for domestic
production in our analysis.

[36] During the first period the coefficient of x'_{fp} proved quite insignificant as compared with its
standard error. Consequently, it was omitted from the equations, and the other coefficients were corrected for this omission.

TABLE 21

COTTON: EQUATIONS SUMMARIZING FACTORS

y = Deflated U.S. farm price. Unit: Cents per pound
x_{dc} = Per capita domestic consumption. Unit: Pounds
x_{dp} = Total domestic production. Unit: 1,000 bales of 500 pounds gross weight
x_{fp} = Total foreign (= world *minus* U.S.) production. Unit: 1,000 bales of 500 pounds gross weight
x_{ds} = Domestic supply. Unit: 1,000 bales of 500 pounds gross weight

(Figures in parentheses are standard errors)

EQUATION No.	PERIOD†		Constant Term	x_{dc}		w	t	t^2
1	I	$y=$	12.8976	−0.5530 (0.1410)	....	+0.0618 (0.0221)	+0.1187 (0.0498)	....
2	II	$y=$	19.5817	−0.6545 (0.2255)	....	+0.0766 (0.0674)	+0.3599 (0.0795)	....
3	III‡	$y=$	7.7573	−0.6745 (0.3438)	....	+0.2389 (0.0916)	....	−0.0663 (0.0318)

			Constant Term	x'_{dc}		w'	§Mt	§Mt^2
4	I	$y'=$	1.0461	−1.1119 (0.2866)	....	+0.6572 (0.2470)	+0.0154 (0.0062)	−0.0010 (0.0006)
5	II	$y'=$	1.7095	−1.3499 (0.5134)	....	+0.6030 (0.6173)	+0.0320 (0.0074)	....
6	III	$y'=$	− 0.9613	−1.4464 (0.7269)	....	+2.0748 (0.7139)	....	−0.0055 (0.0025)

			Constant Term	x'_{dp}	x'_{fp}	w'	§Mt	§Mt^2
7	I‖	$y'=$	2.9251	−0.6697 (0.2070)	¶	+0.3158 (0.2440)	+0.0171 (0.0075)	−0.00082 (0.00077)
8	II	$y'=$	2.4052	−0.6044 (0.2259)	+0.6447 (0.1294)	−0.6938 (0.5107)	....	−0.0019 (0.0013)
9	III	$y'=$	− 0.1215	−0.8432 (0.2737)	+0.7520 (0.4161)	+0.8510 (0.4169)	+0.0114 (0.0104)	−0.0059 (0.0027)

* For eqs. 1–6, 8, and 9 the origins of t are given in Table 19. For eqs. 7, 10, and 11, the origins of t are, respectively, September 1, 1886, February 1, 1918, and August 1, 1924.

† I = 1875–95; II = 1896–1913; III = 1914–29; IV = 1905–29; V = 1918–29; VI = 1920–32.

‡ If the observations for 1914–21 are omitted, eq. 3 becomes:

$$y = 35.7697 - 0.9140x_{dc} + 0.0220w - 0.7479t \, . \quad R' = 0.6948$$
$$(0.6280) \quad (0.2906) \quad (0.3378)$$

If w is dropped because it is not significant, this equation becomes:

$$y = 37.1168 - 0.8772x_{dc} - 0.7491t \, . \quad R' = 0.7652 \, .$$
$$(0.3561) \quad (0.3020)$$

TABLE 21—*Continued*

AFFECTING THE UNITED STATES PRICE OF COTTON

x_{fs} = Total foreign supply. Unit: 1,000 bales of 500 pounds gross weight
w = W. M. Persons' "Index of U.S. Industrial Production and Trade" adjusted, weighted. Normal = 100
v = N. J. Wall's "Index of World Industrial Production" (1923–25 = 100)
x', y', w', v' = Logs of x, y, w, v
t = Time in years*

(Figures in parentheses are standard errors)

DESCRIPTIVE CONSTANTS

Flexibility of Price $\varphi_{yx_{dc}}$	Quadratic Mean Error ϵ (Cents)	Adjusted Multiple Correlation Coefficient R'	\multicolumn{4}{c	}{Percentage of Variance of Price Attributable to}	EQUATION No.
			x_{dc}		w	t	
−0.9058 (0.3290)	0.7513	0.6556	70.33	....	1.38	−20.18	1
−1.5053 (0.7300)	1.2747	0.7125	−1.11	....	0.48	60.08	2
−1.3291 (0.9291)	2.3015	0.6384	7.81	....	22.84	21.95	3

$\varphi_{yx_{dc}}$	ϵ (Per Cent)	R'	x'_{dc}		w'	t	
−1.1119 (0.2866)	91.8–108.9	0.6426	75.18	....	1.68	−23.82	4
−1.3499 (0.5134)	88.8–112.6	0.6950	−2.38	....	0.17	59.63	5
−1.4464 (0.7269)	83.3–120.0	0.6728	4.57	....	29.79	21.85	6

$\varphi_{yx_{dp}}$	ϵ (Per Cent)	R'	x'_{dp}	x'_{fp}	w'	t	
−0.6697 (0.2070)	91.1–109.7	0.5504	62.85	....	0.02	−17.90	7
−0.6044 (0.2259)	89.6–111.6	0.7442	−4.49	70.18	−0.20	0.39	8
−0.8432 (0.2737)	85.3–117.2	0.7667	36.36	−4.72	12.22	28.65	9

§ $M = \log_{10} e = 0.43429$.
‖ This period covers the years 1876–95 because data for foreign production were not available for 1875.
¶ This variable was omitted because it proved statistically insignificant.

TABLE 21—*Continued*

EQUA-TION No.	PERI-OD†		Constant Term	x'_{ds}	x'_{fp}	w'	§Mt		§Mt^3
					EQUATIONS				
10	IV	$y'=$	4.6926	−1.3786 (0.2213)	+0.3277 (0.2077)	+0.4207 (0.2992)	+0.0254 (0.0097)	....	−0.000108 (0.000113)
11	V	$y'=$	2.2787	−1.2771 (0.2113)	+1.0498 (0.2750)	¶	−0.0279 (0.0130)	....	....
			Constant Term	x_{ds}	x'_{fs}	v'			
12	VI	$y'=$	8.1689	−1.3945 (0.1958)	−0.7374 (0.4630)	+0.9486 (0.2355)	....	....	....

3. An increase of 1 per cent in the index of United States industrial production and trade for any year is, on the average, associated with an increase in the price of 0.42 per cent, when the domestic supply and foreign production is fixed (see line $d'_1d'_4$, Fig. 53C).

4. Even when the domestic supply, foreign production, and United States business conditions are kept fixed, the price does not remain fixed but shifts in the manner indicated by the coefficients of Mt and Mt^3 (see $d'_1d'_5$, Fig. 53D). Beginning with 1925 the shift was downward.

5. Judged by R', the fit of equation 10 is better than that of equation 9.

Although hypothesis (3.5) is thus seen to be in somewhat better agreement with the facts than is (3.2) or (3.4), a consideration of the scatter of the points about the curve $d'_1d'_5$ in Figure 53D shows that we were not justified in assuming that the observations for the entire period 1905–29 constituted a homogeneous series for the purpose of testing hypothesis (3.5). The vertiginous rise in the price of cotton which took place between 1914 and 1919 and which is not appreciably reduced when allowance is made for changes in the general trend of prices, in business conditions, in the domestic supply, and in foreign production constitutes a most definite break in our series. Moreover, the level about which prices fluctuated between 1918 and 1929 was reached by such a precipitous climb, and remained so far above the pre-war level, that a separate analysis of the observations since 1918 is clearly called for. Accordingly, it was decided to omit the observations for 1905–17 from the computations and to confine the testing of hypothesis (3.5) to the data from 1918 to 1929.

Equation 11 summarizes the results obtained.

TABLE 21—*Continued*

			DESCRIPTIVE CONSTANTS				
Flexibility of Price $\varphi_{yx_{ds}}$	Quadratic Mean Error ϵ (Per Cent)	Adjusted Multiple Correlation Coefficient R'	Percentage of Variance of Price Attributable to				EQUATION No.
			x'_{ds}	x'_{fp}	w'	t	
−1.3786 (0.2213)	88.2–113.4	0.8106	50.28	1.70	5.51	15.37	10
−1.2771 (0.2113)	90.9–110.1	0.9044	66.72	10.80	....	9.24	11
$\varphi_{yx_{ds}}$	ϵ (Per Cent)	R'	x'_{ds}	x'_{fs}	v'		
−1.3945 (0.1958)	89.9–111.2	0.9536	71.42	8.77	13.00	....	12

As judged by a comparison of the adjusted multiple correlation coefficients, this equation gives a better fit to the data than does equation 10. However, the positive effect of foreign production on the price of cotton remains unchanged.

Changes in United States business conditions proved to have only an insignificant *average* effect on price fluctuations of this period. The coefficient of w' was therefore omitted, and the remaining coefficients and their standard errors were adjusted for this omission.[37]

From the coefficient of Mt it appears that, other things being equal, the price would have kept on falling at the average rate of 2.79 per cent per annum. However, the actual decline was not uniformly downward but followed a pronounced zigzag course, producing a wide scatter of the observations about the trend.

We turn finally to the most probable of our hypotheses, namely, that the domestic price depends on domestic supply, foreign supply, world business conditions, and time:

$$(3.6) \qquad y = y(x_{ds}, x_{fs}, v, t).$$

Since data on world-stocks and world business conditions are available only for the years after 1920, we have decided to test this hypothesis only for the years 1920–32.

Equation 12 summarizes the results obtained.

By far the most important result is the negative sign obtained for the regression of price on foreign supply (see line $d'_1d'_3$, Fig. 54B).

[37] The formulas used were modifications of those given by R. A. Fisher, *Statistical Methods for Research Workers* (6th ed.; Edinburgh: Oliver & Boyd, 1936), § 29.1.

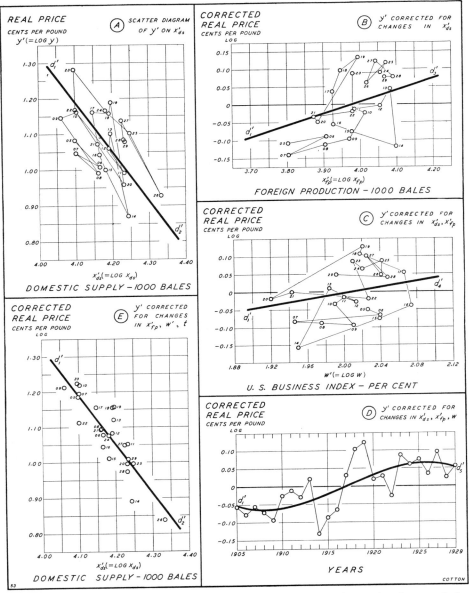

FIG. 53.—Cotton: Four factors affecting the deflated United States farm price of cotton during the period 1905–29 on the assumption that

$$y = 49267\ x_{ds}^{-1.3786}\ x_{fp}^{0.3277}\ w^{0.4207}\ e^{0.0254t-0.000108t^3}.$$

318

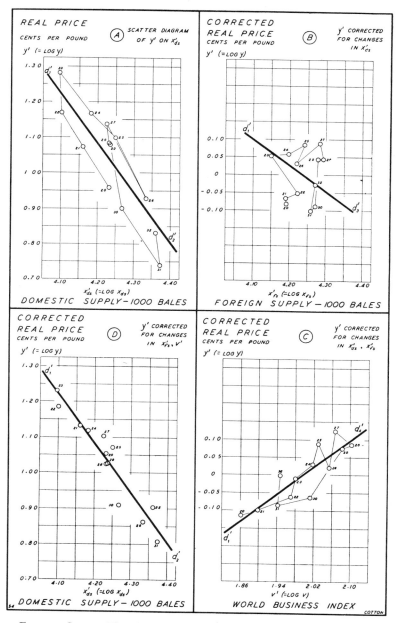

FIG. 54.—Cotton: Three factors affecting the United States farm price of cotton during the period 1920–32 on the assumption that

$$y = 1475(10^5)\ x_{ds}{}^{-1.3945}\ x_{fs}{}^{-0.7374}\ v^{0.9486}\ .$$

A comparison of the coefficients of x'_{ds} and x'_{fs} shows that the farm price was more responsive to domestic supply than to foreign supply: the partial price flexibility with respect to the former is nearly twice that with respect to the latter variable (cf. lines $d'_1d'_2$ and $d'_1d'_3$, Figs. 54A and B).

From the coefficient of v we see that, other things being equal, an increase of 1 per cent in the index of world industrial production was associated with an average increase in the deflated United States farm price of 0.95 per cent (line $d'_1d'_4$, Fig. 54C). (It should be noted that the index of world business conditions is not drawn to the same scale as the index of United States business conditions.)

The regression of price on time proved insignificant. The coefficient of t was therefore omitted, and the remaining coefficients and their standard errors were adjusted for this omission.

VI. SUMMARY OF FINDINGS

Although the demand for cotton has been the subject of several notable studies,[38] none of them had for its object the analysis of the changes that have taken place in the shape, the elasticity, and the rate of shift of the demand curve, and of the factors which account for them. The main findings of the present

---

[38] The studies which have blazed the path for all later investigations into the demand for cotton are. Professor Henry L. Moore's *Forecasting the Yield and the Price of Cotton* (New York: 1917), and his "Empirical Laws of Demand and Supply and the Flexibility of Prices," *Political Science Quarterly*, XXXIV (1919), 546–67.

The more recent investigations are: M. Ezekiel, "A Method of Handling Curvilinear Correlation for Any Number of Variables," *Journal of the American Statistical Association*, XIX (1924), 431–53; "Preisvoraussage bei landwirtschaftlichen Erzeugnissen," *Veröffentlichungen der Frankfurter Gesellschaft für Konjunkturforschung*, Heft IX (1930); A. B. Cox, *Cotton Prices and Market* (U.S.D.A. Bull., No. 1444 [1926]); Hugh B. Killough and Lucy W. Killough, "Price Making Forces in the Cotton Markets," *Jour. Amer. Statist. Assoc.*, XXI (1926), 47–54; Bradford B. Smith, "Forecasting the Volume and Value of the Cotton Crop," *Jour. Amer. Statist. Assoc.*, XXII (1927), 442–59; *Factors Affecting the Price of Cotton* (U.S.D.A. Tech. Bull., No. 50 [January, 1928]); V. P. Timoshenko, "Correlations between Prices and Yields of Previous Years," *Journal of Political Economy*, XXXVI, No. 4 (1928), 510–15; Otto Donner, "Bestimmungsgründe der Baumwollpreise," *Vierteljahrshefte zur Konjunkturforschung*, Sonderheft XV (Berlin, 1930); L. H. Bean, "Some Interrelationships between the Supply, Price and Consumption of Cotton" (mimeographed notes published by the U.S.D.A., Bureau of Agricultural Economics [1928]); "A Simplified Method of Graphic Curvilinear Correlation," *Jour. Amer. Statist. Assoc.*, XXIV (1929), 386–97, esp. Chart V; "Measuring the Effect of Supplies on Prices of Farm Products," *Journal of Farm Economics*, XV (1933), 349–74, esp. Fig. 3; C. Bresciani-Turroni, "Relations entre la récolte et le prix du coton égyptien," *L'Egypte contemporaine*, XXI (1930), 633–89; "L'Influence de la speculation sur les fluctuations des prix du coton," *ibid.*, XXII (1931), 308–42; "Über die Elastizität des Verbrauchs ägyptischer Baumwolle," *Weltwirtschaftliches Archiv*, XXXIII (1931), 46–86; Umberto Ricci, "Die Nachfrage nach ägyptischer Baumwolle und ihre Elastizität," *Weltwirtschaftliches Archiv*, XXXV (1932), 250–61; and J. Roger Wallace, "Factors Affecting American Cotton Prices," Appen. III of Garside's *Cotton Goes to Market* (New York, 1935).

Messrs. Bean and Wallace use only the graphic method in their analyses. Messrs. Ezekiel, Smith, and Cox also make use of mathematical formulas.

chapter center around these topics, although they also embrace an analysis of the factors affecting the price of cotton.

To repeat:

1. The net effect of a 1 cent rise in the (deflated) price per pound of cotton was to decrease the annual per capita consumption by 0.85 pound in 1875–95, by 0.57 pound in 1896–1913, and by 0.27 pound in 1914–29. Translated in terms of elasticities of demand, the foregoing relations mean that, *other things being equal*, the effect of an increase of 1 per cent in the (deflated) price of cotton was to decrease the annual per capita consumption by approximately 0.51 per cent in the first period, by 0.25 per cent in the second, and by 0.12 per cent in the third.

2. But other things did not remain equal. In each of the three periods changes in United States business conditions and shifts in the position of the demand curve with time also had important effects on consumption. An increase of 1 unit in W. M. Persons' "Index of Industrial Production and Trade," other things being equal, was associated with an increase in the per capita consumption of cotton of 0.10 pound in the first period, 0.16 pound in the second, and 0.24 pound in the third. The same findings expressed in terms of relative changes mean that a change of 1 per cent in the index was associated with a change of 0.57 per cent in the first period, 0.69 per cent in the second, and 0.89 in the third.

3. During the first two periods the demand curve shifted upward and to the right, the rate of shift being 0.26 pound per capita per annum (subject to a retardation of 0.02 lb. per capita per annum) during the first period, and 0.35 pound per capita per annum during the second period. During the third period, however, the shift assumed a downward course, *decreasing* by 0.21 pound per capita per annum. If we express these shifts in relative terms, we find that they amounted to 1.64 per cent per annum (subject to a retardation of 0.16 per cent per annum) during the first period, and 1.4 per cent during the second. During the third period the shift was *downward*, the negative rate being 0.75 per cent per annum. *The fact that the domestic per capita demand curve for cotton was shifting downward with time during 1914–29 means that, even if the price of cotton and business conditions had been kept constant, producers of cotton would have been faced with a decrease in the domestic per capita consumption from one year to the next.*

So much for the domestic demand for cotton.

4. Turning next to the factors affecting the price of cotton, we found it desirable, on account of the nature of the available data, to consider the following hypotheses:

a) Price depends on domestic consumption, domestic business conditions, and time.

b) Price depends on domestic production, foreign production, domestic business conditions, and time.

c) Price depends on domestic supply, foreign production, domestic business conditions, and time.

d) Price depends on domestic supply, foreign supply, world business conditions, and time.

Abstracting from the positive regression of price on foreign production, we find a progressive improvement in the fits of the hypotheses to the data.

5. From the specific form (constant elasticity) which we gave to the first hypothesis, it emerges that an increase of 1 per cent in the per capita consumption of cotton was associated with a decrease in the (deflated) farm price of 1.11 per cent in the first period, 1.35 per cent in the second, and 1.45 per cent in the third. An increase of 1 per cent in the index of domestic business conditions was associated with an increase of approximately 0.6 per cent in the first and second periods, and 2.07 per cent in the third. During the first two periods consumers (i.e., the mills) were willing to pay a higher price from one year to the next for the same consumption, business conditions being constant. During the third period, however, this situation no longer obtained.

6. From the specific form in which the second hypothesis was fitted to the data, it appears that, other things being equal, an increase in domestic production tended to lower the domestic price, while an increase in foreign production tended to raise it, in each of the three periods.[39] Thus, if x'_{fp}, w', and t had remained constant, an increase of 1 per cent in the United States production (x'_{dp}) would have lowered the farm price by between 0.6 and 0.8 per cent; while, if x'_{dp}, w', and t had been fixed, an increase in foreign production (x'_{fp}) of 1 per cent would have been associated with an *increase* in the price of between 0.6 and 0.8 per cent. As we have seen, however, this positive regression coefficient is spurious.

Changes in domestic business conditions appear to have had no consistent effect on price. During the first and third periods the net effect of an increase in W. M. Persons' index was to increase the price of cotton. During the second period the net effect was to decrease it. But this negative relation is not very significant statistically.

Even if domestic production, domestic business conditions, and foreign production had been fixed, this analysis suggests that the (deflated) price of cotton would have shown a tendency to decrease with time, this tendency becoming particularly noticeable and significant in the second half of the third period.

7. Proceeding to the third hypothesis, in which the United States supply $(x_{ds} = \text{production} + \text{stocks})$ was substituted for the United States production

[39] In the equation for the first period the regression of price on foreign production was not significant.

(x_{dp}), and confining our attention to the post-war period of 1918–29, the analysis indicates that during this period the net average effect on price of changes in business conditions was negligible; that the most important factors were the size of the American supply, the size of the foreign crop, and time, the three factors accounting, respectively, for 67, 11, and 9 per cent of the variance of price.

The net effect of an increase of 1 per cent in the domestic supply was to decrease the domestic price by 1.28 per cent. The net effect of an increase of 1 per cent in the foreign production was to *increase* the domestic price by 1.05 per cent. We have already pointed out, however, that this regression coefficient is spurious.

Even if domestic supply and foreign production had been fixed, it appears that the price would not have remained constant but would have decreased at the average rate of 2.79 per cent per annum.

8. Turning finally to the fourth hypothesis, in which foreign supply is substituted for foreign production, and world business conditions for domestic business conditions, we find that the net effect of an increase of 1 per cent in the domestic supply was to decrease the domestic price by 1.4 per cent but that the net effect of an equal increase in the foreign supply was to decrease the domestic price by only 0.7 per cent. The net effect of a 1 per cent increase in the index of world industrial production was to increase the domestic price of cotton by 0.95 per cent. There was no significant regression of price on time.

VII. THE BEARING OF THE FINDINGS ON THE FUTURE OF COTTON

If our findings that the demand for cotton is quite inelastic and that the demand curve has been shifting downward since the World War are valid, they are of paramount importance to the farmers of the Cotton Belt and to the American people as a whole.

An inelastic demand means that, *other things being equal*, a bumper crop will sell for less than a moderate crop. This fact, which has long been known to economists, has recently been used as an argument in favor of restriction of output by the A.A.A. Thus, referring to the inelastic demand of such commodities as cotton and potatoes, Ezekiel and Bean correctly observe that

this basic fact has little significance to the individual grower unless the entire group undertakes, in a joint effort, to bring about a condition of moderate supplies. Without that common effort, the individual farmer sees his interest only in producing a larger volume, especially if there is reason to believe that other producers are undertaking to bring about a reduction in supplies and higher prices.[40]

But, if the downward shift of the per capita domestic demand curve does not come to a stop in the near future, then all such plans for restriction of output as were sponsored by the A.A.A. will give only temporary relief, for it will be

[40] Mordecai Ezekiel and Louis H. Bean, *Economic Bases for the Agricultural Adjustment Act* (U.S. Dept. Agric., 1933), p. 50.

a matter of only a few years before the downward shift of the curve will counter-act the gain obtained from the creation of an artificial scarcity. Thus, to take an extreme illustration, suppose that all cotton planters had been induced in 1914 to combine and to charge a monopoly price to the American consumer and to sell the surplus abroad for whatever it would bring. Suppose, furthermore, that no imports of foreign cottons could climb over our tariff wall. If the planters had used equation 3 of Table 20 and assumed "normal" industrial production ($w = 100$) as the basis of their computations, they would have charged a price of 58.0 cents in 1914 and 52.2 cents in 1929, in terms of the 1913 dollar. At these prices the per capita consumption in the United States would have been 15.8 pounds and 14.2 pounds, and the corresponding average receipts from each unit of the population $9.18 and $7.44—a decrease of $1.74 between the two years. Owing, however, to the growth of population, the total receipts would have increased from $905,000,000 in 1914 to $910,000,000 in 1929—an increase of 0.55 per cent in the sixteen years. But, as the rate of growth of the population is rapidly decreasing, this relatively small increase in total receipts would soon become a negative quantity.[41] Total receipts would almost certainly decline if for some reason or other the planters charged a price different from the monopoly price.

That total receipts (in deflated dollars) from the domestic consumers of cotton is bound to decline with time is evident from a consideration of the causes which have brought about the downward shift of the demand curve. These are: (1) the changing styles and habits of dress which have reduced the requirements of cotton and (2) the competition of silk and rayon. Thus, our production of rayon, which was only 2.4 million pounds in 1914, mounted to 36.3 million pounds by 1924, and reached 210.3 million pounds in 1934,[42] an amount which is equal in weight to 420,600 bales of cotton of 500 pounds gross weight. The operation of these causes cannot be stopped. Their effects can only be counteracted through the increased use of cotton in industry.

So far we have failed to take into account in our illustration the effect on the planters' income of receipts from exports. A full consideration of this factor involves a knowledge of the domestic and foreign demand and supply functions for the American and foreign cottons, and most of these functions are not known. As will be shown later, however, the production of cotton abroad has been increasing (stimulated in part by the American restriction program), and foreign buyers have been turning increasingly to other countries for their cotton. The foreign-demand situation does not, therefore, justify the expectation of a higher (deflated) price for American cotton.

[41] The empirical eq. 3 of Table 20 cannot be safely extrapolated much beyond the range of the data.

[42] Moïs H. Avram, *The Rayon Industry* (New York: Van Nostrand Co., Inc., 1929), p. 51; and *U.S.D.A. Yearbook, 1935*, p. 745. (The figures relate to calendar years.)

In view of this finding, the events since 1929 assume a new significance.[43] In October, 1929, the Federal Farm Board announced that it would make loans averaging 16 cents a pound to cotton co-operative marketing associations. Although cotton was then selling at $17\frac{1}{3}$ cents per pound, the price was considered so low in relation to costs of production that the Board justified its action "as a means of preventing a threatened demoralization of the cotton market." In spite of these loans, cotton in February, 1930, fell below 16 cents a pound. Many of the co-operatives, expecting the price to rise, bought "futures" when they sold the cotton they were holding. When the futures matured and they faced a loss, they called for delivery of the cotton. The Cotton Stabilization Corporation, which was formed in June, 1930, under the auspices of the Federal Farm Board, took over the stocks of cotton acquired by the co-operatives. The purchase of the supplies tended to maintain production and to expand the surplus, so that despite this assistance the price of cotton continued to drop, reaching 4.6 cents in June, 1932. The United States carry-over in August, 1932, was 9,921,000 bales, an amount equal to an entire year's normal crop. The stocks were disposed of only at a heavy loss to the government and with dissatisfaction to all concerned.

In 1933 the situation improved somewhat. Although the domestic carry-over of all cotton on August 1 of that year was still high (8,421,000 bales), both prices and plantings increased. This was due primarily to the general belief that "something would be done for cotton." On May 12, 1933, the A.A.A. received the signature of the President.[44] Its main purpose was:

To establish and maintain such balance between the production and consumption of agricultural commodities, and such marketing conditions therefor, as will reestablish prices to farmers at a level that will give agricultural commodities a purchasing power with respect to articles that farmers buy, equivalent to the purchasing power of agricultural commodities in the base period. The base period in the case of all agricultural commodities except tobacco shall be the pre-war period, August 1909–July 1914. In the case of tobacco, the base period shall be the post-war period, August 1919–July 1929.[45]

[43] The more important series showing the changes in the cotton situation since 1929 are given in Tables IIb and V of Appen. A.

[44] This is the first of the series of the New Deal legislation passed in 1933:
Agricultural Adjustment Act, Act of May 12, 1933.
Federal Emergency Relief Act of 1933, Act of May 12, 1933.
Emergency Relief Act of 1933, Act of May 12, 1933.
Tennessee Valley Authority Act of 1933, Act of May 18, 1933.
Securities Act of 1933, Act of May 27, 1933.
Uniform Value of Coins and Currencies, Resolution of June 5, 1933.
Reconstruction Finance Corporation, Act of June 10, 1933.
Home Owners' Loan Act of 1933, Act of June 13, 1933.
National Industrial Recovery Act, Act of June 16, 1933.
Banking Act of 1933, Act of June 16, 1933.
Farm Credit Act of 1933, Act of June 16, 1933.
Emergency Railroad Transportation Act, 1933, Act of June 16, 1933.

[45] Ezekiel and Bean, *op. cit.*, p. 1.

Prices which would give producers the same purchasing power as the commodities enjoyed in the base period were called "parity" prices.[46]

The act aimed particularly to regulate production of certain specific agricultural commodities such as wheat, cotton, corn, hogs, rice, tobacco, and dairy products. But some of its features were broad enough to include other farm products. The act recognized limitation of production as a means of attaining a rise in agricultural prices. The Secretary of Agriculture was authorized to make benefit payments to farmers in return for a reduction of output and to make rental payments to farmers for taking land out of production. The necessary funds for this purpose was to be raised through processing taxes on the commodities in question.

Shortly after the act was passed, the government began a campaign to get farmers to plow under between one-fourth and one-half of the cotton acreage which they had already planted. For every acre withdrawn they were offered cash payments of from $6.00 to $12.00, according to the estimated yield of that acre, plus options to buy government-owned cotton[47] at 6 cents a pound. Instead of this, farmers could take straight cash payments of from $7.00 to $20.00 an acre. Although the government succeeded in removing from production approximately 10,900,000 acres, or one-fourth of the amount planted, the cotton crop in 1933 turned out to be actually larger than the 1932 crop. Presumably only the poorer acreage was plowed under and, restricted to a smaller acreage, some farmers undoubtedly used more fertilizer. Furthermore, the weather and the growing conditions were very favorable in 1933.

In spite of the large yield, the price of cotton improved, the farm price rising from 6.52 cents per pound in 1932 to 9.72 cents per pound in 1933. But it was not high enough to satisfy the planters. Therefore, in October of that year the Commodity Credit Corporation agreed to make loans on cotton at 10 cents a pound. The loans were made without recourse on the borrower. If prices rose above 10 cents, the farmer could sell his cotton in the open market, pay off his debt to the government, and pocket the difference. If prices fell, he could sell his cotton to the government at the loan price. Since prices in 1934 rose well above 10 cents, the government did not lose on this particular venture.

The upshot of the cotton adjustment program for 1933 was that it prevented the crop from becoming a bumper crop, although it did not succeed in reducing it below the level reached in the previous year.

But in view of the size of the 1933 crop it was felt that a more drastic and effective method was needed for curtailing production. It was feared that the

---

[46] As can be seen from a glance at Figs. 48 and 49, both the money and the deflated prices for the base period 1909–13 were the highest prices paid for cotton previous to the war.

[47] This cotton represented for the most part what the Federal Farm Board had acquired in its stabilization purchases.

farmers who did not accept the government contract would take advantage of their neighbors who agreed to curtail production and increase their plantings. The Bankhead Cotton Control Act, which became a law on April 21, 1934, was designed to prevent the occurrence of such a contingency. The act fixed a production quota for 1934 of 10,000,000 bales, or 77 per cent of the average production for the years 1909–13. More specifically, it provided that 10,000,000 bales might be ginned free of the ginning tax. This amount of tax-exempt cotton was allotted to individual farmers on the basis of the production history of each farm. Any cotton raised in excess of the exempt limit was subject to a tax of 50 per cent of the average central market price of $\frac{7}{8}$ inch middling spot cotton. In any case the tax was to be not less than 5 cents a pound. As a result of this act, only 28,400,000 acres were planted to cotton in 1934. And the low yields on this reduced acreage produced a crop of 9,650,000 bales, or the smallest crop since 1921. Primarily in response to the small crop the farm price for 1934–35 rose to 12.6 cents per pound.

That the cotton program of the A.A.A. has temporarily improved the position of the planters appears probable. The farm value of the 1932 cotton and cottonseed crop was $484,000,000 (see Table 22). The farm value of the 1933 crop was $716,000,000. But in 1933 the farmers received benefit payments from the government of $174,000,000, making a gross value of $890,000,000. The farm value of the 1934 crop was $744,000,000, and the benefit payments in that year were $116,000,000. The total amount, or $860,000,000, was nearly double the value of the crop for 1932. Moreover, the long-sought-for "parity" was attained by January, 1934.

The rental benefit payments on the 1933 crop together with the value of options, amounted to about 4 cents per pound on the production of those who participated. This amount added to the current farm price came close to giving the participating cotton farmers pre-war parity on the domestically consumed portion of the crop.[48]

The A.A.A. program, however, was not the only and perhaps not the most important factor in this income improvement. Part of the higher price of cotton since 1932 has been the result of the devaluation of the dollar in 1933, of the government loan policy, and of improvements in general business conditions.

By reducing the dollar to 59 per cent of its former value, the government enabled foreigners to buy it at a large discount. This made the price of our cotton more attractive to them and led to its being bid up. By devaluing the dollar, the government also enabled farmers to buy nonfarm goods at better relative prices and lightened their debt and taxation burdens.

By making loans at 12 cents a pound in 1934 without recourse on the borrower, the A.A.A. virtually guaranteed the cotton planter a price of 12 cents.

[48] *U.S.D.A. Yearbook, 1934*, p. 110.

Although the government as a result of this policy was obliged to take over nearly half of the 1934 crop and although it suffered a great loss, the cotton planters gained at least temporarily from the guaranteed price.

Of even greater importance in the increased farm income from cotton was the improvement in general business conditions which has been going on since

TABLE 22*

COTTON: FARM VALUE AND GROSS INCOME FROM COTTON AND COTTONSEED
IN THE UNITED STATES, 1909–10 TO 1935–36

(In Thousands of Dollars)

YEAR	COTTON Farm Value and Gross Income	COTTONSEED		TOTAL Cotton and Cottonseed		BENEFIT PAYMENT	TOTAL (INCLUDING BENEFIT PAYMENTS)	
		Farm Value	Gross Income	Farm Value	Gross Income		Farm Value	Gross Income
Average (1909–10 to 1913–14).........	783,011	†	88,613	....	871,624	....	....	....
1914–15......	592,830	†	93,100	....	685,930	....	....	....
1915–16......	626,774	†	122,220	....	748,994	....	....	....
1916–17......	992,304	†	186,535	....	1,178,839	....	....	....
1917–18......	1,529,862	†	251,600	....	1,781,462	....	....	....
1918–19......	1,738,071	†	258,058	....	1,996,129	....	....	....
1919–20......	2,020,398	†	245,728	....	2,266,126	....	....	....
1920–21......	1,069,257	†	95,273	....	1,164,530	....	....	....
1921–22......	675,773	†	79,016	....	754,789	....	....	....
1922–23......	1,115,578	†	109,336	....	1,224,914	....	....	....
1923–24......	1,454,320	†	143,338	....	1,597,658	....	....	....
1924–25......	1,561,022	206,212	146,456	1,767,234	1,707,478	....	....	....
1925–26......	1,577,091	220,379	159,257	1,797,470	1,736,348	....	....	....
1926–27......	1,121,185	172,131	127,131	1,293,316	1,248,316	....	....	....
1927–28......	1,308,088	206,940	153,233	1,515,028	1,461,321	....	....	....
1928–29......	1,302,036	226,874	167,215	1,528,910	1,469,251	....	....	....
1929–30......	1,244,846	200,521	143,694	1,445,367	1,388,540	....	....	....
1930–31......	659,041	135,753	92,063	794,794	751,104	....	....	....
1931–32......	483,627	72,412	44,814	556,039	528,441	....	....	....
1932–33......	424,006	59,881	40,323	483,887	464,329	....	....	....
1933–34......	633,507	82,474	53,046	715,981	686,553	173,676	889,657	860,229
1934–35......	595,602	148,987	110,778	744,589	706,380	115,824	860,413	822,204
1935–36‡.....	645,000§	151,000	105,000	796,000	750,000‖	123,000	919,000	873,000

* I am grateful to Dr. O. C. Stine, of the Bureau of Agricultural Economics, for supplying this table.
† Not available.
‡ Preliminary.
§ Based on December 1 estimate of crop.
‖ From Agricultural Adjustment Administration report, March 4, 1936.

March, 1933. In the absence of governmental interference and under normal business conditions, it is probable that the (deflated) price would have continued its downward course.

Perhaps the most important of the long-run effects of the A.A.A. is that it pegged American cotton prices above world-prices and therefore caused foreign buyers to turn to other countries. Our export figures bear eloquent testimony on the point. In the year 1932–33 exports amounted to 8,630,000 bales. In 1933–34 they fell tò 7,770,000 bales. In 1934–35 they were down to 4,857,000 bales.[49] This drop in our exports in the face of a general increase in world-consumption (see Table 23) in all probabilities reflects a real substitution of foreign growths for American cotton.[50]

TABLE 23*

MILL CONSUMPTION OF AMERICAN AND OTHER GROWTHS IN THE WORLD
AND IN FOREIGN COUNTRIES, 1913–14 TO 1935–36

YEAR BEGINNING AUGUST†	WORLD-CONSUMPTION				FOREIGN-CONSUMPTION			
	All Growths	American Cotton‡	Other Growths	Ratio of American to Other Growths§	All Growths	American Cotton‡	Other Growths	Ratio of American to Other Growths§
	(1,000 Bales)§	(1,000 Bales)§	(1,000 Bales)§	(Per Cent)	(1,000 Bales)§	(1,000 Bales)§	(1,000 Bales)§	(Per Cent)
1913–14....	22,200	13,748	8,452	165.1	16,623	8,365	8,258	101.3
1914–15....	20,671	13,249	7,422	178.5	15,074	7,874	7,200	109.4
1915–16....	21,978	13,039	8,939	145.9	15,580	6,958	8,622	80.7
1916–17....	21,109	12,562	8,547	147.0	14,320	6,092	8,228	74.0
1917–18....	18,516	10,871	7,645	142.2	11,950	4,489	7,461	60.2
1918–19....	16,705	9,909	6,796	145.8	10,939	4,319	6,620	65.2
1919–20....	19,300	11,898	7,402	160.7	12,880	5,895	6,985	84.4
1920–21....	16,905	10,268	6,637	154.7	12,012	5,591	6,421	87.1
1921–22....	19,990	12,209	7,781	156.9	14,080	6,596	7,484	88.1
1922–23....	21,325	12,449	8,876	140.3	14,659	6,124	8,535	71.8
1923–24....	19,982	10,917	9,065	120.4	14,301	5,564	8,737	63.7
1924–25....	22,642	13,311	9,331	142.7	16,449	7,394	9,055	81.7
1925–26....	23,930	14,010	9,920	141.2	17,474	7,834	9,640	81.3
1926–27....	25,869	15,748	10,121	155.6	18,679	8,868	9,811	90.4
1927–28....	25,285	15,576	9,709	160.4	18,451	9,041	9,410	96.1
1928–29....	25,782	15,226	10,556	144.2	18,691	8,448	10,243	82.5
1929–30....	24,878	13,021	11,857	109.8	18,772	7,218	11,554	62.5
1930–31....	22,402	11,056	11,346	97.4	17,139	5,972	11,167	53.5
1931–32....	22,896	12,528	10,368	120.8	18,030	7,784	10,246	76.0
1932–33....	24,986	14,385	10,601	135.7	18,849	8,381	10,468	80.1
1933–34....	25,324	13,780	11,544	119.4	19,624	8,227	11,397	72.2
1934–35....	25,283	11,206	14,077	79.6	19,922	5,965	13,957	42.7
1935–36....	27,631	12,539	15,092	83.1	21,280	6,319	14,961	42.2

* Source: U.S. Dept. Agric., *Yearbook of Agriculture, 1935*, p. 432; *Agricultural Statistics, 1936*, p. 82; and letter from the U.S. Department of Agriculture, dated April 9, 1937.

† Year beginning August 1, except 1913, which is the year beginning September 1.

‡ "American Cotton" means cotton which is grown in the United States.

§ According to the *U.S.D.A. Yearbook*, American are in running bales and other growths in bales of 478 lb. net.

The American restriction program has also stimulated the raising of cotton in other parts of the world (see Table 17). Thus the Brazilian crop increased from an average of 568,000 bales during the five-year period from 1921–22 to

[49] See Table II*b*, Appen. A.

[50] True, world-consumption in 1934–35 was 25,283,000 bales as compared with 25,324,000 bales in 1933–34. But this decrease was only 0.16 per cent, while the decrease in our exports was 37.5 per cent.

1925–26 to 969,000 bales in 1933–34, and to 1,361,000 bales in 1934–35. The Russian crop increased from 306,000 bales in the five-year period 1921–22 to 1925–26 to 1,887,000 bales in 1933–34, and to 1,937,000 bales in 1934–35.[51]

Part of the increase in foreign production would, however, have occurred in any event, for the ground was prepared for it by the World War. That tragic event marks a turning-point in our history. We have changed from a debtor to a creditor nation, and therefore we must import more than we export. We are a surplus-producing country, and therefore we must export more than we import. We are surrounded by a high tariff wall, making it virtually impossible for our debtors to bring goods to us or to buy our goods. It is not surprising, therefore, that the producers of cotton—a commodity of which they exported 60 per cent of their production in pre-war years—should never have recovered from this blocking of the normal channels of trade. In 1913–14 the percentage that foreign consumption of American cotton formed of the foreign consumption of other growths was 101.3. By 1933–34 it had dropped to 72.2 (see Table 23).

On January 6, 1936, the Supreme Court declared the tax feature of the A.A.A. unconstitutional. This decision probably prevented us from witnessing a natural economic breakdown of the American experiment in control of production like that which attended the British rubber restriction plan, the attempt of the Brazilian government to raise the price of coffee, and of the Japanese government to bolster the price of silk. For the increase in foreign production and in the consumpton of foreign cotton at the expense of American cotton would in time have brought about such a depressing effect on the industry as would more than offset the benefit payments to the cotton farmers of 120 million dollars a year.

Even if no further attempt is made to reduce cotton production, the *long-run effects* of the A.A.A. will probably tend to reduce the income of the cotton farmers as a group by an amount which may well equal, if not exceed, the increase in income already realized because of the A.A.A. program. While an exact determination of the losses and gains is out of the question, the findings of this chapter strongly suggest that the demand curve for cotton will soon begin to shift downward, if it is not doing so now. And this circumstance, combined with the relative ease with which foreign countries can expand their output, will spell the ultimate failure of production control, notwithstanding the fact that in a given year a small crop may be worth more than a large crop.[52]

[51] *Foreign Commerce Yearbook, 1935*, p. 353.

[52] This chapter was written before the publication by the Brookings Institution of Henry S. Richards' *Cotton and the A.A.A.*, and by the Bureau of Agricultural Economics of the preliminary (mimeographed) analysis of the world cotton situation prepared by a committee of its experts. (Part II of this report, relating to cotton production in the United States, was released on February 4, 1936.) The reader is referred to these studies for a fuller treatment of the present cotton situation.

VIII. NOTE ON THE DEMAND FUNCTION FOR COTTON WHEN THE PRICES RELATE TO THE CROP YEAR AND THE QUANTITIES TO THE SUCCEEDING CALENDAR YEAR

In his comments on the manuscript of this chapter, Mr. L. H. Bean, of the United States Department of Agriculture, made the observation that instead of correlating price and consumption for synchronous crop years we should have correlated the price for the crop year with the consumption for the succeeding calendar year because "the bulk of the cotton crop is purchased during the crop year and the processing of these purchases takes place chiefly during the calendar year." As this suggestion merits careful consideration, it was decided to subject it to a statistical test. Since, however, the prices for the years prior to 1908 are December 1 prices and not season average prices, it seemed best to confine the test to the data for the third period (1914-29).

The following equations are a summary and comparison of the results obtained:

$$x = 13.3728 - 0.6361y + 0.2203w - 0.2627t - 0.0329t^2$$
$$(0.1476) \quad (0.0372) \quad (0.0735) \quad (0.0214)$$

$$x = 6.4026 - 0.2727y + 0.2366w - 0.2100t$$
$$(0.1177) \quad (0.0345) \quad (0.0710).$$

The first of these was computed by following Bean's suggestion. In this equation, y (as well as w and t) relates to the year beginning August 1, while x relates to the year beginning January 1 following. The second equation is equation 3 of Table 20, which is reproduced here for the purpose of facilitating comparison. In it all the variables relate, of course, to the year beginning August 1.

It will be observed that the first equation differs from the second in two respects: (1) It has a numerically larger coefficient of y and (2) it has a term in t^2 which exceeds its standard error, while the second equation shows no corresponding term. (A term in t^2 was originally computed, but it was smaller than its standard error. Consequently, it was eliminated from the equation, and the remaining coefficients were corrected for its omission.) Of these differences, the first is the more important, since it gives rise to a corresponding difference between the elasticities of demand, which are $\eta = -0.2832$ for the first equation, and $\eta = -0.1245$ for the second, the coefficients relating to the "representative points" of the two demand surfaces. Even if we omit the term in t^2 in the first equation and adjust the remaining coefficients for this omission, in order to render the two equations more comparable, the coefficient of y is only reduced (numerically) to -0.5056, and the elasticity of demand to only -0.2308, and these are still twice as large as the corresponding values of the second equation.

The two equations are, however, sensibly equal to each other in all other respects. The adjusted multiple correlations are, respectively, 0.9217 and 0.8843, and the quadratic mean errors are 1.3147 bales and 1.2801 bales. According to the first criterion, the first equation gives a slightly better fit; according to the second criterion, the second equation gives a slightly better fit. It is, therefore, reasonable to conclude that the two equations fit the data equally well. And even the difference in the elasticities of demand does not affect the general conclusions of this chapter.

CHAPTER IX

THE DEMAND FOR HAY

CHAPTER IX

THE DEMAND FOR HAY

I. THE POSITION OF HAY IN THE NATIONAL ECONOMY

The United States Department of Agriculture defines hay as

the entire dry-cured-above-ground parts—that is, the stems and leaves, and in some cases the seed—of relatively fine-stemmed plants harvested especially for feed. Thus hay is distinguished from such roughage as corn fodder or stover largely because of its fineness of stem, and from the fine-stemmed crops cut and fed green or as silage, because it is prepared by dry-curing. Hay should not be confused with straw, as the latter is a by-product of a crop harvested for another purpose.[1]

There are two main classes of hay: "native or wild hay," produced on natural meadows and marshes, and cultivated hay. Although the acreage of wild hay in the United States is large, cultivated plants constitute by far the largest part of our total hay supply and may be considered as a separate commodity. We shall concern ourselves in this study with cultivated hay only.

There are numerous plants which might be grown for hay; only a few, however, are actually used to any great extent. As the United States Department of Agriculture points out, a plant in order to become widely used as a hay crop must (1) be well adapted to the natural conditions where it is grown; (2) fit in with the other farm crops with regard to cultural requirements so that sufficient labor will be available to cut it at the proper time; (3) be of fine enough texture to cure easily and to be palatable for the animal to which it will be fed; (4) give a high yield; (5) give a good stand without too much expense and be easily eradicated when necessary; and (6) be easily baled and stored.

The hay crops which seem to fulfil these requirements best are (1) clover and timothy, (2) alfalfa, and (3) wild hay. Although clover and timothy are usually sown together, either one may be sown separately. When sown separately, timothy is by far the more important hay plant both in value and in acreage. It is especially well adapted to the climate of the northeastern states and, in fact, cannot be grown to advantage in the South because of the high temperatures. Alfalfa is the chief type of hay in the western states. The two states which lead in the production of alfalfa hay are Nebraska and California. Most of the wild hay produced is cut from the meadows of Minnesota, Nebraska, the Dakotas, and the western plains.

---

[1] *U.S.D.A. Agriculture Yearbook, 1924*, article on hay, pp. 286–87. This article (pp. 285–376) is an invaluable source of information on the technological and economic aspects of hay production.

The United States Department of Agriculture has classified hay into the following groups for the purposes of grading:

Group I, Alfalfa and Alfalfa Mixed Hay; group II, Timothy and Clover Hay; group III, Prairie Hay; group IV, Johnson and Johnson Mixed Hay; group V, Grain, Wild Oat, Vetch, and Grain Mixed Hay; group VI, Lespedeza and Lespedeza Mixed Hay; group VII, Soybean and Soybean Mixed Hay; group VIII, Grass Hay; and group IX, Mixed Hay.[2]

These groups are subdivided into "classes"—a term which "is used to describe the kind of hay or the mixtures of various kinds, and has no reference whatever to quality or condition."[3] The grade numbers for the various groups are determined by the color of the hay and the amount of foreign material. In general, hay which has been cured in such a way as to retain its green color is of a higher grade than hay which has been allowed to become brown. An additional criterion for determining the grade of leguminous hay is the percentage of leafiness. For grain hay the maturity at the time of cutting is a factor in determining the grade.

With so many different plants that can be used for the production of hay, lack of a suitable haymaking crop is seldom the reason for limiting the hay production of a given region. Climatic conditions and topography do, however, play a large part in the distribution of the hay crop of the United States. Moisture sufficient for the growing plant and periods of sunshine without showers are needed for the production of hay. In regions where there is less than twenty-five inches of rainfall annually, and where irrigation must be resorted to in order to provide adequate moisture for the growth of the plant, fewer acres are devoted to hay production. Likewise regions with frequent rains and high humidity have smaller hay crops than regions with plenty of sunshine for the proper curing of the hay. In the Cotton Belt, where the annual rainfall is from fifty to sixty inches, with much of it falling during the time of hay-curing, production of hay is not sufficient for local needs. Hillsides can be utilized for hay very profitably, since hay can be grown with very little stirring of the soil. The rough topography of sections of New York, Pennsylvania, and the New England states is one of the reasons for the relatively great importance of hay in these states.

Important as are the natural factors in determining the distribution of the hay crop, the economic factors seem to be far more decisive. Chief among these factors is the competition of hay with corn and with the more important cash crops. Farmers in one section of the country will produce crops in which they have a comparative advantage and, if necessary, buy from others those in which they have a comparative disadvantage. In regions where wheat, corn, or cotton can be grown to better advantage, hay acreage decreases. On the other hand, transportation costs, which form a large percentage of the destina-

---

[2] U.S. Dept. Agric., *Handbook of Official Hay Standards, 1936*, p. 37.   [3] *Ibid.*, p. 39.

tion value of hay, cause it to be produced near localities where it will be used. Therefore, in regions where dairying has been developed on a large scale to serve metropolitan centers, hay competes successfully with corn and other cash crops. This is an important reason for the relatively large acreage devoted to hay in New York and New England. In the range country of the West high transportation costs together with other factors such as rough topography and the lack of important cash crops contribute to the relatively large acreage devoted to hay.

The regions where the percentage of the crop area devoted to hay is high are New England and New York; the western mountain region and the Pacific Coast; the "North Dairy Belt" consisting of New Jersey, West Virginia, Pennsylvania, Michigan, Wisconsin, and Minnesota; and the plains of Kansas, Nebraska, and the Dakotas. In the remaining states the acreage devoted to hay is less than 20 per cent of the total crop acreage, and corn or cotton is the chief crop of the region. Historically, the production of hay spread across the country with the westward movement of the population.

The relative importance of the hay crop may be judged from the fact that it ranked third in farm value for the decade 1924–33—in 1930 and 1931 it was second. During the same period approximately 20 per cent of the total crop acreage of the United States was devoted to hay. Of this, 80 per cent was devoted to tame hay, for which the average yield per acre fluctuated between 1.20 and 1.50 short tons.

Hay is produced chiefly for use on the farm where the hay crop is grown— less than 15 per cent of the crop is sold off the farm. However,

approximately 16,000,000 tons, having a farm value of about $200,000,000, are handled in the commerce of the United States each year. Railroad statistics from Class I railways show that in 1923 about 6,628,472 tons of hay originated on these transportation lines for shipment to the various markets. This portion of the 1923 hay crop had a destination value of between $125,000,000 to $150,000,000.[4]

Prior to the introduction of motor-driven vehicles, a large part of the commercial hay crop was sold for use in cities. Beginning about 1910, the disappearance of the horse in cities caused a change in the direction of hay movement. Dairy farms and cattle ranches have since become the most important consumers of the commercial hay crop.

II. FACTORS INFLUENCING THE DEMAND FOR HAY

Hay is produced exclusively for the use of herbivorous domestic animals. In this it differs from barley, corn, and oats, which are also used as human foods and as raw materials in industry. The demands for these four feed crops are nevertheless interrelated, as will be shown in Part III.

[4] U.S.D.A. Agriculture Yearbook, 1924, p. 353.

The best approximation to the ideal quantity series for hay, as for most of the other commodities which we have studied, would be production, plus imports, minus exports, plus stocks at the beginning of the year, minus stocks at the end of the year. This would leave the amount actually consumed plus the losses incurred, as the quantity series to be used in deriving our demand curve. However, it would not be practicable to compute this series. In the first place, imports and exports are negligible. Imports—chiefly from Canada—seldom amount to as much as 1 per cent of production, and exports are usually even smaller. Second, figures for stocks on hand at the end of the year are not available for tame hay. For the years 1910–24 approximately 12 per cent of all hay produced during the year remained on the farm on May 1—an amount so small that it was no doubt used up before the new crop was cut. To take into consideration imports, exports, and stocks would, therefore, constitute an unnecessary refinement of data which are already subject to considerable error. We shall, therefore, consider production as being equal to consumption.[5]

Since the consumption of hay depends upon the domestic animal population, we shall take into consideration the changes in the number of animals consuming hay. As in our analysis of the demand for corn (chap. vii), we shall use an animal-unit series, both as a deflator of the total consumption series and as an independent variable. The price series which we shall use is the December 1 farm price deflated by the Bureau of Labor Statistics "Index of Wholesale Prices" (1913 = 100).

Our analysis will then proceed by stages as follows:

First, we shall consider consumption per animal unit x, the deflated price y, and time t as the variables of our demand function, and write

$$(2.1) \qquad\qquad x = x\,(y,\,t)\,,$$

and

$$(2.2) \qquad\qquad y = y(x,\,t)\,,$$

using both linear and constant-elasticity equations as specific forms of the foregoing hypotheses.

---

[5] The production series used in our computations was taken from the *U.S.D.A. Statistical Bulletin*, No. 11, for the years 1875–1914 and from the *U.S.D.A. Yearbook of Agriculture, 1931*, for the years 1915–29. The latter series has been revised twice (in 1932 and again in 1933) since our computations were completed. A comparison of the series which we used with that given in the *U.S.D.A. Yearbook* for 1933 shows that the later estimates are from 10 to 25 per cent lower than the earlier ones. For a more detailed discussion of the accuracy of the United States Department of Agriculture estimates of production and prices see chap. v, Secs. III and IV.

Second, we shall consider the number of animal units z as a separate variable and experiment with the hypotheses:

$$(2.3) \qquad\qquad x = x(y, z, t) \, ,$$

and

$$(2.4) \qquad\qquad y = y(x, z, t) \, ,$$

where x is now total consumption.

To obtain a better insight into the changes that have taken place in the shape of the demand curve for hay and in the direction and the rate of its shifting during the fifty-five years from 1875 to 1929, we shall break up the series into the following subdivisions: I, 1875–92; II, 1899–1914; III, 1915–29 (excluding 1917–21), and make the foregoing analyses for each subdivision. The observations for 1893–98 will be eliminated from the computation, since a break occurs in the animal-unit series for those years. This has resulted from adjustments apparently made by the United States Department of Agriculture in order that its estimates of the number of horses and cattle might conform to the census figures for 1899.

In Part III we shall analyze the relation between the demand for hay and the demands for barley, corn, and oats.

III.   DEMAND FUNCTIONS WITH ANIMAL-UNIT CONSUMPTION AS THE DEPENDENT VARIABLE[6]

Table VI of Appendix A gives for the period 1875–1929, inclusive, the consumption (=production) per animal unit, the real price, and the value per animal unit of the hay crop of the United States, together with the trend ratios and the link relatives of the first two series. The animal-unit series and the deflator for the price series are given in Table I, and the basic (unadjusted) data in Table IIa, of the same appendix.

Figure 55 is a graphic representation of the annual consumption and value per animal unit, as well as the real price, of hay from 1875 to 1929. As was explained in chapter vi, the value per animal-unit series is useful in connection with the estimation of the elasticity of demand. When the demand is· *elastic*, the year-to-year changes in total value will tend to be *negatively* correlated with the corresponding changes in price. On the other hand, when the demand is *inelastic*, the changes in total value will be *positively* correlated with the corresponding changes in price. By comparing the value series with the price series (or with the quantity series), we can observe when the correlation changes

---

[6] For a more detailed explanation of the methods used and for definitions of the technical terms employed see chap. vi.

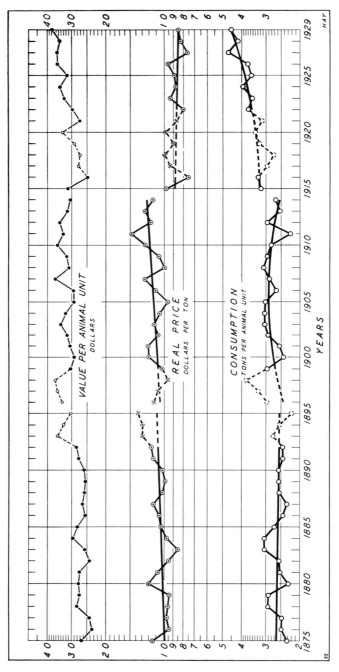

Fig. 55.—Hay: The basic adjusted annual data used in deriving the demand curves for hay in the United States, 1875–1929

sign. That year is generally one in which a disturbing factor has made its appearance. Table 24 is a descriptive summary, by periods, of the animal-unit consumption series and the deflated prices.

As can be seen from Figure 55, there is a marked negative correlation between consumption and price in each of the three periods. The equations in Table 25 represent several measures of this relationship, corresponding to the hypotheses (2.1) and (2.2).

TABLE 24

HAY: SUMMARY BY PERIODS OF THE ADJUSTED DATA USED IN
DERIVING THE DEMAND FUNCTIONS, 1875–1929

PERIOD*	CONSUMPTION PER ANIMAL UNIT $x(t)$				DEFLATED PRICE $y(t)$				CORRELATION COEFFICIENT
	Descriptive Constants								
	Mean (Short Tons)	Median (Short Tons)	Standard Deviation (Short Tons)	Coefficient of Variation	Mean (Dollars)	Median (Dollars)	Standard Deviation (Dollars)	Coefficient of Variation	r_{xy}
I	2.5872	2.5292	0.2298	8.88	10.3236	10.142	0.9201	8.91	−0.7620
II	2.7947	2.9087	0.2475	8.86	11.5384	11.364	1.2500	10.83	−0.7727
III	3.8290	3.7102	0.4700	12.28	8.6341	8.596	0.7622	8.83	−0.4610
	Equations of Trends								Origins
I	$x(t) = 2.5872 - 0.0047t$				$y(t) = 10.3236 + 0.0466t$				July 1, 1884
II	$x(t) = 2.9043 - 0.0095t - 0.0052t^2$				$y(t) = 11.5384 + 0.1062t$				July 1, 1907
III	$x(t) = 3.5417 + 0.0900t + 0.0068t^2$				$y(t) = 8.6716 - 0.0250t$				Jan. 1, 1923

*I = 1875–92; II = 1899–1914; III = 1915–29 (excl. 1917–21).

The coefficients of y in the first three equations mean that, other things being equal, an increase (or decrease) of one dollar per ton in the real price of hay brought about on the average a decrease (or increase) in the consumption per animal unit of approximately 0.20 ton in the first period, 0.16 ton in the second, and 0.20 in the third. These figures are all statistically significant.

The coefficients of t and t^2 in the same equations show that the "other things" which we represented by the catch-all "time" remained substantially equal in the first and second periods, for the curve exhibited no significant upward or downward shift during these periods.[7] During the third period, however, the curve was shifting upward at an average rate of 0.08 ton per animal

---

[7] Since the coefficients of t are also very small, the elimination of the time variable from these equations would not appreciably change the slope of the demand curve.

TABLE 25

Hay: Demand per Animal Unit: The Characteristics

x = Consumption per animal unit in short tons
y = Deflated December 1 farm price in dollars per ton

(Figures in parentheses are standard errors)

Equation No.	Period*		Constant Term	y	t	t^2
1	I	$x=$	4.6193	−0.1968 (0.0428)	+0.0044 (0.0076)	....
2	II	$x=$	4.6612	−0.1550 (0.0349)	+0.0070 (0.0094)	−0.0037 (0.0021)
3	III	$x=$	5.2899	−0.1993 (0.0992)	+0.0845 (0.0169)	+0.0059 (0.0042)

Equation No.	Period*		Constant Term	y'	$\dagger Mt$	$\dagger Mt^2$
4a	I	$x'=$	1.2064	−0.7857 (0.1603)	+0.0020 (0.0027)	....
4b	I	$x'_1\ddagger=$	5.3499	−5.7717 (1.0052)	....	....
5	II	$x'=$	1.1822	−0.6853 (0.1598)	+0.0026 (0.0036)	−0.0012 (0.0008)
6	III	$x'=$	0.9560	−0.4312 (0.2044)	+0.0224 (0.0040)	+0.0013 (0.0010)

Equation No.	Period*		Constant Term	x		t^2
7	I	$y=$	18.0147	−2.9728 (0.6463)	+0.0325 (0.0286)	....
8	II	$y=$	21.7876	−3.6673 (0.8242)	+0.0715 (0.0443)	....
9	III	$y=$	15.0534	−1.7250 (0.8528)	+0.1237 (0.0891)	....

Equation No.	Period*		Constant Term	x'	$\dagger Mt$	$\dagger Mt^2$
10a	I	$y'=$	1.3343	−0.7837 (0.1599)	+0.0034 (0.0027)	....
10b	I	$y'=$	0.9548	−0.1166** (0.0203)	....	....
11	II	$y'=$	1.4260	−0.8240 (0.1865)	+0.0060 (0.0037)	....
12	III	$y'=$	1.4312	−0.8762 (0.4027)	+0.0175 (0.0108)	....

* I = 1875–92; II = 1899–1914; III = 1915–29 (excl. 1917–21).
† $M = \log_{10} e = 0.43429$
‡ $x'_1 = \log (x - 2.2)$
§ No standard error has been computed for this coefficient because the constant 2.2 subtracted from x was not determined by the method of least squares.

TABLE 25—*Continued*

OF THE DEMAND FUNCTIONS, BY PERIODS, 1875–1929

t = Time in years. For origins see Table 24

x', x'_t, y' = Logs of x, $(x - 2.2)$, y

(Figures in parentheses are standard errors)

	DESCRIPTIVE CONSTANTS					EQUA-TION No.
	Elasticity of Demand η	Quadratic Mean Error ϵ (Tons)	Adjusted Multiple Correlation Coefficient R'	Percentage of Variance of Consumption Attributable to y	t	
....	−0.7855 (0.2367)	0.1612	0.7316	60.07	−1.07	1
....	−0.6228 (0.1922)	0.1587	0.7840	60.49	8.68	2
....	−0.4639 (0.2741)	0.2353	0.8800	14.90	70.06	3
	η	ϵ (Per Cent)	R'	y'	t	
....	−0.7857 (0.1603)	94.3–106.0	0.7541	63.12	−1.19	4a
....	−0.7376§	....	−0.8080‖	67.32¶	....	4b
....	−0.6853 (0.1598)	94.1–106.3	0.7704	60.04	7.45	5
....	−0.4312 (0.2044)	94.5–105.8	0.8960	13.83	73.03	6

Flexibility of Price φ	Maximum Value of η $1/\varphi$	ϵ (Dollars)	R'	Percentage of Variance of Price Attributable to x	t	
−0.7450 (0.2232)	−1.3423	0.6263	0.7499	56.56	4.82	7
−0.8883 (0.2818)	−1.1258	0.8033	0.7828	56.12	10.32	8
−0.7650 (0.4729)	−1.3072	0.7158	0.4541	49.04	−10.78	9
φ	$1/\varphi$	ϵ (Per Cent)	R'	x'	t	
−0.7837 (0.1599)	−1.2760	94.3–106.0	0.7722	59.08	5.29	10a
−0.7794§	−1.2830	94.7–105.5	−0.8080‖	67.32¶	....	10b
−0.8240 (0.1865)	−1.2136	93.4–107.0	0.7800	55.86	10.21	11
−0.8762 (0.4027)	−1.1413	92.2–108.4	0.4945	52.12	−10.88	12

‖ This is the simple coefficient of correlation between log $(x - 2.2)$ and log y, adjusted for the number of parameters in the equation.

¶ This is the percentage of the variance of log $(x - 2.2)$ which is attributable to log y. This figure, divided by 100, is the square of the simple coefficient of correlation between log $(x - 2.2)$ and log y.

** This is the coefficient of x'_t = log $(x - 2.2)$.

unit per annum, with an acceleration of 0.01 ton per animal unit per annum. In this period the major part (70 per cent) of the variance of consumption is directly or indirectly attributable to this shift of the demand curve with time. This suggests that our analysis has failed to isolate some very important factor or factors influencing the demand for hay during this period. It should be borne in mind, however, that the consumption figures for the third period have been revised (see n. 5) since our computations were completed, and, further, that the revised figures were all from 10 to 25 per cent less than the figures used. It is probable, therefore, that the shift in question is more apparent than real.

The absolute changes in consumption consequent upon a unit change in price—the coefficients of y—can be converted into relative changes or "elasticities" by multiplying them by representative values of y/x. This yields the first three entries in the column headed "Elasticity of Demand" in Table 25. It is important to observe that the demand for hay was becoming increasingly inelastic from period to period. An increase (or decrease) of 1 per cent in the price brought about a decrease (or increase) in the yearly consumption per animal unit of 0.79 per cent in the first period, 0.62 per cent in the second, and 0.46 per cent in the third.

Equations 4a, 5, and 6 of Table 25 are the logarithmic forms of hypothesis (2.1). (Eq. 4b will be explained later.) The coefficients of y' ($= \log y$) of these equations tell us that, in a given year, an increase (or decrease) of 1 per cent in price was, on the average, associated with a decrease (or increase) in the consumption of hay per animal unit of approximately 0.79 per cent in the first period, 0.69 per cent in the second, and 0.43 per cent in the third. These figures are all statistically significant and are in very close agreement with those derived from the corresponding linear demand functions.

The coefficients of t and t^2 in these equations give the *relative* rate of shift of the demand curve (see chap. vi, n. 20). They show that, during the first and second periods, the demand curve was subject to no significant shift either upward or downward but that, during the third period, it was moving upward at the rate of 2.24 per cent per annum, with an acceleration of 0.26 per cent per annum. It is probable, however, that this shift is more apparent than real.[8]

We return to equation 4b. This equation is an improvement over 4a and may be looked upon as a substitute for it as well as for equation 1. Its fitting was decided upon when a graphical analysis of the data (not reproduced here) showed that neither the straight line (eq. 1) nor the constant-elasticity curve (eq. 4a) gave a good fit to the data: the scatter of consumption on price was too skew to admit of being satisfactorily represented by these curves, notwithstanding the fact that the regression of x on y and the regression of x' on y' are both highly significant as compared with their standard errors. The log-

[8] See n. 5, p. 338.

arithms of consumption were, therefore, plotted against the logarithms of the deflated prices, and the whole scatter was subjected to several trial (graphic) rectifications. These showed that, if 2.2 were subtracted from each observation in x, an equation of the form

(3.1) $$\log (x - 2.2) = a + b \log y,$$

would give a very satisfactory fit to the data. Equation 4b gives the least-square values of the parameters of this equation. (The variable t was excluded because it had proved insignificant in eqs. 1 and 4a.) Figure 56 is a graphic representation of this equation in arithmetic form. A measure of the goodness of fit of this curve to the data is given by the adjusted simple coefficient of correlation between the log of $(x - 2.2)$ and the log of y. This coefficient has the value of -0.8080 as compared to the adjusted multiple correlation coefficients 0.7316 and 0.7541 for equations 1 and 4a of Table 25.

The coefficient of y' in equation 4b is not comparable with the coefficients of y' in the other equations of Table 25. In this equation it measures the regression of log $(x - 2.2)$ on log y, or the percentage change in the quantity $(x - 2.2)$ associated with a 1 per cent change in y. Also, the standard error of this coefficient is not a true least-squares sampling error, since the constant 2.2 was determined by inspection. To get a measure of the percentage change in x associated with a 1 per cent change in y, we must compute the elasticity of demand. For this curve the coefficient of elasticity is not constant but varies from point to point, for

(3.2) $$\eta = \frac{dx}{dy} \cdot \frac{y}{x} = \frac{b(x - 2.2)}{y} \frac{y}{x} = b \left(1 - \frac{2.2}{x} \right).$$

When y is given its mean value, and x is computed from equation 4b, Table 25, and substituted in (3.2) above, the elasticity of demand corresponding to this representative point on the demand curve is found to be -0.7376. That is to say, during the period 1875–92, an increase of 1 per cent in the price of hay was associated with a decrease of approximately 0.7 per cent in the consumption per animal unit. This does not differ greatly from the elasticities of demand computed from equations 1 and 4a.

Figures 57 and 58 are graphic representations of equations 5 and 6 for the second and third periods, respectively. Figure 57A shows the scatter diagram of the logarithms of consumption per animal unit, x', on the logarithms of real price, y'. The line $D_1'D_2'$ is the *net* regression of x' on y'. It gives the relation between that part of the logarithm of consumption per animal unit which is linearly independent of time and that part of the logarithm of real price which is linearly independent of time. The slope of the line (-0.6853), which is

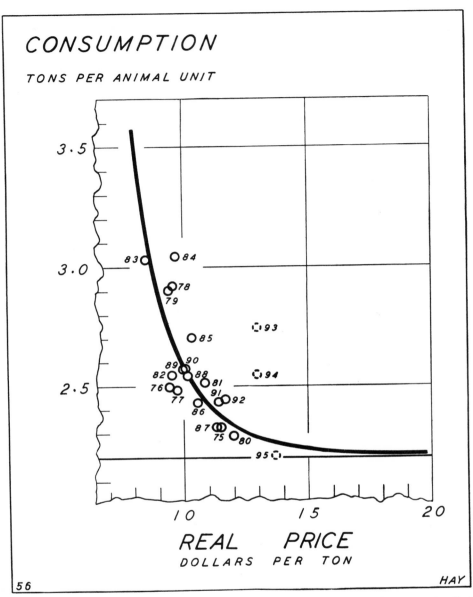

Fig. 56.—Hay: The demand curve for hay during the period 1875–92 on the assumption that

$$(x - 2.2) = 223815 \, y^{-5.7717} \, ,$$

where x is consumption per animal unit.

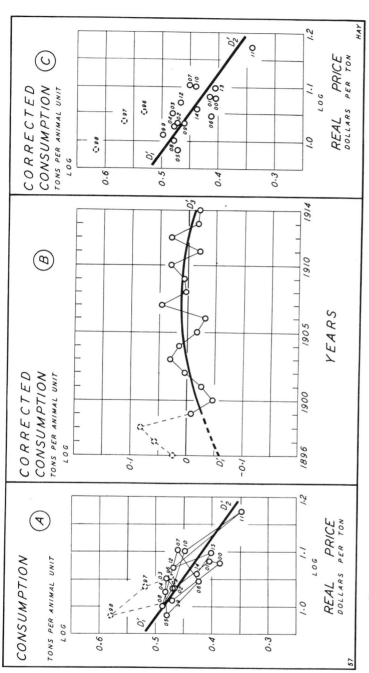

Fig. 57.—Hay: Three aspects of the demand per animal unit during the period 1899–1914 on the assumption that

$$x = 15.21 \; y^{-0.6853} \; e^{0.00261 t - 0.00121 t^2} \, .$$

A: Relation between consumption per animal unit and real price, when the data are not corrected for the effects of "time," with the demand curve $D_1'D_2'$ which results when such correction is made.

B: Relation between consumption per animal unit and time when the former is corrected for the effects of changes in the real price. The slope of the line $D_1'D_3'$ (fitted to the variables x' and t when both are corrected for price) represents the mean rate of shift of the animal-unit demand curve $D_1'D_2'$.

C: The animal-unit demand curve for hay, 1899–1914. Line $D_1'D_2'$ shows the relation between that part of the animal-unit consumption of hay in the United States which is independent of time and that part of the real price which is independent of time. In the scatter, however, only the ordinate is corrected for secular changes, the abscissa being uncorrected.

347

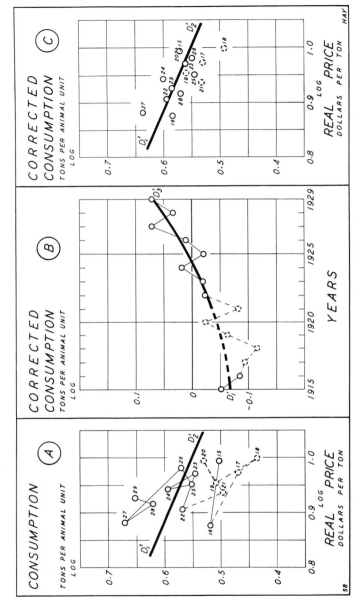

Fig. 58.—Hay: Three aspects of the demand per animal unit for hay during the period 1915–29 (excluding 1917–21) on the assumption that

$$x = 9.036 \, y^{-0.4312} \, e^{0.0224t + 0.0013t^2} \, .$$

given by the coefficient of y' in equation 5, is the elasticity of demand for hay during the second period. Similarly, the slope (-0.4312) of the line $D_1'D_2'$ in Figure 58A, which is the coefficient of y' in equation 6, gives the elasticity of the demand for hay during the third period.

The curve $D_1'D_3'$ in Figure 57B gives the direction and the rate of shift of the demand curve for the second period. It is a graphic representation of the regression of animal-unit consumption on time, after the effect of price has been eliminated. When allowance is made for this shift, we obtain the reduced scatter of Figure 57C. The curve $D_1'D_3'$ in Figure 58B is the net regression of animal-unit consumption on time for the third period. A comparison of the two diagrams brings into clear relief the changes that have taken place in the shift of the demand curves between the two periods. Whereas during the second period the demand curve was apparently shifting upward until 1908 and then downward until 1914, during the third period the demand curve was moving upward at an increasing rate from the very beginning. It is doubtful, however, whether the curve $D_1'D_3'$ in Figure 58B is a true representation of the actual shift of the demand curve in the third period, since a graphical analysis (not reproduced here) shows that the use of the revised production series[9] would have materially reduced, if not entirely eliminated, the upward shift in question.

The fit of equations 4b, 5, and 6 (Figs. 56, 57, and 58) is very good, the coefficient of multiple correlation (corrected for the number of constants in the equation) being approximately 0.8, and the quadratic mean error falling between 94 per cent and 106 per cent, for each equation. The last two figures give the limits below and above the computed consumption within which approximately 68 per cent of the observations actually fall.

IV. DEMAND FUNCTIONS WITH PRICE AS THE DEPENDENT VARIABLE

Equations 7–12 in Table 25 are the regressions of price on animal-unit consumption and time. They measure the degree to which changes in the price of hay may be explained by changes in the other two variables in each of the three periods.

The coefficients of x in equations 7, 8, and 9 mean that in any given year an increase in the annual consumption of hay of one ton per animal unit would, on the average, be associated with a decrease in the real price per ton of $2.97 in the first period, $3.67 in the second, and $1.72 in the third.

The coefficients of t in the same equations signify that, even if the consumption per animal unit had been constant, the real price per ton would have shown a tendency to increase by 3 cents per annum in the first period, by 7 cents in the second, and by 12 cents in the third. But, as the standard errors of these

[9] See n. 5, p. 338.

coefficients are relatively large, no importance should be attached to these figures. This conclusion is also borne out by the figures in the last two columns of Table 25 (eqs. 7, 8, and 9), which show that the time variable accounts at most for 10 per cent of the variance of price, whereas the changes in consumption per animal unit account for at least one-half of the price variance, in each of the three periods.

Equations 10a, 11, and 12 in Table 25 express the relation between price, consumption, and time in terms of relative changes. (Eq. 10b will be explained later.) Thus the coefficients of x' ($= \log x$) in these three equations give the partial "price flexibilities" for the three periods, i.e., the percentage change in price brought about by a 1 per cent change in animal-unit consumption, when the demand curve in question is not permitted to shift with time. The numerical values of these coefficients are all of the order -0.8, which means that a 1 per cent increase in hay consumption per animal unit was associated with a decrease in the deflated price of only 0.8 per cent in each of the three periods. The reciprocal of this number gives the maximum value of the elasticity of demand (chap. vi, n. 40).

Taken at their face value, the coefficients of t of the same equations suggest that, even if the consumption per animal unit had been fixed, the price of hay in terms of the 1913 dollar would have increased by 0.34 per cent per annum in the first period, by 0.60 per cent in the second, and by 1.75 per cent in the third. But these figures are not statistically significant.

We now return to equation 10b. Like its analogue, equation 4b, it was introduced into Table 25 because a graphic analysis of the data (not reproduced here) showed that neither the constant-elasticity curve (eq. 10a) nor the straight line (eq. 7), gave a good fit to the data for the first period: the scatter of price on consumption was too skew to be adequately represented by these curves, notwithstanding the fact that the regression of y on x and of y' on x' are both highly significant as compared with their standard errors. The scatter of the logarithms of price on the logarithms of consumption was, therefore, rectified by the method explained in the previous section, and the straight line

$$(4.1) \qquad\qquad \log y = a + b \log (x - 2.2)$$

was fitted to the data. Equation 10b gives the numerical values of a and b. (The variable t was excluded because it had proved hardly significant in eqs. 7 and 10a.) As can be seen fom the relevant descriptive constants, equation 10b gives a better fit to the data than does either equation 10a or equation 7.

A comparison of the R''s of the equations of Table 25 in which price is the dependent variable with the corresponding R''s of the equations in which consumption is the dependent variable shows that, except in the case of the equations relating to the third period, both sets of equations fit the data equally well. This should put us on our guard against spurious regressions arising from high correlations among the independent variables. We have reason to believe, however, that the equations with consumption as the dependent variable are more trustworthy than those in which price is the dependent variable (see chap. iv, Sec. III).

V. DEMAND FUNCTIONS WITH ANIMAL UNITS AS AN EXPLICIT VARIABLE

The demand functions summarized in Table 25 and discussed in the previous section are all specific forms of the hypotheses (2.1) and (2.2) that we made about the demand for hay. Into these functions, the number of animal units, z, enters only as a deflator of total consumption x. We are now ready to consider the more complex hypotheses

$$(2.3) \qquad\qquad x = x(y, z, t) ,$$

and

$$(2.4) \qquad\qquad y = y(x, z, t) ,$$

into which the number of animal units enters as an explicit variable. Table 26 is a summary of the linear and of the logarithmic forms of these hypotheses. The variable "time" does not appear in this summary, since, in the specific forms which we gave to the foregoing hypotheses, it turned out to be statistically insignificant.[10]

From the coefficients of y in the first three equations we see that, if the number of animal units had been kept constant, an increase (or decrease) of one dollar in the real price per ton of hay would have brought about, on the average, a decrease (or increase) in the annual consumption of 2.95 million tons in the first period, of 3.79 million tons in the second, and of 5.64 million tons in the third.

These coefficients can be converted into relative changes, or elasticities, by multiplying them by representative values of y/x. The results, which are given in the column headed "Elasticity of Demand," are in fairly close agreement with the corresponding elasticities of the first three equations of Table 25.

From the coefficients of z in the same equations we see that, if the deflated price of hay had been kept constant, an increase (or decrease) of 1 million animal units would have brought about, on the average, an increase (or de-

---

[10] Our experiments with the time variable were confined to the equations for the first and second periods. It did not seem advisable to introduce the variable t also into the equation for the third period because the number of observations is too small. Even in the equations for the first and second periods, it is difficult to isolate the net regression on animal units from that on time because the two variables are highly correlated.

TABLE 26

HAY: TOTAL DEMAND: THE CHARACTERISTICS OF THE DEMAND FUNCTIONS IN

x = Total consumption in 1,000,000 short tons
y = Deflated December 1 farm price in dollars per ton

(Figures in parentheses are standard errors)

EQUA- TION No.	PERIOD*		Constant Term	y	z
				EQUATIONS	
1	I	$x=$	30.1923	−2.9523 (0.6482)	+2.6006 (0.2271)
2	II	$x=$	35.4110	−3.7907 (0.8367)	+3.1425 (0.5948)
3	III	$x=$	174.0251	−5.6379 (2.0527)	−1.3153 (0.8557)
			Constant Term	y'	z'
4	I	$x'=$	1.1326	−0.7863 (0.1571)	+1.0622 (0.0844)
5	II	$x'=$	1.0168	−0.6996 (0.1587)	+1.1229 (0.2172)
6	III	$x'=$	2.9282	−0.5158 (0.1872)	−0.3445 (0.2240)
			Constant Term	x	z
7	I	$y=$	9.6537	−0.1966 (0.0432)	+0.5497 (0.1154)
8	II	$y=$	8.6268	−0.1615 (0.0356)	+0.5733 (0.1489)
9	III	$y=$	19.7945	−0.0920 (0.0335)	−0.1058 (0.1199)
			Constant Term	x'	z'
10	I	$y'=$	1.2208	−0.7953 (0.1580)	+0.8941 (0.0849)
11	II	$y'=$	1.1098	−0.8565 (0.1943)	+1.0969 (0.2898)
12	III	$y'=$	3.3457	−1.0086 (0.3661)	−0.3071 (0.3432)

*I = 1875–92; II = 1899–1914; III = 1915–29 (excl. 1917–21).

TABLE 26—*Continued*

WHICH THE NUMBER OF ANIMAL UNITS IS AN EXPLICIT VARIABLE, BY PERIODS, 1875–1929

z = Animal units in millions

x', y', z' = Logs of x, y, z

(Figures in parentheses are standard errors)

	Elasticity of Demand η	Quadratic Mean Error ϵ (1,000,000 Short Tons)	Adjusted Multiple Correlation Coefficient R'	Percentage of Variance of Consumption Attributable to		EQUATION No.
				y	z	
. . . .	−0.7401 (0.2224)	2.4420	0.9411	5.12	84.80	1
. . . .	−0.6573 (0.2036)	4.0626	0.8444	30.07	45.06	2
. . . .	−0.5228 (0.2334)	4.9333	0.6991	44.92	15.32	3
	η	ϵ (Per Cent)	R'	y'	z'	
. . . .	−0.7863 (0.1571)	94.4–105.9	0.9509	5.74	85.80	4
. . . .	−0.6996 (0.1587)	93.7–106.7	0.8374	29.32	44.78	5
. . . .	−0.5158 (0.1872)	94.9–105.4	0.6991	45.02	15.21	6

Flexibility of Price φ	Maximum Value of η $1/\varphi$	ϵ (Dollars)	R'	Percentage of Variance of Price Attributable to		
				x	z	
−0.7841 (0.2524)	−1.2753	0.6301	0.7463	19.84	41.08	7
−0.9315 (0.2998)	−1.0736	0.8386	0.7603	44.19	19.24	8
−0.9922 (0.4569)	−1.0079	0.6302	0.6203	54.06	−1.92	9
φ	$1/\varphi$	ϵ (Per Cent)	R'	x'	z'	
−0.7953 (0.1580)	−1.2574	94.4–106.0	0.7752	23.92	40.88	10
−0.8563 (0.1943)	−1.1675	93.1–107.4	0.7521	42.62	19.73	11
−1.0086 (0.3661)	−0.9915	93.0–107.6	0.6214	54.06	−1.81	12

353

crease) in the annual consumption of 2.60 million tons in the first period, and of 3.14 million tons in the second. In the third period, however, an increase in the number of animal units would, under the same assumption, be associated with a *decrease* in the consumption of hay—which does not make sense. But, as was pointed out in the previous section, the findings for the third period are all to be regarded with suspicion, inasmuch as the consumption data have been subject to such drastic revision by the United States Department of Agriculture since our computations were completed.[11]

Equations 4, 5, and 6 of Table 26 express the same results in terms of relative change. The coefficients of y' in these equations show that, if the number of animal units had been fixed, an increase of 1 per cent in the deflated price would have brought about, on the average, a decrease of 0.79 per cent in the annual consumption in the first period, of 0.70 per cent in the second, and of 0.52 per cent in the third. These coefficients of the elasticity of demand agree fairly closely with the corresponding coefficients of equations 4a, 5, and 6 of Table 25.

The coefficients of z' in the same equations give the percentage change in total consumption of hay corresponding to a 1 per cent change in the number of animal units, in each of the three periods. These percentages are the elasticities of demand with respect to the number of animal units. They show that, even if the deflated price had been kept constant, an increase of 1 per cent in the number of animal units would have increased the annual hay consumption by somewhat over 1 per cent in the first and second periods but that, during the third period, an increase in animal units would, under the same assumption, be associated with a *decrease* in total consumption. However, this finding, like the corresponding finding in equation 3, is in all probability due to errors in the data.

Figures 59, 60, and 61 are, respectively, the graphic representations of equations 4, 5, and 6 of Table 26. In each of these diagrams the slope of the line $D_1'D_2'$ represents the partial elasticity of demand with respect to price (the coefficient of y' in the equation), and the slope of the line $D_1'D_3'$ measures the partial elasticity of demand with respect to the number of animal units (the coefficient of z' in the equation). Thus, in Figure 59, which relates to the first period, the line $D_1'D_2'$ has a slope of -0.7863, and the line $D_1'D_3'$ has a slope of $+1.0622$ (see eq. 4).

A comparison of the slopes of the lines $D_1'D_3'$ for the three periods shows at a glance the change which took place in the third period: the line in Figure 61 slopes downward, thus suggesting that the net effect of an increase in the number of animal units is to decrease the consumption of hay. For the reason already given, this finding casts doubt on the accuracy of the data and not on the correctness of the analysis.

[11] See n. 5, p. 338.

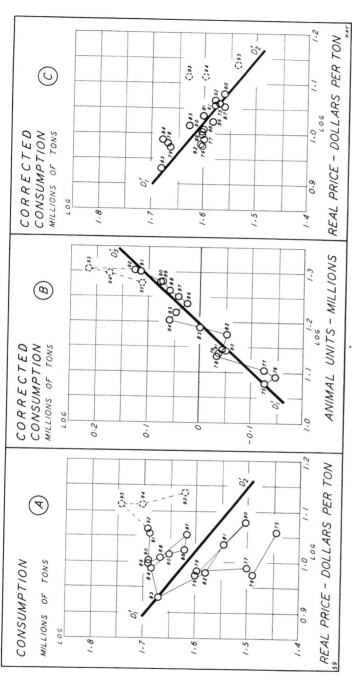

Fig. 59.—Hay: Three aspects of the total demand for hay during the period 1875–92 on the assumption that

$$x = 13.57 \, y^{-0.7863} \, z^{1.0622} \, .$$

A: Relation between total consumption and real price when the data are not corrected for the changes in the animal-unit series, with the demand curve $D_1'D_2'$ which results when such correction is made.

B: Relation between total consumption and the number of animal units when the former is corrected for the effects of changes in the real price. The slope of the line $D_1'D_3'$ (fitted to the variables x' and z' when both are corrected for price) represents the *net* relationship between total consumption and animal units.

C: The total demand curve for hay, 1875–92. Line $D_1'D_2'$ shows the relation between that part of the total consumption of hay in the United States which is independent of changes in the number of animal units and that part of the real price which is independent of the number of animal units. In the scatter, however, only the ordinate is corrected for the number of animal units, the abscissa being uncorrected.

355

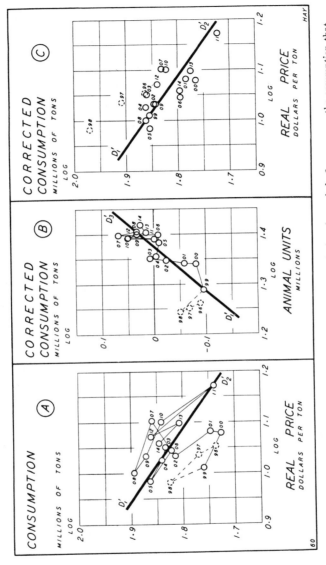

Fig. 60.—Hay: Three aspects of the total demand for hay during the period 1899–1914 on the assumption that

$$x = 10.39 \, y^{-0.6906} \, z^{1.1229} \, .$$

356

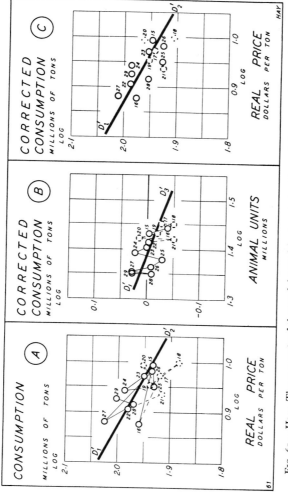

Fig. 61.—Hay: Three aspects of the total demand for hay during the period 1915–29 (excluding 1917–21), on the assumption that

$$x = 847.6\, y^{-0.5158} z^{-0.3445}\,.$$

From the statistical and methodological viewpoint, the most interesting aspect of equations 4, 5, and 6 (or of eqs. 1, 2, and 3) is the improvement in the results obtained in all but the third period by using the number of animal units as an explicit variable instead of as a deflator.[12] (Compare the R'''s of these equations with the R'''s of the corresponding equations of Table 25.) But close inspection of the observations in Figures 59B and 60B reveals the interesting fact that they are ordered in time, the observations for the earlier years being at the lower left corner of the chart, and the observations for the later years at the upper right corner. To the statistician this suggests "spurious correlation." A little reflection will, however, convince us that there is nothing "spurious" in the net positive correlation between the number of animal units and the amount of hay consumed, although both variables may increase in time.

There remain to be explained equations 7–12 in Table 26.

These are the specific forms of hypothesis (2.4), the first triad being the linear equations, and the second triad the logarithmic equations. On account of the difference in units, equations 7, 8, and 9 in this table are not comparable with equations 7, 8, and 9 of Table 25. But the logarithmic equations 10, 11, and 12 of Table 26 are comparable with the equations 10a, 11, and 12 of Table 25 in one respect: the coefficients of x' are the partial elasticities of demand for hay, the first set being the elasticity of the demand per animal unit, and the second the elasticity of the total demand. The two sets of coefficients are in fair agreement.

The fit of the equations in Table 26 in which y or y' is the dependent variable is just as good as the fit of the corresponding equations in Table 25 for the first two periods and is better for the third period.

VI. SUMMARY AND CONCLUSIONS

Although hay is a highly important crop, very few studies of the demand for it can be found in the literature.[13] In this chapter we have attempted to give a first, proximate, quantitative description of the changes that have taken place in the shape, the elasticity, and the rate of shift of the demand curve for hay since 1875.

1. But these properties of the demand function could not have been determined without making a hypothesis about the factors affecting the demand for hay. Probably the most satisfactory hypothesis would be that the quantity of hay demanded is a function not only of the price of hay but also of the prices

---

[12] If the revised data had been available when the computations were made, it is probable that even this period would have proved no exception.

[13] The pioneering study is that by Professor H. L. Moore in his *Economic Cycles* (New York, 1914), chap. iv, pp. 62–88. Correlations between the size of the hay crop and price are also to be found in G. F. Warren and F. A. Pearson, *Interrelationships of Supply and Price* (Cornell Agricultural Experiment Station Bull. No. 466 [Ithaca, 1928]), and V. P. Timoshenko, "Correlations between Prices and Yields of Previous Years," *Journal of Political Economy*, XXXVI, No. 4 (August, 1928), 510–15.

of other feeds, and of the number of horses, cows, and other hay-consuming animals. The interrelations of the prices of four feeds—barley, corn, hay, and oats—and their effect on the demand for hay will be analyzed in Part III. It was impracticable, however, also to take into consideration the effect on the demand for hay of changes in the number of horses, cows, and other animals receiving hay, either because the necessary data were not available or because the resulting equations would have contained too many parameters to justify their application to our relatively short series. All that appeared practicable was to substitute one animal-unit series for the numbers of the different kinds of livestock receiving hay. It is this series which we have used in this chapter both as a deflator and as an explicit variable in our demand equations. The series is, of course, subject to the limitations that it is based on the estimated consumption of hay in only one year (1914), and by only two kinds of live-stock—horses and cows—and does not, therefore, reflect the changes in quantities of hay fed to the different animals as the result of changes in the prices of different kinds of feed. It appears, however, to reflect the more important changes in the number of horses and cows and cannot, therefore, be entirely disregarded.

2. When we wrote the *consumption per animal unit* as a function of the deflated price and of time, we found that the net effect of an increase (or decrease) of one dollar per ton in the price of hay was to reduce (or increase) the average annual consumption per animal unit by 0.20 ton in the first period (1875–92), by 0.16 ton in the second (1899–1914), and by 0.20 ton in the third (1915–29 excluding 1917–21). Stated in terms of relative changes or elasticities, the foregoing figures mean that an increase (or decrease) of 1 per cent in the deflated price of hay brought about a decrease (or increase) in the average annual consumption per animal unit of 0.79 per cent in the first period, of 0.69 per cent in the second, and of 0.43 per cent in the third.

3. When we wrote the deflated price as a function of the consumption per animal unit and of time, we found that an increase (or decrease) of one ton in the annual consumption per animal unit brought about a decrease (or increase) in the deflated price per ton of hay of $2.97 in the first period, of $3.67 in the second, and of $1.72 in the third.

4. There was no evidence of a definite shift of the demand curve with time in any of the three periods.

5. The hypothesis that the *total consumption* of hay is a function of the price and of the number of animal units, showed that, other things being equal, an increase (or decrease) of one dollar per ton in the deflated price of hay brought about a decrease (or increase) of 2.95 million tons in the first period, 3.79 million tons in the second, and 5.64 million tons in the third. But other things did not remain equal: the number of animal units kept changing from year to year. The equations show that, if the deflated price of hay had been

kept constant, an increase of one million animal units would have been associated with an increase in consumption of 2.60 million tons in the first period and 3.14 million tons in the second. In the third period, however, the same increase in the number of animal units would have been associated with a *decrease* in the total consumption. This finding is obviously absurd and suggests that the underlying data for the third period are subject to gross errors. Some support for this hypothesis is lent by the drastic revisions which the United States Department of Agriculture has made in the production estimates of hay for the third period, since our computations were completed.

6. The partial elasticities of the total demand for hay are in very close agreement with the partial elasticities of the demand per animal unit.

7. The two variables, total consumption and the number of animal units, give a fairly good explanation of the changes in the deflated price of hay. The regressions of price on these two variables showed that, if the number of animal units had been fixed, an increase of one million tons in the consumption (=production) of hay, would have been associated with a decrease in the price per ton of hay of 20 cents in the first period, of 16 cents in the second, and of 9 cents in the third. The same equations also showed that if the total production had been kept constant an increase of one million animal units would have brought about an increase of between 50 and 60 cents in the price per ton of hay in all periods except the third, and even in this period the same increase would probably have been obtained, had the revised data been used.

8. The upshot of the various findings is that the demand for hay has been growing increasingly inelastic with time and that the demand curve has not shown any tendency to shift upward or downward with time. It is rather difficult to subject these findings to a statistical test by using the data published since 1929, on account of the drastic changes in production as a result of the droughts in 1934 and 1936 and the reduction in the livestock population by the A.A.A. This difficulty is aggravated by the fact that our analysis is based on the production and on the livestock statistics in the *Yearbook of Agriculture* for 1931, and these have been subjected to extensive revisions in 1932 and in later years. If, however, we subject these revised series to a graphical correlation analysis,[14] we find that our conclusion is strengthened, not weakened. In fact, the new data show that even the animal-unit demand for hay, which appeared to shift upward from 1915 to 1929 (see Fig. 54*B*), is now shifting downward.

9. Further progress in the analysis of the demand for hay awaits the publication of more and better data on production, prices, and distribution of hay as well as the number and kinds of livestock receiving hay.

[14] In this analysis we treated the consumption of hay per animal unit as a function of the deflated price and of time, and used the data for the fourteen years 1922–35 appearing in *Agricultural Statistics, 1937*.

CHAPTER X

THE DEMAND FOR WHEAT

CHAPTER X

THE DEMAND FOR WHEAT[1]

I. THE FACTUAL BACKGROUND

Although wheat is "the world's king of cereals," it is not our most important crop. In respect to farm value it is outranked by corn, hay, and cotton; and in respect to acreage occupied, by corn and sometimes by hay. In the six years 1924–29 gross farm income from wheat was only about 7 per cent of gross income from all farm production—dairy and poultry products combined being far more important than wheat.[2]

Wheat is, however, the great national bread crop and constitutes an important part of our domestic and foreign commerce. It was grown on over 1.2 million farms in 1929—the number exceeded 2.2 millions in 1919—and was "the greatest single focus of interest" in the post-war agitation for agricultural relief which culminated in the passage of the Agricultural Marketing Act of 1929.

A. THE EXTENT OF THE AMERICAN WHEAT BELT

Wheat production began on the Atlantic Coast at least as early as 1618[3] and moved westward with the advance of settlement. The first American wheat belt stretched from Delaware and Maryland to central New York, a region which still grows much wheat. The next center of commercial wheat production was western New York and the Ohio Valley and the eastern lake regions. These regions are still the center of production of the soft red winter wheats. Production in these regions was stimulated by the opening of canals in the period 1783–1840 which facilitated the shipment of wheat to the more populous eastern seaboard and by the waves of railroad construction in the decades after 1830 which extended the acreage devoted to wheat by improving and cheapening still further the process of moving the grain to the seaboard.

The most rapid expansion of American wheat production took place after the Civil War and continued to about 1900. This period saw the steady westward movement of the wheat frontier with an enormous expansion of acreage on the prairies of Minnesota and the eastern parts of the Dakotas (the hard red spring and durum wheat region), and on the plains from the Dakotas south to

[1] I am profoundly grateful to Professors Holbrook Working and Joseph S. Davis, of the Food Research Institute of Stanford University, for reading the manuscript of this chapter and for much valuable criticism and suggestions. Professor Working also patiently replied to many questions relating to the statistics of wheat and supplied the latest corrected series.

[2] Joseph Stancliffe Davis, *Wheat and the AAA* (Washington, 1935), p. 13.

[3] "Wheat Production and Marketing," *U.S.D.A. Yearbook, 1921*, p. 87.

Texas (the hard red winter wheat region). This period also saw a great increase in the dry-land production of Washington, Oregon, and (to a lesser degree) Idaho.[4] The expansion of production in these regions was due to a complex of factors, the most important of which were: (1) the liberal homesteading laws that opened up for settlement the vast stretches of the Great Plains; (2) the development of large-scale harvesting and threshing machinery, which had been the goal of inventors for years prior to the war; (3) the opening up of the British market following the repeal of the Corn Laws in 1846; (4) the improvement and cheapening of ocean transport; (5) the introduction of new varieties of wheat better adapted to the drier areas west of the Mississippi; and (6) the "widespread application of the roller milling process in the 1880's which gave hard wheats the preference in milling bread flour."[5] These factors, together with the favorable soil and climate and the level open fields of these regions, made production profitable, and wheat became the dominant crop of the new inland empire.

The rapid expansion of wheat production which took place after the Civil War is reflected in the official estimates of acreage and production.

1. ACREAGE

In 1870 the wheat acreage harvested was 26.6 million acres. By 1880 it had increased to 40.8 million acres and remained at approximately the same level until 1883. During the next decade it increased almost continually, reaching a new peak of 51.2 million acres in 1892. Acreage declined slightly until 1895, only to resume its upward trend and reach a new peak of 56.4 million acres in 1899. In the following year acreage began a downward secular movement which continued until about 1909. Then began the almost continuous rise which reached a new high of 60.3 million acres in 1915. The highest acreage in American history was 73.7 million acres which was harvested in 1919. From 1919 through 1934 the wheat acreage harvested was 58.3 millions on the average, or about one-sixth of the total crop acreage, and only corn, and sometimes hay, occupied a higher acreage.[6]

2. PRODUCTION

The general trend of production is similar to that of acreage. In 1870 the crop was only 330 million bushels. By 1880 it had reached 535 million bushels. From 1881 to 1885 production fluctuated about a level of 490 million bushels. Production rose from 1886 to 1898, when it reached a high of 831 million bushels. This figure was not exceeded until 1914. In that year the United States happened to have a high yield (16.1 bushels per acre) on a record acreage (55.6 million acres), the production being 897 million bushels. In 1915, with acreage

---

[4] Joseph S. Davis, "Pacific Northwest Wheat Problems and the Export Subsidy," *Wheat Studies of the Food Research Institute* (Stanford University, Calif.), X, No. 10 (August, 1934), 362–64, 414–15.

[5] Davis, *Wheat and the AAA*, pp. 1–2.   [6] *Ibid.*, pp. 12 and 13. Cf. also Table 27.

and yield still higher, the United States harvested an all-time record crop of 1,009 million bushels. This production has never been equaled, not even during the war, in spite of the stimulus of high prices, reinforced by official propaganda to increase wheat production which adopted the slogan, "Food will win the war." Production decreased from 1919 to 1925, when it fell below 700 million bushels. Thereafter it rose rapidly, reaching 937 millions in 1931, when it began

TABLE 27*

DISTRIBUTION OF THE WHEAT ACREAGE HARVESTED IN THE UNITED STATES
BY PRINCIPAL STATES, FOR SELECTED YEARS

STATE AND DIVISION	ABSOLUTE FIGURES (1,000 ACRES)			PERCENTAGE OF TOTAL		
	1913–14	1923–24	1933–34	1913–14	1923–24	1933–34
Total...............	52,012	56,920	49,438	100.00	100.00	100.00
North Atlantic:						
Pennsylvania...........	1,200	1,210	937	2.31	2.13	1.90
North Central:						
Ohio.................	1,875	2,062	2,089	3.60	3.62	4.23
Indiana..............	2,075	2,135	1,577	3.99	3.75	3.19
Illinois..............	2,175	3,429	1,874	4.18	6.02	3.79
Minnesota............	3,610	1,871	1,629	6.94	3.29	3.29
Missouri.............	2,360	2,810	1,362	4.54	4.94	2.75
North Dakota.........	9,280	8,411	10,098	17.84	14.78	20.43
South Dakota.........	3,900	2,883	1,150	7.50	5.06	2.33
Nebraska.............	3,410	3,252	2,437	6.56	5.71	4.93
Kansas...............	7,250	8,299	7,361	13.94	14.58	14.89
South Central:						
Oklahoma............	1,940	3,847	3,093	3.73	6.76	6.26
Texas................	820	1,554	2,105	1.58	2.73	4.26
Western:						
Montana.............	1,300	3,274	3,512	2.50	5.75	7.10
Washington...........	2,160	1,298	2,163'	4.15	3.51	4.37
All other states..........	8,657	9,885	8,051	16.64	17.37	16.28

* Sources: For the years 1913–14 and 1923–24, *Revised Estimates of Wheat Acreage, Yield and Production, 1866–1929* (U.S. Dept. Agric., September, 1934), pp. 3–51; for 1933–34, *General Crop Revisions, Crop Years 1924–1935, Acreage, Yield and Production* (U.S. Dept. Agric., June, 1936), p. 22.

to decline again, reaching the very low level of 526 million bushels in 1934. For the entire period from 1919 to 1934 annual production averaged 807 million bushels.

B. SOIL AND CLIMATE

The extent of the wheat belts are determined by economic as well as geographic factors. As Finch and Baker put it:

So many factors other than geographical enter into the location of wheat-producing areas that the precise nature of the most favorable wheat climate is not easily determined. At present this crop is not grown in regions of warm, humid climate, principally because of wheat diseases which thrive under those conditions. It is not extensively cultivated in regions having a growing season of less than 90 days, nor in regions having less than 9 inches of annual rainfall, except under irrigation; but, on the other hand, most of the important wheat regions of the world have an average annual precipitation of less than 30 inches. The seasonal distribution of the rainfall is as important as the yearly amount, the most favorable conditions being found where a cool, moderately moist season, during which the basal leaves become well developed and tillering proceeds freely, merges gradually into a warm, bright and preferably dry harvest period, which favors the formation of a hard wheat, high in nitrogen, and retards the growth of fungous diseases. These conditions are found in coastal regions possessing the Mediterranean type of climate and also in the interior of continents, so that, unlike the geographic conditions required by corn, those adapted to wheat extend over large areas in various portions of the earth.

Wheat is successfully grown on a wide range of soils. Most of the famous wheat soils of the world, however, are of high fertility and of fine texture, such as silts, silt loams, and clay loams, usually with a large humus content. The quality of wheat is less dependent upon soil than upon climate, but black soils rich in nitrates, such as the chernozem of Russia and the dark-colored soils of the northwestern prairies of the United States and Canada, generally produce a wheat of higher gluten content.[7]

That climate is more important than soil in determining the quality of wheat is evident from the fact that the same type of soil will produce different kinds of wheat in different climates. In the cold, dry lands, where winter kills growth, wheat is usually sown in the spring, although it is normally a winter annual. It is for this reason that practically all the wheat grown in Minnesota, North Dakota, South Dakota, Montana, and Washington are spring sown. In 1919, 82 per cent of the harvested spring wheat acreage of the United States (total: 23,296,000 acres) was located in these states.[8]

South of the spring wheat area, or between latitude 35 and latitude 41, is the winter wheat area. Kansas, Oklahoma, Missouri, Nebraska, Illinois, Ohio, Indiana, and Texas are the leading producers of winter wheat, having harvested 72 per cent of the entire winter wheat acreage (total: 50,404,000 acres) in 1919. In these states a continuous snow covering often protects the grain from hard frosts. It appears and is harvested earlier than spring wheat.

C. CLASSES AND GRADES OF WHEAT

The problems encountered in the classification of wheat constitute an excellent illustration of the difficulties inherent in any attempt to give an unambiguous definition of a commodity. Like many other commodities, wheat is not a homogeneous article but is of many varieties. Being the fruit of a plant that is easily influenced by environment (and therefore particularly unstable in type) and that has always been migrating to new environments and often undergoing a complete change of type although retaining its old name, it has always presented perplexing difficulties of classification. Add to this the fact that

---

[7] V. C. Finch and O. E. Baker, *Geography of the World's Agriculture* (U.S. Dept. Agric., 1917), p. 13.

[8] See dot maps in *U.S.D.A. Yearbook, 1921*, p. 101.

the modern art of breeding wheat has originated many new varieties, and that wheat has been shipped all over the world, not only for commercial purposes but also for seed experiments, and it is not surprising that the nomenclature is tangled.

For commercial purposes the most common and widely used classifications have been those based on time of sowing, as spring and winter wheat; on the firmness of the grain, as hard and soft; on the products into which they are transformed, as bread and macaroni wheats; and on the color of the seed, as red and white. Of special importance are the classifications based on the climatic conditions under which wheat is grown. The product of humid climates is usually soft and yields starchy flours, while drier climates produce a hard grain that yields a flour with a higher protein content. Hard wheat usually gives "strong" flours, which produce well-risen and light loaves of even texture, and which have a greater capacity for absorbing water in the baking process and hence yielding a larger quantity of bread per barrel—an advantage sought by the baker. Soft wheats, on the other hand, are preferable for pastry, crackers, biscuits, cakes, pies, and for other flaky or crumbly products. In breadmaking they produce a more compact loaf, requiring less shortening. Durum wheat yields a hard granular flour with a larger quantity and different quality of protein than can be obtained from hard wheat and in strength is intermediate between soft and hard wheat. These qualities render it especially desirable for macaroni and spaghetti.

To a large extent the different classes of wheat compete with one another in consumption. Although there are consumers who must have a particular class or grade, a larger proportion of the crop is used by manufacturers who can substitute more or less of one class, variety, or quality for another when prices warrant such substitution. In milling it is, therefore, customary to mix different classes and grades of wheats not only for the purpose of meeting the demand for established kinds and qualities of flours but also for the purpose of effecting desired substitutions.

The official wheat standards of the United States, like those of other countries, have varied from time to time. Those now in force recognize seven commercial classes of wheat: (I) Hard Red Spring, (II) Durum, (III) Red Durum, (IV) Hard Red Winter, (V) Soft Red Winter, (VI) White, and (VII) Mixed Wheat.

Hard Red Spring is grown principally in North Dakota, South Dakota, and Montana, where the winter is too severe for the production of winter wheat. It occupies nearly one-fourth of the total wheat acreage. The strongest flour for breadmaking is produced from this wheat.

Durum and Red Durum wheats are grown in almost the same area as Hard Red Spring wheat. The acreage occupied by them forms about one-sixteenth of the total wheat acreage. From them is made the flour from which macaroni, spaghetti, vermicelli, and other edible pastes are manufactured.

Hard Red Winter wheat is grown principally in the Great Plains area and occupies nearly one-third of the total wheat acreage. This wheat ranks next to Hard Red Spring wheat in quality for flour manufacture.

Soft Red Winter wheat is grown largely in the humid sections in the eastern half of the United States. It occupies less than one-third of the total wheat acreage. This wheat is used in the manufacture of both breadmaking and pastry flours. The flour from this wheat is often blended with those from Hard Red Spring and Hard Red Winter wheats in order to make a stronger bread flour.

White wheat is grown in both the eastern and western parts of the United States and occupies about 7 per cent of the total wheat acreage. Washington, California, Oregon, and Idaho lead in its production in the West; New York and Michigan in the East. It is used in making pastry flours and breakfast foods and is exported to South America and the Orient.

Mixed wheat is wheat of one class having more than 10 per cent of another in it.

There are many varieties in each of these classes. Official investigations of the 1919 crop showed twenty-four varieties of Hard Red Spring wheat, about sixty-five of Soft Red Winter, and more than fifty of White.[9]

The quality of the wheat crop is dependent upon the weather and other conditions which prevail during the growing and harvest season. Drought, rain, and rust are the chief factors affecting the quality. Thus the very low quality of spring wheat of 1904, 1916, and 1935 was due chiefly to an epidemic of black stem rust, and the low quality of spring wheat in 1911 and 1914 was due chiefly to severe drought.

Each of the major classes of wheat is divided into several subclasses, and each subclass is divided into five numerical grades (1, 2, 3, 4, 5), dependent upon the following factors: test weight per bushel, moisture content, percentage of damaged kernels, purity, cleanliness, and condition. Wheat failing to meet the specifications for any one of the five numerical grades is graded "Sample Grade."

Table 28 summarizes the United States official classes of wheat.

Wheat, after leaving the farm, in finding its way through channels of interstate commerce to distant mills and to seaboard cities for export is inspected and graded at terminal markets in accordance with the official wheat standards of the United States. There were 92 such inspection points in 1917, 118 in 1918, 143 in 1919, 158 in 1920, and 167 in 1921. The inspectors at terminal markets are not employees of the Government, but are employed by State grain-inspection departments, chambers of commerce, and boards of trade, or in some cases they operate independently on a fee basis. These inspectors, however, are licensed by the United States Department of Agriculture, and use the Federal standards.[10]

---

[9] *Ibid.*, pp. 123–26. [10] *Ibid.*, p. 129.

The great bulk of the wheat crop falls into the three upper grades, Numbers 1, 2, and 3, and more than half of all wheat inspected is graded Number 1 and Number 2.[11]

TABLE 28

WHEAT: UNITED STATES OFFICIAL CLASSES* AND SUBCLASSES†

CLASS

I. Hard Red Spring:
   Subclasses:
   a) Dark Northern Spring
   b) Northern Spring
   c) Red Spring

II. Durum:
    Subclasses:
    a) Hard Amber
    b) Amber
    c) Durum

III. Red Durum:
     Grades Nos. 1, 2, 3, 4, 5, and sample

IV. Hard Red Winter:
    Subclasses:
    a) Dark Hard Winter
    b) Hard Winter
    c) Yellow Hard Winter

CLASS

V. Soft Red Winter:
   Subclasses:
   a) Red Winter
   b) Western Red

VI. White:
    Subclasses:
    a) Hard White
    b) Soft White
    c) White Club
    d) Western White

VII. Mixed Wheat:
     Grades Nos. 1, 2, 3, 4, 5, and sample

* Compiled from U.S. Dept. Agric., *Handbook of Official Grain Standards of the United States, 1935*, pp. 1–12.
† Each subclass is divided into Grades Nos. 1, 2, 3, 4, 5, and sample.

II. INTERNATIONAL TRADE IN WHEAT AND AMERICAN EXPORTS

Of the average annual world-production of about three and three-quarter billion bushels in the so-called "normal" years of 1909 to 1913, Europe produced about 50 per cent, the United States 20 per cent, British India 10 per cent, Canada and Argentina each around 5 per cent, and the remaining 10 per cent was contributed by a large number of countries. About one-fifth of the world's annual production entered into international trade which consisted largely of imports to about seven industrial nations of Europe and of exports from Russia, the United States, Canada, Argentina, and to some extent from British India, Australia, Hungary, and Rumania. The war eliminated the surpluses of Russia and of Rumania, which constituted about one-third of the international exports. In the decade after the war these two countries, as well as other countries of Europe, restored their wheat production; and, while Russia and the Danube Basin have not resumed their pre-war importance in the international trade in wheat, their export shipments have been substantial in occasional years (see Table 29).

[11] Letter of O. C. Stine, of the Bureau of Agricultural Economics, dated October 15, 1937.

TABLE 29*

WHEAT: WORLD-PRODUCTION, ACREAGE, YIELD PER ACRE, AND INTERNATIONAL TRADE

FOR 1909–10 TO 1913–14 AND 1925–26 TO 1929–30

COUNTRY	AVERAGE 1909–10 TO 1913–14						AVERAGE 1925–26 TO 1929–30					
	Production†		Acreage† (Million Acres)	Yield† per Acre in Bushels	International Trade in Millions of Bu.		Production		Acreage (Million Acres)	Yield per Acre in Bushels	International Trade in Millions of Bu.	
	Total in Millions of Bu.	Percentage of World-Total			Net Imports	Net Exports	Total in Millions of Bu.	Percentage of World-Total			Net Imports	Net Exports
World (excluding China)	3,798.3	100.00	278.2	....	559.3‡	663.3‡	4,413.9	100.00	314.3	....	697.1§	770.5§
Russia (U.S.S.R.)	757.3	19.94	74.0	10.2	....	164.3	790.9	17.92	71.0	11.1	....	17.7
United States	690.1	18.17	47.1	14.7	....	105.3	822.5	18.63	58.3	14.1	....	154.3‖
India	351.8	9.26	29.2	12.0	....	50.5¶	320.5	7.26	31.5	10.2	....	1.4¶
France	325.6	8.58	16.5	19.7	42.9	....	291.4	6.60	13.2	22.0	42.4	....
Canada	197.1	5.19	9.9	19.8	....	93.8	430.7	9.76	23.1	18.6	....	306.8
Italy	184.4	4.85	11.8	15.6	52.8	....	229.2	5.19	12.0	19.0	74.2	....
Rumania	158.7**	4.18	9.5**	16.7**	....	54.4	105.5	2.39	7.7	13.6	....	6.4
Argentina	147.1	3.87	16.1	9.2	....	85.2	243.0	5.51	19.0	12.8	....	159.4††
Germany	131.3	3.46	4.0	32.6	68.6	....	119.8	2.71	4.1	29.4	74.1	....
Spain	130.4	3.43	9.5	13.7	5.9	....	146.2	3.31	10.7	13.7	4.7	....
Australia	90.5	2.38	7.6	11.9	....	49.7	136.0	3.08	12.8	10.6	....	83.3
United Kingdom‡‡	59.6	1.57	1.9	36.1§§	215.7	....	53.0	1.20	1.6	36.9§§	222.7	....
Belgium	15.2	0.40	0.4	37.6	50.9	....	14.8	0.34	0.4	39.5	41.0	....
Netherlands	5.0	0.13	0.1	36.1	22.3	....	6.0	0.14	0.1	44.5	29.1	....
All others (excluding China)	554.2	14.59	40.6	....	100.2	60.1	704.4	15.96	48.8	....	208.9	41.2

* Sources: For 1909–13, *U.S.D.A. Yearbook, 1931*, pp. 590–91, for production, acreage, and yield per acre, and p. 599 for international trade; for 1925–29, U.S. Dept. Agric., *Agricultural Statistics, 1936*, pp. 12–13, for production, acreage, and yield per acre, and p. 23 for international trade.

† Where changes in boundary have occurred, averages are estimates for territory within present boundaries.

‡ Total, 42 countries.   § Total, 41 countries.

‖ Imports include all wheat, i.e., dutiable for consumption, free for grinding in bond for export, and dutiable for feed. Exports of flour include flour ground from domestic wheat and from wheat imported in bond.

¶ British India.   †† Imports (which equal only 10,000 bu.) are for three-year average.

** Four-year average.   ‡‡ Includes Irish Free State.

§§ Simple average of yields for (1) England and Wales, (2) Scotland, (3) Northern Ireland, and (4) Irish Free State.

International trade in wheat began on a large scale in the middle of the nineteenth century. As it rose by leaps and bounds, the United States was in most years the world's greatest exporter. At the beginning of the last quarter of the nineteenth century, our net exports were 75 million bushels, representing nearly one-fourth of our wheat production. The general trend of our exports was upward until about 1901, when it reached a peak of 239 million bushels, or nearly one-third of our production, and constituted nearly half of the world-trade in wheat and flour. According to Dr. Davis, the coincidence of good crops here with short crops in Europe in 1879, 1891, and 1897 "led to large exports at attractive prices and gave a pronounced stimulus to business in this country, twice facilitating revival from depression, and once (1891–1892) helping materially to reverse a recession under way."[12]

In the first decade of the twentieth century, our exports tended irregularly downward, reaching a low level of 70 million bushels in 1910. (In 1904 our exports had fallen to 43 million bushels, but that year was exceptional.) This period saw the rise of Russia to pre-eminence as a wheat exporter, followed by Argentina, Canada, and Australia.

During the four years following 1910, our exports expanded sharply, reaching an all-time record of 335 million bushels in 1914–15. In this year a bumper crop here coincided with short or subnormal crops in Europe, Canada, India, and Australia, and with the interference of shipments from Russia and Argentina by the war. This big crop and heavy shipments helped to counteract other factors which were making for a depression.

Exports declined sharply in 1917 to 103 million bushels, increased to 313 million bushels in 1920, and fell again to the low level of 93 millions in 1925. Although they rose in 1926 to 206 millions, they resumed the downward course in the following years, falling to 112 millions in 1930. Beginning with 1932 exports suffered a drastic decline to 32 millions, and a still further drop in 1933 to the low-water mark of 26 millions. In 1934 the drought and the A.A.A., combined, reduced our production to such an extent (it fell to 526 million bushels) that for the first time we had to import 4 million bushels of wheat.[13] In the next two crop years, also marked by short crops in this country, net imports were substantially larger.

III. THE DATA

A. SUPPLY AND DISTRIBUTION

Since our production of wheat greatly exceeds our consumption, a true picture of the demand-supply situation cannot be obtained without a knowledge of: (1) production, carry-over, and imports, which constitute the total United States supply; (2) consumption, stocks, and exports, which constitute the dis-

---

[12] Davis, *Wheat and the AAA*, p. 2.

[13] All import and export figures given here are net.

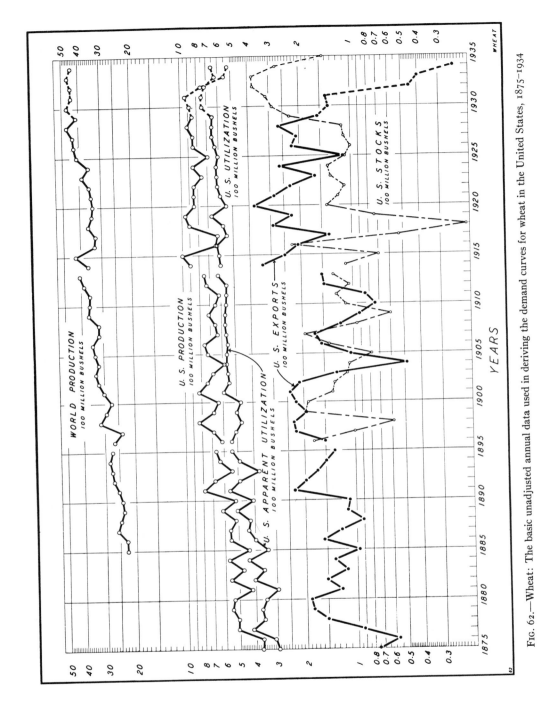

Fig. 62.—Wheat: The basic unadjusted annual data used in deriving the demand curves for wheat in the United States, 1875–1934

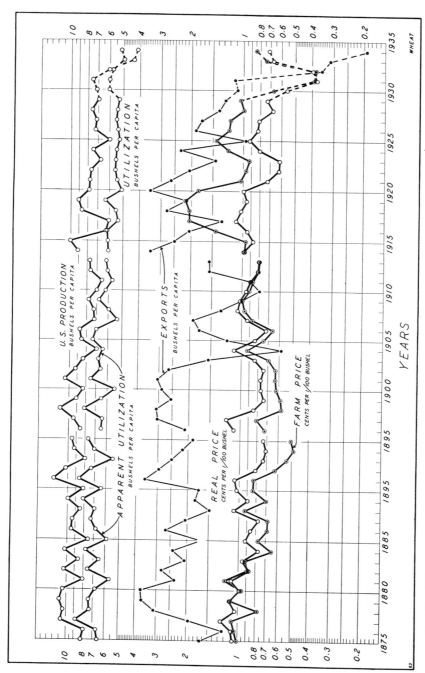

FIG. 63.—Wheat: The basic adjusted annual data used in deriving the demand curves for wheat in the United States, 1875–1934

373

tribution; and (3) prices. World production, supply, and consumption are also very useful. Complete and consistent statistics of all of these series are, however, not available. Table IIc of Appendix A presents the best estimates of these series which we have been able to assemble. It will be observed that two of these series—world-production and United States stocks—do not go back to 1875, the first beginning with 1885, and the second with 1896. In Table VII of Appendix A several of these series are reduced to a per capita basis. Figures 62 and 63 are graphic representations of the more important series, the former relating to the unadjusted, and the latter to the adjusted, data.

To get a correct idea of the limitations of these series and the uses to which they may be put, it is necessary to keep in mind the following definitions and explanations.

1. DOMESTIC PRODUCTION

Despite the great importance of wheat in our national economy, accurate and consistent statistics on the size of the United States wheat crop are not available. A rough-and-ready measure of the inaccuracies in the production data is afforded by the extent of the major revisions which the United States Department of Agriculture made in 1920, 1933, 1935, and 1936.

For example, the revisions of the data for 1879 and 1889–1909, which were published in 1920, vary from 27.2 per cent for 1896 to 0.6 per cent for 1907. For the period as a whole—1889–1909—the original and the adjusted estimates differ in absolute value by 9.3 per cent on the average, the latter being higher than the former in all but the first three and last two years.[14] Minor revisions also appear in succeeding yearbooks.

In 1933, the year of the second major revision, the United States Department of Agriculture adjusted the production data for 1919–28 (1) by revising the former estimates of yield per acre so as to make them comparable with the census figures for 1919, 1924, and 1929 and (2) by revising the acreages for the period 1919–28 to conform to the census acreages of 1919 and 1929.

In 1935 the United States Department of Agriculture made a comprehensive revision of the data for the years prior to 1929, with the view of making its estimates consistent with the decennial census figures and the state enumerations. The adjustments are quite large for the years 1875–95, differing from the 1931 series by more than 10 per cent in eight years, and by more than 15 per cent in five years. For the entire fifty-five-year period, 1875–1929, the 1935 series differs in absolute value from the 1931 series by 4.7 per cent on the average.

---

[14] The adjustments consisted "(1) in using the Department of Agriculture's estimates of average yield per acre to compute, from census acreage, the total production, [and] (2) in adjusting the Department's estimates of acreage for each year so as to be consistent with the following as well as the preceding census acreage" (*U.S.D.A. Yearbook, 1920*, p. 538 and notes to Table 20, p. 551, and to Table 5, p. 538).

In 1936 there were further revisions in the acreage, yield, and production for the years 1924–35.

But *even the revised data are far from accurate.* A study of the wheat acreage and production series made by Professor Holbrook Working, of the Food Research Institute, in 1926 proved conclusively that the official estimates, at least for the years prior to 1902, were invariably too low. In his own words:

> Evidence has accumulated from various sources indicating that the official estimates of acreage and production of wheat in the United States in certain years have been wide of the truth. Further study of the facts, as assembled in the succeeding pages, indicates that in recent years the estimates have been quite reliable, but proves conclusively that prior to 1902, at least, the official estimates were invariably too low, as were also the census figures. *For several years the actual acreage and production are shown to have been as much as 30 to 40 per cent above the official estimates.*[15]

This finding is based on a comparison of the annual "domestic retention" (i.e., the quantity of each crop consumed as food and feed and the quantity wasted) with the quantity of wheat milled for domestic flour consumption. The former is calculated by deducting from the estimated production the calculated seed requirements and the exports of wheat and of flour in terms of its wheat equivalent; the latter is obtained from the Census of Manufactures by (1) deducting flour exports from the total quantity milled, (2) correcting for changes in flour stocks during the year, and (3) converting the barrels of flour into the equivalent number of bushels of wheat on the basis of the census data on the average wheat requirement per barrel of flour. Since the general level of domestic retention corresponds to the general level of domestic consumption and waste, we should expect it to be higher than the level of domestic consumption of wheat in the form of flour. Yet actually the reverse is true! We find, for example, that during the middle nineties the average annual discrepancy amounted to about $1\frac{3}{4}$ bushels per capita, or to more than 15 per cent of the total production for those years.

What is the cause of these striking discrepancies? Since the United States Department of Agriculture estimates of production are equal to their estimates of acreage multiplied by their estimates of yield per acre, the errors in the production data may be due to errors in both component series. Working accepts the estimates of yield per acre as being quite satisfactory, but he believes that the acreage data are subject to large errors, "owing chiefly to the fact that it is very difficult for any individual correspondent to know even approximately what acreage changes have occurred within the county or other geographical

---

[15] "Wheat Acreage and Production in the United States since 1866," *Wheat Studies of the Food Research Institute*, II, No. 7 (June, 1926), 237. (Italics inserted.)

unit for which he is reporting." The nature of these errors is thus described by Working:

Acreage estimates of earlier years have been subject to three kinds of errors: (1) The *general level* of the estimates was subject to error from inadequacies and inaccuracies in the census data on which they were based. (2) The *trend* of the estimates during intercensal periods was likely to deviate considerably from the actual trend of the acreage. (3) The estimated *changes from year to year*, apart from the general trend, were subject to a considerable and quite unknown error, but are probably deserving of consideration. They must be used, however, with the understanding that occasionally a change may indicate the adoption of a new basis for the estimate (as when data from a new general census became available) rather than a belief that the acreage had actually changed as represented.[16]

As a result of these findings Working revised the production data for 1866–1910 as follows:[17]

He adjusted the *level* of the production data year by year to correspond to the *level* of total disposition of wheat in the form of food, feed and waste, seed requirements, changes in stocks and net exports. Dividing the production by the official estimates of yield per acre, he readily obtained the level of the acreage harvested for each year. He then adjusted the acreage to reflect the year-to-year changes in the original acreage estimates of the United States Department of Agriculture after having corrected the latter for errors in the trend and for discontinuities. Multiplying these revised acreage estimates by the official estimates of yield per acre he obtained his revised production estimates.[18]

The possible errors still remaining in these estimates are summarized by Working as follows:

1. The year-to-year changes in the production figures are affected by errors in the year-to-year changes in the yield per acre.

2. The general level and trend of the production estimates are affected by errors in the disposition items (per capita domestic utilization, average per acre seed requirement, exports, and the ratio of wheat ground to flour milled).

3. The trend of the production estimates is affected by the divergence of the trend of actual acreage from the trend of the theoretical acreage.

4. The revised acreage and production estimates for the period 1875–79 are also subject to error in that they reflect changes only in the *trend* of acreage and neglect the year-to-year fluctuations. After 1880 the year-to-year changes shown in the acreage (and therefore in production) are those of the original

---

[16] *Ibid.*, pp. 245–46. For a discussion of the acreage and yield estimates see also chap. v, Sec. III of this book.

[17] The revisions for the years 1910–25 were so slight that Working accepted the U.S. Dept. Agric. estimates for those years.

[18] For a full explanation of the manner in which Working estimated the various disposition items as well as acreage and production see Working, *op. cit.* Working informs us that the methods he used were carefully chosen with a view of leaving the coefficient of elasticity unaffected.

estimates and are subject to all the errors of those estimates except that they have been corrected to show the actual trend of acreage and further corrected to eliminate most, at least, of the errors arising from the discontinuities in the original estimates.[19] The uncertainty in this latter correction is greatest for the period 1896–1901.

Such, in brief, are the adjustments which Working saw fit to make in the official data on wheat production.

Since the appearance of Working's adjusted estimates in 1926 the United States Department of Agriculture has made further revisions in its acreage, yield, and production series which obviously affect his estimates. It appears, nevertheless, that his series give a better picture of the actual production for the years 1875–1910 than do the latest United States Department of Agriculture estimates. For the purposes of our present demand analysis we shall therefore take Working's estimates of production for those years. However, the data for 1875–79 will be omitted from our calculations since they reflect only the changes in the level of acreage and not in the year-to-year fluctuations. The data for 1896–1901 will be included in our analysis, but it should be remembered that they are especially open to suspicion.

The official production estimates of the post-war years which appear in *Agricultural Statistics, 1936*, have been investigated by Dr. M. K. Bennett, of the Food Research Institute.[20] He applied corrections to the United States Department of Agriculture estimates for the years 1921, 1924–27, and 1929 which are based on a comparison of utilization (=production, plus imports, minus exports, and minus changes in stocks) with the sum of (a) Working's recently revised estimates of net mill grindings, (b) official estimates of seed use, and (c) official estimates of wheat fed on farms where grown. These corrections have been incorporated in the series which we shall use (see Table IIc of Appen. A and Figs. 62 and 63). For the remaining years of the post-war period the production data are the latest United States Department of Agriculture estimates available.

2. UNITED STATES STOCKS

Changes in stocks are an important element in absorbing the fluctuations in the size of the crop. As Working put it:

Changes in year-end stocks of wheat have played an equal part with variations in exports in absorbing the fluctuations in the crops. On the average the excess supplies from a large crop are absorbed nearly one-half by increased exports and one-half by additions to stocks, while the deficient supplies from a short crop are met about one-half by increased imports and reduced exports and again one-half by drawing down stocks.

[19] *Ibid.*, pp. 256–57.

[20] "World Wheat Utilization since 1885–86," *Wheat Studies of the Food Research Institute*, XII, No. 10 (1936), 345–46.

. . . . It becomes clear that for an accurate judgment of the supply and demand situation in any year, the need for complete and accurate information on year-end stocks of wheat is nearly as great as the need for accurate statistics of production.[21]

The stock estimates for the years since 1895 which were published by the United States Department of Agriculture in *Wheat and Rye Statistics* (Statistical Bull. No. 12 [1926], pp. 44–47) were carefully investigated by Working and found to be seriously incomplete. As a result of his investigations, he proposed a new series of year-end stocks which include stocks on farms, stocks in terminal elevators, and total (recorded and estimated) outside commercial stocks. Although they are probably the most reliable estimates available, they are nevertheless still subject to numerous errors from various sources. The item of stocks on farms is subject to the errors involved in estimating the percentage of the previous crop remaining on farms July 1, as well as to the errors in the production data. The data on stocks in terminal elevators and the *recorded* estimates of stocks in outside commercial hands are likewise subject to considerable errors of estimation as well as to several inconsistencies. Probably the least reliable of all, however, are the estimates of total changes in outside commercial stocks. Working himself states that the *average error* in these estimates is around 17 million bushels. But this is admittedly a rough guess.[22] In view of the large errors in these stock estimates, we should not be surprised if the adjustment of "apparent utilization" (=production plus imports minus exports) for changes in stocks does not yield any discernible price-quantity relationship for the pre-war years.

[21] Holbrook Working, "Disposition of American Wheat since 1896, with Special Reference to Changes in Year-End Stocks," *Wheat Studies of the Food Research Institute*, IV, No. 4 (1928), 136.

[22] It may be well at this point to sketch briefly the manner in which Working compiled the data on total stocks in all positions. The stocks on farms he derived by applying to his revised estimates of production the official estimates of the percentage of the previous crop remaining on farms July 1. The stocks in terminal elevators (Eastern and Pacific Coast) he compiled from the *Chicago Daily Trade Bulletin* and from *Bradstreet's*. Data on changes in outside commercial stocks east of the Rockies he obtained from the *Daily Trade Bulletin's* monthly statement of "world's available supply of breadstuffs." Working then estimated the total changes in outside commercial stocks as follows:

a) Using the estimates of changes in farm stocks and recorded terminal stocks, he subtracted from the total supply of wheat for each year the disposition for all uses except that for feed and waste. This difference represents:

1. Errors in the data used in the calculations
2. Actual feed and waste
3. Changes in all stocks other than farm stocks (as estimated) and the recorded terminal stocks

b) He then determined the regression of this composite item on the index of outside commercial stocks east of the Rockies and assumed that the correlation between the two series reflects only the influence of the element of stock changes in the former series.

c) Having separated out the element of *changes* in stocks in outside commercial hands, he obtained the totals for individual years by working backwards from the 1927 total (estimated by the United States Department of Agriculture). It is obvious from the computational method employed that these estimates are significant chiefly for the year-to-year changes shown. But even these are subject to considerable error.

It is only for the post-war years, when the official estimates of total stocks are more nearly accurate, that we may hope to obtain fairly reliable results. The data which we shall use for these years appear in *Agricultural Statistics, 1936*, and *Agricultural Outlook Charts, 1937, Wheat and Rye* (November, 1936).[23]

3. DOMESTIC UTILIZATION

This item represents the quantity of wheat used for "food, feed and waste, and seed" in the United States. Theoretically, the utilization for any year may be obtained by subtracting from the total supply of wheat (=production, plus stocks, plus imports of wheat [not wheat and flour]) the disposition of wheat in the form of stocks at the end of the year and exports of wheat and of flour made from that year's supply of wheat. Since we cannot separate the flour exports into flour made from the present year's wheat supply and that made from the previous year's wheat supply, we shall include the total flour exports and flour imports in our data on foreign trade. We thus define "domestic utilization" as production plus stocks of wheat at the beginning of the year, plus imports of wheat and flour in terms of wheat, minus exports of wheat and flour, minus stocks of wheat at the end of the year. For the years 1875–95, when no data on stocks exist, all we can obtain is "apparent utilization" which we define as production, plus imports, and minus exports of wheat and flour. The data on apparent utilization for the period 1875–95, and on utilization for the period 1896–1934 appear in Table IIc of Appendix A. As will be seen later, the utilization series for the period 1896–1913 yields no discernible negative relation between price and quantity. For this period we have, therefore, substituted the series on apparent utilization in our analysis. It is this series which appears in Figures 62 and 63.

It is obvious from the manner in which the series on utilization and apparent utilization are derived that they reflect the errors in all the other supply and disposition items. That these errors are considerable is pointed out by Working.

It appears that there are important errors in the statistics of supplies and disposition of wheat in the United States for even the more recent years. It is not possible to determine with certainty the source of the errors, but in our opinion the larger ones are in the production estimates. The Department of Agriculture has greatly improved its methods of preparing these estimates, but with the radical changes in wheat acreage in recent years, the task of obtaining accurate acreage estimates has been very difficult. It may well be that something approaching an annual census of wheat acreage will be required to remove the danger of occasional serious errors.[24]

[23] Working informs us that he, too, uses the United States Department of Agriculture estimates for the post-war years.

[24] "Disposition of American Wheat since 1896," *op. cit.*, p. 137.

4. WORLD-PRODUCTION

It is impossible to obtain production statistics for the entire world, even for recent years. Thus, only the wildest guesses on production are available for large areas such as China, which may produce 20 to 25 per cent of the total world-crop. Even less is known of the crops of Arabia, Persia, Abyssinia and other wheat-producing countries. For many countries data are available for only a few years or for only a portion of the territory of the country concerned. And even such official statistics as are available for most countries—including as we have already seen, those for the United States—are considerably wide of the truth for many years. Such estimates of world-production as do exist, therefore, make no attempt to represent the whole of world-production but, instead, include only about forty countries of major importance for which data are available. Such a series is that which appears in *Agricultural Statistics*.[25] However, this series is not only incomplete but suffers from numerous gaps and inconsistencies with respect to the areas included and the comprehensiveness of the estimates, as well as from demonstrable errors. It is for this reason that Working and Bennett each developed a new series of world-production. Working broke up the period covered into three subperiods, 1883–92, 1893–1919, and 1920–30. The total area of the countries reporting is the same for all years in each period but varies from period to period.[26] His series does not, however, include estimates of the Russian wheat production, for he found it impossible to obtain a consistent series over the whole period. Bennett's series is designed to show the world-wheat production for the years since 1885 within a land area unchanged from year to year. The number of adjustments which he had to make was largest in the first few years following 1885 and smallest in the years 1908–13. Although it is highly debatable as to whether the data for Russia are consistent, we have decided to use Bennett's series of total world-production including Russia. It is this series which appears in Table IIc of Appendix A.

As Bennett himself points out, the series is subject to the following limitations:

1. It does not represent the whole of the world wheat production. Areas such as China, Asia Minor, Arabia, and Persia may produce over one billion bushels a year. Moreover, since these are old countries with relatively stable populations it is quite likely that wheat production in these areas increased more slowly than it did in the areas included in the world-production series. The trend of wheat production in the world as a whole has, therefore, probably been less steeply upward than the trend shown by this series.

2. The series is subject to all the errors of estimation involved in both the

[25] U.S. Dept. Agric., *Agricultural Statistics, 1936*, p. 11.

[26] Holbrook Working, "Cycles in Wheat Prices," *Wheat Studies*, VIII, No. 1 (November, 1931), 65.

official statistics and in Bennett's adjustments. According to Bennett, these errors tend to exaggerate the actual rate of increase within a country as well as for the world.

Such, in brief, are the quantity series for the United States and the "world" which we shall use in our analysis. For the United States we have the series on apparent utilization for 1875–95, which is equal to production plus imports minus exports. Beginning with 1896 we also have the Working estimates of United States stocks which permit us to obtain estimates of domestic utilization. We have seen, however, that these estimates of stocks are subject to very large errors. It appears, therefore, that it is only from the data for the period since 1921 that we may expect to obtain a fairly accurate determination of the shape and shift of the demand curve for wheat.

The best estimates of world-production appear to be those of Bennett. These do not extend beyond 1885. Estimates of world-stocks are available only since 1922.[27]

B. PRICES

For the purpose of deriving the demand curve for wheat, the price which we should like to have for each year is that which, if it had been maintained throughout the year, would have cleared the market. Such a series is not, however, available. Two series which may be taken as approximations to this ideal series are (1) the prices of basic cash wheat at Chicago and (2) the United States farm price.

The Chicago price, which is available for the years since 1883, is an unweighted average of quotations at weekly intervals of the spot price of such wheat as is being delivered on Chicago futures contracts or is expected to be delivered on them, adjusted for any premiums or discount applicable on delivery.[28] It should be emphasized, however, that this price (1) relates only to the grade eligible for delivery (and nearly always the minimum quality within the grade); (2) is not weighted by sales; and (3) relates to only one market—Chicago—which has long ceased to be the dominant market for cash wheat. Although these limitations are not necessarily decisive against the use of the Chicago price in studies of demand—in the opinion of such a recognized authority on wheat as Holbrook Working they are not—they should be given considerable weight.

The farm price is an average price of all grades and qualities sold in the whole of the United States, weighted according to the production in each state.

[27] For 1922–29: Joseph S. Davis, "The World Wheat Situation, 1934–1935," *Wheat Studies*, XII, No. 4 (1935), 167. For 1930–35: M. K. Bennett *et al.*, "World Wheat Survey and Outlook," *Wheat Studies*, No. 9 (1936), 314.

[28] Holbrook Working, "Prices of Cash Wheat and Futures at Chicago since 1883," *Wheat Studies*, XI, No. 3 (1934), 75–124.

For the years 1875–1907 it is a December 1 price; for the years since 1908 it is also weighted by the estimated sales during the marketing season.[29]

Although the two series are differently constructed and do not represent the same thing, they fluctuate sympathetically for both the pre-war and the post-war years. It is, therefore, largely a matter of indifference as to which price series we should use in our analysis of the demand for wheat. However, since the farm price is a weighted average for the United States as a whole, and since it is the most important price from the standpoint of the farmer, we have decided to use it in all our demand investigations.

It should be noted that the farm price does not include transportation and handling charges and is, therefore, always lower than the Chicago price. The use of this (lower) price should result in a somewhat lower elasticity of demand than would have been obtained from the Chicago price series.[30]

IV. ASSUMPTIONS AND METHODS

The problem of deriving the demand curve for wheat differs from that which we encountered in our analysis of the demand for such a commodity as corn in at least one important respect: there is lacking in the demand function for wheat that symmetry between the quantity demanded and the price paid which we found in the demand for corn.[31] Corn is imported and exported in relatively negligible quantities, the United States being practically a closed economy with respect to it. Moreover, the carry-over is small, so that production and consumption may be taken as approximately equal to each other. Under these conditions, it is a priori a matter of indifference whether we write the demand function for corn as

(4.1) $$x = x(y, t) ,$$

or as

(4.2) $$y = y(x, t) ,$$

---

[29] "Monthly prices received by producers are based on reports from special price reporters, who are mostly country buyers of or dealers in agricultural products. These are prices paid to farmers for all grades and qualities. . . . . Most of these prices relate to the 15th of the month, and for current information and the preparation of index numbers the State averages are weighted by State production to secure a United States weighted average for the date. The seasonal (weighted) prices represent the State prices weighted by estimated sales during the marketing season" (U.S. Dept. Agric., *Agricultural Statistics, 1936*, p. 2).

[30] By definition, the elasticity of demand is $\eta = \dfrac{dx}{dy} \cdot \dfrac{y}{x}$. For fixed values of $\dfrac{dx}{dy}$ and x, this will be numerically smaller, the smaller the y. The use of the farm price series probably does not change $\dfrac{dx}{dy}$ sufficiently to offset this effect on the coefficient of elasticity.

[31] It will be recalled that the identical problem was met in chap. viii, "The Demand for Cotton."

where x is consumption, y is price, and t is time. True, certain *statistical* considerations may turn the scales in favor of one of the two hypotheses, for in fitting (4.1) we generally minimize the sum of the squares of the x-residuals, while in fitting (4.2) we generally minimize the sum of the squares of the y-residuals, and one of these procedures might be preferable to the other in a given situation.[32] But, in theory at least, both (4.1) and (4.2) are equally valid representations of the unique functional relation connecting all the three variables:

$$(4.3) \qquad\qquad f(x, y, t) = 0.$$

A different situation obtains, however, in the case of wheat. Of our total production, a large part is normally sold abroad, where it competes with foreign-grown wheat. Under these conditions it is no longer a matter of indifference whether we write the demand function for wheat in the form (4.1) or (4.2). The former is still a most reasonable hypothesis, for the effect on consumption of a given change in price is not likely to depend on the cause of the price change—whether it be a change in foreign or in domestic production or stocks. The latter is, however, no longer very plausible, since the price of wheat is likely to be more affected by the American and foreign production and stocks than by the American consumption. Consequently, hypothesis (4.2) should be replaced either by

$$(4.4) \qquad\qquad y = y(x_{ds}, x_{fp}, t) ,$$

where x_{ds} stands for the domestic supply and x_{fp} for the foreign production, and t for time; or, better still, by

$$(4.5) \qquad\qquad y = y(x_{ds}, x_{fs}, t) ,$$

in which foreign supply (x_{fs}) takes the place of foreign production.

There are, of course, many other factors which affect the price of wheat, but these factors cannot be conveniently measured and included in our demand equations. In so far, however, as they change slowly and smoothly with time, they are subsumed under the catch-all variable t.

Our statistical analysis will be governed by the foregoing considerations, as well as by the nature of the available data. Whereas in most of the preceding statistical chapters the analysis covered the three periods 1875–95, 1896–1914, and 1915–29, in this chapter the analysis will begin with 1880 and will cover the four periods: (I) 1880–95, (II) 1896–1913, (IIIa) 1921–29, (IIIb) 1921–34. The reason for the omission of the observations for 1875–79 has been explained

[32] See chap. iv, pp. 146–49.

in the previous section: the adjustments made in these observations by Working reflect only changes in the level of acreage and not in the year-to-year fluctuations. The reason for the omission of the observations for 1914–20 is, of course, that all our wheat series for these years are affected by the abnormal conditions of the World War.

It will be recalled that for Period I the data on apparent utilization (production plus imports minus exports) are available. Consequently, we shall assume that, as a first approximation, apparent utilization is equal to actual utilization and write our demand function for this period as

$$(4.6) \qquad\qquad x_{au} = x_{au}(y, t) ,$$

where x_{au} is the apparent utilization. (This assumption is not, however, to be interpreted as supporting the view that statistics of wheat utilization which neglect changes in stocks are sufficiently reliable for deriving elasticities of demand.)

For Periods II, IIIa, and IIIb, we have statistics on United States stocks and, hence, on utilization, although the stocks estimates for the second period are particularly suspect. We shall, therefore, experiment not only with (4.6) but also with the theoretically more valid hypothesis

$$(4.7) \qquad\qquad x_{u} = x_{u}(y, t) ,$$

where x_{u} stands for utilization.

For the periods IIIa and IIIb, when the data on utilization are more reliable than for any other period, we shall also experiment with utilization less seed (x_{u-s}) as a function of price and time:

$$(4.8) \qquad\qquad x_{u-s} = x_{u-s}(y, t) ,$$

and compare the results obtained.

The foregoing equations (4.6) to (4.8) are the most probable hypotheses relating to the *demand* for wheat in the different periods. When we have finished this analysis, we shall take up the investigation of the factors affecting the price of wheat, using hypotheses (4.4) and (4.5). Since reliable estimates of foreign production, let alone foreign supply, are not available for Period I, the investigation will have to be confined to Periods II and III.

But even for Period II data on foreign supply are lacking so that the only hypothesis that can be tested with the available data for this period is hypothesis (4.4). It is only for the third period (or, more accurately, for the period since 1922) that statistics on foreign supply become available. Consequently, it is only for this period that we shall be able to submit the more reasonable hypothesis (4.5) to a statistical test.

Since the quantity data for the first period relate to *apparent* utilization, and those for the second and third periods relate to utilization, a comparison of the relation between absolute changes in quantity and absolute changes in price is not so significant as a comparison of the relation between the corresponding relative changes. Consequently, we shall make use only of the logarithmic forms of hypotheses (4.4) to (4.8).

V. THE DEMAND FUNCTIONS FOR WHEAT[33]

Figure 64A is the scatter diagram of the logarithms of the apparent utilization per capita for 1880–95 against the logarithms of the corresponding deflated prices. Line $D_1'D_2'$ is the net regression of consumption on price. Figure 64B shows the deviations of the apparent utilization from the line $D_1'D_2'$ plotted as a function of time. (The dotted circles indicate observations not used in the computations.)

The two diagrams show at a glance that there is no significant relation between apparent utilization and price and time, the absence of a net negative correlation between quantity and price being apparently due to the effects of the (unknown) changes in stocks and of the errors in the data for 1880–95.

Equation 1 of Table 30 is the equation of regression of the logarithms of apparent utilization on the logarithms of the deflated price and on time. As was to be expected from Figure 64, the regressions of consumption on price and on time are both insignificant, being exceeded by their standard errors. We conclude, therefore, that the data on apparent utilization for 1880–95 enable us to determine neither the elasticity nor the shift of the demand curve for wheat.[34]

Figure 65 relates to the period 1896–1913. The left-side diagram shows the relation between apparent utilization and price, while the right-side diagram shows the relation between utilization and price. (In both diagrams line $D_1'D_2'$ is the net regression of quantity on price.) We should expect the utilization series to yield better results than does the series on apparent utilization because the former is a better measure of the quantity of wheat demanded, since it has apparently taken into account changes in stocks. Actually, the results are worse, the net regression of utilization on price being positive![35] This shows, of course, that the differences between beginning- and end-year stocks are subject to such large errors that the introduction of this series masks the negative relation between quantity and price which was suggested by the presumably less

[33] For an explanation of the statistical methods used and for definitions of the technical terms see chap. vi.

[34] If t is omitted from eq. 1, the elasticity of demand is still insignificant, being -0.1060 ± 0.2273.

[35] The regression equation is

$$x_u' = 0.7161 + 0.0505y' - 0.00886\,Mt\,,$$
$$\quad\quad\quad\quad (0.0861)\quad\ (0.00259)$$

where $M = \log_{10} e$, the adjusted multiple correlation coefficient being 0.6178.

TABLE 30

WHEAT: THE CHARACTERISTICS OF THE PER CAPITA DEMAND FUNCTIONS

x'_{au} = Logs of apparent utilization in bushels per capita
x'_u = Logs of utilization in bushels per capita

(Figures in parentheses are standard errors)

EQUA-TION No.	PERIOD†		Constant Term	y'	$‡Mt$	$‡Mt^2$
1	I	$x'_{au} =$	0.8942	−0.0271 (0.2646)	+0.00515 (0.00824)	. . . .
2	II	$x'_{au} =$	1.1039	−0.1512 (0.1606)	−0.00761 (0.00483)	. . . .
3	IIIa	$x'_u =$	0.8851	−0.0809 (0.0401)	−0.00207 (0.00201)	. . . .
4	IIIb	$x'_u =$	1.0845	−0.1854 (0.0372)	−0.00498 (0.00229)	−0.00137 (0.00059)
5	IIIb	$x'_{u-s} =$	1.0802	−0.2143 (0.0398)	−0.00358 (0.00245)	−0.00163 (0.00063)

* The origin of t is for Period I, July 1, 1888; for Period II, July 1, 1905; for Period IIIa, January 1, 1926; for Period IIIb, July 1, 1928.

trustworthy series of apparent utilization. It follows, therefore, that even for the second period we have no other recourse than to work with apparent utilization.

Equation 2 of Table 30 summarizes this relationship. Figure 66 is a graphic representation of this equation. The equation tells us that, other things being equal, an increase of 1 per cent in the deflated farm price of wheat was associated with a decrease in the annual per capita disappearance of only 0.15 of 1 per cent. This is the slope of line $D'_1D'_2$ in Figure 66A. But other things did not remain equal during this period. The demand curve kept shifting downward at the average rate of 0.76 per cent per annum. This is the slope of line $D'_1D'_3$ of Figure 66B. If the apparent utilization may be considered a good approximation to the quantity of wheat demanded, then the first coefficient is the elasticity of demand. The fit of equation 2 is, however, very poor, as is shown by the large scatter of the observations and by the small R'. Moreover, an examination of the standard errors shows that the elasticity of demand is statistically insignificant, since it is exceeded by its standard error, so that we are not justified in placing any confidence in this finding unless it is supported by other evidence.

TABLE 30—*Continued*

WITH QUANTITY AS THE DEPENDENT VARIABLE, BY PERIODS, 1880–1934

x'_{u-s} = Logs of utilization less seed in bushels per capita
y' = Logs of deflated farm price in cents per bushel
t = Time in years*

(Figures in parentheses are standard errors)

| DESCRIPTIVE CONSTANTS | | | | | EQUA-TION No. |
| | | | Percentage of Variance of Demand Attributable to | | |
Elasticity of Demand η	Quadratic Mean Error ϵ (Per Cent)	Adjusted Multiple Correlation Coefficient R'	y	t	
−0.0271 (0.2646)	87.5–114.3	0.0§	0.39	4.01	I
−0.1512 (0.1606)	90.0–111.2	0.2513	4.22	13.11	2
−0.0809 (0.0401)	98.5–101.5	0.6154	39.43	13.97	3
−0.1854 (0.0372)	96.9–103.2	0.8079	62.41	10.87	4
−0.2143 (0.0398)	96.7–103.4	0.8347	68.82	7.85	5

† I = 1880–95; II = 1896–1913; IIIa = 1921–29; IIIb = 1921–34.

‡ $M = \log_{10} e = 0.43429$.

§R' is to be interpreted as zero whenever R'^2 turns out to be negative. See n. 34 of chap. vi.

We conclude, then, that the data for the second period, like those for the first, are not sufficiently accurate to yield a determination of the coefficient of the elasticity of demand for wheat with a standard error which is at least smaller than the coefficient itself. The series which is subject to the greatest errors is that relating to wheat stocks,[36] although neglecting it does not improve our results—which was to be expected.

It is only in the third period, i.e., in the years beginning with 1921, that the data on stocks and production become sufficiently accurate to enable us to derive the elasticity of demand for wheat with a fairly high degree of prob-

[36] The fact that the standard error of the elasticity for wheat is of the same order of magnitude as the elasticity itself, or even larger, does not necessarily imply that the underlying data relating to wheat are less trustworthy than those relating to the other commodities whose demands we have studied. All that this suggests is that, the smaller the η, the more accurate must be the data on consumption and prices, if it is to be determined with a fair degree of probability. For a small value of η means that the demand curve is nearly parallel to the price axis $\left(\frac{\partial x'}{\partial y'} \to 0\right)$. And, when this condition obtains, a relatively small inaccuracy in the underlying data will bring about a relatively large error in the slope and, consequently, in the elasticity. See Henry Schultz, "A Comparison of Elasticities of Demand Obtained by Different Methods," *Econometrica*, I, No. 3 (1933), 295, n. 32.

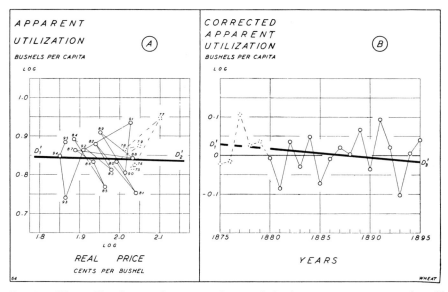

Fig. 64.—Wheat: The absence of a net negative correlation between apparent per capita utilization and the real price of wheat, 1880–95, showing the impossibility of deducing a demand curve for wheat from these series.

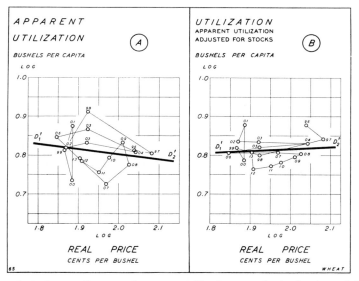

Fig. 65.—Wheat: Scatter diagrams of apparent utilization on real price for the period 1896–1913 (A), and of utilization on real price for the same period (B), showing the impossibility of deducing a demand curve for wheat from the latter, since the net relation between utilization and price (line $D'_1D'_2$) is positively sloped.

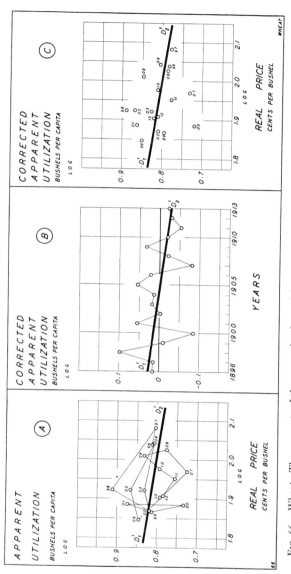

Fig. 66.—Wheat: Three aspects of the per capita demand for wheat during the period 1896-1913 on the assumption that

$$x_{au} = 12.703\, y^{-0.1512}\, e^{-0.00761\,t}\,.$$

A: Relation between per capita apparent utilization and real price when the data are not corrected for the effects of "time" with the demand curve $D_1'D_2'$ which results when such corrections are made. This relation is, however, not significant statistically.

B: Relation between per capita apparent utilization and time when the former is corrected for the effects of changes in the real price. The slope of line $D_1'D_3'$ (fitted to the variables x_{au} and t when both are corrected for price) represents the mean rate of shift of the per capita demand curve $D_1'D_2'$.

C: The per capita demand curve for wheat, 1896-1913. Line $D_1'D_2'$ shows the relation between that part of the per capita apparent utilization of wheat in the United States which is independent of time and that part of the real price which is independent of time. In the scatter, however, only the ordinate is corrected for secular changes, the abscissa being uncorrected.

389

ability. We shall first consider the demand function derived from the data for 1921–29 (Period III*a*). Equation 3, Table 30, is the function in question.

From the coefficient of y' we see that based on the experience of this period an increase of 1 per cent in the deflated farm price (season average, weighted) brings about a decrease in the annual per capita utilization of wheat of only 0.08 of 1 per cent, for

(5.1)
$$\frac{\partial x'}{\partial y'} = \frac{\partial x}{\partial y} \cdot \frac{y}{x} = -0.0809 .$$

Since wheat utilization is the best approximation we have of the amount of wheat demanded (i.e., the amount used for food, feed, and seed, and the amount wasted), we may say that the elasticity for wheat in the United States is −0.08. The standard error of this coefficient is only 0.04, so that the elasticity in question is probably significantly different from zero. The smallness of the standard error is, of course, a marked improvement over the corresponding values of equations 1 and 2.

From the coefficient of Mt we see that the demand curve for wheat shifted downward at the average rate of 0.2, or 1 per cent per annum, for

$$\frac{\partial \log_e x}{\partial t} = \frac{1}{M} \cdot \frac{\partial x'}{\partial t} = \frac{1}{x} \cdot \frac{\partial x}{\partial t} = -0.00207 .$$

But this shift is barely significant; it may well be due to fluctuations of simple sampling.

Figure 67 is a graphic illustration of equation 3. Line $D_1'D_2'$ (Fig. 67*A*) is the demand curve for wheat; the slope of this line is the elasticity of demand, $\eta = -0.08$. Line $D_1'D_3'$ (Fig. 67*B*) gives the change through time of that part of the logarithms of the per capita utilization which is linearly independent of the logarithms of price. The slope of this line measures the relative rate of shift of the demand curve.

Figure 67*C* gives the relation between the quantity demanded and the price of wheat when the former has been corrected for the shifting of the demand curve.

Since the rate of shift of the demand curve derived from the data for 1921–29 is barely significant, it was deemed advisable to extend the period to 1934 in order to see what effect the increase in the number of observations will have on the rate of shift as well as on the elasticity of demand. Equation 4, Table 30, is the demand function obtained. Figure 68 is a graphic illustration of it. According to this equation the elasticity of demand for wheat is −0.19, or more than twice as large as that derived from the data for the shorter period. The demand curve moved upward from 1921 to about 1926 and then began to shift

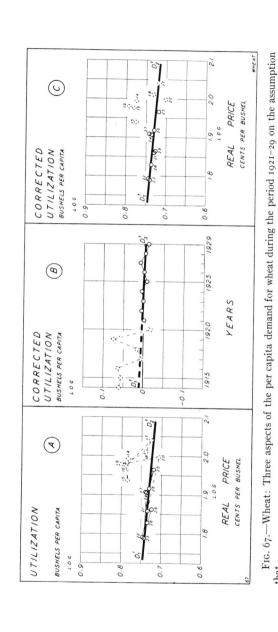

Fig. 67.—Wheat: Three aspects of the per capita demand for wheat during the period 1921–29 on the assumption that

$$x_u = 7.675\, y^{-0.0809}\, e^{-0.00207\, t}.$$

(The dotted observations were not used in the computations.)

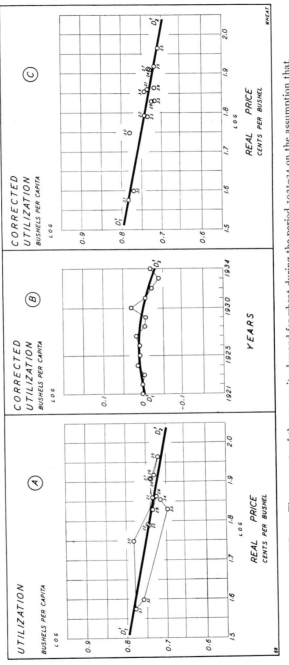

FIG. 68.—Wheat: Three aspects of the per capita demand for wheat during the period 1921–34 on the assumption that

$$x_u = 12.148\, y^{-0.1854}\, e^{-0.00498\, t - 0.00137\, t^2}\,.$$

rapidly downward (see Fig. 68B). All the coefficients of this equation have relatively small standard errors and are, therefore, quite significant. Judged by the adjusted coefficient of multiple correlation, the fit of equation 4 is better than that of any of the preceding equations.[37]

In equation 4 the variable x_u (utilization) includes the quantities used for seed. If we deduct the seed requirements from total utilization, obtaining utilization for food, feed, and waste, and express it as a function of price and time, we obtain equation 5. Judged by the magnitude of R', this equation gives a slightly better fit to the data than equation 4, but this is of comparatively minor significance. What is significant to the economist is that the elasticity of demand yielded by this equation, $\eta = -0.21$, is numerically somewhat higher than that derived from equation 4 ($\eta = -0.19$), for this is what we should expect on theoretical grounds.[38]

VI. FACTORS IN THE PRICE OF WHEAT

As was explained in Section IV, the most plausible, simple hypotheses concerning the factors affecting the price of wheat which it is practicable to submit to a statistical test are (4.4) and (4.5). According to (4.4), the average price of wheat depends on the domestic supply (production plus beginning stocks plus imports), the foreign production, and the catch-all factor, time. According to (4.5), the price depends on the domestic supply, foreign supply, and time. Of course, (4.5) is a more reasonable hypothesis than (4.4), but data on foreign supply are not available prior to 1922. The only procedure open to us, therefore, is to test hypothesis (4.4) by means of the data for 1896–1913 (Period II), and hypothesis (4.5) by means of the data for 1922–34 (Period III). (There are no data on domestic supply for the first period.) Equation (6.1), which re-

---

[37] Professor Holbrook Working suggests that the results obtained from eqs. 3 and 4 of Table 30 (Figs. 67 and 68) hinge in large part on the acceptance of M. K. Bennett's corrections (see Sec. III, A, 1, above), which involve smoothing of the official production statistics. He argues that no reliance can be placed on the standard errors of the computed parameters. It is instructive, therefore, to derive the corresponding equation without using M. K. Bennett's corrections. Of eqs. 3 and 4, to which the objection applies, the first relates to 1921–29 and the second to 1921–34. Since the first period contains only nine observations, the comparison will be confined to the equations for the longer period. For this period the demand equation based on official production data is

$$x' = 1.1202 - 0.2066y' - 0.0036Mt - 0.0016Mt^2. \qquad R' = 0.7362.$$
$$(0.0513) \quad (0.0032) \qquad (0.0008)$$

It will be seen that with the possible exception of the coefficient of Mt the agreement between this equation and eq. 4 of Table 30 is excellent.

[38] By definition, $\eta = \dfrac{\partial x}{\partial y} \cdot \dfrac{y}{x}$. The deduction of seed requirements from total utilization decreases x and tends consequently to increase the absolute value of η; for there is no reason to suppose that $\dfrac{\partial x}{\partial y}$ would be appreciably affected by this modification of x.

lates to the second period, is one specific form—the logarithmic—of hypothesis (4.4):

$$(6.1) \quad y' = 8.3802 - 1.4989\ x'_{ds} - 0.6130\ x'_{fp} + 0.0101\ Mt + 0.00153\ Mt^2,$$
$$\quad\quad\quad (0.2709) \quad\quad (0.3044) \quad\quad (0.0097) \quad\quad (0.00089)$$

the origin being July 1, 1905. The subscripts ds and fp stand for domestic supply and foreign production. The quadratic mean error of this equation is $\epsilon = \pm 0.0384$ units. The antilogarithms corresponding to -0.0384 and $+0.0384$ are, respectively, 91.5 per cent and 109.3 per cent. This means that, if the observations are normally distributed about the surface, approximately 68 per cent of them will lie between 91.5 and 109.3 per cent of the computed prices (see chap. vi, Sec. III, D, 2, c). The adjusted multiple correlation coefficient is $R' = 0.8339$. Of the variance of the dependent variable ($\sigma_{y'}^2$), domestic supply accounts for 57.42 per cent, foreign production for 16.80 per cent, and time for 2.49 per cent.

Equation (6.2), which relates to the period 1922–34, is the logarithmic form of hypothesis (4.5):

$$(6.2) \quad\quad y' = 9.3389 - 2.0122\ x'_{ds} - 0.3920\ x'_{fs} - 0.0120\ Mt^2,$$
$$\quad\quad\quad\quad (0.3321) \quad\quad (0.2997) \quad\quad (0.0034)$$

the origin being July 1, 1928. In this equation foreign supply (x'_{fs}) has been substituted for foreign production. The quadratic mean error is ± 0.0581 units. The antilogarithms of -0.0581 and $+0.0581$ are 87.5 per cent and 114.3 per cent, respectively. The adjusted multiple correlation coefficient, $R' = 0.8677$. Of the variance of the dependent variable ($\sigma_{y'}^2$), domestic supply accounts for 71.53 per cent, foreign supply for 3.75 per cent, and time for 6.18 per cent.[39]

Figures 69 and 70 are graphic representations of certain aspects of (6.1) and (6.2).

Among the more important relations summarized by these equations are the following:

1. Other things being equal, an increase of 1 per cent in the domestic supply for any given year of the period 1896–1913 was, on the average, associated with a reduction in the (deflated) annual price of approximately 1.5 per cent (see line $d'_1 d'_2$, Fig. 69). This is the partial flexibility of the domestic price with respect to the domestic supply.

2. Other things being equal, an increase of 1 per cent in the foreign production for any given year of this period was associated with a reduction in the same price of only 0.6 per cent (see line $d'_1 d'_3$, Fig. 69). This is the partial flexibility of the domestic price with respect to foreign production.

[39] The regression of y' on t was omitted from this equation because it proved insignificant; the remaining coefficients were corrected for this omission.

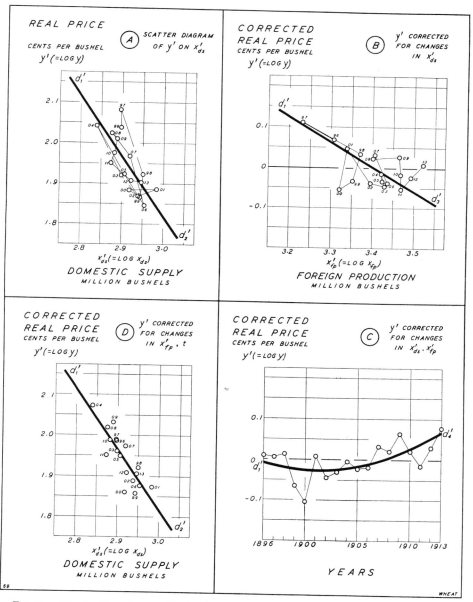

FIG. 6ç.—Wheat: Three factors affecting the United States farm price of wheat during the period 1896–1913 on the assumption that

$$y = 2.400(10^8)\, x_{ds}^{-1.4989}\, x_{fp}^{-0.6130}\, e^{0.01011t+0.00153t^2}.$$

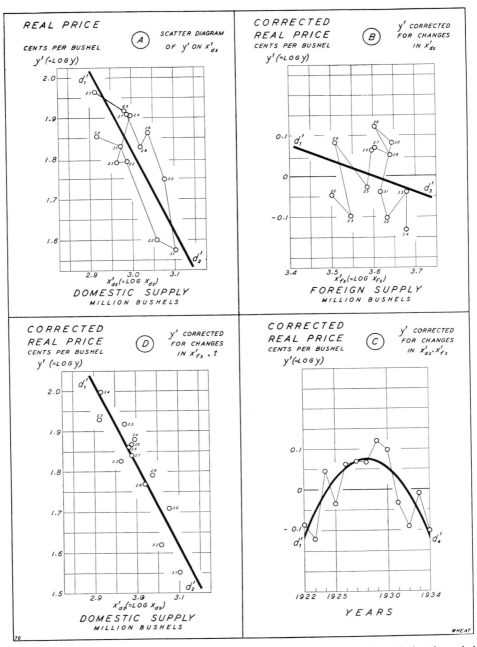

FIG. 70.—Wheat: Three factors affecting the United States farm price of wheat during the period 1922–34 on the assumption that

$$y = 2.182(10^9) \, x_{ds}^{-2.0122} \, x_{fs}^{-0.3920} \, e^{-0.0120 t^2} \, .$$

3. But other things did not remain equal. Even if domestic supply and foreign production had been fixed, the price would have decreased from 1896 to about 1903 and increased very rapidly from 1903 until the end of the period (see curve $d_1'd_4'$, Fig. 69).

4. All the coefficients of this equation are statistically significant, and the fit of the equation, as judged by R', is very good.

Turning now to equation (6.2), we find that during the period 1922–34 the price was more responsive to changes in domestic supply than to changes in foreign supply. The partial flexibility of the deflated farm price with respect to the former was −2.0 (see line $d_1'd_2'$, Fig. 70), whereas its partial flexibility with respect to the latter was only −0.39 (see line $d_1'd_3'$, Fig. 70). However, the standard error of the latter coefficient is not very significant.

The curve $d_1'd_4'$ (Fig. 70) shows that, even if x_{ds} and x_{fs} had been fixed, the price would have increased from 1922 until about 1927 and have decreased from 1927 to 1934.

Since these results are based in part on the observations for 1930–34, when the price of wheat was affected by such special circumstances as the A.A.A. and the devaluation of the dollar, it is instructive to see how the parameters are modified when these years are omitted. For the years 1922–29 the equation which we obtain is

$$(6.3) \quad y' = 13.69 - 2.0255x_{ds}' - 1.6132x_{fs}' + 0.1209Mt. \qquad R' = 0.7541 .$$
$$\quad\quad\quad (0.6171) \quad\quad (0.8363) \quad\quad (0.0445)$$

The regression on x_{ds}' is almost identical with the corresponding coefficient of equation (6.2). The regression on x_{fs}' is about four times as large as that of the corresponding coefficient of (6.2). Unfortunately, the observations for this period are too few to warrant our placing much confidence in this difference.

VII. SUMMARY AND CONCLUSIONS

Although the nature of the demand curve for wheat was discussed by the political arithmeticians of the seventeenth century, as is evidenced from the famous relation between the changes in the crop and the changes in the price of "corn" attributed by Charles Davenant to Gregory King and known as "Gregory King's Law,"[40] it was not until 1914 that the first attempt was made to derive the elasticity of demand for wheat from the actual statistics of crops and prices. In that year Professor Lehfeldt published a study[41] in which he analyzed the relation between the world-crop and the mean price of English imported wheat for the calendar years 1888–1911. Lehfeldt corrected the crop

[40] See Palgrave's *Dictionary of Political Economy*, articles on Charles Davenant and Gregory King as well as W. Stanley Jevons, *The Theory of Political Economy* (1871); 4th ed., 1924, pp. 152–61.

[41] R. A. Lehfeldt, "The Elasticity of Demand for Wheat," *Economic Journal*, XXIV (1914), 212–17.

series by fitting a compound-interest curve to the data and adjusting the annual crop estimates for the secular increase in population; and he corrected the price series by deflating it by Sauerbeck's quinquennial index. He then took the logarithms of the two series, and, to allow at least approximately for the fact that "the full effect of a good or bad harvest is shown on the price a certain number of months afterwards," he correlated the production series with the price series lagged by one year, obtaining a correlation coefficient of $r = -0.44$. Not wishing to fit a curve to the scatter diagram of the two series of logarithms and deducing the elasticity of demand from the curve—he does not even refer to the possibility of using this procedure—he simply took the coefficient of the elasticity of demand to be the ratio of the standard deviation of the logarithms of the quantities to the standard deviation of the logarithms of the prices: $\eta = \sigma_{x'}/\sigma_{y'}$ and obtained a value of -0.6 for this constant.

Although his determination of the elasticity of demand for wheat appears to be the first determination of this important constant to be based on actual observations of quantities and prices, his numerical result is admittedly only the roughest approximation to the true value. Moreover, his underlying series are subject to large (and unknown) margins of error, and his statistical procedure is also open to criticism.[42]

In 1925, Professor Killough correlated the adjusted Chicago price of wheat for the period 1895–1914 with the world-production and carry-over of wheat, the world-production of barley, and the world-production of rye, and obtained a coefficient of multiple correlation of the order of 0.8, whether he used the method of trend ratios or the method of link relatives.[43] But Killough appears not to have been interested in the shape and the elasticity of the demand function for wheat. He does not even give the equations on which his correlations are based and from which the elasticity of demand might perhaps have been computed. In fact, his entire treatment of the price of wheat is brief and inadequate as compared with his analysis of the price of oats.

In 1926, C. C. Bosland correlated the deflated price of wheat with world-production plus carry-over, United States acreage harvested, and United States exports.[44] He obtained the value of 0.59 for the coefficient of multiple correlation.

In 1927, Professors Warren and Pearson made a number of correlation studies for the period 1899–1913 between the prices of various wheats at several markets and the wheat production of the world and of various areas—the

[42] See Henry Schultz, *Statistical Laws of Demand and Supply* (Chicago, 1928), Appen. I, pp. 211–12.

[43] Hugh B. Killough, *What Makes the Price of Oats* (U.S. Dept. Agric. Bull. No. 1351 [September, 1925]), p. 25.

[44] "Forecasting the Price of Wheat," *Journal of the American Statistical Association*, XXI (1926), 149–61.

southern hemisphere, East Europe, West Europe, North America, the United States, British India, Russia, etc.[45] Their equations are of the form log $y = a + b$ log x which yield directly only the coefficients of flexibility of prices with respect to production and not the coefficients of elasticity of demand.

In 1932, we derived arithmetic and logarithmic demand functions for wheat for each of the three periods 1875–95, 1896–1913, and 1922–29, by making use of the then available data on apparent disappearance and disappearance. Expressing quantity as a function of price and time, we obtained coefficients of elasticity of + 0.13 ± 0.17 for the first period; of − 0.01 ± 0.10 for the second; and of − 0.27 ± 0.12 for the third.[46] In a companion publication we called attention to the fact that,

since the demand curve for wheat is practically parallel to the axis of price, a small change in the slope of the curve, due to sampling fluctuations of the data, is associated with a large change in the coefficient of elasticity. The standard errors of the coefficients are, therefore, also large. There is no reasonable doubt, however, about the extreme *inelasticity* of the demand for wheat.[47]

Although this conclusion is still valid, the demand functions are no longer acceptable, since they were derived from the old, unrevised United States Department of Agriculture data on production and stocks and reflect, therefore, the relatively large errors to which those series were subject.

In this chapter, we have attempted to determine the elasticity and the rate of shift of the demand curve for wheat, together with the precisions of these parameters, from the best estimates of the disappearance, supply, and price of wheat that are available. The more important findings may be summarized briefly as follows.

1. The most accurate and complete series are available only since 1921 or 1922. Based on the statistics of per capita utilization less seed and on deflated farm prices from 1921 to 1934, the elasticity of demand for wheat is of the order of − 0.2 ± 0.04. That is, the net effect of an increase of 1 per cent in the deflated average price of any year of this period is to reduce the per capita utilization for the same year by only 0.2 of 1 per cent. If the observations for 1930–34 are omitted, the elasticity of demand drops (in absolute value) to − 0.1 ± 0.04. (This equation does not appear in Table 30.)

The elasticity of demand is slightly smaller numerically if, for utilization less seed, we substitute utilization for all purposes including seed in the demand equation. This is what we should expect on theoretical considerations.

[45] G. F. Warren and F. A. Pearson, *Interrelationships of Supply and Price* (Cornell University Agricultural Experiment Station Bull. No. 466 [Ithaca, N.Y., March, 1928]), pp. 54–68 and 134–37.

[46] Henry Schultz, "The Shifting Demand for Selected Agricultural Commodities, 1875–1929," *Journal of Farm Economics*, XIV (1932), 220–21, Table 2.

[47] "A Comparison of Elasticities of Demand Obtained by Different Methods," *Econometrica*, I, No. 3 (1933), 295, n. 32.

2. Substantially the same value for the elasticity of demand ($\eta = -0.15$) is yielded by the less reliable data (*apparent* utilization and farm price) for the second period (1896–1913), but this value is exceeded by its standard error. The data on apparent utilization for the first period (1880–95) are much too inaccurate to yield even approximations to the elasticity of demand for that period. In fact, the greatest obstacle which has stood in the way of the derivation of the shape, the elasticity, and the rate of shift of the demand curve for wheat even for the second and third periods is the lack of accurate data on utilization and supply.

3. The present findings confirm the elasticities of demand for wheat determined by Professor Holbrook Working, an eminent authority on statistics of wheat. In a recent paper[48] in which he considered several approaches to the problem, Working correlated the first differences of the logarithms of total apparent utilization with the first differences of the logarithms of the prices of basic cash wheat at Chicago for the years 1896–1913 and obtained for his coefficient of elasticity of the demand the value of $\eta = -0.36 \pm 0.21$. By omitting the amount used for seed from his quantity series, the elasticity of demand is increased (in numerical value) to $\eta = -0.43 \pm 0.25$. By making further allowance for changes in stocks, the coefficient becomes $\eta = -0.001 \pm 0.13$. Considering their standard errors, Working's findings for 1896–1913 are in substantial agreement with ours. For the period 1921–35, for which Working used the per capita utilization less seed and less changes in stocks, he obtained an elasticity of demand of $\eta = -0.24 \pm 0.09$. This is almost identical with our determination of $\eta = -0.21 \pm 0.04$ for the period 1921–34.[49]

4. The per capita demand curve for wheat (which for simplicity we assumed to be of constant-elasticity) has been shifting downward at least since 1927 (see Fig. 68). It is probable that the demand curve for wheat was also shifting downward during the period from 1896 to 1913 (see Fig. 66).

5. Coming to the factors influencing the price of wheat, we find that the deflated price is more responsive to changes in the domestic supply than to changes in foreign supply. Based on the experience of 1922–34, the net effect of an increase of 1 per cent in the domestic supply is to decrease the domestic price by 2 per cent; the net effect of the same relative increase in foreign supply is to decrease the domestic price by only 0.4 of 1 per cent. But the latter coefficient is statistically not so significant as the former.

6. Even if the domestic supply and the foreign supply had been kept fixed, the purchasing power of the farm price of wheat (1913 = 100) would have shown a decline from about 1921 to date (see Fig. 70). This is in marked con-

---

[48] "The Elasticities of Demand for Wheat," read before the meeting of the Econometric Society held in Chicago, Illinois, December 28, 1936, and summarized in *Econometrica*, V, No. 2 (1937), 185–86.

[49] See chap. xvii for the elasticity of demand for wheat derived from our data by the methods of link relatives and trend ratios.

trast with the increase in the purchasing power of the price of wheat which took place from 1896 to 1913 (see Fig. 69).

7. The findings that the demand for wheat is very inelastic, and more especially that the demand curve has been shifting downward with time, are of paramount importance to the wheat farmers and to the American people as a whole. An inelastic demand means that, *other things being equal*, a bumper crop will sell for less (in the domestic market) than a moderate crop. This fact has recently been used as an argument in favor of the restriction of output by the A.A.A. If the downward shift of the per capita demand curve does not come to a stop in the near future, then all such plans for restriction of output as were sponsored by the A.A.A., or as are now being sponsored by the United States Department of Agriculture will give only temporary relief, for it will be a matter of only a few years before the downward shift of the curve will counteract the gain obtained from the creation of an artificial scarcity.[50]

[50] For an invaluable and extended account of the politico-economic experiment under the Agricultural Adjustment Administration up to the end of March, 1935, and its bearing on wheat production, prices, and related subjects, see Davis, *Wheat and the AAA*. See also Edwin G. Nourse, Joseph S. Davis, and John D. Black, *Three Years of the Agricultural Adjustment Administration* (Washington, D.C.: Brookings Institution, 1937).

CHAPTER XI

THE DEMAND FOR POTATOES

CHAPTER XI

THE DEMAND FOR POTATOES

I. THE POSITION OF POTATOES IN THE NATIONAL ECONOMY

The potato was first introduced into the United States from Ireland, in 1719, at Londerry, New Hampshire.[1] Since then its production in this country has gradually spread until in 1933 the potato was the sixth most important crop in point of value and the seventh in point of acreage. If compared with table food plants alone, the potato ranks second only to wheat.[2]

Potatoes are more widely grown than any other American crop, some acreage being devoted to it in almost every *county* in the United States.[3] Several reasons may be cited in explanation of this fact.

1. The potato can be grown successfully on almost every variety of land—on soil so light as to require thatching with straw in order to keep it from blowing away, as well as on clay lands so heavy that they require close tiling for underdraining.

2. The potato is a short-season crop. It can therefore, if planted at the proper time, be raised in every section of the country despite the fact that fairly low temperatures are required for its growth.

3. Since the cost of transporting potatoes over long distances would form a large proportion of its value, the crop has to be grown within comparatively short distances from the markets. Potato production must, therefore, be almost as widespread as the population.

4. With the exception of wheat, the potato is the most widely used of the table food crops. Since no further manufacturing process is necessary to convert the crop into a food, a considerable amount of potatoes is grown in farm gardens for home consumption, in addition to that raised as a commercial crop.

Largely because of the differences in climate, the potato crop is made up of two parts: the early or truck crop of the South, which constitutes about 15 per cent of the total, and the late or main crop of the North. Of the latter, approximately 20 per cent is grown in the ten far western states,[4] and 80 per cent in the remaining northern states.

The early or truck crop is supplementary to the late crop in that it bridges over the gap that would otherwise occur during the summer season if only a late crop were grown. In

[1] J. W. Strowbridge, *Origin and Distribution of the Commercial Potato Crop* (U.S. Dept. Agric., Tech. Bull. No. 7 [July, 1927]), pp. 1–2.

[2] *U.S.D.A. Agriculture Yearbook, 1925*, p. 346.

[3] V. C. Finch and O. E. Baker, *Geography of the World's Agriculture* (U.S. Dept. Agric., 1917), p. 67.

[4] Montana, Wyoming, Colorado, New Mexico, Idaho, Utah, Nevada, Washington, Oregon, and California.

addition to this it makes it possible to offset any serious shortage of the late or main crop by increasing the acreage of the early crop particularly in those sections in which the crop is normally marketed from the latter part of March to the latter part of June or early July. The relative ease of such crop expansion is well illustrated by the short crop of 1916, which was followed by a 90 per cent increase in production from the 16 Southern States over that of the preceding year.[5]

As the bulk of the southern crop is marketed at a time when the public is eager for fresh vegetables, these early crop potatoes generally sell at a price sufficiently high to permit their being transported to the North. Some late or

TABLE 31*

AVERAGE ACREAGE AND PRODUCTION OF POTATOES, 1924–28, AND
AVERAGE YIELD PER ACRE, 1919–28, BY STATES

| STATES | ABSOLUTE FIGURES | | | PERCENTAGE OF TOTAL | |
	Average Production (1,000 Bu.)	Average Acreage (1,000 Bu.)	Average Yield per Acre (Bu.)	Production	Acreage
United States...........	361,115	3,081	109.3	100.00	100.00
Maine................	37,684	148	248.0	10.44	4.80
Minnesota............	33,855	321	96.0	9.38	10.42
New York............	28,363	245	114.0	7.85	7.95
Michigan.............	26,510	243	104.0	7.34	7.89
Wisconsin............	26,308	240	104.0	7.29	7.80
Pennsylvania..........	22,872	200	106.0	6.33	6.49
Idaho................	16,503	84	187.0	4.57	2.73
Virginia..............	15,357	115	121.0	4.25	3.73
Colorado.............	13,511	85	145.0	3.74	2.76
Ohio.................	10,285	108	88.0	2.85	3.51
All others............	129,867	1,292	....	35.96	41.92

* Source: U.S. Dept. Agric., *Yearbook of Agriculture, 1932*, pp. 729–30.

main crop potatoes are grown in the South also, but these are largely confined to the northern tier of the southern states and the more elevated sections of the others.

The largest potato-producing states have generally been New York, Minnesota, Michigan, Maine, Wisconsin, and Pennsylvania. In recent years, however, Idaho has also become a leading potato state. The average acreage and production of the leading states for the years 1924–28 are given in Table 31. It is seen that the first six states account for nearly one-half of the total United States production.

It is wrong to assume, however, that because these six states are the leading potato-growers, that they are necessarily better adapted physically to potato

[5] U.S.D.A. *Agriculture Yearbook, 1925*, p. 352.

production than are any of the far western states which produce very small crops. In fact, with the exception of Maine, the six leading potato-producing states ranked fourteenth or lower in point of average yield per acre for the years 1919–28. Moreover, as can be seen from the table, the yields per acre in Minnesota, Michigan, Wisconsin, and Pennsylvania were for the same period lower than the average for the United States as a whole. On the other hand, several of the far western states, such as Washington, Utah, and Nevada, ranked among the first ten with respect to yield per acre.

The chief reason for the heavy production of potatoes in the six states mentioned is that of proximity to large consuming centers. On account of the bulkiness of the crop and its relative cheapness, the potato grower can not afford to transport his crop any considerable distance, with the result that those localities occupying the most favorable position with relation to markets and which at the same time have a suitable soil and climate, possess a decided advantage over less favored localities.[6]

Some regions relatively far removed from the market but with cheap water transportation and excellent railroad facilities are also large centers of potato production. Among these are the eastern counties of Virginia, which supply Baltimore, Washington, Philadelphia, and New York; western Michigan, which is provided with cheap lake transportation to Chicago; central Wisconsin, which sends its potatoes to Milwaukee, Chicago, and the neighboring industrial cities; and the Aroostook (Maine) region, which supplies Boston and New England.

This distribution of heavy potato-producing regions is simply another illustration of the theory of comparative costs, which states that a region will export those commodities in which it has a comparative advantage and import those in which it has a comparative disadvantage. Obviously, the theory applies to trade within a country as well as to trade between countries.

The period from 1875 until after the war years saw—amid wide year-to-year fluctuations—a steady increase in the average acreage and production of potatoes. Since the beginning of this century there has also been continued improvement in the average yield per acre. These changes are in large part due to (1) the increasing population, (2) improved machinery, (3) more intensive cultivation, (4) improved use of fertilizer, (5) better seed strains, and (6) more successful methods of coping with crop diseases. The war years saw a very striking increase in both acreage and production, but since then the potato crop has been characterized by wide changes from year to year without any apparent trend. Thus the total production of potatoes which amounted to 298 million bushels in 1925 rose to 426 million in 1928 and fell to 322 million in 1929.

Of the total production, about 10 per cent, on the average, consists of unsalable stock or culls, about 5 per cent is diseased and frozen stock, another 5

[6] *Ibid.*, pp. 349–50.

per cent is lost in storage shrinkage, and about 10 per cent is used as seed for the ensuing crop. The remaining 70 per cent is used for human consumption in the United States.[7]

II. FACTORS AFFECTING THE DEMAND FOR POTATOES

As explained in chapter v, the demand curve which we have agreed to study is that of the wholesaler-dealer-farmer. For deriving this demand curve, the consumption series needed is the quantity bought each year by the wholesaler-dealer-farmer-consumers from the farmer-producers. As the best approximation to this series, the quantity demanded in any year should be taken as the production of that year plus the stocks at the beginning of the year, minus the stocks at the end of the year, plus the imports and minus the exports.

In our analysis, however, we shall consider production as approximately equal to consumption for the following reasons:

1. Data relating to stocks on hand at the beginning of the year (July 1) are unavailable. Moreover, there is good reason for believing that beginning stocks are negligible.

2. Our imports and exports of potatoes are very small. Thus, it was not until 1904 that our exports of potatoes amounted to as much as one million bushels. Although they have since exceeded the figure for 1904 fairly consistently, they have never been as high as five million bushels. For the years 1920–29 the exports averaged only 0.8 of 1 per cent of the total production. Our imports have, on the whole, been higher than our exports, exceeding a million bushels per annum thirty-five times during the period 1875–1934, and amounting to over thirteen million bushels in 1911. However, they have seldom amounted to as much as 5 per cent, and for the years 1920–29 averaged only 0.9 of 1 per cent, of the total production. Since these percentages are considerably lower than the percentage errors in our production data, the addition of the imports and exports series would only constitute a superrefinement of data admittedly subject to grosser errors.

Because of the wide distribution of the potato crop, and the countless patches of potatoes raised for home use, it has been found very difficult to obtain accurate estimates of the total production. A rough-and-ready measure of the extent of the error in the data may be obtained by a comparison of the unrevised and revised production series in the *Yearbooks of Agriculture* for 1931 and 1935. For the years 1920–29 the two series differ, on the average, by approximately 10 per cent.

In taking production as an approximation to consumption, we must necessarily define the demand for potatoes in its broad sense, as the aggregate of the quantities which will be utilized for all purposes at a given price. This defini-

[7] *Ibid.*, p. 347.

tion includes: (1) seed requirements, (2) losses due to shrinkage, freezing, rot and disease, and (3) the quantities which do not exchange hands but which are consumed by the farmer-producers on the farm.

The price series which we shall take for our analysis is the December 1 farm price. This is an average price for all the United States of all potatoes sold December 1. These potatoes, it should be noted, are of the late or main crop. In 1934 the United States Department of Agriculture in its *Yearbook* published a weighted average farm price for the crop-marketing season, which differs considerably from the December 1 farm price. This series, however, has been carried back only as far as 1919 and, consequently, could not be used in our investigations.[8]

As in the previous studies the consumption data will be reduced to a per capita basis, and the prices will be deflated by the Bureau of Labor Statistics "Index of Wholesale Prices." We shall also investigate the effect of general business conditions by introducing an index of production and trade into our demand function. The other factors which affect the demand for potatoes, such as dietary fads and the demand for substitutes, cannot easily be measured. In so far as they change slowly and smoothly with time, however, they may be subsumed under the catch-all variable, time.

The analysis will then proceed by stages as follows:

We shall at first study the per capita demand as a function of the deflated price and time:

$$(2.1) \qquad\qquad x = x\,(y,\,t)\,,$$

using both the arithmetic and logarithmic (constant-elasticity) forms.

Next we shall introduce Persons' "Index of Industrial Production and Trade" (w) as an independent variable and write the demand function as:

$$(2.2) \qquad\qquad x = x(y,\,w,\,t)\,,$$

in order to see what improvement, if any, results therefrom.

Finally, we shall repeat these analyses with price as the dependent variable and compare the results obtained.

The study will first be made for the three periods into which we have chosen to subdivide the data for all the commodities: (1) 1875–95; (2) 1896–1914; and (3) 1915–29, omitting 1917–21. It will be shown, however, that the series for 1890–1900 are not comparable with the data for either the previous or the subsequent years. We shall, therefore, also experiment with the periods: (4) 1875–89 and (5) 1890–1900.

---

[8] See chap. v, Sec. IV, for a discussion of the farm prices. In 1936 the United States Department of Agriculture carried its season average price back to 1908. See *Agricultural Statistics, 1937*, pp. 188–89.

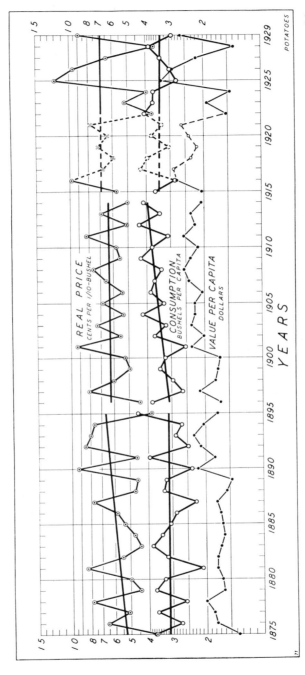

FIG. 71.—Potatoes: The basic adjusted annual data used in deriving the demand curves for potatoes in the United States, 1875–1929, with the computed trends by periods of the real prices and the per capita consumption. The dotted observations in the third period are those which are not used in the computations.

III. DEMAND FUNCTIONS WITH PER CAPITA CONSUMPTION AS THE DEPENDENT VARIABLE[9]

In Table VIII of Appendix A are listed the per capita consumption (= production) and deflated prices of potatoes, together with the link relatives and trend ratios for the years 1875–1929. Tables IIa and I of the same appendix record the basic (unadjusted) data of total consumption and money prices and their deflators. Figure 71 is a graphic representation of the per capita consumption, deflated price, and per capita value series. As can be seen at a glance

TABLE 32

POTATOES: SUMMARY BY PERIODS OF THE ADJUSTED DATA USED IN DERIVING THE DEMAND FUNCTIONS, 1875–1929

PERIOD*	PER CAPITA CONSUMPTION $x(t)$				DEFLATED PRICE $y(t)$				CORRELATION COEFFICIENT
	Descriptive Constants								
	Mean (Bu.)	Median (Bu.)	Standard Deviation (Bu.)	Coefficient of Variation	Mean (Cents)	Median (Cents)	Standard Deviation (Cents)	Coefficient of Variation	r_{xy}
Ia	3.122	3.198	0.6069	19.44	59.685	53.214	17.156	28.74	−0.8887
II	3.522	3.449	0.5198	14.76	62.811	58.021	13.208	21.03	−0.7513
III	3.387	3.490	0.4449	13.14	69.124	60.948	28.318	40.97	−0.9636

PERIOD	Equations of Trends		Origins
Ia	$x(t) = 3.122 - 0.000243t$	$y(t) = 59.685 + 0.683t$	Jan. 1, 1886
II	$x(t) = 3.522 + 0.0472t$	$y(t) = 62.811 + 0.0462t$	Jan. 1, 1906
III	$x(t) = 3.393 - 0.00434t$	$y(t) = 69.124 =$ Arithmetic mean	Jan. 1, 1923

* Ia = 1875–95; II = 1896–1914; III = 1915–29 (excl. 1917–21).

from this diagram, the year-to-year changes in consumption exhibit a high degree of negative correlation with the corresponding changes in price. The last series has been added because of its usefulness in indicating whether the demand is elastic or inelastic.[10] The positive correlation between the price and value series shows clearly that the demand for potatoes is inelastic. Table 32 summarizes the consumption and price data for each of the three periods. Table 33 is a descriptive summary of the important changes which have taken place in the demand for potatoes from 1875 to 1929.

[9] For an explanation of the statistical methods used and for definitions of the technical terms see chap. vi.

[10] See chap. vi, p. 191.

TABLE 33

POTATOES: CHARACTERISTICS OF THE PER CAPITA DEMAND FUNCTIONS

x = Per capita consumption in bushels

y = Deflated December 1 farm price in cents per bushel

(Figures in parentheses are standard errors)

EQUA-TION No.	PERIOD†		Constant Term	y	t	t^2
1	Ia *	$x=$	4.9418	−0.0336 (0.0026)	+0.0227 (0.0075)	+0.0050 (0.0013)
2	Ib	$x=$	5.0734	−0.0352 (0.0029)	−0.0198 (0.0092)	. . . .
3	Ic	$x=$	5.6363	−0.0371 (0.0034)	−0.0595 (0.0200)	−0.0085 (0.0064)
4	II	$x=$	5.5757	−0.0312 (0.0040)	+0.0487 (0.0095)	−0.0031 (0.0020)
5	III	$x=$	4.4403	−0.0155 (0.0014)	+0.0136 (0.0088)	. . . .
			Constant Term	y'	‡Mt	‡Mt^2
6	Ia	$x'=$	1.6291	−0.6587 (0.0560)	+0.0057 (0.0026)	+0.0010 (0.0005)
7	Ib	$x'=$	1.7157	−0.7089 (0.0676)	−0.0048 (0.0036)	. . . .
8	Ic	$x'=$	1.7236	−0.6832 (0.0458)	−0.0101 (0.0043)	−0.0022 (0.0014)
9	II	$x'=$	0.9393	−0.2702§ (0.0261)**	+0.0163 (0.0022)	−0.0016 (0.0005)
10	III	$x'=$	1.0808	−0.3073 (0.0285)	−0.0015 (0.0056)	. . . .

* For the periods Ia, II, and III the origins are given in Table 32. For the periods Ib and Ic the origins are, respectively, January 1, 1883, and January 1, 1896.

† Ia = 1875–95; Ib = 1875–89; Ic = 1890–1900; II = 1896–1914; III = 1915–29 (excl. 1917–21).

‡ M = log₁₀ e = 0.43429.

§ This is the coefficient of log $(y − 35)$. If, instead of log $(y − 35)$, log y is taken as the independent variable, the equation reads:

$$x' = 1.6703 − 0.6220y' + 0.0150Mt − 0.0012Mt^2.$$
$$(0.0647) \quad (0.0023) \quad (0.0005).$$

$\eta = −0.6220.$ ϵ = 94.6 per cent − 105.7 per cent. R' = 0.9349.

TABLE 33—*Continued*

WITH QUANTITY AS THE DEPENDENT VARIABLE, BY PERIODS, 1875–1929

t = Time in years*

x', y' = Logs of x and y

(Figures in parentheses are standard errors)

		DESCRIPTIVE CONSTANTS				
Elasticity of Demand η	Quadratic Mean Error ϵ (Bushels)	Adjusted Multiple Correlation Coefficient R'	Percentage of Variance of Consumption Attributable to		EQUA-TION No.
			y	t	
−0.6827 (0.1443)	0.2012	0.9462	84.40	6.70	I
−0.6295 (0.1246)	0.1542	0.9560	90.00	2.63	2
−0.7309 (0.1759)	0.1860	0.9624	97.87	− 3.04	3
−0.5428 (0.1306)	0.2261	0.9060	59.61	25.45	4
−0.3171 (0.0832)	0.1226	0.9652	95.29	− 0.61	5
η	ϵ (Per Cent)	R'	y'	t	
−0.6587 (0.0560)	93.2–107.3	0.9369	86.61	3.01	6
−0.7089 (0.0676)	94.1–106.3	0.9420	88.75	1.60	7
−0.6832 (0.0458)	96.0–104.2	0.9802	99.22	− 1.96	8
−0.6102‖	94.9–105.4	0.9424	61.08¶	29.60	9
−0.3073 (0.0285)	96.3–103.9	0.9628	94.12	0.20	10

‖ No standard error has been computed for this coefficient because the constant 35 subtracted from y was not determined by the method of least squares.

¶ This is the percentage of variance in log x which is attributable to log $(y - 35)$.

** This is not a true least-squares sampling error, since the constant 35 was determined by inspection.

A. THE PERIOD 1875-95

From the coefficient of y in the first equation we see that, other things being equal, an increase of one (deflated) cent in the price per bushel of potatoes brought about an average decrease in the per capita consumption of 0.03 bushel. Expressing this effect in terms of relative changes for the representative values of y and x, we find that the elasticity of demand during this period was:

$$(3.1) \qquad \frac{\partial x}{\partial y} \cdot \frac{y}{x} = -0.6827 ,$$

which means that, if the real price which prevailed in 1885 ($t = 0$ at 1885) had been increased (or decreased) by 1 per cent, *and if the demand curve had remained fixed for one year*, there would have been a decrease (or increase) of 0.68 of 1 per cent in the annual per capita consumption.

From the coefficients of t and t^2 in this equation we see that the demand curve shifted upward and to the right by 0.02 bushel per capita per annum, subject to an annual acceleration effect of 0.01 bushel per capita.[11]

The sixth equation of Table 33 expresses the demand for potatoes during the years 1875-95 directly in terms of relative changes. From the coefficient of y' we see that, other things being equal, a 1 per cent rise in the price of potatoes brought about a decrease of 0.66 of 1 per cent in the per capita consumption. This value agrees quite well with the coefficient of elasticity derived from the arithmetic equation.

From the antilogarithm of the sixth equation we obtain the *relative* rate of shift of the demand curve. It is

$$(3.2) \qquad \frac{1}{x} \cdot \frac{\partial x}{\partial t} = \frac{\partial \log_e x}{\partial t} = 0.0057 + 2(0.0009)t ,$$

which means that the demand curve shifted upward and to the right at the rate of 0.57 of 1 per cent per annum, subject to an annual acceleration of 0.18 per cent.

The fit of either demand function to the data for this period, if judged by the standard errors of the parameters, by the quadratic mean error, and by the adjusted multiple correlation coefficient, is quite good. It would be erroneous, however, to conclude therefrom—without a supplementary graphical analysis —that the equations do actually give a good fit to the data.

Figure 72 is a graphic representation of the logarithmic equation. Figure 72A is a scatter diagram of the logarithms of per capita consumption (x') on those of the deflated price (y'). The line $D_1'D_2'$ gives the net relation between the logarithm of consumption and the logarithm of price when both are linearly

[11] For definitions of the measures of the rate of shift and the rates of acceleration and retardation see chap. vii, p. 257.

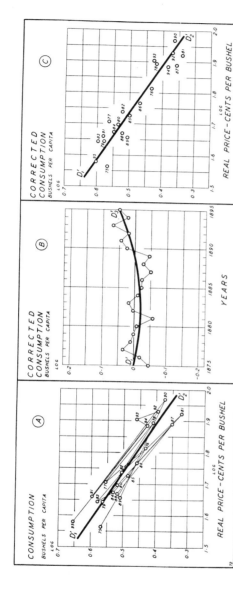

FIG. 72.—Potatoes: Three aspects of the per capita demand for potatoes during the period 1875–95 on the assumption that

$$x = 42.57 \, y^{-0.6587} \, e^{0.0057 \, t + 0.0009 \, t^2} \, .$$

A: Relation between per capita consumption and real price when the data are not corrected for the effects of "time," with the demand curve $D_1'D_2'$ which results when such correction is made.

B: Relation between the per capita consumption and time when the former is corrected for the effects of changes in the real price. The slope of line $D_1'D_3'$ (fitted to the variables x' and t when both are corrected for price) represents the mean rate of shift of the per capita demand curve $D_1'D_2'$.

C: The per capita demand curve for potatoes, 1875–95. Line $D_1'D_2'$ shows the relation between that part of the per capita consumption of potatoes in the United States which is independent of time and that part of the real price which is independent of time. In the scatter, however, the ordinate is corrected only for secular changes, the abscissa being un-corrected.

corrected for changes in time. The slope of this line, i.e., -0.6587, is the elasticity of demand.

In Figure 72B the difference between the observed and computed values of x' are plotted against time. The slope of the curve $D_1'D_3'$ measures the *average* rate of shift of the demand curve given by equation (3.2) above. Figure 72C shows the scatter of the points about the demand curve $D_1'D_2'$ when allowance has been made for changes in t.

An examination of Figure 72B shows that the data for the period are not homogeneous but that a definite break occurs in 1889. For the years subsequent to 1889 the demand curve seems to have been on a higher level than for the period 1875–89. It is this fact which makes it appear that the demand curve shifted upward subject to an annual acceleration effect. The corresponding chart for the arithmetic equation (which is not given here) shows an even more pronounced division of the data. The first explanation which suggested itself was that the break in the series was due to the revision in 1920 of the data for 1889–1909. But a graphical analysis of the data for 1875–95 using the original, unrevised series for 1889–95, yielded the same discontinuity in 1889 that appears in Figure 72B.

The per capita value series of Figure 71, which reflects changes in both per capita consumption and deflated price, indicates that the new level reached in 1890 was maintained until 1900 and that thereafter an even higher level was attained. It would, therefore, have been best to have subdivided the data for 1875–1914 into the following three periods: (1) 1875–89, (2) 1890–1900, and (3) 1901–14. However, since it was desired to study the demand for potatoes for the conventional second period, 1896–1914, and since it was felt that the results would not be substantially modified if the first five years (1896–1900) were omitted from the study, no further analysis for the years 1901–14 was made. We have instead considered the equations derived for the second period (1896–1914) as approximately descriptive of the years 1901–14 and have made supplementary studies only for the periods 1875–89 and 1890–1900.

B. THE PERIOD 1875–89

Equations 2 and 7, Table 33, are, respectively, the arithmetic and logarithmic demand functions for the period 1875–89. The most interesting result is, of course, the negative coefficient of t (and of Mt), which means that for the years 1875–89 the demand curve was shifting *downward* at the rate of 0.02 bushel per capita, or 0.48 per cent per annum. A glance at the year-to-year changes in Figure 72B shows that this was actually the case, for a straight line with negative slope would give an excellent fit to the data for those years. The average upward shift for the entire period 1875–95 described by the parabola $D_1'D_3'$ in this figure is meaningless because of the nonhomogeneity of the data.

As was to be expected, a comparison of the quadratic mean errors, the adjusted multiple correlation coefficients, and the percentage of variance attributable to time shows that equations 2 and 7 give a better fit to the data than do equations 1 and 6, which represent nonhomogeneous series. Nevertheless, the coefficients of the elasticity of demand derived from the former equations (−0.63 and −0.71, respectively) do not differ much from those derived from the latter pair of equations (−0.68 and −0.66).

C. THE PERIOD 1890–1900

The demand functions for the years 1890–1900 are given by equations 3 and 8, Table 33. The coefficients of y and y', which express the relationship between price and consumption in absolute and percentage changes, respectively, do not differ materially from their values for the period 1875–89.

There was, however, a change in the shift of the demand curve during this period, as can be seen from the coefficients of t and t^2 (and of Mt and Mt^2). The demand curve for 1890–1900 shifted downward at the rate of 0.06 bushel per capita or 1.0 per cent per annum (subject, moreover, to a slight negative acceleration annually), as compared with the downward shift of 0.02 bushel per capita or 0.48 per cent during 1875–89.

As judged by the standard errors of the parameters, the quadratic mean error, the adjusted multiple correlation coefficient, and the percentage of variance in x (or x') attributable to the independent variables, both these equations give an excellent description of the data.

D. THE PERIOD 1896–1914

As has already been explained, this period is not homogeneous, since the first five years in reality form the second half of the period which extended from 1890 to 1900. As to be expected, therefore, the equations derived for the period 1896–1914 give a very poor fit to the data for 1896–1900. This is seen both from the graphic representations of these equations (one of which, Fig. 73, is shown here) and from the actual determination of the residuals which for the first five years are from two to four times the quadratic mean error. Although it would have been better to have omitted those years and to have fitted a curve to the data for 1901–14, we felt that the minor modifications of the parameters which would result therefrom were not worth the additional effort involved. We therefore retained the equations of 1896–1914 as approximately descriptive of the years 1901–14, keeping in mind all the while that the parameters should be adjusted for the omission of 1896–1900.

Equation 4, Table 33, is the arithmetic demand function for the period 1896–1914. The slope of the demand curve, given by the coefficient of y, is approximately the same as the slopes for the preceding periods. However, the elasticity of demand—derived by multiplying the coefficient of y by the representative

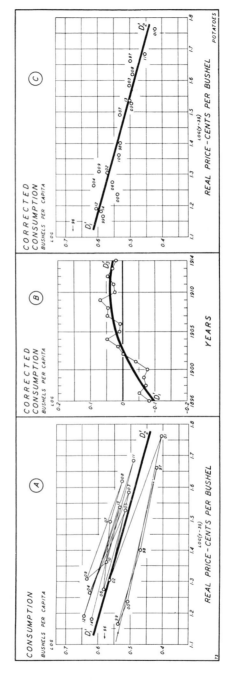

FIG. 73.—Potatoes: Three aspects of the per capita demand for potatoes during the period 1896–1914 on the assumption that

$$x = 8.695(y - 35)^{-0.2702} \, e^{0.0163t - 0.0016t^2} \, .$$

value of y/x—is somewhat less in numerical value than for the preceding years.

From the coefficients of t and t^2 we see that the demand curve shifted upward by 0.05 bushel per capita per annum subject to a slight annual retardation of 0.006 bushel per capita.

Equation 9 expresses the demand function in terms of relative changes. In this equation $(y - 35)$ instead of y is taken as the independent variable. This change was suggested by a scatter diagram on double-logarithmic paper which showed that the net relationship between the logarithm of consumption and the logarithm of price was not linear. It was estimated that, if the scatter were shifted thirty-five units to the left (i.e., if thirty-five cents were subtracted from each observed price), the logarithmic relationship between consumption and the new price series would be approximately linear. Accordingly, the price for each year was diminished by thirty-five cents, and the curve,

$$(3.3a) \qquad\qquad x = A(y - 35)^b\, e^{ct+dt^2} ,$$

in its logarithmic form,

$$(3.3b) \qquad\quad \log x = \log A + b \log (y - 35) + cMt + dMt^2 ,$$

was fitted to the data.[12]

In this equation, unlike the other logarithmic functions, the elasticity of demand is not constant but varies instead from point to point on the curve, for

$$(3.4) \qquad\qquad \eta = \frac{\partial x}{\partial y} \cdot \frac{y}{x} = \frac{bx}{y - 35} \cdot \frac{y}{x} = \frac{b}{1 - \dfrac{35}{y}} .$$

The term listed in the column "Elasticity of Demand" ($-$ 0.6102) is the coefficient of elasticity computed at the mean value of y. It is slightly larger in numerical value than the corresponding coefficient of the arithmetic equation.

As in the other logarithmic functions the relative rate of shift is given by

$$(3.5) \qquad\qquad \frac{1}{x} \cdot \frac{\partial x}{\partial t} = \frac{\partial \log_e x}{\partial t} = 0.0163 - 2(0.0016)t ,$$

which means that the demand curve shifted upward at the rate of 1.63 per cent per annum, subject to an annual retardation effect of 0.32 per cent.

Figure 73 is a graphic representation of the logarithmic equation. Figure 73A

[12] For purposes of comparison the equation $\log x = \log A + b \log y + cMt + dMt^2$, for the period 1896–1914, is given in n. §, Table 33. It will be observed from a comparison of the coefficients of elasticity, the rates of shift, and the measures of goodness of fit that this function does not differ materially from the fifth equation in the table.

TABLE 34

POTATOES: THE CHARACTERISTICS OF THE PER CAPITA DEMAND FUNCTIONS

x = Per capita consumption in bushels

y = Deflated December 1 farm price in cents per bushel

(Figures in parentheses are standard errors)

EQUA-TION No.	PERIOD†		Constant Term	x	t	t^2
				EQUATIONS		
1	Ia	$y=$	138.0560	−25.1066 (2.6073)	+0.6772 (0.2613)	....
2	Ib	$y=$	137.4320	−26.2595 (2.1675)	−0.5245 (0.2548)	....
3	Ic	$y=$	146.7225	−25.4112 (2.3471)	−1.6630 (0.4731)	−0.2033 (0.1703)
4	II	$y=$	156.1721	−25.6654 (3.2977)	+1.2582 (0.3130)	−0.0992 (0.0556)
5	III	$y=$	274.1780	−60.9386 (5.4636)	+0.8923 (0.5401)	....
			Constant Term	x'	$‡Mt$	$‡Mt^2$
6	Ia	$y'=$	2.3936	−1.3070 (0.1184)	+0.0089 (0.0038)	....
7	Ib	$y'=$	2.3528	−1.2721 (0.1212)	−0.0060 (0.0049)	....
8	Ic	$y'=$	2.5000	−1.4190 (0.0952)	−0.0155 (0.0059)	−0.0030 (0.0021)
9	II	$y'=$	2.5635	−1.3832 (0.1440)	+0.0210 (0.0040)	−0.0019 (0.0007)
10	III	$y'=$	3.4194	−3.0690 (0.2848)	−0.0047 (0.0178)	....

* For the periods I*a*, II, and III the origins are given in Table 32. For the periods I*b* and I*c*, the origins are, respectively, January 1, 1883, and January 1, 1896.

TABLE 34—*Continued*

WITH PRICE AS THE DEPENDENT VARIABLE, BY PERIODS, 1875–1929

$t =$ Time in years*

$x', y' =$ Logs of x and y

(Figures in parentheses are standard errors)

DESCRIPTIVE CONSTANTS						EQUA-TION No.
Flexibility of Price φ	Maximum Value of η $1/\varphi$	Quadratic Mean Error ϵ (Cents)	Adjusted Multiple Correlation Coefficient R'	Percentage of Variance of Price Attributable to		
				x	t	
−1.3131 (0.3530)	−0.7616	7.2508	0.9110	78.92	5.77	I
−1.4686 (0.2964)	−0.6809	4.2125	0.9549	92.21	0.23	2
−1.2189 (0.2816)	−0.8204	4.8653	0.9680	83.56	12.03	3
−1.3739 (0.3597)	−0.7278	6.4810	0.8786	75.88	5.11	4
−2.9858 (0.7301)	−0.3349	7.6790	0.9663	92.25	2.61	5
φ	$1/\varphi$	ϵ (Per Cent)	R'	x'	t	
−1.3070 (0.1184)	−0.7651	89.9–111.2	0.9294	83.56	4.17	6
−1.2721 (0.1212)	−0.7861	92.2–108.5	0.9409	90.37	− 0.20	7
−1.4190 (0.0952)	−0.7047	94.2–106.1	0.9817	91.84	5.62	8
−1.3832 (0.1440)	−0.7230	92.1–108.6	0.9179	77.82	9.06	9
−3.0690 (0.2848)	−0.3258	88.7–112.7	0.9628	94.25	0.06	10

† Ia = 1875–95; Ib = 1875–89; Ic = 1890–1900; II = 1896–1914; III = 1915–29 (excl. 1917–21).

‡ $M = \log_{10} e = 0.43429$.

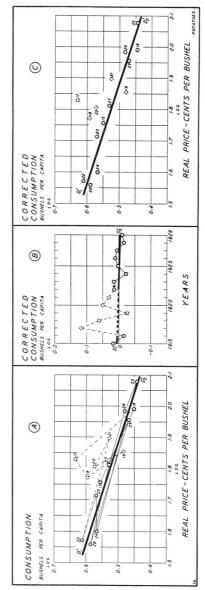

FIG. 74.—Potatoes: Three aspects of the per capita demand for potatoes during the period 1915–29 (excluding 1917–21) on the assumption that

$$x = 12.04\,y^{-0.3073}\,e^{-0.0015t}.$$

422

shows the scatter diagram of the logarithm of x on the logarithm of $(y - 35)$, together with the line of *net* relationship between these variables, $D_1'D_2'$. The slope of this line, -0.2702, measures the percentage change in x associated with a 1 per cent change in the quantity $(y - 35)$. It is evident that the percentage change in x associated with a 1 per cent change in y (i.e., the elasticity) varies from point to point on the curve.

Figure 73*B* shows the relationship between the logarithm of per capita consumption and time, when the former is corrected for changes in the logarithm of $(y - 35)$. The curve $D_1'D_3'$ represents the average rate of shift of the demand curve $D_1'D_2'$. It may be seen that this average shift does not fit the downward trend for 1896–1900.

Figure 73*C* shows the reduced scatter of the points about the demand curve $D_1'D_2'$ when allowance has been made for the average changes in t.

E. THE PERIOD 1915–29

The demand functions for this period are given by equations 5 and 10 in Table 33 and Figure 74. The most important fact to observe here is the decrease in the numerical value of the elasticity of demand to 0.31, a decrease of approximately 50 per cent from its value for the preceding periods. No definite conclusions can be drawn with regard to the shift of the demand curve, since the arithmetic function indicates a slight upward shift, whereas the logarithmic function indicates a slight downward shift. Indeed, the variable t contributes almost nothing to the variance of consumption (σ_x^2).

IV. DEMAND FUNCTIONS WITH PRICE AS THE DEPENDENT VARIABLE

Table 34 gives the regression of price on consumption and time. Equations 1–5 are the arithmetic regressions; equations 6–10 are the corresponding logarithmic regressions.

From the coefficient of x in the first five of these equations we find that, other things being equal, an increase in the per capita consumption of one bushel was associated with a decrease in the deflated price of approximately twenty-five cents during the years 1875–1914, but of nearly two and one-half times that amount during 1915–29. The terms listed in the column "Flexibility of Prices" give the relative change in price associated with a 1 per cent change in the per capita consumption. The reciprocal of the price flexibility is the maximum value of the elasticity of demand.[13]

The coefficients of t (and t^2) indicate roughly the same type of shift in the demand curve (except for an acceleration factor in the period 1875–95) as did the functions with consumption as the dependent variable.

The second set of equations expresses the same relations in relative terms. Thus, the coefficients of x' measure the flexibility or relative change in price

[13] See chap. vi, p. 228.

TABLE 35

POTATOES: EFFECT OF CHANGES IN BUSINESS CONDITIONS ON THE PER CAPITA DEMAND:

x = Per capita consumption in bushels

y = Deflated December 1 farm price in cents per bushel

t = Time in years. For origins see Table 32

(Figures in parentheses are standard errors)

EQUA-TION No.	PERIOD*		Constant Term	y'	w'	†Mt	†Mt^2
1	Ia	$x' =$	1.6302	−0.6589 (0.0576)	−0.0004 (0.1545)	+0.0057 (0.0027)	+0.0010 (0.0005)
2	II	$x' =$	1.4238	−0.2714‡ (0.0263) ¶	−0.2403 (0.2438)	+0.0168 (0.0023)	−0.0019 (0.0006)
3	III	$x' =$	1.3820	−0.3025 (0.0357)	−0.1532 (0.4136)	−0.0030 (0.0051)	. . . .

			Constant Term	x'	w'	†Mt	†Mt^2
4	Ia	$y' =$	2.4025	−1.3069 (0.1217)	−0.0044 (0.2337)	+0.0089 (0.0039)	. . . .
5	II	$y' =$	3.4400	−1.3905 (0.1427)	−0.4343 (0.3819)	+0.0219 (0.0040)	−0.0025 (0.0009)
6	III	$y' =$	3.8372	−3.0902 (0.3329)	−0.2011 (1.2203)	−0.0067 (0.0151)	. . . .

* Ia = 1875–95; II = 1896–1914; III = 1915–29 (excl. 1917–21).

† $M = \log_{10} e = 0.43429$.

‡ This is the coefficient of log $(y − 35)$.

§ No standard error has been computed for this coefficient because the constant 35 subtracted from y was not determined by the method of least squares.

TABLE 35—*Continued*

THE CHARACTERISTICS OF THE DEMAND FUNCTIONS, BY PERIODS, 1875–1929

w = W. M. Persons' "Index of Industrial Production and Trade," adjusted,
weighted, normal = 100

x', y', w' = Logs of x, y, w

(Figures in parentheses are standard errors)

			DESCRIPTIVE CONSTANTS					EQUA-TION No.
	Elasticity of Demand η	Quadratic Mean Error ϵ (Per Cent)	Adjusted Multiple Correlation Coefficient R'	Percentage of Variance of Consumption Attributable to				
				y'	w'	t		
. . . .	−0.6589 (0.0576)	93.0–107.5	0.9331	86.64	. . . .	3.01		I
. . . .	−0.6130§	94.9–105.4	0.9423	61.36‖	−0.61	30.53		2
. . . .	−0.3025 (0.0357)	95.7–104.5	0.9490	92.66	1.41	0.40		3

Flexibility of Price φ	Maximum Value of η $1/\varphi$	ϵ (Per Cent)	R'	Percentage of Variance of Price Attributable to				
				x'	w'	t		
−1.3069 (0.1217)	−0.7651	89.6–111.6	0.9252	83.56	0.02	4.17		4
−1.3905 (0.1427)	−0.7191	92.1–108.5	0.9195	78.23	−1.38	11.14		5
−3.0902 (0.3329)	−0.3236	87.9–113.8	0.9566	94.91	−0.65	0.09		6

‖ This is the percentage of variance in log x which is attributable to log $(y - 35)$.

¶ This is not a true least-squares sampling error, since the constant 35 was determined by inspection.

associated with a 1 per cent change in consumption. It is seen that during the period 1915–29 the price was more than twice as flexible as it was during the preceding periods.

The coefficients of t (and t^2) in these equations indicate for all periods but the last the same direction of shift of the demand curve as did the corresponding arithmetic regressions. In the last period, however, we find the same contradiction in terms that obtained in equations 5 and 10 of Table 33.

It appears, therefore, that the demand functions with price as the dependent variable and those with consumption as the dependent variable give fairly consistent results.

V. THE EFFECT OF CHANGES IN BUSINESS CONDITIONS ON THE DEMAND FOR POTATOES

As in the studies of sugar, corn, cotton, and wheat, we decided to investigate the effect of changes in business conditions on the demand for potatoes. The results obtained from the introduction of Persons' "Index of Industrial Production and Trade" (w) as an independent variable into our logarithmic demand equations are summarized in Table 35.

The results are as disappointing as they were in sugar, corn, and wheat. Except for the fifth equation in this table the coefficients of w' are all exceeded by their standard errors. The adjusted multiple correlation coefficient is, therefore, lower in these equations than it was for the corresponding equations of Tables 33 and 34. Moreover, the variance (σ^2) in the dependent variable which may be imputed to w' is negligible for all three periods.

It appears, therefore, that changes in business conditions as measured by Persons' index had no effect on the demand for potatoes.

VI. SUMMARY OF FINDINGS

Although the demand for potatoes has been the subject of several notable studies,[14] none of them had for its object the analysis of the changes that have

[14] Henry L. Moore, *Economic Cycles: Their Law and Cause* (New York, 1914); "Elasticity of Demand and Flexibility of Prices," *Journal of the American Statistical Association*, XVIII (1922–23), 8–19; "A Moving Equilibrium of Demand and Supply," *Quarterly Journal of Economics*, XXXIX (1924–25), 357–71; Holbrook Working, *Factors Determining the Price of Potatoes in St. Paul and Minneapolis* (University of Minnesota Agricultural Experiment Station Tech. Bull. No. 10 [October, 1922]); *Factors Affecting the Price of Minnesota Potatoes* (University of Minnesota Agricultural Experiment Station Tech. Bull. No. 29 [October, 1925]); F. V. Waugh, *Factors Influencing the Price of New Jersey Potatoes on the New York Market* (State of New Jersey Department of Agriculture Circ. No. 66 [July, 1923]); G. F. Warren and F. A. Pearson, *Interrelationships of Supply and Price* (Cornell Agricultural Experiment Station Bull. No. 466 [Ithaca, 1928]), pp. 23–25; V. P. Timoshenko, "Correlations between Prices and Yields of Previous Years," *Journal of Political Economy*, XXXVI, No. 4 (1928), 510–15; and Mordecai Ezekiel, "Preisvoraussage bei landwirtschaftlichen Erzeugnissen" Frankfurter Gesellschaft für Konjunkturforschung, *Veröffentlichungen*, Heft IX (Bonn: K. Schroeder, 1930). There is also a study on the demand for potatoes in Great Britain by Ruth L. Cohen, *Factors Affecting the Price of Potatoes in Great Britain* (Cambridge University, Department of Agriculture, Farm Economics Branch, Report No. 15 [Cambridge, 1930]).

taken place in the shape, the elasticity, and the rate of shift of the demand curve since 1875, and of the factors which account for them. The main findings of the present chapter center around these topics, although they also embrace an analysis of the factors affecting the price of potatoes.

To summarize:

1. The net effect of a 1 cent increase in the (deflated) price per bushel of potatoes was to decrease the annual per capita consumption by between 0.03 and 0.04 bushel during the years 1875–1914 and by 0.02 bushel in 1915–29. Translated in terms of elasticities these relations mean that, other things being equal, an increase of 1 per cent in the (deflated) price of potatoes was associated with a decrease of between 0.5 and 0.7 bushel per capita during the years 1875–1914 and of 0.3 bushel during 1915–29. Since these coefficients are all less than unity, it follows that a large crop was worth less than a small crop throughout the period 1875–1929.

2. The demand curve shifted downward slowly during 1875–89 and more rapidly during 1890–1900. It began shifting upward thereafter but since 1915 has fluctuated irregularly with no trend being discernible.[15]

3. Changes in business conditions had no measurable effect on the demand for potatoes.

4. The studies of the demand for potatoes from the point of view of the net effect on price of changes in the other variables reinforce our conclusions with respect to the shift and elasticity of the demand curve.

The fact that the demand for potatoes is inelastic gave rise to an attempt, in the form of the Potato Act of 1935, at restricting the output of potatoes. By this act the Agricultural Adjustment Act was amended to designate potatoes as a basic commodity. The aim of the act was to adjust the production of potatoes so as to give them "a purchasing power equal to the purchasing power they had on the average for the period August 1919–July 1929." It provided for national, state, and individual grower sales allotments of potatoes for each year, with a tax of three-quarters of a cent per pound to be levied on all potatoes sold in excess of tax-exempt allotments. It is difficult to surmise what the effects of the adjustment program would have been, for the Potato Act was never really effective. It fell with the invalidation of the Agricultural Adjustment Act by the Supreme Court on January 6, 1936.

[15] An extrapolation of the equations for the third period for the years since 1929 is impossible owing to the drastic revisions by the United States Department of Agriculture of the production data, and the substitution of the season-average price for the December 1 farm price. As this chapter goes to press, the latest year for which the basic production and price series are available is 1935 (the figures for the crop year 1936 are preliminary estimates). A graphical correlation analysis of the latest revised data for 1922–35 indicates that since 1929 or thereabouts the demand curve for potatoes has been shifting downward.

CHAPTER XII

THE DEMAND FOR OATS

CHAPTER XII

THE DEMAND FOR OATS

I. THE FACTUAL BACKGROUND

Although the American oat crop constitutes one-fourth of the total world-supply, it ranks only fifth in importance among our agricultural crops and third among our cereal crops, being exceeded in value by both corn and wheat. Of the total American crop, only 3 per cent is milled for human food; the rest is consumed by livestock, chiefly on farms. The replacement of the horse by motor-driven vehicles has reduced the volume of sales of oats. It has also had a tendency to reduce the size of the crop, but this has been counterbalanced by the increasing importance of the cattle-raising industry, for oats is unsurpassed as a food for young stock and breeding animals.[1]

The history of oat production in the United States is very similar to that of wheat production. Oats were first sown on the Atlantic seaboard about 1630. Following the Revolutionary War, the production of oats shifted westward into the Ohio Valley. The period from 1871 to about 1890, which was a period of rapid expansion for all American agriculture, gave rise to a large increase throughout the Corn Belt in the acreage devoted to oats. However, this expansion in acreage was accompanied by a decrease in the yield per acre. The period from 1890 to 1905 saw a more gradual increase in the production of oats, owing primarily to an increase in the yield per acre. Beginning with 1905 there was a rapid expansion in the upper Mississippi Valley which brought the acreage devoted to oats to its highest point (about 45,500,000 acres) in 1921, although the unfavorable weather of that year reduced the size of the crop to somewhat less than the average (1,234,000 bushels) for the ten years immediately preceding. After 1921 the area harvested fluctuated between 38 and 44 million acres, with a yield of from 26 to 34 bushels per acre. However, hot weather and drought during the early part of the summer drastically reduced the crops of 1933 and 1934. The former was the smallest crop since the turn of the century, or about 60 per cent of the average crop for the previous decade, and the latter was smaller than any crop since 1881. A moderately good crop in 1935 brought production back to the previous level, only to be again cut in half by drought in 1936.

Oat production requires a cool, moist climate, and the distribution of the

[1] *U.S.D.A. Yearbook, 1922*, article on oats and other cereals, pp. 469–568. The section on oats (pp. 471–86) is an invaluable source of information on the technological and economic aspects of oat production.

oat crop is affected to some extent by this requirement. Thus we find that the North Central states produce more than half of the total crop, best represented by such well-known varieties as Swedish Select, Silvermine, Kherson, and White Tartar. True, Iowa and Illinois are the leading oat-producing states in this group, in spite of the fact that the climate of these states is less suited to oat production than that of other states of the same group. But these states are in the heart of the Corn Belt, and, in the system of crop rotation practiced in this belt, oats is one of the best crops to come between corn and wheat, or corn and grass. Certain varieties of oats may be grown successfully in regions of high temperatures, such as the southern United States and California. But in these areas the culture of oats is limited to varieties of the species *Avena byzantina*. This is a distinct type and is represented in this country by the Red Rustproof oat and its relatives. Texas and Oklahoma are the leading producers of this variety.

In addition to its importance in the crop-rotation system, oats may also be used advantageously as a nurse crop for grass and as a cover crop in orchards. Moreover, its production requires a relatively small amount of labor, since under certain conditions it can be grown without plowing. As a nurse crop, oats may be sown with clover, grass, or alfalfa, and cut as hay. But the use of oats as hay is not of interest to us here as such a crop would not be included in figures for the production of oats. However, when oats precede the meadow or pasture crop in the crop-rotation program, it is often desirable to sow some grass or clover with it. In this case an early maturing oat crop may serve as a nurse crop and yet be cut for grain. As a cover crop oats is sometimes sown in orchards to shade the roots of the trees in the late summer and to form a mulch to hold the snow in winter. By checking the growth of the trees, the cover crop also permits the young wood to ripen thoroughly before the weather turns cold. The advantage of an oat crop in economizing farm labor is due to the fact that, when sown following the corn crop, it is usually unnecessary to plow. Moreover, since it matures before wheat and other crops which require much labor, it is possible to harvest it without interfering with the harvesting of the cash crop.[2] These advantages make it a favorite crop, notwithstanding the fact that it is not a cash crop.

For purposes of grading, oats are classified according to color. White (which includes yellow), red, gray, black, and mixed oats are the five different classes. Within each class there are four grades based on the following points: condition and general appearance, test weight per bushel, soundness, percentage

---

[2] In some sections of the Dakotas and Minnesota farmers have turned to barley as a substitute for oats in the crop-rotation system. It is impossible for this tendency to spread into the Corn Belt proper, for the reason that a warm climate is even more unfavorable for barley than for oats and that, when barley is rotated with corn, it is likely to develop scab infection.

damaged by heating, percentage of mixture with wild oats, with other classes of oats, and with foreign material. Oats failing to meet the specifications for any one of the four numerical grades are graded "Sample grade."[3]

II. FACTORS IN THE DEMAND FOR OATS

Since oats are consumed almost exclusively by domestic animals, and since they are also a factor in the production of other crops, the quantity of oats demanded is a function not only of its own price but also of the numbers of the different kinds of livestock and of the prices of other feedstuffs and of other crops. If the period covered by the data is at all considerable, the demand for oats, like that for other staples, also becomes a function of changes in the purchasing power of money and of other factors which we shall club together under the heading "time."

The best approximation to the total quantity demanded for all purposes in any year is "disappearance," i.e., production, plus imports, minus exports, minus changes in stocks. Next to production, the most important of these series are stocks and exports. But data on stocks are available only since 1896, and exports seldom amount to as much as 10 per cent of production for any year (imports are generally negligible). We may, therefore, consider production as a first approximation to consumption and refer to it as "apparent consumption." This series is available for all the three periods. For the second and third periods we also have the estimates of disappearance. Our analysis will make use of both of these series. From the first we shall derive comparable equations for all three periods; and from the second, comparable equations for the last two periods.

The price which we should like to have is that which, if maintained throughout the year, would have cleared the market. The best available approximation to this price is that weighted for the crop-marketing season. But this series has been published only for the years 1919–35 and is therefore of little use for studying the changes which have taken place in the demand for oats since 1875. We shall, therefore, use the December 1 farm price, which is available for the entire period since 1875.[4]

To allow for changes in the purchasing power of money, we shall deflate

---

[3] U.S. Dept. Agric., *Handbook of Official Grain Standards of the United States* (May, 1935), pp. 34–40.

[4] In a study published by the United States Department of Agriculture, Mr. Zapoleon made an interesting investigation of the geographical differences in the price of oats (L. B. Zapoleon, *Geographical Phases of Farm Prices: Oats* [U.S. Dept. Agric. Bull. No. 755 (1919)]). He has shown that a "price divide appears between sections which ship to the East and South and those which ship to the West and South." This "divide" coincides with the region in the North Central states, where prices are lowest and where the bulk of the crop is produced. We look upon the December 1 farm price as an index of the prices for the United States as a whole, since it is derived by averaging the state prices weighted according to the production in each state.

the price series by the Bureau of Labor Statistics "Index of Wholesale Prices" (1913 = 100).

The introduction of the numbers of the different kinds of livestock consuming oats as separate variables into our demand equations, although theoretically desirable, is practically impossible because the number of variables in the equations would become too large and because the underlying data are incomplete and subject to large errors. We shall, therefore, follow the procedure used in our analyses of the demands for corn and hay and make use of only one series— the number of *animal units*. This is a weighted average of the number of milk cows, of cattle other than milk cows, and of horses in the United States, the weights being proportional to the consumption per head of oats by each type of livestock in 1914—the only year for which these estimates are available. And we shall use the animal-unit series both as a deflator of the quantity demanded and as an independent variable in our demand equations.

Attention should be called to the fact that, in addition to the observations for the war years, 1917–21, which we have generally omitted from our previous analyses, we shall also omit the observations for 1893–98 and for 1922 and 1923, so that, in this chapter, the subdivisions of the entire period 1875–1929 will be: (I) 1875–92, (II) 1899–1914, and (III) 1915–29 (excluding 1917–23). The observations for 1893–98 will be eliminated because a break occurs in the animal-unit series for those years. This has resulted from adjustments apparently made by the United States Department of Agriculture in order that its estimates of the number of horses and cattle might conform to the census figures for 1899. The years 1922 and 1923 will be omitted because the unstable conditions resulting from the war appear to have extended to these years.

Our analysis will, therefore, proceed by stages as follows:

First, we shall assume that the apparent consumption (= production) of oats per animal unit or per head (x), the deflated price (y), and time (t) are the variables of our demand function, and we shall write

$$(2.1) \qquad\qquad x = x(y, t) ,$$

and

$$(2.2) \qquad\qquad y = y(x, t) ,$$

using both linear and constant-elasticity equations as specific forms of the foregoing hypotheses, for each of the three periods.

Second, we shall substitute disappearance per animal unit for apparent consumption per animal unit in the foregoing hypotheses for the second and third periods and compare the results obtained.

Third, we shall consider the number of animal units (z) as a separate variable and experiment with the hypotheses:

$$(2.3) \qquad\qquad\qquad x = x(y, z, t) ,$$

and

$$(2.4) \qquad\qquad\qquad y = y(x, z, t) ,$$

where x is now total apparent consumption ($=$production).[5]

Finally, in Part III, we shall also analyze the effect of changes in the prices of four feed crops—barley, corn, hay, and oats—on the demand for oats.

III. THE DEMAND FUNCTIONS WITH APPARENT CONSUMPTION PER ANIMAL UNIT AS THE DEPENDENT VARIABLE[6]

Table IX of Appendix A gives for the period 1875–1929 the apparent consumption ($=$production) per animal unit,[7] disappearance per animal unit, the real price, and value per animal unit of the oat crop of the United States, together with the trend ratios and the link relatives of the apparent consumption and the real price. The animal-unit series and the deflator of the price series are given in Table I, and the basic (unadjusted) data in Table IIa of the same appendix.

Figure 75 is a graphic representation of apparent consumption per animal unit, the deflated price per bushel, and the value per animal unit, from 1875 to 1929. As was explained in chapter vi, the value series is useful in connection with the estimation of the elasticity of demand. When the year-to-year fluctuations in this series are positively correlated with the corresponding fluctuations in the price series, the presumption is that the demand is inelastic.[8]

Table 36 is a descriptive summary, by periods, of apparent consumption per animal unit, disappearance per animal unit, and deflated prices. As can be seen from Figure 75, there is a marked negative correlation between apparent consumption and price in each of the three periods. The equations of Table 37 represent several measures of this relationship for each of the three periods, the first six corresponding to hypothesis (2.1) and the last six to hypothesis (2.2).

[5] It would have been better to have used disappearance rather than apparent consumption in the hypotheses (2.3) and (2.4), but the data on stocks go back only to 1896 and were discovered only after our major computations had already been completed. Consequently, we did not feel it worth while to recompute all our demand functions but decided to substitute disappearance only in hypotheses (2.1) and (2.2). In computing disappearance, we used the latest estimates of production which appear in the U.S. Dept. Agric., *Yearbook of Agriculture, 1935*, pp. 390–91.

[6] For a more detailed explanation of the methods used and for definitions of the technical terms employed see chap. vi.

[7] For the sake of brevity we shall often substitute the expression "per head" for "per animal unit" in what follows.

[8] See chap. vi, p. 191.

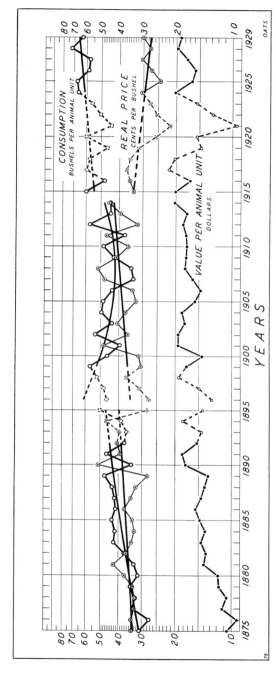

FIG. 75.—Oats: The basic adjusted annual data used in deriving the demand curves for oats in the United States, 1875–1929, with the computed trends by periods of the real prices and the consumption per animal unit. The dotted observations are those which are not used in the computations.

436

TABLE 36

OATS: SUMMARY BY PERIODS OF THE ADJUSTED DATA USED IN DERIVING THE DEMAND FUNCTIONS, 1875–1929

Descriptive Constants

PERIOD*	DEFLATED PRICE $y(t)$				APPARENT CONSUMPTION PER ANIMAL UNIT $x(t)$					DISAPPEARANCE PER ANIMAL UNIT $x(t)$				
	Mean (Cents)	Median (Cents)	Standard Deviation (Cents)	Coefficient of Variation	Mean (Bu.)	Median (Bu.)	Standard Deviation (Bu.)	Coefficient of Variation	Correlation with Price r_{xy}	Mean (Bu.)	Median (Bu.)	Standard Deviation (Bu.)	Coefficient of Variation	Correlation with Price r_{zy}
I	36.0467	34.084	4.9912	13.85	37.8501	37.303	5.6911	15.04	−0.2542	....	....	....	....	....
II	39.4631	38.310	6.6711	16.90	45.4526	44.672	6.8690	15.11	−0.8474	43.9130	44.4925	5.7394	13.07	−0.8419
III	29.7576	30.100	3.2606	10.96	61.8481	61.736	6.9578	11.25	−0.6997	55.8124	57.3095	6.2515	11.20	−0.8385

Equations of Trends†

I: $y(t) = 36.0467 + 0.3258t$
II: $y(t) = 39.4631 + 0.4409t$
III: $y(t) = 30.5800 + 0.4699t$

I: $x(t) = 37.8501 + 0.7980t$
II: $x(t) = 42.4148 - 0.3107t + 0.1430t^2$
III: $x(t) = 60.4324 + 0.8090t$

II: $x(t) = 43.9130 - 0.6033t$
III: $x(t) = 54.0731 + 0.9939t$

* I = 1875–92; II = 1899–1914; III = 1915–29 (excl. 1917–23).
† Origins of trends by periods: I = July 1, 1884; II = July 1, 1907; III = January 1, 1923.

TABLE 37

OATS: APPARENT CONSUMPTION PER ANIMAL UNIT, 1875–1929: EQUATIONS IN WHICH

x = Apparent consumption (=Production) per animal unit in bushels

y = Deflated December 1 farm price in cents per bushel

(Figures in parentheses are standard errors)

EQUA- TION No.	PERIOD*		Constant Term	y	t	t^2
				EQUATIONS		
1	I	$x=$	60.6760	−0.5905 (0.1197)	+0.9904 (0.1134)	−0.0572 (0.0235)
2	II	$x=$	80.5613	−0.8897 (0.1584)	+0.0815 (0.2293)	. . . .
3	III	$x=$	98.5849	−1.2476 (0.9701)	+0.2227 (0.6334)	. . . .
			Constant Term	y'	$†Mt$	$†Mt^2$
4	I	$x'=$	2.4770	−0.5687 (0.1225)	+0.0260 (0.0030)	−0.0018 (0.0006)
5	II	$x'=$	2.9312	−0.8042 (0.1407)	+0.0027 (0.0051)	. . . .
6	III	$x'=$	2.6070	−0.5592 (0.4649)	+0.0054 (0.0103)	. . . .
			Constant Term	x	t	t^2
7	I	$y=$	78.0428	−1.0753 (0.2179)	+1.1838 (0.2255)	−0.0482 (0.0355)
8	II	$y=$	75.6376	−0.7959 (0.1417)	+0.1936 (0.2112)	. . . .
9	III	$y=$	42.6208	−0.1992 (0.1549)	−0.3087 (0.2158)	. . . .
			Constant Term	x'	$†Mt$	$†Mt^2$
10	I	$y'=$	3.2436	−1.0633 (0.2297)	+0.0307 (0.0063)	−0.0015 (0.0010)
11	II	$y'=$	3.0600	−0.8895 (0.1556)	+0.0057 (0.0052)	. . . .
12	III	$y'=$	2.1961	−0.4014 (0.3337)	−0.0096 (0.0078)	. . . .

* I = 1875–92; II = 1899–1914; III = 1915–29 (excl. 1917–23).

TABLE 37—*Continued*

APPARENT CONSUMPTION PER ANIMAL UNIT IS TAKEN AS THE QUANTITY DEMANDED

t = Time in years. For origins see Table 36

x', y' = Logs of x and y

(Figures in parentheses are standard errors)

	DESCRIPTIVE CONSTANTS					EQUATION No.
	Elasticity of Demand η	Quadratic Mean Error ϵ (Bushels)	Adjusted Multiple Correlation Coefficient R'	Percentage of Variance of Apparent Consumption Attributable to		
				y	t	
. . . .	−0.5404 (0.1598)	2.3429	0.9165	13.17	73.65	1
. . . .	−0.7724 (0.2397)	4.0269	0.8233	73.22	− 1.14	2
. . . .	−0.6003 (0.5519)	6.2113	0.5502	40.91	9.28	3
	η	ϵ (Per Cent)	R'	y'	t	
. . . .	−0.5687 (0.1225)	93.9–106.5	0.9168	11.91	74.96	4
. . . .	−0.8042 (0.1407)	91.5–109.3	0.8278	74.36	− 1.64	5
. . . .	−0.5592 (0.4649)	90.0–111.1	0.5402	35.90	13.52	6

Flexibility of Price φ	Maximum Value of η $1/\varphi$	ϵ (Cents)	R'	Percentage of Variance of Price Attributable to		EQUATION No.
				x	t	
−1.0898 (0.3528)	−0.9176	3.1614	0.7881	31.17	37.63	7
−0.9167 (0.2875)	−1.0909	3.8088	0.8333	69.44	4.07	8
−0.4141 (0.3741)	−2.4148	2.4822	0.7021	29.75	34.03	9
φ	$1/\varphi$	ϵ (Per Cent)	R'	x'	t	
−1.0633 (0.2297)	−0.9405	91.8–108.9	0.7614	31.39	34.01	10
−0.8895 (0.1556)	−1.1242	91.1–109.8	0.8404	69.40	5.14	11
−0.4014 (0.3337)	−2.4913	91.4–109.4	0.6517	29.16	29.75	12

† $M = \log_{10} e = 0.43429$.

Equation 1 of Table 37 relates to the first period. From the coefficient of y in this equation we learn that, other things being equal, an increase (or decrease) of one cent in the deflated price per bushel of oats brought about, on the average, a decrease (or increase) in the annual apparent consumption per head of approximately 0.59 bushel. But other things did not remain equal. Even if the price had been fixed, apparent consumption per head would have increased on the average by 0.99 bushel per annum, subject to a retardation effect of 0.11 bushel per annum. The analytic expression for this rate of shift is given by

$$(3.1) \qquad \frac{\partial x}{\partial t} = 0.9904 - 2(0.0572)t.$$

Both the slope of the curve and its rate of shift are statistically significant.

The absolute change in consumption consequent upon a unit change in price —i.e., the coefficient of y—can be converted into a relative change or an "elasticity of demand" by multiplying it by the representative value of y/x. Giving y and t their respective mean values, $\bar{y} = 36.05$ and $\bar{t} = 0$ (Table 36), we may compute from our equation the corresponding representative value of x, $x_c = 39.39$. This is the x-coordinate of the point on the demand surface for which $\bar{y}$ and $\bar{t}$ are the remaining coordinates. Substituting x_c and the mean value of y into the formula for the (partial) elasticity of demand:

$$(3.2) \qquad \eta = \frac{\partial x}{\partial y} \cdot \frac{y}{x},$$

we get $\eta = -0.5404$. This means that in the neighborhood of the point $(x_z, \bar{y}, \bar{t})$ on the demand surface, a 1 per cent increase (or decrease) in the deflated price is associated with a decrease (or increase) in the apparent consumption of oats per head of only 0.54 per cent.

The fit of the demand curve to the data is quite good, as judged by the fairly small quadratic mean error (2.34 bu.) and the large adjusted coefficient of multiple correlation (0.92). However, only 13 per cent of the variance of apparent consumption per head is attributable to price, and approximately 74 per cent to the shift of the demand curve with time. The large percentage of the variance which is thus attributable to the time variable suggests that our analysis has failed to isolate some very important factor or factors influencing the demand for oats during the period 1875–92.

We now turn to the demand curves for the second and third periods, which are given by equations 2 and 3 of Table 37. The most important difference to be observed between these curves and the curve for the first period is that they do not shift upward or downward with time: the coefficients of t in equations 2 and 3 are definitely not significant, since they are exceeded by their standard errors.[9] The curves also differ in slope. Whereas in the first period a one cent increase in the deflated price reduced the annual apparent consumption per head by only 0.59 bushel, in the second and third periods the corresponding reductions were 0.89 bushel and 1.25 bushels (cf. the coefficients of y). As is to be expected, the differences between the slopes of the demand curves for the three periods are reflected in corresponding differences in the elasticities of demand.[10]

Judged by the values of the quadratic mean errors and the adjusted multiple correlation coefficient, the fit of the demand curve for the second period is not so good as that for the first, and the fit of the demand curve for the third period is not so good as that for the second.

The fluctuations in price account for approximately 73 per cent of the variance of apparent consumption in the second period, and 41 per cent in the third. The variance in apparent consumption directly or indirectly attributable to the shift of the demand curve (i.e., to time) is negligible or statistically insignificant.

Equations 4, 5, and 6 of Table 37 are the logarithmic forms of hypothesis (2.1). From the coefficient of y' ($= \log y$) in the first of these equations, we learn that, for any given year in the period 1875–92, an increase (or decrease) of 1 per cent in the price brought about a decrease (or increase) in the apparent consumption of oats per head of approximately 0.57 per cent. This figure, which is also the elasticity of demand for this curve, is in close agreement with the elasticity of demand derived from the arithmetic equation (1).

The coefficients of t and t^2 give the *relative* rate of shift of the demand curve. They show that during this period the demand curve was moving upward at the rate of 2.60 per cent per annum, subject to a retardation of 0.36 per cent per annum, for

$$(3.3) \qquad \frac{\partial \log_e x}{\partial t} = \frac{1}{x} \cdot \frac{\partial x}{\partial t} = 0.0260 - 2(0.0018)t .$$

The fit of this equation to the data is about as good as the fit of the corresponding arithmetic equation (1). The quadratic mean error indicates that approximately 68 per cent of the observations on apparent consumption fall

[9] Elimination of the time variable from these equations would change the slope of the demand curve from −0.8897 to −0.8725 in the second period and from −1.2476 to −1.4931 in the third period. It would also decrease the ϵ's and raise the R''s in the two equations.

[10] It should be recalled that the elasticities are measured at "representative points" on the demand curves. Since our demand curves are straight lines, and since the elasticity of demand of a straight line demand curve varies in numerical value from zero for $y = 0$ to infinity for $x = 0$, it is possible to select triads of points on the three curves at which the elasticities are equal. But these points would not necessarily be "representative points."

It should also be recalled that the standard errors of the elasticities of demand of eqs. 1, 2, and 3 are *maximum* standard errors and are not comparable with the standard errors of the coefficients of y and of t which are least-square standard errors.

within 93.9 per cent and 106.5 per cent of the computed values. The value of the multiple coefficient of correlation is just as high as that of equation (1).

As in the corresponding arithmetic equation (1), the shift of the demand curve accounts for approximately 75 per cent of the variance of apparent consumption, the fluctuations in price accounting for only 12 per cent.

Equations 5 and 6 of Table 37 give the elasticities and the rates of shift of the demand curves for the second and third periods. In general, they confirm the results derived from equations 2 and 3. The coefficients of y' tell us that the elasticity of demand was -0.80 in the second period and -0.56 in the third. The coefficients of t are exceeded by their standard errors, thus showing that there was no significant upward or downward shift of demand during these periods.

Figures 76, 77, and 78 are graphic representations of equations 4, 5, and 6. Figure 76A, which relates to the first period, shows the scatter diagram of the logarithms of apparent consumption per head, x', on the logarithms of real price, y'. The line $D'_1 D'_2$ is the *net* regression of x' on y'. It gives the relation between that part of the logarithm of apparent consumption per head which is linearly independent of time and that part of the logarithm of real price which is linearly independent of time. The slope of the line (-0.5687), which is given by the coefficient of y' in equation 4, is the elasticity of demand for oats during that period.

The curve $D'_1 D'_3$ in Figure 76B gives the direction and the rate of shift of the demand curve for the first period. It is a graphic representation of the regression of apparent consumption per head on time, after the effect of price has been eliminated. When allowance is made for this shift, we obtain the reduced scatter of Figure 76C.

Figure 77 relates to the second period. The slope of the line $D'_1 D'_2$, given by the coefficient of y' in equation 5, is the elasticity of demand. The line $D'_1 D'_3$ (Fig. 77B) gives the average shift of the demand curve $D'_1 D'_2$. It is, however, scarcely different from zero (and statistically insignificant), so that the corrected scatter diagram (Fig. 77C) is practically the same as the original scatter in Figure 77A.

Figure 78, which relates to the third period, is a graphic representation of equation 6, Table 37. The slope of the line $D'_1 D'_2$ gives the elasticity of demand for the third period, and the slope of the line $D'_1 D'_3$ measures the relative rate of shift of the demand curve. But this value, which is given by the coefficient of t in equation 6, is insignificant, so that we would have done better to have omitted the variable t from our equation.

The fit of equation 4 is better than that of equation 5, and the fit of equation 5 is better than that of equation 6. This is evident from a comparison of the corresponding ϵ's and the corresponding R'''s. It should not be forgotten, how-

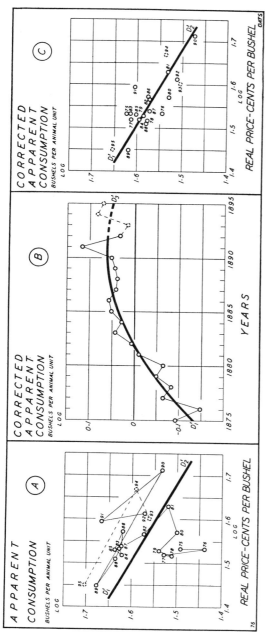

Fig. 76.—Oats: Three aspects of the demand per animal unit for oats during the period 1875–92 on the assumption that

$$x = 299.9\, y^{-0.5687}\, e^{0.02601\, t - 0.00181\, t^2}.$$

A: Relation between consumption per animal unit and real price when the data are not corrected for the effects of "time," with the demand curve $D_1' D_2'$ which results when such correction is made.

B: Relation between consumption per animal unit and time when the former is corrected for the effects of changes in the real price. The slope of the line $D_1' D_3'$ (fitted to the variables x' and t when both are corrected for price) represents the mean rate of shift of the animal-unit demand curve $D_1' D_2'$.

C: The animal-unit demand curve for oats, 1875–92. Line $D_1' D_2'$ shows the relation between that part of the animal-unit consumption of oats in the United States which is independent of time and that part of the real price which is independent of time. In the scatter, however, only the ordinate is corrected for secular changes, the abscissa being uncorrected.

443

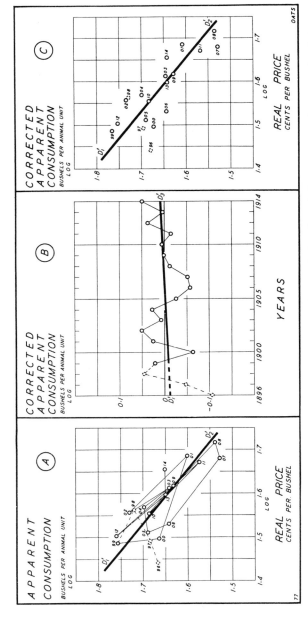

Fig. 77.—Oats: Three aspects of the demand per animal unit for oats during the period 1890–1914 on the assumption that

$$x = 853.5\, y^{-0.8042}\, e^{0.0027\,t},$$

where x is apparent consumption per animal unit.

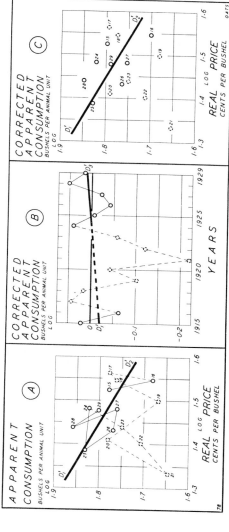

Fig. 78.—Oats: Three aspects of the demand per animal unit for oats during the period 1915–29 (excluding 1917–23), on the assumption that

$$x = 404.5\, y^{-0.5592}\, e^{0.0054\,t},$$

where x is apparent consumption per animal unit.

445

ever, that both ϵ and R' for the second and third periods are affected by the inclusion of the time variable, which turned out to be insignificant, and that the omission of this variable would have lowered the value of ϵ and increased that of R', thus indicating a better agreement between the observed and the computed apparent consumption.

IV. DEMAND FUNCTIONS WITH PRICE AS THE DEPENDENT VARIABLE

Equations 7–12 in Table 37 are the specific forms of demand hypothesis (2.2), the first three being the linear equations and the second three being the logarithmic equations. These equations measure the degree to which changes in the deflated price of oats may be explained by changes in consumption per animal unit and time, in each of the three periods.

The coefficient of x in equation 7, which relates to the first period, means that, in any given year in this period, an increase in the apparent consumption of oats of one bushel per animal unit would, on the average, be associated with a decrease in the real price per bushel of 1.08 cents.

The coefficient of t in the same equation signifies that, even if the apparent consumption per head had been constant, the real price per bushel would have shown a tendency to increase by 1.18 cents per annum, subject to a retardation of 0.10 cents per annum, for

$$(4.1) \qquad \frac{\partial y}{\partial t} = 1.1838 - 2(0.0482)t \,.$$

The absolute change in price consequent upon a unit change in apparent consumption—i.e., the coefficient of x—can be converted into a relative change or into a coefficient of "price flexibility," by multiplying it by the representative value of x/y.[11] At this representative point on the demand surface for the first period, we have for the coefficient of flexibility

$$(4.2) \qquad \varphi = \frac{\partial y}{\partial x} \cdot \frac{x}{y} = -1.0898 \,,$$

which means that an increase of 1 per cent in apparent consumption per animal unit was associated with a decrease of nearly 1.1 per cent in the deflated price of oats.

Equations 8 and 9 are the demand curves for the second and third periods. The most important difference to be observed between these curves and the curve for the first period relates to the shifting of the three curves. Whereas in the first period the demand curve shifted upward by approximately 1.18 cents per annum, in the second period it exhibited no shift, and in the third the shift

[11] See chap. vi, Sec. III, D, 2, b.

was downward at the rate of 0.31 cent per annum, although this shift is hardly significant (compare the coefficients of t). The curves also differ in slope. Whereas in the first period an increase in the annual apparent consumption of one bushel of oats per animal unit was associated with a decrease in the deflated price per bushel of 1.08 cents, in the second and third periods the corresponding figures were approximately 0.80 cent and 0.20 cent (cf. the coefficients of x).

Equations 10, 11, and 12 in Table 37 express the relationship between price, apparent consumption, and time directly in terms of relative changes. Thus from the coefficient of x' in the first of these equations we see that, other things being equal, an increase of 1 per cent in the annual apparent consumption of oats per head was associated with a decrease of approximately 1.06 per cent in the deflated price. But other things did not remain equal: even if the apparent consumption per animal unit had remained constant during this period, the deflated price would have increased by 3.07 per cent per annum subject to an annual retardation of 0.30 per cent for

$$(4.3) \qquad \frac{\partial \log_e y}{\partial t} = \frac{1}{y} \cdot \frac{\partial y}{\partial t} = 0.0307 - 2(0.0015)t .$$

Equations 11 and 12, which relate to the second and third periods, are, of course, to be interpreted in a manner analogous to that of equation 10. The coefficients of x' in equations 11 and 12 give the price flexibilities for the second and third periods. They show that price flexibility decreased in numerical value from period to period. The coefficients of t which give the relative rates of shift of the demand curves barely exceed their standard errors; they show that there was no significant upward or downward shift in the demand curve during these two periods.

The price flexibilities and the rates of shift yielded by the logarithmic equations 10–12 are thus in excellent agreement with the corresponding flexibilities and rates of shift deduced from the linear equations 7–9.

A comparison of the R''s, for equations 7–12, in which price is the dependent variable, with the corresponding R''s in equations 1–6, in which apparent consumption is the dependent variable, shows that the latter set gives a better fit to the data for the first period, while the former gives a better fit to the data for the third period and that both sets of equations fit the data for the second period equally well. However, as we had occasion to point out before,[12] the characteristics of our data are such that the regressions of consumption on price and time give a better approximation to the underlying demand curves than do the corresponding regressions of price on consumption and time.

[12] See chap. iv, pp. 146–49.

V. DEMAND FUNCTIONS WITH DISAPPEARANCE
PER ANIMAL UNIT AS A VARIABLE

As we stated in Section II above, the second step in our analysis will be to substitute disappearance (=production, plus imports, minus exports, minus changes in stocks) for apparent consumption (=production) in hypotheses (2.1) and (2.2). This is a better estimate of the quantity of oats demanded in the United States in any given year than is production. We proceed now to make this substitution.

In Table 38 both the arithmetic and the logarithmic forms of the demand equations are presented. Since the magnitude of the disappearance series is different from that of the apparent consumption series, we shall confine our comparison of results to the logarithmic equations, as, in these, the coefficients are given in relative terms rather than in absolute units.

It will be recalled that the data on disappearance are available for only the second and third periods of our study. We begin, therefore, with a comparison of equation 5 in Table 37 with equation 3 in Table 38. It can be seen immediately that the percentage change in the quantity demanded consequent upon a 1 per cent change in price—i.e., the elasticity of demand—is less than appeared at first sight from the use of the approximate series of apparent consumption, for the coefficient of y' changes from -0.80 to -0.58.

This should serve to warn us against drawing hard-and-fast conclusions from the data for the first period. It is quite likely that apparent consumption is not a good measure of the quantity demanded and that, had estimates of disappearance been available, they would have yielded considerably different results.

An even more striking difference is found in the measures of the shift of the demand curve for the second period. Whereas from the analysis with apparent consumption it appeared that the demand curve had no significant shift, the substitution of the disappearance series shows that the demand curve had a definite shift, given by the relation:

$$(5.1) \qquad \frac{\partial \log_e x}{\partial t} = \frac{1}{x} \cdot \frac{\partial x}{\partial t} = -0.0067 + 2(0.0012)t \, .$$

This means that the demand for oats shifted downward at the rate of 0.67 per cent per annum subject to an annual acceleration of 0.24 per cent per annum. However, a study of Figure 79B, which is a graphical analysis of this equation, reveals that even these coefficients do not accurately measure the shift of the demand curve but that a curve of higher order than that which we have fitted would be required to explain the routine of change involved. In fact, if the observation for 1900 is neglected, a smooth curve with cyclical fluctuations could be drawn through the points in Figure 79B.

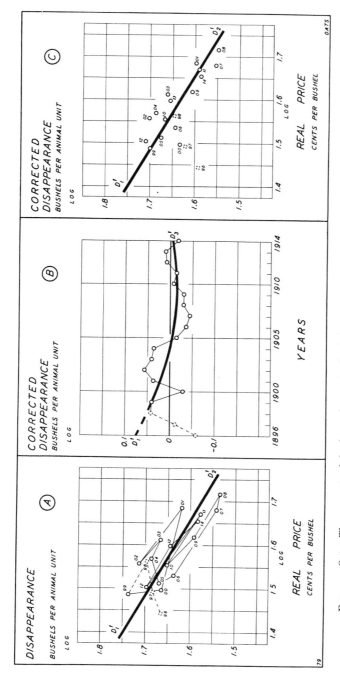

Fig. 79.—Oats: Three aspects of the demand per animal unit for oats during the period 1899–1914 on the assumption that

$$x = 358.7\, y^{-0.5829}\, e^{-0.0067t + 0.0012t^2} ,$$

where x is disappearance per animal unit.

TABLE 38

OATS: DISAPPEARANCE PER ANIMAL UNIT, 1899–1929: EQUATIONS IN WHICH

x = Disappearance* per animal unit in bushels

y = Deflated December 1 farm price in cents per bushel

(Figures in parentheses are standard errors)

EQUA-TION No.	PERIOD†		EQUATIONS			
			Constant Term	y	t	t^2
1	II	$x=$	67.3424	−0.6235 (0.1200)	−0.3284 (0.1701)	+0.0553 (0.0404)
2	III	$x=$	86.5678	−1.0626 (0.5816)	+0.4945 (0.3797)	. . . .
			Constant Term	y'	$\ddagger Mt$	$\ddagger Mt^2$
3	II	$x'=$	2.5548	−0.5829 (0.1156)	−0.0067 (0.0041)	+0.0012 (0.0010)
4	III	$x'=$	2.5265	−0.5378 (0.3194)	+0.0109 (0.0071)	. . . .
			Constant Term	x	t	t^2
5	II	$y=$	82.4346	−0.9786 (0.1677)	. . . .	. . . .
6	III	$y=$	54.1650	−0.4373 (0.1160)	. . . .	. . . .
			Constant Term	x'	$\ddagger Mt$	$\ddagger Mt^2$
7	II	$y'=$	3.3351	−1.0648 (0.1800)	. . . .	. . . .
8	III	$y'=$	2.7790	−0.7501 (0.2208)	. . . .	. . . .

* Disappearance equals production (revised) (U.S. Dept. Agric., *Yearbook of Agriculture, 1935*, pp. 390–91), minus changes in stocks, plus imports, minus exports.

† Periods: II = 1899–1914; III = 1915–29 (excl. 1917–23).

TABLE 38—*Continued*

DISAPPEARANCE PER ANIMAL UNIT IS TAKEN AS THE QUANTITY DEMANDED

t = Time in years. For origins see Table 36

x', y' = Logs of x and y

(Figures in parentheses are standard errors)

	DESCRIPTIVE CONSTANTS					
	Elasticity of Demand η	Quadratic Mean Error ϵ (Bushels)	Adjusted Multiple Correlation Coefficient R'	Percentage of Variance of Disappearance Attributable to		EQUATION No.
				y	t	
. . . .	−0.5757 (0.1761)	2.9807	0.8644	61.01	18.76	1
. . . .	−0.5666 (0.3713)	3.7233	0.8304	46.47	31.36	2
	η	ϵ (Per Cent)	R'	y'	t	
. . . .	−0.5829 (0.1156)	93.1–107.4	0.8542	62.07	16.31	3
. . . .	−0.5378 (0.3194)	93.0–107.5	0.8225	40.34	36.55	4
Flexibility of Price φ	Maximum Value of η $1/\varphi$	ϵ (Cents)	R'	Percentage of Variance of Price Attributable to		
				x		
−1.0889 (0.3295)	−0.9184	3.8491	−0.8294§	70.87‖	. . . .	5
−0.8202 (0.3089)	−1.2192	2.0514	−0.8085§	70.31‖	. . . .	6
φ	$1/\varphi$	ϵ (Per Cent)	R'	x'		
−1.0648 (0.1800)	−0.9391	90.9–110.0	−0.8330§	71.43‖	. . . .	7
−0.7501 (0.2208)	−1.3331	92.8–107.7	−0.7752§	65.79‖	. . . .	8

‡ $M = \log_{10} e = 0.43429$.

§ This is the simple correlation coefficient adjusted for the number of parameters (2) in the equation.

‖ This is 100 times the square of the unadjusted simple correlation coefficient.

Nevertheless, the equations with disappearance per animal unit do yield a somewhat better fit to the data than do those with apparent consumption. The quadratic mean error shows that the observations deviate from the computed values by approximately 7 per cent, as opposed to 9 per cent in the case of apparent consumption, and the adjusted multiple correlation coefficient is 0.85 in place of 0.83.

The substitution of the disappearance series for the apparent consumption series gives rise to less modifications of the results for the third period than it did for the second period. The elasticity of demand (i.e., the coefficient of y') yielded by the analysis of disappearance per animal unit (eq. 4, Table 38, and Fig. 80) is approximately the same as that derived from the analysis of apparent consumption (eq. 6, Table 37, and Fig. 78).

It appears, however, from the former analysis (as opposed to the latter analysis in which the coefficient of t was less than its standard error) that the demand curve for oats shifted upward at the rate of 1.09 ± 0.71 per cent per annum.

From the standard errors of the coefficients, the quadratic mean errors, and especially the adjusted multiple correlation coefficients, it may be seen that the substitution of the disappearance series for the apparent consumption series results in a better fit of the data to the curve.

We shall now substitute disappearance per animal unit for apparent consumption per animal unit in the equations in which price is the dependent variable—hypothesis (2.2). The result is to be found in equations 7 and 8 in Table 38, which should be compared with equations 11 and 12 of Table 37. The former are all simple regressions of deflated price on disappearance per animal unit, the time variable having proved insignificant. The latter are functions both of apparent consumption per animal unit and of time. The equation for the second period in Table 38 does not give quite so good a fit to the data as the corresponding equations of Table 37. The new analysis yields a price flexibility of the order -1.1, whereas the earlier computations yielded a price flexibility of the order -0.9.

The fit of equation 8, Table 38, is better than that of equation 12, Table 37. The quadratic mean error of the former is approximately 7.5 per cent as compared with 9 per cent for the latter. The adjusted coefficient of correlation has the corresponding values -0.78 and -0.65.

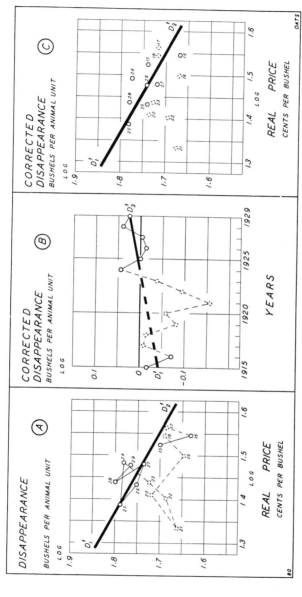

Fig. 80.—Oats: Three aspects of the demand per animal unit for oats during the period 1915–29 (excluding 1917–23) on the assumption that

$$x = 336.1\, y^{-0.5378}\, e^{0.0109\,t},$$

where x is disappearance per animal unit.

VI. DEMAND FUNCTIONS WITH ANIMAL UNITS
AS AN EXPLICIT VARIABLE

In the equations of the preceding section the number of animal units entered only implicitly as a deflator of the total quantity demanded. In this section we shall consider the animal-unit series as an explicit variable and experiment with the demand hypotheses

(2.3) $x = x(y, z, t)$

and

(2.4) $y = y(x, z, t)$,

where x is now total apparent consumption (see n. 5; p. 435 above) and z is the number of animal units. We shall use both linear and constant-elasticity equations as specific forms of the two hypotheses.

Table 39 is a summary, by periods, of the results obtained. The first thing to be observed about the equations of this table is that time does not appear as a variable. Table 39 is a summary, by periods, of the results obtained. The variable "time" has been omitted from the equations because of its very high correlation with the number of animal units ($|r| > 0.9$ in each of the three periods).

The interpretation of the equations of Table 39 is similar to that of the equations in Tables 37 and 38. Thus equation 1 of Table 39 is the arithmetic form of hypothesis (2.3) for the first period. The coefficient of y of this equation means that, if the number of animal units had remained fixed, an increase (or decrease) of one cent in the deflated price per bushel would have brought about on the average a decrease (or increase) in the total annual apparent consumption (=production) of 8.259 million bushels. The change in apparent consumption consequent upon a given change in z varies from point to point on the demand curve with the value of z. If the price remains constant, the effect of changes in the number of animal units on apparent consumption is given by the expression

(6.1) $\dfrac{\partial x}{\partial z} = 233.4 - 2(5.527)z$.

The absolute change in apparent consumption brought about by a unit change in price may be converted into a relative change, or into an elasticity of demand, in the manner explained in a previous section. The value of the elasticity of demand at the representative point on the demand curve turns out to be −0.52, which agrees very well with the corresponding figure derived from equation 1 of Table 37. The fit of this equation is excellent, the coefficient of multiple correlation, R', being 0.9546.

As we might have guessed from the coefficients of this equation, the changes in the number of animal units account for practically all the variance of consumption.

From equations 2 and 3 of Table 39 we see that the slope of the demand curve for oats changed from period to period. The net effect of an increase in price of one cent per bushel was to reduce the annual apparent consumption by 19 million bushels in the second period and by 29 million bushels in the third period (cf. the coefficients of y). However, the net effect of a given increase in the number of animal units on the consumption of oats remained substantially constant during these two periods (cf. the coefficients of z). The fit of equation 2 is not so good as that of equation 1, and the fit of equation 3 is very poor, R' being only of the order of 0.3.

Equations 4, 5, and 6 of Table 39 are the logarithmic forms of hypothesis (2.3). The coefficients of y' and z' are, respectively, the partial elasticities of demand with respect to price and the number of animal units. For the first period the elasticity with respect to price is -0.42 and that with respect to the number of animal units is given by the equation

$$(6.2) \qquad \frac{\partial x'}{\partial z'} = \frac{\partial x}{\partial z} \cdot \frac{z}{x} = 26.0646 - 2(23.9761)Mz' .$$

For the second and third periods the elasticities with respect to price are, respectively, -0.75 and -0.57, while those with respect to animal units are 0.88 and 0.72. But these elasticities are of little significance, since they do not take into account the fact that the number of animal units, as we defined the term, depends on the price of oats, for as the price rises, other feeds are undoubtedly substituted for oats. Figures 81, 82, and 83 are the graphic illustrations of equations 4, 5, and 6. The interpretation of these diagrams is analogous with that of Figures 76, 77, and 78, except that in these diagrams the number of animal units takes the place of time.

Equations 7–12 are the specific forms of hypothesis (2.4), the first three being the arithmetic equations and the second three being the logarithmic equations. The interpretation of these equations is similar to that of the corresponding equations in Table 37 except that z takes the place of t, and x is now total apparent consumption. The two sets of equations, in Tables 37 and 39, fit their respective observations equally well. The differences between the corresponding R''s and between the corresponding ϵ's are quite small.

TABLE 39

Oats: Total Apparent Consumption, 1875–1929: Equations in Which

$x =$ Total apparent consumption ($=$Production) in millions of bushels
$y =$ Deflated December 1 farm price in cents per bushel

(Figures in parentheses are standard errors)

Equation No.	Period*		Constant Term	y	z	z^2
					EQUATIONS	
1	I	$x=$	$-1,338.091$	$-\ 8.259$ (2.268)	$+233.386$ (75.952)	$-\ 5.527$ (2.545)
2	II	$x=$	800.212	-19.049 (3.698)	$+\ 42.943$ (9.069)	. . . .
3	III	$x=$	$1,175.942$	-28.732 (20.627)	$+\ 46.937$ (28.586)	. . . .
			Constant Term	y'	z'	$\dagger M z'^2$
4	I	$x'=$	-12.7890	$-\ 0.4208$ (0.1219)	$+\ 26.0646$ (5.1910)	-23.9761 (5.1380)
5	II	$x'=$	2.9994	$-\ 0.7467$ (0.1420)	$+\ 0.8816$ (0.1849)	. . . .
6	III	$x'=$	3.0054	$-\ 0.5673$ (0.4202)	$+\ 0.7153$ (0.4472)	. . . .
			Constant Term	x	z	z^2
7	I	$y=$	-48.5763	$-\ 0.0589$ (0.0162)	$+\ 11.7968$ (7.6774)	$-\ 0.2484$ (0.2395)
8	II	$y=$	34.3005	$-\ 0.0352$ (0.0068)	$+\ 1.8192$ (0.3999)	. . . .
9	III	$y=$	17.8067	$-\ 0.0097$ (0.0070)	$+\ 1.1369$ (0.4092)	. . . .
			Constant Term	x'	z'	$\dagger M z'^2$
10	I	$y'=$	-10.5322	$-\ 1.0925$ (0.3165)	$+\ 23.8728$ (12.4591)	-21.5206 (11.9187)
11	II	$y'=$	3.0169	$-\ 0.9109$ (0.1732)	$+\ 0.9691$ (0.2059)	. . . .
12	III	$y'=$	1.8393	$-\ 0.4710$ (0.3488)	$+\ 0.8239$ (0.3395)	. . . .

* Periods: I = 1875–92; II = 1899–1914; III = 1915–29 (excl. 1917–23).

456

TABLE 39—*Continued*

TOTAL APPARENT CONSUMPTION IS TAKEN AS THE QUANTITY DEMANDED

z = Animal units in millions

x', y', z' = Logs of x, y, and z

(Figures in parentheses are standard errors)

DESCRIPTIVE CONSTANTS

	Elasticity of Demand η	Quadratic Mean Error ϵ (1,000,000 Bushels)	Adjusted Multiple Correlation Coefficient R'	Percentage of Variance of Apparent Consumption Attributable to		EQUATION No.
				y	z	
. . . .	−0.5150 (0.1992)	45.469	0.9546	0.17	92.53	1
. . . .	−0.7429 (0.2437)	91.297	0.8313	41.55	31.67	2
. . . .	−0.6282 (0.5413)	139.247	0.3267	9.10	27.10	3
	η	ϵ (Per Cent)	R'	y'	z'	
. . . .	−0.4208 (0.1219)	93.9–106.5	0.9749	− 0.03	95.95	4
. . . .	−0.7467 (0.1420)	91.7–109.1	0.8335	42.72	30.82	5
. . . .	−0.5673 (0.4202)	90.3–110.8	0.3130	10.03	25.54	6

Flexibility of Price φ	Maximum Value of η $1/\varphi$	ϵ (Cents)	R'	Percentage of Variance of Price Attributable to		EQUATION
				x	z	
−0.8753 (0.3877)	−1.1425	3.8397	0.6641	1.07	52.90	7
−0.9033 (0.3019)	−1.1070	3.9263	0.8217	43.68	28.18	8
−0.4450 (0.3748)	−2.2471	2.5625	0.6779	5.50	55.90	9
φ	$1/\varphi$	ϵ (Per Cent)	R'	x'	z'	
−1.0925 (0.3165)	−0.9153	90.4–110.7	0.6431	− 0.32	52.02	10
−0.9109 (0.1732)	−1.0978	90.8–110.1	0.8305	43.42	29.69	11
−0.4710 (0.3488)	−2.1231	91.1–109.8	0.6116	6.96	48.33	12

† $M = \log_{10} e = 0.43429$.

457

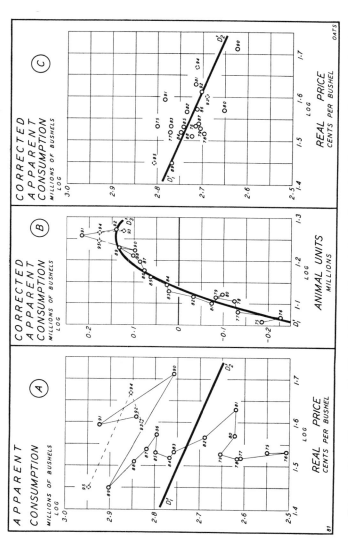

Fig. 81.—Oats: Three aspects of the total demand for oats during the period 1875–92 on the assumption that

$$x = 1625 \left(10^{-16}\right) y^{-0.4208} z^{26.0646} e^{-23.9761} \left(\log z\right)^2.$$

A: Relation between total consumption and real price when the data are not corrected for the changes in the animal-unit series with the demand curve $D_1'D_2'$ which results when such correction is made.

B: Relation between total consumption and the number of animal units when the former is corrected for the effects of changes in the real price. The slope of the line $D_1'D_3'$ (fitted to the variables x' and z' when both are corrected for price) represents the *net* relationship between total consumption and animal units.

C: The total demand curve for oats, 1875–92. Line $D_1'D_2'$ shows the relation between that part of the total consumption of oats in the United States which is independent of changes in the number of animal units and that part of the real price which is independent of the number of animal units. In the scatter, however, only the ordinate is corrected for the number of animal units, the abscissa being uncorrected.

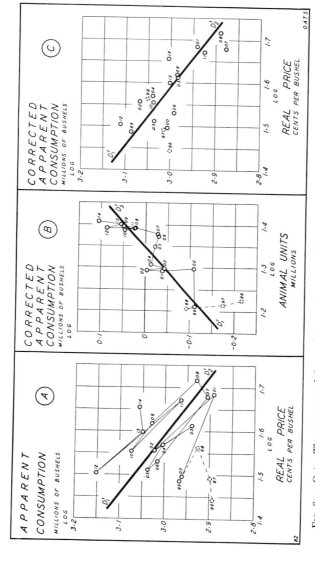

Fig. 82.—Oats: Three aspects of the total demand for oats during the period 1899–1914 on the assumption that

$$x = 998.7 \, y^{-0.7467} \, z^{0.8816} \,,$$

where x is total apparent consumption.

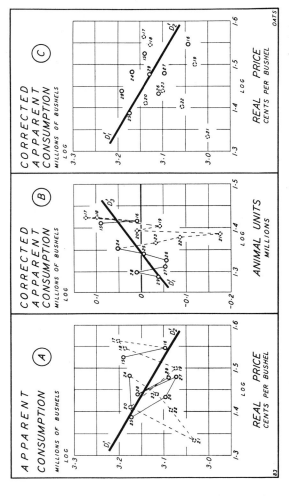

FIG. 83.—Oats: Three aspects of the total demand for oats during the period 1915–29 (excluding 1917–23), on the assumption that

$$x = 1013\, y^{-0.5673}\, z^{0.7153}\ ,$$

where x is total apparent consumption.

460

VII. SUMMARY AND CONCLUSIONS

Although several previous studies have dealt with the demand for oats in the United States, none of them contains an analysis of the changes which may have occurred in the shape, the elasticity, and the rate of shift of the demand curve for this important commodity during the periods covered by them.[13] In this study we have investigated these changes for the period since 1875 and found that the demand for oats exhibits both varying and fixed properties.

1. The slope of the demand curve has varied from period to period. If we deflate the total "apparent consumption" (=production) of oats by the number of "animal units" consuming oats, and write the quantity of oats demanded per animal unit as a function of deflated price (1913 = 100) and of time, we find that, other things being equal, an increase of one cent in price was associated with an average decrease in the annual consumption per animal unit of 0.59 bushel during the first period (1875–92); of 0.89 bushel in the second (1899–1914); and of 1.25 bushels in the third (1915–29, excluding 1917–23). If we translate these relations into terms of relative changes at the "representative points" on the demand surfaces, we find that an increase of 1 per cent in the deflated price was associated with a decrease in the consumption per animal unit of 0.54 per cent during the first period; of 0.77 per cent during the second; and of 0.60 per cent during the third.

2. If for "apparent consumption" we substitute "disappearance" (=production, plus imports, minus exports, minus changes in stocks)—and this series is available only for the second and the third periods—we find that the elasticities of demand for these periods were in fairly close agreement with that for the first. The conclusion is probably justified that the elasticity of demand for oats remained constant throughout the entire period from 1875 to 1929 and that it was of the order of −0.5 or −0.6.

3. During the first period the demand (apparent consumption) per animal unit shifted upward at the average rate of approximately 1 bushel (or 2.6 per cent) per annum but was subject to an annual retardation of $\frac{1}{10}$ of a bushel (or 0.36 per cent). During the second and third periods the demand curve was

[13] The pioneering study is that of Professor Henry L. Moore, who, in his *Economic Cycles* (New York, 1914), derived for the first time the demand curve for oats by applying the method of percentage changes to the data on production and prices from 1866 to 1911. The second investigation is that by Professor Hugh B. Killough. In his *What Makes the Price of Oats* (U.S. Dept. Agric. Bull. No. 1351 [September, 1925]), he experimented with various subdivisions of the quantity and price series for 1881–82 to 1922–23 and with the method of multiple correlation, his variables being (among others) the price of oats, production plus carry-over, and the Bureau of Labor Statistics index number of wholesale prices, each variable being expressed as a ratio to its trend. A third, and extremely brief, study is to be found in G. F. Warren and F. A. Pearson, *Interrelationships of Supply and Price* (Cornell University Agricultural Experiment Station Bull. No. 466 [March, 1928]), pp. 51–52. See also V. P. Timoshenko, "Correlations between Prices and Yields of Previous Years," *Journal of Political Economy*, XXXVI, No. 4 (1928), 510–15.

subject to no significant upward or downward shift. If, however, we substitute "disappearance" for "apparent consumption," we find that during the second period there was a downward shift of the demand curve from 1899 to about 1910 and a slight upward shift from 1910 to the end of the period. But the fluctuations of the observations about the curve which traces the rate of shift (curve $D_1'D_3'$, Fig. 79) exhibit such definite cyclical movements that the average rate given by the curve is of little or no significance. During the third period the curve shifted upward at the average rate of 1/2 bushel (or 1 per cent) per annum.

4. When we used the number of animal units not as a deflator but as an independent variable, it was found desirable to omit the time variable from the equations because of its very high correlation with the number of animal units. In all other respects, however, the demand functions in which the number of animal units appears as an explicit variable yield substantially the same results as did the functions in which this variable appeared as a deflator.

5. Has this shift continued since 1929? It is impossible to answer this question for the reason that the latest data on production and stocks are not comparable with those used in our computations. As we have already pointed out, in 1934 the United States Department of Agriculture discontinued the old series on stocks and constructed a new and radically different series which, however, it has carried back only to 1926. It also constructed a new price series (the season average price) which it has carried back to 1908. These series cannot conveniently be "spliced" on to the series which we have used.

The only procedure that seems practicable is to derive a new demand function for the third period from the new data and extrapolate it over the years 1930–34. This was actually done (graphically), and it was seen (a) that, contrary to our previous findings based on the old data, the demand curve exhibited a very rapid downward shift and (b) that the observations fluctuated violently about the demand function, that for 1932 being the most depressed. Perhaps this extreme deviation is due to the fact that at that time wheat was being substituted in large quantities for oats as a feed for cattle, since the price of wheat dropped to the lowest point in its history—thirty-eight cents per bushel.

The one conclusion that we may state unhesitatingly is that, until continuous series of more accurate data on production, stocks, prices, and distribution of oats, as well as on the number and kinds of livestock receiving oats are available, we shall not be able to make much further progress in the analysis of the demand for this important crop.

6. In Part III the demand for oats will be expressed as a function not only on the price of oats but also of the prices of barley, corn, and hay and of time.

CHAPTER XIII

THE DEMAND FOR BARLEY

CHAPTER XIII

THE DEMAND FOR BARLEY

I. THE FACTUAL BACKGROUND

Barley generally ranks eighth in value among the crops which we selected
for demand analyses and fourth among the cereal crops of the United States.
The production of barley increased from 195 million bushels in 1914 to 302
million bushels in 1932. Its farm value, however, declined from 106 million
dollars to 66 million dollars during the same period.[1]

The regions suitable for barley production are determined by physical and
economic factors. Barley, the "corn of the North," grows best in the cool
regions, directly north of the Corn Belt. It is for this reason that California
barley and the little barley that is grown in the South has to be sown in the fall
and winter to produce good results. Although barley requires well-drained
loam soils for the best yield, it can be grown profitably on poorer soils than can
wheat. Thus, much of the barley acreage in California consists of land which
has become too poor for wheat-growing. Because barley grows rapidly and
matures early, it can be seeded late in the spring when other crops such as
wheat and oats could no longer be sown successfully. This factor accounts for
a good deal of the barley crop of the Dakotas and Kansas especially when the
wheat-seeding has not been successful.

The increasing recognition of the value of barley as a feed has led to a wider
cultivation of the crop for local use. Under suitable conditions barley yields
more pounds of feed and digestible nutrients per acre than does any other
small grain. This factor, together with the decreased demand for oats following
the displacement of the horse by machines, has led many farmers to replace
oats with barley. In many regions barley is grown for the very excellent hay
which it makes when it is cut and cured properly. It is also often grown as a
winter and spring pasture crop which is readily eaten by all stock.

Barley has also several secondary uses. It fits in well in the farm rotation
between corn and wheat, or corn and grasses. It is the best nurse crop for
grasses and clover, for it provides a good shade and matures earlier than oats,
leaving more moisture in the soil for the grass. It is also an excellent cover crop
to keep the surface soil from being washed into the streams. An additional use
of barley is that of an aid in clearing the land of weeds: its growth smothers

[1] Excellent discussions of the economics of barley production may be found in the *U.S.D.A. Yearbook, 1922*, pp. 486–500, and in T. W. Schultz, *The Tariffs on Barley, Oats, and Corn* (Tariff Research
Committee, Madison, Wis.; Freeport, Ill.: Rawleigh Foundation, 1933), pp. 1–40.

many weed species, while its early maturity permits it to be cut before many of the weed seeds ripen. These secondary uses account for a considerable percentage of the barley crop.

Barley was first introduced by the Dutch and English settlers of the seaboard colonies and cultivated as one of their leading grain crops. In the decades which followed, the South gradually replaced barley with wheat, but New York increased its cultivation and became the dominant barley-producing area. Since the transportation of malt was expensive, the cultivation of barley for brewing spread into the interior with the westward movement of population. Following the discovery of gold in 1849, California became as important a barley-producing state as New York. Until the middle of the seventies these two states accounted for nearly one-half of the total annual barley production in the United States. Thereafter Wisconsin, Iowa, and Minnesota became prominent barley regions, producing more than a fourth of the total crop in 1879 and more than a third in 1889.

By 1889 there was a marked concentration of the areas growing barley for the malting market. On the favorable soils of western New York, southeastern Wisconsin, southeastern Minnesota, and northwestern Iowa, and in the central valley of California barley was grown as a money crop. At the same time production was increasing in the Red River Valley of Minnesota and North Dakota. The production of barley about Cincinnati decreased in the face of competition from the northern Mississippi Valley.

In 1890 the tariff on barley was raised to 30 cents per bushel. The malt houses of western New York had been securing part of their barley from Canada, but this tariff made the importation of barley unprofitable. The near-by supplies were insufficient and the malting industry was transferred to Wisconsin and Minnesota. In New York the area devoted to barley decreased after 1890. Production increased notably in Minnesota and California, also in eastern Washington and Oregon, in the Red River Valley, and in the central section of the Great Plains area.[2]

Beginning about 1900 the North Central area was the dominant barley-producing region, with California ranking second and the region of eastern Washington, eastern Oregon, and western Idaho ranking third. After 1910 there began, in all regions but California, a gradual drift away from barley as a money crop to barley as a feed crop. This shift has been most marked in the North Central group of states, where the percentage of barley moved from the county where grown decreased from 60 per cent in 1911 to 20 per cent in 1930. For the United States as a whole, these shipments declined from 55 per cent to 25 per cent during the same period.[3] In California, however, where the barley is of a higher quality and is grown principally for foreign brewers, shipments have increased.

The passage of the Eighteenth Amendment accelerated the shift to barley as a feed crop. The annual consumption of barley in the form of malt or liquor

[2] U.S. Dept. Agric., *Yearbook, 1922*, p. 494.   [3] T. W. Schultz, *op. cit.*, p. 11.

dropped from 21 pounds per capita during 1902–17 to 6 pounds per capita during prohibition.[4] With the brewing industry no longer dominating the barley market, farmers and buyers of feedstuffs increasingly turned to barley as an excellent feed. This process was reflected in the increased number of farms and the wider area devoted to barley and in the decreased percentage of barley moved from the county of origin. Prohibition had little effect on California, however, for, as we have seen, the barley of that state was grown principally for the export trade.

The shift in the areas of production was accompanied by a steady increase in the annual acreage and production of barley from 1875 until about 1910. Thereafter, except for the dip immediately after the passage of the Eighteenth Amendment, the average acreage remained on a fairly stationary level until 1927. Production, however, did fluctuate considerably as a result of changes in yield per acre from year to year. In 1927 a notable increase in acreage yielded the largest crop recorded up to that time—266 million bushels. In 1928 there was a still further increase to 350 million bushels, as a result of the great amount of winter-killed wheat in the Corn Belt. This new high level was maintained until the drought of 1933. In 1934 the acreage harvested dropped to 7 million acres yielding the smallest crop on record since 1900—119 million bushels. What the permanent effects of the repeal of the Eighteenth Amendment will be, we can only surmise.

The historical changes in the disposition of the barley crop have been no less striking than those in its production. Before 1890 the United States was definitely an importing country, the net imports amounting to approximately 15 per cent of the total production. Since then, however, it has become an exporting country with net exports usually amounting to between 10 and 15 per cent of the barley production. (In the last few years our exports have again become almost negligible.) Before the prohibition years, roughly 30 per cent of the crop went to the brewing industry. In the late twenties, however, the barley converted into malt constituted only about 10 per cent of the total production. The proportion of barley used as feed increased from about 55 per cent in 1910 to approximately 80 per cent during the years 1923–27. Of this portion, roughly four-fifths was consumed on the farms where grown. Less than 1 per cent of the total barley crop goes into the manufacture of pearl barley, barley flour, and breakfast foods.

II. FACTORS AFFECTING THE DEMAND FOR BARLEY

Since most of the barley crop is used for feed, it is evident that the quantity of barley demanded is a function not only of its price but also of the prices of

[4] *Ibid.*, p. 10, citing O. E. Baker, "Do We Need More Land?" U.S. Dept. Agric. Address before Agricultural Experimental Conference, University of Minnesota, December 13 and 14, 1929.

the other feeds, and of other factors which may be clubbed together under the heading "time." The interrelations of the prices of four feeds—barley, corn, hay, and oats—and their effect on the demand for barley—will be studied in Part III. In this chapter we shall consider only the simpler demand functions, i.e., those relating the quantity of barley demanded with price and time.

For the present purpose we shall take the quantity demanded in any year as synonymous with the consumption of that year and we shall define it as production, plus net imports (or minus net exports), minus net changes in stocks. Of these items, by far the most important is production. Imports and exports are second in importance, the foreign trade in barley having been appreciable in all years. Data relating to the carry-over from one year to the next are not available for the entire period covered by this study. Estimates of the visible supply on the Saturday nearest the first of each month are available since 1899, or for practically the last two periods, while estimates for old stocks on farms "based on percentage of entire crop as reported by crop reporters" are available only since 1910 or for little more than the third period.[5] The visible supply is negligible during the second period, amounting to only 0.6 of 1 per cent of the total production during the sixteen-year period, 1899–1914. We may, there-fore, neglect the visible supply for this period and consider only the combined effect of visible supply plus stocks on farms during the third period, 1915–29 (excluding 1917–21). For these years the absolute values of the differences be-tween total stocks at the beginning of the year and total stocks at the end of the year average less than 3 per cent of total production. Likewise, the *fluctua-tions* of the production-minus-net-export series, when corrected for net changes in stocks, differ very little from those of the uncorrected series, the former series sometimes lying slightly above and sometimes slightly below the latter series. Moreover, a preliminary graphic analysis indicates that the allowance for changes in net stocks would produce no significant effect on the shape of the demand curve, the production estimates being admittedly subject to greater errors. Accordingly, it was decided to make no allowance for changes in the stocks of barley during the third period. This is equivalent to defining the quantity of barley demanded or consumed as being very nearly equal to produc-tion plus imports, minus exports.

The price which we should like to have for each year is that which, if it had been maintained throughout the year, would have cleared the market. Two approximations to this ideal series are available—the December 1 farm price and the Chicago price. The former is an average price, weighted according to the production in each state, for all barley sold in the United States on Decem-

---

[5] U.S. Dept. Agric., *Statistics of Oats, Barley and Grain Sorghums* (Statistical Bull. No. 29), p. 127, and *Yearbook of Agriculture, 1931*, p. 646.

ber 1.[6] The latter is an August–July average quotation of choice-to-fancy or fair-to-good malting grades in Chicago. The two series have markedly diverging trends during 1875–95. Whereas the Chicago prices fluctuate about a slightly rising level, the farm prices show a definite downward trend. This downward trend appears to be due not to an actual decline in prices throughout the country but to a shifting of the areas of production, with the resulting changes in weights for the farm price series. Thus the farm price of 1875 is heavily weighted by the high-priced producing regions of New York and California, whereas the price of 1895 is more heavily weighted by the low-priced barley areas of the North Central states. This change in weights would be sufficient to give the farm price series a downward trend even though prices in each section throughout the country had actually been rising. After experimenting with the two series, it was decided to use the Chicago price in our investigations of the demand for barley.

As in the analyses of the preceding chapters, we shall deflate the price series by the Bureau of Labor Statistics "Index of Wholesale Prices" (average for year beginning August—1913 = 100) and reduce the consumption series to a per capita basis.

In our statistical analysis we shall first assume that the per capita consumption is a function of the deflated Chicago price and time:

(2.1) $$x = x(y, t) ,$$

and use both the arithmetic and logarithmic (constant-elasticity) equations as specific forms of (2.1). Then we shall repeat our analysis with price as the dependent variable:

(2.2) $$y = y(x, t) ,$$

again using both the arithmetic and the logarithmic equations, and compare the results obtained. In all our analyses we shall divide the data into the three periods: (I) 1875–95, (II) 1896–1914, and (III) 1915–29 (excluding 1917–21), in order to see the changes that have taken place in the shape, the elasticity, and the rate of shift of the demand curve.

III. DEMAND FUNCTIONS WITH PER CAPITA CONSUMPTION AS THE DEPENDENT VARIABLE[7]

Tables IIa and I of Appendix A give, for the period 1875–1929, the total consumption and the Chicago price of barley, together with the deflators of con-

---

[6] In 1934, after our major computations had already been completed, the United States Department of Agriculture published a weighted average farm price for the crop-marketing season. Since this series extends back only as far as 1919, it was not felt worth the while to recompute our equations by substituting the new series for the old.

[7] For an explanation of the statistical methods used and for definitions of the technical terms see chap. vi.

sumption and price. Table X of the same appendix gives the adjusted series—the per capita consumption, the deflated prices, and the per capita values—together with the link relatives and trend ratios of the quantities and prices. To facilitate comparison, the three adjusted series are graphed in Figure 84. Table 40 summarizes the more elementary statistical properties of the consumption and the price series in each of the three periods.

TABLE 40

BARLEY: SUMMARY BY PERIODS OF THE ADJUSTED DATA USED IN
DERIVING THE DEMAND FUNCTIONS, 1875–1929

PERIOD*	PER CAPITA CONSUMPTION $x(t)$				DEFLATED PRICE $y(t)$				CORRELATION COEFFICIENT
	Descriptive Constants								
	Mean (Bu.)	Median (Bu.)	Standard Deviation (Bu.)	Coefficient of Variation	Mean (Cents)	Median (Cents)	Standard Deviation (Cents)	Coefficient of Variation	r_{xy}
I	1.1658	1.138	0.1710	14.67	58.661	52.97	12.4069	21.15	+0.1344
II	1.6631	1.755	0.3115	18.73	70.716	66.83	17.1615	24.27	+0.2731
III	1.7646	1.619	0.3604	20.43	52.999	50.26	10.5274	19.86	−0.2736
	Equations of Trends								Origins
I	$x(t) = 1.1658 + 0.0217t$				$y(t) = 58.6614 + 0.8898t$				Jan. 1, 1886
II	$x(t) = 1.8205 + 0.0431t - 0.0052t^2$				$y(t) = 70.7163 + 1.6141t$				Jan. 1, 1906
III	$x(t) = 1.3528 + 0.0338t + 0.0161t^2$				$y(t) = 55.2501 - 1.5007t$				Jan. 1, 1923

* I = 1875–95; II = 1896–1914; III = 1915–29 (excl. 1917–21).

Figure 84 shows at a glance that even in the first two periods, when the trend of consumption and the trend of price are positively correlated with each other, the year-to-year changes of consumption and price show a negative correlation. Table 41 represents a quantitative measure of this correlation in the form of the equations connecting consumption, price, and time.

A. THE LINEAR REGRESSIONS

Equation 1 of this table, which relates to the first period, is the arithmetic form of the demand hypothesis (2.1). It shows that, other things being equal, an increase in the deflated price of barley of one cent per bushel was associated during this period with an average decrease in the annual per capita consumption of 0.0034 bushel (coefficient of y). But other things did not remain equal: the demand curve kept shifting upward at the rate of 0.0248 bushel per capita per annum (coefficient of t). That is, even if the deflated price had been kept constant, per capita consumption would have shown an average increase of

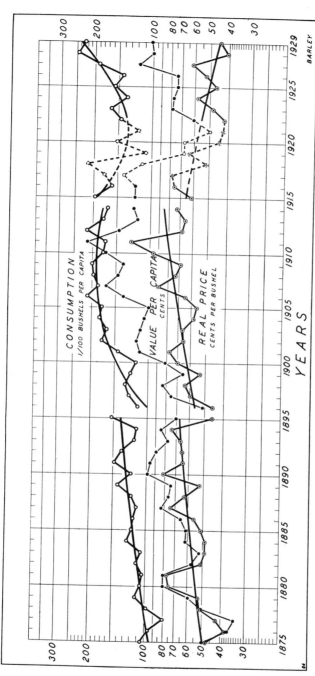

FIG. 84.—Barley: The basic adjusted annual data used in deriving the demand curves for barley in the United States, 1875–1929, with the computed trends by periods of the real prices and the per capita consumption. The dotted observations in the third period are those which are not used in the computations.

TABLE 41

BARLEY: THE CHARACTERISTICS OF THE PER CAPITA

x = Per capita consumption in bushels
y = Deflated Chicago price in cents per bushel

(Figures in parentheses are standard errors)

EQUA-TION No.	PERIOD*		EQUATIONS			
			Constant Term	y	t	t^2
1	I	$x=$	1.3649	-0.0034 (0.0022)	$+0.0248$ (0.0044)	. . . .
2	II	$x=$	2.1614	-0.0046 (0.0023)	$+0.0506$ (0.0072)	-0.0057 (0.0013)
3	III	$x=$	2.0656	-0.0135 (0.0078)	$+0.0143$ (0.0177)	$+0.0175$ (0.0035)
			Constant Term	y'	$\dagger Mt$	$\dagger Mt^2$
4	I	$x'=$	0.3522	-0.1585 (0.1197)	$+0.0213$ (0.0040)	-0.00072 (0.00068)
5	II	$x'=$	0.6573	-0.2151 (0.1142)	$+0.0328$ (0.0044)	-0.0038 (0.0008)
6	III	$x'=$	0.8055	-0.3870 (0.2361)	$+0.0069$ (0.0098)	$+0.0094$ (0.0020)
			Constant Term	x	t	t^2
7	I	$y=$	106.7771	-37.9987 (22.0903)	$+1.7156$ (0.6231)	-0.1041 (0.0738)
8	II	$y=$	155.5750	-45.0839 (22.6340)	$+3.5574$ (1.1495)	-0.3293 (0.1721)
9	III	$y=$	86.1942	-24.6887 (14.2541)	-0.6090 (0.7590)	$+0.5016$ (0.2710)
			Constant Term	x'	$\dagger Mt$	$\dagger Mt^2$
10	I	$y'=$	1.8283	-0.5901 (0.4455)	$+0.0271$ (0.0107)	-0.0021 (0.0013)
11	II	$y'=$	2.0880	-0.8887 (0.3572)	$+0.0470$ (0.0152)	-0.0046 (0.0022)
12	III	$y'=$	1.8294	-0.7991 (0.4875)	-0.0121 (0.0138)	$+0.0087$ (0.0051)

* I = 1875–95; II = 1896–1914; III = 1915–29 (excl. 1917–21).
† $M = \log_{10} e = 0.43429$.

TABLE 41—*Continued*

DEMAND FUNCTIONS, BY PERIODS, 1875–1929

t = Time in years. For origins see Table 40
x', y' = Logs of x and y

(Figures in parentheses are standard errors)

DESCRIPTIVE CONSTANTS

	Elasticity of Demand η	Quadratic Mean Error ϵ (Bushels)	Adjusted Multiple Correlation Coefficient R'	Percentage of Variance of Consumption Attributable to		EQUATION No.
				y	t	
. . . .	−0.1708 (0.1330)	0.1106	0.7756	− 3.31	67.45	1
. . . .	−0.1789 (0.1145)	0.1474	0.8877	− 6.98	89.32	2
. . . .	−0.5300 (0.4171)	0.1935	0.8606	10.79	71.92	3
	η	ϵ (Per Cent)	R'	y'	t	
. . . .	−0.1585 (0.1197)	90.7–110.2	0.7628	− 5.10	69.56	4
. . . .	−0.2151 (0.1142)	91.7–109.1	0.9041	− 8.67	93.46	5
. . . .	−0.3870 (0.2361)	89.7–111.5	0.8494	9.94	71.48	6

Flexibility of Price φ	Maximum Value of η $1/\varphi$	ϵ (Cents)	R'	Percentage of Variance of Price Attributable to		
				x	t	
−0.7090 (0.5605)	−1.4104	11.0199	0.4986	− 7.03	43.17	7
−0.9303 (0.6756)	−1.0749	14.5108	0.5681	−22.34	65.90	8
−1.0220 (0.8581)	−0.9784	8.2749	0.6663	23.13	39.80	9
φ	$1/\varphi$	ϵ (Per Cent)	R'	x'	t	
−0.5991 (0.4455)	−1.6947	82.9–120.6	0.4960	− 9.20	45.11	10
−0.8887 (0.3572)	−1.1252	83.8–119.4	0.6074	−30.01	77.41	11
−0.7991 (0.4875)	−1.2514	85.5–116.9	0.6268	21.67	37.86	12

0.0248 bushel per annum. From these two coefficients it is clear that fluctuations in price had only a slight effect on the changes in per capita consumption during 1875-95, the shift in the demand curve having had a preponderant influence.

The net relation between consumption and price can, perhaps, be stated more significantly when it is converted into an elasticity of demand. True, the coefficient of elasticity of a linear demand function varies from point to point. But, since this function passes through the means of all the variables, we may take as a representative point on it that point whose ordinates are the arithmetic means of x, y, and t.[8] At this point the elasticity of demand is −0.1708. This figure means that, if the average price has been increased (or decreased) by 1 per cent, and *if the demand curve had remained fixed for one year*, there would have been a decrease (or increase) of only 0.17 of 1 per cent in the annual per capita consumption.

That factors other than price (which we designated by the variable "time") had a preponderant effect on the consumption of barley is also evident from the percentages of the variance of consumption which may be imputed to each of the two independent variables—price and time. The direct and indirect contribution of price to the variance of consumption is negligible (−3.31 per cent), whereas the corresponding contributions of the factors represented by t is 67.45 per cent.[9]

Equation 2 of Table 41 gives the slope and the rate of shift of the demand curve for the second period. By comparing the coefficient of y with its standard error, we see that per capita consumption was not significantly more responsive to a unit change in price during this period than during the first. An increase of one cent per bushel was still associated with a decrease of only 0.0046 ± 0.0023 of a bushel in the per capita consumption. However, the shift of the demand curve was even more pronounced during this period than during the first. The coefficients of t and t^2 show that, even if the deflated price of barley had been kept constant, per capita consumption would have increased 0.05 bushel per annum but that this increase would have been subject to a retardation of 0.0114 bushel, for

$$(3.1) \qquad \frac{\partial x}{\partial t} = 0.0506 - 2(0.0057)t .$$

This retardation had the effect of giving the demand curve an upward shift until about 1910 and a downward shift from that date.

---

[8] These are given in Table 40.

[9] The *direct* contribution of y (not shown in Table 41) is 6.06 per cent, and its joint contribution with t is −9.37 per cent, thus yielding −3.31 per cent. See chap. vi for a more detailed explanation of these terms.

Equation 3 relates to the third period. This period saw a decided change in the slope and in the rate of shift of the demand curve. During this period a one cent increase in price, other things being equal, was associated with a decrease in consumption of a little more than 0.01 bushel. But other things did not remain equal, for the curve shifted downward from 1915 to 1922 and upward from 1922 to 1929.[10]

Equations 1, 2, and 3 give equally good fits to their respective observations: the adjusted coefficients of multiple correlation are all of the order of 0.8, approximately.

B. THE LOGARITHMIC REGRESSIONS

Equations 4, 5, and 6 are the logarithmic forms of the demand hypothesis (2.1). From the coefficient of y' in equation 4 we see that, other things being equal, an increase (or decrease) of 1 per cent in the deflated price of barley brought about a decrease (or increase) of 0.16 of 1 per cent in the annual per capita consumption. This value differs only slightly from the coefficient of elasticity of demand from the first equation. The coefficients of t and t^2 (see chap. vi, n. 20) of the same equation express the shift of the demand curve in relative terms, for

$$(3.2) \qquad \frac{1}{M} \cdot \frac{\partial x'}{\partial t} = \frac{\partial \log_e x}{\partial t} = 0.0213 - 2(0.0007)t \, .$$

From this expression we see that the curve shifted upward and to the right at the average rate of 2 per cent per annum but that it was subject to an annual retardation of 0.14 of 1 per cent. But, since this retardation coefficient exceeds its standard error only slightly, it is of little statistical significance.

Figure 85 is a graphic representation of equation 4. Figure 85A is a scatter diagram of the logarithms of per capita consumption (x') on those of real price (y'). The slope of the line $D_1'D_2'$ measures the net regression of x' on y' when both variables are linearly corrected for changes in time. Its numerical value is the elasticity of demand and is given by the coefficient of y'. In Figure 85B the differences between the observed and computed values of x' are plotted against time. The slope of the curve $D_1'D_3'$ measures the *average* rate of shift of the demand curve given by equation (3.2) above. Figure 85C shows the reduced scatter about the demand curve $D_1'D_2'$ after x' has been corrected for changes in t. The large scatter which still remains in Figure 85C is reflected in the comparatively large value of the standard error of the coefficient of y' in equation 4 (or of the slope of $D_1'D_2'$).

Equations 5 and 6 relate, respectively, to the second and third periods.

[10] Since the data for 1917–21 were not included in the computations, the downward shift from 1915 to 1922 does not have much significance.

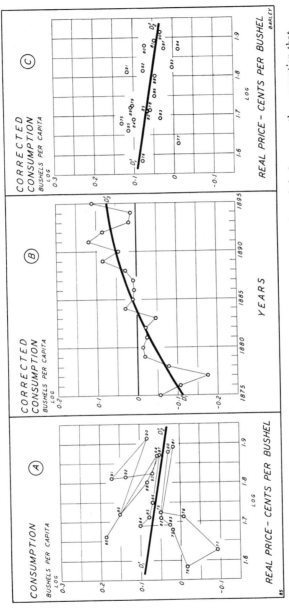

FIG. 85.—Barley: Three aspects of the per capita demand for barley during the period 1875–95 on the assumption that

$$x = 2.250 \, y^{-0.1585} \, e^{0.0213t - 0.0007t^2} \, .$$

A: Relation between per capita consumption and real price when the data are not corrected for the effects of "time," with the demand curve $D_1'D_2'$ which results when such corrections are made.

B: Relation between the per capita consumption and time when the former is corrected for the effects of changes in the real price. The slope of line $D_1'D_3'$ (fitted to the variables x' and t when both are corrected for price) represents the mean rate of shift of the per capita demand curve $D_1'D_2'$.

C: The per capita demand curve for barley, 1875–95. Line $D_1'D_2'$ shows the relation between that part of the per capita consumption of barley in the United States which is independent of time and that part of the real price which is independent of time. In the scatter, however, only the ordinate is corrected for secular changes, the abscissa being uncorrected.

Figures 86 and 87 summarize the three aspects of these equations more clearly than can be done in words. Although the scatter diagram of the observations in Figure 86A gives the appearance of a disorganized swarm, the year-to-year changes in consumption appear to be negatively correlated with the corresponding changes in price. Line $D_1'D_2'$ is a measure of this relationship. It gives the *net* relation between that part of the logarithm of per capita consumption which is linearly independent of time and that part of the logarithm of the deflated price which is linearly independent of time. The slope of this line—given by the coefficient of y' in equation 5—is the elasticity of demand.

In Figure 86B the deviations of the observed values from the computed values of x' are plotted against time. The curve $D_1'D_3'$ fitted to these data traces the direction and the relative rate of shift of the demand curve $D_1'D_2'$. It shows that the demand curve shifted upward until about 1910, and downward from 1910 to 1914. It is this shift which accounts for most of the scatter of Figure 86A. When allowance is made for the trend of this shift, we obtain the reduced scatter of Figure 86C. It should be observed that the reduced scatter about the line $D_1'D_2'$ for the second period (Fig. 86C) is considerably less than the corresponding scatter for the first period (Fig. 85C).

Figure 87 brings into clear relief the changes which took place in the third period. They are: (1) the increase in the numerical value of the elasticity of demand, which is indicated by the greater slope of the line $D_1'D_2'$, and (2) the change in the direction and in the rate of shift of the demand curve, which is indicated by the U-shaped curve $D_1'D_3'$. (The graphs for the three periods have been drawn to the same scale and are, therefore, comparable with one another.) This diagram shows quite clearly the increasing rate at which the demand curve shifted upward despite the ratification of the Eighteenth Amendment. The rapid increase in the demand for barley which took place from 1922 to 1929 was undoubtedly the result of the greater use of barley as a feed crop.

A possible explanation of the increase in the numerical value of the elasticity of demand during the third period is the decrease in the use of barley for brewing purposes and the increase in its use as a feed crop, which took place during this period. But the differences between the elasticities of demand for the three periods are not statistically significant, and it is idle to speculate on the possible causes of these supposed divergences.

The logarithmic equations 4, 5, and 6 fit the data about as well as do the corresponding arithmetic equations 1, 2, and 3. Figures 85C, 86C, and 87C show, however, that even the adjusted observations do not lie very closely about the demand curves. This is probably due to errors in the original production and price series.

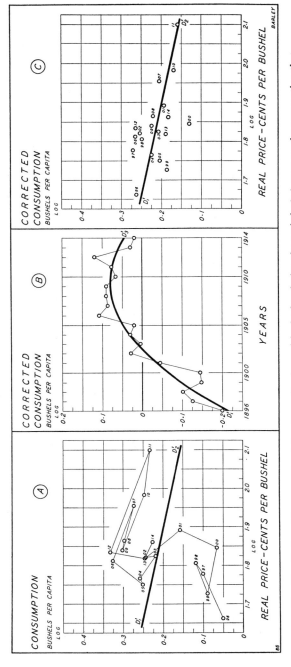

Fig. 86.—Barley: Three aspects of the per capita demand for barley during the period 1896–1914 on the assumption that

$$x = 4 \cdot 542 \, y^{-0.2151} \, e^{0.0328 \, t - 0.0038 \, t^2} \, .$$

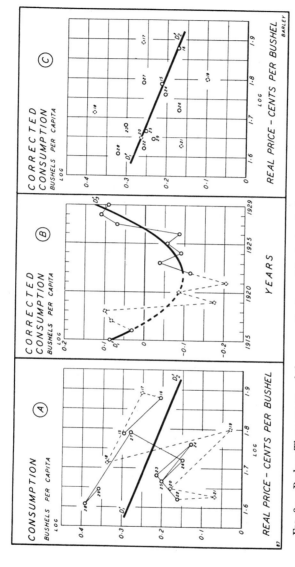

Fig. 87.—Barley: Three aspects of the per capita demand for barley during the period 1915–29 (excluding 1917–21) on the assumption that

$$x = 6.391 \, y^{-0.3870} \, e^{0.0069t + 0.0094t^2} \, .$$

479

IV. DEMAND FUNCTIONS WITH DEFLATED PRICE
AS THE DEPENDENT VARIABLE

Equations 7–12 of Table 41 are the specific forms of the demand hypothesis (2.2), the first three being the arithmetic equations and the last three being the logarithmic equations.

Equation 7, which relates to the first period, signifies that, *other things being equal*, an increase (or decrease) of one bushel in the annual per capita consumption of barley was, on the average, associated with a decrease (or increase) in the deflated price of 38 cents per bushel (coefficient of x). But the other things did not remain equal: the deflated price kept increasing at the average rate of 1.72 cents per annum, although it was subject to an annual retardation of 0.21 cents, for

$$(4.1) \qquad\qquad \frac{\partial y}{\partial t} = 1.7156 - 2(0.1041)t .$$

The quadratic mean error of equation 7 is, however, rather large—11 cents— and the adjusted multiple correlation coefficient is rather small—0.50—so that any price computed from equation 7 would be subject to a large error of estimate. This is clearly brought out by the graph of this equation (not reproduced here), which shows that some of the observations—especially those for the years 1877, 1880, 1881, and 1890—deviate very widely from the computed demand surface.

Equation 8 means that, during the second period, an increase of one bushel in the annual per capita consumption of barley was associated with a net average decrease in the deflated price of 45 cents per bushel; but that, even if the per capita consumption had been kept constant, the deflated price would have increased by 3.56 cents per annum, subject to a retardation of 0.66 cents per annum. This retardation had the effect of giving the demand curve a downward shift since about 1910.

Equation 9 tells us that, during the third period, important changes took place in the reaction of price to changes both in consumption and in the shift of the demand curve with time. During this period an increase of one bushel in the annual per capita consumption, other things being equal, was associated with a decrease in the deflated price of only 25 cents per bushel. However, even if the per capita consumption had been fixed, the deflated price would have decreased until about 1923 and increased from 1923 to 1929.

Equations 10, 11, and 12, Table 41, express the relation between price, consumption, and time for the three periods in relative terms. Thus, equation 10 means that, during the first period, an increase (or decrease) of 1 per cent in the per capita consumption for any given year was associated with an average decrease (or increase) of 0.59 of 1 per cent in the deflated price (coefficient of x').

This is the coefficient of the flexibility of price with respect to consumption. However, even if per capita consumption had been fixed, the deflated price would have increased by 2.71 per cent per annum, subject to a retardation of 0.42 per cent per annum, for

$$(4.2) \qquad \frac{1}{M} \cdot \frac{\partial y'}{\partial t} = \frac{\partial \log_e y}{\partial t} = 0.0271 - 2(0.0021)t.$$

Equations 11 and 12 are interpreted in an analogous manner. They show that the price flexibilities were approximately equal (−0.9 or −0.8) in the second and third periods but that the shift of the demand curve (i.e., the regression of y' on t) was of a radically different nature in the third period from what it was in the second. In the second period, the demand curve moved upward at an average annual rate of 4.7 per cent, subject to a retardation of 0.92 per cent per annum (resulting in a downward shift beginning with 1910). In the third period it moved downward until about 1923 and then upward until 1929, thus describing a U-shaped trace. The upward shift since 1923 is probably the result of the increased use of barley as a feed which followed the adoption of the Eighteenth Amendment.

Equations 7–12 give a poorer fit to the data than do the corresponding equations 1–6. This is in harmony with the conclusion derived in chapter iv, Section III, that, since the price series is relatively more trustworthy than the consumption series, the regression of price on consumption is not so good an approximation to the true demand curve as is the regression of consumption on price.

V. SUMMARY

Although barley is a fairly important crop, we have been able to find no mathematical investigations into the demand for barley. The main findings of the present chapter center around the changes that have taken place in the shape, the elasticity, and the rate of shift of the demand curve since 1875, and of the factors which account for them.

To summarize:

1. The demand curve for barley appears to have undergone fairly large structural changes during the fifty-five years from 1875 to 1929. Thus, our equations show that the net effect of a one cent increase in the price per bushel (in terms of the 1913 dollar) was to decrease the annual per capita consumption by 0.0034 bushel during 1875–95, by 0.0046 bushel during 1896–1914, and by 0.0135 bushel during 1915–29. However, as these figures are subject to comparatively large standard errors, no significance can be attached to differences between them.

2. The partial elasticity of the demand was approximately −0.16 during the first period, −0.22 during the second, and −0.39 during the third, but the

difference between any two of these coefficients is also insignificant, for it is exceeded by its standard error. All that it is safe to assert, on the basis of our findings, is that within the range of our observations the demand for barley is quite inelastic: a 1 per cent increase in price reduces consumption by considerably less than 1 per cent.

3. During the period 1875–95 the demand curve shifted upward at the average rate of 0.0248 bushel per capita per annum. During the period 1896–1914 the upward rate of shift was 0.0506 bushel, but it was being retarded at the average rate of 0.0114 bushel per capita per annum. These figures are statistically significant. During the period 1915–29 the demand curve shifted downward until about 1923 and then upward at a very rapid rate until 1929.

In relative terms, the rate of shift of the demand curve was 2.13 per cent per annum during the first period and 3.28 per cent per annum during the second period, when it was being retarded at the rate of 0.76 per cent per annum. From 1922 to 1929—the curve shifted downward from 1915 to 1922— the upward shift averaged over 2 per cent. This shift was undoubtedly the result of the greater use of barley as a feed crop following the ratification of the Eighteenth Amendment.[11]

4. Changes in the price of barley had a very small effect on consumption as compared with the changes in the position of the demand curve. This indicates, of course, that we have not succeeded in isolating some very important factors affecting the demand for barley.

5. Changes in the price of barley cannot be explained satisfactorily by changes in consumption and by regular shifts in the demand curve. Other important factors were effectively at work, but the existing data do not permit an isolation of them.

[11] It would not do to extrapolate the equations for the third period to 1936–37 since the United States Department of Agriculture has revised its production series. As this chapter goes to press, the latest year for which the basic production and price series are available is 1935. (The figures for the crop year 1936 are preliminary estimates.) A rough graphical analysis of the latest revised data for 1922–35 shows large fluctuations with no discernible trend.

CHAPTER XIV

THE DEMAND FOR RYE

CHAPTER XIV

THE DEMAND FOR RYE

I. THE FACTUAL BACKGROUND

Compared with the other crops which we have studied, rye is of relatively little economic importance in the United States. It forms less than 1 per cent of the total value of all crops and covers at most 2 per cent of the total acreage. It is, however, of considerable importance in the North Central states.

The areas of rye production are determined by physical and economic conditions.

1. Rye, "the grain of poverty," can be grown under conditions too poor for the successful cultivation of wheat, corn, or barley. It germinates and grows when the temperature is just above freezing and may, therefore, be sown later in the fall than can other grains. Because of its ability to grow on sandy, exposed, poor, and acid lands, it is the leading winter grain crop on the acid, lime-requiring soils of northern Pennsylvania and southern New York. It is also frequently sown on newly cleared timberland and drained marshland which are likely to be acid in reaction. Rye uses less nitrogen per pound of crop produced than does wheat and can, therefore, be grown with less exhaustion of the nitrogen supply. In New England it is often the first crop in a rotation designed to build up worn-out soils.

2. Rye is grown in many southern states as a winter cover crop to prevent erosion and leaching, as well as to increase the vegetable matter in the soil.

3. In the Corn Belt rye is frequently sown in the standing corn and plowed under in the spring as a green-manure crop.

4. Rye is used extensively in Michigan as a nurse crop for grass and clover.

5. Rye is the best cereal for pasture, since it grows upright and is more cold-resisting than the other cereals.

6. Rye straw, which is long and tough, is excellent for bedding horses, stuffing horse collars, packing, and manufacturing paper. Near the large cities of New York, New Jersey, and Pennsylvania the demand for rye straw for such purposes often makes it more valuable than the grain.[1]

Rye was introduced into the United States by the early settlers of Massachusetts, New York, Maryland, and Georgia. In New England, where wheat did not thrive well and wheat flour was not available (prior to the development of the wheat industry in western New York), rye and corn meal were the main

[1] C. E. Leighty, *Culture of Rye in the Eastern Half of the United States* (U.S. Dept. Agric., Farmers Bull. No. 756 [October 11, 1916]), pp. 7–8.

breadstuffs. In 1839, the date of the first agricultural census, the total rye production was over eighteen million bushels, a figure higher in proportion to the population than that for any other census year. The area of production was centered in the district covered by southeastern New York, northern New Jersey, eastern Pennsylvania, and central Maryland. In the years following, production fluctuated irregularly, but a new area of rye cultivation was being developed in the central states of Ohio, Illinois, Wisconsin, and Michigan. By 1889, Wisconsin was the leading rye state, producing approximately 15 per cent of the total United States crop (four and one-quarter million bushels). Production continued to fluctuate considerably from year to year as a result of changes in acreage and even greater changes in yield per acre. There was apparent, however, a gradual increase in production from the beginning of our period until about 1911 and a more rapid increase thereafter. Michigan, Wisconsin, and Minnesota now became the leading rye states, averaging approximately five million bushels each in 1909, out of a total of twenty-nine and one-half million bushels for the United States. During the World War there was a marked increase in production, owing to the enlarged foreign demand and the restrictions placed on the use of wheat. In 1919 the United States' production was over seventy-five million bushels, of which North Dakota alone produced over sixteen million bushels, Michigan twelve million, and Minnesota more than eight million. This higher production level persisted until about 1924, the record crop—over one hundred million bushels—being attained in 1922. Thereafter production declined considerably, reaching thirty-two millions in 1931, and the extremely low figure of sixteen millions in the drought year, 1934. In 1935, however, production rose to fifty-eight million bushels.

Rye is of much less importance in the United States than in Europe. During the five-year period 1910–14 approximately 96 per cent of the world rye crop was produced in Europe, and only 2 per cent in the United States. Rye is not very popular in the United States for making flour, the preference being decidedly in favor of the more palatable and attractive breads and cakes made from wheat flour. Although a large portion of the crop is used as food for domestic animals, rye is not a popular feed and is unlikely to replace barley, corn, and oats. Before the war over five million bushels were used annually in distilling alcohols. During the war, however, and after the passage of the Eighteenth Amendment the use of rye for distilling declined rapidly. The decreased demand for these purposes was, however, more than offset by the increased foreign demand. Thus during the years 1914–28 our net exports of rye fluctuated in amount between one-fourth and three-fourths of the entire crop for each year. Since 1928, however, our net exports have been very small, owing to increased production abroad, tariff restrictions, and subsidies of exports by foreign governments.

II. FACTORS AFFECTING THE DEMAND FOR RYE

Since rye has many uses—for making bread, for distilling, and for feeding livestock—the American demand for it must be defined in its broad sense as the aggregate of the quantities which will be utilized for all purposes at a given price. According to this definition, the quantity demanded in any year should be given by the production of that year, minus net exports (or plus net imports), minus net changes in stocks. Unfortunately, it is impossible to take the last item into consideration, since data on the carry-over from year to year do not exist for the entire period (1875–1929) covered by our demand analyses, and such estimates as do exist are incomplete and unreliable.[2] Our exports of rye, however, have been considerable during the period studied. In our demand analyses we shall, therefore, consider the quantity demanded in any year as approximately equal to production minus net exports.

The price series which we shall take for our analysis is the December 1 farm price. This is an average price, weighted according to the production in each state of all rye sold in the United States on December 1. Since 1934 the United States Department of Agriculture has published an average farm price weighted for the crop-marketing season. However, this series has been carried back only as far as 1919 and, consequently, could not be used in our investigations.

As in the preceding chapters, the consumption data will be reduced to a per capita basis and the prices will be deflated by the Bureau of Labor Statistics "Index of Wholesale Prices." The other factors which affect the demand for rye will be clubbed together under the catch-all variable, time.

In our statistical analyses we shall first assume that the per capita consumption is a function of the deflated December 1 farm price and time,

$$(2.1) \qquad x = x(y, t) ,$$

and use both the arithmetic and the logarithmic (constant-elasticity) equations as specific forms of (2.1). Then we shall repeat our analysis with price as the dependent variable,

$$(2.2) \qquad y = y(x, t) ,$$

again using both the arithmetic and the logarithmic equations, and compare the results obtained. As in the preceding chapters, we shall divide the data into the three periods: (I) 1875–95, (II) 1896–1914, and (III) 1915–29 (excluding 1917–21).

---

[2] Figures relating to the visible supply of rye in the United States on the Saturday nearest the first of each month for the years 1909–24 are published in the U.S. Dept. Agric., *Statistical Bulletin*, No. 12, p. 105.

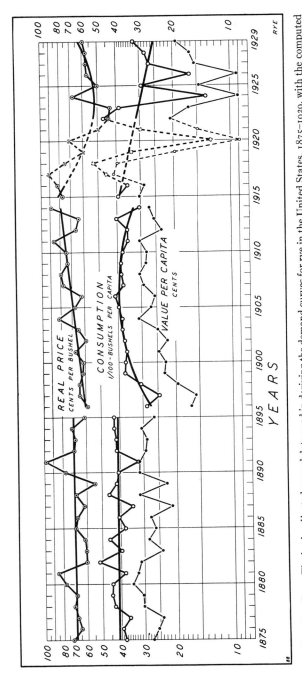

FIG. 88.—Rye: The basic adjusted annual data used in deriving the demand curves for rye in the United States, 1875–1929, with the computed trends by periods of the real prices and the per capita consumption. The dotted observations in the third period are those which are not used in the computations.

III. DEMAND FUNCTIONS WITH PER CAPITA CONSUMPTION AS THE DEPENDENT VARIABLE[3]

Table XI of Appendix A lists for 1875–1929 the per capita consumption (=production plus imports minus exports), the deflated prices, and the per capita value of rye, together with the link relatives and trend ratios of the consumption and the price series. Tables I and IIa of the same appendix give the deflators and the basic (unadjusted) data of total consumption and money prices. Figure 88 is a graphic representation of the per capita consumption, deflated price, and per capita value series. Table 42 summarizes, by periods,

TABLE 42

RYE: SUMMARY BY PERIODS OF THE ADJUSTED DATA USED IN DERIVING THE DEMAND FUNCTIONS, 1875–1929

PERIOD*	PER CAPITA CONSUMPTION $x(t)$				DEFLATED PRICE $y(t)$				CORRELATION COEFFICIENT
	Descriptive Constants								
	Mean (Bu.)	Median (Bu.)	Standard Deviation (Bu.)	Coefficient of Variation	Mean (Cents)	Median (Cents)	Standard Deviation (Cents)	Coefficient of Variation	r_{xy}
I	0.4114	0.419	0.0431	10.48	69.3040	68.372	9.4694	13.66	−0.4422
II	0.3586	0.372	0.0422	11.78	69.8783	66.300	9.0794	12.99	+0.0266
III	0.3054	0.307	0.0973	31.87	59.5310	57.483	12.2630	20.60	−0.1692
	Equations of Trends								Origins
I	$x(t) = 0.4114 + 0.00013t$				$y(t) = 69.3040 + 0.0769t$				Jan. 1, 1886
II	$x(t) = 0.3935 + 0.0032t − 0.0012t^2$				$y(t) = 69.8783 + 1.0313t$				Jan. 1, 1906
III	$x(t) = 0.3202 − 0.0098t$				$y(t) = 52.8204 − 1.3623t + 0.3891t^2$				Jan. 1, 1923

* I = 1875–95; II = 1896–1914; III = 1915–29 (excl. 1917–21).

the more elementary statistical properties of the per capita consumption and deflated price series.

Table 43 is a descriptive summary of the changes that have taken place in the shape, elasticity, and rate of shift of the demand curve from 1875 to 1929. We turn first to the linear forms of hypothesis (2.1).

A. THE LINEAR REGRESSIONS

From the coefficient of y in the first equation we see that, other things being equal, an increase (or decrease) of one cent in the (deflated) price of rye during the first period was associated with an average decrease (or increase) of 0.002

[3] For an explanation of the statistical methods used and for definitions of the technical terms see chap. vi.

TABLE 43

RYE: THE CHARACTERISTICS OF THE PER CAPITA

x = Per capita consumption in bushels
y = Deflated December 1 farm price in cents per bushel

(Figures in parentheses are standard errors)

EQUA-TION No.	PERIOD*		EQUATIONS			
			Constant Term	y	t	t^2
1	I	$x=$	0.5517	$-$ 0.0020 (0.0010)	$+$0.0003 (0.0015)	. . . .
2	II	$x=$	0.5372	$-$ 0.0020 (0.0006)	$+$0.0053 (0.0010)	$-$0.0012 (0.0002)
3	III	$x=$	0.8828	$-$ 0.0108 (0.0023)	$-$0.0244 (0.0049)	$+$0.0044 (0.0013)
			Constant Term	y'	$\dagger Mt$	$\dagger Mt^2$
4	I	$x'=$	0.2742	$-$ 0.3605 (0.1755)	$+$0.0005 (0.0037)	. . . .
5	II	$x'=$	0.4044	$-$ 0.4374 (0.1466)	$+$0.0163 (0.0033)	$-$0.0037 (0.0005)
6	III	$x'=$	3.6298	$-$ 2.4444 (0.4569)	$-$0.0766 (0.0155)	$-$0.0199 (0.0045)
			Constant Term	x	t	t^2
7	I	$y=$	109.3435	$-$ 97.3144 (46.3263)	$+$0.0900 (0.3300)	. . . .
8	II	$y=$	149.2165	$-$ 200.3253 (62.1972)	$+$1.6712 (0.3249)	$-$0.2500 (0.0895)
9	III	$y=$	75.7304	$-$ 72.7953 (15.6517)	$-$2.0689 (0.3399)	$+$0.4061 (0.0753)
			Constant Term	x'	$\dagger Mt$	$\dagger Mt^2$
10	I	$y'=$	1.6326	$-$ 0.5268 (0.2564)	$+$0.0007 (0.0045)	. . . .
11	II	$y'=$	1.5024	$-$ 0.8516 (0.2858)	$+$0.0229 (0.0046)	$-$0.0034 (0.0013)
12	III	$y'=$	1.5241	$-$ 0.3382 (0.0632)	$-$0.0292 (0.0052)	$+$0.0079 (0.0012)

* I = 1875–95; II = 1896–1914; III = 1915–29 (excl. 1917–21).

TABLE 43—*Continued*

DEMAND FUNCTIONS, BY PERIODS, 1875–1929

t = Time in years. For origins see Table 42

x', y' = Logs of x and y

(Figures in parentheses are standard errors)

	DESCRIPTIVE CONSTANTS					EQUA-TION No.
	Elasticity of Demand η	Quadratic Mean Error ϵ (Bushels)	Adjusted Multiple Correlation Coefficient R'	Percentage of Variance of Consumption Attributable to		
				y	t	
. . . .	−0.3408 (0.2072)	0.0417	0.3286	19.64	0.08	1
. . . .	−0.3615 (0.1412)	0.0196	0.8923	− 1.17	84.19	2
. . . .	−2.9645 (1.5561)	0.0521	0.8615	22.92	59.90	3
	η	ϵ (Per Cent)	R'	y'	t	
. . . .	−0.3605 (0.1755)	90.2–110.8	0.3167	18.96	0.06	4
. . . .	−0.4374 (0.1466)	94.0–106.4	0.8842	− 2.79	84.61	5
. . . .	−2.4444 (0.4569)	83.4–119.9	0.8866	29.58	56.15	6
Flexibility of Price φ	Maximum Value of η $1/\varphi$	ϵ (Cents)	R'	Percentage of Variance of Price Attributable to		
				x	t	
−0.5777 (0.3649)	−1.7309	9.1550	0.3314	19.60	0.28	7
−0.9284 (0.3877)	−1.0771	6.1386	0.7530	− 2.48	66.39	8
−0.4333 (0.1754)	−2.3078	4.2862	0.9434	9.78	82.89	9
φ	$1/\varphi$	ϵ (Per Cent)	R'	x'	t	
−0.5268 (0.2564)	−1.8983	88.3–113.2	0.3170	18.96	0.08	10
−0.8516 (0.2858)	−1.1742	91.7–109.1	0.7395	− 5.77	68.01	11
−0.3382 (0.0632)	−2.9569	93.5–107.0	0.9490	13.73	79.65	12

† $M = \log_{10} e = 0.43429$.

bushel in the per capita consumption of rye. Translated in terms of the elasticity of demand for a representative point on the demand curve[4] this relationship means that, if the average price had been increased (or decreased) by 1 per cent, and *if the demand curve had remained fixed for one year*, there would have been a decrease (or increase) of 0.34 of 1 per cent in the annual per capita consumption.

Changes in the position of the demand curve apparently had no effect on the per capita consumption of rye during the first period, for the demand curve exhibited no upward or downward shift.

That "time" had no effect on changes in consumption may also be seen from the percentage of the variance in consumption which is attributable to each of the independent variables. The contribution of "time" to the variance of consumption is negligible, whereas the contribution of price is 19.64 per cent. However, since the reduction in the total variance of consumption attributable to the independent variables is only 19.72 per cent, it is obvious that we have failed to give a full explanation of the factors affecting the consumption of rye during the years 1875–95. This is also evident from the fairly high quadratic mean error, 0.04 bushel per capita, or 10 per cent of the average consumption, and the low value of the adjusted coefficient of multiple correlation, 0.3286. Had we omitted the variable t from our equation, this last coefficient would have been somewhat higher (0.3914), but the coefficient of y and the elasticity of demand would have remained approximately the same.

Equation 2 relates to the second period. The average effect of changes in the (deflated) price on the per capita consumption of rye was the same during this period as in the first period. There was, however, a marked change in the rate of shift of the demand curve. The coefficients of t and t^2 show that the demand curve moved upward at the rate of 0.0053 bushel per capita per annum subject to an annual retardation of 0.0024 bushel per capita, for

$$(3.1) \qquad \frac{\partial x}{\partial t} = 0.0053 - 2(0.0012)t .$$

This retardation had the effect of giving the demand curve a downward shift from about 1907 to the end of the period.

This equation gives a fairly good fit to the data, as can be judged from the fairly high value of the adjusted coefficient of multiple correlation (0.8923). Nevertheless, it is not a very satisfactory explanation of the factors affecting the consumption of rye, for the variance of consumption is attributable entirely to the unspecified factors which we have clubbed together under the variable "time."

[4] As explained in chap. vi (III, D, 2, b), the representative value of y is taken as the arithmetic mean, and the representative value of x is obtained by substituting the mean values of the independent variables y and t in the demand equation. In this equation the representative value of x is also the arithmetic mean.

Equation 3 gives the corresponding information for the third period. During this period striking changes took place both in the elasticity of demand and in the shift of the demand curve. An increase of one (deflated) cent in the price of rye was now associated with a decrease in the per capita consumption of 0.01 bushel, instead of 0.002 bushel as in the first and second periods. If we translate this relationship in terms of relative changes, we see that the demand for rye was definitely elastic during this period, for a 1 per cent increase in the price of rye, other things being equal, was associated with a decrease in the per capita consumption of 2.96 per cent. However, even if the price of rye had remained fixed, the consumption would have decreased from 1915 to 1925 and would have increased from 1925 to 1929, for

(3.2)
$$\frac{\partial x}{\partial t} = -0.0244 + 2(0.0044)t .$$

B. THE LOGARITHMIC REGRESSIONS

Equations 4, 5, 6 are the logarithmic forms of hypothesis (2.1) for the three periods. From the coefficient of y' in equation 4 we see that during the first period a 1 per cent increase (or decrease) in the deflated price of rye, other things being equal, was associated with an average decrease (or increase) of 0.36 of 1 per cent in the per capita consumption. The coefficient of t (see chap. vi, n. 20), gives the rate of shift of the demand curve in relative terms,

(3.3)
$$\frac{1}{M} \cdot \frac{\partial x'}{\partial t} = \frac{\partial \log_e x}{\partial t} = 0.0005 ,$$

which means that the demand curve shifted upward at the negligible rate of 0.05 per cent per annum. But since this coefficient is only one-seventh its standard error, it is of no statistical significance.

Figure 89 is a graphic representation on a logarithmic scale of the relationship between consumption, price, and time for the first period. Figure 89A is a scatter diagram of the logarithms of per capita consumption (x') on those of real price (y'). The line $D_1'D_2'$ gives the net relationship between these variables when each is linearly corrected for changes in time. The slope of this line (-0.3605) is the elasticity of demand. In Figure 89B the differences between the observed and computed values of x' are plotted against time. The almost horizontal line $D_1'D_3'$ shows clearly that the shift of the demand curve was negligible during this period. Figure 89C shows the slightly reduced scatter about the demand curve $D_1'D_2'$ after x' has been corrected for changes in t. The large (and apparently nonrandom) scatter which still remains is reflected in the large quadratic mean error, in the large standard error of the coefficient of t (or of the slope of $D_1'D_3'$), and in the comparatively low value of the adjusted coefficient of multiple correlation.

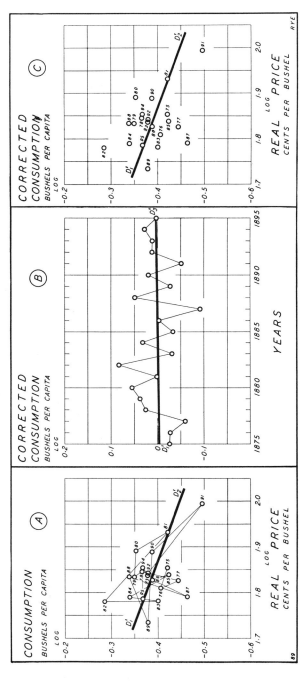

Fig. 89.—Rye: Three aspects of the per capita demand for rye during the period 1875–95 on the assumption that

$$x = 1.880\ y^{-0.3605}\ e^{0.0005t}.$$

A: Relation between per capita consumption and real price when the data are not corrected for the effects of "time," with the demand curve $D_1'D_2'$ which results when such correction is made.

B: Relation between per capita consumption and time when the former is corrected for the effects of changes in the real price. The slope of line $D_1'D_3'$ (fitted to the variables x' and t when both are corrected for price) represents the mean rate of shift of the per capita demand curve $D_1'D_2'$.

C: The per capita demand curve for rye, 1875–95. Line $D_1'D_2'$ shows the relation between that part of the per capita consumption of rye in the United States which is independent of time and that part of the real price which is independent of time. In the scatter, however, only the ordinate is corrected for secular changes, the abscissa being uncorrected.

Equation 5 and Figure 90 relate to the second period. A comparison of the lines $D_1'D_2'$ of Figures 90A and 89A shows that the elasticity of demand (i.e., the slope of the line $D_1'D_2'$) was approximately the same during this period as it was in the first period. There was, however, a striking change in the direction and rate of shift of the demand curve. The curve moved upward at the rate of 1.63 per cent per annum subject to an annual retardation of 0.74 per cent per annum, for

$$(3.4) \qquad \frac{1}{x} \cdot \frac{\partial x}{\partial t} = 0.0163 - 2(0.0037)t \,.$$

This retardation had the effect of giving the curve a downward shift since about 1907. As can be seen both from Figure 90 and from the percentages of the variance of x' attributable to y' and t, in Table 43, equation 5, the shift of the demand curve accounts for most of the original scatter of x' on y'. When allowance is made for this shift, we obtain the considerably reduced scatter of Figure 90C.

Equation 6 and Figure 91 give the corresponding information for the third period. This period saw a decided change in both the elasticity of demand and the shift of the demand curve. The elasticity of demand (given by the coefficient of y' or the slope of the line $D_1'D_2'$) was now -2.444, which means that a 1 per cent change in price was in any given year associated with a change in the opposite direction of 2.44 per cent in the per capita consumption of rye. However, even if the price had remained constant, the per capita consumption would have decreased until about 1924 and would have increased thereafter until 1929.

The logarithmic equations 4, 5, 6, fit the data about as well as do the corresponding arithmetic equations 1, 2, 3. The correlation coefficients are approximately the same in the logarithmic as in the arithmetic equations for each of the three periods. Likewise the percentages of the variance of consumption attributable to the independent variables are roughly the same for the two sets of equations. Figures 89C, 90C, and 91C show, however, that even when the data are adjusted for changes in price and time, the observations do not lie very closely about the demand curves $D_1'D_2'$. This is probably due to errors in the original production, exports, and price series.

IV. DEMAND FUNCTIONS WITH THE DEFLATED PRICE AS THE DEPENDENT VARIABLE

Equations 7–12 of Table 43 are the specific forms of the demand hypothesis (2.2), the first three being the arithmetic equations, and the last three the logarithmic equations.

The coefficient of x in equation 7 means that, other things being equal, an increase (or decrease) of one bushel in the annual per capita consumption of

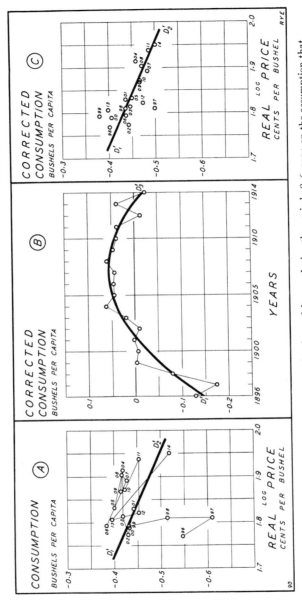

Fig. 90.—Rye: Three aspects of the per capita demand for rye during the period 1896–1914 on the assumption that

$$x = 2.538 \ y^{-0.4374} \ e^{0.01631 - 0.0037t^2} \ .$$

496

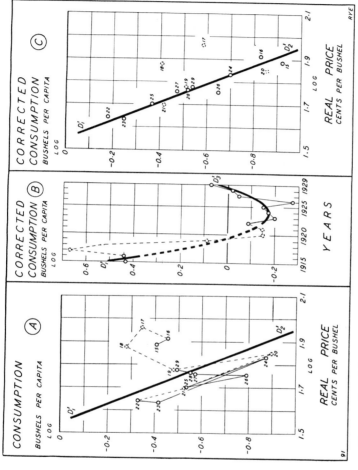

FIG. 91.—Rye: Three aspects of the per capita demand for rye during the period 1915–29 (excluding 1917–21) on the assumption that

$$x = 4264.0 \ y^{-2.4444} \ e^{-0.07661+0.01991t^2} \ .$$

rye during the first period would have been associated with an average decrease (or increase) of 97 cents in the deflated price per bushel. Translated into relative terms this relationship means that a 1 per cent increase in the per capita consumption would in any given year have been associated with a decrease of 0.58 of 1 per cent in the deflated price of rye. Although the reciprocal of the price flexibility is the elasticity of demand, there is no reason to expect that in statistically derived demand curves the elasticity of demand computed from the regression of x on y should equal the reciprocal of the price flexibility[5] computed from the regression of y on x. In fact, from equation 7 it would appear that the demand for rye was elastic during the first period whereas equation 1 indicates that the demand was inelastic.

From the coefficient of t of equation 7 we see that the demand curve shifted upward at the slight rate of 0.09 cent per annum. But this coefficient is less than one-third the size of its standard error and is therefore statistically insignificant.

The quadratic mean error of this equation is rather large—9.2 cents—and the adjusted multiple correlation coefficient is rather small—0.33—so that any price computed from equation 7 would be subject to a large error of estimate. If t were omitted from this equation, the latter coefficient would have been raised somewhat, but the coefficient of x would have been approximately the same.

Equation 8, which relates to the second period, means that, *other things being equal,* an increase of one bushel in the per capita consumption of rye would have been associated with a decrease of 200 cents per bushel in the deflated price. But other things did not remain equal: the demand curve kept shifting upward at the rate of 1.67 cents per annum, subject to an annual retardation of 0.50 cent, for

$$(3.5) \qquad \frac{\partial y}{\partial t} = 1.6712 - 2(0.2500)t.$$

This retardation caused the average price to move upward until about 1908 and shift downward thereafter.

Equation 9 gives the corresponding information for the third period. During this period the deflated price became much less flexible, a 1 per cent increase in the per capita consumption giving rise to a decrease of only 0.43 of 1 per cent in the deflated price of rye. There was likewise a striking change in the shift of the demand curve, for it moved rapidly downward until 1925 and upward thereafter until 1929.

Equations 10, 11, and 12 are the logarithmic forms of hypothesis (2.2). They express the relation between consumption, price, and time for the three periods

---

[5] See chap. vi, pp. 225–28, and esp. n. 40.

in relative terms. Thus, the coefficient of x' in equation 10 means that, other things being equal, a 1 per cent increase in the per capita consumption during the first period was, on the average, associated with a decrease of 0.53 of 1 per cent in the deflated price of rye. The coefficient of t means that the price shifted upward at the negligible rate of 0.07 of 1 per cent per annum. But this coefficient is less than one-sixth its standard error and is therefore of no statistical significance.

Equations 11 and 12 are interpreted in an analogous manner. They show that the price flexibility rose in magnitude to 0.85 in the second period but that it fell to 0.34 in the third period. The shifts of the demand curves were also radically different in the two periods. If the per capita consumption had been kept constant during the second period, the price would have moved upward until about 1908 and downward from 1908 until 1914. During the third period, however, the price would have declined until about 1925 and would have risen thereafter until 1929.

The logarithmic equations 10, 11, and 12 give about as good a fit to the data as do the corresponding arithmetic equations 7, 8, and 9. Likewise the measures of the relative importance which may be attached to consumption and time in explaining price for the three periods are roughly the same in the two sets of equations.

V. SUMMARY AND CONCLUSIONS

Although rye is a fairly important crop, we have been able to find no mathematical investigations into the demand for rye. The main findings of the present chapter center around the changes that have taken place in the shape, the elasticity, and the rate of shift of the demand curve since 1875 and of the factors which account for them.

To summarize:

1. The demand curve for rye underwent important structural changes during the fifty-five years from 1875 to 1929. Thus, the net effect of a one cent increase in the price per bushel (in terms of the 1913 dollar) was to decrease the annual per capita consumption by 0.002 bushel in the first two periods and by 0.01 bushel in the third period.

2. The demand for rye was inelastic during the first two periods but became elastic during the third period. Thus the partial elasticity of demand was of the order −0.4 in the first two periods but changed to −2.4 in the third period.

3. During the period 1875–95 the demand curve had no measurable shift. During the period 1896–1914 the demand curve shifted upward at the average rate of 0.0053 bushel per capita, or 1.63 per cent per annum, subject to an annual average retardation of 0.0024 bushel per capita or of 0.74 per cent. This retardation gave the curve an upward shift from 1896 until about 1907 and then a downward shift until 1914. During the third period the demand curve

shifted rapidly downward until about 1925—probably as a result of the Eighteenth Amendment—and then assumed an upward course until 1929.

4. Except during the first period, changes in the price of rye had a smaller effect on consumption than did changes in the position of the demand curve. This indicates that we have not succeeded in isolating some important factors affecting the demand for rye. Unfortunately, the data for rye are probably not so reliable as for the more important crops and do not permit an isolation of these factors.

5. The equations with price as the dependent variable indicate the same direction of shift of the demand curve as do those with consumption as the dependent variable. The two sets of equations do not, however, give consistent answers to the question whether the demand for rye was elastic during the first two periods: whereas the latter set indicates that the demand was inelastic during those periods, the former suggests that the demand was elastic. Since the price series is relatively more trustworthy than the consumption series, the regression of consumption on price is, in general, a better approximation to the true demand curve than is the regression of price on consumption. In these equations likewise the quadratic mean errors[6] indicate that the regressions of x on y give a better fit to the data than do those of y on x. The former regressions are therefore to be preferred for the purposes of estimating the elasticity of demand. For the third period all equations indicate an elasticity of demand greater than 2 in absolute value.

6. An extrapolation of the equations for the third period for the years since 1929 is impossible, owing to the fundamental revisions by the United States Department of Agriculture of the production data and its substitution of the season average price series for the December 1 farm price. However, a rough graphical analysis of the data indicates that in 1929 the demand for rye had reached its highest level. During the next two years the demand for rye decreased considerably, and, although it rose in 1932 and 1933, it fell again in 1934. It is, however, too early as yet to determine the trend of shift of the demand curve for these later years.

The actual changes in the production and price of rye since 1929 may, however, be briefly reviewed. During the first three years following 1929 there was no discernible decline in the production of rye. However, with net exports becoming negligible as a result of increased foreign production and tariff re-

---

[6] It should be recalled that the quadratic mean errors of eqs. 1 and 7 and of 2 and 8 are not directly comparable, since those of eqs. 1 and 2 are given in bushels per capita, whereas those of eqs. 7 and 8 are given in cents per bushel. When, however, they are expressed as relatives of their means, they take on the values of 10 and 13 per cent, respectively, for eqs. 1 and 7, and of 5.5 and 8.8 per cent for eqs. 2 and 8. It is fairly evident, therefore, that the regressions of x on y are more trustworthy than those of y on x, even though R' for the first period is slightly higher in the latter regressions than in the former.

strictions, farmers experienced a drastic fall in the price of rye. Thus, the season average price fell from 85.7 cents per bushel in 1929 to 27.6 cents in 1932. This fall in price, followed by the drought of 1933, resulted in the very small crop—twenty-one million bushels—of 1933, which made it necessary for us to import approximately twelve million bushels of rye. Although the season average price rose to 61.8 cents in 1933, production decreased even further to sixteen million bushels in 1934 as a result of the severe drought of that year. During that year we again imported over eleven million bushels of rye. In 1935, however, production rose to approximately fifty-eight million bushels. In October of that year the Secretary of Agriculture issued a proclamation setting up a rye-adjustment program under the Agricultural Adjustment Administration. What the effects of the program would have been is difficult to surmise, for it fell with the invalidation of the Agricultural Adjustment Act by the Supreme Court on January 6, 1936.

CHAPTER XV

THE DEMAND FOR BUCKWHEAT

CHAPTER XV

THE DEMAND FOR BUCKWHEAT

I. THE FACTUAL BACKGROUND

Buckwheat, in point of value, is the least important of the commodities whose demand curves we have undertaken to derive in this book.[1] For every bushel of it produced in 1922 there were produced 192 bushels of corn, 57 bushels of wheat, 81 bushels of oats, 12 bushels of barley, 6 bushels of rye, and nearly 3 bushels of rice.[2] It is included in our list primarily for the purpose of determining whether the official data on the production and prices of a relatively unimportant crop yield price-quantity relations of the same order of consistency as do the data for the more important crops.

Since buckwheat is not a grass seed but the fruit of a herbaceous plant, it is not a true cereal. However, it is used for making flour and, as such, may be classed with the cereal grains.

Buckwheat was brought to this country from Europe by the early settlers, and records show that samples of the crop harvested in 1625 were sent back to Holland by the Dutch colonists along the Hudson River.[3] Nevertheless, buckwheat remained of secondary importance, corn, wheat, and rye being the principal crops of colonial days. By 1839, the date of the first agricultural census, the buckwheat crop totaled 7,292,000 bushels, of which approximately three-fifths was grown in New York and Pennsylvania. These two states have continued to produce almost two-thirds of the entire crop.

During the decade from 1875 to 1884 the production of buckwheat was subject to violent fluctuations. From a level of 10 million bushels at the beginning of the decade, it shot up to 15 millions in 1880, only to drop to 8 millions in 1883. Then it began to move upward at a fairly steady rate, reaching the level of 14–15 millions in 1895–97. After declining for three years, the production curve began to increase again but at a slower rate, reaching 17 million bushels in 1909. The record crop for the period 1875–1929 came in 1912. The next few years saw a rapid reduction in the size of the crop to the level of 1885–95,

---

[1] For the list of commodities see Table 4, chap. v, p. 157.

[2] *U.S.D.A. Yearbook, 1922*, pp. 546–47. Although the American buckwheat crop ranks low among American crops it is the third largest buckwheat crop in the world. Our average annual crop of 17,528,000 bushels during 1909–13 was exceeded only by those of Russia (55,000,000 bu.) and of France (21,000,000 bu.).

For a fairly comprehensive discussion of the role of buckwheat in American agriculture see *ibid.*, pp. 546–53 and 559.

[3] *Ibid.*, p. 549.

for between 1919 and 1929 production fluctuated fairly closely about the average of 12 million bushels. From 1930 to date (1936) production has been below the average for the preceding decade.

The area occupied by buckwheat was over 1,600,000 acres in 1869. It dropped to 450,000 acres in 1870 and continued below 600,000 acres until 1875. During the period 1875–1929 the area harvested fluctuated between 600,000 and 1,000,000 acres. From 1930 to 1935 the area harvested has been between 450,000 and 570,000 acres.

Buckwheat may be grown on poor, thin land. A profitable crop may be grown on land unsuitable for wheat or rye. It is a crop which can use relatively insoluble materials. Consequently, a poor grade of fertilizer may be used with it, and hard lands on which it has been sown become mellow and friable. It is often used as the first crop on new land.

Another advantage which buckwheat has over the cereal crops is its short growing season. It may be sown as late as July 1 even in the northern states. This permits the crop to be used as a "catch crop," when earlier crops have failed or have been drowned out. By extending the period in which planting may be done, it permits a more advantageous use of both farm labor and land.

Although buckwheat may be grown on soils unfavorable for other crops, it requires a climate which is cool and moist. Hot weather at blooming time will blast the flowers and destroy the crop. It is, therefore, confined to the higher elevations or to the northern sections of the country.

II.   FACTORS IN THE DEMAND FOR BUCKWHEAT

Like wheat and rye, buckwheat is grown chiefly for human consumption. Buckwheat pancakes are often referred to as the national dish of the United States. The flour is also used for shortbread and shortcake in some sections of the country. In addition, a small amount of groats, grits, and farina are manufactured.

The by-products of the milling process are not so satisfactory a feed for cattle and hogs as corn or hay; they are less palatable, and the hulls are not easily digested. However, middlings, one of the by-products of the milling process, have a high protein, carbohydrate, and fat content and a relatively small proportion of hulls. This makes good feed for dairy cattle.

Only a small amount of the crop is consumed without milling on the farm where it is grown. This portion is used as an ingredient in scratch feed for poultry.

Since we are interested in the demand for buckwheat for all purposes, the series which would be best suited for our needs is production, plus imports, minus exports, plus stocks at the beginning of the year, minus stocks at the end of the year. This would give us a close approximation to the amount of buckwheat actually consumed. However, data on stocks do not exist, and those on exports and imports are available only since 1896. Except for the three years 1896–98, when the exports amounted to well over a million bushels, the foreign trade in buckwheat has been negligible. Thus for the twenty-one years 1909–29 imports minus exports averaged only a little over 1 per cent of our production. Since the latter series is admittedly subject to grosser errors, we shall neglect the foreign trade and consider production as equal to consumption.

The ideal price for our purposes is the one which, if maintained throughout the year, would have cleared the market. The season average farm price first published by the United States Department of Agriculture in the 1934 *Year-book* is, perhaps, the best available approximation to this price. However, the series goes back only to 1919 and, consequently, will not be of use to us, as we must have comparable data for all three periods. We have, therefore, decided to use the December 1 farm price. As in the preceding chapters we shall reduce the production data to a per capita basis and deflate the price series by the Bureau of Labor Statistics "Index of Wholesale Prices" ($1913 = 100$).

In our statistical analysis we shall first assume that the per capita consumption is a function of deflated price and time:

$$(2.1) \qquad\qquad x = x(y, t) \,,$$

and use both the arithmetic and the logarithmic equations as specific forms of (2.1). Then we shall repeat our analysis with time as the dependent variable:

$$(2.2) \qquad\qquad y = y(x, t) \,,$$

again using both the linear and the constant-elasticity equations, and compare the results obtained. To gain a better insight into the changes which have taken place in the shape of the demand curve and in the rate and direction of its shifting during the fifty-five-year period from 1875 to 1929, we shall break up our data into the following subdivisions: (I) 1879–95, (II) 1896–1914, (III) 1915–29 (excl. 1917–21). (The figures for 1875–78 will be omitted from the computations because they do not appear to be homogeneous with the data for the following years.)

III. DEMAND FUNCTIONS WITH PER CAPITA CONSUMPTION AS THE DEPENDENT VARIABLE[4]

Table XII of Appendix A lists for 1875–1929 the per capita consumption (=production), the deflated prices, and the per capita value of buckwheat together with the link relatives and trend ratios of the consumption and the price series. Tables I and IIa of the same appendix give the deflators and the

---

[4] For an explanation of the statistical methods used and for definitions of the technical terms see chap. vi.

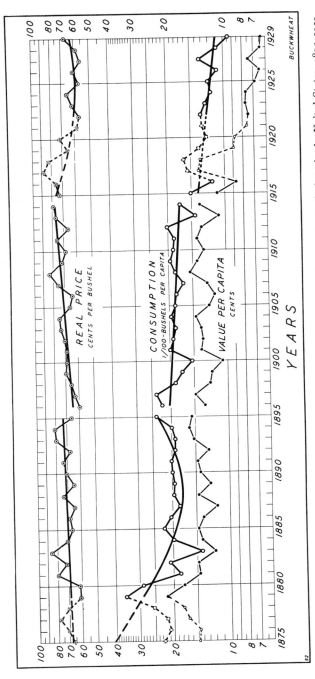

FIG. 92.—Buckwheat: The basic adjusted annual data used in deriving the demand curves for buckwheat in the United States, 1875–1920, with the computed trends by periods of the real prices and the per capita consumption. The dotted observations in the first and third periods are those which are not used in the computations.

basic (unadjusted) data of total consumption and money prices. Figure 92 is a graphic representation of the per capita consumption, deflated price, and per capita value series, the latter series being added for its usefulness in indicating the elasticity of demand.[5] Table 44 summarizes the consumption and price data for each of the three periods. Table 45 is a descriptive summary of the important changes which have taken place in the demand for buckwheat from 1879 to 1929.

TABLE 44

BUCKWHEAT: SUMMARY BY PERIODS OF THE ADJUSTED DATA USED
IN DERIVING THE DEMAND FUNCTIONS, 1879–1929

PERIOD*	PER CAPITA CONSUMPTION $x(t)$				DEFLATED PRICE $y(t)$				CORRELATION COEFFICIENT
	Descriptive Constants								
	Mean (Bu.)	Median (Bu.)	Standard Deviation (Bu.)	Coefficient of Variation	Mean (Cents)	Median (Cents)	Standard Deviation (Cents)	Coefficient of Variation	r_{xy}
I	0.2106	0.1990	0.0457	21.71	70.802	70.119	6.944	9.81	−0.6653
II	0.1869	0.1864	0.0207	11.10	70.419	69.875	5.807	8.25	−0.5334
III	0.1202	0.1190	0.0149	12.40	63.144	60.894	6.596	10.45	+0.0292

	Equations of Trends			Origins
I	$x(t) = 0.1791 - 0.0034t + 0.0013t^2$		$y(t) = 70.802 + 0.2714t$	Jan. 1, 1888
II	$x(t) = 0.1869 - 0.0016t$		$y(t) = 70.419 + 0.6397t$	Jan. 1, 1906
III	$x(t) = 0.1234 - 0.0021t$		$y(t) = 60.449 - 0.9055t + 0.1802t^2$	Jan. 1, 1923

* I = 1879–95; II = 1896–1914; III = 1915–29 (excl. 1917–21).

A. THE FIRST PERIOD, 1879–95

From the coefficient of y in the first equation of Table 45 we see that, other things being equal, an increase of one (deflated) cent in the price per bushel of buckwheat was associated with a decrease in the annual per capita consumption of 0.0038 bushel. Expressed in relative terms this means that, for the representative values[6] of y and x, the elasticity of demand during this period was:

(3.1)
$$\frac{\partial x}{\partial y} \cdot \frac{y}{x} = -1.5044 .$$

[5] See chap. vi, pp. 190–92.

[6] As explained in chap. vi (III, D, 2, b) the representative values of y and t are the arithmetic means of these variables, and the representative value of x is obtained by substituting the mean values of y and t in the demand equation.

TABLE 45

BUCKWHEAT: THE CHARACTERISTICS OF THE PER CAPITA

x = Per capita consumption in bushels
y = Deflated December 1 farm price in cents per bushel

(Figures in parentheses are standard errors)

EQUATIONS

Equation No.	Period*		Constant Term	y	t	t^2
1	I	$x=$	0.4529	$-$ 0.0038 (0.0008)	$-$0.0023 (0.0011)	$+$0.0012 (0.0002)
2	II	$x=$	0.2939	$-$ 0.0015 (0.0009)	$-$0.0007 (0.0010)	. . . .
3	III	$x=$	0.2343	$-$ 0.0017 (0.0006)	$-$0.0038 (0.0009)	. . . .

			Constant Term	y'	†Mt	†Mt^2
4	I	$x'=$	1.6281	$-$ 1.2790 (0.2424)	$-$0.0061 (0.0047)	$+$0.0048 (0.0011)
5a	II	$x'=$	0.3590	$-$ 0.5904 (0.3597)	$-$0.0032 (0.0054)	. . . .
5b	II	$x=$	0.2537	$-$ 0.0599‡ (0.0196)	. . . .	. . . .
6	III	$x'=$	0.8712	$-$ 0.9864 (0.3195)	$-$0.0320 (0.0072)	. . . .

			Constant Term	x	t	t^2
7	I	$y=$	105.6542	$-$189.0447 (34.1673)	$-$0.3082 (0.2521)	$+$0.2063 (0.0216)
8	II	$y=$	87.9043	$-$ 93.5708 (57.4429)	$+$0.4855 (0.2175)	. . . .
9	III	$y=$	100.8747	$-$293.6202 (110.1817)	$-$1.6165 (0.3650)	. . . .

			Constant Term	x'	†Mt	†Mt^2
10	I	$y'=$	1.4572	$-$ 0.5330 (0.1010)	$-$0.0019 (0.0032)	$+$0.0025 (0.0009)
11	II	$y'=$	1.6678	$-$ 0.2441 (0.1487)	$+$0.0070 (0.0030)	. . . .
12	III	$y'=$	1.2747	$-$ 0.5845 (0.1893)	$-$0.0251 (0.0052)	. . . .

* I = 1879–95; II = 1896–1914; III = 1915–29 (excl. 1917–21).
† $M = \log_{10}e = 0.43429$.
‡ This is the coefficient of log $(y - 56)$, the equation being of the type, $x = a + b \log (y - 56)$.

TABLE 45—*Continued*

DEMAND FUNCTIONS, BY PERIODS, 1879–1929

t = Time in years. For origins see Table 44

x', y' = Logs of x and y

(Figures in parentheses are standard errors)

	DESCRIPTIVE CONSTANTS					
	Elasticity of Demand η	Quadratic Mean Error ϵ (Bushels)	Adjusted Multiple Correlation Coefficient R'	Percentage of Variance of Consumption Attributable to		EQUA-TION No.
				y	t	
....	-1.5044 (0.5139)	0.0214	0.8908	38.83	44.39	1
....	-0.5729 (0.4206)	0.0188	0.4668	22.71	7.76	2
....	-0.9007 (0.4425)	0.0098	0.7833	-2.22	72.17	3
	η	ϵ (Per Cent)	R'	y'	t	
....	-1.2790 (0.2424)	91.1–109.8	0.8813	45.90	35.95	4
....	-0.5904 (0.3597)	90.3–110.8	0.4533	22.92	6.45	5a
....	-0.6892	0.0176§	$-0.5632\|$	35.51¶	....	5b
....	-0.9864 (0.3195)	92.7–107.9	0.8159	1.91	72.08	6

Flexibility of Price φ	Maximum Value of η $1/\varphi$	ϵ (Cents)	R'	Percentage of Variance of Price Attributable to		
				x	t	
-0.6045 (0.1681)	-1.6544	4.5305	0.7742	75.33	-7.88	7
-0.2483 (0.1754)	-4.0274	4.6741	0.6215	17.82	27.63	8
-0.5591 (0.2687)	-1.7885	4.0411	0.8137	-1.94	75.66	9
φ	$1/\varphi$	ϵ (Per Cent)	R'	x'	t	
-0.5330 (0.1010)	-1.8760	94.1–106.2	0.7928	76.34	-6.533	10
-0.2441 (0.1487)	-4.0972	93.6–106.8	0.6266	17.52	28.49	11
-0.5845 (0.1893)	-1.7108	94.3–106.0	0.8374	1.71	75.05	12

§ In absolute units, i.e., bushels, since the dependent variable (x) is measured in bushels.

‖ This is the simple correlation coefficient adjusted for the number of parameters (2) in the equation.

¶ This is 100 times the square of the unadjusted simple correlation coefficient.

That is, if the average price had been increased (or decreased) by 1 per cent, and *if the demand curve had remained fixed for one year*, there would have been a decrease (or increase) of 1.50 per cent in the annual per capita consumption. This indicates that the demand for buckwheat was quite elastic during the first period.

From the coefficients of t and t^2 in this equation we obtain the mean rate of shift of the demand curve,

$$(3.2) \qquad \frac{\partial x}{\partial t} = -0.0023 + 2(0.0012)t ,$$

which means that the demand curve shifted downward at the average rate of 0.0023 bushel per annum, subject to an annual positive acceleration of 0.0024 bushel. This acceleration had the effect of giving the curve an upward shift since about 1888.

This curve gives a fairly good fit to the data, as can be judged by the high ratios of the regression coefficients to their respective standard errors, the fairly low quadratic mean error (0.02 bushel per capita, or 10 per cent of the mean consumption), and the fairly high value of the adjusted coefficient of multiple correlation (0.8908). From the percentage of variance in consumption which is attributable to each of the independent variables, it appears that "time" had a slightly greater effect on changes in consumption than did price.

Equation 4 of Table 45 expresses the demand for buckwheat during the first period directly in terms of relative changes. The coefficient of y' means that, other things being equal, a 1 per cent increase in the deflated price of buckwheat was associated with a decrease of 1.28 per cent in the per capita consumption. Although this value of the elasticity of demand is somewhat smaller than that derived from the arithmetic equation 1, it does reinforce the conclusion that the demand for buckwheat was elastic during the first period.

The coefficients of t and t^2 (see chap. vi, n. 20) give the mean rate of shift of the demand curve in relative terms. It is

$$(3.3) \qquad \frac{1}{M} \cdot \frac{\partial x}{\partial t} = \frac{\partial \log_e x}{\partial t} = -0.0061 + 2(0.0048)t ,$$

which means that the demand curve shifted downward at the average rate of 0.61 per cent per annum, subject to an annual positive acceleration of 0.96 per cent. This acceleration had the effect of giving the curve an upward shift after about 1888.

Figure 93 is a graphic representation on a logarithmic scale of the relationship between consumption, price, and time during the first period. Figure 93*A* is a scatter diagram of the logarithms of per capita consumption (x') on those

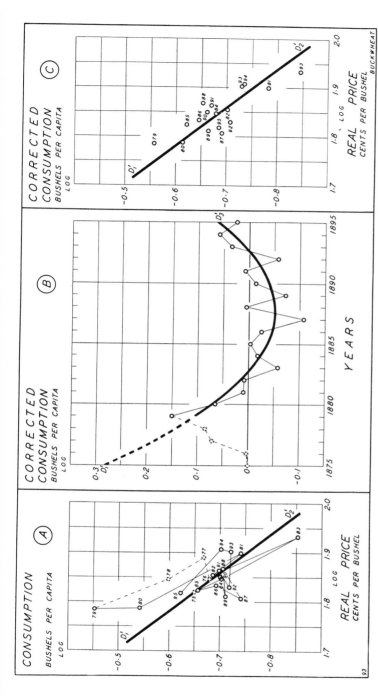

FIG. 93.—Buckwheat: Three aspects of the per capita demand for buckwheat during the period 1875–95 on the assumption that

$$x = 42.47 \; y^{-1.2790} \; e^{-0.0001t + 0.0048t^2}$$

A: Relation between per capita consumption and real price when the data are not corrected for the effects of "time," with the demand curve $D_1'D_2'$ which results when such corrections are made.

B: Relation between per capita consumption and time when the former is corrected for the effects of changes in the real price. The slope of line $D_1'D_3'$ (fitted to the variables x' and t when both are corrected for price) represents the mean rate of shift of the per capita demand curve $D_1'D_2'$.

C: The per capita demand curve for buckwheat, 1875–95. Line $D_1'D_2'$ shows the relation between that part of the per capita consumption of buckwheat in the United States which is independent of time and that part of the real price which is independent of time. In the scatter, however, only the ordinate is corrected for secular changes, the abscissa being uncorrected.

of the real prices (y'). The line $D_1'D_2'$ gives the net relationship between these variables when each is linearly corrected for changes in time. The slope of this line (-1.2790) is the elasticity of demand. In Figure 93B the differences between the observed and the computed values of x' are plotted against time. The curve $D_1'D_3'$ represents the average rate of shift of the demand curve given by the coefficients of t and t^2. Figure 93C shows the considerably reduced scatter about the demand curve $D_1'D_2'$ after x' has been corrected for changes in time.

The logarithmic equation gives almost as good a fit to the data for the first period as does the arithmetic equation. The adjusted multiple correlation is only slightly smaller than for the arithmetic equation, and the quadratic mean error is about 10 per cent. In contrast to the arithmetic equation, however, we see that the percentage of variance of consumption attributable to price is somewhat higher than is the percentage attributable to time.

B. THE SECOND PERIOD, 1896–1914

Equation 2 of Table 45 is the arithmetic form of hypothesis (2.1) for the second period. The coefficient of y shows that consumption was more responsive to changes in price during the first period than during this period. Whereas in 1879–95 a one cent increase in the deflated price in any given year brought about a decrease of 0.0038 bushel in the per capita consumption of buckwheat, during 1896–1914 the same change in price was associated with a decrease in consumption of only 0.0015 bushel per capita. This relation may be seen more clearly when expressed in relative terms. Whereas during the first period a 1 per cent increase in the deflated price was associated with a decrease of 1.50 per cent in the per capita consumption, during the second period it was associated with a decrease of only 0.57 per cent. This means that the demand for buckwheat became inelastic during the second period; a small crop was now more profitable than a large crop.

By comparing the coefficient of t with its standard error, it appears that changes in the position of the demand curve had no effect on the per capita consumption of buckwheat during this period, for the demand curve exhibited no significant upward or downward shift.

Equation 5a gives the relationship between consumption, price, and time directly in terms of relative changes. The coefficient of y' means that during the second period a 1 per cent increase (or decrease) in the deflated price of buckwheat was associated with an average decrease (or increase) of 0.59 of 1 per cent in the per capita consumption. In this equation, as well as in equation 2, the coefficient of t is insignificant, so that we may conclude that the demand curve had no significant upward or downward shift during 1896–1914.

Both the arithmetic and the logarithmic equations give a poor fit to the data, as may be seen from the low value of the adjusted multiple correlation coefficient and the large standard errors of the regression coefficients. A graphical analysis of the data (not reproduced here) likewise shows that neither the arithmetic nor the constant-elasticity curve gives a good fit to the data; the scatter of consumption on price is too skew to admit of being satisfactorily represented by these curves. After several trial (graphic) experiments with the

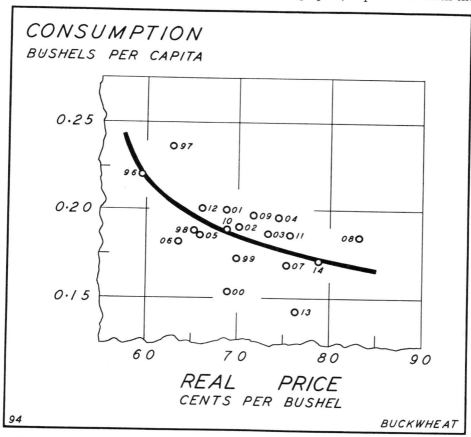

FIG. 94.—Buckwheat: The demand curve for buckwheat during the period 1896–1914 on the assumption that

$$x = 0.2537 - 0.0599 \log (y - 56) ,$$

where x is consumption per capita.

data, it appeared that, if 56 cents were subtracted from each observed price, an equation of the form

(3.4) $$x = a + b \log (y - 56)$$

would give a somewhat improved fit to the data. Equation 5b gives the least-square values of the parameters of this equation. (The variable t was excluded, because it had proved insignificant in eqs. 2 and 5a.) Figure 94 is a graphic representation of this equation in arithmetic form. A measure of the goodness of fit of this curve to the data is given by the adjusted simple coefficient of correlation between x and the logarithm of $(y - 56)$. This coefficient has the value of -0.5631 as compared to the adjusted multiple correlation coefficients 0.4668 and 0.4533 for equations 2 and $5a$ of Table 45.

The coefficient of log $(y - 56)$ gives the absolute change in the per capita consumption associated with a 1 per cent change in $(y - 56)$. To get a measure of the percentage change in x associated with a 1 per cent change in y, we must compute the elasticity of demand. For this curve, the coefficient of elasticity is not constant but varies from point to point, for

$$(3.5) \qquad \eta = \frac{dx}{dy} \cdot \frac{y}{x} = \frac{b \log_{10} e}{y - 56} \cdot \frac{y}{x}.$$

When y is given its mean value, and x is computed from equation $5b$ of Table 45 and substituted in (3.5) above, the elasticity of demand corresponding to this representative point on the demand curve is found to be -0.6892. This coefficient means that during the period 1896–1914 an increase of 1 per cent in the price of buckwheat was associated with a decrease of approximately 0.7 per cent in the per capita consumption. This value is somewhat larger in magnitude than the coefficients of elasticity computed from equations 2 and $5a$.

C. THE THIRD PERIOD, 1915–29

Equation 3 of Table 45 describes the demand for buckwheat during the third period. From the coefficient of y we see that an increase of one (deflated) cent in the price per bushel of buckwheat was in any given year associated with a decrease in the per capita consumption of 0.0017 bushel. When expressed in relative terms for the representative point on the demand curve, this relationship yields a coefficient of ·elasticity of -0.9007.

The coefficient of t shows that during this period the demand curve shifted downward at the average rate of 0.0038 bushel per capita per annum. This shift of the demand curve is in direct contrast to the upward movement during the second half of the first period and the absence of any shift during the second period.

Equation 6 gives the demand function directly in terms of relative changes. The coefficient of y' shows that a 1 per cent increase in the (deflated) price of buckwheat was associated with an average decrease of 0.99 of 1 per cent in the per capita consumption or that the demand for buckwheat was of nearly unitary elasticity.

From the coefficient of t we see that the demand curve shifted *downward* during 1915–29 at the extremely rapid rate of 3.20 per cent per annum. This means that, even if the deflated price had been kept constant, the per capita demand for buckwheat would, on the average, have decreased at the rate of 3.20 per cent per annum. As can be seen from the measures of the percentage of the variance of consumption attributable to price and time, it is this shift of the demand curve which accounts for nearly all the variation in consumption.

Figure 95 is a graphic representation of equation 6 on a logarithmic scale. Figure 95A is a scatter diagram of the logarithms of per capita consumption (x') on those of the real prices (y'), together with the *net* regression of x' on y' when both variables are linearly corrected for changes in time. The slope of this regression line (-0.9864) is the elasticity of demand. Figure 95B gives the direction and mean rate of shift of the demand curve during the third period. When allowance is made for this shift, we obtain the reduced scatter of Figure 95C. As may be seen at a glance from Figure 95B nearly all the variation in consumption is attributable to time.

IV. DEMAND FUNCTIONS WITH THE DEFLATED PRICE AS THE DEPENDENT VARIABLE

Equations 7–12 of Table 45 are the specific forms of the demand hypothesis (2.2), the first three being the arithmetic equations and the last three being the logarithmic equations.

Equation 7, which relates to the first period, means that, other things being equal, an increase (or decrease) of one bushel in the annual per capita consumption of buckwheat during the first period would have been associated with an average decrease (or increase) of 189 cents in the deflated price per bushel. Translated into relative terms this relationship means that a 1 per cent increase in the per capita consumption would in any given year have been associated with a decrease of 0.60 of 1 per cent in the deflated price of buckwheat. This is the coefficient of the flexibility of price; its reciprocal gives the maximum value of the coefficient of elasticity.

From the coefficients of t and t^2 we see that during the first period the deflated price of buckwheat decreased at the rate of 0.31 cent per annum, subject to an annual positive acceleration of 0.41 cent, for

(4.1)
$$\frac{\partial y}{\partial t} = -0.3082 + 2(0.2063)t .$$

This acceleration had the effect of giving the curve an upward shift since about 1888.

This curve gives a fairly satisfactory fit to the data, as can be seen from the quadratic mean error (4.53 cents), from the standard errors of the regression coefficients, and from the adjusted multiple correlation coefficient (0.7742).

Equation 8 gives the corresponding information for the second period. The coefficient of y means that, other things being equal, an increase of one bushel

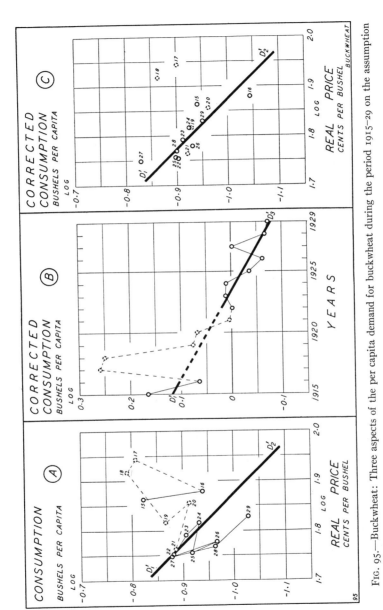

Fig. 95.—Buckwheat: Three aspects of the per capita demand for buckwheat during the period 1915–29 on the assumption

that

$$x = 7.434 \, y^{-0.9864} \, e^{-0.0320t}$$

in the per capita consumption of buckwheat would have been associated with a decrease of only 94 cents per bushel in the deflated price. Translated into relative terms this relationship yields a coefficient of price flexibility of only −0.2483. Its reciprocal (−4.0274), which gives the maximum value of the coefficient of elasticity, is not at all in agreement with the coefficient of elasticity derived from the equations in which x is the dependent variable.

The coefficient of t shows that the (deflated) price shifted upward at the average rate of 0.49 cent per annum. From the measures of the percentage of variance of price attributable to each of the independent variables, it appears that this shift accounted for more of the price variation than did changes in consumption.

Equation 9 relates to the third period. During this period an increase of one bushel in the per capita consumption of buckwheat, other things being equal, would have been associated with a decrease of 294 cents in the deflated price per bushel. But other things did not remain equal, for the price kept shifting downward at the average rate of 1.62 cents per annum. It is this shift which accounts for nearly all the variation in the price.

Equations 10, 11, and 12 are the logarithmic forms of hypothesis (2.2). They express the relation between consumption, price, and time for the three periods in relative terms. Thus equation 10 means that, other things being equal, a 1 per cent increase in the per capita consumption during the first period was, on the average, associated with a decrease of 0.53 per cent in the deflated price of buckwheat but that, even if the consumption had been kept constant, the price would have shifted downward until about 1888 and upward thereafter.

Equations 11 and 12 show that the price flexibility fell in magnitude to 0.2441 in the second period but that it rose again to 0.58 during the third period. The coefficients of t in these equations show that, whereas the price shifted upward during the second period at the rate of 0.70 per cent per annum, during the third period it reversed its trend and shifted downward at the rate of 2.51 per cent.

The logarithmic equations 10, 11, and 12 appear to give a slightly better fit to the data than do the corresponding arithmetic equations 7, 8, and 9. However, the measures of the relative importance which may be attached to consumption and time in explaining price for the three periods are roughly the same in the two sets of equations.

V. SUMMARY AND CONCLUSIONS

This chapter has dealt in the main with the changes that have taken place in the shape, the elasticity, and the rate of shift of the demand curve for buckwheat since 1879. The analysis has brought to light the following facts:

1. The demand curve for buckwheat underwent important structural changes during the period 1879–1929. From the equations with consumption as the dependent variable it appears that the net effect of a one cent increase in the price per bushel (in terms of the 1913 dollar) was to decrease the annual per capita consumption by 0.0038 bushel in the first period, by 0.0015 bushel in the second, and by 0.0017 bushel in the third.

2. The demand for buckwheat was elastic during the first period and inelastic during the second and third periods.

3. During the period 1879–95 the demand curve shifted downward at the average rate of 0.0023 bushel per capita (or 0.61 per cent per annum), subject to an annual average positive acceleration of 0.0024 bushel per capita (or of 0.96 per cent). This acceleration had the effect of giving the curve an upward shift since about 1888 (see Fig. 93B). During the second period the demand curve had no appreciable shift, but during the third period it moved downward at the average annual rate of 0.0038 bushel per capita, or 3.2 per cent.

4. During the first period price and time were about of equal importance in determining variations in consumption. In the second period changes in the factors represented by time did not affect consumption. During the third period, however, they accounted for practically all the variance of the per capita consumption.

5. Except for the second period, the equations with price as the dependent variable indicate the same direction of shift of the demand curve as do those with consumption as the dependent variable. The two sets of equations do not, however, give consistent answers to the question whether the demand for buckwheat was elastic during the second and third periods. The regression of price on consumption and time suggest that the demand was definitely elastic, while regressions of consumption on price and time indicate an inelastic demand. Although our belief that the errors in the consumption data are relatively larger than the errors in the price data should lead us to favor the regressions of consumption on price, the large standard errors of the coefficients of elasticity should warn us against attaching too much confidence to our statistical findings. It is quite possible that the demand for buckwheat was elastic not only in the first period but also in the second and third periods.

6. An extrapolation of the equations for the third period from 1929 to date (1936) is impossible, owing to the fundamental revisions by the United States Department of Agriculture of the production data and its substitution of the season average price series for the December 1 farm price. However, a rough graphical analysis of the data (not reproduced here) indicates that, with the possible exception of 1933 and 1934, the demand for buckwheat continued to shift downward in recent years. This downward trend is of great importance

to cultivators of buckwheat, for it means that a crop of a given size will be worth less and less in each succeeding year.

The foregoing findings perhaps justify the conclusion that, except for the second period, the data on the production and prices of buckwheat yield price-quantity relations of approximately the same order of consistency as do the data for the more important crops. In the second period, however, the equations give a relatively poor fit to the data and yield conflicting results with respect both to the elasticity and to the shifting of the demand. This suggests the need of a thoroughgoing revision of the underlying production and price series with the view of improving their accuracy and consistency.

CHAPTER XVI

DEMAND CURVES IN THE TREND-RATIO
AND IN THE LINK-RELATIVE FORMS

CHAPTER XVI

DEMAND CURVES IN THE TREND-RATIO AND IN THE LINK-RELATIVE FORMS

I. INTRODUCTION

In chapter iv, page 151, we gave an outline of the methods and procedures to be followed in deriving the demand curves of our ten commodities. The plan called for the application of three different methods, each with two types of regression equations, and for a comparison of the results obtained. Table 46, which is a reproduction of Table 3 of chapter iv, is a summary of the typical

TABLE 46

PRINCIPAL METHODS AND TYPES OF EQUATIONS PROPOSED FOR DETER-
MINING THE ELASTICITIES AND THE RATES OF SHIFT OF THE DE-
MAND CURVES OF THE COMMODITIES STUDIED IN PART II

I. The Time-Regression Method
   Type of demand equation assumed

   $\quad$ (1) $\quad x = a + by + ct$ $\qquad\qquad a > 0,\ b < 0,\ c \gtrless 0$

   $\quad$ (2) $\quad x = A y^a e^{\beta t}$ $\qquad\qquad A > 0,\ a < 0,\ \beta \gtrless 0$

II. The Method of Trend Ratios*
   Type of demand equation assumed

   $\quad$ (3) $X = a + bY$ $\qquad\qquad a > 0,\quad b < 0$
   $\quad$ (4) $X = A Y^a$ $\qquad\qquad A > 0,\quad a < 0$

III. The Method of Link Relatives*
   Type of demand equation assumed

   $\quad$ (5) $X = a + bY$ $\qquad\qquad a > 0,\quad b < 0$
   $\quad$ (6) $X = A Y^a$ $\qquad\qquad A > 0,\quad a < 0$

   * Capital letters indicate trend ratios or link relatives in contrast with the small letters which indicate actual quantities and prices.

methods and types of equations proposed. In the statistical chapters vi–xv, the time-regression method was used exclusively. There remains the task of applying the method of trend ratios and the method of link relatives to the same data and of comparing the results obtained by all methods. In this chapter we shall develop the more important properties or characteristics of these methods and illustrate them by means of examples. In chapter xvii we shall apply these methods to the adjusted data for our commodities and compare the results obtained.

Since the discussions in the preceding statistical chapters centered largely on the elasticity and on the rate of shift of the demand curves yielded by the time-regression method, the analysis of this chapter will also be confined largely to the same properties of demand curves yielded by the trend-ratio and the link-relative methods. Fortunately, the task will not be so difficult as that which we have just finished, since the groundwork has already been prepared for it in chapter ii, pages 67–68.

The trend-ratio and the link-relative methods precede the time-regression method in Professor Henry L. Moore's pioneering investigations. The rationale of these methods has already been explained in chapter ii and need not be repeated. Suffice it to say that, when we use the method of trend ratios, we attempt to derive the demand curve not from the absolute prices and the corresponding absolute quantities but from the ratios of these prices and quantities to their respective trends. Similarly, when we use the method of link relatives, which is a slight variant of Professor Moore's "method of relative changes," we attempt to find the relationship not between the absolute prices and the absolute quantities but between the link relatives of the prices and the link relatives of the corresponding quantities.

It is convenient to begin with a résumé of the formulas for the coefficients of elasticity and for the rates of shift of the six equations in Table 46, although this may involve a repetition of some of the relations which we have already studied.

II.   RESUME OF THE THREE METHODS

A.   THE TIME-REGRESSION METHOD

Equation (1) represents a plane. When we fit this equation to data we are assuming that the demand curve is a straight line with slope b, and that it shifts its position upward (or downward) to the right by c units per annum for

$$(2.1) \qquad \begin{cases} \dfrac{\partial x}{\partial y} = b\,, \\[2ex] \dfrac{\partial x}{\partial t} = c\,. \end{cases}$$

According to this assumption, the coefficient of partial elasticity of demand, η, varies from point to point on the demand curve:

$$(2.2) \qquad \eta_{xy.t} = \frac{\partial x}{\partial y} \cdot \frac{y}{x} = b\frac{y}{x}\,.$$

Equation (2) represents a surface. When we fit this equation to data, we are assuming that the demand curve has a constant elasticity at every point, this elasticity being

$$(2.3) \qquad \eta_{xy.t} = \frac{\partial x}{\partial y} \cdot \frac{y}{x} = \frac{\partial \log_e x}{\partial \log_e y} = a\,,$$

and that the demand curve shifts its position not by a constant absolute amount as in (1) but by a constant relative amount, equal to β, for

(2.4)
$$\frac{1}{x} \cdot \frac{\partial x}{\partial t} = \beta .$$

Illustrations of the foregoing properties of equations (1) and (2) have been given in the preceding statistical chapters and especially in chapters vi and vii.

B. THE METHOD OF TREND RATIOS

The trend ratios are defined as $X = x/T_x$ and $Y = y/T_y$, where T_x and T_y are functions of time representing, respectively, the trends of x and y. Substituting in equation (3) and multiplying both sides by T_x, we obtain

(2.5)
$$x = aT_x + b \left(\frac{T_x}{T_y}\right) y .$$

For any given year for which T_x and T_y are known, this is the equation of a straight line in x and y, since we assume T_x and T_y to be time series not depending on the values of x and y.

The slope of the line, namely,

(2.6)
$$\frac{\partial x}{\partial y} = b \left(\frac{T_x}{T_y}\right) ,$$

may, of course, vary from year to year, depending on the ratio of T_x to T_y. If the two trends are linear:

(2.7)
$$\begin{cases} T_x = C_1 + B_1 t \\ T_y = C_2 + B_2 t , \end{cases}$$

then substitution in (2.6) yields

(2.8)
$$\frac{\partial x}{\partial y} = b \left(\frac{C_1 + B_1 t}{C_2 + B_2 t}\right) .$$

Thus we see that the demand curve changes its slope as it shifts with time.

The rate of shift of the curve (2.5) is

(2.9)
$$\frac{\partial x}{\partial t} = a \frac{\partial T_x}{\partial t} + b \left\{ \frac{T_y \left(\frac{\partial T_x}{\partial t}\right) - T_x \left(\frac{\partial T_y}{\partial t}\right)}{T_y^2} \right\} y .$$

Assuming that the two trends are linear, substitution of (2.7) into (2.9) yields

(2.10)
$$\frac{\partial x}{\partial t} = aB_1 + b \left\{ \frac{B_1(C_2 + B_2 t) - B_2(C_1 + B_1 t)}{(C_2 + B_2 t)^2} \right\} y .$$

Since the shift of the demand curve changes not only with time but also with price, it is clear that different points on the demand curve will shift through time at different rates. Consequently, it is very difficult to summarize the rate of shift of the demand curve as a whole, although we can easily measure the rate of shift of a given point on it.

The elasticity of demand of (2.5) for any given year is

$$(2.11) \qquad \eta = \frac{\partial x}{\partial y} \cdot \frac{y}{x} = b\left(\frac{T_x}{T_y}\right)\frac{y}{x} = b\left(\frac{Y}{X}\right).$$

This shows that, if assumption (3) is adopted, η becomes a constant for any given point on the (X, Y) curve and that it changes with time only because the point on the (X, Y) demand curve changes with time. If, however, we consider η as a characteristic of any given point on the (x, y) curve, it will change with time even though the point (x, y) itself does not change.

When we use equation (4), Table 46, we are assuming that the demand curve has a constant elasticity a at every point, both on the (X, Y) curve and on the (x, y) curve regardless of whether the curve is written in the trend-ratio form or in terms of absolute quantities and prices. For, by substituting x/T_x for X and y/T_y for Y in (4) we get

$$(2.12) \qquad x = A\left(\frac{T_x}{T_y^a}\right)y^a ,$$

a being the elasticity of demand. The relative rate of shift of the curve (2.12) is

$$(2.13) \qquad \frac{1}{x} \cdot \frac{\partial x}{\partial t} = \frac{1}{T_x} \cdot \frac{\partial T_x}{\partial t} - a \frac{1}{T_y} \cdot \frac{\partial T_y}{\partial t} .$$

If T_x and T_y are linear functions of time, as in (2.7), this becomes

$$(2.14) \qquad \frac{1}{x} \cdot \frac{\partial x}{\partial t} = \frac{B_1}{C_1 + B_1 t} - a \frac{B_2}{C_2 + B_2 t} .$$

It is evident from (2.13) that it is only when each trend increases (or decreases) by a constant percentage per annum, i.e., when $\frac{1}{T_x} \frac{\partial T_x}{\partial t}$ and $\frac{1}{T_y} \frac{\partial T_y}{\partial t}$ are constants, that the relative shift of the demand curve (4), Table 46, is also a constant.

C. THE METHOD OF LINK RELATIVES

The transformation of the link-relative equations (5) and (6) into equations expressed in terms of actual prices and quantities is similar to the transformation of the trend-ratio equations discussed above. All we have to do, for example, to transform (5) is to substitute in it x_i/x_{i-1} for X_i, and y_i/y_{i-1}, for Y_i, thus obtaining

$$(2.15) \qquad x_i = a(x_{i-1}) + b \frac{x_{i-1}}{y_{i-1}} y_i \, .$$

This is the equation of a straight line in x_i and y_i, if the preceding year quantity x_{i-1} and the preceding year price y_{i-1} are taken as known constants.

For any given year, the slope of this line is constant, namely,

$$b \frac{x_{i-1}}{y_{i-1}} \, .$$

The elasticity of demand, namely,

$$(2.16) \qquad \eta = \frac{\partial x_i}{\partial y_i} \cdot \frac{y_i}{x_i} = b\left(\frac{x_{i-1}}{y_{i-1}} \cdot \frac{y_i}{x_i}\right) = b\left(\frac{Y}{X}\right) \, ,$$

varies from point to point on the (x_i, y_i) curve and also on the (X_i, Y_i) curve. At any given point on the (X_i, Y_i) curve, it is constant over time. But at a given point on the (x_i, y_i) curve it varies with time because the parameters x_{i-1} and y_{i-1} vary with time.

By the same procedure we may transform (6) into an equation in terms of actual prices and thus obtain

$$(2.17) \qquad x_i = A\left(\frac{x_{i-1}}{y_{i-1}^a}\right) y_i^a \, .$$

The slope of this curve varies from point to point, but the coefficient of elasticity of demand has the constant value a at every point, for

$$(2.18) \qquad \eta = \frac{\partial x_i}{\partial y_i} \cdot \frac{y_i}{x_i} = a \, .$$

The rates of shift of (2.15) and (2.17) cannot be expressed analytically, since these functions do not have continuous derivatives in t. However, a general idea of their nature may be obtained by computing these functions for each year and comparing the family of curves obtained from each function. This will be illustrated later.

Formula (2.16) for computing the elasticity of demand from a straight-line demand curve has been criticized by Professor Luigi Amoroso. A consideration and refutation of this criticism will be found in the appendix to this chapter.

III. ILLUSTRATIONS

To give a concrete illustration of the various methods and procedures listed in Table 46, we may use the per capita consumption and the deflated price of sugar for 1896–1914. The application of the time-regression method to such data is fully discussed and illustrated in the preceding statistical chapters, and especially in chapter vi, and need not be repeated here. We shall, therefore, confine our illustrations to the trend-ratio and the link-relative methods.

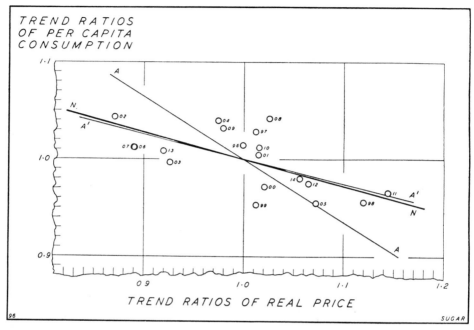

FIG. 96.—The trend ratios of the per capita consumption and the real price of sugar, 1896–1914, with three lines of regression:

Line $A'A'$ = Regression of consumption on price
Line AA = Regression of price on consumption
Line NN = Mutual regression

A. THE METHOD OF TREND RATIOS

The equations to the trends of the per capita consumption and the real price of sugar for 1896–1914 are, respectively,

(3.1) $$T_x = 73.8526 + 1.3558t$$

and

(3.2) $$T_y = 5.6999 - 0.1305t,$$

where T_x is measured in pounds, T_y in cents, and t in years, the origin being at 1905 (see chap. vi, Table 5, p. 180).

The ratios of the per capita consumption and the real price to their respective trends are given in Table III, Appendix A. Figure 96 is a graphic representation of these series. As can be seen from this diagram the two sets of trend ratios are negatively correlated with each other, the coefficient of correlation being −0.6225.

The three lines of regression in Figure 96 are: the regression of x on y (line $A'A'$); the regression of y on x (line AA); and the mutual regression (line NN). Line $A'A'$ was fitted on the assumption that an observed point fails to fall on the line because of an "error" or deviation in the quantity variable, the price variable being allowed no deviation. Line AA was fitted on the assumption that an observed point fails to fall on the line because of an "error" or deviation in the price variable, the quantity variable being allowed no deviation. The assumptions underlying the fitting of line NN are (1) that the failure of any point to fall on the line is due to deviations in both variables and (2) that both deviations have the same *weight* or importance.[1]

Since, in fact, both variables are subject to error, it is evident that line NN is a better approximation to the "true" demand curve than is either of the other two lines. We shall not, however, use it in the statistical testing of the link-relative and the trend-ratio methods, partly because it is more difficult to fit than the primary regressions; partly because in our statistical series it lies rather close to line $A'A'$, the regression of consumption on price, which, as was shown in chapter iv (pp. 146–49) is to be preferred to the other elementary regression, so that the elasticities of the two lines would not differ significantly from each other; but primarily because the curves of the time-regression method with which we wish to compare the curves of the link-relative and the trend-ratio methods are also regressions in which consumption is the dependent variable.[2] Accordingly, we shall use the line $A'A'$. The equation of this line is

(3.3) $$X = 1.251 - (0.2512 \pm 0.0766)\,Y\,,$$

and its quadratic mean error is $\epsilon = \pm\,0.0246$ units.

By (2.5), the equation (3.3) in terms of actual prices and quantities is

(3.4) $$x = 1.251\,T_x - 0.2512\left(\frac{T_x}{T_y}\right)y\,.$$

The values of T_x and T_y for any given year may be obtained from (3.1) and (3.2).

[1] See chap. iv, Sec. III, esp. n. 31. In terms of the symbols of that note, line NN was fitted on the assumption that the ratio of the weight of x to the weight of y is unity:

$$g = \frac{w_x}{w_y} = 1\,.$$

In fitting line $A'A'$, the assumption was made that $g = 0$; while, in fitting the line AA, the assumption was made that $g = \infty$.

[2] It would have been impracticable or impossible to fit all these curves by the method of mutual regression.

Figure 97 is a graphic representation of the function (3.4). Each heavy line of the type D_1D_2 represents the average demand curve for the year in question.[3] A careful examination of the diagram shows that the different points on this demand curve shift at different rates. Curves D_1D_3 and D_2D_4 measure the rates of shift of the demand curve for $y = 0$ and $y = 13$, respectively. The equations to these curves may be obtained by substituting in (2.10) the values of the parameters given by the trend equations (3.1) and (3.2) and then fixing y at $y = 0$ and $y = 13$.

It is important to observe that, while the curve D_1D_3 shows that the demand curve shifted upward throughout the entire period, the curve D_2D_4 shows that it shifted upward until about 1907 and downward from 1907 to 1914. Other curves such as D_1D_3 or D_2D_4 would show still other shifts. This is a quite different result from that yielded by the time-regression method (see Figs. 25, 27, and 28 of chap. vi).

Perhaps a clearer picture of the rate of shift represented by equation (3.4) may be obtained by projecting the demand curves for the individual years in Figure 97 onto the vertical plane erected at the last year, 1914. The result is shown in Figure 98, together with the projections of the observations onto the plane for 1914. It is clear from an examination of this diagram that, if the price is kept fixed at three cents per pound, per capita consumption increases with time, whereas if the price is fixed at twelve cents per pound, per capita consumption first increases and then decreases. (See the arrangement of the terminal points of the nineteen demand curves when the price is three cents and when it is twelve cents.) This result is, of course, what we should expect from (2.9) and illustrates the impossibility of measuring the rate of shift of the demand curve as a whole by a single constant.

So much for the rate of shift of (3.3). To compute the elasticity of demand of the same curve at a representative point, we give X and Y their mean values ($X = 1.0000$ and $Y = 1.0003$) and then make use of (2.11), thus obtaining

$$(3.5) \qquad \eta = \frac{\partial x}{\partial y} \cdot \frac{y}{x} = b\,\frac{Y}{X} = -0.2512 \left(\frac{1.0003}{1.0000}\right) = -0.2512 \,.$$

That is to say, when both consumption and price are at their normal (trend) levels, a change of 1 per cent in price, if maintained for the period in question (one year), would, on the average, be associated with a change of only one-fourth of 1 per cent in the annual consumption. This value of the elasticity of demand happens to be almost identical with the corresponding values derived by the time-regression method. (See the values of the coefficients of elasticity given in chap. vi, eqs. 2 and 5, Table 7, pp. 196–97).

[3] The underlying theoretical curves are probably subject to rather pronounced seasonal fluctuations, but these cannot be determined from annual data.

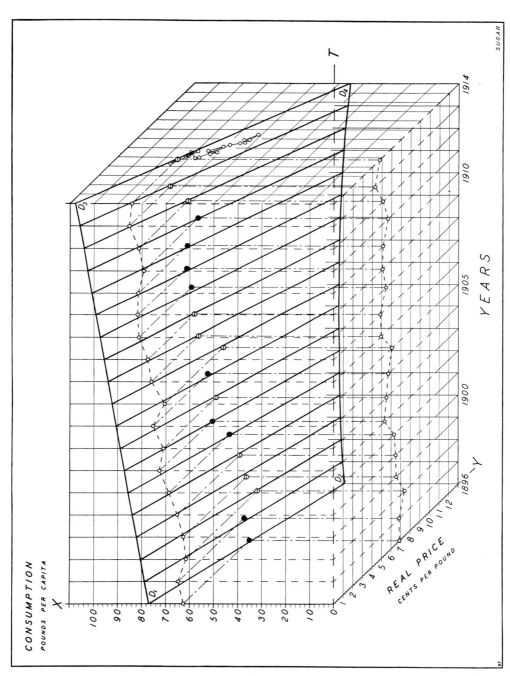

Fig. 97.—The per capita demand for sugar, 1896–1914, derived by the method of trend ratios, and illustrating assumption (3). (See eqs. [3.3] and [3.4].)

If, instead of fitting a straight line, we fit an equation of type (4), we obtain

(3.6) $X = 0.9989 \; Y^{-(0.2575 \pm 0.0774)}$.

The elasticity of demand and the other results derived from this equation are similar to those yielded by (3.3). A graph of this function would resemble that

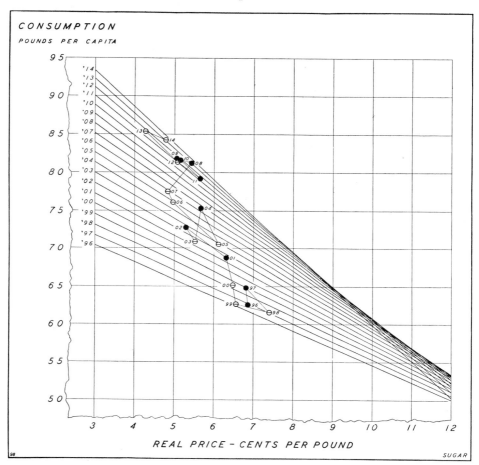

FIG. 98.—The shift of the per capita demand for sugar during 1896–1914, on the assumption that the demand function is given by (3.4). The lines in this diagram are the projections of the demand curves D_1D_2 in Fig. 97 on the vertical plane erected at 1914.

of Figure 97, except that the straight lines would be replaced by curves of constant elasticity (hyperbolas). The projections of these curves onto the vertical plane erected at 1914 would not, however, cross one another as do the straight lines in Figure 98. In fact, if we rectified the curves by taking the logarithms of X on Y we should obtain for the projections a family of *parallel lines* with slope $a = -0.2575$, instead of the family of intersecting lines of Figure 98. However, instead of showing a steady upward progression with time, the curves would shift upward until about 1900 and downward from 1900 to 1914. This follows from the fact that, if we transform (3.6) by substituting x/T_x for X and y/T_y for Y, and take the logarithms of both sides, we obtain

(3.7) $\log x = (\log 0.9989 + \log T_x + 0.2575 \log T_y) - 0.2575 \log y$.

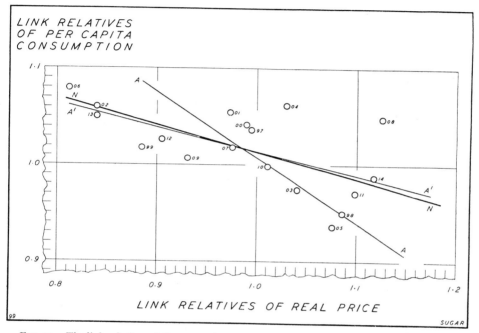

FIG. 99.—The link relatives of the per capita consumption and the real price of sugar, 1897–1914, with three lines of regression:

Line $A'A'$ = Regression of consumption on price
Line AA = Regression of price on consumption
Line NN = Mutual regression

This represents a family of parallel lines with slope of -0.2575 and intercept given by the terms in parentheses.

Within the immediate range of the data there is no significant difference between the two sets of equations, (3.3) and (3.6).

B. THE METHOD OF LINK RELATIVES

The link relatives of consumption and the corresponding link relatives of the prices which are given in Table III, Appendix A, are negatively correlated with one another, the coefficient of correlation being $r = -0.6121$. Figure 99 is a graphical representation of the correlated link relatives together with three lines of regression fitted to the scatter diagram. As in the method of trend ratios, we shall consider only the regression of x on y (line $A'A'$ in Fig. 99) as the best approximation to our demand function. The equation of this line is

$$(3.8) \qquad\qquad X = 1.269 - (0.2551 \pm 0.0824)Y ,$$

its quadratic mean error being $\epsilon = \pm 0.0335$ units.

In terms of actual prices and quantities, the equation is, by (2.15)

$$(3.9) \qquad\qquad x_i = 1.269(x_{i-1}) - 0.2551\left(\frac{x_{i-1}}{y_{i-1}}\right)y_i .$$

Figure 100 is a graphic representation of this function. It corresponds to Figure 97, relating to trend ratios, and is constructed by using the quantity (x_{i-1}) and the price (y_{i-1}) of the preceding year from Table III, Appendix A.

The elasticity of demand when the link relatives are given their mean values $(X = 1.018$ and $Y = 0.9849)$ is by (2.16)

$$(3.10) \qquad\qquad \eta = -0.2469 .$$

We interpret this result to mean that, when the per capita consumption and the deflated price for any year are both "normal" (i.e., when the consumption is 101.8 per cent of the consumption for the previous year and the deflated price is 98.49 per cent of the price for the previous year) an increase (or decrease) of 1 per cent in the price will bring about a decrease (or increase) of one-fourth of 1 per cent in consumption.

The rate of shift of (3.9) does not admit of being expressed in mathematical terms, although a fairly good notion of the way in which the demand curve changed both its position and its slope may be obtained from a study of the broken curves D_1D_3 and D_2D_4 in Figure 100. Perhaps a clearer representation of the changes in both the shift and the slope in question may be obtained by projecting the demand curves for the individual years in Figure 100 onto the vertical plane erected at the last year, 1914. The result is shown in Figure 101. It is clear from a comparison of Figure 101 with Figure 98 that the two methods make quite different assumptions regarding the shift of the demand curve with time and that the method of trend ratios has a greater affinity for the method of time-regression than does the method of link relatives.

So much for the equation of type (5).

If we fit an equation of type (6), we obtain

$$(3.11) \qquad\qquad X = 1.012 Y^{-(0.2447 \pm 0.0789)} .$$

The elasticity of demand (-0.2447) and the other results derived from this equation are similar to those yielded by (3.3), (3.6), and (3.9). A graph of this

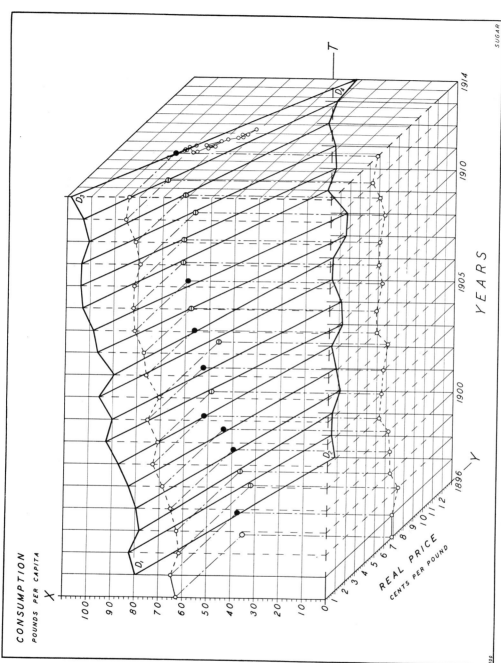

CONSUMPTION
POUNDS PER CAPITA

REAL PRICE
CENTS PER POUND

YEARS

SUGAR

FIG. 100.—The per capita demand for sugar, 1897–1914, derived by the method of link relatives and illustrating assumption (5). (See eqs. [3.8] and [3.9].)

function would resemble that of Figure 100, except that the straight lines would be replaced by curves of constant elasticity (hyperbolas). The projections of these hyperbolas onto the vertical plane erected at 1914 would not, however, cross one another as do the straight lines in Figure 101. In fact, if we rectified

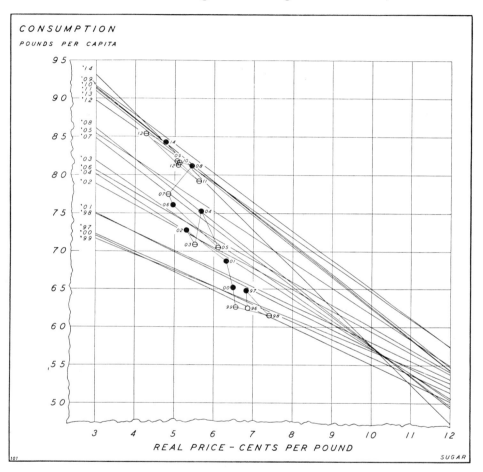

FIG. 101.—The shift of the per capita demand for sugar, 1897–1914, on the assumption that the demand function is given by (3.9). The lines in this diagram are the projections of the demand curves D_1D_2 in Fig. 100 on the vertical plane erected at 1914.

the equilateral hyperbolas by taking the logarithms of X and Y, we should obtain for the projections a family of *parallel lines* with slope $a = -0.2447$, instead of the family of intersecting lines of Figure 101. However, they would still fail to show any regular progression with time, owing to the irregular variation of x_{i-1} and y_{i-1}. This may be seen more clearly if we transform (3.11) by substituting x_i/x_{i-1} for X_i and y_i/y_{i-1} for Y_i, and take the logarithms of both sides. We then obtain

$$(3.12) \quad \log x_i = (\log 1.012 + \log x_{i-1} + 0.2447 \log y_{i-1}) - 0.2447 \log y_i ,$$

which represents a family of parallel lines with slope of -0.2447 and intercept given by the terms in parentheses.

The methods and equations illustrated in this chapter have been applied to the data for each of our commodities for each of the three periods: (I) 1875–95, (II) 1896–1914, and (III) 1915–29 (omitting 1917–21). A comparison of the results obtained will be presented in the next chapter.

APPENDIX

PROFESSOR AMOROSO'S CRITICISM OF THE METHOD OF COMPUTING THE ELASTICITY OF DEMAND WHEN THE DEMAND CURVE IS EXPRESSED IN THE LINK-RELATIVE FORM

Formula (2.16) for deriving the elasticity of demand is considered erroneous by Professor Amoroso[4] because his theory demands that the elasticity of (5) or (2.15) be constant. Referring favorably to an earlier study of mine[5] wherein this formula was first given, he remarks:

in my opinion, the developments on p. 587 are not correct, in so far as $x_0, y_0, x_{i-1}, y_{i-1}$ which are variables with respect to time are considered constant in the differentiation. From this error it follows that the elasticity of demand appears to Schultz as variable from point to point, while it is constant. The contradictions, which Schultz himself points out on pp. 604–606, flow from the same source [p. 77].

As I pointed out no "contradictions" in the pages to which he refers, and as I could not follow his argument because it seemed to me that it was vitiated by a mathematical error, I wrote to him, explaining my difficulties, and asked him to set me right.

In a friendly reply, dated September 10, 1929, Professor Amoroso elaborated his criticism as follows:[6]

Your equation of demand, except for the numerical coefficients, is:

$$(a) \qquad \frac{x + \Delta x}{x} = a \frac{y + \Delta y}{y} + b$$

where x represents the quantity sold, y the price, Δx and Δy are the increments of x and y in the unit of time.

[4] Luigi Amoroso, "Le Equazioni differenziali della dinamica economica," *Giornale degli economisti*, LXIX (February, 1929), 68–79.

[5] "The Statistical Law of Demand as Illustrated by the Demand for Sugar." (See Amoroso, *op. cit.*, n. 3.)

[6] I have taken the liberty to modify one or two of his expressions so as to clarify his meaning.

It is convenient to render the equation homogeneous, referring not to the unit of time, but to the time Δt; (a) must then be written:

(b)
$$\frac{x + \Delta x}{x} = a\,\frac{y + \Delta y}{y} + b\Delta t$$

or, indicating with c a convenient constant:

(c)
$$\frac{\Delta x}{x} = a\,\frac{\Delta y}{y} + c\Delta t\,.$$

Taking an infinitesimal interval of time and giving to the symbols their usual meaning, we can write also:

(d)
$$\frac{dx}{x} = a\,\frac{dy}{y} + cdt\,.$$

Your equation, or equation (a), is therefore, in its substance, equivalent to *my* equation, or equation (d), and is in its very nature a dynamical equation, representing not *one* curve, but a *family of the curves of demand*.

Any one curve of demand can be deduced from (d), supposing in it time constant, or putting $dt = 0$. We obtain then:

(e)
$$\frac{dx}{x} = a\,\frac{dy}{y}\,,$$

an equation which just represents a curve of demand with constant elasticity.

To sum up my reasoning: your (1) [eq. (5) of this study] is a dynamical equation, representing not one curve of demand but a family of curves of demand; all of the curves of the family have a constant elasticity.

If my reasoning leads to conclusions different from yours, this is traceable to the fact that, at a given moment, you differentiate with respect to the time supposing constant the denominators of the ratios:

$$\frac{x + \Delta x}{x}\,,\qquad \frac{y + \Delta y}{y}\,.$$

It is true that you *say* that you consider x_{i-1} and y_{i-1} as constant, but you have by no means the right of making this assumption which contradicts the very structure of your theory.

In my opinion, Professor Amoroso's contentions are not well taken for the following reasons:

1. His equation (b) is true if and only if

(α)
$$\frac{x + \Delta x}{x\Delta t} = a\,\frac{y + \Delta y}{y\Delta t} + b$$

is true. But, if this is true, then his fundamental equation (c) does not follow, since equation (b) can be written as

$$1 + \frac{\Delta x}{x} = a + a\,\frac{\Delta y}{y} + b\Delta t$$

or

(β)
$$\frac{\Delta x}{x} = a\,\frac{\Delta y}{y} + b\Delta t + (a - 1)\,,$$

which is not the same as equation (c).

2. His equation (*c*) is true if

$$\frac{x\Delta t + \Delta x}{x} = a\left(\frac{y\Delta t + \Delta y}{y}\right) + b\Delta t$$

is true, for then we obtain

(γ)
$$\frac{\Delta x}{x} = a\frac{\Delta y}{y} + (a + b - 1)\,\Delta t\,,$$

which is Amoroso's equation (*c*), with *c* set equal to $(a + b - 1)$. But if, with Amoroso, we set $\Delta t = 0$, then $\Delta x = 0$, and $\Delta y = 0$. In terms of the economics of the problem, this means that in an actual economy *there can be no change in consumption and no change in price if no time interval is allowed during which these changes can, and must, take place.* In this, as well as in all my other studies, I have considered the time interval Δt during which consumers adjust their purchases to the new price as a fixed, finite quantity—one year, one month, or one day, depending on the nature of the problem.

In this connection it is necessary to repeat what I have tried to emphasize elsewhere: "The elasticity of demand is a function of the *time interval* between the successive observations on which the demand function is based. Thus the use of annual data might lead to a demand curve which is quite different from that based on monthly figures of the same series."[7]

3. Amoroso's equation (*e*) may arise if $c \equiv (a + b - 1) = 0$, which is a very special case. It corresponds to my constant-elasticity demand function in the link-relative form which is given by equation (6) or (2.17). *Does Professor Amoroso mean that when the variables are in the link-relative form none but the constant-elasticity demand curve (6) should be fitted to the data?*

4. Regarding the argument in the penultimate paragraph in the foregoing quotation from Amoroso, the following observations are in order:

It is true that

$$\frac{x + \Delta x}{x}\,, \qquad \frac{y + \Delta y}{y}$$

are each a function of *t*. But a distinction should be drawn between a function and a functional value. The denominator in each of these expressions is a function on a certain range of *t*. But at every fixed value of *t*, say at $t = t_0$, $x(t_0)$ and $y(t_0)$ are functional values and no longer vary with *t*. This is clearly illustrated by Figures 100 and 101. This is not the same as assuming that *x* and *y* are constants. Since a functional value is fixed, my assumption by no means

---

[7] *Der Sinn der statistischen Nachfragekurven* ("Veröffentlichungen der Frankfurter Gesellschaft für Konjunkturforschung" Heft 10), ed. Dr. Eugen Altschul (Bonn, 1930), p. 55, n. 13.

contradicts the basis of my theory, as Amoroso supposes. On the contrary, it is in agreement with it.[8]

5. Finally, there is the incontrovertible fact (see Table 48, chap. xvii, pp. 548–50) that the elasticities of demand yielded by the link-relative method are remarkably consistent with those yielded by the time-regression method and by the trend-ratio method, which are not questioned by Professor Amoroso. Surely this consistency would have been extremely improbable if my procedure were as erroneous as Professor Amoroso supposes it to be. I conclude, therefore, that, if one accepts the link-relative procedure for deriving demand curves, one must also accept formula (2.16) for computing coefficients of elasticity from such curves.

[8] In my letter of July 20, 1929, I yielded too much to Amoroso on this point. I trust, however, that the foregoing observations will enable him to see the rationale of my approach.

CHAPTER XVII

SUMMARY AND COMPARISONS OF THE STATISTICAL FINDINGS

CHAPTER XVII

SUMMARY AND COMPARISONS OF THE STATISTICAL FINDINGS

The analysis of the preceding chapter has laid bare the assumptions that we make regarding the elasticity and the rate of shift of a demand curve when we represent it by any of the six equations of Table 46. Since there is frequently no a priori reason for preferring one type of equation or method to another, it is instructive to make a comparison of the results obtained by applying the various equations and methods to the same data. To provide such a comparison, we have applied the method of trend ratios and the method of link relatives to the per capita consumption and the real prices of each of our commodities and have put our findings side by side with those yielded by the time-regression methods used in chapters vi–xv. In this chapter we shall summarize the results obtained. This summary will consist of three parts: (1) a comparison of the goodness of fit of the six types of equations of Table 46 as measured by the correlation between the observed and the computed values of the dependent variable (Table 47); (2) a comparison of the elasticities of demand yielded by the different equations (Table 48); and (3) a comparison of the rates of shift of the demand curves for the different commodities (Table 49).

The data on which these comparisons are based have been adjusted for population growth and the purchasing power of money. However, substantially the same results are also obtained by using unadjusted data, i.e., actual consumption and money prices.

I. THE GOODNESS OF FIT OF THE DEMAND CURVES AS MEASURED BY THE COEFFICIENTS OF CORRELATION

Table 47 is designed to indicate the goodness of fit of the various demand equations from which the elasticities of Table 48 have been computed. It gives for each demand equation the coefficient of correlation between the observed values of the dependent variable and the corresponding values computed from the equation. Thus the first entry in Table 47 means that the coefficient of multiple correlation between the per capita consumption of sugar, on the one hand, and real price and time, on the other, when the demand equation is assumed to be of type (1), is $R_{x.yt} = 0.955$. This is also the simple correlation between the observed consumption series and that computed from the regression of type (1). It will be noted that for each of the three methods used there is excellent agreement between the correlation coefficients of the arithmetic and logarithmic forms. This means that *within the range of the observations* there is little difference between the fit of the arithmetic

TABLE 47

COEFFICIENTS OF CORRELATION* BETWEEN THE OBSERVED AND THE COMPUTED DEMANDS FOR THE COMMODITIES STUDIED IN PART II, CLASSIFIED ACCORDING TO THE PERIOD COVERED BY THE DATA AND THE TYPE OF DEMAND EQUATION ASSUMED (ADJUSTED DATA)

COMMODITY AND PERIOD†	TYPE OF DEMAND EQUATION ASSUMED (SEE TABLE 46, CHAP. XVI)					
	(1)	(2)	(3)	(4)	(5)	(6)
Sugar:						
Per Capita "Consumption"						
1875–95	0.955	0.954	−0.581	−0.603	−0.358	−0.373
1896–1914	0.976	0.974	−0.623	−0.628	−0.612	−0.613
1915–29 (excl. 1917–21)	0.948‡	0.960§	−0.706	−0.733	−0.836	−0.866
Corn:						
Per Capita Production						
1879–95	0.897	0.895	−0.887	−0.875	−0.908‖	−0.908‖
1896–1914	0.942¶	0.944**	−0.933	−0.927	−0.882	−0.934
1915–29 (excl. 1917–21)	0.897	0.889	−0.773	−0.751	−0.853	−0.821
Cotton:						
Per Capita Consumption						
1875–95	0.945††	0.951††	−0.464	−0.439	−0.674	−0.724
1896–1913	0.893§§	0.890	−0.591	−0.583	−0.678	−0.679
1914–29	0.909‖‖	0.899	⊤⊤	⊤⊤	⊤⊤	⊤⊤
1922–29	0.824					
Hay:						
Production per Animal Unit						
1875–92	−0.821***	−0.821***	−0.828‖	−0.828‖	−0.744	−0.750
1899–1914	0.832¶	0.821**	−0.779	−0.763	−0.753	−0.754
1915–29 (excl. 1917–21)	0.922¶	0.932**	−0.618	−0.608	−0.646	−0.710
Wheat:						
Apparent Utilization per Capita						
1880–95		0.210	−0.00636	−0.0308	−0.416	−0.407
1896–1913		0.416	−0.259	−0.236	−0.359	−0.372
Utilization per Capita						
1921–29		0.731	−0.658	−0.645	−0.553	−0.559
1921–34		0.856				−0.703

† For notes to this table see p. 550.

TABLE 47—*Continued*

COMMODITY AND PERIOD†	TYPE OF DEMAND EQUATION ASSUMED (SEE TABLE 46, CHAP. XVI)					
	(1)	(2)	(3)	(4)	(5)	(6)
Potatoes:						
Per Capita Production						
1875–89	0.962	0.951	...	...	...	...
1890–1900	0.974¶	0.986**	...	...	...	...
1875–95	0.954¶	0.947**	−0.907	−0.972	−0.898†††	−0.970†††
1896–1914	0.952‡‡‡	0.952‡‡‡	−0.882	−0.900	−0.914†††	−0.964†††
1915–29 (excl. 1917–21)	0.973	0.971	−0.964	−0.971	−0.918	−0.970
Oats:						
Production per Animal Unit						
1875–92	0.932¶	0.932**	−0.755	−0.749	−0.704	−0.781
1899–1914	0.849	0.853	−0.821	−0.836	−0.822	−0.874
1915–29 (excl. 1917–23)	0.708	0.703	−0.478	−0.469	−0.600	−0.595
Disappearance per Animal Unit§§§						
1899–1914	0.893¶	0.885**	...			
1915–29 (excl. 1917–23)	0.882	0.877				
Barley:						
Per Capita "Consumption"						
1875–95	0.801	0.803**	−0.271	−0.263	−0.518	−0.459
1896–1914	0.907¶	0.921**	−0.427	−0.419	−0.418	−0.411
1915–29 (excl. 1917–21)	0.909¶	0.902**	−0.587	−0.598	−0.568	−0.577
Rye:						
Per Capita "Consumption"						
1875–95	0.444	0.436	−0.443	−0.436	−0.410	−0.428
1896–1914	0.911¶	0.905**	−0.604	−0.604	−0.575	−0.509
1915–29 (excl. 1917–21)	0.910¶	0.926**	−0.881	−0.882	−0.798	−0.795
Buckwheat:						
Per Capita Production						
1879–95	0.912¶	0.905**	−0.812	−0.807	−0.694	−0.702
1896–1914	−0.596⊕	−0.596⊕	−0.390	−0.383	−0.305	−0.320
1915–29 (excl. 1917–21)	0.836	0.860	−0.704	−0.707	−0.638	−0.629

TABLE 48†

ELASTICITIES OF DEMAND FOR THE COMMODITIES STUDIED IN PART II, CLASSIFIED ACCORDING TO THE PERIOD COVERED BY THE DATA AND THE TYPE OF DEMAND EQUATION ASSUMED (ADJUSTED DATA)

(Negative values throughout. Figures preceded by ± are standard errors.)

Commodity and Period†	Type of Demand Equation Assumed (See Table 46, Chap. XVI)					
	(1)	(2)	(3)	(4)	(5)	(6)
Sugar:						
Per Capita "Consumption"						
1875–95	0.36 ±0.16	0.38 ±0.12	0.37 ±0.15	0.40 ±0.12	0.31 ±0.23	0.31 ±0.18
1896–1914	0.26 ±0.093	0.27 ±0.084	0.25 ±0.087	0.26 ±0.077	0.25 ±0.094	0.24 ±0.079
1915–29 (excl. 1917–21)	0.34 ±0.11‡	0.31 ±0.077§	0.27 ±0.12	0.28 ±0.093	0.28 ±0.12	0.29 ±0.068
Corn:						
Per Capita Production						
1879–95	0.72 ±0.19	0.77 ±0.11	0.74 ±0.19	0.76 ±0.11	0.84 ‖	0.84 ‖
1896–1914	0.60 ±0.11¶	0.70 ±0.066**	0.57 ±0.099	0.68 ±0.067	0.74 ±0.15	0.77 ±0.074
1915–29 (excl. 1917–21)	0.48 ±0.20	0.49 ±0.16	0.47 ±0.088	0.48 ±0.15	0.81 ±0.32	0.68 ±0.19
Cotton:						
Per Capita Consumption						
1875–95	0.51 ±0.17††	0.44 ±0.11††	0.43 ±0.23	0.37 ±0.17	0.47 ±0.19	0.55 ±0.12
1896–1913	0.25 ±0.11§§	0.24 ±0.093	0.32 ±0.14	0.32 ±0.11	0.30 ±0.12	0.30 ±0.08
1914–29	0.12 ±0.067§§	0.12 ±0.057‡‡	¶¶	¶¶	¶¶	¶¶
1922–29	0.107 ±0.109	....	....	....	....	....
Hay:						
Production per Animal Unit						
1875–92	0.74***	0.74***	0.78‖	0.78‖	0.67 ±0.22	0.69 ±0.16
1899–1914	0.62 ±0.19¶	0.69 ±0.16**	0.64 ±0.19	0.66 ±0.15	0.77 ±0.28	0.74 ±0.18
1915–29 (excl. 1917–21)	0.46 ±0.27¶	0.43 ±0.20**	0.62 ±0.35	0.62 ±0.28	0.53 ±0.33	0.56 ±0.23
Wheat:						
Apparent Utilization per Capita						
1880–95	....	0.027 ±0.26	0.0057 ±0.24	0.029 ±0.26	0.49 ±0.42	0.50 ±0.31
1896–1913	....	0.15 ±0.16	0.16 ±0.17	0.15 ±0.16	0.35 ±0.30	0.35 ±0.23
Utilization per Capita						
1921–29	....	0.081 ±0.040	0.083 ±0.04	0.082 ±0.037	0.084 ±0.058	0.087 ±0.053
1921–34	....	0.19 ±0.037	....	....	....	0.18 ±0.055

† For notes to this table see p. 550.

548

TABLE 48—Continued

Commodity and Period†	Type of Demand Equation Assumed (See Table 46, Chap. XVI)					
	(1)	(2)	(3)	(4)	(5)	(6)
Potatoes:						
Per Capita Production						
1875–89	0.63 ±0.12	0.71 ±0.068	....	....	....	....
1890–1900	0.73 ±0.18¶	0.68 ±0.046**				
1875–95	0.68 ±0.14¶	0.66 ±0.056***	0.64 ±0.16	0.66 ±0.037	0.68 ±0.25†††	0.71 ±0.042†††
1896–1914	0.61±‡‡‡	0.61±‡‡	0.55 ±0.13	0.59 ±0.069	0.59 ±0.17†††	0.62 ±0.043†††
1915–29 (excl. 1917–21)	0.32 ±0.083	0.31 ±0.029	0.31 ±0.084	0.31 ±0.027	0.25 ±0.12	0.27 ±0.028
Oats:						
Production per Animal Unit						
1875–92	0.54 ±0.16¶	0.57 ±0.12**	0.59 ±0.18	0.62 ±0.14	0.47 ±0.20	0.64 ±0.13
1899–1914	0.77 ±0.24	0.80 ±0.14	0.70 ±0.22	0.73 ±0.13	0.80 ±0.31	0.80 ±0.12
1915–29 (excl. 1917–23)	0.60 ±0.55	0.56 ±0.46	0.57 ±0.50	0.54 ±0.42	0.79 ±0.69	0.71 ±0.48
Disappearance per Animal Unit§§§						
1899–1914	0.58 ±0.18¶	0.58 ±0.12**				
1915–29 (excl. 1917–23)	0.57 ±0.37	0.54 ±0.32				
Barley:						
Per Capita "Consumption"						
1875–95	0.17 ±0.13	0.16 ±0.12***	0.13 ±0.12	0.13 ±0.11	0.31 ±0.18	0.31 ±0.14
1896–1914	0.18 ±0.11¶	0.22 ±0.11***	0.20 ±0.13	0.22 ±0.12	0.24 ±0.17	0.23 ±0.13
1915–29 (excl. 1917–21)	0.53 ±0.42¶	0.39 ±0.24***	0.41 ±0.26	0.42 ±0.20	0.59 ±0.50	0.52 ±0.30
Rye:						
Per Capita "Consumption"						
1875–95	0.34 ±0.21	0.36 ±0.18	0.34 ±0.20	0.36 ±0.17	0.42 ±0.30	0.42 ±0.21
1896–1914	0.36 ±0.14¶	0.44 ±0.15***	0.43 ±0.17	0.43 ±0.14	0.42 ±0.21	0.43 ±0.15
1915–29 (excl. 1917–21)	2.96 ±1.56¶	2.44 ±0.46***	1.94 ±0.50	2.40 ±0.45	1.99 ±1.48	2.21 ±0.69
Buckwheat:						
Per Capita Production						
1879–95	1.50 ±0.51¶	1.28 ±0.24***	1.18 ±0.35	1.32 ±0.25	0.97 ±0.44	1.03 ±0.28
1896–1914	0.69 ⊕	0.69 ⊕	0.59 ±0.41	0.60 ±0.35	0.48 ±0.45	0.50 ±0.37
1915–29 (excl. 1917–21)	0.90 ±0.44	0.99 ±0.32	1.17 ±0.53	1.20 ±0.43	1.15 ±0.75	1.04 ±0.53

NOTES TO TABLES 47 AND 48

* Simple correlation (r), multiple correlation (R), or index of correlation (ρ). Only the simple coefficients of correlation are preceded by their sign, which is negative.

† For choice of period and for additional equations for each commodity see the appropriate chapter. When link relatives are used, the number of observations is, of course, reduced by one, except in the third period, in which it is reduced by two on account of the omission of the war years.

‡ Regression equation is of the type:

$$x = a + by + c(1 - h^t) .$$

§ Regression equation is of the type:

$$x = A y^a e^{\beta(1 - h^t)} .$$

‖ Regression equation is of the type: $(X + h) = A Y^a$. The standard error of η is not given, since one of the parameters (h) was not obtained by the method of least squares.

¶ Regression equation is of the type:

$$x = a + by + ct + dt^2 .$$

** Regression equation is of the type:

$$x = A y^a e^{\beta t + \gamma t^2} .$$

†† Regression equation is of the type:

$$x = a + by + cw + dt + et^2 .$$

(w = W. M. Persons' "Index of United States Industrial Production and Trade.")

‡‡ Regression equation is of the type:

$$x = A y^a w^{\beta} e^{\gamma t + \delta t^2} .$$

§§ Regression equation is of the type:

$$x = a + by + cw + dt .$$

‖‖ Regression equation is of the type:

$$x = A y^a w^{\beta} e^{\gamma t} .$$

¶¶ The correlation between price and quantity is positive.

*** Regression equation is of the type: $(x + h) = A y^a$. The standard error of η is not given, since one of the parameters (h) was not obtained by the method of least squares.

††† For these periods, a slight improvement in the fit was obtained by fitting a curve of the type $X = A Y^a e^{\beta t}$. The coefficients of multiple correlation are then 0.974 and 0.971, respectively. The corresponding elasticities of demand are −0.69 ± 0.43 and −0.62 ± 0.55.

‡‡‡ Regression equation is of the type:

$$x = A(y + h)^a e^{\beta t + \gamma t^2} .$$

§§§ This is the term used in chap. xii, "The Demand for Oats." It is synonymous with "Utilization."

⊕ Regression equation is of the type:

$$x = a + b \log (y + h) .$$

TABLE 49

THE SHAPE (ELASTICITY) OF THE PER CAPITA DEMAND CURVE FOR EACH OF THE SELECTED COMMODITIES WITH ITS RELATIVE RATE OF SHIFT AND RELATED CONSTANTS, BY PERIODS

COMMODITY AND PERIOD*	EQUATION OF DEMAND x=Adjusted Quantity Demanded† y=Real Price (1913=100)† t=Time in Years with Origin at Middle of Each Period (Figures Preceded by ± Are *Standard* Errors)	MULTIPLE CORRELATION R‡	PERCENTAGE OF VARIANCE ($\sigma^2_{\log x}$) ATTRIBUTABLE TO	
			Price	Time
SUGAR: x=Per Capita "Consumption"				
1875–95	$x = 113.7\, y^{-(0.3828\pm0.1224)}\, e^{(0.0156\pm0.0044)\,t}$	0.954	42.44	48.66
1896–1914	$x = 117.5\, y^{-(0.2717\pm0.0844)}\, e^{(0.0124\pm0.0022)\,t}$	0.974	33.63	61.17
1915–29 (excl. 1917–21)	$x = 157.8\, y^{-(0.3118\pm0.0775)}\, e^{(0.0090\pm0.0025)\,[1-(2/3)t]}$	0.960	49.63	42.47
CORN: x=Per Capita Production				
1879–95	$x = 550.1\, y^{-(0.7749\pm0.1100)}\, e^{-(0.0032\pm0.0040)\,t}$	0.895	77.10	3.05
1896–1914	$x = 468.8\, y^{-(0.6982\pm0.0663)}\, e^{(0.0149\pm0.0027)\,t-(0.0009\pm0.0004)\,t^2}$	0.044	106.79	−17.77
1915–29 (excl. 1917–21)	$x = 172.8\, y^{-(0.4924\pm0.1563)}\, e^{-(0.0213\pm0.0044)\,t}$	0.889	18.02	60.97
COTTON: x = Per Capita Consumption w = Persons' Index				
1875–95	$x = 3.379\, y^{-(0.4360\pm0.1124)}\, w^{(0.5653\pm0.1206)}\, e^{(0.0164\pm0.0020)\,t-(0.0084\pm0.0037)\,t^2}$	0.951	15.35	56.66§
1896–1913	$x = 1.885\, y^{-(0.2449\pm0.0931)}\, w^{(0.6886\pm0.2000)}\, e^{(0.0149\pm0.0030)\,t}$	0.890	1.16	49.08§
1914–29	$x = 0.594\, y^{-(0.1248\pm0.0570)}\, w^{(0.8936\pm0.1365)}\, e^{-(0.0075\pm0.0028)\,t}$	0.899	2.33	12.46§
HAY: x = Production per Animal Unit				
1875–92	$(x - 2.2) = 223800\, y^{-(5.7717\pm1.0052)}$‖	−0.821¶	......	......
1899–1914	$x = 15.21\, y^{-(0.6853\pm0.1598)}\, e^{(0.0026\pm0.0036)\,t-(0.0012\pm0.0008)\,t^2}$	0.821	60.04	7.45
1915–29 (excl. 1917–21)	$x = 9.036\, y^{-(0.4312\pm0.2044)}\, e^{(0.0224\pm0.0040)\,t+(0.0013\pm0.0010)\,t^2}$	0.932	13.83	73.03

* For explanation of choice of periods see appropriate chapter.

† For definitions of quantity demanded and price see appropriate chapter.

‡ In comparing the coefficients of correlation, allowance should be made for the different number of parameters in the regression equations on which they are based.

§ The variance ($\sigma^2_{\log x}$) attributable to w' is 18.40 per cent for the first period, 31.28 for the second, and 66.06 for the third.

‖ The elasticity of demand for this equation varies from point to point on the demand curve. At the point of means of the independent variables it is −0.74.

¶ This is the coefficient of simple correlation between $\log (x - 2.2)$ and $\log y$.

TABLE 49—Continued

COMMODITY AND PERIOD*	EQUATION OF DEMAND x=Adjusted Quantity Demanded† y=Real Price (1913=100)† t=Time in Years with Origin at Middle of Each Period (Figures Preceded by ± Are *Standard* Errors)	MULTIPLE CORRELATION R‡	PERCENTAGE OF VARIANCE ($\sigma^2_{\log x}$ ATTRIBUTABLE TO) Price	PERCENTAGE OF VARIANCE ($\sigma^2_{\log x}$ ATTRIBUTABLE TO) Time
Hay:—*Continued* x = Total Production z = Animal Units				
1875–92........	$x = 13.57\, y^{-(0.7863\pm0.1571)}\, z^{(1.0622\pm0.0844)}$	0.957	5.75	85.80**
1899–1914.....	$x = 10.39\, y^{-(0.6996\pm0.1587)}\, z^{(1.1229\pm0.2172)}$	0.861	29.32	44.78***
1915–29 (excl. 1917–21)....	$x = 847.6\, y^{-(0.5158\pm0.1872)}\, z^{-(0.3445\pm0.2240)}$	0.776	45.02	15.21**
WHEAT: x = Per Capita Apparent Utilization				
1880–95........	$x = 7.837\, y^{-(0.0271\pm0.2646)}\, e^{(0.00515\pm0.00824)\,t}$	0.210	0.39	4.01
1896–1913.....	$x = 12.70\, y^{-(0.1512\pm0.1606)}\, e^{-(0.00761\pm0.00483)\,t}$	0.416	4.22	13.11
x = Per Capita Utilization				
1921–29........	$x = 7.675\, y^{-(0.0809\pm0.0401)}\, e^{-(0.00207\pm0.00201)\,t}$	0.731	39.43	13.97
1921–34........	$x = 12.15\, y^{-(0.1854\pm0.0372)}\, e^{-(0.00498\pm0.00229)\,t-(0.00137\pm0.00059)\,t^2}$	0.856	62.41	10.87
POTATOES: x = Per Capita Production				
1875–89........	$x = 51.96\, y^{-(0.7089\pm0.0676)}\, e^{-(0.0048\pm0.0036)\,t}$	0.951	88.75	1.60
1890–1900.....	$x = 52.92\, y^{-(0.6832\pm0.0458)}\, e^{-(0.0101\pm0.0043)\,t-(0.0022\pm0.0014)\,t^2}$	0.986	99.22	− 1.96
1875–95........	$x = 42.57\, y^{-(0.6587\pm0.0560)}\, e^{(0.0057\pm0.0026)\,t+(0.0010\pm0.0005)\,t^2}$	0.947	86.61	3.01
1896–1914.....	$x = 8.695\,(y-35)^{-(0.2702\pm0.0261)}\, e^{(0.0163\pm0.0022)\,t-(0.0016\pm0.0005)\,t^2}$††	0.952	61.08	29.60
1915–29 (excl. 1917–21)....	$x = 12.04\, y^{-(0.3073\pm0.0285)}\, e^{-(0.0015\pm0.0056)\,t}$	0.971	94.12	0.20
OATS: x = Production per Animal Unit				
1875–92........	$x = 299.9\, y^{-(0.5687\pm0.1225)}\, e^{(0.0260\pm0.0030)\,t-(0.0018\pm0.0006)\,t^2}$	0.932	11.91	74.96
1899–1914.....	$x = 853.5\, y^{-(0.8042\pm0.1407)}\, e^{(0.0027\pm0.0051)\,t}$	0.853	74.36	− 1.64
1915–29 (excl. 1917–23)....	$x = 404.6\, y^{-(0.5592\pm0.4649)}\, e^{(0.0054\pm0.0103)\,t}$	0.703	35.90	13.52

** This is the percentage of variance ($\sigma^2_{\log x}$) attributable to animal units (z).

†† The elasticity of demand for this equation varies from point to point on the demand curve. At the point of means of the independent variables it is −0.61.

TABLE 49—Continued

Commodity and Period*	Equation of Demand x = Adjusted Quantity Demanded† y = Real Price (1913 = 100)† t = Time in Years with Origin at Middle of Each Period (Figures Preceded by ± Are *Standard* Errors)	Multiple Correlation R‡	Percentage of Variance ($\sigma^2_{\log x}$) Attributable to	
			Price	Time
Oats:—*Continued*				
x = Disappearance per Animal Unit				
1899–1914........	$x = 358.7\, y^{(0.5829 \pm 0.1156)}\, e^{-(0.0067 \pm 0.0041)\,t\,+\,(0.0012 \pm 0.0010)\,t^2}$	0.885	62.07	16.31
1915–29 (excl. 1917–23)....	$x = 336.1\, y^{-(0.5378 \pm 0.3194)}\, e^{(0.0109 \pm 0.0071)\,t}$	0.877	40.34	36.55
x = Total Production				
z = Animal Units				
1875–92........	$x = (10)^{-16}1626\, y^{-(0.4208 \pm 0.1219)}\, z^{(26.0646 \pm 5.1910)}\, e^{-(23.9761 \pm 5.1380)(\log z)^2}$	0.979	− 0.03	95.95**
1899–1914........	$x = 998.7\, y^{-(0.7407 \pm 0.1420)}\, z^{(0.8816 \pm 0.1849)}$	0.858	42.72	30.82**
1915–29 (excl. 1917–23)....	$x = 1013\, y^{-(0.5673 \pm 0.4202)}\, z^{(0.7153 \pm 0.4472)}$	0.596	10.03	25.54**
BARLEY:				
x = Per Capita "Consumption"				
1875–95........	$x = 2.250\, y^{-(0.1585 \pm 0.1197)}\, e^{(0.0213 \pm 0.0040)\,t\,-\,(0.00072 \pm 0.00068)\,t^2}$	0.803	− 5.10	69.56
1896–1914........	$x = 4.542\, y^{-(0.2151 \pm 0.1142)}\, e^{(0.0328 \pm 0.0044)\,t\,-\,(0.0038 \pm 0.0008)\,t^2}$	0.921	− 8.67	93.46
1915–29 (excl. 1917–21)....	$x = 6.391\, y^{-(0.3870 \pm 0.2361)}\, e^{(0.0069 \pm 0.0098)\,t\,+\,(0.0094 \pm 0.0020)\,t^2}$	0.902	9.94	71.48
RYE:				
x = Per Capita "Consumption"				
1875–95........	$x = 1.880\, y^{-(0.3605 \pm 0.1755)}\, e^{(0.0005 \pm 0.0037)\,t}$	0.436	18.96	0.06
1896–1914........	$x = 2.538\, y^{-(0.4374 \pm 0.1466)}\, e^{(0.0163 \pm 0.0033)\,t\,-\,(0.0037 \pm 0.0005)\,t^2}$	0.905	− 2.79	84.61
1915–29 (excl. 1917–21)....	$x = 4264\, y^{-(2.4444 \pm 0.4569)}\, e^{-(0.0766 \pm 0.0155)\,t\,+\,(0.0199 \pm 0.0045)\,t^2}$	0.926	29.58	56.15
BUCKWHEAT:				
x = Per Capita Production				
1879–95........	$x = 42.47\, y^{-(1.2790 \pm 0.2424)}\, e^{-(0.0061 \pm 0.0047)\,t\,+\,(0.0048 \pm 0.0011)\,t^2}$	0.995	45.90	35.95
1896–1914........	$x = 1.794\, (y - 56)^{-(0.0599 \pm 0.0196)}$	0.596‡‡	......	......
1915–29 (excl. 1917–21)....	$x = 7.434\, y^{-(0.9864 \pm 0.3195)}\, e^{-(0.0320 \pm 0.0072)\,t}$	0.860	1.91	72.08

‡‡ This is the coefficient of simple correlation between $\log x$ and $\log (y - 56)$.

and logarithmic surfaces obtained by any one method. For the time-regression method this is shown by Figures 23, 28, and 31 of chapter vi.

All figures in Table 47 to which no signs have been prefixed are either co-efficients of multiple correlation or indexes of correlation. Those to which signs are prefixed are simple correlation coefficients. Except as indicated in the foot-notes to the table, the equations of types (3), (4), (5), and (6) all have two param-eters, and the correlation coefficients of these equations are therefore directly comparable. They are not, however, comparable with those of types (1) and (2), since the equations of these types generally have three or four parameters. To make them all comparable, each correlation coefficient should be adjusted for the number of parameters in the equation from which it has been derived.[1] Although there are important exceptions, even the adjusted coefficients for the equations of types (1) and (2) are generally higher than the unadjusted co-efficients of the equations of types (3) to (6).

Comparing the correlation coefficients obtained by the time-regression method, we find that most of them are of the order of 0.8 or 0.9, indicating a good fit of the equations to the data. The time-regression equations for sugar, corn, cotton, hay, potatoes, and barley are uniformly good; those for oats, rye, and buckwheat yield a correlation coefficient of 0.7 or less in only one period; the equations for wheat, however, are very poor except for the post-war years.

It is difficult to determine the causes of these differences in goodness of fit, but we may offer a partial explanation. For commodities such as sugar, corn, potatoes, and hay the theoretical problem is relatively simple, either because there are no substitutes of importance for these commodities or because the United States is a relatively closed economy with respect to them. There is reason to expect, therefore, that we have been able to isolate and include in our regressions most of the important factors affecting the demand for these commodities. Although cotton represents a more complicated theoretical prob-lem, this difficulty is offset to a certain extent by the fact that the basic data are relatively accurate, since they represent the mill consumption as reported to the Bureau of the Census. The theoretical problem for wheat is not very differ-ent from that for cotton, since they are both international commodities. How-ever, the data on wheat production and stocks are subject to considerable error.[2] It is probable, then, that the differences in the coefficients of correlation are due to the varying complexity of the factors affecting the demands for the different commodities and to the varying degrees of accuracy of the underlying data.

---

[1] The adjusted coefficients derived from the time regressions are given in chaps. vi–xv in the tables of the demand functions. For an explanation of the adjusted and unadjusted coefficients see Part II, chap. vi, pp. 218–19, and also the Mathematical Appendix, Sec. VI, B.

[2] See chap. x, Sec. III.

II. THE ELASTICITIES OF THE DIFFERENT TYPES OF DEMAND CURVES

A. THE REDUCTION OF THE ELASTICITIES TO A COMPARABLE BASIS

In order to be able to compare the elasticities of demand yielded by the different curves, we must dispose of two questions: (*a*) At what point on each demand curve shall the elasticity of demand be computed for the purpose of comparison? and (*b*) What is the standard error of the elasticity of demand?

a) The convention which we have adopted for comparing elasticities that vary from point to point on the demand curve is to consider *those points on two different demand curves (or surfaces) as comparable whose coordinates contain the mean values of the independent variables*. In equations of types (1) and (2) the independent variables for each period whose means we need are price and time; in equations of types (3) and (4) the independent variables whose means we need are the trend ratios of the real prices; and in equations of types (5) and (6) the corresponding independent variables are the link relatives of the real prices. This convention will facilitate the interperiod and the intraperiod comparisons of the elasticities of demand derived by different methods.

b) When the coefficient of elasticity of demand is constant at every point on the demand curve, and when the curve is fitted by the method of least squares, the standard error of that coefficient can be determined by a well-known least-square procedure.[3] It is these standard errors which are attached to the constant coefficients of elasticity of this study. But, when the coefficient of elasticity varies from point to point on the demand curve, its standard error is not given directly by the method of least squares but must be derived from the standard errors of the parameters and of the variables on which it depends. Its exact value cannot be determined.[4] An upper limit to it has, however, been derived and is given in Appendix D. *It is this limiting value which has been attached to the elasticities of demand of equations (1), (3), and (5). These standard errors are not, therefore, strictly comparable with those of the constant elasticity equations (2), (4), and (6).* No standard error is given for those elasticities which are derived from demand curves in which one or more of the parameters was obtained by a method other than the method of least squares.

B. THE FINDINGS

Table 48 is a comparison of the elasticities of demand derived by different methods for the ten commodities studied in Part II. The results shown admit

---

[3] See my "The Standard Error of a Forecast from a Curve," *Journal of the American Statistical Association*, Vol. XXV (June, 1930), and the Mathematical Appendix of this book.

[4] After the book had gone to press, my assistant, Mr. Jacob L. Mosak, succeeded in deriving the exact formula for the standard error of the elasticity of demand. It appears in the last section of Appen. D. A full treatment of this subject is given in a paper which he has submitted to the *Jour. Amer. Statist. Assoc.*

of comparison vertically by periods and horizontally by methods used in any one period. We are primarily interested in the latter comparison.

A study of this table suggests the following observations:

1. For any one commodity in any one period there is reasonably close agreement between the elasticities of demand yielded by the various methods. This agreement is very close for sugar, potatoes, barley (second period), rye (first and second periods), and cotton (second period), and is practically perfect for wheat in the third period.

For most commodities, however, the elasticities of demand yielded by the time-regression method and the trend-ratio method are generally in closer agreement with each other than they are with the corresponding elasticities derived by the link-relative method. The latter method gives considerably higher numerical values for the coefficients of elasticity in the case of corn for all three periods and of wheat for the first two periods. There is need for a number of experiments with artificial series in order to explain the apparently erratic results yielded by the link-relative method.

2. The standard errors of the coefficients of elasticity of demand are all relatively large, generally affecting the accuracy of the first significant figure. This makes it impossible to say with a high degree of probability whether the difference between any two elasticities is significant. It is better, however, to have a numerical, though approximate, value for the elastictiy of demand of a commodity than none at all.

3. With the possible exception of buckwheat (first and third periods), and of rye for the third period, the demand for all the ten commodities is inelastic (i.e., $|\eta| < 1$). A large supply of any one of these commodities is, therefore, worth less than a small supply under normal conditions. This finding is supported by all the different methods.

4. The elasticities of demand for some commodities have remained remarkably constant from period to period. Thus, the elasticity of demand for sugar has been of the order -0.3 or -0.4 during each period. The elasticities of demand of other commodities have, however, fluctuated somewhat from period to period. Thus, the elastictiy of demand for corn seems to have decreased (numerically) in the last period and that for buckwheat seems to have decreased in the second period and to have increased again in the last period. But the standard errors of these coefficients are entirely too large to justify much confidence in these changes.

5. The fact that one method yields a lower correlation between the variables in question as compared with another does not necessarily mean that the elasticity of demand derived by it is materially different from that yielded by the method which gives the better description of the data (cf., e.g., the elasticities of demand for sugar, first period, with the corresponding coefficients of cor-

relation). This does not mean that in determining the coefficient of elasticity of demand the choice of curve is immaterial. In general, that coefficient is to be preferred which is deduced from the demand curve that fits the data with the highest degree of probability.[5] As has already been indicated, the curves which give the best fit, as measured by the correlation coefficient, generally belong to type (1) or to type (2), although there are important exceptions (see, e.g., the correlations relating to corn, first period). These curves also have another advantage in that they express the direct relations between the quantities (consumption, price, etc.) with which we are primarily concerned rather than between the trend ratios or the link relatives of these quantities. They afford, therefore, the best measure of the degree of elasticity of demand. It should be emphasized, however, that they cannot always be relied upon to give the best results. The careful statistician should not, therefore, pin his faith on any one method.

6. The question still remains, however, "Why do the different types of curves yield substantially the same degree of elasticity of demand?" The answer has already been given in the statistical chapters of Part II: *Within the neighborhood of the representative point* on the demand curves there is no very significant difference between the fits of several types of curves (see esp. Figs. 23, 28, and 31 of chap. vi, which shows this clearly).

III. THE SHIFTS OF THE DEMAND CURVES

A. REDUCTION OF THE SHIFTS TO A COMPARABLE BASIS

As we saw in the previous chapter, the concept of the shift of a demand curve through time is not a simple one. If we think of the quantity demanded at any given time as the dependent variable, and of the price as the independent variable, then the shifts of the demand curves which we have studied may take one of the following forms:

1. Between two given dates the *entire* demand curve may increase or decrease by the same *absolute amount*, this amount being either a constant through time or a continuous function of time.

2. Between two given dates the *entire* demand curve may increase or decrease by the same *relative amount*, this percentage being either a constant through time or a continuous function of time.

3. Between two given dates *different points* on the demand curve may increase or decrease by *different absolute* amounts, these amounts being continuous functions of price (as well as of time).

[5] This criterion does not dispose of the prior question whether we should compare regressions of x on y, or of y on x, or mutual regressions; for the selection of one of these regressions involves important assumptions regarding the weights or errors of the different variables (see chap. iv, Sec. III, and esp. n. 31). A change from one type of regression to the next generally involves a much greater change in the elasticity of demand than does a change from one type of curve to the next, which does not involve the substitution of a new dependent variable.

4. Between two given dates *different points* on the demand curve may increase or decrease by *different relative* amounts, these percentages being continuous functions of price (as well as of time).[6]

These four forms represent, respectively, the rates of shift of the first four equations of Table 46. All of them have in common the property that the rate of shift of each point on the demand curve is a continuous function of time. They differ from types (5) and (6) for which the rate of shift is discontinuous through time.

In view of the radically different ways in which the six types of demand functions shift through time, a comparison of all these rates of shift is an exceedingly difficult task even when all the demand curves relate to one and the same commodity. The task becomes insuperable when we also have to deal with the demands for different commodities measured in different units. This limits our comparison to *relative* rates of shift. Of the three types of demand functions whose rates of shift are given in relative terms—types (2), (4), and (6)—the simplest and most convenient is type (2), which assumes that each point on the demand curve shifts by the same (fixed or varying) *percentage* per annum. If we generalize this equation somewhat by writing it as

$$(3.1) \qquad\qquad x = A y^\alpha e^{\beta t + \gamma t^2} ,$$

we obtain for the varying relative rate of shift per unit per annum

$$(3.2) \qquad\qquad \frac{1}{x} \cdot \frac{\partial x}{\partial t} = \frac{\partial \log_e x}{\partial t} = \beta + 2\gamma t ,$$

in which β is the relative rate of shift, and 2γ its relative rate of acceleration. To express the rate of shift as a *percentage* per annum, we multiply (3.2) by 100.

B. THE FINDINGS

Table 49 brings together all the demand equations of type (2). The rate of shift can easily be read off by differentiating with respect to t the exponents of e. For example, the relative rate of shift of the demand curve for corn during the period 1896–1914 may be obtained from the fifth equation of Table 49:

$$(3.3) \qquad\qquad \frac{1}{x} \cdot \frac{\partial x}{\partial t} = 0.0140 - 2(0.0009)t ,$$

which, when multiplied by 100, shows that the demand was increasing at 1.4 per cent per annum but was subject to an annual retardation of 0.18 per cent. In chapter vii this was illustrated graphically in Figure 40B by the curve $D_1' D_3'$.

---

[6] Another classification of the different types of shift to which a demand curve may be subject can be obtained by considering the price as the dependent variable, i.e., by interchanging the words "quantity demanded" and "price" in the foregoing classification. But, as we have pointed out several times, the nature of our data is such that the demand curves which have the greatest significance are those giving the regression of consumption on price. Consequently, this alternative classification will not be used.

Figures 102a and 102b are a convenient summary of the rates of shift of
the demand curves of all ten of our commodities during each of the three periods

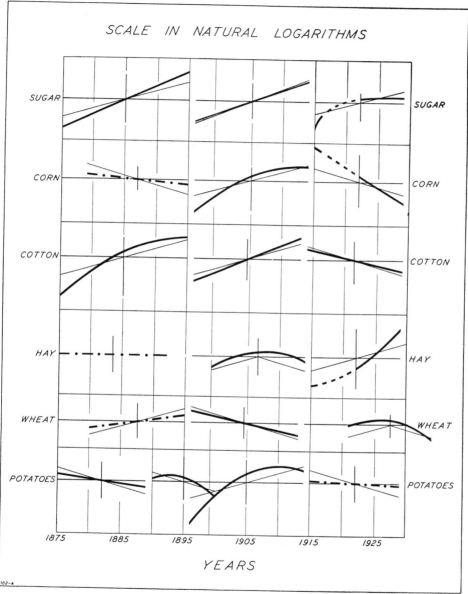

FIG. 102a.—The relative rates of shift of the demand curves for selected commodities, by periods,
1875–1929.

into which we have divided our data. These curves are simply the reproduction
on a natural-logarithm scale of the curves $D'_1 D'_3$ which we have studied in the

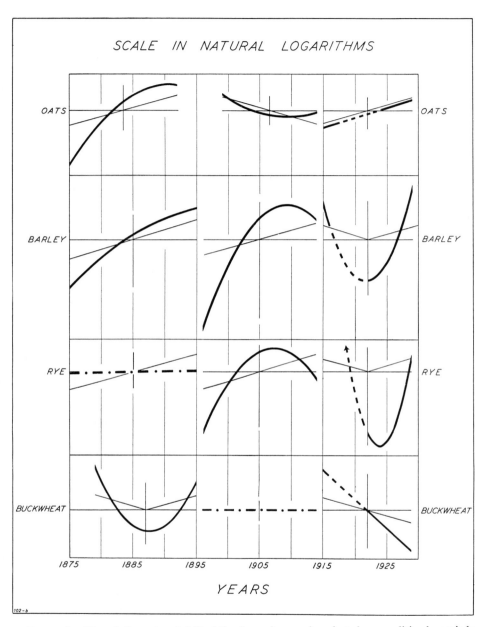

SCALE IN NATURAL LOGARITHMS

YEARS

FIG. 102b.—The relative rates of shift of the demand curves for selected commodities, by periods, 1875–1929.

preceding chapters and which measure the computed average rate of shift. The broken segments of these curves relate to years omitted in our study of the period in question, and the dot-dash lines represent rates of shift which are exceeded by their standard errors. Each of the thin lines through the origin, drawn in to facilitate the reading of the diagrams, represents a rate of shift of 1 per cent per annum.

The three curves at the top of Figure 102a relate to sugar. The first of these shows that during the period 1875–95 the demand curve shifted upward at the rate of 1.56 per cent per annum. The second curve shows that during the second period (1896–1914) it shifted upward at the somewhat lower rate of 1.24 per cent. The third curve shows that in the latter part of the third period (1915–29) the demand curve ceased to shift upward. In fact, the analysis of the data for 1922–36 (see chap. vi, Sec. VI) shows that the demand curve for sugar had not only reached its "ceiling" in the middle of the third period but has been shifting *downward* since 1922.

The second set of curves, which relates to corn, shows that the demand curve for corn had no significant shift during the first period, that it shifted upward but at a decreasing rate during the second period, and that it shifted downward at the average rate of 2.12 per cent per annum during the third period.

The per capita demand curve for cotton shifted upward, but at a decreasing rate, during the first period. During the second period it shifted upward at the constant rate of 1.40 per cent per annum. During the third period the trend was reversed; the demand curve shifted downward at the rate of 0.75 per cent per annum.

The fourth set of curves shows that the demand curve for hay (when demand is expressed in terms of tons per animal unit) remained fixed during the first period, shifted first upward and then downward during the second, and showed a tendency to shift upward again during the third period.

There are, however, at least two ways of allowing for the effects of changes in the number of animal units: (1) to divide the total consumption by the number of animal units or (2) to introduce the number of animal units as an additional variable in the demand equation, i.e., to write total consumption (x) as a function of the number of animal units (z) as well as of price (y) and time (t):

(3.4) $$ x = A y^\alpha z^\beta e^{\gamma t} . $$

When this procedure is adopted, the coefficient γ turns out to be statistically insignificant: the catch-all "time" disappears as a factor in the study of demand.[7] (The resulting equations are shown in Table 49.) Moreover, a rough graphical correlation analysis of the demand for hay for 1922–35 shows that in

[7] See, however, chap. ix, n. 10.

1927 or thereabouts even the apparent upward shift in the per animal unit demand for hay was reversed, and that the curve has been shifting downward since then.

Coming to wheat, we must first recall that there are no estimates of stocks for the first period and that even for the second period the data on stocks and production are subject to exceedingly large errors. It is, therefore, impossible to obtain even an approximate value of the rate of shift of the demand curve during these two periods. For the third period, however, the data are more reliable. They show that, based on the observations for 1921–34, the demand curve for wheat moved upward from 1921 to about 1926 and then began to shift rapidly downward.

As was shown in chapter xi, the demand for potatoes cannot properly be subdivided into the usual three periods, since the data for 1890–1900 are not comparable with the data for either the previous or the subsequent years. We have, therefore, divided our series into the periods 1875–89 and 1889–1900, and have considered the equations already derived for the period 1896–1914 as approximately descriptive of the years 1901–14. The first curve shows that during the period 1875–89 the demand curve for potatoes shifted downward at the rate of 0.48 per cent per annum. The second curve shows that during the period 1890–1900 the demand curve shifted downward at an increasing rate. During the years 1901–14 the demand curve shifted upward but at a decreasing rate. During the last period, 1915–29, the demand curve came to a standstill. The slight downward shift shown here is probably not significant. In fact, a graphical correlation analysis of the latest revised data for 1922–35 indicates that since 1929 or thereabouts the demand for potatoes has been subject to a downward shift.

Turning now to Figure 102b, it should be recalled (see chap. xii) that data relating to stocks for oats are available only since 1896. The three curves for oats are, therefore, not comparable with one another. The first one is based on production which we consider as being only approximately equal to consumption; the second and third are based on "disappearance" (i.e., production plus imports, minus exports, minus changes in stocks). In all the three periods the quantities are reduced to an animal-unit basis. The first curve shows that the "consumption" (=production) per animal unit had a marked upward shift during the first period. During the major part of the second period the demand (=disappearance per animal unit) shifted downward but at a decreasing rate, turning slightly upward only in the last few years of the period. During the third period it shifted upward at the rate of 1.09 per cent per annum. As was shown in chapter xii, however, a graphical correlation analysis of the latest revised data for the third period, including the years 1930–34, shows a definite reversal of this upward shift.

The curves for barley show that during the first period the per capita demand curve shifted upward at a decreasing rate, the average being approximately 2.1 per cent per annum; that during the second period, the shift was first upward and then downward, the turning-point being at 1910 or thereabouts; and that during the third period the shift was first downward and then upward. A graphical correlation analysis of the revised data for 1922–35 shows no discernible trend, but large up-and-down fluctuations.

The demand curve for rye had no upward or downward shift during the first period. During the second and third periods, however, its movements resembled those of the demand curve for barley.

The path followed by the shifting demand for buckwheat during the first period was U-shaped. During the second period there was no significant shift. During the third period the shift was downward at the rate of 3.2 per cent per annum.

Interest naturally centers on the changes that have taken place in the demand for these commodities during recent years. A glance at Figures 102a and 102b brings out the interesting fact that during the last period the demand curves for at least six of the commodities have either ceased to shift upward (sugar) or have shifted downward. The four apparent exceptions are hay, oats, barley, and rye. But, as we have already indicated, an analysis of the latest revised data shows that *the demands for even these commodities either have ceased to shift upward or have been shifting downward since 1929.*

IV: GENERAL CONCLUSIONS

Throughout the vast field of economics there are but few abstractions that are more common, more valid, or more useful than the elasticity of demand and the shift of the demand curve. Yet even these abstractions are imperfectly represented by vague words and are rarely stated in quantitative, statistical terms.

In this book we have attempted to give these concepts an approximate statistical significance. It is approximate because it depends not only upon the inaccuracies and incompleteness of the underlying data but also upon deliberate neglect of variables that are known to be involved in demand phenomena, such as the effects of substitutes, of changes in income, etc. In a first attack on such difficult problems as the elasticity of demand and the shift of demand, such simplifications are very desirable, if not indispensable.

If we accept the data at their face value, the conclusion emerges that the per capita demand curves of some of the basic farm crops have either ceased to shift upward or have begun to shift downward. The only upward shift in demand for these commodities to be expected in the near future is that due to the normal increase in population. But this increase is declining at a rapid rate.

The secular decrease of the per capita demand for these commodities is probably due to physiological causes. The shift of the population from country to city, the increasing use of the automobile, and the growing proportion of old people in the population—factors which have been at work for several decades —all have favored a smaller consumption of calories per capita. This has had an effect on the demand for the "heavier" foods. This explanation has been advanced independently by several students of the problem. In the words of Dr. Joseph S. Davis, of the Food Research Institute:

> Greater average longevity, shorter hours of labor, mechanization of industry and agriculture, increased transportation facilities, better housing and heating, have reduced per capita food requirements for energy and heat to quite a marked degree. . . . . The restriction of immigration, by the war and after, and the higher level of incomes after the war, made for a reduction in per capita use of certain staple food products and an increased use of sugar, fruits and vegetables, of which some are produced abroad, some on truck farms near cities, and only a part by organized agriculture. . . . . Here, in short, we have . . . . a tendency, present but obscured during the war and continuing since, for a reduced per capita demand at home.[8]

This decreasing per capita demand for some of the basic crops, coupled with the significant technical changes which American agriculture has witnessed since the war and which will probably lead to a veritable agricultural revolution, have an important bearing on the agricultural policies behind the A.A.A. and the "Ever Normal Granary" program. As long as the demand curves for these crops continue to shift downward, crop-restriction programs will give only temporary relief, for it is only a matter of a few years before the downward shift of the demand curve will counteract the gain obtained from the creation of an artificial scarcity. If this downward shift is not retarded, we shall in the future need relatively fewer farmers and probably fewer farms. Agriculture will have to adjust itself to these conditions or seek outlets in foreign countries.

[8] "America's Agricultural Position and Policy," *Harvard Business Review*, VI, No. 2 (1928), 146.

PART III

INTERRELATIONS OF DEMAND

CHAPTER XVIII

THE SPECIAL THEORY OF RELATED DEMANDS

CHAPTER XVIII

THE SPECIAL THEORY OF RELATED DEMANDS[1]

I. THE PROBLEM

In the statistical demand functions derived in Part II we neglected to take into consideration the effect on the demand for a commodity of changes in the prices of related commodities. There are two methods of overcoming this defect: (1) the purely empirical method, which consists of the introduction of the prices of the related goods as new variables into the demand function and the comparison of the changes effected, and (2) the rational method, which attempts, first, to deduce certain *theoretical* conditions which demand functions for related (completing and competing) goods must satisfy and, then, to see whether these relations are observed in fact. It is this second procedure which we shall follow in Part III.

More specifically, our objectives in Part III will be: (1) to define completing, competing, and independent goods; (2) to deduce and to compare the theoretical properties of demand functions for completing and competing goods; (3) to see whether these properties are satisfied by the concrete, statistical demand curves for (*a*) beef, pork, and mutton; (*b*) sugar, tea, and coffee; and (*c*) barley, corn, hay, and oats; (4) to call attention to certain new problems in statistical methodology; and (5) to indicate the practical significance of studies in the interrelations of demand. The analysis will proceed by stages as follows: In this chapter we shall present a special theory of the demand for related goods, which neglects the effect on demand of changes in income, and we shall subject it to a statistical test. In chapter xix, after reviewing the attempts which have been made to overcome the limitations of the special theory, we shall develop a more general theory, in which the effects of changes in income are directly taken into account, and we shall also submit it to a concrete test.

II. LIMITING CASES OF RELATED DEMANDS

In very few treatises on economics is the concept of related goods defined, although an attempt is often made to exemplify it. In developing our definitions, it will be convenient, first, to define the limiting cases of perfectly com-

[1] This and the following chapter are based largely on my studies, "Interrelations of Demand," *Journal of Political Economy*, XLI (1933), 468–512, and "Interrelations of Demand, Price, and Income," *ibid.*, XLIII (1935), 433–81.

I am profoundly grateful to Mr. Milton Friedman for invaluable assistance in the preparation and writing of these chapters and for permission to summarize a part of his unpublished paper on indifference curves in Sec. III, chap. xix.

pleting and perfectly competing goods and, then, to proceed to the definitions
of the intermediate cases of related goods, which are much more numerous and
important.

A. PERFECTLY COMPLETING AND PERFECTLY COMPETING GOODS

The first step in making more precise the general common-sense meanings of
competing and completing goods was taken by Professor Irving Fisher when he
defined in terms of indifference curves the extreme cases of *perfectly* completing
and *perfectly* competing commodities.[2]

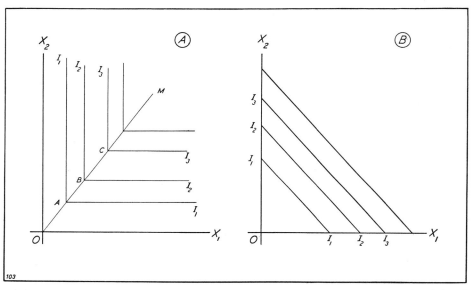

Fig. 103.—Indifference maps of two commodities illustrating perfect complementarity (*A*) and
perfect competitiveness (*B*).

According to Professor Fisher, two commodities are *perfectly completing* if
they cannot be used separately but only jointly in a fixed ratio. Left shoes and
right shoes are examples of this type of relation: they can be used only in the
ratio of one to one. In fact, perfectly completing goods may be looked upon as
constituting one commodity. The indifference curves for perfectly completing
goods reduce to pairs of straight lines meeting at right angles, such as I_1AI_1,
I_2BI_2, in Figure 103*A*. The slope of the line *OM* connecting the vertices of the
right angles equals the ratio in which the commodities must be consumed, and
every point on this line is a point of possible equilibrium. If the individual
possesses any combination of X_1 and X_2 represented by a point on *OM*—say,
the point *A*—an increase in only x_1 or in only x_2 is of no use to him. This is indi-

[2] "Mathematical Investigations in the Theory of Value and Prices," *Transactions of the Connecticut
Academy of Arts and Sciences* (New Haven), IX (July, 1892), 76–85. Reprinted in 1925 by the Yale
University Press. See also Pareto, *Manuel d'économie politique* (Paris, 1909), pp. 275–81.

cated by the fact that the two branches of each indifference curve are parallel to the x_1—and the x_2—axes, respectively.

Two commodities are *perfectly competing* if they can be substituted one for the other in a certain constant ratio. Thus, one-cent stamps and three-cent stamps are perfectly competing, since they can be substituted one for the other in the ratio of 3 to 1.[3] Indifference curves for perfectly competing goods reduce to parallel straight lines, such as I_1I_1 and I_2I_2 in Figure 103B; the slope of the indifference curves equals the ratio in which the commodities can be substituted for one another.

B. ROUGH TESTS FOR DISTINGUISHING BETWEEN COMPLETING AND COMPETING GOODS

While these extreme cases by themselves do not suggest a precise definition of the intermediate cases, they do suggest conditions that would be satisfied by the observed price and quantity data for perfectly competing and completing goods, and, by analogy, a rough statistical test for determining whether the goods of any given pair compete with or complete each other in consumption.

As we have just seen, if two goods are perfectly completing, they will be consumed in a constant ratio. The ratio of their prices is, however, subject to no restriction. We may then assume that when two goods are completing—even though not perfectly completing—the ratio of the quantity demanded of one of them to that of the other (x_i/x_j) fluctuates relatively less than the corresponding price ratios (y_i/y_j).

If, however, the two goods are perfectly competing (perfect substitutes), their prices must bear a given constant ratio. If the ratio is other than that at which the two goods can be substituted one for the other, only one of them will be consumed. As long as both goods are purchased, the price ratio must be constant and equal to the ratio in which one good can be substituted for the other. But with this constant price ratio the quantity ratio is completely indeterminate, and a small change in the price ratio will lead to a large change in the quantity ratio. We may, then, assume that, even when the goods are not perfectly competing, the quantity ratio fluctuates relatively more than the price ratio.

Of the various measures of fluctuation which suggest themselves, the coefficient of variation of the ratios is probably the most appropriate.[4] If, then, the coefficient of variation of the price ratios is significantly greater than the corresponding coefficient of the quantity ratios, the presumption is that the two

[3] There are, of course, instances in which one three-cent stamp cannot replace three one-cent stamps.

[4] While theory does not indicate whether the absolute variation or the relative variation in the ratios should be compared, statistical considerations suggest that it is the relative variations that are significant. For, by changing the units of measurement, it is possible to make the absolute magnitude of the fluctuations any size whatsoever.

commodities are completing; if it is significantly less than that of the quantity ratios, the presumption is that the two commodities are competing.

III. INTERMEDIATE CASES OF RELATED DEMANDS

A. THE EDGEWORTH-PARETO DEFINITION OF COMPLEMENTARITY

There remains the problem of defining the intermediate cases of complementarity.[5] The classic definition is that suggested by Edgeworth and Pareto and given in chapter i.[6] For ready reference it is convenient to restate it in terms of the symbols of Part II.

Let x_i and y_i be, respectively, the quantity and price of the commodity (X_i) $(i = 1, \ldots, n)$, and let

$$(3.1) \qquad\qquad \varphi = \varphi(x_1, \ldots, x_n)$$

be the total utility function for an individual. Denote the partial derivative of φ with respect to x_i by φ_i:

$$(3.2) \qquad\qquad \varphi_i = \frac{\partial \varphi}{\partial x_i},$$

and the second partial derivative with respect to x_i and x_j by φ_{ij}:

$$(3.3) \qquad\qquad \varphi_{ij} = \frac{\partial^2 \varphi}{\partial x_j\, \partial x_i}.$$

According to the Edgeworth-Pareto definition, the commodities (X_i) and (X_j) are said to be completing, independent, or competing, in consumption, according as an increase in the quantity of one of them augments, maintains constant, or diminishes the marginal degree of utility of the other,[7] i.e., according as

$$(3.4) \qquad\qquad \varphi_{ij} \gtrless 0 .$$

The sign of φ_{ij} need not, of course, be the same for the whole range of consumption combinations in question. This means that, according to this definition, two commodities may be completing for one range of combinations, independent for another, and competing for yet a third range.

---

[5] For want of a better expression, we shall use this term to designate competing, completing, or independent demands.

[6] See pp. 22–24.

[7] Pareto distinguishes between two kinds of dependence: (1) that which arises from the fact that the utility derived from the consumption of a particular good is *associated with* the utilities derived from the consumption of other goods and (2) that which arises from the fact that one good may be *substituted* for another in order to produce utilities which, if not identical, are at least approximately

The economic significance of the mathematical definitions (3.4) may perhaps be more easily grasped from the hypothetical illustration (Table 50), which I am adapting from Pareto.[8]

TABLE 50

HYPOTHETICAL ILLUSTRATION OF THE DIFFERENCE BETWEEN
COMPLETING AND COMPETING GOODS

QUANTITIES OF THE COMMODITIES (X_1) AND (X_2)		TOTAL UTILITY YIELDED BY THE COMBINATION	QUANTITIES OF THE COMMODITIES (X_1) AND (X_2)		TOTAL UTILITY YIELDED BY THE COMBINATION
x_1	x_2	$(x_1 x_2)$	x_1	x_2	$(x_1 x_2)$
Completing Goods					
10	10	5.0	10	11	5.15
11	10	5.1	11	11	7.00
Increase in total utility due to an increase of 1 unit in x_1		0.1	. . . .		1.85

Difference between the two increases in total utility. . . . . +1.75

Competing Goods					
10	10	5.0	10	11	6.0
11	10	5.9	11	11	6.1
Increase in total utility due to an increase of 1 unit in x_1		0.9	. . . .		0.1

Difference between the two increases in total utility. . . . . −0.8

equal. The two types of dependence differ only quantitatively, the first possessing in a less pronounced manner the same characteristics as the second. (See *Manuel*, p. 252.)

In the first type of dependence, Pareto finds it useful to distinguish the following extreme cases:

α) The dependence which arises from the fact that we appreciate more or less the use or the consumption of a thing, depending on the state in which we find ourselves. Thus a starving man cares little or nothing for knives, forks, spoons, napkins, etc., although under normal conditions of hunger the pleasure which he gets from a meal depends in part on the way in which it is served.

β) The dependence which arises from the fact that certain things must, in general, be used jointly if they are to yield us pleasure, irrespective of the condition in which we find ourselves. These are called *complementary* goods.

In the present chapter, goods which exhibit Pareto's first type of dependence (of which [α] and [β] are special cases) are referred to as *completing* goods, and those which exhibit the second type of dependence are referred to as *competing* goods.

[8] *Ibid.*, p. 269.

The upper part of this table shows that, when the quantity x_2 of (X_2) is kept constant at 10 units, the marginal degree of utility of (X_1)—i.e., the increase in total utility due to a unit increase in the quantity of (X_1)—is 0.1 when 10 units of (X_1) are consumed.[9] But when the quantity of (X_2) is increased to 11 units, the marginal degree of utility of the *same quantity* of (X_1) becomes 1.85. Since the increase in the marginal degree of utility is positive $(+1.75)$, the two commodities are said to be *completing*.

The lower part of Table 50 shows that, when the quantity x_2 of (X_2) is 10 units, the marginal degree of utility of (X_1) when 10 units of (X_1) are consumed is 0.9; and that, when the quantity of (X_2) is raised to 11 units, the marginal degree of utility of (X_1) is 0.1, although the quantity of (X_1) consumed has not changed. Since the difference between the two marginal degrees of utility is negative (-0.8), the commodities are said to be *competing*.[10]

Table 50 is, of course, nothing more than a numerical illustration of the fundamental definition of $\varphi_{12} = \dfrac{\partial^2 \varphi}{\partial x_2\, \partial x_1}$, which is

$$
(3.5) \quad \varphi_{12} = \lim \frac{\dfrac{\varphi(x_1 + \Delta x_1,\, x_2 + \Delta x_2) - \varphi(x_1,\, x_2 + \Delta x_2)}{\Delta x_1} - \dfrac{\varphi(x_1 + \Delta x_1,\, x_2) - \varphi(x_1,\, x_2)}{\Delta x_1}}{\Delta x_2} ,
$$

where the limit is found by letting, first, Δx_1 and, then, Δx_2 approach zero. If Δx_1 and Δx_2 are reasonably small, the fraction can be taken as approximately equal to the limit. Thus, if we substitute in this expression the values of φ from Table 50, and recall that $\Delta x_1 = \Delta x_2 = 1.0$, we obtain

$$\varphi_{12} = [7.00 - 5.15] - [5.1 - 5.0] = +1.75 ,$$

when the goods are completing, and

$$\varphi_{12} = [6.1 - 6.0] - [5.9 - 5.0] = -0.8 ,$$

when they are competing.

In this illustration we have compared the marginal degrees of utility of (X_1) corresponding to different values of (X_2). The same conclusions would have

[9] A distinction must be drawn between *marginal degree of utility* and *marginal utility*. The former is the partial derivative $\varphi_i \left(= \dfrac{\partial \varphi}{\partial x_i} \right)$. The latter is the increment $\varphi_i dx_i$. The two measures are numerically equal, though still different in meaning, and in dimension, when dx_i, the increase in the quantity of (X_i), is equal to unity, as is true in the present illustration. Thus, $dx_1 = 11 - 10 = 1$, and $\varphi_1 = (5.1 - 5.0)/1.0 = 0.1$.

[10] Strictly speaking, the commodities have this property *only within the range in question*, for, as we have already indicated, two commodities may be competing within one range of values for x_1 and x_2 and completing or independent within another range.

been reached from a comparison of the marginal degrees of utility of (X_2) for different values of (X_1), since, by assumption, the order of differentiation is immaterial, φ_{12} being equal to φ_{21}.

B. PROPERTIES OF DEMAND FUNCTIONS FOR RELATED GOODS

But utility functions cannot be used directly in the study of demand. It is desirable, therefore, to translate definition (3.4), which involves the subjective (and perhaps the nonexistent) total utility function, into operations on demand functions, i.e., on the objective magnitude of prices and quantities.

We begin by relating the degree of utility of a commodity to its price. By the fundamental equation of mathematical economics,[11] the relation is

$$(3.6) \qquad \varphi_i = m y_i$$

where m is the marginal degree of utility of money expenditure. Differentiating this equation with respect to x_j, we obtain

$$(3.7) \qquad \varphi_{ij} = m \frac{\partial y_i}{\partial x_j} + y_i \frac{\partial m}{\partial x_j} .$$

If we could eliminate the terms m and $\dfrac{\partial m}{\partial x_j}$ from the right-hand member of this equation, then we could define completing and competing goods in terms of the properties of $\dfrac{\partial y_i}{\partial x_j}$, which can be determined statistically. One way of doing this is to assume that the marginal degree of utility of money is approximately constant with respect to a small change in x_j consumed. The expression $\dfrac{\partial m}{\partial x_j}$ then becomes zero, and (3.7) becomes

$$(3.8) \qquad \varphi_{ij} = m \frac{\partial y_i}{\partial x_j} .$$

Since m is assumed constant and positive, the sign of φ_{ij} is the same as the sign of $\dfrac{\partial y_i}{\partial x_j}$. We may then say that the commodities (X_i) and (X_j) are completing, independent, or competing according as

$$(3.9) \qquad \frac{\partial y_i}{\partial x_j} \gtrless 0 ,$$

where

$$(3.10) \qquad y_i = y_i(x_1, \ldots, x_n, r) ,$$

[11] See chap. i, pp. 28–29, 34, 36–37.

is the demand function, in which x_i is the quantity of (X_i) demanded by the individual, and r is his income.[12]

Thus, for example, if we have two commodities with linear demand functions:

(3.11a)
$$\begin{cases} y_1 = a_1 + b_{11} x_1 + b_{12} x_2 + b_{1r} r \\ y_2 = a_2 + b_{21} x_1 + b_{22} x_2 + b_{2r} r , \end{cases}$$

then by (3.9), $b_{12} > 0$, and $b_{21} > 0$, if the commodities are completing; and $b_{12} < 0$, $b_{21} < 0$, if they are competing. (The coefficients b_{11} and b_{22} are always negative, since the demand curve is negatively sloped.) Of course, if the commodities are independent in consumption, $b_{12} = b_{21} = 0$.

If, for example, beef and pork are completing goods, it is clear from the properties of the related demand functions (3.11a) that an increase in the quantity demanded of either of the commodities should *increase* the price of the other. If, however, they are competing goods, an increase in the quantity demanded of any one of them should *decrease* the price of the other.

If we solve equations (3.11a) so as to express the quantities as functions of the prices, we obtain

(3.11b)
$$\begin{cases} x_1 = h_1 + c_{11} y_1 + c_{12} y_2 + c_{1r} r \\ x_2 = h_2 + c_{21} y_1 + c_{22} y_2 + c_{2r} r . \end{cases}$$

Condition (3.9) now assumes the form

(3.12)
$$\frac{\partial x_i}{\partial y_j} \gtrless 0$$

according as the commodities x_i and x_j are completing, independent, or competing. Thus $c_{12} < 0$, $c_{21} < 0$, if the commodities are completing, and $c_{12} > 0$, $c_{21} > 0$, if they are competing. (Of course, $c_{11} < 0$, $c_{22} < 0$, always, on account of the negative slopes of the demand curves.)

To take our previous illustration, if beef and pork are completing goods, an increase in the price of either one of them should decrease the demand for the other good; while, if they are competing, an increase in the price of either one of them should increase the demand for the other.

The properties of the related demand functions (3.11a) and (3.11b) can be most clearly grasped from the eight diagrams of Figure 104. The first group of four diagrams is a graphic representation of the demand functions when the price is taken as the dependent variable, as in (3.11a); the second group of four

[12] It is assumed that (3.10) can be subjected to the inverse transformation yielding
$$x_i = x_i(y_1, \ldots, y_n, r) .$$

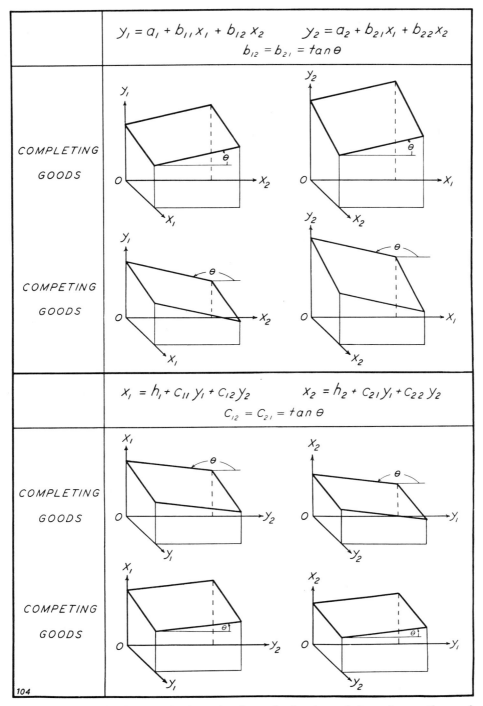

FIG. 104.—Relation between the demand surfaces of pairs of completing and competing goods when either the prices or the quantities are taken as the dependent variables.

diagrams is the corresponding graphic representation of the demand functions when quantity is taken as the dependent variable, as in (3.11b).

Other properties of the demand functions may be derived from the second-order conditions on the utility functions.[13]

Since φ is assumed to be finite and to have continuous second derivatives, at least in the region in which we happen to be interested, the order of differentiation is immaterial[14] so that

$$(3.13) \qquad \varphi_{ij} = \varphi_{ji} .$$

Substituting j for i in (3.6) and differentiating both sides of the resultant equation with respect to x_i, we have

$$(3.14) \qquad \varphi_{ji} = m \frac{\partial y_j}{\partial x_i} + y_j \frac{\partial m}{\partial x_i} .$$

By virtue of (3.13) we can equate the right-hand members of (3.7) and (3.14), obtaining

$$(3.15) \qquad m \frac{\partial y_i}{\partial x_j} + y_i \frac{\partial m}{\partial x_j} = m \frac{\partial y_j}{\partial x_i} + y_j \frac{\partial m}{\partial x_i} .$$

Again assuming m to be constant for small changes in x_j and x_i, we obtain from (3.15) an important condition which the demand equations (3.10) must satisfy:

$$(3.16) \qquad \frac{\partial y_i}{\partial x_j} = \frac{\partial y_j}{\partial x_i} .$$

If we multiply and divide the first member of (3.16) by x_j/y_i and the second member by x_i/y_j, we obtain an expression for (3.16) in terms of elasticities:

$$(3.17) \qquad x_i y_i \eta_{y_i x_j} = x_j y_j \eta_{y_j x_i} ,$$

which, when divided by the income

$$r = \Sigma x_i y_i ,$$

---

[13] See Pareto, *Manuel*, "Mathematical Appendix," §§ 47–48 and §§ 121–25; "Economie mathématique," *Encyclopédie*, Tome I, Vol. IV, Fasc. 4, p. 613; W. E. Johnson, "The Pure Theory of Utility Curves," *Economic Journal*, XXIII, No. 92 (December, 1913), 483–513; A. W. Zotoff, "Notes on the Mathematical Theory of Production," *Economic Journal*, XXXIII (March, 1923), 115–21; F. Y. Edgeworth, *Papers Relating to Political Economy*, II, 450–91; and R. G. D. Allen, "The Foundations of a Mathematical Theory of Exchange," *Economica*, XII (May, 1932), 219–23.

The second-order conditions are of particular importance in the consideration of the stability of the equilibrium of exchange. In a paper to which I shall refer later, Professor Harold Hotelling has also used these conditions to derive theorems in connection with the incidence of taxation.

[14] What this means is that two commodities are related in the same manner whether we consider the quantity of one of them as increasing while the quantity of the other remains constant, or the reverse.

yields

(3.18)
$$k_i \, \eta_{v_i \, x_j} = k_j \, \eta_{v_j \, x_i} \, ,$$

where $k_i = x_i y_i / r$ is the proportion of his income the individual spends on the commodity (X_i).[15]

Equation (3.16) means that, if the related demand functions are linear equations such as (3.11a), the coefficients b_{12} and b_{21} in these equations must be equal to each other. They are both positive if the commodities are completing and both negative if they are competing.

It can be shown that condition (3.16) involves the condition

(3.19)
$$\frac{\partial x_i}{\partial y_j} = \frac{\partial x_j}{\partial y_i}.$$

This means that in the transformed demand equations (3.11b) the coefficients c_{12} and c_{21} must be equal to each other. They are both negative if the commodities are completing and both positive if they are competing.

By multiplying and dividing the first member of (3.19) by y_j/x_i and the second member by y_i/x_j, we obtain an expression for (3.19) in terms of elasticities:

(3.20)
$$x_i \, y_i \, \eta_{x_i \, v_j} = x_j \, y_j \, \eta_{x_i \, v_j} \, ,$$

which, when divided by the income

$$r = \Sigma x_i \, y_i \, ,$$

yields:

(3.21)
$$k_i \, \eta_{x_i \, v_j} = k_j \, \eta_{x_j \, v_i} \, ,$$

which corresponds to (3.18).

If the demand functions (3.10) are not linear, the integrability conditions (3.16) yield, of course, different restrictions on the parameters. Thus, if instead of the linear form (3.11a) our demand functions are of the type

(3.22)
$$\begin{cases} y_1 = A_1 \, x_1^{a_{11}} \, x_2^{a_{12}} \, r^{a_{1r}} \\ y_2 = A_2 \, x_1^{a_{21}} \, x_2^{a_{22}} \, r^{a_{2r}} \end{cases}$$

where $a_{11} < 0$, $a_{22} < 0$; and $a_{12} \gtrless 0$, $a_{21} \gtrless 0$, depending upon whether the commodities are completing or competing, the condition (3.16) becomes

$$A_1 \, a_{12} \, x_1^{a_{11}} \, x_2^{a_{12}-1} \, r^{a_{1r}} = A_2 \, a_{21} \, x_1^{a_{21}-1} \, x_2^{a_{22}} \, r^{a_{2r}} \, ,$$

[15] These elasticities correspond to what Professor H. L. Moore has called "price flexibilities." They are not necessarily the reciprocals of the ordinary elasticities of demand.

which can be put in the form

$$(3.23) \qquad A_1 a_{12} = A_2 a_{21} x_1^{a_{21}-a_{11}-1} x_2^{a_{22}-a_{12}+1} r^{a_{2r}-a_{1r}} .$$

If (3.16) is to hold for all values of x_1 and x_2 (but not for all values of r), then (3.23) must be independent of changes in x_1 and x_2. This necessitates that

$$(3.24a) \qquad a_{21} - a_{11} - 1 = 0 ,$$

$$(3.24b) \qquad a_{12} - a_{22} - 1 = 0 .$$

We have, then,

$$A_1 a_{12} = A_2 a_{21} r^{a_{2r}-a_{1r}} .$$

If (3.16) is to hold also for all values of r, we must have

$$(3.24c) \qquad a_{1r} = a_{2r}$$

and

$$(3.24d) \qquad A_1 a_{12} = A_2 a_{21} .$$

Since the a's are price flexibilities

$$a_{ij} = \frac{\partial y_i}{\partial x_j} \cdot \frac{x_j}{y_i} ,$$

the foregoing conditions constitute an important restriction on their numerical values.

By the same reasoning we may determine the relations that must obtain between the parameters of any other set of nonlinear demand functions, if the integrability conditions are to hold.

Although the integrability conditions (3.16) and (3.19) relate to the demand function of an individual, they also hold when the individual demand functions are combined in the usual manner to yield the market demand function. Also, when two commodities are completing in the consumption of one individual (or group) and competing in that of another, then the combined demand function of the two individuals (or groups) for each of the two commodities may have the properties of either completing, competing, or independent demands, depending upon the shapes of the component individual demand functions. Of course, the numerical values of the partial derivatives in (3.16) and (3.19) of the combined demand function will be different from the corresponding values of the individual demand functions, but the integrability conditions will still hold.

The conditions (3.16) and (3.19) were first deduced by Professor Harold Hotelling, who followed a different procedure. In a very suggestive and important study[16] he not only pointed out the significance of these "integrability conditions" for the study of demand but also deduced similar conditions for supply and used them as tools with which to blaze new paths in the field of the incidence of taxation. In deriving these and other related conditions, Professor Hotelling began with the assumption that each entrepreneur or purchaser of goods tries to maximize his net profit and, by analogy from mechanics, made use of the notion of "price potential," whose partial derivatives are the quantities of the various commodities. It is therefore appropriate to refer to (3.16) and (3.19) as the "Hotelling conditions." I prefer, however, to adopt as my point of departure the fundamental classical definitions of related and independent commodities in terms of the utility functions, for these functions seem to me to lead more directly to the characteristics of the related demand equations with which we shall be primarily concerned in this chapter, and to have other heuristic properties as well.[17]

Such is the special theory of related demands. It provides us with clear definitions of competing, independent, and completing goods; with rough tests of complementarity requiring only a comparison of the coefficients of variation of the price ratios and the quantity ratios; and with the more refined tests (3.16) and (3.19) or their equivalent forms. It has some very desirable features: (1) it is a simple theory; (2) it defines complementarity solely in terms of the individual's tastes and preferences and without reference to the market situation; and (3) it gives explicit recognition of the fact that two commodities may be completing for a certain set of consumption combinations and competing or independent for another set. True, it has some serious limitations which will

[16] "Edgeworth's Taxation Paradox and the Nature of Demand and Supply Functions," *Journal of Political Economy*, XL, No. 5 (October, 1932), 577 ff.

[17] I had deduced conditions (3.9) and (3.12) (but not [3.16] and [3.19]) several years ago and had completed much of the statistical work of this chapter before I saw Professor Hotelling's manuscript. A reading of his paper then suggested that his conditions (3.16) and (3.19), as well as other conditions, could also be deduced from the inequality $d^2\varphi > 0$, which is the sufficient condition for a maximum of φ.

The work which first aroused my interest in the study of the demand for related goods is Professor Marco Fanno's memoir, "Contributo alla téoria economica dei beni succedanei," *Annali di economia*, Vol. II (1926); also published in book form by Università Bocconi Editrice (Milan, 1926). In 1928–29, Dr. Hans Staehle, of the International Labour Office at Geneva, who was then studying at the University of Chicago, was about to undertake a translation of this memoir—and I gave him my heartiest support—when the discovery of a few errors or inconsistencies compelled him to forego the project. Communication with Professor Fanno established the fact that he had already discovered and corrected these errors. A revised, abridged, and corrected version of his theory appears in his "Die Elastizität der Nachfrage nach Ersatzgütern," *Zeitschrift für Nationalökonomie*, I, Heft I (1929), 51–74. With the help of Dr. Edward Theiss of Hungary, I have re-examined Professor Fanno's memoir and have also read the German article. I have been forced to the conclusion that, consistent as his theory is, it is almost impossible to apply it and that, also, it lacks the heuristic properties which I believe are possessed by the theory which Professor Hotelling and I have been attempting to develop. I am indebted to Dr. Staehle, Professor Fanno, and Dr. Theiss for their interest and co-operation.

form the subject matter of the following chapter. But, as we shall see later, these constitute a good reason why we should subject the theory to a statistical test. Accordingly, we shall make use of the simple theory in the analysis of the interrelations of the following groups of commodities:

    A. Beef and Pork in the United States.
    B. Tea, Coffee, and Sugar in Canada.
    C. Barley, Corn, Hay, and Oats in the United States.

IV. APPLICATIONS

A. INTERRELATIONS OF THE DEMANDS FOR BEEF AND PORK

    As the first application of this theory we shall consider the extent to which the demand of the American consumers for beef and pork satisfy the condition

TABLE 51*

DATA USED IN THE ANALYSIS OF THE INTERRELATIONS OF THE DEMANDS FOR
BEEF AND PORK IN THE UNITED STATES, 1922–30

YEAR	BEEF AND VEAL		PORK		INCOME
	Total Consumption, Federally Inspected (Billion Lb.)	Composite Retail Price† (Cents per Lb.)	Total Consumption, Federally Inspected (Billion Lb.)	Composite Retail Price† (Cents per Lb.)	Index of Payrolls Lagged Three Months (1923–25 = 100)
	x_b	y_b	x_p	y_p	I
1922..........	4.94	24.1	5.78	34.7	76.3
1923..........	5.13	24.9	7.06	33.2	100.2
1924..........	5.28	25.3	7.20	33.2	97.4
1925..........	5.53	26.1	6.30	39.8	97.9
1926..........	5.74	27.0	6.15	42.3	105.6
1927..........	5.36	28.2	6.71	39.5	102.8
1928..........	4.81	32.4	7.33	37.5	100.1
1929..........	4.85	34.5	7.30	38.4	107.3
1930..........	4.77	31.6	6.92	37.1	93.4
Mean......	5.157	28.23	6.750	37.3	97.89
Standard deviation	0.324	3.509	0.524	2.94	8.62

  * Source: Mordecai Ezekiel, "Some Considerations on the Analysis of the Prices of Competing or Substitute Commodities," *Econometrica*, I (1933), 180.
  † Average of monthly prices weighted by consumption.

of consistency (3.16) or (3.19). Although the demands for these commodities were not analyzed in Part II, the fact that they are generally taken as competing makes them a suitable pair for this test. For this purpose we shall use the data of Table 51. It should be observed that the consumption figures relate not to total consumption but only to that part which is federally inspected.

Let us first apply the rough test. The coefficient of variation of the ratios of x_b to x_p is $V(x_b/x_p) = 12.2$ per cent, and the corresponding coefficient of variation of the price ratios is $V(y_b/y_p) = 11.7$ per cent. The coefficient of variation of the quantity ratios is greater than that of the price ratios, and neither series of ratios is subject to secular changes. If the difference between the two coefficients is significant, then we may conclude that beef and pork are probably competing in consumption.

It remains to be seen whether the test based on the demand equations will confirm this conclusion. Although theoretically it is a matter of indifference whether we write our demand equations with the quantities or with the prices as the dependent variables, in practice only one set of regressions may have significance. In the present illustration, however, either set of regressions may be used to test our theory. Table 52 gives the regressions of quantity on the prices (and income), as well as the regressions of price on the quantities (and income).

The time variable was introduced into each of these equations and found insignificant. To judge from the magnitude of R', the equations with quantity as the dependent variable give a better fit to the data than do those in which price is the dependent variable.

The relations shown by equations 1 and 2 may also be expressed in relative terms, or elasticities, at the representative points on the demand surfaces.[18] We obtain from equation 1:

$$\eta_{x_b \, v_b} = -0.49 , \qquad \eta_{x_b \, v_p} = +0.46 , \qquad \eta_{x_b I} = +0.36 ,$$

and from equation 2:

$$\eta_{x_p \, v_p} = -0.81 , \qquad \eta_{x_p \, v_b} = +0.35 , \qquad \eta_{x_p I} = +0.60 .$$

It will be observed that the demand for beef is more responsive to a 1 per cent change in the price of beef than it is to the same relative change in either the price of pork or the size of the income (payrolls). Similarly the demand for pork is more responsive to the price of pork than it is to the price of either of the other two variables.

Let us now apply our tests (3.19) and (3.16) to these equations and see whether they agree with the findings of the rough criterion.

The test appropriate to the first set of equations is by (3.19):

$$\frac{\partial x_b}{\partial y_p} = \frac{\partial x_p}{\partial y_b} .$$

[18] See chap. vi, pp. 215–17, for definitions and methods of computation.

TABLE 52

THE RELATED DEMAND FUNCTIONS FOR BEEF AND PORK IN THE UNITED STATES, 1922–30

x_b, x_p = Total consumption of federally inspected beef and pork (unit: 1 billion pounds)
y_b, y_p = Composite retail prices of beef and pork (unit: cents per pound)
I = Index of payrolls, lagged by three months

(The figures in parentheses are standard errors)

EQUATION NUMBER		Constant Term	y_b	y_p	I	Quadratic Mean Error ε (Billion Pounds)	Adjusted Multiple Correlation Coefficient R'	EQUATION NUMBER
1	$x_b =$	3.4892	−0.0899 (0.0086)	+0.0637 (0.0104)	+0.0187 (0.0037)	0.0791	0.9732	1
2	$x_p =$	5.7729	+0.0829 (0.0176)	−0.1457 (0.0212)	+0.0416 (0.0077)	0.1621	0.9565	2

EQUATION NUMBER		Constant Term	x_b	x_p	I	Quadratic Mean Error ε (Cents per pound)	Adjusted Multiple Correlation Coefficient R'	EQUATION NUMBER
3	$y_b =$	77.4347	−13.3040 (3.3159)	−4.2838 (2.3235)	+0.4936 (0.1325)	1.8078	0.8741	3
4	$y_p =$	68.7746	−5.3652 (3.2979)	−7.5333 (2.3109)	+0.4806 (0.1318)	1.7980	0.8169	4

EQUATIONS — DESCRIPTIVE CONSTANTS

This condition is satisfied approximately by these equations, for we have:

$$+0.0637 \doteqdot +0.0829 .$$
$$(0.0104) \quad (0.0176)$$

From the fact that both coefficients are positive, we conclude that the commodities are competing in consumption.

The test appropriate to the second set of equations is by (3.16):

$$\frac{\partial y_b}{\partial x_p} = \frac{\partial y_p}{\partial x_b},$$

which is also satisfied approximately, for

$$-4.2838 \doteqdot -5.3652 .$$
$$(2.3235) \quad (3.2979)$$

The fit of this pair of equations, however, is not so good as that of the first pair. Since both coefficients are negative, we conclude as before that beef and pork are competing in consumption.

Tests (3.19) and (3.16) thus confirm the results of the rough test.

B. INTERRELATIONS OF THE DEMANDS FOR SUGAR, TEA, AND COFFEE IN CANADA

As a second test of the special theory, we shall analyze the demands for sugar, tea, and coffee. Since sugar is probably complementary to both tea and coffee, and since tea and coffee are probably competing in consumption, it is instructive to apply our tests to this triad of commodities. However, such a large part of the sugar consumed is used for other purposes than for sweetening tea and coffee that we may find it difficult to verify the theoretical relationship existing between sugar and tea and coffee. In the United States, moreover, the per capita consumption of tea is very small as compared with that of coffee, so that the known and large errors in the data on consumption and prices would almost certainly mask the theoretical relationships. We have therefore decided to analyze the Canadian, rather than the American, demands for sugar, tea, and coffee.

There are no data on the actual consumption of sugar, tea, and coffee in Canada. We are, therefore, compelled to treat imports as being approximately equal to consumption, hoping that the changes in stocks have not been sufficiently great to upset the expected relationships. Table 53 shows the per capita imports (=consumption) and the deflated prices of the three commodities which we shall use in our analysis. The basic unadjusted quantity and price series, as well as the deflators of the quantities and prices from which Table 53 has been derived, are shown in Table XIII of the Appendix.

TABLE 53*

DATA USED IN THE ANALYSIS OF THE INTERRELATIONS OF THE CANADIAN
DEMANDS FOR SUGAR, TEA, AND COFFEE, 1922–33

YEAR	SUGAR		TEA		COFFEE	
	Per Capita Net Imports (Pounds)	Deflated Price (Dollars per Cwt.)	Per Capita Net Imports (Pounds)	Deflated Price (Cents per Pound)	Per Capita Imports (Pounds)	Deflated Price (Cents per Pound)
	x_s	y_s	x_t	y_t	x_c	y_c
1922	87.91	4.523	4.319	22.63	2.580	12.54
1923	82.36	5.426	4.282	27.52	2.095	14.20
1924	77.24	6.092	4.187	30.16	2.419	14.79
1925	79.23	4.438	3.905	32.80	2.218	19.36
1926	82.77	3.740	3.949	33.56	2.460	17.90
1927	84.60	4.067	3.926	33.33	2.636	16.26
1928	80.58	3.966	3.922	33.25	2.887	16.70
1929	82.62	3.595	3.856	32.43	2.618	19.68
1930	82.36	3.450	4.546	30.77	2.798	16.80
1931	86.39	3.747	4.124	27.43	3.200	13.88
1932	78.97	4.145	3.675	30.01	2.992	14.61
1933	76.58	4.677	3.582	31.83	2.987	18.20
Means	81.80	4.322	4.023	30.48	2.658	16.24
Standard deviations	3.32	0.748	0.266	3.11	0.316	2.18

* Source: Basic data and deflators given in Append. A, Table XIII. I am grateful to the Dominion Statistician, Mr. R. H. Coats, for special compilations.

TABLE 54

ROUGH TEST FOR THE TYPE OF RELATIONS EXISTING BETWEEN THE
DEMANDS FOR COFFEE, TEA, AND SUGAR IN CANADA,
FISCAL YEARS, 1922–33

COMMODITIES	COEFFICIENT OF VARIATION		PROBABLE TYPE OF RELATION
	Quantity Ratios	Price Ratios	
Coffee and tea	15.4	7.4	Competing
Sugar and tea	5.6	23.5	Completing
Sugar and coffee	12.7	25.8	Completing

Before proceeding with the derivation of the demand curves, it is instructive to apply our rough tests for the type of relations existing between the demands for the three commodities. Table 54 is a summary of the results obtained.

The results are what we should expect. Coffee and tea are presumably competing in consumption, while sugar is complementary both to tea and to coffee. The coefficients of variation relating to sugar and coffee are, however, to be suspected because both the quantity ratios and the price ratios have a pronounced downward secular trend.

Will the more refined tests (3.16) and (3.19) bear out the findings of Table 54? Table 55 provides an answer. This table is a summary of the regressions of the prices on the quantities. Most of the regressions of quantity on price turned out to be insignificant.

The first three groups of equations represent the demand functions for each pair of commodities which can be formed from our triad of commodities. Each of these pairs is in turn looked upon as a closed set, and the price of each member of the pair is expressed as a linear function of the two quantities and of time. In the ·fourth group of equations all three commodities are considered as a closed set, and the price of each is expressed as a function of the three quantities and of time.

In all four groups of equations the regression of the price of any commodity on the quantity of the same commodity is negative and probably significant. However, *in all but the first pair of equations, the regression of the prices on the quantities of the other commodities are probably insignificant as compared with their standard errors.*[19] The two equations in Group I are, therefore, the only equations which satisfy the integrability condition:

$$(3.16) \qquad \frac{\partial y_c}{\partial x_t} = \frac{\partial y_t}{\partial x_c},$$

at least approximately, for they yield

$$-2.3318 \doteq -5.5509 .$$
$$(1.9864) \qquad (2.3985)$$

The negative sign of both of these coefficients indicates, of course, that tea and coffee are competing in consumption.

The results yielded by the other equations are quite disappointing. They indicate that, although the fluctuations in the Canadian statistics of imports of tea, coffee, and sugar are sufficiently close to the fluctuations in the (unknown) statistics of consumption to yield negative regressions of price on consumption, the data are not sufficiently accurate for the purpose of obtaining

[19] This statement is based on the rather liberal interpretation of "significance" which we have made in this work, namely, that a regression coefficient is considered significant if it exceeds its standard error. (We have not taken $P = 0.05$ or $P = 0.01$ in R. A. Fisher's t-test as the limit of significant deviation.) The extreme difficulty of getting more reliable data for demand analysis seems to dictate this unorthodox interpretation.

TABLE 55

The Interrelations of the Demands for Sugar, Tea, and Coffee in Canada, 1922–33

x_s, x_t, x_c = Per capita consumption (imports) of sugar, tea, and coffee (in pounds)
y_s = Deflated price of sugar (dollars per cwt.)
y_t, y_c = Deflated price of tea and coffee (in cents per pound)
t = Time in years, the origin being at January 1, 1928

(The figures in parentheses are standard errors)

Equation Number		Constant Term	x_s	x_c	x_t	t	t^2	Quadratic Mean Error ϵ^*	Adjusted Multiple Correlation Coefficient R'	Equation Number
1	$y_c =$	43.0820	....	−6.1842 (2.6054)	−2.3318 (1.9864)	+0.5613 (0.2633)	−0.0859 (0.0425)	1.5175	0.7447	1
2	$y_t =$	65.4313	....	−5.5509 (2.3985)	−4.4499 (1.8287)	+0.5653 (0.2424)	−0.1932 (0.0391)	1.3970	0.9031	2
3	$y_s =$	14.4118	−0.1402 (0.0455)		+0.2564 (0.6290)	−0.1402 (0.0441)	+0.0291 (0.0125)	0.4551	0.8128	3
4	$y_t =$	77.4043	−0.3697 (0.1220)		−3.5013 (1.6873)	+0.0787 (0.1184)	−0.2182 (0.0335)	1.2206	0.9269	4
5	$y_s =$	14.8228	−0.1531 (0.0497)	+0.6424 (0.9018)	....	−0.2023 (0.0856)	+0.0266 (0.0127)	0.4446	0.8222	5
6	$y_c =$	39.6852	−0.0699 (0.1839)	−6.2881 (3.3360)	....	+0.6401 (0.3168)	−0.0853 (0.0470)	1.6446	0.6905	6
7	$y_s =$	14.4523	−0.1596 (0.0562)	+0.6258 (0.9649)	+0.0358 (0.6576)	−0.1937 (0.0946)	+0.0266 (0.0136)	0.4752	0.7937	7
8	$y_c =$	43.3177	−0.0058 (0.1939)	−6.1244 (3.3312)	−2.3112 (2.2701)	+0.5560 (0.3266)	−0.0862 (0.0469)	1.6404	0.6925	8
9	$y_t =$	77.2092	−0.2758 (0.1383)	−3.0205 (2.3765)	−3.4020 (1.6195)	+0.3374 (0.2330)	−0.2063 (0.0334)	1.1702	0.9330	9

* The units are the same as the corresponding prices.

the *interrelations* of the demands of these commodities. And it is these inter-relations which constitute the keystone of our theory.

Since the Canadian data are admittedly defective as measures of the consumption of sugar, tea, and coffee, it is impossible to tell from this experiment whether the assumption of the rationality of human behavior in the market place, which underlies condition (3.16), is congruent with experience.

C. INTERRELATIONS OF THE DEMANDS FOR BARLEY, CORN, HAY, AND OATS

For our third illustration we shall make use of the data for the four feed crops—barley, corn, hay, and oats—the demands for which have already been derived in Part II.

1. THE ROUGH TEST

Table 56 gives the coefficients of variation of the quantity ratios and the price ratios of each of the six pairs of commodities that can be formed from our

TABLE 56

ROUGH TEST FOR THE TYPE OF RELATIONS EXISTING BETWEEN THE
DEMANDS FOR BARLEY, CORN, HAY, AND OATS IN
THE UNITED STATES, 1896–1914

| COMMODITIES | COEFFICIENT OF VARIATION OF | | APPARENT TYPE OF RELATION |
	Quantity Ratios	Price Ratios	
Barley and corn............	21.6	19.6	Competing
Barley and hay............	20.6	15.5	Competing
Barley and oats............	21.3	18.2	Competing
Corn and hay..............	12.9	20.8	Completing
Corn and oats..............	11.4	11.4	?
Hay and oats..............	15.6	17.1	Completing

set of four. The apparent types of relation indicated by the magnitudes of these coefficients are, however, of little significance because an examination of the graphs of the ratios of the quantities and of the ratios of the corresponding prices (not shown here) shows that they are not free from secular movements. Thus for barley and corn the quantity ratios have a pronounced upward trend. If allowance were made for this trend, the coefficient of variation of the quantity ratios would be materially reduced, and the commodities would be classified as *completing*.

In the case of barley and hay, both sets of ratios have upward trends, that of the quantity ratios being steeper than that of the price ratios. Apparently the larger coefficient of variation of the quantity ratios is due to this steeper trend. If the data were corrected for their trends, the test would suggest another relation between the commodities—perhaps one of independence.

The quantity ratios for barley and oats have a parabolic trend which is concave downward. Elimination of this trend is likely to indicate a different type of relationship.

In corn and hay it is the price ratios which move upward with time, while the quantity ratios appear to have no trend. It is doubtful, however, whether the test with the adjusted ratios would yield a different type of relationship.

The ratios for corn and oats have no secular trends, but the coefficients of variation are so close to each other that the differences between them are insignificant. The approximate equality between them might perhaps be taken as an index of independence, but our rough criterion provides no definition of independent goods.

The ratios for hay and oats have no trends, so that there exist no obvious grounds, other than that of statistical significance, for suspecting the relationship of complementarity suggested by the larger coefficient of variation of the price ratios.

It may be asked, "Why not eliminate the secular trends from all the ratios and compare the coefficients of variation of the adjusted data?" The answer is the one which we have already given in the sugar-tea-coffee example, namely, that the criterion is a rough one at best, hardly warranting the time and labor that would have to be expended in the adjustment of the data, especially since we shall be applying the more refined tests (3.16) and (3.19) to the same data. We turn, therefore, to the functions expressing the *interrelations* of the demands for the crops in question, which are indispensable for the application of the more refined tests.

2. THE RELATED DEMAND FUNCTIONS

Table 57 summarizes the equations in which the quantities are expressed as a function of the prices as well as those in which the prices are expressed as a function of the quantities. These equations differ from the corresponding equations in Part II in that they express each quantity as a function of all the four prices and of time, and each price as a function of all four quantities and of time.[20] Table 58 is a corresponding summary for the logarithmic equations.

In fitting the equations of the first set of Tables 57 and 58, the assumption was made that the prices are free from error, that the failure of the observations to fall on the demand surface is due to errors or deviations in the quantities. In fitting the equations of the second set of Tables 57 and 58, the assumption was made that the quantities are free from error, that the failure of the observations to fall on the demand surface is due to errors or deviations in the prices.

---

[20] One source of inaccuracy of our equations is the fact that the quantity series for oats is that of production and not disappearance (we saw in chap. xii that the disappearance figures give better results), but the equations of Tables 57 and 58 were computed before we discovered the statistics on disappearance, and it was not believed worth while to recompute all the equations.

TABLE 57

THE INTERRELATIONS OF THE DEMANDS FOR BARLEY, CORN, HAY, AND OATS IN THE UNITED STATES, 1896–1914 (ARITHMETIC EQUATIONS)

x_b, x_c, x_h, x_o = Per capita consumption of barley, corn, hay, and oats, respectively (in bushels)
y_b, y_c, y_h, y_o = Real price (in cents per bushel)
t = Time in years (origin: January 1, 1906)

(The figures in parentheses are standard errors)

EQUATION No.		Constant Term	y_b	y_c	y_h	y_o	t	t^2	Quadratic Mean Error ε (Bushels)	Adjusted Multiple Correlation Coefficient R'	EQUATION No.
1	$x_b =$	2.245	− 0.0056 (0.0049)	− 0.0121 (0.0080)	+ 0.0044 (0.0592)	+ 0.0143 (0.0132)	+ 0.0601 (0.0094)	− 0.0053 (0.0015)	0.1484	0.8860	1
2	$x_c =$	49.066	− 0.0216 (0.0452)	− 0.3551 (0.0728)	− 0.0256 (0.5415)	+ 0.0327 (0.1209)	+ 0.3223 (0.0863)	− 0.0123 (0.0133)	1.3573	0.9189	2
3	$x_h =$	1.295	− 0.0002 (0.0013)	− 0.0047 (0.0020)	− 0.0473 (0.0150)	+ 0.0075 (0.0034)	+ 0.0020 (0.0024)	− 0.0004 (0.0004)	0.0377	0.8788	3
4	$x_o =$	24.163	+ 0.0317 (0.0231)	+ 0.0693 (0.0373)	− 0.6074 (0.2773)	− 0.2971 (0.0619)	+ 0.1218 (0.0442)	− 0.0070 (0.0068)	0.6951	0.8675	4

EQUATION No.		Constant Term	x_b	x_c	x_h	x_o	t	t^2	ε (Cents)	R'	EQUATION No.
5	$y_b =$	212.309	−13.6012 (26.1816)	+ 0.5099 (1.2793)	−90.4983 (56.0220)	−4.9378 (2.9254)	+ 1.9864 (1.4762)	− 0.2452 (0.1650)	13.2911	0.6571	5
6	$y_c =$	131.419	− 1.6228 (7.4008)	− 2.3992 (0.3616)	− 0.1919 (15.8358)	− 0.3603 (0.8269)	+ 1.0197 (0.4173)	− 0.0434 (0.0466)	3.7570	0.9487	6
7	$y_h =$	2.316	+ 0.6087 (1.3872)	+ 0.0400 (0.0678)	−13.7885 (2.9682)	− 0.2777 (0.1550)	+ 0.0187 (0.0782)	− 0.0037 (0.0087)	0.7042	0.8306	7
8	$y_o =$	81.378	− 0.9888 (5.3914)	− 0.7899 (0.2634)	+17.1496 (11.5362)	− 2.5992 (0.6024)	+ 0.6597 (0.3040)	− 0.0451 (0.0340)	2.7369	0.9222	8

TABLE 58

THE INTERRELATIONS OF THE DEMANDS FOR BARLEY, CORN, HAY, AND OATS IN THE UNITED STATES, 1896–1914 (LOGARITHMIC EQUATIONS)

x'_b, x'_c, x'_h, x'_o = Logs of per capita consumption of barley, corn, hay, and oats, respectively
y'_b, y'_c, y'_h, y'_o = Logs of real price
t = Time in years (origin: January 1, 1906)

(The figures in parentheses are standard errors)

EQUATION No.		Constant Term	y'_b	y'_c	y'_h	y'_o	t	t^2	Quadratic Mean Error ε (Per Cent)	Adjusted Multiple Correlation Coefficient R'	EQUATION No.
1	$x'_b =$	0.8043	−0.2106 (0.2177)	−0.3383 (0.2595)	−0.0924 (0.3626)	+0.3269 (0.3169)	+0.01646 (0.00264)	−0.00154 (0.00039)	91.4–109.4	0.8985	1
2	$x'_c =$	2.7772	+0.0006 (0.1169)	−0.7076 (0.1393)	−0.1346 (0.1947)	+0.0311 (0.1701)	+0.00644 (0.00142)	−0.00033 (0.00021)	95.3–104.9	0.9224	2
3	$x'_h =$	0.6943	−0.0321 (0.1354)	−0.3131 (0.1013)	−0.7291 (0.2255)	+0.3570 (0.1970)	+0.00129 (0.00164)	−0.00033 (0.00024)	94.6–105.7	0.8528	3
4	$x'_o =$	2.3668	+0.2282 (0.1414)	+0.3083 (0.1685)	−0.6172 (0.2355)	−1.1107 (0.2058)	+0.00387 (0.00172)	−0.00020 (0.00025)	94.4–106.0	0.8781	4
		Constant Term	x'_b	x'_c	x'_h	x'_o	t	t^2	ε (Per Cent)	R'	
5	$y'_b =$	2.4761	−0.2327 (0.5512)	+0.0248 (0.4127)	−0.7467 (0.5329)	−0.6311 (0.3996)	+0.01078 (0.00841)	−0.00140 (0.00093)	85.0–117.7	0.6827	5
6	$y'_c =$	3.6457	−0.1803 (0.2198)	−1.2176 (0.1645)	+0.1694 (0.2124)	−0.0694 (0.1593)	+0.01204 (0.00335)	−0.00071 (0.00037)	93.7–106.7	0.9597	6
7	$y'_h =$	1.0570	+0.1267 (0.0682)	+0.0942 (0.1395)	−0.8750 (0.1348)	−0.2533 (0.1351)		....	94.5–105.8	0.8522	7
8	$y'_o =$	3.2953	−0.0891 (0.2261)	−0.5938 (0.1693)	+0.3761 (0.2185)	−0.7249 (0.1639)	+0.00840 (0.00345)	−0.00060 (0.00038)	93.5–106.9	0.9304	8

Actually, both variables are subject to error, but it is exceedingly difficult, if not impossible, to make allowance for this fact in the curve-fitting process when the demand functions which we wish to fit are nonlinear.[21] Since, however, the prices are known more accurately than the quantities, the regressions of the quantities on the prices give a better approximation to the true relation than do the regressions of the prices on the quantities. It is, therefore, appropriate that we should devote most of our attention to the first four equations of Tables 57 and 58.

Before proceeding to a consideration of the extent to which these equations satisfy the integrability conditions (3.19), let us pause to note the more important differences between these equations and the corresponding simpler, unrelated demand equations for barley, corn, hay, and oats given in Part II.

1. The diagonal terms of the first four equations of Table 57 which are all negative, and which give the regressions of the various quantities on their respective prices, are practically the same as in the corresponding simpler unrelated equations of Part II. The standard errors of these terms are, however, larger than the standard errors of the corresponding equations in Part II. This shows that the precision of the *slopes* of the demand curves determined in Part II on the assumption that the quantity demanded of each commodity is a function only of its price and time has not been improved through the introduction of the other prices into the demand equation.

2. The introduction of the additional variables (prices) has, however, resulted in an improvement in the "fits" of some of the curves. Judged by the magnitudes of the corresponding R'''s the "fits" of the demand curves for hay and oats are definitely better, while those for barley and corn are not significantly worse.[22]

3. Of the twelve remaining regression coefficients, each of which gives the change in the quantity demanded of a given commodity corresponding to an increase in the price of *another* commodity, some are positive, and some are negative, thus indicating that some of the commodities supplement one another in consumption (completing), while others are correlated by way of rivalry (competing).

4. Turning to Table 58, which gives directly the elasticities of demand of the various commodities with respect to each of the four prices (first group of equations), and the flexibilities of the various prices with respect to each of the four quantities (second group of equations), we observe that the demand for each of the four commodities with respect to the price of any other commodity is

[21] See chap. iv, Sec. III, pp. 146–49 for a discussion of this question.

[22] Judged by the same standard, the improvement has been even greater in the regressions of y on x. It must be remembered, however, that R' is not necessarily a reliable measure of goodness of fit when the independent variables are highly correlated with one another, as they are in these equations.

inelastic. With the single exception of oats, the demand for each of these commodities is also inelastic with respect to its own price.

5. With the exception of barley, the elasticity of demand of a commodity with respect to its own price (the diagonal terms) is numerically greater than its elasticity with respect to the price of any other commodity.

6. The coefficients in the first four equations of Table 58 have the same signs as the corresponding coefficients of Table 57, with two exceptions: the regression of the quantity of corn (x_c) on the price of barley (y_b) and the regres-

TABLE 59

COMPARISON OF THE THEORETICAL AND THE OBSERVED PROPERTIES OF THE RELATED
DEMAND FUNCTIONS FOR BARLEY, CORN, HAY, AND OATS, 1896–1914

| PAIRS OF COMMODITIES | INTEGRABILITY CONDITIONS | | PROBABLE TYPE OF RELATION |
	Theoretical	Calculated	
Barley and corn.........	$\dfrac{\partial x_b}{\partial y_c} = \dfrac{\partial x_c}{\partial y_b}$	$\begin{array}{cc} -0.0121 = & -0.0216 \\ (0.0080) & (0.0452) \end{array}$	? Completing
Barley and hay.........	$\dfrac{\partial x_b}{\partial y_h} = \dfrac{\partial x_h}{\partial y_b}$	$\begin{array}{cc} +0.0044 = & -0.0002 \\ (0.0592) & (0.0013) \end{array}$	Independent
Barley and oats.........	$\dfrac{\partial x_b}{\partial y_o} = \dfrac{\partial x_o}{\partial y_b}$	$\begin{array}{cc} +0.0143 = & +0.0317 \\ (0.0132) & (0.0231) \end{array}$	Competing
Corn and hay..........	$\dfrac{\partial x_c}{\partial y_h} = \dfrac{\partial x_h}{\partial y_c}$	$\begin{array}{cc} -0.0256 = & -0.0047 \\ (0.5415) & (0.0020) \end{array}$	Completing
Corn and oats.........	$\dfrac{\partial x_c}{\partial y_o} = \dfrac{\partial x_o}{\partial y_c}$	$\begin{array}{cc} +0.0327 = & +0.0693 \\ (0.1209) & (0.0373) \end{array}$	Competing
Hay and oats..........	$\dfrac{\partial x_h}{\partial y_o} = \dfrac{\partial x_o}{\partial y_h}$	$\begin{array}{cc} +0.0075 = & -0.6074 \\ (0.0034) & (0.2773) \end{array}$	?

sion of the quantity of barley (x_b) on the price of hay (y_h). But, as these two regressions are practically negligible, compared with their standard errors, the difference in sign is of no significance.

7. Turning to the second part of Table 58, we find that, with one exception, the signs of the coefficients are in agreement with the signs of the corresponding coefficients of Table 57. The exception is the regression of the price of corn on the consumption of hay, which is positive in Table 58 and negative in Table 57. The positive sign is consistent with the interpretation that corn and hay are completing goods. In all other respects, this part is as disappointing as the corresponding part of Table 57. There are more inconsistencies between the regressions of y on x (logarithmic or arithmetic) than between the regressions of x

on y. A more detailed analysis of the interrelations involved shows, however, that the conclusions of Table 59 are not improbable.

The main fact that emerges from a comparison of the arithmetic and the logarithmic equations is that, while the former enable us more easily to verify the integrability conditions, the latter are more advantageous for computing the elasticities of the related demands.

3. THE TESTS OF RATIONAL CONSUMER BEHAVIOR

With these facts in mind, let us proceed to examine the degree to which the equations of Table 57 satisfy the integrability conditions

$$(3.19) \qquad \frac{\partial x_i}{\partial y_j} = \frac{\partial x_j}{\partial y_i}$$

or

$$(3.16) \qquad \frac{\partial y_i}{\partial x_j} = \frac{\partial y_j}{\partial x_i},$$

(3.19) applying to the first group of equations and (3.16) to the second.

It should be recalled that condition (3.19)—and the same is true of condition (3.16)—is a condition on the signs, as well as on the absolute magnitudes, of the coefficients. When both terms of this condition are negative (and statistically significant), the commodities are definitely completing. When they are positive, the commodities are competing. When one of the signs is negative, and the other positive, the condition is not satisfied, no matter how many times each coefficient exceeds its standard error. Our comparison of the coefficients of the first four equations of Table 57 may, therefore, take the form of deriving an answer to the question, "To what extent is condition (3.19) satisfied?" If this condition is satisfied, then we may conclude that the consumers act in the market as though they were rational or consistent.

Table 59 gives an answer to this question.

1. In all but the second and the last equations of condition in this table, both terms have the same signs, indicating a *qualitative* verification of the integrability condition (3.19).

If we confine our attention to the signs, neglecting the absolute magnitudes of the regression coefficients, and compare these signs with those required by theory for completing and competing goods—see (3.12)—we find that, out of the six pairs into which the four commodities may be combined, two are completing (barley and corn, hay and corn), two are competing (barley and oats, corn and oats), and two yield contradictory results (barley and hay, oats and hay). But this conclusion may not be valid because some of the coefficients are even exceeded by their standard errors.

2. The probable type of relation indicated by Table 59 agrees with that indicated by the rough test (Table 56) only in the case of barley and oats, and corn and hay. We have seen, however, that in the present example the rough test is likely to be misleading because most of the quantity ratios and price ratios have secular trends. It is probable, therefore, that, if allowance had been made for these trends in computing the coefficients of variation, the agreement between the criterion of Table 56 and that of Table 59 would have been closer.

3. The terms in the second equation (barley and hay) are both so small with respect to their standard errors as to be statistically equivalent to zero. Based on the data for 1896–1914, barley and hay may, therefore, be considered as independent commodities; that is, the demand for either one of them does not depend on the price of the other.

This conclusion appears also to be borne out by additional statistical experiments with the same data. If we omit the price of hay from the variables in the demand function for barley, and the price of barley from the variables in the demand function for hay, and determine the parameters anew, we find that the R'''s are greater, and the standard errors of the coefficients are smaller, than in the first and third equations of Table 57.

4. The terms in the third equation both exceed their standard errors and are both positive. They indicate, therefore, that barley and oats are probably competing goods, or that an increase in the price of either one of them will increase the quantity demanded of the other.

5. In each of the first, fourth, and fifth equations, in which there is agreement between the signs of the two terms, one of the terms is so small compared with its standard error as not to be statistically significant. Other evidence is, therefore, needed in order to determine the most probable type of relation between each of the three pairs of commodities.

To throw some light on this problem, we proceeded as follows: We recomputed the demand equations for the first pair of commodities—barley and corn —by omitting successively the price of hay, then the price of oats, and finally both of these prices from the equations of the commodities as given in Table 58, thus obtaining three additional pairs of equations. We then examined the various coefficients of these equations with a view of determining whether the omission of either one or of both of the other prices caused a change in the signs of the suspected coefficients. We then analyzed the demand equations for corn and hay, and corn and oats in a similar manner. We also extended the analysis to the regressions of the prices on the quantities of the commodities in question.[23] From these analyses, which are not reproduced here, it appears that corn and hay are completing, and corn and oats are competing, as is indicated

[23] In making these analyses and comparisons, we used only the logarithmic equations. The results would not, however, have been materially different had we worked with the arithmetic equations.

in Table 59. The evidence with respect to barley and corn is, however, conflicting.[24]

6. The last (sixth) equation of condition gives rise to a difficult problem. The terms are statistically significant, notwithstanding the fact that they do not agree in sign. Furthermore, the significance is not destroyed by eliminating one or both of the other prices from the demand equations. If this finding can be accepted at its face value, it represents a striking phenomenon for which some explanation is required. It is as though the relation between the two commodities were such that the utility of hay to farmers *increases* as the quantity of oats is increased, while the utility of oats *decreases* as the quantity of hay is increased! But such an explanation cannot be entertained, for there is no reason to suppose that the order of purchase of the feed crops in question affects their utility to the farmers.

The most plausible explanation is that the data are not sufficiently accurate for the purpose in view, although they may be tolerably accurate for the purpose of deriving the ordinary, simpler demand functions.[25] This appears to be supported by our experiments with the same data for the first period, 1879–95, and for the third, 1915–29 (omitting 1917–23). If we derive demand functions like those of Table 57 for these periods, we obtain for the theoretical condition

$$\frac{\partial x_h}{\partial y_o} = \frac{\partial x_o}{\partial y_h}$$

the value

$$+0.0085 \doteq -0.2488$$
$$(0.0043) \quad (0.2193)$$

for the first period, and

$$+0.0137 \doteq +0.2406$$
$$(0.0110) \quad (0.6592)$$

for the third. It should be observed that there is no contradiction in the signs of the coefficients for the third period, although one of them is definitely insignificant.

[24] In order to determine which, if any, of the variables should be eliminated from the demand functions, the set of correlations between the various prices and quantities was also subjected to an analysis by a method recommended by Professor Ragnar Frisch. Unfortunately, the method has failed to yield conclusive results, and the conclusion has been forced on us that it has no advantages over the combined least-squares and graphic methods used in this book. See Ragnar Frisch and Bruce D. Mudgett, "Statistical Correlation and the Theory of Cluster Types," *Jour. Amer. Statist. Assoc.*, December, 1931, and the reference to Frisch's earlier work therein given. See also Ragnar Frisch, *Statistical Confluence Analysis by Means of Complete Regression Systems* (Oslo, 1934); and T. Koopmans, *Linear Regression Analysis of Economic Time Series* (Netherlands Economic Institute, Nr. 20 [Haarlem: De Erven F. Bohn N.V., 1937]).

[25] See, however, n. 19, p. 587.

7. Turning to the regressions of the prices on the quantities (the second part of Table 57), and examining them for condition (3.16), and comparing the signs of the coefficients with those of the coefficients in (3.11a), we find that the coefficients in only three out of the six combinations—barley and oats, corn and oats, and hay and oats—have signs which are consistent with those of the regressions of the quantities on the prices, the last pair being consistent in its inconsistency! Thus, for the theoretical condition

$$\frac{\partial y_o}{\partial x_h} = \frac{\partial y_h}{\partial x_o}$$

we obtain

$$+17.1496 \doteq -0.2777 .$$
$$(11.5362) \qquad (0.1550)$$

In other words, the contradiction is still there!

8. Turning finally to the logarithmic equations of Table 58, we must first recall that *in their logarithmic form* these equations cannot satisfy the integrability conditions (3.16) or (3.19). To derive the integrability conditions for these equations, each of the first group must be transformed into the form

(4.1) $x = A y_b^{a_b} y_c^{a_c} y_h^{a_h} y_o^{a_o} e^{F(t)} ,$

and each of the second group must be transformed into the form

(4.2) $y = B x_b^{a_b} x_c^{a_c} x_h^{a_h} x_o^{a_o} e^{f(t)} .$

For (4.2), which is of the same form as (3.22), the integrability condition (3.16) $\frac{\partial y_i}{\partial x_j} = \frac{\partial y_j}{\partial x_i}$ is applicable, and, if it is to hold for all the values of the x's, it is necessary that conditions a, b, and d of (3.24) be satisfied. (Condition [3.24c] is not applicable, since the income r is not one of the variables of [4.2].) *But the integrability condition (3.19)* $\frac{\partial x_i}{\partial y_j} = \frac{\partial x_j}{\partial y_i}$ *does not hold for the nonlinear demand functions (4.1), since these functions are not the inverse transformations of (4.2).* Conditions which demand functions of type (4.1) must satisfy will be developed in chapter xix. Meanwhile we may compare the *signs* of the regression coefficients of the logarithmic equations of Table 58 with the *signs* of the corresponding regressions of the arithmetic equations of Table 57: the corresponding coefficients should agree in sign. Allowing for the fact that a relatively large standard error throws doubt on the sign, as well as the magnitude, of the coefficient in question, we find that the probable type of relations existing between the six pairs of commodities is the same, whether we use the signs of the equations of Table 58 or of Table 57. Barley and corn, and barley and hay, are probably independent in consumption, although there is a bare possibility that the first pair is completing. Barley and oats, and corn and oats, are competing. Corn and hay are completing. The hay-oats combination leads to contradictory results, as in Table 57.

V. RATIONAL CONSUMER BEHAVIOR
IN THEORY AND PRACTICE

In order to bring out the relations between the theoretical and the statistical parts of this chapter, it is desirable to summarize the more important findings and to offer a few interpretations.

1. The statistical studies of demand which have been carried on in the last decade have reached the point where they can advantageously begin to embrace analyses of the interrelations existing among the demands for *related* commodities.

2. The attack on this problem need not be wholly empirical—for economic theory lays down certain conditions which the demand functions for any two related goods must fulfil. These are the conditions of the rationality or consistency of consumer behavior which may be stated as follows: *The demand behavior of a rational or consistent individual with respect to any two commodities* (X_1) *and* (X_2) *is such that a one cent increase in the price of* (X_1) *brings about the same change in his demand for* (X_2) *that a one cent increase in the price of* (X_2) *brings about in his demand for* (X_1). This is the meaning of the "integrability condition" (3.19). (An analogous condition—condition [3.16]—holds for changes in the price of any one of the goods brought about by a change in the quantity of the other good.) The quantities change in the same direction as the prices of the related goods if the commodities are competing and in the opposite direction if they are completing.

3. These conditions may be deduced, as Professor Hotelling has first deduced them, from the postulate that each purchaser attempts to maximize his net profits, or (as I believe) more directly from the fundamental definitions of competing and completing goods in terms of the properties of the utility functions and from the equilibrium relations obtaining between these functions and the prices when the marginal degree of utility of money is constant. When these conditions are satisfied, we may be reasonably certain that the market behavior of the consumers in question is consistent or rational.

4. The demands for three groups of commodities: (*a*) beef and pork; (*b*) tea, coffee, and sugar; and (*c*) barley, corn, hay, and oats have been analyzed with the view of determining for each group which combinations of commodities are completing, and which competing, and to what extent the demand for

these commodities indicates rational, consistent behavior on the part of the purchasers. The analysis shows that with respect to no combination of these commodities is the behavior of consumers *perfectly* rational. Most of the terms of the calculated conditions agree in sign but differ in absolute value, while the others differ also with respect to sign. Furthermore, the standard errors of the statistical parameters are so large that no conclusion about the integrability conditions of the *true*, underlying demand functions has a large degree of probability. But while the findings are thus weakened, the following conclusions have, nevertheless, a fair degree of probability:

Beef and pork are competing in consumption. Also the demand functions for these commodities give a good approximation to those characteristic of perfect rational behavior.

Coffee and tea are competing in consumption in Canada. The relations existing between the demands for sugar, tea, and coffee in Canada cannot be determined from the inadequate data.

Barley and hay are independent in consumption. Barley and corn, and corn and hay, are completing. Barley and oats, and corn and oats, are competing. Hay and oats have a contradictory type of relation; an increase in the price of oats increases the demand for hay, but an increase in the price of hay decreases the demand for oats.

5. Although, when the integrability conditions are satisfied, we may conclude that the consumers behave in an apparently consistent manner, the converse of this proposition is not necessarily true. Even if we postulate a perfect correspondence between the statistical results and the properties of the true demand functions, the fact that the integrability conditions are not satisfied does not necessarily mean that the market behavior of the consumers is inconsistent or irrational. The following explanations of the phenomenon suggest themselves:

a) The commodities may be such that the total utility yielded by them depends on the order in which they are consumed. Thus the pleasure which we get from a meal depends in part on whether we consume our dessert at the end or at the beginning of the meal. When the order of consumption influences the utility, it is no longer true that $\varphi_{ij} = \varphi_{ji}$, and consequently the integrability conditions (3.16) and (3.19) do not hold. But this explanation does not, we submit, apply to the demand functions of this chapter. All that we know about our three groups of commodities seems to belie it. Even if it were true, for example, that the utility which a farmer derives from his cattle is affected by the order in which the various feeds are consumed, some one order of consumption having a more desirable effect on the cattle than some other, it does not follow that this order will reflect itself in the purchases and that, consequently, the integrability conditions will not be satisfied. The whole discussion of order of consumption, a subject which naturally appeals to the mathematician, seems to me to be of little significance for the economist.[26]

b) *The marginal degree of utility of money may not have been constant to each consumer.* A general theory of the interrelations of demand which does not assume the constancy of the marginal utility of money will be developed and applied in the next chapter. We shall see, however, that it is extremely improbable that the corrections introduced by that theory would account for the failure of the statistical demand functions of this chapter to satisfy the theoretical conditions.

c) *A change may have taken place in the state of demand during the period covered by the data, so that the same commodities were considered as completing during one part of the period and competing during the other, or vice versa.* Such a change in demand is always possible, and it is difficult to detect it except possibly by subdividing the data and making a separate analysis of each part. Since articles may be competing at some combinations and completing at others, a marked increase or decrease in the quantity demanded of one of the articles may change its relation to the other commodity from a completing good to a competing good or vice versa. There is no evidence, however, that such a change took place in the demand for any of the commodities in the three groups whose demands we analyzed in this chapter.

6. More plausible reasons why failure to obtain a statistical verification of the integrability conditions is not necessarily an indication of inconsistent or irrational behavior on the part of consumers are to be found in the very nature of the inductive approach and the data used. We may list three of them:

a) *The commodities considered may be only a part of a group of related goods, some of which have been neglected in the analysis.* This possibility is worthy of serious consideration. It means that if in studying a group of related goods we neglect some, and calculate from the statistical data the demand functions for the rest, the coefficients in the calculated demand functions may not satisfy the integrability conditions even though they are satisfied by the true demand functions. This difficulty—and many others—is likely to arise when the correlations between some of the prices (or quantities) approach unity.[27] Thus, suppose that we have a closed system of three commodities—bread, butter, and margarine—which we shall denote by the subscripts 1, 2, 3, and that the true demand functions for these goods are:

$$x_i = a_i + \sum_j b_{ij} y_j \qquad\qquad (i, j = 1, 2, 3) .$$

---

[26] See, however, the interesting analogy with the line integral of the second law of thermodynamics, to which Professor H. T. Davis calls attention in *Econometrica*, I (1933), 211–12. See also chap. i, pp. 16–18.

[27] In fact, it was an analysis of the effects of the fairly high correlations between the price series used which suggested this possibility. This possibility was also discovered independently by Dr. Eric Lundberg and communicated to me through Professor Hotelling. This particular example is theirs.

Now if the makers of margarine maintain their price at half that of butter, then there is perfect correlation between the two prices, for we always have $y_3 = \frac{1}{2} y_2$. The two demand functions then become

$$x_1 = a_1 + b_{11} y_1 + (b_{12} + \tfrac{1}{2} b_{13}) y_2$$
$$x_2 = a_2 + b_{21} y_1 + (b_{22} + \tfrac{1}{2} b_{23}) y_2 .$$

It follows, therefore, that if the statistical demand functions were obtained for bread and butter, without considering margarine, the last two equations would be the ones found from accurate data. For these two equations the integrability conditions are not satisfied, even though for the three commodities the integrability conditions $b_{ij} = b_{ji}$ are in all cases satisfied. Both coefficients of y_2 are exaggerated in absolute value. The difficulty is a serious one: To include y_3 is to render the parameters quite meaningless, since the perfect correlation between y_3 and y_2 gives rise to large or indeterminate standard errors. To omit it is to destroy the validity of the integrability conditions.

I doubt, however, whether there exists a commodity which is related to any of our three groups and which we have overlooked whose price is so highly correlated with the price of one of the commodities of the group as to give rise to the difficulty in question. Even sugar, which is used jointly with tea and with coffee, and which is a favorite illustration of a complementary good, is also employed in other uses, so that the correlation between the price of sugar and the price of tea (or between the price of sugar and the price of coffee) is far from perfect. Nor is the correlation between any two of our price series sufficiently high to be suspected,[28] even in Group C, in which we observed a flagrant disagreement between theory and observation. We conclude, therefore, that, although this explanation is not to be ruled out, it is not very probable.

b) The related demand functions may represent the aggregate demand of two groups of consumers, the component demand functions being such that they satisfy the integrability conditions only with respect to sign, one pair being positive, and the other negative. As an illustration of this phenomenon, let us assume that the demand functions of the two groups for two commodities are as follows:

Group 1	Group 2
$x_1 = 40 - 5y_1 - 8y_2$	$x_1 = 10 - 8y_1 + 10y_2$
$x_2 = 60 - 10y_1 - 10y_2$	$x_2 = 15 + 7y_1 - 5y_2$

[28] The correlations between the price series used (b = barley, c = corn, h = hay, o = oats) are as follows, all correlations being positive:

$r_{bc} = 0.52$	$r_{bh} = 0.80$	$r_{bo} = 0.59$
$r_{ch} = 0.41$	$r_{co} = 0.85$	$r_{ho} = 0.32$

The partial correlations for constant time (t) are:

$r_{bc.t} = 0.27$	$r_{bh.t} = 0.74$	$r_{bo.t} = 0.46$
$r_{ch.t} = 0.17$	$r_{co.t} = 0.82$	$r_{ho.t} = 0.13$

It will be observed that the integrability conditions are satisfied *with respect to sign* in the equations for each group, the commodities being considered completing by the consumers of Group 1 and competing by Group 2. Now let us construct the combined demand of the two groups for each commodity. We obtain

$$\Sigma x_1 = X_1 = 50 - 13y_1 + 2y_2$$
$$\Sigma x_2 = X_2 = 75 - 3y_1 - 15y_2 .$$

In these equations the integrability conditions are not satisfied *even with respect to sign*.

Possibly the demand functions of the various users of hay and oats are of the type illustrated in this hypothetical example.

c) *The data may not be reliable.* Although this claim that the data are unreliable has too often served the purpose of covering up weaknesses in one's analysis, yet I believe that in the statistical demand functions of this chapter, the data must be blamed for most, if not all, of our difficulties and disappointments. No one who has studied the way in which the estimates of prices and quantities are made will doubt for a minute that they are subject to considerable error. Furthermore, even if the data on production are tolerably accurate, the data on stocks are either lacking entirely or are quite unreliable. More progress in the analysis of the interrelations of demand must, therefore, await the development of more adequate and accurate data.

7. The discoveries of the properties of the theoretical demand functions for related goods give rise to new problems. We may mention two of them.

a) *Different methods of fitting the demand curves may lead to different conclusions regarding the type of relations connecting the demands for the commodities in question.* Thus the regressions of the quantities on the prices may lead to the conclusion that two commodities are connected by way of rivalry (competing), while the regressions of the prices on the quantities may suggest that the same commodities are connected by way of combination (completing). Furthermore, if, as is generally true of statistical demand functions, the integrability conditions are satisfied only with respect to sign, it does not follow that the integrability conditions calculated from the inverse transformations of the same functions will also be satisfied with respect to sign.

b) The second problem is that suggested by Professor Hotelling. *Assuming that we know that the integrability conditions hold, how can we fit the demand functions to data subject to this condition?* This is especially difficult when the demand functions are not linear and when it is desired to take into consideration errors in all the variables. Here are problems worthy of the best attention of the most skilled mathematicians and statisticians.

8. The upshot of the foregoing is that, although the special theory of related demands provides a simple test of the rationality of human behavior in the

market place, in practice the results are not likely to be unequivocal. Nevertheless, it is an intriguing theory, and one likely to have practical utility. For it defines and gives simple criteria for distinguishing between completing, independent, and competing pairs of goods, and it happens that competing commodities like beef and pork, or corn and oats, are of particular interest today when the various plans for relieving the farmers are under discussion. If the commodities which are competing in consumption should also turn out to be competing in production, then subject to a condition proved by Professor Hotelling,[29] a tax on one of them may lower the prices of both of them. These properties of competing goods should have important applications to the theory of international trade and to several other branches of economics.

9. The greatest obstacle in the way of determining the extent to which actual human behavior is rational—in the sense of the theory of this chapter—is the lack of accurate statistics on the consumption and prices of related goods. There is need, however, for a more satisfactory definition of rational market behavior, and for a better theory of choice.

[29] Hotelling, *op. cit.*, pp. 600–608.

CHAPTER XIX

THE GENERAL THEORY OF RELATED DEMANDS

CHAPTER XIX

THE GENERAL THEORY OF RELATED DEMANDS

The object of this chapter is to generalize the special theory of related demands developed in the preceding chapter and to apply it to the anaysis of the interrelations existing between the demands for beef, pork, and mutton in the United States.[1]

I. THE LIMITATIONS OF THE SPECIAL THEORY OF RELATED DEMANDS

Although the special theory of related demands admits of a ready test when we have accurate statistics of the consumption and the prices of the related goods, this advantage is in part counterbalanced by two limitations. These have their origin in the two underlying assumptions of the theory: (1) that there exists a unique total utility function $\varphi\ (x_1, \ldots, x_n)$ for each individual and (2) that the amount which the individual spends on the commodity in question forms such a small proportion of his total income that the marginal degree of utility of his money expenditure, m, remains practically constant.

The first assumption is unnecessary, if all that we wish to do is to develop a general theory of the pricing process,[2] for then we may work with an index of utility:

$$(1.1) \qquad I = F[\varphi(x_1, \ldots, x_n)] ,$$

where F is quite arbitrary except for the condition that it increases with φ; and this does not imply that utility is measurable.[3] If, however, we wish to retain the Edgeworth-Pareto definition that two commodities (X_i) and (X_j) are completing, independent, or competing, according as

$$(1.2) \qquad \varphi_{ij} \gtreqless 0 ,$$

then we can no longer assume that the index I is arbitrary, for

$$(1.3) \qquad I_{ij} \equiv \frac{\partial^2 I}{\partial x_i\, \partial x_j} = \varphi_{ij} F'(\varphi) + \varphi_i \varphi_j F''(\varphi) ,$$

[1] The first three sections of this chapter have no direct bearing on the statistical applications which follow. The reader who is interested primarily in the bearing of the theory on the interpretation of statistical demand curves will do well to review Secs. III*A* and III*B* of chap. i and then to turn to Sec. IV of the present chapter.

[2] Irving Fisher, *Mathematical Investigations in the Theory of Value and Prices* (New Haven, 1892), p. 89. (For complete reference see n. 2, chap. xviii.)

[3] Vilfredo Pareto, *Manuel*, Appendix, § 4, pp. 541–42, and his "Economie mathématique," *Encyclopédie des sciences mathématiques*, Tome I, Vol. IV, Fasc. 4 (1911), p. 597.

may not have the same sign as φ_{ij}, since it varies with the form assumed for $F(\varphi)$.

The second assumption appears to be necessary in order to translate the Edgeworth-Pareto definition (1.2) into conditions on the market demand functions. If we give up this assumption, we apparently give up the possibility of defining complementarity in terms of the aggregate objective market behavior of consumers (see Sec. V of the present chapter).

Of the two limitations, the first is the basic one, since without it the Edgeworth-Pareto definition of complementarity (1.2) falls. For Slutsky has proved, the values of the second partial derivatives of the utility function *cannot be obtained from empirical data*.[4]

It is these considerations, coupled with the desires to develop an objective "theory of choice," which have led to several attempts to replace the Edgeworth-Pareto definition of complementarity (1.2) by one which is independent of the assumption that utility is measurable. In the following pages we shall analyze three such definitions: (1) the Johnson-Allen definition, (2) the Friedman modification of the Johnson-Allen definition, and (3) the Slutsky and the Hicks-Allen definitions. We shall find that only the last is of practical significance, and we shall, therefore, submit it to a statistical test by analyzing with its aid the interrelations of the demand for beef, pork, and mutton. Since all these definitions are found implicitly in the writings of Pareto and of Slutsky, which we have discussed at some length,[5] it will be convenient to take these writings as our point of departure.

II. THE JOHNSON-ALLEN DEFINITION OF COMPLEMENTARITY

In a remarkable article published in 1913,[6] W. E. Johnson suggested that the competitive or complementary relation between any two goods (X_i) and (X_j) be defined in terms of the variation in the *ratio* of their marginal degrees of utility φ_i/φ_j, or, what amounts to the same thing, in terms of the variation of the slope $V_{ji} = \dfrac{\partial x_j}{\partial x_i}$ of the indifference curves of (X_i) and (X_j), for we know from the theory of implicit functions that

$$(2.1) \qquad V_{ji} = \frac{\partial x_j}{\partial x_i} = -\frac{\varphi_i}{\varphi_j},$$

[4] For proof see Eugenio Slutsky, "Sulla teoria del bilancio del consumatore," *Giornale degli economiste*, LI (1915), 19–23.

[5] See chap. i, pp. 12–50, and chap. xviii, pp. 572–81.

[6] "The Pure Theory of Utility Curves," *Economic Journal*, XXIII (1913), 483–513. See, however, Professor Luigi Amoroso's review, "Sulla teoria delle curve di utilità," *Giornale degli economisti*, LII (1916), 409–12, in which he takes Johnson to task for failing to refer to Pareto's fundamental contributions to this field.

a relation which we have already studied in chapter i, Section II*B*. The advantage of the Johnson definition is that it is invariant for a transformation of φ into $F(\varphi)$.

Now the changes in the slope V_{ji} corresponding to changes in x_i and x_j constitute the second characteristic of the utility function which we discussed in chapter i, Section II*B*. That characteristic, it will be recalled, is that the slope (with respect to the x_i-axis) of the indifference curves of (X_i) and (X_j) should decrease (in absolute value) when the quantity x_i of (X_i) is increased, while the quantity x_j of (X_j) is held constant; but should increase (in absolute value) when x_j is increased, while x_i is held constant. These conditions expressed mathematically (eqs. [2.13] of chap. i) are:

$$(2.2a) \qquad -\frac{\partial V_{ji}}{\partial x_i} = \frac{\partial}{\partial x_i}\left(\frac{\varphi_i}{\varphi_j}\right) = \frac{\varphi_j \varphi_{ii} - \varphi_i \varphi_{ji}}{\varphi_j^2} < 0 \,,$$

and

$$(2.2b) \qquad \frac{\partial V_{ji}}{\partial x_j} = \frac{\partial}{\partial x_j}\left(-\frac{\varphi_i}{\varphi_j}\right) = \frac{\varphi_i \varphi_{jj} - \varphi_j \varphi_{ij}}{\varphi_j^2} < 0 \,.$$

As was pointed out in chapter i, these conditions are invariant under the transformation of φ into $F(\varphi)$. Moreover, they are always satisfied when $\varphi_{ij} \geq 0$, but not necessarily for $\varphi_{ij} < 0$. That is, they are satisfied when, according to the Edgeworth-Pareto criterion, the commodities are completing or independent, but not necessarily when they are competing. This was also pointed out by Pareto.[7]

Johnson refers to (X_i) and (X_j) as complementary goods when $(2.2a)$ and $(2.2b)$ are satisfied—this is his "standard case"—and as competitive goods when either $(2.2a)$ or $(2.2b)$ is not satisfied (i.e., when one or the other of the expressions is positive).[8]

Johnson does not clearly indicate whether he wishes to define two commodities as competing *everywhere* when $(2.2a)$ or $(2.2b)$ is not satisfied at one or more points, or only *within the range* for which $(2.2a)$ or $(2.2b)$ is not satisfied. Mr. R. G. D. Allen, of the London School of Economics, who in a later paper puts forward the Johnson definition, is quite explicit on this point.[9] He calls a position in which both $(2.2a)$ and $(2.2b)$ are satisfied—Johnson's "standard case"—a "normal" position; and one at which one of the inequalities is reversed a "nonnormal" position; and then defines two goods as "*complementary* if they are normally related at all positions, and *competitive* if they are non-

[7] See *Manuel*, p. 573.

[8] By virtue of eq. (2.16) in chap. i, it is not possible for both the expressions to be positive.

[9] "A Comparison between Different Definitions of Complementary and Competitive Goods," *Econometrica*, II (1934), 168–75; "Nachfragefunktionen für Güter mit korreliertem Nutzen," *Zeitschrift für Nationalökonomie*, V, Heft 4 (1934), 486–506.

normally related at some (but not necessarily at all) positions."[10] It follows that, according to this definition, two commodities are considered to have the same relationship at all points.

In order to understand the meaning of this definition, it is necessary to consider more at length the meaning of "normal" and "nonnormal" positions. The satisfaction of the inequalities (2.2a) and (2.2b) means that, other things being equal, the more of one good possessed by an individual, the more of it he will be willing to give up to obtain a unit of another good; i.e., the more of (X_i) possessed with a constant quantity of (X_j), the lower the ratio of the marginal degree of utility of (X_i) to that of (X_j). Now it would seem a priori that this situation would be the usual one and, moreover, that it would *always* obtain in the case of completing and independent goods—using these terms in the sense of chapter xviii. If, for example, (X_i) and (X_j) are used jointly, and the quantity x_i of (X_i) is kept constant, this should cause the individual's relative desire for x_i to increase, as x_j is increased, because of the smaller relative amount of (X_i) which he possesses. It is only for substitutes that the inequalities (2.2a) and (2.2b) may conceivably not be satisfied. For in this case, the fact that, the greater the quantity x_j, the less the need for x_i (and vice versa), might offset his desire that the good (X_i) (whose quantity is kept constant) should be increased.

It should be noted that, at a "nonnormal" position, the relationship between the two commodities is not reciprocal. As an illustration, we may consider a "nonnormal" position at which an increase in the quantity of (X_i) possessed *raises* the ratio of the marginal degree of utility of (X_i) to that of (X_j)—i.e., (2.2a) is positive. It does not follow that an increase in the quantity of the other good (X_j) will raise the ratio of the marginal degree of utility of (X_j) to that of (X_i). Indeed, it cannot do so; it must lower the ratio.[11] When such a relation exists between the two goods, Pareto and Allen would refer to (X_i) as the "superior" good and to (X_j) as the "inferior" good. In Johnson's terminology we are, then, in an (X_i)—urgent region. It seems reasonable to suppose that "nonnormal" positions in which (X_i) is the superior good are likely to occur when little of (X_i) and much of (X_j) is possessed and that nonnormal positions in which (X_j) is the superior good are likely to occur when the situation is reversed. In short,

a normal position is characterized by the fact that either good loses in relative importance when the individual gets more of it, while, at a non-normal position, it is always one definite good (the inferior) that loses in relative importance whenever the individual increases his possession of the goods in any way.[12]

[10] "A Comparison between Different Definitions of Complementary and Competitive Goods," *op. cit.*, p. 170. (Italics are his.)

[11] See n. 8 above.   [12] Allen, "A Comparison . . . . , " *op. cit.*, p. 170.

The invariance of $(2.2a)$ and $(2.2b)$ under the transformation of φ into $F(\varphi)$ indicates that it should be possible to express them in terms of the parameters of the demand functions without making any additional assumptions. And this can be done.

From (3.6) of chapter xviii we have for the commodities (X_i) and (X_j):

$(2.3a)$
$$\varphi_i = m y_i$$

$(2.3b)$
$$\varphi_j = m y_j .$$

Differentiating the first with respect to x_i and the second with respect to x_j, we obtain

$(2.4a)$
$$\varphi_{ii} = m \frac{\partial y_i}{\partial x_i} + y_i \frac{\partial m}{\partial x_i}$$

and

$(2.4b)$
$$\varphi_{jj} = m \frac{\partial y_j}{\partial x_j} + y_j \frac{\partial m}{\partial x_j} .$$

From (3.7) and (3.14) of the preceding chapter, we also have

$(2.5a)$
$$\varphi_{ij} = m \frac{\partial y_i}{\partial x_j} + y_i \frac{\partial m}{\partial x_j} .$$

and

$(2.5b)$
$$\varphi_{ji} = m \frac{\partial y_i}{\partial x_i} + y_j \frac{\partial m}{\partial x_i} .$$

Substituting from these six equations into $(2.2a)$ and $(2.2b)$, we obtain

$(2.6a)$
$$-\frac{\partial V_{ji}}{\partial x_i} = \frac{1}{y_j} \cdot \frac{\partial y_i}{\partial x_i} - \frac{y_i}{y_j^2} \cdot \frac{\partial y_j}{\partial x_i} < 0 ,$$

and

$(2.6b)$
$$\frac{\partial V_{ji}}{\partial x_j} = \frac{y_i}{y_j^2} \cdot \frac{\partial y_j}{\partial x_j} - \frac{1}{y_j} \cdot \frac{\partial y_i}{\partial x_j} < 0 .$$

We can express $(2.6a)$ and $(2.6b)$ in terms of elasticities by multiplying the first by $y_j \, x_i/y_i$ and the second by $y_j \, x_j/y_i$. Since both of these expressions are positive, the inequality sign is not affected. Neglecting the first members, this gives:

$(2.7a)$
$$\eta_{y_i \, x_i} - \eta_{y_j \, x_i} < 0 ,$$

and

$(2.7b)$
$$\eta_{y_j \, x_j} - \eta_{y_i \, x_j} < 0 ,$$

respectively.

The Johnson-Allen definition may now be stated as follows:

If (2.6a) *and* (2.6b) (*or* [2.7a] *and* [2.7b]) *are satisfied for the whole region for which none of the commodities possessed has reached the point of satiety* ($\varphi_i = 0$), *then the commodities* (X_i) *and* (X_j) *are completing, and, if one or the other of the inequalities is reversed at some one or more points within that region, the commodities are competing.*

If we knew the "true" demand functions of our commodities, it would be possible to discover from the elasticities of demand whether the inequalities (2.7a) and (2.7b) were everywhere satisfied, or were reversed at some points. We could then classify the commodities as competing or completing.[13] In practice, however, we never know the "true" demand curves. Our statistical analysis yields at best only the first few terms of a Taylor's expansion of the "true" function about some point. The statistical demand curves are thus valid only in the neighborhood of this point, which ordinarily will be quite removed from the extremes of the effective region. But the Johnson-Allen test gives an unequivocal determination of the relationship existing between the two commodities only in the neighborhood of the *boundaries* of the effective region, for which the empirically derived demand curve is not valid. In regions removed from the boundaries, we should expect the inequalities (2.7) always to be satisfied, no matter whether the goods are completing or competing (i.e., the absolute value of $\eta_{y_j x_i}$ will ordinarily be smaller than that of $\eta_{y_i x_i}$). The Johnson-Allen test, therefore, gives us no clue as to the nature of the relationship existing between the commodities. It follows that, while the Johnson-Allen definition theoretically enables us to express the criteria of complementarity in terms of the parameters of the demand curve, in practice it is of no aid whatsoever. The only use which the inequalities (2.6), or (2.7), serve in practice is as conditions which the statistically obtained demand curves should satisfy in the neighborhood for which they are valid.

We may verify this conclusion by applying conditions (2.7a) and (2.7b) to the demand functions for the three groups of commodities which we analyzed in chapter xviii: (1) beef and pork; (2) coffee and tea; and (3) barley, corn, hay, and oats. Of the various demand functions considered in that chapter, those appropriate for this test are equations 3 and 4 of Table 52 for the first group of commodities; equations 1 and 2 of Table 55 for the second; and equations 5–8 of Table 58 for the third. For the purpose of this test sugar will not be included in the second group of commodities because all the regressions of the price of sugar on the quantities of coffee and tea are quite insignificant (see eqs. 3, 5, and 7 of Table 55).

[13] The foregoing test must, as was indicated in the definition given above, be confined to the "effective" region, i.e., the region within which the commodities are desired (*ibid.*, p. 171).

This is the region on the utility surfaces (or indifference varieties) for which φ_i is not negative. The corresponding region on the demand curve is that for which the prices and quantities are positive.

Table 60 is a summary of the results obtained. Of the price flexibilities entering into this table, those relating to the first two groups of commodities are derived from arithmetic demand functions (Tables 52 and 55 of chap. xviii); these are computed at the points on the demand functions corresponding to the means of the independent variables. The price flexibilities relating to the

TABLE 60

THE LAXITY OF THE JOHNSON-ALLEN CONDITIONS OF COMPLEMENTARITY (2.7)
AS ILLUSTRATED BY THE DEMAND FUNCTIONS FOR BEEF AND PORK;
COFFEE AND TEA; AND BARLEY, CORN, HAY, AND OATS

PAIRS OF COMMODITIES	CONDITIONS (2.7a) AND (2.7b)	
	Theoretical	Calculated
Beef and pork...........	$\begin{cases} \eta_{y_b x_b} - \eta_{y_p x_b} < 0 \\ \eta_{y_p x_p} - \eta_{y_b x_p} < 0 \end{cases}$	$\begin{cases} -2.429 - (-0.742) < 0 \\ -1.364 - (-1.024) < 0 \end{cases}$
Coffee and tea...........	$\begin{cases} \eta_{y_c x_c} - \eta_{y_t x_c} < 0 \\ \eta_{y_t x_t} - \eta_{y_c x_t} < 0 \end{cases}$	$\begin{cases} -1.012 - (-0.484) < 0 \\ -0.587 - (-0.577) < 0 \end{cases}$
Barley and corn.........	$\begin{cases} \eta_{y_b x_b} - \eta_{y_c x_b} < 0 \\ \eta_{y_c x_c} - \eta_{y_b x_c} < 0 \end{cases}$	$\begin{cases} -0.233 - (-0.180) < 0 \\ -1.218 - (+0.025) < 0 \end{cases}$
Barley and hay..........	$\begin{cases} \eta_{y_b x_b} - \eta_{y_h x_b} < 0 \\ \eta_{y_h x_h} - \eta_{y_b x_h} < 0 \end{cases}$	$\begin{cases} -0.233 - (+0.127) < 0 \\ -0.875 - (-0.747) < 0 \end{cases}$
Barley and oats.........	$\begin{cases} \eta_{y_b x_b} - \eta_{y_o x_b} < 0 \\ \eta_{y_o x_o} - \eta_{y_b x_o} < 0 \end{cases}$	$\begin{cases} -0.233 - (-0.089) < 0 \\ -0.725 - (-0.631) < 0 \end{cases}$
Corn and hay...........	$\begin{cases} \eta_{y_c x_c} - \eta_{y_h x_c} < 0 \\ \eta_{y_h x_h} - \eta_{y_c x_h} < 0 \end{cases}$	$\begin{cases} -1.218 - (+0.094) < 0 \\ -0.875 - (+0.169) < 0 \end{cases}$
Corn and oats...........	$\begin{cases} \eta_{y_c x_c} - \eta_{y_o x_c} < 0 \\ \eta_{y_o x_o} - \eta_{y_c x_o} < 0 \end{cases}$	$\begin{cases} -1.218 - (-0.594) < 0 \\ -0.725 - (-0.069) < 0 \end{cases}$
Hay and oats...........	$\begin{cases} \eta_{y_h x_h} - \eta_{y_o x_h} < 0 \\ \eta_{y_o x_o} - \eta_{y_h x_o} < 0 \end{cases}$	$\begin{cases} -0.875 - (+0.376) < 0 \\ -0.725 - (-0.253) < 0 \end{cases}$

third group of commodities are constant at every point on the demand surfaces. They should correspond very closely to the flexibilities which we might have computed from the corresponding arithmetic demand functions of Table 57.

A glance at Table 60 is sufficient to show that the Johnson-Allen conditions (2.7a) and (2.7b) are satisfied by the demand functions for each and every pair of the commodities in question—even those which, by the tests of chapter xviii, compete with one another in consumption (beef and pork, coffee and tea, and barley and oats). This merely confirms our a priori conclusion that the conditions (2.6) or (2.7) are too lax to be of much use in practice.

We conclude, therefore, that the Johnson-Allen definition, while it is independent of the assumption that utility is measurable and thus overcomes one of the disadvantages of the Edgeworth-Pareto definition, is nevertheless of little or no practical importance. Moreover, it has the further disadvantage— although Mr. Allen considers it an advantage—that it requires two commodities to have the same type of relationship over the whole region considered: it rules out the possibility that two commodities will be completing at some points and competing at others. Finally, it does not provide a criterion for the borderline relationship of independence.

III. THE FRIEDMAN MODIFICATION OF THE JOHNSON-ALLEN DEFINITION OF COMPLEMENTARITY

A variant of the Johnson-Allen definition, which is not subject to the last two disadvantages, has been suggested by Mr. Milton Friedman.[14] He designates as a "satiation point" for x_i a point on an indifference curve where additional quantities of (X_i) do not increase the total utility of the individual. At such a point the individual is satiated with (X_i); he is not willing to sacrifice additional units of some other commodity to obtain additional units of it. At that point his marginal degree of utility is $\varphi_i = 0$, and the tangent to the indifference curve is parallel to the x_i-axis. (The slope with respect to the x_i-axis $\dfrac{dx_j}{dx_i} = -\dfrac{\varphi_i}{\varphi_j} = 0$.) The x_i-coordinate of such a point is "the satiation quantity" of (X_i); and the locus of satiation points for (X_i), the "satiation curve" of (X_i). If the satiation curves of two commodities (X_i) and (X_j) meet in a point, this is the "point of total satiety."[15] The region inclosed by the satiation curves is what has been called the "effective" region.

Figure 105 is a graphic illustration of these relations. In this diagram I_1, I_2, and I_3 are three indifference curves of (X_1) and (X_2). GM is the satiation curve of (X_1); it is the locus of all points at which the indifference curve has a horizontal tangent, or at which the price of (X_1) in terms of (X_2) is $-\dfrac{dx_2}{dx_1} = 0$.

HM is the satiation curve of (X_2); it is the locus of all points at which the indifference curve has a vertical tangent, or at which the price of (X_2) in terms

[14] Mr. Friedman arrived at his definition independently of both Allen and Johnson and presented it in an unpublished paper on "The Fitting of Indifference Curves as a Method of Deriving Statistical Demand Curves," which was written in January, 1934. The following treatment is based largely on this paper.

[15] These terms are used in this way by Marcel Lenoir in *Etudes sur la formation et la mouvement des prix* (Paris, 1913).

of (X_1) is $-\dfrac{dx_1}{dx_2} = 0$. M is the "point of total satiety" (bliss). The region $OHMG$ is the "effective" region.

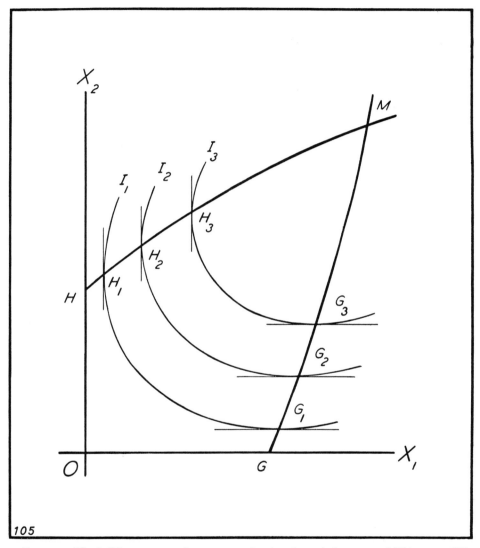

105

FIG. 105.—The indifference map of a consumer showing the satiation curve of (X_1): curve GM; the satiation curve of (X_2): curve HM; the point of total satiety: M; and the effective region: $OHMG$.

Friedman then suggests that "two commodities be defined as completing, competing, or independent according as the satiation quantity of each commodity increases, decreases, or remains the same when the quantity possessed of the other commodity increases."[16] When the satiation curves for two commodities slope positively the whole of their length as in Figure 105, the commodities are completing; when they slope negatively, the commodities are competing; and when they are perpendicular to the axes to which they pertain, the commodities are independent.

Mathematically, the equation of the satiation curves for (X_i) is

$$(3.1a) \qquad V_{ji} = -\frac{\varphi_i}{\varphi_j} = K(x_1, x_2, \ldots, x_n) = 0,$$

and for (X_j)

$$(3.1b) \qquad V_{ij} = -\frac{\varphi_i}{\varphi_i} = P(x_1, x_2, \ldots, x_n) = 0.$$

Consider the slopes of these curves with respect to, say, the x_i-axis:

$$(3.2a) \qquad \frac{\partial x_j}{\partial x_i} = -\frac{K_i}{K_j} = \frac{\varphi_j \varphi_{ii} - \varphi_i \varphi_{ij}}{\varphi_i \varphi_{jj} - \varphi_j \varphi_{ij}},$$

and

$$(3.2b) \qquad \frac{\partial x_j}{\partial x_i} = -\frac{P_i}{P_j} = \frac{\varphi_j \varphi_{ii} - \varphi_i \varphi_{ij}}{\varphi_i \varphi_{jj} - \varphi_j \varphi_{ij}}.$$

"For the range for which both $(3.2a)$ and $(3.2b)$ are positive, the commodities (X_i) and (X_j) are completing; for the range for which both are negative, the commodities are competing; and for the range for which $(3.2a)$ is zero, and $(3.2b)$ is infinite, the commodities are independent."[17]

The last members of (3.2) are identical in form, and it would appear as if they must have the same value. But it must be remembered that they are evaluated for different sets of x_i's and x_j's; $(3.2a)$ is evaluated for the set of values of the variables on the curve $(3.1a)$, and $(3.2b)$ for the set on the curve $(3.1b)$.

The relationship between this definition and the Johnson-Allen definition may be deduced from the fact that the right-hand members of (3.2) are equal to the ratio of $(2.2a)$ to $(2.2b)$. According to the Friedman definition, two commodities are said to be competing if the satiation curves are negatively sloped. The mathematical translation of this condition is that the numerator and the denominator of the right-hand members of (3.2) must differ in sign. But this means that $(2.2a)$ and $(2.2b)$ must differ in sign. In the Johnson-Allen terminology this means that "nonnormal" points occur along the boundaries. The commodities are, therefore, also competing according to their criterion. Similarly the two commodities are said to be completing according to the Friedman

[16] *Op. cit.*   [17] *Ibid.*

definition if the satiation curves are positively sloped. The analytical condition for this is that the numerator and the denominator of (3.2) should agree in sign. But then the expressions in (2.2) must also agree in sign. And, since it is almost certain that, if no "nonnormal" positions are found on the boundaries of the effective region, none will exist elsewhere,[18] the commodities are completing also by the Johnson-Allen criterion.

It is also easy to see the relationship between this definition and the Edgeworth-Pareto definition. Along the satiation curve for (X_i), $\varphi_i = 0$, and along the satiation curve for (X_j), $\varphi_j = 0$, so that the right-hand members of (3.2a) and (3.2b) reduce to

(3.3a)
$$\frac{\partial x_j}{\partial x_i} = -\frac{\varphi_{ii}}{\varphi_{ij}},$$

(3.3b)
$$\frac{\partial x_j}{\partial x_i} = -\frac{\varphi_{ij}}{\varphi_{jj}}.$$

Now along the satiation curves the signs of the second partial derivatives of the utility function are determinate,[19] and φ_{ii} and φ_{jj} are negative. It follows that (3.3a) and (3.3b) have the same sign as φ_{ij}. But, when $\varphi_{ij} \gtrless 0$ along the satiation curves, the latter slope positively, negatively, or are perpendicular to their respective axes. We see, then, that the Friedman and the Edgeworth-Pareto definitions yield the same conclusions along the boundaries.

Thus far we have concerned ourselves with the situations in which the slopes of the satiation curves have the same sign *throughout their entire length.* This is equivalent to the assumption that the commodities retain the same relation to each other *irrespective of changes in their quantities.* There is, however, no reason for supposing this to be the only, or even the predominant, type of relationship. It may well be, for example, that, until a certain point, the more butter an individual possesses, the greater the amount of bread he can use; but that, after that point has been reached, an increase in the amount of butter will decrease the maximum amount of bread he can use. To represent such a case, the satiation curves of Figure 105 should be modified so that they will not be inclined positively to their respective axes throughout their extent. Figure 106, which is due to Friedman, represents such a modification. In this diagram the satiation curve GEM for (X_1) is positively inclined to the x_1-axis from the point G to the point E and is negatively inclined from the point E to the point M; and the satiation curve HDM for (X_2) is positively inclined to the x_2-axis between the points H and D and negatively inclined between the points D and M. If the perpendiculars DA and EB be dropped to the x_1-axis and the x_2-axis, respectively, the entire region inclosed by the satiation curves is divided into a

[18] See above, p. 610; Allen, "A Comparison . . . . ," *op. cit.,* pp. 172–73.
[19] See the appendix at the end of this chapter, p. 652.

number of areas. These can be classified into three types: Type I are areas such as *ACBO*, which lie under positively sloping portions of both satiation

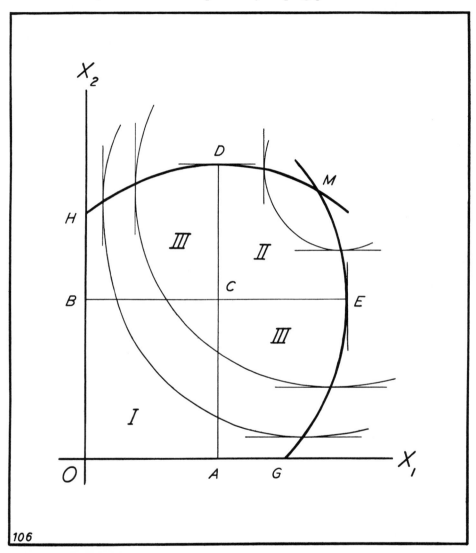

FIG. 106.—Principal subdivisions of the effective region inclosed by the satiation curves *HDM* and *GEM* showing the range within which the relation between the two commodities is one of complementarity, competitiveness, or is indeterminate.

curves. For the range of values included in such areas it is clear that the commodities should be defined as completing. Type II are areas such as *CDME*, which lie under negatively sloping portions of both curves; within these areas the commodities are defined as competing. Type III are areas such as $BCDH$ and $ACEG$ which lie under a positively sloping portion of one curve and a negatively sloping portion of the other. The areas of the third type can be further subdivided into those for which only one of the curves is an actual boundary (Type IIIa), and those for which both or neither of the curves are actual boundaries (Type IIIb). In Figure 106 the area $BCDH$ and the area $ACEG$ are both illustrations of Type IIIa. The chart does not contain areas of Type IIIb. They arise when the satiation curve of one of the commodities is *convex* to the axis of the other. If, for example, the satiation curve GEM has been concave to the x_2-axis (i.e., if the curve had a *negative* slope from G to E and a *positive* slope from E to M), the areas $DCEM$ and $OBCA$ would have been of Type IIIb. Whether the commodities should be considered completing or competing within areas of Type III it is difficult to say. For areas of Type IIIa, however, it seems reasonable to consider the commodities as completing or competing for the relevant range of values according as the bounding curve is positively or negatively sloped. For areas of Type IIIb it is not possible to say whether the commodities are completing or competing. But there is good reason to suppose that such situations will, in fact, rarely (possibly never) occur.[20]

Like the Johnson-Allen definition, the Friedman definition can be translated into a condition on the "true" demand functions. All we have to do is to substitute $m \dfrac{\partial y_i}{\partial x_j}$ for φ_{ij}, and $m \dfrac{\partial y_i}{\partial x_i}$ for φ_{ii} in (3.3). (And the result can easily be converted into price flexibilities.) But this procedure, while theoretically valid, is of no practical consequence, since (3.3) holds only for the boundaries of the effective region, at which the prices are zero. And statistically derived demand curves are not valid at the boundaries.

We conclude that the Friedman definition and the Johnson-Allen definition of complementarity have a very intimate theoretical connection. If two commodities are everywhere completing according to the former definition, they are likewise completing according to the latter; and, if they are competing at any points according to the former definition, they are considered everywhere competing by the latter. Both definitions are independent of the assumption that utility is measurable. The Friedman definition has the very definite advantages, first, that it does, where the Johnson-Allen definition does not, enable the relationship between two commodities to vary according to the quantities of the commodities possessed and, second, that it provides a criterion of independence. But, like the Johnson-Allen definition, it is of no use in practice: Both definitions suffer from the same basic limitation that it is impossible to translate them into terms applicable to statistically derived demand curves.

[20] These definitions are due to Friedman, *op. cit.*

IV. THE SLUTSKY AND THE HICKS-ALLEN
DEFINITIONS OF COMPLEMENTARITY

We come finally to an examination of definitions of completing and competing goods which can be applied to the analysis of statistical demand curves.

In a very important paper published in 1934, Hicks and Allen suggested a definition of complementarity which diverges from the Edgeworth-Pareto definition to a much greater degree than does the Johnson-Allen definition or the Friedman modification of it.[21] It is more than a formal change designed to render the criteria of competitiveness and complementarity independent of the assumption that utility is uniquely measurable; it involves a radical recasting of our conceptions of these terms at the same time that it yields conditions on the demand function of which the theory of the preceding chapter is a special case. As was pointed out in chapter i,[22] Hicks and Allen derived their results quite independently of Slutsky's paper, which was published in 1915 and which was discovered by Dr. Hicks and myself in 1934. Yet, basically, the two approaches are identical. Since we have already summarized and illustrated Slutsky's analysis in chapter i, we shall take his concepts as the point of departure and relate them to Hicks and Allen's.[23]

A. NEW CONDITIONS ON THE DEMAND
FUNCTIONS FOR RELATED GOODS

It will be convenient for the present purpose to reverse the procedure followed in the discussion of the Pareto and the Johnson-Allen definitions. Instead of first giving the Slutsky and the Hicks-Allen definitions and then translating them into conditions on the demand curve, we shall first derive conditions on the demand curve and then use these conditions to define the notion of complementarity.

Consider equation (3.16) of chapter i which, in the new notation, becomes

$$(4.1) \qquad \frac{\partial x_i}{\partial y_j} = m \, \frac{M_{j+1,\, i+1}}{M} - x_j \, \frac{\partial x_i}{\partial r},$$

where M is the determinant (3.5) of chapter i:

$$(4.2) \qquad M = - \begin{vmatrix} 0 & y_1 & y_2 & y_3 & \cdots \\ y_1 & \varphi_{11} & \varphi_{12} & \varphi_{13} & \cdots \\ y_2 & \varphi_{21} & \varphi_{22} & \varphi_{23} & \cdots \\ y_3 & \varphi_{31} & \varphi_{32} & \varphi_{33} & \cdots \\ \cdots & \cdots & \cdots & \cdots & \cdots \end{vmatrix}$$

[21] J. R. Hicks and R. G. D. Allen, "A Reconsideration of the Theory of Value," *Economica*, XIV (1934), 52–76 and 196–219.

[22] See p. 46.

[23] See pp. 37–50. The symbolism of this chapter differs from that of chap. i in that here the quantities of the different commodities are designated by x_1, x_2, x_3, . . . (instead of by x, y, z), and the corresponding prices by y_1, y_2, y_3, . . . (instead of by p_x, p_y, p_z, . . .). The present symbolism is in agreement with that employed in the statistical chapters of Part II.

By symmetry, we also have

(4.3)
$$\frac{\partial x_j}{\partial y_i} = m \frac{M_{i+1,\ i+1}}{M} - x_i \frac{\partial x_j}{\partial r}.$$

Since $\varphi_{ij} = \varphi_{ji}$,[24] the determinant M is symmetrical, $M_{i+1,\ i+1} = M_{i+1,\ i+1}$, and the first terms on the right side of (4.1) and (4.3) are equal to each other. We have then

(4.4a)
$$m \frac{M_{j+1,\ i+1}}{M} = m \frac{M_{i+1,\ j+1}}{M},$$

or

(4.4b)
$$\frac{\partial x_i}{\partial y_j} + x_j \frac{\partial x_i}{\partial r} = \frac{\partial x_j}{\partial y_i} + x_i \frac{\partial x_j}{\partial r},$$

as the general conditions which the demand curves for related commodities must satisfy, and which do not depend for their validity on the constancy of the marginal degree of utility of money, or on the measurability of utility.[25] We shall refer to (4.4b) as the "Slutsky condition."

If, for example, we have two commodities (X_1) and (X_2) with linear demand functions:

(4.5)
$$\begin{cases} x_1 = h_1 + c_{11} y_1 + c_{12} y_2 + c_{1r} r \\ x_2 = h_2 + c_{21} y_1 + c_{22} y_2 + c_{2r} r, \end{cases}$$

condition (4.4b) assumes the simple form:

(4.6)
$$c_{12} + x_2 c_{1r} = c_{21} + x_1 c_{2r}.$$

Conditions (4.4) may also be expressed in terms of elasticities:

(4.7)
$$k_i(\eta_{x_i y_j} + k_j\ \eta_{x_i r}) = k_j(\eta_{x_j y_i} + k_i\ \eta_{x_j r}),$$

where $k_i = x_i y_i / r$ is the proportion of the total income which the individual spends on x_i.

[24] This is true whether or not utility is uniquely measurable. All that is required is that the function indexes be continuous.

[25] See Slutsky, *op. cit.*, p. 15. Slutsky makes use of (4.4b) to derive more general conditions. Probably the most significant of these from an economic point of view is his equation (56), p. 16, which, when converted into elasticities, becomes

$$\eta_{x_i y_1} + \eta_{x_i y_2} + \eta_{x_i y_3} + \ldots = -\eta_{x_i r}.$$

This equation indicates very clearly the fallacy involved in taking the negative of the elasticity of demand for (X_i) with respect to income $(-\eta_{x_i r})$ as an approximation to its elasticity of demand with respect to its own price $(\eta_{x_i y_i})$. For, even if each of the other elasticities is negligible, their sum is not necessarily negligible, since there are many of them.

Conditions (3.19) and (3.21) of chapter xviii are special cases of (4.4b) and (4.7), respectively.

B. NEW DEFINITIONS OF COMPLEMENTARITY

Although Slutsky does not give a definition of completing and competing goods, the conditions (4.4a) which he deduced enable us to define these notions in the following terms:

Two commodities (X_i) *and* (X_j) *are completing, independent, or competing, according as*

$$(4.8a) \qquad m\,\frac{M_{j+1,\,i+1}}{M} = m\,\frac{M_{i+1,\,j+1}}{M} \lesseqgtr 0\,;$$

or, from (4.4b), according as

$$(4.8b) \qquad \frac{\partial x_i}{\partial y_j} + x_j\,\frac{\partial x_i}{\partial r} = \frac{\partial x_j}{\partial y_i} + x_i\,\frac{\partial x_j}{\partial r} \lesseqgtr 0\,.$$

In the special case of the linear demand functions (4.5) considered above, the definition (4.8b) states that the two commodities are completing, independent, or competing, according as

$$(4.9) \qquad c_{12} + x_2\,c_{1r} = c_{21} + x_1\,c_{1r} \lesseqgtr 0\,.$$

The economic significance of this definition may be understood most easily from (4.8b). As was explained in chapter i, the first term in this equation, i.e., $\dfrac{\partial x_i}{\partial y_j}$, measures the *total* effect on the demand for (X_i) of a unit change in the price of (X_j). This effect, it should be recalled, is made up of two parts: (1) a *direct* effect, or that resulting from the opportunity which the price change offers of using more (or less) of (X_i) in place of other goods, and (2) an *indirect* effect, or that resulting from the change in the real income of the individual which the change in price entails.[26] Now the latter is measured by $-x_j\,\dfrac{\partial x_i}{\partial r}$. Consequently, when this quantity is subtracted from the *total* effect, the difference $\dfrac{\partial x_i}{\partial y_j} + x_j\,\dfrac{\partial x_i}{\partial r}$ measures the *direct* effect on the demand for (X_i) of a unit change in the price of (X_j). Similarly, the right-hand member of (4.8b) measures the *direct* effect on the demand for (X_j) of a unit change in the price of (X_i).

[26] The *direct* effect is the change in consumption corresponding to a compensated variation in price. See eqs. (3.16), (3.17), (3.20), (3.21) of chap. i and the explanation given on pp. 40–46 in chap. i.

The economic meaning of the general definition of complementarity (4.8) may then be stated as follows:

If the *direct* effect of a reduction in the price of one of the goods is to increase the quantity demanded of the other good (both members of [4.8b] negative), the commodities are completing in consumption; and, if the *direct* effect of a decrease in the price of one of the goods is to decrease the quantity demanded of the other (both members of [4.8b] positive), the commodities are competing in consumption.

The general definitions (4.8b) may also be translated in terms of elasticities, as follows:

Two commodities (X_i) *and* (X_j) *are completing, independent, or competing, according as*

(4.10) $$k_i(\eta_{x_i v_j} + k_j \, \eta_{x_i r}) = k_j(\eta_{x_j v_i} + k_i \, \eta_{x_j r}) \lesseqgtr 0 .$$

This follows from (4.8b) and (4.7).

Hicks and Allen do not employ the concept of the elasticity of demand with respect to a compensated variation of price (the expressions in parentheses in eq. [4.7]). They use, instead, the notion of the elasticity of substitution. As I pointed out in chapter i,[27] the Hicks-Allen elasticity of substitution between (X_j) and the pair (X_i) and (X_h) which they denote by $\sigma/_{ih}\sigma_{ih}$ is equal to the negative of $1/(1 - k_j)$ times the elasticity of demand for (X_j) with respect to a compensated variation in the price of (X_j):

$$\frac{\sigma}{ih\sigma_{ih}} = - \frac{1}{1 - k_j} (\eta_{x_j v_j} + k_j \, \eta_{x_j r}) .$$

Similarly the Hicks-Allen elasticity of complementarity of (X_i) with (X_j) against (X_h), which they denote by $\sigma/_{jh}\sigma_{ih}$, is equal to the negative of $(1/k_j)$ times the elasticity of demand for (X_i) with respect to a compensated variation in the price of (X_j):

$$\frac{\sigma}{jh\sigma_{ih}} = - \frac{1}{k_j} (\eta_{x_i v_j} + k_i \, \eta_{x_i r}) .$$

Hicks and Allen do not, however, explicitly define the elasticities of substitution and complementarity for more than three variables.

Since the k's are positive and less than one, the Hicks-Allen elasticities and the elasticities with respect to compensated variations in price are opposite in sign. But, since Hicks and Allen define two commodities as complementary or competitive according as the elasticity of complementarity is positive or negative, it is evident that *their definition is identical with* (4.8). They do not, however, employ the definition of independence given in (4.8). In their theory the relation between any two commodities can only be one of rivalry. To consider

[27] P. 46.

independence, they introduce a third commodity and then define (X_j) and (X_h) as independent of (X_i) if the ratio of the marginal degrees of utility of (X_j) and (X_h) is unaffected by the quantity of (X_i) possessed.[28]

The second term of each member of (4.8b) will ordinarily be positive, since an increase in income ordinarily gives rise to an increase in the quantity demanded of any commodity.[29] It follows, therefore, that the two terms of each member of (4.4b) will differ in sign when the goods are completing in consumption, since the sum of the terms must then be negative. The two terms may also differ in sign when the goods are competing, and the indirect effect of the change in price outweighs the direct effect.

The simpler Hotelling conditions

(4.11) $$\frac{\partial x_i}{\partial y_j} = \frac{\partial x_j}{\partial y_i},$$

or

(4.12) $$k_i\,\eta_{x_i v_j} = k_j\,\eta_{x_j v_i},$$

(conditions [3.19] and [3.21] of chap. xviii) are, respectively, special cases of (4.8b) and (4.10) and are satisfied only if the indirect (or income) effect of a change in price either is negligible as compared with the direct effect or is of equal importance for the two commodities. This is easily seen by putting $x_j\,\dfrac{\partial x_i}{\partial r} = x_i\,\dfrac{\partial x_j}{\partial r}$ in (4.8b), and $\eta_{x_i r} = \eta_{x_j r}$ in (4.10). However, it is only when the indirect effects are negligible that the sign of the members of (4.11) and (4.12) may be taken as a definition of complementarity. If the indirect effects are equal but not negligible, then the members of (4.11) (or of [4.12]), though equal to each other, may differ in sign from the members of (4.8b). That is, the second term in each member of (4.8b) may be sufficiently large to determine the sign of the entire expression.[30]

---

[28] Hicks and Allen, *op. cit.*, pp. 74–76 and 214–18.

[29] In the exceptional cases in which $\dfrac{\partial x_i}{\partial r}$ is negative, the demand curve may have a positive slope. See Slutsky, *op. cit.*, p. 14, or Hicks and Allen, *op. cit.*, pp. 68–69.

[30] If the elasticities of demand with respect to income are of the same order of magnitude as the cross-elasticities of demand, the indirect effect would presumably be negligible as compared with the direct effect. For then the second term in each member of the Slutsky condition (4.7) will be of a smaller order of magnitude than the first term (or the whole expression), since it is multiplied by two factors, k_i and k_j, each of which is less than unity and ordinarily quite small, while the first term contains only one such factor.

The Hicks and Allen equations corresponding to (4.1) and (4.3) contain the elasticity of complementarity instead of the elasticity of demand with respect to a compensated variation of price,

$$m\left(\frac{M_{j+1,\,i+1}}{M}\right)\left(\frac{y_j}{x_j}\right).$$

Since their elasticity of complementarity is $-1/k_j$ times our elasticity of demand with respect to a compensated variation of price, it follows, if our assumption that $\eta_{x_i r}$ is of the same order of magni-

C. COMPARISON OF THE NEW DEFINITIONS OF COMPLEMENTARITY WITH THE CLASSICAL DEFINITION

Although the new definition of complementarity (4.8), which does not involve the assumption that utility is a measurable quantity, appears as a natural generalization of the Edgeworth-Pareto definition that two commodities (X_i) and (X_j) are completing, independent, or competing, according as (4.13) $\varphi_{ij} \gtreqless 0$, the two definitions do not become equal to each other, even when the assumption is made that utility is measurable, i.e., that a definite sign can be given to such expressions as φ_{ij}. Consider, first, the special and limiting case in which the individual purchases only two commodities. According to definition (4.13), the two commodities may be completing, independent, or competing in consumption; but, according to definition (4.8), they can only be competing. This is evident from Figure 4, chapter i, which shows that any fall in the price of Y $(= X_2$ in the present notation) that is accompanied by a compensating variation in the individual's income must cause a decrease in the quantity of X $(= X_1$ in the present notation) that is demanded. The amount of the decrease is measured in that diagram by the difference between the distance OX_2 and OX_1 on the X-axis. In other words, the *direct* effect of a fall in the price of (X_j) is to decrease the consumption of (X_i)—which is the test for competing goods according to definition (4.8).[31]

The two definitions also yield different results when the number of commodities exceeds two. If, for example, the commodities (X_i), (X_j), (X_h), . . . , are independent in consumption according to definition (4.13):

$$\varphi_{ij} = \varphi_{ik} = \varphi_{jk} = \ldots = 0 ,$$

tude as $\eta_{x_i y_j}$ is fulfilled, that the elasticity of demand with respect to a compensated variation of price will also be of the same order of magnitude as $\eta_{x_i r}$, and the elasticity of complementarity will be very much greater in magnitude than $\eta_{x_i r}$. Similarly, if, as Hicks and Allen suggest in their paper (*op. cit.*, p. 72, n. 2; p. 202; pp. 213–14; and p. 213, n. 2), the elasticity of complementarity is of the same order of magnitude as the income elasticity, then the elasticity of demand with respect to a compensated variation of price will be much smaller in magnitude than the income elasticity; that is to say, the second term of each member of (4.7) will be of the same order of magnitude as the first term (or the whole expression).

The question of which of the two assumptions is the more nearly satisfied in practice is, of course, one that can be settled only by obtaining the numerical values of the various elasticities. For the commodities considered in this book whose demand functions contain income among the variables, it will be shown that it is the income elasticities and the elasticity with respect to a compensated variation in price (rather than the elasticity of complementarity) which are of about the same order of magnitude and that, consequently, the conditions are such that the simple integrability conditions should be satisfied and that they should also indicate by their sign the type of relation existing between the two commodities.

[31] Hicks and Allen, *op. cit.*, pp. 69 and 202.

they are *competing* with one another, according to definition (4.8), for the sign of $m \dfrac{M_{i+1,\,i+1}}{M}$ is then positive. Again, if according to definition (4.13) a pair of commodities is competing, and all the other pairs are independent:

$$\varphi_{ij} < 0, \qquad \varphi_{ik} = 0, \qquad \varphi_{jk} = 0, \dots,$$

the given pair must also be competing according to (4.8). Finally, if according to definition (4.13), one pair of commodities is completing and all the other pairs independent:

$$\varphi_{ij} > 0, \qquad \varphi_{ik} = 0, \qquad \varphi_{jk} = 0, \dots,$$

the given pair may be completing, independent, or competing according to (4.8).

The foregoing anomalous results are all traceable to the essential difference in the *operations* by which the relation existing between any two commodities is determined. According to (4.13), if we wish to know whether two commodities are completing, independent, or competing to an individual, we must ask him (and he must be able to tell us) whether, as we increase the quantity of one of the goods, his marginal degree of utility for the other increases, remains constant, or decreases. The operation calls for an *introspective comparison* of marginal degrees of utility on his part. The size of his income and the number of commodities in the economy do not affect his ability to make the comparison in question. According to (4.8), if we wish to know whether the individual considers two commodities as completing, independent, or competing, we must note his income and observe whether a fall in the price of one of the goods, accompanied by a compensating variation in his income, will cause him to increase, maintain constant, or decrease his purchases of the other. Instead of *observing* his behavior, we may, of course, *ask* him what his demand would be under various price and income conditions and thus derive our test from replies which are based on introspection. The point is, however, that the answers called for by (4.8b) do not require a comparison of marginal degrees of utility and *may* be obtained by observing the individual's market behavior, whereas the answers called for by (4.13) *cannot* be so obtained.[32]

Another, and possibly more significant, way of stating the difference between (4.13) and (4.8) is this: The former places no restriction on the way in which the various goods are to be combined in consumption. It simply compares the changes in the marginal degree of utility of a good, due to increases in the quantity of another good. The latter presupposes a *limited range* of alternative combinations—that given by the line $t_2 T_2$ in Figure 4, chapter i—which can be

[32] See Slutsky, *op. cit.*, pp. 19–23, for a proof of this statement.

purchased with an income adjusted so as to compensate for the price change, and the selection of the most favorable combination from this range. In view of the more restricted nature of the choices allowed by (4.8), it is not surprising that it should classify a wider range of goods as competing than (4.13).

D. SUMMARY

The classical definition of complementarity (4.13) has two major advantages: first, it defines the relationship between commodities solely in terms of individuals' tastes and preferences and without reference to the market situation and, second, if the individual's expenditure forms a small proportion of his income, it is translatable into quantitatively definite relationships which must exist between demand functions for related goods and which can be tested statistically.

However, at about the time of the first statistical application of that definition[33] the assumptions underlying it were re-examined, and it was discovered (see chap. i, n. 26) that the classical definition is based on the assumption that utility is uniquely measurable, for otherwise the sign of the second partial derivative φ_{ij} is indeterminate.[34]

The two principal definitions suggested which are independent of the assumption that utility is uniquely measurable achieve this result by sacrificing one or the other of the advantages of the classical definition. One procedure—that followed by Johnson, Allen, and Friedman—directs attention to the extremities or boundaries of the "effective region," where the signs of the second partial derivatives of the utility function are determinate. The definitions formulated in this way bear a very close relationship to the classical definition and retain the first of its advantages, namely, they are independent of the market situation. They cannot, however, be applied to statistically derived demand functions and are thus only of theoretical interest. The other procedure—that which we have found essentially at hand in Slutsky's theory and which we have elaborated in the previous section, as well as that followed by Hicks and Allen—makes use of the individual's response to market phenomena. This procedure yields results which do not depend on the assumption of the measurability of utility and yields the conditions on the demand functions derived from the classical theory, as a special case. But, as we shall show later, this definition is not, strictly speaking, applicable to the aggregate market demand functions and is not independent of the market situation. Moreover, the classification of commodities according to this definition does not coincide with that of the classical definition, even when the assumption is made (in the new theory) that utility is measurable.

[33] Henry Schultz, "Interrelations of Demand," *Journal of Political Economy*, XLI (1933), 468–512.

[34] See, however, the appendix to this chapter for a demonstration of the fact that the assumption of the principle of declining marginal utility involves the assumption that utility is measurable.

No definition has yet been suggested which corrects the basic limitation of the classical definition and which retains all its advantages. Of those which have been suggested, the Slutsky and the Hicks-Allen definitions are the most promising. But the testing of it encounters several difficulties.

V. DIFFICULTIES ENCOUNTERED IN THE STATISTICAL
TESTING OF THE THEORY

In addition to the technical, statistical difficulties which were pointed out in the previous chapter, the attempt to subject a theory of rational consumer behavior like (4.4) to a statistical test also encounters difficulties of another type, of which three demand our immediate attention.

1. There is, first, the question, "What values are we to assign to the dependent or the independent variables of the conditions (4.4b)?" If we had the "true" demand functions, these conditions would be identities, satisfied for any consistent set of the variables. The statistical demand functions are, however, only approximations to the "true" demand functions. At best they may be considered as giving the first few terms of a Taylor's expansion of the "true" functions about a particular point. Geometrically, they may be thought of as surfaces tangent to the "true" demand surfaces at the point about which the expansion is made. It follows that if the conditions (4.4b) hold for the "true" demand functions at every point, they need hold for the statistical functions only at the point of tangency. But what is this point? We don't know. All that we can assert about it is that it cannot be zero (no consumption), for the problem would then be meaningless. There is, however, some justification for considering it as the point whose coordinates include the arithmetic means of the independent variables, since that is in a sense a "representative point." We shall, therefore, make all our statistical tests at this point.[35]

The difference between considering the conditions (4.4b) as identities that hold for all consistent sets of the variables, or as equalities that are satisfied for only one set, may be illustrated by applying the condition to the two types of demand functions used in this book—linear and logarithmic (constant elasticity).

The application of (4.4b) to linear demand functions such as (4.5) has already been made. We have seen that it takes the form

$$(5.1) \qquad\qquad c_{12} + x_2 c_{1r} = c_{21} + x_1 c_{2r} \, .$$

[35] It might seem that by using the same conditions expressed in terms of elasticities (conditions [4.7]) and using constant elasticity curves, we could escape the difficulty of defining the point of tangency, since these conditions hold apparently at every point on the demand surface. But these conditions involve the proportions spent on the various commodities, and these proportions vary from point to point on the demand surface, unless the latter has an elasticity of -1 at every point. The difficulty cannot be dodged: a "representative point" must also be selected in this case.

To obtain the necessary conditions for (5.1) to be an identity, we substitute for x_1 and x_2 from (4.5) and equate coefficients on either side of the equation. This gives,

(5.2a)
$$c_{12} + h_2 c_{1r} = c_{21} + h_1 c_{2r}$$

(5.2b)
$$\frac{c_{11}}{c_{21}} = \frac{c_{12}}{c_{22}} = \frac{c_{1r}}{c_{2r}} .$$

The equalities (5.2b) mean that changes in any or all of the independent variables (y_1, y_2, r) will always change x_1 and x_2 in a fixed ratio. *But this is the basic characteristic of perfectly completing goods.*[36] It follows, therefore, that the "true" demand functions can be linear functions only for *perfectly* completing goods. When the goods are related in other ways, linear demand functions can only serve as approximations to the "true" functions, in which case there is no reason to suppose that statistically derived functions will satisfy (5.2a) or (5.2b). All that we can expect of our statistical demand functions is that, if we substitute for x_1 and x_2 their values at the assumed point of tangency of the "true" demand function to the statistical function, the two members of (5.1) should be (approximately) equal to each other.[37]

As a second illustration of the difference between the treatment of the Slutsky condition (4.4b) as an equality and as an identity, we may take the constant-elasticity demand functions:

(5.3)
$$\begin{cases} x_1 = A_1 \, y_1^{n_{11}} \, y_2^{n_{12}} \, r^{n_{1r}} \\ x_2 = A_2 \, y_1^{n_{21}} \, y_2^{n_{22}} \, r^{n_{2r}} , \end{cases}$$

where the n's, it will be remembered, are the elasticities of demand. Thus $n_{11} = \eta_{x_1 v_1}$; $n_{12} = \eta_{x_1 v_2}$; $n_{1r} = \eta_{x_1 r}$, etc.

Condition (4.4b) requires that, for at least one consistent set of values of the variables,

(5.4) $A_1 y_1^{n_{11}} y_2^{n_{12}-1} r^{n_{1r}-1} (n_{12} r + n_{1r} x_2 y_2) = A_2 y_1^{n_{21}-1} y_2^{n_{22}} r^{n_{2r}-1} (n_{21} r + n_{2r} x_1 y_1) .$

[36] See chap. xviii, pp. 570–71.

[37] In this connection it is important to keep in mind the fact that when we have only two commodities they can never be completing by the criterion (4.8b). If they are *perfectly* completing in the sense that the indifference curves for them reduce to perpendicular lines, (4.8b) will equal zero, and we should, according to this criterion, list them as independent goods.

It is of interest to note that, if (5.2b) is satisfied, the determinant of the coefficients of y_1 and y_2 in (4.5) vanishes, and it is impossible to solve these equations for the prices as functions of the quantities. That is, the two equations of (4.5) are not independent. For all practical purposes we have but one commodity, composed of c_{1r}/c_{2r} units of x_1 to every unit of x_2, and with a price of

$$\left(\frac{c_{1r}}{c_{2r}} y_1 + y_2 \right) .$$

To find the conditions which must be satisfied in order that this should be an identity, we substitute for x_1 and x_2 their values from (5.3) and simplify. We then obtain:

(5.5a) $n_{11} - n_{21} + 1 = 0$

(5.5b) $n_{12} - n_{22} - 1 = 0$

(5.5c) $A_1 n_{12} = A_2 n_{21}$

(5.5d) $n_{1r} = n_{2r}$.

Now we have seen that if the Hotelling conditions (4.11) are to be satisfied the income elasticities of the two commodities must be equal to each other. Equation (5.5d) shows that, if the Slutsky integrability conditions are to be identically satisfied for the demand equations (5.3), the equality between the income elasticities must obtain and that, consequently, the Hotelling conditions must likewise be satisfied.

2. The second major difficulty which we encounter in the application of the theoretical relations to statistical data is that the Slutsky conditions (4.4b) relate to the demand of a single individual, while our statistical results are the aggregated demands of a large number of individuals. The question arises: If the conditions (4.4b) are satisfied for the demand curves of each individual, are they also satisfied for the aggregated market demand curve? It can be proved that the simpler Hotelling conditions (4.11) have this property. But the more complex Slutsky conditions (4.4b) do not appear to have this property except under extremely rigid assumptions.

The source of the difficulty is, of course, traceable to the impossibility of defining uniquely a procedure for aggregating individual demands with respect to changes in income when the relations which exist between these incomes are not given. A unit change in income and a unit change in price do not have the same significance. There is a certain objectivity about the latter which is quite lacking in the former. An increase of one unit in the price of a given commodity affects all consumers, rich and poor, alike: They all have to pay the higher price if they purchase the commodity. An increase of one unit in the national income is not distributed equally among the different consumers: some get more, some less. Consequently, when we aggregate the individual demands corresponding to a unit change in price, we obtain something which is independent of the base from which the change is measured. On the other hand, when we aggregate the individual demands corresponding to a unit change in the income—assuming that such demands were available—the result depends on the level from which the income change is measured, i.e., on the distribution of income. It follows, therefore, that, when we are dealing with aggregate figures $\frac{\partial x_i}{\partial y_i}$ gives the sum of the responses of the consumers to a unit change in price *which falls on each purchaser;* $\frac{\partial x}{\partial r}$ does not have this property.

It may appear at first blush that this difficulty can be overcome by dividing the consumption and income figures by the population and by considering the resulting data as holding for a "representative individual." Although the use of the total population as a deflator may be desirable for technical, statistical considerations, it is not a solution of the present difficulty.

If, therefore, the conditions (4.4b) are not satisfied by the (market) demand curves derived from statistics, it does not necessarily follow that they are not satisfied by the individual demand curves. But the indirect income effect is, in general, likely to be very small as compared with the direct effect, so that the simple conditions (4.11) are not seriously modified by them, and these hold for the market, as well as for the individual, demand curves.

3. A third difficulty is that which arises when the variables in the statistical demand equations are not actual consumption and actual income but only indexes of consumption and income, or when the price and the income variables are not measured in the same units, as, for example, when we express income in dollars and prices in cents. If indexes rather than actual consumption and actual income are used, the conditions (4.4b) need not be satisfied; and, if income and prices are measured in different units, the income effect—the second term in each member of (4.4b)—will appear distorted.

If, however, we assume that the total demand may be obtained from the partial demand (e.g., federally inspected slaughter) by multiplying the latter by a suitable constant, the difficulties can be overcome by an adjustment of the partial derivatives in (4.4b).

As an illustration of these adjustments we may consider the first two equations of Table 52 of chapter xviii, which give the demands for beef and pork in the United States from 1922 to 1930:

(5.6)
$$\begin{cases} x_b' = 3.4892 - 0.0899y_b + 0.0637y_p + 0.0187I \\ x_p' = 5.7729 + 0.0829y_b - 0.1457y_p + 0.0416I . \end{cases}$$

In these equations the quantity variables x_b' and x_p' refer not to total consumption but to the consumption of federally inspected slaughter and are measured in billions of pounds; the price variables y_b and y_p are measured in cents per pound; and the index of payrolls I has for its base average 1923–25 = 100.

Let us first adjust the consumption figures so that they relate, at least approximately, to total consumption (or to total per capita consumption) as theory demands. The per capita consumption of federally inspected slaughter averaged (from 1922 to 1930) 44.28 pounds for beef and 57.92 pounds for pork. The total per capita consumption averaged 65.4 pounds for beef and 70.4 pounds for pork. Federally inspected slaughter thus constitutes for beef $44.28/65.4 \times 100 = 67.71$ per cent, and for pork $57.92/70.4 \times 100 = 82.27$ per cent, of the total. Letting x stand for total consumption, we have:

$$(5.7a) \qquad x_b' = 0.6771x_b, \qquad \text{and} \qquad x_p' = 0.8227x_p,$$

or

$$(5.7b) \qquad \frac{\partial x_b'}{\partial y} = 0.6771 \frac{\partial x_b}{\partial y}, \qquad \text{and} \qquad \frac{\partial x_p'}{\partial y} = 0.8227 \frac{\partial x_p}{\partial y};$$

from which we obtain:

$$(5.7c) \qquad \frac{\partial x_b}{\partial y} = 1.477 \frac{\partial x_b'}{\partial y}, \qquad \text{and} \qquad \frac{\partial x_p}{\partial y} = 1.216 \frac{\partial x_p'}{\partial y}.$$

The payroll index used is presumably the Federal Reserve Board index with the average for $1923-25 = 100$. The average national income for the three-year period was 72,587 million dollars, or 7,258,700 million cents. Since the index for the base period is taken as 100 (not as 1), we have

$$r = (7,258,700,000,000) \frac{I}{100} = (72,587,000,000)I,$$

where r is the national income in cents. Therefore

$$(5.8a) \quad \begin{cases} \dfrac{\partial x_b}{\partial r} = \dfrac{\partial x_b}{\partial I} \cdot \dfrac{dI}{dr} = 1.477 \dfrac{\partial x_b'}{\partial I} \cdot \dfrac{dI}{dr} = \dfrac{1.477}{72,587,000,000} \cdot \dfrac{\partial x_b'}{\partial I} \\[2ex] \dfrac{\partial x_p}{\partial r} = \dfrac{\partial x_p}{\partial I} \cdot \dfrac{dI}{dr} = 1.216 \dfrac{\partial x_p'}{\partial I} \cdot \dfrac{dI}{dr} = \dfrac{1.216}{72,587,000,000} \cdot \dfrac{\partial x_p'}{\partial I}. \end{cases}$$

This gives the effect on total consumption of a one-cent change in the *national* income. But, as we have pointed out above, a one-cent change in national income is not comparable with a one-cent change in the market price. The latter represents the price change *for every individual;* the former constitutes only a negligible change in the income of every individual, since it may be considered as distributed among the entire population. What is comparable, therefore, to the effect of a one-cent change in price is the effect of a *one-cent change in the income of every individual.* Assuming that (5.8a) measures the average effect of a one-cent change in the income of a "typical" individual, we have merely to multiply this equation by the population to obtain the corresponding change in the aggregate demand. Using the average population P for 1922–33 ($P =$ 116,532,000), we obtain from (5.8a):

(5.8b)
$$\begin{cases} P\,\dfrac{\partial x_b}{\partial r} = 0.002371\,\dfrac{\partial x_b'}{\partial I} \\[2mm] P\,\dfrac{\partial x_p}{\partial r} = 0.001952\,\dfrac{\partial x_p'}{\partial I}\,. \end{cases}$$

In terms of the symbols of (5.6) the Slutsky condition for the aggregated market demand function becomes

(5.9)
$$\frac{\partial x_b}{\partial y_p} + x_p \left(P\,\frac{\partial x_b}{\partial r} \right) = \frac{\partial x_p}{\partial y_b} + x_b \left(P\,\frac{\partial x_p}{\partial r} \right).$$

The mean values of x_b and x_p are:

(5.10)
$$\begin{cases} \bar{x}_b = \bar{x}_b' \cdot 1.477 = (5.156)(1.477) = 7.615 \text{ billion pounds} \\ \bar{x}_p = \bar{x}_p' \cdot 1.216 = (6.750)(1.216) = 8.208 \text{ billion pounds}\,. \end{cases}$$

Substituting from (5.6), (5.7c), (5.8b), and (5.10) in (5.9) we obtain:

$$(0.0637)\,(1.477) + (8.208)\,(0.002371)\,(0.0187)$$
$$= (0.0829)\,(1.216) + (7.615)\,(0.001952)\,(0.0416)\,,$$

or

$$0.09408 + 0.00036 = 0.10081 + 0.00062\,,$$

and finally

$$0.09444 \qquad = \qquad 0.10143\,.$$

This is in much better agreement with the theory than we had a right to expect, considering the errors in the data and the nature of the assumptions which we have been compelled to make. The result is due primarily to the fact that the indirect income effect is so small that the Slutsky condition practically reduces to the Hotelling condition.

VI. APPLICATION: INTERRELATIONS OF THE DEMANDS FOR BEEF, PORK, AND MUTTON

As a further statistical test and illustration of the general theory of related demands as summarized by condition (4.4), we shall deduce the concrete, statistical demand functions for beef and veal, pork, and mutton and lamb from estimates of total consumption and total income, as contrasted with the estimates of the federally inspected slaughter and index of income, and compare the observation with the theory.

More specifically, we shall express the demand for each of the three commodities in two forms:

$$(6.1) \qquad x_i = c_i + c_{i1} y_1 + c_{i2} y_2 + c_{i3} y_3 + c_{ir} r + c_{it} t,$$

and

$$(6.2) \qquad x_i = A_i \, y_1^{a_{i1}} \, y_2^{a_{i2}} \, y_3^{a_{i3}} \, r^{a_{ir}} \, e^{a_{it} t},$$

and then study the extent to which the simple Hotelling conditions (4.11) and the more complex Slutsky conditions (4.4b) are satisfied by each set of demand equations. In these equations the independent variables are the prices of the three commodities, income, and time.

TABLE 61

DATA USED IN THE ANALYSIS OF THE INTERRELATIONS OF THE DEMANDS FOR BEEF, PORK, AND MUTTON IN THE UNITED STATES, 1922–33

| YEAR | BEEF AND VEAL | | PORK | | MUTTON AND LAMB | | INCOME | | DEFLATORS |
	Per Capita Consumption* (Lb.)	Deflated Retail Price† (Cents per Lb.)	Per Capita Consumption* (Lb.)	Deflated Retail Price† (Cents per Lb.)	Per Capita Consumption* (Lb.)	Deflated Retail Price† (Cents per Lb.)	Per Capita‡ (Deflated Dollars)	Population§ (Thousands)	Index of Cost of Living‖ (1923–25 = 100)
	x_b	y_b	x_p	y_p	x_m	y_m	r		
1922.......	67.7	24.92	66.1	41.71	5.0	37.69	573.5	109,873	97.1
1923.......	69.1	25.20	74.7	38.77	5.2	37.15	628.8	111,537	98.8
1924.......	69.8	25.35	74.7	38.13	5.2	37.32	639.0	113,202	99.4
1925.......	70.9	25.64	67.6	44.50	5.2	37.92	654.7	114,867	101.8
1926.......	71.8	26.37	65.7	47.95	5.5	38.09	661.3	116,532	102.4
1927.......	65.8	28.04	68.5	46.21	5.4	38.82	675.9	118,197	100.2
1928.......	58.5	32.73	73.9	44.34	5.6	39.80	688.1	119,862	99.0
1929.......	58.2	34.89	72.8	45.74	5.8	40.67	686.8	121,526	98.6
1930.......	56.9	33.40	69.3	46.26	6.6	36.99	648.4	123,191	94.9
1931.......	56.5	30.29	69.6	43.39	7.1	34.50	596.7	124,070	85.5
1932.......	54.2	27.94	72.2	34.99	7.0	30.94	519.8	124,822	76.6
1933.......	60.0	25.34	73.1	32.79	6.9	29.54	504.5	125,693	73.8
Mean......	63.28	28.34	70.68	42.06	5.88	36.62	623.12	....	....
Standard deviation..	6.20	3.45	3.14	4.64	0.76	3.22	59.41	....	....

* *Yearbook of Agriculture, 1934*, p. 623.

† For 1922–28, *Bureau of Labor Statistics Bulletin*, No. 495 (1929), pp. 4 and 32–35; and for 1928–33, *Retail Prices and Cost of Living* (B.L.S. Bull. R. 70 [December, 1933]), pp. 5–7; deflated by cost-of-living index (last column).

‡ Total income: For 1922–25, W. I. King, *The National Income and Its Purchasing Power* (New York, 1930), p. 74. For 1926–28, Leven, Moulton, and Warburton, *America's Capacity To Consume* (Washington, 1934), pp. 152–53, column "All Income" *minus* column "Business Savings" *minus* imputed income as given by King, *op. cit.*, p. 74. For 1929–33, R. F. Martin, "The National Income, 1933," *Survey of Current Business* (January, 1935), p. 17. Total income was then deflated by population and by cost of living.

§ Population: *Statistical Abstract of the U.S., 1933*, p. 10.

‖ Cost-of-living index: For 1922–26, Paul H. Douglas, *Real Wages in the United States, 1890–1926* (Boston and New York, 1930; New York, 1934), p. 60; and for 1926–33, National Industrial Conference Board, *Survey of Current Business*, 1931 supplement and later issues.

A. THE DATA

Table 61 gives the quantity, price, and income series for 1922–33 which we shall use in deriving our statistical demand curves.

The quantity series are all total yearly per capita consumption as estimated by the United States Department of Agriculture. The data for 1933 are preliminary unofficial estimates.

Estimates of the total per capita consumption in the United States of each of the three kinds of meats are available annually from 1900. Estimates of apparent per capita consumption of federally inspected meats are available monthly since 1916 and are probably more reliable. For our purposes, however, it is better to work with the total consumption data, since, as we have seen, the integrability conditions (4.11) and (4.4b) apply directly only when the variables in the demand equations are total consumption and total income. But a preliminary analysis of these data showed that they are not homogeneous over the entire period from 1900. Consequently, it was decided to confine this analysis only to the data for the twelve years from 1922 to 1933.

The definition of "consumption" and the adequacy and reliability of the data for our purposes may be inferred from the following statement of Mr. Preston Richards, of the Bureau of Agricultural Economics:

The meat production and consumption estimates . . . . have been computed . . . . on a dressed weight or fresh meat basis with the edible offal excluded. The estimate of total meat production includes the estimate of meat produced from livestock slaughtered under Federal inspection, meat produced from slaughter in wholesale establishments not having Federal inspection, meat produced from slaughter in retail establishments, and meat produced from farm slaughter. . . . .

Data on slaughter of livestock under Federal inspection are of course available each year, but estimates of livestock slaughtered outside of Federally inspected plants were estimated on the basis of such information as was available, using of course the census data for the years reported.

The estimates of consumption of the various meats represent the disappearance of such meats in continental United States. . . . . It is necessary to convert exports and imports to their equivalent carcass weight in order to reduce all figures to a comparable basis. The ratios used . . . . were determined from information supplied by those familiar with packing-house operations. . . . . The exports and imports used . . . . include shipments to the non-contiguous territories, Alaska, Hawaii, and Puerto Rico. . . . .

. . . . allowance was made for the differences in the quantities of meats . . . . in storage at the beginning and end of each year. . . . . The actual quantities reported in storage were converted to a fresh or dressed weight basis by using conversion factors similar to those used in converting the exports and imports.

In computing meat production from Federally inspected slaughter, allowance was made for animals condemned as unfit for human food but no such allowance was made with respect to other slaughter or for spoilage of any kind.

Per capita consumption . . . . was computed by dividing the estimated total consumption by the total population in continental United States on July 1 of each year as estimated by the Bureau of the Census.[38]

The greatest source of error in these estimates of per capita consumption is admittedly in the estimates of noninspected slaughter; but, since the former are very highly correlated with the presumably more reliable series of consumption from federally inspected slaughter, it is probable that the same results would be obtained from both series.

The price data are all derived from the average annual retail prices collected by the Bureau of Labor Statistics. These prices are computed "by dividing the sum of all prices for an article . . . . by the total number of reporting firms."[39] The composite prices used for beef and pork are weighted averages of five grades of beef and three pork products. The weights are in each case the estimated proportions which the cuts or products represent of the carcass of the animal in question.[40] The price used for mutton is that of leg of lamb, since this is the only grade of mutton for which prices are quoted.[41] The prices of the various grades of beef and pork fluctuate in such close sympathy that a high degree of reliability can be attached to the year-to-year movement of the composite prices. The only effect of different systems of weighting, or (presumably) of including more grades, would be to change the level of the entire series.

The income estimates which served as the basis for the per capita real income series given in Table 61 are the estimates of total national income (excluding imputed income) prepared for the National Bureau of Economic Research. While this series is probably less sensitive to short-time fluctuations in income than is such a series as the Bureau of Labor Statistics index of industrial payrolls, it was chosen (1) because it gives actual estimates of income rather than indexes of changes in income and (2) because it is much more inclusive.[42] The

[38] Letter of Dr. O. C. Stine, of April 23, 1935. I am grateful to Dr. Stine and to Mr. Richards for this information, as well as for many other courtesies.

[39] *Bureau of Labor Statistics Bulletin*, No. 495 (1929), p. 12.

[40] For beef the cuts and weights are: sirloin steak, 7; round steak, 15; rib roast, 9.5; chuck roast, 17; plate beef, 15. For pork the products and weights are: pork chops, 1; bacon, 1; and ham, 1.

These weights, which were supplied by Mr. Preston Richards through Dr. L. H. Bean, of the United States Department of Agriculture, differ considerably from those used by the Bureau of Labor Statistics in computing its retail price index (see *Bureau of Labor Statistics Bulletin*, No. 495, p. 13). The Bureau of Labor Statistics weights represent family consumption as determined by the 1918 budget study. The marked difference between the two sets of weights is strange, since it should be expected that the proportion in which the various cuts are consumed tends to be the same as the proportion which they form of the carcass. The explanation of the divergence probably lies in the relatively small and biased sample from which the Bureau of Labor Statistics weights were secured.

[41] The price series actually used have been adjusted for changes in the cost of living. The deflator used will be discussed below.

[42] The Bureau of Labor Statistics index gives no representation to income from other than industrial sources. This, combined with the pronouncedly greater growth of the service industries relative

income figures were reduced to a per capita basis by dividing by the population of Continental United States on July 1 of each year as estimated by the Bureau of the Census.

The three price series and the income series were deflated by a cost of living index obtained by combining the index computed by Professor Paul H. Douglas in his *Real Wages in the United States* and the National Industrial Conference Board monthly index of the cost of living. The former was used for 1922–26, the latter for 1926–33.[43]

B. THE ROUGH CRITERION

Before proceeding with the mathematical calculations, it is instructive to apply the rough criterion of complementarity which we developed and il-

TABLE 62

ROUGH CRITERION FOR THE TYPE OF RELATIONS EXISTING BETWEEN
THE DEMANDS FOR BEEF AND VEAL, PORK, AND MUTTON AND
LAMB IN THE UNITED STATES, 1922–33

COMMODITIES	COEFFICIENT OF VARIATION		PROBABLE TYPE OF RELATION
	Quantity Ratios	Price Ratios	
Beef and pork............	12.2	11.7	Competing
Beef and mutton..........	20.6	12.3	Competing
Pork and mutton..........	12.3	6.6	Competing

lustrated in the previous chapter. As the reader will recall, according to that criterion two commodities are considered as completing or competing when the coefficient of variation of the ratios of the two quantity series is less than or greater than the coefficient of variation of the ratios of the corresponding price series. Table 62 is a summary of the results obtained. It shows that all the three meats compete with one another in consumption.

Will the more refined test (4.4b) bear out these findings? To answer this question we must, of course, have the statistical demand functions.

---

to manufacturing industries during the twenties, probably accounts for the steeper upward trend of the National Bureau income series. However, the year-to-year fluctuations of the two series are quite similar.

[43] Douglas' index, which extends only to 1926, is based very largely on the data used in computing the Bureau of Labor Statistics cost-of-living index. The procedure used in computing it differs, however, from that used by the Bureau of Labor Statistics in two important respects: (1) the Bureau of Labor Statistics weights retail prices by the average consumption of workers for the country as a whole, while Douglas weights the prices for each city by the average consumption of workers in that city and computes an index for each city; (2) the Bureau of Labor Statistics, in computing the average price, does not weight the price quotations, while Douglas obtains his average index by weighting the

C. THE STATISTICAL DEMAND FUNCTIONS

As we have seen in the previous chapters, the answer to this question involves an assumption regarding the relative accuracy of the price and quantity variables. Since, in the present investigation, the quantity series are known less accurately than the price and income series, the selection of the quantities for the dependent variables of our demand equations is likely to yield better approximations to the true demand relations. Moreover, the general theoretical conditions (4.4b) and (4.7) can be calculated more easily when the quantities are taken as the dependent variables. Consequently, we shall confine our investigations to this type of demand function.

In Table 63 linear demand functions of this type for beef, pork, and mutton are arranged in groups. In the first group, the demand for each of the three commodities is expressed as a function of the three prices and of income; the three commodities are here considered as a closed set. In the other groups each pair of commodities which can be formed from the original set of three is in turn looked upon as a closed set, and the demand for each member of the pair is expressed as a linear function of the two prices and of income. Time is not included among the independent variables because it turned out to be of no significance.[44]

Attention naturally centers on the first group. The diagonal terms in this group are all negative, which shows that, other things being equal, an increase in the price of any of the commodities is associated with a decrease in its consumption. Since these terms are between 8.5 and 12.5 times their respective standard errors, they are almost certainly significant. The other terms (includ-

---

cost-of-living indexes for the several cities by the population of those cities. For the period from 1926 to date the National Industrial Conference Board series was chosen in preference to the Bureau of Labor Statistics index because it is more convenient to get a yearly average from it, since it is a monthly index, the Bureau of Labor Statistics index being given only for June and December. The two series fluctuate in close sympathy for the period 1926–33. The National Industrial Conference Board index was spliced on to the Douglas index by multiplying each item by the ratio of the 1926 value of the Douglas series to the 1926 value of the National Industrial Conference Board series. The items in the final series were adjusted so that the average for 1923–25 equals 100.

[44] If we add the additional time variable t to the independent variables of each of the first three equations of Table 63 and recompute the equations, we obtain for the coefficients of the t values

$$-0.0041, \qquad -0.2748, \qquad \text{and} \qquad -0.0394,$$
$$(0.6005) \qquad (0.2768) \qquad (0.0498)$$

respectively, and for the three R'''s the values

$$0.9632, \qquad 0.9697, \qquad \text{and} \qquad 0.9836,$$

respectively.

It will be observed that the regression coefficients are all less than their standard errors, with the result that the R'''s are less than the corresponding R'''s of the first three equations in Table 63. It is clear, therefore, that t is a superfluous variable.

TABLE 63

THE INTERRELATIONS OF THE DEMANDS FOR BEEF, PORK, AND MUTTON IN THE UNITED STATES, 1922–33 (ARITHMETIC EQUATIONS)

x_b, x_p, x_m = Per capita consumption of beef, pork, and mutton, respectively (in pounds)
y_b, y_p, y_m = Deflated retail price of beef, pork, and mutton (in cents per pound)
r = Deflated per capita income (in dollars)

(The figures in parentheses are standard errors)

EQUATION NUMBER		Equations					Descriptive Constants		EQUATION NUMBER
		Constant Term	y_b	y_p	y_m	r	Quadratic Mean Error ε (Pounds)	Adjusted Multiple Correlation Coefficient R'	
1	$x_b =$	63.3140	−1.8560 (0.1589)	+0.1575 (0.1866)	+0.4976 (0.4056)	+0.0445 (0.0238)	1.6109	0.9686	1
2	$x_p =$	71.0080	+0.4340 (0.0790)	−1.1672 (0.0928)	−0.1302 (0.2017)	+0.0662 (0.0118)	0.8010	0.9698	2
3	$x_m =$	10.2925	+0.1323 (0.0137)	+0.0518 (0.0161)	−0.3037 (0.0351)	+0.0012 (0.0021)	0.1394	0.9845	3
4	$x_b =$	66.3955	−1.8999 (0.1596)	+0.1987 (0.1892)	....	+0.0680 (0.0145)	1.6610	0.9666	4
5	$x_p =$	70.2017	+0.4455 (0.0741)	−1.1780 (0.0879)	....	+0.0600 (0.0067)	0.7713	0.9720	5
6	$x_b =$	62.8571	−1.8224 (0.1511)	....	+0.5592 (0.3917)	+0.0507 (0.0222)	1.5817	0.9697	6
7	$x_m =$	10.1426	+0.1433 (0.0196)	....	−0.2835 (0.0568)	+0.0033 (0.0029)	0.2049	0.9661	7
8	$x_p =$	77.3543	....	−1.0397 (0.1936)	−0.3799 (0.4235)	+0.0818 (0.0247)	1.7265	0.8505	8
9	$x_m =$	12.2270	....	+0.0907 (0.0551)	−0.3798 (0.1206)	+0.0060 (0.0070)	0.4917	0.7847	9

ing the regressions on income) do not have such relatively small standard errors, and three of them are even smaller than their respective standard errors, thus increasing the difficulties of interpretation. The coefficients of multiple correlation are all very high, and the quadratic mean errors are all very small—which indicates that the fitted curves are in good agreement with the observations. The demand for any of the three commodities is more influenced by its own price than by any other factor or by all the other factors taken together. Thus the three prices and income account for 96 per cent of the variance ($\sigma^2_{x_b}$) of x_b (beef), for 96 per cent of the variance of x_p (pork), and for 98 per cent of the variance of x_m (mutton). But y_b, y_p, and y_m singly account for 71 per cent, 97 per cent, and 94 per cent of the variances of x_b, x_p, and x_m, respectively, the rest of the variance being imputed (positively or negatively) to all the other variables. It is the relatively small influence on demand of all variables other than the price of the commodity in question, coupled with the errors in the data, which makes the analysis of complementarity so difficult and so inconclusive.[45]

Although the fit of these demand curves to the data appears excellent, thus verifying the assumption that all the regressions are linear, a graphic analysis of the observations brought to light the fact that the net relation between the quantity of beef and its price is not linear and that the coefficient of regression, -1.8560, does not give a very good fit. From the scatter it appeared that a constant-elasticity curve might give a better fit, without increasing the number of parameters of the curve.[46] Accordingly, we fitted such a curve to the data for beef, and for comparative purposes also fitted constant-elasticity curves to the data for pork and mutton.

Table 64, which corresponds to Table 63, is a summary of the results obtained. While the constant-elasticity curves give, on the whole, better fits (cf. the values of R or R' in the two tables), a graphic analysis of the scatter diagram of x'_b and y'_b (when allowance is made for the fluctuations in the other variables) indicates that the relation between these two variables is also nonlinear and that the constant-elasticity curve does not give a measurably better fit than the straight line. It is inadvisable, however, to experiment with more complex curves, since we have only twelve observations. Furthermore, the constant-elasticity equations yield directly all the elasticities of demand. Although these could also have been computed from the entries in Table 63—and the corresponding elasticities would have approximately the same values in the two sets—the use of constant-elasticity curves has the additional advantage of yielding a direct determination of the least-square standard errors of these constants.

[45] Part of the difficulty is also traceable to the correlations which exist among the independent variables, but a full treatment of this technical problem is not appropriate here.

[46] With only twelve observations, we should not be justified in fitting more complex curves.

TABLE 64

The Interrelations of the Demands for Beef, Pork, and Mutton in the United States, 1922–33 (Logarithmic Equations)

x_b', x_p', x_m' = Logs of per capita consumption of beef, pork, and mutton, respectively
y_b', y_p', y_m' = Logs of real price
r' = Log of deflated per capita income

(The figures in parentheses are standard errors)

Equation Number		Equations						Descriptive Constants		Equation Number
		Constant Term	y_b'	y_p'	y_m'	r'	Quadratic Mean Error ε (Per Cent)	Adjusted Multiple Correlation Coefficient R'	
1	$x_b' =$	1.2302	−0.8576 (0.0679)	+0.0955 (0.1142)	+0.2010 (0.2139)	+0.4810 (0.2095)	97.7–102.4	0.9741	1
2	$x_p' =$	1.1948	+0.1945 (0.0322)	−0.7009 (0.0543)	−0.0037 (0.1017)	+0.5422 (0.0996)	98.9–101.1	0.9716	2
3	$x_m' =$	1.5377	+0.6347 (0.0704)	+0.3669 (0.1186)	−1.7951 (0.2220)	+0.1851 (0.2175)	97.6–102.4	0.9830	3
4	$x_b' =$	1.0864	−0.8754 (0.0647)	+0.1212 (0.1101)	....	+0.6392 (0.1238)	97.7–102.3	0.9745	4
5	$x_p' =$	1.1975	+0.1948 (0.0290)	−0.7014 (0.0493)	....	+0.5393 (0.0554)	99.0–101.0	0.9752	5
6	$x_b' =$	1.1615	−0.8412 (0.0637)	....	+0.2439 (0.2037)	+0.5285 (0.1978)	97.8–102.3	0.9751	6
7	$x_m' =$	1.2735	+0.6980 (0.0970)	....	−1.6302 (0.3103)	+0.3676 (0.3013)	96.6–103.5	0.9644	7
8	$x_p' =$	1.1597	....	−0.6059 (0.1210)	−0.1747 (0.2274)	+0.6962 (0.2241)	97.5–102.6	0.8345	8
9	$x_m' =$	1.4231	....	+0.6771 (0.3767)	−2.3531 (0.7081)	+0.6876 (0.6981)	92.3–108.3	0.7925	9

D. THE THEORETICAL CONDITIONS AND
THEIR OBSERVED VALUES

We are now ready for the testing of the theoretical conditions by our statistical findings. These conditions, it should be recalled, may be stated either in terms of the slopes of the curves (eqs. [4.11] and [4.4b]) or in terms of their elasticities (eqs. [4.12] and [4.7]). Although the two ways of stating the conditions must yield the same conclusions,[47] since they are equivalent, the slope relations lend themselves to a somewhat simpler interpretation.

Table 65 is a summary of the integrability conditions in terms of these relations. It is based on the first three equations of Table 63. As an illustration of the economic meaning of the calculated conditions, we may consider the first line of this table. The entries in columns 1, 3, and 5 all show different aspects of the effect on the demand for beef of a one-cent increase in the price of pork. The first entry (col. 1) shows that the *total* effect of a one-cent increase in the price of pork is to raise the per capita consumption of beef by 0.1575 pounds per annum. As we have already shown, this total effect is made up of two parts: one direct and the other indirect. These are entered in columns 3 and 5 (line 1). The entry in column 3 shows that, *if* the rise in price of pork were accompanied by a compensating rise in income, the *direct* effect would be for the decrease in the consumption of pork (which, by Table 63, eq. 2, is 1.1672 pounds) to be partly counterbalanced by the substitution of 0.1890 pound of beef.[48] But, in fact, the increase in the price of pork is not automatically accompanied by an increase in income. That is, the rise in the price of pork when money income (in terms of the 1923–25 dollar) is held constant is equivalent to a fall in real income.[49] The effect of this fall is to *decrease* the per capita consumption of beef by 0.0315 pound, as can be seen from column 5 (line 1). This is the *indirect* effect on the demand for beef of the one-cent increase in the price of pork. From this it follows that column 1 = column 3 + column 5; or that the total effect on the demand for beef of a one-cent change in the price of pork (0.1575 pound) is equal to the direct effect (0.1890 pound) plus the indirect effect (−0.0315 pound).

Similarly, the entries in line 1, columns 2, 4, and 6, give, respectively, the total, the direct, and the indirect effect on the demand for pork of a one-cent change in the price of beef: (0.4340 pound) = (0.4759 pound) + (−0.0419 pound).

The Hotelling condition is that the two *total* effects should be equal to each

---

[47] Eqs. (4.12) and (4.7) will not yield the same numerical results as eqs. (4.11) and (4.4b) because they have been multiplied by $y_i y_j$ and divided by the income, r.

[48] There will, of course, also be other substitutes for pork. Thus from col. 4, line 3, we see that 0.0526 pound of mutton will be substituted for pork.

[49] Chap. i, pp. 40–46.

TABLE 65

THE THEORETICAL AND THE OBSERVED CONDITIONS ON THE DEMAND FUNCTIONS AS CALCULATED FROM THE ARITHMETIC DEMAND EQUATIONS FOR BEEF, PORK, AND MUTTON IN THE UNITED STATES, 1922–33

x_i, x_j = Quantities demanded of any two commodities y_i, y_j = The corresponding prices

(The figures in parentheses are standard errors)

PAIRS OF COMMODITIES	HOTELLING CONDITION* $\dfrac{\partial x_i}{\partial y_j} = \dfrac{\partial x_j}{\partial y_i}$		SLUTSKY CONDITION†‡ $\dfrac{\partial x_i}{\partial y_j} + x_j \dfrac{\partial x_i}{\partial r} = \dfrac{\partial x_j}{\partial y_i} + x_i \dfrac{\partial x_j}{\partial r}$		INDIRECT (INCOME) EFFECT‡ $-x_j\dfrac{\partial x_i}{\partial r}$	$-x_i\dfrac{\partial x_j}{\partial r}$	PROBABLE TYPE OF RELATION
	(1)	(2)	(3)	(4)	(5)	(6)	(7)
Beef and pork..........	0.1575 (0.1866)	0.4340 (0.0790)	0.1890 =	0.4759	−0.0315	−0.0419	Competing
Beef and mutton........	0.4976 (0.4056)	0.1323 (0.0137)	0.5002 =	0.1331	−0.0026	−0.0008	Competing
Pork and mutton........	−0.1302 (0.2017)	0.0518 (0.0161)	−0.1263 =	0.0526	−0.0039	−0.0008	? Independent

* Equation (4.11).
† Equation (4.4b).
‡ The unit of income (dollars) has been changed to cents in order to put it on a comparable basis with the unit in which the prices are expressed.

other. The Slutsky condition is that the two *direct* effects should be equal to each other. Actually the two conditions are satisfied only approximately, the more general Slutsky condition, which is free from the assumption of the measurability of utility and the constancy of the final utility of money, yielding approximately the same results as the simple Hotelling condition. The explanation of this fact is, of course, to be found in the smallness of the indirect effect (cf. col. 5 with col. 3, and col. 6 with col. 4).

For beef and pork, the two terms of the Slutsky condition are positive: the direct effect of an increase in the price of one of the goods is to increase the quantity demanded of the other. Disregarding the question of statistical significance, we may perhaps conclude that the two commodities are competing in consumption. The same statement also applies to the Hotelling condition. By the same test we may say that beef and mutton are also competing. The type of relationship which exists between pork and mutton is, however, difficult to determine, since the two terms in the condition equation have different signs. But, since the standard error of the negative term is nearly twice as large as the term itself, the latter may be taken as zero, and the two commodities may be considered independent in consumption.

We now turn to Table 66. In this table the relations of Table 65, which are deduced from the first three (arithmetic) equations of Table 63, are converted into elasticities and compared with the corresponding conditions deduced from the first three (constant-elasticity) equations of Table 64. The conditions derived from the linear and from the constant-elasticity demand curves are in fairly close agreement. In the latter, as in the former, the indirect or income effect is small as compared with the direct effect, so that the Hotelling conditions and the corresponding Slutsky conditions are of approximately the same order of magnitude.

This result is to be expected whenever the elasticities of demand with respect to income are of the same order of magnitude as the cross-elasticities of demand. For then the second term in each member of the Slutsky condition (4.7) will be of a smaller order of magnitude than the first term (or the whole expression), since it contains two factors each of which is less than unity and ordinarily quite small, while the first term contains only one such factor.[50]

VII. CONCLUSIONS

1. With the development of his general law of demand, Pareto has corrected, completed, and extended the work of Walras and others on the relation of utility to demand; with the explicit introduction of income into the demand function Slutsky and, later, Hicks and Allen have rendered a similar service to Pareto. Given the tastes (utility function) of an individual, we now know

[50] See n. 30 above.

TABLE 66

THE THEORETICAL AND THE OBSERVED CONDITIONS ON THE DEMAND FUNCTIONS IN TERMS OF ELASTICITIES AS CALCULATED FROM THE ARITHMETIC AND FROM THE LOGARITHMIC (CONSTANT-ELASTICITY) DEMAND EQUATIONS FOR BEEF, PORK, AND MUTTON IN THE UNITED STATES, 1922–33

x_i, x_j = Quantities of any two commodities y_i, y_j = The corresponding prices

(The figures in parentheses are standard errors)

PAIRS OF COMMODITIES AND TYPE OF DEMAND EQUATION*	HOTELLING CONDITION† $100 k_i \eta_{x_i y_j} = 100 k_j \eta_{x_j y_i}$		SLUTSKY CONDITION‡ $100\left(k_i \eta_{x_i y_j} + k_i k_j \eta_{x_i r}\right) = 100\left(k_j \eta_{x_j y_i} + k_j k_i \eta_{x_j r}\right)$		INDIRECT (INCOME) EFFECT		PROBABLE TYPE OF RELATION
	(1)	(2)	(3)	(4)	$-100 k_i k_j \eta_{x_i r}$ (5)	$-100 k_j k_i \eta_{x_j r}$ (6)	(7)
Beef and Pork Equation:							
Arithmetic.........	0.3015 =	0.8305	0.3617 =	0.9107	−0.0602	−0.0802	....
Logarithmic.........	0.2750 = (0.3289)	0.9278 (0.1536)	0.3410 =	1.0022	−0.0660 (0.0288)	−0.0744 (0.0137)	Competing
Beef and Mutton Equation:							
Arithmetic.........	0.8294 =	0.2202	0.8338 =	0.2215	−0.0044	−0.0013	....
Logarithmic.........	0.5789 = (0.6160)	0.2190 (0.0243)	0.5838 =	0.2207	−0.0049 (0.0002)	−0.0017 (0.0022)	Competing
Pork and Mutton Equation:							
Arithmetic.........	−0.3220 =	0.1280	−0.3124 =	0.1301	−0.0096	−0.0021	....
Logarithmic.........	−0.0176 = (0.4851)	0.1266 (0.0409)	−0.0087 =	0.1296	−0.0089 (0.0016)	−0.0030 (0.0036)	? Independent

* The arithmetic equations used are the first three in Table 64; the constant-elasticity equations are the first three in Table 63. The proportion k of income spent on each commodity is an average for 1922–33 obtained by multiplying the mean quantity and dividing by the mean income. This yielded the values $k_b = 0.0288$, $k_p = 0.0477$, and $k_m = 0.00345$.

† Equation (4.12).

‡ Equation (4.7).

how to express his demand for any commodity as a function of its price, of all the other prices, and of his income.

2. In this chapter we have: (*a*) given a proof of the interrelations of demand, price, and income in a simple manner; (*b*) developed the implications of these interrelations on the demand for related (completing and competing) goods and on the elasticity of substitution; (*c*) pointed out some unsolved problems in this field; and (*d*) compared the theoretical findings with those yielded by the concrete, statistical demand functions for beef, pork, and mutton.

3. The equations summarizing the interrelations in question constitute a category of laws which is comparatively rare in the social sciences: they specify *quantitatively definite relations* which must exist between the variables—if the theory is true. They thus enable us to test the extent of the agreement between theory and fact.

4. Probably the most important of these relations is that given by the Slutsky condition, which is essentially a test of the rationality or consistency of human behavior in the market place, and which may be stated as follows: *The demand behavior of a rational or consistent individual is such that the* DIRECT *effect of a one-cent increase in the price of* (X_1) *brings about the same change in his demand for* (X_2) *that the* DIRECT *effect of a one-cent increase in the price of* (X_2) *brings about in his demand for* (X_1).

The Hotelling condition, which was used in the previous chapter, is a special case of this one and may be derived from it simply by substituting the word "total" for the word "direct." The Slutsky condition is valid, whether or not utility is measurable, and whether or not the final utility of money is constant to the individual; but it does not necessarily hold for the aggregate demand function of two or more individuals except under rather rigid assumptions. The Hotelling condition assumes either that the final utility of money is constant or that the indirect (income) effect is the same for the two commodities; but it can be applied to the aggregate market demand function.

5. The application which we have made of the two conditions in testing the consistency of the behavior of the American consumer with respect to his demand for beef, pork, and mutton shows that the indirect effect is so small that the Slutsky and the Hotelling conditions are both satisfied equally well (or equally poorly). It is probable that the income effect is also small for most articles of wide consumption on which only a small proportion of the income is spent. We may, therefore, expect the simpler Hotelling conditions to be satisfied by a large number of demand phenomena. But this supposition needs to be fortified by more extensive statistical investigations.

6. In terms of the Slutsky conditions, two commodities may be defined as completing or competing, according as the *direct* effect of an increase in the price of one of the goods is to bring about a decrease or an increase in the demand for the other. (We have seen that the two increases or decreases must be

equal to each other.) The corresponding definition in terms of the Hotelling condition is a special case of the foregoing and may be derived from it by substituting the word "total" for the word "direct."

7. These are not, however, the only definitions of complementarity that might be given, nor do the various definitions necessarily lead to the same conclusions when applied to the same demand functions. In fact, we have seen that even so apparently simple a concept as independent consumption turns out to be a complex and elusive notion.

8. Whichever definition is adopted, the statistical demand functions for beef, pork, and mutton show that beef competes with mutton and also with pork but that the demand relation between pork and mutton cannot be determined from the data, since the statistical evidence is conflicting. Thus, one equation apparently leads to the conclusion that the direct (and also the total) effect of an increase in the price of mutton is to *decrease* the quantity demanded of pork, while the other equation shows that the direct (and also the total) effect of an increase in the price of pork is to *increase* the quantity demanded of mutton, when, according to our theory, the two net effects must be both positive or both negative. However, the amount of the decrease in the demand for mutton is so insignificant statistically that without additional evidence we should be justified in considering it equal to zero. Under these conditions, perhaps the best guess is that pork and mutton are independent in consumption, although when tested by the rough criterion (Table 63) they were found to be competing.

9. It is greatly to be desired that criteria for distinguishing between complements and substitutes should be developed which will apply not only to pairs of commodities, as do the criteria of this and the preceding chapter, but also to groups of three or more commodities, for the present criteria tend to become complex and elusive when applied to such groups.

APPENDIX

POSTULATES OF THE THEORY OF CHOICE AND THEIR BEARING ON THE PROBLEM OF THE MEASURABILITY OF UTILITY

I

In his *Manuel d'économie politique*, and later in his article, "Economie mathématique," Pareto attempted to develop a completely objective "theory of choice" by taking as the basis of his analysis the indifference curve instead of the utility function. As he himself tells us in the *Manuel*:

He [Professor F. Y. Edgeworth] assumes the existence of *utility* (ophelimity) and deduces from it the indifference curves; I consider, on the other hand, the indifference curves as an empirical datum [*donnée de fait*], and I deduce from them all that is necessary for the theory of equilibrium, without having recourse to ophelimity.[51]

[51] P. 169.

The indifference curves are ordered as follows: Designate the different combinations of the n quantities of the n commodities (X_1), (X_2), . . . , (X_n) by
$(x'_1, x'_2, x'_3, \ldots)$, $(x''_1, x''_2, x''_3, \ldots)$, . . . , $(x'''_1, x'''_2, x'''_3, \ldots)$, etc. Each
combination may be thought of as a point in n-space. To each point is assigned
an index which satisfies the following conditions but which is otherwise quite
arbitrary:

1. Two points representing combinations between which the choice is indifferent have the same index.

2. Of two points, that representing the preferred combination has a higher
index.

The locus of all points having the same index is an indifference curve. The
family of the indifference curves of an individual constitutes his indifference
map (see Fig. 1, chap. i, p. 15).

As we have already pointed out,[52] it is generally possible by integrating the
differential equation of the indifference curves to obtain a function whose contour lines give the indifference curves. This function is, however, not unique.
If we obtain one integral:

$$\varphi = \varphi (x_1, x_2, \ldots , x_n) ,$$

then any arbitrary function of φ, say,

$$F = F(\varphi) ,$$

is also an integral of the differential equation of the indifference curves.

Pareto restricted the arbitrariness of the function F by positing two conditions which any "eligible" utility function must satisfy,[53] and which have been
studied by Dr. Oskar Lange.

Postulate 1.—If φ is the individual's utility function and $(x'_1, x'_2, x'_3, \ldots)$
and $(x''_1, x''_2, x''_3, \ldots)$ are two combinations of the goods (X_1), (X_2), (X_3),
. . . , possessed by him, we must have

$$\varphi (x'_1, x'_2, x'_3, \ldots) \gtreqless \varphi (x''_1, x''_2, x''_3, \ldots) ,$$

according as the utility derived from the first combination is greater than,
equal to, or less than, the utility derived from the second combination. In other
words, the utility function must change in *the same direction* as the utility does.

Postulate 2.—If $(x'_1, x'_2, x'_3, \ldots)$, $(x''_1, x''_2, x''_3, \ldots)$, and $(x'''_1, x'''_2, x'''_3, \ldots)$ are three combinations of goods possessed by the individual, we must have

$$\varphi (x''_1, x''_2, x''_3, \ldots) - \varphi (x'_1, x'_2, x'_3, \ldots) \gtreqless \varphi (x'''_1, x'''_2, x'''_3, \ldots) - \varphi (x''_1, x''_2, x''_3, \ldots)$$

---

[52] Chap. i, pp. 13–18.   [53] *Manuel*, pp. 169, 265, 556.

according as the change in utility caused by the transition from the combination $(x_1', x_2', x_3', \ldots)$ to the combination $(x_1'', x_2'', x_3'', \ldots)$ is greater than, equal to, or less than, the change in utility caused by the transition from combination $(x_1'', x_2'', x_3'', \ldots)$ to combination $(x_1''', x_2''', x_3''', \ldots)$. In other words, a *change* in the utility function must move in the same direction as a change of utility moves.[54]

Pareto makes use of both postulates. But, as Dr. Lange clearly shows,

if [in constructing the utility function] postulate (1) alone is used the utility function is an *index* of total utility and only the signs of its first derivatives have a meaning while the numerical values of these derivatives have no meaning. If both postulates are used the signs of the second derivatives of the utility function acquire a meaning, too, and the values of the first derivatives may be interpreted as *indices of marginal utility* just as the values of the utility function are interpreted as indices of total utility. The law of diminishing marginal utility is then defined by the negative sign of the pure partial second derivatives. This law is entirely dependent on the use of postulate (2) for if postulate (1) alone is used the marginal utility concept is not capable of numeral representation by a system of indices, being only a "preference direction."[55]

Pareto's definition of complementarity in terms of the mixed second derivative φ_{ij} of the utility function φ thus requires for its justification the second postulate. Now, as Dr. Lange points out, there is a fundamental inconsistency between the use of the second postulate and Pareto's repeated assertions to the effect that he is assuming utility to be not a measurable but only an ordered quantity. For the second postulate implies that utility is measurable except for a scale constant and a zero point. And these are arbitrary in any system of measurement.[56]

The validity of this proposition is apparent from the following considerations. If postulate (2) is to be satisfied by all the permissible utility functions, then if for one function the difference between the utilities of two combinations of goods is equal to the corresponding difference for two other combinations, the same must be true for the identical combinations of goods when we use another function. That is, "the ratio of the differences between various degrees of the index function"[57] must be invariant under the transformation of one utility function into another. The choice of the zero point obviously does not affect the differences between the values of the utility function, nor does the choice of a scale constant affect the ratios of differences, for the scale constant will be

[54] Oskar Lange, "The Determinateness of the Utility Function," *Review of Economic Studies*, I (1934), 219. I have taken the liberty of modifying Lange's wording and symbols.

[55] *Ibid.*

[56] *Ibid.*, p. 221; R. G. D. Allen, "A Note on the Determinateness of the Utility Function," *Review of Economic Studies*, II (1934–35), 155–58.

[57] H. Bernardelli, "Notes on the Determinateness of the Utility Function, Part II," *Review of Economic Studies*, II (1934–35), 70, n. 1.

contained in numerator and denominator. But any other arbitrary element will affect these ratios.[58]

A mathematical proof of the proposition that the second postulate implies the measurability of utility was given by Dr. Lange in a later note. It is so elegant and brief as to warrant reproduction in full:

First let us consider utility functions defined by postulate (1) alone. Let $\varphi(x_1, x_2, x_3, \ldots)$ be such a function and [let] $G(x_1, x_2, x_3, \ldots) = F[\varphi(x_1, x_2, x_3, \ldots)]$. G is a utility function, i.e., satisfies postulate (1) if and only if $G(x_1'', x_2'', x_3'', \ldots) - G(x_1', x_2', x_3', \ldots)$ has the same sign as $\varphi(x_1'', x_2'', x_3'', \ldots) - \varphi(x_1', x_2', x_3', \ldots)$ for any values of the variables. According to the mean-value theorem:

$$(1) \qquad \varphi(x_1'', x_2'', x_3'', \ldots) - \varphi(x_1', x_2', x_3', \ldots) = d\varphi(\zeta_1, \zeta_2, \zeta_3, \ldots)$$

where

$$(2) \qquad \begin{cases} \zeta_1 = x_1' + \theta(x_1'' - x_1') \\ \zeta_2 = x_2' + \theta(x_2'' - x_2') \\ \zeta_3 = x_3' + \theta(x_3'' - x_3') \\ \text{etc.} \end{cases} \qquad (0 < \theta < 1)$$

Similarly:

$$(3) \quad G(x_1'', x_2'', x_3'', \ldots) - G(x_1', x_2', x_3', \ldots) = dG(\zeta_1, \zeta_2, \zeta_3, \ldots)$$
$$= F'(\varphi) \, d\varphi(\zeta_1, \zeta_2, \zeta_3, \ldots),$$

where $\zeta_1, \zeta_2, \zeta_3, \ldots$ have the meaning defined by (2). The necessary and sufficient condition that (1) and (3) be of the same sign is obviously $F'(\varphi) > 0$. This is the well-known result due to Pareto.

Now let us consider utility functions defined by both postulates. Let φ be such a function, then $G = F(\varphi)$ is a utility function if and only if for any values of $(x_1, x_2, x_3, \ldots)$,

$$(4) \qquad \text{sign}(\Delta_2 G - \Delta_1 G) = \text{sign}(\Delta_2 \varphi - \Delta_1 \varphi),$$

where

$$\Delta_1 G = G(x_1'', x_2'', x_3'', \ldots) - G(x_1', x_2', x_3', \ldots),$$
$$\Delta_2 G = G(x_1''', x_2''', x_3''', \ldots) - G(x_1'', x_2'', x_3'', \ldots)$$

and $\Delta_1 \varphi$ and $\Delta_2 \varphi$ are defined similarly for the function φ.

Denote by $\varphi(I)$ and $G(I)$ the value of the function φ and G respectively for:

$$(5) \qquad \begin{cases} x_1 = x_1' + \theta_1(x_1'' - x_1') \\ x_2 = x_2' + \theta_1(x_2'' - x_2') \\ x_3 = x_3' + \theta_1(x_3'' - x_3') \\ \text{etc.} \end{cases} \qquad (0 < \theta_1 < 1)$$

and by $\varphi(II)$ and $G(II)$ denote the value of φ and G respectively for:

$$(6) \qquad \begin{cases} x_1 = x_1'' + \theta_2(x_1''' - x_1'') \\ x_2 = x_2'' + \theta_2(x_2''' - x_2'') \\ x_3 = x_3'' + \theta_2(x_3''' - x_3'') \\ \text{etc.} \end{cases} \qquad (0 < \theta_2 < 1)$$

[58] *Ibid.* Bernardelli states the same thing as follows:

"φ being a 'suitable' index system, only those systems can be considered as 'suitable,' too, which can be derived from φ by means of a transformation which leaves the ratio of the differences of corresponding values of the index function invariant. Now the only transformations which satisfy this condition are extensions and translations, that is to say, transformations having the form $A\varphi + B$."

By the mean-value theorem we have

(7a)
$$\Delta_2\varphi - \Delta_1\varphi = d\varphi(II) - d\varphi(I)$$

and

(7b)
$$\Delta_2 G - \Delta_1 G = dG(II) - dG(I) = F'[\varphi(II)]d\varphi(II) - F'[\varphi(I)]d\varphi(I) .$$

The equality (4) must hold also for the special case in which the sign is zero, i.e.:

(8)
$$\Delta_2 G - \Delta_1 G = \Delta_2\varphi - \Delta_1\varphi = 0 .$$

By substitution of (7a) and (7b) into (8) we have:

(9)
$$F'[\varphi(II)]d\varphi(II) - F'[\varphi(I)]d\varphi(I) = d\varphi(II) - d\varphi(I) = 0 .$$

Hence $d\varphi(II) = d\varphi(I)$ and:

(10)
$$F'[\varphi(II)] = F'[\varphi(I)] ,$$

i.e., $F'(\varphi)$ does not depend on the value of φ, i.e., is a constant. And reversely: the equality (9) can hold only if $F'(\varphi)$ is a constant. The condition (10) is, therefore, both necessary and sufficient. Denoting $F'(\varphi) = A$ and integrating we get

(11)
$$G(x_1, x_2, x_3, \ldots) = A\varphi(x_1, x_2, x_3, \ldots) + B ,$$

where B is the constant of integration. Thus the theorem is proved that all utility functions defined by both postulates are mutually in linear relationship. The constant A is to be chosen positively because of the condition $F'(\varphi) > 0$ imposed by postulate (1).[59]

It follows, therefore, that if we accept the second postulate we can determine the signs of the second-order derivatives uniquely. For we then have

$$G_{ij} = A\varphi_{ij} ,$$

which means that the second-order derivatives of all the "eligible" utility functions will have the same sign as those of $\varphi(x_1, \ldots, x_n)$.

As Dr. Lange points out, there are thus two possible approaches to the theory of value. One is to accept the second postulate and thereby admit the measurability of utility. With this approach we may give a psychological interpretation in terms of the marginal utility concept to the equations of consumers' equilibrium. As we have already pointed out in chapter xix,[60] our theory then relies on psychological introspection for information with respect to the signs of the second-order derivatives, since these cannot be determined from objective market behavior. The second method is to reject the second postulate with its implication that utility is measurable and to restate the theory in terms which

---

[59] "Notes on the Determinateness of the Utility Function, Part III," *Review of Economic Studies*, II (1934–35), 76–77. I have taken the liberty to modify Dr. Lange's symbols.

The conclusion that the only "suitable" transformation of φ is $A\varphi + B$, where A and B are constants, was also reached independently and communicated to me early in 1934 by Dr. Georges Lutfalla, of Paris.

[60] Pp. 607–8, 626.

do not make use of the marginal utility concept, especially those based on the signs of the second derivatives. We should, then, have to reject the law of diminishing marginal utility and the Edgeworth-Pareto definition of complementarity in terms of the signs of the second-order derivatives φ_{ij}. Our theory would be expressed solely in terms of the objective aspects of human behavior.

But, if we adopt this second method and assume that utility is not measurable, we must be certain that the conclusions we reach are invariant under the transformation of φ into $F(\varphi)$, where F is entirely arbitrary except that $F'(\varphi) > 0$.

II

To test this invariance, we must express the various derivatives of F in terms of the derivatives of φ and then substitute these expressions for the derivatives of φ in the function whose invariance is being tested.

As an illustration of the procedure we shall prove that the Slutsky equations (3.13), (3.14), (3.16), and (3.17) of chapter i are invariant under the transformation of φ into $F(\varphi)$—something which was asserted without proof several times in chapter i.

In terms of the symbolism of chapter xix, the four equations are included in the expressions

$$(12) \qquad \frac{\partial x_i}{\partial r} = \frac{M_{1,\,i+1}}{M},$$

and

$$(13) \qquad \frac{\partial x_i}{\partial x_j} = m\,\frac{M_{i+1,\,j+1}}{M} - x_j\,\frac{\partial x_i}{\partial r}.$$

In these equations x_i is the quantity of the commodity (X_i) purchased by an individual, y_i is the price, $r = \Sigma x_i y_i$ is the individual's income, $m = \varphi_i/y_i$ is the marginal degree of utility of money to the individual, and

$$(14) \qquad M = -\begin{vmatrix} 0 & y_1 & y_2 & \cdots \\ y_1 & \varphi_{11} & \varphi_{12} & \cdots \\ y_2 & \varphi_{21} & \varphi_{22} & \cdots \\ \cdot & \cdot & \cdot & \cdot & \cdot & \cdot \end{vmatrix}.$$

We wish to prove that (12) and (13) are invariant under the transformation of φ into $F(\varphi)$, where $F'(\varphi) > 0$.

We first derive the values of the partial derivatives[61] of F:

$$(15) \qquad F_i = F' \cdot \varphi_i$$

$$(16) \qquad F_{ij} = F'\,\varphi_{ij} + F''\,\varphi_i\varphi_j.$$

[61] From eq. (16) it is evident that, if either φ_i or φ_j is zero, i.e., if we are on one of the satiation curves, the sign of F_{ij} is equal to the sign of φ_{ij}. This is the statement made above (chap. xix, p. 617).

We then substitute these values into (14) in place of the corresponding deriva-tives of φ. Let us designate by a prime any expression in which F has been substituted for φ. Then

$$(17) \qquad M' = - \begin{vmatrix} \circ & y_1 & & y_2 & \cdots \\ y_1 & F'\varphi_{11} + F''\varphi_1^2 & F'\varphi_{12} + F''\varphi_1\varphi_2 & \cdots \\ y_2 & F'\varphi_{21} + F''\varphi_1\varphi_2 & F'\varphi_{22} + F''\varphi_2^2 & \cdots \\ \cdot & \cdot & \cdot & \cdot & \cdot & \cdot & \cdot \end{vmatrix}.$$

Multiply each element of the first column of M' by $F''(\varphi_1^2/y_1)$ and subtract it from the corresponding element of the second column; multiply each element of the first column by $F''(\varphi_2^2/y_2)$ and subtract it from the corresponding element of the third column; and (in general) multiply each element of the first column by $F''(\varphi_i^2/y_i)$ and subtract it from the corresponding element of the $i + 1$ col-umn. Making use of the fact that $\varphi_i/\varphi_j = y_i/y_j$, we obtain

$$(18) \qquad M' = - \begin{vmatrix} \circ & y_1 & y_2 & \cdots \\ y_1 & F'\varphi_{11} & F'\varphi_{12} & \cdots \\ y_2 & F'\varphi_{21} & F'\varphi_{22} & \cdots \\ \cdot & \cdot & \cdot & \cdot & \cdot & \cdot \end{vmatrix}.$$

Consider first the cofactors $M'_{1,\,i+1}$

$$(19) \quad M'_{1,\,i+1} = -(-1)^{2+i} \begin{vmatrix} y_1 & F'\varphi_{11} & F'\varphi_{12} & \cdots & F'\varphi_{1,\,i-1} & F'\varphi_{1,\,i+1} & \cdots \\ y_2 & F'\varphi_{21} & F'\varphi_{22} & \cdots & F'\varphi_{2,\,i-1} & F'\varphi_{2,\,i+1} & \cdots \\ \cdot & \cdot & \cdot & \cdot & \cdot & \cdot & \cdot & \cdot & \cdot & \cdot & \cdot \end{vmatrix}$$

$$(20) \qquad = (F')^{n-1} \cdot M_{1,\,i+1},$$

where n is the number of commodities. Now

$$(21) \qquad M' = \sum_i y_i M'_{1,\,i+1},$$

or, from (20),

$$(22) \qquad M' = (F')^{n-1} M.$$

From (12),

$$(23) \qquad \left(\frac{\partial x_i}{\partial r}\right)' = \frac{M'_{1,\,i+1}}{M'}.$$

Substituting from (20) and (22) into (23), we obtain

$$(24) \qquad \left(\frac{\partial x_i}{\partial r}\right)' = \frac{(F')^{n-1}M_{1,\,i+1}}{(F')^{n-1}M} = \frac{M_{1,\,i+1}}{M} = \frac{\partial x_i}{\partial r} \qquad \text{Q.E.D.}$$

We now proceed to prove that $\dfrac{\partial x_i}{\partial y_j}$ is invariant under the transformation of φ into $F(\varphi)$.

Consider the cofactors $M'_{i+1,\,j+1}$:

$$(25)\quad M'_{i+1,\,j+1} = -(-1)^{i+j}\begin{vmatrix} 0 & y_1 & \cdots & y_{j-1} & y_{j+1} & \cdots \\ y_1 & F'\,\varphi_{11} & \cdots & F'\,\varphi_{1,\,j-1} & F'\,\varphi_{1,\,j+1} & \cdots \\ \cdot & \cdot & \cdots & \cdot & \cdot & \cdot \\ y_{i-1} & F'\,\varphi_{i-1,\,1} & \cdots & F'\,\varphi_{i-1,\,j-1} & F'\,\varphi_{i-1,\,j+1} & \cdots \\ y_{i+1} & F'\,\varphi_{i+1,\,1} & \cdots & F'\,\varphi_{i+1,\,j-1} & F'\,\varphi_{i+1,\,j+1} & \cdots \\ \cdot & \cdot & \cdot & \cdot & \cdot & \cdot \end{vmatrix}$$

If this determinant is expanded according to the elements of the first column it is evident that, since the first element in the column is o, $(F')^{n-2}$ can be factored from each of the cofactors, leaving the corresponding cofactors of M:

$$(26)\qquad M'_{i+1,\,j+1} = (F')^{n-2} \cdot M_{i+1,\,j+1}\,.$$

Further,

$$(27)\qquad m' = \frac{F_i}{y_i} = \frac{F'\,\varphi_i}{y_i} = F'\,m\,.$$

Substituting from (22), (24), (26), (27), into the equation corresponding to (13) with F substituted for φ, we obtain:

$$(28)\qquad \left(\frac{\partial x_i}{\partial y_j}\right)' = \frac{F'\,m(F')^{n-2}\,M_{i+1,\,j+1}}{(F')^{n-1}\,M} - x_j\,\frac{\partial x_i}{\partial r}$$

$$= \frac{m\,M_{i+1,\,j+1}}{M} - x_j\,\frac{\partial x_i}{\partial r}$$

$$= \frac{\partial x_i}{\partial y_j}\,. \qquad\qquad \text{Q.E.D.}$$

CHAPTER XX

RETROSPECT AND PROSPECT

CHAPTER XX

RETROSPECT AND PROSPECT

I. RETROSPECT

The history of the statistical study of demand is essentially a recital of neglected opportunities crowned by a few belated and partial successes.

A century ago Cournot urged that

commercial statistics should . . . . be required to separate articles of high economic importance into two categories, according as their current prices are above or below the value which makes a maximum $pF(p)$ [i.e., according as the elasticity of demand is numerically greater or less than unity]. We shall see that many economic problems have different solutions, according as the article in question belongs to one or the other of these two categories.[1]

But Cournot was much too far ahead of his time. Although he made two gallant attempts to state the gist of his theory in nonmathematical terms, his work was forgotten.

In 1871 Jevons wrote:

I know nothing more strange and discreditable to statists and economists than that in so important a point as the relation of price and supply of the main article of food, we owe our most accurate estimates to writers who lived from one to two centuries ago.[2]

Jevons was undoubtedly referring to the famous estimate of the relation between a defect in the harvest and the corresponding increase in the price of corn made in 1696 and attributed to Gregory King.[3] When it is recalled that in seventeenth-century England there existed neither a public nor a private agency for determining the size of the annual corn crop and that even today, with our vastly greater resources for gathering such information, the official estimate of a wheat crop may deviate from the true value by as much as one-third, it becomes obvious that the oft-quoted "Gregory King's Law" must be only a plausible guess and that Jevons had actually understated the sterility of the economics of his day. Yet Jevons himself did nothing more to improve the situation than to fit an empirical curve to Gregory King's guesses!—the same Jevons who excelled in other branches of statistical economics and who

[1] Augustin Cournot, *Researches into the Mathematical Principles of the Theory of Wealth*, trans. Bacon (New York, 1897), p. 54.

[2] W. S. Jevons, *The Theory of Political Economy* (1871; 4th ed.; London, 1924), p. 154.

[3] Charles Whitworth, *The Political and Commercial Works of That Celebrated Writer Charles D'Avenant* (London, 1771), II, 224–25.

complained of the great extent and complexity of the statistical data that were available in his day.[4]

In 1885 Marshall took up the theme. Addressing himself to the statisticians of the world, he declared: "I believe that inductions with regard to the elasticity of demand, and deductions based on them, have a great part to play in economic science."[5] Five years later, in his *Principles*, he published the first general, systematic treatment of the law of demand, which has since become classic, and included in it his valuable "Note on Statistical Consumption," which contains some penetrating observations on the difficulties of the statistical study of demand. But he himself steered clear of inductive investigations in this field.

In 1907 Pareto wrote:

The progress of political economy in the future will depend in great part upon the investigation of empirical laws, derived from statistics, which will then be compared with known theoretical laws, or will suggest derivation from them of new laws.[6]

In the same year, Professor Benini,

. . . . stimulated by the fact that the economists were holding their sessions as one section of a general association of physical and natural scientists, urged that economists should adopt in their investigations methods of research employed by the natural scientists. In particular, he advised the use of methods of interpolation for the discovery of empirical laws from statistical data, and instanced the utility of the evaluation of laws of demand and supply. In his inaugural address as Professor of Statistics at Rome, he returned to the subject, proposing that the equations to the demand curves of the most important commodities be determined, their elasticities of demand be calculated, and the commodities be classified according to their respective elasticities.[7]

Benini promised to carry out his program in his academic work at Rome and, as we have already pointed out, actually derived the demand for coffee in Italy

---

[4] " 'But where,' the reader will perhaps ask, 'are your numerical data for estimating pleasures and pains in Political Economy?' I answer, that my numerical data are more abundant and precise than those possessed by any other science, but that we have not yet known how to employ them. The very abundance of our data is perplexing. There is not a clerk nor bookkeeper in the country who is not engaged in recording numerical facts for the economist. The private-account books, the great ledgers of merchants and bankers and public offices, the share lists, price lists, bank returns, monetary intelligence, Custom house and other Government returns, are all full of the kind of numerical data required to render Economics an exact mathematical science. Thousands of folio volumes of statistical, parliamentary, or other publications await the labour of the investigator. *It is partly the very extent and complexity of the information which deters us from its proper use. But it is chiefly a want of method and completeness in this vast mass of information which prevents our employing it in the scientific investigation of the natural laws of Economics*" (Jevons, *op. cit.*, pp. 10–11). (Italics inserted.)

[5] Alfred Marshall, "On the Graphic Method of Statistics," *Jubilee Volume of the Royal Statistical Society* (London, 1885), p. 260.

[6] Vilfredo Pareto, "L'Interpolazione per la ricerca della leggi economiche," *Giornale degli economisti*, XXXIV (May, 1907), 366.

[7] Henry L. Moore, "The Statistical Complement of Pure Economics," *Quarterly Journal of Economics*, XXIII (1908), 24–25.

as a function of its price and the price of sugar.[8] But he soon lost interest in the subject, and today he is even apologetic for his youthful indiscretion.

It was not until 1914 that the first definitive attack on the problem of deriving demand curves from statistics was made. In that year Professor Henry L. Moore published his *Economic Cycles: Their Law and Cause,*[9] in which he obtained equations expressing the relations between the quantities demanded and the prices of corn, hay, oats, and potatoes; determined the precision of these equations as formulas for estimating prices; and measured the elasticity of demand for each crop. True, we now know that Moore's attempt to derive the numerical values of the elasticities of demand of the different commodities was anticipated not only by Benini but also by Pigou, by Tschayanow, by Lehfeldt, and by Arthur B. and Henry Farquhar.[10] But, as we have already pointed out, none of these writers attracted so much attention, none covered so wide a field, and none succeeded so well in wringing fresh knowledge from the accumulated masses of data. Moore's work has served as the point of departure for practically all the demand studies that have been carried on in the last generation. The investigations of Mordecai Ezekiel, L. H. Bean, G. F. Warren, F. A. Pearson, Holbrook Working, E. J. Working, and others have been directly and indirectly influenced by Professor Moore.[11]

The present work is the first systematic treatise on the subject. It begins with a résumé of the modern mathematical theory of demand and then proceeds to summarize, compare, and evaluate the various methods and procedures that have been suggested for deriving demand curves from statistics (Part I). Finally, it utilizes some of these methods and procedures in deriving the American demand functions for sugar, corn, cotton, hay, wheat, potatoes, oats, barley, rye, buckwheat, and for beef, pork, and mutton; and the Canadian demand functions for sugar, tea, and coffee (Parts II and III). An important feature of this work is the comparison of the elasticities of demand and the rates of shift of the demand curves of the various commodities obtained by the different methods.

The keystone of this treatise is the "Law of Rational Consumer Behavior," which may be stated as follows:

The demand behavior of a rational or consistent individual with respect to any two commodities (X_1) and (X_2) is such that the DIRECT effect of a one-cent increase in the price of (X_1) brings about the same change in his demand for (X_2) that the DIRECT effect of a one-cent increase in the price of (X_2) brings about in his demand for (X_1).[12]

To test this law, we must express the statistical demand for each commodity as a function of all the prices and of income and compare certain properties of

[8] See chap. ii, n. 11.   [9] New York, 1914.
[10] See chap. ii, pp. 63–64, for references.
[11] See the Bibliography at the end of this book.   [12] See chap. xix, pp. 622–24, and esp. p. 646.

these functions. This frees the statistical study of demand from much of its former empiricism and gives it greater significance and utility.

The foregoing summary strongly suggests that the success of a new method or idea depends on the social and intellectual milieu in which it is launched. At best, statistical research is difficult, expensive, time-consuming, and not so productive of doctoral dissertations as is historical or literary research. A student may spend several years in an effort to determine the factors affecting the demand for or the supply of a commodity and have little to show for his work, while the same time and effort spent on antiquarian research would almost certainly have yielded material for one or more publications. Unless, therefore, conditions are exceptionally favorable to statistical research in economics, it will fail to take root and proliferate.

For the last decade or two, the American intellectual weather has, on the whole, been favorable to the development of this subject. The United States Department of Agriculture discovered in the early 1920's that *economic* research, and more especially analysis of the factors affecting the prices of farm goods, is just as useful as research in animal husbandry and, under the leadership of the late Secretary Henry C. Wallace and of Dr. Henry C. Taylor, inaugurated a program of research which is notable for its scope and achievement. Some of the more important state agricultural colleges collaborated with the United States Department of Agriculture in promoting this research. Then the great foundations discovered in this research a worthy object for their interest and contributed generously to its development. Finally, some of the more progressive brokerage houses, advertising agencies, and department stores began to realize the advantage of having quantitatively definite information on demand as a basis for making business decisions and encouraged their statisticians to gather and analyze this information. With the advent of the economic depression, this development was greatly retarded but not permanently checked.

II. PROSPECT

What of the future?

We may render our forecast both more definite and more true if we consider separately the immediate future and the more distant future. In the immediate future conditions will probably not be so favorable for the development of our subject as they were in the 1920's. The last depression has brought to the forefront social, political, and economic problems of pressing importance, and this has tended to draw young investigators and promoters of research away from such slow and prosaic work as the statistical analysis of demand to the more alluring field of "economic planning." Scientific research in this branch of econometrics is, therefore, likely to be confined to a very small number of investigators having also other duties and interests and operating on very modest budgets. Consequently, they will have to proceed slowly and to avoid large-scale undertakings.

In the more distant future, however, the prospects are more favorable. Of the factors which are likely to promote the development of our subject, probably the most important are the continuous improvement which is being made in the quality and quantity of the basic data; the rapid progress which is being made in the art of computation through the development of calculating machines and other aids to computers; the advances in statistical theory and in general economic theory; and last, but not least, the increasing number of young economists with a mastery of higher mathematics and higher statistics. The effect of these forces may well be to initiate a new era not only in the statistical study of demand but also in the entire field of statistical economics.

What form will this development take?

This question does not admit of a definite answer. We may, however, sketch a program of research which, because of its intrinsic importance, will probably receive increasing attention.

A. A PROGRAM OF RESEARCH IN DEMAND

This program falls into four fields as follows:

1. Investigations in the demands for nonagricultural commodities.
2. Investigations in family expenditure.
3. Investigations in the demands for completing and competing goods.
4. Investigations in the demands for stock-exchange securities.

1. The first field is a natural extension of the one covered by this book. It is concerned with the demands of important commodities and groups of commodities which have thus far defied mathematical analysis. It should be the aim of research in this field to derive the statistical demand functions for such representative producers goods as iron, steel, copper, and coal; and for such groups of representative consumers goods as food, clothing, and housing.

The chief difficulty to be overcome in this field is the lack of reliable data on prices and sales. Thus, according to Professors Stratton and de Chazeau, the composite prices of finished steel published in the *Iron Age* were, before the Code period,

not filed prices but represented the judgment of the journal's representative as to the going price. They were recognized as nominal and important producers could purchase steel at prices under the published price by upwards of $2 to $4 per ton. Even if accurate as base prices, they did not represent actual cost to the consumer for this would vary with the extras, imposed or waived, relative to quantity or specification and the transportation charges, made or absorbed by the mills, used in calculating delivered price. Even if accurate in all these respects, they could hardly be considered as motivating total "sales" unless it could be assumed that no changes took place in inter-basing point differentials; in other words, that changes in Pittsburgh prices accurately measured changes at all basing points. Finally, as an unweighted average, it must be assumed not only that the prices of products included in the index are representative of steel prices generally but also that no shifts in demand from one type of steel to another type had taken place over the period studied.[13]

Similarly, the monthly figures of steel ingot production published by the United States Steel Corporation are inadequate even as indices of the quantities demanded because:

(1) The steel ingot is a raw material for all other finished steel products, the production of each of which varies in quantity, according to conversion losses associated with further processing, and in value, according to the labor and processing associated with finishing operations and requirements;

(2) Steel is usually purchased on a contract basis, the contract being regarded by both parties as an option within maximum and minimum amounts to be taken up or not within the contract period (generally three months although often longer) either at the contract price or the going price, whichever is lower, at the time at which specifications are issued by the customer. Actual shipment is not billed at existing price at time of shipment and actual specifications issued by consumers are not billed at the then existing price unless the price trend has been downward. Specifications are issued more nearly with reference to the expected trend of prices (and sometimes price changes have been announced a month in advance) rather than with reference to existing actual prices. This imparts an apparent inverse character to production data—an increase with a rise in price, a decrease with a fall—which is a product of the contract relations on the one hand and the derived nature of the demand for steel on the other and is not properly associated with true elasticity but with speculation;

(3) Finally, it has been the practice of many steel companies to quote special price concessions to jobbers during off-peak periods which would confuse the relation of either production or shipment data to apparent price.[14]

Stratton and de Chazeau conclude, therefore, that

. . . . no matter how carefully one may correct for seasonal factors, time lags, the direction of price movement, and the general business situation, such data as these are inadequate to provide either a measure or an indication of elasticity of demand having significance for the formulation of pricing policy within the industry or even for the evaluation of any existing pricing policy.[15]

Similar obstacles to the intelligent analysis of demand are also to be found in the inadequacies of the data relating to coal, clothing, and many other commodities.[16] The first step in the development of this field should, therefore, be the improvement of the basic data.

[13] S. S. Stratton and M. G. de Chazeau, "Preliminary Report on a Program for Research on the Price Structure and Pricing Policies of the Iron and Steel Industry" (submitted to the Conference on Price Research and discussed at the December 1937 meeting of the American Statistical Association [mimeographed]), p. 11; the final report will be published by the National Bureau of Economic Research.

[14] Ibid., p. 12.   [15] Ibid., pp. 12–13.

[16] See reports submitted to the Committee on Price Research on oil, bituminous coal, and textile industries, which will be published by the National Bureau of Economic Research. See, also, the informative paper by Frederick C. Mills, "Price Data and Problems of Price Research," Econometrica, IV, No. 4 (1936), 289–309.

2. The field of family expenditure is much older than that of statistical demand curves. Estimates of expenditures of families and classes were made by the political arithmeticians and by the physiocrats in the seventeenth and eighteenth centuries. While some of these were merely systematic observations taken at a distance, others involved contact between the observer and the family through a third person. In the nineteenth century, largely through the influence of E. Ducpétiaux, F. Le Play, and E. Engel, the techniques of gathering and classifying the information were greatly improved, and the findings were found to have social and economic implications of the highest importance. Today there exist records of hundreds of investigations of various degrees of accuracy and completeness relating to different times and countries and constituting a veritable mine of interesting and significant material.[17]

These investigations are, however, quite empirical. They were all made without the inspiration of the modern integrated theory of choice,[18] for the adequate and simple reason that that theory was not then in existence. Yet it is the only theory which provides a rational explanation of the interrelations of consumption, income, and price and which lends itself to statistical testing. It is, therefore, ideally suited not only for organizing the masses of accumulated data but also for giving unity and coherence to future investigations. The first study of family budgets to be definitely based on this theory is that by Mr. Allen and Professor Bowley.[19] It is to be hoped that it will be followed by more and better studies of the same type, for the results are likely to be of great practical, as well as of theoretical, importance.

3. The study of the demands for completing and competing goods falls partly in Field 1 and partly in Field 2. However, it is desirable to refer to it as a separate field because it is likely to grow in importance. The investigations summarized in chapters xviii and xix merely scratch the surface.[20] Future investigations will do well to begin with the demands for a small group of related commodities and then extend their range to include larger and larger groups. As we have seen in chapters xviii and xix, such investigations should enable us to test the rationality or consistency of human behavior in the market place.

4. The fourth field is a veritable *terra incognita*. Nothing is known about the characteristics of the demand functions for securities—at least nothing has

[17] See Faith M. Williams and Carle C. Zimmerman, *Studies of Family Living in the United States and Other Countries: An Analysis of Material and Method* ("U.S. Dept. Agric. Misc. Publication," No. 223 [December, 1935]). See also Carle C. Zimmerman, *Family and Society* (New York, 1935), and *Consumption and Standards of Living* (New York, 1936).

[18] See chaps. iii, xviii, and xix and the references given therein.

[19] R. G. D. Allen and A. L. Bowley, *Family Expenditure: A Study of Its Variations* (London, 1935). For a review of this book by the present author see *Journal of the American Statistical Association*, XXXI (1936), 316–17.

[20] See also the study by W. R. Pabst, *Butter and Oleomargarine: An Analysis of Competing Commodities* (New York, 1937).

been published on this subject. As we have already pointed out,[21] millions upon millions of dollars have been spent on the elaboration of stock-exchange statistics for the purpose of "beating the market" and developing get-rich-quick formulas, but not a cent for determining the characteristics of the demand curves for the more important stocks. Yet specific exploration of the available and potential statistics relating to stock-market transactions are quite necessary if we are ever to learn the nature of the demand curves for the more important stocks and the changes which they undergo from time to time. Perhaps the information contained in the books of the specialists and of their brokers on the New York Stock Exchange, supplemented by a judicious use of the questionnaire method, might be made to yield something of value in this connection.[22] By observing the changes which take place in these functions from time to time, we should be able to learn about changes in "anticipations" and their relations to that complex of events which is designated by the term "business cycle." The many difficulties to be encountered in such a study are formidable but not insurmountable. This is a field which should challenge the best efforts of research institutes.

B. A PROGRAM OF RESEARCH IN COST AND SUPPLY

The four fields outlined above, as well as that covered by the investigations of this book, are all parts of the great field of consumption. But demand is only one of the great fields of economics, the others being cost and supply. It is beyond the scope of this chapter to provide detailed outlines of investigations in these fields. We may, however, make a few observations on the need for statistical research in these fields.

These investigations, if they are to have theoretical as well as practical significance, should have for their object the determination of the production functions, the cost functions, and the supply functions of the more important commodities and industries. In spite of the practical utility of such investigations, only two have been published in the United States.[23] The explanation of the aridity of this field is undoubtedly to be found in the circumstance that records of cost and output are generally considered trade secrets and that the engineers and accountants who compile these records and use them do not speak the language of the economists and do not, as a rule, recognize the importance for

---

[21] Chap. iv, pp. 134–35.

[22] A confidential weekly statistical survey of specialists' books in twenty New York Stock Exchange stocks is being currently made by Dr. Paul P. Gourrich, director of the research division of the Securities and Exchange Commission. I am grateful to Dr. Gourrich and to Mr. B. B. Smith, economist of the New York Stock Exchange, for valuable information.

[23] H. R. Tolley, J. D. Black, and M. J. B. Ezekiel, *Input as Related to Output in Farm Organization and Cost-of-Production Studies* (U.S. Dept. Agric. Bull. No. 1277 [1924]); and Joel Dean, *Statistical Determination of Costs, with Special Reference to Marginal Costs* ("University of Chicago Studies in Business Administration," Vol. VII, No. 1 [1936]).

their work of such a tool as the marginal cost curve. They compute the average cost of production of an article to six or more decimals and then attempt to convince the entrepreneur—against his better business judgment—that he ought not to sell it at a price which does not cover this average cost. The result of this practice has been not only an uneconomical adjustment of output to cost and price but also the prevention of the establishment of such accounting and production records as would yield the economists' marginal cost functions and production functions. Without a knowledge of these functions, much of our economic theory and business-cycle theory must remain vague and indefinite.

The following outline indicates in somewhat greater detail the character of the studies which would help to improve the situation.

1. Investigations in the production and cost functions of representative commodities
   a) The role of fixed and variable services in production
   b) The marginal productivities of the different factors
   c) Direct and indirect costs
   d) The special position of labor
   e) Size and efficiency of different kinds of business units
   f) Economies of large-scale production
   g) Variation in costs with the different phases of the business cycle
2. Investigations in supply
   a) Restatement of the received theory of supply so that it will have meaning in terms of statistical operations
   b) Derivation of the supply curves of the more important commodities, and the classification of the commodities according to their elasticities of supply
   c) Relation between shifts in supply and changes in business conditions
   d) Relation between shifts in demand and shifts in supply

The *practical* significance of the proposed investigations in the fields of consumption and production would be great. They would enable us not only to make economic theory more quantitative and realistic but also to throw light on many questions of importance, of which the following are representative:

1. What are the objective criteria of free competition and monopoly? (E.g., can we tell from the behavior of the prices of any commodity whether it is produced under conditions of free or monopolistic competition?)

2. In view of the supply and demand conditions obtaining for a given commodity, would it be advantageous to the individual producer to modify his production policy, or to the selling co-operative to modify its sales policy?

3. What is the effect of the tariff on the conditions of supply of the commodity under consideration?

4. How is industrial productivity affected by price changes?

5. What is the relation between changes in the interest rate and changes in commodity prices?

6. To what extent is the business cycle a price phenomenon?

III. SCOPE OF SYNTHETIC ECONOMICS

It should be clear by this time that the main objective back of the proposed investigations is the development and unification of the theoretical-quantitative and the empirical-quantitative approaches to economics. The emphasis on the quantitative aspects of economics has a profound significance. Economic life is a complex of relationships operating in all directions. Therefore, as long as we confine ourselves to general statements as to the "effect" that one factor may have on another, almost any sort of relationship may be selected and "explained" by plausible arguments. Such explanations not only are inadequate but may be even thoroughly misleading. As Professor Ragnar Frisch, of the University of Oslo, put it:

.... they may be just as deceptive as to say that when a man tries to row a boat forward, the boat will be driven backward because of the pressure exerted by his feet. The rowboat situation is not, of course, explained by finding out *that* there exists a pressure in one direction or other, but only by comparing the relative *magnitudes* of the number of pressures and counterpressures. It is this comparison of magnitudes that gives a real significance to the analysis. Many, if not most, of the situations we have to face in economics are just of this sort.[24]

The full usefulness and significance of a large part of economic theory await the development of quantitative relations between the more important economic variables.

But there are several aspects of the quantitative approach to economics. There is, first, that part of the general nonmathematical theory which is quantitative, although not necessarily numerical. There is, second, the large body of economic statistics, which shows the historic changes in the more important economic forces. There is, third, the science of mathematics, which is indispensable both in the formulation of the general propositions of economic theory and in the handling of statistical data. Each of these approaches is a necessary, but not sufficient, condition for understanding the quantitative relations of economic life. The investigations in consumption and production sketched in the foregoing pages call for the unification of all three aspects and for the development of what Professor Moore has called *"Synthetic Economics* [which] is both deductive and inductive; dynamic, positive and concrete."[25]

The attainment of this objective would also constitute a fine program for adequately equipped research institutes. The most that any one worker can do is, of course, to break up the main task into its component parts and attack as many of these as he can in his lifetime. He must not get discouraged before the enormity of the task, for, as Aristotle tells us:

The search for truth is in one way hard and in another easy, for it is evident that no one can master it fully nor miss it wholly. But each adds a little to our knowledge of Nature, and from all the facts assembled there arises a certain grandeur.[26]

---

[24] "Editorial," *Econometrica*, I (1933), 1–2. [25] *Synthetic Economics* (New York, 1929), p. 6.

[26] *Metaphysics* ia. 993a. 30— 993b. 4. Quotation inscribed in Greek on the façade of the National Academy of Sciences Building in Washington.

APPENDIXES

APPENDIX A

BASIC DATA

BASIC DATA

TABLE I

INDEXES AND DEFLATORS

YEAR	INDEX OF U.S. WHOLESALE PRICES* (B.L.S., 1913 = 100)				INDEX OF U.S. INDUSTRIAL PRODUCTION AND TRADE† (W. M. PERSONS, ADJUSTED)		
	Dec.¶	Average for Year Beginning			Average for Year Beginning		
		Jan.**	July††	Aug.‡‡	Jan.§§	July|| ||	Sept.¶¶
1875	94†††	113	....	106.8	112	108	105.3
1876	95†††	103	....	101.8	101	93	91.7
1877	86†††	99	....	87.3	91	88	87.1
1878	75†††	82	....	77.5	85	85	85.7
1879	99	82	....	94.4	92	102	104.5
1880	97	98	....	97.8	105	108	110.2
1881	109	103	....	110.3	114	113	111.8
1882	102	111	....	105.4	110	110	109.6
1883	96	100	....	95.6	106	101	98.0
1884	84	93	....	85.8	92	85	84.0
1885	84	82	....	81.6	85	90	93.3
1886	80	80	....	80.2	98	104	103.7
1887	88	81	....	84.8	105	101	101.2
1888	86	87	....	84.0	101	106	106.7
1889	78	80	....	80.1	108	112	114.0
1890	81	82	....	80.5	116	109	107.9
1891	78	79	....	77.1	107	114	113.6
1892	77	76	....	76.7	113	110	107.0
1893	73	76	....	72.2	96	82	81.7
1894	69	70	....	68.8	87	93	95.1
1895	69	69	....	67.6	98	100	98.2
1896	66	66	....	65.4	90	84	82.9
1897	67	66	....	66.8	87	93	93.2
1898	69	67	....	70.5	93	96	97.7
1899	80	75	....	80.7	101	101	100.1
1900	81	82	....	80.0	96	96	97.1
1901	82	80	....	82.2	101	102	102.1
1902	85	84	....	84.6	102	104	103.7
1903	83	84	....	83.8	102	98	95.7
1904	84	84	....	84.0	97	100	101.4
1905	89	86	....	88.8	104	106	106.2
1906	94	91	....	94.0	107	109	109.6
1907	93	96	....	93.2	106	92	88.3
1908	91	91	91.2	91.5	86	92	94.5
1909	98	94	96.7	97.0	99	103	102.9
1910	96	97	95.8	95.7	101	98	97.8
1911	96	95	97.2	97.5	98	99	100.3
1912	100	99	99.7	99.8	103	104	103.2
1913	99	100	99.1	98.8	101	98	96.5
1914	97	98	98.8	99.0	92	89	89.0

TABLE I—*Continued*

Used, 1875–1936

Index of World Industrial Production‡ (N. J. Wall, 1923-25 = 100)	Population§ of U.S. Jan. 1 of Following Year (Millions)	Animal Units‖ Jan. 1 of Following Year (Millions)			Year
		Corn	Hay	Oats***	
. . . .	45.034	16.572	12.004	11.432	1875
. . . .	46.193	17.636	12.354	11.693	1876
. . . .	47.353	19.321	12.724	12.043	1877
. . . .	48.513	20.921	13.557	12.741	1878
. . . .	49.673	21.079	13.744	13.002	1879
. . . .	50.902	21.586	13.938	13.225	1880
. . . .	52.181	23.390	13.969	12.611	1881
. . . .	53.460	23.655	14.994	13.072	1882
. . . .	54.740	23.953	15.456	13.460	1883
. . . .	56.019	24.294	15.942	13.916	1884
. . . .	57.298	24.740	16.549	14.497	1885
. . . .	58.577	24.640	17.202	14.994	1886
. . . .	59.856	24.815	17.812	15.701	1887
. . . .	61.136	26.331	18.340	16.246	1888
. . . .	62.415	26.959	19.140	16.898	1889
. . . .	63.709	26.937	19.077	16.741	1890
. . . .	65.013	28.507	20.041	18.067	1891
. . . .	66.318	27.484	20.161	18.662	1892
. . . .	67.623	27.576	20.225	18.591	1893
. . . .	68.928	27.217	19.819	18.367	1894
. . . .	70.232	26.395	18.965	17.565	1895
. . . .	71.537	25.456	18.274	16.798	1896
. . . .	72.842	25.097	17.854	16.387	1897
. . . .	74.146	24.764	17.563	16.072	1898
. . . .	75.451	26.164	19.428	16.228	1899
. . . .	76.938	28.673‡‡‡	21.912‡‡‡	19.797‡‡‡	1900
. . . .	78.556	27.419	21.955	19.541	1901
. . . .	80.174	27.710	22.270	19.608	1902
. . . .	81.792	28.336	22.493	19.825	1903
. . . .	83.410	29.057	22.730	20.229	1904
. . . .	85.028	30.705	24.156	22.296	1905
. . . .	86.646	31.997	25.065	23.643	1906
. . . .	88.264	32.777	25.044	23.889	1907
. . . .	89.882	32.245	25.411	24.634	1908
. . . .	91.500	30.589	25.145	24.908	1909
. . . .	92.975	31.478	24.680	24.402	1910
. . . .	94.390	31.467	24.616	24.601	1911
. . . .	95.805	31.248	24.721	24.670	1912
. . . .	97.220	31.392	25.403	25.150	1913
. . . .	98.635	33.036	26.182	25.504	1914

TABLE I—*Continued*

YEAR	INDEX OF U.S. WHOLESALE PRICES* (B.L.S., 1913 = 100)				INDEX OF U.S. INDUSTRIAL PRODUCTION AND TRADE† (W. M. PERSONS, ADJUSTED)		
	Dec.¶	Average for Year Beginning			Average for Year Beginning		
		Jan.**	July††	Aug.‡‡	Jan.§§	July‖ ‖	Sept.¶¶
1915	108	101	110.6	112.5	97	108	109.4
1916	149	127	151.9	157.3	115	118	118.6
1917	182	177	186.7	187.3	118	116	116.5
1918	202	195	199.9	201.2	116	110	104.2
1919	223	207	226.9	229.3	107	111	105.0
1920	179	227	183.7	175.3	106	91	83.2
1921	140	147	142.4	143.6	82	87	87.8
1922	156	149	155.8	155.4	95	104	106.4
1923	151	154	150.3	150.0	106	102	102.4
1924	157	150	154.8	155.9	98	99	104.9
1925	156	159	155.8	155.1	103	105	110.2
1926	147	151	147.2	146.6	105	105	109.9
1927	149	144 ⊕	146.9	147.3	102	100	105.9
1928	149	148 ⊕	148.0	148.1	101	103	111.8
1929	145	146 ⊕	142.0	140.2	101	94	98.2
1930	....	130 ⊕	119.7	118.6	....	....	77.5
1931	....	110 ⊕	103.7	102.7	....	....	58.4
1932	....	98 ⊕	95.6	96.3	....	....	55.3
1933	....	100 ⊕	109.5	110.1	....	....	63.7
1934	....	113 ⊕	118.5	119.2	....	....	62.3
1935	....	121 ⊕	....	....	....	....	....
1936	....	122 ⊕	....	....	....	....	....

NOTES TO TABLE I

* Taken from Carl Snyder, *Business Cycles and Business Measurements* (New York: Macmillan Co., 1927), p. 288. "The sources for . . . . this index are as follows: Commodity Prices at Wholesale: 1875–1889, Monthly Index of Basic Commodities compiled by Federal Reserve Bank of New York; 1890–1899, monthly figures interpolated from quarterly series of the United States Department of Labor; 1900 to date [1926], Department of Labor monthly index" (*ibid.*, p. 137). For the years following 1926, the index is taken from the Bureau of Labor Statistics *Bulletins*. In 1928 the Bureau of Labor Statistics made several modifications in its index numbers of wholesale prices and changed the base to 1926 = 100. The new index numbers for the years beginning with 1928 were, therefore, spliced on to the old series as follows: The new index (1926 = 100) was first shifted to 1913 as a base by dividing by the 1913 average. Then the figures thus obtained for the years beginning with 1928 were multiplied by the ratio for 1927 of the old index to the new index with 1913 as a base. For the specific series used in deflating the prices of the various commodities see nn. ¶, **, ††, and ‡‡ of this table.

† Taken from Warren M. Persons, *Forecasting Business Cycles* (New York: John Wiley & Sons, Inc., 1931), pp. 93–167. This index is adjusted for trend and seasonal variation. For the period since 1931 the monthly figures may be found in *Barron's National Financial Weekly*. For brief descriptions of the annual and monthly indexes as well as the new weekly index see Warren M. Persons, "Gauging Business Activity," *Barron's*, January 18, 1937, pp. 3 and 6. For the specific series used in connection with the various commodities see nn. §§, ‖ ‖, and ¶¶.

‡ This index was used in the cotton computations. It is taken from Norman J. Wall, *Monthly Index of World Industrial Production, 1920–1935* (U.S. Dept. Agric. Preliminary Report [June, 1936]), p. 18. The index represents only the following ten countries: United States, United Kingdom, France, Germany, Italy, Japan, Canada, Czechoslovakia, Belgium, and Poland.

§ The data for 1875–1919 were supplied by Clarence E. Batscheldt, geographer, Department of Commerce. The data for 1920–29 were computed by straight-line interpolation from the population figures for July 1, supplied by Mr. Batscheldt. The data for 1930–34 are from *Agricultural Statistics, 1936*, p. 18. These population figures were used in reducing quantity figures to a per capita basis for all commodities except sugar. The per capita consumption series for sugar was taken directly from the source quoted in Table III.

‖ The animal-unit series for hay and oats is a weighted index of the number of milk cows, of other than milk cows, and of horses and mules for each year, the weights being the consumption of the commodity by each of these groups in 1914. The animal-unit series for corn is a weighted index of the number of hogs, of milk cows, of other than milk cows, and of horses and mules (see U.S. Dept. Agric., *Farmers' Bulletin*, No. 629, p. 9).

¶ This index was used to deflate the price series as of December 1 of the following commodities: corn, hay, potatoes, oats, rye, and buckwheat. It was also used to deflate the December 1 prices for 1875–1907 of cotton and wheat.

** This index was used to deflate the price of sugar, which is a New York currency price for the year beginning January.

†† This index was used to deflate the season average prices of wheat for the years beginning with 1908. Prior to that date the December index was used (see n. ¶).

TABLE I—*Continued*

Index of World Industrial Production‡ (N. J. Wall, 1923-25 = 100)	Population§ of U.S. Jan. 1 of Following Year (Millions)	Animal Units‖ Jan. 1 of Following Year (Millions)			Year
		Corn	Hay	Oats***	
. . . .	100.050	34.121	26.956	25.728	1915
. . . .	101.465	34.035	27.665	26.022	1916
. . . .	102.880	35.406	28.240	26.524	1917
. . . .	104.296	35.829	28.148	26.526	1918
. . . .	105.711	34.300	26.930	25.345	1919
72.62	107.375	33.529	26.398	24.786	1920
79.05	109.040	33.499	26.248	24.372	1921
93.42	110.705	35.018	25.889	23.891	1922
95.48	112.370	33.956	25.369	23.273	1923
104.07	114.035	31.134	24.710	22.586	1924
107.23	115.700	29.783	23.934	21.956§§§	1925
113.12	117.364	29.626	23.144	21.193	1926
116.74	119.029	30.223	22.608	20.489	1927
126.66	120.694	29.331	22.365	19.887	1928
121.02	122.359	28.434	22.414	19.416	1929
102.92	123.630	. . . .	. . . .	. . . .	1930
87.42	124.511	. . . .	. . . .	. . . .	1931
88.47	125.197	. . . .	. . . .	. . . .	1932
100.00	126.128	. . . .	. . . .	. . . .	1933
104.02	126.791	. . . .	. . . .	. . . .	1934
. . . .	. . . .	. . . .	. . . .	. . . .	1935
. . . .	. . . .	. . . .	. . . .	. . . .	1936

NOTES TO TABLE I—*Continued*

‡‡ This index was used to deflate the price of barley, which is a Chicago currency price for the year beginning August. It was also used to deflate the price of cotton for the years since 1908. Since the August index (rounded off to the nearest whole number) is identical with the September index for the years 1908-13, it is permissible to use the former for these years even though the "cotton year" began September 1 until 1913.

§§ This index was used in all the sugar computations except those for the period 1922-36 (which were made as chap. vi went to press), for which the following *revised* figures were used:

1922.	95.8	1930.	87.6
1923.	107.9	1931.	71.6
1924.	100.4	1932.	53.4
1925.	109.2	1933.	59.3
1926.	110.5	1934.	61.8
1927.	106.5	1935.	66.9
1928.	108.7	1936.	78.3
1929.	109.4		

For the years 1922-32 these are taken from W. M. Persons and Le Baron R. Foster, "A New Index of Industrial Production and Trade," *Review of Economic Statistics*, XV (1933), 155 and 160. For the years 1933-34 the data were supplied by W. M. Persons (letter of November 23, 1935). For the years 1935-36 I am indebted to Mr. L. C. Duncan of *Barron's National Financial Weekly* (letter of January 20, 1938).

‖ ‖ This index was used in the computations for both corn and potatoes.

¶¶ This index was used in the cotton computations. The series relates to the year beginning September only for the years 1875-1913. For the years 1914-29 it relates to the year beginning August. This conforms with the "cotton year" for those years. The figures for 1918-29 are the revised series given in the *Review of Economic Statistics* for August 15, 1933, and supplemented by data contained in a letter from W. M. Persons dated November 23, 1935.

*** In the actual computations one more significant figure was used.

††† Reduced to a gold base, since the farm prices as given in the *Yearbooks of Agriculture* are on a gold base. The method followed was to divide the December index on a currency base by the average price of gold in greenbacks for December. See W. C. Mitchell, *Gold, Prices, and Wages* (Berkeley: University of California Press, 1908), pp. 4-13.

‡‡‡ After the computations were completed, the U.S. Department of Agriculture revised the figures for milk cows and other than milk cows for 1900-29 and for horses and mules for 1919-29 (see *Yearbook of Agriculture, 1932*, p. 770, Table 313; p. 818, Table 378; and p. 825, Table 386). A comparison shows, however, that the revisions would not materially affect our conclusions.

§§§ The incorrect figure, 21.950, was used in the computations.

⊕ Through an oversight, a slight inconsistency crept into the method of splicing the index used to deflate sugar prices. The figures for 1927-29 (1913=100) were multiplied by the ratio for 1926, instead of for 1927, of the old index to the new index with 1913 as base (see n. *). This method was continued in the later computations for the figures for 1930-36.

YEAR‡	SUGAR		CORN		HAY	
	"Consumption" 1,000 Short Tons§	Price Cents per Lb.‖	Production 10,000 Bu. ¶	Price Cents per Bu.**	Production 1,000 Short Tons¶	Price Dollars per Ton**
1875	886.6	10.718	132.107	36.7	27,874	10.78
1876	868.6	10.468	128.383	34.0	30,867	8.97
1877	834.7	11.312	134.256	34.8	31,629	8.37
1878	866.3	9.484	138.822	31.7	39,608	7.20
1879	931.7	8.785	154.790‖‖‖	37.5‖‖‖	39,862	9.31
1880	1072	9.602	171.744	39.6	31,925	11.65
1881	1134	9.667	119.492	63.6	35,135	11.82
1882	1271	9.234	161.702	48.5	38,138	9.73
1883	1371	8.506	155.107	42.4	46,864	8.19
1884	1467	6.780	179.553	35.7	48,470	8.17
1885	1454	6.441	193.618	32.8	44,732	8.71
1886	1634	6.117	166.544	36.6	41,796	8.46
1887	1548	6.013	145.616	44.4	41,454	9.97
1888	1702	7.007	198.779	34.1	46,643	8.76
1889	1586	7.640	199.865	27.4	49,181	7.76
1890	1654	6.171	146.041	50.0	49,057	8.18
1891	2116	4.641	205.582	39.7	48,759	8.89
1892	2076	4.346	171.369	38.8	49,238	8.95
1893	2136	4.842	170.757	35.9	55,575	9.48
1894	2254	4.120	133.968	45.1	50,468	8.96
1895	2184	4.152	231.095	25.0	41,838	9.46
1896	2195	4.532	250.348	21.3	54,380	7.48
1897	2319	4.503	214.455	26.0	58,878	7.28
1898	2243	4.965	226.112	28.4	66,772	6.63
1899	2327	4.919	245.463	29.9	57,450	8.20
1900	2486	5.320	250.515	35.1	53,231	9.72
1901	2657	5.050	160.729	60.0	55,819	9.91
1902	2874	4.455	262.070	40.0	65,296	9.19
1903	2856	4.638	233.942	42.1	68,154	9.35
1904	3099	4.772	252.068	43.7	69,192	8.91
1905	2948	5.256	274.433	40.7	72,973	8.59
1906	3208	4.515	289.582	39.2	66,341	10.43
1907	3353	4.649	251.206	50.9	72,261	11.78
1908	3568	4.957	254.496	60.0	78,440	9.14
1909	3649	4.765	257.234	58.6	74,384	10.58
1910	3752	4.972	288.626	48.0	69,378	12.14
1911	3754	5.345	253.149	61.8	54,916	14.29
1912	3925	5.041	312.475	48.7	72,691	11.79
1913	4192	4.278	244.699	69.1	64,116	12.43
1914	4212	4.683	267.280	64.4	70,071	11.12
1915	4258	5.559	299.479	57.5	85,920	10.63
1916	4098	6.862	256.693	88.9	91,192	11.22
1917	4126	7.663	306.523	127.9	83,308	17.09
1918	3915	7.834	250.266	136.5	76,660	20.13
1919	4556	9.003	281.130	134.5	86,997	20.05
1920	4575	11.390	320.858	67.0	89,785	17.66
1921	4600	6.207	306.857	42.3	82,458	12.10
1922	5704	5.904	290.602	65.8	95,748	12.55
1923	5354	8.441	305.356	72.6	89,250	14.13
1924	5437	7.471	230.941	98.2	97,224	13.76
1925	6171	5.483	291.611	67.4	85,431	13.93
1926	6352	5.473	269.153	64.2	86,144	14.10
1927	5933	5.828	276.309	72.3	106,001	11.35
1928	6208	5.540	281.890	75.2	93,351	12.27
1929	6508‡‡‡	5.025‡‡‡	261.413	78.1	100,893	12.22

QUANTITIES AND PRICES†

POTATOES		OATS					YEAR‡
Production 1,000,000 Bu.¶	Price Cents per Bu.**	Production 1,000,000 Bu.¶	Revised Production 1,000,000 Bu.††	Stocks Aug. 1 1,000,000 Bu.‡‡	Net Exports 1,000,000 Bu.††	Price Cents per Bu.**	
166.877	34.4	354.318	. . . .	. . . .	. . . .	32.0	1875
124.827	61.9	320.884	. . . .	. . . .	. . . .	32.4	1876
170.092	43.7	406.394	. . . .	. . . .	. . . .	28.4	1877
124.127	58.7	413.579	. . . .	. . . .	. . . .	24.6	1878
181.626	43.6	450.745	. . . .	. . . .	. . . .	33.3	1879
167.660	48.3	417.885	. . . .	. . . .	. . . .	36.0	1880
109.145	91.0	416.481	. . . .	. . . .	. . . .	46.4	1881
170.973	55.7	488.251	. . . .	. . . .	. . . .	37.5	1882
208.164	42.2	571.302	. . . .	. . . .	. . . .	32.7	1883
190.642	39.6	583.628	. . . .	. . . .	. . . .	27.7	1884
175.029	44.7	629.409	. . . .	. . . .	. . . .	28.5	1885
168.051	46.7	624.134	. . . .	. . . .	. . . .	29.8	1886
134.103	68.2	659.618	. . . .	. . . .	. . . .	30.4	1887
202.365	40.2	701.735	. . . .	. . . .	. . . .	27.8	1888
201.200	35.4	801.586	. . . .	. . . .	. . . .	21.9	1889
150.494	75.3	572.671	. . . .	. . . .	. . . .	41.7	1890
256.122	35.6	839.995	. . . .	. . . .	. . . .	30.6	1891
164.516	65.5	695.277	. . . .	. . . .	. . . .	31.5	1892
195.040	58.4	676.151	. . . .	. . . .	. . . .	29.1	1893
183.841	52.9¶¶	715.535	. . . .	. . . .	. . . .	32.1	1894
317.114	26.2	885.959	924.858	. . . .	15.117	19.4	1895
271.769	29.0	780.124	774.929	129.702	37.613	18.3	1896
191.025	54.2	791.442	829.525	90.177	73.855	20.8	1897
218.772	41.5	842.747	842.205	56.318	33.506	25.2	1898
260.257	39.7	925.555	937.173	66.939	44.095	24.5	1899
247.759	42.3	913.800	945.483	73.784	42.237	25.4	1900
198.626	76.3	778.392	799.812	62.936	13.240	39.7	1901
293.918	46.9	1,053.489	1,076.899	35.437	8.233	30.6	1902
262.053	60.9	869.350	885.469	87.221	1.857	34.0	1903
352.268	44.8	1,008.931	1,011.556	50.438	8.339	31.1	1904
278.885	61.1	1,090.236	1,104.395	70.458	48.395	28.9	1905
331.685	50.6	1,035.576	1,022.715	85.082	6.379	31.9	1906
322.954	61.3	805.108	801.144	77.240	2.195	44.5	1907
302.000	69.7	850.540	829.308	43.224	− 4.252	47.3	1908
394.553	54.2	1,068.289	1,013.909	32.805	1.704	40.6	1909
349.032	55.7	1,186.341	1,106.162	71.790	3.707	34.4	1910
292.737	79.9	922.298	885.527	80.861	0.030	45.0	1911
420.647	50.5	1,418.337	1,353.273	36.447	35.695	31.9	1912
331.525	68.7	1,121.768	1,039.131	123.568	− 18.858	39.2	1913
409.921	48.7	1,141.060	1,066.328	70.529	100.158	43.8	1914
359.721	61.7	1,549.03	1,435.270	57.677	98.648	36.1	1915
286.953	146.1	1,251.84	1,138.969	125.310	94.348	52.4	1916
442.108	122.8	1,592.74	1,442.519	55.630	122.273	66.6	1917
411.860	119.3	1,538.12	1,428.611	91.505	108.167	70.9	1918
322.867	159.5	1,184.03	1,106.603	114.178	37.365	70.4	1919
403.296	114.5	1,496.28	1,444.291	59.217	5.831	46.0	1920
361.659	110.1	1,078.34	1,045.270	203.256	19.422	30.2	1921
453.396	58.1	1,215.80	1,147.905	112.737	25.087	39.4	1922
416.105	78.1	1,305.88	1,227.184	76.859	4.550	41.4	1923
419.560	62.5	1,502.53	1,424.422	69.632	13.926	47.7	1924
320.915	187.0	1,487.55	1,410.336	118.199	39.565	38.0	1925
354.458	141.4	1,246.85	1,141.941	142.406	14.988	39.8	1926
402.741	96.5	1,182.59	1,093.097	73.507	9.611	45.0	1927
465.350	53.9	1,439.41	1,318.977	44.840†††	15.825	40.9	1928
359.048	130.9	1,228.37	1,118.414	94.442	7.680	43.5	1929

	BARLEY		RYE		BUCKWHEAT	
YEAR‡	"Consumption" 1,000,000 Bu.§	Price Cents per Bu.§§	"Consumption" 1,000,000 Bu.§	Price Cents per Bu.**	Production 1,000,000 Bu.¶	Price Cents per Bu.**
1875	47.117	51	17.083	67.1	10.082	62.0
1876	44.462	39	18.141	61.4	9.669	66.6
1877	38.212	37	17.011	57.6	10.177	66.9
1878	47.644	40	20.896	52.5	12.247	52.6
1879	55.636	50	22.236	67.6	17.530	60.3
1880	54.424	74	22.599	75.6	14.618	59.4
1881	54.160	86	19.798	93.3	9.486	86.5
1882	59.772	54	27.738	61.5	11.019	73.0
1883	58.113	47	21.721	58.1	7.669	82.2
1884	70.861	42	25.620	51.9	11.116	58.9
1885	68.535	42	21.629	57.9	12.626	55.9
1886	68.584	45	23.995	53.8	11.869	54.5
1887	67.204	63	20.590	54.5	10.844	56.5
1888	73.878	53	28.106	58.8	12.050	63.3
1889	88.248	42	26.137	42.3	12.109	50.5
1890	76.842	66	26.074	62.6	12.678	57.3
1891	96.342	50	20.756	77.1	13.013	57.0
1892	90.837	50	27.768	53.6	12.643	52.0
1893	79.164	48	28.343	50.2	12.866	58.3
1894	78.456	51	29.594	49.4	13.721	55.7
1895	107.696	31	30.128	42.2	16.748	45.3
1896	80.373	30	20.339	38.8	15.805	39.3
1897	91.801	40	17.904	43.2	17.260	42.1
1898	97.356	45	22.719	44.5	13.961	45.0
1899	92.793	43	27.952	49.6	13.001	55.9
1900	89.596	56	28.446	49.8	11.810	55.8
1901	112.765	64	28.391	55.4	15.693	56.4
1902	140.703	56	29.811	50.5	15.286	59.6
1903	135.677	56	31.239	54.0	15.248	60.8
1904	151.084	49	31.796	68.9	16.327	62.5
1905	151.679	50	33.781	60.4	15.797	58.6
1906	183.638	61	35.790	58.5	15.734	59.7
1907	165.638	84	33.012	72.5	14.858	70.0
1908	178.132	67	34.473	72.8	16.541	75.7
1909	183.524	67	35.194	72.2	17.983	70.2
1910	164.512	92	35.084	71.5	17.598	66.1
1911	161.357	122	33.222	83.2	17.549	72.6
1912	205.965	68	33.810	66.3	19.249	66.1
1913	171.595	65	39.145	63.4	13.833	75.5
1914	166.344	72	29.899	86.5	16.881	76.4
1915	198.068	69	39.366	83.4	15.056	78.7
1916	162.452	119***	35.587	122.1	11.662	112.7
1917	183.559	146	46.581	166.0	16.022	160.0
1918	226.924	104	55.212	151.6	16.905	166.5
1919	113.252	145	35.029	133.2	14.399	146.1
1920	162.098	78	13.605	126.8	13.142	128.3
1921	127.408	61	32.431	69.7	14.207	81.2
1922	160.197	65	51.798	68.5	14.564	88.5
1923	183.833	72	43.177	65.0	13.965	93.3
1924	153.080	90	15.279	106.4	13.357	102.6
1925	183.468	72	33.810	78.2	13.994	88.8
1926	165.300	77	19.052	83.4	12.676	88.2
1927	226.652	91	31.819	85.3	15.755	83.5
1928	297.238	60	33.879	86.0	13.148	87.5
1929	278.879	62	39.312	86.4	11.474	97.7

NOTES TO TABLE IIa

* The arrangement follows the order of the chapters in Part II except for cotton and wheat which are given separately in Tables IIb and IIc.

† The data for all commodities except sugar (and stocks for oats) are taken from the *Yearbooks of Agriculture* for 1920, 1921, 1927, and 1931. Revisions of these data appeared in the later *Yearbooks* after our analyses were completed (see chap. v and the sections relating to the data in the other chapters of Part II). The data for sugar are taken from Palmer's *Concerning Sugar*, a loose-leaf service formerly published by the U.S. Beet Sugar Association, then by the United States Sugar Manufacturers' Association, and now discontinued. They are based on the statistics published in Willett and Gray, *Weekly Statistical Sugar Trade Journal*.

‡ The year begins July 1 for all commodities except sugar, for which the year begins January 1.

§ These figures represent "consumption," i.e., production minus net exports. The "consumption" series for sugar is given by the United States Sugar Manufacturers' Association. The "consumption" series for barley and rye are based on U.S. Department of Agriculture data.

|| Average New York wholesale price of refined sugar for year beginning January 1.

¶ The U.S. Department of Agriculture estimates for production have been used (see text).

** December 1 farm price (see text).

†† Taken from the *U.S.D.A Yearbook of Agriculture, 1935*, p. 391.

‡‡ Figures for 1895–1928 are for total stocks as given in U.S. Dept. Agric., *Statistical Bulletin*, No. 29, p. 56; for 1929 the figure is the sum of stocks on farms and visible supply as given in the *U.S.D.A. Yearbook of Agriculture, 1931*, pp. 634–35.

§§ An August–July average of quotations for choice to fancy or fair to good malting grades in Chicago.

|| || Revisions of these figures may be found in the *Yearbook of Agriculture, 1927*, p. 774, Table 47.

¶¶ The incorrect figure, 52.8, was used in our computations.

*** This is the correct figure and is taken from the *Yearbook of Agriculture* for 1927. In recent *Yearbooks* it is given as 191 through a typographical error (letter of July 7, 1931, from Dr. O. C. Stine, of the Division of Statistical and Historical Research).

††† Disagrees with the figure in *Statistical Bulletin*, No. 29, since an error was made there in addition.

‡‡‡ The data for the years 1930–36 which were used in equations (6.1), (6.2), (6.3), and (6.4) of chap. vi, Sec. VI, are as follows:

Year	Sugar Consumption (1,000 Short Tons)	Price of Sugar (Cents per Lb.)
1930	6,271	4.634
1931	6,132	4.425
1932	5,840	3.992
1933	5,903	4.308
1934	5,751	4.123
1935	5,981	4.302
1936	6,184	4.660

Source: Willett and Gray, *op. cit.*, 62d year, No. 2 (January 13, 1938), pp. 13, 19 (annual number).

YEAR*	WORLD-PRODUCTION† (1,000 BALES)‡	FOREIGN (=WORLD minus U.S.) PRODUCTION (1,000 BALES)‡	U.S. SUPPLY (1,000 BALES)‡			
			Production§	Stocks at Beginning of Year‖	Net Imports§	Total Supply¶
1875	. . . .	3,153	4,303	. . . .	4	4,307
1876	7,271	3,153	4,118	. . . .	5	4,123
1877	7,214	2,720	4,494	. . . .	5	4,499
1878	7,037	2,292	4,745	. . . .	5	4,750
1879	8,252	2,786	5,466	. . . .	8	5,474
1880	9,285	2,928	6,357	. . . .	5	6,362
1881	8,538	3,402	5,136	. . . .	3	5,139
1882	10,280	3,446	6,834	. . . .	5	6,839
1883	9,028	3,506	5,522	. . . .	11	5,533
1884	8,876	3,408	5,468	. . . .	7	5,475
1885	9,396	3,026	6,370	. . . .	8	6,378
1886	10,077	3,763	6,314	. . . .	8	6,322
1887	10,623	3,738	6,885	. . . .	12	6,897
1888	10,413	3,490	6,923	. . . .	15	6,938
1889	11,376	3,903	7,473	. . . .	18	7,491
1890	12,522	3,960	8,562	. . . .	46	8,608
1891	12,842	3,902	8,940	. . . .	64	9,004
1892	10,590	3,932	6,658	. . . .	86	6,744
1893	11,771	4,341	7,430	. . . .	59	7,489
1894	13,619	3,594	10,025	. . . .	99	10,124
1895	11,923	4,777	7,146	. . . .	112	7,258
1896	13,501	4,986	8,515	. . . .	115	8,630
1897	15,959	4,970	10,989	. . . .	106	11,095
1898	16,442	4,996	11,446	. . . .	103	11,549
1899	14,394	5,040	9,354	. . . .	135	9,489
1900	15,931	5,787	10,144	. . . .	117	10,261
1901	15,292	5,488	9,804	. . . .	190	9,994
1902	16,948	6,294	10,654	. . . .	149	10,803
1903	16,253	6,392	9,861	. . . .	100	9,961
1904	20,079	6,628	13,451	. . . .	130	13,581
1905	16,925	6,342	10,583	1,951	133	12,667
1906	21,357	8,075	13,282	1,380	203	14,865
1907	17,458	6,354	11,104	1,521	141	12,766
1908	21,267	8,017	13,250	1,252	165	14,667
1909	19,329	9,319	10,010	1,475	151	11,636
1910	21,915	10,299	11,616	1,044	231	12,891
1911	25,356	9,640	15,716	1,389	229	17,334
1912	25,043	11,328	13,715	1,807	225	15,747
1913	26,259	12,100	14,159	1,530	266	15,955
1914	28,687	12,548	16,139	1,386	364	17,889
1915	20,689	9,482	11,207	3,985	421	15,613
1916	19,900	8,441	11,459	3,166	288	14,913
1917	19,700	8,405	11,295	2,731	217	14,243
1918	20,900	8,845	12,055	3,493	197	15,745
1919	21,300	9,879	11,421	4,323	683	16,427
1920	21,100	7,662	13,438	3,608	211	17,257
1921	15,400	7,455	7,945	6,507	352	14,804
1922	19,300	9,530	9,770	2,844	450	13,064
1923	19,700	9,550	10,150	2,320	272	12,742
1924	25,000	11,361	13,639	1,556	303	15,498
1925	27,900	11,777	16,123	1,610	314	18,047
1926	28,400	10,422	17,978	3,587	382	21,947
1927	24,000	11,030	12,970	3,817	321	17,108
1928	26,800	12,324	14,476	2,568	442	17,486
1929	26,500	11,678	14,822	2,356	368	17,546

QUANTITIES AND PRICES USED, 1875-1934

U.S. DISTRIBUTION (1,000 BALES)‡				FOREIGN CARRY-OVER OF AMERICAN COTTON AT BEGINNING OF SEASON** (1,000 BALES)‡	AVERAGE NET WEIGHT PER BALE†† (LB.)	PRICE RECEIVED BY PRODUCERS DEC. 1‡‡ (CENTS PER LB.)	FARM VALUE OF CROP§§ (1,000 DOLLARS)	YEAR*
Consumption§	Stocks at End of Year‖	Exports of Domestic Cotton§	Total Distribution¶					
1,167	......	2,822	3,989	......	444	10.5‖‖	215,958	1875
1,210	......	2,613	3,823	......	440	9.7	190,953	1876
1,374	......	3,010	4,384	......	450	8.5	182,600	1877
1,363	......	3,077	4,440	......	447	8.2	185,988	1878
1,426	......	3,555	4,981	......	454	10.3	269,132	1879
1,796	......	4,285	6,081	......	460	9.8	297,787	1880
1,741	......	3,179	4,920	......	450	10.7	262,709	1881
2,004	......	4,514	6,518	......	470	9.12	297,894	1882
1,753	......	3,608	5,361	......	462	9.13	240,986	1883
1,623	......	3,641	5,264	......	460	9.19	240,201	1884
2,029	......	4,069	6,098	......	463	8.39	255,437	1885
1,990	......	4,176	6,166	......	464	8.06	243,280	1886
2,154	......	4,415	6,569	......	467	8.55	281,369	1887
2,304	......	4,720	7,024	......	477	8.50	281,313	1888
2,518	......	4,929	7,447	......	478	8.55	305,394	1889
2,577	......	5,789	8,366	......	473	8.59	351,561	1890
2,817	......	5,835	8,652	......	473	7.24	309,418	1891
2,401	......	4,457	6,858	......	475	8.34	265,435	1892
2,281	......	5,263	7,544	......	474	7.00	248,618	1893
3,021	......	7,048	10,069	......	484	4.59	219,962	1894
2,495	......	4,752	7,247	......	477	7.62	260,287	1895
2,835	......	6,111	8,946	......	477	6.66	271,069	1896
3,501	......	7,876	11,377	......	482	6.68	350,885	1897
3,757	......	7,803	11,560	......	489	5.73	313,518	1898
3,672	......	6,142	9,814	......	476	6.98	312,089	1899
3,619	......	6,835	10,454	......	480	9.15	443,684	1900
4,174	......	7,028	11,202	......	489	7.03	329,415	1901
4,213	......	6,957	11,170	......	481	7.60	387,064	1902
3,998	......	6,260	10,258	......	480	10.49	494,455	1903
4,523	......	9,057	13,580	......	478	8.98	577,391	1904
4,918	1,360	7,033	13,311	......	482	10.78	545,321	1905
5,088	1,550	9,028	15,666	1,485	489	9.58	608,214	1906
4,512	1,241	7,813	13,566	2,291	480	10.36	549,883	1907
5,156	1,503	9,002	15,661	1,879	484	9.01	570,660	1908
4,593	1,033	6,451	12,077	2,197	475	13.60	650,698	1909
4,517	1,381	8,060	13,958	1,340	480	13.95	774,616	1910
5,183	1,795	11,197	18,175	1,391	483	9.60	721,165	1911
5,575	1,536	9,353	16,464	2,586	486	11.49	753,219	1912
5,647	1,466	9,372	16,485	1,925	484	12.50	845,960	1913
5,679	3,994	8,445	18,118	2,512	485	7.36	567,775	1914
6,478	3,179	5,970	15,627	2,962	484	11.22	601,055	1915
6,846	2,743	5,344	14,933	1,879	482	17.34	949,782	1916
6,593	3,464	4,306	14,363	1,079	480	27.12	1,464,251	1917
5,838	4,341	5,662	15,841	885	484	28.93	1,667,160	1918
6,474	3,593	6,600	16,667	2,165	482	35.41	1,932,999	1919
4,954	6,616	5,817	17,387	2,832	484	15.92	1,022,565	1920
5,885	2,820	6,158	14,863	2,938	476	17.01	645,942	1921
6,694	2,335	4,843	13,872	2,535	480	22.87	1,068,044	1922
5,669	1,553	5,644	12,866	1,187	477	28.69	1,391,873	1923
6,193	1,610	8,005	15,808	1,272	478	22.91	1,493,648	1924
6,456	3,543	8,051	18,050	1,877	478	19.59	1,509,716	1925
7,280	3,809	11,064	22,153	2,114	484	12.47	1,071,604	1926
6,934	2,573	7,650	17,157	4,244	485	20.19	1,251,742	1927
7,180	2,341	8,145	17,666	2,816	484	17.99	1,244,823	1928
6,221	4,615	6,816	17,652	2,431	487	16.79	1,189,534	1929

TABLE IIb—*Continued*

YEAR*	WORLD-PRODUCTION † (1,000 BALES)‡	FOREIGN (=WORLD *minus* U.S.) PRODUCTION (1,000 BALES)‡	U.S. SUPPLY (1,000 BALES)‡			
			Production§	Stocks at Beginning of Year‖	Net Imports§	Total Supply¶
1930	25,800	11,871	13,929	4,587	99	18,615
1931	27,500	10,384	17,116	6,557	107	23,780
1932	23,700	10,671	13,029	9,921	124	23,074
1933	26,100	13,039	13,061	8,421	137	21,619
1934¶¶	23,622	13,972	9,650	7,890	107	17,647

NOTES TO TABLE IIb

* The cotton year is as follows: for the years 1875–1913, September 1–August 31; for the years 1914–34, August 1–July 31. For foreign production for 1900–1934 "data . . . . are for crops harvested between about Aug. 1 and July 31 of the following year. This applies to both Northern and Southern Hemispheres" (*U.S.D.A. Yearbook, 1924*, p. 754). The source for the data on foreign production prior to 1900 does not indicate the beginning of the year. U.S. production relates to the year of growth.

† Figures for the years 1876–99 have been taken from *Jones' Annual Cotton Handbook* as quoted on p. 395 of John A. Todd's *The World's Cotton Crops* (London: A. and C. Black, Ltd., 1915); no indication is there given whether figures include those for China. Beginning with 1900 and continuing through 1915 the figures are from p. 754 of the *U.S.D.A. Yearbook, 1924*; for 1916–33 they are from p. 429 of the *U.S.D.A. Yearbook, 1935*; for 1934 they are from *Agricultural Statistics, 1936*, p. 79. U.S. Department of Agriculture figures are for an estimated world total crop including China.

For the years beginning with 1920 there are also available data on world-stocks. These estimates (in thousands of bales) are:

1920............	11,454	1928............	9,817
1921............	14,591	1929............	9,632
1922............	9,983	1930............	11,324
1923............	6,873	1931............	14,128
1924............	5,977	1932............	17,649
1925............	7,276	1933............	16,582
1926............	9,705	1934............	17,057
1927............	11,926		

This series was used in estimating the foreign supply in eq. (12) of Table 21, chap. viii. Source: *Cotton Yearbook of the New York Cotton Exchange, 1935*, p. 171, for the years 1920–33; *ibid., 1936*, p. 173, for the year 1934. American cotton is in running bales; foreign cottons are in equivalent bales of 478 pounds net weight. American linters are not included.

TABLE II*b*—*Continued*

U.S. Distribution (1,000 Bales)‡				Foreign Carry-Over of American Cotton at Beginning of Season** (1,000 Bales)‡	Average Net Weight per Bale†† (Lb.)	Price Received by Producers Dec. 1‡‡ (Cents per Lb.)	Farm Value of Crop§§ (1,000 Dollars)	Year*
Consumption§	Stocks at End of Year‖	Exports of Domestic Cotton§	Total Distribution¶					
5,329	6,450	6,845	18,624	1,888	484	9.46	629,816	1930
5,009	9,961	8,963	23,933	2,792	492	5.66	463,068	1931
6,291	8,370	8,630	23,291	3,775	490	6.52	406,048	1932
5,879	7,987	7,770	21,636	3,845	493	9.72	606,855	1933
5,462	7,344	4,889	17,695	3,110	487	12.36	570,151	1934

NOTES TO TABLE II*b*—*Continued*

‡ Bales are 500 lb. gross, or 478 lb. net, weight (for conversion factor used see n. ††).

§ Data for 1875–1930 have been taken from the U.S. Department of Commerce Bureau of the Census *Bulletin*, No. 168 (1931), pp. 57–58; for 1931–34 from *Census Bulletin*, No. 172 (1935), p. 42

‖ Data for 1905–12 from *U.S.D.A. Yearbook, 1921*, p. 393; for 1913–33 from *U.S.D.A. Yearbook, 1935*, p. 430; for 1934 from *Agricultural Statistics, 1936*, p. 80. The tables in the agricultural yearbooks are summaries of material appearing yearly in the U.S. Department of Commerce bulletins "Cotton Production and Distribution."

The figure for any one year in the column headed "Stocks at End of Year" does not agree with the figure for the following year in the column headed "Stocks at Beginning of Year" because the factors used in converting running bales to bales of 500 lb. gross weight ("Average Net Weight per Bale") differ from year to year. The "Stocks at Beginning of Year" series is the one used in the computations.

¶ The figures in this column are the sums of the figures in the three preceding columns.

** Taken from the New York Cotton Exchange, *Cotton Year Book, 1935*, p. 168.

†† Used to convert running bales to bales of 500 lb. gross, or 478 lb. net, weight by multiplying running bales by the average net weight per bale and dividing by 478. For source see n. §.

‡‡ Prices for 1876–81 are from a letter from Dr. O. C. Stine, of the Bureau of Agricultural Economics, dated January 21, 1936 (see n. ‖ ‖). Prices for the years 1882–1933 are from the *U.S.D.A. Yearbook, 1935*, pp. 425–26; for the year 1934, from *Agricultural Statistics, 1936*, p. 76 (revised figures). "Calculations of average price . . . . not completed. Beginning with 1908 prices are weighted average prices for crop-marketing season."

§§ U.S. Production multiplied by price.

‖ ‖ Our estimate.

¶¶ The data for 1934 were inserted after our computations were completed. It appears that the series which we have taken from the U.S. Department of Agriculture have, for the later years, been subjected to slight revisions in *Agricultural Statistics, 1936*.

TABLE IIc

YEAR BEGINNING JULY 1	WORLD-PRODUCTION* (MILLION BUSHELS)	FOREIGN PRODUCTION† (MILLION BUSHELS)	UNITED STATES SUPPLY (MILLION BUSHELS)			
			Production‡	Imports of Wheat and Flour§, ‖	Stocks at Beginning of Year¶	Total Supply**
1875	. . . .	. . . .	368.5	1.664	. . . .	370.164
1876	. . . .	. . . .	365.4	0.366	. . . .	365.766
1877	. . . .	. . . .	508.7	1.391	. . . .	510.091
1878	. . . .	. . . .	504.4	2.074	. . . .	506.474
1879	. . . .	. . . .	549.2	0.487	. . . .	549.687
1880	. . . .	. . . .	535.0	0.212	. . . .	535.212
1881	. . . .	. . . .	417.8	0.867	. . . .	418.667
1882	. . . .	. . . .	553.7	1.088	. . . .	554.788
1883	. . . .	. . . .	469.3	0.033	. . . .	469.333
1884	. . . .	. . . .	571.4	0.213	. . . .	571.613
1885	2,260.3	1,828.0	432.3	0.389	. . . .	432.689
1886	2,273.9	1,718.9	555.0	0.283	. . . .	555.283
1887	2,558.2	1,999.4	558.8	0.596	. . . .	559.396
1888	2,467.7	1,951.4	516.3	0.136	. . . .	516.436
1889	2,365.7	1,747.3	618.4	0.163	. . . .	618.563
1890	2,404.3	1,888.6	515.7	0.586	. . . .	516.286
1891	2,515.0	1,727.9	787.1	2.463	. . . .	789.563
1892	2,687.7	2,007.0	680.7	0.968	. . . .	681.668
1893	2,746.9	2,207.6	539.3‡	1.183	. . . .	540.483
1894	2,830.6	2,169.4	634.2	1.439	. . . .	635.639
1895	2,730.9	2,062.0	668.9	2.117	. . . .	671.017
1896	2,639.3	2,026.7	612.6	1.545	175.234	789.379
1897	2,389.1	1,704.1	685.0	2.060	100.436	787.496
1898	3,177.0	2,345.4	831.6	1.875	58.730	892.205
1899	2,928.7	2,246.5	682.2	0.320	195.833	878.353
1900	2,730.2	2,091.6	638.6	0.603	188.171	827.374
1901	3,003.4	2,174.5	828.9	0.121	134.158	963.179
1902	3,221.1	2,483.2	737.9	1.080	130.368	869.348
1903	3,364.2	2,682.7	681.5	0.229	109.689	791.418
1904	3,214.6	2,633.6	581.0	3.296	106.336	690.632
1905	3,377.5	2,650.3	727.2	0.273	78.085	805.558
1906	3,488.2	2,728.5	759.7	0.602	139.667	899.969
1907	3,177.9	2,541.1	636.8	0.530	192.447	829.777
1908	3,170.8	2,516.3	654.5	0.475	95.492	750.467
1909	3,627.8	2,915.1	712.7	0.845	59.781	773.326
1910	3,585.2	2,934.7	650.5‡	1.175	110.121	761.796
1911	3,557.8	2,939.6	618.166	3.445	125.950	747.561
1912	3,835.5	3,105.5	730.011	1.304	104.598	835.913
1913	4,069.8	3,318.7	751.101	2.402	130.516	884.019
1914	3,617.6	2,720.1	897.487	0.728	109.537	1,007.752
1915	4,279.3	3,270.7	1,008.637	7.254	69.718	1,085.609
1916	3,294.4	2,659.8	634.572	24.960	226.347	885.879
1917	3,253.8	2,634.0	619.790	31.215	52.841	703.846
1918	3,580.8	2,676.7	904.130	11.289	20.879	936.298
1919	3,406.8	2,454.7	952.097	5.511	73.301	1,030.909
1920	3,363.9	2,520.6	843.277	57.682	138.385	1,039.344

TABLE IIc—*Continued*

QUANTITIES AND PRICES USED, 1875–1934

Stocks at End of Year¶	Total Exports of Wheat and Flour‖, ††	Utilization‡‡	Seed Requirements§§	SEASON AVERAGE PRICE RECEIVED BY U.S. PRODUCERS‖ ‖ (CENTS PER BUSHEL)	YEAR BEGINNING JULY 1
		UNITED STATES DISTRIBUTION (MILLION BUSHELS)			
. . . .	74.751	295.413	51.504	101.0	1875
. . . .	57.044	308.722	54.168	103.6	1876
. . . .	92.142	417.949	56.980	108.5	1877
. . . .	150.503	355.971	58.904	77.2	1878
. . . .	181.807	367.880	60.443	110.7	1879
. . . .	188.308	346.904	60.621	95.2	1880
. . . .	123.371	295.296	60.251	119.6	1881
. . . .	150.113	404.675	59.881	88.8	1882
. . . .	113.822	355.511	65.046	91.4	1883
. . . .	135.232	436.381	61.524	64.5	1884
. . . .	96.611	336.078	66.245	77.2	1885
. . . .	156.685	398.598	68.346	68.7	1886
. . . .	122.616	436.780	68.835	68.1	1887
. . . .	90.944	425.492	70.951	92.7	1888
. . . .	112.488	506.075	68.761	69.8	1889
. . . .	109.640	406.646	75.154	83.7	1890
. . . .	231.303	558.260	75.746	83.1	1891
. . . .	196.640	485.028	70.640	62.4	1892
. . . .	168.714	371.769	71.647	53.4	1893
. . . .	149.179	486.460	71.218	48.9	1894
. . . .	132.462	538.555	73.112	50.5	1895
100.436	150.270	538.673	76.220	72.1	1896
58.730	223.024	505.742	81.504	80.9	1897
195.833	229.176	467.196	83.442	57.9	1898
188.171	192.757	497.425	80.778	58.8	1899
134.158	222.371	470.845	79.683	62.1	1900
130.368	240.412	592.399	77.806	63.1	1901
109.689	211.087	548.572	74.316	63.0	1902
106.336	127.034	558.048	71.618	69.3	1903
78.085	48.624	563.923	70.358	92.6	1904
139.667	103.158	562.733	69.020	74.7	1905
192.447	153.380	554.142	67.502	66.0	1906
95.492	168.963	565.322	66.155	86.6	1907
59.781	118.679	572.007	64.979	96.7	1908
110.121	91.710	571.495	70.706	99.1	1909
125.950	73.826	562.020	74.007	90.8	1910
104.598	84.438	558.525	76.888	86.9	1911
130.516	147.909	557.488	74.048	80.7	1912
109.537	151.348	623.134	78.359	79.4	1913
69.718	338.377	599.657	84.681	97.4	1914
226.347	249.532	609.730	80.461	96.1	1915
52.841	208.574	624.464	79.961	143.4	1916
20.879	136.001	546.966	92.868	204.7	1917
73.301	290.319	572.678	103.068	205.0	1918
138.385	225.160	667.364	90.858	216.3	1919
119.196	373.003	547.145	89.269	182.6	1920

TABLE IIc—*Continued*

Year Beginning July 1	World-Production* (Million Bushels)	Foreign Production† (Million Bushels)	United States Supply (Million Bushels)			
			Production‡	Imports of Wheat and Flour§, ‖	Stocks at Beginning of Year¶	Total Supply**
1921	3,426.	2,577.	848.964	17.375	119.196	985.535
1922	3,515.	2,668.	846.649	20.031	109.617	976.297
1923	3,855.	3,096.	759.482	28.079	132.312	919.873
1924	3,538.	2,688.	850.091	6.201	137.087	993.379
1925	4,131.	3,437.	694.142	15.679	108.401	818.222
1926	4,289.	3,440.	848.544	13.264	100.225	962.033
1927	4,334.	3,484.	849.733	15.734	109.506	974.973
1928	4,699.	3,785.	914.373	21.442	112.372	1,048.187
1929	4,137.	3,285.	852.180	12.956	228.373	1,093.509
1930	4,683.	3,797.	886.470	19.059	288.879	1,194.408
1931	4,406.	3,469.	936.831	12.886	313.288	1,263.005
1932	4,437.	3,680.	756.927	9.382	375.152	1,141.461
1933	4,623.	4,071.	551.683	11.494	377.942	941.119
1934	4,422.	3,896.	526.393	25.134	274.328	825.855

NOTES TO TABLE IIc

* Sources: For 1885–1920, M. K. Bennett, "World Wheat Crops, 1885–1932," *Wheat Studies of the Food Research Institute*, IX, No. 7 (1933), 264. For 1921–34, the sum of "World Excluding Russia," as given by M. K. Bennett, "World Wheat Utilization since 1885–1886," *Wheat Studies*, XII, No. 10 (1936), 392, col. (1), and "Russia" as given in *Wheat Studies*, IX, No. 7 (1933), 265, for 1921–30, and in U.S. Dept. Agric., *Agricultural Statistics, 1936*, for 1931–34. These "World" estimates do not include large wheat-producing areas in China and southwestern Asia, and also numerous insignificant producing areas.

For the years beginning with 1922 there are also available data on "World" (excluding Russia) stocks. These estimates in millions of bushels are:

1922	615	1928	707
1923	552	1929	976
1924	687	1930	921
1925	528	1931	1,010
1926	612	1932	1,002
1927	654	1933	1,106
		1934	1,158

Sources: For 1922–29, Joseph S. Davis, "The World Wheat Situation, 1934–1935," *Wheat Studies*, XII, No. 4 (December, 1935), 167. For 1930–34, M. K. Bennett, *et al.*, "World Wheat Survey and Outlook," *Wheat Studies*, XII (May, 1936), 314. The foregoing series was used in estimating the foreign supply in eq. (6.2) of chap. x. It should be noted, however, that foreign production and foreign stocks, which were added to obtain the foreign supply, do not relate to exactly the same areas, since the former includes Russia and the latter does not.

† "Foreign Production" = "World" production *minus* U.S. production.

‡ Sources: For 1875–1910, Holbrook Working's estimates, taken from "Wheat Acreage and Production in the United States since 1866," *Wheat Studies*, II, No. 7 (1926), 260–61. The figures for 1893 and 1910 are corrections confirmed by Holbrook Working in his letter of February 3, 1937. For 1911–27 and 1929, official estimates taken from *Agricultural Statistics, 1936*, pp. 5–6, except for years 1921, 1924–27, and 1929, for which M. K. Bennett's corrections have been used. These were taken from his "World Wheat Utilization since 1885–1886," *op. cit.*, p. 395. For the remaining years the figures are the latest official revisions taken from *General Crop Revisions, Crop Years 1924–1935, Acreage, Yield, and Production* (U.S. Dept. Agric., Bureau of Agricultural Economics, Crop Reporting Board [1936]), pp. 19–22.

§ Source: U.S. Dept. Agric., *Agricultural Statistics, 1936*, pp. 5–6.

‖ Barrels of flour are expressed in terms of equivalent number of bushels of wheat by applying the following conversion factors (i.e., the average number of bushels of wheat per barrels of flour): 1875–78, 5; 1879–1907, 4.75; 1908–16, 4.7; 1917–18, 4.5; 1919, 4.6; 1920–34, 4.7. These conversion factors are for fiscal years and are derived by adjusting the conversion factors for calendar years which are given in *Agricultural Statistics, 1936*, n. 4 of Table I (confirmed by letter of R. E. Post, of the U.S. Department of Agriculture, March 3, 1937).

TABLE IIc—*Continued*

UNITED STATES DISTRIBUTION (MILLION BUSHELS)				SEASON AVERAGE PRICE RECEIVED BY U.S. PRODUCERS‖ ‖ (CENTS PER BUSHEL)	YEAR BEGINNING JULY 1
Stocks at End of Year¶	Total Exports of Wheat and Flour‖, ††	Utilization‡‡	Seed Requirements§§		
109.617	285.653	590.265	88.322	103.0	1921
132.312	228.017	615.968	85.140	96.6	1922
137.087	162.944	619.842	74.103	92.6	1923
108.401	263.767	621.211	79.903	124.7	1924
100.225	111.089	606.908	78.843	143.7	1925
109.506	222.340	630.187	83.279	121.7	1926
112.372	209.002	653.599	89.879	119.0	1927
228.373	166.914	652.900	83.677	99.8	1928
288.879	156.294	648.336	83.353	103.6	1929
313.288	134.345	746.775	80.886	67.1	1930
375.152	139.458	748.395	80.049	39.0	1931
377.942	44.690	718.829	81.161	38.0	1932
274.328	39.802	626.989	75.511	74.1	1933
145.618	24.474	655.763	82.467	84.7	1934

NOTES TO TABLE IIc—*Continued*

¶ Sources: For 1896–1918, Holbrook Working's estimates, taken from "Disposition of American Wheat since 1896, with Special Reference to Changes in Year-End Stocks," *Wheat Studies*, IV, No. 4 (1928), 180. In Working's opinion the estimates for these years are more significant for the year-to-year changes than for the absolute values (see *ibid.*, pp. 135–77, and esp. pp. 138 and 169–70).

For 1919–22 the series is taken from *Agricultural Statistics, 1936*, p. 18, except that, in order to make the estimates comparable with those for 1923–35, the item "In Transit to Merchant Mills and Bought To Arrive" has been excluded from the stock total and 3,000,000 bushels have been added to the total for each year as estimates of stocks stored for others.

The data for 1923–35 have been taken from U.S. Dept. Agric., *Agricultural Outlook Charts 1937, Wheat and Rye* (1936), p. 1. The stocks at the beginning of a given year are the same as those at the end of the preceding year.

** The figures in this column are the sums of the figures in the three preceding columns. For the years 1875–95 these figures are *apparent* total supply, since they do not include stocks at the beginning of the year.

†† Sources: For 1875–89, U.S. Dept. Agric., *Agricultural Statistics, 1936*, p. 5. For 1890–1918, U.S. Dept. Agric., *Statistical Bulletin*, No. 12 (1926), Table 43, except that barrels of flour are expressed in equivalent number of bushels of wheat by using the conversion factors described in n. ‖ to this table, instead of 4.5 bushels of grain per barrel of flour as is done there. For 1919–34, U.S. Dept. Agric., *Agricultural Statistics, 1936*, p. 18. Data include re-exports and shipments to possessions, except for 1875–89, when they consist of domestic exports only.

‡‡ The figures in this column are equal to total supply, *minus* stocks at the end of the year, *minus* total exports, and represent utilization for food, feed and waste, and seed requirements for the next year's crop. The data for 1875–95 are *apparent* utilization, since they are not adjusted for changes in stocks. (In Table VII of this appendix, relating to the adjusted data, the series used for the second period, 1896–1913, is also apparent utilization.)

§§ Sources: For 1896–1909, Holbrook Working, *Wheat Studies*, IV, No. 4 (1928), 178; for 1919–22, *Agricultural Statistics, 1936*, p. 18; for 1923–34, U.S. Dept. Agric., *Agricultural Outlook Charts, 1937, Wheat and Rye* (1936), p. 3; other years, our calculations.

For the years 1875–1909 the data are based on Working's acreage estimates (see *Wheat Studies*, II, No. 7 [1926] 260–61), and for subsequent years on the latest official estimates.

To allow for the average winter wheat acreages abandoned in the absence of estimates of such abandonment for the years prior to 1900, the seed requirements for the years 1875–99 were calculated on the basis of 1.48 bushels of seed per acre harvested in the following year. The figures for 1900–1918 are calculated on the basis of 1.38 bushels per acre of winter wheat sown and spring wheat harvested. For 1919–34 the amount of seed used is based upon per acre returns to the Bureau of Agricultural Economics from inquiries sent to crop reporters.

‖ ‖ Source: U.S. Dept. Agric., *Agricultural Statistics, 1936*, pp. 5–6. Prior to 1908 prices are as of December 1.

TABLE III

SUGAR: ADJUSTED SERIES OF QUANTITIES AND PRICES, WITH LINK
RELATIVES AND TREND RATIOS, 1875–1936

YEAR BEGINNING JAN. 1	PER CAPITA CONSUMP- TION* (LB.)	REAL PRICE† (CENTS PER LB.)	VALUE PER CAPITA‡ (DOLLARS)	LINK RELATIVES		TREND RATIOS§	
				Per Capita Consump- tion	Real Price	Per Capita Consump- tion	Real Price
1875	40.3	9.485	3.82	....	....	1.069	0.873
1876	38.5	10.163	3.91	0.955	1.071	0.984	0.958
1877	46.1	11.426	5.27	1.197	1.124	1.138	1.103
1878	38.6	11.566	4.46	0.837	1.012	0.920	1.145
1879	38.1	10.713	4.08	0.987	0.926	0.879	1.088
1880	42.7	9.798	4.18	1.121	0.915	0.954	1.022
1881	44.2	9.385	4.15	1.035	0.958	0.957	1.005
1882	48.4	8.319	4.03	1.095	0.886	1.017	0.916
1883	51.1	8.506	4.35	1.056	1.022	1.043	0.964
1884	53.4	7.290	3.89	1.045	0.857	1.059	0.851
1885	51.8	7.855	4.07	0.970	1.078	0.999	0.945
1886	56.9	7.646	4.35	1.098	0.973	1.068	0.949
1887	52.7	7.423	3.91	0.926	0.971	0.964	0.951
1888	56.7	8.054	4.57	1.076	1.085	1.011	1.067
1889	51.8	9.550	4.95	0.914	1.186	0.901	1.310
1890	52.8	7.526	3.97	1.019	0.788	0.896	1.070
1891	66.3	5.875	3.90	1.256	0.781	1.099	0.867
1892	63.8	5.718	3.65	0.962	0.973	1.033	0.877
1893	64.4	6.371	4.10	1.009	1.114	1.020	1.017
1894	66.7	5.886	3.93	1.036	0.924	1.033	0.979
1895	63.4	6.017	3.81	0.951	1.022	0.961	1.045
1896	62.5	6.867	4.29	....	....	1.014	0.999
1897	64.8	6.823	4.42	1.037	0.994	1.028	1.012
1898	61.5	7.410	4.56	0.949	1.086	0.956	1.120
1899	62.6	6.559	4.11	1.018	0.885	0.953	1.012
1900	65.2	6.488	4.23	1.042	0.989	0.972	1.021
1901	68.7	6.312	4.34	1.054	0.973	1.004	1.014
1902	72.8	5.304	3.86	1.060	0.840	1.043	0.871
1903	70.9	5.521	3.91	0.974	1.041	0.997	0.926
1904	75.3	5.681	4.28	1.062	1.029	1.039	0.974
1905	70.5	6.112	4.31	0.936	1.076	0.955	1.072
1906	76.1	4.962	3.78	1.079	0.812	1.012	0.891
1907	77.5	4.843	3.75	1.018	0.976	1.012	0.890
1908	81.2	5.447	4.42	1.048	1.125	1.042	1.026
1909	81.8	5.069	4.15	1.007	0.931	1.032	0.979
1910	81.6	5.126	4.18	0.998	1.011	1.012	1.016
1911	79.2	5.626	4.46	0.971	1.098	0.966	1.144
1912	81.3	5.092	4.14	1.027	0.905	0.975	1.064
1913	85.4	4.278	3.65	1.050	0.840	1.008	0.919
1914	84.3	4.779	4.03	0.987	1.117	0.980	1.056

* Source: For the years 1875–1929, *Concerning Sugar* (loose-leaf service by U.S. Sugar Manufacturers Assoc.), pp. E-54-A, B, C, D. These statistics are derived from Willett & Gray, *Weekly Statistical Sugar Trade Journal.* For the years 1930–36, Willett & Gray, *ibid.*, Annual No. 62d year, No. 2, Jan. 13, 1938, p. 13.

† For deflator see Table I of this appendix.

‡ "Per Capita Consumption" multiplied by "Real Price."

§ For the trend equations used see Table 5, chap. vi.

TABLE III—*Continued*

YEAR BEGINNING JAN. 1	PER CAPITA CONSUMPTION* (LB.)	REAL PRICE† (CENTS PER LB.)	VALUE PER CAPITA‡ (DOLLARS)	LINK RELATIVES		TREND RATIOS§	
				Per Capita Consumption	Real Price	Per Capita Consumption	Real Price
1915	83.8	5.504	4.61	. . . .	. . . .	1.017	0.984
1916	79.3	5.403	4.28	0.946	0.982	0.941	0.991
1917	78.6	4.329	3.40	. . . .	. . . .	. . . .	. . . .
1918	73.4	4.017	2.95	. . . .	. . . .	. . . .	. . . .
1919	85.4	4.349	3.71	. . . .	. . . .	. . . .	. . . .
1920	86.6	5.018	4.35	. . . .	. . . .	. . . .	. . . .
1921	84.5	4.222	3.57	. . . .	. . . .	. . . .	. . . .
1922	103.2	3.962	4.09	. . . .	. . . .	1.076	0.865
1923	95.6	5.481	5.24	0.926	1.383	0.978	1.236
1924	95.9	4.981	4.78	1.003	0.909	0.961	1.161
1925	107.5	3.448	3.71	1.121	0.692	1.057	0.832
1926	109.3	3.625	3.96	1.017	1.051	1.055	0.906
1927	101.0	4.047	4.09	0.924	1.116	0.957	1.049
1928	104.3	3.743	3.90	1.033	0.925	0.970	1.008
1929	108.1	3.442	3.72	1.036	0.920	0.988	0.965
1930	99.4	3.551	3.53	. . . .	. . . .	. . . .	. . . .
1931	98.5	4.015	3.95	. . . .	. . . .	. . . .	. . . .
1932	93.3	4.082	3.81	. . . .	. . . .	. . . .	. . . .
1933	93.6	4.330	4.05	. . . .	. . . .	. . . .	. . . .
1934	90.7	3.645	3.31	. . . .	. . . .	. . . .	. . . .
1935	93.8	3.561	3.34	. . . .	. . . .	. . . .	. . . .
1936	96.3	3.820	3.68	. . . .	. . . .	. . . .	. . . .

TABLE IV

CORN: ADJUSTED SERIES OF QUANTITIES AND PRICES, WITH LINK RELATIVES AND TREND RATIOS, 1875–1929*

YEAR BEGINNING JULY 1	CONSUMPTION Per Capita (Bu.)	Per Animal Unit (Bu.)	REAL PRICE (CENTS PER BU.)	VALUE PER CAPITA† (DOLLARS)	LINK RELATIVES Per Capita Consumption	Real Price	TREND RATIOS‡ Per Capita Consumption	Real Price
1875	29.335	79.717	39.043	11.45	. . . .	. . . .	. . . .	. . . .
1876	27.793	72.796	35.789	9.95	. . . .	. . . .	. . . .	. . . .
1877	28.352	69.487	40.465	11.47	. . . .	. . . .	. . . .	. . . .
1878	28.615	66.355	42.267	12.09	. . . .	. . . .	. . . .	. . . .
1879	31.162	73.433	37.879	11.80	. . . .	. . . .	1.012	0.879
1880	33.740	79.562	40.825	13.77	1.083	1.078	1.105	0.938
1881	22.899	51.087	58.349	13.36	0.679	1.429	0.757	1.326
1882	30.247	68.359	47.549	14.38	1.321	0.815	1.008	1.069
1883	28.335	64.755	44.167	12.51	0.937	0.929	0.953	0.983
1884	32.052	73.908	42.500	13.62	1.131	0.962	1.088	0.936
1885	33.791	78.261	39.048	13.19	1.054	0.919	1.157	0.852
1886	28.432	67.591	45.750	13.01	0.841	1.172	0.982	0.988
1887	24.328	58.681	50.455§	12.27	0.856	1.103	0.848	1.079
1888	32.514	75.492	39.651	12.89	1.336	0.786	1.144	0.839
1889	32.022	74.137	35.128	11.25	0.985	0.886	1.138	0.737
1890	22.923	54.216	61.728	14.15	0.716	1.757	0.822	1.282
1891	31.622	72.116	50.897	16.09	1.379	0.825§	1.145	1.047
1892	25.840	62.352	50.390	13.02	0.817	0.990	0.945	1.027
1893	25.251	61.922	49.178	12.42	0.977	0.976	0.932	0.993
1894	19.436	49.222	65.362	12.70	0.770	1.329	0.724	1.307
1895	32.905§	87.553	36.232	11.92	1.693	0.554	1.239	0.718
1896	34.996	98.346	32.273	11.29	. . . .	. . . .	1.110	0.827
1897	29.441	85.451	38.806	11.42	0.841	1.202	0.940	0.959
1898	30.495	91.307	41.159	12.55	1.036	1.061	0.980	0.983
1899	32.533	93.817	37.375	12.16	1.067	0.908	1.052	0.864
1900	32.561	87.370	43.333	14.11	1.001	1.159	1.059	0.970
1901	20.460	58.619	73.171	14.97	0.628	1.689§	0.670	1.587
1902	32.688	94.576	47.059	15.38	1.598	0.643	1.077	0.991
1903	28.602	82.560	50.723	14.51	0.875	1.078	0.949	1.037
1904	30.220	86.750	52.024	15.72	1.057§	1.026	1.009	1.034
1905	32.276	89.377	45.730	14.76	1.068	0.879	1.085	0.884
1906	33.421	90.503	41.702	13.94	1.035	0.912	1.131	0.785
1907	28.461	76.641	54.731	15.58	0.852	1.312	0.969	1.003
1908	28.314	78.926	65.934	18.67	0.995	1.205	0.971	1.178
1909	28.113	84.093	59.796	16.81	0.993	0.907	0.970	1.042
1910	31.043	91.691	50.000	15.52	1.104	0.836	1.079	0.850
1911	26.819	80.449	64.375	17.26	0.864	1.288	0.939	1.069
1912	32.616	99.998	48.700	15.88	1.216	0.756	1.149	0.790
1913	25.170	77.949	69.798	17.57	0.772	1.433	0.893	1.107
1914	27.098	80.906	66.392	17.99	1.077§	0.951	0.968	1.030

* For deflators see Table I of this appendix.
† "Per Capita Consumption" multiplied by "Real Price."
‡ For the trend equations used see Table 10, chap. vii.
§ Owing to inconsistencies in rounding-off, the following figures were used in our computations:

1887—Real price	50.454	1914—Link relatives—consumption	1.076
1895—Per capita consumption	32.904	1891—Link relatives—real price	0.824
1904—Link relatives—consumption	1.056	1901—Link relatives—real price	1.688

TABLE IV—*Continued*

YEAR BEGINNING JULY 1	CONSUMPTION Per Capita (Bu.)	CONSUMPTION Per Animal Unit (Bu.)	REAL PRICE (CENTS PER BU.)	VALUE PER CAPITA† (DOLLARS)	LINK RELATIVES Per Capita Consumption	LINK RELATIVES Real Price	TREND RATIOS‡ Per Capita Consumption	TREND RATIOS‡ Real Price
1915	29.933	87.770	53.241	15.94	....	....	1.062	0.981
1916	25.299	75.420	59.664	15.09	0.845	1.121	0.911	1.108
1917	29.794	86.574	70.275	20.94	....	....	....	....
1918	23.996	69.850	67.574	16.22	....	....	....	....
1919	26.594	81.962	60.314	16.04	....	....	....	....
1920	29.882	95.696	37.430	11.18	....	....	....	....
1921	28.142	91.602	30.214	8.50	....	....	....	....
1922	26.250	82.986	42.179	11.07	....	....	1.044	0.824
1923	27.174	89.927	48.079	13.06	1.035	1.140	1.099	0.947
1924	20.252	74.176	62.548	12.67	0.745	1.301	0.834	1.243
1925	25.204	97.912	43.205	10.89	1.245	0.691	1.057	0.866
1926	22.933	90.850	43.673	10.02	0.910	1.011	0.980	0.883
1927	23.214	91.423	48.523	11.26	1.012	1.111	1.010	0.990
1928	23.356	96.107	50.470	11.79	1.006	1.040	1.036	1.039
1929	21.364	91.937	53.862	11.51	0.915	1.067	0.966	1.119

TABLE V

COTTON: ADJUSTED SERIES OF QUANTITIES AND PRICES, WITH LINK RELATIVES AND TREND RATIOS, 1875–1934*

YEAR†	PER CAPITA PRODUCTION (LB.)	PER CAPITA EXPORTS (LB.)	PER CAPITA CONSUMPTION (LB.)	REAL PRICE (CENTS PER LB.)	LINK RELATIVES Per Capita Consumption	LINK RELATIVES Real Price	TREND RATIOS‡ Per Capita Consumption	TREND RATIOS‡ Real Price
1875	45.671	29.949	12.380	11.170	....	....	0.932	1.114
1876	42.617	27.046	12.521	10.211	1.011	0.914	0.920	1.018
1877	45.366	30.386	13.862	9.884	1.107	0.968	0.996	0.986
1878	46.753	30.316	13.427	10.933	0.969	1.106	0.944	1.090
1879	52.603	34.208	13.716	10.404	1.022	0.952	0.943	1.038
1880	59.696	40.246	16.862	10.103	1.229	0.971	1.135	1.008
1881	47.052	29.119	15.949	9.817	0.946	0.972	1.051	0.979
1882	61.100	40.365	17.921	8.941	1.124	0.911	1.157	0.892
1883	48.219	31.509	15.309	9.510	0.854	1.064	0.969	0.949
1884	46.658	31.067	13.854	10.940	0.905	1.150	0.860	1.091
1885	53.135	33.944	16.926	9.988	1.222	0.913	1.031	0.996
1886	51.528	34.073	16.236	10.075	0.959	1.009	0.970	1.005
1887	54.980	35.259	17.206	9.716	1.060	0.964	1.009	0.969
1888	54.134	36.906	18.017	9.884	1.047	1.017	1.038	0.986
1889	57.228	37.748	19.287	10.962	1.070	1.109	1.091	1.093
1890	64.240	43.434	19.337	10.605	1.003	0.967	1.075	1.058
1891	65.737	42.902	20.711	9.282	1.071	0.875	1.132	0.926
1892	47.991	32.125	17.304	10.831	0.835	1.167	0.930	1.080
1893	52.522	37.201	16.124	9.589	0.932	0.885	0.852	0.956
1894	69.525	48.882	20.951	6.652	1.299	0.694	1.089	0.663
1895	48.637	32.339	16.978	11.043	0.810	1.660	0.868	1.101
1896	56.895	40.834	18.946	10.091	....	....	0.847	1.098
1897	72.112	51.686	22.977	9.970	1.213	0.988	1.013	1.063
1898	73.794	50.298	24.218	8.304	1.054	0.833	1.054	0.867
1899	59.259	38.910	23.262	8.725	0.961	1.051	1.000	0.893
1900	63.025	42.465	22.482	11.296	0.966	1.295	0.954	1.134
1901	59.650	42.767	25.399	8.573	1.130	0.759	1.064	0.844
1902	63.524	41.477	25.120	8.941	0.989	1.043	1.040	0.864
1903	57.629	36.583	23.360	12.639	0.930	1.414	0.955	1.199
1904	77.086	51.905	25.921	10.690	1.110	0.846	1.047	0.996
1905	59.494	39.542	27.649	12.112	1.067	1.133	1.104	1.100
1906	73.273	49.807	28.073	10.191	1.015	0.841	1.107	0.917
1907	60.135	42.307	24.434	11.140	0.870	1.093	0.953	0.985
1908	70.466	47.870	27.417	9.793	1.122	0.879	1.057	0.851
1909	52.290	33.701	23.993	14.021	0.875	1.432	0.914	1.198
1910	59.724	41.436	23.224	14.531	0.968	1.036	0.875	1.222
1911	79.586	56.704	26.247	9.796	1.130	0.674	0.978	0.811
1912	68.425	46.665	27.816	11.490	1.060	1.173	1.025	0.936
1913	69.612	46.080	27.767	12.626	0.998	1.099	1.012	1.012

* For deflators see Table I*a*.

† The cotton year begins, for the years 1875–1913 with September 1; for the years 1914–29, with August 1.

‡ For the trend equations used see Table 19, chap. viii.

TABLE V—*Continued*

YEAR†	PER CAPITA PRODUCTION (LB.)	PER CAPITA EXPORTS (LB.)	PER CAPITA CONSUMPTION (LB.)	REAL PRICE (CENTS PER LB.)	LINK RELATIVES		TREND RATIOS‡	
					Per Capita Consumption	Real Price	Per Capita Consumption	Real Price
1914	78.211	40.924	27.523	7.434	....	....	0.904	0.754
1915	53.543	28.521	30.949	10.018	1.124	1.348	1.041	0.915
1916	53.983	25.175	32.248	11.045	1.042	1.103	1.109	0.929
1917	52.480	20.008	30.637	14.503	0.950	1.313	1.075	1.145
1918	55.254	25.952	26.758	14.393	0.873	0.992	0.956	1.084
1919	51.640	29.844	29.271	15.463	1.094	1.074	1.062	1.125
1920	59.820	25.895	22.054	9.097	0.753	0.588	0.811	0.647
1921	34.826	26.996	25.799	11.812	1.170	1.298	0.958	0.831
1922	42.185	20.910	28.903	14.755	1.120	1.249	1.082	1.038
1923	43.174	24.009	24.113	19.127	0.834	1.296	0.908	1.360
1924	57.172	33.555	25.961	14.686	1.077	0.768	0.980	1.068
1925	66.608	33.264	26.672	12.639	1.027	0.861	1.007	0.951
1926	73.221	45.061	29.649	8.483	1.112	0.671	1.116	0.670
1927	52.087	30.723	27.846	13.735	0.939	1.619	1.042	1.156
1928	57.331	32.256	28.436	12.155	1.021	0.885	1.056	1.110
1929	57.902	26.626	24.302	11.993	0.855	0.987	0.893	1.216
1930	53.852	26.464	20.604	7.950	....	....	....	....
1931	65.708	34.408	19.228	5.495	....	....	....	....
1932	49.743	32.952	24.021	6.792	....	....	....	....
1933	49.527	29.450	22.293	8.836	....	....	....	....
1934§	36.344	18.431	20.570	10.387	....	....	....	....

§ The data for 1934 were inserted after our computations were completed. It appears that the series which we have taken from the U.S. Department of Agriculture have, for the later years, been subjected to slight revisions in *Agricultural Statistics, 1936.*

TABLE VI

HAY: ADJUSTED SERIES OF QUANTITIES AND PRICES, WITH LINK RELATIVES AND TREND RATIOS, 1875–1929*

YEAR BEGINNING JULY 1	CONSUMPTION PER ANIMAL UNIT (SHORT TONS)	REAL PRICE (DOLLARS PER TON)	VALUE PER ANIMAL UNIT† (DOLLARS)	LINK RELATIVES Per Animal Unit Consumption	LINK RELATIVES Real Price	TREND RATIOS‡ Per Animal Unit Consumption	TREND RATIOS‡ Real Price
1875	2.3221	11.468	26.63	. . . .	. . . .	0.884	1.155
1876	2.4985	9.442	23.59	1.076	0.823	0.953	0.947
1877	2.4858	9.733	24.19	0.995	1.031	0.950	0.971
1878	2.9216	9.600	28.05	1.175	0.986	1.118	0.954
1879	2.9003	9.404	27.27	0.993	0.980	1.112	0.930
1880	2.2905	12.010	27.51	0.790	1.277	0.880	1.182
1881	2.5152	10.844	27.27	1.098	0.903	0.968	1.062
1882	2.5436	9.539	24.26	1.011	0.880	0.980	0.930
1883	3.0321	8.531	25.87	1.192	0.894	1.171	0.828
1884	3.0404	9.726	29.57	1.003	1.140	1.176	0.940
1885	2.7030	10.369	28.03	0.889	1.066	1.048	0.998
1886	2.4297	10.575	25.69	0.899	1.020	0.943	1.013
1887	2.3273	11.330	26.37	0.958	1.071	0.905	1.080
1888	2.5432	10.186	25.91	1.093	0.899	0.991	0.967
1889	2.5695	9.949	25.56	1.010	0.977	1.003	0.940
1890	2.5715	10.099	25.97	1.001	1.015	1.006	0.950
1891	2.4330	11.397	27.73	0.946	1.129	0.954	1.068
1892	2.4422	11.623	28.39	1.004	1.020	0.959	1.084
1893	2.7478	12.986	35.68	. . . .	. . . .	. . . .	. . . .
1894	2.5464	12.986	33.07	. . . .	. . . .	. . . .	. . . .
1895	2.2061	13.710	30.25	. . . .	. . . .	. . . .	. . . .
1896	2.9758	11.333	33.72	. . . .	. . . .	. . . .	. . . .
1897	3.2977	10.866	35.83	. . . .	. . . .	. . . .	. . . .
1898	3.8019	9.609	36.53	. . . .	. . . .	. . . .	. . . .
1899	2.9571	10.250	30.31	. . . .	. . . .	1.101	0.954
1900	2.4293	12.000	29.15	0.822	1.171	0.884	1.106
1901	2.5424	12.085	30.72	1.047	1.007	0.908	1.103
1902	2.9320	10.812	31.70	1.153	0.895	1.031	0.978
1903	3.0300	11.265	34.13	1.033	1.042	1.054	1.009
1904	3.0441	10.607	32.29	1.005	0.942	1.051	0.941
1905	3.0209	9.652	29.16	0.992	0.910	1.039	0.848
1906	2.6468	11.096	29.37	0.876	1.150	0.910	0.966
1907	2.8854	12.667	36.55	1.090	1.142	0.996	1.093
1908	3.0869	10.044	31.00	1.070	0.793	1.072	0.859
1909	2.9582	10.796	31.94	0.958	1.075	1.039	0.915
1910	2.8111	12.646	35.55	0.950	1.171	1.001	1.062
1911	2.2309	14.885	33.21	0.794	1.177	0.809	1.239
1912	2.9405	11.790	34.67	1.318	0.792	1.091	0.973
1913	2.5240	12.556	31.69	0.858	1.065	0.962	1.027
1914	2.6763	11.464	30.68	1.060	0.913	1.052	0.929

* For deflators see Table I of this appendix.
† "Consumption per Animal Unit" multiplied by "Real Price."
‡ For the trend equations used see Table 24, chap. ix.

TABLE VI—*Continued*

Year Beginning July 1	Consumption per Animal Unit (Short Tons)	Real Price (Dollars per Ton)	Value per Animal Unit† (Dollars)	Link Relatives		Trend Ratios‡	
				Per Animal Unit Consumption	Real Price	Per Animal Unit Consumption	Real Price
1915	3.1874	9.843	31.37	. . . .	. . . .	0.983	1.113
1916	3.2963	7.530	24.82	1.034	0.765	1.016	0.854
1917	2.9500	9.390	27.70	. . . .	. . . .	. . . .	. . . .
1918	2.7235	9.965	27.14	. . . .	. . . .	. . . .	. . . .
1919	3.2305	8.991	29.05	. . . .	. . . .	. . . .	. . . .
1920	3.4012	9.866	33.56	. . . .	. . . .	. . . .	. . . .
1921	3.1415	8.643	27.15	. . . .	. . . .	. . . .	. . . .
1922	3.6984	8.045	29.75	. . . .	. . . .	1.044	0.928
1923	3.5181	9.358	32.92	0.951	1.163	0.867	1.082
1924	3.9346	8.764	34.48	1.118	0.937	1.050	1.016
1925	3.5694	8.929	31.87	0.907	1.019	0.822	1.039
1926	3.7221	9.592	35.70	1.043	1.074	0.928	1.119
1927	4.6887	7.617	35.71	1.260	0.794	1.127	0.891
1928	4.1740	8.235	34.37	0.890	1.081	0.965	0.966
1929	4.5013	8.428	37.94	1.078	1.023	1.000	0.992

TABLE VII

WHEAT: ADJUSTED SERIES OF QUANTITIES AND PRICES,

YEAR BEGINNING JULY 1	PER CAPITA U.S. PRODUCTION (BUSHELS)	PER CAPITA U.S. EXPORTS (BUSHELS)	PER CAPITA U.S. UTILIZATION† (BUSHELS)	REAL PRICE (CENTS PER BU.)
1875	8.1827	1.6599	6.5598	107.45
1876	7.9103	1.2349	6.6833	109.05
1877	10.7427	1.9459	8.8262	126.16
1878	10.3972	3.1023	7.3376	102.93
1879	11.0563	3.6601	7.4060	111.82
1880	10.5104	3.6994	6.8151	98.14
1881	8.0067	2.3643	5.6591	109.72
1882	10.3573	2.8079	7.5697	87.06
1883	8.5733	2.0793	6.4945	95.21
1884	10.2001	2.4140	7.7899	76.79
1885	7.5448	1.6861	5.8654	91.90
1886	9.4747	2.6749	6.8047	85.88
1887	9.3357	2.0485	7.2972	77.39
1888	8.4451	1.4876	6.9598	107.79
1889	9.9079	1.8023	8.1082	89.49
1890	8.0946	1.7209	6.3829	103.33
1891	12.1068	3.5578	8.5869	106.54
1892	10.2642	2.9651	7.3137	81.04
1893	7.9751	2.4949	5.4977	73.15
1894	9.2009	2.1643	7.0575	70.87
1895	9.5241	1.8861	7.6682	73.19
1896	8.5634	2.1006	6.4844	109.24
1897	9.4039	3.0618	6.3704	120.75
1898	11.2157	3.0909	8.1501	83.91
1899	9.0416	2.5547	6.4911	73.50
1900	8.3002	2.8903	5.4178	76.67
1901	10.5517	3.0604	7.4929	76.95
1902	9.2037	2.6329	6.5843	74.12
1903	8.3321	1.5531	6.7818	83.49
1904	6.9656	0.5830	6.4222	110.24
1905	8.5525	1.2132	7.3425	83.93
1906	8.7679	1.7702	7.0046	70.21
1907	7.2147	1.9143	5.3064	93.12
1908	7.2818	1.3204	5.9667	106.03
1909	7.7891	1.0023	6.7960	102.48
1910	6.9965	0.7940	6.2151	94.78
1911	6.5491	0.8946	5.6910	89.40
1912	7.6198	1.5439	6.0895	80.94
1913	7.7258	1.5568	6.1937	80.12

* For deflators see Table I of this appendix.

† This series represents per capita utilization only for the years beginning with 1914. For 1875–1913 it represents *apparent* utilization, i.e., it does not allow for changes in stocks. For the period 1875–95 data on stocks are not available. For the period 1896–1913 estimates of stocks are available (see Table IIc of this appendix), but they are subject to such large errors that we found it advisable to discard them (see chap. x, Sec. V).

TABLE VII—*Continued*

WITH LINK RELATIVES AND TREND RATIOS, 1875–1934*

LINK RELATIVES		TREND RATIOS‡		YEAR BEGINNING JULY 1
Per Capita U.S. Utilization†	Real Price	Per Capita U.S. Utilization†	Real Price	
. . . .	. . . .	. . . .	. . . .	1875
. . . .	. . . .	. . . .	. . . .	1876
. . . .	. . . .	. . . .	. . . .	1877
. . . .	. . . .	. . . .	. . . .	1878
. . . .	. . . .	. . . .	. . . .	1879
. . . .	. . . .	1.019	0.995	1880
0.830	1.118	0.841	1.127	1881
1.338	0.794	1.118	0.906	1882
0.858	1.094	0.953	1.004	1883
1.200	0.807	1.137	0.820	1884
0.753	1.197	0.851	0.995	1885
1.160	0.935	0.982	0.943	1886
1.072	0.901	1.047	0.861	1887
0.954	1.393	0.993	1.217	1888
1.165	0.830	1.150	1.025	1889
0.787	1.155	0.900	1.200	1890
1.345	1.031	1.204	1.256	1891
0.852	0.761	1.020	0.970	1892
0.752	0.903	0.762	0.889	1893
1.284	0.969	0.973	0.874	1894
1.087	1.033	1.051	0.917	1895
. . . .	. . . .	0.939	1.184	1896
0.982	1.105	0.929	1.313	1897
1.279	0.695	1.198	0.916	1898
0.796	0.876	0.961	0.805	1899
0.835	1.043	0.808	0.843	1900
1.383	1.004	1.125	0.849	1901
0.879	0.963	0.996	0.821	1902
1.030	1.126	1.033	0.928	1903
0.947	1.320	0.986	1.230	1904
1.143	0.761	1.136	0.940	1905
0.954	0.837	1.092	0.789	1906
0.758	1.326	0.833	1.051	1907
1.124	1.139	0.944	1.201	1908
1.139	0.967	1.084	1.165	1909
0.915	0.925	0.999	1.082	1910
0.916	0.943	0.922	1.024	1911
1.070	0.905	0.994	0.931	1912
1.017	0.990	1.020	0.925	1913

‡ The trend equations used are:

I: 1880–95   II: 1896–1913   IIIa: 1921–1929

$$x_{au} = 6.9919 + 0.0401t \qquad x_{au} = 6.4889 - 0.0488t \qquad x_u = 5.4172 - 0.0175t$$
$$y = 89.2181 - 1.2547t \qquad y = 89.4378 - 0.3323t \qquad y = 74.7567 + 0.9955t$$

The origins for t are in each case at the middle of the period.

TABLE VII—*Continued*

Year Beginning July 1	Per Capita U.S. Production (Bushels)	Per Capita U.S. Exports (Bushels)	Per Capita U.S. Utilization† (Bushels)	Real Price (Cents per Bu.)
1914	9.0991	3.4306	6.0796	98.58
1915	10.0813	2.4941	6.0943	86.89
1916	6.2541	2.0556	6.1545	94.40
1917	6.0244	1.3219	5.3165	109.64
1918	8.6689	2.7836	5.4909	102.55
1919	9.0066	2.1300	6.3131	95.33
1920	7.8536	3.4738	5.0956	99.40
1921	7.7858	2.6197	5.4133	72.33
1922	7.6478	2.0597	5.5640	62.00
1923	6.7588	1.4501	5.5161	61.61
1924	7.4546	2.3130	5.4475	80.56
1925	5.9995	0.9601	5.2455	92.23
1926	7.2300	1.8944	5.3695	82.68
1927	7.1389	1.7559	5.4911	81.01
1928	7.5760	1.3830	5.4095	67.43
1929	6.9646	1.2773	5.2986	72.96
1930	7.1703	1.0867	6.0404	56.06
1931	7.5241	1.1200	6.0107	37.61
1932	6.0459	0.3570	5.7416	39.75
1933	4.3740	0.3156	4.9711	67.67
1934	4.1517	0.1930	5.1720	71.48

TABLE VII—*Continued*

LINK RELATIVES		TREND RATIOS‡		YEAR BEGINNING JULY 1
Per Capita U.S. Utilization†	Real Price	Per Capita U.S. Utilization†	Real Price	
. . . .	. . . .	. . . .	. . . .	1914
. . . .	. . . .	. . . .	. . . .	1915
. . . .	. . . .	. . . .	. . . .	1916
. . . .	. . . .	. . . .	. . . .	1917
. . . .	. . . .	. . . .	. . . .	1918
. . . .	. . . .	. . . .	. . . .	1919
. . . .	. . . .	. . . .	. . . .	1920
. . . .	. . . .	0.987	1.022	1921
1.028	0.857	1.017	0.864	1922
0.991	0.994	1.012	0.847	1923
0.988	1.308	1.002	1.092	1924
0.963	1.145	0.968	1.234	1925
1.024	0.896	0.994	1.091	1926
1.023	0.980	1.020	1.056	1927
0.985	0.832	1.008	0.867	1928
0.980	1.082	0.991	0.927	1929
. . . .	. . . .	. . . .	. . . .	1930
. . . .	. . . .	. . . .	. . . .	1931
. . . .	. . . .	. . . .	. . . .	1932
. . . .	. . . .	. . . .	. . . .	1933
. . . .	. . . .	. . . .	. . . .	1934

TABLE VIII

POTATOES: ADJUSTED SERIES OF QUANTITIES AND PRICES, WITH LINK
RELATIVES AND TREND RATIOS, 1875–1929*

YEAR BEGINNING JULY 1	PER CAPITA CONSUMPTION (BU.)	REAL PRICE (CENTS PER BU.)	VALUE PER CAPITA† (DOLLARS)	LINK RELATIVES		TREND RATIOS‡	
				Per Capita Consumption	Real Price	Per Capita Consumption	Real Price
1875	3.706	36.596	1.36	. . . .	. . . .	1.186	0.692
1876	2.702	65.158	1.76	0.729	1.780	0.865	1.217
1877	3.592	50.814	1.83	1.329	0.780	1.150	0.937
1878	2.559	78.267	2.00	0.712	1.540	0.819	1.426
1879	3.656	44.040	1.61	1.429	0.563	1.171	0.792
1880	3.294	49.794	1.64	0.901	1.131	1.055	0.885
1881	2.092	83.486	1.75	0.635	1.677	0.670	1.466
1882	3.198	54.608	1.75	1.529	0.654	1.024	0.947
1883	3.803	43.958	1.67	1.189	0.805	1.218	0.754
1884	3.403	47.143	1.60	0.895	1.072	1.090	0.799
1885	3.055	53.214	1.63	0.898	1.129	0.979	0.892
1886	2.869	58.375	1.67	0.939	1.097	0.919	0.967
1887	2.240	77.500	1.74	0.781	1.328	0.718	1.269
1888	3.310	46.744	1.55	1.478	0.603	1.061	0.757
1889	3.224	45.385	1.46	0.974	0.971	1.033	0.727
1890	2.362	92.963	2.20	0.733	2.048	0.757	1.473
1891	3.940	45.641	1.80	1.668	0.491	1.263	0.716
1892	2.481	85.065	2.11	0.630	1.864	0.795	1.319
1893	2.884	80.000	2.31	1.162	0.940	0.955	1.228
1894	2.667	76.667§	2.04	0.925	0.958	0.855	1.165
1895	4.515	37.971	1.71	1.693	0.495	1.448	0.571
1896	3.799	43.939	1.67	. . . .	. . . .	1.227	0.704
1897	2.622	80.896	2.12	0.690	1.841	0.834	1.296
1898	2.951‖	60.145	1.77	1.125	0.743	0.924	0.963
1899	3.449	49.625	1.71	1.169	0.825	1.065	0.794
1900	3.220	52.222	1.68	0.934	1.052	0.980	0.834
1901	2.528	93.049	2.35	0.785	1.782	0.758	1.486
1902	3.666	55.176	2.02	1.450	0.593	1.085	0.880
1903	3.204	73.373	2.35	0.874	1.330	0.935	1.170
1904	4.223	53.333	2.25	1.318	0.727	1.216	0.850
1905	3.280	68.652	2.25	0.777	1.287	0.931	1.093
1906	3.828	53.830	2.06	1.167	0.784	1.073	0.856
1907	3.659	65.914	2.41	0.956	1.224	1.012	1.048
1908	3.360	76.593	2.57	0.918	1.162	0.917	1.217
1909	4.312	55.306	2.38	1.283	0.722	1.162	0.878
1910	3.754	58.021	2.18	0.871	1.049	0.999	0.920
1911	3.101	83.229	2.58	0.826	1.434	0.815	1.319
1912	4.391	50.500	2.22	1.416	0.607	1.140	0.800
1913	3.410	69.394	2.37	0.777	1.374	0.874	1.098
1914	4.156	50.206	2.09	1.219	0.723	1.053	0.794

* For deflators see Table I of this appendix.
† "Per Capita Consumption" multiplied by "Real Price."
‡ For the trend equations used see Table 32, chap. xi.
§ In our computations for the period 1890–1900, 76.522 was used.
‖ In our computations 2.950 was used, except for the period 1890–1900.

TABLE VIII—*Continued*

YEAR BEGINNING JULY 1	PER CAPITA CONSUMPTION (BU.)	REAL PRICE (CENTS PER BU.)	VALUE PER CAPITA† (DOLLARS)	LINK RELATIVES		TREND RATIOS‡	
				Per Capita Consumption	Real Price	Per Capita Consumption	Real Price
1915	3.595	57.130	2.05	. . . .	. . . .	1.050	0.826
1916	2.828	98.054	2.77	0.787	1.716	0.827	1.419
1917	4.297	67.473	2.90	. . . .	. . . .	. . . .	. . . .
1918	3.949	59.059	2.33	. . . .	. . . .	. . . .	. . . .
1919	3.054	71.525	2.18	. . . .	. . . .	. . . .	. . . .
1920	3.756	63.966	2.40	. . . .	. . . .	. . . .	. . . .
1921	3.317	78.643	2.61	. . . .	. . . .	. . . .	. . . .
1922	4.096	37.244	1.53	. . . .	. . . .	1.207	0.539
1923	3.703	51.722	1.92	0.904	1.389	1.093	0.748
1924	3.679	39.809	1.46	0.994	0.770	1.087	0.576
1925	2.774	119.872	3.33	0.754	3.011	0.821	1.734
1926	3.020	96.190	2.90	1.089	0.802	0.895	1.392
1927	3.384	64.765	2.19	1.121	0.673	1.004	0.937
1928	3.856	36.174	1.39	1.139	0.559	1.145	0.523
1929	2.934	90.276	2.65	0.761	2.496	0.872	1.306

TABLE IX

OATS: ADJUSTED SERIES OF QUANTITIES AND PRICES, WITH LINK RELATIVES AND TREND RATIOS, 1875–1929*

YEAR BEGINNING JULY 1	APPARENT CONSUMPTION PER ANIMAL UNIT (BU.)	DISAPPEARANCE PER ANIMAL UNIT (BU.)	REAL PRICE (CENTS PER BU.)	VALUE PER ANIMAL UNIT† (DOLLARS)	LINK RELATIVES Consumption per Animal Unit	Real Price	TREND RATIOS‡ Consumption per Animal Unit	Real Price
1875	30.994	....	34.043	10.55	....	....	•0.998	1.023
1876	27.443	....	34.105	9.36	0.885	1.002	0.861	1.015
1877	33.744	....	33.023	11.14	1.230	0.968	1.033	0.973
1878	32.461	....	32.800	10.65	0.962	0.993	0.970	0.958
1879	34.666	....	33.636	11.66	1.068	1.025	1.012	0.973
1880	31.599	....	37.113	11.73	0.912	1.103	0.901	1.063
1881	33.025	....	42.569	14.06	1.045	1.147	0.921	1.208
1882	37.350	....	36.765	13.73	1.131	0.864	1.019	1.034
1883	42.443	....	34.063	14.46	1.136	0.927	1.133	0.949
1884	41.938	....	32.976	13.83	0.988	0.968	1.096	0.911
1885	43.417	....	33.929	14.73	1.035	1.029	1.112	0.929
1886	41.625	....	37.250	15.51	0.959	1.098	1.045	1.011
1887	42.011	....	34.545	14.51	1.009	0.927	1.034	0.929
1888	43.193	....	32.326	13.96	1.028	0.936	1.042	0.862
1889	47.435	....	28.077	13.32	1.098	0.869	1.123	0.742
1890	34.208	....	51.481	17.61	0.721	1.834	0.795	1.349
1891	46.493	....	39.231	18.24	1.359	0.762	1.061	1.019
1892	37.256	....	40.909	15.24	0.801	1.043	0.835	1.054
1893	36.369	....	39.863	14.50	....	....	....	....
1894	38.957	....	46.522	18.12	....	....	....	....
1895	50.438	....	28.116	14.18	....	....	....	....
1896	46.443	46.247	27.727	12.88	....	....	....	....
1897	48.296	48.179	31.045	14.99	....	....	....	....
1898	52.435	49.655	36.522	19.15	....	....	....	....
1899	57.036	54.613	30.625	17.47	....	....	1.081	0.847
1900	46.158	46.173	31.358	14.47	0.809	1.024	0.914	0.857
1901	39.834	41.658	48.415	19.29	0.863	1.544	0.822	1.307
1902	53.726	51.860	36.000	19.34	1.349	0.744	1.150	0.961
1903	43.851	46.426	40.964	17.96	0.816	1.138	0.969	1.080
1904	49.875	48.603	37.024	18.47	1.137	0.904	1.131	0.965
1905	48.898	46.707	32.472	15.88	0.980	0.877	1.132	0.837
1906	43.801	43.318	33.936	14.86	0.896	1.045	1.028	0.865
1907	33.703	34.869	47.849	16.13	0.769	1.410	0.797	1.206
1908	34.526	34.260	51.978	17.95	1.024	1.086	0.817	1.295
1909	42.890	39.073	41.429	17.77	1.242	0.797	1.008	1.021
1910	48.617	44.808	35.833	17.42	1.134	0.865	1.129	0.874
1911	37.491	37.800	46.875	17.57	0.771	1.308	0.854	1.131
1912	57.891	49.876	31.900	18.34	1.533	0.681	1.277	0.762
1913	44.604	44.177	39.596	17.66	0.776	1.241	0.961	0.935
1914	44.740	38.387	45.155	20.20	1.003	1.140	0.930	1.056

* For deflators see Table I of this appendix.

† "Consumption per Animal Unit" multiplied by "Real Price."

‡ For trend equations used see Table 36, chap. xii.

TABLE IX—*Continued*

YEAR BEGINNING JULY 1	APPARENT CONSUMPTION PER ANIMAL UNIT (Bu.)	DISAPPEARANCE PER ANIMAL UNIT (Bu.)	REAL PRICE (CENTS PER BU.)	VALUE PER ANIMAL UNIT† (DOLLARS)	LINK RELATIVES		TREND RATIOS‡	
					Consumption per Animal Unit	Real Price	Consumption per Animal Unit	Real Price
1915	60.207	50.100	33.426	20.12	. . . .	. . . .	1.099	0.987
1916	48.107	42.822	35.168	16.92	0.799	1.052	0.866	1.053
1917	60.049	48.423	36.593	21.97	. . . .	. . . .	. . . .	. . . .
1918	57.985	48.924	35.099	20.35	. . . .	. . . .	. . . .	. . . .
1919	46.716	44.355	31.570	14.75	. . . .	. . . .	. . . .	. . . .
1920	60.369	52.225	25.698	15.51	. . . .	. . . .	. . . .	. . . .
1921	44.245	45.805	21.571	9.54	. . . .	. . . .	. . . .	. . . .
1922	50.890	48.499	25.256	12.85	. . . .	. . . .	. . . .	. . . .
1923	56.112	52.845	27.417	15.38	. . . .	. . . .	. . . .	. . . .
1924	66.524	60.299	30.382	20.21	. . . .	. . . .	1.072	1.025
1925	67.750	61.346	24.359	16.50	1.018	0.802	1.078	0.835
1926	58.834	56.428	27.075	15.93	0.868	1.111	0.924	0.943
1927	57.718	54.280	30.201	17.43	0.981	1.115	0.895	1.070
1928	72.379	63.033	27.450	19.87	1.254	0.909	1.109	0.989
1929	63.266	58.191	30.000	18.98	0.874	1.093	0.957	1.099

TABLE X

BARLEY: ADJUSTED SERIES OF QUANTITIES AND PRICES, WITH LINK RELATIVES AND TREND RATIOS, 1875–1929*

YEAR BEGINNING JULY 1	PER CAPITA CONSUMPTION (BU.)	REAL PRICE (CENTS PER BU.)	VALUE PER CAPITA† (CENTS)	LINK RELATIVES		TREND RATIOS‡	
				Per Capita Consumption	Real Price	Per Capita Consumption	Real Price
1875	1.0463	47.75	49.96	....	....	1.103	0.960
1876	0.9625	38.31	36.87	0.920	0.802	0.992	0.756
1877	0.8070	42.38	34.20	0.838	1.106	0.813	0.822
1878	0.9821	51.61	50.69	1.217	1.218	0.969	0.984
1879	1.1200	52.97	59.33	1.140	1.026	1.082	0.993
1880	1.0692	75.66	80.89	0.955	1.428	1.011	1.396
1881	1.0379	77.97	80.93	0.971	1.031	0.962	1.415
1882	1.1181	51.23	57.28	1.077	0.657	1.016	0.915
1883	1.0616	49.16	52.19	0.950	0.960	0.946	0.864
1884	1.2649§	48.95	61.92	1.192	0.996	1.106	0.847
1885	1.1961	51.47	61.56	0.946	1.051	1.026	0.877
1886	1.1708	56.11	65.70	0.979	1.090	0.986	0.942
1887	1.1228	74.29	83.41	0.959	1.324	0.929	1.229
1888	1.2084	63.10	76.25	1.076	0.849	0.982	1.029
1889	1.4139	52.43	74.13	1.170	0.831	1.129	0.843
1890	1.2061	81.99	98.89	0.853	1.564	0.946	1.299
1891	1.4819	64.85	96.10	1.229	0.791	1.143	1.013
1892	1.3697	65.19	89.29	0.924	1.005	1.039	1.005
1893	1.1707	66.48	77.83	0.855	1.020	0.874	1.011
1894	1.1382	74.13	84.38	0.972	1.115	0.836	1.112
1895	1.5334	45.86	70.32	1.347	0.619	1.109	0.679
1896	1.1235	45.87	51.54	....	....	1.115	0.816
1897	1.2603	59.88	75.47	1.122	1.305	1.106	1.036
1898	1.3130	63.83	83.81	1.042	1.066	1.041	1.074
1899	1.2298	53.28	65.53	0.937	0.835	0.896	0.873
1900	1.1645	70.00	81.52	0.947	1.314	0.790	1.117
1901	1.4355	77.86	111.77	1.233	1.112	0.918	1.212
1902	1.7550	66.19	116.16	1.223	0.850	1.068	1.005
1903	1.6588	66.83	110.86	0.945	1.010	0.968	0.990
1904	1.8113	58.33	105.66	1.092	0.873	1.022	0.844
1905	1.7839	56.31	100.45	0.985	0.965	0.980	0.796
1906	2.1194	64.89	137.53	1.188	1.152	1.140	0.897
1907	1.8766	90.13	169.14	0.885	1.389	0.995	1.219
1908	1.9818	73.22	145.11	1.056	0.812	1.042	0.969
1909	2.0057	69.07	138.54	1.012	0.943	1.051	0.895
1910	1.7694	96.13	170.09	0.882	1.392	0.929	1.220
1911	1.7095	125.13	213.91	0.966	1.302	0.904	1.556
1912	2.1498	68.14	146.49	1.258	0.545	1.153	0.831
1913	1.7650	65.79	116.12	0.821	0.966	0.965	0.787
1914	1.6865	72.73	122.66	0.955	1.105	0.946	0.853

* For deflators see Table I of this appendix.

† "Per Capita Consumption" multiplied by "Real Price."

‡ For trend equations used see Table 40, chap. xiii.

§ Owing to an inconsistency in rounding-off, 1.2650 was used in our computations.

TABLE X—*Continued*

Year Beginning July 1	Per Capita Consumption (Bu.)	Real Price (Cents per Bu.)	Value per Capita† (Cents)	Link Relatives		Trend Ratios‡	
				Per Capita Consumption	Real Price	Per Capita Consumption	Real Price
1915	1.9797	61.33	121.42	....	....	1.040	0.933
1916	1.6011	75.65	121.12	0.809	1.233	0.926	1.177
1917	1.7842	77.95	139.08	....	....	....	....
1918	2.1758	51.69	112.47	....	....	....	....
1919	1.0713	63.24	67.75	....	....	....	....
1920	1.5096	44.50	67.18	....	....	....	....
1921	1.1685	42.48	49.64	....	....	....	....
1922	1.4471	41.83	60.53	....	....	1.070	0.757
1923	1.6360	48.00	78.53	1.130	1.148	1.166	0.893
1924	1.3424	57.73	77.50	0.821	1.203	0.904	1.105
1925	1.5857	46.42	73.61	1.181	0.804	0.992	0.915
1926	1.4084	52.52	73.97	0.888	1.131	0.807	1.066
1927	1.9042	61.78	117.64	1.352	1.176	0.990	1.294
1928	2.4627	40.51	99.76	1.293	0.656	1.154	0.876
1929	2.2792	44.22	100.79	0.925	1.092	0.959	0.988

TABLE XI

RYE: ADJUSTED SERIES OF QUANTITIES AND PRICES, WITH LINK RELATIVES
AND TREND RATIOS, 1875–1929*

YEAR BEGINNING JULY 1	PER CAPITA CONSUMPTION (Bu.)	REAL PRICE (CENTS PER BU.)	VALUE PER CAPITA † (CENTS)	LINK RELATIVES		TREND RATIOS‡	
				Per Capita Consumption	Real Price	Per Capita Consumption	Real Price
1875	0.37934	71.383	27	. . . .	. . . .	0.925	1.042
1876	0.39272	64.632	25	1.035	0.905	0.957	0.942
1877	0.35924	66.977	24	0.915	1.036	0.875	0.975
1878	0.43073	70.000	30	1.199	1.045	1.049	1.018
1879	0.44765	68.283	31	1.039	0.975	1.090	0.992
1880	0.44397	77.938	35	0.992	1.141	1.081	1.131
1881	0.37941	85.596	32	0.855	1.098	0.923	1.241
1882	0.51886	60.294	31	1.368	0.704	1.262	0.873
1883	0.39680	60.521	24	0.765	1.004	0.965	0.875
1884	0.45734	61.786	28	1.153	1.021	1.112	0.893
1885	0.37748	68.929	26	0.825	1.116	0.917	0.995
1886	0.40963	67.250	28	1.085	0.976	0.995	0.969
1887	0.34399	61.932	21	0.840	0.921	0.836	0.892
1888	0.45973	68.372	31	1.336	1.104	1.116	0.983
1889	0.41876	54.231	23	0.911	0.793	1.016	0.779
1890	0.40927	77.284	32	0.977	1.425	0.993	1.109
1891	0.31926	98.846	32	0.780	1.279	0.774	1.417
1892	0.41871	69.610	29	1.312	0.704	1.015	0.997
1893	0.41913	68.767	29	1.001	0.988	1.016	0.984
1894	0.42935	71.594	31	1.024	1.041	1.040	1.023
1895	0.42898	61.159	26	0.999	0.854	1.039	0.873
1896	0.28431	58.788	17	. . . .	. . . .	1.051	0.970
1897	0.24579	64.478	16	0.865	1.097	0.837	1.046
1898	0.30641	64.493	20	1.247	1.000	0.975	1.029
1899	0.37047	62.000	23	1.209	0.961	1.114	0.973
1900	0.36973	61.481	23	0.998	0.992	1.061	0.950
1901	0.36141	67.561	24	0.977	1.099	0.998	1.027
1902	0.37183	59.412	22	1.029	0.879	0.996	0.890
1903	0.38193	65.060	25	1.027	1.095	0.999	0.959
1904	0.38120	82.024	31	0.998	1.261	0.980	1.191
1905	0.39729	67.865	27	1.042	0.827	1.010	0.971
1906	0.41306	62.234	26	1.040	0.917	1.044	0.878
1907	0.37401	77.957	29	0.905	1.253	0.946	1.084
1908	0.38354	80.000	31	1.025	1.026	0.977	1.096
1909	0.38463	73.673	28	1.003	0.921	0.992	0.996
1910	0.37735	74.479	28	0.981	1.011	0.992	0.993
1911	0.35197	86.667	31	0.933	1.164	0.949	1.139
1912	0.35290	66.300	23	1.003	0.765	0.983	0.860
1913	0.40264	64.040	26	1.141	0.966	1.168	0.820
1914	0.30313	89.175	27	0.753	1.392	0.924	1.127

* For deflators see Table I of this appendix.
† "Per Capita Consumption" multiplied by "Real Price."
‡ For trend equations used see Table 42, chap. xiv.

TABLE XI—*Continued*

Year Beginning July 1	Per Capita Consumption (Bu.)	Real Price (Cents per Bu.)	Value per Capita† (Cents)	Link Relatives		Trend Ratios‡	
				Per Capita Consumption	Real Price	Per Capita Consumption	Real Price
1915	0.39346	77.222	30	....	....	1.011	0.948
1916	0.35073	81.946	29	0.891	1.061	0.925	1.093
1917	0.45277	91.209	41	....	....	....	....
1918	0.52938	75.050	40	....	....	....	....
1919	0.33137	59.731	20	....	....	....	....
1920	0.12671	70.838	9	....	....	....	....
1921	0.29742	49.786	15	....	....	....	....
1922	0.46789	43.910	21	....	....	1.461	0.831
1923	0.38424	43.046	17	0.821	0.980	1.238	0.830
1924	0.13399	67.771	9	0.349	1.574	0.446	1.312
1925	0.29222	50.128	15	2.181	0.740	1.005	0.960
1926	0.16233	56.735	9	0.556	1.132	0.578	1.059
1927	0.26732	57.248	15	1.647	1.009	0.986	1.027
1928	0.28070	57.718	16	1.050	1.008	1.075	0.984
1929	0.32128	59.586	19	1.145	1.032	1.278	0.956

TABLE XII

BUCKWHEAT: ADJUSTED SERIES OF QUANTITIES AND PRICES, WITH LINK
RELATIVES AND TREND RATIOS, 1875–1929*

YEAR BEGINNING JULY 1	PER CAPITA CONSUMPTION (BU.)	REAL PRICE (CENTS PER BU.)	VALUE PER CAPITA † (CENTS)	LINK RELATIVES Per Capita Consumption	LINK RELATIVES Real Price	TREND RATIOS ‡ Per Capita Consumption	TREND RATIOS ‡ Real Price
1875	0.22388	65.957	14.77	. . . .	. . . .	. . . .	. . . .
1876	0.20932	70.105	14.67	. . . .	. . . .	. . . .	. . . .
1877	0.21492	77.791	16.72	. . . .	. . . .	. . . .	. . . .
1878	0.25245	70.133	17.71	. . . .	. . . .	. . . .	. . . .
1879	0.35291	60.909	21.50	. . . .	. . . .	1.217	0.887
1880	0.28718	61.237	17.59	0.814	1.005	1.076	0.889
1881	0.18179	79.358	14.43	0.633	1.296	0.737	1.147
1882	0.20612	71.569	14.75	1.134	0.902	0.901	1.031
1883	0.14010	85.625	12.00	0.680	1.196	0.656	1.228
1884	0.19843	70.119	13.91	1.416	0.819	0.987	1.002
1885	0.22036	66.548	14.66	1.111	0.949	1.153	0.947
1886	0.20262	68.125	13.80	0.919	1.024	1.103	0.966
1887	0.18117	64.205	11.63	0.894	0.942	1.012	0.907
1888	0.19710	73.605	14.51	1.088	1.146	1.113	1.036
1889	0.19401	64.744	12.56	0.984	0.880	1.093	0.907
1890	0.19900	70.741	14.08	1.026	1.093	1.101	0.988
1891	0.20016	73.077	14.63	1.006	1.033	1.073	1.017
1892	0.19064	67.532	12.87	0.952	0.924	0.978	0.936
1893	0.19026	79.863	15.19	0.998	1.183	0.923	1.103
1894	0.19906	80.725	16.07	1.046	1.011	0.906	1.110
1895	0.23847	65.652	15.66	1.198	0.813	1.010	0.900
1896	0.22093	59.545	13.16	. . . .	. . . .	1.095	0.921
1897	0.23695	62.836	14.89	1.073	1.055	1.185	0.962
1898	0.18829	65.217	12.28	0.795	1.038	0.949	0.989
1899	0.17231	69.875	12.04	0.915	1.071	0.876	1.049
1900	0.15350	68.889	10.57	0.891	0.986	0.787	1.025
1901	0.19977	68.780	13.74	1.301	0.998	1.032	1.014
1902	0.19066	70.118	13.37	0.954	1.019	0.994	1.024
1903	0.18642	73.253	13.66	0.978	1.045	0.980	1.059
1904	0.19574	74.405	14.56	1.050	1.016	1.038	1.066
1905	0.18579	65.843	12.23	0.949	0.885	0.994	0.935
1906	0.18159	63.511	11.53	0.977	0.965	0.981	0.894
1907	0.16834	75.269	12.67	0.927	1.185	0.917	1.050
1908	0.18403	83.187	15.31	1.093	1.105	1.012	1.150
1909	0.19654	71.633	14.08	1.068	0.861	1.090	0.982
1910	0.18928	68.854	13.03	0.963	0.961	1.060	0.935
1911	0.18592	75.625	14.06	0.982	1.098	1.050	1.018
1912	0.20092	66.100	13.28	1.081	0.874	1.146	0.883
1913	0.14229	76.263	10.85	0.708	1.154	0.819	1.010
1914	0.17115	78.763	13.48	1.203	1.033	0.995	1.034

* For deflators see Table I of this appendix.

† "Per Capita Consumption" multiplied by "Real Price."

‡ For trend equations used see Table 44, chap. xv.

TABLE XII—*Continued*

YEAR BEGINNING JULY 1	PER CAPITA CONSUMPTION (BU.)	REAL PRICE (CENTS PER BU.)	VALUE PER CAPITA † (CENTS)	LINK RELATIVES		TREND RATIOS‡	
				Per Capita Consumption	Real Price	Per Capita Consumption	Real Price
1915	0.15048	72.870	10.97	. . . .	. . . .	1.091	0.964
1916	0.11494	75.638	8.69	0.764	1.038	0.846	1.045
1917	0.15573	87.912	13.69	. . . .	. . . .	. . . .	. . . .
1918	0.16209	82.426	13.36	. . . .	. . . .	. . . .	. . . .
1919	0.13621	65.516	8.92	. . . .	. . . .	. . . .	. . . .
1920	0.12239	71.676	8.77	. . . .	. . . .	. . . .	. . . .
1921	0.13029	58.000	7.56	. . . .	. . . .	. . . .	. . . .
1922	0.13156	56.731	7.46	. . . .	. . . .	1.066	0.938
1923	0.12428	61.788	7.68	0.945	1.089	1.025	1.035
1924	0.11713	65.350	7.65	0.942	1.058	0.983	1.101
1925	0.12095	56.923	6.88	1.033	0.871	1.033	0.959
1926	0.10801	60.000	6.48	0.893	1.054	0.939	1.005
1927	0.13236	56.040	7.42	1.225	0.934	1.172	0.927
1928	0.10894	58.725	6.40	0.823	1.048	0.983	0.955
1929	0.09377	67.379	6.32	0.861	1.147	0.862	1.071

TABLE XIII

CANADIAN DATA: BASIC DATA FOR THE ANALYSIS OF THE INTERRELATIONS OF THE
CANADIAN DEMANDS FOR SUGAR, TEA, AND COFFEE, FISCAL YEARS 1922–33

YEAR ENDING JUNE 30	POPULA-TION JANU-ARY 1* (THOU-SANDS)	WHOLE-SALE PRICE INDEX† 1913 = 100	SUGAR		TEA		COFFEE	
			Net Imports (Refined)‡ (Million Pounds)	Granulated Standard, Price per 100 Lb. at Montreal§ in Dollars	Net Imports‖ (Million Pounds)	Pekoe, Ceylon and India, Price per Lb. Delivered at Ware-house Duty Paid in Cents¶	Total Imports of Green Coffee (Million Pounds)**	Santos, Green, Good Quality, per Pound at Toronto, Freight and Duty Paid in Cents§
1922	8,864	155.8	779.2	7.047	38.28	35.25	22.865	19.54
1923	8,972	152.9	738.9	8.297	38.42	42.08	18.800	21.71
1924	9,087	153.6	701.9	9.358	38.05	46.32	21.977	22.71
1925	9,230	158.8	731.3	7.048	36.04	52.08	20.468	30.75
1926	9,385	159.4	776.8	5.962	37.06	53.50	23.089	28.54
1927	9,558	152.7	808.6	6.210	37.52	50.90	25.194	24.83
1928	9,750	152.2	785.7	6.037	38.24	50.61	28.152	25.41
1929	9,946	148.0	821.7	5.320	38.35	48.00	26.035	29.12
1930	10,131	147.3	834.4	5.082	46.06	45.33	28.343	24.75
1931	10,304	121.5	890.2	4.552	42.49	33.33	32.975	16.86
1932	10,451	108.3	825.3	4.489	38.41	32.50	31.273	15.82
1933	10,598	102.1	811.6	4.775	37.96	32.50	31.656	18.58

* Sources: Population as of June 1 is given in the *Canadian Yearbook, 1932*, p. 110, for the years 1922–31, and in a letter from R. H. Coats, Dominion statistician, September 22, 1933, for the years 1932–33. Population as of January 1 was obtained by linear interpolation.

† Sources: For the years 1922–28 the data are taken from *Prices and Price Indexes, 1913–1929*, pp. 21–23, for 1929, *ibid., 1913–1930*, p. 17, for 1930–31, *ibid., 1913–1931*, p. 17, and for 1932–33 from R. H. Coats, September 22, 1933.

‡ Sources: Supplied by W. A. Warne, chief, External Trade Branch, Dominion Bureau of Statistics, Canada, July 20, 1933. "Sugar, n.o.p. not above No. 16 Dutch Standard" and "Sugar above No. 16 Dutch Standard . . . . for refining purposes only" were converted to a refined-sugar base and added to "all sugar, above No. 16 Dutch Standard . . . . and all refined sugars" to arrive at an import figure. To obtain net imports, domestic exports (refined) were subtracted from total imports.

§ Sources: For the years 1922–24 and 1932–33 the data were supplied by R. H. Coats, August 9, 1933. For 1925–31 the data are taken from *Prices and Price Indexes* for the respective years.

‖ Source: Supplied by W. A. Warne, July 20, 1933. "Net Imports" are imports of tea *minus* exports of foreign tea.

¶ Source: Supplied by R. H. Coats, August 9, 1933.

** Source: Supplied by W. A. Warne, July 20, 1933.

APPENDIX B

THE USE OF UNADJUSTED DATA IN
THE STUDY OF DEMAND

APPENDIX B

THE USE OF UNADJUSTED DATA IN
THE STUDY OF DEMAND

When the statistical investigations underlying this book were planned, comparatively little was known in the concrete about the relative advantages and limitations attaching to the use of unadjusted (i.e., undeflated), as compared with adjusted, quantity and price series as variables in the demand equation, although on general theoretical considerations economic statisticians preferred to work with adjusted data. It was, therefore, deemed instructive to subject the total-consumption and the money-price series to the same analyses as were decided upon for the per capita consumption and the real-price series (see Table 46, of chap. xvi) and to compare the results obtained.

After most of the work was done and summary tables of the coefficients of correlation, of the elasticities of demand, of the price flexibilities, and of the time rates of shift of the demand curves were prepared, the United States Department of Agriculture began publishing its revisions of the underlying data on production and prices. Since the task of recomputing all of our equations would have been enormous, and since it was evident from the analyses already made that the results yielded by the unadjusted data are in general harmony with those obtained from the adjusted data, we decided to do no more work on the unadjusted series but to confine all future changes and revisions to the adjusted data.

Although the two sets of findings are thus not comparable for all commodities and for all periods, there remain a sufficiently large number of comparable items—especially those relating to the first and second periods—to warrant a brief summary.

1. Of the three aspects of a demand curve in which we are primarily interested—its fit, its elasticity, and its time shift—the first is the most difficult to measure and to compare. If, however, we agree to take the correlation between the observed and the computed values (i.e., the coefficient of multiple correlation between the dependent variable and the set of the independent or determining variables) as a measure of goodness of fit, and if we confine our comparison to curves of the same type and with the same number of parameters, then we are struck by the surprising fact that *in a large number of cases the unadjusted data give a better fit than the adjusted data.* This is particularly true of the demand curves relating to the first and second periods. For sugar, corn, and potatoes, the coefficients of multiple correlation derived from the logarithmic time-regression equations with quantity as the dependent variable are given in the following table. The larger coefficients of the unadjusted data are, however, generally due to the greater importance of the time variable in these data. When the time shift of the demand curve is very pronounced, the multiple coefficient of correlation will be quite large, although the year-to-year fluctuations may deviate markedly from the curve.

2. With respect to the second characteristic—the elasticity of demand—the curves derived from the unadjusted data do not differ significantly from those based on the adjusted data (Table 48, of chap. xvii). This is true not only of the time regression equations but also of the link-relatives and the trend-ratio equations.

3. From the equations in which price is the dependent variable it also appears that the price flexibilities obtained from the unadjusted data do not differ significantly from the corresponding flexibilities based on the adjusted data.

4. It is only with respect to their time rates of shift that the two sets of demand curves yield different results, the total demand curve shifting at higher rates. Thus

SAMPLE OF COEFFICIENTS OF MULTIPLE CORRELATION OF DEMAND
FUNCTIONS DERIVED FROM UNADJUSTED DATA (UPPER FIG-
URES) AND FROM ADJUSTED DATA (LOWER FIGURES)

Commodity	Period I	Period II	Period III
Sugar.....................	$\begin{cases}0.984\\0.954\end{cases}$	$\begin{cases}0.993\\0.974\end{cases}$	$\begin{cases}0.986\\0.960\end{cases}$
Corn......................	$\begin{cases}0.875\\0.895\end{cases}$	$\begin{cases}0.948\\0.944\end{cases}$	$\begin{cases}0.814\\0.889\end{cases}$
Potatoes..................	$\begin{cases}0.951\\0.947\end{cases}$	$\begin{cases}0.978\\0.952\end{cases}$	$\begin{cases}0.994\\0.971\end{cases}$

for sugar for the second period (1896–1914) the equations based on the adjusted data and on the unadjusted data are, respectively,

$$x = 117.5y^{-(0.2717 \pm 0.0844)} e^{(0.0124 \pm 0.0022)t}$$

and

$$x = 391.8y^{-(0.2488 \pm 0.1010)} e^{(0.0382 \pm 0.0011)t}.$$

These show that, while the time shift of the per capita demand curve was 1.24 per cent per annum, that of the total demand curve was 3.82 per cent per annum, or three times as large. The computations also show that in the first equation the time variable accounts for 61.2 per cent of the variance of the logarithm of x, while in the second equation it accounts for as much as 98.3 per cent of the variance. *But a higher time shift of demand is just what we should expect to obtain from the unadjusted data.* And it is in this characteristic that the use of the revised data would introduce significant modifications.

We conclude, therefore, that the more important findings of the book are confirmed by the analysis of the unadjusted data. It is, however, generally preferable to work with adjusted data in analyses of demand, since the process of deflating the quantities and the prices removes much, if not most, of the unanalyzed and troublesome factor—time.

APPENDIX C

ELEMENTS OF CURVE-FITTING AND CORRELATION: SUMMARY OF STATISTICAL METHODS AND TECHNIQUES USEFUL IN ANALYSIS OF DEMAND

APPENDIX C*

ELEMENTS OF CURVE-FITTING AND CORRELATION: SUMMARY OF STATISTICAL METHODS AND TECHNIQUES USEFUL IN ANALYSIS OF DEMAND

In chapters iv and vi the principal statistical methods and procedures used in this work were explained in nontechnical terms with a minimum of mathematical symbols. These notes supplement those explanations with a brief, mathematical treatment of some of the topics. Since the methods and procedures in question center around the problem of fitting a curve to data and determining its "goodness of fit," we may begin our treatment with this problem.

I. THE GENERAL METHOD OF LEAST SQUARES: ALL VARIABLES SUBJECT TO ERROR

Let the variables be

$$X_1, X_2, \ldots, X_k .$$

Thus in the demand functions considered in this book, X_1 may stand for consumption, X_2 for price, X_3 for time, X_4 for time squared, etc. Corresponding to each of the k variables there is a given series of n observations, so that

$$(1.1) \qquad X_i^{(\tau)} , \qquad i = 1, 2, \ldots, k , \qquad \tau = 1, 2, \ldots, n ,$$

stands for the value of the τth observation on the ith variable. If we knew the multivariate frequency distribution of our variables, we would have a *complete description* of the relationship existing between them. But we don't. Suppose that, on grounds not exclusively derived from the observations, we can assume that there exists a *linear* relation between these variables:

$$(1.2a) \qquad A_0 + \sum_i A_i X_i = 0 .$$

From this equation we obtain the computed value $X_i'^{(\tau)}$ of X_i corresponding to the τth observation, and hence

$$(1.2b) \qquad A_0 + A_1 X_1'^{(\tau)} + \ldots + A_i X_i'^{(\tau)} + \ldots + A_k X_k'^{(\tau)} = 0 ,$$

for every $\tau = 1, 2, \ldots, n$. The observations, however, fail to satisfy this relation exactly; there exist differences, called *residuals*, between the observed and the computed values:

$$(1.3) \qquad V_i^{(\tau)} = X_i^{(\tau)} - X_i'^{(\tau)} ,$$

---

* Based on lecture and laboratory notes. I am grateful to my assistants, Jacob L. Mosak and Elizabeth J. Slotkin, for help in preparing these notes for publication, and to my former assistant, Dr. Yue Kei Wong, for reading the final draft of the manuscript.

715

which give rise to the *observation equations:*

(1.4) $\quad A_0 + A_1(X_1^{(\tau)} - V_1^{(\tau)}) + \ldots + A_i(X_i^{(\tau)} - V_i^{(\tau)})$
$$+ \ldots + A_k(X_k^{(\tau)} - V_k^{(\tau)}) = 0.$$

The problem is to estimate the coefficients A_i and to judge the reliability of these estimates.

This problem does not admit of a solution unless we (1) adopt a definite criterion for estimation and (2) assign *weights* to the different variables, reflecting our judgment of their relative accuracy or importance. Moreover, *the weight assigned to any one variable must be taken as constant for all the observations on that variable.* Adopting the least squares criterion, we reduce our problem to that of determining the values of the coefficients A_i which minimize the sum of the weighted squares of the residuals.

The problem may be stated as follows:

Let w_i stand for the (constant) weight of $X_i^{(\tau)}$ for every τ. Then for the τth observation, the sum of the weighted squares of the residuals is

(1.5a) $\qquad\qquad w_1 V_1^{(\tau)2} + \ldots + w_i V_i^{(\tau)2} + \ldots + w_k V_k^{(\tau)2} ,$

or

(1.5b) $$\sum_{i=1}^{k} w_i V_i^{(\tau)2} .$$

For all n observations, the weighted sum is

(1.6) $$\sum_{\tau=1}^{n} \sum_{i=1}^{k} w_i V_i^{(\tau)2} .$$

The problem is to determine the values of the A's which minimize (1.6).

The weights represent our estimate of the relative accuracies of the different variables. They may have any value between zero and infinity. *A zero weight does not mean, however, that the variable to which it is attached is to be discarded. On the contrary, that variable is the one whose sum-square residuals are to be minimized.* All that the zero weight signifies is that, with respect to the variable to which it is attached, all the other variables have infinite weights; for it is the *relative*, and not the absolute, weights which are significant. To assign a zero weight to more than one variable is to render the problem indeterminate.

Since it is the relative weights which matter, we may, without loss of generality, divide all the weights by any one of them—say w_1—thus obtaining

(1.7a) $\qquad f^{(\tau)} = V_1^{(\tau)2} + \ldots + \dfrac{w_i}{w_1} V_i^{(\tau)2} + \ldots + \dfrac{w_k}{w_1} V_k^{(\tau)2}$

in place of (1.5), and

(1.8a) $\qquad F \equiv \Sigma f^{(\tau)} = \Sigma V_1^{(\tau)2} + \ldots + \dfrac{w_i}{w_1} \Sigma V_i^{(\tau)2} + \ldots + \dfrac{w_k}{w_1} \Sigma V_k^{(\tau)2}$

in place of (1.6), the summation extending from $\tau = 1$ to $\tau = n$.

If now we let w_1 approach zero, then, since the other weights are finite and different from zero, the ratios $w_i/w_1, \ldots, w_k/w_1$ approach infinity, which means that the variables $X_i, \ldots, X_k$ are thus given infinite weights. But when we assign an infinite weight to a variable, we are assuming that its residuals are zero: that the failure of any observed point to fall on the curve is brought about by inaccuracies in the other variables, the variable in question being measured with perfect accuracy. Consequently all the residuals in (1.7a) and (1.8a) except V_1 vanish; and it can be shown that the products of these residuals by their infinite weights also vanish,[1] so that equations (1.7a) and (1.8a) reduce to

(1.7b)
$$f^{(\tau)} = V_1^{(\tau)2}$$

and

(1.8b)
$$F \equiv \Sigma f^{(\tau)} = \Sigma V_1^{(\tau)2},$$

respectively.

The weights have also a geometric meaning. They determine the *direction* in which an observed point must be moved in order to become adjusted. If, for example, $w_1 = 0$, the point is moved along a line which is parallel to the X_1-axis. If all the weights are equal, the point is moved along a line which is perpendicular to the curve (i.e., the hyperplane [1.2a]). The assignment of relative weights to the variables constitutes, therefore, the first step in the curve-fitting process.

II. A SPECIAL CASE OF THE METHOD OF LEAST SQUARES: ONLY ONE VARIABLE SUBJECT TO ERROR

The solution of the problem when all the weights are finite may be designated as the *generalized least-squares procedure*. For two variables the solution is given in chapter iv, footnote 31. The solution becomes progressively more difficult as we increase the number of variables. For this reason, as well as for the fact that in most of our demand analyses the variables price and time were so much more accurate than con-

---

[1] If we minimize (1.8a), we obtain the following relation between the residuals and the weights of any two variables X_1 and X_i:

(i)
$$\frac{w_i}{w_1} = \frac{V_1^{(\tau)}}{V_i^{(\tau)}} b,$$

where $b = - \dfrac{\partial F}{\partial X_i} \Big/ \dfrac{\partial F}{\partial X_1}$ is the slope of the curve at the point under consideration. Now $V_1^{(\tau)}$ and $V_i^{(\tau)}$ cannot both be zero for all the observations. Since b and all the V's must be finite or the problem is meaningless, it follows that, as w_1 approaches zero, $V_i^{(\tau)}$ also approaches zero, and the terms $\frac{w_i}{w_1} \Sigma V_i^{(\tau)2}$ in (1.8a) assume the form $\infty \cdot 0^2$. To evaluate this expression, we multiply (i) by $V_i^{(\tau)2}$ and sum for all the observations, obtaining

(ii)
$$\frac{w_i}{w_1} \Sigma V_i^{(\tau)2} = \Sigma V_1^{(\tau)} V_i^{(\tau)} \cdot b.$$

When w_1 and hence $V_i^{(\tau)}$ approach zero, the right-hand side of (ii) vanishes, and $\frac{w_i}{w_1} \Sigma V_i^{(\tau)2} = 0$. This holds for all values of i $(i = 2, \ldots, k)$, and (1.8a) thus reduces to (1.8b).

sumption, we felt quite justified in giving price and time infinite weights as compared with consumption, i.e., in minimizing the sum of the squares of the consumption residuals.[2] It will, therefore, be quite sufficient for our purposes if we consider only the special case in which all the weights but one are infinite, i.e., in which the sums of the squares of the residuals of all variables but one are zero. That variable will be referred to as the *dependent variable*, and its regression on all the other variables as the *elementary regression equation*. From the purely mathematical point of view, anyone of the k variables may be considered as the dependent variable. There are, then, as many elementary regression equations as there are variables. It is one of the main objects of this appendix to show how to deduce all the elementary regression equations simultaneously. For convenience, however, we shall first consider the derivation of only one of these equations.

A. DEFINITIONS

Let X_1 be the dependent variable. Then all the residuals except $V_1^{(\tau)}$ are put equal to zero, and the observation equation (1.4) becomes

$$(2.1) \quad A_0 + A_1(X_1^{(\tau)} - V_1^{(\tau)}) + A_2 X_2^{(\tau)} + \ldots + A_i X_i^{(\tau)} + \ldots + A_k X_k^{(\tau)} = 0.$$

We can put this equation in the more conventional form by transposing all the terms not involving $V_1^{(\tau)}$ to the right side of the equality sign, dividing all coefficients by A_1. Designating the constant term $-A_0/A_1$ by b_{11} and the regression coefficients $-A_i/A_1$ of X_1 on X_i by b_{1i}, $(i = 2, \ldots, k)$, we obtain

$$(2.2) \quad V_1^{(\tau)} = X_1^{(\tau)} - (b_{11} + b_{12} X_2^{(\tau)} + \ldots + b_{1i} X_i^{(\tau)} + \ldots + b_{1k} X_k^{(\tau)}),$$

which is the definition (1.3) applied to this special case, the expression in parenthesis being equal to the computed value $X_1'^{(\tau)}$.

Substituting this expression in (1.8b), we obtain

$$(2.3) \quad F = \sum_{\tau=1}^{n} V_1^{(\tau)2} = \sum_{\tau=1}^{n} [X_1^{(\tau)} - (b_{11} + b_{12} X_2^{(\tau)} + \ldots + b_{1i} X_i^{(\tau)}$$
$$+ \ldots + b_{1k} X_k^{(\tau)})]^2.$$

We are to determine the values of the b's so that this expression becomes a minimum.

Differentiating F partially with respect to $b_{11}, b_{12}, \ldots, b_{1k}$, and setting each derivative equal to zero, we obtain

$$(2.4a) \quad -2\Sigma V_1 = 0, \quad -2\Sigma X_2 V_1 = 0, \ldots, -2\Sigma X_i V_1 = 0, \ldots, -2\Sigma X_k V_1 = 0.$$

Since all the summations are over the entire range of the observations, from $\tau = 1$ to $\tau = n$, it would be pedantic to indicate the limits in each equation. Consequently they are omitted together with the superscript of X_i.

---

[2] Although, in the statistical chapters, we have also given the regressions of price on quantity and time, we have repeatedly indicated that, in general, these equations are not of as great importance as the regressions of quantity on price and time.

Substituting for V_1 from (2.2), we have the following k equations, called *normal equations:*

$$(2.4b) \begin{cases} b_{11}n + b_{12}\Sigma X_2 + \ldots + b_{1i}\Sigma X_i + \ldots + b_{1k}\Sigma X_k - \Sigma X_1 = 0 \\ b_{11}\Sigma X_2 + b_{12}\Sigma X_2^2 + \ldots + b_{1i}\Sigma X_2 X_i + \ldots + b_{1k}\Sigma X_2 X_k - \Sigma X_1 X_2 = 0 \\ \cdot \quad \cdot \quad \cdot \quad \cdot \quad \cdot \quad \cdot \quad \cdot \quad \cdot \quad \cdot \quad \cdot \quad \cdot \quad \cdot \quad \cdot \quad \cdot \quad \cdot \\ b_{11}\Sigma X_i + b_{12}\Sigma X_2 X_i + \ldots + b_{1i}\Sigma X_i^2 + \ldots + b_{1k}\Sigma X_i X_k - \Sigma X_1 X_i = 0 \\ \cdot \quad \cdot \quad \cdot \quad \cdot \quad \cdot \quad \cdot \quad \cdot \quad \cdot \quad \cdot \quad \cdot \quad \cdot \quad \cdot \quad \cdot \quad \cdot \quad \cdot \\ b_{11}\Sigma X_k + b_{12}\Sigma X_2 X_k + \ldots + b_{1i}\Sigma X_i X_k + \ldots + b_{1k}\Sigma X_k^2 - \Sigma X_1 X_k = 0 \end{cases}$$

from which to determine the k unknown b's.

B. EVALUATION OF THE REGRESSION COEFFICIENTS BY DETERMINANTS

Let

$$(2.5) \qquad D = \begin{vmatrix} n & \Sigma X_2 & \ldots \Sigma X_i & \ldots \Sigma X_k \\ \Sigma X_2 & \Sigma X_2^2 & \ldots \Sigma X_2 X_i & \ldots \Sigma X_2 X_k \\ \cdot & \cdot & \cdot & \cdot & \cdot & \cdot \\ \Sigma X_i & \Sigma X_2 X_i & \ldots \Sigma X_i^2 & \ldots \Sigma X_i X_k \\ \cdot & \cdot & \cdot & \cdot & \cdot & \cdot \\ \Sigma X_k & \Sigma X_2 X_k & \ldots \Sigma X_i X_k & \ldots \Sigma X_k^2 \end{vmatrix}$$

and let D_{rc} denote the cofactor of the element in the rth row and the cth column. It will be observed that the determinant D is symmetric. Then the solution of $(2.4b)$ is

$$(2.6) \qquad b_{1i} = \frac{1}{D} \begin{vmatrix} n & \Sigma X_2 & \ldots \Sigma X_1 & \ldots \Sigma X_k \\ \Sigma X_2 & \Sigma X_2^2 & \ldots \Sigma X_1 X_2 & \ldots \Sigma X_2 X_k \\ \cdot & \cdot & \cdot & \cdot & \cdot & \cdot \\ \Sigma X_i & \Sigma X_2 X_i & \ldots \Sigma X_1 X_i & \ldots \Sigma X_i X_k \\ \cdot & \cdot & \cdot & \cdot & \cdot & \cdot \\ \Sigma X_k & \Sigma X_2 X_k & \ldots \Sigma X_1 X_k & \ldots \Sigma X_k^2 \end{vmatrix}, \qquad (i = 1, \ldots, k).$$

Expanding the determinants in the numerators of (2.6), we have:

$$(2.7) \begin{cases} b_{11} = \frac{D_{11}}{D} \Sigma X_1 + \frac{D_{21}}{D} \Sigma X_1 X_2 + \ldots + \frac{D_{i1}}{D} \Sigma X_1 X_i + \ldots + \frac{D_{k1}}{D} \Sigma X_1 X_k \\ \cdot \quad \cdot \quad \cdot \quad \cdot \quad \cdot \quad \cdot \quad \cdot \quad \cdot \quad \cdot \quad \cdot \quad \cdot \quad \cdot \quad \cdot \\ b_{1i} = \frac{D_{1i}}{D} \Sigma X_1 + \frac{D_{2i}}{D} \Sigma X_1 X_2 + \ldots + \frac{D_{ii}}{D} \Sigma X_1 X_i + \ldots + \frac{D_{ki}}{D} \Sigma X_1 X_k \\ \cdot \quad \cdot \quad \cdot \quad \cdot \quad \cdot \quad \cdot \quad \cdot \quad \cdot \quad \cdot \quad \cdot \quad \cdot \quad \cdot \quad \cdot \\ b_{1k} = \frac{D_{1k}}{D} \Sigma X_1 + \frac{D_{2k}}{D} \Sigma X_1 X_2 + \ldots + \frac{D_{ik}}{D} \Sigma X_1 X_i + \ldots + \frac{D_{kk}}{D} \Sigma X_1 X_k, \end{cases}$$

where $D_{rc} = D_{cr}$, since the determinant D is symmetric.

C. EVALUATION OF THE WEIGHTS AND STANDARD ERRORS OF THE REGRESSION COEFFICIENTS BY DETERMINANTS

Having determined the probable values of the regression coefficients, we proceed to derive their standard errors and the standard error of any computed value of the dependent variable, i.e., the standard error of the function. This necessitates the determination of the following auxiliary values: (1) the quadratic mean error or "the standard error of a single observation of unit weight," (2) the weight of each parameter, and (3) the weight of the function. The weights of the parameters and the weight of the function are not to be confused with the weights w_i assigned to the variables X_i $(i = 1, \ldots, k)$ in Section I. The latter are the givens of the problem; the former have to be computed.

1. THE QUADRATIC MEAN ERROR

Let $\bar{\epsilon}$ denote the standard error, or "the quadratic mean error"[3] of a single observation of unit weight. "Each observation has its own individual error and when we refer to a 'single observation' in this connection, we mean an observation such as those in the set which is being discussed, not any single one of them, but a hypothetical one which is never evaluated, but which is typical of the entire set in so far as precision is concerned."[4] In this sense only may it be taken as the common or mean error of the observed values, $X_1^{(1)}, \ldots, X_1^{(\tau)}, \ldots, X_1^{(n)}$. Its exact value is given by the equation

$$(2.8) \qquad \bar{\epsilon}_1^2 = \frac{1}{n} \sum_{\tau=1}^{n} E_1^{(\tau)2} ,$$

where E_1 is the error, or the difference between the *true* value of the unknown and its observed value. It may also be written as

$$(2.9) \qquad \bar{\epsilon}_1^2 = \frac{1}{n-k} \cdot \frac{\displaystyle\sum_{s=1}^{N} \sum_{\tau=1}^{n} V_1^{(\tau)2}}{N} ,$$

where N is the number of samples, s (assumed to be indefinitely large). In most investigations N is small, frequently not exceeding unity. We therefore substitute for $\bar{\epsilon}_1^2$ the approximate value,

$$(2.10a) \qquad \epsilon_1^2 = \frac{\displaystyle\sum_{\tau=1}^{n} V_1^{(\tau)2}}{n-k} .$$

If in computing the well-known "standard error of estimate," S_1, where

$$S_1^2 = \frac{\displaystyle\sum_{\tau=1}^{n} (X_1^{(\tau)} - X_1'^{(\tau)})^2}{n} ,$$

[3] The term "quadratic mean error" is that used by Whittaker and Robinson. Gauss calls ϵ simply the "mean error," a term still employed by German writers on the method of least squares.

[4] Ora Miner Leland, *Practical Least Squares* (New York, 1921), p 161.

we divide the sum of the squares of the difference not by n, but by n less the number of "constants" in the regression equation, the result is equal to ϵ_1^2, or

(2.10b)
$$\epsilon_1^2 = \frac{n}{n-k} S_1^2 .$$

It will be seen from (2.10a) that, to determine ϵ_1, we must know the sum of the squares of the residuals of X_1. This is given by the convenient formula[5]

(2.11) $\Sigma V_1^2 = \Sigma X_1^2 - b_{11} \Sigma X_1 - b_{12} \Sigma X_1 X_2 - \ldots - b_{1i} \Sigma X_1 X_i - \ldots$
$$- b_{1k} \Sigma X_1 X_k .$$

2. THE WEIGHTS AND THE STANDARD ERRORS OF THE REGRESSION COEFFICIENTS

Since in (2.7) the b's are linear in $X_1^{(1)}, \ldots, X_1^{(\tau)}, \ldots, X_1^{(n)}$, we may write equations (2.7) as

(2.12)
$$\begin{cases} b_{11} = a_{1.1}^{(1)} X_1^{(1)} + \ldots + a_{1.1}^{(\tau)} X_1^{(\tau)} + \ldots + a_{1.1}^{(n)} X_1^{(n)} = \sum_{\tau=1}^{n} a_{1.1}^{(\tau)} X_1^{(\tau)} \\ \cdot \quad \cdot \quad \cdot \quad \cdot \quad \cdot \quad \cdot \quad \cdot \quad \cdot \quad \cdot \quad \cdot \quad \cdot \quad \cdot \\ b_{1i} = a_{1.i}^{(1)} X_1^{(1)} + \ldots + a_{1.i}^{(\tau)} X_1^{(\tau)} + \ldots + a_{1.i}^{(n)} X_1^{(n)} = \sum_{\tau=1}^{n} a_{1.i}^{(\tau)} X_1^{(\tau)} \\ \cdot \quad \cdot \quad \cdot \quad \cdot \quad \cdot \quad \cdot \quad \cdot \quad \cdot \quad \cdot \quad \cdot \quad \cdot \quad \cdot \\ b_{1k} = a_{1.k}^{(1)} X_1^{(1)} + \ldots + a_{1.k}^{(\tau)} X_1^{(\tau)} + \ldots + a_{1.k}^{(n)} X_1^{(n)} = \sum_{\tau=1}^{n} a_{1.k}^{(\tau)} X_1^{(\tau)} \end{cases}$$

in which the a's are functions of the X_i's of equation (2.2) to be defined later.

In these equations the unknown b's have been expressed as linear functions of $X_1^{(1)}, \ldots, X_1^{(\tau)}, \ldots, X_1^{(n)}$. Since these observations are, by assumption, independent of each other, and since $\bar{\epsilon}_1^2$ is the mean square error of each X_1, we have, by the formula for "the mean square error" or the square of the standard error of a linear function of several independent quantities,[6]

(2.13)
$$\begin{cases} \sigma_{b_{11}}^2 = a_{1.1}^{(1)2} \cdot \bar{\epsilon}_1^2 + \ldots + a_{1.1}^{(\tau)2} \cdot \bar{\epsilon}_1^2 + \ldots + a_{1.1}^{(n)2} \cdot \bar{\epsilon}_1^2 = \bar{\epsilon}_1^2 \sum_{\tau=1}^{n} a_{1.1}^{(\tau)2} \\ \cdot \quad \cdot \quad \cdot \quad \cdot \quad \cdot \quad \cdot \quad \cdot \quad \cdot \quad \cdot \quad \cdot \quad \cdot \quad \cdot \\ \sigma_{b_{1i}}^2 = a_{1.i}^{(1)2} \cdot \bar{\epsilon}_1^2 + \ldots + a_{1.i}^{(\tau)2} \cdot \bar{\epsilon}_1^2 + \ldots + a_{1.i}^{(n)2} \cdot \bar{\epsilon}_1^2 = \bar{\epsilon}_1^2 \sum_{\tau=1}^{n} a_{1.i}^{(\tau)2} \\ \cdot \quad \cdot \quad \cdot \quad \cdot \quad \cdot \quad \cdot \quad \cdot \quad \cdot \quad \cdot \quad \cdot \quad \cdot \quad \cdot \\ \sigma_{b_{1k}}^2 = a_{1.k}^{(1)2} \cdot \bar{\epsilon}_1^2 + \ldots + a_{1.k}^{(\tau)2} \cdot \bar{\epsilon}_1^2 + \ldots + a_{1.k}^{(n)2} \cdot \bar{\epsilon}_1^2 = \bar{\epsilon}_1^2 \sum_{\tau=1}^{n} a_{1.k}^{(\tau)2} . \end{cases}$$

[5] The proof is simple. Multiply (2.2) by $V_1^{(\tau)}$ and sum all n observation equations, making use of (2.4a). The result is

(i)
$$\Sigma V_1^2 = \Sigma X_1 V_1 .$$

Now multiply (2.2) by $X_1^{(\tau)}$ and sum all n equations. Substituting in (i), we obtain (2.11).

[6] T. W. Wright and J. F. Hayford, *The Adjustment of Observations* (2d ed.; New York, 1906), Art. 53, pp. 62–63.

Let us designate the sums on the right-hand side of (2.13) by $c_{1.11}, \ldots, c_{1.ii}, \ldots,$ $c_{1.kk}$. Their reciprocals, which we may designate by $w_{1.11}, \ldots, w_{1.ii}, \ldots, w_{1.kk}$, are the *weights* of $b_{11}, \ldots, b_{1i}, \ldots, b_{1k}$, respectively.[7] Thus

$$(2.14) \quad \begin{cases} c_{1.11} = \dfrac{1}{w_{1.11}} = \displaystyle\sum_{\tau=1}^{n} a_{1.1}^{(\tau)2} \\[2ex] \cdots \cdots \cdots \cdots \\[1ex] c_{1.ii} = \dfrac{1}{w_{1.ii}} = \displaystyle\sum_{\tau=1}^{n} a_{1.i}^{(\tau)2} \\[2ex] \cdots \cdots \cdots \cdots \\[1ex] c_{1.kk} = \dfrac{1}{w_{1.kk}} = \displaystyle\sum_{\tau=1}^{n} a_{1.k}^{(\tau)2} . \end{cases}$$

Hence by (2.13):

$$(2.15a) \quad \begin{cases} \sigma_{b_{11}}^2 = c_{1.11}\,\bar{\epsilon}_1^2 \\[1ex] \cdots \cdots \cdots \\[1ex] \sigma_{b_{1i}}^2 = c_{1.ii}\,\bar{\epsilon}_1^2 \\[1ex] \cdots \cdots \cdots \\[1ex] \sigma_{b_{1k}}^2 = c_{1.kk}\,\bar{\epsilon}_1^2 . \end{cases}$$

As was pointed out above, the true value $\bar{\epsilon}_1^2$ is unknown in most investigations, and we must substitute for it the approximate value ϵ_1^2. It follows, therefore, that we cannot obtain the true values $\sigma_{b_{1i}}^2$ but only the approximate values

$$(2.15b) \quad \begin{cases} s_{b_{11}}^2 = c_{1.11}\,\epsilon_1^2 \\[1ex] \cdots \cdots \cdots \\[1ex] s_{b_{1i}}^2 = c_{1.ii}\,\epsilon_1^2 \\[1ex] \cdots \cdots \cdots \\[1ex] s_{b_{1k}}^2 = c_{1.kk}\,\epsilon_1^2 . \end{cases}$$

To evaluate the c's, we must first evaluate the a's. These quantities are the coefficients of $X_1^{(1)}, \ldots, X_1^{(\tau)}, \ldots, X_1^{(n)}$ in (2.12).

Comparing (2.12) with (2.7), it is clear that the a's can be evaluated by equating

[7] In these quantities the subscript to the left of the period designates the dependent variable, while the subscripts to the right of the period designate the independent variables. For the sake of symmetry, the reciprocal of the weight of the constant term b_{11} is designated $c_{1.11}$. The doubling of the subscripts relating to the independent variables will prove useful later in our discussion of the standard error of the function.

the coefficients of $X_1^{(1)}, \ldots, X_1^{(\tau)}, \ldots, X_1^{(n)}$ in these two sets of equations. Thus, by expanding the first equation of (2.7), we obtain:

$$(2.16a) \quad b_{11} = \frac{D_{11}}{D} (X_1^{(1)} + \ldots + X_1^{(\tau)} + \ldots + X_1^{(n)})$$

$$+ \frac{D_{21}}{D}(X_1^{(1)} X_2^{(1)} + \ldots + X_1^{(\tau)} X_2^{(\tau)} + \ldots + X_1^{(n)} X_2^{(n)})$$

$$+ \ . \quad . \quad . \quad . \quad . \quad . \quad . \quad . \quad . \quad . \quad .$$

$$+ \frac{D_{i1}}{D}(X_1^{(1)} X_i^{(1)} + \ldots + X_1^{(\tau)} X_i^{(\tau)} + \ldots + X_1^{(n)} X_i^{(n)})$$

$$+ \ . \quad . \quad . \quad . \quad . \quad . \quad . \quad . \quad . \quad . \quad .$$

$$+ \frac{D_{k1}}{D}(X_1^{(1)} X_k^{(1)} + \ldots + X_1^{(\tau)} X_k^{(\tau)} + \ldots + X_1^{(n)} X_k^{(n)}) .$$

Collecting the coefficients of $X_1^{(1)}, \ldots, X_1^{(\tau)}, \ldots, X_1^{(n)}$, we may write this equation as:

$$(2.16b) \quad b_{11} = \left(\frac{D_{11}}{D} + \frac{D_{21}}{D} X_2^{(1)} + \ldots + \frac{D_{i1}}{D} X_i^{(1)} + \ldots + \frac{D_{k1}}{D} X_k^{(1)} \right) X_1^{(1)}$$

$$+ \ . \quad . \quad . \quad . \quad . \quad . \quad . \quad . \quad . \quad . \quad . \quad . \quad .$$

$$+ \left(\frac{D_{11}}{D} + \frac{D_{21}}{D} X_2^{(\tau)} + \ldots + \frac{D_{i1}}{D} X_i^{(\tau)} + \ldots + \frac{D_{k1}}{D} X_k^{(\tau)} \right) X_1^{(\tau)}$$

$$+ \ . \quad . \quad . \quad . \quad . \quad . \quad . \quad . \quad . \quad . \quad . \quad . \quad .$$

$$+ \left(\frac{D_{11}}{D} + \frac{D_{21}}{D} X_2^{(n)} + \ldots + \frac{D_{i1}}{D} X_i^{(n)} + \ldots + \frac{D_{k1}}{D} X_k^{(n)} \right) X_1^{(n)} .$$

By the same procedure we may determine the coefficients of $X_1^{(1)}, \ldots, X_1^{(\tau)}, \ldots,$ $X_1^{(n)}$ in all the other equations of (2.12).

Comparing $(2.16b)$ with (2.12), we see that

$$(2.17) \quad \begin{cases} a_{1.1}^{(1)} = \dfrac{D_{11}}{D} + \dfrac{D_{21}}{D} X_2^{(1)} + \ldots + \dfrac{D_{i1}}{D} X_i^{(1)} + \ldots + \dfrac{D_{k1}}{D} X_k^{(1)} \\[6pt] . \quad . \quad . \quad . \quad . \quad . \quad . \quad . \quad . \quad . \quad . \\[6pt] a_{1.1}^{(\tau)} = \dfrac{D_{11}}{D} + \dfrac{D_{21}}{D} X_2^{(\tau)} + \ldots + \dfrac{D_{i1}}{D} X_i^{(\tau)} + \ldots + \dfrac{D_{k1}}{D} X_k^{(\tau)} \\[6pt] . \quad . \quad . \quad . \quad . \quad . \quad . \quad . \quad . \quad . \quad . \\[6pt] a_{1.1}^{(n)} = \dfrac{D_{11}}{D} + \dfrac{D_{21}}{D} X_2^{(n)} + \ldots + \dfrac{D_{i1}}{D} X_i^{(n)} + \ldots + \dfrac{D_{k1}}{D} X_k^{(n)} . \end{cases}$$

Multiplying the first equation of (2.17) by $a_{1.1}^{(1)}$, the τth by $a_{1.1}^{(\tau)}$, etc., and adding the equations, we have

$$(2.18) \quad \Sigma a_{1.1}^{(\tau)2} = \frac{D_{11}}{D} \Sigma a_{1.1}^{(\tau)} + \frac{D_{21}}{D} \Sigma a_{1.1}^{(\tau)} X_2^{(\tau)} + \ldots + \frac{D_{i1}}{D} \Sigma a_{1.1}^{(\tau)} X_i^{(\tau)}$$

$$+ \ldots + \frac{D_{k1}}{D} \Sigma a_{1.1}^{(\tau)} X_k^{(\tau)} ,$$

the summations being from $\tau = 1$ to $\tau = n$.

To obtain $\Sigma a_{1.1}^{(\tau)}$ we add (2.17). The result is

$$(2.19a) \quad \Sigma a_{1.1}^{(\tau)} = \frac{D_{11}}{D} n + \frac{D_{21}}{D} \Sigma X_2^{(\tau)} + \ldots + \frac{D_{i1}}{D} \Sigma X_i^{(\tau)} + \ldots + \frac{D_{k1}}{D} \Sigma X_k^{(\tau)}$$

or, multiplying by D,

$$(2.19b) \quad D\Sigma a_{1.1}^{(\tau)} = D_{11} n + D_{21} \Sigma X_2^{(\tau)} + \ldots + D_{i1} \Sigma X_i^{(\tau)} + \ldots + D_{k1} \Sigma X_k^{(\tau)} .$$

The right-hand side of this equation is the expansion of the determinant D—see (2.4) —in terms of the elements in the first column. Hence (2.19b) may be written as

$$D\Sigma a_{1.1}^{(\tau)} = D ,$$

or

$$(2.20) \qquad\qquad \Sigma a_{1.1}^{(\tau)} = 1 .$$

To find $\Sigma a_{1.1}^{(\tau)} X_2^{(\tau)}$, we multiply both sides of the equations in (2.17) by $X_2^{(\tau)}$. ($\tau = 1, \ldots, n$), and add. We have

$$(2.21a) \quad \Sigma a_{1.1}^{(\tau)} X_2^{(\tau)} = \frac{D_{11}}{D} \Sigma X_2^{(\tau)} + \frac{D_{21}}{D} \Sigma X_2^{(\tau)2} + \ldots + \frac{D_{i1}}{D} \Sigma X_2^{(\tau)} X_i^{(\tau)}$$
$$+ \ldots + \frac{D_{k1}}{D} \Sigma X_2^{(\tau)} X_k^{(\tau)} .$$

When this is multiplied by D, we obtain

$$(2.21b) \quad D \Sigma a_{1.1}^{(\tau)} X_2^{(\tau)} = D_{11} \Sigma X_2^{(\tau)} + D_{21} \Sigma X_2^{(\tau)2} + \ldots + D_{i1} \Sigma X_2^{(\tau)} X_i^{(\tau)}$$
$$+ \ldots + D_{k1} \Sigma X_2^{(\tau)} X_k^{(\tau)} ,$$

The right-hand side of (2.21b) is the expansion of a determinant in which two columns are identical. Therefore,

$$\Sigma a_{1.1}^{(\tau)} X_2^{(\tau)} = 0 .$$

In like manner it can be shown that $\Sigma a_{1.1}^{(\tau)} X_k^{(\tau)} = 0$.
Substituting in (2.18), we obtain

$$(2.22a) \qquad\qquad \Sigma a_{1.1}^{(\tau)2} = \frac{D_{11}}{D} .$$

In like manner it can be shown that

$$(2.22b) \qquad\qquad \Sigma a_{1.2}^{(\tau)2} = \frac{D_{22}}{D} , \qquad \Sigma a_{1.i}^{(\tau)2} = \frac{D_{ii}}{D} .$$

Comparing these results with (2.14), we have for the reciprocals of the weights of $b_{11}, \ldots, b_{1i}, \ldots, b_{1k}$,

$$(2.23a) \qquad \begin{cases} c_{1.11} = \dfrac{D_{11}}{D} \\ \quad \cdot \quad \cdot \quad \cdot \quad \cdot \\ c_{1.ii} = \dfrac{D_{ii}}{D} \\ \quad \cdot \quad \cdot \quad \cdot \\ c_{1.kk} = \dfrac{D_{kk}}{D} \; . \end{cases}$$

In a similar way it can be shown that the reciprocal of the weight $c_{1.ij}$ relating to the covariance[8] of b_{1i} and b_{1j}, i.e.,

$$(2.24) \qquad p_{b_{1i} b_{1j}} \equiv r_{b_{1i} b_{1j}} \sigma_{b_{1i}} \sigma_{b_{1j}},$$

which we shall need in the formula for the standard error of the function, is

$$(2.23b) \qquad c_{1.ij} = \frac{D_{ij}}{D} \; .$$

It should be observed that *the reciprocals of the weights depend only on the independent variables: for the same set of values of the independent variables the weights are the same, no matter what the values of the dependent variable may be.*

Substituting (2.23a) in (2.15), we obtain for the true variances of the regression coefficients

$$(2.25a) \qquad \begin{cases} \sigma_{b_{11}}^2 = \dfrac{D_{11}}{D} \bar{\epsilon}_1^2 \\ \quad \cdot \quad \cdot \quad \cdot \quad \cdot \quad \cdot \\ \sigma_{b_{1i}}^2 = \dfrac{D_{ii}}{D} \bar{\epsilon}_1^2 \\ \quad \cdot \quad \cdot \quad \cdot \quad \cdot \quad \cdot \\ \sigma_{b_{1k}}^2 = \dfrac{D_{kk}}{D} \bar{\epsilon}_1^2 \, , \end{cases}$$

[8] In general, if x and y are two variables measured from their respective means, then their variances are the mean squares

$$\sigma_x^2 = \frac{\Sigma x^2}{n} \, , \quad \text{and} \quad \sigma_y^2 = \frac{\Sigma y^2}{n} \, ;$$

and their covariance is the mean product

$$p_{xy} = \frac{\Sigma xy}{n} = r_{xy} \sigma_x \sigma_y \, .$$

and for the approximate values of the variances

(2.25b)
$$\begin{cases} s^2_{b_{11}} = \dfrac{D_{11}}{D}\, \epsilon_1^2 \\ \cdot\quad\cdot\quad\cdot\quad\cdot\quad\cdot \\ s^2_{b_{1i}} = \dfrac{D_{ii}}{D}\, \epsilon_1^2 \\ \cdot\quad\cdot\quad\cdot\quad\cdot\quad\cdot \\ s^2_{b_{1k}} = \dfrac{D_{kk}}{D}\, \epsilon_1^2 \,. \end{cases}$$

Likewise we have for the true covariance of b_{1i} with b_{1j}

(2.26a)
$$\pi_{b_{1i} b_{1j}} = \frac{D_{ij}}{D}\, \bar{\epsilon}_1^2 \,,$$

and for its approximate value

(2.26b)
$$p_{b_{1i} b_{1j}} = \frac{D_{ij}}{D}\, \epsilon_1^2 \,.$$

D. EVALUATION OF THE COEFFICIENTS AND THEIR WEIGHTS BY GAUSS'S METHOD OF SUBSTITUTION

It is a consideration in favor of the determinantal method of solving the normal equations that, as D, $D_{11}, \ldots, D_{ii}, \ldots, D_{kk}$, are calculated in order to find $b_{11}, \ldots, b_{1i}, \ldots, b_{1k}$, the method furnishes the weights without any fresh calculation.[9] We have found it more convenient, however, to use a modified form of Gauss's method of substitution which also furnishes the weights (or their reciprocals) at the same time as the parameters $b_{11}, \ldots, b_{1i}, \ldots, b_{1k}$, and provides a very convenient check on the arithmetic.

From (2.7) it is clear that the reciprocal of the weight of b_{11}, i.e., $D_{11}/D \equiv c_{1.11}$, is what the value of b_{11} becomes when ΣX_1 is replaced by 1, and $\Sigma X_1 X_2, \ldots, \Sigma X_1 X_k$ are each replaced by 0. When these substitutions are made, the values of $b_{12}, \ldots, b_{1k}$ become $D_{12}/D \equiv c_{1.12}, \ldots, D_{1k}/D \equiv c_{1.1k}$.

Also, the reciprocal of the weight of b_{12}, i.e., $D_{22}/D \equiv c_{1.22}$, is what the value of b_{12} becomes when $\Sigma X_1 X_2$ is replaced by 1, and ΣX_1 and $\Sigma X_1 X_3, \ldots, \Sigma X_1 X_k$ are each replaced by 0. When these substitutions are made, the values of b_{11} and b_{13}, $\ldots, b_{1k}$ become $D_{21}/D \equiv c_{1.21}, \ldots, D_{2k}/D \equiv c_{1.2k}$, respectively.

And similarly for each of the unknowns in succession.

But since the values $\Sigma X_1, \Sigma X_1 X_2, \ldots, \Sigma X_1 X_k$ form the last column of the normal equations (2.4b), we may summarize the foregoing conclusions in the following.

Rule:[10] In the first normal equation (2.4b) write 1 for ΣX_1, and in the other normal equations put 0 for each $\Sigma X_1 X_2, \ldots, \Sigma X_1 X_k$; the value of b_{11} found from these equations will be the reciprocal of the weight of b_{11}, and the values of $b_{12}, \ldots, b_{1k}$

---

[9] E. T. Whittaker and G. Robinson, *The Calculus of Observations* (New York, 1924), p. 241.

[10] See Wright and Hayford, *op. cit.*, Art. 98, p. 124.

found will be the values of $D_{12}/D \equiv c_{1.12}, \ldots, D_{1k}/D \equiv c_{1.1k}$. In the second normal equation write 1 for $\Sigma X_1 X_2$, and 0 for each of ΣX_1, and $\Sigma X_1 X_3, \ldots, \Sigma X_1 X_k$; the value of b_{12} found from these equations will be the reciprocal of the weight of b_{12}, and the values of $b_{11}, \ldots, b_{1k}$ found will be $D_{21}/D \equiv c_{1.21}, \ldots, D_{2k}/D \equiv c_{1.2k}$. Similarly for each of the unknowns in succession. Thus, for four unknowns, the weight

A

$c_{1.11}$	$c_{1.12}$	$c_{1.13}$	$c_{1.14}$	R
n	ΣX_2	ΣX_3	ΣX_4	-1
ΣX_2	ΣX_2^2	$\Sigma X_2 X_3$	$\Sigma X_2 X_4$	0
ΣX_3	$\Sigma X_2 X_3$	ΣX_3^2	$\Sigma X_3 X_4$	0
ΣX_4	$\Sigma X_2 X_4$	$\Sigma X_3 X_4$	ΣX_4^2	0

B

$c_{1.12}$	$c_{1.22}$	$c_{1.23}$	$c_{1.24}$	S
n	ΣX_2	ΣX_3	ΣX_4	0
ΣX_2	ΣX_2^2	$\Sigma X_2 X_3$	$\Sigma X_2 X_4$	-1
ΣX_3	$\Sigma X_2 X_3$	ΣX_3^2	$\Sigma X_3 X_4$	0
ΣX_4	$\Sigma X_2 X_4$	$\Sigma X_3 X_4$	ΣX_4^2	0

C

$c_{1.13}$	$c_{1.23}$	$c_{1.33}$	$c_{1.34}$	T
n	ΣX_2	ΣX_3	ΣX_4	0
ΣX_2	ΣX_2^2	$\Sigma X_2 X_3$	$\Sigma X_2 X_4$	0
ΣX_3	$\Sigma X_2 X_3$	ΣX_3^2	$\Sigma X_3 X_4$	-1
ΣX_4	$\Sigma X_2 X_4$	$\Sigma X_3 X_4$	ΣX_4^2	0

D

$c_{1.14}$	$c_{1.24}$	$c_{1.34}$	$c_{1.44}$	U
n	ΣX_2	ΣX_3	ΣX_4	0
ΣX_2	ΣX_2^2	$\Sigma X_2 X_3$	$\Sigma X_2 X_4$	0
ΣX_3	$\Sigma X_2 X_3$	ΣX_3^2	$\Sigma X_3 X_4$	0
ΣX_4	$\Sigma X_2 X_4$	$\Sigma X_3 X_4$	ΣX_4^2	-1

FIG. I.—Subsidiary sets of equations for solving for the weights of the parameters of a regression equation.

Line No.	b_{11}	b_{12}	b_{13}	b_{14}		R	S	T	U	Sum-Check
I	n	ΣX_2	ΣX_3	ΣX_4	$-\Sigma X_1$	-1	0	0	0	Σ_1
II		ΣX_2^2	$\Sigma X_2 X_3$	$\Sigma X_2 X_4$	$-\Sigma X_1 X_2$	0	-1	0	0	Σ_2
III			ΣX_3^2	$\Sigma X_3 X_4$	$-\Sigma X_1 X_3$	0	0	-1	0	Σ_3
IV				ΣX_4^2	$-\Sigma X_1 X_4$	0	0	0	-1	Σ_4

FIG. II.—Combined form for obtaining the regression coefficients and their weights.

equations are shown in Figure I. The negative sign is attached to the digit 1 in the R, S, T, U columns because in our normal equations $(2.4b)$ we have put all terms to the left of the equality signs.

To solve these weight equations directly would be excessively troublesome. It is possible, however, to combine the solution of all these subsidiary sets of normal equations with the ordinary solution for the unknowns, as in Figure II.

The double vertical line divides Figure II into two parts. The entries in the first five columns are the normal equations (2.4b), with the unknown b's put at the head of the columns. Since the coefficients of the b's in (2.4b) constitute a determinant which is symmetrical about the principal diagonal, and since the method of solution causes terms to the left of the diagonal to become zero as the variables are eliminated, we have omitted these terms[11] in Figure II. The entries in the last four columns— those headed R, S, T, U—are the final columns of diagrams A, B, C, and D in Figure I. Figure II shows, therefore, the arrangement of the equations for the simultaneous solution of both the b-coefficients and their weights.

When the R, S, T, and U columns have been added to the normal equations as in Figure II, any of the customary methods for solving the b's may also be made to yield the reciprocals of the weights.[12] The procedure followed in solving many of the equations of the statistical chapters of this book was incorporated in a special form which, together with specially prepared computation sheets, proved very convenient for both laboratory and classroom purposes. We shall not, however, reproduce that form because we replaced it in 1935–36 by a modified form which we shall present later, and which has the advantage of yielding in one solution *all the elementary regressions*, together with their standard errors, all the multiple correlations, and most of the other descriptive constants which we have used. Suffice it to observe that the solution for the c's and the solution for the b's are related to each other. Thus, the line giving the value of b_{14}—the first unknown to be determined—will also give the values of

$$c_{1.14} = \frac{D_{14}}{D}, \quad c_{1.24} = \frac{D_{24}}{D}, \quad c_{1.34} = \frac{D_{34}}{D}, \text{ and } c_{1.44} = \frac{D_{44}}{D}.$$

These will appear as entries in the columns R, S, T, and U, respectively. Similarly, the line from which the value of b_{13} is derived will also yield, by substitution,

$$c_{1.13} = \frac{D_{13}}{D}, \quad c_{1.23} = \frac{D_{23}}{D}, \text{ and } c_{1.33} = \frac{D_{33}}{D};$$

and the line from which b_{12} is derived will yield

$$c_{1.12} = \frac{D_{12}}{D}, \text{ and } c_{1.22} = \frac{D_{22}}{D}.$$

Finally, the last substitution will yield not only b_{11} but also

$$c_{1.11} = \frac{D_{11}}{D}.$$

[11] They must, however, be included in the entries of the "Sum" column or the check cannot be applied. E.g., Σ_2 is the sum of ΣX_2 plus all the items in line II (including the -1).

[12] For convenient forms for solving normal equations see esp. Wright and Hayford, *op. cit.*, arts. 79–97, pp. 101–24, wherein the method of solution due to M. H. Doolittle is explained and illustrated. It is a combination of improvements on the Gaussian method of substitution whose advantage lies mainly in the arrangement of the work in a very convenient form for the computer. The so-called "Doolittle Solution" as given in most textbooks is a misnomer.

If it is desired to compute another regression with a different set of values of the dependent variable *but with the same sets of values of the independent variables*, it is not necessary to solve this form anew. For as we have already seen (p. 725) the weights $c_{1.ij} = D_{ij}/D$ are then identical in the two regressions. And the regression coefficients may readily be computed from (2.7), once we have obtained the new values[13] ΣX_1, $\Sigma X_1 X_2$, ..., $\Sigma X_1 X_k$. This is the method which we used in getting the interrelated demands for beef, pork, and mutton in chapter xix, except that the computations were further simplified by expressing the variables in "standard units" (see Sec. VI).

E. RESTATEMENT OF THE PRECEDING DEVELOPMENTS IN MATRIX FORM

The developments of the preceding sections may be stated more compactly in matrix notation.

Write the *observation equations* (2.2) in the expanded form:

$$(2.2) \quad \begin{cases} V_1^{(1)} = X_1^{(1)} - (b_{11} + b_{12} X_2^{(1)} + b_{13} X_3^{(1)} + \ldots + b_{1k} X_k^{(1)}) \\ V_1^{(2)} = X_1^{(2)} - (b_{11} + b_{12} X_2^{(2)} + b_{13} X_3^{(2)} + \ldots + b_{1k} X_k^{(2)}) \\ \quad \cdot \quad \cdot \quad \cdot \quad \cdot \quad \cdot \quad \cdot \quad \cdot \quad \cdot \quad \cdot \quad \cdot \\ V_1^{(n)} = X_1^{(n)} - (b_{11} + b_{12} X_2^{(n)} + b_{13} X_3^{(n)} + \ldots + b_{1k} X_k^{(n)}) , \end{cases}$$

in which $k < n$.

In matrix notation this may be written as

$$(2.2M) \qquad V_1 = X_1 - X_{)1(} B_1$$

$$\begin{bmatrix} V_1^{(1)} \\ V_1^{(2)} \\ \cdot \\ \cdot \\ \cdot \\ V_1^{(n)} \end{bmatrix} = \begin{bmatrix} X_1^{(1)} \\ X_1^{(2)} \\ \cdot \\ \cdot \\ \cdot \\ X_1^{(n)} \end{bmatrix} - \begin{bmatrix} 1 & X_2^{(1)} & X_3^{(1)} & \ldots & X_k^{(1)} \\ 1 & X_2^{(2)} & X_3^{(2)} & \ldots & X_k^{(2)} \\ \cdot & \cdot & & & \cdot \\ \cdot & \cdot & & & \cdot \\ \cdot & \cdot & & & \cdot \\ 1 & X_2^{(n)} & X_3^{(n)} & \ldots & X_k^{(n)} \end{bmatrix} \times \begin{bmatrix} b_{11} \\ b_{12} \\ \cdot \\ \cdot \\ \cdot \\ b_{1k} \end{bmatrix}$$

$$V_1 \qquad\qquad X_1 \qquad\qquad\qquad X_{)1(} \qquad\qquad\qquad B_1$$

the subscript $)1($ indicating that the observations on the dependent variable are missing from the matrix in question. (In this development we shall retain the equation numbers used in the preceding pages and add the letter M to indicate that the equations are restated in matrix notation.)

The sum of the squares of the residuals is

$$(2.3M) \qquad\qquad V_1' V_1 = \left(X_1' - B_1' X_{)1(}' \right) \left(X_1 - X_{)1(} B_1 \right) .$$

By following the rule (given in H. W. Turnbull and A. C. Aitken, *An Introduction to the Theory of Canonical Matrices* [London and Glasgow, 1932], p. 173) for differen-

---

[13] This fact is also pointed out by R. A. Fisher in his *Statistical Methods for Research Workers* (6th ed.; Edinburgh and New York, 1936), sec. 29.

tiation with respect to a vector, we differentiate $(2.3M)$ with respect to the vector B, set the derivative equal to zero, divide by two, and thus obtain

$(2.4M)$ $$\left(X'_{1(}X_{)1(}\right)B_1 - \left(X'_{1(}X_1\right) = 0 .$$

$$\begin{bmatrix} n & \Sigma X_2 & \Sigma X_3 & \ldots & \Sigma X_k \\ \Sigma X_2 & \Sigma X_2^2 & \Sigma X_2 X_3 & \ldots & \Sigma X_2 X_k \\ \Sigma X_3 & \Sigma X_3 X_2 & \Sigma X_3^2 & \ldots & \Sigma X_3 X_k \\ \cdot & \cdot & \cdot & \ldots & \cdot \\ \cdot & \cdot & \cdot & \ldots & \cdot \\ \cdot & \cdot & \cdot & \ldots & \cdot \\ \Sigma X_k & \Sigma X_k X_2 & \Sigma X_k X_3 & \ldots & \Sigma X_k^2 \end{bmatrix} \times \begin{bmatrix} b_{11} \\ b_{12} \\ b_{13} \\ \cdot \\ \cdot \\ \cdot \\ b_{1k} \end{bmatrix} - \begin{bmatrix} \Sigma X_1 \\ \Sigma X_1 X_2 \\ \Sigma X_1 X_3 \\ \cdot \\ \cdot \\ \cdot \\ \Sigma X_1 X_k \end{bmatrix} = 0 .$$
$$\left(X'_{1(}X_{)1(}\right) \qquad\qquad B_1 \qquad\qquad \left(X'_{1(}X_1\right)$$

Equations $(2.4M)$ are the *normal equations* $(2.4b)$ in matrix form. This form shows clearly their relation to the observation equations.

The solution of $(2.4M)$ is

$(2.7M)$ $$B_1 = \left(X'_{1(}X_{)1(}\right)^{-1}\left(X'_{1(}X_1\right) ,$$

which corresponds to (2.7).

To determine the weight reciprocals $c_{1.ij}$ of the regression coefficients, we proceed as follows: First we write $(2.7M)$ in the form

$(2.12M)$ $$B_1 = \left[\left(X'_{1(}X_{)1(}\right)^{-1}X'_{1(}\right]X_1 \equiv A'_1 X_1 .$$

Then, designating by C_1 the matrix of the weight reciprocals, we see from (2.13) and (2.14) that

$(2.23M)$ $$C_1 = A'_1 A_1 .$$

Substituting for A'_1 its value from $(2.12M)$ and multiplying by its transpose, we obtain

$$A'_1 A_1 = \left[\left(X'_{1(}X_{)1(}\right)^{-1}X'_{1(}\right]\left[X_{)1(}\left\{\left(X'_{1(}X_{)1(}\right)^{-1}\right\}'\right]$$
$$\equiv \left(X'_{1(}X_{)1(}\right)^{-1}\left(X'_{1(}X_{)1(}\right)\left[\left(X'_{1(}X_{)1(}\right)^{-1}\right]' .$$

But

$$\left(X'_{1(}X_{)1(}\right)^{-1}\left(X'_{1(}X_{)1(}\right) = I$$

and

$$\left[\left(X'_{1(}X_{)1(}\right)^{-1}\right]' = \left(X'_{1(}X_{)1(}\right)^{-1} ,$$

since the matrix is symmetric. The value of C_I therefore reduces to

$$(2.23M) \qquad C_I = A_I' A_I \equiv \left(X_{)I(}' X_{)I(}\right)^{-1}$$

$$\begin{bmatrix} c_{1.11} & \cdots & c_{1.1k} \\ \cdot & \cdots & \cdot \\ \cdot & \cdots & \cdot \\ \cdot & \cdots & \cdot \\ c_{1.k1} & \cdots & c_{1.kk} \end{bmatrix} = \begin{bmatrix} \hat{D}_{11} & \cdots & \hat{D}_{1k} \\ \cdot & \cdots & \cdot \\ \cdot & \cdots & \cdot \\ \cdot & \cdots & \cdot \\ \hat{D}_{k1} & \cdots & \hat{D}_{kk} \end{bmatrix}$$

$$C_I \qquad\qquad \left(X_{)I(}'(X_{)I(}\right)^{-1}$$

where $\hat{D}_{ij} = D_{ij}/D$, and D is defined by (2.5).

Similarly we may use the algebra of matrices to derive most of the other formulas of this appendix in a more elegant and compact form. We shall not, however, make further use of the matrix notation, as we prefer to derive our results by the more elementary and, hence, better-known methods.

III.   THE STANDARD ERROR OF THE REGRESSION EQUATION

When the weights of the regression coefficients and ϵ_I have been determined, their standard errors may be found from (2.15). There remains the problem of combining the weights and standard errors of the coefficients so as to obtain the weight and standard error of the computed values of the dependent variable X_I.

The standard error of the dependent variable is what we have called elsewhere "the standard error of a function."[14] Like the standard error of a regression coefficient, its true value may be computed from the formula

$$(3.1a) \qquad \sigma_{f_I}^2 = \bar{\epsilon}_I^2 \, c_{f_I}$$

and its approximate value from the formula

$$(3.1b) \qquad s_{f_I}^2 = \epsilon_I^2 \, c_{f_I} \, ,$$

where c_{f_I} is the reciprocal of the weight of the function X_I'. This is no longer a constant but is a function of the independent variables of the linear equation and of the weights of the regression equations. In terms of the symbols of this appendix it may be written as follows:

Let the computed value of X_I be

$$(3.2) \quad f_I(b_{11}, \ldots, b_{1i}, \ldots, b_{1k}) \equiv X_I' = b_{11} + b_{12} X_2 + \ldots + b_{1i} X_i$$
$$+ \ldots + b_{1k} X_k \, .$$

[14] Henry Schultz, "The Standard Error of a Forecast from a Curve," *Jour. Amer. Statist. Assoc.*, XXV, No. 170 (1930), 139–85.

Then the reciprocal of the weight of X'_1 is

$$(3.3) \quad c_{f_1} = c_{1.11}\left(\frac{\partial f_1}{\partial b_{11}}\right)^2 + \ldots + c_{1.ii}\left(\frac{\partial f_1}{\partial b_{1i}}\right)^2 + \ldots + c_{1.kk}\left(\frac{\partial f_1}{\partial b_{1k}}\right)^2$$

$$+ 2c_{1.12}\frac{\partial f_1}{\partial b_{11}}\frac{\partial f_1}{\partial b_{12}} + \ldots + 2c_{1.ij}\frac{\partial f_1}{\partial b_{1i}}\frac{\partial f_1}{\partial b_{1j}}$$

$$+ \ldots + 2c_{1.(k-1)k}\frac{\partial f_1}{\partial b_{1(k-1)}}\frac{\partial f_1}{\partial b_{1k}},$$

$$i, j = 1, \ldots, k; \quad i < j.$$

The proof for (3.3) appears in the article referred to in footnote 14.

Substituting for the c's their values from (2.23) and for the partial derivatives their values derived from (3.2), and inserting the resulting expression in (3.1b), we obtain for the variance of (3.2)

$$(3.4) \quad s_{f_1}^2 = \epsilon_1^2\left\{\frac{D_{11}}{D} + \frac{D_{22}}{D}X_2^2 + \ldots + \frac{D_{ii}}{D}X_i^2 + \ldots + \frac{D_{kk}}{D}X_k^2\right.$$

$$+ 2\frac{D_{12}}{D}X_2 + \ldots + 2\frac{D_{1i}}{D}X_i + \ldots + 2\frac{D_{1k}}{D}X_k$$

$$\left.+ 2\frac{D_{23}}{D}X_2X_3 + \ldots + 2\frac{D_{ij}}{D}X_iX_j + \ldots + 2\frac{D_{(k-1)k}}{D}X_{(k-1)}X_k\right\}.$$

$$i, j = 2, \ldots, k; \quad i < j.$$

The square root of this expression gives the standard error of any computed value of X_1.

The standard error s_{f_1} has the interesting and important property that it increases without limit as we extrapolate X'_1 beyond the range of the observations.

Although we did not use it in our computations, the value of s_{f_1} enters in the formula for the standard error of the elasticity derived from a linear demand function (see Appen. D: "The Standard Error of the Coefficient of Elasticity of Demand").

IV. STANDARD ERRORS AND TESTS OF SIGNIFICANCE OF REGRESSION COEFFICIENTS

If we knew the true value $\bar{\epsilon}_1^2$, of X_1, we could substitute it in (2.25a) and (2.26a) and obtain the variances and the covariances of the regression coefficients. It can be shown that each coefficient b is normally distributed with a standard deviation σ_b. Consequently, the significance of any deviation of an observed regression b from the assumed true value $\bar{b}$ could be tested by computing $u = (b - \bar{b})/\sigma_b$ and using the Tables of the Normal Probability Integral.[15] Generally the assumption is made that $\bar{b} = 0$.

In practice we rarely, if ever, know $\bar{\epsilon}_1^2$. All that we know is its *approximate value*, ϵ_1^2, and therefore the approximate value s_b. Since ϵ_1 as well as s_b are subject to error, we can no longer use the u-test but must satisfy ourselves with the t-test. This con-

---

[15] To test the significance of the difference between two observed regression coefficients, we need also their co-variance, $\pi_{b_{1i} b_{1j}}$.

sists of computing $t = (b - \bar{b})/s_b$ and judging its significance from "Student's" distribution, which takes into account the number of degrees of freedom from which the b has been computed. The probability that a ratio of $b - \bar{b}$ to s_b greater than or equal to t in absolute value will arise by chance in a sample of size n from which k parameters have been computed, is given by the area under "Student's" distribution (for $n - k$ degrees of freedom) outside of the range $\pm t$. This probability can be conveniently obtained from Table IV of R. A. Fisher's *Statistical Methods for Research Workers*.

A nontechnical explanation of the rationale of statistical tests of significance, and of the difference between the u-test and the t-test, is given in chapter vi, Section III, under the heading, "The Standard Errors," and need not be repeated. It may be useful, however, to give here another interpretation of these subjects—the concepts associated with the names of J. Neyman and E. S. Pearson.[16]

The test of the hypothesis that $\bar{b} = $ o consists in a rule of rejecting the hypothesis tested in certain circumstances specified by some particular criterion, and in non-rejecting it (= "accepting" it, for short) in others. In our particular case the criterion is the sample regression b calculated by least squares. If the hypothesis tested be true, then the distribution of b is normal about a mean of zero.

Now the same value of b may be observed both when $\bar{b} = $ o and when $\bar{b} \neq $ o. Therefore, the test of the hypothesis that $\bar{b} = $ o (and indeed of any other statistical hypothesis) may lead to wrong conclusions. The fallacy of the conclusion may be of two kinds: (1) we may reject the hypothesis tested while it is true and (2) we may accept it though it is wrong. We may reduce the probability of the error (1) to any desired level, say a, by making a rule of rejecting the hypothesis tested, H, when the criterion chosen exceeds a limit, say b_a, such that the chances of its being exceeded, calculated on the assumption of H being true, be equal to a. The proper choice of the criterion minimizes the probability of committing a fallacy of kind (2).

In the particular case described above, if it were desired to reduce the probability of rejecting the hypothesis tested, H, when it is true, to the level $a = $ 4.55 per cent, it would be sufficient to make a rule of rejecting H when the sample regression b differs from zero by more than 2σ. In order to apply this rule, the value of the true standard error σ_b of b must be known. Since it is generally unknown, some other method of testing must be devised having the two essential properties described above: (i) it should reject the hypothesis tested when it is true with a prescribed frequency a and (ii), when the hypothesis tested is wrong, it should detect this circumstance more frequently than any other devisable test.

The criterion having these properties is provided by the ratio $t = (b - \bar{b})/s_b$. If the "true" or population value is $\bar{b} = $ o, then t is distributed according to the law found by "Student," and the excellent tables calculated by R. A. Fisher give the values of t, say t_a, exceeded by chance with specified frequencies 0.9, 0.8, etc., 0.1, 0.05, 0.02, and 0.01. The values of t_a depend on the number of degrees of freedom on which the calculation of s_b is based. When a is fixed—and this is done arbitrarily by the re-

[16] I am indebted to Dr. Neyman for enlightening discussions of these subjects on the occasion of his visit to Chicago in May, 1937. The following explanation is a somewhat condensed version of a brief memorandum which he drew up for my benefit.

search worker—the value of t_a is obtained from the Fisher tables, and then the test of the hypothesis that $\bar{b} = 0$ consists in the rule of rejecting it when $t > t_a$.

Regarding the difference between the u-test and the t-test, Dr. Neyman makes the following important observations:

1. The value of the criterion t may be calculated in both cases, when the true standard error σ_b of b is known, and when it is not. When σ_b is known, then it can be shown that the most sensitive criterion to test H is b and not t, and that under these circumstances the t-test will be less powerful in detecting cases when the hypothesis tested is false.

2. It must be clearly understood that in any particular statistical hypothesis it is possible to devise an infinity of tests all of which will have the same property of rejecting (falsely) the hypothesis tested when it is true with the same frequency a which may be chosen in advance. Among those tests there exists one (maybe more than one) having the property of detecting cases when the hypothesis tested is wrong more frequently than any other. Once such a "most powerful" test is chosen (in the examples above they were b and t, respectively), it is useless and indeed harmful to combine any such test with some other desirable test. This is a warning against the use of the so-called "additional information provided by the sample," consisting in the alternative application of several tests some of them being suggested by the character of the sample obtained. If one of these tests, say ζ, has the property of being the most powerful, then the combination of this test with some other or others, which in fact is equivalent to a new test, is found to be less powerful than ζ itself. Besides, it is possible to prove[17] that, if we are allowed to adjust our test *after* the sample has been drawn, then having a certain mathematical skill, we shall be able to adjust it so as to reject any hypothesis or any sample and, the result of the test being known in advance, *it is useless to perform* any experiments and calculations.

V. SIMPLIFICATION OF THE FORMULAS WHEN THE VARIABLES ARE MEASURED FROM THEIR RESPECTIVE MEANS

The formulas for the regression coefficients, their standard errors, and the standard error of the regression equation developed in the preceding sections do not depend for their validity on the origins of the variables. These may be quite arbitrary. We may, however, effect a simplification in the results if we shift the origins of the several variables to their respective means.

Recalling that X_i denotes the deviation of the variable X_i from an arbitrary origin —say, zero—let us designate the deviation of X_i from its arithmetic mean M_i by x_i or

$$(5.1) \qquad\qquad X_i = x_i + M_i .$$

Substituting this expression for X_i in the *first* of the normal equations $(2.4b)$, and recalling that $\sum_{\tau=1}^{n} x_i^{(\tau)} = 0$, we obtain for the value of the constant term b_{11}

$$(5.2) \qquad\qquad b_{11} = M_1 - b_{12}M_2 - \ldots - b_{1i}M_i - \ldots - b_{1k}M_k ,$$

[17] J. Neyman, "Méthodes nouvelles de vérification des hypothèses statistiques," *C. R. Premier Congrès Math. Pays Slaves* (Warsaw, 1929).

which shows that the hyperplane (2.1) passes through the mean of the dependent variable.

Substituting (5.1) and (5.2) in all of the k normal equations of (2.4b), we reduce them to the form:

$$(5.3) \begin{cases} M_1 n + & \circ & + \ldots + & \circ & + \ldots + & \circ & = M_1 n \\ \circ + b_{12} \Sigma x_2^2 & + \ldots + & b_{1i} \Sigma x_2 x_i & + \ldots + & b_{1k} \Sigma x_2 x_k & = \Sigma x_1 x_2 \\ & & \cdots & & & & \\ \circ + b_{12} \Sigma x_2 x_i & + \ldots + & b_{1i} \Sigma x_i^2 & + \ldots + & b_{1k} \Sigma x_i x_k & = \Sigma x_1 x_i \\ & & \cdots & & & & \\ \circ + b_{12} \Sigma x_2 x_k & + \ldots + & b_{1i} \Sigma x_i x_k & + \ldots + & b_{1k} \Sigma x_k^2 & = \Sigma x_1 x_k . \end{cases}$$

Since the first of these is an identity, we see that the number of normal equations has been reduced by one. But the number of unknowns has also been reduced by one (since M_1 takes the place of b_{11}), so that the system is determinate.

Although the first equation of (5.3) is an identity, it is desirable to retain it in that system in order not to overlook the need for computing the variance of M_1 and the covariances of $M_1 b_{1i}$—quantities which enter into the formula for the standard error of the regression equation (formula [3.4]).

Like the system (2.4b) the system (5.3) together with the subsidiary equations involving the reciprocals of the weights may be solved as in Figure II by Gauss's method of substitution. It will be instructive, however, to express the results in terms of the correlation determinant.

Let D denote the determinant of (5.3):

$$(5.4a) \qquad D = \begin{vmatrix} n & \circ & \ldots \circ & \ldots \circ \\ \circ & \Sigma x_2^2 & \ldots \Sigma x_2 x_i & \ldots \Sigma x_2 x_k \\ \cdot & \cdot & \cdot & \cdot \\ \circ & \Sigma x_2 x_i & \ldots \Sigma x_i^2 & \ldots \Sigma x_i x_k \\ \cdot & \cdot & \cdot & \cdot \\ \circ & \Sigma x_2 x_k & \ldots \Sigma x_i x_k & \ldots \Sigma x_k^2 \end{vmatrix}.$$

Substituting $n r_{ik} \sigma_i \sigma_k$ for $\Sigma x_i x_k$, and factoring out multipliers of the same row or of the same column, we can reduce (5.4a) to the form:

$$(5.4b) \qquad D = n^k \sigma_2^2 \ldots \sigma_i^2 \ldots \sigma_k^2 \begin{vmatrix} 1 & \circ & \ldots \circ & \ldots \circ \\ \circ & 1 & \ldots r_{2i} & \ldots r_{2k} \\ \cdot & \cdot & \cdot & \cdot \\ \circ & r_{i2} & \ldots 1 & \ldots r_{ik} \\ \cdot & \cdot & \cdot & \cdot \\ \circ & r_{k2} & \ldots r_{ki} & \ldots 1 \end{vmatrix},$$

where $1 = r_{ii}$ and $i = 2, \ldots, k$. It should be observed that this expression does not contain correlations involving the dependent variable. These appear in the expressions on the right-hand side of the equality signs of (5.3).

In terms of D, the value of b_{1i} is the ratio of two determinants, the numerator being the determinant (5.4a) with the ith column replaced by the quantities on the right-hand side of (5.3) (i.e., by n, $\Sigma x_1 x_2, \ldots, \Sigma x_1 x_i, \ldots, \Sigma x_1 x_k$), and the denominator being D. Reducing the numerator to a form analogous to (5.4b), and dividing by (5.4b), we obtain:

$$(5.5) \qquad b_{1i} = \frac{\sigma_1}{\sigma_i} \frac{\begin{vmatrix} 1 & 0 & \cdots & 1 & \cdots & 0 \\ 0 & 1 & \cdots & r_{12} & \cdots & r_{2k} \\ \cdot & \cdot & \cdot & \cdot & \cdot & \cdot \\ 0 & r_{i2} & \cdots & r_{1i} & \cdots & r_{ik} \\ \cdot & \cdot & \cdot & \cdot & \cdot & \cdot \\ 0 & r_{k2} & \cdots & r_{1k} & \cdots & 1 \end{vmatrix}}{\begin{vmatrix} 1 & 0 & \cdots & 0 & \cdots & 0 \\ 0 & 1 & \cdots & r_{2i} & \cdots & r_{2k} \\ \cdot & \cdot & \cdot & \cdot & \cdot & \cdot \\ 0 & r_{i2} & \cdots & 1 & \cdots & r_{ik} \\ \cdot & \cdot & \cdot & \cdot & \cdot & \cdot \\ 0 & r_{k2} & \cdots & r_{ki} & \cdots & 1 \end{vmatrix}}, \qquad (i = 2, \ldots, k).$$

This can be expressed in more compact form as follows: Let Δ denote the correlation determinant:

$$(5.6) \qquad \Delta = \begin{vmatrix} 1 & r_{12} & \cdots & r_{1i} & \cdots & r_{1k} \\ r_{21} & 1 & \cdots & r_{2i} & \cdots & r_{2k} \\ \cdot & \cdot & \cdot & \cdot & \cdot & \cdot \\ r_{i1} & r_{i2} & \cdots & 1 & \cdots & r_{ik} \\ \cdot & \cdot & \cdot & \cdot & \cdot & \cdot \\ r_{k1} & r_{k2} & \cdots & r_{ki} & \cdots & 1 \end{vmatrix},$$

so that from (5.4b)

$$(5.7) \qquad D = n^k \sigma_2^2 \ldots \sigma_i^2 \ldots \sigma_k^2 \Delta_{11},$$

where Δ_{11} is the cofactor of the element in the first row and the first column of the correlation determinant Δ.

The values of the regression coefficients when x_1 is the dependent variable may now be expressed by

$$(5.8) \qquad b_{1i} = -\frac{\sigma_1}{\sigma_i} \frac{\Delta_{1i}}{\Delta_{11}}, \qquad (i = 2, \ldots, k).$$

The reciprocals of the weights necessary for the variances of M_1, b_{1i}, and for the covariance of b_{1i} with b_{1j}, are, by (2.23),

$$(5.9) \qquad \begin{cases} c_{1.11} \equiv \dfrac{D_{11}}{D} = \dfrac{1}{n} \\[2mm] c_{1.ii} \equiv \dfrac{D_{ii}}{D} = \dfrac{1}{n\sigma_i^2} \cdot \dfrac{\Delta_{11ii}}{\Delta_{11}} \\[2mm] c_{1.ij} \equiv \dfrac{D_{ij}}{D} = \dfrac{1}{n\sigma_i \sigma_j} \cdot \dfrac{\Delta_{11ij}}{\Delta_{11}}, \end{cases} \qquad (i, j = 2, \ldots, k)$$

where Δ_{ijkl} is obtained from Δ by striking out the ith and kth rows and the jth and lth columns and multiplying by $(-1)^{i+j+k+l}$.

The variances of M_1 and b_{1i}, and the covariance of b_{1i} with b_{1j} are, by (2.25) and (2.26)

$$(5.10) \quad \begin{cases} s^2_{M_1} = \dfrac{\epsilon_1^2}{n} \\ \qquad . \qquad . \qquad . \qquad . \\ s^2_{b_{1i}} = \dfrac{\epsilon_1^2}{n\sigma_i^2} \cdot \dfrac{\Delta_{11ii}}{\Delta_{11}} \\ \qquad . \qquad . \qquad . \qquad . \\ p_{b_{1i}b_{1j}} = \dfrac{\epsilon_1^2}{n\sigma_i\,\sigma_j} \cdot \dfrac{\Delta_{11ij}}{\Delta_{11}} . \end{cases} \qquad (i, j = 2, \ldots, k)$$

It is clear from the preceding sections that, if we had the true value $\bar{\epsilon}_1^2$, we would obtain the true values of the variances (σ^2) and of the covariance (π) by substituting $\bar{\epsilon}_1^2$ for ϵ_1^2 in (5.10). From this point on, however, we shall refer only to the approximate values obtained from the sample and not to the true values.

Since all the elements except the first in the first line and the first column of D are zero, the reciprocals of the weights of M_1, b_{1i} $(i = 2, \ldots, k)$ are all zero, for they involve the terms D_{1i}, which are zero (when the origins of the variables are at their respective means). We have, then,

$$(5.11) \qquad c_{1,1i} = \frac{1}{n\sigma_i} \cdot \frac{\Delta_{111i}}{\Delta_{11}} = 0 .$$

Finally, making use of (5.10), we reduce the formula for the variance of the function (i.e., of the dependent variable x_1') to

$$(5.12) \quad s^2_{f_1} = \epsilon_1^2 \left\{ \frac{D_{11}}{D} + \frac{D_{22}}{D}x_2^2 + \ldots + \frac{D_{ii}}{D}x_i^2 + \ldots + \frac{D_{kk}}{D}x_k^2 \right.$$
$$\left. + 2\frac{D_{23}}{D}x_2 x_3 + \ldots + 2\frac{D_{ij}}{D}x_i x_j + \ldots + 2\frac{D_{(k-1)k}}{D}x_{(k-1)} x_k \right\}$$

in which $i, j = 2, \ldots, k$, $i < j$ and in which the D_{ij}/D have the values defined by (5.9).

VI. FURTHER SIMPLIFICATION OF THE FORMULAS WHEN THE VARIABLES ARE MEASURED IN "STANDARD UNITS"

It is possible to simplify still further the solution for the regression coefficients, their weights, and related parameters, and to deduce additional relations and descriptive constants, if in addition to measuring the variables from their respective means we divide each variable by its standard deviation.

A. THE BETA-COEFFICIENTS AND THEIR STANDARD ERRORS

Instead of writing the linear relation between the variables as

$$(6.1) \qquad x_1' = b_{12}x_2 + \ldots + b_{1i}x_i + \ldots + b_{1k}x_k$$

(the prime indicating a *computed* value of the variable), let us write it as

$$(6.2) \qquad z_1' = \beta_{12}z_2 + \ldots + \beta_{1i}z_i + \ldots + \beta_{1k}z_k ,$$

where

$$(6.3) \qquad z_i = \frac{x_i}{\sigma_i} = \frac{X_i - M_i}{\sigma_i} .$$

Comparing (6.1) and (6.2), we see that

$$(6.4) \qquad b_{1i} = \beta_{1i} \frac{\sigma_1}{\sigma_i} .$$

If we let $z_i^{(\tau)}$ stand for the value of the τth observation on the ith variable, the observation equations become

$$(6.5) \qquad \nu_1^{(\tau)} = z_1^{(\tau)} - (\beta_{12} z_2^{(\tau)} + \ldots + \beta_{1i} z_i^{(\tau)} + \ldots + \beta_{1k} z_k^{(\tau)}) .$$

(It should be noted that the residual ν_1 is measured in units of z_1, and not of X_1, and should not, therefore, be confused with V_1. The relation between the two is, of course, $\nu_1 = V_1/\sigma_1$.) If now we designate by ϕ_1 the sum of the squares of the residuals:

$$(6.6) \quad \phi_1 = \sum_{\tau=1}^{n} \nu_1^{(\tau)2} = \sum_{\tau=1}^{n} [z_1^{(\tau)} - (\beta_{12} z_2^{(\tau)} + \ldots + \beta_{1i} z_i^{(\tau)} + \ldots + \beta_{1k} z_k^{(\tau)})]^2$$

we obtain for our normal equations

$$(6.7) \quad \begin{cases} \beta_{12} \Sigma z_2^2 + \ldots + \beta_{1i} \Sigma z_2 z_i + \ldots + \beta_{1k} \Sigma z_2 z_k = \Sigma z_1 z_2 \\ \cdot \quad \cdot \quad \cdot \quad \cdot \quad \cdot \quad \cdot \quad \cdot \quad \cdot \quad \cdot \quad \cdot \quad \cdot \quad \cdot \quad \cdot \quad \cdot \\ \beta_{12} \Sigma z_2 z_i + \ldots + \beta_{1i} \Sigma z_i^2 + \ldots + \beta_{1k} \Sigma z_i z_k = \Sigma z_1 z_i \\ \cdot \quad \cdot \quad \cdot \quad \cdot \quad \cdot \quad \cdot \quad \cdot \quad \cdot \quad \cdot \quad \cdot \quad \cdot \quad \cdot \quad \cdot \quad \cdot \\ \beta_{12} \Sigma z_2 z_k + \ldots + \beta_{1i} \Sigma z_i z_k + \ldots + \beta_{1k} \Sigma z_k^2 = \Sigma z_1 z_k . \end{cases}$$

Since $\Sigma z_i z_k = n r_{ik}$ and $r_{ii} = 1$, this system of equations reduces, upon division by n, to the form

$$(6.8) \quad \begin{cases} \beta_{12} + \ldots + \beta_{1i} r_{2i} + \ldots + \beta_{1k} r_{2k} = r_{12} \\ \cdot \quad \cdot \quad \cdot \quad \cdot \quad \cdot \quad \cdot \quad \cdot \quad \cdot \quad \cdot \quad \cdot \quad \cdot \quad \cdot \quad \cdot \\ \beta_{12} r_{2i} + \ldots + \beta_{1i} + \ldots + \beta_{1k} r_{ik} = r_{1i} \\ \cdot \quad \cdot \quad \cdot \quad \cdot \quad \cdot \quad \cdot \quad \cdot \quad \cdot \quad \cdot \quad \cdot \quad \cdot \quad \cdot \\ \beta_{12} r_{2k} + \ldots + \beta_{1i} r_{ik} + \ldots + \beta_{1k} = r_{1k} . \end{cases}$$

The solution of this system is exactly analogous to the solution of system (5.3). In terms of the correlation determinant it is[18]

$$(6.9) \qquad \beta_{1i} = \frac{-\Delta_{1i}}{\Delta_{11}} ,$$

[18] See, e.g., Truman Kelley, *Statistical Method* (New York, 1923), pp. 295 ff.

where Δ is defined by (5.6) and Δ_{ij} is the cofactor of r_{ij}. Comparing (6.9) with (5.8), we see that

(6.10)
$$\beta_{1i} = b_{1i} \frac{\sigma_i}{\sigma_1},$$

which is in agreement with (6.4).

Since the conversion of the b's into β's involves simply multiplication by a constant, it follows that the conversion of the σ_b's into σ_β's can be effected by multiplying by the same constant.[19] Now the variance of b_{1i} is given by (5.10). Multiplying it by σ_i^2/σ_1^2, we obtain immediately

(6.11a)
$$s^2_{\beta_{1i}} = \left(\frac{\epsilon_1}{\sigma_1}\right)^2 \frac{1}{n} \frac{\Delta_{11ii}}{\Delta_{11}}.$$

Similarly, by multiplying the covariance of b_{1i} with b_{1j} given in (5.10) by $\sigma_i\sigma_j/\sigma_1^2$, we obtain

(6.11b)
$$p_{\beta_{1i}\beta_{1j}} = \left(\frac{\epsilon_1}{\sigma_1}\right)^2 \cdot \frac{1}{n} \cdot \frac{\Delta_{11ij}}{\Delta_{11}}.$$

The expression $\left(\dfrac{\epsilon_1}{\sigma_1}\right)$ is, of course, the quadratic mean error of z_1, which we will

[19] This presumably obvious proposition hides a fundamental difficulty which is generally overlooked. When we determine $\sigma_{b_{1i}}$ by (2.13) or by the equivalent formulas (2.15) or (2.25), we assume, of course, that b_{1i} varies from sample to sample as a result of variations in the dependent variable X_1, while the independent variables, which are assumed to be perfectly accurate, are kept fixed at given values. Since X_1 has a sampling error, it follows that σ_1 also has a sampling error. However, when we determine $\sigma_{\beta_{1i}}$—this may be done by substituting $\bar{\epsilon}_1$ for ϵ_1 in (6.11a)—we assume that σ_1 is constant from sample to sample, which contradicts the first assumption.

To obtain the value of $\sigma_{\beta_{1i}}$ under the more plausible assumption that σ_1 has a sampling error, we should have to consider σ_i as the only constant in (6.10), and write

$$d\beta_{1i} = \frac{\partial \beta_{1i}}{\partial b_{1i}} db_{1i} + \frac{\partial \beta_{1i}}{\partial \sigma_1} d\sigma_1,$$

and then make use of methods similar to those of Appen. D (see also Sewall Wright, "The Method of Path Coefficients," *Annals of Mathematical Statistics*, V (1934), esp. 204–13). We should then have obtained the formula

$$\sigma^2_{\beta_{1i}} = \frac{\sigma_i^2}{\sigma_1^2} \cdot \sigma^2_{b_{1i}} - \frac{\bar{\epsilon}_1^2}{n\sigma_1^2} \cdot \beta^2_{1i},$$

which allows for the sampling variation of X_1 and, hence, of σ_1. (To obtain the corresponding formula for $s^2_{\beta_{1i}}$ we substitute the approximate ϵ_1 for the true $\bar{\epsilon}_1$.) It will be observed that formula (6.11a) is a special case of the foregoing formula, obtained by neglecting the second term on the right-hand side of the equality sign.

But this limitation of formula (6.11a)—and this holds also for formula (6.11b)—does not invalidate any of our statistical findings, since the latter are all based on the b's and the σ_b's. The only use which we made of formulas (6.11) and of the related formulas (6.12) and (6.13) was as a means of facilitating the computations of the b's and the σ_b's.

henceforth designate by ϵ_I^*. The coefficients of ϵ_I^* in (6.11) are the reciprocals of the weights of the parameters in question, and may be defined as follows:

(6.12)
$$\begin{cases} \gamma_{I.ii} = \dfrac{1}{n} \cdot \dfrac{\Delta_{IIii}}{\Delta_{II}} \\ \gamma_{I.ij} = \dfrac{1}{n} \cdot \dfrac{\Delta_{IIij}}{\Delta_{II}} \end{cases}.$$

Comparing (6.12) with (5.9), we obtain

(6.13)
$$\begin{cases} \gamma_{I.ii} = \sigma_i^2 \, c_{I.ii} \\ \gamma_{I.ij} = \sigma_i \, \sigma_j \, c_{I.ij} \end{cases}.$$

With the β's, their variances, and the covariances determined in terms of the correlation determinant Δ, we may next consider the remaining descriptive constants used in this study—the multiple correlation coefficient, the "coefficients of determination," and the partial correlation coefficient.

B. THE COEFFICIENT OF MULTIPLE CORRELATION

By definition, the coefficient of multiple correlation between the dependent variable X_1 and the independent or determining variables $X_2, \ldots, X_k$ is

(6.14)
$$R_1 = \left(1 - \frac{S_1^2}{\sigma_1^2} \right)^{1/2}.$$

This is also the simple coefficient of correlation between the computed and the observed values of X_1. It is also the ratio of the standard deviation of the computed X_1's to the standard deviation of the observed X_1's.

First we shall prove that

(6.15)
$$R_1^2 = 1 - \frac{\Delta}{\Delta_{II}}.$$

By analogy from (2.11) the sum of the squares of the z_1-residuals is

(6.16)
$$\Sigma v_1^2 = \Sigma z_1^2 - \beta_{12} \Sigma z_1 z_2 - \ldots - \beta_{1i} \Sigma z_1 z_i - \ldots - \beta_{1k} \Sigma z_1 z_k.$$

Dividing both sides by n, and substituting for β_{1i} from (6.9), we obtain

(6.17)
$$\frac{\Sigma v_1^2}{n} \equiv \left(\frac{S_1}{\sigma_1} \right)^2 = 1 - \beta_{12} r_{12} - \ldots - \beta_{1i} r_{1i} - \ldots - \beta_{1k} r_{1k}$$
$$= \frac{\Delta_{II} + \Delta_{12} r_{12} + \ldots + \Delta_{1i} r_{1i} + \ldots + \Delta_{1k} r_{1k}}{\Delta_{II}}.$$

But the numerator of this expression is the expansion of Δ. Hence

(6.18)
$$S_1^{*2} \equiv \frac{S_1^2}{\sigma_1^2} = \frac{\Delta}{\Delta_{II}}.$$

By substituting from (6.18) in (6.14), we immediately obtain (6.15).

When the distribution of each of the variables entering into a given equation is normal, the multiple correlation coefficients R_i complete the description of the frequency surface in question. That is, when the means, the standard deviations, and the multiple (and simple) correlation coefficients are known, all the other properties of the frequency surface, such as the equations of regression, the standard errors of estimate, can be derived from these constants: the surface is perfectly described. When, however, the distributions are not normal, R does not have this property and is simply another measure of goodness of fit. Since the curves which we wish to compare do not have the same number of parameters, and since the number of observations is generally small, it is advisable to adjust R for the number of constants in the curve from which it is derived. This adjustment involves the correction of both S^2 and σ^2 in (6.14) for the number of constants upon which they are based.[20] We then have

$$(6.19) \qquad \begin{cases} \epsilon_1^2 = \dfrac{nS_1^2}{n - k} \\[2mm] \mu_1^2 = \dfrac{n\sigma_1^2}{n - 1} \end{cases}$$

(see [2.10b] above), and

$$(6.20) \qquad R_1' = \left(1 - \frac{\epsilon_1^2}{\mu_1^2}\right)^{1/2} .$$

C.   THE COEFFICIENTS OF DETERMINATION

From (6.14) we have

$$(6.21a) \qquad S_1^2 = \sigma_1^2(1 - R_1^2) .$$

It is clear from this equation that R_1^2 is the relative amount by which the variance σ_1^2 of X_1 is reduced through the use of the independent variables in the regression equation (6.1). It may, therefore, be taken as a measure of the "total determination" of X_1 by the independent variables $X_2, \ldots, X_i, \ldots, X_k$. The higher R_1^2, the greater the degree of determination. When R_1 is unity, the variables are said to be causally related.

Formula (6.21a) does not, however, enable us to measure the relative importance of the several variables as "determinants" of X_1. One such measure may be obtained by using the value of S_1^2 derived in (6.17):

$$(6.21b) \qquad S_1^2 = \sigma_1^2(1 - \beta_{12} r_{12} - \ldots - \beta_{1i} r_{1i} - \ldots - \beta_{1k} r_{1k}) .$$

The sum of the product terms in the parenthesis equals R_1^2, and each of these measures the *total* (direct and indirect) importance of the indicated independent variable as a "determinant" of the dependent variable. Thus $\beta_{1i} r_{1i}$ measures the proportion of the total variance of X_1 which is attributable to X_i. It is the sum of the *direct* effect of

---

[20] This adjustment is perfectly general and may be applied to the simple as well as to the multiple correlation coefficient.

X_i on the variance of X_1, and of the *indirect* effect of X_i through its influence on the other variables.

But $\beta_{1i}\, r_{1i}$ may be negative. This suggests that instead of diminishing σ_1^2 it *increases* it, which suggests that we would have gotten a better estimate of X_1 from our regression equation if we had not used X_i at all!

This anomaly is due to the interrelations of the independent variables and may be resolved by separating $\beta_{1i}\, r_{1i}$ into its two components—the direct and the indirect. It then develops that the direct effect of X_i can be only positive, so that when it is subtracted from unity in (6.21b) it reduces the variance σ_1^2. However, the indirect effect of X_i, i.e., its joint effect with the other variables, may be negative and may exceed numerically the direct effect. This would give a negative sign to the "total coefficient of determination" $\beta_{1i}\, r_{1i}$ of X_i.

To resolve the total coefficients of determination into their direct and indirect components, we multiply the first of the normal equations (6.8) by β_{12}, the second by β_{13}, etc., thus obtaining

$$(6.22) \quad \begin{cases} \beta_{12}\, r_{12} = \beta_{12}^2 \qquad\quad + \ldots + \beta_{12}\, \beta_{1i}\, r_{2i} + \ldots + \beta_{12}\, \beta_{1k}\, r_{2k} \\ \ldots \ldots \ldots \ldots \ldots \ldots \ldots \ldots \\ \beta_{1i}\, r_{1i} = \beta_{12}\, \beta_{1i}\, r_{2i} + \ldots + \beta_{1i}^2 \qquad\quad + \ldots + \beta_{1i}\, \beta_{1k}\, r_{ik} \\ \ldots \ldots \ldots \ldots \ldots \ldots \ldots \ldots \\ \beta_{1k}\, r_{1k} = \beta_{12}\, \beta_{1k}\, r_{2k} + \ldots + \beta_{1i}\, \beta_{1k}\, r_{ik} + \ldots + \beta_{1k}^2 \end{cases} ,$$

in which the coefficients of the β^2's are $r_{ii} = 1$. In these equations the total coefficients of determination of $X_2, \ldots, X_i, \ldots, X_k$ appear to the left of the equality signs; their direct and indirect components appear to the right of the equality signs. Thus (from the i-th equation), $\beta_{1i}\, r_{1i}$, or the proportion of the variance of σ_1^2 which may be imputed to X_i, is made up of the *direct* effect of X_i: β_{1i}^2; of its indirect effect through its correlation with X_2: $\beta_{12}\, \beta_{1i}\, r_{2i}$; of its indirect effect through its correlation with X_j: $\beta_{1i}\, \beta_{1j}\, r_{ij}, j = 3, \ldots,)i(, \ldots, k$. The direct effects, being squares, can be only positive. The indirect effects may be positive, negative, or zero, and may exceed the direct effect in numerical value.

Adding the equations (6.22), and recalling that the sum of the product terms in (6.21b) is R_1^2, we obtain

$$(6.23) \qquad\qquad R_1^2 = \Sigma\beta_{1i}^2 + 2\Sigma\beta_{1i}\, \beta_{1j}\, r_{ij} ,$$

where $i, j = 2, \ldots, k, i < j$. Substituting in (6.21a), we get

$$(6.21c) \qquad\qquad S_1^2 = \sigma_1^2(1 - \Sigma\beta_{1i}^2 - 2\Sigma\beta_{1i}\, \beta_{1j}\, r_{ij}) ,$$

where $i, j = 2, \ldots, k, i < j$.

If, for example, our regression equation has only three independent variables, then the relations between (6.21a), (6.21b), and (6.21c) may be shown conveniently in Figure III. This figure brings into clear relief an interesting property of (6.22): *the indirect or joint effect of any two independent variables is distributed equally between them.* This should put us on our guard against an uncritical acceptance of the results yielded by the coefficients of determination. In the absence of a theory of the inter-relations to be expected among our variables, the coefficients of determination might be quite misleading.[21]

	PROPORTION OF σ_1^2 DUE TO			
	X_2	X_3	X_4	Total
Directly	β_{12}^2	β_{13}^2	β_{14}^2	$\sum_{i=2}^{4}\beta_{1i}^2$
Jointly X_2 and X_3 X_2 and X_4 X_3 and X_4	$\beta_{12}\beta_{13}r_{23}$ $\beta_{12}\beta_{14}r_{24}$	$\beta_{12}\beta_{13}r_{23}$ $\beta_{13}\beta_{14}r_{34}$	 $\beta_{12}\beta_{14}r_{24}$ $\beta_{13}\beta_{14}r_{34}$	$2\beta_{12}\beta_{13}r_{23}$ $2\beta_{12}\beta_{14}r_{24}$ $2\beta_{13}\beta_{14}r_{34}$
Total	$\beta_{12}r_{12}$	$\beta_{13,}r_{13}$	$\beta_{14}r_{14}$	R_1^2

FIG. III.—Imputation of σ_1^2 to the independent variables. (For a concrete illustration see chap. vii, Table 15.)

VII. ADJUSTMENT OF THE REGRESSION PARAMETERS FOR THE OMISSION OF A VARIABLE

After the regression equation has been computed, it is often found that a certain independent variable is statistically insignificant and that it should therefore be elimi-nated. Of course the new regression may be determined from the correlations between the remaining variables by recomputing (6.8). As was first shown by R. A. Fisher,[22] however, it is not necessary to recompute (6.8), for the variable may be eliminated more conveniently with the aid of a few simple formulas.

Let X_g represent the variable to be omitted. Then the new correlation determinant from which the coefficients of correlation between X_g and the other variables have been eliminated, and which we shall denote by $\Delta_{)g(}$, is

$$(7.1) \qquad \Delta_{)g(} = \Delta_{gg}.$$

By (6.9) the new regression coefficients are

$$(7.2) \qquad \beta_{1i)g(} = -\frac{\Delta_{1i)g(}}{\Delta_{11)g(}} = -\frac{\Delta_{gg1i}}{\Delta_{gg11}}.$$

[21] See chap. vi, Sec. III D, part e. For an extended treatment of the problem of imputation and the meaning that can be attached to the correlation coefficients and beta-coefficients see Sewall Wright, "Correlation and Causation," *Jour. Agric. Res.* XX (1921), 557–85; "Corn and Hog Correla-tions," *U.S.D.A. Bulletin No. 1300* (1925); "The Method of Path Coefficients," *Annals of Mathe-matical Statistics* V (1934), 161–215.

[22] *Op. cit.*, sec. 29.1. It should be noted that Fisher deals with original and not with "standard units." However, the relationship between the two is, as we have seen, simple.

The difference between the new and the old coefficients is

$$(7.3) \qquad \beta_{1i)\varrho(} - \beta_{1i} = -\frac{\Delta_{\varrho\varrho 1i}}{\Delta_{\varrho\varrho 11}} + \frac{\Delta_{1i}}{\Delta_{11}} = -\left(\frac{\Delta_{11}\Delta_{\varrho\varrho 1i} - \Delta_{1i}\Delta_{\varrho\varrho 11}}{\Delta_{11}\Delta_{\varrho\varrho 11}}\right).$$

By the use of a well-known theorem in determinants[23] which states that

$$(7.4) \qquad \Delta\Delta_{ijkl} = \Delta_{ij}\Delta_{kl} - \Delta_{il}\Delta_{kj},$$

we have

$$(7.5) \qquad \Delta_{11}\Delta_{\varrho\varrho 1i} - \Delta_{1i}\Delta_{\varrho\varrho 11} = -\Delta_{\varrho 1}\Delta_{11i\varrho}.$$

Substituting (7.5) into (7.3), we obtain

$$(7.6) \qquad \beta_{1i)\varrho(} - \beta_{1i} = -\left(-\frac{\Delta_{\varrho 1}\Delta_{11i\varrho}}{\Delta_{11}\Delta_{\varrho\varrho 11}}\right).$$

But from (6.9) we know that

$$(7.7) \qquad -\frac{\Delta_{\varrho 1}}{\Delta_{11}} = \beta_{1\varrho},$$

and from (6.12) we know that

$$(7.8) \qquad \frac{\Delta_{11i\varrho}}{\Delta_{\varrho\varrho 11}} = \frac{\Delta_{11i\varrho}}{n(\Delta_{11})} \cdot \frac{n(\Delta_{11})}{\Delta_{11\varrho\varrho}} = \frac{\gamma_{1.i\varrho}}{\gamma_{1.\varrho\varrho}}.$$

Substituting into (7.6), we obtain, finally

$$(7.9) \qquad \beta_{1i)\varrho(} = \beta_{1i} - \frac{\gamma_{1.i\varrho}}{\gamma_{1.\varrho\varrho}} \beta_{1\varrho},$$

which expresses the new regression coefficient as a function of the known constants. By similar reasoning we may also obtain a formula for adjusting the *weights*, $\gamma_{1.ij}$, of the β-coefficients for the omission of a variable. It is

$$(7.10) \qquad \gamma_{1.ij)\varrho(} = \gamma_{1.ij} - \frac{\gamma_{1.i\varrho}}{\gamma_{1.\varrho\varrho}} \gamma_{1.j\varrho}.$$

Having adjusted the regression coefficients for the omission of X_ϱ from the set of variables, we may, of course, compute the new coefficient of multiple correlation by using the formulas of Figure III. Thus:

$$(7.11) \qquad R^2_{1)\varrho(} = \beta_{12)\varrho(} r_{12} + \ldots + \beta_{1i)\varrho(} r_{1i} + \ldots + \beta_{1k)\varrho(} r_{1k}$$

or

$$(7.12) \qquad R^2_{1)\varrho(} = \Sigma\beta^2_{1i)\varrho(} + 2\Sigma\beta_{1i)\varrho(}\beta_{1j)\varrho(} r_{ij},$$

[23] See Máxime Bocher, *Introduction to Higher Algebra* (New York, 1924), corollary 3, p. 33.

where $i, j = 2, \ldots,)g(, \ldots, k$, and $i < j$. It is possible, however, also to derive the new R_i^2 by applying a simple correction to the old. By (6.15) we have

$$(7.13) \qquad R_{1)g(}^2 = 1 - \frac{\Delta_{gg}}{\Delta_{11gg}},$$

or

$$(7.14) \qquad R_{1)g(}^2 - R_1^2 = \frac{\Delta}{\Delta_{11}} - \frac{\Delta_{gg}}{\Delta_{11gg}} = \frac{\Delta \Delta_{11gg} - \Delta_{11} \Delta_{gg}}{\Delta_{11} \Delta_{11gg}}.$$

By the use of (7.4) we obtain

$$(7.15) \qquad R_{1)g(}^2 - R_1^2 = -\frac{\Delta_{1g}^2}{\Delta_{11} \Delta_{11gg}} = -\frac{\Delta_{1g}^2}{\Delta_{11}^2} \cdot \frac{\Delta_{11}}{\Delta_{11gg}},$$

or by (6.9) and (6.12)

$$(7.16) \qquad R_{1)g(}^2 = R_1^2 - \frac{\beta_{1g}^2}{n\gamma_{1.gg}}.$$

The method of adjustment of the regression parameters given here was used in the study of the interrelations of demand, price, and income.

VIII. SIMULTANEOUS DETERMINATION OF ALL THE ELEMENTARY REGRESSIONS AND THEIR STANDARD ERRORS

As we stated in Section II, D, of this appendix, it is possible to obtain all of the k elementary regressions with little more work than was formerly required to obtain a single regression. As a first step in the explanation of the new procedure it is desirable to generalize the formulas for the regression coefficients, the standard errors, and the other descriptive constants which we have obtained in Section VI.

Let the k elementary regression equations in standard units be written

$$(8.1) \quad z_h' = \beta_{h1} z_1 + \beta_{h2} z_2 + \ldots + \beta_{hh-1} z_{h-1} + \beta_{hh+1} z_{h+1} + \ldots + \beta_{hk} z_k,$$

where $h = 1, \ldots, k$.

Generalizing (6.9), (6.11a), (6.11b), (6.18), and (6.15), we obtain:

$$(8.2) \qquad \beta_{hi} = -\frac{\Delta_{hi}}{\Delta_{hh}},$$

$$(8.3) \qquad s_{\beta_{hi}}^2 = \epsilon_h^{*2} \frac{1}{n} \cdot \frac{\Delta_{hhii}}{\Delta_{hh}} = \epsilon_h^{*2} \cdot \frac{1}{n} \cdot \frac{\Delta_{hh} \Delta_{ii} - \Delta_{hi}^2}{\Delta \Delta_{hh}},$$

$$(8.4) \qquad p_{\beta_{hi} \beta_{hj}} = \epsilon_h^{*2} \frac{1}{n} \frac{\Delta_{hhij}}{\Delta_{hh}} = \epsilon_h^{*2} \cdot \frac{1}{n} \cdot \frac{\Delta_{hh} \Delta_{ij} - \Delta_{hi} \Delta_{hj}}{\Delta \Delta_{hh}},$$

$$(8.5) \qquad S_h^{*2} = \frac{\Delta}{\Delta_{hh}},$$

where

$$S_h^* = \frac{S_h}{\sigma_h},$$

and

(8.6)
$$R_h^2 = 1 - \frac{\Delta}{\Delta_{hh}}.$$

We also have for the coefficient of partial correlation

(8.7)
$$r_{hi.[1\ldots)hi(\ldots k]} = -\frac{\Delta_{hi}}{(\Delta_{hh}\Delta_{ii})^{1/2}}.$$

Let

(8.8)
$$P_{hi} = \frac{\Delta_{hi}}{\Delta}.$$

Substituting (8.8) in equations (8.2) to (8.7), we obtain:

(8.9)
$$\beta_{hi} = -\frac{P_{hi}}{P_{hh}},$$

(8.10)
$$s_{\beta_{hi}}^2 = \epsilon_h^{*2} \cdot \frac{1}{n} \cdot \frac{P_{hh}P_{ii} - P_{hi}^2}{P_{hh}},$$

(8.11)
$$p_{\beta_{hi}\beta_{hj}} = \epsilon_h^{*2} \cdot \frac{1}{n} \cdot \frac{P_{hh}P_{ij} - P_{hi}P_{hj}}{P_{hh}},$$

(8.12)
$$S_h^{*2} = \frac{1}{P_{hh}},$$

(8.13)
$$R_h^2 = 1 - \frac{1}{P_{hh}},$$

and

(8.14)
$$r_{hi.[1\ldots)hi(\ldots k]} = -\frac{P_{hi}}{(P_{hh}P_{ii})^{1/2}}.$$

It is obvious from these equations that all we need do to obtain all the elementary regressions and the descriptive constants is to determine the $k(k+1)/2$ values P_{hi}. (The reader who is familiar with the elements of matrix algebra will immediately recognize the P_{hi} as the elements of the reciprocal matrix of Δ.)

To determine P_{hi}, we first recall that the determinant Δ may be expanded in the k ways:

(8.15)
$$\Delta_{h1} r_{h1} + \ldots + \Delta_{hi} r_{hi} + \ldots + \Delta_{hk} r_{hk} = \Delta,$$

where $(h = 1, \ldots, k)$.

We also have the $k(k-1)$ equations which involve the expansion of a determinant, two rows or columns of which are identical:

(8.16)
$$\Delta_{h1}\, r_{j1} + \ldots + \Delta_{hi}\, r_{ji} + \ldots + \Delta_{hk}\, r_{jk} = 0$$
$$(j, h = 1, \ldots, k), \qquad j \neq h.$$

Dividing each of the equations in (8.15) and (8.16) by Δ, we obtain the following k^2 equations.

$$(8.17)\begin{cases}
P_{h1}\, r_{11} + P_{h2}\, r_{12} + \ldots + P_{hi}\, r_{1i} + \ldots + P_{hk}\, r_{1k} = & 1, & 0, & \ldots, & 0, & \ldots, & 0, \\
P_{h1}\, r_{21} + P_{h2}\, r_{22} + \ldots + P_{hi}\, r_{2i} + \ldots + P_{hk}\, r_{2k} = & 0, & 1, & \ldots, & 0, & \ldots, & 0, \\
\quad \cdot \quad\quad\quad \cdot \quad\quad\quad\quad \cdot \quad\quad\quad\quad \cdot \quad \\
P_{h1}\, r_{i1} + P_{h2}\, r_{i2} + \ldots + P_{hi}\, r_{ii} + \ldots + P_{hk}\, r_{ik} = & 0, & 0, & \ldots, & 1, & \ldots, & 0, \\
\quad \cdot \quad\quad\quad \cdot \quad\quad\quad\quad \cdot \quad\quad\quad\quad \cdot \quad \\
P_{h1}\, r_{k1} + P_{h2}\, r_{k2} + \ldots + P_{hi}\, r_{ki} + \ldots + P_{hk}\, r_{kk} = & 0, & 0, & \ldots, & 0, & \ldots, & 1.
\end{cases}$$

The column headers over the right-hand side read: $(h=1)\ (h=2) \quad (h=i) \quad (h=k)$.

Solving the set of equations for which $h = 1$, we obtain P_{1i} ($i = 1, \ldots, k$), with $h = 2$ we obtain P_{2i}, etc. We may solve all k sets of equations by Gauss's method of substitution in a manner analogous to that outlined in Section II, D, above.[24]

The method of solution for four variables is set forth in detail in Figure IV. The form consists of the four columns containing Δ which are headed A, B, C, D, and an equal number of columns R, S, T, U in which the diagonal elements are -1 and all the remaining elements are zero. These are the terms which, in equations (8.17), appear to the right of the equality signs.

Performing the computations indicated in the column headed "Directions," we obtain in the last line of the form the values P_{14} in column R, P_{24} in column S, P_{34} in column T, and P_{44} in column U. The remaining values of P_{ij} are given from the last line of each section by means of the following equations. Line 11 yields:

$$(8.18a)\begin{cases}
P_{13} = \dfrac{\Delta_{34}}{\Delta_{44}}\, P_{14} + \dfrac{\Delta_{1344}}{\Delta_{44}}, \\[2ex]
P_{23} = \dfrac{\Delta_{34}}{\Delta_{44}}\, P_{24} + \dfrac{\Delta_{2344}}{\Delta_{44}}, \\[2ex]
P_{33} = \dfrac{\Delta_{34}}{\Delta_{44}}\, P_{34} + \dfrac{\Delta_{3344}}{\Delta_{44}}.
\end{cases}$$

Line 6 yields:

$$(8.18b)\begin{cases}
P_{12} = \dfrac{\Delta_{2344}}{\Delta_{3344}}\, P_{13} - \dfrac{\Delta_{2334}}{\Delta_{3344}}\, P_{14} - \dfrac{r_{12}}{\Delta_{3344}}, \\[2ex]
P_{22} = \dfrac{\Delta_{2344}}{\Delta_{3344}}\, P_{23} - \dfrac{\Delta_{2334}}{\Delta_{3344}}\, P_{24} + \dfrac{1}{\Delta_{3344}}.
\end{cases}$$

[24] In fact, we saw that there the solution of the subsidiary sets of normal equations which were combined in Fig. II yielded the reciprocals of the weights, D_{ij}/D. It is obvious that we may deal with the determinant Δ in a similar way and obtain the values $P_{ij} = \Delta_{ij}/\Delta$.

Line No.	Directions	A	B	C	D
I		I	r_{12}	r_{13}	r_{14}
II			I	r_{23}	r_{24}
III				I	r_{34}
IV					I
I	I	I	r_{12}	r_{13}	r_{14}
2	$-(1)$	$-I$	$-r_{12}$	$-r_{13}$	$-r_{14}$
3	II		I	r_{23}	r_{24}
4	$-r_{12}\cdot(1)$		$-r_{12}^2$	$-r_{12}r_{13}$	$-r_{12}r_{14}$
5	$(3)+(4)$		Δ_{3344}	$-\Delta_{2344}$	Δ_{2334}
6	$\dfrac{-I}{\Delta_{3344}}\cdot(5)$		$-I$	$\dfrac{\Delta_{2344}}{\Delta_{3344}}$	$-\dfrac{\Delta_{2334}}{\Delta_{3344}}$
7	III			I	r_{34}
8	$(-r_{13})\cdot(1)$			$-r_{13}^2$	$-r_{13}r_{14}$
8A	$(7)+(8)$			Δ_{2244}	$-\Delta_{2234}$
9	$\dfrac{\Delta_{2344}}{\Delta_{3344}}\cdot(5)$			$-\dfrac{(\Delta_{2344})^2}{\Delta_{3344}}$	$\dfrac{\Delta_{2344}\cdot\Delta_{2334}}{\Delta_{3344}}$
10	$(8A)+(9)$			$\dfrac{\Delta_{44}}{\Delta_{3344}}$	$-\dfrac{\Delta_{34}}{\Delta_{3344}}$
11	$-\dfrac{\Delta_{3344}}{\Delta_{44}}\cdot(10)$			$-I$	$\dfrac{\Delta_{34}}{\Delta_{44}}$
12	IV				I
13	$(-r_{14})\cdot(1)$				$-r_{14}^2$
13A	$(12)+(13)$				Δ_{2233}
14	$\dfrac{-\Delta_{2334}}{\Delta_{3344}}\cdot(5)$				$\dfrac{-(\Delta_{2334})^2}{\Delta_{3344}}$
14A	$(13A)+(14)$				$\dfrac{\Delta_{33}}{\Delta_{3344}}$
15	$\dfrac{\Delta_{34}}{\Delta_{44}}\cdot(10)$				$\dfrac{-(\Delta_{34})^2}{\Delta_{44}\Delta_{3344}}$
16	$(14A)+(15)$				$\dfrac{\Delta}{\Delta_{44}}$
17	$\dfrac{-\Delta_{44}}{\Delta}\cdot(16)$				$-I$

FIG. IV.—Form for the simultaneous evaluation of the coefficients in all of the regression

R	S	T	U	Sum-Check		Line No.
$-I$	o	o	o	Σ_I		I
o	$-I$	o	o	Σ_2		II
o	o	$-I$	o	Σ_3		III
o	o	o	$-I$	Σ_4		IV
$-I$	o	o	o	Σ_I	√	I
I	o	o	o	$-\Sigma_I$	√	2
o	$-I$	o	o	Σ_2		3
r_{12}	o	o	o	$-r_{12}\cdot\Sigma_I$		4
r_{12}	$-I$	o	o	Σ'_2	√	5
$\dfrac{-r_{12}}{\Delta_{3344}}$	$\dfrac{I}{\Delta_{3344}}$	o	o	$\dfrac{-\Sigma'_2}{\Delta_{3344}}$	√	6
o	o	$-I$	o	Σ_3		7
r_{13}	o	o	o	$-r_{13}\cdot\Sigma_I$		8
r_{13}	o	$-I$	o	$\Sigma_3-r_{13}\cdot\Sigma_I$		8A
$\dfrac{\Delta_{2344}\cdot r_{12}}{\Delta_{3344}}$	$\dfrac{-\Delta_{2344}}{\Delta_{3344}}$	o	o	$\dfrac{\Delta_{2344}}{\Delta_{3344}}\cdot\Sigma'_2$		9
$\dfrac{-\Delta_{1344}}{\Delta_{3344}}$	$\dfrac{-\Delta_{2344}}{\Delta_{3344}}$	$-I$	o	Σ'_3	√	10
$\dfrac{\Delta_{1344}}{\Delta_{44}}$	$\dfrac{\Delta_{2344}}{\Delta_{44}}$	$\dfrac{\Delta_{3344}}{\Delta_{44}}$	o	$\dfrac{-\Delta_{3344}}{\Delta_{44}}\cdot\Sigma'_3$	√	11
o	o	o	$-I$	Σ_4		12
r_{14}	o	o	o	$-r_{14}\cdot\Sigma_I$		13
r_{14}	o	o	$-I$	$\Sigma_4-r_{14}\cdot\Sigma_I$		13A
$\dfrac{-\Delta_{2334}\cdot r_{12}}{\Delta_{3344}}$	$\dfrac{\Delta_{2334}}{\Delta_{3344}}$	o	o	$\dfrac{-\Delta_{2334}}{\Delta_{3344}}\cdot\Sigma'_2$		14
$\dfrac{\Delta_{1334}}{\Delta_{3344}}$	$\dfrac{\Delta_{2334}}{\Delta_{3344}}$	o	$-I$	$\Sigma_4-r_{14}\cdot\Sigma_I-\dfrac{\Delta_{2334}}{\Delta_{3344}}\Sigma'_2$		14A
$\dfrac{-\Delta_{34}\Delta_{1344}}{\Delta_{44}\Delta_{3344}}$	$\dfrac{-\Delta_{34}\Delta_{2344}}{\Delta_{44}\Delta_{3344}}$	$\dfrac{-\Delta_{34}}{\Delta_{44}}$	o	$\dfrac{\Delta_{34}}{\Delta_{44}}\Sigma'_3$		15
$\dfrac{-\Delta_{14}}{\Delta_{44}}$	$\dfrac{-\Delta_{24}}{\Delta_{44}}$	$\dfrac{-\Delta_{34}}{\Delta_{44}}$	$-I$	Σ'_4	√	16
$\dfrac{\Delta_{14}}{\Delta}$	$\dfrac{\Delta_{24}}{\Delta}$	$\dfrac{\Delta_{34}}{\Delta}$	$\dfrac{\Delta_{44}}{\Delta}$	$\dfrac{-\Delta_{44}}{\Delta}\Sigma'_4$	√	17

equations and related parameters in terms of the correlation determinant and its cofactors

And the last line of the first section yields:

(8.18c) $$P_{11} = -r_{12}P_{12} - r_{13}P_{13} - r_{14}P_{14} + 1\,.$$

It will also be noted that the value of Δ is given by the product of the first entries in the next to last line of each section:

(8.18d) $$\Delta = 1 \cdot \Delta_{3344} \cdot \frac{\Delta_{44}}{\Delta_{3344}} \cdot \frac{\Delta}{\Delta_{44}}\,.$$

Having obtained P_{hi}, we substitute in equations (8.9) to (8.14) to obtain the regression coefficients, their standard errors, and the remaining descriptive constants.[25]

Turning now to the problem of determining the parameters in *subsets* of the whole set of k variables, we readily observe that by correcting the P_{hi} values for the omission of a variable we may obtain all the remaining constants adjusted for this omission. The correction of the P_{hi} values is simple. By (8.8) we have

(8.19a) $$P_{hi)g(} = \frac{\Delta_{hi\,gg}}{\Delta_{gg}}\,,$$

or, applying (7.4),

(8.19b) $$P_{hi)g(} = \frac{\Delta_{hi}\,\Delta_{gg} - \Delta_{hg}\,\Delta_{gi}}{\Delta\Delta_{gg}}\,,$$

or

(8.19c) $$P_{hi)g(} = P_{hi} - \frac{P_{hg}}{P_{gg}}\,P_{gi}\,.$$

In some problems it may be a satisfactory procedure to drop the variable z_i from the set of variables under consideration if the regression coefficient β_{hi} of z_h on z_i turns out to be statistically insignificant. In that event it is not necessary to wait until the entire regression equation has been computed in order to determine whether β_{hi} is, or

[25] In an unpublished paper entitled, "A Method for Finding the Inverse of a Matrix," Mr. Ledyard R. Tucker shows how the method described above may be modified so as to yield all the P's directly without substitutions. When the number of variables is small—say less than six—our method is less time-consuming than Tucker's.

The method explained in this appendix seems to me to be superior to the methods developed by the following authors: Paul Horst, "A General Method for Evaluating Multiple Regression Constants," *Jour. Amer. Statist. Assoc.*, XXVII (1932), 270–78; Ragnar Frisch, *Statistical Confluence Analysis by Means of Complete Regression Systems* (Universitetets Økonomiske Institutt, Publikasjon Nr. 5 [Oslo, 1934]); Frederick V. Waugh, "A Simplified Method of Determining Multiple Regression Constants," *Jour. Amer. Statist. Assoc.*, XXX (1935), 694–700.

While the proofs of this appendix were being corrected, my attention was called to an article by Godfrey H. Thomson, entitled, "Some Points of Mathematical Technique in the Factorial Analysis of Ability," *Journal of Educational Psychology*, XXVII No. 1 (1936), 37–54, in which he presents a method for calculating the reciprocal of the determinant devised by Dr. A. C. Aitken, of Edinburgh University. This method, which appears to be based on the Chiò method of evaluating a determinant (see E. T. Whittaker and G. Robinson, *The Calculus of Observations* [New York, 1924], chap. v), is very neat and appears to have practically the same advantages as are possessed by my form.

is not, insignificant, and whether, therefore, z_i should, or should not, be dropped. If we agree to consider β_{hi} (and, hence, b_{hi}) as statistically insignificant if

$$(8.20) \qquad\qquad s^2_{\beta_{hi}} > a\beta^2_{hi} ,$$

where $s^2_{\beta_{hi}}$ is defined by (6.11a), and a is an arbitrary positive constant, then there exists a criterion which will tell us *in advance* whether the value of β_{hi} will satisfy this inequality. This criterion, which is due to Jacob L. Mosak,[26] is that

$$(8.21) \qquad\qquad P_{hh}P_{ii} > [a(n - k) + 1]P^2_{hi} .$$

The method outlined in this section for determining the regression coefficients and for adjusting them for the omission of a variable was used in the studies of cotton and wheat. Wider application would undoubtedly have been made of the method had it been developed earlier.

IX. NUMERICAL ILLUSTRATION

Figures Va, Vb, and Vc, and Figures VIa and VIb constitute a numerical illustration of the simultaneous evaluation of the coefficients in all the regression equations. The data relate to the demand for cotton for the period 1914–29, which was discussed in chapter viii. The variables are:

$X_1 = x'_{dc}$ = logs of per capita U.S. consumption of cotton

$X_2 = y'$ = logs of deflated U.S. season average farm price of cotton

$X_3 = w'$ = logs of Persons' "Index of United States Industrial Production and Trade"

$X_4 = t$ = time in years

and

$X_5 = t^2$.

The notation $X_1, \ldots, X_5$ is more convenient in the computations. The other notation given above is that used in chapter viii. Arithmetic values of the first three variables are given in Appendix A.

Figure Va is a numerical illustration of the computational form given in Figure IV. The entries in lines I to V, columns A to E are the elements of the correlation determinant, Δ. Since the determinant is symmetric, it is convenient to omit the elements below the diagonal.[27] The entries in lines I to V, columns R to V are the quantities which are needed for determining the P_{hi} values. These are the terms which in equations (8.17) appear to the right of the equality signs. Only the diagonal entries are shown, since the rest are all zero (see Fig. IV). The computations shown

[26] Jacob L. Mosak, "On the Simultaneous Determination of the Elementary Regression and Their Standard Errors in Subsets of Variables," *Jour. Amer. Statist. Assoc.*, XXXII (1937), 517–24.

[27] We are not showing here the set of forms which we have developed for deriving and checking the simple correlation coefficients. For a form similar to ours see Francis McIntyre, "Automatic Checks in Correlation Analysis," *Jour. Amer. Statist. Assoc.*, XXXII (1937), 119–23.

Line No.	Directions	A	B	C	D	E
I		I.	− .07689	.74737	− .35305	.25863
II			I.	.35321	.24219	− .50096
III				I.	.08292	.10543
IV					I.	O
V						I.
1	Line I	I.	− .07689	.74737	− .35305	.25863
2	−1·line 1	−I.	.07689	− .74737	.35305	− .25863
3	Line II		I.	.35321	.24219	− .50096
4	.07689·line 1		− .00591	.05747	− .02715	.01989
5	Sum		.99409	.41068	.21504	− .48107
6	−(.99409)⁻¹·line 5		−I.	− .41312	− .21632	.48393
7	Line III			I.	.08292	.10543
8	− .74737·line 1			− .55856	.26386	− .19329
9	− .41312·line 5			− .16966	− .08884	.19874
10	Sum			.27178	.25794	.11088
11	−(.27178)⁻¹·line 10			−I.	− .94908	− .40798
12	Line IV				I.	O
13	.35305·line 1				− .12464	.09131
14	− .21632·line 5				− .04652	.10407
15	− .94908·line 10				− .24481	− .10523
16	Sum				.58403	.09015
17	−(.58403)⁻¹·line 16				−I.	− .15436
18	Line V					I.
19	− .25863·line 1					− .06689
20	.48393·line 5					− .23281
21	− .40798·line 10					− .04524
22	− .15436·line 16					− .01392
23	Sum					.64114
24	−(.64114)⁻¹·line 23					−I.

$$\Delta = .10117$$

Fig. Va.—First step in the evaluation of the P_{hi}'s by Gauss's
are not numerically accurate and are

in the lines 1–24 of the form are carried out according to the instructions given in the "Directions" column to the left. (The subsidiary sums in lines 8A, 13A, 14A, 19A, 20A, and 21A of Fig. IV are omitted from this form.)

Before solving for the P's in Figure Vb, equations (8.18) must be extended to cover the case of five variables. This may be done by referring to Figure IV (which is designed for four variables) and comparing it with Figure Va. Reasoning by analogy, we conclude that the values P_{15} to P_{55} must be given in line 24 in columns R, S, T, U, and V, respectively. The value P_{14}, which is

$$P_{14} = \frac{\Delta_{45}}{\Delta_{55}} P_{15} + \frac{\Delta_{1455}}{\Delta_{55}},$$

R	S	T	U	V	Sum	Check	Line No.
-1.					.57606		I
	-1.				.01755		II
		-1.			1.28893		III
			-1.		- .02794		IV
				-1.	- .13690		V
-1.					.57606		I
1.					- .57606	- .57606	2
	-1.				.01755		3
- .07689					.04429		4
- .07689	-1.				.06184	.06185	5
.07735	1.00595				- .06221	- .06221	6
		-1.			1.28893		7
.74737					- .43053		8
.03176	.41312				- .02555		9
.77913	.41312	-1.			.83285	.83285	10
-2.86677	-1.52005	3.67945			-3.06443	-3.06443	11
			-1.		- .02794		12
- .35305					.20338		13
.01663	.21632				- .01338		14
- .73946	- .39208	.94908			- .79044		15
-1.07588	- .17576	.94908	-1.		- .62838	- .62838	16
1.84216	.30094	-1.62505	1.71224		1.07594	1.07593	17
				-1.	- .13690		18
.25863					- .14899		19
- .03721	- .48393				.02993		20
- .31787	- .16854	.40798			- .33979		21
.16607	.02713	- .14650	.15436		.09700		22
.06962	- .62534	.26148	.15436	-1.	- .49875	- .49874	23
- .10859	.97536	- .40784	- .24076	1.55972	.77791	.77789	24

method of substitution. (In this, and in all related forms, figures in italics retained only for checking purposes.)

is computed in lines 17a, 17b, and 17c of Figure Vb and is the sum of the item in line 17, column R, of Figure Va plus the product of P_{15} with the item in column E of line 17 (i.e., $1.84216 - 0.15436 \times P_{15}$). Similarly, equations (8.18) are extended to yield the remaining P-values.

After the P's have been computed, they may be checked in equations (8.17). In the present illustration, the maximum disagreement in the check was only three units in the fifth place.

We now have all the values for computing all the regression equations and their related parameters by means of the formulas (8.9) to (8.14). In the present illustration, however, we shall compute only two elementary regressions—that of z_1 [$z_i = (X_i - M_i)/\sigma_i$] on the remaining variables and that of z_2 on the remaining

Line No.	Derivation of P_{5i} ($i = 1, \ldots, 5$):	P_{51}	P_{52}	P_{53}	P_{54}	P_{55}
24a	From line 24, cols. R, S, T, U, V	$-.10859$ $= P_{51}$	$.97536$ $= P_{52}$	$-.40784$ $= P_{53}$	$-.24076$ $= P_{54}$	1.55972 $= P_{55}$

	Derivation of P_{4i} ($i = 1, \ldots, 4$):	P_{41}	P_{42}	P_{43}	P_{44}
17a	From line 17, cols. R, S, T, U	1.84216	$.30094$	-1.62505	1.71224
17b	$-.15436$(l. 17, col. E)$\cdot P_{5i}$	$.01676$	$-.15056$	$.06295$	$.03716$
17c	Total	1.85892 $= P_{41}$	$.15038$ $= P_{42}$	-1.56210 $= P_{43}$	1.74940 $= P_{44}$

	Derivation of P_{3i} ($i = 1, \ldots, 3$):	P_{31}	P_{32}	P_{33}
11a	From line 11, cols. R, S, T	-2.86677	-1.52005	3.67945
11b	$-.40798$(l. 11, col. E)$\cdot P_{5i}$	$.04430$	$-.39793$	$.16639$
11c	$-.94908$(l. 11, col. D)$\cdot P_{4i}$	-1.76426	$-.14272$	1.48256
11d	Total	-4.58673 $= P_{31}$	-2.06070 $= P_{32}$	5.32840 $= P_{33}$

	Derivation of P_{2i} ($i = 1, 2$):	P_{21}	P_{22}
6a	From line 6, cols. R, S	$.07735$	1.00595
6b	$.48393$(l. 6, col. E)$\cdot P_{5i}$	$-.05255$	$.47201$
6c	$-.21632$(l. 6, col. D)$\cdot P_{4i}$	$-.40212$	$-.03253$
6d	$-.41312$(l. 6, col. C)$\cdot P_{3i}$	1.89487	$.85132$
6e	Total	1.51755 $= P_{21}$	2.29675 $= P_{22}$

	Derivation of P_{11}:	P_{11}
2a	From line 2, col. R	$1.$
2b	$-.25863$(l. 2, col. E)$\cdot P_{51}$	$.02808$
2c	$.35305$(l. 2, col. D)$\cdot P_{41}$	$.65629$
2d	$-.74737$(l. 2, col. C)$\cdot P_{31}$	3.42798
2e	$.07689$(l. 2, col. B)$\cdot P_{21}$	$.11668$
2f	Total	5.22903 $= P_{11}$

Fig. Vb.—Second step in the evaluation of the Phi's by Gauss's method of substitution

variables, since the other regressions have no significance for us. The computations are shown in Figure VI*a*.

A comparison of the β-coefficients of Figure VI*a* with their standard errors shows that $\beta_{15} = 0.020767$ is only one-eighth as large as its standard error, $s_{\beta_{15}} = 0.16455$. The coefficient of the variable z_5 is therefore statistically insignificant in this equation, and the variable may be omitted. The omission of a variable for which the regression coefficient is less than its standard error will increase the value of the adjusted multiple correlation coefficient.[28]

Since z_5 is the last variable in the regression equation, the procedure for omitting it does not require the use of equation (8.19*c*) and is not shown in the figure. All that need be done is to ignore the entire section in Figure V*a* which pertains to this variable (cols. E and V and ll. 18–24), and solve for $P_{ij)5(}$ in exactly the same manner as we would have solved for the P_{ij}'s in a four-variable problem. (See Fig. IV and eqs. [8.18]). The values $P_{i4)5(}$ ($i = 1, \ldots, 4$) are then, respectively, obtained from line 17, columns R, S, T, and U. The value $P_{13)5(}$ is given by the entry in line 11, column R, plus 0.94908 (l. 11, col. D) times P_{14}. The remaining P's are computed in the same way by formulas (8.18). This adjusted set of P's is then used in the computation of the β's. The final step (not shown in our forms) consists of converting the β's into b's by multiplying by σ_1/σ_i ($i = 1, \ldots, 4$). This yields, in the symbols of chapter viii,

$$(9.1) \qquad x'_{dc} = -0.2264 - 0.1248y' + 0.8936w' + 0.0075Mt,$$
$$(0.0570) \qquad (0.1365) \qquad (0.0028)$$

which is equation 6 of Table 20 of that chapter.

Turning next to the regression of z_2 on the remaining variables (second part of Fig. VI*a*), we see that the coefficient $\beta_{24} = -0.065475$ has a value only one-fourth of its standard error, $s_{\beta_{24}} = 0.26240$. The variable z_4 in this equation is therefore statistically insignificant and may be omitted. Since we desire only one regression equation of the variables z_1, z_2, z_3, and z_5—that of z_2 on the remaining variables—the most convenient way to eliminate z_4 from the original equation is to adjust the β_{ij}'s of this equation directly. A form similar to the first section of Figure V*c* may be drawn up and equation (7.9) applied systematically to the β_{ij}'s. In many problems it is, however, desirable to eliminate the same variable from more than one of the elementary regression equations. In that case it is best to adjust the P's for the omission of the variable, for then all of the elementary regressions may be derived from this new set of P's without further adjustments. As an illustration of the method we shall adjust the P's for the omission of z_4, notwithstanding the fact that, since we are interested in only one regression, it would be more convenient to adjust the β's directly.

The formula which we need has already been given. It is

$$(8.19c) \qquad\qquad P_{hi)4(} = P_{hi} - \frac{P_{h4}}{P_{44}} P_{4i} .$$

[28] Fisher, *op. cit.*, sec. 29.1.

First Elementary Regression Equation: $z_1 = \beta_{12}z_2 + \beta_{13}z_3 + \beta_{14}z_4 + \beta_{15}z_5$

$n = 16, \quad k = 5$		$i = 2$	$i = 3$	$i = 4$	$i = 5$
$S_1^{*2} \equiv P_{11}^{-1} =$ .19124.	$\beta_{1i} = -P_{1i}/P_{11} =$	— .29022	.87717	— .35550	.020707
$R_1^2 \equiv 1 - S_1^{*2} =$ .80876					
$\epsilon_1^{*2} \equiv \dfrac{n}{n-k} S_1^{*2} =$ .27817	$P_{ii} =$	2.29675	5.32840	1.74940	1.55972
	$\beta_{1i} P_{1i} =$	— .44042	— 4.02334	— .66085	— .002255
$\epsilon_1^{*2}/n =$ .017386	$s_{\beta_{1i}}^2 = \dfrac{\epsilon_1^{*2}}{n}(P_{ii} + \beta_{1i} P_{1i}) =$	.032274	.022690	.018926	.027078
$R_1 =$ .89931	$s_{\beta_{1i}} =$	.17965	.15063	.13757	.16455

Second Elementary Regression Equation: $z_2 = \beta_{21}z_1 + \beta_{23}z_3 + \beta_{24}z_4 + \beta_{25}z_5$

$n = 16, \quad k = 5$		$i = 1$	$i = 3$	$i = 4$	$i = 5$
$S_2^{*2} \equiv P_{22}^{-1} =$ .43540	$\beta_{2i} = -P_{2i}/P_{22} =$	.66074	.89722	— .065475	.42467
$R_2^2 \equiv 1 - S_2^{*2} =$ .56460					
$\epsilon_2^{*2} \equiv \dfrac{n}{n-k} S_2^{*2} =$ .63331	$P_{ii} =$	5.22903	5.32840	1.74940	1.55972
	$\beta_{2i} P_{2i} =$	— 1.00271	— 1.84890	— .00985	— .41421
$\epsilon_2^{*2}/n =$ .039582	$s_{\beta_{2i}}^2 = \dfrac{\epsilon_2^{*2}}{n}(P_{ii} + \beta_{2i} P_{2i}) =$	.16729	.13773	.068855	.045342
$R_2 =$ .75140	$s_{\beta_{2i}} =$	.40901	.37112	.26240	.21294

FIG. VIa.—Derivation of the coefficients in the elementary regression equations with their standard errors and the multiple correlation coefficients

NOTE.—In this illustration only two regression equations are derived, because the regressions of z_3 (business conditions), z_4 (time), and z_5 (time squared) on the remaining variables have no economic meaning.

Figure V*c*, which is self-explanatory, shows how this formula is applied systematically to all of the P_{ij}'s in the set. The new P's are then checked in all sets of equations (8.17) except that for which $h = 4$. In our illustration these checks agreed to three digits in the fifth place. Once the P's have been adjusted for the omission of z_4, the β's of the subset, as well as their standard errors, may be computed in the same way as the original regressions and their standard errors. Figure VI*b* is an illustration of the method.

When the β_{2i}'s shown in Figure VI*b* are converted into the corresponding b_{2i}'s, and the symbols of chapter viii are substituted for those used in the computations, the regression equation becomes:

$$(9.2) \qquad y' = -0.9613 - 1.4464 x'_{dc} + 2.0748 w' - 0.0055 M l^2 .$$
$$\qquad\qquad (0.7269) \qquad (0.7139) \qquad (0.0025)$$

This is equation 6 of Table 21, chapter viii.

X. THE ACCURACY OF THE NUMERICAL RESULTS

We now turn to one of the most important, yet one of the most neglected, problems in social and economic statistics, namely, the determination of the number of significant figures to be retained in statistical constants. This is quite a different problem from that of determining the intrinsic accuracy of the underlying data, which was treated in chapter v. For this problem we assume that the basic data are correct to within one unit in the last place, and attempt to determine the number of significant figures which we are justified in retaining in the derived constants—the means, the coefficients of correlation, the coefficients of regression, etc. The problem is important because not only is much time wasted on computations, owing to the retention of more figures than the precision of the data warrants, but results expressed to many decimal places without regard to their precision give a very misleading impression of accuracy.

For physical and engineering computations there are definite and consistent rules covering the retention of significant figures. These have been briefly summarized by Professor Bartlett as follows:

RULE 1. In casting off places of figures increase by 1 the last figure retained, when the following figure is 5 or over.

RULE 2. In the precision measure[29] retain two significant figures.

RULE 3. In any quantity retain enough significant figures to include the place in which the second significant figure of its precision measure occurs.

RULE 4. When several quantities are to be added or subtracted, apply Rule 3 to the least precise and keep only the corresponding figures in the other quantities.

RULE 5. When several quantities are to be multiplied or divided into each other, find the percentage precision of the least precise. If this is

> 1 per cent or more, use four significant figures.
> .1 per cent or more, use five significant figures.
> .01 per cent or more, use six significant figures.

in all the work. If the final result obtained in this way conflicts with Rule 3, apply the latter.

[29] In engineering computations the precision measure is generally taken to be the mean deviation. When the errors are normally distributed, this quantity bears a definite relation to the standard error.

Directions	$P_{51)4(}$	$P_{52)4(}$	$P_{53)4(}$	$P_{55)4(}$
P_{5i} [i = 1, ... ,)4(5] $-(P_{54}/P_{44})P_{4i} = .13762 \cdot P_{4i}$	− .10859 .25582	.97536 .02070	− .40784 − .21498	1.55972 − .03313
Total	.14723 $= P_{51)4(}$	.99606 $= P_{52)4(}$	− .62282 $= P_{53)4(}$	1.52659 $= P_{55)4(}$

	$P_{31)4(}$	$P_{32)4(}$	$P_{33)4(}$
P_{3i} (i = 1, ... , 3) $-(P_{34}/P_{44})P_{4i} = .89293 \cdot P_{4i}$	−4.58673 1.65989	−2.06070 .13428	5.32840 −1.39485
Total	−2.92684 $= P_{31)4(}$	−1.92642 $= P_{32)4(}$	3.93355 $= P_{33)4(}$

	$P_{21)4(}$	$P_{22)4(}$
P_{2i} (i = 1, 2) $-(P_{24}/P_{44})P_{4i} = -.085961 P_{4i}$	1.51755 − .15979	2.29675 − .01293
Total	1.35776 $= P_{21)4(}$	2.28382 $= P_{22)4(}$

	$P_{11)4(}$
P_{11} $-(P_{41}/P_{44})P_{41} = -1.06260 P_{41}$	5.22903 −1.97529
Total	3.25374 $= P_{11)4(}$

FIG. Vc.—Adjustment of the P_{hi}'s for the omission of z_4 by the formula $P_{hi)4(} = P_{hi} - \dfrac{P_{h4}}{P_{44}} \cdot P_{4i}$.

NOTE.—If the variable to be omitted happens to be the last—z_5 in our illustration—it is not necessary to make use of the equation for the adjustment of the P's. For the procedure to be used see the text.

RULE 6. When logarithms are used, retain as many places in the mantissae as there are significant figures retained in the data under Rule 5.[30]

[30] Dana P. Bartlett, *General Principles of the Method of Least Squares* (3d. ed.; Boston, 1915), p. 24. I am grateful to the late Professor Bartlett's family (Mrs. J. Gardner Bartlett) for permission to quote.

For a general discussion of the subject and for a justification of these rules see Silas W. Holman, *Discussion of the Precision of Measurements with Examples Taken Mainly from Physics and Electrical Engineering* (New York, 1892), pp. 76–85. For a briefer treatment of the same subject see Harry M. Goodwin, *Elements of the Precision of Measurements and Graphical Methods* (New York, 1919), pp. 21–38.

Second Elementary Regression Equation (Adjusted): $z_2 = \beta_{21)4(} z_1 + \beta_{23)4(} z_3 + \beta_{25)4(} z_5$

$n = 16, \quad k = 4$		$i = 1$	$i = 3$	$i = 4$	$i = 5$
$S^{*2}_{2)4(} = P^{-1}_{22)4(} =$	.43786				
$R^2_{2)4(} \equiv 1 - S^{*2}_{2)4(} =$	.56214	$\beta_{2i)4(} = -P_{2i)4(}/P_{22)4(} =$	$-$ .59451	.84351		$-$ .43614
$\epsilon^{*2}_{2)4(} \equiv \dfrac{n}{n-k} S^{*2}_{2)4(} =$	.58381	$P_{ii)4(} =$	3.25374	3.93355	(X_4 is the omitted variable)	1.52659
		$\beta_{2i)4(} \cdot P_{2i)4(} =$	$-$ .80720	$-$ 1.62495		$-$ .43442
$\epsilon^{*2}_{2)4(}/n =$	.036488	$s^2_{\beta_{2i)4(}} = \dfrac{\epsilon^{*2}_{2)4(}}{n}[P_{ii)4(} + \beta_{2i)4(}\, P_{2i)4(}] =$	.089269	.084236		.039851
$R_{2)4(} =$	.74976	$s_{\beta_{2i)4(}} =$	.29878	.29023		.19963

FIG. VI*b.*—Derivation of the second elementary regression with z_4 omitted

NOTE.—The other elementary regressions of the subset z_1, z_2, z_3, and z_5 (z_4 omitted) may be computed in the same way. However, only two of these regressions—those with z_1 and z_2 as the dependent variables—have economic meaning, and only the latter is of interest in this subset (see text). If only one regression of the subset is desired, much labor may be saved by adjusting the β's of the original set directly by means of formula (7.9). Figures VI*c* and VI*b* are convenient when two or more regressions of the subset are desired.

Of these, the most important for our immediate purposes is Rule 2, which may be stated more definitely as follows:

In all deviation and precision measures retain two, and only two, significant figures .... the place of figures corresponding to the *first* significant figure of the deviation measure is somewhat uncertain (from 1 to 9 units), while the place corresponding to the *second* significant figure in the deviation measure is uncertain by ten times this amount (10 to 90 units, or more exactly, 10 to 99 units). Beyond this place the significance of additional figures is so slight as to be of no value.[31]

For the adjustment of social, economic, and biological observations, which are subject to much greater errors than are physical observations, no such general rule has been adopted by statisticians, although different modifications of the physical rule have been suggested from time to time. The latest suggestion appears to be that of Professor Roessler, who recommends the following "definite, simple, yet mathematically sound rule" to workers in the social and biological sciences: "*In a final published constant retain no figures beyond the position of the first significant figure in the standard error; keep one more place in all computations.*"[32]

If, for example, the mean and the standard error of the heights of a group of men (given to the nearest inch) are found to be 68.6435 inches and 0.0797 inch, respectively, then, according to this rule, the result should be given as 68.64 inches $\pm$ 0.08 inch, and all computations should be carried to three decimals.

Although the rule is simple, it is not always convenient or even possible to apply it for the following reasons: (1) The standard error may be either unattainable or known only at the end of the computations. (2) When the underlying data differ considerably in the number of significant figures, and the work is done on an electric calculating machine, it may be more convenient to carry all computations to a larger number of *decimals* than would be justified by the rule, and then to round off the results. This is especially true when the computer is not a mathematician and cannot be trusted to apply the rule correctly to each step in the computations. (3) Some computations, especially those involving the solution of normal equations, may well require decimals considerably in excess of the number that proved to be significant in the results.

The first two reasons are quite obvious. The third requires an explanation. It is due to the fact that very often some of the significant figures of the observations are lost in the determination of the statistical constants. Consider, for example, the formula for the simple coefficient of correlation:

$$(10.1) \qquad r_{12} \equiv \frac{p_{12}}{\sigma_1 \sigma_2} = \frac{\dfrac{\Sigma X_1 X_2}{n} - M_1 M_2}{\left(\dfrac{\Sigma X_1^2}{n} - M_1^2\right)^{1/2} \left(\dfrac{\Sigma X_2^2}{n} - M_2^2\right)^{1/2}}$$

---

[31] Goodwin, *op. cit.*, pp. 23–24. I am grateful to the author and his publishers, McGraw Hill Book Co., Inc., for permission to quote.

[32] Edward B. Roessler, "Significant Figures in Statistical Constants," *Science* (N.S.), LXXXIV, No. 2178 (September 25, 1936), 289–90. (Italics are Roessler's.)

and suppose that each observation in X_1 and X_2 is determined to four significant figures and is positive. Then $(\Sigma X_1 X_2)/n$ and $M_1 M_2$ will be determined to four or five significant figures. If, however, the first three digits of the two terms are the same, r_{12} will be determined to only one or two significant figures. In this case any additional figures obtained from the division of the numerator by the denominator of (10.1) are wholly illusory, and the labor spent on the additional computation is a waste of time.

Consider next the normal equations (2.4b). We know from elementary algebra that these linear equations have a unique solution for the coefficients $b_{11}, \ldots, b_{1i}$, $\ldots, b_{1k}$, if the determinant D of the coefficients—see (2.5)—is not zero. (If the determinant is zero, at least one of the coefficients may be assigned an arbitrary finite value.) This solution is given by (2.6) or (in more explicit form) by (2.7). If all the elements of D were perfectly accurate, and if the equations were solved in terms of common fractions, the resulting b's would satisfy the normal equations absolutely.

In practical problems the elements of D are known only approximately; that is, to some number of significant figures, and the question arises: To how many significant figures are the b's determined? The answer is contained in a paper by Moulton published twenty-five years ago and recently summarized in a discussion of this subject.[33] It is that *the number of significant figures in the solution for the regression coefficients cannot exceed the number of significant figures in the determinant D, but usually equals it.* Since the determinant is a sum of products, the number of significant figures in it is obtained by applying the engineering rules 4 and 5 given above to each element and to the final sum. Thus if each element $\Sigma X_i X_k$ is given to six significant figures, the product of such elements will be determined to at least six significant figures. But the sum of such products may be determined only to a smaller number of significant figures. It is this number of significant figures which determines the limit of accuracy of the regression coefficients.

The following example, which I am taking from a paper by Deming, with his permission,[34] should make this clear. Suppose that our normal equations are

$$(10.2a) \quad \begin{cases} 1.994009b_{11} + 1.998994b_{12} + 1.997000b_{13} = 11.982997 \\ 1.998994b_{11} + 6.004004b_{12} + 0.002000b_{13} = 14.013002 \\ 1.997000b_{11} + 0.002000b_{12} + 3.000000b_{13} = 11.001000 \ . \end{cases}$$

If we solve these equations by eliminating first b_{11} and then b_{11} and b_{12}, we obtain, respectively,

$$(10.2b) \quad \begin{cases} 4.000013b_{12} - 1.999992b_{13} = 2.000048 \\ 0.000016b_{13} = 0.000046 \ . \end{cases}$$

[33] F. R. Moulton, "On the Solutions of Linear Equations Having Small Determinants," *American Mathematical Monthly*, XX (1913), 242–49; "Memoir on the Theory of Determining Orbits," *Astronomical Journal*, XXVIII (1913–15), 103–27; and "Significant Figures in Statistical Constants," *Science* (N.S.), LXXXIV, No. 2191 (1936), 574–75.

[34] W. Edwards Deming, "On the Significant Figures of Least Squares and Correlation," *Science* (N.S.), LXXXV, No. 2210 (May 7, 1937), 451–54. I have taken the liberty to modify Dr. Deming's symbols.

It will be seen immediately that, since 0.000016 contains only two figures, b_{13} is determined only to two significant figures, no matter how many decimals are carried to the right. If we had carried three or even four decimals in (10.2a), we could then have assigned *any* value to b_{13} and have obtained values for b_{11} and b_{12} which would satisfy (10.2). It is also clear from (10.2) that the inaccuracy in b_{13} will be passed on to b_{12} and b_{11} in the substitutions. This example illustrates the effect on the significance of the regression coefficients of a small number of significant figures in the determinant of (10.2a), for this determinant has a value of only 0.00013, indicating that, when six decimals are carried throughout in the solution, not more than two can be significant in the values of the regression coefficients, no matter what the order of their solution may be.

We are now in a position to explain why some computations require decimals considerably in excess of the number significant. *If it is desired to satisfy the normal equations to six decimals, the regression coefficients must be computed to six decimals, although no more than two can be significant.* Thus, in the present example, we must have

$$b_{11} = 1.187844 , \qquad b_{12} = 1.937500 , \qquad b_{13} = 2.875000 .$$

The presence of all the figures written is required for the satisfaction of the normal equations to six decimals.

Does this mean that we have somehow evolved accuracy out of inaccuracy? Not at all. As Dr. Deming shows, we can round off b_{13} to 2.9 and obtain

$$b_{11} = 1.150275 , \qquad b_{12} = 1.950000 , \qquad b_{13} = 2.900000 ,$$

which satisfy the equations equally well. In fact, the set

$$b_{11} = 0.774586 , \qquad b_{12} = 2.075001 , \qquad b_{13} = 3.150000$$

also satisfies the equations to six decimals, although it differs from the other set in the first figure! There is, in fact, an infinite number of sets of parameters which satisfies the normal equations (10.2a) to six decimals; the set which satisfies them *absolutely* is

$$b_{11} = 1 , \qquad b_{12} = 2 , \qquad b_{13} = 3 .$$

Deming explains the infinitude of solutions as follows:

So long as D differs from zero by any finite number, however small, there is one and only one value of b_{11}, one of b_{12}, and one of b_{13}, that will satisfy the normal equations absolutely. These values can be found by holding to common fractions throughout the solution; and when this is done, any two procedures for solution will give identical and perfect results. There will nevertheless be a band of b_{11} values, a band of b_{12} values and a band of b_{13} values, not necessarily of the same width, from which can be picked any number of sets b_{11}, b_{12}, b_{13} that will satisfy the equations to the number of decimals required—the greater the accuracy required, the narrower the bands. Moreover, for satisfaction of the equations to a specified number of decimals, the bands can be made wider and wider as D diminishes; in the limit when D is zero the equations are completely indeterminate, which means that b_{11} or b_{12} or b_{13}—one of them (two if D is of rank one)—can be assigned any value whatever for absolute satisfaction of the equations.

The width of each band is in fact the interval within which the corresponding unknown is significantly determined. Different methods of solution are merely devices for picking out from these bands different sets for b_{11}, b_{12}, b_{13} that will satisfy the equations as far as required. If D is small, the bands will be wide, and the results of two different methods of solution may appear alarmingly discrepant, yet be consistent with the equations to the last decimal.[35]

Although the solution of (10.2) is, as we have seen, determinate to only two places, the equations will not be satisfied to six decimals if we vary the parameters arbitrarily even in the sixth decimal alone. Thus, it is not permissible to round off b_{11}, b_{12}, and b_{13} to two figures simply because they are significant to only two figures. Six decimals are required if the equations are to be satisfied to six decimals.

The discussion of this section has centered about the solution for the b's and their determinant D. The conclusions are equally applicable to the evaluation of the β's and the correlation determinant Δ defined by (5.6).

In 1928–29, when the investigations of which this book is a partial summary were being planned, we experimented with different methods and procedures for solving normal equations and discovered empirically that some computations may well require decimals considerably in excess of the number significant, if the results are to check to a required number of places. At that time we did not know of Moulton's important paper but related the phenomenon to the existence of high correlations between the independent variables and to the effect which this had on the correlation determinant Δ.

This discovery, combined with the necessity of developing procedures and checks which could be followed by students and assistants with varying mathematical and statistical backgrounds, working with series of varying degrees of accuracy, led us to adopt the practice of retaining more places in the computations than is warranted by the numerical accuracy of the data, and then rounding off the results.

It is exceedingly difficult to give a concise and accurate evaluation of the numerical accuracy of our published results, for it probably differs considerably from chapter to chapter, and perhaps also from one group of equations to the next in the same chapter. The chief sources of inaccuracy are the varying number of significant figures in the underlying series of quantities and prices (see Appen. A), and the varying number of significant figures lost in the computations.

As an example of the type of difficulty encountered, we may consider the numerical accuracy of the series used in the numerical illustration of Section IX: (1) the per capita United States consumption of cotton; (2) the deflated United States farm price of cotton; and (3) W. M. Persons' "Index of United States Industrial Production and Trade." Of these, only the third was given; the other two had to be derived from the basic data on total consumption and money prices.

The per capita consumption is, of course, the result obtained by dividing the total consumption (given in bales) by the population of the United States and multiplying the quotient by the average number of pounds per bale. Thus for 1915 this yielded

$$\frac{6,397,613 \text{ bales} \times 484 \text{ lb./bale}}{100,050,000 \text{ individuals}} = 30.949 \text{ lb./capita} .$$

[35] *Ibid.*, pp. 452–53. I have taken the liberty to modify his symbols. I learn from Dr. W. E. Deming that Dr. L. B. Tuckerman, of the National Bureau of Standards, has been making a study of this problem and will have something important to add later on.

We don't know the degree of precision of either the total consumption or the population series. Certainly the last two digits, and probably the last three, are not significant. The net weight per bale is subject to an error of at least one unit in the last place, or of 0.2 per cent. Even if the total consumption and the population series were entirely accurate, this error alone would render the consumption per capita correct to only three significant figures. In our computations, however, we have taken it to five figures, and also used five-place logarithms.

The prices are given in general to four significant figures. The deflator (Bureau of Labor Statistics "Index of Wholesale Prices") is given to only three. We have, however, taken both the deflated price and its logarithm to five figures.

Persons' "Index of Industrial Production and Trade" is given to four places. According to Rule 6, four-place logarithms should have been used for this series. However, we thought it more convenient to use the same number of places—five—in the logarithms for all of the series.

The product terms which enter into the formula for the simple coefficients of correlation were computed on a United Calculating Machine, which prints and adds the products to the full number of places. For the purpose of checking, it was convenient to carry all of the places given by the machine, and then round off the results.

Although the logarithms were assumed to be correct to five places, the coefficients of correlation between some pairs of the logarithmic series were found correct to a smaller number of places. The least accurate of these turned out to be r_{12}, for

$$\frac{\Sigma X_1 X_2}{n} - M_1 M_2 \qquad \text{(See eq. [10.1])}$$

was

$$1.564296 - 1.564637 = -0.000341 ,$$

which is correct to only three significant figures. (We have assumed that the means are correct to one more place than the items in the series.) Dividing by $\sigma_1\sigma_2 = 0.004433$, we obtain $r_{12} = -0.07689$.

Although this correlation coefficient is correct to only three significant figures, we have allowed one additional place for rounding-off purposes in making entries in the correlation determinant, Figure Va. The remaining correlation coefficients are correct to four significant figures, except r_{24} and r_{25}, which are correct to five. This justifies us in carrying five *decimals* throughout the computations of Figure Va. The figures in italics are those which would have been dropped by the application of Rules 4 and 5 given above, if we did not wish our equations to be satisfied to five decimals.

This illustration shows the impossibility of determining the numerical accuracy of derived statistical parameters without a careful examination of each step in the computations. From an examination of the computations underlying the equations of this book we conclude that it is unlikely that we have lost more than one or two decimals in the process. The regression coefficients presented are, therefore, numerically correct to at least two significant figures.

APPENDIX D

THE STANDARD ERROR OF THE COEFFICIENT OF
ELASTICITY OF DEMAND

THE STANDARD ERROR OF THE COEFFICIENT OF ELASTICITY OF DEMAND

Let the demand function be

(1)
$$x = x(y, z, w, \ldots, t),$$

where x stands for quantity, y for price, z, w, . . . , for other variables, and t for time. The partial elasticity of demand is then

(2)
$$\eta = \frac{\partial x}{\partial y} \cdot \frac{y}{x}.$$

It is required to determine the standard error of η, given the standard errors of the parameters of (1).

It will be sufficient for present purposes to consider two special cases of demand functions: (1) that in which η is the same at every point on the curve and (2) that in which η varies from point to point on the curve.

As an example of the first case we may cite the equation

(3a)
$$x = A y^\alpha e^{\beta t + \gamma t^2},$$

which becomes, upon taking logarithms,

(3b)
$$\log_e x = \log_e A + \alpha \log_e y + \beta t + \gamma t^2.$$

Here the elasticity of demand is a constant:

(4)
$$\eta = \frac{\partial x}{\partial y} \cdot \frac{y}{x} = \frac{\partial \log x}{\partial \log y} = \alpha.$$

If the demand equation (3b) is fitted by the method of least squares, the process of fitting may be easily modified so that it will also yield the standard errors of all the parameters.[2] Then by (4)

$$\sigma_\eta = \sigma_\alpha.$$

[1] In the preparation of this appendix I have had the benefit of discussions with my friend and colleague, Professor Walter Bartky of the Department of Astronomy, University of Chicago. The proof of (10b) is his, and is somewhat neater than the one which I had developed. Professor Bartky also deduced another upper limit for σ_η, but, as that limit gave consistently higher values than (10b), it was considered less satisfactory than the latter.

I am also grateful to my assistant, Mr. Jacob L. Mosak, for permission to give the *exact* formula for the standard error of the coefficient of the elasticity of demand, which he developed while reading the proofs of this book, and which should be substituted for my formula (18) in all future work.

[2] See my "Standard Error of a Forecast from a Curve," *Jour. Amer. Statist. Assoc.*, XXV (June, 1930), 139–85.

The only difficulty that may arise in this connection is that when we fit $(3b)$ we are minimizing the sum of the squares of the logarithmic residuals of x, while we may really wish to minimize the sum of the squares of the residuals of x. The former procedure gives greater weight to the low values of x. But this can be overcome by properly weighting the observation equations of $(3b)$. In any event, the use of the second method of fitting is not likely materially to affect the value of a or its standard error when the data used are annual consumption and average annual prices, for the reason that the scatter of quantity on price (both variables being corrected for secular trend) is generally too small to enable us to say that the two values of a obtained by the two different methods of fitting are significantly different from each other.

As an example of the second case, we may take the equation

$$(5) \qquad x = a + by + ct + dt^2 .$$

The fitting of this equation by the method of least squares yields the standard error of b, as well as the standard errors of the other parameters. But the elasticity of demand, η, derived from this equation, namely,

$$(6a) \qquad \eta = \frac{\partial x}{\partial y} \cdot \frac{y}{x} = b \frac{y}{x} ,$$

is a function of y and x, as well as of b. We are required to determine the error of this function.

Denote the foregoing expression by

$$(6b) \qquad \eta = \eta(b, y, x) .$$

Then we know that errors Δb, Δy, and Δx in b, y, and x, respectively, are related to a corresponding error $\Delta \eta$ in the function, by the equation

$$(7) \qquad \Delta \eta = \eta_b \, \Delta b + \eta_y \, \Delta y + \eta_x \, \Delta x ,$$

where

$$(8) \qquad \eta_b = \frac{\partial \eta}{\partial b} , \qquad \eta_y = \frac{\partial \eta}{\partial y} , \qquad \eta_x = \frac{\partial \eta}{\partial x} .$$

This expression for $\Delta \eta$, which assumes that the squares and higher powers of the errors may be neglected, holds for any kind of errors whatever. Thus, if Δb, Δy, and Δx are actual errors of measurement, with known signs, the magnitude and the sign of $\Delta \eta$ could be determined by (7).

In most statistical investigations, however, we are concerned with the *sampling* errors of the several variables, which are given approximately by the standard errors σ_η, σ_b, σ_y, and σ_x.

If the correlations between b, y, and x were known, the value of σ_η would be given by the well-known relation

$$(9)\quad \sigma_\eta = \sqrt{\eta_b^2 \sigma_b^2 + \eta_y^2 \sigma_y^2 + \eta_x^2 \sigma_x^2 + 2r_{by}\, \eta_b\, \eta_y\, \sigma_b\, \sigma_y + 2r_{bx}\, \eta_b\, \eta_x \sigma_b\, \sigma_x + 2r_{xy}\, \eta_x\, \eta_y\, \sigma_x\, \sigma_y}\,,$$

where the r's are the coefficients of correlation between the variables indicated by the subscripts. But since they are not known, and since it is generally not safe to neglect them, it is desirable to determine an upper limit to σ_η, so that we may have at least some estimate of the sampling fluctuations of η. A simple expression for an upper limit may be obtained from (9) by treating all the partial derivatives as positive and replacing each correlation coefficient by unity. Since r_{by}, r_{bx}, and r_{xy} are actually less than unity, we have

$$(10a)\quad \begin{cases} \sigma_\eta^2 < \eta_b^2 \sigma_b^2 + \eta_y^2 \sigma_y^2 + \eta_x^2 \sigma_x^2 + 2\,|\eta_b\, \eta_y\, \sigma_b\, \sigma_y| + 2\,|\eta_b\, \eta_x \sigma_b\, \sigma_x| + 2\,|\eta_x\, \eta_y\, \sigma_x\, \sigma_y| \\ < (|\eta_b\, \sigma_b| + |\eta_y\, \sigma_y| + |\eta_x \sigma_x|)^2 \end{cases}$$

or

$$(10b)\quad \sigma_\eta < |\eta_b\, \sigma_b| + |\eta_y\, \sigma_y| + |\eta_x \sigma_x|\,.$$

To apply this equation, we need the values of the partial derivatives and of the standard errors of b, y, and x.

The partial derivatives are obtained from (6a), which gives

$$(11)\quad \eta_b = \frac{y}{x}\,,\qquad \eta_y = \frac{b}{x}\,,\qquad \eta_x = \frac{-by}{x^2}\,.$$

The standard error σ_b offers no difficulty, since it is determined in the curve-fitting process. There remains the determination of σ_y and σ_x.

The determination of σ_y gives rise to an interesting question. Since in fitting such a demand curve as (5) we generally minimize the sum of the squares of the residuals in x,

$$\sum_1^n v^2 = \sum_1^n \{x_o - (a + by + ct + dt^2)\}^2\,,$$

we thereby assume that the independent variables y and t are free from errors. Shall we, therefore, put $\sigma_y = 0$ in (10a)? There could be no objection to this procedure if y were actually free from errors. But this is not true in general. The primary reason for making this assumption is that the assumption that both x and y are subject to error would either make it impossible to fit the demand curve (5) by the method of least squares, or would enormously complicate the process. It is clear, therefore, that under these conditions to put $\sigma_y = 0$ is to underestimate σ_η. But this is not so objectionable as it appears, since the standard error of the constant elasticity $\eta = a$ deduced from (3b) is also subject to the same limitation, for in fitting (3b), the assumption is made that $\log y$ is free from error; the two standard errors would, therefore, be comparable to this extent.

We may, however, make some allowance for the standard errors in y, if we agree to compute our elasticity of demand for that point on the demand curve for which y has its mean value[3] $y = \bar{y}$. Now the standard error of $\bar{y}$ has the well-known value

$$(12) \qquad \sigma_{\bar{y}} = \frac{\sigma'_y}{\sqrt{n-1}},$$

where n is the number of observations, and σ'_y is the *standard deviation* of y, and is to be distinguished from σ_y, which, in this appendix, is used to denote the *standard error of sampling* of a particular value of y. This assumption permits us to write

$$(13) \qquad \sigma_y = \sigma_{\bar{y}}$$

in $(10b)$.

For σ_x we should take

$$(14) \qquad \sigma_x = \sigma_f,$$

where σ_f is the "standard error of a function."[4] For the regression equation

$$x = a + by + \ldots + mt,$$

it gives the error in the *computed* values of x, and is a function of the errors in the parameters $a, b, \ldots, m$. Thus, if we write the regression in the form

$$x = f(a, b, \ldots, m),$$

we obtain for the standard error of the function x,

$$(15) \qquad \sigma_x \equiv \sigma_f = \epsilon_x \left\{ [aa]\left(\frac{\partial f}{\partial a}\right)^2 + [\beta\beta]\left(\frac{\partial f}{\partial b}\right)^2 + \ldots + [\mu\mu]\left(\frac{\partial f}{\partial m}\right)^2 \right.$$
$$\left. + 2[a\beta]\frac{\partial f}{\partial a} \cdot \frac{\partial f}{\partial b} + \ldots + 2[a\mu]\frac{\partial f}{\partial a} \cdot \frac{\partial f}{\partial m} + \ldots + 2[\beta\mu]\frac{\partial f}{\partial b} \cdot \frac{\partial f}{\partial m} \right\}^{1/2}.$$

In this equation ϵ_x is the quadratic mean error

$$(16) \qquad \epsilon_x = \sqrt{\frac{[vv]_x}{n-m}},$$

where n = number of sets of observations and m = number of parameters. This is an approximation to the hypothetical "standard error of a single observation" of least-square theory, which is assumed to be typical of the entire set of observations,

[3] Even if the elasticity is desired for any other point on the demand curve, it may still be worth while arbitrarily to assume that the (unknown) standard error of y is approximately given by the standard error of the mean of y.

[4] For a full treatment of this concept see the paper cited in n. 2.

in so far as precision is concerned. The quantities in the square brackets in (15) are the reciprocals of the weights of the parameters and can be calculated from the normal equations.[5] This function increases with $x = f(y, z, w, \ldots, t)$ as we extrapolate x beyond the range of the observations. Thus, if x is a linear function of two variables y and t,

$$x = a + by + ct,$$

$$\sigma_f = \sigma_x = \epsilon_x \{[aa] + [\beta\beta]y^2 + [\gamma\gamma]t^2 + 2[a\beta]y + 2[a\gamma]t + 2[\beta\gamma]yt\}^{1/2}.$$

This is a hyperboloid of two sheets with its minimum at the arithmetic means.

If we agree to compute η at that point on the demand surface, $x = x(y, z, \ldots, t)$, for which the independent variables assume their mean values: $y = \bar{y}$, $z = \bar{z}$, $\ldots$, $t = \bar{t}$, then in the special case, when the demand function is linear, $x = \bar{x}$, and the formula for σ_f reduces to $\sigma_f = \dfrac{1}{\sqrt{n}} \epsilon_x$. If, however, the demand function is non-linear (as in [5]), the dependent variable x is not equal to its mean value when the independent variables are given their mean values. At that point on this function, σ_f is not equal to $\dfrac{1}{\sqrt{n}} \epsilon_x$, and the evaluation of it becomes a more or less laborious task. We have, therefore, decided to substitute in both linear and nonlinear demand functions the constant ϵ_x for σ_f and to make use of the approximate relation

$$(17) \qquad\qquad \sigma_x = \epsilon_x.$$

[5] Thus, for the regression equation,

$$x = a + by + \ldots + mt,$$

the determinant of the coefficients in the normal equations is:

$$D = \begin{vmatrix} n & \Sigma y & \ldots & \Sigma t \\ \Sigma y & \Sigma y^2 & \ldots & \Sigma yt \\ \cdot & \cdot & \cdot & \cdot \\ \Sigma t & \Sigma yt & \ldots & \Sigma t^2 \end{vmatrix}$$

If now we let D_{ij} denote the cofactor of the element in the ith row and the jth column, we have

$$[aa] \equiv \frac{1}{W_a} = \frac{D_{11}}{D} \qquad\qquad [a\beta] \equiv \frac{1}{W_{ab}} = \frac{D_{12}}{D}$$

$$[\beta\beta] \equiv \frac{1}{W_b} = \frac{D_{22}}{D} \qquad\qquad [a\mu] \equiv \frac{1}{W_{am}} = \frac{D_{1m}}{D}$$

$$[\mu\mu] \equiv \frac{1}{W_m} = \frac{D_{mm}}{D} \qquad\qquad [\beta\mu] \equiv \frac{1}{W_{bm}} = \frac{D_{2m}}{D}$$

See reference in n. 2 of this appendix and the mathematical appendix (Appen. C). In the latter the quantities in the square brackets are designated by the symbol $c_{h \cdot ij}$.

Making the substitutions (11), (13), and (17), in equation (10b), and using the least-squares value for σ_b, we obtain for the upper limit[6] of σ_η

(18a)
$$\sigma_\eta < \left|\frac{y}{x}\sigma_b\right| + \left|\frac{b}{x}\sigma_{\bar{y}}\right| + \left|\frac{by}{x^2}\epsilon_x\right|,$$

or

(18b)
$$\sigma_\eta < \left|\eta\right|\left(\left|\frac{\sigma_b}{b}\right| + \left|\frac{\sigma_{\bar{y}}}{y}\right| + \left|\frac{\epsilon_x}{x}\right|\right).$$

By substituting (17) instead of (14) in (10b), we have in the case of linear demand functions increased the upper limit of σ_η at the point of the means of the variables by $\eta\frac{\epsilon_x}{x}\left(1 - \frac{1}{\sqrt{n}}\right)$. But since this value of σ_η will only be used in comparison with other values of σ_η computed by different methods, no serious objection can be raised against a formula which increases the upper limit of σ_η beyond its correct value, especially when allowance is made for the time saved in computing.

As an illustration, we may compute by (18b) the upper limit to the standard error of the elasticity of demand for sugar.

It was shown in chapter vi that the demand for sugar for the first period (1875–95) is described excellently either by

(19)
$$x = 113.7y^{(-0.3828\pm0.1224)} e^{(0.0156\pm0.0044)t}$$

or by

(20)
$$x = 70.62 - (2.2588 \pm 0.7322)y + (0.8371 \pm 0.2152)t,$$

where x is the per capita consumption in pounds, y is the real (deflated) price in cents per pound, and t is time in years, the origins of x and y being at o, o, and the origin of t being at July 1, 1885. The figures preceded by $\pm$ are least-square standard errors.

From (19) the elasticity of demand with its standard error is easily seen to be the exponent of y, for

(21)
$$\eta = \frac{\partial x}{\partial y}\cdot\frac{y}{x} = \frac{\partial \log x}{\partial \log y} = -0.3828,$$

and

(22)
$$\sigma_\eta = \pm0.1224.$$

This value of η is, of course, a constant, independent of y, x, and t.

From (20), the elasticity of demand is

(23a)
$$\eta = \frac{\partial x}{\partial y}\cdot\frac{y}{x} = -2.2588\frac{y}{x},$$

[6] Formula 18b was suggested to me by Mr. Jacob L. Mosak.

which is an explicit function of y and x, and an implicit function of t. To determine its numerical value we must fix y and x; and to determine x we must fix t, as well as y.

If we fix y and t by giving them their mean values $y = \bar{y} = 8.313$ and $t \equiv \bar{t} = 0$ (since the origin was taken at 1885), we derive the value[7] $x = 51.8429$. Substituting these values of y and x in $(23a)$, we have

$$(23b) \qquad \eta = -2.2588 \frac{8.313}{51.8429} = -0.3622 .$$

To obtain the standard error of this value, we must know the values of the terms on the right-hand side of $(18b)$. The least-square procedure which was used in fitting (20) yields, or can be made to yield,

$$|\sigma_b| = 0.7322 , \qquad |\sigma_{\bar{y}}| = 0.3980 , \qquad \text{and} \qquad |\epsilon_x| = 2.9472 .$$

Substituting in $(18b)$ the values of b, y, and x used in $(23b)$, we obtain for the three terms

$$\left|\frac{\sigma_b}{b}\right| = 0.3242 , \qquad \left|\frac{\sigma_{\bar{y}}}{y}\right| = 0.0479 , \qquad \text{and} \qquad \left|\frac{\epsilon_x}{x}\right| = 0.0568 .$$

Their sum, 0.4289 multiplied by the absolute value of η (0.3622), is an upper limit of σ_η, or $\sigma_\eta < 0.1553$. This may be compared with the standard error derived from (19), namely, $\sigma_\eta = \pm 0.1224$.

Generally the term involving $\sigma_{\bar{y}}/y$ adds little to the value of σ_η. Several random comparisons indicate that its inclusion rarely increases the standard error by as much as 30 per cent.

If for σ_x we substitute not ϵ_x but the standard error of the function (see [15]), which, for a linear curve equals $\epsilon_x/\sqrt{n}$ at the point corresponding to the means of the independent variables, we obtain 0.0124 as the value of $\left|\dfrac{\epsilon_x}{x\sqrt{n}}\right|$ and 0.1393 as the upper limit to the value of σ_η. This represents a reduction of 10 per cent in the value of σ_η computed with the help of the approximate relation (17).

It is formula (18) which was used in computing the standard errors of the elasticities of demand of the demand equations (1), (3), (5) given in Table 3, chapter iv.

A formula for the upper limit of the standard error of the coefficient of price flexibility

$$(24) \qquad \varphi = \frac{\partial y}{\partial x} \cdot \frac{x}{y} ,$$

may also be derived by following the methods explained above.

---

[7] This happens also to be the arithmetic mean of x because (20) is a plane, and we know that a plane, fitted by the method of least squares, must pass through the center of gravity of the observations. If the demand function (20) had not been linear, then the value of x obtained by giving the independent variables y and t their mean values would not have been equal to its mean value.

Thus if our demand function is of the type

(25) $$y = a + bx + ct + dt^2 ,$$

the price flexibility (24) becomes

(26) $$\varphi = b\,\frac{x}{y} ,$$

and the upper limit for σ_φ becomes:

(27a) $$\sigma_\varphi < \left|\frac{x}{y}\,\sigma_b\right| + \left|\frac{b}{y}\,\sigma_{\bar{x}}\right| + \left|\frac{bx}{y^2}\,\epsilon_y\right| ,$$

or

(27b) $$\sigma_\varphi < \left|\varphi\right|\left\{\left|\frac{\sigma_b}{b}\right| + \left|\frac{\sigma_{\bar{x}}}{x}\right| + \left|\frac{\epsilon_y}{y}\right|\right\}.$$

NOTE: THE EXACT VALUE OF THE STANDARD ERROR OF THE COEFFICIENT OF THE ELASTICITY OF DEMAND

After the book had gone to press, my assistant, Mr. Jacob L. Mosak, succeeded in deriving the exact formula for the standard error of the elasticity of demand. A full treatment of this subject will be found in the paper which he is submitting to the *Journal of the American Statistical Association*. In the special case in which the demand function is

(28) $$x = a + by + ct ,$$

Mosak's formula for the standard error of $\eta = b(y/x)$ takes the form

$$(29)\quad \sigma_\eta = \eta\epsilon_x \left\{ \frac{D_{11}}{D}\frac{1}{x^2} + \frac{D_{22}}{D}\left(\frac{\eta-1}{b}\right)^2 + \frac{D_{33}}{D}\left(\frac{t}{x}\right)^2 + 2\,\frac{D_{12}}{D}\cdot\frac{\eta-1}{bx} \right.$$
$$\left. + 2\,\frac{D_{13}}{D}\cdot\frac{t}{x^2} + 2\,\frac{D_{23}}{D}\cdot\frac{(\eta-1)t}{bx} \right\}^{1/2} ,$$

where D and D_{ij} are defined in footnote 5. It is clear from this formula that, like η itself, σ_η varies from point to point on the demand curve.

When the origins of the variables in the demand function (28) are taken at their respective means and η is evaluated at the point $(\bar{x}, \bar{y}, \bar{t})$, then formula (29) reduces to the very simple form

(30) $$\sigma_\eta = \eta\left\{ \left(\frac{\sigma_{\bar{x}}}{\bar{x}}\right)^2 + \left(\frac{\sigma_b}{b}\right)^2 \right\}^{1/2}.$$

Applying this formula to the demand function (20), for which $\eta_{\bar{x}\bar{y}} = -0.3622$, we obtain for the standard error the value $\sigma_\eta = 0.1175$. The ratio of η to this standard error is

$$t = -\frac{0.3622}{0.1175} = -3.083 .$$

When the upper limit of σ_η yielded by (18) is substituted in the foregoing expression, the ratio reduces to

$$t = -\frac{0.3622}{0.1553} = -2.332 \,.$$

When both η and σ_η are determined directly from a constant-elasticity curve fitted to the same data by the method of least squares—see equation (19)—the ratio is

$$t = -\frac{0.3828}{0.1224} = -3.127 \,.$$

It is clear from these results that the elasticity of demand derived from the linear equation (20) is statistically just as significant as the elasticity of demand yielded by the constant-elasticity equation (19): in both cases $t \equiv \eta/\sigma_\eta$ is of the order 3.1.

In using the upper limit of σ_η in our computations we have underestimated the statistical significance of the coefficients of elasticity of demand derived from the linear demand functions.

SELECTED BIBLIOGRAPHY

SELECTED BIBLIOGRAPHY

This bibliography is divided into three parts: (A) "Works Cited in the Text," (B) "Related Works," and (C) "Sources of Data." A few of the works listed in Part B have been taken from the following bibliographies, to which the reader may turn for further references:

WORKING, HOLBROOK. "The Statistical Determination of Demand Curves," *Quarterly Journal of Economics*, Vol. XXXIX (August, 1925).

BERCAW, L. O. "Factors Affecting Prices [A Selected Bibliography]" (mimeographed). Agricultural Economics Bibliography No. 14. Washington, D.C.: U.S. Department of Agriculture, Bureau of Agricultural Economics, March, 1926.

BLACK, J. D. "Research in Prices of Farm Products," *Journal of Farm Economics*, X, No. 1 (January, 1928), 42–70.

WARREN, G. F., and PEARSON, F. A. *Interrelations of Supply and Price.* Cornell University Agricultural Experiment Station Bull. 466. Ithaca, 1928.

WELLS, O. V. *Farmers' Response to Price.* A selected bibliography. Washington: Bureau of Agricultural Economics, 1933.

BERCAW, L. O. "Price Analysis" (mimeographed). Agricultural Economics Bibliography No. 48. Washington, D.C.: U.S. Department of Agriculture, Bureau of Agricultural Economics, 1933.

———. "Price Analysis: Selected References on the Theoretical Aspects of Supply and Demand Curves and Related Subjects, *Econometrica*, II (1934), 398–421.

A. WORKS CITED IN THE TEXT

ALLEN, R. G. D. "The Foundations of a Mathematical Theory of Exchange," *Economica*, XII (1932), 219–23.

———. "On the Marginal Utility of Money and Its Application," *ibid.*, XIII (1933), esp. 187–94.

———. "A Comparison between Different Definitions of Complementary and Competitive Goods," *Econometrica*, II (1934), 168–75.

———. "A Critical Examination of Professor Pigou's Method of Deriving Demand Elasticity," *ibid.*, pp. 249–57.

———. "Nachfragefunktionen für Güter mit korreliertem Nutzen," *Zeitschrift für Nationalökonomie*, V, Heft 4 (1934), 486–506.

———. "The Nature of Indifference Curves," *Review of Economic Studies*, I (1934), 110–21.

———. "A Note on the Determinateness of the Utility Function," *ibid.*, II (1934–35), 155–58.

ALLEN, R. G. D., and BOWLEY, A. L. *Family Expenditure: A Study of Its Variations.* London: P. S. King & Son, Ltd., 1935.

AMOROSO, LUIGI. "Le Equazioni differenziali della dinamica economica," *Giornale degli economisti e rivista di statistica*, LXIX (February, 1929), 68–79.

———. *Lezioni di economia matematica.* Bologna: Nicola Zanichelli, 1921.

———. "Bulla teoria delle curve di utilità," *Gior. degli econ.*, LII (1916), 409–12.

AVRAM, MoÏS H. *The Rayon Industry.* New York: Van Nostrand Co., Inc., 1929.

BAKER, O. E. "Do We Need More Land?" U.S.D.A. Address before Agricultural Experimental Conference, University of Minnesota, December, 1929.

BARONE, E. "Sul trattamento di questioni dinamiche," *Gior. degli econ.*, Vol. IX (1894 II).

BARTLETT, DANA P. *General Principles of the Method of Least Squares.* 3d ed. Boston, 1915.

BEAN, L. H. "Some Interrelationships between the Supply, Price, and Consumption of Cotton" (mimeographed). Washington: U.S. Department of Agriculture, Bureau of Agricultural Economics, 1928.

――――. "A Simplified Method of Graphic Curvilinear Correlation," *Journal of the American Statistical Association*, XXIV (1929), 386–97, esp. Chart V.

――――. "Measuring the Effect of Supplies on Prices of Farm Products," *Journal of Farm Economics*, XV (1933), 349–74, esp. Fig. 3.

BENINI, RODOLFO. "Sul'uso delle formole empiriche nell'economia applicate," *Gior. degli econ.*, XXXV (1907 II), 1052–63.

――――. "Una possibile creazione del metodo statistico: l'economia politica induttiva," *ibid.*, XXXVI (1908 II), 11–34.

BENNETT, M. K., *et al.* "World Wheat Survey and Outlook," *Wheat Studies of the Food Research Institute*, Vol. XII, No. 9 (1936).

――――. "World Wheat Utilization since 1885–86," *ibid.*, No. 10 (1936).

BERNARDELLI, H. "Notes on the Determinateness of the Utility Function. Part II," *Review of Economic Studies*, Vol. II (1934–35).

BOSLAND, C. C. "Forecasting the Price of Wheat," *JASA*, XXI (June, 1926), 149–61.

BOWLEY, ARTHUR L. *F. Y. Edgeworth's Contributions to Mathematical Statistics.* London: Royal Statistical Society, 1928.

――――. *The Mathematical Groundwork of Economics.* Oxford: Clarendon Press, 1924.

BRESCIANI-TURRONI, C. "L'Influence de la speculation sur les fluctuations des prix du coton," *L'Egypte contemporaine*, XXII (1931), 308–42.

――――. "Relations entre la récolte et le prix du coton égyptien," *ibid.*, XXI (1930), 633–89.

――――. "Über die Elastizität des Verbrauchs ägyptischer Baumwolle," *Weltwirtschaftliches Archiv*, XXXIII Heft 1 (January, 1931), 46–86.

BRIDGMAN, P. W. *The Logic of Modern Physics.* New York: Macmillan Co., 1927.

BROWN, E. H. PHELPS, BERNARDELLI, H., and LANGE, O. "Notes on the Determinateness of the Utility Function," *Review of Economic Studies*, II (1934), 66–77.

BURGESS, ROBERT W. *Introduction to the Mathematics of Statistics.* Boston: Houghton Mifflin Co., 1927.

BURK, A. "Real Income, Expenditure Proportionality, and Frisch's 'New Methods of Measuring Marginal Utility,'" *Review of Economic Studies*, IV, No. 1 (1936), 33–52.

BURTT, EDWIN. "Two Basic Issues in the Problem of Meaning and of Truth" in *Essays in Honor of John Dewey.* New York, 1929.

CASSEL, GUSTAV. *The Theory of Social Economy*, Chap. iv, "The Mechanism of Pricing." New York: Harcourt, Brace & Co., 1932.

CASSELS, J. M. "A Critical Consideration of Prof. Pigou's Method for Deriving Demand Curves," *Economics Journal*, XLIII (1933), 575–87.

COHEN, MORRIS R. *Reason and Nature: An Essay on the Meaning of Scientific Method*, Book III, chap. i, "The Social and the Natural Sciences." New York: Harcourt, Brace & Co., 1931.

COHEN, RUTH L. *Factors Affecting the Price of Potatoes in Great Britain.* University of Cambridge, Department of Agricultural Farm Economics, Branch Report No. 15 (issued July, 1930). Cambridge: W. Heffer & Sons, Ltd., 1930.

COURNOT, AUGUSTIN. *Researches into the Mathematical Principles of the Theory of Wealth* (1838), trans. BACON. New York, 1897. 2d ed., 1927.

——. *Principes de la théorie des richesses.* Paris: L. Hachette, 1863.

COX, A. B. *Cotton Prices and Markets.* U.S.D.A. Bull. 1444. Washington, 1926.

COX, REX W. *Factors Influencing Corn Prices.* University of Minnesota Agric. Exper. Station, Univ. Farm, St. Paul, Minn. Tech. Bull. 81. St. Paul, 1931.

DALTON, JOHN E. *Sugar: A Case Study of Government Control.* New York: Macmillan Co., 1937.

DARWIN, C. G. *The New Conceptions of Matter.* London: Macmillan & Co., Ltd., 1931.

DAVIS, JOSEPH S. "America's Agricultural Position and Policy," *Harvard Business Review,* VI, No. 2 (1928), 146.

——. "Some Observations on Federal Agricultural Statistics," *JASA,* XXIII (March, 1928, Suppl.), 6–8.

——. "Pacific Northwest Wheat Problems and the Export Subsidy," *Wheat Studies.* Vol.X, No. 10, (August, 1934).

——. *Wheat and the AAA.* Washington: Brookings Institution, 1935.

——. "The World Wheat Situation 1934–35," *Wheat Studies,* Vol. XII, No. 4 (1935).

DEAN, JOEL. *Statistical Determination of Costs, with Special Reference to Marginal Costs,* "Studies in Business Administration," Vol. VII, No. 1. University of Chicago, 1936.

DEMING, W. EDWARDS. "The Chi-Test and Curve Fitting," *JASA,* Vol. XXIX (1934).

——. "On the Significant Figures of Least Squares and Correlation," *Science* (N.S.) LXXXV, No. 2210 (May 7, 1937), 451–54.

DEMING, W. EDWARDS, and BIRGE, RAYMOND T. "On the Statistical Theory of Errors," *Reviews of Modern Physics,* VI, No. 3 (July, 1934), 119–61, and their note bearing same title in *Physical Review,* XLVI, No. 11 (December, 1934), 1027, both reprinted by U.S. D.A., Washington, 1937.

DIVISIA, FRANÇOIS. *Economique rationnelle.* Paris: Gaston Dion, 1928.

DOMINEDO, VALENTINO. "Considerazioni intorno alla teoria della domanda," *Gior. degli econ.* LXXIII (January, 1933), 30–48, and *ibid.* (November, 1933), pp. 765–807.

DONNER, OTTO. *Bestimmungsgründe der Baumwollpreise.* Berlin Institut für Konjunkturforschung Vierteljahrshefte zur Konjunkturforsch, Sonderheft 15. Berlin, 1930.

EDGEWORTH, F. Y. "Demand Curves," in *Palgraves' Dictionary of Political Economy.*

——. *Mathematical Psychics.* London: C. Kegan Paul & Co., 1881.

(Reprinted as No. 10 of "Series of Reprints of Scarce Tracts in Economics and Political Science" by the London School of Economics and Political Science, 1932).

——. "On the Representation of Statistics by Mathematical Formulae," *Journal of the Royal Statistical Society,* Vol. LVI (December, 1898).

——. *Papers Relating to Political Economy,* Vol. II. London: Macmillan & Co., Ltd., 1925.

ELDERTON, W. PALIN. *Frequency Curves and Correlation.* London, 1906. 3d ed., 1937.

ENGELBRECHT, TH. H. *Die geographische Verteilung der Getreidepreise in Indien von 1861 bis 1905.* Berlin: Paul Parey, 1908.

——. *Die geographische Verteilung der Getreidepreise in den Vereinigten Staaten von 1862 bis 1900.* Berlin: Paul Parey, 1903.

EVANS, GRIFFITH C. "The Dynamics of Monopoly," *American Mathematical Monthly*, XXXI (1924), 77–83.

———. *Mathematical Introduction to Economics*, chaps. XI and XII. New York: McGraw-Hill Book Co., Inc., 1930.

———. "The Role of Hypothesis in Economic Theory" *Science* (N.S.), LXXV, No. 1943 (March 25, 1932), 321–24.

———. "A Simple Theory of Economic Crises," *JASA*, XXVI (March, 1931, Suppl.), 61–68.

EZEKIEL, MORDECAI. "A Method of Handling Curvilinear Correlation for Any Number of Variables," *JASA*, XIX (1924), 431–53.

———. "Statistical Analyses and the 'Laws' of Price," *Quarterly Journal of Economics*, XLII (1928), 199–227.

———. *Methods of Correlation Analysis*, esp. chaps. xiv, xvi, xx, & xxi. New York: John Wiley & Sons, Inc., 1930.

———. *Preisvoraussage bei landwirtschaftlichen Erzeugnissen*. Frankfurter Gesellschaft für Konjunkturforschung. Veröffentlichungen Heft 9. Bonn: K. Schroeder, 1930.

———. "Some Considerations on the Analysis of the Prices of Competing or Substitute Commodities," *Econometrica*, Vol. I (April, 1933).

EZEKIEL, MORDECAI, and BEAN, LOUIS H. "Economic Bases for the Agricultural Adjustment Act." Washington: U.S.D.A., 1933.

FANNO, MARCO. "Contributo alla téoria economica dei beni succedanei," *Annali di economia*, Vol. II (1926); also published in book form by Università Bocconi Editrice. Milan, 1926.

———. "Die Elastizität der Nachfrage nach Ersatzgütern," *Zeitschrift für Nationalökonomie*, I, Heft I (1929), 51–74.

FARQUHAR, ARTHUR B., and HENRY. *Economic and Industrial Delusions*. New York: G. B. Putnam's Sons, 1891.

FERGER, WIRTH. "Notes on Pigou's Method of Deriving Demand Curves," *Econ. Jour.*, XLII (1932), 17–26.

———. "The Static and the Dynamic in Statistical Demand Curves," *Quar. Jour. Econ.*, XLVII (1932), 36–62.

FINCH, V. C., and BAKER, O. E. *Geography of the World's Agriculture*. Washington: U.S. D.A., 1917.

FISHER, IRVING. "Mathematical Investigations in the Theory of Value and Prices," *Transactions of Connecticut Academy of Arts and Sciences*, IX, Part I (New Haven, 1892), 1–124. (Reprinted in 1925 by the Yale University Press.)

———. "A Statistical Method for Measuring 'Marginal Utility' and Testing the Justice of a Progressive Income Tax," in *Economic Essays Contributed in Honor of John Bates Clark*, ed. JACOB H. HOLLANDER. New York: Macmillan Co., 1927.

FISHER, R. A. *Statistical Methods for Research Workers*. Edinburgh and London: Oliver & Boyd, 1925. 6th ed., 1936.

FRÉCHET, MAURICE. "Sur l'existence d'un indice de désirabilité des biens indirects," *Comptes rendus des séances de l'académie des sciences*, CLXXXVII (1928), 589–91.

FRIEDMAN, MILTON. "The Fitting of Indifference Curves as a Method of Deriving Statistical Demand Curves." January, 1934 (unpublished).

———. "Marginal Utility of Money and Elasticities of Demand. II," *Quar. Jour. Econ.*, L (1935–36), 532–33.

———. "Professor Pigou's Method for Measuring Elasticities of Demand from Budgetary Data," *ibid.* (November, 1935), pp. 151–63.

FRISCH, RAGNAR. "Sur un problème d'économie pure," *Norsk Matematisk Forenings Skrifter*, Series 1, No. 16 (1926), pp. 1–40.

———. *New Methods of Measuring Marginal Utility.* "Beiträge zur ökonomischen Theorie," No. 3. Tübingen: J. C. B. Mohr, 1932.

———. "Editorial," *Econometrica*, Vol. I (1933).

———. "Pitfalls in the Statistical Construction of Demand and Supply Curves," *Veröffentlichungen der Frankfurter Gesellschaft für Konjunkturforschung*, ed. EUGEN ALTSCHUL. Neue Folge, Heft 5. Leipzig, 1933.

———. "More Pitfalls in Demand and Supply Analysis"—"a Reply"; LEONTIEF, W., "A Final Word"; MARSCHAK, JACOB, "Some Comments," *Quar. Jour. Econ.*, Vol. XLVIII (1934).

———. *Statistical Confluence Analysis by Means of Complete Regression Systems.* Oslo, 1934. (Separate impression from *Nordic Statistical Journal*, Vol. V.)

FRISCH, RAGNAR, and MUDGETT, BRUCE D. "Statistical Correlation and the Theory of Cluster Types," *JASA*, XXVI (December, 1931), 375–92.

FRISCH, RAGNAR, and WAUGH, FREDERICK V. "Partial Time Regressions as Compared with Individual Trends," *Econometrica*, I (1933), 387–401.

FUOCO, FRANCESCO. *Saggi economici.* Pisa, 1825–27.

GARSIDE, ALSTON HILL. *Cotton Goes to Market.* New York: Frederick A. Stokes Co., 1935.

GEORGESCU-ROEGEN, N. "Marginal Utility of Money and Elasticities of Demand. III," *Quar. Jour. Econ.*, L (1935–36), 533–39.

GILBOY, ELIZABETH WATERMAN. "The Leontief and Schultz Methods of Deriving 'Demand' Curves," *Quar. Jour. Econ.*, XLV (1931), 218–61.

GOODWIN, HARRY M. *Elements of the Precision of Measurements and Graphical Methods.* New York: McGraw-Hill Book Co., 1919.

HARTKEMEIER, HARRY PELLE. *The Supply Function for Agricultural Commodities: A Study of the Effect of Price and Weather on the Production of Potatoes and Corn.* "University of Missouri Studies," Vol. VII, No. 4. Columbia, Mo., October 1, 1932.

HICKS, J. R., and ALLEN, R. G. D. "A Reconsideration of the Theory of Value," *Economica*, XIV (1934), 52–76, 196–219.

HOLMAN, SILAS W. *Discussion of the Precision of Measurements with Examples Taken Mainly from Physics and Electrical Engineering.* New York: John Wiley & Sons, 1892.

HORST, PAUL. "A General Method for Evaluating Multiple Regression Constants," *JASA*, XXVII (1932), 270–78.

HOTELLING, HAROLD. "Edgeworth's Taxation Paradox and the Nature of Demand and Supply Functions," *Journal of Political Economy*, XL (1932), 577–616.

JEVONS, STANLEY (W. S.). *The Theory of Political Economy.* London: Macmillan & Co., Ltd., 1871. 4th ed., 1924.

JOHNSON, W. E. "Pure Theory of Utility Curves," *Econ. Jour.*, XXIII (1913), 483–513.

JONES, HERBERT E. "Some Geometrical Considerations in the General Theory of Fitting Lines and Planes," *Metron*, XIII, No. 1 (28-II-1937), 21–30.

KILLOUGH, HUGH B. *What Makes the Price of Oats?* U.S.D.A. Bull. No. 1351. Washington, 1925.

KILLOUGH, HUGH B., and LUCY W. "Price Making Forces in Cotton Markets," *JASA* (N.S.), CLIII (1926), 47–54.

KING, GEORGE. *Textbook of the Institute of Actuaries*, Part II, chap. vi. London: C. & E. Layton, 1887–1901.

KOOPMANS, T. *Linear Regression Analysis of Economic Time Series*. "Netherlands Economic Institute," Nr. 20. Haarlem: De Erven F. Bohn N.V., 1937.

KRICHEWSKY, S. *Interpretation of Correlation Coefficients*. Cairo: Government Press, 1927.

KUZNETS, SIMON S. *Secular Movements in Production and Prices*. New York: Houghton Mifflin Co., 1930.

LANE, E. P. *Projective Differential Geometry of Curves and Surfaces*. Chicago: University of Chicago Press, 1932.

LANGE, O. "The Determinateness of the Utility Function," *Review of Economics Studies*, I (1934), 218–25.

————. "Notes on the Determinateness of the Utility Function. Part III," *ibid.*, II (1934–35), 76–77.

LEHFELDT, R. A. "The Elasticity of Demand for Wheat," *Econ. Jour.*, XXIV (1914), 212–17.

————. "The Normal Law of Progress" *Jour. Roy. Statist. Soc.*, LXXIX (1916), 329–32.

LEIGHTY, C. E. *Culture of Rye in the Eastern Half of the United States*. Farmers Bull. No. 756. Washington: U.S.D.A., October, 1916.

LELAND, ORA MINER. *Practical Least Squares*. New York: McGraw-Hill Book Co., 1921.

LENOIR, MARCEL. *Etudes sur la formation et le mouvement des prix*. Paris: M. Giard, 1913.

LEONTIEF, WASSILY. "Ein Versuch zur statistischen Analyse von Angebot und Nachfrage," *Weltwirtschaftliches Archiv*, XXX, Heft I (July, 1929), 1*–53*.

————. "Pitfalls in the Construction of Demand and Supply Curves. A Reply," *Quar. Jour. Econ.*, XLVIII (1934), 352–63.

LLOYD, GENERAL HENRY. *An Essay on the Theory of Money*. London, 1771.

LOTKA, A. J. *Elements of Physical Biology*. Baltimore: Williams & Wilkins Co., 1925.

LUTFALLA, GEORGES. "Compte rendu de la IIIe réunion européenne de la Société internationale d'Econométrie," *Revue d'économie politique*, II (1934), 414–15.

MACH, ERNST. *The Science of Mechanics*, chap. iii. English trans. Chicago, 1919.

McINTYRE, FRANCIS. "Automatic Checks in Correlation Analysis," *JASA*, XXXII (1937), 119–23.

MARSCHAK, JACOB. *Elastizität der Nachfrage*. "Beiträge zur ökonomischen Theorie," No. 2. Tübingen, 1931.

MARSHALL, ALFRED. "On the Graphic Method of Statistics," *Jubilee Volume of the Roy. Statist. Soc.* London, 1885.

————. *Principles of Economics*. 8th ed. London: Macmillan & Co., Ltd., 1920.

MILL, JOHN STUART. *Principles of Political Economy*, ed. W. J. ASHLEY, Book III, chap. xviii. London: Longmans, Green & Co., 1929.

MILLS, FREDERICK C. "Price Data and Problems of Price Research," *Econometrica*, IV, No. 4 (1936), 289–309.

MOLINA, E. C., and WILKINSON, R. I. "The Frequency Distribution of the Unknown Mean of a Sampled Universe," *Bell System Technical Journal*, VIII (1929), 632–45.

MOORE, HENRY L. "The Statistical Complement of Pure Economics," *Quar. Jour. Econ.*, Vol. XXIII (1908–9).

————. *Economic Cycles: Their Law and Cause*. New York: Macmillan Co., 1914.

————. *Forecasting the Yield and Price of Cotton*. New York: Macmillan Co., 1917.

———. "Empirical Laws of Demand and Supply and the Flexibility of Prices," *Political Science Quarterly*, XXXIV (1919), 546–67.

———. "Elasticity of Demand and Flexibility of Prices," *JASA*, XVIII (1922), 8–19.

———. "A Moving Equilibrium of Demand and Supply," *Quar. Jour. Econ.*, XXXIX (1925), 357–71.

———. "Partial Elasticity of Demand," *ibid.*, XL (1926), 393–401.

———. "A Theory of Economic Oscillations," *ibid.*, XLI, No. 1 (1926), 1–29.

———. *Synthetic Economics*. New York: Macmillan Co., 1929.

MORET, JACQUES, and FRISCH, RAGNAR. "Méthodes nouvelles pour mesurer l'utilité marginale," *Revue d'économie politique*, XLVI, Part II (1932), 14–28.

MOSAK, JACOB L. "The Least-Squares Standard Error of the Coefficient of Elasticity of Demand." (Submitted to the *Journal of the American Statistical Association*.)

———. "On the Simultaneous Determination of the Elementary Regressions and Their Standard Errors in Subsets of Variables," *JASA*, XXXII (1937), 517–24.

MOULTON, F. R. "Memoir on the Theory of Determining Orbits," *Astronomical Journal*, XXVIII (1913–15), 103–27.

———. "On the Solution of Linear Equations Having Small Determinants," *Amer. Math. Monthly*, XX (1913), 242–49.

———. "Significant Figures in Statistical Constants," *Science* (N.S.), LXXXIV, No. 2191 (1936), 574–75.

NATIONAL BUREAU OF ECONOMIC RESEARCH, COMMITTEE ON PRICE RESEARCH. Reports on the oil, coal, automobile, and textile industries (1938).

NEYMAN, J. "Méthodes nouvelles de vérification des hypothèses statistiques," *Comptes rendus premier congrès math. pays slaves*. Warsaw, 1929.

———. "Sur la vérification des hypothèses statistiques composées," *Bulletin de la société mathématique de France*, LXIII (1935), 1–21.

———. "Outline of a Theory of Statistical Estimation Based on the Classical Theory of Probability," *Philosophical Transactions of the Royal Society of London*, Ser. A, CCXXXVI (1937), 333–80.

NEYMAN, J., and PEARSON, EGON S. "On the Use and Interpretation of Certain Test Criteria for Purposes of Statistical Inference," *Biometrika*, XX^A (1928), 175–240.

———. "On the Problem of the Most Efficient Test of Statistical Hypotheses," *Phil. Trans. Roy. Soc. London*, Ser. A., CCXXXI (1933), 289–337.

———. "The Testing of Statistical Hypotheses in Relation to Probabilities *a priori*," *Proceedings of the Cambridge Philosophical Society*, XXIX, Part IV (1933), 492–510.

———. "Contributions to the Theory of Testing Statistical Hypotheses. (I) Unbiassed Critical Regions of Type *A* and Type *A₁*" and "Sufficient Statistics and Uniformly Most Powerful Tests of Statistical Hypotheses," *Statistical Research Memoirs*, Vol. I. Department of Statistics, University of London, University College, 1936.

NORTON, J. P. *Statistical Studies in the New York Money Market*. New York: Macmillan Co., 1902.

NOURSE, EDWIN G., DAVIS, JOSEPH S., BLACK, JOHN D., *Three Years of the Agricultural Adjustment Administration*. Washington, D.C.: Brookings Institution, 1937.

PABST, W. R. *Butter and Oleomargarine: An Analysis of Competing Commodities*. New York: Columbia University Press, 1937.

Palgrave's Dictionary of Political Economy. Articles on Charles Davenant, Simon Gray, and Gregory King.

PARETO, VILFREDO. "Considerazioni sui principii fondamentali dell'economia pura," *Gior. degli econ.*, IV (2d ser., 1892), 389–420; V (1892), 119–57; VI (1893), 1–37; VII (1893), 279–321.

———. "La Legge della domanda," *ibid.*, Vol. X (2d ser., January, 1895).

———. *Cours d'économie politique.* Lausanne: F. Rouge, 1896–97.

———. "Le nuove teorie economiche," *Gior. degli econ.*, Vol. XXIII (2d ser., 1901).

———. "L'Interpolazioni per la ricerca della leggi economiche," *ibid.*, Vol. XXXIV (May, 1907).

———. *Manuale di economia politica.* Milan: Società Editrice Libraria, 1907.

———. *Manuel d'économie politique.* Paris: V. Giard & E. Brière, 1909.

———. "Economie mathématique," in *Encyclopédie des sciences mathématiques*, Tome I, Vol. IV, Fasc. 4 (1911).

PEABODY, LEROY E. "Growth Curves and Railway Traffic," *JASA*, XIX (1924), 476–83.

PEARL, RAYMOND. *Studies in Human Biology*, chaps. xxiv–xxv. Baltimore: Williams & Wilkins Co., 1924.

PEARSON, KARL(ed.). *Tables for Statisticians and Biometricians*, Parts I and II. Cambridge: University Press, Part I, 2d ed., 1924; Part II, 1931.

PERSONS, WARREN M. "The Correlation of Economic Statistics," *Quarterly Publications of the American Statistical Association*, XII (1910), 287–322.

PIETRA, G. "Interpolating Plane Curves," *Metron*, III (1923–24), 311–28.

———. "Dell'interpolazione parabolica nel caso in cui entrambi i valori delle variabili sono affetti da errori accidentali," *ibid.*, IX, Nos. 3–4 (1932), 77–85.

PIGOU, A. C. "A Method of Determining the Numerical Value of Elasticities of Demand," *Econ. Jour.*, XX (1910), 636–40; and reprinted in his *Economics of Welfare*, Appen. II. London: Macmillan & Co., Ltd., 1920.

———. "The Statistical Derivation of Demand Curves," *Econ. Jour.*, XL (1930), 384–400, and reprinted in A. C. PIGOU and DENNIS H. ROBERTSON, *Economic Essays and Addresses.* London: P. S. King & Co., Ltd., 1931.

———. "Marginal Utility of Money and Elasticities of Demand. I," *Quar. Jour. Econ.*, L (1935–36), 532.

PLANCK, MAX. *A Survey of Physics*, essay, "The Principle of Least Action." London: Methven & Co., Ltd., 1925.

PRESCOTT, R. B. "Laws of Growth in Forecasting Demand," *JASA*, XVIII (1922), 471–79.

REED, LOWELL J. "A Form of Saturation Curve," *JASA*, XX (1925), 390–96.

RICCI, UMBERTO. "Elasticità dei bisogni, della domanda e dell'offerta," *Gior. degli econ.*, Vol. LXIV (1924).

———. "La Loi de la demande individuelle et la rente de consommateur," *Revue d'économie politique*, XL (1926), 5–24.

———. "Courbes de la demande et courbes de la dépense," *L'Egypte contemporaine*, XXII (1931), 556–88.

———. "Klassifikation der Nachfragekurven auf Grund des Elastizitätsbegriffes," *Archiv für Sozialwissenschaft und Sozialpolitik*, LXVI (1931), 36–61.

———. "Die Nachfrage nach ägyptischer Baumwolle und ihre Elastizität," *Weltwirtschaftliches Archiv*, XXXV (1932), 250–61.

RICHARDS, HENRY S. *Cotton and the A.A.A.* Washington: Brookings Institution, 1936.

ROESSLER, EDWARD B. "Significant Figures in Statistical Constants," *Science* (N.S.), LXXXIV, No. 2178 (September 25, 1936), 289–90.

ROOS, CHARLES F. "A Dynamical Theory of Economics," *Jour. Pol. Econ.*, XXXV (1927), 632–56.

———. "A General Invariant Criterion of Fit for Lines and Planes Where All Variables Are Subject to Error," *Metron*, XIII, No. 1 (28-II-1937), 3–20.

———. "A Mathematical Theory of Competition," *American Journal of Mathematics*, XLVII (1925), 163–75.

———. "A Mathematical Theory of Price and Production Fluctuations and Economic Crises," *Jour. Pol. Econ.*, XXXVIII (1930), 501–22.

ROSENSTEIN-RODAN, P.N. "La Complementarietà: prima delle tre tappe del progresso della teoria economica pura," *Riforma sociale*, XLIV (1933), 257–308.

———. "Grenznutzen," *Handwörterbuch der Staatswissenschaft*. 4th ed. January, 1927.

———. "The Role of Time in Economic Theory," *Economica* (N.S.), No. 1 (1934), pp. 77–97.

ROY, RENÉ. *Contribution aux recherches économétriques*. Paris: Hermann & Cie, 1936.

———. "La Demande dans ses rapports avec la répartition des revenus," *Metron*, VIII, No. 3 (1930), 101–53.

———. *Etudes économétriques*. Paris: Recueil Sirey, 1935.

———. "Les Index économiques," *Revue d'économie politique*, XLI (1927), 1251–91, 1493–1527. (Also published separately and reprinted in *Etudes économétriques*. Paris: Recueil Sirey, 1935.)

———. "Les Lois de la demande," *ibid.*, XLV (1931), 1190–1218. (Reprinted in *Etudes économétriques*. Paris: Recueil Sirey, 1935.)

SARLE, CHARLES F. *Reliability and Adequacy of Farm-Price Data*. U.S.D.A. Bull. 1480. Washington, D.C., 1927.

SAY, JEAN BAPTISTE. *Catéchisme d'économie politique*, chap. xi. 4th ed. Paris, 1835.

SCHMECKEBIER, LAWRENCE F. *The Statistical Work of the National Government*. Baltimore: Johns Hopkins Press, 1925.

SCHNEIDER, ERICH. Über den Einfluss von Änderungen der Nachfrage auf die Monopolpreisbildung," *Archiv für Sozialwissenschaft und Sozialpolitik*, LXIV, No. 2 (October, 1930), 281–315.

———. "Über die Nachfrage nach Produktionsmitteln und ihre Elastizität," *Jahrbücher für Nationalökonomie und Statistik*, 137–III. Folge, 82 (1932), 801–14.

SCHULTZ, HENRY. "An Extension of the Method of Moments," *JASA*, XX (1925), 242–44.

———. *Statistical Laws of Demand and Supply with Special Application to Sugar*. Chicago: University of Chicago Press, 1928.

———. "Marginal Productivity and the General Pricing Process," *Jour. Pol. Econ.*, Vol. XXXVII (1929).

———. "The Standard Error of a Forecast from a Curve," *JASA*, XXV (1930), 139–85.

———. *Der Sinn der statistischen Nachfragekurven*, ed. EUGEN ALTSCHUL. "Veröffentlichungen der Frankfurter Gesellschaft für Konjunkturforschung," Heft 10. Bonn, 1930.

———. Discussion of Evans' "A Simple Theory of Economic Crises," *JASA*, XXVI (March, 1931, Suppl.), 68–72.

———. Review of Evans' *Mathematical Introduction to Economics*, *ibid.*, pp. 484–91.

———. "The Shifting Demand for Selected Agricultural Commodities, 1875–1929," *Jour. Farm Econ.*, Vol. XIV (1932).

SCHULTZ, HENRY. Review of Marschak's *Elastizität der Nachfrage*, in *Weltwirtschaftliches Archiv*, XXXVII, Heft I (1933), 29*-38*.

——. "Frisch on the Measurement of Utility," *Jour. Pol. Econ.*, XLI (1933), 95-116.

——. "The Standard Error of the Coefficient of Elasticity of Demand," *JASA*, XXVIII, (1933), 64-69.

——. "A Comparison of Elasticities of Demand Obtained by Different Methods," *Econometrica*, Vol. I, No. 3 (1933).

——. "Interrelations of Demand," *Jour. Pol. Econ.*, XLI (1933), 468-512.

——. "Interrelations of Demand, Price, and Income," *ibid.*, XLIII (1935), 433-81.

——. Review of R. G. D. Allen and A. L. Bowley, *Family Expenditure: A Study of Its Variations* (London, 1935), *JASA*, XXXI (1936), 316-17.

SCHULTZ, THEODORE W. *The Tariffs on Barley, Oats and Corn*. Madison, Wis.: Tariff Research Committee; Freeport, Ill.: Rawleigh Foundation, 1933.

SHEPHERD, G. S. *The Secular Movement of Corn Prices*. Agric. Exper. Station, Iowa State College of Agriculture and Mechanic Arts, Research Bull. No. 140. Ames, Iowa, 1931.

——. *The Trend of Corn Prices*. Agric. Exper. Station, Iowa State College of Agriculture and Mechanic Arts, Bull. No. 284. Ames, Iowa, July, 1931.

SHEPHERD, GEOFFREY, and WILCOX, WALTER W. *Stabilizing Corn Supplies by Storage*. Agric. Exper. Station, Iowa State College of Agriculture and Mechanic Arts, Bull. No. 368. Ames, Iowa, December, 1937.

SLUTSKY, EUGENIO. "Sulla teoria del bilancio del consumatore," *Gior. degli econ.*, LI (1915), 1-26.

SMITH, BRADFORD B. "The Error in Eliminating Secular Trend and Seasonal Variation before Correlating Time Series," *JASA*, XX (1925), 543-45.

——. *Factors Affecting the Price of Cotton*. U.S.D.A. Tech. Bull. No. 50. Washington, January, 1928.

——. "Forecasting the Volume and Value of the Cotton Crop," *JASA*, XXII (1927), 442-59.

SPILLMAN, W. J. *The Law of Diminishing Returns*. Chicago: World Book Co., 1924.

STAEHLE, H. "International Comparison of Food Costs," *International Comparisons of Cost of Living*. "Studies and Reports of the International Labour Office," Ser. N (Statistics), No. 20, esp. Appen. I, pp. 74-92. Geneva, 1934.

Statistical Work of the United States Government. Report on House Document 394. 67th Cong., 2d sess., Washington, 1922.

STRATTON, S. S. and DE CHAZEAU, M. G. *Preliminary Report on a Program for Research on the Price Structure and Pricing Policies of the Iron and Steel Industry* (mimeographed). Submitted to the Conference on Price Research and discussed at the December, 1937, Meeting of the American Statistical Association (final report to be published by the National Bureau of Economic Research).

STROWBRIDGE, J. W. *Origin and Distribution of the Commercial Potato Crop*. U.S.D.A. Tech. Bull. No. 7. Washington, 1927.

TAYLOR, ALONZO E. *The Corn and Hog Surplus of the Corn Belt*. Stanford University, Calif.: Stanford University Press, 1932.

THOMSON, GODFREY H. "Some Points of Mathematical Technique in the Factorial Analysis of Ability," *Journal of Educational Psychology*, XXVII (1936), 37-54.

THURSTONE, L. L. "The Indifference Function," *Journal of Social Psychology*, II (1931), 139-67.

TIMOSHENKO, V. P. "Correlations between Prices and Yields of Previous Year," *Jour. Pol. Econ.*, XXXVI, No. 4 (1928), 510–15.

TINBERGEN, J. "L'Utilization des équations fonctionnelles et des nombres complexes dans les recherches économiques," *Econometrica*, Vol. I (1933).

TODD, JOHN A. *The Cotton World*. London: Pitman & Son, 1927.

TOLLEY, H. R., BLACK, J. D., and EZEKIEL, M. J. B. *Input as Related to Output in Farm Organization and Cost-of-Production Studies*. U.S.D.A. Bull. No. 1277. Washington, 1924.

TRUESDELL, LEON E. "Discussions of Dr. Davis' Paper. II," *JASA*, Vol. XXIII (March, 1928, Suppl.).

TSCHAYANOW, ALEX. *Essays on the Theory of Labor Economics* (in Russian). Moscow, 1912.

———. *Die Lehre von der bäuerlichen Wirtschaft*. Berlin, 1923.

TUCKER, LEDYARD R. "A Method for Finding the Inverse of a Matrix" (unpublished paper).

TURNBULL, H. W., and AITKEN, A. C. *An Introduction to the Theory of Canonical Matrices*. London and Glasgow: Blackie & Son, Ltd., 1932.

UNITED STATES DEPARTMENT OF AGRICULTURE. "World Cotton Situation [Part II—U.S.]" (mimeographed—preliminary). Washington, 1936.

———. *Yearbooks of Agriculture*. "The Corn Crop" (1921), "The Cotton Situation," (1921), "Wheat Production and Marketing" (1921), "Barley" (1922), "Buckwheat" (1922), "Oats" (1922), "Sugar" (1923), "Hay" (1924), "Potatoes" (1925). Washington.

UNITED STATES DEPARTMENT OF AGRICULTURE, BUREAU OF AGRICULTURAL ECONOMICS. *Service and Regulatory Announcements, Nos. 124* (May, 1931), *125* (May, 1931) [these supersede *Nos. 105* and *115*, respectively], and *117* (November, 1929).

VALERIANI, L. M. *Del prezzo delle case tutte mercatabili*. Bologna, 1806.

———. *Operette concernenti quella parte del gius delle genti e pubblico che dicesi pubblica economia*. Bologna, 1815–24.

VERRI, PIETRO. *Meditazioni sull'economia politica*, 1st ed. Livorno, 1771.

VINCI, FELICE. "L'Elasticità dei consumi," *Rivista italiana di statistica*, III (1931), 30–91.

VINER, JACOB. "The Utility Concept in Value Theory and Its Critics," *Jour. Pol. Econ.*, XXXIII (1925), 369–87, 638–59.

VOLTERRA, VITO. Review of Pareto's *Manuale di economia politica* in *Gior. degli econ.*, XXXII (2d ser., 1906), 296–301.

WALD, A. *Über die eindeutige positive Lösbarkeit der neuen Produktionsgleichungen*. Ergebnisse eines mathematischen Kolloquiums, ed. KARL MENGER, Vol. VI. Leipzig and Wien, 1933–34.

———. *Über die Produktionsgleichungen der ökonomischen Wertlehre II*. "Ergebnisse eines mathematischen Kolloquiums," ed. KARL MENGER, Vol. VII. Leipzig and Wien, 1934–35.

WALLACE, HENRY A. "Forecasting Corn and Hog Prices," chap. xvii of W. M. PERSONS, W. T. FOSTER, and A. J. HETTINGER, JR. (eds.), *The Problem of Business Forecasting*. Boston, 1924.

WALLACE, J. ROGER. "Factors Affecting American Cotton Prices," Appen. III of GARSIDE, *Cotton Goes to Market*.

WALRAS, LÉON. *Eléments d'économie politique pure*. 4th ed. Lausanne and Paris, 1900.

WARREN, G. F., and PEARSON, F. A. *Interrelations of Supply and Price*. Cornell University Agric. Exper. Station Bull. 466. Ithaca, 1928.

WATKINS, JAMES L. "Production and Price of Cotton for 100 Years," U.S.D.A., Div. of Statistics, Misc. Series, Bull. No. 9. Washington, 1895.

WAUGH, FREDERICK V. *Factors Influencing the Price of New Jersey Potatoes on the New York Market*. New Jersey Department of Agriculture Circ. No. 66. Trenton, 1923.

————. "A Simplified Method of Determining Multiple Regression Constants," *JASA*, XXX (1935), 694–700.

WHEWELL, W. "Mathematical Exposition of Some Doctrines of Political Economy," *Transactions of the Cambridge Philosophical Society*, Vol. III (1830).

————. "Mathematical Exposition of Some of the Leading Doctrines in Mr. Ricardo's 'Principles of Political Economy and Taxation,' " *ibid.*, Vol. IV (1833).

————. "Mathematical Exposition of Some Doctrines of Political Economy. Second Memoir," *ibid.*, Vol. IX, Part I (1856); "Third Memoir," *ibid.*, Part II (1856).

WHITEHEAD, ALFRED N. "On Foresight." Introduction to W. B. DONHAM, *Business Adrift*. New York: McGraw-Hill Book Co., Inc., 1931. (Reprinted in A. N. WHITEHEAD, *Adventures of Ideas*, chap. vi. New York: Macmillan Co., 1933.)

WHITMAN, ROSWELL H. "Statistical Investigations in the Demand for Iron and Steel." Doctor's dissertation, University of Chicago, 1933.

————. "The Problem of Statistical Demand Techniques for Producers' Goods: An Application to Steel," *Jour. Pol. Econ.*, XLII (1934), 577–94.

————. "The Cabbage Industry and the Price System" (unpublished).

————. "The Statistical Law of Demand for a Producer's Good as Illustrated by the Demand for Steel." *Econometrica*, IV (1936), 138–52.

WHITTAKER, E. T., and ROBINSON, G. *The Calculus of Observations*. New York: D. Van Nostrand Co., 1924.

WHITWORTH, CHARLES. *The Political and Commercial Works of That Celebrated Writer Charles d'Avenant*, Vol. II. London, 1771.

WICKSELL, KNUT. "Vilfredo Pareto's *Manuel d'économie politique*," *Zeitschrift für Volkswirtschaft, Sozialpolitik und Verwaltung*, XXII (1913), 132–51, and esp. 138.

WILLIAMS, FAITH M., and ZIMMERMAN, CARLE C. *Studies of Family Living in the United States and Other Countries: An Analysis of Material and Method*. U.S.D.A. Misc. Publ. No. 223. Washington, December, 1935.

WILSON, EDWIN B. Review of Pareto's "*Manuel d'économie politique*," *Bulletin of the American Mathematical Society*, Vol. XVIII (1912).

WORKING, ELMER J. "What Do Statistical 'Demand Curves' Show?" *Quar. Jour. Econ.*, XLI (1927), 212–35.

WORKING, HOLBROOK. Factors Determining the Price of Potatoes in St. Paul and Minneapolis. University of Minnesota Agric. Exper. Station Tech. Bull. No. 10. St. Paul, October, 1922.

————. "Factors Affecting the Price of Minnesota Potatoes." University of Minnesota Agric. Exper. Station Tech. Bull. No. 29. St. Paul, October, 1925.

————. "Wheat Acreage and Production in the United States since 1866," *Wheat Studies*, Vol. II, No. 7 (June, 1926).

————. "Disposition of American Wheat since 1896, with Special Reference to Changes in Year-end Stocks," *ibid.*, Vol. IV, No. 4 (1928).

————. "Cycles in Wheat Prices," *ibid.*, Vol. VIII, No. 1, November, 1931.

————. "Prices of Cash Wheat and Futures at Chicago since 1883," *ibid.*, Vol. XI, No. 3 (1934).

————. "The Elasticities of Demand for Wheat." A paper read before the meeting of the

Econometric Society held in Chicago, Ill., December 28, 1936, and summarized in *Econometrica*, Vol. V, No. 2 (1937).

WRIGHT, PHILIP G. Review of Henry Schultz, *Statistical Laws of Demand and Supply*, in *JASA*, XXIV (1929), 207–15.

——. *The Tariff on Animal and Vegetable Oils*. Appen. B. New York, 1928.

WRIGHT, SEWALL. "Correlation and Causation," *Journal of Agricultural Research*, XX (1921), 557–85.

——. *Corn and Hog Correlations*. U.S.D.A. Bull. No. 1300. Washington, January, 1925.

——. "The Method of Path Coefficients," *Annals of Mathematical Statistics*, Vol. V (1934).

WRIGHT, T. W., and HAYFORD, J. F. *The Adjustment of Observations*. 2d ed. New York: D. Van Nostrand Co., 1906.

Yearbooks of Agriculture. *See* United States Department of Agriculture.

YOUNG, ALLYN A. "English Political Economy," *Economica*, Vol. VIII (1928).

ZAPOLEON, L. B. *Geography of Wheat Prices*. U.S.D.A. Bull. No. 594. Washington, 1918.

——. *Geographical Phases of Farm Prices: Corn*. U.S.D.A. Bull. No. 696. Washington, 1918.

——. *Geographical Phases of Farm Prices: Oats*. U.S.D.A. Bull. No. 755. Washington, 1919.

ZIMMERMAN, CARLE C. *Consumption and Standards of Living*. New York: D. Van Nostrand Co., 1936.

——. *Family and Society*. New York: D. Van Nostrand Co., 1935.

ZAWADZKI, WL. *Les Mathêmatiques appliquées à l'économie politique*. Paris, 1914.

ZOTOFF, A. W. Notes on the Mathematical Theory of Production," *Econ. Jour.*, XXXIII (March, 1923), 115–21.

B. RELATED WORKS

ALLEN, R. G. D. "Professor Slutsky's Theory of Consumers' Choice," *Review of Economic Studies*, III (1935–36), 120–29.

ALT, F. "Über die Messbarkeit des Nutzens," *Zeitschrift für Nationalökonomie*, VII (1936), 161–69.

AMOROSO, LUIGI. "Equazione differenziale della domanda e teoria matematica delle crisi economiche," *Gior. degli econ.* XLV (i.e., XLVI), No. 1 (January, 1931), 39–40.

——. "Intorno all determinazione empirica delle leggi della domanda e dell'offerta," *ibid.*, XLV, No. 11 (November, 1930), 941–44.

BAUER, WILLY. "Einkommen und Fleischverbrauch," in *Vierteljahrshefte zur Konjunkturforschung*, XXVIII (1932), 20–42. Berlin: Reimar Hobbing (S.W. 61).

BAURY, ROGER. *La Prévision du prix du coton américain*. Paris: Epinal, 1930.

BEAN, L. H. "Agriculture and the Nation's Business," *Jour. Farm Econ.*, IX (1927), 340–45.

——. "Factors Affecting the Yearly Average Price of Cranberries," *U.S.D.A. Bureau of Agric. Econ.*, *Agric. Situation*, XII, No. 8 (August, 1928), 17–18.

——. "Helping the Farmer To Make His Plans. Interrelationships between Supply, Price, and Consumption," *Commercial American Cotton Annual Review*, August 30, 1928, pp. 17–18.

——. "The Farmers' Response to Price," *Jour. Farm Econ.*, XI (1929), 368–85.

BEAN, L. H. "Relation between Production, Prices and Acreage of Potatoes on the Eastern Shore of Maryland," Washington, D.C.: Bureau of Agricultural Economics, November, 1929 (mimeographed).

——. "Factors Bearing on the Price of Apples." *U.S.D.A. Bureau of Agric. Econ., Agric. Situation*, XIII, No. 11 (November, 1929), 10–13.

——. "Post-war Interrelations between Agriculture and Business in the U.S.," *Proceedings of the Second International Conference of Agricultural Economics* (1930) or mimeographed report of U.S.D.A. (1930).

——. "Potato Prices and Acreage Stability," *Proceedings of the Seventeenth Annual Meeting of the Potato Association of America*, December, 1930, pp. 53–61.

——. "Relation between Production, Prices, and Acreage of Potatoes in North Carolina," (mimeographed). Washington: Bureau of Agricultural Economics, 1930.

——. "Relation between Acreage, Production and Prices of Potatoes in Florida" (mimeographed). Washington: Bureau of Agricultural Economics, February, 1931.

——. "Relation between Production, Prices and Acreage of Potatoes in Idaho" (mimeographed). Washington: Bureau of Agricultural Economics, February, 1931.

——. "Factors Related to Production, Prices and Acreage of Potatoes in Maine" (mimeographed). Washington: Bureau of Agricultural Economics, February, 1931.

——. "Characteristics of Agricultural Supply and Demand Curves" (10 pp. diagrams; typewritten). Reported in *Econometrica*, I (1933), 102–4.

BEAN, L. H., and THORNE, G. B. "The Use of 'Trends in Residuals' in constructing Demand Curves," *JASA*, XXVII (March, 1932), 61–67.

BENNER, C. L., and GABRIEL, H. S. *The Marketing of Delaware Eggs*. Delaware Agric. Exper. Station Bull. 150. Newark, N.J., 1927.

BJORKA, K. *Some Statistical Characterizations of the Hog Market*. Iowa Agric. Exper. Station Research Bull. No. 102. Ames, 1927.

BLACK, J. D. *Agricultural Reform in the United States*. New York: McGraw-Hill Book Co., Inc., 1929.

——. "The Outlook for American Cotton," *Review of Economic Statistics*, XVII (1935), 68–78.

——. "Social Implications of Restriction of Agricultural Output," *American Economic Review* (March, 1931, Suppl.).

BLOXOM, J. *Some Determining Factors in Apple Prices*. "New York Food Marketing Research Council, Food Marketing Studies," No. 10. 1926.

BORDIN, ARRIGO. "La Legge della domanda dal punto di vista della statica e della dinamica," *Gior. degli econ.*, XLV, No. 5 (May, 1930), 421–71.

——. "Il significato di alcune moderne teorie matematiche della dinamica economica," *ibid.*, LXXV (1935), 161–210, 369–421, 580–611.

BOWLEY, A. L. "The Action of Economic Forces in Producing Frequency Distributions of Income, Prices, and other Phenomena: A Suggestion for Study," *Econometrica*, I (1933), 358–72.

BRAUN, E. W. "Analysis of the Principal Factors Affecting the Price of Fancy Gravenstein Apples in Sonoma County, California, 1923–1930" (mimeographed). Berkeley: California College of Agriculture, Agricultural Extension Service, 1931.

——. "Price Analysis as a Guide in Marketing Control," *Jour. Farm Econ.*, XIX (1937), 691.

BRETHERTON, R. F. "A Note on the Law of Diminishing Elasticity of Demand," *Econ. Jour.*, XLVII (September, 1937), 187, 574–77.

Broster, E. J. "Railway Passenger Receipts and Fares Policy," *Econ. Jour.*, XLVII (1937), 451–64.

———. "A Simple Method of Deriving Demand Curves," *Jour. Royal Statist. Soc.*, Vol. C, Part IV (1937), pp. 625–41.

Brown, E. H. P. "Demand Functions and Utility Functions: A Critical Examination of Their Meaning," *Econometrica*, II, No. 1 (January, 1934), 51–58.

Brown, T. H. "The Law of Demand and the Theory of Probability," *JASA*, (N.S.), XX (June, 1925), 223–30.

Buechel, F. A., and Kedzierski, S. L. "Analysis of the Price-making Forces in the New York Egg Market." A preliminary report (mimeographed). Washington, D.C.: U.S. D.A., Bureau of Agric. Econ., Division of Dairy and Poultry Products, April, 1932.

Burgess, R. W. "A Statistical Approach to Mathematical Formulation of Demand-Supply-Price Relationship," *Annals of Mathematical Statistics*, III, No. 1 (February, 1932), 10–19.

Bye, R. T. "Composite Demand and Joint Supply in Relation to Public Utility," *Quar. Jour. Econ.*, XLIV, No. 1 (November, 1929), 40–62.

Campbell, C. E. *Factors Affecting the Price of Rice.* U.S.D.A. Tech. Bull. No. 297. Washington, D.C., 1932.

Card, D. G. *Some Factors Affecting the Price of White Burley Tobacco.* Kentucky Agric. Exper. Station Bull. 323. Lexington, 1931.

Clark, J. M. "The Bullion Market and Prices: An Inductive Study of Elasticity of Demand," Appendix to "Possible Complications of the Compensated Dollar" in *Amer. Econ. Review*, III, No. 3 (September, 1913), 584–88.

Clarke, R. W. B. "Production, Output per Head, Prices and Costs in the Iron and Steel Industry, 1924–1931," *Jour. Royal Statist. Soc.*, XCVI (1933), 637–50.

Coase, R. H., and Fowler, R. F. "Bacon Production and the Pig-Cycle in Great Britain, *Economica* (N.S.), II (1935), 142–67.

———. "The Pig-Cycle: A Rejoinder," *ibid.*, pp. 423–28.

Cohen, Ruth, and Barker, J. D. "The Pig-Cycle: A Reply," *Economica* (N.S.), II (1935), 408–22.

Cover, John H. *Consumption of Meat and Meat Products with Particular Reference to Price.* "University of Chicago Bureau of Business and Economic Research Studies in the Packing Industry." Chicago: University of Chicago, 1930.

———. *Retail Price Behavior.* "Studies in Business Administration," Vol. V, No. 2. Chicago: University of Chicago, School of Business, January, 1935.

———. "Some Investigations in the Sampling and Distribution of Retail Prices," *Econometrica*, V (1937), 263 ff.

Cowden, T. K. "Supply and Utilization of Milk in Pennsylvania," *Jour. Farm Econ.*, XIX (1937), 501.

Cox, A. B. "The Relation of the Price and Quality of Cotton," *Jour. Farm Econ.*, XI, No. 4 (October, 1929), 542–49.

Crawford, G. L., and Gabbard, L. P. *Relation of Farm Prices to Quality of Cotton.* Texas Agric. Exper. Station Bull. 383. College Station, 1928.

"Crops and Markets: Effect of the Supply of Potatoes on Farm Prices and Crop Values," *U.S.D.A. Crops and Markets*, III (October, 1926), 325.

Daggit, E. M. "Flaxseed Price Largely Influenced by Argentine Crop," *U.S.D.A. Yearbook, 1926.* Washington, 1927.

DAGGIT, E. M. "A Method of Estimating the May Price of Spring Wheat," *Foreign Crops and Markets*, May 11, 1925, pp. 549–52.

———. "Peach Prices Are Mainly Governed by Size of Crop," *U.S.D.A. Yearbook, 1926*. Washington, 1927.

———. "Potato Supply—Effect on Markets," *ibid*.

DAVIS, H. J. "Mathematical Adventures in Social Science," *American Mathematical Monthly*, XLV, No. 2, 93–104.

DAVIS, JOSEPH S. "Wheat, Wheat Policies, and the Depression," *Review of Economic Statistics*, XVI (1934), 80–88.

DERKSEN, J. B. D., and ROMBOUTS, A. "The Demand for Bicycles in the Netherlands," *Econometrica*, V, No. 3 (July, 1937), 295–301.

DOMINEDO, V. "Ancora in tema di curve di domanda," *Gior. degli econ.*, LXXIV (1934), 115–16.

DOUGLAS, P. H. "Elasticity of Supply as a Determinant of Distribution," in *Economic Essays Contributed in Honor of John Bates Clark*, ed. JACOB H. HOLLANDER. New York: Macmillan Co., 1927.

DUDDY, E. A. "The Potential-Supply Area of the Chicago Livestock Market," *Jour. Farm Econ.*, XIII (July, 1931), 410–25.

DUDDY, E. A., and REVZAN, DAVID. "Potential Supply Areas of Pacific Coast Markets for Hogs," *Jour. Farm Econ.*, XIV (October, 1932), 586–98.

———. *The Supply Area of the Chicago Livestock Market*. "Studies in Business Administration," Vol. II, No. 1. Chicago: University of Chicago, School of Business, 1931.

ELLIOTT, F. F. *Adjusting Hog Production to Market Demand*. Illinois Agric. Exper. Station Bull. 293. Urbana, 1927.

ELLIOTT, F. F., and WELLS, O. V. "Farmer's Response to Price in the Production of Flax." A preliminary report (mimeographed). Washington, D.C.: U.S.D.A., Bureau of Agric. Econ., Div. of Farm Management and Costs, December, 1930.

ELLIS, LIPPERT S. *The Tariff on Sugar*. Madison, Wis.: Tariff Research Commission; Freeport, Ill.: Rawleigh Foundation, 1933.

ENGLÄNDER, OSKAR. "Elastizität der Nachfrage," *Schmöllers Jahrbuch für Gesetzgebung, Verwaltung und Volkswirtschaft im Deutschen Reiche*, LIII, No. 3 (June, 1929), 1–28.

EZEKIEL, MORDECAI. "A Statistical Examination of Factors Relating to Lamb Prices," *Jour. Pol. Econ.*, XXXV (April, 1927), 233–60.

———. "A Statistical Examination of the Problem of Handling Annual Surpluses of Nonperishable Farm Products," *Jour. Farm Econ.*, XI, No. 2 (1929), 193–226.

———. "Two Methods of Forecasting Hog Prices," *JASA* (N.S.), XXII (March, 1927), 22–30.

EZEKIEL, M., RAUCHENSTEIN, E., and WELLS, O. V. "Farmers' Response to Price in the Production of Market Milk" (mimeographed). Washington, D.C.: Bureau of Agricultural Economics, May, 1932.

FANNO, MARCO. "Correlazioni tra prezzi e curve statistische di domanda e offerta," *Rivista italiana de statistica economia e finanza*, IV, No. 2 (June, 1932), 223–37.

———. "Interrelations des prix et courbes statistiques de demande et d'offre," *Econometrica*, I (1933), 162–71.

FENTON, J. M. *A Statistical Study of Egg Marketing*. New Jersey Department of Agriculture Circ. No. 148. Trenton, 1928.

FOÀ, BRUNO. "In tema di curve di domanda," *Gior. degli econ.*, XLVIII, No. 8 (August, 1933), 571–79.

FUBINI, RENZO. "Sull'influenza dell'imposta sulla domanda e sull'offerta," *Gior. degli econ.*, XLIV, No. 1 (January, 1929), 12–22.

GANS, A. R. "The Relation of Quality to the Price of Eggs in New York City," *Farm Economics* (N.Y.), No. 79 (February, 1933), pp. 1846–49.

GARVER, RAYMOND. "The Edgeworth Taxation Phenomenon," *Econometrica*, I (1933), 402–7.

GEORGESCU-ROEGEN, N. "Note on a Proposition of Pareto," *Quar. Jour. Econ.*, XLIX (1934–35), 706–14.

———. "The Pure Theory of Consumer's Behavior," *ibid.*, L (1935–36), 545–93.

GILBOY, E. W. "Demand Curves in Theory and Practice," *Quar. Jour. Econ.*, XLV, No. 2 (February, 1931), 218–61.

———. "Demand Curves by Personal Estimate," *ibid.*, XLVI, No. 2 (February, 1932), 376–84.

———. "Studies in Demand: Milk and Butter," *ibid.*, XLVI (August, 1932), 671–97.

———. "Time Series and the Derivation of Demand and Supply Curves: A Study of Coffee and Tea, 1850–1930," *ibid.*, XLVIII (August, 1934), 667–85.

GUIN, MARVIN. *Relation of Price to Quality of South Carolina Cotton, 1929–1930 Season.* South Carolina Agric. Exper. Station Bull. 279. Clemson Agricultural College, August, 1931.

GRAAFF, A. DE. "Grundsätzliches zur Messbarkeit der Nachfrage-elastizität," *Weltwirtschaftliches Archiv*, XXXIX, No. 1 (January, 1934), 94–150.

GRANT, H. C. *Barley Survey: A Study of Barley Production, Exports, Imports, Marketing and Prices in the Principal Exporting and Importing Countries in the World.* London: H. M. Stationery Office (Great Britain Empire Marketing Board [Publ.] E.M.B. 62), 1933.

HAAS, G. C., and EZEKIEL, M. *Factors Affecting the Price of Hogs.* U.S.D.A. Dept. Bull. No. 1440. Washington, 1926.

———. "What Makes Hog Prices?" (mimeographed). Washington: U.S.D.A., 1925.

HALL, O. J. *Relation of Central Market Prices of Strawberries to Production Planning.* Arkansas Agric. Exper. Station Bull. 275. Fayetteville, 1932.

HANAU, ARTHUR. *Die Prognose der Schweinepreise.* "Berlin Institut für Konjunkturforschung. Vierteljahrshefte zur Konjunkturforschung," Sonderheft 18. Berlin, 1930.

———. "Wie lange wird die Preisbaisse am Schweinemarkt noch dauern?" *Blätter für Landwirtschaftliche Marktforschung, Institut für Landwirtschaftliche Marktforschung* II (July, 1931), 77–82.

HARLAN, C. L. "Relation between the Weekly Receipts and Prices of Western Dressed Lamb at New York City," *U.S.D.A. Bureau of Agric. Econ., Agric. Situation*, XII, No. 5 (May, 1928), 17–19.

HARTKEMEIER, H. P. "Notes on Shifts in Demand and Supply Curves," *Econometrica*, III (1935), 428–34.

HEDDEN, W. P. "Studies of Market Supplies, Price, and Sales as a Basis for Control of Distribution of Perishables," *Jour. Farm Econ.*, VIII (April, 1926), 220.

HEDDEN, W. P., and CHERNIACK, N. "Measuring the Melon Market." Preliminary report, U.S.D.A. and Port of New York Authority co-operating. Washington, 1924.

HEFLEBOWER, R. B. *Factors Relating to the Price of Idaho Potatoes.* Idaho Agric. Exper. Station Bull. 166. Moscow, Idaho, 1929.

HOPKINS, J. A. "Forecasting Cattle Prices," *Jour. Farm. Econ.*, IX, No. 4 (October, 1927), 433–46.

——. *A Statistical Study of the Prices and Production of Beef Cattle.* Iowa Agric. Exper. Station, Research Bull. 101. Ames, 1926.

HOTELLING, HAROLD. "Demand Functions with Limited Budgets," *Econometrica*, III (1935), 66–78.

——. "Note on Edgeworth's Taxation Phenomenon and Professor Garner's Additional Condition on Demand Functions," *ibid.*, I (1933), 408–9.

HOWARD, R. H. *Relation of Quality to Price of Cotton.* "Florida College of Agriculture, Agricultural Extension Survey, Florida Agric. Exper. Econ.," Vol. II, No. 4. April, 1932.

HOWELL, L. D., and FULLILOVE, W. T. *Farm Prices of Cotton Related to Quality: Georgia Crop 1928–29.* Georgia Agric. Exper. Station Bull. 165. Athens, Ga., 1930.

——. *Farm Prices of Cotton Related to Its Grade and Staple Length in Georgia, Seasons 1929–1930 and 1930–31.* Georgia Agric. Exper. Station Bull. 174. Athens, 1933.

JENKIN, FLEEMING. *The Graphic Representation of the Laws of Supply and Demand, and Other Essays on Political Economy.* "London School of Economics and Political Science, Reprints of Scarce Tracts," No. 9. London, 1931.

JORDAN, G. L. "Factors Affecting the Price of Fresh First Eggs at New York, 1919–1928," *Poultry Science*, IX, No. 5 (July 1, 1930), 283–90.

KANTOR, HARRY S. *Factors Affecting the Price of Peaches in the New York Market.* U.S.D.A. Tech. Bull. No. 115. Washington, 1929.

LEONTIEF, WASSILY. "Composite Commodities and the Problem of Index Numbers," *Econometrica*, IV, No. 1 (1936), 39 ff.

——. "Price-Quantity Variations in Business Cycle," *Review of Economic Statistics*, XVII, No. 4 (1935), 21–27.

LERNER, A. P. "The Diagrammatical Representation of Elasticity of Demand," *Review of Economic Studies*, I, No. 1 (October, 1933), 39–44.

LEWIS, E. E. "Note on Inter-commodity Relationships in Demand," *Review of Economic Studies*, V, No. 1 (October, 1937), 53–59.

——. "Intercommodity Relationships in Stable Demand," *Econometrica*, VI, No. 2 (April, 1938), 130–42.

McBRIDE, R. S. "Some Factors Affecting Supply and Price of Butter," *Food Industry*, IV, No. 12 (December, 1932), 406–9 (charts).

MAJEROTTO, SERAFINO. "Un nuovo metodo per la determinazione empirica delle curve di domanda e offerta," *Rivista internazionale di scienze sociali e discipline ausitiarie*, III, No. 4 (July, 1932), 528–39.

MALLORY, L. D., SMITH, S. R., and SHEAR, S. W. "Factors Affecting Annual Prices of California Fresh Grapes, 1921–1929," *Hilgardia*, VI, No. 4 (September, 1931), 101–30. Berkeley: University of California Agric. Exper. Station.

MASCI, GUGLIELMO. "Sulla determinazione statistica della curva di domanda," *Rivista italiana di statistica economia e finanza*, IV, No. 3 (September, 1932), 476–514.

MORETTI, VINCENZO. "Sopra alcuni problemi di dinamica economica," *Gior. degli econ.*, XLIV, No. 7 (July, 1929), 449–88.

MURRAY, JANET. "A Study of Factors Affecting the Price of Dry Edible Beans in the United States by Classes, 1922–23 to 1934–35" (mimeographed). Washington: U.S.D.A., 1938.

MURRAY, K. A. H. *Factors Affecting the Price of Livestock.* Oxford: Oxford University Press, 1931.

NICHOL, A. J. "Measures of Average Elasticity of Demand," *Jour. Pol. Econ.*, XXXIX, No. 2 (April, 1931), 249–55. Further note in *ibid.*, No. 5 (October, 1931), pp. 658–61.

PANKRAZ, OTOMAR. "Sur la loi de la demande," *Econometrica*, IV, No. 2 (April, 1936), 153–56.

PIGOU, A. C. "Demand Supply Equations," in A. C. PIGOU and D. H. ROBERTSON, *Economic Essays and Addresses*, pp. 84–94. London: P. S. King & Son, Ltd., 1931.

RAUCHENSTEIN, EMIL. *Economic Aspects of the Apple Industry*. University of California Agric. Exper. Station Bull. 445. Berkeley, 1927.

———. *Economic Aspects of the Cantaloupe Industry*. University of California Agric. Exper. Station Bull. 419. Berkeley, 1927.

———. *Economic Aspects of the Fresh Plum Industry*. University of California Agric. Exper. Station Bull. 459. Berkeley, 1928.

———. *Economic Aspects of the Watermelon Industry*. University of California Agric. Exper. Station Bull. 449. Berkeley, 1928.

———. "Factors Affecting the Milk Supply in the Twin Cities Area." Doctor's dissertation, University of Minnesota, 1928.

———. "Factors Affecting the Price of Gravenstein Apples at Sebastopol," *Hilgardia*, III, No. 12 (June, 1928), 325–38. Berkeley: University of California Agric. Exper. Station.

———. "Factors Affecting the Price of Watermelon at Los Angeles," *ibid.*, pp. 305–23.

RICCI, UMBERTO. "Ancora sull'offerta del risparmio," *Gior. degli econ.*, XLII, No. 9 (September, 1927), 482–504.

———. "Die 'Synthetischeökonomie' von Henry Ludwell Moore," *Zeitschrift für National-ökonomie*, I, No. 5 (April, 1930), 649–88.

———. "Die statistischen Gesetze des Gleichgewichtes nach Henry Schultz," *ibid.*, II, No. 3 (January, 1931), 305–33.

———. "Può una curva di domanda esser crescente?" *Gior. degli econ.*, XLVII, No. 4 (April, 1932), 194–240.

———. "The Psychological Foundation of the Law of Demand," *Jour. Pol. Econ.*, XL, No. 2 (April, 1932), 145–85 (translated from the Italian by H. J. WADLEIGH).

———. "On the Demand for Rival (or Substitute) Commodities," *Econometrica*, I, No. 2 (April, 1933), 181–89.

———. "Modifications of the Utility Curve for Money," *Economica* (N.S.), II (1935), 168–97.

ROBBINS, LIONEL. "On the Elasticity of Demand for Income in Terms of Effort," *Economica*, X (June, 1930), 123–29.

ROOS, C. F. "Theoretical Studies of Demand," *Econometrica*, II, No. 1 (January, 1934), 73–90.

ROSS, H. A. *The Demand Side of the New York Milk Market*. Cornell University Agric. Exper. Station Bull. 459. Ithaca, 1928.

———. "Effect of Price Changes on Sales of Milk in the New York Metropolitan Area, 1919–1924," *Farm Econ.* (N.Y.), No. 43 (March, 1927), pp. 649–50.

———. *Some Factors Affecting the Demand for Milk and Cream in the Metropolitan Area of New York*. U.S.D.A. Tech. Bull. 73. Washington, 1928.

ROSSI, LIONELLO. L'Elasticità della domanda e la traslazione dell'imposta in regime di monopolio," *Gior. degli econ.*, XLVII, No. 8 (August, 1932), 600–607.

RUSSELL, S. W. "Forecasting Hog Production and Marketing," *JASA*, XXIV (1929 Suppl.), 225–33.

SAMUELSON, PAUL A. "A Note on Measurement of Utility," *Review of Economic Studies*, IV, No. 2 (February, 1937), 155–61.

SARLE, CHARLES F. "Forecasting the Price of Hogs," *Amer. Econ. Review*, XV, No. 3, Suppl. No. 2 (September, 1925), 1–22.

SCHMIDT, ROBERT. "Die Prägnanz der Elastizitätskoeffizienten," *Weltwirtschaftliches Archiv*, XXXII, No. 1 (July, 1930), 264–73.

SCHNEIDER, ERICH. "Kostenanalyse als Grundlage einer statistischen Ermittlung von Nachfragekurven," *Archiv für Sozialwissenschaft und Sozialpolitik*, LXVI, No. 3 (1931), 585–605.

——. "Kostentheoretisches zum Monopolproblem," *Zeitschrift für Nationalökonomie*, III, No. 2 (December, 1931), 185–211.

SCHOENBERG, E. H. "The Demand Curve for Cigarettes," *Journal of Business of the University of Chicago*, VI, No. 1 (January, 1933), 15–35.

SCHULTZ, HENRY. "The Statistical Measurement of the Elasticity of Demand for Beef," *Jour. Farm Econ.*, VI, No. 3 (July, 1924), 254–78.

——. "The Statistical Law of Demand," *Jour. Pol. Econ.*, XXXIII (October–December, 1925), 481–504 and 577–637.

——. "Cost of Production, Supply, Demand, and the Tariff," *Jour. Farm Econ.*, IX (April, 1927), 192–209.

——. "Theoretical Considerations Relating to Supply," *Jour. Pol. Econ.*, XXXV (August, 1927), 438–39.

——. "Henry L. Moore's Contribution to the Statistical Law of Demand." Analysis No. 46 (pp. 645–61) in *Methods in Social Science*, ed. STUART A. RICE. Chicago: University of Chicago Press, 1931.

SHAUL, J. R. H. "The Demand Curve for Beef and Veal in Great Britain," *Econ. Jour.*, XLV, No. 179 (September, 1935), 493–500.

SHEAR, S. W., and HOWE, R. M. "Factors Affecting California Raisin Sales and Prices, 1922–1929," Berkeley: University of California Agric. Exper. Station. *Hilgardia*, VI, No. 4 (September, 1931), 73–100.

SHEPHERD, G. S. "The Incidence of the Cost of the AAA Corn-Hog Program," *Jour. Farm Econ.*, XVI (1934), 417–30.

——. "The Incidence of the AAA Processing Tax on Hogs," *ibid.*, XVII (1935), 321–24.

——. "Supply and Production, Demand and Consumption," *ibid.*, XIII (October, 1931), 639–42.

——. "Vertical and Horizontal Shifts in Demand Curves," *ibid.*, XV (October, 1933), 723–29.

——. "Vertical and Horizontal Shifts in Demand Curves," *Econometrica*, IV, No. 4 (October, 1936), 361–67.

SINGER, H. W. "Income and Rent: A Study of Family Expenditure," *Review of Economic Studies*, IV, No. 2 (February, 1937), 145–54.

SMITH, B. B. "The Adjustment of Agricultural Production to Demand," *Jour. Farm Econ.*, VIII (April, 1926), 145–65.

——. "Forecasting the Acreage of Cotton," *JASA*, XX (1925), 31–47.

STACKELBERG, HEINRICH VON. "Die grundlegenden Hypothesen der neueren Preisanalyse," *Archiv für mathematische Wirtschafts- und Sozialforschung* (Leipzig), Heft 2 (1935), 84–103.

STAEHLE, HANS. *Die Analyse der Nachfragekurven in ihrer Bedeutung für die Konjunkturforschung.* Frankfurter Gesellschaft für Konjunkturforschung, ed. EUGEN ALTSCHUL. Veröffentlichungen, Heft. 2, Bonn: K. Schroeder, 1929.

———. "Family Budgets—Source Materials," *Econometrica*, III (1935), 106–18.

———. "The Reaction of Consumers to Changes in Prices and Income: A Quantitative Study in Immigrants' Behavior," *ibid.*, II (1934), 59–72.

———. "Short-Period Variations in the Distribution of Incomes," *Review of Economic Statistics*, XIX, No. 3 (1937), 133–43.

———. "Sopra alcuni problemi di dinamica economica," *Gior. di econ. e rivista di statistica*, XLV, No. 3 (March, 1930), 243–49.

———. "Die statistische Analyse von Angebot und Nachfrage und die Klausel *ceteris paribus*," *Weltwirtschaftliches Archiv*, XXXII, No. 1 (July, 1930), 135–49.

STITTS, T. G. "Economic Factors Affecting the Price of Butter." Doctor's dissertation, University of Minnesota, 1926.

STOKER, H. M. "World Production and Price of Merino and Crossbred Wool," *Second International Conference on Agricultural Economics*, pp. 746–61. Ithaca, N.Y.: Cornell University, 1930.

STOVER, H. J. "Relation of the Production of Grapes in Western New York and in California to Price," *Farm Econ.* (N.Y.), No. 59 (June, 1929), pp. 1111–1113.

SZELISKI, VICTOR S. VON, and PARADISO, L. J. "Demand for Boots and Shoes as Affected by Price Levels and National Income," *Econometrica*, IV, No. 4 (October, 1936), 338–55.

THOMPSON, C. D. "A Note on the Elasticity of Demand Calculated from a Demand Schedule or from Statistics," *Indian Journal of Economics*, XIV (July, 1933), 105–9.

THOMSEN, F. L. " 'Vertical' and 'Horizontal' Shifts of Demand," *Jour. Farm Econ.*, XV, No. 3 (July, 1933), 566–70.

THOMSEN, F. L., and FANKHANEL, W. R. *Factors Affecting Sweet Potato Prices in Missouri.* Missouri Agric. Exper. Station Bull. 302. Columbia, 1931.

TINTNER, GERHARD. "A Note on Distribution of Income over Time," *Econometrica*, IV, No. 1 (January, 1936), 60–66.

VARGA, STEFAN. "Die Preisbestimmungsfaktoren des ungarischen Weizens," *Zeitschrift für Nationalökonomie*, II, No. 5 (May, 1931), 780–92.

VECCHIO, GUSTAVO DEL. "La Dinamica economica di H. L. Moore," *Gior. degli econ.*, XLV, No. 6 (June, 1930), 545–53.

VINCI, FELICE. "La Derivazione statistica delle curve di domanda," *Rivista italiana di statistica*, III, No. 1 (January–March, 1931), 98–100.

———. "Sui fondamenti della dinamica economica," *ibid.*, II, No. 3 (July–September, 1930), 232–68.

———. "Sui metodi di studio della dinamica economica," *ibid.*, IV, No. 2 (June, 1932), 238–47.

WAITE, W. C. "The Effect of a Business Depression on the Demand for Livestock Products and the Outlook for These Products," *Jour. Farm Econ.*, XIV, No. 2 (April, 1932), 228–38.

———. "A Study of the Demand for Eggs in Selected Chain Stores of Metropolitan New York, 1929," *ibid.*, No. 3 (July, 1932), pp. 373–83.

———. "On the Term 'Change in Demand,' " *ibid.*, XII, No. 4 (October, 1930), 620–21.

———. "Some Developments in the Techniques of Studying Consumer Demand," *JASA*, XXV (March, 1930), 140–45.

WAITE, WARREN C., and COX, REX W. *Seasonal Variations of Prices and Marketings of Minnesota Agricultural Products, 1921–1935.* University of Minnesota Agric. Exper. Station Tech. Bull. 127. Minnespolis, March, 1938.

WAITE, W. C., and STURGES, ALEXANDER. "On Certain Mathematical Properties of Demand Curves of Constant Elasticity," *Jour. Farm. Econ.*, XII, No. 1 (January, 1930), 181–82.

WALLACE, H. A. *Agricultural Prices*. Des Moines: Wallace Publishing Co., 1920.

———. "Supply and Price Interactions in Farm and City Products," *Annals of the American Academy of Political and Social Science*, CXVII, No. 206 (January, 1925), 243–47.

WALLACE, H. A., and BRESSMAN, E. N. *Corn and Corn-growing*. Des Moines: Wallace Publishing Co., 1925.

WARREN, G. F., and PEARSON, F. A. "Apple Prices," *Farm Econ.*, No. 48 (October, 1927), pp. 777–79.

———. "Relation of Supply to Price," *Jour. Farm. Econ.*, XL (December, 1926), 559–71.

WATKINS, JAMES L. *King Cotton*. New York: Watkins & Sons, 1908.

WAUGH, A. E. "'Elasticity of Demand' from Budget Studies," *Quar. Jour. Econ.*, XLVII, No. 1 (November, 1932), 134–37.

———. *Forecasting Prices of New Jersey White Potatoes and Sweet Potatoes*. New Jersey Dept. of Agric. Circ. No. 78. Trenton, 1924.

———. "Quality Factors Influencing Vegetable Prices," *Jour. Farm Econ.*, X, No. 2 (April, 1928), 185–96.

———. *Quality as a Determinant of Vegetable Prices: A Statistical Study of Quality Factors Influencing Vegetable Prices in the Boston Wholesale Market*. "Studies in History, Economics, and Public Law," ed. Faculty of Political Science, Columbia University, No. 312. New York: Columbia University Press, 1929.

———. "The Relation of Quality to the Price of Farm Products," *Second International Conference on Agricultural Economics*. Ithaca, N.Y.: Cornell University, 1930.

———. "The Marginal Utility of Money in the United States from 1917 to 1921 and from 1922 to 1932," *Econometrica*, III (1935), 376–99.

WAUGH, F. V., BURTIS, E. L., and WOLF, A. F. "The Controlled Distribution of a Crop among Independent Markets," *Quar. Jour. Econ.*, LI (November, 1936), 1–41.

WAUGH, F. V., WHITE, C. M., and HERSEY, M. R. *Maine Potato Quality Related to Market Prices*. Maine Development Commission Bull. 3. Augusta, Me., 1931.

———. *Market Preferences and Premiums for Maine Potatoes*. Maine Development Commission Bulls. 2 and 3. Augusta, Me., 1930 and 1931.

WELLMAN, H. R. "Factors That Affected the Annual Average Prices of Canned Apricots, 1923–24 to 1930–31 (a Preliminary Report)" (mimeographed). Berkeley: University of California, College of Agriculture, Agricultural Extension Service, 1931.

———. "Factors That Affected the Annual Average Prices of Canned Clingstone Peaches, 1921–22 to 1930–31" (mimeographed). Berkeley: University of California, College of Agriculture, Agricultural Extension Service, June, 1931.

———. "Factors That Affected the Annual Average Prices of Canned Pears, 1921–22 to 1930–31 (a Preliminary Report)" (mimeographed). Berkeley: University of California. College of Agriculture, Agricultural Extension Service, 1931.

———. *Supply, Demand and Prices of California Peaches*. University of California Agric. Exper. Station Bull. 547. Berkeley, 1932.

WELLMAN, H. R., and BRAUN, E. W. *Beans*. University of California Agric. Exper. Station Bull. 444. Berkeley, 1927.

———. *Oranges*, University of California Exper. Station Bull. 457. Berkeley, 1928.

———. *Lemons*. University of California Agric. Exper. Station Bull. 460. Berkeley, 1928.

———. *Grapefruit*. University of California Agric. Exper. Station Bull. 463. Berkeley, 1928.

————. *Asparagus*. University of California Agric. Exper. Station Bull. 487. Berkeley, 1930.

————. *Cherries*. University of California Agric. Exper. Station Bull. 488. Berkeley, 1930.

WENTWORTH, E. N., and ELLINGER, T. U. "The Determination of Hog Prices at Public Markets." *Jour. Farm Econ.*, VI, No. 3 (July, 1924), 279–82.

WICKSTEED, P. H. "Buyer and Seller, Demand and Supply," in *The Common Sense of Political Economy and Selected Papers and Reviews on Economic Theory*, ed. LIONEL ROBBINS, Vol. II, chap. iv, pp. 493–526. London: George Routledge & Sons, Ltd., 1933.

WILLIAMS, F. M. "The Measurement of the Demand for Food," *JASA*, XXIV (September, 1929), 288–95.

WILLIAMS, J. B. "Speculation and the Carryover," *Quar. Jour. Econ.*, L (1935–36), 436–55.

WIŚNIEWSKI, J. "Demand in Relation to the Income Curve," *Econometrica*, III (1935), 411–15.

WOLFE, P. DE. "The Demand for Passenger Cars in the United States," *Econometrica*, VI, No. 2 (April, 1938), 113–29.

WORKING, E. J. "Evaluation of Methods Used in Commodity Price Forecasting," *Jour. Farm Econ.*, XII, No. 1 (January, 1930), 119–38.

————. "Statistical Demand Curves," *Encyclopedia of the Social Sciences* (1931), V, 72–75.

————. "Indications of Changes in the Demand for Agricultural Products," *Jour. Farm Econ.*, XIV (1932), 239–56.

————. *Production and Demand: Contrasts between Agriculture and Other Industries*, chap. xi, pp. 160–91. (Reprinted from *Stabilization of Employment*, ed. C. F. ROOS. A symposium held under the auspices of the American Association for the Advancement of Science. Bloomington, Ind.: Principia Press, 1933.)

————. "Demand Studies during Times of Rapid Economic Change," *Econometrica*, II, No. 2 (April, 1934), 140–51.

————. "New Indices of Agricultural Supplies and Carry-Over, *Review of Economic Statistics*, XIX, No. 3 (1937), 144–53.

WORKING, HOLBROOK. "The Statistical Determination of Demand Curves," *Quar. Jour. Econ.*, XXXIX (August, 1925), 503–43.

————. "Factors Influencing Price Differentials between Potato Markets," *Jour. Farm Econ.*, VII (October, 1925), 377–98.

————. "Forecasting the Price of Wheat," *ibid.*, XI (July, 1927), 273–87.

————. "Materials for a Theory of Wheat Prices," *Second International Conference on Agricultural Economics*. Ithaca, N.Y.: Cornell University, 1930.

————. "Differential Price Behavior as a Subject for Commodity Price Analysis," *Econometrica*, III (1935), 416–27.

WRIGHT, P. G. *The Tariff on Animal and Vegetable Oils*. New York: Macmillan Co., 1928.

WRIGHT, SEWALL. "The Theory of Path Coefficients: A Reply to Niles' Criticism," *Genetics*, VIII (May, 1923), 239–55.

YOUNGBLOOD, BONNEY. "Analysis of the Relation of Quality to Price of Cotton," *Jour. Farm Econ.*, XI, No. 4 (October, 1929), 525–41.

ZAHRA, M. A., and EL-DARWISH, M. *The Statistical Study of Some of the Factors Affecting the Price of Egyptian Cotton*. Egypt Ministry of Finance, Cotton Bureau Tech. Bull. 1. Cairo: Government Press, 1930.

ZEUTHEN, F. "On the Determinateness of the Utility Function," *Review of Economic Studies*, IV, No. 3 (June, 1937), 236–39.

ZIMMERMAN, CARLE C. "Ernst Engel's Law of Expenditures for Food." *Quar. Jour. Econ.*, XLVII, No. 1 (November, 1932), 78–101.

C. SOURCES OF DATA

Barron's National Financial Weekly. New York, 1931——.

BUREAU OF LABOR STATISTICS. *Retail Prices, 1890 to 1928*. Bull. No. 495. Washington, 1929.

——. *Retail Prices and Cost of Living*. Bull. R. 70. Washington: December, 1933.

Commercial and Financial Chronicle (weekly). 1897——.

DOMINION BUREAU OF STATISTICS. *Prices and Price Indexes*. Ottawa, Can., 1923——.

——. *The Canada Yearbook*. Ottawa, Can., 1932.

DOUGLAS, PAUL H. *Real Wages in the United States 1890–1926*. Boston and New York: Houghton Mifflin Co., 1930.

Foreign Commerce Yearbook, 1935. Washington: Bureau of Foreign and Domestic Commerce, 1935.

KING, W. I. *The National Income and Its Purchasing Power*. New York: National Bureau of Economic Research, 1930.

LEVEN, M., MOULTON, H. G., and WARBURTON, C. *America's Capacity To Consume*. Washington: Brookings Institution, 1934.

MARTIN, R. F. "The National Income, 1933." *Survey of Current Business*, January, 1935, pp. 16–18.

MITCHELL, W. C. *Gold, Prices, and Wages*. Berkeley: University of California Press, 1908.

NEW YORK COTTON EXCHANGE. *Cotton Year Book*. New York, 1928——.

PERSONS, W. M. *Forecasting Business Cycles*. New York: John Wiley & Sons, Inc., 1931.

——. "Gauging Business Activity," *Barrons*,' January 18, 1937.

PERSONS, W. M., and LE BARON, R. FOSTER. "A New Index of Industrial Production and Trade," *Review of Economic Statistics*, XV (1933), 145–60.

SHEPPERSON PUBLISHING COMPANY. *Cotton Facts*. New York, 1878——.

SNYDER, CARL. *Business Cycles and Business Measurements*. New York: Macmillan Co., 1927.

Standard Statistical Bulletin Basebook. New York, 1929——.

STANFORD UNIVERSITY, FOOD RESEARCH INSTITUTE. *Wheat Studies*. Stanford, Calif., 1924–25——.

UNITED STATES BEET SUGAR ASSOCIATION. *Concerning Sugar* (a loose-leaf publication).

UNITED STATES DEPARTMENT OF AGRICULTURE. *Agricultural Outlook Charts*. Washington, 1937.

——. *Agricultural Statistics*. Washington, 1936——.

——. *The Crop and Livestock Reporting Service of the U.S.* Misc. Publication No. 171. Washington, 1933.

——. *Farmer's Bulletin, No. 629*. Washington, 1914.

———. *General Crop Revisions, Crop Years 1924–1935, Acreage, Yield, and Production.* Washington, 1936.

———. *Handbook of Official Grain Standards of the U.S.* Washington, 1935.

———. *Handbook of Official Hay Standards.* Washington, 1936.

———. *Hay and Feed Statistics.* Stat. Bull. No. 11. Washington, 1925.

———. *Revised Estimates of Wheat Acreage, Yield, and Production, 1866–1929.* September, 1934.

———. *Statistics of Oats, Barley, and Grain Sorghums.* Stat. Bull. No. 29. Washington, 1930.

———. *Wheat and Rye Statistics.* Stat. Bull. No. 12. Washington, 1926.

———. *Yearbooks of Agriculture* especially from 1920 to 1935. (Beginning with 1936 the statistical series appear in a separate annual publication entitled *Agricultural Statistics.*)

UNITED STATES DEPARTMENT OF COMMERCE. *Census Bulletins. Cotton Production and Distribution.* Washington, 1905———.

———. *Statistical Abstract of the United States.* Washington, 1931———.

WALL, N.J. *Monthly Index of World Industrial Production, 1920–1935, Preliminary Report.* Washington: U.S. Department of Agriculture, June, 1936.

WILLETT and GRAY. *Weekly Statistical Sugar Trade Journal.* New York, 1937———.

INDEXES

AUTHOR INDEX

SUBJECT INDEX

(See also the tables of contents for the individual chapters as well as the List of Tables (p. xxv and List of Charts (p. xix)

A[gricultural] A[djustment] A[ct]
    and corn, 280–81
    and cotton, 323–30
    and potatoes, 427
    and shifts of demand curves, 563–64
    and sugar, 233–34
    and wheat, 401

Accuracy
    of data, 157–73
    of quantity series, 167–69
    of price series, 172
    of numerical results, 757–64

Acreage, method of estimating, 166–67

Adjustment of data, 149–50

Agricultural statistics, collection of, 164–69

Allen and theory of related demands; see Hicks-Allen definition of complementarity; Johnson-Allen definition of complementarity; see also Author Index

Amoroso, criticism of link-relative method, 539–42

Animal units
    and demand for corn, 269–74
    and demand for hay, 339–58
    and demand for oats, 435–62

Bankhead Cotton Control Act, 327

Barley
    Chicago price of, 172
    definition of demand for, 468
    demand for, 463–82
    demand functions for, with consumption the dependent variable, 469–70
    demand functions for, with price the dependent variable, 480–81
    elasticity of demand for, 474, 475–77
    factors affecting the demand for, 467–69
    factual background of, 465–67
    flexibility of price of, 480–81
    production of, 465–67
    shift of demand for, 470, 474, 475–77, 481
    stocks, 468
    summary of demand for, 481–82

Barley-corn-hay-oats interrelations of demand, 589–99

Beef and pork, interrelations of demand, 582–85

Beef-mutton-pork interrelations of demand, 633–44

Beta-coefficients and their standard errors, 737–40, 743–45, 745–51

Bridgman, operational procedure of, 10–12

Buckwheat
    definition of demand for, 506–7

demand for, 503–21
demand functions for, with consumption the dependent variable, 507–17
demand functions for, with price the dependent variable, 517–19
elasticity of demand for, 500, 514, 516
factors affecting the demand for, 506–7
factual background of, 505–6
flexibility of price of, 517–19
production of, 505–6
shift of demand for, 512–17, 517–19
summary of demand for, 519–21

Budget data, derivation of demand curves from, 105–29

Budgetary investigations, 663

Business conditions
    and demand for corn, 269
    and demand for cotton, 302–10
    and demand for potatoes, 426
    and demand for sugar, 220–21, 225
    and price of cotton, 310–20

Carry-over
    barley, 468
    buckwheat, 506–7
    corn, 239–40
    cotton, 294
    hay, 338
    oats, 433
    potatoes, 408
    rye, 487
    sugar, 178
    wheat, 377–79

Classification of commodities, 22–24, 570–82. See also Complementarity

"Cob-web" theorem, 78–80

Coefficient of complementary; see Complementarity

Coefficient of correlation, see Correlation; Correlation coefficients, comparison of

Coefficients of determination, 741–42

Coefficient of elasticity of demand; see Elasticity of demand

Cofactors, 719, 748–49, 771

Coffee-sugar-tea interrelations of demand, 585–89

Commodities, classification of, 22–24, 570–82. See also Complementarity

Commodity Credit Corporation and cotton, 326

Commodities, demands for, analyzed, 157–61

Competing goods
    mathematical criteria for, 22–24, 572–82